PURPOSE AND POWER

Across the full span of the nation's history, Donald Stoker challenges our understanding of the purposes and uses of American power. From the struggle for independence to the era of renewed competition with China and Russia, he reveals the grand strategies underpinning the nation's pursuit of sovereignty, security, expansion, and democracy abroad. He shows how successive administrations have projected diplomatic, military, and economic power, and mobilized ideas and information to preserve American freedoms at home and secure US aims abroad. He exposes the myth of American isolationism, the good and ill of America's quest for democracy overseas, and how too often its administrations have lacked clear political aims or a concrete vision for where they want to go. Understanding this history is vital if America is to relearn how to use its power to meet the challenges ahead and to think more clearly about political aims and grand strategy.

Donald Stoker is Professor of National Security and Resource Strategy at the National Defense University's Dwight D. Eisenhower School in Washington, DC. He is the author or editor of thirteen books, including *The Grand Design: Strategy and the US Civil War, 1861–1865* (2010), winner of the Fletcher Pratt award, and *Why America Loses Wars: Limited War and US Strategy from the Korean War to the Present* (2022).

PURPOSE AND POWER

*US Grand Strategy from
the Revolutionary Era to the Present*

Donald Stoker
National Defense University, Washington, DC

Shaftesbury Road, Cambridge CB2 8EA, United Kingdom

One Liberty Plaza, 20th Floor, New York, NY 10006, USA

477 Williamstown Road, Port Melbourne, VIC 3207, Australia

314–321, 3rd Floor, Plot 3, Splendor Forum, Jasola District Centre, New Delhi – 110025, India

103 Penang Road, #05–06/07, Visioncrest Commercial, Singapore 238467

Cambridge University Press is part of Cambridge University Press & Assessment, a department of the University of Cambridge.

We share the University's mission to contribute to society through the pursuit of education, learning and research at the highest international levels of excellence.

www.cambridge.org
Information on this title: www.cambridge.org/9781009257275
DOI: 10.1017/9781009257268

© Donald Stoker 2024

This publication is in copyright. Subject to statutory exception and to the provisions of relevant collective licensing agreements, no reproduction of any part may take place without the written permission of Cambridge University Press & Assessment.

First published 2024

A catalogue record for this publication is available from the British Library

Library of Congress Cataloging-in-Publication Data
Names: Stoker, Donald, author.
Title: Purpose and power : US grand strategy from the revolutionary era to the present / Donald Stoker, National Defense University, Washington, DC.
Description: Cambridge ; New York, NY : Cambridge University Press, 2024. | Includes bibliographical references and index.
Identifiers: LCCN 2022040999 | ISBN 9781009257275 (hardback) | ISBN 9781009257268 (ebook)
Subjects: LCSH: National security – United States – History. | United States – Military policy. | United States – Foreign relations. | United States – Economic policy.
Classification: LCC UA23 .S818 2024 | DDC 355/.033573–dc23/eng/20230206
LC record available at https://lccn.loc.gov/2022040999

ISBN 978-1-009-25727-5 Hardback

Cambridge University Press & Assessment has no responsibility for the persistence or accuracy of URLs for external or third-party internet websites referred to in this publication and does not guarantee that any content on such websites is, or will remain, accurate or appropriate.

To Carol – Who Made It Possible

Contents

List of Figures	page ix
List of Maps	x
List of Abbreviations	xi
Thinking about Grand Strategy in Peace and War	1

PART I: FROM BACKWATER TO GREAT POWER

1	The Fight for Sovereignty, 1775–1801	15
2	Expansion, Sovereignty, and War, 1801–1817	50
3	Seeking a Continent: Expansion, Indian Removal, and the Mexican War, 1817–1849	77
4	Schism, Civil War, and Reconstruction, 1849–1877	118
5	Conquering a Continent: The Indian Wars, 1865–1897	156
6	American Empire, 1897–1913	191

PART II: FROM GREAT POWER TO SUPERPOWER

7	Stepping upon the Global Stage, 1913–1921	227
8	The Interwar Interlude, 1921–1939	258
9	Moving Astride the World: The Second World War, 1939–1945	294
10	The Hot Peace and the Korean War, 1945–1953	344
11	The Hot Peace: The Eisenhower, Kennedy, and Johnson Years, 1953–1969	390
12	The Vietnam War, 1961–1969	416
13	Détente and Defeat: Nixon, Ford, and Vietnam, 1969–1977	446
14	For Want of a Vision: The Carter Years, 1977–1981	477
15	Winning the Hot Peace: Reagan's Great-Power Competition, 1981–1990	497

CONTENTS

PART III: THE POST-COLD WAR WORLD

16 The Gulf War, or First Iraq War, 1990–1991   537
17 The New World Disorder: Bush and Clinton, 1991–2001   560
18 Wilsonian Revolutionaries: The Bush Administration, 2001–2009   589

PART IV: RETREAT AND DEFEAT

19 Retrenchment, Engagement, and War:
    The Obama Years, 2009–2017   633
20 Retrenchment, Engagement, and Weakness:
    Trump and Biden, 2017–2022   661

Conclusion   696

Acknowledgements   704
Notes   705
Index   824

Figures

0.1 A framework for strategic analysis   *page* 2
12.1 North Vietnamese Army infiltration into South Vietnam, 1965–75 (in thousands)   421

Maps

1.1	Principal battles of the American Revolutionary War, 1775–83. Universal Images Group North America LLC / Alamy	*page* 14
2.1	An expanding country: US territorial acquisitions and growth	51
2.2	The Eastern United States, 1812	55
3.1	Florida and the Second Seminole War, 1835–42	93
3.2	The Mexican War, 1846–48	102
4.1	Principal campaigns of the American Civil War, 1861–65	123
5.1	The US army in the West, 1860–90	157
6.1	Santiago de Cuba and vicinity, 1898	193
6.2	Expansionism: The United States in the Spanish–American War, 1898–1902	194
7.1	The First World War, 1914–18	236
9.1a	Major operations in Europe, 1939–45	295
9.1b	Central Europe, 1944: Allied Occupation Zones	321
9.2a, 9.2b	Pacific axes of advance, 1942–45	324
10.1	The Korean War, 1950–51	363
12.1	North and South Vietnam	441
16.1a, 16.1b	Operation DESERT STORM, 1991	546
18.1	Major US operations, Afghanistan, 2001–02	593
18.2	Southern Iraq and vicinity, 2003	605

Abbreviations

AMH	*American Military History*
B&L	*Battles and Leaders of the Civil War*
CWL	*The Collected Works of Abraham Lincoln*
FRUS	*Foreign Relations of the United States*
NYT	*New York Times*
OR	*Official Records of the Civil War*
ORN	*Official Records of the Civil War, Navy*
ORS	*Official Records of the Civil War, Supplemental*
PWR	*The Papers of George Washington, Revolutionary War Series*
USGPO	United States Government Printing Office
WSJ	*Wall Street Journal*
WW	*The Writings of George Washington*

THINKING ABOUT GRAND STRATEGY IN PEACE AND WAR

INTRODUCTION

On February 24, 2022, Vladimir Putin's Russia escalated the war it began against Ukraine with its 2014 invasion of Crimea. This occurred at a time when tensions with China had increased as Beijing began openly seeking regional hegemony and to replace the United States as the world's most powerful state. Totalitarian, revisionist states were on the march. "Great-power competition" was back.

Will the United States emerge victorious from this new contest as it did during the Cold War? To do so, American leaders need to understand the purposes for which American power has been used and learn how to *think* about utilizing this power effectively. Examining the nation's past actions – good and ill – is the best preparation for overcoming today's challenges and tomorrow's.

"WHAT SHOULD AMERICAN GRAND STRATEGY BE?"

The advent of America's post–Second World War rivalry with the Soviet Union moved "grand strategy" firmly into the US political-military lexicon. The latest wave of interest arose in the 2010s in the face of revisionist and expansionist Chinese and Russian regimes.

"What should American grand strategy be?" became a common query in political, defense, and academic circles.

But this is the wrong question.

Strategy is about the use of power. Grand strategy is the coordinated use of the various elements of national power. But to use power absent a political aim – and without understanding the effects of the aim or aims – is to flail, to expend at times both blood and treasure for no clear purpose. Proper analysis rests on asking "What is our aim? What do we want to achieve?" The political aim should be decided *first*. The wise use of power flows from this. Few works on grand strategy rest on such a solid foundation.[1]

The aim is the most important element in proper strategic analysis, but it is only a part. The first step is to learn how to *think* about the use of power and its purpose.

A FRAMEWORK FOR STRATEGIC ANALYSIS

Having a clear analytical approach is fundamental. (See Figure 0.1.) How we *think* about a challenge drives how we address it. Grand strategy works frequently conflate terms, confusing the aims being sought with the ways and means of achieving them and the underpinning interests. One critic of American grand strategy wrote: "Instead of pursuing a more restrained grand strategy, US leaders opted for liberal hegemony."[2] Grand strategies are implemented, political aims (such as hegemony) are pursued. This is more than a semantic problem: it is broken theory. This statement has the added weakness of being historically inaccurate, as no US administration has ever sought hegemony, and writers insisting upon this usually confuse war plans for addressing hypotheticals or the creation of regional military preponderance with a desire to achieve political dominance. Other works attempt encapsulation of American grand strategy in a single term. The urge is understandable as this could provide an instantly grasped concept,

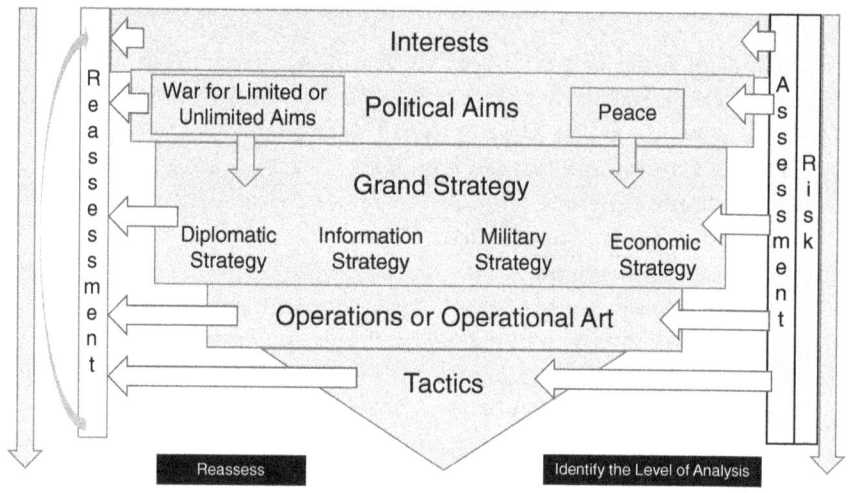

0.1 A framework for strategic analysis

but America's historical challenges are generally too complex for this.[3] "Containment" in the Cold War comes the closest, one unsurpassed for branding success. But even this fails to paint a complete picture, nor was it meant to as it was initially directed at the Soviet Union. A critical examination of any topic requires a clear methodology based on solid definitions.

INTERESTS

We begin with interests. These are often issues relating to a state's survival or prosperity. Interests depict part of the why and how of the behavior of state and nonstate actors and are often underpinned by ideas and values. Ideally, both become involved in issues because their leaders judge it necessary – in the *interests*, or national interests – of the state or organization.

We must avoid confusing interests with political aims. Interests usually underpin why nations select certain political aims and drive the actions of leaders. But this is not an absolute; there are few absolutes in such matters.[4] Some things can be both interests and aims, complicating the analytical problem. For example, it is in the interest of the United States to have security, but the security of the nation is also a political aim.

Interests can be subjective because leaders have different views and prejudices, they can vary over time as the international and domestic situations are in constant flux, and are sometimes determined by unique events. Administrations at times don't see acting in some areas as in the US interest until a new threat arises. In 1950, fighting a war in Korea wasn't viewed as in the American interest until Communist North Korea invaded non-Communist South Korea and threatened American credibility. Interests aren't fixed and change as circumstances change. This can drive alteration of political aims, which means the grand strategy should be reassessed and changed where necessary to address the new environment.

How then do we determine what is in the nation's interests? Interests, like so many aspects of foreign affairs, remain frustratingly subjective. Sometimes this is easy: countering a threat to the nation's survival is clearly in the national interest. Sometimes this is difficult. Is it in the US interest to defend Taiwan against aggression from Beijing? Theorist Bernard Brodie wrote: "A sovereign nation determines for itself what its vital interests are (freedom to do so is what the term 'sovereign' means) and its leaders accomplish this exacting task largely by using their highly fallible and inevitably biased human judgment to interpret the external political environment."[5] Some advise ranking, but this suffers from subjectivism and sometimes poor judgment.[6] As with so many things in politics and war, the answer depends upon circumstances, the conditions under which the assessment is made, and the views and goals of the individuals performing the assessments and making the decisions. As elsewhere, as our graphic shows, risk is a factor.

Some argue that "a nation's interests are determined by its power." This is backward reasoning. A nation's interests have little to do with its power, but power has everything to do with the achievement of its aims. The leaders of all states see regime survival as in the nation's interest. But the nation may lack the power to assure it. President Abraham Lincoln decided it was in the country's interest to resist secession despite the great costs, and mustered the power to suppress the rebellion.[7] Interests should drive the creation of political aims, though this isn't always the case.

AMERICA'S HISTORIC POLITICAL AIMS: SECURITY, SOVEREIGNTY, EXPANSION (AND DEMOCRACY)

Political aims provide a foundation for analysis and the point toward which a nation's power is directed. Ideally, the aims being sought are rationally founded upon what is best for the state – or at least what the leaders decide is best. But there are potentially many aims – in peace and in war – and these change. Possessing multiple aims often means states need *multiple grand strategies* to achieve them, a challenge overlooked in most works on grand strategy. We see in American history predominant aims in particular eras. The pursuit of these leads to the formulation of additional aims (sometimes), which then, ideally, drive the development of different and *multiple* grand strategies (coordinated uses of power) for pursuing these disparate aims. This is not always clear or even systematic. But methodically examining past aims and related uses of power teaches future leaders and their advisors how to think critically while providing a historical foundation for crafting future aims and grand strategy.

From the time of their first settlements, the people who came to be called "Americans" sought security. For the infant United States, security became a critical political aim. Until the 1890s, Native American peoples constituted the most persistent though withering threat. Early settlers also worried about foreign intrusions, particularly from Spain and France. The danger of their destroying what became the United States evaporated with Britain's victory in the French and Indian War in 1763. They remained a threat, though Britain became a greater one. The hazards evolved as the country grew, but the desire to achieve security has remained a dominant aim driving the creation of US grand strategy.

The second key political aim is sovereignty. Americans were first concerned with achieving sovereignty during their war for independence: they wanted to control their own affairs without interference from abroad. After achieving independence in 1783, securing sovereignty against external enemies, particularly the European powers, as well as the neighboring Native American nations, became important. America has also faced internal threats to sovereignty such as the 1794 Whiskey Rebellion, the Confederacy, and domestic organizations using terrorism. In each case, Federal power was wielded to defeat threats.

A third aim was expansion. Americans were land hungry from the beginning, and American expansion was dominated by taking land from Native American nations. This desire to expand underpinned wars against European powers and their former colonies as Americans enthusiastically sought British (Canadian), French, Spanish, and Mexican lands.

The American trinity of security, sovereignty, and expansion altered after President Theodore Roosevelt's acquisition of what became the Panama Canal Zone in 1903. Afterward, the US no longer pursued territorial expansion using military force. Instead, the US added a new political aim toward which it directed power. "Security, Sovereignty, and Expansion" became "Security, Sovereignty, and Democracy." The US would go abroad in search of monsters to slay. There were tinges of this in US foreign relations dating to Thomas Jefferson, but Woodrow Wilson made it a core political aim by weaponizing Progressivism to spread democracy.

All aims can produce troubles at home. Politics as a blood sport was present from the republic's birth. A myth arising during the Cold War was "politics stops at the water's edge," meaning America's political parties unite against a foreign danger. Republican Senator Arthur Vandenberg, perhaps Congress' foremost internationalist in his day, used the phrase to illustrate how he and Democratic president Harry Truman worked in a bipartisan fashion. Their relationship, even at the time, was "an aberration."[8] Bitter partisanship marked disagreements over the Quasi-War of 1798–1800 with France. American resistance to the War of 1812 reached full-fledged treason. The American Civil War marked the bloodiest partisan discord. Schisms over neutrality and preparedness for war prevented national political unity at the dawns of both world wars. Disagreement over the Vietnam War became noxious. In 2007, Democratic Senator Harry Reid enthused upon how Republican George W. Bush's errors in Iraq would help Democrats win Senate seats.[9] America's foreign relations – especially its wars – have always provoked division.

IF AT WAR…

If not attacked, one of the most important decisions of American leaders is whether it's in the nation's interest to go to war. The nation's chiefs should determine the political aim or aims before doing so, and if the US has been forced into a conflict, its leaders should quickly determine the political aims sought. The course for achieving them – the grand strategy – should follow. In the American experience, the aims generally involve some version of the quadrumvirate detailed above, but not always. There may be multiple political aims, and these can vary by opponent. Aims that are pursued via war can always be classified as two types: unlimited aims – meaning the overthrow of the enemy state, or limited aims – something short of regime change, such as seizing territory. The political aims and the planning associated with them should include a vision of the postwar situation and a peace treaty – when possible – as this is ideally a war's final act.[10]

Critical to the decision regarding what political aims are being sought is an assessment of the situation to see whether the nation possesses the power to achieve the aims, or what resources must be mobilized or obtained to succeed, as well as the potential roles of other powers. A thorough appraisal can increase the chances of success or show that the aims need to change. Thucydides, the historian of the Peloponnesian War, observed: "It is a common mistake in going to war to begin at the wrong end, to act first, and wait for disaster to discuss the matter."[11]

Prussian soldier and theorist Carl von Clausewitz cut a clear path for performing assessments, one useful in both peace and war:

> we must first examine our own political aim and that of the enemy. [It is important to understand what the foe wants.] We must gauge the strength and situation of the opposing state. We must gauge the character and abilities of its government and people and do the same regarding our own. Finally, we must evaluate the political sympathies of other states and the effect the war may have on them.[12]

Clausewitz also had no illusions regarding the difficulty of doing this well. Ideally, reassessment should occur continuously despite the challenges of doing so. It should certainly take place whenever there is significant change, such as a battlefield victory or defeat or the entry of a third party into the war.

Leaders should also decide how to bring the war to a victorious conclusion. The paths here are innumerable, but Clausewitz marks the dominant routes:

> We can now see that in war many roads lead to success, and they do not all involve the enemy's outright defeat. They range from *the destruction of the*

enemy's forces, the conquest of his territory, to a temporary occupation or invasion, to projects with an immediate political purpose, and finally to passively awaiting the enemy's attacks. Any one of these may be used to overcome the enemy's will: the choice depends on circumstances.[13]

GRAND STRATEGY

The path for tapping American power to accomplish the desired aims – both in peace and in war – is grand strategy. Grand strategy – as a concept and a necessity – has its skeptics.[14] The term has been with us since the early 1800s, but no common definition has emerged.[15] Grand strategy is how nations use their power, ideally in a coordinated manner. This should be directed at specific political aims. Some works on grand strategy mix the political aim being sought with the strategy being pursued to obtain it, making the analytical error of not distinguishing between them.[16] Others deem the political aim grand strategy.[17] Some discuss the advantages of specific grand strategies, and *then* examine the nation's interests and political aims.[18] This places the grand strategy cart before the political horse.

The elements of national power can be divided into four dominant realms: diplomatic, informational, military, and economic, which are sometimes represented by the acronym DIME. There are numerous additions made to this, finance, intelligence, and law (FIL) being the most common, but intelligence is part of the "I," and other add-ons generally mark tools for implementing or "operationalizing" the DIME's respective elements. Finance, for example, is an economic strategy tool, while law is part of all four. Grand strategy is *not* the end being sought but the course for getting there – the ways – that considers the necessary means.[19] "National strategy" is sometimes used as a synonym.[20] "Doctrine" often serves as another, but this also describes the methods military forces use to implement operations.

Some insist grand strategy must necessarily be for the long term, an artificial requirement ignoring the reality of changing political aims and an international environment in perpetual flux. If the aims and situation change, the grand strategy might need to as well. Other artificial requirements include the insistence that grand strategy only applies to wartime and that small states can't have one. All countries (and even non-state actors) can have a grand strategy, or even multiple grand strategies, as all nations have interests and threats, and these usually generate political aims. Different aims often require different utilizations of national power. The reality of the possession of multiple political aims, combined with how nations variously use their elements of national power, destroys a basic conceit of much grand strategy literature: that a nation can simply pick a grand strategy that addresses all its strategic challenges. This mistake arises from analysis mistakenly rooted in the ways or means used to pursue an aim rather than the aim itself.

THE ELEMENTS OF GRAND STRATEGY

By beginning with the political aims, this book examines US diplomatic, informational, military, and economic strategies, though it emphasizes the diplomatic and military. US actions in any of these arenas are invariably intertwined with the others and cannot be adequately considered in isolation from one another or the political aims being sought. This provides a picture of how America has used its power and for what purposes.

DIPLOMATIC STRATEGY

In diplomatic strategy (or foreign affairs) the key question is: how has the US used its diplomatic power in pursuit of its political aims? There are, of course, many variables, but among the most important are alliance relations, interactions with friendly or partner nations, and dealings with rivals, bad actors, and enemies. When examining American debates over foreign affairs, one must also keep in mind the effects of domestic politics.[21]

A related myth is America's supposed isolationist tradition, meaning that the United States sought at times to separate itself from the world and remains in danger of doing so again. The US has never done this. A trading nation from its inception, America has always engaged abroad. Trade, evangelism, immigration, and the currency of ideas characterized America's internationalism from its founding. Its struggle for independence against Britain saw the nascent republic forge with France its first military alliance. What alarmed American statesmen was foreign *entanglement*. Don't confuse reluctance to being dragged into Europe's internecine struggles with burying one's head in the international sand.[22]

The isolationist canard first appeared in the 1890s as an imperialist bludgeon used against political foes. One of its most important propagators was expansionist and naval theorist Alfred Thayer Mahan. Politicians and pundits continue Mahan's approach. When President Bill Clinton failed to get his Nuclear Test Ban Treaty through the Senate, he claimed to see "signs of a new isolationism." President George W. Bush, in defense of his war in Iraq, wrote in 2006: "We choose leadership over isolationism."[23] The period often deemed the most isolationist – the years between the world wars – were marked by particularly intense US action abroad. America has always been involved with the world beyond – both in peace and in war. What follows makes this clear.

INFORMATION STRATEGY

The information realm can be viewed as a stool with four legs: ideas (which can include values), intelligence, strategic communication or propaganda, and public affairs or public information. The ideas underpinning America – liberty, personal freedom, democracy, and others – are critical for motivating Americans and telling the nation's story abroad. Intelligence is key for understanding others and threats. Strategic communication (*propaganda* is what other states do) is usually directed at competitors. Public affairs efforts, which are often aimed internally, provide information on the nation's activities. The latter two are sometimes branded narrative creation. Having the world see the picture we wish to present – not that painted by enemies – is important for the preservation of American freedoms at home, and the building and maintenance of respect for them abroad. It is also a tool for achieving the political ends that secure US interests. So-called "soft power" is a nebulous form of influence difficult to wield in the pursuit of political aims.[24] Information strategy is inextricably tied to diplomacy.

MILITARY STRATEGY

Much of US grand strategy has been driven by preparation for war, waging it, and its aftermath. It is a myth to think Americans historically rejected Clausewitz's dictum that war is a political tool used in pursuit of the nation's aims.[25] The key question here: how has the US used its military power – in peace and in war (in war one uses military force) – to achieve its political aims? This, of course, has many facets, all based upon the circumstances and the aims being pursued. We also consider the ideas driving the development and application of American military power. Military strategy is exemplified by such things as attrition and simultaneous pressure, and is "the link between military means and political ends, the scheme for how to make one produce the other."[26] Plans and strategy are not the same. War plans are the tools by which nations execute strategy.[27]

It is impossible to talk about an "American way of war." First, Americans were originally Europeans, predominantly English, and derived their warfighting methods from a European military heritage. Second, Americans have always absorbed warfighting ideas and techniques from other places, just like everyone else. Adaptation is a hallmark of military learning. Third, war has a certain perverse logic no matter who is fighting.[28] Examples of

American tactical innovation, which are generally the basis of such arguments, demonstrate not a uniquely American way of war but tactical innovation.

ECONOMIC STRATEGY

So much of America's power, particularly since the 1890s, derives from and rests upon American economic strength. Preserving and strengthening America's economic situation is critical and a perennial presidential concern. Domestic industrial and raw material production, foreign trade, technology investment, and infrastructure construction are among the key economic activities. The important question: how has the US developed and used its economic power in pursuit of its political aims?

A related myth is that the US became a great power because of dedication to free trade. The truth is more complex. George Washington and Alexander Hamilton supported tariffs to protect nascent American industries – particularly those important to national defense. In the late 1800s, "a protectionist America and a protectionist Germany both outperformed free trade Britain." "Free trade does not assure prosperity," historian Alfred Eckes wrote, "nor does protectionism automatically produce ruin."[29] Economic power is a critical tool of grand strategy. But economic conditions and connections remain in constant flux. Grasping what has worked, when, and under what circumstances is critically important.

Another myth among critics of US foreign relations is that America goes to war for economic reasons. Supporters of American intervention abroad have rarely pushed for action because of economic motivations, though their opponents generally accuse them of it. Other reasons weighed more heavily, particularly during the Cold War when credibility and maintaining commitments influenced US involvement in Korea, Vietnam, and other parts of what was then called the Third World. Developing states were never significant markets for US exports, which have gone overwhelmingly to developed nations. Washington certainly promotes foreign US business interests and has sometimes protected them with force, but US leaders rarely voice such things publicly from a fear of eliciting opposition from the American public, which exhibits an amusing *schadenfreude* toward the overseas business losses of wealthy Americans.[30] Economic sanctions, such as those placed upon Russia in 2022 because of its war against Ukraine, can fall into this realm, though they are inextricably tied to diplomacy.

ASSEMBLING THE PARTS

Ideally, the grand strategy realms work together in harness in pursuit of the aims. But this isn't always the case as sometimes administrations lack clear political aims and provide little guidance. The American machine of state then runs on its own. At other times there are clear aims and firm direction. Deciding these aims, and constructing coherent grand strategies for achieving them, demands leaders who are educated to think creatively and in a disciplined manner about the uses of American power and the purposes toward which it should be directed. Where do the nation's interests lie? How do we decide this? What should be achieved? How can American power be used to do this? What are the risks of action or inaction? What are the rewards? What, in the end, do we want the future America to look like? And what should be its role in the world?[31]

A FINAL WORD BEFORE WE BEGIN...

It would be incorrect to insist the US has always possessed a grand strategy or developed clear strategic paths. It's equally false to say it never has. Some may find it surprising that although past American leaders didn't always use terms recognizable to us or define their actions in the same manner, they thought and acted in ways familiar to and often more coherent than what we see today. The framework provided here is useful for analyzing the actions of any nation. I have applied it to the United States to paint a clearer picture of the nation's aims and strategic history. I hope it will teach readers how to *think* about political aims and grand strategy. We begin by examining America's first efforts to use its power.

PART I

FROM BACKWATER TO GREAT POWER

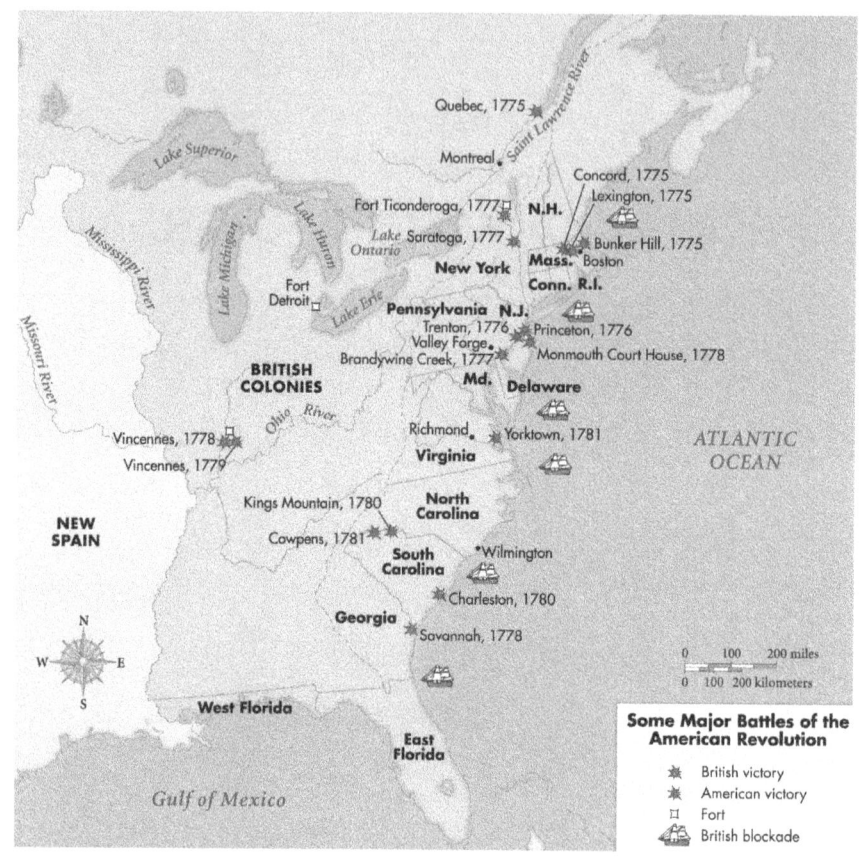

Map 1.1 Principal battles of the American Revolutionary War, 1775–83.
Universal Images Group North America LLC / Alamy.

1

THE FIGHT FOR SOVEREIGNTY, 1775–1801

THE INSURRECTIONISTS

America's founders were insurrectionists, rebels against the greatest imperial overlord of their age. The Americans, like most rebels, were weak and initially bereft of diplomatic, military, or economic power. But in the informational realm, the Americans had something of immense value – a powerful, infectious idea.

THE ORIGINS OF THE WAR FOR AMERICAN INDEPENDENCE, 1776–83

The most important Colonial idea was that the Americans should have a say in ruling themselves. Britain had long practiced "salutary neglect" toward the colonies, but 1763's conclusion of the French and Indian War (or Seven Years' War) left a victorious but indebted Britain eager to right its fiscal ship via a once traditional means: taxation. London expected its subjects to do their duty, including those in America, a demand made after Britain took France's Canadian lands, removing the primary threat to American security. The drive for a common response knit together thirteen colonies.[1]

Britain's Parliament passed the Sugar Act in April 1764, reducing the molasses tax by half, but this half London intended to collect. The Americans' reply was novel: Parliament had no right to tax them because the colonists hadn't elected any of its members. March 1765's Stamp Act imposed a levy on anything the Colonials printed. Opposition groups known as the Sons of Liberty formed; a protest petition followed. Parliament dropped the Stamp Act but insisted upon its authority over the colonies. The 1767 Townshend Acts followed, taxing imports such as tea, paint, and glass, and feeding the Colonial political awakening. Riots and protests produced tragedies like the 1770 Boston "Massacre," while Pennsylvanian John Dickinson argued the colonists could only be taxed by assemblies they elected. Parliament eventually repealed the taxes – except that on tea.[2]

On December 16, 1773, Americans dressed as Indians famously staged the Boston Tea Party by dumping tea into the harbor. Parliament acted against growing Colonial lawlessness by closing Boston harbor pending restitution, occupying the city, and suspending Massachusetts' government. The colonists replied with Philadelphia's September 1774 Continental Congress. It branded British actions the "Intolerable Acts," dispatched a petition listing thirteen grievances, and used trade as a weapon for the first time by halting British imports and restricting American exports. Colonial committees formed to enforce Congress' rulings began seizing local reins of power, including over the militia. The British attempted conciliation. The colonists prepared for war by stealing British gunpowder and stockpiling military supplies.[3]

Under the direction of Lord Frederick North, first minister to the king and head of government, Parliament declared Massachusetts in rebellion on February 9, 1775, ordered its leaders arrested and Colonial arsenals seized, and authorized Lieutenant General Thomas Gage, Massachusetts' military governor, to use force to reassert control. On April 18, 1775, Gage dispatched 800 soldiers from Boston to seize powder and weapons stored at a village named Concord. American militia assembled on the green at Lexington blocked their advance. A firefight ensued from which the Americans fled. Another skirmish at Concord followed. On their return march to Boston, the British endured numerous, uncoordinated attacks from Colonial militia (who proved exceptionally poor marksmen) and retaliated by looting the homes of suspected attackers and killing the occupants. The Americans put their version of events on a fast ship and had it to the London newspapers two weeks before the British government received Gage's report.[4]

The violence enflamed the Americans, who overthrew the Royal governors in the lower thirteen colonies. Even in areas where they were a minority, the insurrectionists seized control.[5]

AN INSURRECTION LIKE NO OTHER

America first learned to use its power – slight though it was – in war's crucible. That the War for American Independence began as an insurrection shaped its nature. It also became a revolutionary struggle as the Americans sought to rule themselves in a manner and on a scale not attempted since ancient Rome. But doing this required the revolt succeed. Insurrections generally hinge upon three factors: the support of the people; the control of internal or external insurgent sanctuary; and whether the rebels have outside aid.

THE FIGHT FOR SOVEREIGNTY, 1775–1801

THE POLITICAL AIMS

At the Second Continental Congress convened in Philadelphia on May 10, 1775, its members disagreed upon *the* fundamental issue: for what purpose were the Americans fighting? The core dispute: should they pursue reconciliation or independence? Moderates wanted "redress of grievances." Radicals wanted independence but balked at open advocacy; public opinion sat not in their camp. Congress adopted Jefferson's Declaration of the Causes and Necessity of Taking Up Arms. It listed American grievances, expressed loyalty to the Crown, and insisted upon self-government but not independence. The key complaint: Parliament's insistence it could "of right make Laws to bind us in all Cases whatsoever." The colonists fought not for independence, but "in defence of the Freedom that is our Birthright."[6]

Congress declared a trade embargo, created a Continental Army in June 1775 and navy in October, improved the militia, raised defense funds, and, in November, a committee to communicate with European states. Congress believed Canada should be part of "the American union" and wanted control over the lands between the Appalachian Mountains and Mississippi River. Its actions and expansionist territorial aims didn't align with seeking "redress of grievances."[7]

To Britain, the value of the object was high. London insisted the rebels recognize Parliament's supremacy and right to rule; the shape of British constitutionalism was at stake. King George III and others saw the American lands as the Empire's jewel and believed losing them threatened national survival. On August 23, 1775, London issued a Proclamation of Rebellion. It forbade all trade with the rebellious colonies and allowed the capture of American ships, but London never abandoned efforts to craft a political solution.[8]

The conflict established one of the great traditions of American grand strategy: entering a war unprepared. Here, the Americans had little choice, but it took the nation's leaders generations to correct this. When the war began, America possessed neither army nor navy. Each state had a regulated militia, but preparation varied, and their appearance when summoned was as unpredictable as their performance in battle. The presence of Continental Army troops usually helped both, but, if not used quickly, militia often went home.[9] The seafaring Americans also had an enormous merchant fleet.

ASSESSMENT AND PREPARATION

When fighting began, 2.5 million people lived in the thirteen colonies. (See Map 1.1.) Perhaps 15 to 20 percent were Loyalists. Others were pacifists, another 600,000 were African-American, generally slaves. Legions preferred neutrality. On June 14, 1775, Congress approved an army of 30,000. Theoretically, the Colonials could raise several hundred thousand soldiers, but this assumes widespread support for rebellion and a willingness to serve. Congress named as the army's head Virginian George Washington, a militia veteran of the French and Indian War, respected political figure, and the only representative to wear a uniform to the Continental Congress. It established a board of war to run the conflict, one replaced by a secretary of war in 1781, and three military departments with their own armies, essentially the northern, middle, and southern, all under Washington's overall command.[10]

London was unprepared, which gave the Americans a year to build their force. The British army in April 1775 numbered 27,000; 7,000 in North America. The population of England, Scotland, and Wales was 8 million, Ireland around 4 million. Britain possessed an enormous colonial empire and hired some 30,000 soldiers from six German states, a common practice. London's task became subduing a vast area stretching from Maine to Georgia, and from the Atlantic Ocean to the Appalachians. The British estimated that with 50,000 men, and three to four years, they could defeat the rebels.[11]

In May 1775, Gage received 6,500 reinforcements and three Major Generals, Sir William Howe, Sir Henry Clinton, and Sir John Burgoyne. The Americans discovered the enemy's plan to fortify the Dorchester Heights dominating Boston, and replied by entrenching on Breed's and Bunker Hills on the Charlestown peninsula on the night of June 16. The British took the position on June 18 on the third assault but suffered 40 percent casualties.[12] The British nearly always captured any Colonial position they wanted, whether field, fort, or city, but always paid a price in casualties their small army could hardly bear. Britain's manpower limits made it susceptible to an attritional strategy.

COLONIAL GRAND STRATEGY: THE FIRST PHASE

Ideally, a government uses its elements of national power to achieve its political aims. But with their political aim being "redress of grievances," meaning Britain addressing differences over taxation and political rights, some Colonials' actions made questionable strategic sense.

Canada refused to rise despite Congressional appeals, and in June 1775 Congress prohibited its invasion. But Congress grew fearful that Britain controlling Canada would mean London raising the Indians, invading, and potentially isolating New England, and threatening the American army besieging Boston. Word that Canada's governor general, Sir Guy Carleton, intended to recapture Fort Ticonderoga in upstate New York (which the Americans had seized in May 1775), and the same region's Caughnawaga Indians deciding to fight for King George galvanized Congress to act. It approved an invasion on June 27, 1775, aiming to convince Canada to join the rebellion. Driving Britain from Canada also meant Indian neutrality, while taking Montreal and Quebec would force London to abandon its forts in the American interior. American intelligence reported a light British hold on Canada and that its people would welcome the rebels as liberators. There were also fewer than 700 British troops.[13]

On August 20, 1775, Washington proposed supplementing Congress' invasion with what became Benedict Arnold's expedition up Maine's Kennebec River to Quebec. To Washington, this would divert Carleton from Congress's primary offensive under the capable Brigadier General Richard Montgomery. Montgomery departed Ticonderoga for Montreal in September with 1,000 men, took the city's surrender on November 13, 1775, and, on New Year's Eve, after uniting with Arnold, attacked the fortified city of Quebec in a blinding snowstorm. It was a debacle. Montgomery was killed and Arnold wounded.[14]

Meanwhile, Washington fought the war in Massachusetts. He had been promised an army of 20,000 but found on July 2 an unkept rabble of 14,000. Congress instructed him "to destroy or make prisoners of all persons, who now are, or who hereafter shall appear in arms against the good people of the United Colonies." He was told to use his best judgment and given a directive that governed much of how he formulated strategy over the next eight years: to hold a council of war with his generals before conducting operations. Washington, who respected British skill and professionalism, and thought Colonial success required the same, began melding the militia and volunteers into a British-style army. Others believed the militia sufficient and a standing army a threat to Colonial freedoms, hurdles Washington had to overcome. He relied on militia in innumerable ways, including for internal security and local defense, but quickly realized their limits.[15]

Washington's weakness in comparison to the enemy meant he could do little beyond prepare. But at the end of summer 1775, he launched naval forces by recruiting privateers (government-licensed raiders) to attack British merchant shipping, which Congress encouraged. Their primary task: seize vessels bringing provisions to the British in Boston. American privateers eventually took about 2,000 British ships. State navies and the establishment of the Continental Navy followed, as did the conversion of merchant ships to vessels of war and construction of new ones. The Colonials used sea power primarily to attack British commerce, as defensive military action on inland waterways, and in a few spectacular raids by John Paul Jones on the British Isles. After 1778, America's French ally brought desperately needed naval power.[16]

Washington's immediate concern remained Boston, where the guns of Britain's fleet protected its entrenched force. In July 1775, Congress told Washington to expel the British from Boston; he searched for a way to win the war "by some decisive Stroke." After nearly a year, and consideration of several risky schemes, the Americans placed cannon on Dorchester Heights, threatening the garrison and its ships. The British abandoned the city on March 17, 1776, sailing for Nova Scotia.[17]

The Colonials failed in Canada, but demonstrated creativity in contesting British power, particularly at sea. Something generally overlooked is that early in the war the Americans constructed a military strategy with related arms: the siege of Boston, commerce raiding at sea, and a two-pronged invasion of Canada.

BRITAIN'S WAR: REASSESSMENT AND STRATEGY

After being driven from the thirteen colonies, Britain faced the challenge of conquering a territory of 360,000 square miles. The nearly 1,000 miles from Boston to Charleston is the distance between Antwerp and Madrid. Britain's ocean supply line stretched 3,500 miles. Lord George Germain, the colonial secretary, dominated Britain's war effort. He believed a rebel minority controlled America and that a quick, heavy blow would force the Americans into line and break Congress. This, combined with a blockade, would encourage people to turn to the Loyalists, who would secure British control.[18]

In October 1775, William Howe took command of the British forces stretched from Nova Scotia to Florida; Carleton held a separate Canada command. In February 1776, Lord Richard Howe, the general's brother, was appointed to head the North American fleet. King George III failed to appoint a commander-in-chief of the army in America until 1778, producing a divided command. New England was considered the rebellion's heart, and its recapture the quickest path to victory. In an offensive approved in January 1776, Howe planned to seize New York City, advance up the Hudson River, America's most important water route, and link with Carleton's forces pushing from Canada while securing the river crossings, a plan fed by French and Indian War experience. A two-pronged attack against Massachusetts would follow. Howe hoped to force a battle in New York, where Washington had moved his force, to crush the American army. This, he believed, was the quickest way to end the war.[19]

A NEW AIM: SOVEREIGNTY

As Howe and Washington prepared, the Continental Congress changed America's political aim. On July 4, 1776, it became independence. Congress was now convinced both of its possibility and necessity. The failed Canada invasion furnished one catalyst. Britain's determination to fight provided another. The king refused Congress' Olive Branch Petition calling for an Anglo-American Union and virtual American autonomy and declared Congress illegal. Public opinion had also shifted, fed by Virginia governor Lord Dunmore offering freedom to slaves willing to fight the rebels, Britain hiring German mercenaries, and Thomas Paine's *Common Sense*, which argued vehemently for independence. Foreign assistance – meaning French – now proved indispensable. Only by declaring independence could America hope to secure this. France gained nothing helping an America that planned to reconcile with its mercantilist master; an independent America could at least offer its trade.[20]

The Declaration of Independence spelled out the Colonial political aims:

> the Representatives of the united [sic] States of America, in General Congress ... do, in the Name, and by Authority of the good People of these Colonies, solemnly publish and declare, That these united Colonies are, and of Right ought to be Free and Independent States, that they are Absolved from all Allegiance to the British Crown, and that all political connection between them and the State of Great Britain, is and ought to be totally dissolved; and that as Free and Independent States, they have full Power to levy War, conclude Peace, contract Alliances, establish Commerce, and to do all other Acts and Things which Independent States may of right do.[21]

The changing of the political aim alters the war's nature, which means reassessment should occur, with particular attention paid to the internal and external effects. This isn't escalation. Aims change. Means escalate.

DIPLOMATIC AND ECONOMIC STRATEGY

In July 1776, Congress sought recognition from abroad using the lure of American trade. The US sought "free trade," which meant trading "on equal terms with other nations." Benjamin Franklin and John Adams drafted a treaty with two options to guide US representatives: reciprocal national treatment, which meant US trade would be treated as if conducted by citizens of that nation, and unconditional most-favored-nation status, meaning Americans paid the same tariff rates as others with this standing.[22]

COLONIAL MILITARY STRATEGY: THE SECOND PHASE

In late May 1776, Washington and the Continental Congress decided General Washington "would make a maximum effort to defend New York." Washington believed Britain's major blows would fall in Canada and New York, with the enemy trying to seize the lakes in upstate New York and the Hudson, both critical for movement, communication, and supply, and unite their prongs. Worse, he thought America unprepared to meet them in manpower and armaments.[23]

But Washington believed surviving the 1776 campaign season would place the Americans "on such a footing as to bid defiance to the utmost malice of the British Nation and those in alliance with her." The question was how. Washington hoped that if not victorious in the field he could at least force the British "to wade through much blood & Slaughter before they can carry any part of our Works, If they carry 'em at all." He planned to fight what he later called a "War of Posts." He would sap British strength via attrition by fighting from fixed positions in New York City as the Americans had at Bunker Hill. American forces lacked the training and discipline to stand against the enemy in the open, but American leaders believed they had a chance behind fortifications. But as summer wore on, Washington grew pessimistic about defending New York City and its environs with forces dispersed sometimes 15 miles apart. Major General Henry Knox, Washington's artillery chief, later described the flaw in the American decision to fight here: "Islands separated from the main by navigable waters are not to be defended by a people without a navy against a nation who can send a powerful fleet to interrupt the communications."[24]

Howe's troops began landing on Staten Island on June 3, 1776. They sat until August 22 – seven weeks – as the summer unwound. Instead of quickly forcing a battle, Howe waited for additional troops and equipment. He also faced a critical constraint: he had the bulk of Britain's army and would receive only a few reinforcements, which fed his caution. He had intended to land on Manhattan and compel a battle but changed his operational plan after learning Washington divided his army between Long Island and Manhattan. As Britain controlled the waterways, Howe could choose where to fight. He also remembered Bunker Hill and knew the Americans had had nearly a year to fortify. He decided to first strike Long Island, methodically grind away the American forces (lowering his casualties by bringing superior numbers to bear), destroy the American army, seize territory, and erode Colonial morale. Combined with a blockade, his campaign would bring the Americans to the negotiating table, which aligned with his own desire for reconciliation, another factor underlying the shift. But this would take longer than his original plan, and time benefits the defender.[25]

On August 21, 1776, Washington reported intelligence that the British were finally "upon the point of striking the long-expected Stroke." Washington had 19,000 troops, the British 31,000, who began landing on Long Island the next day. Howe then attacked Washington's strategy. Instead of assaulting the American fortifications on Brooklyn Heights, he waged a cautious campaign that preserved his forces while decimating the Colonials. By the end of August, he had taken their Long Island posts and broken their morale. The militia proved particularly despondent and left in large numbers. On the night of August 29, 1776, Washington's Long Island force escaped across the East River to Manhattan, protected by what many saw as a providential fog.[26]

Washington's "War of Posts" was an example of scriptwriting in that success depended upon the enemy doing *exactly* as the Americans wanted as well as "the tacticization of strategy," meaning substituting tactical, battlefield action for military strategy, meaning a larger idea for the use of military force.[27] It is nearly impossible to achieve a political aim by depending upon tactical results.

While Washington fought Howe, the Northern Army, now led by Benedict Arnold, a former merchant and pharmacist from Connecticut, countered the British offensive from Canada. Arnold didn't believe Carleton could advance up Lake Champlain before September because of the quantity of supplies needed for the fleet being built. Arnold advised fighting a delaying action to thwart the British until the following year by reinforcing Fort Ticonderoga and building a fleet on Lake Champlain. Arnold was ordered to delay the enemy until winter. On October 4, 1776, he fought the British to a standstill off Lake Champlain's Valcour Island, slipping the noose under a night fog. He escaped southward to Crown Point, New York, burned his ships, and led his men to Ticonderoga. On October 20, the first snow fell. Carleton reached Ticonderoga, refused to attack, and withdrew north in early November. British and American commentators have credited Arnold with saving the Colonial cause.[28] One wonders about the result if Carleton's army had joined Howe's.

PART I: FROM BACKWATER TO GREAT POWER

A STRATEGIC SHIFT: PROTRACTING THE WAR WITH A FABIAN STRATEGY

On September 7, 1776, Major General Nathanael Greene launched the line of thought underpinning a new American strategy:

> The City and Island of New York are no objects for us; we are not to bring them in Competition with the General Interest of America. Part of the army already has met with a defeat; the Coungry [sic] is struck with a pannick; any Cappital loss at this time may ruin the cause. Tis our business to study to avoid any considerable misfortune, and to take post where the Enemy will be obliged to fight us and not we them.[29]

In this last sentence of the lapsed Quaker merchant from Rhode Island we find the beginnings of the American Fabian strategy: fight where advantageous and avoid a decisive defeat that would fatally wound the cause. The idea, a form of a strategy of protraction, came from Roman history. Fabius Maximus Cunctator, or Fabius Maximus "the Delayer," was a Roman general during the Second Punic War (218–201 BC). During Hannibal's invasion of Italy, unable to defeat the Carthaginians in the field, Fabius simply refused to fight a major battle. He kept his army in hilly terrain to thwart Hannibal's cavalry superiority, while bleeding the enemy with small detachments and raids to erode their strength and prevent their recruiting.[30]

Washington valued Greene's advice. This – and not a little desperation – produced a new strategy. Washington informed Congress of its risks and rewards:

> I am sensible a retreating Army is incircled with difficulties, that the declining an Engagement subjects a General to reproach and that the Common cause may be in some measure affected by the discouragements which it throws over the minds of many; nor am I insensible of the contrary effects, if a brilliant stroke could be made with any Probability of success, especially after our loss upon Long Island: but when the fate of America may be at stake on the Issue; when the Wisdom of cooler moments and experienced Men have decided that we should protract the War if Possible; I cannot think it safe or wise to adopt a different System, when the season for Action draws so near a close.[31]

Washington's shift was perhaps the war's critical strategic move. In summer 1777 his aide, Alexander Hamilton, penned a cogent assessment of American strategy and its effects on the British, one worth quoting:

> I know the comments that some people will make on our Fabian conduct. It will be imputed either to cowardice or weakness: But the more discerning,

I trust, will not find it difficult to conceive that it proceeds from the truest policy.... The liberties of America are an infinite stake. We should not play a desperate game for it or put it upon the issue of a single cast of the die. The loss of one general engagement may effectually ruin us, and it would certainly be folly to hazard it, unless our resources for keeping an army were to end, and some decisive blow was absolutely necessary; or unless our strength was so great as to give certainty of success. Neither is the case. America can in all probability maintain its army for years.... It is therefore Howe's business to make the most of his present strength, and as he is not numerous enough to conquer and garrison as he goes, his only hope lies in fighting us and giving a general defeat in one blow.... Their affairs will be growing worse – our's [sic] better; – so that delay will ruin them. It will serve to perplex and fret them, and precipitate them into measures, that we can turn to good account. Our business then is to avoid a General engagement and waste the enemy away by constantly goading their sides, in a desultory teazing way.[32]

Washington chose a tough path, one for a weaker force. Success required cooperation from other commanders and support from political leaders and the people. A Fabian strategy strains the state's fibers by demanding an irreplaceable commodity: time. Success requires resisting the temptation to fight a major battle too early or under disadvantageous circumstances. This was difficult for the aggressive Washington. It also demands incremental successes. Protracting a war means betting your people will support the war longer than the enemy's. The clock is ticking. Successes slow your clock and accelerate the enemy's. It also requires keeping an army in the field to threaten the opponent and limit his or her options. Victories help here as no one joins an army that only loses and runs away. It also requires sanctuary, someplace to run to, which the colonial vastness provided. Timely flight requires good intelligence. Washington did his utmost to secure agents and information, and unknowingly echoed Sun Tzu's *Art of War*: "I beg you to take every possible means in your power, to find out the designs of the Enemy and What their plan of Operation is – do not hesitate at Expence." This observation on Fabius' war fits Washington's: "Nothing makes greater demands on loyalty and morale than a plea for patience, a promise of a long war, and a failure to strike back while a foreign army occupies territory of your friends and threatens your own."[33]

Though the Americans decided in September 1776 to adopt a Fabian strategy, both Washington and Greene initially failed to restrain their natural aggressiveness or abandon the War of Posts. During September's second week they dithered over defending New York City and Manhattan Island's Fort Washington. Greene's insistence helped assure the latter and the Americans fought for a fixed position, suffering one of their worst defeats of the war when it fell on November 16. Brigadier General Thomas Mifflin complained bitterly that the Colonials should have "adhered to the Fabian plan."[34]

Howe, meanwhile, mounted a cautious campaign on Manhattan. His forces landed at Kip's Bay on September 15, between the divided Americans. But Howe's pauses and dilatoriness squandered several opportunities to destroy the fractured American forces. Washington began abandoning Manhattan on October 18. After 125 days, Howe achieved the operational aim of his campaign – the capture of New York City – but he failed in his most important task: to destroy Washington's army. Tench Tilghman, Washington's secretary, wrote: "we have done greatly in stopping the career of Monsr Howe with the finest army that ever appeared in America, opposed to as bad a one as ever appeared in any part of the Globe."[35]

In autumn 1776, Washington's army fled Howe's pursuit by retreating across New Jersey, which passed into British hands. Washington, beaten but not defeated, looked for opportunities to strike back. He pushed his commanders to gather troops and information in the hope of recovering their fortunes. He looked for chances to hurt the enemy with militia, issuing mid December orders to various commanders to use detachments to harass the British whenever possible. The partisan war was about to heat up.[36]

Washington and his generals possessed great familiarity with the military manuals addressing "Partizan Warfare" or *Petite Guerre* (Little War). Washington first suggested this mode of fighting in July 1776, proposing a "Partizan Party" for operations against the British on Staten Island.[37] It fed his Fabian strategy. The Americans used militia and detachments of regular troops to harass the British, ambush their messengers and foraging parties, attack their supply lines, and so on, stretching, tying down, and depleting the enemy's resources and, more importantly – manpower. "Partisan War" should not be confused with modern-day theory on guerrilla warfare, a common mistake because the tactical implementation is similar.

In December 1776, the American effort reached its lowest ebb. On December 12, a desperate Congress entrusted Washington with near-dictatorial powers on defense issues for the next six months. Thomas Paine's *The American Crisis* appeared on December 19. His words again decisively strengthened public opinion favoring the American cause. On December 20, Washington told Congress: "We find Sir, that the Enemy are daily gathering strength from the disaffected; This strength, like a Snowball by rolling, will increase, unless some means can be devised to check effectually, the progress of the Enemy's Arms."[38]

Facing the dissolution of his army because of expiring enlistments, Washington famously crossed the Delaware River from his Pennsylvania base and attacked Trenton and Princeton in late December, scoring two victories that proved enormous boons to Colonial morale and the American cause. Supplementing Washington's offensive was militia with orders to prosecute a partisan war against the British occupation of New Jersey. In the winter campaign that followed, Washington excelled. He maintained his regular army, which forced Howe to concentrate his, and used intense partisan activity to recover most of New Jersey. By winter's end, Howe retained only Brunswick and Amboy on New Jersey's shore, and had only 14,000 troops fit for duty.[39]

THE 1777-78 CAMPAIGN

By mid January 1777, Howe planned to take Philadelphia, the erstwhile Colonial capital, and defeat Washington's army, seeing here the keys to victory. Meanwhile, Major General Burgoyne proposed a plan for an advance from Canada supported by a light push down the Mohawk Valley. He intended to take the lakes in upstate New York and Fort Ticonderoga, and then, depending upon circumstances, move down the Hudson to link with Howe, thus reducing New England. Germain approved both plans. Accompanying his failure to coordinate between the commanders was an understanding that Howe would *not* support Burgoyne's march on Albany. Britain also lacked a plan for after reaching the city.[40]

Washington's preservation of his army and ability to hang on Britain's heels and strike detachments made it impossible for Howe to safely move the roughly 100 miles overland against Philadelphia. To hedge against Washington attacking Burgoyne and enable him to operate on the Hudson if Washington moved north, Howe took his army to Philadelphia by sea via the Delaware River. Howe hoped to destroy Washington's army by forcing a fight for Philadelphia. In concentrating his force, he abandoned New Jersey and its Loyalists to insurgent retribution.[41]

Washington, unsure of British plans, feared the Canada drive was a feint to draw off his army. Taking the bait would leave Philadelphia to Howe, which he suspected was the general's operational objective. He dispatched some regulars northward and ordered them supplemented with militia. Howe, meanwhile, spent the spring and summer preparing, and landed south of Philadelphia on August 25. Washington wanted to avoid battle and not risk his army for any geographical position, even Philadelphia. But public opinion and political pressure dictated otherwise. He met Howe's

16,000 men with 14,000 of his own at Brandywine on September 11, 1777. Washington lost, but Howe failed to destroy the American army. Howe dispatched Lord Charles Cornwallis to seize Philadelphia. Howe's slowness and decision to move by sea meant he ended the campaigning season in Philadelphia instead of helping Burgoyne.[42]

Burgoyne certainly needed it. His campaign began in late June. Determined American resistance and a relief column stopped the Mohawk Valley arm. Meanwhile Burgoyne, commanding 8,000 men, took Forts George and Ticonderoga, then Fort Edwards on the Hudson River, 30 miles north of Albany. He could have advanced immediately and seized the city, but paused to gather thirty days of supplies, then pushed southward on September 13. The rough terrain and an unnecessarily large baggage and artillery train slowed his movements. The American response from the beginning was to dispatch militia to hang on his haunches and tail. They soon numbered in the thousands, driven by Burgoyne's threats to unleash the Indians and the murder of Jane McCrea by Burgoyne's Indian allies, something American leaders heavily publicized. They cut Burgoyne's communications and destroyed foraging parties as the Americans massed 11,000 regular troops and militia. Burgoyne launched the Battle of Bemis Heights on September 19 and attacked the Americans again at Freeman's Farm on October 7. The Americans under Major General Horatio Gates delivered key Colonial victories and Burgoyne surrendered at Saratoga on October 17, 1777.[43]

If what came to be called Britain's Hudson Valley plan had resulted in control of the Hudson line and the highlands as hoped, Benedict Arnold insisted it would have allowed the British to strangle Washington's army by depriving it of supplies and reinforcements. Even if true, Britain would have lacked sufficient troops to subdue New England and exploit their success. Moreover, Washington's army proved quite capable of starving on its own. It went into winter quarters at Valley Forge shortly before Christmas 1777 and was soon reduced to famine and rags. Congress lacked the authority to tax to fund the army, and most of the states refused to levy their people to support it or fill their enlistment quotas. Despite the obstacles, a drilled American army of 12,000 emerged in the spring.[44]

GLOBAL WAR, 1778–83

It is a common misconception that Burgoyne's surrender at Saratoga produced the French decision to enter the war. Paris had already concluded that March 1778 was its optimal entry time as its naval rearmament plan would be complete. France also needed Spain by its side, and Spain proved a tough sell. Madrid feared the American revolt set a bad example for its extensive empire and saw no reason to join. Word of the British surrender at Saratoga helped France's argument.[45]

DIPLOMATIC AND ECONOMIC STRATEGY

In January 1778, in response to French inquiries, the Americans replied that a treaty of commerce and friendship with Paris would stop any Colonial accord with London granting less than independence. The French proposed this treaty and a military alliance allowing France to decide when it entered the war. The Americans preferred immediately but grasped the offer, signing two treaties on February 4, 1778. France recognized US independence, and both agreed to not make peace until America secured this aim. Later, France sealed its recruitment of Spain with a covert April 1779 pact. The coalition's members had different political aims, some disliked by their allies, a reality of coalition warfighting. For example, Spain sought Gibraltar (among other things) but viewed American independence as a threat to its imperial possessions. France sought chiefly to weaken Britain and strengthen its position in Europe. Upon learning of America's secret treaties with France, Lord North tried to end the war by repealing the "Intolerable Acts," granting the colonies freedom from Parliament's taxes, and dispatching what became known as the Carlisle Commission to negotiate. The Americans rebuffed it all. France broke relations with Britain in May; its war began on June 16, 1778.[46]

With the entry of France, Spain, and later the Netherlands, which Britain attacked in 1780, partially because of its support for the colonists, a localized colonial rebellion became a global war. Clandestine French economic and military assistance had already helped secure the victories that led to Burgoyne's Saratoga surrender. But now Paris and Madrid provided the outside support key to an insurrection's success and everything the Colonials lacked: money, skilled troops, and naval power. After 1778, America's finances were so shattered it's doubtful it could have maintained anything other than guerrilla forces without French funds. The Colonial cause might have perished without foreign assistance.[47]

Financing the war proved difficult. Congress had no authority to tax, yet financial responsibility, and Americans weren't ready to give them power to do what they were rebelling against. Congress resorted to printing money – $241,550,000 – before stopping in 1780. Abundance destroyed the currency's value and fueled inflation, something Franklin justified as a fair form of taxation because it hit everyone's purchasing power. Subsidies came from France and Spain, and later loans, including from Holland and private sources. Congress eventually began issuing certificates – essentially IOUs – for goods needed by the army. Meanwhile, the war's pressures encouraged the expansion of the American industrial base, particularly in iron and steel.[48]

Efforts to place the new nation on a sound economic footing presaged future arguments about government's economic role. In 1780, Hamilton proposed a national bank with no hope of approval. Financier Robert Morris suggested Congress assume the public debt and gain the power to levy taxes. He also called for a national bank, which Congress established. It opened in January 1782, though undercapitalized and thus incapable of fulfilling Morris' hope that its notes become a national currency. The 1778 Franco-American Treaty of Amity and Commerce granted France most-favored-nation trading rights, but the US only received this in French national ports and not its colonial ones. From the US side, the problem was that each of the thirteen states regulated its own trade.[49]

THE WAR IN THE NORTH

In the wake of Burgoyne's surrender at Saratoga, certain of France's entry and fearing Spain's as well, the British reassessed and concluded America could not be reconquered, partially because this would require 80,000 men, a number impossible to raise. They believed the navy had spent too much time cooperating with the army instead of halting shipping going to and from America. Both needed expanding. Britain concluded, correctly, that France had no interest in regaining its colonies in America and would instead strike the West Indies. This led to the decision to take 10,000 soldiers from America, which forced Howe's evacuation of Philadelphia, and redeployment of most of Britain's heavy ships from America.[50] Outside support quickly paid dividends for the rebels.

Washington believed London needed another blow on the scale of Saratoga before it would quit. By 1779, he had chosen New York City, London's primary stronghold and base in North America. Washington wanted a French fleet to blockade the harbor while an American army reduced the city. This remained his focus for the next three years, but his French ally prioritized Europe and the Caribbean. Poverty limited Washington's ability to mount offensive operations.[51]

Circumstances, though, pushed Washington to act against the Iroquois Confederation. Throughout 1778, fighting between Loyalists, Colonials, and their respective Indian allies engulfed the frontiers of New York and Pennsylvania. Atrocities by both sides were common. Washington hoped to drive the Iroquois into neutrality, eliminate their lands as British supply sources, and force London to deploy more men to defend Canada. Washington successfully feinted an invasion of Canada and sent an army of 4,000 into Iroquois territory. Its orders were to "lay waste all the settlements around ... that the country may not be merely *overrun* but *destroyed*," and to take as many prisoners as possible, regardless of age or sex. The August–September campaign didn't achieve Washington's objective but maimed the Iroquois ability to make war. The 1779 campaign broke the Iroquois Confederation and helped ensure America dominated the Trans-Allegheny. Similarly, in 1776–77, the four southern states – Virginia, the Carolinas, and Georgia – crushed a Cherokee rising.[52]

BRITAIN'S SOUTHERN CAMPAIGN

Britain's Southern Strategy emerged from its post-Saratoga reassessment. London judged the southern colonies more valuable than their northern brethren because they supplied naval stores and food. The northern states were a market for British goods, one London believed would return after the war. Britain's leaders decided to seize America south of the Potomac River. They believed it harbored numerous Loyalists who would turn out for the king – if enough British troops appeared to protect them – and saw the region's Indians and slaves as potential allies. Controlling the south would cut the primary transit routes for overseas trade supporting the rebellion, rob the north of desperately needed resources, demoralize it, and make it easier to reduce. Under Germain's plan, a small British force would liberate an area, train Loyalist troops to hold it, then push north and repeat. This was a version of what later eras called "Clear, Hold, and Build." Germain also ordered raids on the New England coast to destroy rebel supplies and impress upon Americans the war's reality.[53]

The British offensive began in South Carolina (they seized sparsely populated Georgia in 1778). Major General Benjamin Lincoln commanded the Americans. He had served under Washington and understood Fabian War but disliked this and decided to hold Charleston rather than preserve the army by withdrawing into the interior. Sir Henry Clinton, who now commanded in America, began landing troops near Charleston on February 11, 1780. He wanted Charleston intact as a point for gathering Loyalists, and exploited Britain's technical superiority by besieging the city. It began on April 1, 1780. The 5,500 defenders surrendered on May 12. Banastre

Tarleton's British force then defeated the Americans at Waxhaws on May 29, killing prisoners to terrorize the Americans. The twin victories secured a base for Britain's campaign and destroyed America's army in the south, enabling Britain to disperse its troops to hold down the cleared area. Clinton began pacifying South Carolina and implementing Germain's plan.[54]

Clinton believed Loyalist vengefulness would undermine the reestablishment of Royal rule and issued two proclamations to thwart this. On June 1, 1780, he offered pardons to anyone taking an oath of allegiance. This angered Loyalists, who wanted rebels punished. On June 3, Clinton released prisoners of war from their paroles and restored their rights while requiring an oath of loyalty and their support. Clinton's proclamation forced them to choose between serving the king or fighting him. After setting the house on fire, Clinton gave the keys to Cornwallis and his 4,000 men and sailed for New York. South Carolina erupted in a Colonial–Loyalist civil war. The British fed the conflagration by attacking the plantations of Thomas Sumter and Andrew Pickens, bringing back into the field two former partisan leaders. Congress, meanwhile, dispatched Gates south with an army. Gates, like Lincoln, also abandoned Washington's Fabian strategy. Cornwallis crushed Gates' force of 4,000 with one half the size on August 16 at Camden, South Carolina.[55]

The British had again destroyed formal Colonial resistance in the most southern colonies. But Gates' presence had inspired insurrection and Britain's pacification effort began coming apart. Cornwallis became skeptical about the Loyalists gaining the ability protect themselves without regular troops and concluded that securing South Carolina required controlling North Carolina. He led his main force toward Hillsborough, North Carolina, crossing the state line on September 26. A second prong of 1,000 Tory militia marched north from the post of Ninety-Six on the South Carolina frontier under the command of Major Patrick Ferguson. Ferguson's force was a diversion that also cleared the rebels from eastern South Carolina, many of whom fled over the Appalachian Mountains. On September 12, 1780, Ferguson threatened them with hangings and fire unless they submitted. This provoked one of the strangest incidents of the war. The inhabitants decided to save Ferguson the trip and formed an army in the Appalachian wilderness. Ferguson began withdrawing toward Cornwallis but decided to make a stand at King's Mountain, South Carolina. On October 6, the Over the Mountain Men killed Ferguson and scattered his army. Cornwallis retreated into South Carolina to hold it.[56]

Washington, meanwhile, worried that if Britain conquered North Carolina, Virginia would soon fall. On October 14, 1780, Washington offered command of the Southern Department to Nathanael Greene. Greene had served with Washington since the siege of Boston and for the two years prior was his quartermaster general. In this era, this meant not only managing logistics but also everything pertaining to moving and deploying the army. Before going south, Greene arranged the supplies and weapons he would need, a difficult task. The war in the south was different from that in the north, which Greene understood. There were fewer men to recruit, fewer artisans to help keep the army going, and large numbers of Loyalists. Most supplies had to come from the north, organized American resistance was all but gone, and the region suffered from war weariness. Georgia and South Carolina lacked Colonial governments, which were critical for furnishing troops and supplies; North Carolina had a weak one. Cornwallis now had 8,000 men, reinforcements coming, and plans to recruit more Loyalists and extend his conquest to North Carolina and Virginia while holding South Carolina and Georgia with a string of fortified positions.[57]

In Hillsborough Greene found a small detachment of Continental troops and 1,200 more at Charlotte with about 1,000 militia. Greene began rebuilding. An asset he did possess were partisan bands.[58] The question for Greene was how to use his scant forces to overcome the enemy. As one architect and a chief implementer of America's Fabian strategy, Greene knew very well what to do. He was accustomed to acting from a position of weakness and making – he said in a biblical allusion – "bricks without straw." In January 1780, he wrote:

> The Salvation of this country don't depend upon little strokes, nor should the great business of establishing a permanent army be neglected to pursue them. Partizan strokes in war are like the garnish of a table …They are most necessary and should not be neglected, and yet, they should not be pursued to the prejudice of more important concerns. You may strike a hundred strokes and reap little benefit from them, unless you have a good Army to take advantage of your success.… It is not a war of posts but a contest for states.[59]

He also understood how to use his regular and irregular forces, and what he risked:

> if both are employed in the partizan way until we have a more permanent force to appear before the enemy with confidence, happily we may regain all our losses. But if we put things to the hazard in our infant state before we have gathered sufficient strength to act with spirit and activity and meet a second misfortune all may be lost and the tide of sentiment among the people turn against you.[60]

Greene realized the tough constraints under which he operated. He faced dire logistical challenges which he made herculean efforts to overcome, and his enemy was superior both in numbers and skill. Greene did what few would advise: he divided his army, placing a significant element under Brigadier General Daniel Morgan. He explained why:

> It makes the most of my inferior force, for it compels my adversary to divide his, and holds him in doubt as to his own line of conduct. He cannot leave Morgan behind him to come at me, or his posts of Ninety-Six and Augusta would be exposed. And he cannot chase Morgan far, or prosecute his views upon Virginia, while I am here with the whole country open before me.[61]

Cornwallis replied by sending 1,150 men under Tarleton to eliminate Morgan while marching to block the retreat of any survivors. He would then move against Greene. Morgan destroyed Tarleton's force at the Cowpens on January 17, 1781. Greene united his forces and retreated north. Cornwallis pursued. Greene began massing troops and supplies with the intention of fighting at Guilford Courthouse. He dispatched his partisan leaders to lead militia against Cornwallis' rear areas and prevent the Loyalists in South Carolina from gathering. Cornwallis suffered the same problem as other British generals: the strength of the Continental Army was not a mortal threat, but wherever it appeared clouds of militia often turned out in support. And when Cornwallis concentrated against the Continentals, he left the countryside to American militia and irregulars.[62]

Greene resolved to retreat to Virginia, if needed. Cornwallis' aggressive pursuit combined with Greene's rapid withdrawal to rupture Cornwallis' supply lines, a devastation Greene furthered by sweeping the countryside of food. Bolstered by reinforcements, on March 15, 1781, Greene's 4,200 men met Cornwallis' 2,000 at Guilford Courthouse. Cornwallis' victory proved pyrrhic; he suffered 25 percent casualties, losses almost impossible to replace. Tarleton considered Greene's decision to give battle wise: an American victory would see Cornwallis' destruction while defeat meant little.[63]

Cornwallis withdrew to Wilmington, North Carolina, to resupply. Greene plunged into South Carolina as Cornwallis marched to Virginia to join the British forces there. Greene fought the British on several occasions, losing every time. But he forced British abandonment of many South Carolina posts. Greene implemented an aggressive form of Washington's Fabian War. He preserved his army and maintained the initiative despite being on the defense. He took much greater risks than Washington and could do so because neither he nor his army weighed on American public opinion as much as Washington and his.[64]

MILITARY VICTORY: YORKTOWN

Cornwallis' arrival in Virginia helped set the stage for the war's dénouement. He received orders to choose a safe post and send all the troops he could to New York City because Clinton feared a descent by Washington and French General Jean-Baptiste Rochambeau. Washington certainly wanted to take the city and kept his attention on it into the summer of 1781 despite pleas from the governors of South Carolina and Virginia to march south. Rochambeau received word on May 6 that a French fleet was heading to North America. Rochambeau convinced Washington to abandon their plans for attacking New York City and instead strike the British in Virginia. Washington agreed. On September 5, 1781, the French fleet wrested control of the Chesapeake from the British while the Franco-American forces moved to besiege Cornwallis at Yorktown. Cornwallis surrendered on October 19, 1781.[65]

POLITICAL VICTORY: THE PEACE

Lord North told the king it was impossible to continue the war because there was no political support. King George remained convinced losing America would destroy Britain as a great power and resisted making peace. Germain believed they could fight on and secure a settlement based upon what Britain held. By March 1782, North had lost the backing of the House of Commons and resigned. The replacement government ended with the death of its leader in four months, but July saw William Petty, Lord Shelburne, become first minister. He and his predecessor were both determined to make peace.[66]

The problem for all the powers was how. The complexities of peacemaking demand consideration of three key, intertwined factors: the political aims of the combatants, how military force should be used, and how the peace will be secured. The number of nations involved, and that each prioritized its own political aims, complicated the process. For example, the Americans wanted independence, but Spain preferred a colonial dependency that kept Britain and America bickering and was exploitable by Paris and Madrid.[67]

The Americans insisted they had achieved their aim of independence and wanted this enshrined in the final accord. Congress instructed America's delegates to consider France's views but to secure recognition of independence before negotiating with Britain to end the war. John Adams advised his fellow delegate, John Jay, to demand "a sovereignty universally acknowledged by all the world." In the end, the US representatives seized the chance London offered and made peace with Britain without France – a contravention of the 1778 accord. Franklin at least notified France's foreign minister the evening before the signing. The September 20, 1783 treaty awarded America substantial territory, and Britain acknowledged the "United States" as "free, sovereign & Independent States."[68]

SOME CONCLUSIONS

The American triumvirate of sovereignty, security, and expansion all mattered. But sovereignty – especially after July 1776 – mattered most of all. American strategy became largely reactive, something not unusual for a weaker power. Washington and others eventually developed a military strategy that helped deliver independence – protraction via a Fabian approach. Sticking to it produced incremental successes and tactical defeats, diverging produced tactical, operational, and strategic disasters in New York and South Carolina. But this strategy alone may not have brought the US success without France, something secured by American diplomacy. The insurgent almost always needs outside support. French economic, military, and diplomatic assistance proved pivotal and arguably indispensable.

TOWARDS CONSTITUTIONAL GOVERNMENT, 1783–89

The United Colonies achieved independence, but the footings were shaky. It was governed via the 1781 Articles of Confederation, which restrained Federal control and vested power in a state-appointed Congress that could impose neither tax nor tariff. But imbuing the independence generation was "a certainty of their future greatness and destiny." It believed their new government would be an example to the world and agreed with Thomas Paine that "We have it in our power to begin the world over again." Idealism. Religious faith. Pragmatism. Ambition. A refusal to play by a corrupt Old World's rules. These underpinned much of what the fledgling US would do and shaped what it would become.[69]

This new nation was weak but fortunate that among its adversaries – Britain, Spain, and the Indians – only Britain could mount an existential threat. The US also enjoyed enormous geographical advantages. An assessment better fitted for later days makes this point: "On the north she had a weak neighbor; on the south, another weak neighbor; on the east, fish, and on the west, fish." Historian C. Vann Woodward argued America often enjoyed "free security" because of its geographic position and the British navy, which someone else paid for.[70] There is some truth to this, but the British fleet didn't protect US commerce from predation – particularly British.

Even before the peace terms were implemented, the US embarked upon what became a traditional element of American grand strategy: disarming at the end of a war. Four days after the September 20, 1783 signing of the Treaty of Paris, Congress ordered Washington to begin demobilization. After the British withdrew from New York, the army shrank to 600. By June 1784, it numbered only eighty-three privates and a handful of officers above captain's rank. Maintaining even a small postwar army provoked bitter Congressional debates related to costs and traditional Colonial fears of a standing military. The navy was disbanded, Congress selling the last ship in 1785.[71]

Britain attempted to beggar the US via trade. A weak Confederation government proved to London it had no reason to grant America's demand for trade reciprocity. London prohibited direct US imports into the West Indies from July 1783, mauling New England's fishing and shipping industries. British merchants buried the US with cheaper manufactured goods while London prevented export of anything that would help the US develop native industry. British dumping contributed to "an economic depression worsened by the massive debt accumulated during the war." One reason John Adams pressed for a stronger central government was the desperate need to regulate trade.[72]

Adams was far from alone. American weakness underpinned a litany of troubles – fear of the Indians; an inability to enforce treaties and field military forces; an incapacity to address economic and trade issues; fears of secession and disintegration; and Daniel Shay's Rebellion in 1786–87, a revolt by destitute farmers unable to pay their debts – all of which helped bring about the Constitutional Convention (1787–89).[73]

The new nation's ideological foundation rested upon an emphasis on God-given natural rights detailed in the Declaration of Independence: "Life, Liberty, and the pursuit of Happiness." But "Liberty," which free peoples particularly valued, always faced threats from a lack of individual restraint and government temptation toward oppressive control. Only the "rule of law" protected free people from both dictatorship and chaos. The Constitution addressed these fears via the separation of powers between Congress and the president, particularly by dividing control of the military between the two. Forestalling fear of Congress having too much power over the states was an amendment to the new Articles of Confederation granting the states sovereignty in everything not expressly allotted to Congress, which was composed of a proportionally elected House of Representatives and a Senate of two appointed (until 1913) representatives from each state. The Constitution granted Congress many powers, including the "power of the purse," the right to tax, and pass customs duties. Treaty-making lay with the president, but the Senate held ratification rights. An independent judiciary formed the third branch. Up to the time of the Civil War, the US possessed no institution dedicated to war planning or the crafting of anything today considered military strategy.[74]

THE GEORGE WASHINGTON ADMINISTRATION, 1789–97

George Washington assumed office as the first president on April 30, 1789. What his administration wanted most was peace. This was necessary to consolidate American sovereignty over its possessions, particularly in the Northwest, and to firmly establish the new government. The nation was also too broke to fight.[75] The first cabinet was small: Thomas Jefferson as secretary of state, Henry Knox as secretary of war, and Alexander Hamilton as secretary of the treasury. Hamilton's brilliance, energy, and intimate relations with Washington developed through service with the general during the war, made him the dominant figure of the administration. He was also arguably America's first grand strategist.

THE ASSESSMENT

In his first annual message, delivered on January 8, 1790, Washington said the security of the US meant the nation needed to be armed but also "promote such manufactories as tend to render them independent of others for essential, particularly military supplies." For this, it needed its own industrial base. What ensued was a struggle over government support for industrial development between commercial and industrial interests in New England and the mid Atlantic states against Southern agriculturalists. Washington believed it a governmental and personal duty to support US industry and encouraged Americans to do the same.[76]

Overall, Hamilton's ideas on government and commerce had more effect than those of anyone else of his time other than Thomas Jefferson. Hamilton saw near limitless potential in America's future and believed America would become a great naval and merchant marine power, giving it leverage economically and in foreign relations and, eventually, "by a steady adherence to the Union, we may hope, ere long, to become the arbiter of Europe in America, and to be able to incline the balance of power in this part of the world as our interest may dictate." Historian Edward Meade Earle wrote of Hamilton's approach: "Surely, this is Realpolitik of a high order and shows that a strategy for America in world politics was evolved by the fathers of the Republic."[77]

ECONOMIC STRATEGY

The economic challenges were enormous and can be divided into intertwined internal and external threats. Hamilton brought to the task a driving intellect and deep knowledge of economic thought, including the ideas of Adam Smith. His greatest test was the national debt crisis, but America also lacked a liquid money supply. Hamilton saw that he could use the debt to create and back money by allowing banks holding government bond debt to issue currency. These same bonds also collateralized loans, increasing available capital. Hamilton successfully fought for the Federal government to assume state debts from the war as a means of binding the new union.[78]

The Founders preferred a version of commerce they called free trade, one perhaps better branded reciprocity or open trade. America's leaders did not expect tariff-free trade as tariffs were a standard source of government revenue, but they wanted the ability to trade anywhere without having to pay higher duties than anyone else. This desire bumped against the closed, mercantilist system of the British Empire in which Britain preferred to import raw materials from its colonies and export to them finished goods. Simultaneously, American leaders worried about national defense and its provision, a lesson derived from the war.[79]

Tariffs can raise revenue as well as protect key industries; the first tariff, signed into law on July 4, 1789, did both. But Hamilton wanted a diverse tax structure because in wartime import revenue would disappear. Tariffs became the primary source of government income for more than 100 years – and among the most contentious. Every region had its own interests and thus varying ideas regarding what should or shouldn't suffer a tariff. Only slavery proved more politically divisive.[80]

Hamilton secured the chartering of a national bank – the Bank of the United States. He stressed the necessity of firm finances that gave the country sound credit, factors critical for national security and development. Banking was unfamiliar to most Americans, which made Hamilton's national bank revolutionary. The Bank's most important function was issuing paper money. Its notes were essentially loans to private citizens and provided a circulating currency for a people lacking silver and gold specie. Government backing, based upon tax revenue, kept currency from depreciating or being exchanged for hard money. The Bank regulated the money supply by overseeing state banks.[81]

Building domestic industry was to Hamilton not only a source of national wealth, but a key element of national security. The nation's defense ability hinged upon its capacity to arm and supply itself against foreign threats. Hamilton thought that as long as America lacked a navy to protect its commerce, it relied on overseas trade it could not protect. Hamilton's 1791 Report on Manufactures proposed an economic program to make America "independent of foreign nations for military and other essential supplies." Washington supported it and urged Congress to do the same. The report "imaginatively contested much conventional wisdom by suggesting that domestic commerce, that is, Americans trading with one another, might be as valuable to the prosperity of the country as international commerce." This would help create a larger internal market for goods and agricultural products as agricultural workers became industrial laborers. Hamilton wanted an America strong enough to face the Europeans as an equal but knew this would take at least three or four decades. He disagreed with the physiocrats – economists who believed commerce brought peace – thinking trade more likely to cause than prevent wars. Hamilton believed that since fledgling US industry stood no hope of competing with developed British counterparts, American business should be protected and encouraged through tariffs and other restrictions. Annual purchasing contracts could support American arms manufacturers. Hamilton preferred targeted subsidies to tariffs, but tariffs were politically palatable.[82]

The new system – a national bank and government funded by tariffs that were sometimes protective – made possible administration borrowing during emergencies such as wars. Tariff revenue enabled payment of US debts, and between 1789 and 1794 America transformed from financial pariah to having a higher credit rating than any European nation, but it took until 1796 before revenue covered government expenses and debt service.[83]

DIPLOMATIC STRATEGY

The French Revolution began in 1789. When Britain declared war on France in February 1793, Washington put to his cabinet the question of how the US should respond under the terms of the 1778 alliance with France as it required America to help defend France's colonies in the West Indies. Hamilton insisted that it only committed the US to a defensive war, and that the alliance and the other treaties were as dead as the French government and monarchy with which they had been made. Secretary of State Jefferson argued the agreements were between France and the US, regardless of government. Paris rescued Washington from having to act. A weak US ally with no substantive navy was no help to Paris against London, but a US at peace meant American ships supplying the West Indies and France. Washington declared US neutrality on April 22, a decision most Americans supported, including Hamilton and Jefferson.[84]

The Anglo-French war produced internal political division that birthed America's first political parties. The Democratic-Republicans, agrarians led by Jefferson and James Madison, hated Britain and favored France. The Federalists, led by Alexander Hamilton and John Jay, and supported by the merchant class, particularly from New England, leaned British. They despised the French Revolutionaries, especially their violence, and feared Britain's power to destroy American trade and deny capital for economic development. Their battles were bitter, giving immediate lie to American political disputes having ever stopped at the water's edge.[85]

The Anglo-French War created dangers for America. Early 1794 saw Britain begin seizing US ships and forbidding American trade with French possessions in the Caribbean. Congress responded with a thirty-day embargo on all US shipping to foreign ports. Paris retaliated against American vessels destined for Britain by taking their cargos. Anti-British sentiment grew, and war clouds loomed, but Hamilton encouraged Washington to negotiate as war would be disastrous economically. In the 1794 Jay Treaty, London agreed to evacuate the frontier forts it had earlier refused to abandon, open some of its West Indian ports to US trade, and grant America most-favored-nation trade status with the British Isles. But American concessions included recognizing Britain's right to confiscate material transported by an enemy nation on a neutral ship. The deal also failed to protect US sailors from being forced into the Royal Navy via impressment. The concessions made the deal politically dicey, and Washington kept it secret as long as possible. Washington's Democratic-Republican political opponents accused the administration of subordinating US sovereignty to Britain, but in the treaty's wake US overseas trade boomed, feeding an economic revival.[86]

MILITARY STRATEGY

Militarily, Hamilton and other Federalists argued for a small, peacetime professional army as a nucleus for wartime expansion, an example for the militia, and indispensable for preserving the republic. If America possessed effective government, remained united, and developed its strength, it could "choose peace or war as our interest guided by justice shall dictate." Waiting until a war's outbreak to raise troops was not the answer. Lacking military strength left one susceptible to attack and at the invader's mercy. Neutrality meant having enough military strength to prevent another state from forcing your hand.[87]

In 1793, Algerian corsairs began seizing American merchant ships. The Naval Act of 1794 marked a reborn US navy but included a provision funding the ships only if the Algerian problem persisted. In 1795, word that peace had been made with Algiers, one that included the payment of tribute, was followed by Congress establishing a peacetime navy.[88]

FRONTIER EXPANSION, 1783–1801

The Peace of Paris gave the Americans vast tracts of land they didn't control and over which they were too weak to exert sovereignty. The British refused to give up their border forts because the US hadn't fulfilled its treaty obligation to ensure Britons recovered wartime claims against Americans. Britain used its Canadian border forts and those in the Northwest as bases for encouraging Indian resistance to American land hunger while helping create Indian coalitions. In the south, the border with Spain was unclear. Spain controlled the vast Louisiana territory, which it had received from France in 1762 for joining the Seven Years' War. Spain disliked American encroachment west of the Appalachians and closed the Mississippi River to American navigation in 1784 to discourage this by preventing settlers from moving their goods down the river. Some Americans in the region connived with Madrid about leaving the Union, impulses Spain fed with bribes and trading licenses.[89]

The British didn't consult their Indian allies when they made peace. Many Indian leaders had feared abandonment and were shocked by a betrayal in which London gave Indian lands to the American and Spanish victors. The 1783 treaty brought only a lull in hostilities. Many Indians and Whites were not ready for peace, and the traditional, vendetta-like frontier violence continued. The Americans imposed treaties on the region's Indians at the end of the war that essentially drew an east–west line through the middle of Ohio, allocating the Indians its north. At the end of 1786, the United Indian Nations, a coalition of fourteen tribes, nullified any agreement not made with all its members. The next year saw Indians repudiating treaties some members had been forced to sign and raiding White settlements. They insisted the Ohio River was the boundary. The January 1789 Fort Harmar Treaty was supposed to resolve issues but did little more than pay the Indians for land the Americans had claimed by right of conquest and establish the same territorial division.[90]

There were perhaps 100,000 Indians between the Appalachian Mountains and the Mississippi River. American leaders wanted orderly settlement of western lands, but Americans poured in. The Northwest Ordinance of 1787 assured settlers retained their political and legal rights as Americans and could establish new states in these territories that were equal to the old. Until they were ready for statehood, a Federally named governor ruled. A population of 60,000 made it eligible for statehood.[91]

Americans generally saw Indian lands as fruit for plucking. A postwar land rush ensued, particularly in the Northwest, one fed by the poverty and indebtedness of the Confederation government (its best source of revenue was the sale of Indian lands), and land grants to veterans. US leaders realized the Indians weren't ready to abandon these areas, but they considered them enemies who had aided the hated British. Taking their land was a way to extract compensation for wartime Indian destruction. Even Indian nations that had fought beside the Americans would be pushed off their lands. Many Americans believed their actions toward Indians could combine "expansion with honor" and thought having too much land caused Indian idleness and kept them from becoming "civilized." Taking their territory did the Indians a favor by forcing them to change. A pattern soon underpinned US expansion against the Indians. New settlers or prospectors, often illegal, provoked Indian reprisals, sometimes because Indian leaders had no more success controlling their people than the US government. Americans then demanded Federal protection from the Indians, sometimes threatening to turn to Britain or Spain if they didn't get it. Federal troops, and sometimes wars, then followed.[92]

The Washington administration temporarily defused problems along its southern frontiers via a treaty with the Creek Indians in 1790, one the Spanish supported as it meant their Indian trade continued. Resolving the situation in the Northwest proved more difficult. In 1789, Washington and Secretary of War Knox tried to gain control of the escalating crisis. Washington preferred to purchase Indian lands, and Knox dealt with the Indians as sovereign nations. Both wanted to prevent the Indians from being exterminated as they had in the east, and Knox hoped to convince them to become farmers like White Americans. This offends the modern conscience but was then the cutting-edge of enlightened thinking. Alternatives included dispossession and death. The continuing military threat led to placing Indian affairs in War Department hands. State legislatures and free-spirited settlers disagreed with the administration, and it lacked the power to do anything about it.[93]

PART I: FROM BACKWATER TO GREAT POWER

THE WAR AGAINST THE WESTERN CONFEDERACY

In January 1790, in his first annual address to Congress, Washington called for defense of the frontiers against Indians. Washington preferred peace, but since this hadn't happened, he urged Congress to better prepare militarily to protect the frontiers and "punish aggression" if needed. Congress increased the army to 1,283 men. As the undeclared frontier war intensified, the pressure upon the administration to act became unbearable. In June 1790, Knox ordered a "rapid and decisive" punitive campaign against the Miami Indians of the Ohio region. Its two prongs were supposed to utilize the effects of surprise to crush Indian forces and destroy their food supplies. The slow, bumbling campaign accomplished little more than burning a few villages and destroying the reputation of one of the commanders. The Indians replied by escalating their attacks. Knox ordered another campaign that culminated in September 1791 with approximately 1,000 Indians ambushing and decimating a US force of 1,400, killing over 600 of them.[94]

In the aftermath, US negotiators offered to make peace based on the Fort Harmar Treaty line, the *de facto* border when the war began. The Indians refused. The Americans now took seriously the prosecution of the war. Overconfidence, underestimation of the opponent, debacle, reassessment: this became a too often repeated pattern of American war-making. Washington named as commander "Mad" Anthony Wayne, an experienced Revolutionary War veteran. Wayne's campaign was well planned and well led, and better prepared as the army was expanded and the troops properly trained. It didn't begin until September 1793 as the administration wanted to first exhaust all efforts at negotiations. After these failed, Wayne broke the Indian forces at the Battle of Fallen Timbers on August 20, 1794. His victory allowed the Americans to attack an Indian critical vulnerability – food – by burning their cornfields. The signing of Jay's Treaty compounded the Indians' disasters as their British ally abandoned its forts in the region. The August 1795 Treaty of Greenville ended the war and established a boundary little changed. Wayne's campaign ended British influence over the Indians of the Northwest until the War of 1812 and increased the credibility of the Federal government.[95]

As Wayne consolidated the nation's northwestern periphery, American representative Thomas Pinckney negotiated a treaty with Spain in 1794 that fixed Florida's boundary at the 31st parallel and granted America navigation rights on the Mississippi. It also robbed the southern Indian tribes of their Spanish support against American expansion. Congress reorganized and reduced the army in 1796, but a standing force survived.[96]

THE FIGHT FOR SOVEREIGNTY, 1775–1801

WASHINGTON'S FAREWELL ADDRESS

George Washington's September 17, 1796 "Farewell Address" is famously known as a foundation for elements of American foreign relations. It can also be viewed as a grand strategy document (one heavily crafted by Hamilton), a shot at their pro-French Democratic-Republican political opponents, and an effort to dampen political division.[97]

Washington urged people to strive for the preservation of the Union and the freedoms it bestowed upon Americans. He believed achieving this depended upon many things, one of the most important being unity. Economically, the US should "cherish its public credit" by not borrowing unnecessarily and using times of peace to repay debts accumulated in "unavoidable wars," thus "not ungenerously throwing upon posterity the burden which we ourselves ought to bear." He considered trade important and believed such relationships should be impartial. On defense, he urged the building of the necessary forces, maintenance of the alliance with France, and reliance upon temporary leagues during wars.[98]

Famously, he cautioned the US against becoming involved in Europe's affairs as the conflicting interests of its nations rarely concerned the United States. America should honor its current ties but create no more. Why, he asked, "by interweaving our destiny with that of any part of Europe," should Americans "entangle our peace and prosperity in the toils of European ambition, rivalship, interest, humor or caprice?" "It is our true policy [strategy] to steer clear of permanent alliances with any portion of the foreign world; so far, I mean, as we are now at liberty to do it; for let me not be understood as capable of patronizing infidelity to existing engagements." If these things were done, and Americans stood together, Washington said, the result would be decisive:

> Our detached and distant situation invites and enables us to pursue a different course. If we remain one people under an efficient government, the period is not far off when we may defy material injury from external annoyance; when we may take such an attitude as will cause the neutrality we may at any time resolve upon to be scrupulously respected; when belligerent nations, under the impossibility of making acquisitions upon us, will not lightly hazard the giving us provocation; when we may choose peace or war, as our interest, guided by justice, shall counsel.[99]

Washington didn't advocate isolationism as some have claimed but disentanglement and the building of the nation's strengths to secure its security and sovereignty. He closed with this: "There can be no greater error than to expect or calculate upon real favors from nation to nation. It is an illusion, which experience must cure, which a just pride ought to discard."[100]

THE JOHN ADAMS ADMINISTRATION, 1797–1801

John Adams, Washington's vice president, succeeded him. His greatest challenge was revolutionary France. "My entrance into office is marked by a misunderstanding with France," Adams told his son, future president John Quincy Adams, "which I shall endeavor to reconcile."[101]

THE POLITICAL AIM

Adams sought to do what was best for the security of the United States and said clearly that he believed peace with all states, including "the aboriginal nations of America," was in the nation's best interests. He believed this best achieved by following the path of neutrality in Europe's wars, particularly the ongoing struggle between Britain and France. This proved a difficult course to chart, especially since the US was a trading nation and entwined economically with both – especially Britain.[102] Stormy political seas at home, including numerous forms of political subversion that threatened to rip the country apart, made Adams' task difficult.

DIPLOMATIC AND MILITARY STRATEGY

Jay's Treaty lowered tensions with Britain but angered revolutionary France (not a difficult task), which began seizing American merchant ships. Adams responded by calling the first special session of Congress and asking it to expand America's defense capabilities. Money for harbor fortifications and the completion of a trio of frigates was forthcoming, as was approval for the president to summon up to 80,000 militia to the colors.[103]

The Federalists, Adams' party, pushed for war with France. Adams tried to defuse the situation by dispatching a diplomatic mission, one his pro-French political rival Jefferson tried to torpedo by advising the French to extend the negotiations as long as possible because Adams would only be president for four years. In October 1797, the trio of French representatives made a series of demands that included bribes for themselves and a loan for France. Further negotiations brought nothing, and in March 1798 Adams called for the US to arm its merchant ships. When the dispatches for what became known as the XYZ Affair (the corrupt French officials were denoted X, Y, and Z) were published in April 1798, the contents enraged Americans. It also turned many against the Democratic-Republicans, who sympathized with revolutionary France, and made Adams and his administration popular.[104]

It also spurred a drive toward war, which Adams didn't want. Not only did he fear he lacked the necessary votes in Congress for a declaration, but he also had information that the French didn't want war. Adams mounted a firm response, hoping to convince France to negotiate or push Congress into acting on a declaration. The Quasi-War followed. Congress embargoed trade with France and canceled all treaties with Paris, including the alliance, permitted the navy to attack armed French ships preying on US vessels, strengthened the army, funded coastal patrol ships and fifteen larger vessels, and created a separate Department of the Navy and a reborn Marine Corps. Further legislation in 1799 established that the navy's roles would be to protect commerce and project power. American success at sea, especially against French warships, fed support for a permanent US navy.[105]

But there was also the issue of whether the US was *at war* with France. The French were using violence against a foe to achieve their own political aims and the US was doing the same, the very definition of war. Behind closed doors, the French admitted to being at war with America but refused to issue a formal declaration and secretly plotted to destabilize Adams' administration and provoke rebellion in America. Adams made the political decision to not acknowledge that the US was at war while fighting a war at sea against France. The struggle resulted in an important legal precedent regarding the terms of an American president's ability to use force: the US was judged to be at war because of France's attacks on America. Thus, war existed even though the US hadn't declared it.[106]

Americans became fearful of a French invasion and Federalists saw in this crisis the chance to get the standing army they wanted. Congress approved a force of 50,000 in case of war. Washington was brought out of retirement to command it and insisted on Hamilton as his second in command. Washington's age and declining health meant it would be Hamilton's army. Adams was suspicious of Hamilton's ambitions. Hamilton saw in the creation of a large standing army a means of accelerating the nation's power and influence, as well as his own. It could enable the seizure of Spanish Florida and Louisiana alongside Britain. Hamilton and Washington selected the officers for the new force, which took a long time because they wanted them to be politically reliable (meaning Federalists) to thwart French political machinations and suppress any internal rebellion. But things moved slowly, partially because Hamilton argued over nearly everything with nearly everyone.[107]

Fears of a French invasion, and that Irish and French emigrants would be tools of foreign influence in the expected war with France, allowed the Federalists to pass the Alien and Sedition Acts in 1798. These gave the government the authority to punish "seditious libel." Democratic-Republicans charged this violated the Constitution's First Amendment free speech protections and that political criticism could not be legally restricted, an argument they won. Many of the French who had fled the revolution for America departed, and the laws produced no deportations. The government believed the press should be restrained and used the laws to arrest twenty-five and indict seventeen Democratic-Republican journalists and editors. Technically, these Federal statutes liberalized many state codes on seditious libel. But in the end, all of this helped destroy the Federalist Party's reputation.[108]

In February 1799, Adams took the risky political move of again trying to make peace. His decision to request negotiations met a frenzy of criticism – including from his own cabinet – which Adams ignored. He received France's agreement to talk in August. Members of Adams' cabinet again fought the move, as did Hamilton, with whom they intrigued against the president. Adams stayed his course and the next year fired one plotter and forced another to resign. The dissension split and helped break the Federalist Party.[109]

The US and France signed an agreement to end the Quasi-War on September 30, 1800. Adams secured peace and the ending of the alliance with France. This cut the legs from under Hamilton as the US no longer needed either an army or a commander. But these events helped ensure Adams wasn't reelected.[110]

SOME CONCLUSIONS

The American colonists secured their independence from Great Britain and revived the republic as a form of government. The postwar leaders, despite often intense debate and political factionalism, secured American sovereignty and built the core of a government that has endured, though with many bumps. Diplomatically, Washington and the Federalists succeeded in securing access to the Mississippi River for American trade, an agreed border with Spain, the removal of the British from their frontier forts, and treaties with various Indian nations. They also bungled a war by entering unprepared, and half-fought one with France. Critically, they strengthened the government's foundations – particularly its economic footing – while presiding over great increases in trade and the rebirth of a war-torn American economy.[111]

2

EXPANSION, SOVEREIGNTY, AND WAR, 1801–1817

ASSESSMENT AND POLITICAL AIMS

In 1801, Thomas Jefferson assumed office as America's third president. He sought a nation built by and upon the yeoman farmer. Jefferson preferred "a wise and frugal Government," meaning small, "which shall restrain men from injuring one another," but "leave them otherwise free to regulate their own pursuits of industry and improvement, and shall not take from the mouth of labor the bread it has earned. This is the sum of good government." In his inaugural, Jefferson listed his administration's "essential principals." These included "peace, commerce, and honest friendship with all nations, entangling alliances with none." This was perhaps Jefferson's ideal, but the purposes toward which he and James Madison that followed directed American power were sovereignty, security, and expansion, especially the latter as Jefferson was "the most expansion-minded president in American history." In 1801, Jefferson saw a United States covering the Western Hemisphere's northern if not also southern continents. Americans were pouring into the new lands faster than expected, and Congress created new territories that soon became states.[1] (See Map 2.1.)

Disputes over how to use national power to pursue aims fed a vitriolic partisan divide that, under the pressures of the War of 1812, threatened to rip apart the republic.

ECONOMIC STRATEGY

Jefferson's economic views differed vastly from the Federalists and Hamilton. The Federalists sought a more diversified economy. Jefferson wanted the US to remain predominantly agricultural, though farmers needed markets abroad in case domestic consumption was insufficient. In 1785, Jefferson the idealist essentially believed in free trade, but that trade with Europe would result in war and America should be closed in its

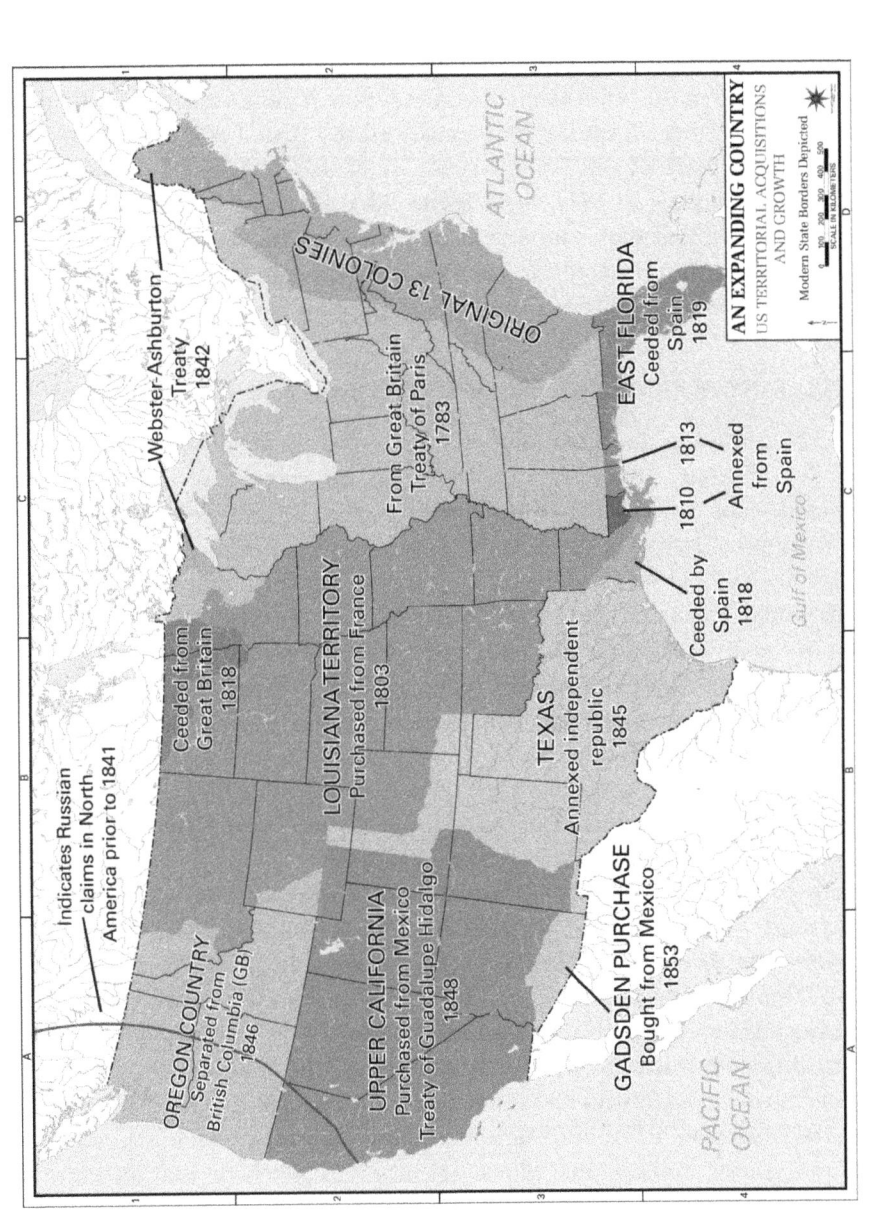

Map 2.1 An expanding country: US territorial acquisitions and growth

relations with Europe. Jefferson the politician realized the impossibility of this and the necessity of opening foreign markets to America.[2]

Jefferson began dismantling Hamilton's national financial system. He eliminated excise taxes and shrank the involvement of government in American lives to the point where the interaction of most was receiving mail. Treasury Secretary Albert Gallatin convinced the bank hating Jefferson to preserve the Bank of the United States but failed to persuade Congress to renew its charter in 1811. State banks filled its roles. A banking boom followed, providing paper money to fuel commercial expansion. The US economy grew, but became the most unpredictable in the West, suffering economic chaos roughly every twenty years over the next century.[3]

MILITARY AFFAIRS AND JEFFERSON'S BARBARY WAR, 1801–07

The US essentially disarmed after the Quasi-War as the Napoleonic Wars engulfed Europe. To Jefferson, reducing the power of government included – most importantly – shrinking the military. Democratic-Republicans saw a large military as a threat to the government. Jefferson cut the army's budget by half and struck at Federalist domination of the officer ranks. The 1802 establishment of the United States Military Academy at West Point was one means of this. Jefferson preferred relying upon state militias in a crisis until a regular army was raised.[4] Jefferson kept a naval core to protect America's Mediterranean trade from Barbary pirates. North Africa's corsair kingdoms terrorized Mediterranean shipping and imprisoned sailors. The US and others paid them protection money instead of solving the problem. The US spent 15 percent of its 1796 budget to buy peace with Algiers and paid $2 million in tribute to the Barbary states by 1800.[5]

In June 1801, Jefferson dispatched what he called "a squadron of observation," but hoped it would deter attacks on American shipping. Commodore Robert Dale reached Gibraltar on July 1, 1801, and discovered Tripoli had declared war. Dale's orders in this event instructed him to protect US commerce, "chastise their insolence – by sinking, burning or destroying their ships and Vessels," and blockade the enemy's primary port while convoying American merchant ships – if time. He had four ships.[6]

Dale sailed to Tunis and Algiers to intimidate them, while striving to escort shipping and conduct blockades, none of which he had sufficient forces to do. Jefferson went to Congress for approval to do more. On February 6, 1802, it recognized America was at war. The administration dispatched a second, slightly larger squadron, but it accomplished little. The administration wanted a more aggressive war. Its new commander, Edward Preble, made Gibraltar in September 1803. He united the US forces and blockaded Morocco, forcing its ruler to reaffirm a 1796 commitment to stop attacking US ships, but this time without America paying tribute. Preble moved to tackle Tripoli but found that the *Philadelphia* had run aground in Tripoli harbor and surrendered to the Algerians. Preble dispatched Lieutenant Stephen Decatur Jr. to burn *Philadelphia* in February 1804. To take Tripoli, Preble reinforced his fleet with vessels borrowed from the Kingdom of the Two Sicilies, shelled the city on August 3, 1804, launched further attacks, and continued his blockade.[7]

Meanwhile, the US mounted a land campaign against Tripoli. The several-hundred-man force of Americans and mercenaries (today we call them contractors) marched from Alexandria, Egypt, 600 miles away. Threatened from land and sea, the pasha struck a deal on June 10, 1805, receiving $60,000 for returning 300 American prisoners. The final act of the first Barbary War came when Commodore John Rodgers sailed a flotilla into Tunis on August 1, 1805. Its ruler granted the US most-favored-nation trading status. Naval patrols continued for another two years.[8]

Despite the navy's success, Jefferson remained determined to change its shape for political reasons. He believed the existence of an oceangoing fleet invited attack from and thus war with Britain. Naval strategy for Jefferson became coastal defense based upon fortifications and a "mosquito fleet" of several hundred shallow-draft coastal gunboats with a single sail and one cannon to swarm and overwhelm enemy warships in coastal waters. Inspired by Barbary pirate vessels, Jefferson insisted his gunboats would prevent the US from fighting an offensive war while not provoking attack. Privateers would be used on the high seas, if needed. Jefferson's gunboats were to be cheap to build and maintain, being mothballed when not in use, and manned by naval militia. The 170 built proved of little military value and cost twice what was projected.[9]

TECUMSEH'S WAR, 1811–13

The settlers flooding the Northwest, and Jefferson's acquisitions of Indian lands, fueled creation of an Indian coalition under Shawnee chief Tecumseh, who opposed ceding any Indian land, and his brother Tenskwatawa. Indiana's territorial governor, William Henry Harrison, insisted the US needed to respond to rising frontier violence and Tecumseh's threats. The administration feared acting because it worried war with Britain was on the horizon, but pressure from other governors pried the government from its stump. It reinforced Harrison's largely militia army with regular troops and approved his plan to march on Prophetstown and force a peace. If the

Indians refused, he would strike. On November 6, 1811, near Tippecanoe Creek, Harrison's army was attacked by an Indian force led by Tenskwatawa. The Americans repelled the assault and burned Prophetstown, but the war against Tecumseh's confederation bled into another.[10]

DIPLOMATIC STRATEGY

Jefferson told Virginia's governor, James Monroe, "it was impossible, not to look forward to distant times, when our rapid multiplication will expand itself beyond those limits, and cover the whole northern, if not southern continent, with a people by similar laws." Jefferson was far from alone in his vision. But obstacles remained. Jefferson didn't see Spain as a threat and believed pieces of Madrid's American empire would gradually fall to the United States. During a 1790 crisis between Spain and Britain, Jefferson made clear his willingness to fight Spain for Florida and the right to navigate the Mississippi, and Britain to keep it from taking Spain's New World holdings. Any additional British presence was intolerable.[11]

Spanish fears of America helped push Madrid to transfer Louisiana back to France in 1800, creating a French buffer between Spain and the United States. This frightened Jefferson. Unlike Spain, France was strong. New Orleans was a critical American trade outlet and Jefferson described any foreign owner of it as America's "natural and habitual enemy." Though he hated Britain, French control would force the Americans to "marry ourselves to the British fleet and nation." Jefferson knew US representatives would pass along this remark (perhaps a bluff) with the question of whether France might sell New Orleans and "the Floridas" (which were still held by Spain) for $6 million. The Americans negotiated a deal for all of Louisiana for $15 million. Jefferson was elated. Acquiring 900,000 square miles of territory fulfilled his "greatest dream of having sufficient land for generations to come of his yeoman farmers," while removing a danger to peace as neither Britain nor France now threatened the Mississippi's access to the sea.[12]

One can't overestimate the strategic importance of the Louisiana Purchase. It gave America control of the Mississippi River and poured the foundation for its dominance of North America and the Western Hemisphere. Jefferson revealed how the Louisiana Purchase underpinned his vision for America: "But who can limit the extent to which the federative principle may operate effectively? The larger our association, the less will it be shaken by local passions; and in any view, is it not better that the opposite bank of the Mississippi should be settled by our own brethren and children, than by strangers of another family?"[13]

EXPANSION, SOVEREIGNTY, AND WAR, 1801–1817

Map 2.2 The Eastern United States, 1812

THE ORIGINS OF THE WAR OF 1812

Jefferson's triumph removed the French threat, but Spain and Britain remained, and the latter was dangerous. The American pursuit of sovereignty, security, and expansion all played a role in the new war's arrival, though sovereignty proved most influential. One cause was Britain's insistence upon the right to take British subjects and deserters from American ships and impress them into the Royal Navy. Driving this was their desperate need for sailors in their protracted war against Napoleon, their arrogance toward Americans, and differing definitions of citizenship. Britain took perhaps 6,000 men from US ships from 1803 to 1812.[14] This was a sovereignty issue as Britain violated American rights.

Running a close second as a cause were trade issues related to America's insistence upon sovereignty. The Napoleonic Wars complicated American trade while creating opportunities. In 1812, partly because of its massive merchant fleet (981,000 tons in 1810), the US was the largest neutral trading nation. The US wanted to trade freely, but Britain and France imposed restrictions. France pushed for neutral trading rights while making it illegal to trade with Britain, a result of Napoleon's Continental System designed to isolate London from European trade. London insisted all ships trading with the continent secure a British license. American vessels following French rules risked capture by British ships. Obeying British decrees risked French confiscation of American cargo.[15] British impositions were more deeply resented, partially because the power of the Royal Navy brought them home to Americans.

On June 22, 1807, the Royal Navy fired upon the US warship *Chesapeake*, boarded it, and seized four crewmen. This threw Americans into a frenzy, and Jefferson averted an early meeting of Congress because he feared a declaration of war. The US retaliated economically via the Embargo Act of 1807, which forbade US ships from going to foreign ports, and barred British and French craft from US ports. The law killed American trade, ruined many merchants, and drove smuggling to epidemic levels while little affecting Britain or France. An unintended effect was spurring American industrial development to replace lost imports. The Embargo Act was repealed in March 1809 by the new James Madison administration.[16]

When Madison became president, the weak US government could do little against the Europeans. The US passed the Non-Intercourse Act of 1809 to restore trade with all nations except France and Britain, and renewed trade with both in 1810 with the odd caveat that if either stopped harassing American shipping, the US would reimpose import restrictions on the other. Napoleon suggested France would do so, and Madison banned British imports. After discovering France had no intention of altering its behavior, Madison kept the prohibition. John Quincy Adams, then America's ambassador to Russia, believed France "had laid the trap which she concluded would catch us in an English war."[17]

Impressment and seizures of American ships continued. Between 1803 and 1812, Britain took 917 US vessels, and conducted searches and seizures near major US ports that became a *de facto* blockade. Madison's Democratic-Republican Party began calling for war to defend American rights. War would stop Britain's injurious behavior while providing an opportunity to solve the "Indian problem," something important in the Northwest. The conquest of Canada, or Britain's defeat here, would cut their ties with the Indians. War would also reaffirm American independence in the face of a Britain determined to have America serve London's interests. The government's failure to protect people's rights undermined the fragile republican experiment, while a successful war would unify the ruling party and silence the administration's Federalist critics as they would rally to the flag. Madison believed failing to go to war meant America sacrificed "the neutral guarantee of an Independent flag" and placed its trade under foreign authority.[18]

Madison decided in July 1811 to begin preparing for war but did little. He called Congress to meet in early November 1811 to consider a declaration of war and dispatched his annual message on November 5. His Democratic-Republican Party held Congress, which was controlled by its War Hawk faction, twelve younger congressmen led by Speaker of the House Henry Clay. Madison denounced Britain's restrictions as a war on US trade and urged war preparations. Accepting it as a war message, Congress approved recruiting the regular army to its complement of 10,000, enlisting 25,000 more regulars and 50,000 one-year volunteers, gave the president authority to call out 100,000 militia for six months, and appropriated $1,900,000 for ordnance. Madison opposed increasing the regulars, believing not enough could be raised in time for an 1812 spring campaign, and planned to use militia and volunteers. Congress failed to expand the navy but voted for coastal fortifications.[19]

But the Bank of the United States was closed in March 1811, which forced the government to borrow on the open market. Treasury Secretary Gallatin intended to finance the war via loans while tax revenue funded the government. Gallatin recommended borrowing $10 million and doubling import duties, and adding new taxes to cover the expected costs. The War Hawks approved a loan for $11 million, of which only $6.5 million was subscribed, and eventually overcame fears of electoral punishment to approve the taxes. Madison and the War Hawks thought this prepared the American people for war militarily and psychologically.[20]

Britain, meanwhile, charted a conciliatory course. Late in 1811, London cleaned up matters related to the *Chesapeake* affair, ordered the Royal Navy to start treating US ships and citizens cordially, and pulled warships from US shores. In May 1812, Britain offered to give the US half of the 10,000 licenses granted annually for continental trade, but the Madison administration rejected this, arguing "that accepting it would be tantamount to surrendering American independence."[21]

FEAR, HONOR, INTEREST: THE POLITICAL AIM

In his June 1, 1812 message to Congress, Madison denounced Britain's impressment, violation of American territorial waters, harassment of US shipping, use of "mock blockades" to disrupt and seize American trade, blockades resulting from Britain's trade restrictions, London's refusal to address these issues, and its incitement of Indian war. Madison didn't ask Congress to declare war but left no doubt about what he wanted. On June 16, Britain repealed the trade restrictions, and eliminated the blockades and licenses a week after. Madison said later that had he known, it would have prevented conflict. The US declared war on June 18.[22] (See Map 2.2.)

To Madison, the underlying problem was Britain's failure to respect the US as an independent, sovereign nation; it needed to be taught to do so. Madison had long advocated using economic tools to correct British behavior, but by 1812 saw war as the most useful instrument for ensuring London respected American sovereignty. To Madison, this meant the invasion and occupation of Britain's Canadian provinces. But was taking Canada part of a strategy for achieving Madison's political aims, or as a political aim in and of itself? To some American leaders, it was both. Congressman Henry Clay said: "Canada was not the end but the means, the object of the war being redress of injuries, and Canada being the instrument by which the redress was to be obtained." Secretary of State Monroe wrote in June 1812 that the US would invade Canada "not as an object of the war but as a means to bring it to a satisfactory conclusion." But Monroe told others it would be very difficult to return any Canadian lands. Jefferson told Madison that, to make the war popular, he needed "to stop Indian barbarities. The conquest of Canada will do this." Many Americans supported annexing Canada. It would rob Britain of timber for its navy and break London's connections to Indians blocking expansion. Others feared enlargement would make the union too big or give the North too much influence in comparison to the South (a bigger problem to come). Congress debated the future of a conquered Canada in the American union but made no decisions.[23]

Was invading Canada wise? If Madison intended to force Britain to bend by taking all or part of Canada, in theory, this was not a bad idea.

Canada was important to Britain in its war against Napoleon. It was also thinly populated, making it vulnerable. Clausewitz urged seizing the enemy's territory as a way of bringing them around to your point of view.[24] But it is doubtful Madison would have returned any land seized unless forced to. But preparing would have been helpful.

THE ASSESSMENT

Politics, geography, a weak Federal government, and poor internal transportation made it difficult for the administration to coordinate and control the war while regional concerns influenced its prosecution. The Northwest feared Tecumseh's coalition; the Southwest feared the Creeks; the coastal areas feared British raids. Internal intra-party political issues sometimes dictated strategy, as did regional concerns.[25]

A glance at the map of the border explains the locations of much of the fighting. Upper Canada, bordered on the west by Lake Huron and the south by Lake Erie and Lake Ontario, could only be attacked between Lakes Huron and Erie in the west, and Lakes Erie and Ontario in the east – unless you controlled Lakes Erie or Huron or the St. Lawrence waterway spilling out of Lake Ontario to form the border between New York state and Ontario and Quebec. Lower Canada, which is largely present-day Quebec, could be attacked from Lake Champlain along the Richelieu River and on the St. Lawrence. All, of course, could be used by both, had poor infrastructure, including bad roads, and most lacked population enough to feed an army attempting to forage, dictating large supply trains. Controlling the lakes and rivers enabled movement and supply.

The route from Lake Champlain to the Richelieu River reached into the most heavily populated part of Canada, including the strategically important city of Montreal. Its fall would give America control of Britain's communications with Upper Canada, isolating it from supplies and reinforcements. But using this route meant American forces fought in the region most against the war and thus provided the least support. In the west, the war was more popular, which sometimes eased the raising of volunteer forces and operations, but it was a theater where military success would not mean victory.[26]

The war was fought on three fronts. The Canadian front had three areas of land operations and significant action on Lakes Erie and Ontario. The Western Theater had two primary arenas: the old Northwest, as it was known, especially areas of present-day Michigan, Ohio, and Indiana where Americans primarily fought Indians, and the southern borderlands where the US battled the Creeks and the British. The third front was the high seas.

Though most Americans supported the conflict, Madison took to war a politically divided nation. The northeast was particularly resistant, and many of its inhabitants rendered more aid to Britain than their homeland and supplied the British. Madison's Democratic-Republicans saw the war as a second fight for American independence. Their Federalist political opponents, who dominated politics in much of the northeast, didn't, and posed numerous problems for the administration. It's sometimes necessary to lead a divided nation to war, but those doing so should understand the corrosive effects and prepare to counter them. Winning quickly can defuse troubles. Waiting for the enemy to declare war can too, but sometimes leaders lack such luxuries.

Compounding Madison's problems were military and economic unpreparedness despite months of effort. America had a poor army. The government's primary revenue source was trade, especially seaborne, which evaporated. The US, a seafaring trading nation possessing a miniscule navy, whose most populous cities lay on the coast or navigable rivers, went to war with the world's greatest naval power, one that since 1793 had been blockading much of Europe and fighting – often successfully – against one of history's great military powers: Napoleonic France.

Americans expected a quick and easy war. The US had 7.7 million people, Canada 300,000. The Democratic-Republicans banked upon residents of Upper Canada seeing Americans as liberators, not conquerors. Jefferson wrote: "the acquisition of Canada this year, as far as the neighborhood of Quebec, will be a mere matter of marching," and would within a year produce "the final expulsion of England from the American continent."[27] The Americans failed to consider the risks or make a rudimentary effort to assess the enemy or themselves. They wrote a script for the war they wanted to fight.

AMERICAN GRAND STRATEGY

The primary tools of grand strategy the Americans planned to use were economic and military. They maintained restrictive trade measures, and Congress passed a law forbidding trade with the enemy, defeating proposals to reopen trade with Britain made even though the US had just declared war.[28]

American conventional wisdom held that seizing Montreal would mean the fall of western Canada as it depended upon supplies and reinforcements coming via the St. Lawrence River. Madison intended to use what troops could be quickly raised to mount an immediate surprise attack on Montreal. Early success would bring Britain to terms or provide a foundation for continued operations in Lower Canada, perhaps even against Quebec.

Major General Henry Dearborn, a veteran of the War for Independence and Jefferson's secretary of war, had a plan for invading Canada ready in early April 1812 that aligned with Madison's ideas: taking Lower Canada (essentially present-day Quebec's lower half) using a volunteer force to overwhelm the enemy, seizing Montreal, then marching on Quebec. But the Americans lacked the necessary troops in summer 1812. Dearborn also suggested dividing British strength by launching two supporting invasions from sites on the Niagara Peninsula and Detroit against Upper Canada, the area west of Quebec and north of Lake Ontario. He insisted speed would bring rapid victory. Privately, he thought things would move slowly and the US wouldn't win quickly.[29]

William Hull, governor of the Michigan Territory and soon brigadier general, believed trying to take Montreal left Detroit and the west vulnerable. Its loss would open Indiana and Ohio to attack. In March 1812, he insisted on invading Upper Canada to remove the Indian threat and "probably induce the Enemy to abandon the province of Upper Canada without Opposition." He rejected insistence America needed to control key Great Lakes to successfully invade Upper Canada, believing the army could march on the British ports and destroy their ships, winning command of the lakes without the expense of ship-building.[30]

Madison didn't like choosing between competing plans and advisors, and approved two attacks from New York under Dearborn and another based at Detroit under Hull, dissipating America's faint military power. The three armies formed addressed the fears and sensibilities of different regions, and the administration lacked the political strength and logistical ability to concentrate its scant forces.[31] The operational objectives in the east were Montreal and Upper Canada, the other two prongs sought Lower Canada. These arms were theoretically related. Reality proved different, and America lacked the strength to properly swing either of them.

THE ENEMY

The strategic situation at the outbreak of the war heavily favored the United States, especially if it moved quickly. Canada was thinly populated and suffered from internal divisions. Many residents were former Americans uninterested in fighting the US; others thought this hopeless. Canada's governor general, Lieutenant General Sir George Prevost, kept most of the 6,500 British regular troops in Quebec to hold this key port controlling the St. Lawrence River's mouth. Prevost gave Major General Sir Isaac Brock 1,200 regulars to hold seven forts stretching from the St. Lawrence River to Lake Huron. Brock also brilliantly used Canadian militia and Indians. Quebec and Ontario provinces raised around 10,000 militia during the war; Indian support in autumn 1813 was perhaps 3,500.[32]

AMERICA GOES TO WAR

America's timing was in some respects good, though accidental, and nearly the only thing the US got right.[33] Its titanic struggle with France was London's *real* war. In theory, the Americans had a window between their declaration of war in June 1812 and the abdication of Napoleon in June 1814 before Britain could significantly reinforce Canada. The Americans could not know this, but it demonstrates that time is always limited. The job of America's military and political leaders was to slow America's clock and speed Britain's.

Despite its war with France, by September 1812 London dispatched eleven ships of the line, thirty-four frigates, and many smaller vessels to America and began implementing a blockade from Spanish Florida to Charleston, South Carolina, by autumn 1812. This was extended to the Chesapeake and Delaware Bays by early 1813, and to America south of New England by November. Britain left open New England's ports because the region opposed the war and London needed its grain to feed its troops fighting on the Iberian Peninsula.[34]

THE 1812 CAMPAIGN

Between 1812 and 1814, the US launched ten invasions of Canada. Madison approved three for 1812: one from Michigan, a second on the Niagara front, and a third from the Lake Champlain area aimed at Montreal. These three offensives were supposed to deliver the Americans a weak and poorly defended Canada; the uncoordinated US efforts gave Britain time to defeat each in detail.[35] But the US also fought at sea.

NAVAL STRATEGY IN 1812

Shortly before the war, Secretary of the Navy Paul Hamilton decided his force of a dozen, unprepared vessels would operate far from America against British trade to force London to divert warships to protect its commerce. This didn't happen initially due to poor direction from Hamilton and the disobedience of ship commanders, but the navy's actions did force Britain to protect its merchant shipping. By September 1812, though, the

US navy achieved little beyond the famous victory of the *Constitution* over the British frigate *Guerrière*.[36]

THE DETROIT FRONT

Hull, commanding one American prong, reached Fort Detroit on July 5, 1812. A week later, he led 300 regulars and 1,500 Ohio militia into Canada against a British-Canadian-Indian force of 700, including Tecumseh. Instead of striking Fort Malden or the enemy forces arrayed against him, an aged and infirm Hull simply sat across from Detroit.[37]

Unfortunately for the Americans, the Canadians were led by Major General Brock, whose inspiring leadership proved pivotal. Early in the war, Brock impressed his Indian allies by urging immediate assaults upon the American Forts Michilimackinac and Detroit. He also prodded Prevost to be more aggressive, but Prevost had orders to sit on the defensive to minimize the number of troops Britain would have to dispatch and believed waiting would allow US political divisions to grow. Historian Alan Taylor wrote that "Where Brock sought to unite Upper Canadians, Prevost believed that dividing the Americans was the true key to British victory. In fact, the British needed to do both."[38]

Hull began withdrawing on August 7. Brock followed. By August 15, Hull was in Fort Detroit being shelled by Brock's artillery. Brock crossed the river the next morning to attack the fort, but Hull immediately struck his colors. As Forts Michilimackinac and Dearborn were already in British hands, the American defenses in the region had been destroyed. "It was impossible to overrate the importance of this success," British Undersecretary for War Henry Goulburn wrote about Brock's victory. "By retarding for a year the American invasion, it gave time to supply such reinforcements as could be collected from other quarters & for organizing the Militia & Volunteers of the Provinces." The US consul in London said it would cause the British to work harder to hold Canada, something they had considered impossible. Madison replaced Hull with William Henry Harrison.[39]

THE NIAGARA FRONT

On the Niagara Front, the Americans also blundered. Dearborn was in charge, but two subordinates divided command of the forces. Major General Stephen van Rensselaer was at Lewistown, New York, on the Niagara River, with 900 regulars and 2,300 militia. In Buffalo, New York, was Brigadier General Alexander Smyth with 1,650 regulars and 400 militia. Another 1,300 troops held Fort Niagara. Rensselaer outranked Smyth, but Rensselaer was a militia general, not a regular officer, and a Federalist. Smyth refused to cooperate with him and even share an encampment.[40]

After Madison's August 15 cancellation of a truce Dearborn had made with the enemy, Dearborn ordered Rensselaer to attack. Rensselaer decided seizing Queenstown, Ontario, would give him command of the area and allow him to push the British out of the Niagara Peninsula. Having been forced to call off his first attack (Rensselaer blamed the "weak and despicable" administration and local Democratic-Republican politicians), Rensselaer finally gathered enough boats for his October 13 assault. He intended not to defeat the Canadians but to put to the test his "blustering" Democratic-Republican force; its defeat and dishonor would prove the Federalists correct in opposing the war.[41]

Rensselaer brought about 500 men across the river. Led by Lieutenant Colonel Winfield Scott, they seized Queenstown. Eighteen hundred American militia refused to cross the river into Canada because they didn't trust Rensselaer, who led from the American side when the fighting was on the other, and they weren't legally required to do so. The delays in launching the offensive had meanwhile allowed Brock to reinforce the Niagara Peninsula. Brock was killed leading the British counterattack, but they routed the Americans and Scott surrendered to prevent a massacre.[42]

Rensselaer resigned and Smyth took command but did little and his army began coming apart. Disease, mismanagement, and hunger killed and sickened perhaps one-third of it. Poor discipline produced riots and clashes with locals. Smyth's men despised him intensely for his failure to act and some tried to kill him. Smyth's force went into winter quarters in November, and the government used his leave request to quietly force him from the army.[43]

DEARBORN'S "OFFENSIVE"

Two hundred and fifty miles away near Albany, New York, was Major General Henry Dearborn's force. Dearborn was 61, "Insecure, fat, slow, and accident-prone." His troops called him "Granny." He had haggled over the terms of his command and waited in Boston until late July worrying about imaginary Federalist plots. Instead of marching on Montreal simultaneous to Rensselaer's assault to relieve pressure on Hull, Dearborn sat. After Rensselaer's defeat, he "belatedly realized that he alone could save the nation from total disgrace," and decided to mount a winter campaign against Montreal, something particularly difficult in the pre-industrial era because the weather could kill the animals moving supplies. Dearborn reached Plattsburgh to find half the army he expected. He pushed into Lower Canada to establish a position for future operations with a force of raw regulars and short-term volunteers, bungled a November 19 attack on La Cole Mill, and withdrew. A contemporary branded his offensive a "miscarriage, without even [the] heroism of a disaster."[44]

THE 1813 CAMPAIGN

The debacles of 1812 forced some reassessment. By the end of the year, Madison's Cabinet agreed to raise a large, regular army under the direction of the War Department as quickly as possible, removing reliance on militia and volunteers. Despite the calamity that had been the war thus far, Madison managed to win reelection and his party kept both houses of Congress, though with smaller majorities. Madison then reluctantly bowed to the pressure to replace his secretaries of war and navy.[45]

THE NAVAL WAR OF 1813

In February 1813, Secretary of the Navy William Jones promulgated a naval strategy mirroring his predecessor's original proposal: single ships making long commerce-raiding cruises. Jones believed this would draw British vessels from America's shore while forcing London to protect its commercial fleet, pressuring the enemy while taking it from America. Britain replied by operating in large squadrons with ships of the line to chase down American frigates.[46] This demonstrated one value of a "fleet in being" for the Americans. Even a weak navy forced Britain – a maritime power dependent upon shipping – to devote substantial resources to protect its commerce and counter American warships.

The Great Lakes began playing an increasingly important role. One reason for Hull's defeat was Brock's use of the lakes, but only after Hull's surrender did the administration decide it had to control them. Captain Isaac Chauncey took command of the US naval forces on Lakes Ontario and Erie in September 1812 with orders to win domination of the lakes that fall. He established a base at Presque Isle (now Erie, Pennsylvania) to complement the one on Lake Ontario at Sackets Harbor, New York, and began building new ships and converting existing ones. Oliver Hazard Perry was given command at Presque Isle in the spring of 1813 so Chauncey could focus on Lake Ontario. The British launched their own building programs as they knew control of the area depended upon this contest. They matched the Americans on Lake Ontario but fell behind on Lake Erie.[47]

THE CAMPAIGN OF 1813

In January 1813, Secretary of the Treasury Gallatin argued that since the focus of 1813 should be moving against Canada from New York rather than New England, the new secretary of war should have connections there. Madison chose John Armstrong, a prickly intriguer who alienated colleagues and had authored the 1783 Newburgh Letter calling for mutiny in the Continental Army, an urge Washington defused with a famous speech.[48]

Four days after his February 4, 1813 arrival in Washington, Armstrong presented a campaign plan for an April 1813 joint army–navy attack on the important British naval base at Kingston, followed by attacks upon York (now Toronto) and Fort George. This would win control of Lake Ontario and lay the foundation for an attack on Montreal. He also hoped success would aid the Democratic-Republicans in the April 1813 New York governor's race. Madison approved the plan, and Armstrong ordered Dearborn to mass 4,000 men at Sackets Harbor for the Kingston assault and 3,000 at Buffalo for attacks against York and Fort George, the latter on the Niagara Peninsula.[49]

The administration also expanded the army. In January 1813, Congress gave Madison the authority to fill the army to its legal number of 35,000 while not recruiting more than 20,000 new men. Meanwhile, the government approached bankruptcy and had trouble raising the $16 million it needed for 1813. By March, Armstrong was comparing the situation with Washington's at the end of 1776 when the national cause hung by a thread. He told Dearborn that if defeat greeted the new campaign "The public will lose all confidence in us, and we will even cease to have any in ourselves." The Americans couldn't fight in Lower Canada before summer 1813, if then. Fighting around Niagara became the only choice for 1813.[50]

THE NIAGARA AND LAKE ONTARIO FRONT

Secretary of War Armstrong altered his plan after the British reinforced Kingston in March 1813, believing the psychological and political results of success here more important than the physical. He reinforced Dearborn and "advised him to deliver a concentrated blow against the enemy's western posts." The politicized nature of this campaign is driven home by Armstrong's use of troops from outside New York to not weaken that state's voter base. Additionally, he made upstate New York a key army supply source.[51]

An ailing Dearborn turned over his command to the explorer Brigadier General Zebulon Pike. The Americans made an unopposed landing at York and seized the fortifications. A powder magazine exploded as they advanced through the works, killing Pike and soldiers on both sides. Discipline among the Americans broke down; the looting and burning of government buildings followed. The US suffered 20 percent casualties.[52]

Meanwhile, Prevost showed the Americans the danger of not first taking Kingston. On the night of May 26, 1813, he sailed from Kingston and attacked Sackets Harbor, New York, the base for the US offensive against York, an assault the Americans repelled. The same day, a recovered Dearborn attacked Niagara with 4,000 men. Two of his subordinates, Colonel Winfield Scott, recently freed from British captivity, and Commander Oliver Hazard Perry, captured Queenstown and Fort George after an amphibious landing. Instead of pursuing and destroying the enemy force (something common in the era's Napoleonic battles), Dearborn stayed a few days at Fort George and then dispatched 2,000 men after the enemy. The British routed them in a night attack by only 700 troops. An again ill Dearborn resigned in July.[53]

THE DETROIT AND LAKE ERIE FRONT

With bankruptcy looming, Secretary of the Treasury Gallatin urged in March 1813 only defensive operations in the west. Armstrong agreed; he wanted to use America's scant resources elsewhere. Harrison was ordered to hold until the completion of a new army base at Cleveland and a fleet at Presque Isle. After the fleet was built (completion was planned for mid May), they were to cross the lake and attack Fort Malden, Ontario. The Americans intended to control Lake Erie, a task falling to Perry who, barring a short interlude to support Dearborn, spent 1813's spring and summer building a fleet at Presque Isle. Perry scored a stunning victory over the British on September 10, 1813, a triumph marked by the only British surrender of an entire fleet during the war. The US thereafter kept control of the lake, making it impossible for Britain to supply its troops in the area.[54]

The Americans could now attack Fort Malden, south of Detroit. Perry moved Harrison's army while another American force marched along the shore toward Detroit. The outnumbered British abandoned both. Harrison left garrisons and pursued, fighting the Battle of the Thames on October 5, 1813. Harrison's 3,500 Americans defeated 2,900 British and Indians, killing Tecumseh. The successful joint use of land and sea forces broke British and Indian power in the region. July 1814 saw some Northwestern Indians sign a treaty to fight Britain. The campaign proved what the Americans could do with solid leadership and preparation.[55]

THE MONTREAL CAMPAIGN

Secretary Armstrong delivered a review of the military situation on July 23, 1813. It provided three options: destroying the British forces on the Niagara (which he thought pointless); attacking Kingston; and a two-pronged attack on Montreal with a fleet sailing down the Saint Lawrence while an army marched overland. He would leave the decision to the new general.[56] The problem was the new general.

A fourth option was severing Britain's communication on the Saint Lawrence River connecting Lake Erie with Montreal. The British remained amazed the Americans hadn't contested London's control of the waterway. Severing it would rob British forces west of Montreal of supplies and support. America's failure here derived from the influence exerted over President Madison by David Parish. Parish became rich selling farms along the Saint Lawrence and his loan of several million dollars kept the government afloat during the war. He had large holdings in the area and wanted the Saint Lawrence Valley neutral, something supported by many regional Federalists and often the British.[57]

Major General James Wilkinson assumed the Lake Ontario command in late August 1813. Renowned for corruption (he was for many years secretly in the pay of Spain), Wilkinson's military career dated to the War for Independence. Wilkinson possessed charm and a knack for impressing people, and for throwing plotting associates such as Aaron Burr under the wagon wheels to save himself. Wilkinson had successfully marched into Spanish West Florida from Louisiana in spring 1813. Louisiana's governor didn't want him back because of his venality, so Secretary Armstrong ordered him north in mid March. Wilkinson meandered, finally reaching his new command at Sackets Harbor on August 20.[58]

As Armstrong and Wilkinson debated the campaign objective, Britain reinforced Kingston in October 1813. Armstrong decided Kingston was now too hard a target and ordered Wilkinson to attack Montreal; neither probably expected success. Wilkinson sailed on November 2, late for launching a campaign in Canada. A 4,500-man army under Wade Hampton was supposed to cooperate, but it was defeated by a force of 1,500, and went into winter quarters in Plattsburgh. Wilkinson used this as an excuse to halt his campaign and enter winter quarters. Removing the primary American army from the war allowed Britain to shift troops to the Niagara front. Wilkinson mounted a failed attack in March 1814 in a vain effort to restore his reputation. Armstrong relieved him.[59]

THE 1814 CAMPAIGN

The British blockade bankrupted the US government by 1814 because it depended upon trade revenue, a wartime problem Hamilton had predicted. The government lacked sufficient money to fight the war and doubted it could borrow what was needed. Madison shocked Congress and many in his party with his March 31, 1814 request to repeal both the trade embargo and the Non-Importation Act. Washington needed money. And the trade situation in Europe had changed. The October 1813 Battle of Leipzig had shattered Napoleon's army and his restrictive Continental System. Congress agreed.[60]

THE NAVAL WAR OF 1814

By 1814, the bulk of American naval personnel served on the coast (6,512) or on the lakes (3,250). Only 450 manned ships at sea. Secretary of the Navy Jones still saw hitting British commerce as the best naval strategy. The US navy achieved little between late 1813 and the end of spring 1814. Growing British strength, poor allocation of American manpower that kept ships in port from a lack of crews, and an unwillingness to take risks to get ships to sea injured its effectiveness. In spring and summer 1814, Jones began laying up ships and dispatching sailors to the lakes. But he prepared to send cruisers back to sea in the fall against British commerce.[61]

THE 1814 CAMPAIGN

The army in June 1814 suffered from nearly every imaginable weakness, but younger, more vigorous leaders now held its operational commands. Many enlistments had expired in January 1814, but the army still had 31,000 men, 27,000 considered effective. When concentrating troops and resources, the administration tended to do so to meet the desires of political supporters. Parish wanted none on the St. Lawrence as this would endanger his financial kingdom. Powerful New York politician Peter B. Porter wanted troops on the Niagara front, producing a concentration where there was no hope of winning the war.[62] This alien influence shaped strategy.

For 1814 the administration again intended to invade Canada, specifically an army–navy expedition to capture Macadash and St. Josephs on Lake

Huron. Using Lake Erie, they would push into Upper Canada to drive off the enemy below Burlington Heights on the shore of Lake Ontario south of York. If this succeeded, and if the navy gained sufficient control of Lake Ontario, the Americans would move against York and other towns on the lake. Meanwhile, the US would grow its fleet at Sackets Harbor to block the St. Lawrence and cut Kingston's communications with Montreal, while the army at Plattsburgh tried to pin British forces by mounting a demonstration against Montreal or perhaps provoke Prevost into a disadvantageous fight.[63]

This campaign was plagued by many of the same earlier problems. There was no area commander. The various army and navy leaders were their own masters and cooperated if they wished and if they liked one another, which was rare. The two primary army commanders, Jacob Brown and George Izard, refused to work together. Isaac Chauncey, who commanded the naval forces on Lake Ontario, did as he wished.[64]

Brown, attacking on the Niagara peninsula, intended to take Fort Erie, then Fort George, and then sweep the rest of the British settlements on Lake Ontario to Kingston. He assumed the navy's movements would be subordinated to his because the army had defended Sackets Harbor. He told Chauncey to meet him with the fleet at Lake George on July 10. Chauncey took offense and refused. Brown crossed into Canada on July 1, 1814, took Fort Erie on July 3, defeated a larger British force at Chippewa on July 5, and pushed on to Queenstown and Fort George. Since Chauncey had not joined him even after a second invitation, Brown withdrew. On July 25, his forces clashed with the British at Lundy's Lane. The Americans retreated to Fort Erie where they were besieged by the British. Chauncey and the fleet appeared off Fort George on August 5, but it no longer mattered. The plan for Brown's offensive had been decided in Madison's cabinet, which had failed to resolve the command problem.[65]

Chauncey had preferred sitting in Sackets Harbor to risking his fleet, though his orders were "to give priority to contesting control of Lake Ontario." He was replaced by Stephen Decatur at the end of July because of illness. Decatur had the same orders, though with an addendum "to cooperate with the army on the Niagara" if he thought it feasible. Secretary Armstrong believed Brown could only secure Lake Ontario if the navy helped and asked Madison to change the orders. Madison refused, and said the real problem was the failure of Brown and Izard to cooperate. Armstrong had sent them identical orders, with no result. The army did little the remainder of the summer. Madison reprimanded Armstrong and seized control of the War Department in mid August by requiring Armstrong to consult on all substantive issues.[66]

THE BRITISH STRIKE

Madison worried in May 1814 that Britain might take the war to the south, even to Washington itself. But neither Madison nor Armstrong did much to prepare for this. Armstrong believed it unlikely, the militia commander, William Winder, was incompetent, and Congress never voted funds for the city's defenses.[67]

Britain's war against the US intensified in 1814 as the war against Napoleon ended with the emperor's April abdication. The same month, Vice Admiral Sir Alexander Cochrane extended the blockade to the rest of the US coast to deny the US tax revenue from trade. In the summer, Britain dispatched experienced units from Europe with the intention of mounting a summer and fall 1814 campaign along the route of their 1776 and 1777 Canada offensives. The British hoped to gain a secure position to force border revisions in New York or perhaps Maine. Attacks on America's seaboard to divert its attention from Canada supported this.[68]

Britain launched its diversionary raids in the Chesapeake in August 1814. Revenge for America's 1813 burning of York was a motivator, as was Britain's belief that a stunning military victory might bring America to terms. The British defeated the Americans at Bladensburg, Maryland, took the American capital, Washington, burned the government buildings, and withdrew. An attack against Baltimore followed in early September 1814. Stubborn resistance and the refusal of Fort McHenry's defenders to surrender forced a British withdrawal. Simultaneously, the British invaded Maine on September 2, 1814, while hoping to stir antiwar sentiment in New England. Seizing most of the sate east of the Penobscot River gave them a territorial bargaining chip.[69]

Britain also attacked New York, pushing south an army of 12,000 supported by warships. Waiting for them at Plattsburgh was an American army of 1,700 regulars and 3,200 militia under Alexander Macomb, and a naval squadron under Thomas Macdonough. The War Department weakened the US defense by ordering troops away, having been tricked by an enemy deception operation. The British tried mounting simultaneous land and naval attacks, but the naval assault went in several hours before the land attack. By the time Prevost began his offensive, he realized the navy verged on defeat. He couldn't maintain his army without naval support, cancelled his assault, and retreated.[70]

The victory at Plattsburgh was a rare American bright spot. Madison pushed out Armstrong after Washington's burning, and Monroe again carried the portfolios for both State and Defense. Secretary of the Navy Jones quit on December 1, 1814. Treasury Secretary Gallatin resigned because of the collapse of the nation's finances. Monroe now believed he needed 100,000 men to conquer Canada but in December 1814 had 40,000 and little hope of raising more. Conscription was politically impossible, and men don't join armies that won't be paid. Some troops went unpaid for a year, and the army's logistical system began collapsing because America couldn't pay the suppliers. The new secretary of the treasury said the government needed $56 million to fund the war in 1815 but would only have $15.1 million in revenue. Borrowing the shortfall was unlikely because no one had faith in the government. The US had a shortage of hard money (specie) because it had been consumed buying smuggled British imports. With no cash, the banking system teetered on collapse, because there was no national bank to support it.[71]

ANDREW JACKSON'S WAR IN THE SOUTH

On June 27, 1813, a group of settlers in the Mississippi Territory attacked a party of Creek Indians they believed were arming to assault White settlers. They were actually preparing to fight other Creeks in their own civil war, but the unprovoked assault produced war with the Creeks. The Americans gathered in forts throughout the region. Those at Fort Mims, about 40 miles north of Mobile, Alabama, were massacred at the end of August, stunning the region.[72]

Even before this, the administration believed that since it would take a large tranche of Canada in 1813, Britain would retaliate by attacking the vulnerable Southwest, where its Spanish ally controlled ports in Florida, and raise the Creeks against the Americans. If London or Madrid aided the Creeks, the US would have an excuse to take Spanish Florida. In July 1813, the secretary of war ordered the governors of Tennessee and Georgia to each recruit 1,500 troops to put down the Creeks. But the administration never had a strategy for fighting the Creeks, primarily because it lacked forces.[73]

Tennessee responded by raising an army of 5,000. The head of the West Tennessee Militia, a planter named Andrew Jackson, was given command. Jackson pursued the war with a single-mindedness demonstrated by no other American commander. About 2,500 men gathered in early October and marched into what is now Alabama. Jackson pushed deep into Creek territory, advancing to the junction of the Coosa and Tallapoosa Rivers about 10 miles north of present-day Montgomery, winning battles along the way and building forts to establish control. He wanted to drive to Pensacola if he found evidence of Spanish support for the Creeks but didn't believe he had the forces. He stopped, built Fort Strother at Ten Islands on the Coosa River, and waited for more troops.[74]

Jackson's force dwindled to 130 men by the end of January 1814. He was eventually reinforced, went on the offensive, and broke Creek power on March 27, 1814, at Horseshoe Bend. He built Fort Jackson on the site and negotiated a treaty with the Creeks granting America most Creek lands in the region. Jackson's victory proved among the war's most significant and greatly increased Britain's difficulties in invading the south.[75]

But Jackson's war wasn't over. London hoped to take New Orleans and possibly even tear away Louisiana. Britain offered to negotiate in late 1813, and the commencement of talks encouraged Britain to try to take the city. Vice Admiral Sir Alexander Cochrane had 10,000 men and his fleet, and planned to take Mobile and advance on New Orleans, supported by attacks inland from Apalachicola, Florida.[76]

Jackson was named a major general in May 1814 and given command of the region. Initially, Jackson didn't believe the British threatened New Orleans but were instead helping the Creeks, and considered it more important to remove what he saw as a coalition of British, Indians, and former slaves gathering in Spanish territory. He concentrated his forces at Mobile and took Pensacola from Spain on November 7, 1814. He then moved to New Orleans to defend the city and became famous for inflicting a heavy defeat on the attacking British on January 8, 1815.[77]

ENDING THE WAR

When the British offered to negotiate in 1813, the US dispatched a team of five representatives that included Gallatin, Clay, and John Quincy Adams. They were to secure an end to impressment and the cession of Canada. Even though Britain held more of the US than the US did of Canada, Monroe wanted his representatives to convince London of the inevitability of Canada's loss. Napoleon's abdication cost the Americans what little leverage they possessed. They reduced their demands in June 1814 to ending the conflict at the prewar boundaries. The administration believed Napoleon's fall would end impressment and accepted that they couldn't win on one of the war's key causes.[78]

The negotiations began in Ghent in August 1814. No longer strapped for resources, the British raised the ante. They demanded restrictions on US fishing in Canadian waters, border revisions at America's expense to make Canada more defensible, and an Indian buffer composed of American lands stretching from the Great Lakes to the Ohio River. Britain had promised the Indians this for joining the war and argued for it by representing the Indians as a sovereign people needing protection from American speculators and settlers. The Americans refused to recognize the Indians as anything other than, as Clay said, "savage tribes, scattered over our acknowledged territory."[79]

In October 1814, the Americans learned Britain's new terms. Monroe believed the union was too shaky to make concessions affecting one region more heavily, and the results of an Indian buffer zone would fall on the west. Moreover, the breakup of the country seemed possible in late 1814 as British naval power was driving US coastal areas out of the war. Britain had occupied much of Maine and forced the neutralization of Nantucket Island. New England suffered deep disaffection with the war. Some Federalists called for states to take control of their own defense and sign separate peace agreements with Britain. A secret Federalist convention met in Hartford, Connecticut, sparking speculation of secession and civil war.[80]

Events in Europe saved the Americans from themselves. Problems at the Congress of Vienna threatened to sink Europe's negotiations and renew the Napoleonic Wars. Britain's leaders didn't believe they could guarantee a victorious end to the American war in another campaign and decided to end it. As it had in 1783 and 1794, Britain abandoned its Indian allies. London dropped the demand for an Indian buffer and pushed a vague proposal granting the Indians rights they possessed in 1811. The US accepted because it required nothing. Britain agreed to American fortifications and warships on the Great Lakes and recognition of most prewar boundaries. The accord was signed on December 24, 1814. It wasn't a true status quo antebellum agreement, because the US kept Mobile and its environs, which it had seized from Spain. Both sides thought it a temporary truce. The administration agreed with Britain's insistence on returning lands taken from the Indians under the treaty of Fort Jackson and ordered Jackson to do so in June 1815. He refused. The administration feared opposing the Southwest's hero and Britain looked the other way.[81]

CONCLUSION

The Democratic-Republicans had hoped the war would end intraparty factionalism. It didn't.[82] Going to war can be one of the most politically contentious things a nation can do, and this war, like most later US conflicts, sparked internal opposition. The resistance, though, went beyond simple protest to deep treason for which no one was held accountable.

America's execution of the war suffered from horrendous and often nonexistent strategic and operational planning and disastrous operational leadership. Moreover, the Americans seem to have learned few of the tactical and operational lessons of the French Revolutionary and Napoleonic Wars. The small size of America's armies certainly would have made adoption of the Napoleonic corps system impossible, but they could have selected energetic and youthful leaders based on merit. Considering the utter incompetence with which American political and military leaders approached and waged the war, it could have been worse. Concentration of forces, good leadership, solid planning and preparation, unified command: fixing these problems could have produced a different war.

Jackson's victory in New Orleans laid the foundation for future American growth and possibly spared the severance of some of the south from the country as the British recognized neither the Louisiana Purchase nor America's Florida conquests. The Treaty of Ghent ending the war addressed neither of these. The New Orleans victory also shaped American memory of the war. Most learned of it before the peace treaty and thus drew a false connection between the two. The antiwar Federalists also made the mistake of appearing in Washington at the same time with their Hartford Convention demands for various changes to the Constitution. Federalists were rounded upon as treasonous in every election thereafter and suffered severe electoral defeats.[83]

Despite its incompetence, Madison's Democratic-Republican Party emerged from the war with a tighter grip on power. His party's method of waging war – doing so on a shoestring – stood in contrast to the thinking of his Federalist predecessors. Though dangerous, it proved "politically safe."[84]

THE SECOND BARBARY WAR, 1815

The US wasted no time before going to war again. After Madison's request, Congress authorized war against Algiers on March 3, 1815, after the Algerians seized a US merchantman and imprisoned the crew. Stephen Decatur and William Bainbridge led two naval squadrons into the Mediterranean. Decatur forced the Algerians to release their US prisoners, pay compensation they so often extorted from others, and grant the US most-favored-nation trading status. He then sailed to Tunis and Tripoli, freeing prisoners, and extracting payment for ships the pirates had taken. When Bainbridge joined him, the flotillas cruised the Mediterranean together to make a point. Success here drove the two other Barbary governments to stop demanding tribute from America.[85]

AFTER THE WAR OF 1812

Madison seized upon the nationalistic feelings generated by the war's end to launch the Madisonian Platform. Militarily, he wanted to maintain some wartime military structures, improve the militia, complete ships under construction, and build coastal defenses. But his economic proposals were the most ambitious: he wanted a new national bank, protective tariffs, and infrastructure improvements. Pushing for and securing the second Bank of the United States was a change for the party of Jefferson. Madison saw tariffs primarily as protection for US industry, particularly those for defense and that had sprung up during the war as the result of the loss of British imports. Internal improvements such as canals and roads were meant to support economic development and tie the nation together. Congress gave Madison his protective tariff in 1816.[86]

The War of 1812 shows how badly the US can wage war and must be judged a defeat for the United States. The administration not only failed to achieve its stated political aims, but its staggering military and political incompetence forced the nation to incur costs in money, blood, and internal political dissension outweighing the scant territorial gains. Jefferson's Louisiana Purchase acquired vastly more, peacefully, and paved the road to American continental domination.

3

SEEKING A CONTINENT: EXPANSION, INDIAN REMOVAL, AND THE MEXICAN WAR, 1817–1849

INTRODUCTION

America's drives for expansion and security were often intertwined. And also used all elements of national power, scant though they may have been. The 1817 to 1849 period gave the US leaders who were masters at this, and some who weren't. The most successful possessed a blaring clarity in their political aims – both in peace and war – and pushed the machine of state to achieve them. But trying to act on the cheap risked disaster.

THE JAMES MONROE AND JOHN QUINCY ADAMS ADMINISTRATIONS, 1817–29

James Monroe's service to the nation stretched from being wounded at Trenton during the War for Independence, to Virginia's governorship, to being secretary of state and of war in the Madison administration, sometimes simultaneously, to the presidency. His key advisor, and one of America's grand strategists, was his secretary of state, John Quincy Adams, a son of the nation's second president, who succeeded Monroe as president in 1825. Some regard Adams as America's greatest secretary of state. He was certainly among the most intelligent and qualified. Having spent seventeen years in Europe in his father's train or as a diplomat, he had exceptional knowledge of the continent and its political machinations and spoke six European languages. Critically, Adams possessed vision. He knew where he wanted the US to go and wasn't afraid to move the country in that direction. He was a devout Christian who shared the view of many early American leaders that God had a special role for America in the world; his faith shaped his revulsion to slavery. Monroe and Adams shared political aims, and Monroe could lead strongminded subordinates to achieve his purposes together. Adams, during his own single-term presidency, proved less successful, but his presence in both administrations links them.[1]

PART I: FROM BACKWATER TO GREAT POWER

THE POLITICAL AIMS

Monroe and Adams relentlessly pursued territorial expansion. Acquiring Spanish Florida was particularly important. Securing one aim – expansion – was necessary for obtaining another – security. Sovereignty intertwined all of this, as did slavery, which influenced expansion's results. Adams sought security by replacing European powers in North America. He believed the US should control North America, its natural domain. In a contentious January 1821 meeting on Britain's global claims, Adams brushed aside Britain's insistence upon title to the Oregon territory and other parts of North America, provoking a distressed British envoy to inquire whether US ambitions aimed at Canada. Adams said they didn't but added: "Keep what is yours and leave the rest of the continent to us."[2]

THE ASSESSMENT: THREATS, RISKS, DANGERS, CHALLENGES

To properly construct and implement a grand strategy, it is critical to first understand the purpose one seeks, then assess the situation to discover the obstacles to achieving this. Challenges and constraints arise from your position and actions, and from states with which pursuit of your aims creates cross-purposes. There are many questions to consider. Who are the enemies? What are their aims? What are the challenges? What are the risks and costs? Are they worth the rewards? And will the people pay them?

Internal dangers took flight in political division and the struggle over slavery and its extension, which became linked to expansion. The establishment of new states challenged traditional power blocks while upsetting the delicate political balance between slave and free states. Externally, Britain controlled Canada and embarked upon naval building on the Great Lakes. The US acquired Louisiana, but Spain disputed its borders. Spanish Florida harbored Creek Indians that endangered US settlements. The revolutions sweeping Latin and South America threatened to provoke French or Spanish interventions. Russia eyed the Pacific Northwest. The War of 1812 proved oceans didn't guarantee security, especially when one lacked a navy; military weakness left one open to aggression. America required more military strength and internal improvements, which necessitated a more activist government. To achieve its aims, America needed to stay uninvolved in Europe's quarrels and keep out the Europeans.[3]

Adams foresaw another danger: America involving itself beyond its capabilities, a possibility arising from America's internal debate over recognizing the independence of former Spanish colonies and supporting

European liberation movements. Adams urged patience on recognition: "The principle of neutrality in *all* foreign wars is, in my opinion, fundamental to the continuance of our liberties and of our Union." To Adams, a successful American republican experiment would be a beacon to other nations. Americans had begun something that would one day overthrow tyranny everywhere. But supporting republican and independence movements abroad didn't mean intervention. In his most famous speech, he said the US supported others seeking freedom, but America "goes not abroad, in search of monsters to destroy." The US wished them well, but involvement meant assuming a responsibility the nation couldn't bear. America

> knows that by once enlisting under other banners than her own, were they even the banner of foreign Independence, she would involve herself beyond the power of extrication, in all the wars of interest and intrigue ... which assume the colors and usurp the standard of freedom. The fundamental maxims of her policy would insensibly change from *liberty* to *force*.... She might become the dictatress of the world. She would be no longer the ruler of her own spirit.[4]

GRAND STRATEGY

Adams worked to undermine European claims in North America. He believed some of this would occur as areas on America's edges were inexorably pulled into Washington's orbit and annexed. The distance to Europe was too great, the costs and problems of keeping them too large, and the attraction of the United States too strong. As historian Charles Edel wrote: "Such a gravitational strategy dictated that the United States expand where it could, bide its time elsewhere, and make sure that its commitments not exceed its capabilities."[5]

In his 1825 presidential inaugural address, Adams looked back at the Monroe administration and described its grand strategic approach:

> The great features ... have been to cherish peace while preparing for defensive war; to yield exact justice to other nations and maintain the rights of our own; to cherish the principles of freedom and of equal rights wherever they were proclaimed; to discharge with all possible promptitude the national debt; to reduce within the narrowest limits of efficiency the military force; to improve the organization and discipline of the Army; to provide and sustain a school of military science; to extend equal protection to all the great interests of the nation; to promote the civilization of the Indian tribes, and to proceed in the great system of internal improvements within the limits of the constitutional power of the Union.[6]

DIPLOMATIC STRATEGY

Adams wanted to reduce security risks. He pushed neutrality in foreign affairs but knew this was impossible unless the US possessed sufficient military strength to keep from being forced to choose a side. Continental expansion reduced risks from foreign powers, meaning European. Adams believed a stable peace with Britain necessary. Both found it useful economically and signed the Rush–Bagot Agreement in 1817, establishing an unfortified border and demilitarizing the Great Lakes. An 1818 agreement established a 48th parallel boundary from today's Minnesota to the Rocky Mountains and opened western lands to settlement.[7]

Diplomatic strategy rested on the Monroe Doctrine. This was rooted in fears of Russian Pacific expansion. Moscow claimed much of the Pacific Northwest and had approached fur trader John Jacob Astor in September 1809 about assuming the Russian American Company's shipping of furs to China. Astor gained President Jefferson's support to establish the Pacific Fur Trading Company and built a fort on the Columbia River in 1810. It became Astoria in 1811, the first permanent American Pacific settlement. Jefferson foresaw not a colony, but a future sibling republic "bound to the United States by ties of blood, language and friendship." Pacific Fur sold the settlement to Britain in 1813 because it couldn't be protected, but President Madison ensured its return in the Treaty of Ghent.[8]

During the War of 1812, Russia expanded its trading posts along the Pacific Coast and to Hawaii. Tsar Alexander I's 1821 edict excluding foreign ships from sailing within 115 miles of Russian territory provoked a reaction. The administration insisted "the United States would contest the right of Russia to any territorial establishment on the American continent and ... distinctly assume the principle that the American continents are no longer subjects for any new European colonial establishments." Adams insisted it was unimaginable "in the present condition of the world, *any* European nation should entertain the project of settling a *colony* on the Northwest coast of America." Adams first sought to shrink Russia's territorial claims and secure freedom for US trade in Russia's American lands, but on July 15, 1823, wrote: "But what right has Russia to *any* colonial footing on the continent? And is it not time for the American *Nations* to inform the Sovereigns of Europe, that the American continents are no longer open to the settlement of new European colonies?"[9]

The threat of further European intrusions provided the underpinning, but a November 1823 Russian statement about suppressing republican government furnished the catalyst, feeding US fears of Europe's monarchist

Holy Alliance helping Madrid regain its rebellious colonies in the Americas. London also disliked what it heard and approached Washington about issuing an opposing joint statement. Adams saw little chance of invasion, thought America looked stronger with an independent pronouncement, and believed its replies should form part of an integrated strategy. He also saw London's proposal as a trap for containing America and wanted it clear Washington opposed not only Europeans using force in South America, but also sought "to disclaim all interference on our part with Europe."[10]

In Monroe's December 2, 1823 Annual Message to Congress, he declared America's intention to maintain the Western Hemisphere as its sphere of influence. Adams' accompanying paper (technically a response to Russian and British notes) laid out America's desire for friendship with all, noninvolvement in European political combinations, and an insistence the US couldn't stand by if Europe attempted to impose European control over former Spanish colonies.[11] The US declared any European attempt:

> to extend their system to any portion of this hemisphere as dangerous to our peace and safety. With the existing colonies or dependencies of any European power we have not interfered and shall not interfere, but with the Governments who have declared their independence and maintained it, and whose independence we have, on great consideration and on just principles, acknowledged, we could not view any interposition for the purpose of oppressing them, or controlling in any other manner their destiny, by any European power in any other light than as the manifestation of an unfriendly disposition toward the United States.... It is impossible that the allied powers should extend their political system to any portion of either continent without endangering our peace and happiness; nor can anyone believe that our southern brethren, if left to themselves, would adopt it of their own accord. It is equally impossible, therefore, that we should behold such interposition in any form with indifference.[12]

The Monroe Doctrine was born, though largely by Adams' hand. America now considered any future European colonization in the Western Hemisphere hostile, but the US wouldn't involve itself with European nations wrestling independence forces. At the time of the Doctrine's pronouncement, America lacked the ability to enforce it and the tsar had already repealed his edict, but one sees it first applied in 1824. America secured trading privileges for a decade and a commitment from Moscow to not cede Alaska to a third nation. The Monroe Doctrine became important for asserting an American sphere of influence and shaping US foreign relations and public opinion.[13]

ECONOMIC STRATEGY

Monroe saw protecting American manufacturing a necessity. Adams believed a republic best provided people the chance to prosper. To ensure and stabilize it, and give the US political system more appeal, he pursued economic growth to improve people's lives, and attacked slavery because it made the US system less attractive morally.[14] The question was how to build America's economic strength.

By 1814, the Embargo and Non-Intercourse Acts and the War of 1812 shrank American imports and exports to one-tenth and one-fifteenth, respectively, of 1807. These functioned as protective tariffs for the American textile industry while forcing some self-sufficiency as the nation sprouted industrial and textile manufacturers. Producers correctly feared a flood of cheap British goods as London tried to crush nascent American industry to remove a competitor. Henry Clay and John C. Calhoun passed America's first purely protective tariff in 1816, launching a century of tariff arguments. This proved inadequate against more efficient British manufacturers while Southern agriculture was unhappy because it risked retaliation against its exports.[15]

An economic crisis hit the US in 1818–19. Agricultural prices stood high, but those for manufactures plummeted. Hamilton's argument to build a domestic market and greater urban population to sustain agricultural prices while expanding industry behind a protective tariff reentered the national conversation. Negotiations, threats, embargos, and war had failed to gain the US equal trading rights. American leaders of all political stripes, even Jefferson, became supporters of building a manufacturing base to protect the nation during wars.[16]

This era gave the US its first true economist, Daniel Raymond, who published *Thoughts on Political Economy* in 1820. He focused upon how to promote national wealth, not individual. He pushed long-term thinking, arguing that leaders should "consider the nation immortal, and … legislate for it as though it was to exist forever." He argued it was government's duty to help the employment situation and believed allowing importation of goods merely because they were cheaper for consumers was wrong if it cost American jobs.[17]

In Federalist Paper 11, Hamilton suggested using trade as a foreign relations tool for influencing how European powers dealt with US neutrality. Adams supported this, though disliked Hamilton. Trade could help grow the country, making relations with it attractive, or be used to punish. But the US couldn't remain neutral on trade matters if it lacked the military means to protect its commerce at sea. Monroe and Adams pushed hard for bilateral trade reciprocity treaties, including one with Britain. Reciprocity deals avoided the complications of considering third states, were simpler than most-favored-nation agreements, and often worked to America's advantage because US merchant and shipping skills trumped competitors.[18]

Clay supported "free trade of perfect reciprocity" but believed access to cheap consumer goods didn't outweigh one-sided agreements with foreign nations wishing to export to America. He also incorrectly thought foreign trade competition caused wars. To Clay, free trade required two conditions that don't exist: "perpetual peace" and every state trading freely. He observed that European states had no romantic ideas about trade and restricted imports to protect their industries. The Tariff Act of 1824 followed. Clay modified Hamilton's ideas, relaunching them as his American System. He believed a home market always better: foreign powers can't close it. This could be built with a protective tariff that grew US industry, helped stabilize agricultural prices, and raised revenue for internal improvements, uniting industry and agriculture while helping develop both.[19]

MILITARY STRATEGY

Under the Monroe administration, Secretary of War Calhoun won the argument that the regular army should provide the foundation of American military planning and not the militia, and addressed the army's command problems by establishing a commanding general. In 1816, Congress approved the nation's first peacetime extended naval building program. Its core included nine ships of the line and twelve frigates. The US began permanently deploying a warship in the Pacific in 1816, established a small Pacific force in 1821, and the East Asia Squadron in 1835. The postwar willingness to spend on defense was short-lived. The 1819 financial crisis saw the naval budget cut and the construction timeline lengthened. The envisioned ships were completed, but most were mothballed and smaller vessels filled out the navy. The army was soon slashed to 6,000.[20]

Calhoun brought energy and creativity to the office of secretary of war. His most ambitious undertaking was securing the Western frontier with a 1,600-mile chain of forts stretching from Sault Sainte Marie, Minnesota, to St. Louis, Missouri. This would make impossible Britain inciting the Indians, show Native Americans Washington's power, and give America dominance over the fur trade. Calhoun didn't get all his forts, but those built cemented authority over the Northwest. Congress also began funding a coastal fortification system.[21]

Adams believed the most important lesson of the War of 1812 was that it was "the primary duty of the nation to place itself in a state of permanent preparation for self-defence." He thought America should have realized its need for a strong navy to protect its trade, and the necessity of supporting domestic industry and sound finance. American freedom depended upon being able to defend itself with military force. He wasn't afraid to use military power when he deemed it appropriate. He had a navy sloop seize Astoria in Oregon after Britain refused to surrender it as the Treaty of Ghent dictated. Britain protested but cared more about its trading relations with America.[22]

THE FIRST SEMINOLE WAR, 1817-19

The most important military event in the Monroe–Adams administrations was its war against the Seminole, an amalgamation of Creek tribes in Florida.[23] Indian cross-border raids, attacks against White squatters on Indian lands, and the insistence of Indian leaders in Fowltown, Georgia, that the Flint River was the border, created a volatile mix. Major General Edmund Gaines, the officer charged with controlling the borderland, dispatched an expedition to destroy Fowltown. The Seminoles fled and replied with a brutal massacre of Whites.[24]

On December 26, 1817, Secretary of War Calhoun ordered Jackson, who commanded the southern military district, to "adopt the necessary measures to terminate a conflict." Jackson saw an opportunity to end Indian attacks from Florida and forestall any possible foreign invasion in the area. He wrote Monroe urging the seizure of East Florida, receiving through a designated third party permission to do what he already wanted. The intrigue gave Monroe what later eras called "plausible deniability."[25]

Jackson left Tennessee on January 22, 1818. In 45 days, he was 450 miles away at Fort Scott with his army. Failing to bring the Indians to battle, and low on supplies, he struck for the Gulf coast and the mouth of the Apalachicola River, rendezvousing with his supply ships on March 15, 1818. He had 3,000 troops and 2,000 Indians, primarily Creek. Jackson decided the way to win the war was to take Spain's posts. The Seminoles, meanwhile, appealed to Britain and Spain for help. Jackson marched from Fort Gadsden on March 26, heading for St. Marks on the Gulf coast. The Spanish fort at St. Marks offered no resistance but provided evidence of Spanish support for the Seminoles. Jackson also tried and executed two Britons caught aiding the Seminoles. This should have been decided by Washington, but Jackson told Calhoun he wanted to make clear to London the cost of inciting the Indians to war.[26]

Jackson decided to reduce the rest of Florida by taking Pensacola. He believed that if the Spanish held Florida, the departure of his army would see the Indians return to attacking American settlements. He reached Pensacola on May 24, easily seizing the town because the Spanish had withdrawn most of their forces to adjacent Fort Carlos de Barrancas. When the Spanish refused to surrender, Jackson began shelling the fort and prepared an assault. The Spanish gave way. The surrender terms included cession of Spanish Florida. Jackson established a provisional government, sent his Spanish prisoners to Cuba, and wrote Calhoun: "The Seminole War, may now be considered at a close."[27]

Whether or not Monroe approved Jackson's actions is in dispute, but Monroe and Adams certainly approved the result. There is also the question of whether Monroe had the constitutional authority to launch this war. Adams argued Monroe acted within his presidential powers, because it was a defensive response to an attack on the US, and thus Congress' approval wasn't needed. The Quasi-War example and court precedent agreed.[28]

During Jackson's campaign, Adams had been negotiating with Spain's representative, discovering Spain had decided to cede West Florida, but news of Jackson's seizure of the territory saw negotiations on boundaries halted until Washington dealt with Jackson. Adams saw a chance to make the nation's borders more secure by driving Spain from Florida and grasped it. He insisted Spain not controlling its territory and meeting its obligation to control the Indians made US actions acceptable. By its failures, "Spain had forfeited its right to inviolable sovereignty."[29] The George W. Bush administration made a similar argument regarding states and terrorism after the 9/11 attacks.

In February 1819, the Transcontinental Treaty settled the borders between the US and Spain in the New World as Florida was officially transferred and Madrid recognized the American boundary stretching to the Pacific. Washington's price was agreeing Texas' border was the Sabine River and not the Rio Grande. The treaty inflamed sectional tensions and fears of additional slave states, and the Texas boundary upset Southerners. Adams understood the sectional frictions but feared acquiring Texas too soon and firing internal division. The 1820 Missouri Compromise temporarily defused matters. Maine entered as a free state, Missouri as a slave one, and slavery was prohibited in the Louisiana Purchase territories.[30]

EXPANSION: INDIAN REMOVAL

Monroe noted in his March 1817 inaugural address that: "With the Indian tribes it is our duty to cultivate friendly relations and to act with kindness and liberality in all our transactions. Equally proper is it to persevere in our efforts to extend to them the advantages of civilization."[31] This was preferred; reality proved different.

The idea of Indian removal from the East originated with Jefferson in 1803 after the Louisiana Purchase. His proposed constitutional amendment was never considered, but Congress voted the president authority to trade eastern tribal lands for territory beyond the Mississippi River. Another impetus for removal was the failure of government programs to educate and "civilize" the Indians, and the injurious effects of White civilization. To early advocates, removal seemed the only way to preserve Indian culture. Putting them beyond the worst White influences would gain time to educate, civilize, and Christianize them. The Monroe and Adams administrations encouraged voluntary emigration to resolve tensions over territorial control. White settlements sometimes now surrounded Indian lands.[32]

The government's primary tool for addressing the Indians continued to be Andrew Jackson. In June 1818, Monroe detailed him to negotiate with the Chickasaw for control of their remaining Kentucky and Tennessee lands. Jackson pressured the reluctant Chickasaw by secretly withholding a $12,000 annuity promised in 1816, one already in arrears, in the hopes of having a full delegation with which to negotiate. The Chickasaw still resisted. Jackson bribed the key chiefs to make a deal. The Cherokee, who lived primarily in Georgia, and some other non-nomadic nations, were not so quickly swayed. The Cherokee had rights to their lands via 1802 and 1816 agreements and were acculturated in a manner that included their own written language and newspapers. Monroe wanted Indian removal but rejected forced expulsion, as did Adams when president. Jackson told the government the Cherokees wanted to go west and should be encouraged to do so. He believed treaties weren't the best way to deal with the Indians because they could be arranged only by bribing the leaders, something he detested and found dishonorable, but still did. He preferred legislation. In 1827, the Cherokee alarmed both Federal and Georgia officials by promulgating a constitution modeled after America's in which they declared themselves a sovereign state.[33] Resolution awaited Jackson's presidency.

Jackson was asked to help negotiate Choctaw removal from the Mississippi area. Jackson told their chiefs in October 1820 that if they didn't go west, they would lose their culture, identity, and religion, and become like White men – which frightened the chiefs – and the Whites would take their land anyway. Jackson asked for about half their territory, 5 million acres, in exchange for 13 million acres in what is now Oklahoma, insisting the US needed their land for national security. Tough negotiations culminated in threats from Jackson that if they waited, Washington would negotiate with their Choctaw brothers in Arkansas, producing only an acre-for-acre exchange. Bribing important chiefs helped seal the October 20, 1820 treaty.[34]

ASSESSING THE MONROE AND ADAMS ADMINISTRATIONS

Adams had great plans when he became president. In his 1825 address to Congress, he proposed a greater national role in the Americas, a larger navy, a naval academy, a national university, and other things. Most important was a national system of canals and roads to tie the nation together and aid industrial development. Adams accomplished little. He didn't understand the shifting political landscape and the burgeoning partisanship that prevented him from selling his agenda and underestimated the growing divisiveness of slavery and how this poisoned issues that strengthened the Federal government. He made the error he feared his country would make: reaching beyond the ability to grasp.[35]

Monroe and Adams achieved their expansionist purposes and made the nation more capable of maintaining its security and sovereignty. They secured Florida, formalized the nation's southern border, and made the US a Pacific power by anchoring it in Oregon. They reduced the chances of foreign intervention, though Britain remained a continental rival and potential threat. Part of their success was industrial, some arising from the use of protective tariffs, particularly for the textile, iron, and steel industries. Tariffs are useful economic strategy tools when facing a superior or predatory rival. Here, they helped the nation leap into the industrial revolution. The 1824 and 1828 tariffs fed textile and iron manufacturing growth. In 1824, 2 million Americans worked in manufacturing, a tenfold increase in five years.[36]

―――――♦―――――

THE AGE OF ANDREW JACKSON, 1829–41

To Andrew Jackson, life had always been a struggle. Orphaned at 14 after barely surviving imprisonment, smallpox, near-starvation, and being sabered by a British officer (Jackson and his brother had been serving as Patriot couriers), he went on to train in the law, serve as a congressman, senator, and judge, and, most famously, a soldier. Upon taking up the presidency, he approached its challenges with deadly seriousness.

PART I: FROM BACKWATER TO GREAT POWER

THE ASSESSMENT AND THE POLITICAL AIMS

The most important thing to Jackson was protecting the Union from external and internal dangers – security. For example, externally, in 1814, during the War of 1812, making peace with the Creeks fell to him as the regional military commander. He sought to link the various White settlements in Tennessee, Georgia, and the Mississippi Territory as a "bulwark against foreign invasion" that would also prevent future Spanish and British efforts to provoke the region's Indians against Whites. Doing this meant appropriating Creek, Cherokee, and Chickasaw land, including from Creek who fought alongside Jackson. The war with Britain was ongoing. US security demanded this. Jackson acted. On internal threats, Jackson supported the Union above all things, but respected the rights of states delineated in the Constitution.[37] Changing these to the Union's harm was intolerable.

DIPLOMATIC STRATEGY

Though unafraid to fight, Jackson didn't look for wars, and used negotiations and diplomacy to resolve disputes and achieve his ends. In his inaugural address, he laid out his desire to resolve disputes with France, Britain, and Spain, and wasted no time dispatching new representatives to these three largest export markets and tasking them with increasing American trade. When an agreement to reopen trade with Britain's possessions in the West Indies was slow in coming, Jackson considered a nonintercourse act with Canada. But his diplomats renewed trade with the West Indies, settled claims with Spain, and resolved damage claims against France from the Napoleonic period. French backpedaling provoked nasty exchanges and fears of war when Jackson severed relations in November 1835. Jackson accepted London's mediation offer but also asked Congress to ban French goods and vote more money for defense. The French paid. Jackson resolved problems confounding his supposedly more sophisticated predecessors.[38]

Jackson tried to gain Texas via diplomacy, branding it a border adjustment to avoid offending Mexico. Diplomacy failed because of Mexican governmental instability, the incompetence of Jackson's agent, and Jackson's refusal to bribe Mexican officials. He was willing to pay Mexico's government a fixed sum but considered direct bribery injurious to national honor and no guarantee of a deal. Jackson wanted a geographical barrier between American immigrants to Texas and native Mexicans and disliked Mexico's thin authority over Texas. Political vacuums invited problems that could threaten American security, and he thought the Americans in Texas would eventually seize upon an incident to declare independence. Antonio López de Santa Anna's assumption of power in Mexico and massing of authority in his hands frightened Texans into declaring independence. Santa Anna's war to regain Texas saw the famous 1836 Battle of the Alamo and Texas' successful independence fight. Jackson kept the US neutral.[39]

INDIAN REMOVAL

George Washington's administration had dealt with the Indians as though they were sovereign. This changed under Jackson. He reasoned that since the US was no longer weak it could dictate to the Indians what they did within the bounds of the United States. When he became president in 1829, Jackson wanted to immediately launch Indian removal but needed Congressional support. He was genuinely concerned about the possible destruction of the Indians and believed moving them west would allow the government to protect them. His haste was encouraged by Georgia declaring in December 1828 that Indians in the state would fall under its jurisdiction in six months, something certain to create trouble. Jackson intended for the Indians to become US citizens when they adopted White culture but knew White greed for Indian land was unstoppable, producing violence and the extermination of any Indians in the way. The administration failed to convince the Cherokee and Creek to go west. Jackson saw removal as the only answer but failed to anticipate what would happen.[40]

In his December 1829 address to Congress, Jackson declared the impossibility of the Cherokee forming their own state as the Constitution forbid this within another jurisdiction without approval of the original state's legislature. Jackson "advised them to emigrate beyond the Mississippi or submit to the laws of those states" where they resided. Only voluntary removal to an area not controlled by any state and where the Indians enjoyed their own domains could prevent their destruction by White culture. Here, "the benevolent may endeavor to teach them the arts of civilization."[41]

Jackson's suggestion met heavy protest. He ignored it and pushed for an Indian removal bill. Bitter debate produced the May 28, 1830 Indian Removal Act authorizing the president to exchange Indian lands for territory in the west and payments for improvements in the ceded areas. The government would fund removal and one year of subsistence. The act didn't order Indian removal, but remaining meant assimilation, and Jackson knew the Indians wouldn't accept this. Removal became enormously corrupt, fraudulent – murderous. Jackson wanted it done more quickly than reasonable or safe. And cheaply, which was impossible. The government spent

$68 million and signed more than seventy treaties. For 32 million acres in the west, the US acquired 100 million acres in the east. The Cherokee had two years to leave. Some 2,000 did. Around 18,000 were forcibly removed under the Martin Van Buren administration in 1838. Some 4,000 to 8,000 died, and the "Trail of Tears" became synonymous with Indian removal. During Jackson's presidency over 45,000 Indians were forced beyond the Mississippi, including those from northern states. Despite removal's appalling nature, Jackson saved the Five Civilized Nations (Choctaw, Cherokee, Chickasaw, Creek, and Seminole) from extinction.[42]

MILITARY STRATEGY

The land and naval forces Jackson inherited remained small, badly funded, and poorly trained. West Point produced a professional officer corps, but the navy lacked an equivalent until the 1845 founding of the Naval Academy. The frontier army spent more time building forts and infrastructure than training and suffered heavily from desertion – around 20 percent in 1830. But it was called upon to fight, supported by militia.[43]

In February 1836, Secretary of War Lewis Cass proposed a cordon of forts connected by a military road running from Fort Towson in southern Oklahoma to Fort Snelling in Minneapolis, with troops patrolling between. This would defend the western frontier, reduce tensions between Indians and Whites and among the tribes, overawe the Indians by demonstrating American power, and prevent Indian raids, helping keep peace. Congress approved the plan in July 1836. Cass soon departed and successive secretaries of war weren't eager to follow his scheme, but Congress had voted the money, so the work began. Secretary of War Joel Roberts Poinsett began implementing elements of Cass' plan while overseeing creation of another during the Van Buren administration. To protect Whites from Indians on the frontier, the government began constructing an exterior line of forts in Indian territory to encourage peaceful behavior. An interior line of posts provided sanctuaries in troubled times and bases for soldiers. Jefferson Barracks near St. Louis, Missouri, hosted a large reserve.[44]

Jackson wasn't eager to use force, but he also never flinched from it if necessary. He improved the navy to protect overseas trade and used it to defend American interests abroad. In 1831, he dispatched the USS *Potomac* to deal with Malay pirates in Sumatra who had attacked an American merchant ship. The *Potomac*'s captain, instead of demanding restitution as ordered, attacked the town of Quallah Battoo, killing about 200 people.[45]

THE BLACK HAWK WAR, 1832

Black Hawk and his Sac and Fox followers were upset with the terms of an 1804 treaty awarding the US large tracts of southern Wisconsin and western Illinois. In 1830, the government decided to sell the ceded lands. To stop this, in 1831 Black Hawk led 2,000 followers across the Mississippi into Illinois to reclaim their lands. Black Hawk insisted his intentions were peaceful and negotiated with the local army commander, who asked the governor to raise militia as regular troops assembled. Negotiations produced nothing, and the Americans attacked Black Hawk's village, but he had retreated during the night. More negotiations followed. Black Hawk and his people were promised land west of the Mississippi and agreed to stay there.[46]

The peace was short-lived. Fueled by a Sac and Fox revenge massacre against another tribe, and rumors of British aid and Indian support, Black Hawk recrossed the Mississippi in April 1832. Jackson wanted the perpetrators of the massacre in irons, fearing it would spark an Indian war. The army, dispatched in March, stumbled across Black Hawk on April 11. The Illinois governor summoned the militia as the army fruitlessly negotiated. Black Hawk marched north to his old territory. Disheartened by discovering aid promises false, he resolved to surrender and sent out a party under a flag of truce, which startled militiamen attacked. Black Hawk then routed the Americans.[47]

Emboldened by Black Hawk's victory, other Indians raided White settlements. The governor called for another 2,000 militia, the army raised 1,000 volunteers, and Black Hawk withdrew to protect his people. In June, upset that the war continued, Jackson sent Winfield Scott to take command and dispatched troops from around the United States. Cholera kept this army from the field and the present forces fought the war. During July, they pursued Black Hawk's hungry band into Wisconsin and then to the Mississippi River. In early August, the army attacked and killed most of them. Others were massacred by the Sioux and Wabasha. Black Hawk was captured. Indian power in the Northwest was broken.[48]

THE SECOND CREEK WAR, 1836–37

The first conflict caused by Indian removal was the Second Creek War. The Creeks in Alabama signed a March 1832 treaty ceding their lands east of the Mississippi, though it permitted allotments to which they could receive title within five years or sell. But White squatters and speculators were soon taking Creek land. The government failed to secure a new treaty for immediate removal while dispossessed and sometimes destitute Creek went where they could, including to Georgia, where a group was attacked by that state's militia in May 1836. The Creeks replied in kind and the Federal government dispatched troops – eventually 10,000. The war ended by July 1837, and the Creeks were forcibly moved west.[49]

THE SECOND SEMINOLE WAR, 1835–42

The Second Seminole War (see Map 3.1) proved not so easily won, and frequently frustrated Jackson. On paper the "Florida War" looked easy. The 5,000 Seminoles had perhaps only 1,200 warriors, often armed only with bows. But a sparsely populated and undeveloped Florida, its climate, Seminole toughness, and the presence of determined escaped slaves in the Seminole ranks, made paper calculations fantasy. And, like other American wars, this one evoked partisan political attack.[50]

When the government began relocating the Seminoles in 1835, they anticipated resistance and gave Brigadier General Duncan Clinch command. But there emerged a Seminole leader opposing removal, Osceola. He promised punishment to Indians supporting removal, killed a departing chief, and informed Clinch the Seminoles would fight to the end. The war began in earnest in December 1835 when the Seminoles seized Florida south of St. Augustine.[51]

Osceola's promise didn't faze Jackson. He ordered Clinch to refuse all negotiations until the Seminoles were "unconditionally subdued" and agreed to go west. Jackson put Scott in command in January 1836, adding responsibility of recapturing the escaped slaves fighting alongside the Seminoles. Jackson told Scott the key to victory was what had become a standard strategy against the Indians: find where they had their families and target this, thus forcing the warriors to fight. Scott instead attempted a three-pronged encirclement campaign, about which Jackson groaned that Scott couldn't surround the Indians without knowing the location of their families. Scott's efforts were undermined by the head of the Western Department, Major General Gaines, who pushed troops into Florida, fought an inconclusive battle with the Seminoles, told them they didn't have to leave, and marched away. Scott eventually abandoned his campaign. He blamed its failure on Gaines, the poor quality of his volunteer troops, and panic caused by Florida's inhabitants. Demands for his removal followed and Scott happily departed Florida in May 1836.[52]

Jackson put Florida Governor Richard Keith Call in command. He planned a summer campaign that only launched in September, fought

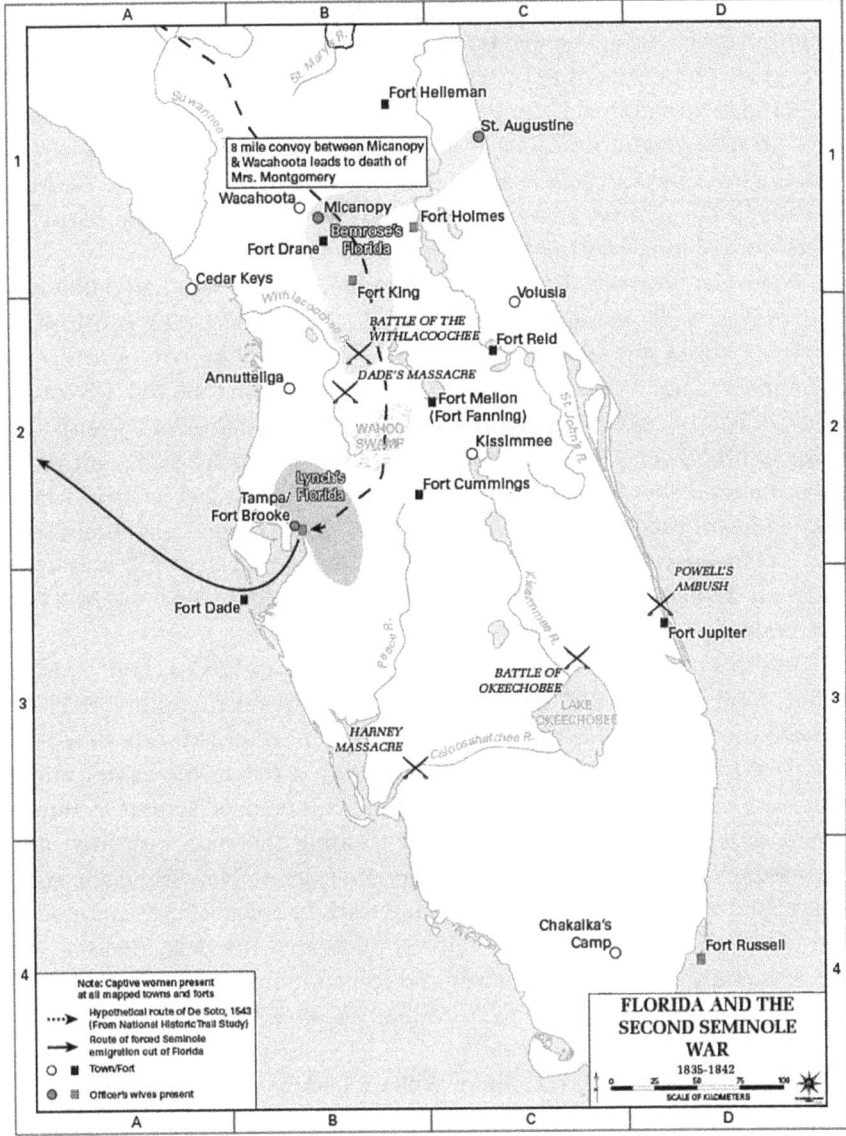

Map 3.1 Florida and the Second Seminole War, 1835–42

the Battle of Wahoo Swamp in November, and was replaced in December. Major General Thomas Jessup next took the reins. He built posts across Florida from the St. Johns River to Tampa Bay and followed with continuous military pressure upon the Seminoles using multiple detachments, driving them to sign a March 6, 1837 truce and agree to go west – if the Blacks could go as well. Jessup agreed but was then brow-beaten into allowing slave catchers to enter the camps of Seminoles awaiting shipment. This reignited the war. Jessup changed his mind again and allowed the Black Seminoles to go west, removing most within a year. Osceola and other chiefs refused to sign the truce but used the breathing space to grow food. Osceola restarted the war in the summer, the most difficult time to campaign; perhaps 700 others joined him. Martin Van Buren was now president.[53]

Over the next year Jessup broke Seminole power. He had 5,000 regular troops, 4,000 volunteers and militia, and a small Creek contingent. Jessup captured several Seminole leaders, including Osceola, by arresting them under flags of truce. A December 1837 offensive followed. US forces won two battles, and numerous Seminoles abandoned the field. Jessup and many of his officers concluded the war would continue for years unless the government let the Seminoles have the parts of Florida they wanted, which were lands in which Whites had no interest. Jessup urged the administration to change its aims and stop the war. Van Buren refused. Jessup soon resigned. In eighteen months, his forces killed or shipped westward 3,000 Seminoles.[54]

Jessup's replacement, Brigadier General Zachary Taylor, built a string of forts and roads from Tampa Bay to the Atlantic during winter 1838–39 to keep the Seminoles south of this. He divided northern Florida above the Withlacoochee River into 20-mile squares with a fort in the center and a half company of infantry to patrol the grid. This enabled settlers to return home, and he encouraged emigration. Dotting the state with forts and increasing White numbers gradually imposed control. Meanwhile, the army negotiated an agreement allowing Seminoles to remain and announced the war over. Secretary of War Poinsett abrogated the deal: removal was the aim and the administration refused to bend. Taylor was succeeded by Brigadier General Walker Keith Armistead, who tried both bribery and violence with equal lack of success.[55]

The final commander, Colonel William Jenkins Worth, served under a new president: John Tyler, and a new secretary of war, John Bell. The aim didn't change and Bell, one designer of the Indian Removal Act, believed his predecessor had failed to properly fight the war. He wanted it won quickly at the least possible cost. Worth launched his 5,000 men in a summer campaign against perhaps 1,500 Seminoles. A summer campaign had been considered too difficult because of climate and disease. But this was when the Seminoles raised their crops. Worth burned their fields, used small detachments fighting in a "partisan character" to keep constant pressure on the Seminoles, and attacked the most intransigent groups with waterborne patrols in the Everglades. His campaign drove many to reconsider transportation, giving Worth the chance to seize an important leader under a flag of truce and force others to surrender by threatening to hang him.[56]

In February 1842, Worth recommended allowing the few hundred remaining Seminoles to stay. Hearing through back channels that the army's leaders didn't agree, Worth continued the war, winning a battle producing the death or capture of nearly half the remaining Seminoles. In May, Tyler agreed that chasing down the few survivors wasn't worth it. Worth negotiated the removal of some; about 600 stayed. The war, which cost $30–$40 million, was declared over by President Tyler on August 18, 1842. To secure the peace, the administration brought in settlers.[57]

The Second Seminole War demonstrates the worst aspects of American warfighting: entering unprepared, not understanding the enemy or the environment, and failing to commit sufficient troops and resources to ensure the achievement of the aims in a timely manner. These weaknesses have never disappeared.

ECONOMIC STRATEGY

Economic matters in the Jackson–Van Buren era swirled around two major issues producing domestic and sometimes international fallout: the tariff and the Bank of the United States. The Jackson administration benefited from a post-1830 economic boom, one partially driven by cotton. This helped fuel banking and industry growth.[58]

THE TARIFF AND THE NULLIFICATION CRISIS

Jackson favored agricultural over business and industrial interests but wanted the tariff for revenue to retire the $49 million debt, most from the War of 1812. He believed that if the US didn't have tariffs, it would make Americans poorer to benefit Europe. He was skeptical of government infrastructure projects from fear of corruption via contractor bribes to Congressmen who also voted for projects in one another's districts. Tariffs varied by administration but were generally high. From 1821 to 1861, the rates fluctuated from 1832's 57 percent to 1861's 14.21 percent. In 33 of these 40 years, the rates were higher than the 17.5 percent fixed by the famous Smoot–Hawley tariff of 1931. In 1828, the year before Jackson took office, protectionist efforts produced the "Tariff of Abominations." A dog's breakfast providing no economic groundwork and designed to injure

Adams' reelection, it set the highest average tariff rate in US history – 61.7 percent – and provoked the Nullification Crisis in South Carolina.[59]

Henry Calhoun and the nullifiers insisted state sovereignty granted veto power over the Federal government, giving states power to "nullify" Federal laws with which they didn't agree. The Nullification Crisis was complicated by the fact that Calhoun, Jackson's vice president, secretly authored the movement's key text. In the wake of Jackson's 1832 reelection, Calhoun resigned as vice president to join the Senate.[60]

To Jackson, whatever threatened American security had to be dealt with. The stakes were high: preservation of the Union. To insure he had the right people to crush nullification, Jackson took the unprecedented step of overturning his entire cabinet. He made it clear he would fight to preserve the Union, began preparing militarily, and wrote a confidant: "The Union must be preserved…. I will die with the Union." He told the nullifiers via proclamation: "Disunion by armed force is *treason*." At a public political dinner in Washington dominated by nullifiers, at a time when toasting was an art and an expectation, Jackson used his to make clear his purpose: "Our Federal Union. It *must* be preserved."[61]

Jackson threatened, but also negotiated, and gave the nullifiers an escape hatch. When they postponed the effective date of their doctrine, Jackson quietly supported Calhoun's efforts to renegotiate the Tariff of Abominations. This defused the crisis. Jackson's second inauguration occurred two days after signing the replacement legislation, and his address relayed what he saw as the foundation stones of American liberty: "the preservation of the rights of the several states and the integrity of the Union."[62]

THE BATTLE WITH THE BANK OF THE UNITED STATES

Jackson's seriousness about defending the Union extended to renewing the charter of the Bank of the United States. Jackson hated banks from reading about the British South Sea bubble and its ruination of so many. By 1830, the Bank was very powerful, particularly in relation to the size of the American economy. He disliked that it was run by men unaccountable to the people and thus not subject to their will. Five directors were appointed by the government, but its stockholders appointed the other twenty. The government owned 20 percent of the stock; 4,000 investors held the rest and sometimes used this position for their own political ends. The Bank's $16 million in deposits was one-quarter of all US bank holdings. It regulated and supported state banks and insured a functioning currency by controlling the money supply, a power resting constitutionally with Congress. All of this,

Jackson believed, meant an organ operating against the public interest. Most importantly, Jackson the lawyer considered it unconstitutional.[63]

In 1831, Jackson decided to let Congress recharter the bank, but expected changes that included the sale of the government's holdings. Unhappy with the final bill, he vetoed it in July 1832 while noting four years remained in the charter, giving ample time to make changes. This burnished Jackson's "reputation as the defender of the common man against moneyed interests." There was fear the Bank was so powerful it could break the national economy. Jackson was uncertain of this (economics was not his strong suit), but this made him even more sure of his actions. "If this despotism be now partially fixed upon the country," he said, "a struggle must be made to cast it off, or our people will be forever enslaved." Jackson's suspicions of banks were confirmed by discovering that Nicholas Biddle, the Bank's director, paid newspapers to push the charter's renewal.[64]

Jackson ordered the government's deposits withdrawn and placed in state banks on October 1, 1833. Biddle reacted by tightening credit, calling in loans, and reducing the money supply. Banks began collapsing, igniting a panic from which the country didn't recover until summer 1834. Jackson shrugged off the alarm and the criticism, and as deposits flowed into the state banks the economy regained liquidity and the panic subsided. Jackson won his battle against the Bank and claimed another victory on January 1, 1835, when he announced the government was out of debt. But there was an unintended consequence. Banks were no longer bound by currency controls and printed money wildly, fueling a speculative economy, particularly in commodities and land. Jackson could do little about the first, but he burst the land bubble in July 1836 by requiring purchase of government lands in gold or silver specie. This helped tank the economy.[65]

THE MARTIN VAN BUREN ADMINISTRATION, 1837-41

Known as the "Little Magician" because of his ability to seamlessly switch his position on political issues, Martin Van Buren was Jackson's chosen successor. Van Buren aimed for "peace, both foreign and domestic," and his inaugural address was "a charter for inaction."[66] This can avoid leading the nation into problems but produce an administration with no focus.

Domestically, Van Buren rode the rising sectionalism related to slavery. He drew back from expansion and convinced Southern leaders to abandon calls for Texas' immediate annexation to cool sectional tensions. But he also vowed to veto any bill dealing with slavery lacking the South's consent. Van Buren considered growing abolitionist action a source of disorder, something many saw in the era's increasingly common political mobs, and thus a threat to the Union. While prosecuting the Second Seminole War, Van Buren made improvements to the army and grew it from 8,000 to 12,000.[67]

ECONOMIC STRATEGY

Van Buren's first crisis was the Panic of 1837. This began two months into his administration when the Bank of England began demanding payment in specie from American banks. They couldn't comply, partly because an unfavorable trade balance had caused specie flight. Bank collapses followed. Jackson's withdrawal of money from the Second Bank of the United States and the resulting speculative bubble worsened the situation. Everyone assumed Van Buren would decrease the currency in circulation and banks began calling in loans, adding another layer to the panic. The collapse of public works projects in the southern and midwestern states fed more bank failures, further shrinking the money supply. The depression that gripped America ensured the defeat of Van Buren's Whig Party in 1840. The Federal government's lacking any means to control the currency greatly contributed to the debacle.[68]

DIPLOMATIC STRATEGY

Van Buren faced problems with both Britain and Mexico that could have produced wars. He was more than once advised to take the nation into conflict, including on the eve of the 1840 elections. He refused. Problems with Britain arose from the November 1837 eruption of a rebellion in Canada, one some Americans supported despite Federal efforts. Britain's seizure and burning of an American ship used to bring supplies and men from New York fed war fears. Van Buren dispatched Winfield Scott, who defused the crisis through rhetoric and force of will, and later prevented an explosion over the disputed Maine–New Brunswick border that brought the administration as close as it came to a new war.[69]

In the last days of Jackson's administration, Congress recognized Texas' independence, something Van Buren opposed. This fed sectional fears by raising the specter of its annexation as a slave state, and annexation meant war with Mexico. Van Buren mounted an about-face from Jackson's support of Texas annexation to insure peace and happily accepted arbitration of various Mexican claims against Washington.[70]

THE WILLIAM HENRY HARRISON AND JOHN TYLER ADMINISTRATIONS, 1841-45

The Van Buren administration marked a short interlude in American expansion, one quickly scrapped by his successors. President John Tyler succeeded to the office upon the death of William Henry Harrison a mere month into his predecessor's term, the first vice president to do so. He brought to the office a long political résumé that included service as a congressman, governor of Virginia, and in the Senate.

ASSESSMENT AND THE POLITICAL AIMS

Tyler's single term fit the pattern of most of his predecessors: territorial expansion remained an aim, but he also wanted to open doors abroad for American commerce. Economic power is not an aim but a tool for obtaining political ends. Despite this logical weakness, versions of Tyler's approach became standard for American leaders. To Tyler, territorial expansion and commercial growth would ensure America remained a slave-holding republic. Here, he followed a standard, ancillary line of thinking. Expansion would diffuse the Black population into new territory, perhaps eventually making it politically acceptable to implement gradual emancipation in areas of the upper South such as Virginia. Territorial expansion could feed slavery's demise.[71]

ECONOMIC STRATEGY

Tyler's efforts to increase America's overseas commerce mirrored previous presidents, particularly Jackson, who had sent agents to Asia. Jackson had failed to open Japan, but his agents made contacts around the Indian Ocean, established communication with Vietnam, and signed Washington's first treaty with Siam (Thailand). As senator, Tyler advocated free trade and envisioned an America stretching to the Pacific and trading in Asia's markets, but he also wanted to protect American manufacturing. As president, he signed the high protective tariff of 1842, probably because he saw it as a first step in pulling the US from its economic doldrums. This also denoted his transformation to a protector of industry as well as agriculture. The economy recovered during Tyler's administration and entered a period of spectacular growth. The growing domestic market helped immensely, as did new technologies increasing American agricultural production, making the US a competitor with Russia for the greatest producer of food. Cotton exports grew dramatically, and mining and manufacturing expanded.[72]

PART I: FROM BACKWATER TO GREAT POWER

Tyler's 1841 inauguration aligned with the publication by German-American economist Friedrich List of his *National System of Political Economy*. Influenced by the 1820s work of Daniel Raymond, List believed in protecting domestic manufacturing with tariffs. He preached protectionism to develop native industry, believing this improved society and that industrialization tapped its most intelligent members. But his protectionism wasn't random. Only native industries possessing the potential to compete with similar fields abroad deserved it, and then only until they could compete internationally. He saw free trade as suitable only for industrially mature nations and pointed out how Britain had achieved its dominant economic station via protectionism. He thought free trade was where the world should ultimately move, but industrially weaker nations would have their businesses crushed by states like Britain that could bury them with cheap goods. He argued that "a nation which should succeed in monopolizing the entire manufacturing of the globe ... would necessarily achieve universal dominion."[73]

DIPLOMATIC AND INFORMATION STRATEGY

Tyler's territorial ambitions were specific: Texas, the Oregon country, and California. Diplomatically, he began pushing Texas annexation in October 1841 and asked Secretary of State Daniel Webster about gaining it via negotiations. Webster was more interested in settling the Maine border dispute. Tyler used government money to fund a ten-month information campaign in Maine to convince the inhabitants to agree to a border compromise. The British cooperated, using their funds for bribes. Tyler used spies in a manner not done by his predecessors and his agents infiltrated an ultra-nationalist group advocating war with Britain. The administration secured the 1842 Webster–Ashburton Treaty fixing Maine's border and that between Lake Superior and Lake of the Woods. Tyler probably delayed settlement of Oregon's border in hopes of securing the 49th parallel and clandestinely funded American settlers.[74]

The 1830s and 1840s saw numerous Americans urging expansion to the Pacific coast. Tyler wanted US influence to not only reach the Pacific, but Hawaii, China, and Japan. On December 30, 1842, he dispatched to Congress a message regarding Hawaii that included what became known as the Tyler Doctrine. He draped the Monroe Doctrine over Hawaii, claiming "an American sphere of influence" over islands 2,500 miles from the Pacific coast, an action fueled by fears of British control and his anti-British bent. He also stressed the necessity of establishing relations with China to gain the same trading privileges Britain secured with its Opium War victory. But, on February 23, 1843, Hawaii's king ceded his nation to Britain under threat of bombardment by a British fleet. The British retreated from this in July, and Britain and France recognized Hawaiian independence. In 1844, Tyler recognized Hawaii and secured the first US treaty with China.[75]

Tyler's great ambition, indeed, obsession, was Texas, and he hoped to balance the admission of slave Texas with free California. He thought this would lessen the threat to the South from antislavery forces but also saw it as a step toward national greatness. Annexation emerged as a key issue in the 1844 presidential election, and James K. Polk's Democratic Party platform called for adding Texas to the Union and securing Oregon. Tyler used Polk's victory to acquire Congressional approval for annexing Texas and signed the measure on March 1, 1845, achieving his aim before departing the White House. Five days later, Mexico's ambassador demanded his passport and departed.[76]

THE JAMES K. POLK ADMINISTRATION AND THE MEXICAN WAR, 1845–49

When James K. Polk accepted his party's nomination, the former Speaker of the House and Tennessee governor promised to serve only one term. He believed this better fitted the Jacksonian spirit and thought (mistakenly) it would heal schisms in his Democratic Party. Polk proved a strong president who kept a tight rein on his cabinet, generals, and the war he launched against Mexico (see Map 3.2). Machiavelli would have blushed at his use of American power. His campaign platform included expansionist aims toward Texas and Oregon.[77]

Several factors underpinned this era's expansionist sentiment. Merchants and farmers wanted larger markets for their goods and ports for trade to Asia. Polk, like Jeffersonians and Jacksonians, wanted expanded agrarian opportunities to counter the baleful influence of cities and industry. Some thought expansion would increase the nation's "racial and cultural homogeneity," particularly in the Southwest, by growing to the Pacific. Still others saw a means of furthering liberty and freedom.[78]

Expansionism became inextricably tied to Manifest Destiny. The phrase came from Democrat journalist John O'Sullivan's magazine *Democratic Review* in 1845. He wrote that "the boundless future will be an era of American greatness. In its magnificent domain of space and time, the nation

PART I: FROM BACKWATER TO GREAT POWER

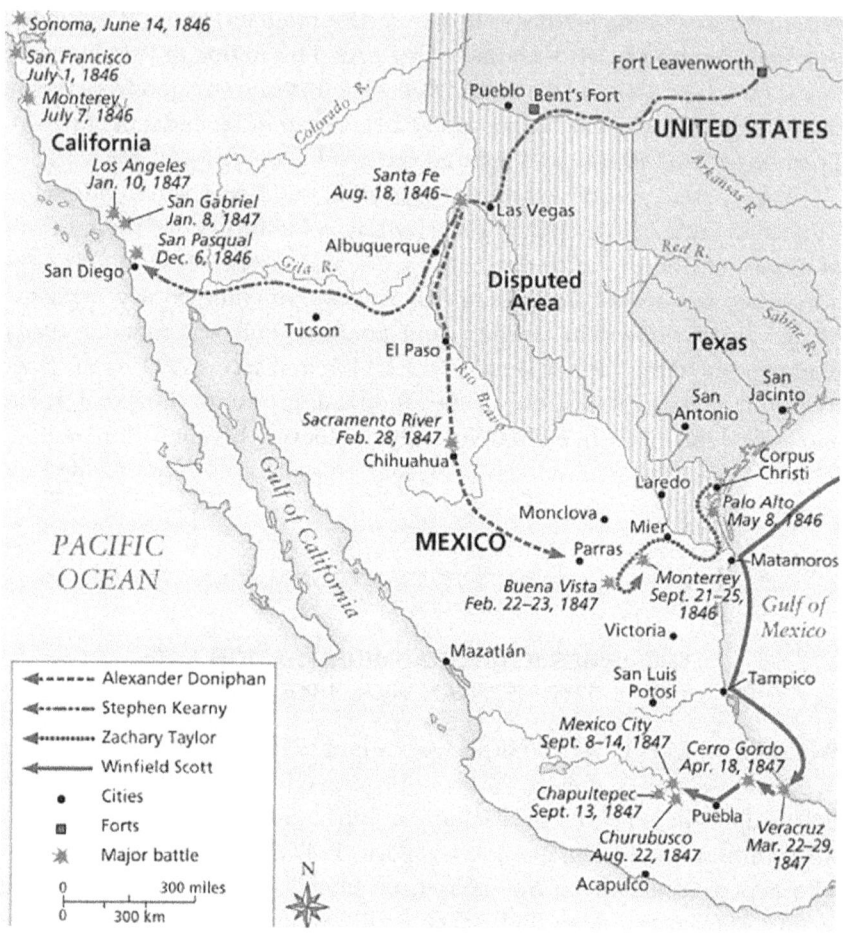

Map 3.2 The Mexican War, 1846–48

of many nations is *destined* to *manifest* to mankind the excellence of divine principles." America's purpose was "to overspread the continent allotted by Providence for the free development of our yearly multiplying millions." Manifest Destiny was "the cloud by day and the pillar of fire by night that guided the westward thrust of the nation." Polk tapped this spirit.[79]

THE POLITICAL AIMS

In his March 4, 1845 inaugural address, Polk spoke of expansion in relation to Texas and Oregon (he only mentioned California privately). The administration wanted ports on the Pacific, which meant seizing California, but would need New Mexico, the territory between Texas and California. Polk insisted Texas had once belonged to the US (a possible allusion to the Louisiana Purchase), that only the US and Texas had any right to determine its fate (a sovereignty issue), and cast annexation as a security matter because "the safety of New Orleans and of our whole southwestern frontier against hostile aggression, as well as the interests of the whole Union, would be promoted by it." If the US didn't have it, "None can fail to see the danger to our safety and future peace if Texas remains an independent state or becomes an ally or dependency of some foreign nation more powerful than herself." Polk insisted it was his "duty to assert and maintain by all Constitutional means the right of the United States to that portion of our territory which lies beyond the Rocky Mountains," meaning Oregon.[80]

Oregon proved easiest to obtain; the value of the object wasn't as high for London as Washington. Polk made what he saw as a "generous" offer to settle the border at the 49th parallel, the line America claimed. This offended the equally nationalistic British. An angry Polk withdrew his offer, demanded all of Oregon, which stretched to the 54° 40′ line, and asked Congress to kill the 1827 Anglo-American Treaty of joint occupation. American jingoists cried "54° 40′ or fight!" Polk defused the issue by quietly telling London he was prepared to compromise. A treaty settled the border largely along the 49th parallel. The war against Mexico had already begun.[81]

THE MEXICAN WAR, 1846–48

If any American president understood – viscerally – Clausewitz's insistence that "war is politics by others means," it was Polk. He had clear political aims and saw military force as one of the tools for achieving them. In his December 1846 Congressional message, Polk insisted – falsely – "The war has not been waged with a view to conquest." It is true that he didn't intend to take all of Mexico, a point he made clear in 1847. He had a limited political aim – Mexican territory – lots of it. In an October 24, 1845 meeting with Senator Thomas Hart Benton, Polk invoked the Monroe Doctrine. "The conversation then turned on California," Polk wrote,

> on which I remarked that Great Britain had her eye on that country and intended to possess it if she could, but that the people of the US would not willingly permit California to pass into the possession of any new colony planted by Great Britain or any foreign monarchy, and that in reasserting Mr. Monroe's doctrine, I had California & the fine bay of San Francisco as much in view as Oregon.

Polk wanted California south to the 26th parallel but by June 30, 1846 had decided to settle for the 32nd. But any treaty had to give the US New Mexico and Upper California (essentially the current state). Polk intended to conquer "an honorable and permanent peace."[82]

DIPLOMATIC AND INFORMATIONAL STRATEGIES

Polk first tried to secure his aims diplomatically, which included Mexico agreeing to Texas' annexation, resolving the boundary issue, and selling California and New Mexico. On September 16, 1845, after reports Mexico understood its weakness and was amenable to agreement, Polk dispatched Louisiana politician John Slidell, instructing him to offer assumption of the $3 million in American debt claims against Mexico, $5 million for Texas and New Mexico ($25 million if California was included), and to demand a border from the Gulf of Mexico along the Rio Grande to El Paso, then to the Pacific along the 32nd parallel. If Mexico refused, Slidell was to assure them Washington would use other means to "redress ... the wrongs and injuries we have suffered." Mexico's political instability delayed Slidell's work. On March 1, 1846, he gave the new government two weeks to decide whether it wanted peace or war. Mexico's foreign minister refused to see him. Simultaneously, Polk practiced subversion. America's California consul's false report of British-financed Mexican troops moving against California prodded Polk to order his consul and other agents to stir the people against foreign influence and Mexican rule while leading them to US control.[83] Meanwhile, Polk finished setting the stage for war.

MILITARY STRATEGY

In June 1845, Polk had ordered Taylor's army into Texas. August rumors (later proven false) of Mexican forces advancing toward the Rio Grande led Polk to reinforce Taylor's 1,500-man army and dispatch more naval forces to the Gulf. Polk didn't see his actions as aggressive, but he and his cabinet began planning eight months before launching the war and issued contingency orders to the army and navy on August 31, 1845. Taylor was ordered to the Rio Grande in January 1846 and arrived in March. The Mexican commander demanded Taylor's withdrawal over the Nueces River, which Mexico considered the border, within twenty-four hours. Taylor refused. Polk intended Taylor's presence to provoke an incident as a pretext for declaring war.[84]

On April 4, Mexico City secretly ordered an attack on Taylor. On April 23, Mexico declared it was at war because the US had invaded. The first clash occurred the next day. Taylor learned of the fight on April 26, and immediately dispatched word to Washington. Mexico's army crossed the

Rio Grande on April 30. The two forces fought to a standstill at Palo Alto on May 8, but Taylor held the field; the Mexican force withdrew. Taylor broke the enemy at the Battle of Resaca de la Palma on May 9. Taylor's impressive, early victories bought the administration time to prepare.[85]

Polk and his cabinet agreed on May 9, 1846, to ask Congress for a declaration of war before any military action occurred. That same evening Taylor's dispatches arrived reporting the Mexicans had crossed the Rio Grande and attacked American troops. On Monday, May 11, Polk told Congress the war had already begun, retraced the history of US problems with Mexico, and insisted (without evidence) the Rio Grande was the traditional Texas border. He made no mention of California. Five hours later, the House voted for war. The not-as-eager Senate bent to public opinion, which was believed to favor conflict. Politically, Polk and the Democratic Party placed the opposition Whigs in the position of voting against support for the troops.[86]

THE ASSESSMENT

Mexico sought to hold the territory it had, but there was also a push to regain Texas. It probably had 20,000 troops. Many Mexicans approached the conflict with optimism, something shared by not a few European observers. They saw a United States divided by arguments over tariffs and slavery and believed American slaves and Indians would rebel if given the chance. Others believed Mexico's geography and climate insurmountable by an invader with a pitifully small professional army supplemented by nearly worthless volunteers. Meanwhile, European aid would strengthen Mexico while privateers devastated American merchant shipping.[87]

In comparison to the United States, though, Mexico was weak. The US had a population above 20 million, Mexico 7 million. The nation was riven by social, class, and racial divides, sporadic peasant revolts, and a political factionalism marked by a willingness to use violence to overthrow any government. Its military was poorly armed, and 87 percent of its meager tax revenue went to service foreign debt. The Polk administration recognized Mexico's weaknesses but didn't grasp the geographical obstacles or the dangers to US forces from disease, and underestimated the willingness of the people to resist the invader.[88]

Polk, realizing public opinion would tolerate nothing less, wanted a quick, short war for limited political aims that cost the US little, and he intended to win. The administration took the rare step of prewar planning but made scant military preparations and went to war unprepared. If there is an "American Way of War," this is it. Polk planned to seize and annex New Mexico and California, but the army numbered only 8,000 and the navy had only 13 ships. Eschewing the state militias because of their abysmal War of 1812 record, Polk instead began raising 20,000 volunteers from the states and Congress granted a temporary increase in the army's size, but this would go slowly. Critically, Polk "began the war with no clear strategy beyond supporting Taylor and initiating operations to seize California." Polk worried the war would create a Whig hero that could run for president. His two most important generals – Zachary Taylor and Winfield Scott – were Whigs. Polk was deeply suspicious of both and exploited every opportunity to tear down their reputations once he no longer needed them. He ensured the thirteen generals appointed to lead the volunteers were fellow Democrats.[89]

American public opinion generally supported the war, but there was a strong current of resistance obscured by the initial uproar of national approval. Public opinion sometimes ran to extremes. A version of the All-Mexico Movement (supported by Walt Whitman) argued for the US occupying all of Mexico to reform it so that Mexicans could enjoy the blessings of liberty and good governance. Others branded the war "unconstitutional, corrupt, and, in fact, immoral." Pacifist groups and some churches opposed it. Abolitionists feared slavery's expansion, though that was not Polk's intent, and openly wished for Scott's defeat.[90]

MILITARY STRATEGY

The administration eventually constructed a *de facto* multi-pronged military strategy. Polk planned to raise the 50,000 men allowed by Congress, 20,000 immediately from the south and southwest. After the declaration of war, Polk offered Scott command of the field forces, which Scott accepted. Polk didn't think him suitable, but believed he deserved the post if he wanted it because he led the army. On May 14, 1846, Polk, Scott, and Secretary of War William L. Marcy met to decide strategy. Polk believed they should march into the northern provinces of Mexico, seize them, particularly California and New Mexico, and the areas around where Taylor was fighting, and hold them until the enemy made peace. Scott and Marcy agreed. On May 26, Polk added another operational prong: a force under Colonel Stephen W. Kearny to seize New Mexico and advance to California. Polk wrote: "I stated that if the war should be protracted for any considerable time, it would in my judgment be very important that the US should hold military possession of California at the time peace was made." Kearny's force would march from Santa Fe, and a new one come behind to hold Santa Fe and then strike for California if circumstances permitted. Simultaneously, the administration encouraged Taylor to advance into Mexico but failed to give him operational objectives. Commodore John D. Sloat, off California, was told to mount a blockade, seize what ports he could, and "conciliate" the locals. Commodore David Connor was ordered to blockade Mexico's Gulf coast and take Tampico if needed to maintain communications with Taylor, and encourage Mexican secession movements along the littoral. Polk attacked on the information front to win over the Catholic Church in Mexico. He approached the bishops of New York to gain aid thwarting rumors the US intended to destroy Catholic religion and property, and was well received. Among Polk's suggestions was that Catholic priests accompany the army as chaplains.[91]

Polk intended to keep a tight rein on the war effort and at a meeting with the secretaries of war and the navy told them to report anything significant, watch matters closely, and not expect their subordinates to act on their own. Polk also had to move the war along, because of resistance from the opposition Whigs. Polk encountered a dichotomy regarding the constraints under which he had to wage war. The aim for Polk and his Democratic Party was territory, but internal political circumstances and public opinion necessitated a quick war and a cheap one. But Scott insisted upon properly preparing and planning while Polk demanded immediate action. Polk's failure to understand the necessity of preparation combined with his political partisanship to poison the relationship between the president and Scott. Polk "urged the most energetic and prompt action" and was angered that Scott didn't intend to depart for the front until around September 1. Polk ordered Secretary of War Marcy to push Scott along only a week after the general's May 13 appointment and said that if Scott didn't soon leave for his command, he would be replaced. Scott's explosive, political response critical of the administration included a reference to preventing "*a fire upon my rear, from Washington.*" An enraged Polk decided to keep Scott in Washington.[92]

DIPLOMATIC STRATEGY

During the summer, Polk launched peace efforts. He first bargained with the exiled Santa Anna, who convinced the Americans he was amenable to peace. He was soon invited home and reached Veracruz from Havana on August 16. Let through the blockade on Polk's orders, Santa Anna assumed command of the Mexican army and rebuilt its ability to resist, probably lengthening the war by more than a year. Simultaneously, having received word Mexico might be receptive to making peace, the administration relayed its willingness. But the government was overthrown, and the offer rejected. Polk pushed harder for military action and warned Mexico he would increase the tempo while relaying willingness to make peace.[93]

ZACHARY TAYLOR'S CAMPAIGN

After Taylor won the battles of Palo Alto and Resaca in early May 1846, he took Matamoros. Many of his enlistments expired, forcing him to await new troops. He besieged Monterrey on September 20. After four days of bloody, house-to-house fighting, the Mexican commander offered to surrender if Taylor granted an armistice and didn't advance for eight weeks. Taylor agreed, arguing it saved lives, that he had been told Mexico was about to make peace, and because he couldn't have pushed for eight weeks regardless. In October, when word of Taylor's victory at Monterrey and the truce reached Washington, Polk and his cabinet decided Taylor had thrown away a chance to end the war. An enraged Polk told Taylor to abrogate the armistice and fight the war "with energy and vigor."[94]

Taylor's army was soon weakened to provide forces for the Veracruz campaign (discussed below), leaving him a poorly trained almost entirely volunteer force of 6,000. Santa Anna had just taken power and was cobbling together an army, even mortgaging his own lands to raise funds. He assembled 20,000 poorly armed men and marched them 240 miles; thousands died. Instead of waiting, Taylor advanced. Santa Anna's 15,000 troops met 5,000 mostly inexperienced Americans at Buena Vista. Despite knowledge of the impending US landing at Veracruz, Santa Anna attacked on February 22, 1847, and again on the 23rd. Taylor's forces held, though Santa Anna might have prevailed if he had struck again. Polk rewarded Taylor with criticism for fighting an unnecessary battle and wasting lives. Taylor blamed Polk, Marcy, and Scott for leaving him with a small force that invited attack.[95]

THE CALIFORNIA CAMPAIGN

Commodore Sloat, commander of the US Pacific Squadron, was dispatched orders in June 1845 to take San Francisco in the event of war with Mexico. US army captain and western explorer John C. Frémont began leading an overland expedition to California the same month. He was in Monterey, California, in March 1846, posing as an explorer while secretly plotting with the American consul, Thomas Larkin. In April, word arrived that if California followed Texas' example, it would be welcomed into the United

States. Frémont then launched a successful revolt in the thinly populated state. The rebels declared California's independence on July 4, 1846.[96]

Sloat sailed into Monterey Bay on July 7 and took the town. Eager to avoid the 1842 mistake of his predecessor, who had seized Monterey when there were no hostilities, Sloat made sure the US and Mexico were at war. He announced California's annexation, an act for which he lacked authority. The navy occupied San Francisco the next day. Sloat's replacement, Commodore Robert Stockton, teamed with Frémont to seize the state's remaining key areas. The *californios* – California's Hispanic population – launched a revolt that recaptured much of southern California. The combined forces of Stockton, Frémont, and Kearny's overland expedition secured US control.[97]

WINFIELD SCOTT'S WAR

In August 1846, while awaiting the results of peace feelers, Polk and his advisors reassessed and concluded they needed a new operation to force Mexico to make peace. The campaign had many fathers and resembled Hernán Cortés' 1519 expedition. On October 27, 1846, Scott presented his plan. The Gulf coast city of Veracruz would be seized, an operation requiring 10,000 men. A march of 260 miles to the capital with 20,000 men would follow. The plan included a willingness to stop and negotiate peace, threats to take the capital, and leaving the coast before yellow fever descended. Before germ theory and antibiotics, disease was usually war's biggest killer. Scott said ending the war required the Americans "to strike, effectively, at the vitals of the nation" and aimed at a Mexican center of gravity – meaning source of power – the capital. Seizing this necessitated defeating and possibly destroying another enemy center of gravity – its army. Scott also went after a third – public opinion – by trying to undermine the people's support for their government. All would be done via a campaign intended to impose as little damage as necessary on the Mexican people and nation. Scott understood he would be surrounded by a potentially hostile population. To keep alienation to a minimum, he intended to establish martial law wherever his forces marched and enforce strict behavior among his men. He punished all crimes against Mexican citizens and paid for supplies taken.[98]

The November 17, 1846 cabinet strategy review discussed the campaign and who would command. Polk liked it but wanted a Democrat general. Taylor was considered too stupid and politically threatening. Four cabinet members believed Scott the best choice. Polk concluded he had no choice.

He offered Scott command but required him to demonstrate support for the administration. Scott promised to include some senior Democrats among his commanders. Word of the planned expedition to Veracruz soon leaked to the press; Polk blamed Scott.[99]

Receiving word on March 20, 1847 of a final negotiation attempt convinced Polk "No alternative was now left but the most energetic crushing movement of our arms upon Mexico." Scott's army of 11,000 had begun landing 2 miles south of Veracruz on March 9, 1847. Scott besieged Veracruz rather than assault this fortified bastion. This took more time but meant lower casualties. Scott had to tame numerous constraints. He knew American public opinion wouldn't appreciate using time instead of blood to take Veracruz, but his army was small. He also faced a long campaign, Polk's impatience, and yellow fever season.[100]

Veracruz surrendered on March 29, 1847. In its occupation Scott established an American military tradition of improving seized foreign places. He put the city in order, organized its cleaning, fed captured Mexican soldiers and many civilians, reopened the port, and, as Polk instructed, collected duties to help pay the war's costs. Scott issued General Order No. 20 establishing martial law to maintain order among his troops, some of whom got out of hand at the end of the siege. This applied to both Americans and Mexicans, though Scott allowed Mexicans to be tried in their own courts.[101]

General Order No. 20 formed an informational wing of Scott's strategy. He knew his march to Mexico City couldn't succeed against a hostile populace and wanted to avoid a guerrilla war, and told his men they had to depend upon the people for supplies. They faced partisan bands, guerrillas, and bandits, but these never threatened the campaign or the army's survival. Order No. 20 was partly why. It made his soldiers behave, treat the population with respect, and work within Mexican culture; Scott executed violators, American and Mexican, and never hesitated to kill brigands and guerrillas. He was particularly insistent upon respecting Catholic churches and heritage, reopened the churches, and attended a public mass even though he was Protestant. Mexican civilians quickly saw the Americans would pay for everything they wanted, markets reopened, and Scott benefited from Mexican dissatisfaction with their government.[102]

In early April 1847, Jane Storms, one of Polk's agents in Mexico City, brought news that Veracruz's fall and the rebellion of National Guard troops (which she helped finance) had caused uproar in Mexico City. She also revealed that her espionage partner, Moses Beach, had obtained limited support from the Catholic Church for the invader. Storms confirmed Scott's method of dealing with civilians, predicting they would either support him or at least remain passive, because he fought their oppressors. Scott, a man known for his vanity, disliked his strategy being affirmed by "a plenipotentiary in petticoats."[103]

On April 10, 1847, word of Veracruz's fall reached Washington. The administration dispatched Nicholas Trist with a draft peace treaty demanding a Rio Grande border, cession of New Mexico and Upper and Lower California (present-day California and Baja California, respectively), and transit rights across the Isthmus of Tehuantepec, while Mexico received up to $30 million. But these were maximum demands and Polk made clear peace didn't require transit rights or Lower California. If Trist couldn't secure transit rights, he could pay $25 million. If he didn't get Lower California, $20 million. In all cases, he was to try to pay less. When Trist departed, Polk tried to shape the national debate on negotiations by leaking word of the mission to friendly newspapers.[104]

On April 8, 1847, Scott departed Veracruz. He dispatched a proclamation to Mexico City. He began with the sword, announcing the advance of two powerful armies, his and Taylor's (Taylor's wasn't moving), then extended the olive branch, insisting Americans weren't enemies of the Mexican people but the rulers misgoverning them who caused the war. The Americans were friends of the people and the Catholic Church, and would protect peaceful citizens while punishing any Americans who committed crimes. He pledged to pay for any livestock the inhabitants would sell but punish civilians injuring American property or citizens.[105]

Scott's army advanced along the National Road, roughly following Cortés' route, a fact not lost on some of his men. The initial objective was Jalapa (Xalapa), 65 miles away at 4,700 feet elevation, beyond the yellow fever zone. The Americans bought supplies along the way, including from Santa Anna, who secretly sold them cattle through an agent while planning to stop Scott's army. Success would force the Americans back into the yellow fever region (and protect one of his haciendas). Santa Anna brought his army south, installing it in mountainous positions at Cerro Gordo. He enjoyed numerical superiority, 12,000 to 8,500. But the Americans inflicted a quick, severe defeat on April 18, 1847. The Mexican army collapsed, but Scott lost 3,000 volunteers whose enlistments expired on May 6 and had 2,000 sick and wounded. Scott did all he could to keep down his casualties; he could afford to do no less.[106]

Scott continued to Jalapa, about 180 miles from Mexico City. He learned of chaos in the Mexican government and delayed because he needed a government with which to make peace. He also wanted to give Mexico time to offer peace. It didn't. The Mexican Congress reacted to defeat at

Cerro Gordo by making it illegal for the executive to negotiate with the Americans if this meant ceding territory, something arising from their distrust of Santa Anna. On April 28, interim Mexican president Pedro Maria Anaya tried to provoke a guerrilla uprising by authorizing creation of units to attack Scott's supply lines. Some guerrilla forces formed spontaneously, but government-authorized units had to be raised by wealthy men, furthering the class divide and undermining the effort. This began producing problems for Scott within several weeks, just when his force size had fallen to 5,000.[107]

In Jalapa, Scott continued benefitting from his respectful treatment of the Mexican people. The poorer classes were indifferent as to whether they were ruled by Americans or from Mexico City. The middle classes were happy because the Americans helped their businesses. The rich were angry because the Americans broke their power. Many places accepted the American presence, and Scott let locals manage their affairs and police themselves – if they didn't support resistance. By May 6, 1847, he had 7,100 of the promised 20,000 men.[108]

Scott issued another proclamation before departing Jalapa, one attempting to further separate the people from their rulers by denouncing the government's conduct of the war and its failure to tell the people the truth about it. He cautioned the inhabitants about resorting to guerrilla warfare, warning it would harm their nation. He also issued General Order No. 127. This levied a $300 fine on local leaders who failed to deal with guerrillas or bandits in their areas. Scott worried about guerrillas because a mass uprising would sever his supply line to Veracruz and paralyze his army. The fear was real as guerrillas began harassing US forces.[109]

When he reached Puebla, Scott decided to await reinforcements. Dysentery sickened 2,000 men and killed many. He couldn't advance without new units, the first of which reached Veracruz in May. Since he would never have the promised 20,000 men, Scott decided in early June to consolidate his forces and made the unconventional decision to abandon his supply lines. This created his strongest possible force while eliminating targets for guerrillas. Being able to buy food from Mexicans enabled Scott's decision.[110]

On May 15, Scott's army reached Puebla, about halfway between Jalapa and Mexico City. He remained three months preparing an attack on the capital. In Jalapa, Scott had received word from Secretary of War Marcy to consider any instruction from Trist to halt military operations a presidential order. Scott exploded at being subordinated to a minor government official who understood nothing about when an army should fight. He refused to allow Trist to decide a ceasefire and wrote him an angry letter, something done despite Scott's April note welcoming administration officials handling negotiations. Trist, who matched the general in stubbornness and arrogance, responded – in eighteen pages. When Trist arrived in Jalapa, Scott refused to meet him. They eventually worked well together, something aided by their joint participation in bribing Santa Anna $10,000 to discuss peace. Santa Anna pocketed the money and insisted he couldn't talk because negotiating with the Americans was treason. He also said attacking Mexico City would break everyone opposed to peace, allowing Santa Anna to again take power and negotiate the war's end.[111]

By summer, the guerrilla problem was becoming more serious, necessitating American movements in columns of 1,000 or more. But the guerrillas never hindered Scott's operations: they only troubled supply shipments from Veracruz. The guerrillas were also generally awful soldiers. One American observed: "One hundred riflemen would consider it an amusement to fight a thousand guerrillas."[112]

Scott had 10,700 men when he left Puebla. Before departing, he dispatched a letter to the Mexican government announcing his advance on the capital and telling them he would "either defeat the enemy in view of the city, if they would give him battle, or he would take a strong position from the enemy, and then, if he could restrain the enthusiasm of his troops, he would halt outside of the city and take measures to give those in the city an opportunity to save the capital by making a peace." Five days later, on August 12, he established his headquarters at Ayolta on the National Road on the approach to Mexico City. Scott had to preserve his force, while Santa Anna hoped Scott would bleed his army assaulting the city, but Scott didn't intend to do this. He attacked Santa Anna's strategy by unexpectedly striking from the south and west.[113]

The Americans besieged the city on August 20, 1847. By scoring a victory at Pedregal (which included fighting at Padierna and Churubusco), Scott broke Mexico City's outer defenses. This cost Scott more than 1,000 men and the Mexicans over 4,000. Many Mexican leaders wanted to surrender, but Santa Anna suggested a truce. The terms forbid either army from being reinforced or to improve its defenses, and either could cancel it with forty-eight hours' notice. It also allowed Scott's army to buy supplies and the Mexicans to bring their own into the city. By granting the armistice, Scott was doing what he had promised in his Puebla proclamation: giving the government time to make peace. He also knew Polk wanted to end the war quickly because of its political and financial costs.[114]

Trist and Scott agreed to hear Santa Anna's terms, which arrived on August 26. Negotiations began on August 27. Santa Anna consented to

Texas independence, but with a border on the Nueces. He demanded the departure of all US forces, lifting of the blockade, that America pay the war's costs and cancel Mexico's debts, and recognition of Mexican land grants in Texas. His terms were refused but negotiations continued. The Texas border was the most contentious issue; both sides refused to bend here.[115]

When Scott agreed to the truce, he thought it might be a ruse but decided the risk worthwhile. This proved a mistake – an opinion his troops generally held. Santa Anna wanted time to strengthen his defenses. Scott only had two days of food, which may have contributed to his decision, but the armistice didn't resolve this as Santa Anna ordered Mexicans to sell no supplies to the Americans but instead feed his force. Scott took over mills, seized cattle, and paid the workers and owners.[116] Scott should have immediately attacked the city, making clear the costs of continued resistance. His approach, as we will see, became a norm for American military and political leaders. They are so eager to end a war they seize upon any negotiation offer, regardless of validity, and with little consideration as to whether doing so might lengthen the war, increasing the blood costs because the enemy is allowed to recover strength.

Scott realized on September 5 that Santa Anna was reinforcing the city and gave notice the armistice would end the next day. The Americans took Molino del Rey on September 8 and started shelling Chapultepec Castle on September 12. Mexico City fell the next day. Santa Anna resigned as president and left Mexico City with his army. US forces mustered in the main square on September 14. Disorder and looting erupted in the city. Three days of fighting against looters, 30,000 freed prisoners, and Mexican army deserters followed, and citizens joined the breakdown of order occurring in the absence of firm government. Scott responded by cannonading any house from which the Americans took fire and ransacking it with infantry who killed any armed Mexican encountered. After about 500 deaths, order was restored.[117]

ENDING THE WAR, SECURING THE PEACE

Yet another Mexican government formed in Querétaro 100 miles to the north. Its factions argued over whether to make peace and disagreed upon political aims. One insisted upon continuing the struggle *until Washington agreed to annex all of Mexico*. Some thought a guerrilla war the route to victory but feared unleashing class or race conflict while giving common people power and arms. The army's decimation meant the leaders couldn't suppress peasants who were already in revolt, and not just against the Americans. For example, Yucatán's Indians had rebelled against their White masters and asked the US to intervene and annex the area. Washington refused. The regional civil war killed 200,000 people. Mexico's elites eventually concluded surrender to and occupation by the Americans was better than a race war some feared had already begun.[118]

The Americans, though, now had an occupation for which they hadn't planned. Scott established martial law and forced Mexico City's 200,000 people to pay $150,000 to cover occupation costs. The city's officials were restored to their offices and the stores reopened. The priests closed the churches to drive a wedge between the people and the Americans. The city's military governor told the clergy he would remove the American flags flying over churches as a sign of US protection unless they reopened. His threat worked. The Polk administration continued dispatching troops to reinforce Scott and reopen his supply lines. By October 1847, Scott had heavily garrisoned five locations between Mexico City and Veracruz. These strongholds, and the men escorting supply trains, soon comprised 26 percent of forces. He gave guerrillas no quarter and in areas suffering heavy guerrilla activity built fortified outposts garrisoned by 500–750 men who launched sorties. By February 1848, guerrilla activity fell dramatically. By the end of November, Scott had around 24,000 troops, perhaps 25 percent involved in counterguerrilla action. The guerrillas remained uncoordinated, lacked the people's support, and failed to stop Scott from supplying his men from the population. American forces often defended Mexican lives and property.[119]

Meanwhile, Polk grew increasingly unhappy with Scott and Trist, angered by the two-week armistice and Trist's willingness to consider deals Polk didn't like. In October, Polk ordered Trist home. Trist received the command on November 16 and ignored it. He believed he could soon negotiate with a new government and wanted to finish what he had begun. In a *65-page reply*, he explained to Washington its lack of understanding of events. The order for Trist's return frightened the Mexicans into action. They feared his departure would pause peace moves. It also created the appearance of an America not so eager for peace; and a new representative might mean new demands. A growing fear that Mexico would come apart convinced the political elite to end the war. The newest president began talks in January 1848. Trist's ignoring Polk's order fed the president's anger and propensity to see conspiracies. Polk concluded Trist and Scott were working against him and decided in early January to relieve Scott.[120]

Polk grew increasingly furious over the war's continuance, especially after so many victories and Mexico City's fall. In December 1847 he asked Congress to extend American rule over the seized parts of California and New Mexico and said the US should continue to occupy the other areas of Mexico "as a means of coercing Mexico to accede to just terms of peace." He also issued a threat: "What further provision may become necessary and what final disposition it may be proper to make of them must depend on the future progress of the war and the course which Mexico may think proper hereafter to pursue." He promised the war would be "vigorously prosecuted ... to obtain an honorable peace." He complained that one reason America hadn't secured peace was the constant overthrow of Mexican governments and suggested it might be necessary for American generals to aid formation of a "free republican government" serious about making peace.[121]

The Treaty of Guadalupe Hidalgo, signed on February 2, 1848, gave the US California, New Mexico, and the Rio Grande border (529,000 square miles of territory), and paid Mexico $15 million. Polk now suffered doubts about how much territory to take. But he couldn't find an acceptable way of refusing to submit the treaty to Congress. It was approved on March 10. Mexico's legislature did the same on March 30. Mexico suffered extensive postwar chaos in the form of several rebellions. The treaty committed America to fighting antigovernment forces and the US protected areas where it had troops. American troops began leaving Mexico City in mid June 1848. The last departed at the end of July.[122]

THE LESSONS OF THE WAR

One must applaud Scott's generalship, as many did at the time. After landing in Veracruz, he fought a six-months campaign that won the war and achieved the administration's political aims. In five major battles, Scott defeated Mexican forces sometimes three times larger in a hostile land with half the troops he had been promised under constant attack from civilian superiors while surrounded by a potentially hostile population.[123]

But Scott proved too eager to grasp any Mexican offer to negotiate, however insincere. He slackened the pressure upon his opponent, gave him time to recover his strength, and made renewal of the offensive more difficult and perhaps more costly. But the war proved to Americans the value of a regular army led by professional officers, and its performance permanently stilled voices calling for West Point's closure.[124]

The US had yet again gone to war unprepared and tried to fight on the cheap. This made Scott's task much more difficult and forced him to run risks he wouldn't have had to take if supplied sufficient means. The US could have learned much from its experience in Mexico that applied to Afghanistan in 2001 and Iraq in 2003: have sufficient forces to maintain order in the captured enemy capital; continue to flow troops into the nation after the military victory seemed ensured but no peace had been secured; prepare for postwar chaos and commit sufficient forces to address it.

For American soldiers, the war was the deadliest US conflict as a percentage of those serving. In less than two years, 10 percent were killed or died of disease (mostly the latter). Nearly a second 10 percent were invalided home. The war cost nearly $100 million and 12,518 men. But "the occupation of so much of Mexico's vast territory by a comparatively small army in less than two years represented an astonishing feat of arms. The extent of this military achievement has never been fully appreciated." The territorial acquisitions, though, fed US sectional rivalry. Would the new states be free or slave?[125] The fallout from the answers to this produced one of America's defining events.

4

SCHISM, CIVIL WAR, AND RECONSTRUCTION, 1849–1877

INTRODUCTION

The United States now entered an intense period of sectional rivalry culminating in its most destructive, self-inflicted tragedy: the Civil War. American expansion fed the tensions. New territory meant new states. This meant additional representatives in the House and Senate, which threatened old power blocks and created new ones. Security retained its importance, and despite internal problems expansion remained key while the industrial revolution and national growth accelerated.

SCHISM: THE ZACHARY TAYLOR, MILLARD FILLMORE, FRANKLIN PIERCE, AND JAMES BUCHANAN ADMINISTRATIONS, 1849–61

As Polk feared, Taylor's military success made the general a Whig presidential contender. Momentum built for his nomination, but Taylor wasn't interested unless the people called him. Party maneuvering saw his nomination and election. Whig congressman and future Confederate Vice President Alexander H. Stephens predicted a difficult time in Washington for Taylor because he owed his office to the people and not the "schemers and intriguers," producing "bitter hostility by a set of leeches who look upon the public offices as nothing but spoils for political hacks to revel on." Stephens proved exceedingly correct. Taylor's lack of establishment contacts also hampered filling administration posts.[1]

THE ZACHARY TAYLOR AND MILLARD FILLMORE ADMINISTRATIONS, 1849–53

In his inaugural address, Taylor cautioned Americans to heed the "voice of our own beloved Washington to abstain from entangling alliances with foreign nations." He wanted: "encouragement and protection to the great interests of agriculture, commerce, and manufactures, to improve our rivers and harbors, to provide for the speedy extinguishment of the public debt." He hoped to work with Congress to do whatever "may harmonize conflicting interests and tend to perpetuate that Union." Taylor made the common error of seeing economic growth as an end, but preserving the nation – security – truly mattered.[2]

Taylor helped conquer a continent (the war nearly doubled the nation's size), but the internal political battle over incorporating the new lands – which boiled down to whether they formed slave states or free – was a greater challenge. Taylor didn't face it long. He died after sixteen months in office and was succeeded by his vice president, Millard Fillmore. Taylor's significant achievements were resolving a dispute with Britain over Nicaraguan canal-building rights and hindering British expansion by standing against London's Mosquito Coast claims in Nicaragua and Honduras.[3]

The victorious war against Mexico didn't slake expansionist desires. Democrats saw slavery's extension as necessary for maintaining the Senate's North–South balance. Others thought it essential for security, or that dispersing the Black population would address "the nation's race problem." Race constrained expansion. Efforts to annex Yucatán and Hawaii collapsed because Mexican Indians and native Hawaiians were deemed unworthy of US citizenship. "Young America," an aggressive, nationalistic Democratic Party faction that disliked the domination of older leaders, pushed Manifest Destiny beyond North America, and supported revolutionary forces in the Old World. Stephen A. Douglas was its spokesman.[4]

The growing stream of settlers westward also fed expansion. In the 1850s, settlement of the Southwest and the Pacific coast convinced American leaders of the impossibility of establishing a permanent border between Indians and White settlers. Instead, the Indians would be moved into two primary Western areas to protect them from White encirclement, support "civilizing" efforts, and clear passage for settlers. The 1851 Treaty of Laramie outlined zones for plains tribes and provided US posts along the immigrant trails, rights for which the government paid annuities. An 1853 agreement established a similar Santa Fe Trail system. The birth of interest in a transcontinental railroad also worked against the Indians.[5]

The key achievement of the Taylor–Fillmore years was the Compromise of 1850. This omnibus bill effort to defuse the sectional crisis brought California into the Union as a free state, ended the slave trade in Washington, DC, strengthened fugitive slave legislation, created territories with no restrictions on slavery from lands seized from Mexico, and resolved the Texas–New Mexico boundary. Taylor threatened a veto, but Stephen Douglas broke the measure into five bills and secured each individually. Taylor died unexpectedly, and Fillmore signed them into law.[6]

The expansionists included the Filibusters. The name derived from the Spanish word for freebooter, *filibustero*; these privately funded adventurers launched ultimately failed attacks on Ecuador, Honduras, and Nicaragua, and plotted more. A failed 1851 attempt in Cuba saw Spain execute about fifty perpetrators. Fillmore could probably have obtained a declaration of war against Madrid but was uninterested. He was happy to have Cuba – if it joined the US on its own – but believed its addition would fuel sectional tensions as it had slavery. Both Taylor and Fillmore tried to stop filibustering, which became a Southern hobby. It broke the Whig Party and eased Democrat Franklin Pierce's 1852 presidential election. Pierce and James Buchanan were quietly supportive but stayed neutral. Filibustering helped deter Britain in Central America but convinced Cuba and Mexico to not sell territory to the United States while creating fear of the US throughout Central and South America.[7]

Fillmore's secretary of state, Daniel Webster, insisted in 1851 that America was destined to "command the oceans, both oceans, all the oceans." Webster blocked French ambitions in Hawaii (which threatened American ambitions) via a secret deal with King Kamehameha II in which Hawaii surrendered its sovereignty to the US in the event of war, and a July 1851 note guaranteeing Hawaiian sovereignty even if it meant conflict.[8]

THE FRANKLIN PIERCE ADMINISTRATION, 1853–57

Fillmore's successor, Democrat Franklin Pierce, was a weak president and had the misfortune to become president as the sectional crisis approached its zenith. Northern voters would no longer tolerate slavery's extension, while Southern leaders were unwilling to abandon slavery or "the power disproportionate to the southern voting population" it granted. Expansion remained a political aim. Pierce was among those eager for more Mexican territory, preferably without a war. Others wanted a boundary adjustment because the best route for a transcontinental railroad was through Mexican lands. William Walker's failed Baja California filibustering expedition complicated negotiations and probably resulted in Washington getting less than it wanted. Fortunately for the Americans, Santa Anna again led Mexico. The Gadsden Purchase agreement gained Santa Anna $15 million for 39 million acres and may have prevented another war. The 1854 Kansas–Nebraska Act, Douglas' brainchild, organized Kansas and Nebraska from Indian lands and granted inhabitants the right to decide whether their states would be slave or free. The political battle for its passage pushed America to a breaking point, fueled secession, drove a stake through the Whig Party, and ensured more Indian lands passed into American hands.[9]

Relations with Pacific nations grew increasingly important. In the wake of the Mexican War, Polk's secretary of the treasury, Robert Walker, said, "Asia has suddenly become our neighbor, with a placid intervening ocean inviting our steamships upon the trade of commerce greater than all of Europe combined." Hope of tapping the region as a great market always underpinned America's Asia relations. Reality never matched the dream. Plans to acquire Hawaii came to nothing, but Pierce secured America's first overseas possession: Baker Island, a guano-covered rock useful for fertilizer a few hundred miles south of Hawaii.[10]

The nineteenth century's first half saw a weak US penetrate Asia economically by following Britain and securing most-favored-nation trading agreements. In 1853 Humphrey Marshall, America's Qing court commissioner during the Taiping rebellion, was instructed to remain neutral in China's civil war. But Marshall believed neutrality dangerous to US interests, backed the Chinese court, and worked to block European imperialist expansion harmful to America, while helping maintain the region's balance of power. This, in his view, propagated what became a pillar of US Asia strategy: "there must be *one* China."[11] Partition would be resisted.

Fillmore's navy secretary, John P. Kennedy, envisioned a series of coaling stations stretching across the Pacific supporting military and commercial vessels, and urged exploration to support this. The commander of the navy's Far East Squadron, Commodore Mathew Perry, had a similar view and developed a maritime strategy that included a post in Japan and hoped to establish independent republics in the region. Perry and others thought Japan ripe for republicanism, which would mean its alignment with Washington. Perry arrived in July 1853 with a fleet large enough to demonstrate American power, and told Japan the US had no connection with European states and wouldn't interfere with its religion. He returned with twice as many ships in 1854 and struck a deal opening Japan to limited US trade.[12]

Pierce's secretary of state, Marcy, pursued free trade and the administration scored an 1854 commercial treaty with Canada allowing both to import many raw materials duty-free while expanding US fishing rights and diffusing tensions many feared would lead to war. Pierce believed this agreement the first step toward eventual merger of the two lands.[13]

PART I: FROM BACKWATER TO GREAT POWER

THE JAMES BUCHANAN ADMINISTRATION, 1857–61

Democrat James Buchanan also had expansionist aims. He wanted Cuba and believed it America's destiny to control North America. He hoped to resolve the slavery issue, but that was beyond any man. He aggressively defended American honor abroad and opened areas to US trade. For example, China peacefully granted the US the same commercial terms France and Britain had wrested from it during the Opium Wars.[14]

The civil war in Mexico, claims for damages to US property, and fears of Napoleon III's ambitions led Buchanan to ask Congress in December 1859 for the right to invade Mexico. He wanted to establish a military colony and promote annexation. The antislavery John Brown raid was consuming Congress' attention and Buchanan was ignored. In January 1860, Buchanan launched yet another effort to buy Cuba, but Congress refused funding. John Brown, Abraham Lincoln's presidential campaign, and the secession crisis were more important.[15]

THE CIVIL WAR, 1861–65

The decades-long struggle over slavery and its extension produced a convergence of paranoia and fear during the 1860 presidential campaign. Radical Southerners saw in Lincoln's election, America's first Republican Party president, a threat to slavery, which Lincoln never made. The president-elect made clear his desire for peace in speeches delivered on his journey from Springfield to Washington and again in his March 4, 1861 inaugural address. He tried to conciliate the South by making it clear the Constitution protected slavery, assuring all, including Southern leaders, that the Constitution prevented him from touching it. The real point, Lincoln insisted, was slavery's extension, which he refused to countenance.[16]

Cooler heads didn't prevail. South Carolina's legislature called a convention that voted unanimously for secession on December 20, 1860. Buchanan denied any right to this but blamed the crisis on Northern agitation of the slavery issue and insisted all problems would be resolved if the South were left alone. Buchanan, a Democrat, also pointed out that Lincoln's election didn't endanger slavery as the president only executed the laws and Congress wouldn't pass legislation obstructing the right to own slaves. He insisted upon secession's unconstitutionality, the Union's perpetual nature, and that Jackson's 1833 Nullification Crisis arguments provided precedent. His solution to the crisis was a constitutional convention passing

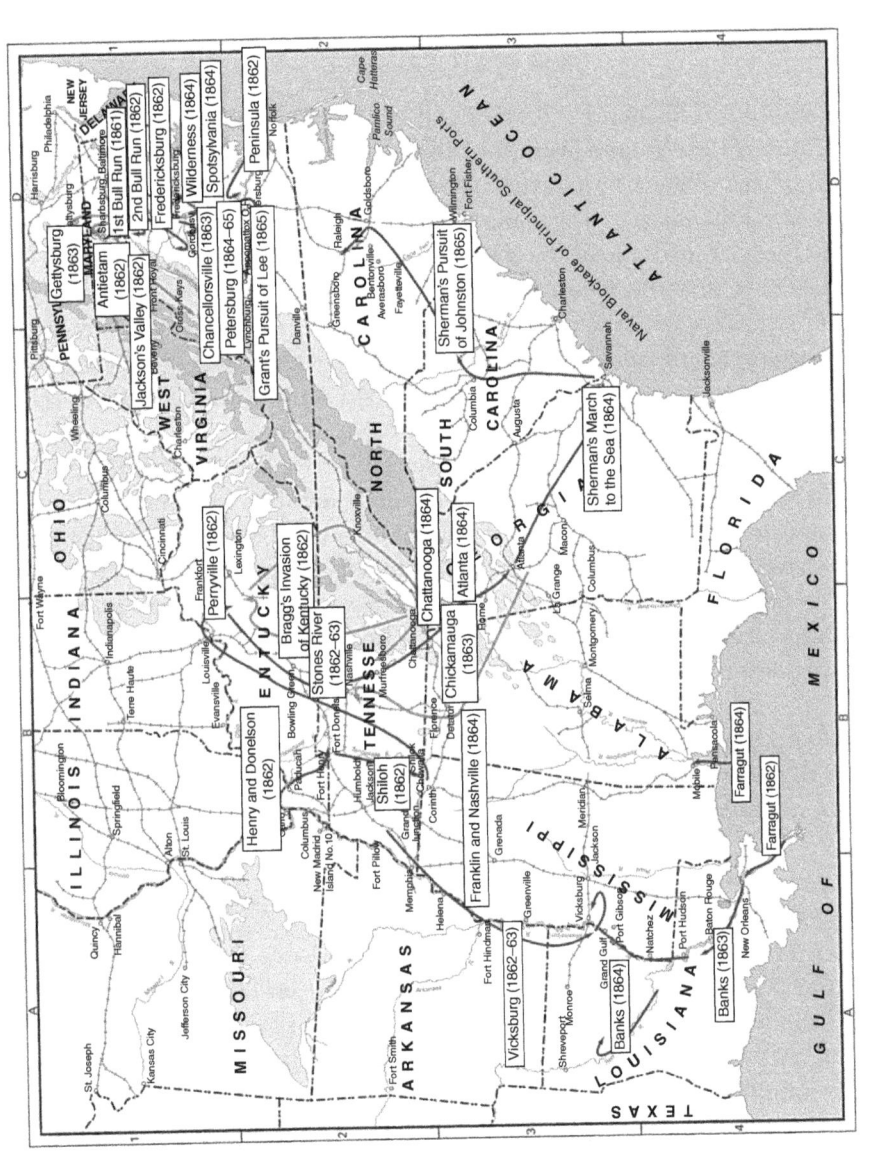

Map 4.1 Principal campaigns of the American Civil War, 1861–65

an amendment guaranteeing slavery where it existed and Federal enforcement of related laws. Seven other states followed South Carolina out of the Union by February 1, 1861.[17]

THE POLITICAL AIMS

Lincoln said in his inaugural address that "The Government will not use force unless force is used against it." But he was also adamant that no state could depart voluntarily and that acts of violence "against the authority of the United States, are insurrectionary or revolutionary, according to circumstances." Lincoln believed it his duty to protect the Union and assured his listeners that the Union "*will* constitutionally defend, and maintain itself." Lincoln closed with this: "In *your* hands, my dissatisfied fellow countrymen, and not in *mine*, is the momentous issue of civil war.... You can have no conflict, without being yourselves the aggressors."[18] Lincoln's political aim was clear: preserve the Union.

In an April 1861 message, Davis declared the South sought "peace at any sacrifice save that of honor and independence ... no conquest, no aggrandizement, no concession of any kind from the States with which we were lately confederated; all we ask is to be left alone." But the South also had imperial ambitions. Davis named the West Indies, northern Mexico, and Cuba as possibilities. The Confederate Congress authorized a Southern version of the Union's Arizona Territory and launched an ultimately failed 1862 offensive to win it.[19] The South's political aims were contradictory. Davis insisted it wanted "to be left alone," while simultaneously seeking new territory. The Confederacy, though, possessed a clear, primary political aim – independence.

STARTING THE WAR: AN ISSUE OF TIMING

When Lincoln was inaugurated on March 4, 1861, the Confederate States of America held an unusually strong position for an insurrection. It had functioning federal, state, and local governments, a significant and growing army, and control over most of the land it claimed. Its position was a historical anomaly as rebels usually must fight to establish territorial control and governmental structures.[20] But there were still forts on the Confederate coast held by Union troops, ones Lincoln resolved to maintain.

On April 6, Lincoln informed South Carolina's governor that the Union would resupply one of these bastions, Fort Sumter, but not try to reinforce it. Fearing inaction would "revive Southern Unionism," Davis decided to eliminate the Federal presence. On April 12, 1861, after negotiations failed, Confederate guns opened on Sumter. It surrendered the next day. The South acted despite knowing Sumter's critical supply situation, and its commander's commitment to abandon the fort by noon on April 15 – unless he received new orders or more supplies. But the Confederates worried about this. The attack enraged the North. Allowing Sumter to surrender without a shot being fired wouldn't have produced such a dramatic effect. The attack also made the South the aggressor, which was probably what Lincoln had in mind.[21]

Lincoln replied with an April 15 proclamation calling for 75,000 volunteers to enforce the laws of the United States. Davis considered this a declaration of war, which it essentially was, called for volunteers and privateers, and dispatched commissioners to Belgium, Great Britain, France, and Russia seeking recognition and trade and friendship treaties. Four more states joined the Confederacy.[22]

Deciding *when* to begin a war is crucial. The South went to war too early. It could have suffered Northern possession of a speck of South Carolina, shipped its cotton through unblockaded ports, and imported war material it lacked. Instead, the Confederates launched a war for which they were unprepared – in American fashion – while emboldening a reluctant enemy. But this didn't guarantee Confederate failure.

STRATEGY AND THE CIVIL WAR

In the Civil War, as in many conflicts pre-dating the First World War, a method of differentiating the levels of war – tactical, operational, and strategic – didn't exist as we understand it today. (See Map 4.1.) Most military and civilian leaders looked only at the prospective battle (tactical issues), not at how each individual engagement fit into a campaign (the operational level of war), and how this related to the nation's military strategy (the methods for prosecuting it). Few could envisage an extended campaign (or operation); almost none looked beyond their theater. The education of Civil War officers hadn't prepared them to think strategically. But some did.

THE ASSESSMENT

Winfield Scott, the 300 plus–pound septuagenarian army general in chief, believed winning the war would take two or three years and require 300,000 men. He anticipated enormous costs in Southern life and property for which the North would gain $250 million in debt and devastated states it would have to hold down for "generations." Scott also thought that if the North invaded the South, the war would be no further advanced a year later. Robert E. Lee thought the war might last ten years, and that the Confederacy had to rely on its own strengths.[23]

The South faced an unequal contest. The 1860 census put the inhabitants of the 11 Confederate states at 9,103,332, including 3,521,110 slaves. Many White southerners feared slave unrest, but slavery kept the economy going, enabling heavy Southern mobilization. Almost 80 percent of the adult, White, male population of the Confederacy between 15 and 40 took up arms, nearly 900,000 of 1,140,000 men. But the North had 4,010,000 men between 15 and 40. Perhaps 2.8 million served. The Union retained a population of 22,339,991, including inhabitants of the critical border states of Delaware, Kentucky, Maryland, and Missouri, the District of Columbia, and the New Mexico Territory, whose combined population was 3,305,557, including 432,586 slaves. In the Rocky Mountain and Pacific coast areas lived 525,660 people, but they contributed little military strength.[24] The US army was miniscule – just over 16,000. Volunteers and militia, almost always raised at the state level, created both armies. Conscription came later but was more important to the South.

In 1860, America was second only to Britain industrially. The number of cotton mills went from 8 in 1800 to 1,091 in 1860, pig iron production from 40,000 to 821,000 tons. Technology helped, as did the rapidly increasing domestic market, the primary outlet for US goods. Americans moved from making most of their needs to consuming manufactured goods. Specialization and the beginning of agricultural mechanization combined with the development of better transportation in the form of railroads, steamboats, and internal improvements spurred demand for manufactures. Of the nation's 128,300 industrial firms, the Confederacy had only 18,206, and these generally small. The value of the South's industrial output was but 7.5 percent of America's total. The North's agricultural production also outstripped the South's. Putting skilled industrial workers in the ranks further undermined Confederate industry.[25]

Railroads – their locations and carrying capacity – heavily influenced the war's prosecution. The Union had 22,085 miles of rails, the South 8,541. General William Tecumseh Sherman compared the value of rail and wagon transportation in his 1864 Atlanta campaign, using as a measure a single-track railroad running 160 cars of supplies a day for 100,000 men and their 35,000 animals. He concluded the campaign couldn't have occurred without railroads. Supplying his force required 36,000 wagons pulled by

220,800 mules hauling 2 tons a day for 20 miles, which the area's roads made impossible. About 1,000 steamboats worked Western waterways in 1861. The Confederates took a few; the Union built hundreds. One 500-ton steamboat carried enough material per trip to provide nearly two days' supplies for 40,000 men and their 18,000 animals.[26]

DIPLOMATIC STRATEGY

The primary targets of Union and Confederate diplomacy were Britain and France. The Confederacy sought recognition and intervention; the Union sought to prevent this. British leaders sympathized with the Confederacy, but the population, particularly the growing middle class, didn't. Most Britons, like most Frenchmen, opposed slavery, and the Confederates injured their cause by sending poor representatives. The closest they came to achieving anything significant was when a Union navy captain seized the *Trent*, a British vessel bearing the South's representatives. Lincoln famously said, "one war at a time," and defused the situation by apologizing to Britain and returning the Confederates. There was scant chance of British and French recognition or intervention. The French wanted to recognize the Confederacy but only if Britain went first. Secretary of State Henry Seward made it clear to London that intervention meant war. London believed this would injure its economic interests and might cost Britain its Western Hemisphere possessions.[27]

ECONOMIC STRATEGY

Davis and many other Southern leaders believed in the power of King Cotton and labored under the illusion that French and British demand for American cotton would translate into political recognition. Davis thought that if the South stopped shipping its cotton, it would be at most a year before this provoked a crisis resulting in recognition. Many Southerners thought similarly and spontaneously instituted a self-imposed and unofficial embargo on cotton exports. Davis' administration didn't support this and bought cotton to underpin Confederate finances but didn't stop it. The South lost the chance to export its cotton before the Union blockade became effective, and Davis didn't understand that the embargo *reduced* the chances of foreign recognition and intervention as no European government could survive such economic blackmail, especially a British one. Plus, India and Egypt could grow cotton, though Britain suffered while production shifted. London also found it expedient to recognize the Union blockade; it might later need the same consideration. And London needed Union grain. The Confederate government recognized its failure in mid 1862, and took control of cotton exports in 1863, but 2.5 million bales had been burned to prevent capture.[28] Davis and other Southern leaders made the common mistake of believing economic relations trumped interests and political aims.

Relatedly, while the Confederate dollar held its value during the war's first two years, it didn't thereafter. The Confederacy refused to tax its people and raised a smaller percentage of its income from taxation than any modern wartime government. The solution: print money. This, combined with scarcity, helped produce rampant inflation that destroyed the economy. Richmond's income up to October 1864 clearly depicts Confederate finances: paper money, 60 percent; bond sales, 30 percent; taxation, about 5 percent; miscellaneous, 5 percent. The states, municipalities, banks, corporations, and even individuals also printed notes. The Union, by the same month of 1864, derived 13 percent of its income from paper money; bonds generated 62 percent; taxes 21 percent; and other sources 4 percent. The Union increased tariffs, which mixed with protectionist sentiment to push the average duty from around 20 percent in 1860 to 47 percent in 1864. Except from 1861–65, until the First World War tariffs provided most government revenue.[29]

MYTH AND THEORY

An error in Civil War writing is that the South pursued an offensive–defensive strategy. This comes largely from historian Frank E. Vandiver, who misunderstood the sources he used, and the theoretical ideas of the Swiss military theorist Baron Antoine-Henri Jomini. Related is the question of how much Jomini's ideas penetrated. No one has delivered a decisive answer. Davis, by using the term "offensive–defensive" (or its inverse), followed a common *tactical* usage of his day of one of Jomini's terms. Generals from both sides used the term, invariably in reference to *tactical* matters. There is clear knowledge of Jomini's ideas (if not necessarily understanding) in the writings of Union Major General Henry Wager Halleck. Nicknamed "Old Brains," Halleck made a name for himself before the war as a military intellectual by writing *Elements of Military Art and Science* (in many respects a poor translation of Jomini's *Art of War*) and translating Jomini's multivolume biography of Napoleon.[30] One arguably sees Jomini's influence in military operations because of the emphasis on securing bases for mounting them.

GROPING TO DESTRUCTION

Confederate President Davis, a West Point graduate, hero of the Battle of Buena Vista in the Mexican War, and a former secretary of war, was an obstacle to Southern strategy creation. The Confederacy's constitution, largely copied from the US document, designated its president the military commander in chief. Davis saw himself as general in chief as well. This prevented creation of a Confederate general staff and ensured no Confederate general in chief until 1865, when it was too late. Davis tightly controlled the war effort, essentially functioning as his own secretary of war, of which he had five. He burrowed into the military weeds and struggled to distinguish between tactical and strategic matters. His leadership, the poor Confederate command system, and the possession of a determined opponent, all weighed against the South.[31]

The Confederacy initially implemented a *cordon strategy* or *cordon defense*, meaning it tried to defend the entirety of the Confederacy and soon had troops scattered from Virginia to Texas. This was ad hoc and reactive, but politically Davis had little choice. Governors worried about Union descents and Southerners expected to see their army. Davis also feared that Union penetrations, even if the territory were recovered, would destroy the slave system in the area. Dispersing forces for a cordon or perimeter defense left the South weak everywhere. Plus, the Confederate's military departmental system, one derived from the extant structure, divided the Confederacy into supposedly militarily self-supporting entities. This increased dispersion and created inefficient compartmentalization of forces. The number of departments and their limits were constantly altered. The South also had an extensive and accessible coastline, and insufficient population to guard it.[32]

The Union's most important initial strategic plan came from Scott, who proposed what became known as the "Anaconda Plan." Scott foresaw a Union column pushing down the Mississippi River, severing the Confederacy in twain while the navy suffocated the South with a blockade. Underlying Scott's strategy was his belief (common among Union military and civilian leaders) that most Southerners were pro-Union and suppressed by a troublesome minority. A slow approach to the war would allow time for latent Unionism to reclaim its rightful place. Scott overestimated Southern Unionism and underestimated Southern support for secession. Lincoln imposed the blockade, a consistent element of Union strategy, but didn't support Scott's slow squeeze. He wanted a quick war and pushed for action. Believing it militarily feasible, he ordered an offensive in Virginia by the armies of Robert "Granny" Patterson and Irvin McDowell that culminated in Union defeat at Manassas on the banks of Bull Run Creek.[33] The Southern cordon held, for now.

THE BORDER STATES

Critical to the successful prosecution of any war is division of responsibility between the military and political realms. Both have distinctive roles to ensure the war is waged efficiently, effectively, and at the least cost. If the government fails to provide clear political aims or ambiguous guidance on when and where military commanders may act, the war may develop in unwanted ways. If military leaders exceed their responsibility and begin to make political decisions, they can unnecessarily widen a conflict. How Union and Confederate leaders dealt with the Border States reveals the dangers and benefits here.

The Border States of Missouri, Kentucky, Maryland, and Delaware were slave-holding states that didn't secede, though all had residents eager to join the Confederacy, and possessed the strength to shift the material balance. Winning over Missouri, Kentucky, and Maryland "would have added 45 percent to the white population and military manpower of the Confederacy," and increased its industry by 80 percent. But the strategic position mattered as well. Gaining Missouri would have given the South the important city of St. Louis. A Confederate Kentucky would create a potentially defensible border along the Ohio River while denying Union access to the Cumberland and Tennessee Rivers, two key waterways into the South.[34]

Lincoln exercised restraint on border state neutrality, especially with Kentucky. "I think to lose Kentucky is nearly the same as to lose the whole game," he wrote. "Kentucky gone, we can not hold Missouri, nor, as I think, Maryland. These all against us, and the job on our hands is too large for us. We would as well consent to separation at once, including the surrender of this capitol." He didn't flinch from acting in Maryland. Geography and necessity demanded it as Maryland's secession meant losing the capital.[35]

Missouri had endured its own pre-Civil War civil war and had troops from both sides fighting in the state. Lincoln created the Department of the West on July 1, 1861, placed John C. Frémont in command, and tasked him with raising an army for a push down the Mississippi. Frémont began establishing political aims via an August 30, 1861 proclamation confiscating the property of anyone in the state fighting against the Union, including their slaves, who "are hereby declared freemen." Frémont belonged to the Republican Party's Radical section, which wanted abolition made a political aim. But Lincoln determined Union political purposes. By attacking slavery,

Frémont crossed the line from a military matter to a political one. Making the war about abolition would also upset Lincoln's dance with the border states, particularly Kentucky. Lincoln alerted Frémont and asked him to reverse himself. Frémont refused unless ordered and Lincoln told him to rescind the seizure of slaves. Frémont also proved a poor commander; Lincoln relieved him in November.[36]

When Kentucky declared its neutrality, Lincoln refused to concede its right to do so but agreed to observe it. Lincoln also saw here a chance to test the Union's strategy of reconciliation. If the North made no aggressive moves, suppressed Southern Unionism might revive. In June 1861, the state's Congressional elections resulted in Unionists in nine of Kentucky's ten districts. The Confederates also rewarded Lincoln's restraint. Davis committed to respecting Kentucky's neutrality, but Confederate Brigadier General Gideon J. Pillow insisted upon occupying Columbus, Kentucky, to block future Union moves. Leonidas K. Polk, Pillow's superior, an old friend of Davis', believed (incorrectly) the Union was preparing to take Columbus and told Pillow to act first, branding it "a *paramount military necessity.*" On September 3, 1861, Pillow's troops landed at Hickman, Kentucky, south of Columbus. Davis initially ordered a withdrawal but bent to Polk's pleas and pressure from prominent Kentucky and Tennessee citizens, decreeing "The necessity justifies the action." The Confederates then failed to immediately seize the entire state, though Albert Sidney Johnston extended the *cordon* into Kentucky. A local Union commander, Ulysses S. Grant, took Kentucky's capital, Paducah. The state declared for the Union, vindicating Lincoln's prudence.[37] Invading Kentucky proved a cataclysmic Confederate mistake. It undermined the South's strategic position by removing a buffer. It eased advances down the Mississippi or overland and opened the Tennessee and Cumberland Rivers into the South's interior. The South needed to forestall Union offensives and gather strength, waiting, while preparing a riposte.

McCLELLAN'S GRAND PLAN

The month before the invasion of Kentucky, in August 1861, Lincoln brought to Washington the successful commander of Union forces in what became West Virginia, George B. McClellan. Though not yet general in chief (he assumed this post on November 1, 1861), McClellan immediately proposed one of the most far-reaching American strategic plans. It called for offensive action against a variety of points of the Confederacy simultaneously, and even urged considering Mexican assistance – all after properly preparing. His plan's key components included clearing Missouri with the troops there; sending a force of 20,000, plus those raised in eastern Tennessee and Kentucky (once it abandoned its neutrality), down the Mississippi River; the seizure of Nashville and eastern Tennessee and the state's rail lines; a move from Kansas and Nebraska against the Red River and western Texas, all intended to take advantage of supposed Union and free state sentiment; and consideration of a drive from California via New Mexico. Most importantly, a force of 273,000 would be raised for an advance into Virginia (the main theater, in McClellan's view), and then into the Deep South in conjunction with the western armies. Naval forces would support these moves and help seize key Confederate ports. What modern military parlance defines as *jointness*, meaning joint army–navy operations, was a consistent characteristic of McClellan's planning.[38]

In his initial grand plan, McClellan insisted victory demanded defeating Confederate forces, taking strong points, and demonstrating the futility of resistance (while protecting private property). McClellan urged reassertion of government authority through "overwhelming physical force" while arguing for light measures against civilians and their property. This was a contradiction. The North couldn't protect people and property while using "overwhelming physical force." He wanted to wage a war that couldn't be waged (though most didn't yet realize it). This demonstrated one of McClellan's problems: he didn't understand the nature of the war. "The contest began with a class; now it is with a people," he wrote.[39] In fact, however, it had always been with "a people." The only masses in thrall were the slaves. McClellan, like many Union leaders, chased the mirage of suppressed Southern Unionism.

Would McClellan's plan have worked? His proposal had weaknesses, the biggest being the small numbers of troops in the western prongs, particularly the Mississippi River advance. But executed by someone with talent for implementation, McClellan's plan stood an excellent chance of success. What Grant proposed for the 1864 campaign was not dissimilar. Nonetheless, McClellan, for all his gifts, lacked sufficient ability to decisively use the army operationally or tactically. The Peninsula Campaign showed this, as did Antietam. The obvious problem was raising his 273,000-man force. This, though difficult, was not beyond Union means, and McClellan's army in 1862 numbered over 220,000.

This plan became the cornerstone of McClellan's strategic thinking, and the fact that the administration never gave him *exactly* what he wanted or allowed him to act *exactly* when and where he wanted, and under the conditions *he* desired, became excuses for inaction. Moreover, weakening this plan and its revisions was McClellan's intention to deliver the decisive punch with the army he personally commanded. Other Union offensive moves were subservient to his.[40] Thus, if McClellan didn't move, strategic paralysis could grip the Union, and as McClellan acquired greater influence, this happened, for a time. Moreover, McClellan didn't sufficiently weigh the war's political elements, particularly the Union public's demand for action, and the administration's necessity of demonstrating progress to satisfy supporters and quiet detractors.

NAVAL STRATEGY

McClellan's plan was reinforced by the Blockade Board, one of the few Civil War institutions dedicated to studying a problem and offering advice. In three months, beginning in late June 1861, it developed the navy's strategic concept for implementing the blockade. Its core planks were building and deploying naval squadrons and seizing Southern ports as bases to support warships. The board's demise after filing its September 1861 report damaged the Union war effort. Between August 1861 and April 1862, its recommendations produced the capture of seven sites from Virginia to Mississippi. To secure the vessels to implement the blockade, the navy grew exponentially. In nine months, the Union commissioned 76 ships, bought 136, and had 52 built. Within a year there were 300. In seizing and holding coastal posts, the Union implemented parts of an enclave strategy. The enclaves tied down Confederate troops, undermined the South's social structure by destabilizing the slave system, and provided bases for raiding Southern resources, railroads, and industry.[41]

The South took the traditional strategic paths of a weaker naval power: commerce raiding and advanced technology. Davis called for privateers in the first days of the war, but the British declaration of neutrality meant that to London the South had to obey an international treaty against privateering while the North had to make the blockade effective to give it standing under international law. Privateering died. Confederate Secretary of the Navy Stephen Mallory believed technological superiority would allow the South to overcome disparity in numbers. He wanted fast, propeller-driven, lightly armed raiders "to harass the enemy's commerce," forcing the Union to commit ships to pursue raiders instead of blockading Southern ports. The result was two deadly, British-built raiders: *Florida* and *Alabama*. He also built a vessel inspired by the old ship of the line but possessing modern twists: an ironclad, steam-powered ram with rifled guns to "prevent all blockades, and encounter, with a fair prospect of success, their entire navy." The *Virginia's* success at Hampton Roads in March 1862 spurred similar efforts. The South also invested in mines (then called torpedoes) and primitive submarines. An innovative scheme for a mosquito fleet of steam-powered boats with spar-mounted mines for coastal defense to swarm enemy vessels never got off the ground. Innovative weapons at times produced tactical successes, but the Confederacy lacked the industrial capacity to build very many. The Union also captured the ports constructing ships or countered with better technology, such as the *Monitor* ironclad.[42]

All of this meant the Confederates couldn't break the blockade. It was firmly in place by the middle of 1862 and its effectiveness stemmed from the Union's occupation of Confederate ports. One Confederate response was to build (or nationalize) industries necessary for supplying and equipping one of the world's largest armies. The Confederacy's chief of army ordnance, Josiah Gorgas, accomplished the amazing feat of building an internal Southern armaments industry. Trade still got through: often privately owned, fast blockade runners brought in valuable luxury goods, importation the government banned in early 1864.[43]

The blockade dramatically reduced Southern trade. In 1862, 1863, and 1864, cotton exports via Confederate ports were one-tenth of prewar levels, though the crops were smaller because of Davis' 1863 call to grow foodstuffs. The inability to export severely damaged the economy. The blockade fed inflation via specie flight and by creating shortages in luxury items and necessities such as needles and shoes. Scarcity and money-printing fueled hyperinflation, diminishing Confederate warfighting ability and will. The price of flour, for example, increased 2,800 percent. Combined with Union military successes, the blockade limited Richmond's ability to raise money overseas through selling bonds. The 5 percent of Union military effort devoted to the blockade paid hefty dividends.[44]

UNION STRATEGY: McCLELLAN IN COMMAND

When McClellan became general in chief in November 1861, he reorganized the Western Theater, establishing two commands under Henry Halleck and Don Carlos Buell, respectively. McClellan knew what he wanted done in the west and had clear operational objectives, some driven by Lincoln's concerns: an immediate advance into eastern Tennessee, severing "communication between the Mississippi Valley and Eastern Virginia," protecting Tennessee Unionists, and reestablishing Union government in East Tennessee, and he wanted Buell to advance on Knoxville, Tennessee. But McClellan suffered a problem with which Lincoln became intimately familiar: subordinates who refused to act. McClellan attempted to coordinate western moves with his, but his generals insisted nothing could be done.[45]

Lincoln, frustrated and besieged politically, pushed his commanders to move. This produced a January 13, 1862 letter showing Lincoln absorbing the ideas of his military-related reading and commanders – and taking them further. "I state my general idea of this war to be that we have the *greater* numbers," the president began,

> and the enemy has the *greater* facility of concentrating forces upon points of collision; that we must fail, unless we can find some way of making *our* advantage an overmatch for *his*; and that this can only be done by menacing him with superior forces at *different* points, at the *same* time; so that we can safely attack, one, or both, if he makes no change; and if he *weakens* one to *strengthen* the other, forbear to attack the strengthened one, but seize, and hold the weakened one, gaining so much.

What followed was Lincoln's Order No. 1 of January 27, 1862, designating February 22 as "the day for a general movement of all the land and naval forces of the United States against the insurgent forces."[46] "Simultaneous pressure" describes Lincoln's approach, the strategy ultimately implemented, and aligns with McClellan's ideas, but Lincoln's prongs were potentially of equal importance.

None of this made Union generals move.

THE CONFEDERACY REACTS

As the Union dithered, the Confederacy scrambled to gather strength. Albert Sidney Johnston assumed command of the bulk of Confederate western forces. Joseph E. Johnston controlled the most important troops in the east. Both worried about the growing Union threat. Strategically, the defense held sway. The Union war machine finally uncoiled on February 2, 1862, when Grant and US navy flag officer Andrew H. Foote moved to take Fort Henry and Fort Donelson on the Tennessee and Cumberland Rivers, respectively. The impetus came from Halleck's subordinate, Grant. This, combined with Don Carlos Buell's drive into Kentucky and Central Tennessee, shattered the *cordon* and the South's strategic position in the west.[47]

The South responded by adopting a strategy of concentration. Confederate General Braxton Bragg recommended abandoning Texas, Florida, and all posts on the Gulf of Mexico (except Pensacola, Mobile, and New Orleans) to gather forces. "A small loss of property would result from their occupation by the enemy," he wrote, "but our military strength would not be lessened thereby, whilst the enemy would be weakened by dispersion. We could then beat him in detail, instead of the reverse." The same month, in the east, both Davis and Joseph Johnston worried over the exposed position of Johnston's forces in northern Virginia. When McClellan launched his Virginia Peninsula campaign in March 1862, Johnston pushed for concentrating his department's forces.[48]

In the east, the South had to concentrate against McClellan. But in the west, the question of where was more difficult. Albert Sidney Johnston, with Davis' advice and assistance, gathered an army at Corinth, Mississippi, to protect the Mississippi River valley. Davis urged a counteroffensive, hoping to recoup the South's losses.[49] Concentration was the correct response, but choosing Corinth was an error. It left the Confederacy's vital center unprotected. Only Union failure could save the South from a quick defeat.

A portion of Buell's force entered Nashville on February 25, 1862. McClellan, as general in chief, wired Halleck on March 2: "Buell thinks the enemy intends uniting behind the Tennessee River, so as to be able to concentrate either on you or Buell." He therefore emphasized that it was "doubly important" to hold Nashville and to take Decatur, Alabama, thereby isolating Memphis and Columbus and making them ripe to fall. Critically, he noted "Chattanooga is also a point of great importance for us." McClellan wanted the Union to take Chattanooga, Tennessee, the doorway to the Deep South and then the only railroad connection linking the Confederacy's east and west. It was virtually undefended and Union forces under Ormsby Mitchel were within striking distance in mid April, but Mitchel's pleas for reinforcements to help him take the city went unheeded. This situation dragged on through the spring and into the summer. But McClellan was no longer Union general in chief. Lincoln relieved him on March 11, 1862.[50] Halleck now commanded in the west. He had charge of Buell, and Buell had charge of Mitchel. But neither Halleck nor Buell possessed the vision to grasp what was important, and they let an astounding opportunity slip through their fingers by failing to take Chattanooga. The Union's western focus shifted to opening the Mississippi River, returning to Chattanooga and its environs only in October 1863.

Meanwhile McClellan, having received permission to try to destroy the Confederate threat via his Virginia Peninsula Campaign, put his army in motion. What is nearly universally overlooked is that McClellan saw his Peninsula Campaign as one element of a larger offensive strategy with multiple tentacles striking the Confederacy at various points simultaneously. But when McClellan went to the Peninsula, Lincoln relieved him as general in chief and put no one else in the job. With the help of Secretary of War Edwin Stanton, Lincoln tried to do it himself.[51] The result: Union strategy collapsed. McClellan, despite his sloth using the forces under his direct command, was solidly directing the Union tentacles crushing the South. He realized the importance of Chattanooga and its rail net, and that it was the gateway into the Confederate core, and understood the value of supporting operations and clear operational objectives. But Union forces no longer had a guiding hand. The Union lost a chance to secure an early victory in the war or at least lay its foundation.

HALLECK'S HALF-HEARTED WAR

When he removed McClellan as general in chief, Lincoln reorganized the departmental structure. One mistake was placing Halleck in command of the west. Halleck possessed some talent as an operational planner but none as a strategist. When he took command in March 1862, he had two primary options: he could drive on Corinth and the Confederate army, or he could follow McClellan's plan and take Chattanooga and push deeper into the Confederacy. He probably had the strength to do both. When advising commanders to go after enemy centers of gravity – sources of strength – Clausewitz includes among these the enemy's army. Indeed, to him, this is the most important point at which to strike. But he also says that sometimes an opportunity arises that is so advantageous that a commander could divert some of his strength to grasp it.[52]

Such was the Union's strategic position in the west in spring 1862. Halleck could strike the enemy's main western army or seize Chattanooga. Doing either would again crack the Confederacy's strategic position in the west and lay the groundwork for capturing the Deep South and Union victory. Halleck did neither. He marched on Corinth but aimed at the city as a valuable point, as a railroad junction; he didn't go intending to destroy the Confederate army. And he did this slowly, ignoring the critical factor of time and giving the enemy a chance to extract his army and rebuild Chattanooga's defenses. At the end of May 1862, the Confederates stole a march on Halleck, evacuating their army to Tupelo, Mississippi. They did it again at the end of July when Bragg shifted this force to central Tennessee. Halleck compounded his failure in the summer by refusing to send some of his more than 100,000 men to help Union Flag Officer David Farragut capture nearly undefended Vicksburg. It controlled passage of the Mississippi River, which the Union navy penetrated after taking New Orleans.[53]

None of this prevented Lincoln from appointing Halleck general in chief in July 1862. His tactical and operational success stood in stark contrast to McClellan's perceived indolence and supposed lack of enthusiasm for the Union cause. Halleck received *carte blanche* over strategy, but his indecisiveness became quickly apparent. Lincoln soon branded Halleck little better than a "first-rate clerk." Lincoln failed to relieve him, likely because he felt he had to use the tools at hand, and Union strategy suffered.[54] The greatest obstacle to Union victory remained a lack of firm, aggressive, strategic leadership consistently exercised.

Halleck's appointment destroyed Union strategy. In early August 1862, he ordered McClellan's army from the Peninsula after a hard campaign, giving Lee and his army freedom to maneuver, and then failed to exercise command over the various Union forces in Virginia, directly contributing to the Union debacle that was the Battle of Second Manassas. In the west, Buell refused to move. Grant's army was left without orders. The Confederacy was given time to breathe, plan, and strike.

THE SOUTH'S OFFENSIVE STRATEGY

By July 1862, Davis' military thoughts had turned to the offensive, and he had generals – Braxton Bragg and Robert E. Lee – eager to give his intentions life. There arose nearly simultaneously among Southern leaders the belief that only offensive action could redeem their strategic situation. The result was a three-pronged, multi-army offensive that stretched from Mississippi to Maryland. Davis intended to regain Tennessee and bring Kentucky and Maryland into the Confederacy. Nothing went as planned. The Confederates headed north believing Kentuckians and Marylanders awaited freedom from Union bondage. Moreover, particularly in the west, the offensive was plagued by poor operational planning and an unclear command structure. Sterling Price was defeated at Iuka, Mississippi, on September 17. Earl Van Dorn was repulsed at nearby Corinth a few days later. Bragg and Kirby Smith forced the Union to surrender some of its gains in Alabama and eastern Tennessee at heavy cost to their forces, but failed to regain Kentucky, partially because of poor coordination. Lee accomplished even less. He went north and nearly had his army destroyed at Antietam, Maryland, in September 1862. Only McClellan's failure to act in the battle's aftermath kept Lee's defeat from becoming a disaster.[55]

But was this a good idea strategically? The Confederates needed to regain lost territory in the west for supply and recruiting. And a *cordon defense* had not served well, especially in the west's vast reaches, but offensive war badly planned and executed proved no better. Indeed, under concerted Union pressure the South failed even to hold its original territory in the west and struggled to do so in the east. The offensives wasted human and material resources and demonstrated the Confederacy's inability to project power in a sustained manner. This was the only time the Confederacy launched a series of simultaneous offensive operations.

ESCALATION AND DESTRUCTION

The 1862 Confederate offensives corresponded to a hardening Union response. Clausewitz wrote about the tendency of a war's violence and means to escalate; the Civil War was no exception. Lincoln had been awaiting a victory like McClellan's at Antietam before issuing the Preliminary Emancipation Proclamation announcing his intention to free the slaves in areas in rebellion on January 1, 1863. This was an effort to take one of the enemy's strengths and use it against them. It was also part of a general attack on Southern property, for such is what the slaves were. McClellan had tried to wage war without enraging the Southern people or destroying their property. But after the failure of the Peninsula Campaign, Union leaders decided the Rebels should feel what Sherman called "the hard hand of war."[56] Union armies began taking useful Southern food, supplies, and animals, and burning facilities of military value. The tempo of destruction continually increased, becoming an element of a Union strategy of exhaustion: it would destroy or erode the South's material ability and will to resist.

JOSEPH JOHNSTON'S WESTERN WAR

After the failure of the Confederate combined offensive, Davis sought to establish better command and control over the Western Theater. Though he disliked doing so, he put Joseph Johnston in charge. Effectively running this vast area necessitated a leader with vision and decisiveness. Johnston possessed neither. His many wounds in three wars attest to his physical bravery, but he lacked the moral courage to exercise his command. In Johnston's defense was that he faced a nearly impossible situation. Grant's troops bore down on Vicksburg, Nathanial Banks pressed Port Hudson, Louisiana, on the Mississippi River, William S. Rosecrans threatened Chattanooga and thus the gateway into Georgia (though not as much as he should have). Johnston lacked the troops to meet these dangers.[57]

Johnston's immediate problem in spring 1863 was trying to save Vicksburg, the South's primary position on the Mississippi and the key to its control. To do this, he believed – correctly – that he needed a larger field army to attack. Johnston assessed the situation and told Davis to decide between saving Vicksburg or Tennessee. This was a tough question, one Johnston was right to push up the chain of command. Davis said the Mississippi was the priority. He also addressed Johnston's complaints: his command area was too large, and the distance between the primary Confederate armies too great for him to manage. Johnston's Division of the West was indeed big, comprising Alabama, Mississippi, parts of eastern Tennessee, the eastern area of Louisiana, and bits of Georgia and South Carolina. Davis consistently told him he had the right to move the troops in his area as he saw fit, including Bragg's army in Tennessee. Johnston consistently refused to listen, undermining the Confederate effort to save Vicksburg.[58]

Strategically, what mattered most for the Confederacy: Vicksburg or the army defending it? Johnston knew the answer: the army of John Pemberton holding the city. Vicksburg mattered little. Its fall wouldn't dramatically affect the Confederacy's ability to resist. Losing Pemberton's army would. But Davis ordered Vicksburg held. On May 17, Johnston told Pemberton to abandon the city and save the army if nearby Haines Bluff became untenable. Pemberton elected to stay.[59] This cumulative failure of Confederate leadership not only cost the South Vicksburg when it surrendered to Grant on July 4, 1863, but also Pemberton's army (though some of it fought again).

Related to this was debate around whether the Union should strike Confederate armies or "strategic centers." Historian James McPherson delivered the decisive blow: "The Confederate nation was carried on the back of its armies. So long as those armies existed, so did the Confederacy. When they surrendered, the Confederacy ceased to exist." The question for the Union was: how do you get at Confederate armies? One way was moving against points the Confederacy considered imperative for survival. This, historian Steven Woodworth tells us, forced Confederate armies to fight.[60]

LEE'S OFFENSIVE

In the summer of 1863, as Grant's forces were attempting to take Vicksburg, Lee again went north. Just what he hoped to accomplish is debated, but it's clear Lee was thinking both strategically and operationally. He believed the Confederacy could win the war only by convincing the North to stop fighting. In other words, the South had to break the Union's will, thus convincing the Northern people to stop supporting the war. This was an apt assessment. But if public opinion was the Union center of gravity, how should the Confederacy go about crushing it? Lee believed the answer was defeating Union armies, particularly doing so in the North, perhaps even destroying a Union force in the field. This was probably what he hoped to do when he crossed the Potomac. It was a misreading. The South's best chance was to protract the war, thus raising its costs (particularly in blood) beyond what the Union populace was willing to pay, but Lee believed he lacked the time for this. Operationally, Lee's objectives were clear. He wanted to upset the Union's plans, throw their forces north of the Potomac, clear the Shenandoah, and feed his army on the enemy for the summer to save Southern resources.[61] The rub was, doing any of this.

As Lee's campaign unwound, Lincoln named a tough Pennsylvanian named George Gordon Meade head of the Army of the Potomac. In a three-day slugfest, Meade defeated Lee at Gettysburg, Pennsylvania. Strategically, what was perhaps most critical was what happened after the battle. Union cavalry destroyed the Confederate bridges over the Potomac and high waters prevented Lee's army from crossing. Lincoln prodded, cajoled, and begged, but Meade wouldn't attack Lee's mangled force. Meade missed a chance to destroy Lee's army, a clear element of Confederate strength. Lincoln believed that such a blow landed against the South, combined with Grant's simultaneous capture of Vicksburg, would have ensured a Union victory.[62]

STRIKING THE PERIPHERY – DEFENDING THE CENTER

After the twin Union triumphs of Vicksburg and Gettysburg, and Rosecrans's relatively bloodless near-simultaneous securing of Murfreesboro, Tennessee, and its environs, the Union gave the Confederacy the most important strategic gift: *time*. The Confederacy was succumbing to the effects of simultaneous pressure. Instead of continuing the strain, the Union flailed at the edges. Two things drove this: Lincoln's insistence upon countering French political influence deriving from Napoleon III's Mexican adventure, and Halleck's insistence upon "cleaning up" the Confederacy's peripheral areas. This led to Union moves against Arkansas, Texas, and other regions. Grant and Sherman, meanwhile, launched what became a Union raiding strategy aimed at destroying Southern resources and transportation.[63]

The South strengthened itself as best it could, and Confederate leaders looked to recoup their territorial losses in the west, particularly in Tennessee. A convoluted and often irrational discussion revolving around unrealistic operational plans followed.[64] This typical Confederate debate didn't address the key issue: how could the South win the war? The Confederacy's leaders never seriously tackled this. The Union gave the Confederacy a breather when it didn't have to, one the South failed to exploit.

PART I: FROM BACKWATER TO GREAT POWER

LINCOLN, STRATEGY, AND SECURING THE PEACE

In December 1863, Lincoln reviewed the Union position in his annual Congressional address. He noted success in keeping foreign powers out of the war, the reinforcing of the blockade, and the navy's seizure of more than 1,000 blockade runners. In the previous eleven months, the Union had cut the Confederacy in half by seizing the Mississippi and cleared most of Tennessee and Arkansas, while emancipation made Confederate slaves Union soldiers. Lincoln spoke of reconstruction and returning rebellious states to the Union, issuing a proclamation on this the same day with an amnesty for anyone taking an oath of allegiance.[65] The proclamation was Lincoln at his best – action directly supporting the aim of maintaining the Union.

Lincoln's political decisions, as always, influenced military events, some his generals didn't like. Reconstruction was one of these. For example, in February 1864 Brigadier General James H. Wilson complained to Grant of the diversion of troops to help reestablish loyal state governments. Wilson believed the priority should be destroying Confederate forces.[66] In terms of strategy, Wilson was correct. But Lincoln determined the administration's priorities and never let his generals forget this.

GRANT'S STRATEGY

On February 29, 1864, Lincoln nominated Grant to the army's then highest rank: lieutenant general, which had previously been held only by George Washington and Winfield Scott. Lincoln didn't do this lightly. He always kept an eye on his political back and first ensured Grant had no political ambitions. With the 1864 presidential election approaching, Lincoln didn't want to create a political rival. Both Republicans and Democrats tried unsuccessfully to bring the general into their camps. Grant said: "Nothing likely to happen would pain me so much as to see my name used in connection with a political office."[67]

Like McClellan and Lincoln, Grant came early to understand the necessity and advantage of Union armies moving in unison. He branded the operations of the eastern and western armies the work of a "balky team, no two ever pulling together." He also believed securing a lasting peace impossible "until the military power of the rebellion was entirely broken." On March 15, 1864, he wrote that it was critical that "all the armies act as much in concert as possible." Grant described his strategy more fully after the war:

> I therefore determined, first, to use the greatest number of troops practicable against the armed force of the enemy, preventing him from using the

same force at different seasons against first one and then another of our armies, and the possibility of repose for refitting and producing necessary supplies for carrying on resistance; second, to hammer continuously against the armed force of the enemy and his resources, until by mere attrition, if in no other way, there should be nothing left to him but an equal submission with the loyal section of our common country to the constitution and laws of the land.[68]

This was Grant's strategy: offensive action to pin the enemy, kill his armies, and destroy his resources, thus eliminating his ability to prosecute the war.

Grant developed an offensive plan composed of multiple, simultaneously moving prongs. "It is my design," he told Sherman, "if the enemy keep quiet and allow me to take the initiative in the spring campaign, to work all parts of the army together and somewhat toward a common center." Grant wanted Major General Nathaniel Banks to quickly finish his operation against Shreveport, Louisiana, and move against Mobile, Alabama, assisted by a fleet under Farragut. He was to strengthen his forces by abandoning Texas, except for a garrison at the Rio Grande's mouth, and strip his other posts to gather an army of at least 25,000. Major General Benjamin Butler was to land on the Virginia coast south of the James River, aiming at Richmond while cooperating with the advance of the Army of the Potomac. Major General Franz Sigel was to march up the Shenandoah Valley to pin the forces there or destroy enemy resources. Sherman was to move against Johnston's army in Georgia and get as deeply into Southern territory as possible, wreaking havoc on their resources. Sherman would keep the enemy from shifting troops to Lee while Grant repaid the favor in the east. Initially, Grant hoped for all these forces to move on April 25, 1864, except for Banks. Subsequently, he ordered "a general movement of the armies" no later than May 4. To gather the necessary troops, Grant ordered the stripping of nonessential areas. Grant rode with the Army of the Potomac, though Meade remained its commander. Grant designated Lee's army as this force's "objective point," telling Meade "that wherever Lee went he would go also." Grant intended for Meade's army to fight Lee between the two capitals, but if Lee fell back to Richmond, Meade would link with Butler. As McClellan before him, Grant ordered pre-campaign preparations to besiege Richmond. Grant also launched raids against Confederate supply and industrial sites.[69]

Lincoln liked Grant's idea. It coincided with his view of how to fight the war: simultaneous pressure at different points. "Those not skinning can hold a leg," Lincoln said. Sherman was also pleased: "That we are now all to act in a common plan, converging on a common center, looks like enlightened war." But success depended upon each commander doing his job. Because only Grant and Sherman proved competent, the plan fell apart almost immediately, destroying Grant's hope of winning the war by the November 1864 election.[70]

On May 5, Grant launched his offensive arm, embarking upon a campaign lasting until Lee's surrender on April 9, 1865. Both Grant and Lee hoped to catch their enemy in motion and force a battle. The armies stumbled into each other, producing a confused May 5–6 struggle, the Battle of the Wilderness. It was a Union defeat. But Grant had immediately accomplished one purpose of his advance: pinning Lee's army. In the battle's wake, Grant raised the whole spirit of the Army of the Potomac when he turned Lee's flank to the east and headed south. Grant also inaugurated something new for the Civil War: continuous battle. Previously, particularly in the Eastern Theater, the armies had tangled for a few days and then withdrew. No more.[71]

Some have branded Grant's fight against Lee a strategy of annihilation. This was not the case. The Union was pursuing attrition; Grant said so. He was not seeking a single, climactic battle. Moreover, Grant had no illusions about his campaign. He realized the bitter necessity of desperate fighting to bring the war to a close. He wrote later: "The losses inflicted, and endured, were destined to be severe; but the armies now confronting each other had already been in deadly conflict for a period of three years, with immense losses ... and neither had made any real progress toward accomplishing the final end." What lay ahead was a campaign that "was destined to result in heavier losses, to both armies, in a given time, than any previously suffered; but the carnage was to be limited to a single year, and to accomplish all that had been anticipated or desired at the beginning in that time."[72] Grant understood the key point: the sooner the war ended, the sooner the dying did as well.

There was great risk in Grant's approach. Attrition takes time, the greatest enemy of political leaders waging war. There can come a point when the populace cries "no," the value of the object having exceeded the cost they're willing to pay. A people can reach this point more quickly if they don't see battlefield results demonstrating progress on the road to success. The side choosing to implement an attrition strategy must prove able to outlast the opponent in terms of will and resources. The weaker, in either arena, may yield first.

In Georgia, Joseph Johnston, by standing on the defensive, surrendered the initiative to the enemy and gave Sherman time to prepare at his leisure. But a full-scale attack against Sherman's army, which outnumbered

Johnston's by two to one, was not the answer. Johnston's best option for offensive action was the raids he launched on Sherman's supply lines; these produced constant worry. Any substantial success here could have delayed the start of Sherman's campaign, or at least limited its strength and thus the Union's ability to sustain an offensive. The South needed to buy time to allow war weariness in the North to grow. After three years of fighting, the North seemed no closer to victory in summer 1864 than after First Bull Run in 1861. Plus, in the two months after the beginning of Grant's offensive, the Union suffered 90,000 casualties – without producing any clear gains.[73] Inflicting upon Sherman's army cumulative delays of one month might have placed the fall of Atlanta after the 1864 Union elections. With Sherman stalled at Atlanta, and Grant stuck before Richmond and Petersburg, Lincoln might have gone down to defeat and his Democratic rival, George McClellan, become president. There is little doubt McClellan would have failed to prosecute the war with sufficient vigor to secure victory.

As Sherman gradually pushed to Atlanta, an increasingly frustrated Davis pressed Johnston to attack. Johnston replied that since the enemy outnumbered him two to one, the defensive remained the only choice. Davis fired Johnston on July 17, 1864 for failing to stop Sherman's advance. John Bell Hood replaced him.[74]

THE 1864 PRESIDENTIAL ELECTION

As August's end drew near, Grant's army remained stalled outside Richmond and Petersburg; Sherman's forces stood before Atlanta. The November elections loomed. Lincoln, though a Republican, campaigned as the National Union Party representative on a platform including a constitutional amendment outlawing slavery. With the inclusion of abolition in the party's platform, emancipation, which had begun as a military measure, became a second political aim. The election platform also provided terms for ending the war: "the determination of the government of the United States not to compromise with rebels, or to offer them any terms of peace, except such as may be based upon an unconditional surrender of their hostility and a return to their just allegiance to the Constitution and laws of the United States."[75]

Lincoln believed the election would decide the "weal or woe of this great nation." His opponent officially favored continuing the war, but Lincoln believed McClellan's election meant Union defeat. Lincoln argued that "the rebel armies cannot be destroyed by Democratic strategy" because the Democrats intended to prosecute the war by turning out of the army between 100,000 and 200,000 Blacks bearing arms for the Union. "These men will be disbanded," Lincoln insisted,

> returned to slavery & we will have to fight two nations instead of one.... You cannot concilliate the South, when you place yourself in such a position, that they see they can achieve their independence.... Abandon all the posts now possessed by black men[,] surrender all these advantages to the enemy, & we would be compelled to abandon the war in 3 weeks.... But no human power can subdue this rebellion without using the Emancipation lever as I have done.[76]

Lincoln would do what he felt necessary to win the war.

Davis saw an opportunity in the presidential election. He had tried to exploit Northern dissent during the 1862 Congressional elections. The proclamation he gave Bragg and Lee to use in their 1862 invasions, which encouraged Northern states to withdraw from the Union and thus spare themselves the war's ravages was part of this. It was also an effort to split what he seems to have viewed as a coalition of Union states. Many Southerners believed a presidential victory by a peace Democrat their best hope of securing independence; emboldening Davis and others were the anti-Union, anti-war, and anti-Lincoln activities of the Copperheads of the Northwest. In the spring and summer of 1864, the Confederates hatched a plan to influence the presidential race. Davis dispatched agents to Canada and the North to negotiate with figures amenable to peace, meddle in Union politics, attempt to free Confederate prisoners, bribe newspapers to push for peace, and plot an uprising at the Democratic convention in Chicago.[77]

These were worthy, low-cost elements of information strategy, though with scant potential for great gains. But Davis expected little and mismanaged the effort. He feared a peace candidate's election would *discourage* Southerners from continuing the war. Seceded states might see in McClellan's victory and conciliation a chance to return to the Union with slavery intact. This would kill the Confederacy. There was also the issue of linkage between the military and diplomatic strategies and between the strategies and the political aim. Grant wrote in his memoirs that the South needed to "protract the war, which was all that was necessary to enable them to gain recognition in the end." The North, he correctly observed, "was growing weary."[78] Its optimal course was the strategic defensive.

Sherman's opponent, Hood, adopted a more direct path. Over an eight-day period beginning on July 20, 1864 he launched three furious assaults, suffering 15,000 irreplaceable casualties to Sherman's 6,000. Sherman now had a vastly superior force and could stretch around Hood's Atlanta positions, trapping him. He focused on cutting Atlanta's last rail links to isolate and capture it. He preferred to destroy Hood's army but as this "Gate-City of the South" was "full of foundries, arsenals, and machine-shops," he believed its fall the "death-knell of the Southern Confederacy." Sherman was wrong about Atlanta but right about what was important: Hood's army. After another failed assault, realizing he faced being cornered and destroyed, Hood abandoned Atlanta on September 1, 1864. Sherman had delivered a triumph the Union desperately needed, one that heartened the Union and ensured Lincoln's reelection.[79]

Hood's army, though, still survived. Sherman resolved to move south, believing, mistakenly, that Hood would be forced to follow. Additionally, Sherman wrote Grant:

> I propose to act in such a manner against the material resources of the South as utterly to negative Davis's boasted threat and promises of protection. If we can march a well-appointed army right through his territory, it is a demonstration to the world, foreign and domestic, that we have a power which Davis cannot resist.... This may not be war, but rather statesmanship.[80]

Sherman's plan struck directly at the Confederacy's will, leaders, and ability to wage war. Sherman reached Savannah in December, then turned north.

Meanwhile, the attritional struggle in Virginia continued. In October 1864, Grant began pushing westward, south of Petersburg, forcing Lee to further thin his lines to meet the Union move. As winter descended, the armies dug in. They skirmished some, but mostly fought the weather. The Confederates also battled hunger. Grant waited for spring.[81]

ENDING THE WAR

Lincoln always maintained control of political matters; this was especially true in negotiating with the Confederates. Reluctantly, Lincoln agreed to an early February 1865 conference with a trio of Confederate delegates but made it clear this shouldn't interfere with Grant's plans. Lincoln insisted upon fighting while negotiating. He dispatched Secretary of State Seward but gave him little leash, instructing him to ensure the Rebels understood three things were "indispensable": "1st, the restoration of the national authority throughout all the States; 2d, no receding by the Executive of the United States on the slavery question," meaning its end; and "3d, no cessation of hostilities short of an end of the war and the disbanding of all the forces hostile to the Government." Anything not clashing with the above would be considered. Lincoln wanted the words of the Confederate negotiators reported to him and told Seward: "You will not assume to definitely consummate anything."[82]

Seward arrived at Fortress Monroe to meet the Confederates on February 1. The whole effort nearly collapsed over whether the Confederates had come to negotiate the fate of "one common country" or "two countries." Lincoln had insisted upon the former; Davis wanted the latter. Grant believed not seeing the Rebel commissioners would have ill-effects on the Union and telegraphed Lincoln. The president bent and rendezvoused with the emissaries at Hampton Roads on February 3, 1865. Some of the press pilloried him for agreeing to the meeting. The Confederates made no commitments but pressed for an armistice. Lincoln held fast. He would grant no halt that didn't end the war, disband Confederate armies, and include Southern recognition of slavery's end.[83]

Nothing came of the Hampton Roads Conference, but one must give Lincoln credit for understanding the danger of granting the Confederacy's wish. "An armistice," he had written in September 1864, "a cessation of hostilities – is the end of the struggle, and the insurgents would be in peaceable possession of all that has been struggled for." He realized this would give the South a breather and might make it difficult to restart the fighting should the South still insist upon secession.[84] Lincoln kept his political aims clearly in view and aligned negotiations and military pressure with these. Davis, for his part, was not ready to end the war. He negotiated because it might gain the South an advantage.

On March 24, 1865, Grant issued orders for an offensive against Lee to begin on the 29th. Cavalry would attack Lee's communications while major elements of the Army of the Potomac moved south of Petersburg. Sherman, by this time, had his army at Goldsboro, North Carolina, and he and Grant had discussed Sherman moving to help against Lee. Despite the immensity of Union progress, Grant still had fears. "I was firmly convinced that Sherman's crossing the Roanoke would be the signal for Lee to leave. With Johnston and him combined, a long, tedious, and expensive campaign, consuming most of the summer, might become necessary.... I therefore determined not to delay the movement ordered."[85]

On March 29, 1865, the Army of the Potomac unwound itself one last time. Lincoln was there. "I hope you will stay to see it out," Secretary of War Edwin Stanton told him. "If you are on the ground there will be no pause." Grant didn't pause. His lines broken, Lee abandoned Petersburg and Richmond on the night of April 2. Grant ordered a pursuit. On April 9, Lee wrote that he had received Grant's terms and would talk. He surrendered his forces the same day.[86]

Sherman met with Joe Johnston in Durham, North Carolina, on April 18. Sherman presented an agreement including a ceasefire, disbandment of Confederate forces, recognition of the governments of the states of the South (if their respective leaders took the oath of allegiance), restoration of the Federal court system, and a general amnesty. An armistice was secured, which lasted from April 18 to 26, but an armistice doesn't necessarily mean peace. A reluctant Davis bowed to his cabinet and told Johnston to accept Sherman's terms.[87]

The political powers, though, intervened. John Wilkes Booth shot Lincoln on the evening of April 14. He died the next morning and Andrew Johnson became president. Sherman had given General Johnston generous terms that essentially allowed state government in the South to remain in Confederate hands. President Johnson disapproved and demanded Johnston's capitulation based upon the articles given Lee at Appomattox: surrendering their arms, accepting paroles, and going home. Sherman gave Johnston forty-eight hours to comply. Johnston and Davis had prepared for the possible failure of the talks by determining a retreat route for Johnston's army, but Johnston elected to end the war by taking Sherman's offer and surrendered on April 26, 1865. The Confederates in the Trans-Mississippi quit a month later.[88] The few remaining Rebel forces soon left the field.

ASSESSING GRAND STRATEGY DURING THE CIVIL WAR

In the end, the decisive element in Union victory was its construction and implementation of a coherent grand strategy utilizing its national power that addressed the nature of the war, one the North tenaciously pursued for as long as it took. Simultaneous advances; destroying Confederate armies and resources; attacking the people's will; blockade; diplomatic isolation: these became the primary strategic actions feeding Union success. From the conflict's beginning, Lincoln sought a way to win the war and pushed his subordinates to act; Davis never tried to construct a strategy for achieving the South's political aim of independence, and never asked what victory demanded. This was the Confederacy's greatest error.

SECURING THE PEACE: THE RECONSTRUCTION ERA, 1865–77

The war was over. The Union preserved. And slavery extinguished. But the Union had to consolidate its victory by securing the peace. Victory had high costs. The Federal government spent $3 billion and had $2.8 billion in debt. And the Union had the world's highest tax rates. Perhaps 752,000 Americans died in the war. At least 110,000 Union servicemen had been killed, another 250,000 perished from disease. The South was devastated. At least 240,000 soldiers died, though this number is probably higher, another 260,000 were wounded or seriously disabled. Union military campaigns destroyed tracts of the South, its industry, railroads, and large sections of most major cities. The end of slavery overturned the agricultural economy and the war destroyed King Cotton. Some areas of the South only avoided starvation because of Union army food distributions. The US immediately began disarming. At the time of Lee's surrender, the army numbered around 1 million. By end of 1865, it was 150,000. Nearly half of these were Black troops. The force reached its new Congressionally authorized strength of 54,000 in October 1866. The US navy dropped from over 600 ships to 115 by fall 1865.[89]

Though the US followed its habit of gutting its military forces this hardly meant it lacked power or ambition. The Monroe Doctrine Committee and other groups pushed for enlargement southward. The expansionists, though, were now the Republicans and former Whigs who had blocked such prewar impulses. With slavery dead, so was the argument over whether new lands would be slave or free, including Indian lands, something examined in the next chapter. But the tenor of national politics from the end of the Civil War to 1889, characterized by dominance of the Senate, constrained administration ambitions. Presidential weakness "translated into passivity and inaction in foreign policy." And some Americans were uneager for new lands "populated by alien races."[90]

THE ANDREW JOHNSON AND ULYSSES S. GRANT ADMINISTRATIONS, 1865–77

The first and most important aim was securing sovereignty. The grand strategy for doing this was Reconstruction. It is apt to characterize Reconstruction so, because it describes how the Federal government used its power to achieve its purpose: reasserting sovereignty over the rebellious South. Reconstruction required reintegration of the former Confederate states and ensuring the citizenship rights of former slaves. How to do this, and what exactly Reconstruction meant for the South, Black Americans, and the nation proved contentious. Union leaders didn't agree on what either of these looked like, which meant they disagreed on what to do. Reconstruction directly or indirectly affected every government initiative and led to Andrew Johnson's impeachment.

WARTIME RECONSTRUCTION

During the war, Lincoln strove to restore normal government as quickly as possible in recaptured areas. He appointed military governors beginning in 1862, usually lawyers and politicians instead of soldiers. In 1863, Lincoln promulgated a plan allowing Confederate states in which 10 percent of the population took the oath of allegiance to form state governments and send representatives to Congress. Congress found this too lenient and refused to seat them. The Republican-controlled Congress regarded Reconstruction as a legislative issue. In July 1864, it disenfranchised Confederate leaders and required among other things abolition of slavery and 50 percent of inhabitants pledging loyalty. Lincoln pocket-vetoed the measure, believing Reconstruction demanded more flexibility. Lincoln proposed other ideas, but nothing was set before he died.[91]

POSTWAR RECONSTRUCTION

The Confederate armies surrendered by early May 1865 and the Johnson administration then focused on Reconstruction. This can be broken into two parts: Presidential Reconstruction (1865–67) and Radical Reconstruction (1867–77). The first postwar phase was lenient, and the army controlled military governments until Washington allowed new state authorities.[92]

PRESIDENTIAL RECONSTRUCTION

Johnson supported soft Reconstruction. He believed the states had no right to secede; thus they remained in the Union. Though he supported emancipation, he didn't support Black political rights and thought Whites should govern the South. He joined the Republican Party but described himself as a Jacksonian Democrat. He supported limited Federal power but planned to impose conditions such as abolition on former Confederate states as a price for reintegration.[93]

Johnson's program was clear by May 1865. He recognized the governments created by Lincoln in Virginia, Tennessee, Arkansas, and Louisiana, though allowed the governor of the last to open the wartime administration to prewar Southern leaders. He issued a pair of May 29, 1865, proclamations outlining his program. Taking the oath of loyalty and agreeing to emancipation gained Confederates pardon, amnesty, and the return of property (not including slaves). But the proclamations excluded fourteen groups, especially Rebel leaders and those with $20,000 in taxable property. In Johnson's mind, this would break the Southern aristocracy's political control and empower White farmers. He appointed a provisional governor for North Carolina, instructing him to call a convention to construct a new government, and soon did the same for other states. Johnson also allowed the raising of Southern militia to address the near-anarchy engulfing much of the region. The governors, exercising patronage, appointed mostly non-Unionist officials as there were insufficient Unionists. The result of Johnson's program was to leave Reconstruction generally in Southern hands, undermining Black suffrage and political rights. November 1865 marked the passage in Mississippi and South Carolina of the first Black Codes, laws intended to maintain White control over the Black population. The result was often slavery in all but name.[94]

In his December 1865 message to Congress, Johnson said he lacked the right to impose Black suffrage on the South, relayed his hope that Southern legislators would address its expansion, and essentially declared "restoration" of the former Confederate states – not Reconstruction – complete. He failed to realize many Northerners supported Black voting rights, particularly in the South, and saw the South as unrepentant and arrogant in defeat. They liked seeing Southerners, particularly elites, forced to act properly, particularly toward freed slaves.[95]

The tensions between Congress and the president escalated when Johnson vetoed the widely supported Freedmen's Bureau Bill, believing it unconstitutional and likely to promote Black "indolence." This garnered Southern support for the president and was a way of isolating the Radical Republicans and potentially destroying them. It only angered them, and overriding the veto fell only two votes short, something Johnson should have seen as a warning regarding Congressional opinion on rights for Blacks. Johnson vetoed the Civil Rights Bill guaranteeing Blacks citizenship and equality under the law, one heavily supported by Republicans. He refused to support the Fourteenth Amendment, which granted Blacks equality and "constituted the peace terms of the North, of Congress, and the Republican party." The Republicans declared a state's ratification of the amendment meant readmission to the Union. Not ratifying meant "they could expect something more drastic." Overall, Johnson destroyed his support in the Republican Party. In July 1866, Congress passed another Freedmen's Bureau Bill and overrode Johnson's veto.[96]

Johnson's soft Reconstruction changed little politically and socially in the South. Few Confederate leaders were punished (Davis spent only two years in prison), and 15,000 disenfranchised Confederates were allowed to apply for pardons. Johnson granted 7,000 by 1866, undermining efforts to achieve his own goal of taking political power from the South's prewar elite.

This was probably an effort by Johnson to maintain Southern White rule and support his reelection.[97]

RADICAL RECONSTRUCTION

Congress now grasped control of Reconstruction. It passed the Tenure of Office and Command of the Army Acts to ensure Stanton remained Secretary of War and Grant head of the army even though Johnson wanted changes, especially Stanton's firing. Congress disbanded Southern militias and forbade new ones. Congress passed the Reconstruction Act of 1867 over Johnson's veto. This established legal authority for the army's occupation, divided the South into five military districts, and reimposed martial law. It gave the military authority over the construction of local and state government, the courts, and elections, and the power to remove and appoint officials. This produced Republican Party governments, but even after the readmission of all rebellious states, these required the army to survive.[98]

Many Republicans believed Reconstruction couldn't succeed with Johnson as president. Many of these same men wanted his job. In February 1868, the Republicans brought eleven charges against Johnson and voted to impeach him. The Senate acquitted him by one vote, though others stood willing to prevent his ouster. The Fifteenth Amendment was approved by Congress in February 1869. It forbade racial discrimination in the right to vote and became part of the Constitution in 1870.[99]

Resistance to Reconstruction in the South took many forms, but the most dangerous wore robes: the Ku Klux Klan. A loosely organized group at best, especially in its early days, the Klan was essentially "a military force serving the interests of the Democratic party, the planter class, and all those who desired the restoration of white supremacy." Its aims were clear: "to reverse the interlocking changes sweeping over the South during Reconstruction: to destroy the Republican party's infrastructure, undermine the Reconstruction state, reestablish control of the Black labor force, and restore racial subordination in every aspect of Southern life." In today's parlance, the Klan should be considered an insurgent group using terrorism as part of its strategy for achieving its political aims. It originated in Tennessee and became the armed wing of the insurgency against Union rule. Murder, whippings, lynching, rape, and every possible form of violence was directed at Blacks and their White supporters. The Klan hoped carnage would undermine the Reconstruction governments by suppressing votes for Republicans and intimidating the party's members and supporters into leaving. The Klan proved particularly effective in lowering Republican voting numbers.[100]

The violence overwhelmed local governments. The only way to suppress an active, armed insurgency is with regular troops. But the US made one of its common errors: it failed to commit sufficient forces. The army only had 17,657 men in the South in 1868, and only 8,038 in 1871. Moreover, the readmission of a state to the Union meant the army could only intervene if the state's officials requested help, something they were often reluctant to do from fear of violence – or support for it. Congress passed helpful Enforcement Acts in the early 1870s; the most important outlawed the Ku Klux Klan and similar organs of violence. President Grant was given authority to institute martial law and suspend habeas corpus, and broad enforcement powers. But application was weak, except in South Carolina, where army forces broke the Klan. The Klan's indiscriminate violence began costing it support while disrupting the Black labor supply upon which much of the Southern economy depended. Democratic Party leaders also couldn't find a way Klan actions could help them win elections and thus return to power.[101]

By 1870, the former Confederate states had rejoined the Union with Republican governments led by White politicians who owed their positions to the Black vote. Democratic leaders turned to other groups in the mid 1870s to end Republican rule where it still existed in the South. Militia-style, openly Democratic Party–controlled organs such as South Carolina's Red Shirts and Louisiana's White League took up the Klan's mantle. They used threats, violence, and economic measures in pursuit of their aims, but never enough to provoke Federal intervention. Moreover, "Democrats planned race riots and battled Republican militia prior to elections, in time to keep Republicans from the polls but too late for Washington to send regulars to police the voting." Critically, what transpired in the South "between 1874 and 1877 was not indiscriminate Klan-style violence, but a calculated insurrection as the last unredeemed states fell to Democrats."[102]

ENDING RECONSTRUCTION

The election of 1876 between Republican Rutherford B. Hayes and Democrat Samuel J. Tilden was marked by staggering corruption and complete abandonment of any principle by both sides. The electoral results in numerous Southern states were protested by the candidates – with good reason. A Federal Election Commission composed of members of the Supreme Court, Senate, and House was created to resolve disputes. It awarded Hayes 185 electoral votes and Tilden 184. But the Democrats controlled the House and had to ratify the result. A deal was cut where Hayes agreed to not enforce the civil rights laws in the South or use Federal troops there, essentially sacrificing the political rights of southern Blacks in exchange for the presidency.[103] Hayes withdrew the remaining US troops after his 1877 inauguration.

ASSESSING RECONSTRUCTION AS GRAND STRATEGY

Reconstruction secured the primary aim of restoring Federal sovereignty over the South but failed to achieve full sovereignty for the Federal system as the political rights of Blacks were restricted by Black Codes and what became the Jim Crow structure. The Lincoln and Johnson administrations had lacked solid plans for securing the peace, which was what Reconstruction – or nation building – was supposed to do. This was partially understandable as US leaders had never faced this before and the idea of planning for postwar occupation didn't exist in the era's theoretical teachings. Moreover, Johnson's vision of a postwar South wherein Whites maintained power differed from that of the more broadminded Republican Party members controlling the government's arms. But once they wrested Reconstruction from Johnson and imposed reform, they never committed the military means required to ensure success while the army's commander in chief – Johnson – didn't support the military's use. All of this, combined with Southern resistance, lengthened the occupation. Time works against democratic governments here as public opinion wearies of the task and events divert attention.[104]

But securing the political reforms necessary to ensure Black political rights could have been beyond the Federal government's ability to achieve because it required changing the "hearts and minds" of the majority of White Southerners, many embittered by a bloody war. Sherman believed the problem was bigger than the Federal government's failures and as early as September 1865 concluded the North could not change Southern attitudes with military force. One analyst believed Reconstruction "demonstrated the hazards of using military force to impose fundamental changes in social values and institutions, no matter how virtuous those changes might be. This was a cautionary lesson for any future soldier or politician charged with such a mission, whether it be in the realm of social engineering at home or nation building abroad."[105] Americans soon attempted both.

5

CONQUERING A CONTINENT: THE INDIAN WARS, 1865–1897

INTRODUCTION

America's post–Civil War development resembles streams of wild horses – or more appropriately steam engines – all rushing forward with few clear aims and fewer guiding hands. For the first time, America faced no existential threat. Between 1865 and 1897, the United States became dominant in the Western Hemisphere. (See Map 5.1.) The US population doubled to more than 71 million. American steel production equaled Britain's and was twice that of the next power, Germany. Exports quadrupled to nearly $250 million annually, and the mid 1870s brought the first positive trade balance. By the next decade, the US led the world in manufactures.[1]

THE ANDREW JOHNSON AND ULYSSES S. GRANT ADMINISTRATIONS, 1865–77

While in the throes of Reconstruction, expansion remained a political aim. When examining foreign relations during this or any era, we must remember the domestic political effects. A president's strength or weakness vis-à-vis Congress and popular support exercise potentially determinative effects upon whether an administration achieves its aims.

THE POLITICAL AIMS

One of the most ambitious American expansionists was William Henry Seward, secretary of state from 1861 to 1867. A former New York senator and governor, Seward was a great admirer of John Quincy Adams. Like Adams, Seward envisioned a larger, more powerful America. But to Seward and Johnson, expansion abroad should take place peacefully. Seward sought "possession of the American continent and the control of the world." The last part was hyperbole (maybe); the first wasn't. Seward thought strong nations would and should expand, and believed in convergence theory,

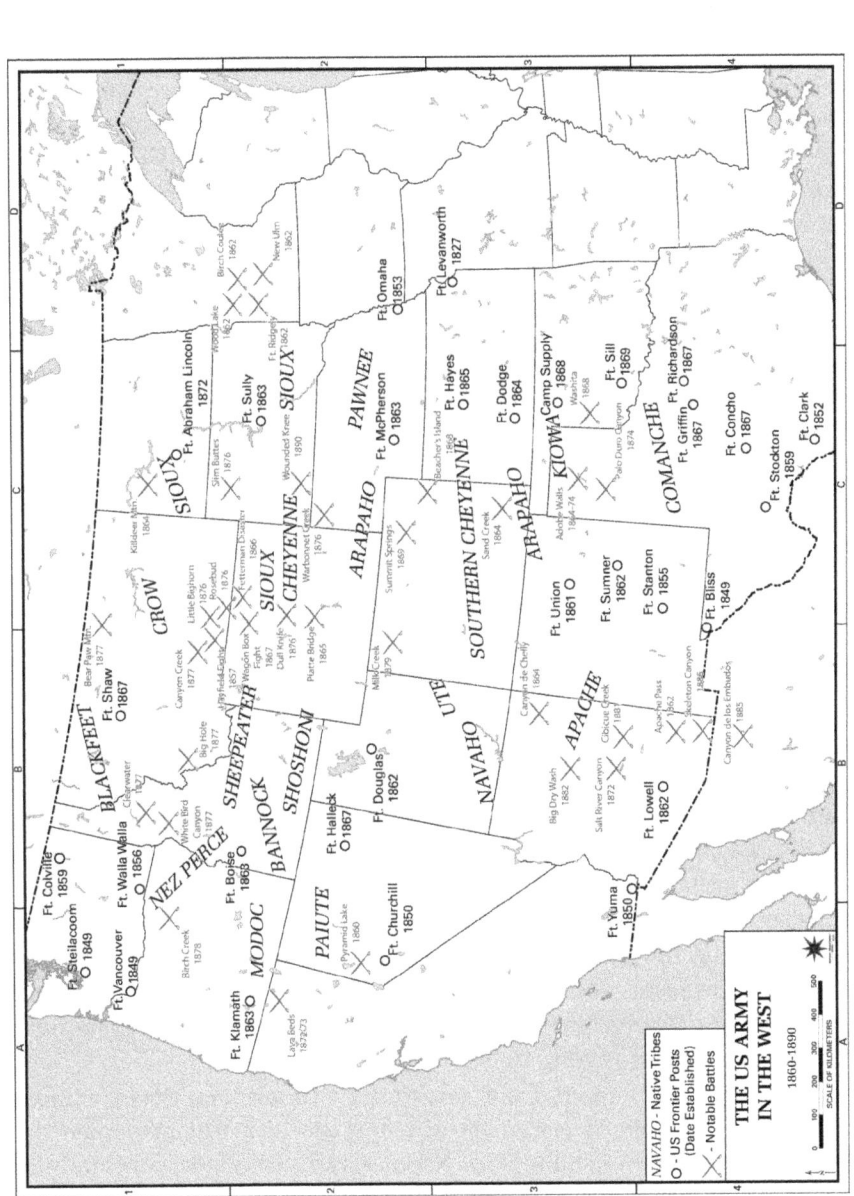

Map 5.1 The US army in the West, 1860–90

meaning economic and cultural ties would see the US unite with Canada and Mexico. He dreamed of a United States including Canada, Mexico, Alaska, and island bases in the Caribbean and Pacific, and looked toward Asia, where he believed the center of global power was shifting. He studied acquiring numerous places, including Iceland and Greenland. Both Seward and Johnson saw the Pacific coast and Caribbean as necessary areas for expansion. This would deny future bases to imitators of Confederate commerce raiding while providing the navy coaling bases for protecting American trade. In the Caribbean, Seward secured the Danish West Indies and the Virgin Islands, rights for a base in the Dominican Republic, and a treaty with Colombia (of which Panama was a part) for a canal. He wanted a port in Formosa (now Taiwan) and laid the foundation for a later mission to Korea, but only acquired uninhabited Midway atoll (1867). He explored annexing Hawaii but was only agreeable if the Hawaiians were interested. They weren't.[2]

THE GRAND STRATEGY

To achieve Seward's vision, the US needed to be strong and secure economically and militarily. Seward supported industrial growth by advocating infrastructure improvements like transcontinental telegraph and railroad lines, cheap labor through foreign immigration, and a protective tariff. Trade was also critical. In the 1850s, he insisted foreign trade would spread American republican virtues abroad, altering international behavior "in ways that would preserve American preeminence." He believed America had to win the competition against Britain, France, and Russia in the Pacific, which he called "the Far West." He insisted that "the nation that draws the most materials and provisions from the earth, and fabricates the most and sells the most of productions and fabrics to foreign nations, must be, and will be, the great power of the earth." He supported a unified China while the Europeans were trying to *de facto* dismember it and took the unusual step for a Western nation of treating China as an equal by granting it most-favored-nation trading rights.[3]

Keeping great powers from the Western Hemisphere was traditionally a way to deliver American security, but the Civil War prevented the US from stopping French Emperor Napoleon III's installation of Habsburg Archduke Maximilian as emperor of Mexico. But after the Confederacy's defeat, the US possessed an enormous military machine. Grant thought aiming it at Mexico a good next step and asked Johnson to send him even further south. Grant dispatched 52,000 men to the Rio Grande in May 1865, and ordered recruitment of Union and Confederate veterans to support Benito Juarez's anti-Maximilian forces. The US invoked the Monroe Doctrine to push France to stop supporting Maximilian while groups known as "Defenders of the Monroe Doctrine" pressed for action. The public, Congress, and Johnson supported Grant's moves. Seward didn't. Johnson left foreign affairs in Seward's hands, and he sank Grant's gambit and pressured Napoleon III to remove his troops from Mexico. Public outcry against the French became so great that Johnson considered taking matters into his own hands. A worried Seward told France peace couldn't be maintained if French forces remained in Mexico. Napoleon III decided to leave in January 1866, partially because of the costs, and withdrew his forces over 1866 and 1867.[4]

Seward's greatest expansionist achievement was gaining Alaska. Its possession would help prevent raids against US shipping, potentially provide a step toward controlling trade with East Asia, and push Canada to join America. Russia couldn't defend it and feared America taking it. Moscow also needed money after its Crimean War defeat and saw the deal as a means of affirming Russo-American friendship. "Seward's folly," as it was known at the time (1867), cost $7.2 million. Russia's open support of the Union during the Civil War had gained it many friends and was perhaps decisive in securing the approval of a House of Representatives that had just impeached Johnson. Bribing enough congressmen also helped. Charles Sumner shepherded it through the Senate, his ardent expansionism trumping his hatred of Seward and Johnson. Seward succeeded, but the power struggle between Congress and Johnson, and the desire to pay down war debt, often tied his hands.[5]

THE GRANT ADMINISTRATION: POLITICAL AIMS AND GRAND STRATEGY

President Grant also sought expansion, as did his secretary of state, Hamilton Fish. But Grant took office amidst the ongoing battle between the executive branch and a Senate seeking dominance.[6] His administration's rampant corruption, which didn't include Grant himself, injured his political standing.

One of the administration's aims was replacing European influence in Latin America. Fish foresaw a time when "America shall be wholly America" and the US position preeminent. He expanded the Monroe Doctrine's umbrella to encompass an 1808 pronouncement by Jefferson that territory "on this continent" couldn't be transferred to a European power.

The administration negotiated a treaty annexing Santo Domingo (now the Dominican Republic), one Sumner ensured didn't pass the Senate to humiliate the administration and assert Senate dominance. Grant unsuccessfully urged Congress to negotiate a new treaty. He warned of possible acquisition of Santo Domingo's harbor by a European power, offered numerous economic, political, and social arguments for annexation, and linked this to American security and "adherence" to the Monroe Doctrine. Additional negotiations for a harbor also failed.[7]

Twice during Grant's administration, the US considered war with Spain over Cuba. Grant and many Congressmen wanted it; Fish didn't, and defused efforts in 1870 to recognize Cuba's rebels. He averted war a second time after Spain's November 1873 seizure of the *Virginius*, a ship flying the American flag that was probably part of a filibustering effort. The Spanish executed its captain and fifty-two passengers and crew, many of whom were American, causing uproar in the United States. The administration began preparing for war, but Fish and the Spanish ambassador resolved the crisis. The economic depression that hit in 1873 dampened aggressive desires.[8]

In Asia, the Grant administration sought to open Korea to US trade. An armed American merchant ship employed by Britain tried this in 1866. The Koreans burned the ship and executed its crew; why is debated. A lack of Korean response to American inquiries resulted in an American attack on the Hermit Kingdom's forts at the mouth of the Han River that killed 200. Grant secured a treaty with Hawaii granting the US dominant influence on the islands, something Congress only approved because it, like Grant, feared British or French control. Grant inked an 1878 treaty with Samoa for naval basing rights.[9]

ECONOMIC STRATEGY

In the post–Civil War era, the United States had a laissez-faire economic system. Federal economic involvement was dominated by trade and tariffs. At the end of the Civil War, the government owed $2.7 billion, 30 percent of GDP. Tariffs increased to fund the war and remained high to pay down the debt. The rates changed in the following decades but stayed elevated through the First World War. The 1890 tariff gave the US the top duty rates among industrialized states. Between 1861 and 1933 only Russia rivaled the US in protectionism, while European states, except Britain, abandoned "free trade" for protectionism.[10]

The tariff morphed into a Republican Party underpinning. Tariffs – and their revenue – were supported by a coalition of party groups: businesses needing protection from foreign competition, Union army pensioners (tariffs funded pensions), the sugar industry, and occasionally producers of agricultural products America didn't export, like wool. Tariffs both hurt and helped, depending upon where one stood. Any industry using a tariffed raw material suffered unless it could find an alternative. Moreover, "Then as now, the benefits of tariff on a particular good, if produced in the domestic economy in any significant amount, were concentrated on a fairly small number of industries, sectors, and regions while the liabilities tended to be widely distributed but relatively minor." But tariffs protected some industries.[11]

Tariffs, though, couldn't protect the increasingly globalized American economy from tremors abroad and speculation at home. The Panic of 1873 was rooted in the collapse of the stock market in Vienna, Austria; the investments from Germany feeding it ceased. The spillover was international. The bubble in American railroad-building burst as European investors began abandoning these often-speculative ventures. The railroads owed vast sums to banks. When important banks began failing, Washington responded with weak use of bonds and some currency printing to restore liquidity. The correct course was doing more. It took the nation four years to climb out of the downturn. The crisis altered the attitudes of US leaders toward foreign trade. Exports were only 7 percent of GDP, but there arose a fear America was producing too much for its market and needed more clients abroad. The search involved the government in a sporadic fashion and was sometimes hindered by high US tariffs.[12]

THE CONQUEST OF THE WEST

In the introduction to his 1892 work Edward S. Ellis wrote: "The history of the Indian wars of the United States is a history of one continuous series of blunders, frauds, oppression, injustice, and crime that is a reproach to our nation."[13] America fought many wars to conquer the West, too many to cover them all, but it is critical to examine the most significant, their respective political aims, their shape, and results, particularly those America lost.

Many American uses of military force against the Indians conform to what were once called "punitive expeditions." British army officer C. E. Callwell, author of *Small Wars*, describes this: "Hostilities entered upon to punish an insult or to chastise a people who have inflicted some injury." This usually entailed attacks on specific Indian tribes or bands and were often responses to raids upon Whites. Sometimes they followed attacks Indians were provoked into making by prospectors, settlers, or the army.

Occasionally, so-called "punitive expeditions" were massacres of innocent Indians, such as the killing of a group of Montana Piegans in January 1870.[14] It is important to remember these were wars fought for the limited political aim of showing a perpetrator the costs of their acts. Today, sometimes drone attacks and airstrikes are the same. These often denote wars of short duration for limited political aims.

The Federal approach toward the Indians lacked coherence. Many Westerners favored killing them. Many Easterners wanted assimilation that destroyed Indian culture. "The government muddled along a middle course," refusing to simply decree their extermination, "while doing virtually everything in its power – sometimes by design but more often by incompetence – to ensure that conflict was all but inevitable." The army cleaned up the mess. The absence of a border meant Whites and Indians became increasingly entangled. The army had the job of protecting Whites from Indians but also Indians from Whites. It was trapped between two chairs: criticized for killing Indians by Easterners; criticized for not killing them by Westerners.[15]

The issue of sovereignty regarding Indians was complex and ever evolving. Generally, Indians were not considered American citizens as they belonged to their own nations whose relationships with the US were governed by treaties endlessly revised to shrink Indian power and lands. American grand strategy toward the Indians in the post–Civil War era was directed at achieving two primary purposes: obtaining as much land as possible for White settlement and assimilating the Indians.[16]

THE ASSESSMENT

In the mid nineteenth century, perhaps 275,000 Indians in 125 separate entities inhabited the lands West of the Mississippi River. Between October 1865 and October 1898, the US army fought over 1,000 engagements against them. Disease was a constant American ally as epidemics tended to sweep Indian tribes every six to eight years, eroding their populations, sometimes dramatically. The Great Plains Indians were nomadic, warrior peoples skilled in the use of horses who lived in an environment where daily life was training in fieldcraft and warfare. As individual warriors they were invariably better than their American opponents. But there were few of them, and they generally lacked anything beyond rudimentary organization. Tribes could not afford the loss of warriors and couldn't fight an attritional war against the US, which could easily replace its losses. They were also dangerous. General George Crook called the Sioux "the finest light cavalry in the world." Colonel Richard I. Dodge, a veteran of thirty years of fighting and studying Indians, called them "the finest soldiers in the world." But the inability of the Indian nations to work together for long, if at all, was a great weakness. This was exacerbated by factionalism as each nation possessed war and peace groups, something the US exploited. The lack of a sense of "Indianness" and a proclivity to constant warfare with one another also weakened them.[17]

The Indians, though, faced few American soldiers (one can't say "Whites" because so many of the troops were Black or other Indians). In 1874, the size of the army was reduced to 27,442. The 116 posts held by the army in the West had miniscule contingents that sometimes took their lives in their hands leaving their forts. Mounting any operation required stripping garrisons to concentrate troops. The army lacked the men to provide the protection it was expected to. Moreover, its few troops generally received virtually no training before joining their units, which suffered high turnover.[18]

POLITICAL AIMS AND GRAND STRATEGY: THE LINCOLN, JOHNSON, AND GRANT ADMINISTRATIONS, 1861–77

Abraham Lincoln, understandably, spent little time on Indian issues. He did face the Sioux Uprising, about which we will hear more shortly. Andrew Johnson gave this even less attention. The government generally dealt with the Indians via "subjugation, removal, and acculturation."[19] These actions supported establishment of US sovereignty over the West and expansion.

MILITARY STRATEGY

The Americans generally struck at the Indian will to resist, partially via an approach developed before the Civil War and taught at West Point by Dennis Hart Mahan. One or more columns of troops would push into Indian territory, often joined by irregulars, volunteers, and allied Indians. This force would bring the Indians to battle or destroy their camps and food supplies. Using this offensive strategy to accomplish either of these operational objectives – it was hoped – would force the Indians to make peace.[20]

Before the Civil War, these attacks were generally mounted in late summer to destroy crops and food supplies, or in the spring before there was sufficient grass for Indian ponies. But this wouldn't work against Plains Indians. The army began mounting winter campaigns. The army's logistical capabilities gave it the advantage as it could supply its men and animals. The army's winter attacks, even if they failed to kill or capture Indian warriors, destroyed their food supplies and homes, which subjected them to the risk of death from starvation, disease, and exposure. It also endangered Indian families – the Indian's great critical vulnerability. American forces rarely found the Indians without Indian scouts – unless the Indians wanted them to. General Nelson Miles called the army practice: "find, follow, and defeat."[21]

Since the Indians didn't abide by traditional Western laws of war, it was considered acceptable to treat them harshly. But American troops, particularly officers trained at West Point, were taught to treat Indian prisoners well because not doing so put them on the level of their enemies.[22] It was also common for US generals to order captured Indians treated as prisoners of war. Moreover, in what may seem counterintuitive, American military officers, though tasked with conquering the Indians, were among their staunchest defenders and sometimes protectors, particularly from corrupt businessmen and Federal Indian agents.

The Americans targeted the Indians' material ability and will to wage war by destroying the buffalo. For the Plains Indians, the buffalo was life. It supplied food, shelter, clothing, tools, and weapons; its dung fueled fires. General Philip Sheridan said buffalo hunters did more than the army in thirty years "to settle the vexed Indian question." The near-extinction of the buffalo, as their numbers declined from 13 million to perhaps only 1,000, forced many Native Americans to become wards of the Indian Bureau. White settlers also killed the other game upon which Indians depended.[23] This eroded Indian will to resist by making it impossible for them to fight and feed their families.

THE INDIAN WARS – THE LINCOLN AND JOHNSON ADMINISTRATION

After the Civil War, one of America's primary political aims remained expansion. This usually (but not always) translated into limited political aims toward the Indian nations, meaning the US wanted their land, but only the best parts. The grand strategy for achieving this can be branded "concentration." This should not be confused with concentration of forces in a military sense. The US sought to concentrate Indians on reservations. This allowed the seizure of their lands and – in theory – the chance to adapt them to White culture. Concentration could sometimes be accomplished via diplomacy or threats, but it usually required war.[24]

THE CIVIL WAR INDIAN WARS

The Homestead Act of 1862 fed Western migration, which accelerated with the building of railroads. The Indians faced an inexorable tide of explorers and settlers who pushed into Indian lands, even the reservations. The Indians would complain but be ignored. Too often, they were driven to their last recourse: taking up arms. This nearly always ended badly.[25]

The Civil War initially created opportunities for Indian Nations as the US stripped its forces from the frontier. But by 1862, the Union had raised large numbers of volunteer units, and by 1865, 20,000 US soldiers were in the West where only 4,000 had been in 1860. A Sioux uprising in Minnesota in August 1862, one spurred by a decade of anger and White encroachment on Sioux lands, proved one of the bloodiest and most brutal Indian wars as the Sioux killed over 400 Whites in the initial frenzy, 800 within a week. Army units under Henry Hastings Sibley defeated the Sioux in September. He captured, tried, and hanged 38 of the leaders (Lincoln having commuted the death sentences of over 260 others). The seat of the war shifted to the Dakotas, marked by expeditions in 1863 and 1864. The war lasted until Union troops broke the Dakota and Lakota Sioux in 1864.[26]

During the Civil War, American frontier politicians and military commanders operated without sufficient political direction or control from Washington. In Colorado in 1864, Governor John Evans, having failed to convince the Cheyenne and Arapaho to trade their hunting grounds for a reservation, decided to take them by force, a decision supported by the local military commander, Colonel John Chivington. Chivington responded to Indian raids by declaring the Cheyenne were at war and raising the Third Colorado Cavalry regiment. He told them to "burn villages and kill Cheyennes wherever and whenever found." His force then conducted what became known as the Sand Creek Massacre when they attacked a village of the peace chief Black Kettle on November 29, 1864. The Southern Cheyenne, Lakota Sioux, Arapaho, Kiowa, and Comanches responded with an enormous raid along the Platte River Road in January and February 1865. This included a July 1865 attack by 1,000–3,000 warriors – the largest Indian war party ever gathered on the Great Plains.[27]

The Indians separated in the autumn for the buffalo hunt. A new American commander then led a September campaign that killed some Indians but collapsed from an inability to deal with the early onset of harsh winter weather. It also cost the government $20 million, and orders came to just protect the travel routes. The army was now also shrinking as the Civil War ended and the volunteer soldiers wanted to go home. Dakota

Territory governor Newton Edmunds needed peace to attract settlers. He found some powerless chiefs to sign a treaty in October 1865 and declared the war over. A temporary calm descended on the northern plains.[28]

In the Southwest, the outbreak of the Civil War opened the door for Indian attacks. Mangas Coloradas, Cochise, and other Apache destroyed nearly every settlement in Arizona except Tucson. Confederate Colonel John R. Baylor was appointed governor of the Confederate areas of Arizona. Baylor urged the killing of all Apache men and the selling of the women and children into slavery. This didn't go over well with Davis and led to Baylor's dismissal. The Union's Southwest commander, J. H. Carleton, assisted by troops under Kit Carson, launched a brutal campaign against the Apache, Mescalero, and Navajo, killing the men and imprisoning the women and children. Carleton also encouraged miners to enter Indian lands. The resulting inevitable provocations would force the government to dispatch troops to protect civilians, resulting in the Indians being killed or driven from their lands. The Apache were defeated by superior American weapons, destruction of their provisions and strongholds, greater American manpower, and the occupation of their waterholes. This broke their will and ability to resist, though the latter cracked first. The war ended in fall 1866.[29]

In February 1865, the War Department created the enormous Military Division of the Missouri, which included Texas, the Great Plains, and the Rocky Mountains, and stretched from Iowa to Idaho, and from Canada to Mexico. The other western department was the Military Division of the Pacific (essentially all territory west of the Continental Divide). Both were subdivided into departments.[30] The strategy for holding the area was to establish forts throughout, but the US lacked the troops to properly garrison them. Sherman and others favored concentration in a few posts, but officials wanted their areas and settlers protected. Sherman wrote in 1868: "It is a physical impossibility for the small army [that] Congress maintains, to guard the exposed settlements any more than we can catch all the pickpockets in our cities." Even as the Indian wars intensified, Congress slashed the army's size to reduce war debt, shrinking it from 54,000 in 1866 to 25,000 in 1874. One-third of the army was in the South. When the Southern states reentered the Union, their Congressional representatives took vengeance by decreasing it further.[31]

THE SNAKE WAR, 1864–68

The deadliest struggle with the Indians was the Snake War against the Bannocks, Shoshone, and Northern Paiutes, who Whites collectively referred to as "Snakes." It was sparked by an increasing influx of settlers and miners into Indian lands in the Great Basin, the nexus of Idaho, Nevada, and Oregon. Sporadic fighting occurred in 1862 and 1863 between the Shoshone and Whites. By 1864 the Shoshone, led by 7-feet-tall Chief Ouluck, whom the Whites called Big Foot, refused to endure any more. The War Department established Fort Boise to protect Americans, but more attacks followed, as did increased traffic to California. During 1864–65, the army built additional forts, brought in more troops, and sporadically fought.[32]

At the end of the Civil War, regular troops replaced the volunteers. The Shoshone routed them at the May 1866 Battle of Three Forks, losing only a single man killed. The violence intensified with the Indian massacre of two groups of Chinese miners. Volunteers were raised to supplement the army and two campaigns followed. The Indians besieged one group in Boulder Creek for six days in July; the army rescued them. The other campaign killed perhaps a dozen Indians and destroyed their supplies. The army then built more posts and garrisoned old ones, increasing its presence and thus control. In late 1866, the aggressive George Crook took command and applied unrelenting pressure against the Indians from January 1867 through the winter of 1867–68. Indian attacks on stagecoaches and settlers continued, but Crook won several battles, weakening Indian resolve enough to make peace in September 1868. More than 1,200 Indians had been killed and wounded, while 378 soldiers, Indian scouts, and American civilians died.[33]

THE RED CLOUD WAR, 1866–68

In June 1865, Sherman assumed command of the Military Division of the Missouri and its 12,000 troops. He hoped for a year of peace to prepare his forces to "be ready to go and visit the Indians where they live." He didn't get it. Gold had been discovered in southwestern Montana in 1862. John Bozeman established a trail to the area in 1863; legions of Whites entered Sioux lands, destroying the buffalo and antelope. Sherman ordered construction of two forts on the Bozeman Trail while the government negotiated for peaceful passage and assured Oglala Sioux leader Red Cloud and his allies that the US had no intention of placing troops along the Bozeman Trail, which it did in June 1866, at Laramie, Wyoming. Red Cloud accused American commissioners of "treating the assembled chiefs as children."[34]

Red Cloud launched the war on July 17 with attacks along the Bozeman Trail. He proved among the most effective Indian leaders. He "set general objectives and organized large war parties but delegated their conduct to younger men of merit" such as Crazy Horse. His Arapaho allies supported him, as did other Sioux factions and even some of their ancestral enemy, the Crow. Red Cloud assembled 1,500 warriors but couldn't prevent the construction of posts such as Fort Kearny, from which he lured out a force commanded by Captain William Fetterman, annihilating it on December 21, 1866.[35]

Afterward, Sherman insisted: "We must act with vindictive earnestness against the Sioux, even to their extermination, men, women, and children." Newspapers cried for vengeance against the "savages." Sherman ordered a summer campaign prepared. Johnson, though, wanted to end the war. Meanwhile, Senator James Doolittle's committee published a report in January 1867 urging removal of Indians from White travel routes and settlements, and their concentration on remote reservations and remolding into Christian farmers. This was nothing new, but it became the Federal government's guidebook on Indian treatment for the next decade and a half.[36]

Military failure, pressure from Eastern peace advocates, and a war with the Cheyenne (examined below) encouraged the government to negotiate and Congress to act. On July 20, 1867, Johnson signed a law establishing a Peace Commission to negotiate permanent peace treaties with Plains Indians. Sherman laughed at the inability of such a commission to deal with the Indians. Being appointed its chair was not so amusing, though he quickly handed the leadership responsibilities to Nathaniel G. Taylor, the Indian Affairs commissioner.[37]

Red Cloud refused to make peace unless the US abandoned the Bozeman Trail forts. The army lacked the troops to fight Indians, occupy the South, protect the Union Pacific Railroad, and guard the Trail. Advocates of ending the war argued peace and feeding the Indians was cheaper on the national pocketbook and conscience. Moreover, the Union Pacific Railroad was almost complete, providing safe passage to Montana's goldfields. On April 29, 1868, the Peace Commission agreed to Red Cloud's demands. The US closed the Bozeman Trail, abandoned the forts, removed its soldiers, created the Great Sioux Reservation, and granted hunting rights, supplies, and an annuity for thirty years, and excluded Whites from settling in an area designated Unceded Indian Territory (large tracts of northeast Wyoming and southeast Montana) without Indian permission. The Indians agreed to become farmers and not disturb the Northern Pacific Railroad's construction. Red Cloud wouldn't sign until US troops withdrew.[38]

During the Red Cloud War, both sides fought for limited political aims as neither sought to overthrow the enemy government. The value of the object was higher for the Indians. Preserving their hunting grounds necessitated keeping out the Whites. They were on Death Ground (as Sun Tzu would put it) and knew it. They fought hard and were well led, and the Americans decided the war wasn't worth the cost. One must judge Red Cloud the victor as he achieved his political aims. This, like all Indian victories against the Americans, was short-lived. Red Cloud couldn't secure the peace.

Red Cloud agreeing to allow railroad construction was unfortunate for the Sioux. Sherman and Sheridan considered railroads critical to breaking the Indians, and the army protected building crews. Peace Commission agreements ensured the construction of the transcontinental railroad lines, the first being completed in 1869, "which for better or worse," Sherman wrote, "have settled the fate of the buffalo and the Indian forever." In 1872, Sherman told Sheridan the Northern Pacific line would "help to bring the Indian problem to a final solution." Grant, Sherman, Sheridan, and other American leaders all used the rhetoric of extermination, but "the physical extermination of the Indians as an ethnic group never became a military goal." Railroads allowed Whites to penetrate even the deserts, overwhelmed the Indians with settlers, and eased the army's communication, transportation, and logistical challenges while producing a kind of oil-spot strategy as settlements sprang up at every railroad watering stop, quickening US control and the buffalo's demise.[39]

THE CHEYENNE-ARAPAHO-KIOWA-SIOUX WAR, 1867

Major General Winfield Scott Hancock took command of the Department of the Mississippi in fall 1866. Some minor raids and breathlessly false claims by Kansas' governor and others convinced Hancock a major Indian uprising was set for 1867. In March 1867, he proposed to his superior, Sherman, a western Kansas expedition to intimidate the Indians. He thought war with the Cheyenne would benefit his region's situation and believed the Indians needed chastising. Sherman disagreed with Hancock's assessment but supported his subordinate.[40]

Hancock met Cheyenne and Sioux chiefs at Fort Larned, Kansas, on April 12, 1867. He had the largest American force yet assembled on the Great Plains, 1,400 men. He insulted and threatened the Cheyenne, and promised to march to one of their villages, essentially daring them to fight. Despite the pleadings of others in his command, Hancock set off the next day. After a parley in which unknown to Hancock he avoided assassination only because his Indian opponents prevented it, he burnt the abandoned Cheyenne villages at Pawnee Fork, bungled negotiations with the Kiowa, and provoked war with the Cheyenne and Oglala Sioux. The Kidder Massacre, the annihilation of a small American detachment under Lieutenant Lyman Kidder, followed on July 1, 1867.[41]

The Kiowa, Southern Arapaho, and some Comanche met the Peace Commission at Medicine Lodge Creek, Kansas, in mid October 1867 and were given a treaty built on a simple point: the buffalo would soon be extinct (which was almost right). This meant the Indians had no choice but to become farmers. Largely through swaying the chiefs with gifts, the government secured a treaty confining them to a 2.9-million-acre reservation consisting of perhaps half of southwestern Oklahoma. Later in October, the commission secured a treaty placing the Cheyenne and Arapaho on a 4.3-million-acre Oklahoma reservation. The treaty had no validity in the eyes of many Cheyenne leaders, and they never took it seriously, which is fair because the American representative never kept his promise to change certain provisions. Sherman had no faith in the treaties bringing peace and concentrated on protecting the railroads and waiting.[42]

THE CHEYENNE-ARAPAHO-KIOWA WAR, 1868

In August 1868, a drunken Cheyenne Dog Soldier band, fresh from being defeated by Pawnee, were fired upon by a White posse. The Cheyenne responded with raiding and rapine from central Kansas to eastern Colorado. The Dog Soldiers, a particularly bellicose Cheyenne faction, "fought to save their country and their way of life the only way they knew how – with horrific raids calculated to terrorize the whites into keeping away." Sherman ordered Sheridan "to drive the Cheyennes from Kansas."[43]

The army failed to produce a quick resolution. In October, Sherman and Sheridan escalated the level of force, fighting what Sherman termed "a predatory war." He sympathized with the Indians because of their poor treatment by the government, the dominant view of senior army officers fighting them. But Sherman possessed little patience (he once threatened to hang all the reporters in his camp during the Civil War), and now believed the only solution was to kill the Indians or reduce them to penury. He insured the government honored its commitments to the Kiowa to keep them out of the war but dealt with the warring Arapaho and Cheyenne as he had the Confederates, giving "them enough of war to satisfy them to their heart's content."[44]

Having found it nearly impossible to catch and kill the Indians, Sheridan developed a plan not unlike earlier efforts. Realizing the Indians were most vulnerable in winter when they were with their families, Sheridan mounted a winter campaign to "disabuse their minds of the idea that they were secure from punishment, and to strike them at a period when they were helpless to move their stock and villages." In November 1868, Sheridan launched three columns against the Cheyenne and Arapaho. In a November 27 attack on Washita, Oklahoma, a force under George Armstrong Custer destroyed the village and killed or captured its inhabitants. The Kiowa surrendered in mid December. The winter campaign didn't end the war but broke the bonds of the Cheyenne tribe. In March 1869, Sheridan again dispatched his cavalry. Some of the Cheyenne went to the reservation. The army destroyed the Dog Soldiers at Summit Springs, Colorado, in July 1869, essentially ending the war. Southern Nebraska and western Kansas "were cleared of hostile Indians."[45]

THE GRANT ADMINISTRATION: POLITICAL AIMS AND GRAND STRATEGY

President-elect Ulysses S. Grant revealed the nation's new approach toward the Indians to a reporter the week prior to his 1869 inauguration: "All Indians disposed to peace will find the new policy a peace-policy." The others would meet "a sharp and severe war-policy." In December 1869, Grant formally proposed his peace policy. He noted that railroads were "rapidly bringing civilized settlements into contact with all the tribes" and "the fact is they do not harmonize well, and one or the other has to give way in the end." Grant feared the current system would lead to the extinction of the Indians, something "too horrible for a nation to adopt without entailing upon itself the wrath of all Christendom and engendering in the citizen a disregard for human life and the rights of others, dangerous to society." To prevent this, Indians would be required to move to reservations (an assimilation tool) where they would be protected and put on the path to forming their own territorial governments. Sherman described Grant's approach as "peace within, or war without." Meaning the Indians would have peace on the reservation but war if they left it. But the strategy could deliver only if the government kept its commitments to the Indians and they remained on their allotted lands.[46]

To serve as the agents guiding the reservation Indians, Grant chose the Quakers, or the Society of Friends, because of their past good relations with Native Americans, nonviolence, honesty, and trustworthiness (the latter two traits being particularly rare in Grant appointees). Having a religious organization controlling Indian affairs would help achieve the government's aim of Americanizing and Christianizing the Indians. Public outcry over the aforementioned January 1870 massacre of Piegan Indians ruined Grant's plan to have the War Department assume control of Indian affairs and led to a law that forbade military personnel acting as Indian agents. The administration began appointing representatives of various religious denominations, putting 73 agencies and 240,000 Indians in their hands by 1872. The army remained responsible for keeping open the lines of communication, protecting the inhabitants, and keeping order. Indians who didn't settle on reservations would be forced to.[47]

The government had dealt with the Indians as sovereign states since independence. This changed on March 3, 1871; they were redefined as the government's wards. This freed administration hands because treaties with sovereign states required approval by two-thirds of the Senate. Agreements, though, were still subject to House and Senate authorization.[48]

THE COMANCHE WAR AND THE RED RIVER WAR, 1867-75

Despite success against various Indian tribes, neither the Johnson administration nor Congress constructed a functioning system for dealing with the Indians. The system, particularly before Grant's efforts at reform, relied upon Indian agents distinguished by corruption and incompetence. They couldn't curb the Kiowa and Comanches, who saw the restraint of army leaders as weakness. Additionally, under the terms of Grant's peace policy, troops weren't allowed on reservations unless requested by the Indian agent. The Kiowa and Comanches exploited this by slipping off the reservation to raid the Texans and sneaking back.[49]

Sherman was slow to take the complaints of Texans seriously; he suspected an attempt to divert troops from Reconstruction. His attitude changed when he was almost killed in a May 1871 raid: a Kiowa medicine man, bidden by a dream, told his tribe's warriors to not attack Sherman's party. Sherman had the leaders arrested. Kiowa and Comanches continued raiding in Texas and Mexico. A chain of forts "intended to enclose the Texas frontier from the Red River to the Rio Grande" failed to protect White settlements. In April 1872, bored, and no longer feeling constrained by the imprisonment of their chiefs, the Kiowa again began raiding Texas, their numbers fed by the poor situation on the reservation. Cheyenne and Comanche joined them. The army was authorized to attack the Indians wherever necessary, even on the reservation. The Kiowa were quelled by a visit of some of their leaders to Washington to negotiate and a promise to free their imprisoned chiefs, but this didn't end their raids. The Comanche War morphed into the Red River War.[50]

Starving because of government failure to deliver promised food and the destruction of the buffalo, Kiowa, Comanche, and Cheyenne continued attacking White settlements in Texas. Sheridan launched a five-pronged operation against perhaps 4,500 Indians encamped at the Washita River's headwaters. He had little luck bringing them to battle, but a clash in the Palo Duro Canyon destroyed vast numbers of tipis and took much important food and material, including 1,400 horses. Follow-on pursuit campaigns in the winter weakened and exhausted the Comanche and their allies. They returned to their reservations. Sheridan treated captured Indians as prisoners of war, and had the leaders tried and jailed in Florida. The Indian wars on the Southern plains were over.[51]

THE MODOC WAR, 1872–73

The Modoc and the Klamath were placed on the same reservation on Klamath land in the Klamath Lake region of the Oregon–California border. In 1870, weary of paying tribute, the Modoc returned to their territory on Oregon's Lost River. The White settlers protested, and the Interior Department ordered out the Modoc. Their leader, Kintpuash, called Captain Jack by Whites, refused. The army was dispatched, and fighting erupted on November 28, 1872. The Modoc fled to a rugged labyrinth of caves and lava flows, some raiding White settlements along the way. A slowly assembled army force attacked what they called Captain Jack's Stronghold on January 17, 1873, drew back defeated, and decided to talk.[52]

Grant was eager to negotiate as this threatened his peace policy. Brigadier General Edward R. S. Canby and others met with the Modoc in April. But Captain Jack, goaded by his more brutal comrades, promised to kill Canby if the general refused to give the Modoc their own reservation. Canby had no authority to grant anything, refused to lie to them, and said the Modoc had no option but surrender. Jack shot him in the eye.[53]

An enraged American public demanded vengeance. Sherman appointed Jefferson C. Davis to Canby's post. Davis, a Union Civil War veteran (no relation to the Confederate president), had murdered a fellow officer during the war and escaped punishment. It was two weeks before he took command, and the battle for the lava beds began without him. A messy struggle ensued in which White numbers forced the Modoc from their stronghold. Pursued, they eventually surrendered. Jack hadn't wanted the war, but those who did were among the first taken and helped capture him. They escaped the noose. Jack didn't.[54]

PART I: FROM BACKWATER TO GREAT POWER

THE GREAT SIOUX WAR, 1876–77

The 1868 treaty with Red Cloud held until 1876. The government failed to keep Whites from Indian lands after the discovery of gold in the Black Hills. Negotiations to buy the land failed. The Great Sioux War followed. It's the best known of the Indian Wars because of the Battle of Little Bighorn – or the Greasy Grass, as the victors call it. The Sioux and Cheyenne went to war because of broken treaties and anger over efforts to keep them on reservations. Moreover, the Red Cloud Agency, where they were supposed to farm, was unsuitable.[55]

The Grant administration had exploited the deteriorating situation. At a November 3, 1875 conference, he and his advisors developed a two-phase plan to achieve their aims: moving all Indians to reservations and forcing them from lands they hadn't ceded. This was partially driven by public pressure to tap the Black Hills' resources. They would continue allowing Whites to illegally enter the Black Hills, knowing this would provoke the Indians. Then they would tell the non-treaty Indians (those who had no agreements with the US) to report to their respective agencies, while not giving them time to do so, and while the Indian Bureau created fake complaints against them. Sheridan, meanwhile, would prepare a winter campaign to win the war sure to follow. This would break the non-treaty Indians, thus forcing the reservation Indians to yield. To spin up public support for war, they released a fake report blaming the Indians for attacks on unarmed White settlers. On December 3, 1875, Sioux chief Sitting Bull and his allies were told to move to the Indian agencies by January 31, 1876, or face war.[56]

The Black Hills were a valuable object for the Indians. The area was holy ground, particularly to the Cheyenne, but also teemed with game and was thus an important source of food. The Sioux and Northern Cheyenne formed a coalition and developed centralized leadership in a way unusual for the Indians. Sitting Bull led them, assisted closely by Gall and Crazy Horse. They abandoned attacking Whites outside of the lands they claimed stretching from the Yellowstone River to the Black Hills. This area they defended tenaciously. A winter (March 1876) army campaign failed to inflict many casualties on the Indians but did burn their village on the Powder River.[57]

In the spring, Sheridan responded with a multi-pronged offensive using three independent columns, each considered strong enough to defeat any Indian force encountered. Their commanders, respectively George Crook, John Gibbon, and Alfred Terry, set out with a combined force of over 2,400 soldiers supported by 300 Indian scouts. The operational objective was to disarm and dismount the tribes. The government would then feed the Indians until they learned to farm. In this instance having multiple columns led to the rare situation where American units risked being overwhelmed and defeated in detail by superior Indian numbers. The Americans understood neither the scale of the enemy force nor that it was concentrated. Crook's column, the largest of the three, discovered this on June 17 when they got the worst of a six-hour fight with perhaps 2,000 Indians at the Battle of the Rosebud. Crazy Horse forced Crook to withdraw, something 7th Cavalry commander Custer didn't know.[58]

What became known as the Battle of Little Bighorn was supposed to be a hammer-and-anvil attack, with Custer's column acting as the hammer pushing the Indians into Gibbon's anvil. The intent was to keep the Indians from escaping. But Custer (part of Terry's command) reached Little Bighorn on June 25, a day before his comrades, and expected to find only 800 Indians. There were perhaps 7,000, including 1,800 warriors. Custer divided his force and the Indians drove back Major Marcus Reno's initial attack at Little Bighorn. Custer, knowing he had been spotted, launched his attack – unsupported – before Gibbon arrived. Instead of fleeing, the Indians counterattacked, annihilating Custer's unit. His other detachments survived by concentrating, digging in, and holding out until Terry and Gibbon relieved them. The Indians then dispersed. The destruction of Custer's command marked the greatest single loss of American forces in the conquest of the West: 265 killed, including three Indian scouts and five civilians.[59]

The Greasy Grass victory didn't end the war. Miles' Fifth Infantry pursued Sitting Bull and his Sioux, one of the most effective things to do as this kept the Indians moving and made it impossible for them to accumulate enough food for the winter. Then, taking advantage of the army's material and technical advantages, Miles scouted the area where he intended to launch his "systematic campaign" and stockpiled supplies. He planned to apply constant pressure and keep the Indians moving, even through the winter. He launched his campaign in October 1876. Crazy Horse and most others were forced back to reservations by May 1877. Some were coaxed back. The government secured its aims as the agency chiefs were forced to surrender the unceded lands, including the Black Hills. War against the Cheyenne continued until January 1879. Sitting Bull and his followers marched into Canada until the hostility of local Indians combined with hunger to drive them to the reservations. He surrendered on July 20, 1881.[60]

PART I: FROM BACKWATER TO GREAT POWER

THE NEZ PERCE WAR, JUNE–OCTOBER 1877, AND THE UTE WAR, 1879

The ancestral lands of the Nez Perce were in the junction of Idaho, Washington, and Oregon, an area holy to the Nez Perce and guaranteed them by an 1855 treaty. But in 1860, after the discovery of gold, Whites began illegally settling the area, abetted in 1863 by corrupt Indian agents bribing leaders to sign a treaty dispatching the Nez Perce to an Oregon reservation. Some remained, including one band led by Chief Joseph. In January 1877, the Grant administration decreed all Nez Perce bound by the treaty and ordered them to the reservation. Facing an unwinnable war, Joseph led his people to Oregon.[61]

In early June 1877, Chief Joseph's band camped a few miles from the reservation. A young warrior from the Nez Perce White Bird Band, angry over the murder of his father by Whites, killed four Whites in revenge. Chief Joseph hoped to negotiate with the army for the punishment of only the guilty man, but an overzealous army captain led an attack on the Nez Perce on June 17, 1877. The Indians killed 34 of the 110 soldiers while suffering only 3 wounded. Another army attack pushed other Nez Perce into the war.[62]

General O. O. Howard launched what became a pursuit of Chief Joseph and the Nez Perce, who accepted the leadership of Looking Glass and were encumbered with their women, children, elderly, and livestock. They refused to attack civilians or murder women and children, and consistently outmarched, outmaneuvered, and often outfought the Americans for 1,700 miles through Montana, back into Idaho, across the Continental divide twice, then back into Montana and Wyoming via Yellowstone National Park. They crossed the Yellowstone River near Billings, trekked past Lewistown and Bear Paw Mountain, making for Canada.[63]

Though the Nez Perce individually were better warriors, they couldn't match White numbers, organization, transportation, technology, and logistics. These enabled the army to continue fighting in winter, the great Indian enemy. Miles cornered the Nez Perce at Bear Paw, Montana. After a five-day battle, Chief Joseph surrendered after being promised his people could return to the Northeast, but over 200 escaped and joined Sitting Bull in Canada. The government spent $1,800,000 and suffered 180 men killed to secure an agreement it had before the fighting, one it didn't keep because it forced the Nez Perce to go to Oklahoma. Most of the survivors returned to the Northwest between 1883 and 1885.[64]

In 1879, the Utes of Colorado were driven to revolt by an abusive and incompetent Indian agent who tried to push them into farming too quickly. The agent called upon the army to enforce his demands, producing a skirmish at Milk Creek, Colorado, on September 29, 1879, where the Utes killed several soldiers. Other Utes killed the Indian agent, nine of his employees, and raped the women they took captive. Sherman dispatched more troops and began preparing a campaign, but Interior Secretary Carl Schurz wanted a negotiated resolution and restrained the army. The situation was defused in October. The Rocky Mountain Indians rose no more.[65]

THE APACHE WARS, 1871–86

On April 30, 1871, a group of Whites, Mexican Americans, and Papago Indians attacked an Apache village at Camp Grant in revenge for raids perpetrated by the area's Indians (though probably not these). They killed 144 Apache, mostly women and children. Arizonans rejoiced, as the Apache were hated for their brutality and propensity for gruesome torture. An unhappy Grant dispatched a peace negotiator.[66]

The Apache leader, Cochise, had been fighting a desultory war against the Americans in the Arizona–New Mexico area since 1861. But by April 1870 had lost most of his men and been ground down by constant army pursuit. He was also suffering from stomach cancer. He offered to make peace, but local officials lacked the authority, and Cochise couldn't control his men. The war went on. Brigadier General Crook prepared campaigns on two occasions in 1871, but Peace Commissioners stopped him. The last of these granted Cochise's request for a reservation in Chokonen. The war ended in April 1873.[67]

But other areas' Indians continued raiding. Crook hunted the Western Apache and their Yavapais allies, applied constant pressure, and fought them nineteen times in the Tonto Basin area over the 1872–73 winter. His destruction of a Yavapais camp at Turret Peak on March 27, 1873, finished the war. The peace lasted six weeks. A group of Western Apache on the White Mountain Reservation were provoked by a corrupt Indian agent and were joined by some of the Yavapais who had just surrendered. Crook pursued them in the same dogged manner. The war was ended when some of the warriors accepted Crook's offer of peace if they killed the rebellious leaders and brought him their respective heads.[68]

In late 1874, Washington began applying concentration to Arizona. Western Apache, Yavapais, and Chiricahua were gathered on the expanded White Mountain Reservation in eastern Arizona. The direction from Washington's Board of Indian Commissioners was to avoid posting traditional enemies together, guidance the Indian Bureau ignored. Appointing a 22-year-old Indian agent worsened matters. The Indians lost their best land and concentration continued.[69]

The Chihennes Apache were forced to move to a particularly unhealthy and inhospitable region (an almost normal occurrence) known as San Carlos. On September 1, 1877, facing starvation, 300 Indians under Victorio, a chief particularly skilled in guerrilla warfare, left the reservation. The army pursued them across New Mexico until they surrendered on October 11, but they were allowed to return to their original lands at Ojo Caliente. The government then decided to move them back to San Carlos. After a year of unsuccessfully negotiating a reversal of this decision, Victorio and his followers again left the reservation and went to war. The US army chased them for four months, including into Mexico. The Mexican army trapped and destroyed them in October 1880.[70]

Among warriors who were perhaps the toughest and deadliest, Chiricahua Chief Geronimo (Goyahkla) was the most dangerous. He combined bravery and intelligence with experience and ruthlessness. He had ridden with Victorio and only returned to San Carlos in early 1880 because he had no other options. He didn't stay long. Fighting broke out at the reservation in October 1880 after the army's bungled arrest and killing of an Indian holy man. Geronimo and seventy-four others left the reservation, joined some survivors of Victorio's band, and raided the reservation in April 1882, killing Whites and forcing other Apache to join them. Possessing sanctuary in Mexico was key to Apache ability to resist. US troops couldn't cross the border before a July 29, 1882 agreement granting both nations pursuit rights.[71]

The army responded by returning Crook to command. He realized abysmal conditions and treatment contributed to uprisings and understood the importance of controlling the population, which he did by issuing the Apache identity tags and requiring rollcalls. Crook organized five companies of Apache scouts to support his units, used mules to haul his supplies instead of cumbersome wagons, and struck out after the Apache in wake of their March 1883 raid in Arizona and New Mexico. He pursued them into Mexico in May, even into the rugged Sierra Madre Mountains the Apache considered a sanctuary. Crook successfully negotiated – partly through bluff – the return of Geronimo and his band to San Carlos, though it was March 1884 before the last Apache arrived.[72]

But Geronimo and his followers chafed under the rules and returned to raiding in May 1885 with their normal brutality. Crook again applied unrelenting pressure in his pursuit, driving them to accept two years in Florida before returning to San Carlos. But the deal quickly collapsed.

An unprincipled army sutler (trader) sold the Apache's mescal and told them to expect brutal treatment on their return. Geronimo and his followers, after a bout of heavy drinking, fled again for the Sierra Madre. Crook's superior, Sheridan, ordered the new terms be unconditional surrender. Crook refused to go back on his word and resigned.[73]

The government had had enough of Geronimo and the Chiricahua. President Cleveland ordered no more negotiations. Death or unconditional surrender were the only solutions allowed. Sheridan developed a plan to ensure Geronimo's destruction. The New Mexico and Arizona territories were divided into twenty-seven districts. Infantry units were placed at key mountain passes and cavalry were mobilized to chase down the fugitives. Perhaps 5,000 troops were deployed on the border with Mexico. Miles readied a force to push into Mexico for the third time. Geronimo's band probably had twenty men.[74]

Miles was one of the most experienced US Indian fighters. He established flying columns like Crook's led by picked officers but manned by Indians and others accustomed to the desert. He established twenty-seven heliograph stations; using mirrors, these stations could flash Morse Code messages up to 50 miles away. This communications advantage allowed him to constantly harry the Apache, who were driven to negotiate. Informed the Indians from San Carlos were being shipped to Florida, Geronimo and his band surrendered on September 4, 1886.[75]

THE "INDIAN QUESTION"

The question for the government remained: what to do with the Indians on the reservations? Some, of course, proved more resistant than others. Indian agents called chiefs who followed the government's programs "progressives." Those failing to see the wisdom of their betters were branded "non-progressive." The government continued trying to turn them into farmers, with mixed success. General Terry suggested: "The first step toward the solution of the Indian question is to give the Indian cattle and let them lead a pastoral life, which is closely allied to their own natural life." The Hayes administration tried to improve the quality of Indian agents and remove the domination of corrupt contractors who were the middlemen between the government and the Indians. Hayes and Senator Schurz wanted Indian assimilation. They were uninterested in saving Indian culture but did want to save Indian lives.[76]

On February 8, 1887, Cleveland signed the Dawes Act (or General Allotment Act), a part of the reform movement's assimilation push. It allowed the government to divide land between the Indians and then buy the rest, which effectively abrogated the various treaties and gave the government power to take more Indian land. This produced further White settlement in Sioux territory beginning in February 1890 under President Benjamin Harrison. This, combined with an Indian religious revival, laid the foundation for the Ghost Dance War. An army effort to disarm some Lakota led to the Battle of Wounded Knee on December 29, 1890, where large numbers of women and children were killed. Other Sioux responded by taking to the field from fear of the army or a desire for revenge. Most were soon convinced to surrender or return. By mid January 1891 the Indian Wars were over.[77]

The conquest of the Plains cost the army probably 919 soldiers killed from 1865 to 1898. Nearly all the Indian wars were fought on the cheap. How the army protected the nation now changed. With the internal threat gone, the US no longer needed its extensive system of frontier forts and began abandoning them in 1889.[78]

FROM RUTHERFORD B. HAYES TO GROVER CLEVELAND, 1877–97

Gilded Age America faced a situation where its power and influence was increasing while threats to its sovereignty and security declined. The Indian nations fell to American suzerainty while the Europeans backed away from the Western Hemisphere. Americans became more interested in and connected to the larger world, something partially fed by a booming Protestant foreign missionary movement that sometimes produced government involvement in new regions. Most businessmen remained more concerned with the domestic than the foreign market. But for the first time, US businesses had the capital to invest abroad and began doing so, particularly in Mexico. In general, Gilded Age politicians devoted little time to foreign affairs. Domestic issues were more important. Actions and reactions toward events abroad were generally improvised.[79]

AIMS AND STRATEGY

Some scholars consider the Republican administration of Rutherford B. Hayes (1877–81) a low point as his administration attempted almost nothing in foreign affairs. The corruption surrounding his elevation to the presidency also severely weakened him. Hayes involved his administration in the promotion of trade and little else. The army was only funded for

25,000 of the men allowed, and the navy was small and obsolete. Hayes himself desired the annexation of Canada, but only if the Canadians wanted it. He opposed Ferdinand de Lesseps' canal-building efforts in Panama because it smacked of French imperialism and supposedly threatened Western Hemisphere nations. De Lesseps' efforts, which were private, fueled invocations of the Monroe Doctrine. In March 1880 Hayes wrote: "The policy of this country is a canal under American control." He condemned foreign efforts here, warning overseas companies they couldn't count on the intervention of their nations in support of their work as this would force America's hand.[80]

In the 1880s, three new powers entered the global stage: Germany, Japan, and the United States. They also became Pacific powers, overturning the region's geopolitical calculus. The United States, as we have seen, had a Pacific presence dating from 1805. Hayes' Pacific ambitions related to trade. He secured a treaty with Samoa for a coaling station that included a promise to provide Washington's "good offices" if Samoa were threatened, but Congress wouldn't fund the station. An 1880 expedition to Korea secured diplomatic relations, most-favored-nation trading status, and extraterritorial rights. Korea didn't receive a reciprocal trade agreement, partially because of Japanese and Chinese influence.[81]

Hayes benefited from the nation's return to financial health. After several tax cuts, the administration enjoyed annual surpluses of over $100 million beginning in 1880. It "could have reduced tariffs, thereby eliminating most of the surplus, but strong domestic constituencies – many of them Republican – favored protecting indigenous industries." Surpluses encouraged spending on things such as a navy. Hayes renewed use of trade reciprocity treaties, partially to keep from being shut out of European markets. These could open the door for US agricultural and manufactured goods and, as was supposedly the case with Hawaii, bind a place to America. Seeing how trade reciprocity helped tie the islands to Washington led some, like Alfred Thayer Mahan, to insist American influence in Asia "would increasingly depend on the further reduction of tariffs with other nations so as to bind them to the United States as well."[82]

In the 1880s, the US had no ability to project power to another continent and American foreign relations were "composed of incidents, not policies – a number of distinct events, not sequences that moved from a source toward a conclusion." Republican Chester A. Arthur became president (1881–85) when James Garfield was assassinated after only 100 days in office. Arthur took up reform and expansion of America's dilapidated navy. The initial recommendations boiled down to expanding the force built primarily around mining, coastal fortifications, and commerce raiders. But as support from a growing "Navalist" faction increased, so did consideration of new ideas, though nothing was encapsulated until 1889. International prestige also underpinned this effort as a modern navy was a manifestation of national power and a tool for exerting influence abroad. Relatedly, the Arthur administration signed a treaty with Hawaii granting an exclusive basing concession at Pearl Harbor.[83]

Reciprocity was the core of Arthur's trade strategy, particularly in Latin America. He sought "to tie Latin economies to the United States, weaken European influence, and promote larger US political aims." Reciprocity deals with Spain removed nearly all trade barriers with Cuba and Puerto Rico. Arthur successfully fought protectionist Republicans and Democrats – both hated reciprocity – to pen several deals. His successor, Grover Cleveland, scrapped them. Cleveland opposed high duties and pushed tariff reduction. He believed tariffs favored certain businesses while increasing the cost of living and saw reciprocity as a conspiracy against tariff reduction. The Benjamin Harrison administration hoped to increase American exports to Latin America and shifted strategy again, eventually concluding eight reciprocity deals. It fought hard to win over Congress.[84]

Democrat Cleveland and his first administration (1885–89) were described thus: "He pursued no grand geopolitical strategy; instead, he reacted – or overreacted – to foreign-policy developments as they occurred." In his March 1885 inaugural, Cleveland's themes were "independence, unilateralism, avoidance of overseas conflicts, and defense of the American state system against European encroachment," essentially security and sovereignty. Cleveland broke with his predecessors with his anti-expansionism and took seriously (arguably to extremes) Washington's warning against foreign entanglements, refusing even to support a treaty with Nicaragua for rights to build a canal. Cleveland believed in a moralistic form of foreign relations long before Woodrow Wilson became famous for it. He wanted an America respected overseas, but the nation should be just in its foreign relations and not opportunistic like many European states. Simultaneously, he protected American interests, particularly in the Western Hemisphere, in line with the Monroe Doctrine, and wouldn't tolerate European construction of or control over a canal in Central America, or European expansion into the New World. He preferred arbitration for solving international disputes.[85]

The administration of Republican Benjamin Harrison (1889–93) marked another foreign relations shift as the US became more aggressive. Harrison insisted America be respected by other nations, and supported acquisition of foreign naval stations and the expansion of American trade. Harrison wasn't an expansionist but became convinced of the need to increase American influence over Hawaii. His secretary of state, James G. Blaine, had greater ambitions and was cut from the traditional expansionist cloth. Known as "Jingo Jim," Blaine had "a vision of empire that included US preeminence in the hemisphere, commercial domination of the Pacific, an American-owned canal, and even the acquisition of Hawaii, Cuba, and Puerto Rico." The anti-expansionist sentiments dominating part of the Republican party, illness, and his own poor diplomacy limited his achievements.[86]

The South American states had tighter links with Europe than the US, and America began trying to shift the region toward Washington. Harrison sought to supplant Britain as the region's dominant outside economic force. Blaine used the 1889–90 Pan-American Conference to grow diplomatic and economic influence. Harrison appointed a bipartisan delegation to represent the US that included distinguished political and business figures such as steel baron Andrew Carnegie. The five months of travel and meetings that ensued achieved little beyond establishing the precedent for future meetings. This did convince Harrison to push for commercial reciprocity in the region, which the administration secured with all but three states. Additional conferences in 1901 and 1906 spawned the Pan-American Union, which was established in Washington in 1910 with Carnegie's financial support. The administration helped establish a three-power protectorate over Samoa with Britain and Germany. The relationship proved fraught. In 1899, the US and Germany divided Samoa.[87]

European bans on importing American pork (implemented to protect their own markets) created tensions and threats of retaliation, and a so-called "trade war." By 1890, American leaders refused to tolerate blatantly discriminatory measures. The Harrison administration established meat inspection rules to remove reasons for a ban and promised retaliation. Negotiations and lifting the bans defused the crisis.[88]

In the immediate aftermath of the 1891 Chilean civil war, two American sailors were killed in a barroom brawl in Chile. There had been much anti-Americanism in Chile because of US efforts to prevent annexations in the 1879–83 War of the Pacific, which Chile convincingly won. Harrison had no patience for extended diplomatic negotiations. In disagreements he took up his position, "left little room for compromise," and "relied on the ultimatum to achieve his objectives." In the Chilean dispute, Harrison insisted Chile issue regrets and make reparation for the deaths. The Chileans refused and dispatched a reply considered offensive. Harrison began preparing for war. Negotiations continued until Chile received Harrison's ultimatum demanding an apology for the deaths of the sailors and repudiation of parts of their letter. Barring this, the US would sever diplomatic relations, the acknowledged precursor to war. On January 25, 1892, Harrison invited Congress to act as it deemed appropriate. Chile's apology arrived the same day.[89]

The Panic of 1893, which was rooted in a British bank failure, brought America's biggest economic downturn yet and produced 17 percent unemployment. Militant labor unrest ensued the next year. This fed anger against giant American corporations and their heads – who were branded Robber Barons. Despite periodic downturns, American industrial and agricultural growth was spectacular. From 1870 to 1900, American steel production leapt from 77,000 to 11,270,000 tons annually. The production of corn and wheat doubled. American goods became better, the nation's transportation networks grew and improved, and exports surged from $234 million to $1.5 billion annually between 1865 and 1900. Increased banking control of industry fed industrial stability by decreasing competition, which produced industrial monopolies by concentrating control, particularly in the railroad, steel, and oil industries.[90]

Cleveland managed the unique presidential success of two, nonconsecutive terms (1885–89 and 1893–97). His second administration took a broad view of the Monroe Doctrine. It not only "forbid new European colonies but declared an American interest in any matter within the hemisphere." In January 1893, shortly before Cleveland's inauguration, there was a coup in Hawaii by Americans who controlled its sugar trade, one supported by the American minister to the islands and which succeeded because of his use of Marines from a navy vessel. The Harrison administration sent the Senate a treaty of annexation on its final day. Cleveland recalled the treaty when he took office. He wasn't interested in annexation unless the populace wanted it and suspected they didn't, a fact confirmed by investigation. Cleveland tried to protect both sides by seeking the ousted queen's return and amnesty for the rebels. She preferred to behead the rebels, who refused to surrender control. Cleveland passed the matter to Congress, urging it to disapprove annexation. Congress advised extending recognition to the rebel government and Cleveland agreed. He didn't oppose acquiring Hawaii but wanted the US to have clean hands.[91]

Washington grew increasingly assertive abroad as the nineteenth century neared its end. In 1895, Britain was pressuring Venezuela regarding its border with British Guiana. Cleveland feared this would provoke a conflict and regretted inadvertently causing an outbreak of American war fever by submitting the matter to Congress. Cleveland's secretary of state, Richard Olney, and others feared successful British bullying of Venezuela could mark the first steps toward European partition of yet another continent (the Europeans were then dividing Africa), this time in America's hemisphere. Such a violation of the Monroe Doctrine couldn't be tolerated. Olney told Britain: "Today the United States is practically sovereign on this continent, and its fiat is law upon the subjects to which it confines its interposition." In other words, stop. The British didn't take the US seriously, but rumblings in South Africa that became the Boer War helped convince them to compromise. Senator Henry Cabot Lodge insisted the US had to stand firm behind the Monroe Doctrine or abandon it.[92]

Yet another rebellion against Spanish rule in Cuba erupted in spring 1895. Cleveland thought it better for US security if Spain continued its rule and feared Cuba would be even more badly governed if the rebels won. He mistrusted Americans who sympathized with the rebels, suspecting they wanted to involve the US in a war over Cuba, and tried to stop American arms flowing illegally to the island. Congress wanted Cleveland to abandon neutrality and support the rebels and Cuban independence. Cleveland instead sought to convince Spain to offer reforms and accept US mediation. Madrid refused, and Cleveland soon left office.[93]

In Asia, by the mid 1890s America had developed a fine reputation among the continent's nations, one undoubtedly due to it not seeking conquests. Japanese leaders remarked happily about how America never interposed itself in arguments between other states. By 1895, "the Americans were indeed seen as the friendliest of powers," something Grant had hoped would be the case in the region.[94]

MILITARY DEVELOPMENTS AND STRATEGIC CONCERNS

In the post–Civil War era, the reunited Democratic Party became an antimilitary party in the Jeffersonian mold. This paralyzed military modernization for a generation.[95] But it didn't stop it. By the 1880s, and with the winding down of the Indian Wars, the American military forces began an intellectual and material rebirth, much of it because of William Tecumseh Sherman.

THE ARMY

Many Americans remained hostile to a significant standing army. Some considered it a threat to American liberties, but more thought it wasteful.

Pacifists were of course against it, and labor leaders and members objected to the army's use for strike-breaking in 1877 and 1894. But more than a few considered soldiers "servants of the republic," while the newspapers generally supported use of the army against striking workers. Moreover, nearly every president from Grant to McKinley had served in the Union army.[96]

July 1868 saw the army's size established at 54,000. The law of March 1869 cut it to 37,000. In 1877, Congressional infighting over further reductions saw delays in the passage of funding that resulted in troops going unpaid from July through November. The 1880s marked the beginning of reform in an army plagued by poor pay, desertion, and inadequate funding. The drive for increased professionalism came from Sherman when he headed the army (1869–83). He believed West Point should be only the beginning of officer education and hoped that one day the US would have a European-style war college. His encouragement of Civil War veteran and author Emory Upton helped promote modernization. In 1881, the army instituted four months of basic training for recruits and added specialist training for cavalry and artillery. In 1882, officer retirement at age 64 was made mandatory to open space for younger officers. The army established the School for the Application for Infantry and Cavalry at Fort Leavenworth, Kansas, in 1881. A Department of Military Art was added after 1887. The Military Information Division was launched in 1885 to gather intelligence on other nation's armies.[97]

THE NAVY

The US navy, which was the strongest in the world in 1865, was among the weakest by 1881. Its 200 ships were almost entirely obsolete. Some South American nations possessed larger and more modern fleets. The force was officer heavy, and these too often superannuated; its civilian employees and its bureaucracy were renowned for inefficiency, incompetence, and sloth. Some voices in the 1870s began calling for a modern navy as it was needed as a foreign relations tool. Grant observed in December 1870 that the navy's funding was only adequate for repairs to old vessels and said – correctly – it would be destroyed without funding for new ships and repairs.[98]

Fear provided the catalyst for change: fear of foreign descents in the form of Chile, Germany, or Britain, the loss of seaborne trade, and an inability to protect American overseas outposts. Prestige also fed reform, as did a desire for a Central America canal. Chile threatened to destroy America's Pacific Squadron if the US continued diplomatically backing Peru, Chile's opponent in the War of the Pacific (1879–84), a threat it could have easily enacted. President Garfield's secretary of the navy, William H. Hunt, proved critical to the navy's rebirth. He discovered upon taking up his post the service's baleful state and launched a reform and rebuilding program that called for the construction of sixty-eight modern ships. Most were smaller, steel vessels for protecting America's coasts and trade.[99]

When Arthur became president in 1881, he launched Hunt's program. The equally capable William E. Chandler replaced Hunt in 1882. He reorganized and shrank the officer corps, founded the Office of Naval Intelligence (1882), and established the Naval War College in Newport, Rhode Island (1884). He closed superfluous shipyards, guided plans for foundries to manufacture guns, and oversaw a replacement for Hunt's naval program as it became clear Congress wouldn't underwrite sixty-eight ships. Arthur secured passage of the 1883 Navy Act funding construction of three modern steel cruisers. The 1886 Endicott Board studied America's coastal defenses and proposed a program to improve twenty-nine sites on the nation's seaboard and the Great Lakes. Congress began funding this in 1890.[100]

Republican leaders worked to shape American public opinion in support of a modern navy, and the Harrison administration was instrumental, particularly his secretary of the navy, Benjamin Franklin Tracy. In 1889, Tracy began pushing for the construction of twenty battleships to protect both coasts of the United States. Congress immediately funded eight. Tracy launched an energetic effort to win support for his fleet in January 1890, a campaign interrupted for some time after fire swept through his house, killing his wife, youngest daughter, a maid, and nearly Tracy as well. The Naval Act of 1890 that passed in June was not nearly what Tracy or other big navy supporters wanted: it funded only three battleships. By the time of the Spanish–American War (1898), the US had four modern battleships in service and others building.[101]

When the 1891 crisis with Chile intensified, the secretary of the navy assembled a small coterie of advisors, including Mahan, to plan for war. This "marked the start of a more comprehensive approach to naval war planning." When the Naval War College resumed teaching in 1893, classes were given a strategic challenge that required construction of a war plan. The College also began formulating plans that were passed to Washington.[102]

Civil War experience had laid the foundation for this and for teaching strategic thinking in the United States. Stephen B. Luce, a career naval officer and Civil War veteran, had a wartime conversation with Sherman regarding the seizure of Charleston. Sherman noted that the navy had been pounding Charleston for three years with no result. He told Luce that as soon as he cut the city's communications, it would fall. Luce wrote, "After hearing General Sherman's clear exposition of the military situation the scales seemed to fall from my eyes." Luce realized there were higher principles at work in war beyond brute force. He embarked upon a quest to establish an institution that would seek strategic principles for warfare at sea and teach them to the service's officers, thus creating a cadre of leaders who could think critically and analytically; he also hoped to discover a "naval Jomini." This produced the 1884 founding of the Naval War College in Newport, Rhode Island. Its survival was in doubt for years; it was shuttered in 1890, 1891, and 1893.[103]

The Naval War College benefited from the assignment of another Civil War veteran, Alfred Thayer Mahan, as a faculty member. He published *The Influence of Sea Power upon History, 1660–1783* in 1890. It profoundly shaped American naval thinking and that of other nations for decades, convincing, among others, Assistant Secretary of the Navy Theodore Roosevelt to expand the country's naval power. The book was hailed in Britain and Japan, and Kaiser Wilhelm II ordered a copy placed on every German naval vessel.[104]

To Mahan, sea power was necessary for growth, security, and national prosperity. His definition of "sea power" remained fuzzy, but it boiled down to command of the sea through a superior navy, combined with control of overseas trade, possessions, and markets, which, in turn, produced wealth.[105] This latter part is derivative of the mercantilist ideas that dominated European political and economic development up to the nineteenth century. Since Mahan studied this period to get his ideas, it is unsurprising he reached this conclusion. Mercantilism was basically having an empire to control natural resources and have a market for your manufactures.

An important part of Mahan's work was his insistence that there were six elements determining the development of sea power.

1. Geographical Position: This meant that the nation had a beneficial geographical position in regard to the sea and didn't have to defend itself against a large, continental power. Britain was the example. It possessed advantages over a nation like France because its geographic position gave it the freedom to emphasize sea power and focus on naval forces.
2. Physical Conformation: The ease with which a nation's geography allows access to the sea from the interior of the country contributes greatly to its ability to develop sea power.
3. Extent of Territory: By this Mahan meant the length of the coastline and the quality of its harbors, meaning natural bays, inlets, and so on. Good,

accessible bays and harbors were necessary for developing sea power. But having these could be a weakness if the nation lacked the population to defend them. Mahan gave the Confederacy as an example.

4. Number of Population: This was the number of people engaged in seaborne occupations or who could be put to doing such jobs.
5. National Character: Mahan argued that if the people were interested in commercial pursuits, this would lead them to seaborne trade, one of the foundational elements of sea power.
6. Character of Government: Governments and a nation's rulers mattered for the development of sea power and must encourage and aid its development. There will be no naval forces unless the government builds them.

Mahan's archetype was Great Britain.[106]

Mahan distinguished between strategy and tactics, and this elevated him above other previous writers of naval history. To Mahan, sea power could do for the US what it had done for Great Britain: serve as a political instrument that could "enhance the nation's power and prestige." He wrote that "Naval strategy has for its end to found, support, and increase, as well in peace as in war, the sea power of a country." Moreover, Mahan insisted, human nature remained the same.[107]

The essence of naval strategy was control of the sea. This necessitated naval power, which allowed one to drive the enemy's commerce from the ocean, damaging the foe's economic strength and allowing blockade of his ports. But faced by an enemy with a strong fleet, overcoming it with your own naval force in what became known as a "Mahanian" decisive battle was the most important course of action. This necessitated keeping the fleet concentrated at critical points and never dispersed or divided. Mahan also examined the concept of a "fleet in being." Here, an inferior naval power holds its forces in port as a way of restricting the enemy's use of its own fleet because it must counter the potential threat of the enemy's "fleet in being." Mahan believed the value of such a force "much overstated."[108]

Mahan's work – and the worldwide acclaim it received – helped catalyze American naval development that had already begun. The US had the sixth largest fleet in the world in 1898. Mahan was originally anti-imperialist, but navies needed bases and coaling stations, and this drove his imperialism, which included pressing for a canal across Panama. His arguments don't lack critics. His conception of concentration is operational and not strategic, and he blends the operational and strategic realms in a manner common in theoretical writing prior to the Second World War. Others see Mahan as a "gross oversimplifier" because he promoted "a single explanation for the complex sweep of history" – sea power.[109]

CONCLUSION

As the nineteenth century ended, the US had firm control over a continental space that soon encompassed forty-eight states. It was organized into territories, linked by railroads, and tied together under the sovereignty of an American government. The Indians that had inspired fear among Americans since the first settlers arrived in the New World were grouped on reservations and were in many ways wards of the state. There were minor outbursts of violence to come, but Indians never again posed a threat. But the United States would continue expanding, though in a way novel for America.

6

AMERICAN EMPIRE, 1897–1913

INTRODUCTION

Theodore Roosevelt referred to "imperialism" as "Americanism." Senator Henry Cabot Lodge described it as the "large policy." Mahan called it what it was: "the extension of national authority over alien communities." But why did America become an imperial power? America faced no threat that encouraged expansion in self-defense. Secretary of State Richard Olney wrote in 1895: "Today, the United States is practically sovereign on this continent ... [i]ts infinite resources combined with its isolated position render it master of the situation and practically invulnerable as against any or all other powers." It didn't arise from the desire to increase foreign markets by government or business. The domestic market was more important. Overseas expansion was partly a continuation of the ongoing pattern of seizing geographic positions deemed necessary for the nation's future security. Relatedly, a stronger US with expanding interests involved itself in disputes Western Hemisphere states had among themselves and with Europe. The US also began doing what John Quincy Adams advised against: going abroad in search of monsters to slay. And first did so "to free a damsel in distress."[1]

THE WILLIAM J. McKINLEY ADMINISTRATION, 1897–1901

William McKinley ran for president on an 1896 Republican Party platform depicting his political aims: he wanted US control of the West Indies and Hawaii, and a canal across Nicaragua. He was a great believer in the power and necessity of American foreign trade. It relieved fears of overproduction at home while spreading American capitalist values abroad, something he saw in US interests. But he also believed in the traditional American diplomatic strategy of disentanglement and praised Washington's warning to keep out of other's affairs. McKinley believed "greater power and influence for his nation would also promote the betterment of mankind."

His platform pledged laboring for peace or independence in Cuba. He deflected intervention upon becoming president and tried to resolve tensions diplomatically.[2] This worked for a while.

THE SPANISH–AMERICAN WAR: APRIL TO DECEMBER 1898

The catalyst for the Spanish–American War was yet another rebellion in Cuba (see Maps 6.1 and 6.2); 1895's grew increasingly bloody. Spain's *reconcentrado* – concentrating civilians in camps or fortified towns – killed perhaps 100,000 Cubans. An enraged American public was not driven by economic or imperialist conspiracies but sympathy for Cubans fighting for independence. America's financial community opposed the war, fearing inflation or the gold standard's abandonment. American support for war was as an early manifestation of the liberal crusading impulse. John C. Spooner, a Republican senator from Wisconsin, said, "we intervene for humanity's sake ... to aid a people who have suffered every form of tyranny and who have made a desperate struggle to be free." Republican Senator Shelby M. Cullom of Illinois said he would back war "*only* if it was fought in the name of liberty."[3]

But why did McKinley take America to war? The effects of American "Yellow Journalism" have been exaggerated. The atrocity stories they played up (some even true) reflected more than shaped American feeling. McKinley understood public sentiment and the possible economic effects, but these weren't decisive. Both parties used Cuba as a whip. The Democrats – the party out of power – cried for war, seeing support for Cuba's rebels as a bludgeon against Republicans and a tool for regaining power. McKinley's Republicans were split. Some were expansionist, others feared the economic effects and discouraged action. Supporters of the war such as Mahan thought US control of the Caribbean necessary to protect a future isthmian canal. McKinley would have avoided the war if possible. The accidental sinking of the *Maine* in Havana Harbor, and the public's reaction, made peace politically impossible. Moreover, "McKinley's ability to postpone war for as long as he did and to control the terms on which the United States commenced hostilities indicates that his presidential leadership ... was more courageous and principled than his critics have realized."[4]

PREWAR STRATEGY

The Cleveland administration tried and failed to negotiate a settlement leaving Spain in control of Cuba. McKinley dispatched a new ambassador

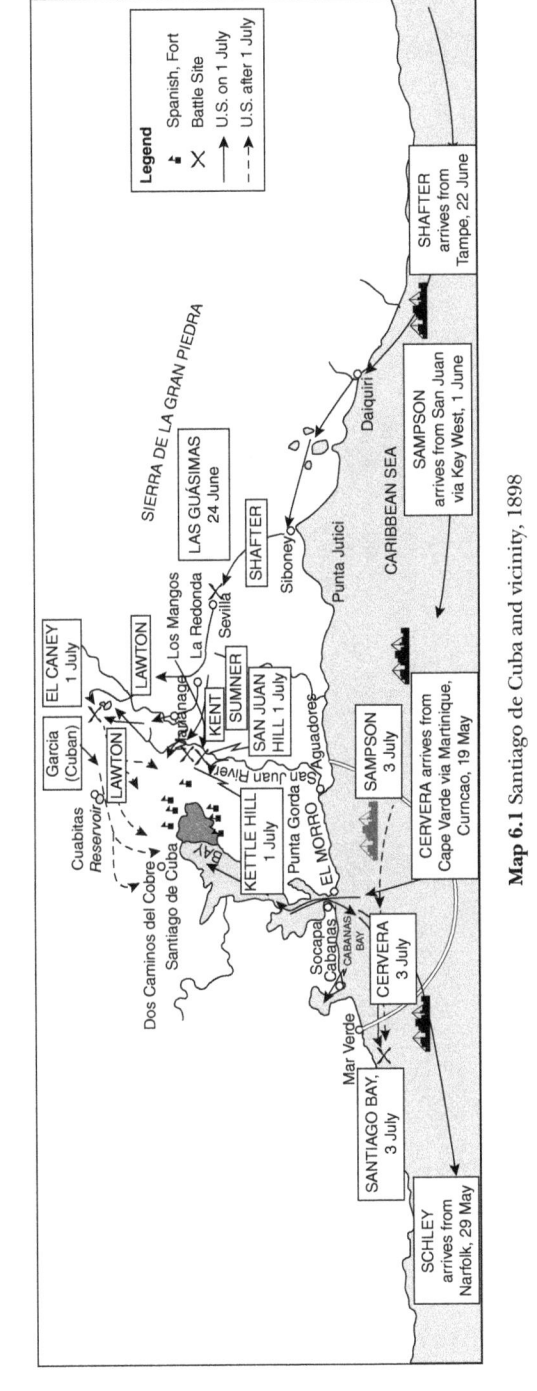

Map 6.1 Santiago de Cuba and vicinity, 1898

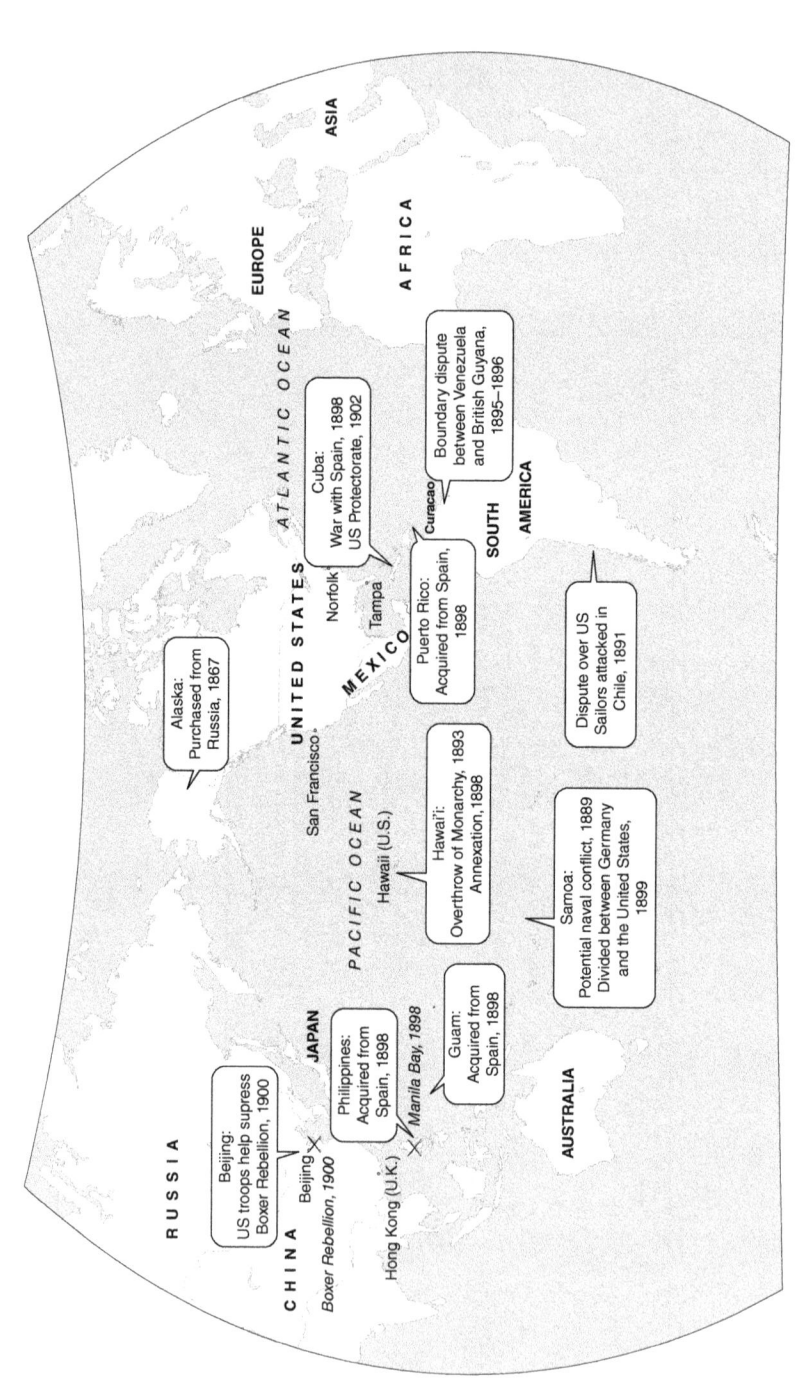

Map 6.2 Expansionism: The United States in the Spanish–American War, 1898–1902

to warn that if the war weren't soon settled, public opinion would force McKinley to act. He wanted a reply by November 1, 1897. McKinley was pressuring Spain to abandon Cuba without a war, assuming that since Americans believed it was in Spain's interest to let Cuba go, Madrid would see the same thing.[5] This is poor reasoning. The other side decides its interests and material factors aren't the only variables. Prestige and honor can be important.

McKinley's message, though, had an effect, undoubtedly partly because a liberal government replaced Spain's conservative one, albeit one publicly insisting it wouldn't surrender Cuba. It ended *reconcentrado*, granted autonomy, an amnesty, and freedom to US citizens jailed in Cuba. The administration claimed success. McKinley wanted to give Spain's reforms time to work but didn't remove the diplomatic thumb. He ensured the fleet was in the Caribbean in January 1898 and issued what we now call a "stop loss" order to keep sailors with expiring enlistments. Other issues fed desire for resolving the Cuba situation. Berlin's occupation of Kiaochow, China, and its "gunboat diplomacy" against Haiti convinced officials Germany aimed at New World acquisitions. Instability could create problems.[6]

Riots met Spanish reform efforts, and McKinley faced Democratic Congressional pressure to act. This, combined with fears of attacks on Americans in Cuba and belief more pressure should be put on Madrid, produced the dispatch of a US warship. The *Maine* arrived in Havana, Cuba, on January 25, 1898. Spain rushed war preparations and rejected, on February 1, 1898, McKinley's insistence on monitoring progress of Spain's autonomy program and Washington's right to fix a deadline for Spanish action. Uproar followed the leaking of a letter purloined from Spain's minister to Washington, Enrique Dupuy de Lôme, in which he criticized McKinley as "weak and a bidder for the admiration of the crowd." De Lôme's resignation and Spain's apology (albeit a slow one) were penance enough for McKinley; many others disagreed.[7]

Then came the mysterious February 15, 1898 explosion that sank the *Maine*. Most Americans saw Spanish perfidy. McKinley preferred to let an investigation determine the cause while pressuring Spain and preparing. On March 25, the enquiry concluded *Maine* had suffered an external explosion, implying a mine. Modern investigators believe the cause was an internal detonation, "perhaps the spontaneous combustion of coal adjacent to the ship's ammunition magazines."[8] Several nations suffered unexplained explosions in the early battleship era.

McKinley didn't want war and tried desperately to avoid it. A Civil War veteran of Antietam and other fields, McKinley said: "I shall never get into a war until I am sure that God and man approve. I have been through one war; I have seen the dead pile up; and I do not want to see another." McKinley tried diplomacy yet again. The Spanish bent on arbitration regarding the *Maine*, but refused to grant Cuba independence, which was what mattered. McKinley still sought a peaceful solution, twice postponing his Congressional "war message," which he finally delivered on April 11. McKinley asked Congress to "authorize and empower the President to take measures to secure a full and final termination of hostilities between the Government of Spain and the people of Cuba," the leeway to establish a government on the island, and approval to use the military to do this. But he didn't ask for war and mentioned Spain's recent decision to grant a suspension of fighting. If this didn't bear fruit, though, he believed it even more necessary for Congress to act.[9]

On April 19, Congress declared Cuba independent, authorized McKinley to drive out the Spanish, and forbade American annexation of Cuba via the Teller Amendment. Congress sent McKinley the bill on April 20. He signed it the same day. Spain severed relations. The US blockaded Cuba on April 22 and McKinley asked for a declaration or war on the 25th. Congress declared a state of war had existed since the 21st.[10]

THE POLITICAL AIMS

An oddity about the US war against Spain was that the primary political aim was *Cuban* independence. Congress specifically authorized the president to intervene to establish an independent government. The US had no intention of annexing the island (which McKinley publicly opposed) and barred itself from doing so. But once the war began, McKinley said: "While we are conducting war and until its conclusion we must keep all we get; when the war is over we must keep what we want." The administration annexed Hawaii to forestall a feared future Japanese effort. McKinley said: "We need Hawaii as much and a good deal more than we did California. It is manifest destiny."[11]

ASSESSMENT, PREPARATION, AND PREWAR PLANNING

As usual, the US wasn't prepared militarily. The miniscule army numbered 28,000 personnel scattered on bases stretching the continent. It hadn't trained in units larger than a regiment and possessed no mobilization plan. Supplementing it were 100,000 poorly trained and equipped National Guard forces. Congress eventually allowed the recruitment of 210,000 volunteers, some drawn from the Guard, and doubled the official size of the army to 65,000. But the US lacked the equipment and organization to effectively manage such growth and training proved inadequate. The navy had benefited from various modernization programs and was in better shape.[12]

On February 25, 1898, after the *Maine*'s sinking, Assistant Secretary of the Navy Theodore Roosevelt ordered Commodore George Dewey to concentrate his vessels at Hong Kong and, if war broke out, destroy the Spanish fleet in the Philippines. This incident is sometimes portrayed as Roosevelt usurping the position of a weak superior. Roosevelt's February 25 order was part of the navy's prewar preparations, and the "actual directive to attack the Spanish at Manilla Bay was based on McKinley's decision."[13]

The first plan for war against Spain emerged from the Naval War College in 1894; others followed from various sources. Because of the new insurrection, Secretary of the Navy John Long formed a War Board under Rear Admiral Montgomery Sicard, and its proposals became fodder for elements of American strategy: a blockade of Cuba, supporting the insurgents, attacking Spanish forces in Puerto Rico and the Philippines, dispatching a naval force to Spanish waters, and chartering civilian vessels for logistical and transportation needs. Neither the army nor navy spent much time learning about Cuba or its defenders, and there was no logistical preparation for what must by necessity be an expeditionary war. America's unpreparedness was one reason McKinley resisted war.[14]

GRAND STRATEGY

As we saw above, the navy had long planned for operations against Spain's colonies. Military force aligned with diplomacy proved the primary American strategic tools. These would be used to try to end the war quickly. But McKinley also wanted US casualties kept low. There would be no attacks on Spain itself or heavily defended Havana.[15]

When the war began, McKinley quickly lost confidence in Secretary of War Russell M. Alger, Commanding General of the Army Nelson Miles, and Secretary of the Navy Long. Adjutant General Henry C. Corbin became McKinley's most important military advisor. McKinley set up a war room in the White House for running the conflict, the first president to do so. It had twenty telegraph lines and could exchange messages with Major General William Shafter in Cuba within 20 minutes. For the first time, a US president could intervene directly in a war zone without leaving the capital. And McKinley did. For example, during negotiations for surrender of Spain's Cuba forces, he ensured inclusion of tougher language.[16]

PART I: FROM BACKWATER TO GREAT POWER

MILITARY STRATEGY

In March 1898, Secretary of the Navy Long organized a formal Naval War Board to provide advice on strategy and operations and create a new war plan. Roosevelt led it. Mahan joined in May and proved influential, though the board's recommendations drew upon previous work. On April 21, William T. Sampson, commander of the North Atlantic Squadron acting rear admiral, was ordered to blockade Cuba, which became preparation for concentrating the navy to strike Spain's fleet. Sampson saw as his primary task defeating Spanish naval forces entering the theater, a rational concern, as Spain dispatched a fleet under Admiral Pascual Cervera. Sampson also planned to support the army. The blockade began on April 23. It severed Spanish troops from resupply, interrupted Madrid's Caribbean trade, ensured its navy couldn't use Havana's port, and gained Washington time to build invasion forces.[17]

After war was declared, McKinley hesitated to order an attack by Dewey. No one knows why. He approved the fleet's dispatch on April 24. Dewey reached Manilla Bay on May 1 and destroyed the seven obsolescent Spanish vessels without losing a man. But no one had planned what to do afterward. After two weeks in the Bay, Dewey requested 5,000 troops to take the city. McKinley expected this, knowing the neutrality laws made Manilla Dewey's only useable port. Major General Wesley Merritt's force was dispatched to take Manilla. Merritt asked McKinley if he was "to subdue and hold all of the Spanish territory in the islands, or merely to seize and hold its capital." He was told that making peace with Spain necessitated the occupation of the islands to break Spanish power (seizing Spanish possessions was part of American strategy). Merritt was to ensure order while the islands remained in US hands.[18]

Dewey and Miles were unsure why the US was in the Philippines, and the army had no plan to conquer the islands. Being uncertain about the objectives of the mission, and ignorant of the Philippines in general, produced disagreement over the force necessary for the task, whatever that might be. Miles, who anticipated little opposition, thought 5,000 National Guard troops sufficient. Merritt wanted more, especially regulars, insisting Spain hadn't been defeated and that the Filipinos would oppose the Americans. Meanwhile, Dewey blockaded Manilla and waited. Another complicating issue was the arrival of French, British, and German naval squadrons. Berlin had imperialist designs on the islands, and its commander had orders to take part or all of the Philippines if the Americans granted it independence. The first US troops arrived on July 4. By month's end, there were 15,000 preparing to attack Manilla. The commander of the Spanish garrison refused to surrender as he had orders to mount at least a token defense. A deal was struck, and an American–Filipino attack launched, but confusion produced more gunfire and casualties than anticipated. The Spanish surrendered on August 13, 1898.[19]

Meanwhile, to remove the Spanish from Cuba, Miles wanted to raise 80,000 troops built around the regular army and didn't want to land in Cuba before October because of the danger of disease. This stunned McKinley, who said: "God willing and not failing us, we shall end the war before the General would have us begin operations. He little understands me; no more does he know the temper of our people. I deplore the war, but it must be short and quick to the finish." The army had no war plans for Cuba and no intelligence on the enemy or the island. The raising of the necessary force is a case study in disorganization, incompetence, and widespread mismanagement.[20]

After Dewey's destruction of the Spanish fleet, and while the invasion preparations continued, McKinley attempted – secretly – to negotiate peace. If Spain would abandon Cuba, which the US would guide to independence, and give the US Puerto Rico, the US wouldn't take the Philippines, though it did want a coaling station there or in the Caroline Islands. Spain refused. McKinley gambled with his peace effort as there were many – including Theodore Roosevelt – already pleading the necessity of taking the Philippines, something McKinley had no desire to do.[21]

The secretary of the navy ordered the fleet concentrated at Key West. Fear about an inopportune arrival of Spain's fleet delayed the invasion, but it slipped through the blockade and arrived in Santiago de Cuba on May 19, 1898. Its arrival ended debate on where to attack as landing either side of Santiago would trap the Spanish between the army and navy. The joint army–navy operation mounted near Santiago lacked an overall commander. Sampson and Shafter cooperated, but one couldn't order the other to act, and they disagreed upon how to strike Santiago. Shafter worried about Spanish naval gunfire against his troops if they attacked the city and wanted the navy to destroy this threat first. The navy was concerned about mines and shore batteries and wanted the army to reduce the guns before it fought Spain's warships. Sampson's orders forbid risking ships in a mined passage protected by guns. The poor health of both plagued the Americans as much of the time they were too ill to consult one another.[22]

The army honored the navy's request (and public pressure to act) by ordering the dispatch of forces from Tampa Bay, Florida. The city, chosen because of its geographical proximity to Cuba, was unsuitable as a departure port. A single rail line fed the harbor, which had one pier for loading. The order to sail for Santiago went out on May 31, but since there was no plan, it took two weeks to load the units, their supplies, and equipment. A fleet carrying 17,000 men sailed on June 14 and arrived off Santiago on the 20th. Lacking the necessary heavy guns to assault Santiago, Shafter took the advice of insurgent leader General Calixto Garcia and landed east of the city at Daiquiri and Siboney between 22 and 24 June. It was conducted so slowly and ineptly that significant resistance could have probably stopped it. The Spanish had 36,000 troops in Santiago province of their 200,000 in Cuba. Some 5,000 guerrillas fought beside 17,000 Americans.[23]

The Americans made two advances toward Santiago, one lightly opposed, and were soon 5 miles from San Juan Heights on the edge of the city. The near-immediate effects of tropical disease combined with the coming hurricane season to convince Shafter to mount a quick attack against Santiago on July 1, one including the Rough Riders' assault on San Juan Heights. Its coordination came apart under impoverished organization, rough terrain, and the effects of tropical heat. The latter debilitated the obese Shafter, who handed over control to subordinates. US troops carried the day.[24]

Fearing the effects of illness upon his men, Shafter told his superiors he was considering a 5-mile withdrawal to better ground. Secretary of War Alger told him "the effect upon the country would be much better" if he held his position. Shafter then tried unsuccessfully to get the navy to penetrate the bay. Spain resolved America's problems. Shafter, driven by McKinley, mounted demonstrations against Santiago. Believing the city would soon fall, Admiral Cervera, who had orders to sortie the fleet if this appeared inevitable, did so. Knowing the blockaders' routine, he chose a time on Sunday morning, July 3, when the enemy was farthest from the harbor. Coincidentally, Sampson was heading ashore to meet with Shafter. In Sampson's absence, his captains did as they had been taught and pursued. The Americans, possessing superior ships, quickly caught, sank, or immobilized the Spanish vessels.[25]

Shafter proved particularly irresolute, and only pressure from Alger and McKinley prevented him from retreating from Santiago after the fleet's destruction. But he convinced Santiago's defenders their position was hopeless. Terms were agreed on July 16 and Santiago capitulated the next day. The Cuban insurgents played a key role in the victory, having weakened the Spanish before the US landed and made them dependent upon imported supplies, thus increasing the blockade's effectiveness.[26]

ENDING THE WAR WITH SPAIN

The American victories placed the US in a position to make demands. Washington had destroyed most of the Spanish navy and could now attack Spain's coastline. Madrid couldn't reinforce or resupply its garrisons abroad. And it wanted peace. In reply to Spain's July 30 armistice request, McKinley demanded Madrid evacuate and relinquish sovereignty over Cuba, surrender Puerto Rico and its other West Indian possessions, an island to be named later in the Marianas (this became Guam), and the right to hold Manilla, its bay, and harbor until a peace treaty decided the Philippines' destiny. Madrid released Cuba but refused to cede Puerto Rico, Guam, or the Philippines. McKinley maintained a hard line. Lacking options, Spain buckled (though one can't blame them for trying – delay can be a useful negotiating tool). Modifications addressed Spanish concerns regarding the ambiguity of the Philippines and added an agreement appointing Peace Commissioners. McKinley decided to annex Puerto Rico, on which the Americans had landed on July 25 and fought a short campaign, believing it too dangerous to have it in foreign hands if the US built an isthmian canal. An armistice (not peace treaty) was signed on August 12, 1898. McKinley tightly controlled negotiations and the terms conformed to ones he penned upon receiving Spain's negotiation offer.[27]

But this left the Philippines. Many factors complicated McKinley's decision here. Germany eyed the archipelago. Filipino insurgents had declared their own government. McKinley didn't want the islands. He understood empire allured some, but he thought they would find it unattractive upon learning the costs and challenges. McKinley exerted enormous effort trying to decide what to do. He dispatched Brigadier General Francis Vinton Greene (a grandson of Nathanael Greene) on a factfinding mission, read extensively, consulted his cabinet, Dewey, and others in the Philippines, and prayed. He concluded US occupation was the least bad option. Returning the islands to Spain meant another power taking them and probably another war, one for which the US would be responsible because it had failed to do its duty regarding the Philippines. It couldn't hand the islands to Emilio Aguinaldo's Filipino rebels because until there was a peace treaty, the islands remained Spain's under international law. McKinley decided the islands would be moved to self-government, just like Cuba, and dispatched a commission to help do this. But war broke out between the Americans and Filipinos before the commission assumed its offices. It tried anyway and offered a form of self-government under American suzerainty. Aguinaldo pushed the rebels toward an arrangement but failed. The Filipinos would fight.[28]

Meanwhile, negotiations with Madrid over the Philippines continued, and Spain held firm. As the negotiations dragged on, the Spanish began hoping in November 1898 that the results of the Congressional elections would hurt McKinley. The opposite proved the case. The Republican Congressional majority shrank, but state victories gave them control over the then appointed Senate. An empowered McKinley demanded annexation by right of conquest. Madrid bent, domestic unrest and fear of a potential US attack driving them. The December 10, 1898 treaty gave the US the Philippines, Guam, and Puerto Rico; Spain got $20 million. Cuba received its independence. McKinley ensured ratification by wisely including a Democratic Party anti-imperialist Senator in the negotiating team.[29]

THE AFTERMATH

To finance the war, Congress increased taxes, relying heavily upon "sin" and luxury taxes, but even more so on – of all things – a stamp tax on financial transactions. Debt covered $48 million of the $274 million price tag. In 1902, the total war cost was estimated at $211 million, roughly 1 percent of US GDP.[30]

America for the first time acquired lands it never intended to make states, while also believing it "had a mission to transplant civilization," meaning American civilization. This created a strange dichotomy: "the United States acted both on the racial assumption that its colonies were not fit to participate fully in national life and on the nonracial assumption that they could, in time, be taught the American way. One historian shrewdly observed: 'The imperialist compromise was to allow the flag to advance *but to deny that the Constitution followed the flag.*'"[31]

The war coincided with the rise of what we call the Progressive era, meaning a time of great governmental and social reform lasting until the 1920s. Progressivism and imperialism were intertwined and laced with a similar utopianism. Herbert Croly, founder of the Progressive journal *The New Republic*, cheered the Spanish–American War, insisting it "had *launched* the whole Progressive Era because it delivered 'a tremendous impulse to the work of reform.'" McKinley and others believed America could establish freedom and good governance in these new lands, and Progressives swept in to perform every imaginable reform whether the inhabitants wanted it or not.[32]

The US now dominated the Caribbean and Central America, and its relationship with Cuba became quasi-colonial. To end American occupation, Cuba was required to include the terms of the 1901 Platt Amendment in its constitution. This prevented Cuba from linking itself to a foreign state, gave the US a base at Guantanamo, and the right (obligation, really) to intervene to maintain a Cuban government that guaranteed "the protection of life, property and individual liberty." A trade reciprocity agreement followed in 1903. In the Pacific, the US occupied and claimed uninhabited Wake Island. In 1900, McKinley ordered a coaling station built in American Samoa. The control of these territories and Hawaii secured America's sea lines of communication with the Philippines.[33]

THE WAR FOR THE PHILIPPINES

McKinley's decision to take the Philippines sparked a national debate on America's role in Asia. Some see here an example of mission creep; it was really a problem created by having unclear political aims. Opposition came from the Anti-Imperialist League and its allies, an odd coalition including industrialist cum philanthropist Andrew Carnegie, populist politician William Jennings Bryan, labor figure Samuel Gompers, racists, and anti–big business and anti-immigrant groups. The leaders were primarily east coast intellectuals who saw in American imperialism an attack on the "real" America. They critiqued on constitutional grounds seizing lands the US never intended to make states and saw here the harbingers of militarism, the corruption of democracy, and what they deemed the unfortunate addition to America of more non-Whites. On the other side were the imperialists, or "jingoists." They grounded their argument in a supposedly *Realpolitik* belief that securing the Philippines was necessary for American defense. Some of their reasons bore the racial overtones of an American civilizing mission. Religious beliefs sometimes played a part. Teddy Roosevelt sat initially among the *Realpolitik* group but later branded the Philippines "a military Achilles heel and an economic drain." Most Americans simply didn't care.[34]

THE ASSESSMENT

American involvement in the Philippines was marked by many classic decision-making mistakes: the political, strategic, and operational objectives were unclear; there was neither a plan for seizing the islands nor for what to do afterward; and US leaders understood nothing about the Philippines or its people. It had an ethnically, linguistically, and religiously diverse population of over 7 million on 7,000 islands scattered across 500,000 square miles, Luzon the largest. The inhabitants spoke numerous languages and were often separated by water, jungle, and rugged terrain. The population was Catholic, except for the Muslim Moros on Mindanao and Sula. The educated classes often spoke Spanish. The *principales*, landowners and businessmen, along with government officials, dominated local politics.[35]

An anti-Spanish independence movement began in the mid nineteenth century. Andrés Bonifacio's *Katipunan*, or Society of the Sons of the People, was created in 1892. An active insurgency began in 1896. Emilio Aguinaldo became leader by having Bonifacio accused of treason and executed. On the same day, May 10, 1897, Aguinaldo declared the Biak-na-Bato Republic. The rebellion intensified and Spain agreed to negotiate. Madrid amnestied the leaders, allowed them to go into exile, and paid reparations. Washington invited Aguinaldo to the Philippines after Dewey's victory, hoping he would help against Spain. Aguinaldo reached Manilla on May 19, 1898. He insisted Dewey told him the Philippines would become independent (which Dewey denied) and asked Aguinaldo to encourage insurrection. On May 23, Aguinaldo named himself dictator until order was restored, declared the Philippines independent on June 12, and established a revolutionary government on June 23. But Aguinaldo's revolution was political, not social. Power would remain in the *principales*' hands.[36]

THE WAR BEGINS

Aguinaldo's forces complicated America's position. They wanted to enter Manila, but the Americans stopped them. Dewey and Merritt also had unclear direction from Washington. Merritt's poor health saw his August 29 replacement by Elwell S. Otis, an Indian expert, graduate of Harvard Law School, and "one of the Army's Armed Progressives." Otis finally received clear instructions on December 21: extend official American control over the entire archipelago. The army was to behave benevolently, forcing rebels to submit but also protecting Filipino rights and property. McKinley wrote: "the mission of the United States is one of benevolent assimilation, substituting the mild sway of justice and right for arbitrary rule." But Aguinaldo and his followers wanted independence. The political aims were irreconcilable.[37]

Fighting began on February 4, 1899, with an exchange of fire between US and Filipino patrols (how is unclear), and developed into a battle for control of Manila the next day. The eruption surprised Aguinaldo, but the Philippine Army of Liberation (15–40,000) had maintained a porous ring of positions around US forces in Manila for months. The Americans had around 20,000 troops in Manila and its environs and won the two-week struggle for the city. This was probably Aguinaldo's best chance to succeed; the Filipinos were never this strong again.[38]

STRATEGY

To emerge victorious, the counter-insurrectionist must separate the enemy from sanctuary, support from the people, and external aid. The US – slowly – implemented a strategy that did so. Otis decided controlling Northern Luzon was the path to success. It held the rebel capital of Malolos, its government, leaders, and primary army. The destruction or capture of these, Otis believed, meant victory. Otis decided to cut the Filipino army's lines of supply and communication to the south, keep the enemy forces in these areas off-balance with raids, and launch a campaign to encircle Aguinaldo's army and destroy it while seizing Luzon's northern, non-Tagalog areas.[39]

Otis's strategy had problems. First, it suffered from a poor assessment that gave him a flawed understanding of the nature of the war. Otis believed most Filipinos would gladly accept US sovereignty if not for the machinations of Aguinaldo and the Tagalog, and that non-Tagalog awaited freedom from Tagalog oppression. Secondly, Otis didn't have enough men to hold Manilla and drive into Luzon. His force had risen to about 26,000, but garrisoning Manilla and other places left him a maneuver strength of only 16,000. As he drove deeper into Luzon, this number fell because of the need to protect his lines of communication. Otis consistently underestimated his manpower requirements. His November 1898 estimate of 25,000 went to 30,000 when the war began, then 60,000 in late June 1899. The expiration of volunteer enlistments also plagued him. Otis had to make do until fall 1899 when the army had expanded. He hoped to then have 70,000 troops.[40]

THE CONVENTIONAL WAR

Otis took Caloocan outside of Manilla, but then delayed for a month a push against Aguinaldo's capital of Malolos because he hoped the enemy's army would mass there. He also began isolating the insurrectionists from their sources of food and supplies. Intelligence from the army and the municipal police revealed the extent to which Manilla and its environs acted as a fount for rebel material and financial support. Otis instituted controls to stop this.[41]

The campaign for Malolos jumped off on March 25. Opposing Otis was Antonio Luna, the commander of the Filipino army. Temperamental, driven, and sometimes cruel, Luna worked to build a Filipino army capable of battling the Americans conventionally and chose to fight a positional war against a better-trained, -armed, and -led opponent. The Filipinos were battered and outmaneuvered, suffering crippling and irreplaceable losses in trained men, weapons, and material. The twin-pronged campaign restarted in earnest on April 24, 1899, but the harsh terrain and weather wore down the Americans, forcing them to stop by mid May. The offensive didn't destroy the Filipino army or force a surrender, but did demoralize it.[42]

Aguinaldo requested a three-week armistice to gather his officials and discuss terms. Otis refused unless the Filipinos put aside their weapons, but he did order a pause while he deduced what was going on. Aguinaldo's representatives arrived in Manilla on May 2 proposing a ceasefire for three months wrapped in terms requiring recognition of a sovereign Filipino republic. Otis believed the negotiations an attempt to stall, and this confirmed it. He rebuffed the effort but handed the representatives the administration's plan for a Filipino government. The subsequent negotiations convinced many this was a good idea. They returned to Aguinaldo, ousted the hardline president of their council of advisors, and dispatched delegates to discuss surrender. Luna intervened, seized the delegates, and sent his own, which destroyed the talks and saw Otis restart the offensive. As the enlistments of some volunteer units were expiring, Otis had to settle for holding areas roughly 40 miles north of Manilla until reinforcements arrived in autumn.[43]

The stalemate that descended in 1899's summer saw Otis reassess. He believed the revolt still possessed strength but that another six months would finish the Army of Liberation. But defeating their military forces wouldn't itself deliver victory. The US had to demonstrate to the people that it wasn't leaving, and that American rule was advantageous. Otis pressed McKinley and Congress for a postwar governance plan. Meanwhile, in July 1899, Otis seized upon a civilian governance program composed by one of his officers, believing its implementation would help convince Filipinos of American good offices while preparing the shift to civilian control. Each town would be run by a council composed of a mayor, vice mayor, and a representative from each *barrio*. The council could pass only taxes necessary to fund the municipal staff and services, including a police force, and were required to show their books to the local army commander monthly to prevent corruption. This became General Order No. 43.[44]

The Americans knew they couldn't control the entire archipelago without Filipino assistance and began raising Filipino police and military units, a common colonial practice. Many officers were suspicious of building Filipino police forces. Despite a push from Washington for this, Otis resisted paying them from his funds, as well as arming them, which retarded their development. When Arthur MacArthur succeeded Otis in command in May 1900, he created city police forces and mounted constabulary but resisted properly arming them until the departure of some of his volunteers in December 1900 left him no choice. He expanded local forces, and they became some of the most effective counterinsurgency tools.[45]

In August 1899, Americans took advantage of their sea control and implemented a blockade to halt waterborne traffic defined as "illicit." Most seaborne trade became illegal, and the US closed all but three ports: Cebu City, Iloilo City, and Manilla. The blockade isolated Filipino forces and separated them from reinforcements, money, and supplies, especially food. Resistance collapsed in a few areas because of the danger of starvation. The blockade, though, sometime hindered reestablishing local order and commerce.[46]

The arrival of reinforcements and the departure of the rainy season allowed Otis to launch what he hoped would be the war's final campaign. He planned to destroy Filipino forces in northern Luzon by encircling and trapping them via a three-pronged offensive, eliminating Aguinaldo's government and army. He would then turn south, clear Luzon, and occupy the rest of the archipelago. The terrain, transportation problems, and enemy attacks ensured Otis' plan didn't work as intended, though it succeeded operationally. By November 19, 1899, the Filipino army and government were nearly destroyed. By December, Otis believed the war was essentially over and began dispersing his forces for pacification and reconstruction. He believed he needed only to finish the few remaining enemy forces and garrison the major towns. He began clearing the Tagalog areas south of Manila in January 1900, but the resistance proved greater than anticipated, and the guerrilla struggle had already begun.[47]

COUNTERINSURGENCY AND NATION BUILDING

Luna died in mysterious circumstances after a scuffle with Aguinaldo's bodyguard. Defeat and the Filipino army's wilting spirits reduced its numbers to about 4,000 by summer 1899's end. Aguinaldo could have used the American summer pause to prepare for a guerrilla struggle but did little. Local leaders were shifting to guerrilla war on their own. Aguinaldo's February 1899 creation of political-military command areas eased this. On November 13, 1899, Aguinaldo finally abandoned conventional resistance. The Filipinos now tried to wear down their opponents to convince them to grant Filipino independence. The main planks of Filipino strategy: attrition via guerrilla war, forbidding the people from working with the enemy, and (later) a fall 1900 offensive intended to undermine McKinley's reelection bid by helping his opponent, who supported Filipino independence.[48] The best chance the Filipinos had of achieving their aim was protracting the war, but they bet on something they didn't control and had little power to affect: an American presidential election.

The Filipinos also undermined their support among the people. They failed to secure the help of the *ladrones*, essentially bandit groups operating in the countryside, and concentrated on winning over the *principales*, the large landowners, who considered the *ladrones* a threat. The result was they fought the *ladrones* and the Americans. Aguinaldo ignored the bulk of the population, which the US won over by demonstrating it was there to help. The *principales* became native leaders dedicated to American success because this preserved their political and economic positions. Their banditry and corruption enabled the Americans to paint the Filipino guerrillas as criminals and seize the law-and-order mantle. The insurgency was strongest in January 1900 and declined thereafter.[49]

Local American garrison commanders carried pacification's burdens. As the Americans secured areas and built local governance and intelligence networks, this destroyed the guerrillas' sources of supply and separated them from their native areas. Their personalities, ability to convince the local population of their sincerity, and their will to succeed proved instrumental. One US officer noted a classic problem: "This business of fighting and civilizing and educating at the same time doesn't mix very well. Peace is needed first." Local elites soon concluded it was in their interests to side with America to keep their lands. Food control also became an important pacification tool. The Americans also made mistakes. They proved slow to develop intelligence networks and exploit captured documents. Army leaders gradually realized they needed intelligence to break the insurgent infrastructure and began running secret agents in the winter of 1899. All intelligence actions quickly expanded.[50]

Otis underestimated the resistance's scale but understood victory required controlling the population and separating them from the insurrectionists. Otis and other army leaders also knew that here the enemy's dispersal required their own. When Aguinaldo shifted to a guerrilla war, the army drastically expanded its outposts on the Archipelago to 639. These provided bases for launching units against the guerrillas and their territory. Dispersal protected the population and established civilian governance that could eventually replace military control. Building roads and telegraph systems was important. The army believed establishing schools immensely valuable and founded at least 1,000 by August 1900.[51]

At the time of his departure in May 1900, Otis declared the US faced virtually no organized guerrilla resistance, only bandits. Despite this obvious error, Otis had constructed a solid strategy that left his successor the building blocks for victory. Colonel William E. Birkhimer described it:

> The object was to make things as uncomfortable as possible for the enemy, thus pursuing the policy [strategy] which alone, apparently, will break down the rebel resistance, namely, the wearing-out policy [exhaustion strategy]; pounding away until the bandit chiefs get tired of living in hiding in the far distant mountains, and the people wearying of their importunate demands for money and their impotent military efforts, withdraw their material and moral support.[52]

When MacArthur took command, he inherited a rapidly progressing program of civic action that was restoring stability and peace to the countryside. But Otis had of late ignored counterinsurgency's military aspects. MacArthur watched his casualties climb nearly to the levels suffered during the conventional fights to clear Luzon. He also didn't have enough men. MacArthur's May 28, 1900 plan projected holding the islands with a force of 45,000 by March 1, 1901, reducing the number of posts, and concentrating forces in areas from which they could move against rural threats. Instead, he eventually increased posts by one-third. He expanded the constabulary and native scouts, asked for money for roads, and granted an amnesty, one with meager results.[53]

One of the difficulties facing US forces was determining how they could and should deal with guerrillas and their supporters. One commander found the solution in May 1900 in the Civil War's 1863 General Order No. 100, also known as the Lieber Code after its author, Francis Lieber. Though neither Otis nor MacArthur officially promulgated it, their subordinates began operating under its guidelines. This combined conciliation with violence, and allowed harsh treatment of guerrillas and their supporters. It obligated government forces to treat civilians properly but also committed them to establishing order. Resistance to this effort was criminal, and guerrillas and those supporting them faced confiscation or destruction of their property, imprisonment, or execution. This was also used by officers who believed the brutality of the guerrilla war being waged meant the army needed to do less conciliating and more killing. The army generally behaved within the bounds authorized by General Order No. 100, but as the war extended and became more violent, there were examples of American excesses, including torture. But the number of such incidents has been exaggerated.[54]

In dealing with the population, Otis initially used light measures and just treatment recommended in Birkhimer's *Military Government and Martial*

Law to gain the population's trust. The army was to respect local customs, not loot, and treat the people well, actions partially inspired by Winfield Scott's strategy in Mexico. Accompanying the good behavior was building of schools, roads, and other infrastructure and establishing local government under Filipino leaders. MacArthur, though, came to doubt the belief shared by Otis and the administration that most Filipinos were happy to accept US rule. He found the inhabitants cooperated to receive everything the US would build for them, but then provided little help with military pacification efforts and supported the rebels. Moreover, insurgent violence proved more convincing to the average Filipino than American benevolence. As is nearly always the case in such situations, if the counterinsurgent cannot prove they can protect the population from the guerrillas, the people will not truly support them. Filipino rebel leaders saw no reason to join the Americans; they could modernize on their own.[55]

September 1900 saw the Filipinos launch Aguinaldo's planned offensive. They concentrated their forces and attacked US patrols and outposts to influence the election. They inflicted two of the worst defeats suffered by the Americans, forcing one unit to surrender and killing or wounding one-third of another. But the Filipinos suffered heavily from the US riposte. And as it became clear that conciliation wasn't the answer, the Americans moved to harsher measures. MacArthur waited until after McKinley's reelection and shifted American strategy via a December 1900 order to concentrate on breaking the networks furnishing guerrillas' supplies and information, and announced that anyone caught violating the laws of war described in General Order No. 100 would be subject to severe punishment. MacArthur still wielded the civic action carrot but gave precedence to the stick. The US cracked down on insurgents and their supporters, breaking their networks, and MacArthur let commanders recruit as many Filipino volunteers as they needed.[56]

MacArthur's winter 1900 and spring 1901 campaigns were successful. He benefited from now having 70,000 men, the largest force the US deployed during the war, and McKinley's reelection severely injuring Filipino morale. MacArthur's strategy aimed at separating the people from the guerrillas, and robbing them of recruits, information, and logistical support. Food control devastated guerrilla-controlled countryside. He attacked the enemy's will by making them feel the war's pain. Civilians began offering to help fortify their own villages to protect them from hungry guerrillas and bandits. The US also launched its own form of concentration, moving civilians to areas where American forces could protect them. The army was exceedingly careful in implementation to avoid comparisons to Spain's brutal *reconcentrado*. MacArthur also went after the Filipino upper class, which furnished the insurgency's leaders. They began falling into American hands, including Aguinaldo. Only Luzon, Samar, and Cebu had active insurgencies by September 1901.[57]

The McKinley administration, as part of its plan to make US control more palatable, began shifting to civilian rule. McKinley appointed William Howard Taft head of a commission to oversee the transfer beginning in September 1900. As each province was declared pacified, it was transferred to civilian governance. MacArthur resented being subordinate to Taft, who mistrusted the senior US commanders. MacArthur handed control of the Philippines to now Governor Taft on July 4, 1901. Taft's hatred of the general guaranteed his relief despite his success, a change MacArthur read about in the newspaper.[58]

Secretary of War Elihu Root ordered Adna R. Chaffee, MacArthur's replacement, to get the army out of civic action and make it an effective fighting force. While preparing to finish the pacification of Batangas on Luzon, an army unit there was attacked in September 1901 and suffered heavy casualties. Chaffee drew upon his Civil War experience, intensified the methods already in use, and made sure the remaining areas in rebellion felt Sherman's "hard hand of war." Sherman believed failing to use sufficient violence in the beginning needlessly prolonged a struggle. Chaffee launched an effective campaign in Batangas and against the rebels on Samar. By April 1902, the last rebel leader had surrendered. President Theodore Roosevelt declared the war over on July 4, 1902, but sporadic guerrilla action continued, particularly against the Moro, until 1913.[59]

ENDING THE WAR AND SECURING THE PEACE

In his final report on the war, Secretary of War Root wrote: "It is evident that the insurrection has been brought to an end by making a war distressing and hopeless on the one hand and by making peace attractive." Using the carrot and the stick had succeeded. The Americans won when they broke the will of the insurrectionists, something impossible via conciliation. But there was also recognition that good actions influenced people toward US rule while bad actions pushed them away. The primary lesson army leaders drew was that conciliation alone was insufficient and that the refusal to use necessary violence prolonged the war. The struggle cost the US $400 million, 4,243 killed, and 2,818 wounded. The conflict's costs and nastiness dulled imperialism's shine for many while blunting expansionism. McKinley's Schurman Commission recommended preparing the Philippines for self-rule.[60]

CHINA AND THE BOXER REBELLION

In the 1890s, China became a target of European and Japanese imperialism. China's defeat in the Sino-Japanese War of 1894–95 was followed by Germany, Britain, and France securing territorial cessions as well. America had little interest in China beyond missionary work and the perennially unfulfilled businessmen's dreams of tapping China's market. But a coterie of Americans feared China's partition and sought its entry into the Western world. This "Open Door constituency" pushed for US defense of Chinese sovereignty and American trade interests. This led to Secretary of State John Hay's first Open Door note in September 1899. Hay, who began his career as Lincoln's secretary, saw this as a means of reassuring American businessmen, countering American anti-imperialists, and gaining favor with the Chinese. Influenced by a British idea, Hay insisted upon equal access to Chinese trade, meaning most-favored-nation status in the trading spheres various states carved out in China. Hay's second Open Door note of July 1900 stressed bringing about peace in China and announced maintaining its territorial integrity as a political aim. The US lacked the means to enforce any of this. The importance of Hay's notes has been exaggerated, but they mark the start of America's independent role in Asia.[61]

The notes had no effect on the nationalist and anti-imperialist Boxers, who trapped a foreign, multinational force of 600 soldiers and civilians in Beijing's legation area. The reluctant McKinley (it was an election year) agreed to support the relief expedition and dispatched troops from the Philippines, eventually sending 2,500 soldiers and Marines and supporting naval vessels. What became known as the China Relief Expedition numbered 19,000 troops from eight countries. It took Tianjin on July 13, 1900, and then marched on Beijing, 70 miles away. It reached the capital on August 12, mounted an uncoordinated and unsuccessful attack the next day, and then fought its way into the city on the 14th and 15th. After China's dowager empress sued for peace, the US left a small detachment as part of the occupation force but withdrew it in September 1901 when the treaty was signed. The intervention against the Boxers "marked the first time since the American Revolution" America "joined with other powers in an allied military operation." Hay tried to temper international reaction to the rebellion by limiting the indemnities demanded and encouraging quick troop withdrawals.[62]

THE STRATEGIC RESULT

Historian David Trask wrote that McKinley "emerges as a serious strategist who effectively related the use of force to the achievement of larger political goals." He was also a reluctant one. It is a rare leader that struggles so hard to prevent a war that his nation wants and then delivers success at a low cost in blood and treasure. McKinley was also exceedingly reluctant to take up what Rudyard Kipling called "the White Man's Burden" and assume the mantle of imperialism. He wouldn't have taken the Philippines if he thought he could have avoided it and kept a clear conscience. Doing so marked a shift in America's role in the world, one Woodrow Wilson noted at the time. But the Philippines War convinced many that empire wasn't the best path. Meanwhile, the navy grew, and Americans became nation builders abroad first in Cuba and the Philippines.[63]

Interservice coordination problems in the Spanish–American War helped produce the 1903 Joint Army and Navy Board. It lacked command or planning authority but reviewed respective service plans. Until 1917, its primary concern was the Color Plans, war plans developed to fight potential enemies, each represented by a specific color. For example, Germany was black, Japan was orange, Mexico was green. German action in Latin America was deemed the most likely threat.[64]

With the acquisition of imperial possessions, the army's role changed. Secretary of War Root pushed army reform. He secured a National Guard Act to help professionalize it, replaced the position of commanding general with an army chief of staff who advised the secretary of war, created a general staff to consider future conflicts, and helped establish the Army War College to provide education in strategic thinking. Brigadier General Tasker H. Bliss, a brilliant, multilingual officer who had served as one of the Naval War College's first instructors, headed the board appointed in February 1900 to design the college. Bliss defined its job as preparing plans "relating to the question of military preparations and movement in time of war." It was soon supporting the general staff and assisting preparation of war plans.[65]

THE THEODORE ROOSEVELT AND WILLIAM HOWARD TAFT ADMINISTRATIONS

Occasionally, the US has leaders deserving the title grand strategist. They possess a vision for the nation with clear aims, ideas for getting there, and the intelligence, drive, and creativity to move the country. Theodore Roosevelt was one of them. Prolific author, naturalist, political figure, explorer, reformer, soldier: Roosevelt was all of these. But he was also a grand strategist. His meteoric political career placed him in McKinley's administration as the assistant secretary of the navy. He left to fight in Cuba as a volunteer officer, winning fame at San Juan Hill. He was elected governor of New York, chosen as McKinley's vice-presidential candidate for the 1900 campaign, and became president after McKinley's September 1901 assassination. He was only 42. He was also an expansionist, the last to serve as president, but a different kind. He also governed an America becoming a global power.

POLITICAL AIMS AND GRAND STRATEGY

Roosevelt's primary aims were peace and security. Diplomatic and military power were the primary tools for achieving these and were intertwined with the Monroe Doctrine. Enforcing the Monroe Doctrine necessitated a strong navy, which ensured the US could defend its rights and privileges abroad. America also needed a more professional army. On April 2, 1903, Roosevelt quoted a West African proverb: "*Speak softly and carry a big stick; you will go far.* If the American nation will speak softly, and yet build, and keep at a pitch of the highest training, a thoroughly efficient navy, the Monroe Doctrine will go far." He inveighed the benefits of quiet diplomacy backed by resolve and military strength. But delivering security for the US in the Western Hemisphere required a bigger navy. With this, Roosevelt insisted, "no foreign power will ever quarrel with us about the Monroe Doctrine." Roosevelt also believed economic and political interdependence meant "all civilized and orderly powers" had "to insist on the proper policing of the world," and claimed the right to act as "an international police power" in the hemisphere.[66]

Roosevelt saw the Monroe Doctrine in its traditional role as a tool for blocking new European territorial acquisitions in the Western Hemisphere and hoped it would also protect the independence of the smaller states. But it wasn't a cover for aggression by American nations, and neither relieved them from responsibility for their commitments nor protected them from retaliation by outside powers, "provided that punishment does not take the form of the acquisition of territory by any non-American power." He said in 1905 that the US wouldn't use the Monroe Doctrine "as an excuse for aggrandizement on our part at the expense of the republics to the south."[67] This was achieved via other means.

THE CANAL

Roosevelt's "aggrandizement" became known as the Panama Canal Zone. By the time of Hayes' administration, desire for control of an isthmian canal had intensified among American leaders. Arthur's administration negotiated a canal treaty with Nicaragua, but Cleveland killed it as an "entangling alliance." Britain abandoned any claim to building a Central American canal, and Roosevelt helped bring about a second Hay–Paunceforte Treaty in 1901 giving Washington building rights.[68]

In December 1901, Roosevelt insisted nothing was more important to America than the canal. The long-term material and economic benefits made it in the nation's interests, as did its value as a monument to America's "constructive ability." It would improve America's military position while benefiting other nations. After engineers determined Panama preferable to Nicaragua, the administration negotiated a treaty with Colombia and, in June 1902, secured Congressional funding and approval. Roosevelt was immensely proud of this, predicting the canal would be "the great bit of work of my administration, and from the material and constructive standpoint one of the greatest bits of work that the twentieth century will see."[69]

But the canal question wasn't smoothly resolved. Panama was part of Colombia, and Colombia's senate decided it wanted more money and balked at ratifying the treaty to which it had agreed. The administration replied that if the treaty was not signed, Washington would be forced to take actions Colombia might find regrettable. Roosevelt launched conversations with supporters of Panamanian secession, stressing his willingness to deal with the leaders of a Panamanian republic if Colombia refused to meet its commitment. When word of this appeared in the press, Roosevelt said nothing. When Colombia rejected the canal treaty on August 12, 1903, Roosevelt charted a cautious course, telling Secretary of State Hay: "What we do now will be of consequence, not merely decades, but centuries hence, and we must be sure that we are taking the right step before we act."[70]

Panama had a troubled relationship with Colombia's rulers. It seceded from the New Granadian Federation upon its collapse in 1830 only to find itself back under Bogotá's rule a dozen years later. The US had treaty obligations under an 1846 agreement to protect the railroad across the isthmus and had prevented rebel movements on the railroad ten times during fifty-three incidences of insurrection or riot since 1846. Some Colombian leaders launched another attempt to get the US to pay $40 million for what it had already agreed to pay $10 million. Hay ignored them; Roosevelt was finished with the Colombian government.⁷¹ It was cheaper and easier to wait for the Panamanian Revolution.

In his late 1903 message to a special session of Congress called to obtain the legislative power to act in Panama if needed, Roosevelt pitched the canal as being of global and not just American importance. Because of Colombia's refusal to keep its word, Roosevelt insisted the US should either build the canal in Nicaragua or purchase the assets of the failed French company and build in Panama while ignoring the Colombian government. He favored the latter but put it to Congress to decide. The Panamanian Revolution occurred in the first week of November. The US neither directly supported nor discouraged the plot, but stationing warships on both of Panama's coasts with orders to prevent a Colombian response helped ensure it. Washington quickly extended recognition. European and Latin American nations followed.⁷²

The treaty gave to the US – "as if it were sovereign" – control over a 10-mile stretch of territory from Colón to Panama City where it would build its canal. Moreover, as the treaty bound the US to guarantee Panama's independence, the new nation became a US protectorate. A 1939 treaty ended this. Roosevelt declared the canal in the "vital interests of civilization" but believed American security and the threat from rising global tensions demanded it. The canal increased American power by enabling the navy's concentration. Roosevelt promulgated some questionable arguments on the matter but also provided a clear explanation: "I took Panama."⁷³

THE VENEZUELA CRISIS, 1902–03

By 1896, Roosevelt wanted to protect South America from European encroachment but urged adoption of the political aim of removing European states from their Western Hemisphere colonies. As president, he didn't expect problems from Britain but remained suspicious of Germany. This proved justified. Roosevelt saw the Venezuela crisis building for eleven months. Venezuela was heavily indebted to a German–British consortium, and corruption and civil war left the country unable to pay. London and Berlin were uninterested in excuses and intended to blockade Caracas to force payment. Both assured Roosevelt they sought no territorial foothold. Roosevelt sympathized with the Europeans, believing people and nations should live up to their responsibilities. But Roosevelt worried German threats might produce foreign occupation. This he wouldn't allow as the US could face paying the debt or going to war.⁷⁴

When the British and Germans decided to act against Venezuela, Roosevelt sent the fleet to the West Indies and told Kaiser Wilhelm "that

I should be obliged to interfere, by force, if necessary, if Germany took actions resembling acquisition of territory in Venezuela or elsewhere along the Caribbean." He insisted Berlin state within ten days that it had no territorial ambitions. If he didn't receive this, he promised to send the navy "to observe matters along Venezuela."[75]

The Anglo-German action against Venezuela began on December 9, 1902 with the seizure of four Venezuelan gunboats, three of which the Germans sank, unnecessarily in Roosevelt's eyes. Venezuela's President Cipriano Castro pled for American arbitration. Roosevelt hadn't received an answer to his ultimatum and was told Germany wouldn't accept mediation. He emphasized his seriousness by cutting a day from his ultimatum's timeline. The British wanted to preserve their good relations with America and shifted to supporting arbitration. The Germans finally got the message and, on December 19, both London and Berlin formally asked Washington to arbitrate. Roosevelt had handled the entire situation quietly, and neither the press nor the public ever knew the seriousness of the crisis.[76]

Roosevelt declined to handle the arbitration himself. Castro asked the US ambassador to Venezuela to represent him. Roosevelt's reaction marked the birth of the Roosevelt Corollary to the Monroe Doctrine: "The debts will be paid. I'll do whatever's necessary to ensure that. There's the Monroe Doctrine to consider. Since we can't, on the one hand, tolerate permanent seizure of territory by a European power in any of the American republics ... I, on the other, can't let *them* hide behind the Monroe Doctrine in order to shirk obligations." Roosevelt intended to force Venezuela to keep any arbitration agreement. The Germans proved truculent but became more reasonable with renewed news that the US navy had been ordered to "hold itself in readiness." Roosevelt scored a great diplomatic coup when an agreement was signed, and the Europeans sailed away.[77]

The official announcement of the Roosevelt Corollary to the Monroe Doctrine was made by Secretary of War Root, who "believed the United States must be the judge of the behavior of Central America's states." He read Roosevelt's letter on this at a May 20, 1904 New York meeting. "It is not that the United States has any land hunger or entertains any projects as regards other nations, *save such as are for their welfare*," it said.

> If a nation shows that it knows how to act with decency in industrial and political matters, if it keeps order and pays its obligations, then it need fear no interference from the United States. Brutal wrongdoing, or an importance which results in a general loosening of the ties of a civilized society, may finally require intervention by some civilized nation, and in the Western

Hemisphere the United States cannot ignore this duty; but it remains true that our interests, and those of our southern neighbors, are in reality identical.

Roosevelt insisted in December 1904 that peace and order were in the interests of all Western Hemisphere states. Those who disturbed this would find themselves subject to American-sponsored arbitration or policing.[78]

THE DOMINICAN REPUBLIC CRISIS, 1902–04

The Dominican Republic's inability to pay its debts threatened repetition of the Venezuela Crisis. A corrupt dictatorship that had plunged the country deeply into debt had just been overthrown; meanwhile, the French, Germans, and Italians threatened intervention. Amid rumors of a German naval force sailing for the island, Dominica's new president asked the US to make his nation a protectorate. In early 1904, American papers were generally supportive. Roosevelt balked, saying, "I have about the same desire to annex it as a gorged boa constrictor might have to swallow a porcupine wrong end to." By December, he had developed the Roosevelt Corollary, and, after the election, an agreement with Dominica placed its trade receipts under US management.[79]

THE CUBAN INTERVENTION, 1906–09

In September 1906, after an invitation from Cuba's leaders, and to meet America's treaty commitment to ensure a functioning Cuban authority, Roosevelt reluctantly intervened, but as an honest broker between revolutionary groups. Roosevelt was eager to avoid bloodshed and insisted America's role was to keep the country solvent until it could govern itself. The insurgents proved amenable to compromise and didn't resist the American troops. The US arranged elections for a new government, installed an American provisional governor, and prepared Cuba for self-rule via a 1906–09 nation-building operation.[80]

THE PACIFIC

Roosevelt believed the nation's future was more dependent upon the Pacific than Europe and remarked in a 1900 speech: "I wish to see the United States the dominant power on the shores of the Pacific Ocean." US leaders focused upon power, America's and that of its potential adversaries in the region, and how the region's geography and geopolitical situation affected American power. Trade with the region was not a significant portion of America's economy. For example, the China trade in 1890 was 0.3 percent of US exports.[81]

Roosevelt, though, looked toward the Pacific as a kind of new frontier for American economic penetration: "In the century that is opening the commerce and the command of the Pacific will be factors of incalculable moment in the world's history." America, in his view, must take up the Pacific Ocean region's challenges, which included Russia and Japan, and how European powers planted themselves on its shores. Roosevelt pointedly described the problems facing China after its defeat in the Sino-Japanese War (1894–95): "China by her misfortune has given us an object-lesson in the utter folly of attempting to exist as a nation at all, if both rich and defenseless." The answer: "We infinitely desire peace, and the surest way of obtaining it is to show that we are not afraid of war."[82]

The Russo-Japanese War of 1904–05 overturned Asia's strategic situation. It offers a rare glimpse at planning a war's end. Before launching the struggle, the Japanese decided they would ask the US to mediate its conclusion and dispatched to Washington Kaneko Kentaro, who had attended Harvard University with Roosevelt. His missions: convince Roosevelt to negotiate peace at the right time and cultivate American popular support for Japan. The Japanese request came on May 31, 1905. Roosevelt had suggested mediation to the Russians and Japanese before the war began, worked hard to secure this during the war, and later exerted himself brilliantly at the peace conference he hosted in Portsmouth, New Hampshire. When approached, Roosevelt assumed the Japanese were exhausted but didn't want the Russians to know this. Secretly, he summoned the Russian ambassador, told him he thought Russia's military situation hopeless, and said that if the tsar agreed, Roosevelt thought he could arrange a peace conference. He then had America's ambassador to St. Petersburg give the tsar the same message, as he doubted Russia's Washington representative would convey it. Roosevelt feared Russia being driven off the Pacific coast and Japan becoming so strong this upset the region's balance of power and threatened US interests. Roosevelt's achievement, for which he received the Nobel Peace Prize, marked further American ascension onto the world stage.[83]

Japanese success against Russia in the war both amazed and alarmed Roosevelt. He believed that unless the US pursued the proper grand strategy in Asia it would eventually face war with Japan. To prevent this, the US and the other Western powers had to treat Japan fairly, respectfully, and as a racial and political equal – not as they had traditionally treated China. Doing otherwise would provoke disaster. Roosevelt concentrated upon diplomatic reassurance and military deterrence. He sought to reassure Japan of Washington's peaceful intentions while protecting what he now called America's Achilles' Heel: the Philippines. State exclusionary laws against Chinese and Japanese immigration, particularly in California, caused Roosevelt diplomatic troubles. The Gentleman's Agreement of 1907 smoothed over some of these. The Root–Takahira Agreement of 1908 calmed relations further and committed Washington and Tokyo to maintaining the Pacific status quo. The administration also acquiesced to Japan's annexation of Korea, about which it could have done nothing.[84]

But Roosevelt knew that military strength – particularly naval strength – was the most potent tool in the strategy box. He exerted himself mightily as president to expand and modernize the navy, and determined to build a force strong enough to protect US shores and possessions and achieve the nation's political aims abroad.[85] He secured a steady stream of funding for new ships, especially battleships, and made the US navy a global force.

INFORMATIONAL STRATEGY

In 1907, the navy suggested a training exercise to move the fleet from the Atlantic to the Pacific. Roosevelt seized upon the idea as a way to make an impact as dramatic as that of the Panama Canal. He saw dispatching a fleet halfway around the world as a diplomatic and strategic move and a demonstration of raw power. And Britain and Germany didn't think it possible. He launched into preparations for the fleet to sail in October from Hampton Roads, Virginia, bound for San Francisco. He was already secretly planning to have the "Great White Fleet" circumnavigate the world. By the time it reached the Straits of Magellan in February, it was a global diplomatic and press event.[86]

ECONOMIC STRATEGY

Roosevelt signed into law on June 17, 1902 the National Reclamation Act. This funded dams and aqueducts to increase the nation's prosperity and growth, and served as a conservation act. Roosevelt secured an anti-trust Commerce and Labor Bill that made him known as a "trust-buster." His war against trusts – monopolies – slackened during 1903 and 1904 when he was running for reelection, but he intensified his campaign for more regulation afterward.[87]

Early in his administration, McKinley had secured passage of the 1897 Dingley Act, a tariff primarily intended to protect US industry and provide revenue. Protectionists praised it, "and when prosperity returned in the second half of 1897, the Dingley Act, in the minds of high-tariff Republicans, became irrevocably associated with the maintenance of economic health." Roosevelt wasn't interested in the tariff (or most economic issues) but some leaders in his party wanted reductions because they believed America was producing too much for its own markets and needed more access to overseas markets. Roosevelt agreed. Residents of wheat- and corn-growing areas also wanted lower tariffs. Roosevelt was unsure what rates were best. In his view, the most expedient thing was to do nothing. He supported trade agreement reciprocity, particularly for Cuba and the Philippines, insisting it "must be treated as the handmaiden of protection" and should "be sought for so far as it can safely be done without injury to our home industries."[88]

In his last address to Congress, in December 1908, Roosevelt said: "This Nation's foreign policy is based on the theory that right must be done between nations precisely as between individuals, and in our actions for the last ten years we have in this matter proven our faith by our deeds."[89] Except perhaps in the case of Panama (though Roosevelt would have insisted Colombia was at fault for breaking its word), one must judge this generally correct.

THE WILLIAM HOWARD TAFT ADMINISTRATION, 1909–13

Roosevelt's handpicked successor, his vice president, William Howard Taft, took office in 1909. Taft was uninterested in being president. A devout jurist, his dream (eventually realized) was to sit on the Supreme Court. His wife, Helen Herron Taft, wanted him to be president, so he became president. Her political skills and instincts helped put him there.[90]

Taft's primary political aim, inasmuch as he had one, was peace. He said in his inaugural address: "Our international policy is always to promote peace. We shall enter into any war with a full consciousness of the awful consequences that it always entails, whether successful or not, and we, of course, shall make every effort consistent with national honor and the highest national interest to avoid a resort to arms." He was a dedicated advocate of world peace and believed general acceptance of international arbitration the cure for war.[91]

A GRAND STRATEGY OF ECONOMICS

Taft's grand strategy was framed by Dollar Diplomacy, a form of Progressivism insisting stability and good government were best achieved by economic means. This didn't mean government providing money but encouraging and arranging private financial involvement. Dollar Diplomacy assumed "financial rehabilitation eventually brought political stability" and that "Central America's perennially warring factions would cease quarreling in their common desire to encourage foreign investment." Dollar Diplomacy would also allow the US to undermine European economic influence in Latin America. He elaborated in 1912:

> This policy [strategy] has been characterized as substituting dollars for bullets. It is one that appeals alike to idealistic humanitarian sentiments, to the dictates of sound policy and strategy, and to legitimate commercial aims. It is an effort frankly directed to the increase of American trade upon the axiomatic principle that the Government of the United States shall extend all proper support to every legitimate and beneficial American enterprise abroad.[92]

Additionally, Taft pushed for lower tariffs when running for president, something his Republican Party generally refused. Carnegie remarked that US industry no longer needed protective tariffs as it could undersell any competitor. Taft launched into tariff reduction after his election, but the measure passed wasn't what he wanted and changed little.[93]

LATIN AMERICA

Nicaragua provided the first test case for Dollar Diplomacy. It suffered a rebellion in October 1909 against José Santos Zelaya's regime, one encouraged without permission by Thomas Moffat, the US consul in the largely American-populated town of Bluefields, Nicaragua. Zelaya enjoyed success against the rebels, and by spring 1910 threatened Bluefields. Moffat begged for help after being told by the rebel commander the town would fall. US Marine Corps Major Smedley Butler, under the command of Rear Admiral W. W. Kimball, was dispatched from Panama with 250 Marines to protect its American residents and other foreign nationals. This also shielded the rebels, which Butler resented. Also, Zelaya had secured a British loan, raising in the eyes of Secretary of State Philander Knox the specter of European meddling if Nicaragua defaulted.[94]

Under pressure from the US and Mexico and believing he couldn't destroy the rebellion because of the presence of US forces (his army numbered only 1,500), Zelaya agreed to resign and hand power to Dr. José Madriz. Madriz continued the war, but American naval protection allowed the rebels to bring in arms and launch a counteroffensive bringing them near the capital of Managua by summer 1910. Madriz fled Nicaragua, and rebel leader Juan J. Estrada became president. His promise of economic reform and immediate elections was music to Knox, and he and Taft believed Nicaragua could be saved via a Dominican Republic-style financial restructuring. This would also allow the US to "achieve its goal of a stable Caribbean without resort to armed intervention or military occupation."[95]

Knox negotiated a series of treaties with troubled Nicaragua in which the US helped reform its financial system and secure a loan for paying its debts and development. The US, in return, established a custom's receivership like Santo Domingo's. A similar agreement negotiated with Honduras fell apart due to the nation's civil war. Private Americans backed investment in both. A plan negotiated for Guatemala also collapsed.[96]

In summer 1912, the administration began substituting bullets for dollars. Knox explained to Taft that Nicaragua wanted US forces to protect American property and citizens. By September 4, the US had 1,000 Marines and sailors in the country to protect US consulates and the American-owned Corinto–Managua rail line. Six US warships were off the coast. More troops followed and facilitated restoration of government control, primarily by securing key railroad lines. US military power helped establish a peace that lasted for fifteen years. Events in Nicaragua helped demonstrate the bankruptcy of Dollar Diplomacy as a strategy.[97]

CHINA AND JAPAN

In Asia, the administration aimed for regional stability. In China, Dollar Diplomacy manifested in Taft's backing American investment to thwart growing Japanese economic influence and control, particularly in Manchuria; it was feared this would injure Chinese territorial integrity while undermining the Open Door. The Americans pushed to help finance China's efforts to buy back control of its railroads, helping it regain sovereignty while creating a buffer between Russia and Japan. The result was to drive the owners of the railroads, Russia and Japan, into cooperating against interlopers.[98]

In 1912, China's Qing dynasty fell and was replaced by a republic. Normally, the US would recognize such a state, but the administration thought preserving most-favored-nation trading status more important and backed the bankers supporting the imperialist nations, including Russia and Japan. One author provides this apt summary: "in three years, Taft's Asia strategy had gone from unilateral balance of power against the other imperial powers in northern China, to a concert of power with the Europeans that was aimed at Japan and Russia, to a concert that included Japan and Russia, and finally to abandonment of the principle of Chinese sovereignty that had animated Taft's strategy in the first place." Additionally, the administration abandoned Roosevelt's strategy of conciliating Japan. In China, Russia and Japan killed Dollar Diplomacy by making foreign investment exceedingly difficult.[99]

CONCLUSION

Taft and Knox saw themselves as returning to a traditional Republican Party approach of "peace and commerce with all nations." But instead of using economic tools as a part of a larger grand strategy, they made this the core. Dollar Diplomacy failed, producing military involvement in Latin America and few deals, while marking the first effort by an American administration to construct grand strategy on economic issues. Taft's Asia failure, particularly the angering of Japan, helped fuel Roosevelt's decision to run against Taft as an independent, easing Democrat Woodrow Wilson's 1912 election victory.[100] This proved a watershed event as Wilson authored one of the greatest course changes in American strategic history, one still underpinning American foreign relations.

PART II

FROM GREAT POWER TO SUPERPOWER

7

STEPPING UPON THE GLOBAL STAGE, 1913–1921

INTRODUCTION

President Woodrow Wilson believed in a strong executive because this provided the power to do what was "right." A historian and political scientist, his New Jersey governorship was preceded by a professorship at Princeton University and a stint as its president, where "he acquired a Cromwellian reputation for being a bold reformer and thorough authoritarian." Wilson believed America was obligated to spread democracy and individual freedom, and his moralism led him to use force to impose upon other nations his vision of how they should govern themselves. Wilson insisted he was a noninterventionist and criticized his Republican predecessors' "gunboat diplomacy" in Latin America, lambasted the treaties Knox made with Nicaragua and Honduras, and condemned Taft's Dollar Diplomacy. The 1912 Democratic platform reproached America's imperialist "blunder" in the Philippines. But Wilson's conduct of American grand strategy was not what his criticism implied. Progressives of his stripe intended to teach people – especially non-Whites – what was best for them. Wilson said of the people of Puerto Rico and the Philippines: "They are children and we are men in these deep matters of government and justice."[1]

WILSON'S POLITICAL AIMS: THE GREAT SHIFT

American political aims, both in war and peacetime, assumed a new form when McKinley took the US to war seeking *Cuban* independence, but Wilson fathered more dramatic change. On October 27, 1914, he declared America would never again expand via territorial conquest. He proved correct, though the US made its final territorial acquisition with Wilson's 1916 purchase of Denmark's Caribbean Virgin Islands.[2] Wilson ended US expansion. Achieving democracy abroad took its place alongside sovereignty and security. The McKinley, Roosevelt, and Taft administrations tried to build a democracy in Cuba, but that was not the original aim. Sovereignty, security, and democracy weren't America's only political aims, but these drove or influenced the establishment of most others.

The idea of pursuing democracy as a political aim creates some semantic mayhem. Seeking to establish a democratic government is an aim. A strategy of democratization is taking the actions necessary to create a democratic or republican government (the aim), such as establishing basic freedoms.

ASSESSMENT

Before the First World War, the US exercised little influence on the world stage despite its preponderance of economic strength and possessed scant ability to project power militarily or diplomatically. The navy was the world's third largest, but the army numbered only 90,000, and the diplomatic service only 663. Wilson recognized America's enormous power and sought to tap it for the world's betterment. He saw the nation's purpose as the exportation of its values (or his version of them), a drive underpinned by Progressive ideas and a version of Christianity. He supported the burgeoning international peace movement, and believed nations such as the US and Great Britain could educate other states about democracy. Wilson disparaged the idea of nations acting in line with their interests and insisted in October 1913 that it was "a very perilous thing to determine the foreign policy of a nation in terms of material interest. It is not only unfair to those with whom you are dealing, but it is degrading as regards your own actions."[3]

Acting based upon material and strategic interests can be regarded as selfish and self-centered (because it is), but the advantage this holds over acting based upon utopian assumptions that fail to acknowledge other nations act in their interests, is that it has a better chance of delivering benefits to the state, though this isn't assured. Wilson possessed no grand strategy when he entered office, but what emerged we now call Wilsonianism.

ECONOMIC STRATEGY

Wilson opposed protectionism and gave tariff reform and anti-trust action pride of place. To Wilson, tariffs were for revenue. He argued US industries no longer needed protection and tariff levels hadn't been sufficiently adjusted to represent America's industrial growth. He believed lower rates would force American businesses to be more competitive and prevent the formation of monopolies. The 1913 Underwood–Simmons tariff law lowered the average import duty from 40 to 27 percent. It also included an income tax. The Sixteenth Amendment was ratified in February 1913. A 1 percent income tax on couples earning over $4,000 annually and individuals $3,000 followed to compensate for lost revenue. In 1913, tariffs supplied 40 percent of government revenue; this fell to 28 percent in 1916, to under 5 percent after the First World War. Later, the enormous income tax stream fueled dramatic growth in government expenditures.[4]

DIPLOMATIC STRATEGY

Wilson, though a historian and political scientist, had scant knowledge of foreign affairs. He had little respect for the State Department and was known to correct poorly written dispatches and return them to their authors. The international environment faced the spirit of revolution. China and Mexico were in turmoil; many Latin American nations joined them. The First World War began during his second year in office. The Russian Revolution struck in 1917.[5]

LATIN AMERICA

Wilson and his first secretary of state, William Jennings Bryan, possessed a paternalistic attitude toward Latin America underpinned by the same sense of racial superiority they exhibited toward African-Americans. Bryan called these states "our political children," and both he and Wilson wanted to guide them to democracy.[6] Wilson's actions in the region are generally termed "interventions." "Wars" is more accurate. The administration used military force in pursuit of its political aims.

In March 1913, the administration issued its "Declaration of Policy in Regard to Latin America." This foreswore any American regional ambitions but noted Washington sought "the security of governments intended for the people and for no special group or interest, and the development of personal and trade relationships between the two continents." The administration committed the common error of seeking economic growth as an end in itself. More important was the democracy emphasis. Wilson and Bryan insisted "just government rests always upon the consent of the governed, and that there can be no freedom without order based upon law and upon the public conscience and approval." America would use "influence of every kind to the realization of these principles." When Wilson didn't get the expected democracy and order, he began to "police" the Latin American nations in a manner far beyond his predecessors to teach them to rule in an orderly fashion – like Americans. The Marines branded the subsequent Caribbean struggles "banana wars." American economic dominance wasn't the point. Progressive politics drove America's actions.[7]

The administration tried securing peace in the Western Hemisphere via a Pan-American Pact guaranteeing the territorial limits of states "under republican government." But some states feared Washington using this to force them to change their governments and create American economic domination. Wilson's Mexican adventures finally killed it.[8] Wilson, though, needed no treaties to justify action.

THE HAITI WAR, 1915–21

Unsubstantiated rumors of French and German influence and Haiti's instability (seven governments since 1911 and a brutal 1915 coup) underpinned Wilson's invasion. Bryan's State Department tried to thwart European penetration by demanding a customs receivership similar to that Washington imposed on the Dominican Republic. Haiti refused. Wilson dispatched troops to restore order. The Marines landed on July 28, 1915. They stayed for almost twenty years. The US faced little initial resistance and controlled Haiti by year's end, but endured bandits and guerrilla attacks until 1921. The administration was unsure about the legality of its occupation and what to do there. It ruled through martial law until 1929, established a client government nominally controlled by Haitians, and negotiated a treaty instituting financial reforms. The Marines built a Haitian constabulary and improved the infrastructure as Haiti became an American protectorate.[9]

WILSON'S MEXICAN WARS, 1914–17

The Mexican Revolution began in 1910 after President Porfirio Díaz reneged on his promise to retire and arrested his most powerful political opponent, Francisco Madero, who was bailed from jail and escaped to Texas. Madero's forces triumphed the next year and he was elected president. But violence and plotting continued, and Madero was betrayed by one of his generals, Victoriano Huerta. The US ambassador helped negotiate a power-sharing agreement with Huerta's primary rival, Felix Díaz, a nephew of the former president, and Huerta then had Madero murdered. This didn't prevent Washington's ambassador from urging recognition of Huerta's regime. Taft, then president, balked, insisting upon settlement of US financial claims first. Wilson refused to recognize the rule of a man he considered a murderer but also wanted Mexico to have better government and sought to educate its people toward this.[10]

In October 1913, Wilson declared Washington had no territorial ambitions in Mexico. He wanted Huerta to accept mediation with the rebels, establish a new government (without Huerta), and hold elections. Huerta insisted upon recognition first. Huerta held elections but the irregularities caused Wilson to reject the results. In October 1914, Wilson delivered a speech promising the US "will never again seek one additional foot of territory by conquest," and denounced European economic intrusion in Latin America. As the Europeans began shifting to Wilson's view on Mexico, he again demanded Huerta's exit and lifted the arms embargo he had imposed to pressure Huerta, permitting the dictator's opponent to arm, and deployed naval forces to patrol Mexico's Gulf coast.[11]

Wilson remained insistent Huerta leave and sought regime change in Mexico – an unlimited political aim – and tapped military, diplomatic, and economic power to achieve this. A State Department message delineated the aim and the strategy:

> Usurpations like that of General Huerta menace the peace and development of America as nothing else could.... It is the purpose of the United States therefore to discredit and defeat such usurpations whenever they occur. The present policy [strategy] of the Government of the United States is to isolate General Huerta entirely; to cut him off from foreign sympathy and aid from domestic credit, whether moral or material, and to force him out.

Secretary of State Bryan (a pacifist) said that if Huerta didn't go, "it will become the duty of the United States to use less peaceful means to put him out."[12]

Wilson insisted America had no right to intervene in Mexico or tell Mexicans how to run their affairs but told London's ambassador to Washington: "I am going to teach the South American republics to elect good men." Wilson, though, wouldn't act without a provocation. He soon had several. A Mexican officer arrested some American officers in Tampico. The local commander immediately ordered their release and apologized, but the American admiral demanded more, including a salute to the American flag. The mistaken arrest of an American sailor in Veracruz fueled the fire. Wilson rebuffed Huerta's proposed compromise of simultaneous salutes and had already begun massing troops and ships. Word of the imminent arrival in Veracruz of a vessel with arms for Huerta galvanized Wilson to ask Congress not for a declaration of war but for a resolution approving US armed action. The House agreed, "justifying" but not "authorizing" Wilson to use force. The arrival of the munitions vessel led Wilson to order Veracruz's seizure before the Senate voted approval. The administration branded the attack a "reprisal."[13]

PART II: FROM GREAT POWER TO SUPERPOWER

As was too frequently true when Washington used military power in the region, the American commander received unclear instructions regarding what he was there to do. What began as an effort to take the customs house became seizure of the entire city when it proved unsafe to do merely the former. The US soon had 7,150 troops holding Veracruz, who cleaned up the city and reorganized its administration. In line with US war planning, on June 20, 1914 the occupation force commander asked permission to push inland. The administration didn't want a bigger commitment.[14]

Wilson expected to injure Huerta and receive praise from his enemies. Huerta became more popular, and his enemies denounced Wilson and America's war against Mexico. Wilson gladly accepted a Latin American mediation offer producing a May 20 peace conference tackling the American landing and the Mexican civil war. It solved nothing but Huerta's forces suffered defeat and he resigned on July 15, 1914. Venustiano Carranza became Mexico's new ruler, accepted Wilson's demands for no reprisals against Mexicans in Veracruz who aided the Americans, and US forces departed on November 23, 1914.[15]

Wilson denied Carranza's government recognition to force democratic reforms. Carranza replied in early 1915 with the Plan of San Diego calling for insurrection and the establishment of a new government in America's southwest by Indians, Hispanics, and Blacks. In summer 1915, he launched guerrilla and bandit raids into Texas. The locals sometimes harbored the raiders, and Wilson's refusal to declare martial law limited the army's response. It spread its forces over every town, leaving it too weak to act, then massed infantry in key places and patrolled with cavalry. Wilson recognized Carranza's government in October; Carranza's punitive war had achieved its aim. Wilson later allowed Carranza to ship troops through the US to mount a successful attack on one of his rivals, Pancho Villa.[16]

On March 9, 1916, Villa's forces raided Columbus, New Mexico. Wilson retaliated with his own punitive war into Mexico with the aim of destroying Villa's army. US forces were to avoid fighting Carranza and pursue Villa wherever he went. It was pointed out that if Villa took a train to Guatemala, this meant the army should follow. The War Department changed the orders to pursuing Villa until his force was dispersed or the Mexican government assumed the task. But the first order's wide publication later led many to see the expedition as a failure. Carranza saw violation of Mexico's sovereignty, while the US army was appalled at dispatching 12,000 men into the wilds of Mexico in the face of what they estimated as 180,000 men under arms. A force under Brigadier General John J. "Black Jack" Pershing departed on March 15, 1916. It pushed 175 miles into Mexico, relentlessly pursued Villa, and forced his army to disperse to survive. But Carranza's troops and local civilians soon opposed Pershing. An April 12 fight at Parral pushed Pershing to request permission to occupy the state of Chihuahua as the first step in a war to pacify Mexico. Wilson refused as this would mean a war with Mexico he didn't want.[17] In reality, he was already fighting one.

Pershing was ordered to hold parts of northern and western Chihuahua. The administration intended to use this as it had Veracruz: to extract concessions. When negotiations reached an impasse, Carranza revived his Plan of San Diego, urged bandit raids into the US, and sent a team into Texas to foment insurrection. The US mobilized 100,000 National Guard units to protect the border while Carranza pushed troops into Chihuahua. An American patrol was defeated by Mexican forces at Carrizal but both sides refused further escalation or to declare war. A staring contest ensued, and Pershing began clearing Villa supporters from his command areas. The approach of war with Germany, and Carranza's decisive defeat of Villa in January 1917, saw Wilson abandon his demands and order Pershing home. Additionally, Wilson deployed a small troop detachment to Panama from 1918 to 1920 to ensure free elections.[18]

THE DOMINICAN REPUBLIC WAR, 1916–21

In December 1900, the navy's General Board planners saw in Hispaniola's instability a strategic problem. It sat between Cuba and Puerto Rico and its chronic chaos could enable a foreign power to gain concessions such as naval bases. Roosevelt created a Dominican customs revenue receivership but left it to its civil wars and political assassinations. Wilson personally controlled relations with Mexico but Bryan handled Dominican issues. A vociferous critic of Roosevelt, Taft, and American businessmen in the Caribbean, Bryan became an ardent interventionist, partially because of the Panama Canal's strategic importance, and implemented Public Dollars Diplomacy, a version of Taft's flawed economic strategy. US government funding instead of private underpinned American strategy. Bryan failed to thwart a rebellion by telling the insurgents that even if they won, the US wouldn't give them the customs revenue, recognize them, or allow them to borrow more to pay any obligations incurred.[19] Bryan didn't understand the dominance of the political over economics.

The Dominicans suffered rampant corruption and endemic government turnovers as political groups vied to control the customs revenue. The administration demanded financial and military reforms and elections conducted by American rules. Securing none of these, and aware of a pending military coup, Wilson dispatched troops in May 1916 to protect the legation. The Dominican leaders still refused to bend. Wilson ordered the nation occupied. Washington disbanded Dominica's assembly, overthrowing the regime, established US military rule, and began disarming the people and army. American troops were soon fighting bandits and a guerrilla opposition. A five-year war followed. In 1917, the Americans created a Dominican National Guard as a constabulary force as a social experiment to educate its members on the larger needs of the nation. The US also invested in public works and education.[20]

CUBA, 1917–22

In February 1917, the Wilson administration began supporting Cuba's government against an insurgency to "protect American strategic and economic interests." Supplies of arms and munitions were followed by landing parties of sailors and Marines, a naval blockade of rebel-held areas, and protection of sugar and mining facilities. Following the American declaration of war on Germany in April 1917, American forces deployed in August to provide stability for the planters to prepare for the 1918 sugar crop, which was important for the war effort. The administration insisted it was helping the Cuban government against insurgents who had been largely defeated.[21]

A fraudulent November 1919 presidential election saw the defeated Liberals appeal for American help. The political dissension grew as a postwar sugar glut destroyed the crop's price, decimating Cuba's economy. The administration dispatched representatives to help Cuba "maintain a government that would protect life and property," action driven partially by a State Department official with investments in Cuba's sugar industry. The US cajoled a new election producing the same corrupt result. Cuba's new leader ruled with the Americans at his back pushing reforms, often financial, underwritten by J. P. Morgan's bank. In 1925, Gerardo Machado became president. He excelled at telling Cubans and Americans what they wanted to hear and conned Washington into believing Cuba now possessed a good leader. His dictatorial rule proved brutal.[22] American troops departed in 1922.

ASIA

Wilson thought he had a better grasp of US Asian interests than his predecessor. He and Bryan believed China easily molded by Westerners and pushed toward Christianity and democracy. Wilson thought Europeans desired a divided China and countered diplomatically with recognition of the Chinese Republic, and declared Hay's Open Door a portal of "friendship and mutual advantage." Economically, he reversed Taft's Dollar Diplomacy by withdrawing from the international consortium underwriting loans to China. None of this helped China. Its new government was weak and didn't represent its people, and the Europeans and Japan remained undeterred, particularly Japan, against whose imperial ambitions the Chinese sought US support. Wilson reentered the banking consortium in 1916; China generally received only American sympathy. The First World War soon consumed the administration and Tokyo used participation on the Allied side to seize Germany's China territories. The May 1917 Lansing–Ishi agreement gave Japan endorsement of its "special interests" in China and haunted later American Asia actions. Wilson secured the 1916 Jones Act assuring future Philippines' independence. It gave no date but was history's "first case of decolonization."[23]

WOODROW WILSON AND THE FIRST WORLD WAR, 1914–18

At the outbreak of the First World War in 1914, America had 90 million people, was the world's richest nation, and its greatest financial and industrial power. Its manufacturing production surpassed Germany, France, and Britain – *combined*. Despite this strength, America involved itself little in great-power politics, though there was a growing sense it could and should take on a larger world role.[24]

The spark igniting the First World War was the assassination of the heir to the Austro-Hungarian crown by a Serbian nationalist on June 28, 1914. Europe was divided into two alliance blocs. The key Central Powers were Germany, Austria, and Italy, but Rome refused to enter the war in 1914 because the alliance was defensive. Turkey joined the Central Powers in October. The major Entente or Allied powers were Great Britain, France, and Russia. Italy joined them in 1915. The Germans famously tried to knock out France with a quick offensive beginning in August 1914, hoping then to focus on Russia. This failed. And within a few months the fighting on what became known as the Western Front evolved into trench warfare marked by titanic attritional battles. (See Map 7.1.) Huge campaigns were fought along a Russian front stretching from the Baltic to the Black Sea, in Serbia and the Balkans, the Middle East and Central Asia, and Italy. Around 9.7 million military personnel were killed. Perhaps 10 million civilians died.

PART II: FROM GREAT POWER TO SUPERPOWER

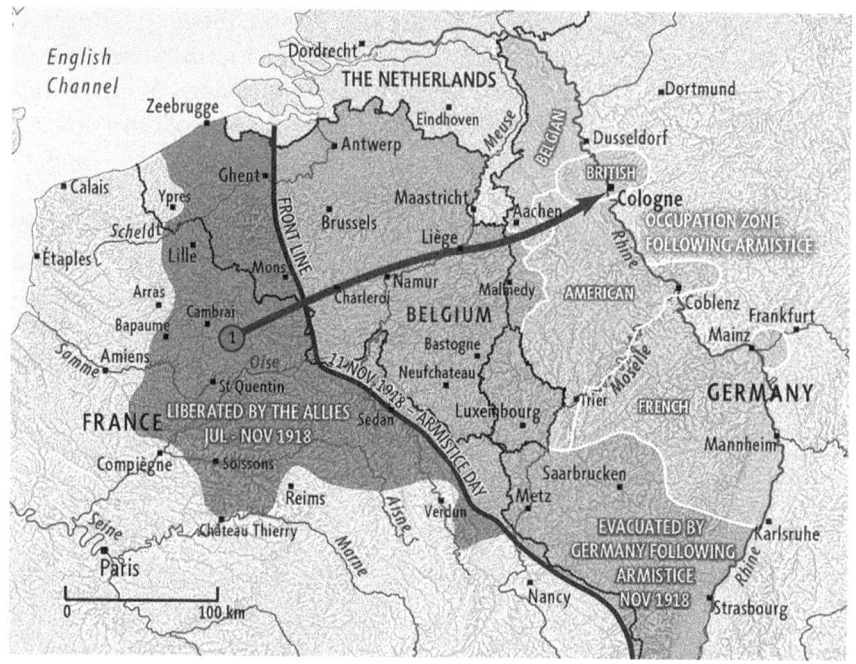

Map 7.1 The First World War, 1914–18

PREWAR POLITICAL AIMS AND DIPLOMATIC STRATEGY

Wilson tightly controlled foreign relations and often composed key notes himself. Important advisors were Secretary of State (from 1915) Robert Lansing and Edward M. House, a Texas politico and diplomat, and Wilson's special advisor. Both Lansing and House believed "America's security in large part rested on retaining amicable Anglo-American relations and preventing Germany from dominating the European continent." But House had his own ambitions for creating an international system in conjunction with Britain to bring world peace – regardless of the possibility of this – and would misrepresent Wilson's views and others.[25]

When the First World War began, most Americans saw a European affair. Wilson insisted upon neutrality and that Americans "be impartial in thought as well as in action." Nevertheless, American neutrality came to favor the Allies even as Wilson and Bryan defended neutral rights and worked to deny belligerents US help. But as the war provided a means of avoiding economic downturn, American loans and goods flowed to

Europe, especially the Allies. Active promotion of US trade followed, producing problems with the warring powers, particularly Britain and Germany.[26]

The Anglo-German struggle produced danger points. Britain, though it never officially imposed a blockade because much of the continent's trade passed through neutral ports, implemented one. One enforcement tool was stopping ships at sea, searching them for goods London labeled contraband, and sometimes seizing or forcing them into British ports. In November 1914, Britain declared the North Sea a war zone and began mining areas. Germany replied on February 4, 1915 with a submarine blockade of the British Isles, designating its waters a war zone where all merchant ships were liable to sinking without warning. Berlin's first unrestricted submarine warfare campaign opened on February 28. Washington replied with a stiff protest insisting upon Berlin's culpability if Americans were killed; Germany then limited its attacks on neutral ships. Wilson attempted to use international law to negotiate restrictions on the actions of both powers, but this was inadequate for Germany's innovative use of a new weapon and restraining a Britain determined to do whatever necessary to win. Lansing, then State Department counselor, was pro-Allied and believed Germany's submarine campaign threatened US interests; a German victory even more so.[27]

A German submarine sank the British liner *Lusitania* on May 7, 1915, killing 1,201 people, including 128 Americans. Appalled Americans voiced thoughts of war. German actions early in the conflict, such as the burning of Louvain, Belgium, and revelations of German spying in the US in 1915, made most Americans favor the Allies. The sinking in such fashion of a passenger liner (even one carrying munitions) was received as a new kind of German barbarity. We forget the shock of the then innovative use of a new weapon. The weight of public opinion forced Wilson to act. He demanded an apology and reparations, asserted the right of Americans to travel aboard the non-military vessels of belligerents, and insisted Germany use its submarines in line with the era's cruiser rules; this meant warning merchant vessels before attacking. Wilson's refusal to heed Bryan's insistence that the US must just as vociferously protest British violations of neutral rights produced the secretary of state's resignation.[28] Lansing replaced him.

The core of Wilson's diplomatic strategy during 1916 was an effort to negotiate a settlement of the war allowing America to remain neutral before events forced it into the war. Wilson tried to stay above the fray, believing this the only way to "exert the moral authority needed to end the war on terms that would make for a lasting peace." He dispatched House on a mediation effort in 1916 based upon Anglo-American cooperation. It achieved nothing.[29] But Wilson's desire to secure a "lasting peace" shows his purpose.

The German sinking of the merchant ship *Sussex* in March 1916 produced an April 1916 threat from Wilson to sever relations with Berlin, the traditional step before declaring war, unless it abandoned unrestricted submarine warfare. The Germans bent and returned to operations based on cruiser or prize rules, but Wilson realized this was a concession made from expediency and liable to change. The Germans soon recalled their submarines, judging a campaign conducted under cruiser rules pointless.[30]

Wilson capitalized politically on his keeping the US neutral. His Democratic Party's campaign slogan for 1916 – "He kept us out of war" – helped him win reelection. He then launched another mediation effort. Wilson saw British "navalism" and German militarism as synonymous. If the Germans replied positively to his overture and Britain didn't, he intended to press the British to bend by using London's dependence upon American credit as leverage and weakened Allied access to US financing before offering the proposal. Wilson was unaware of a late 1916 British study concluding London couldn't continue the war bereft of US munitions and financing, but he knew halting business with the Allies would injure America's economy. Wilson's offer was dispatched on December 18. The new British government of David Lloyd George refused to bend, viewing a compromise peace equal to defeat. Germany felt the same. Both London and Paris also concluded – correctly – that Wilson wouldn't force them to make peace by tightening the economic screws.[31]

Wilson remained undeterred. On January 22, 1917, he delivered his "Peace without Victory" speech to try to spark negotiations, proposing a revolution in how nations conducted war and peacemaking. Wilson sought a League of Peace where all nations joined together to guarantee peace and to end the war via "a peace without victory," meaning one not forced upon any defeated powers and absent humiliation of opponents. He believed only "a peace among equals" would last. He called for an independent Poland, freedom of the seas for trade, no entangling alliances, and limiting armaments. He proposed what he deemed a version of the Monroe Doctrine in that "no nation should seek to extend its polity over any other nation or people." The Allies replied with anger and ridicule, and saw here proof America wouldn't fight.[32]

At the time of Wilson's speech, the Germans had already decided to return to unrestricted submarine warfare. In October 1916, Berlin had resumed its submarine campaign under cruiser rules but was now willing to assume more risk. Germany believed an unrestricted campaign could sink or frighten away enough neutral shippers to make Britain unable to feed itself, forcing it to make peace. This would break France and Italy, producing a German victory. The proclamation delivered on January 9, 1917 declared all ships in a designated war zone around the British Isles subject to attack. Unrestricted submarine warfare began on February 1. The US severed relations on February 3. Wilson continued searching for an honorable way to stay out of the war, something American public opinion supported, believing he had to be a neutral actor to achieve the peace he wanted.[33]

Then London produced an intercepted January 1917 telegram from German Foreign Minister Arthur Zimmerman. Berlin wanted a military alliance with Mexico and promised help recapturing territory lost in the 1846–48 war. An appalled Wilson gave the press the note. Americans now saw war as more likely, but this didn't provoke a declaration. News of the March 8 overthrow of Russia's tsar arrived shortly after. Now, if America entered the war, it wouldn't be fighting alongside an autocratic regime against an autocratic regime but as part of a democratic coalition.[34]

Wilson continued searching for a way to stay out but learned on March 18, 1917 of German submarines sinking three American merchant ships. Wilson now saw war as the only means of securing a just peace. He insisted "war was thrust upon us" (ignoring who declared war upon whom) and believed he could enter the struggle with his conscience clear because America wouldn't fight for its material benefit but "to vindicate the principles of peace and justice in the life of the world." When Wilson signed the April 6 declaration "The United States found itself fully entwined in European and world affairs. It never again would be able to extricate itself."[35]

PREPARATION AND ASSESSMENT

As usual, the US was unprepared militarily. Wilson found planning for an offensive war against Germany incompatible with neutrality. Planning was delayed until the US entered the war, and a preparedness campaign accomplished little for the army. Congress's 1916 National Defense Act further paralyzed preparation by restricting the general staff to forty-five officers. The Naval Act of 1916 would make the US navy the largest in the world, but it funded a battleship-heavy navy years in the building, scant help against submarines. And Wilson's secretaries of the army and navy in late 1916, Newton D. Baker and Josephus Daniels, respectively, had pacifist leanings. The active army numbered 128,000, the National Guard, 80,000. Most of the navy's ships were undermanned, and it lacked antisubmarine forces and support vessels. The Marine Corps had expanded from its 1899 strength of 3,142 to 10,601 in 1916. After Wilson severed relations with Germany in February 1917, the War Department began planning the army's expansion and gave the president a program in early March to grow it to 500,000. By the end of the month, Secretary of War Baker argued for raising an additional 1 million. The administration thought it wouldn't have to deploy a large army to Europe, believing material and financial support enough to win.[36]

British and French military missions soon met Secretary of War Baker, Army Chief of Staff General Hugh Scott, and his deputy, Tasker Bliss. London wanted 500,000 men shipped to Europe to train and equip them and amalgamate them with its army. The French initially didn't favor this but were soon pushing the same. Paris also wanted an immediate token US force. The amalgamation schemes, which essentially meant Americans being reinforcements for Allied armies, received no support in Washington. Bliss insisted upon an independent US army and didn't think the American public would tolerate amalgamation.[37]

In October 1917, to help pay for the war, Congress passed the War Revenue Act. It included traditional "sin taxes" on alcohol and tobacco, luxury goods and postal taxes, "a sharply progressive surtax to the income tax," and "a graduated excess profits tax on corporations and individuals." Only about 30 percent of the war's costs were paid by taxes and other government revenue. The rest came from borrowing (about 40 percent) and the creation (or printing) of money. The latter two hid the war's costs.[38]

Wilson had concluded peace couldn't be made without America entering the war but also thought US finances and naval strength meant the war would end within two years with little sacrifice of US blood. He joined the war on the Entente side but tried to stay above the fray morally while entering the fight physically, something impossible and unrealistic.[39] This marked the oddest element of Wilson's grand strategy for waging the war: assuming he could take the nation to war and remain a detached peace broker. The unreality of this comes through in Wilson making the US an "associated power," not an "allied" one. Germany found here, and in Wilson's unilateral acts in regard to the Entente's relations with Berlin, openings for trying to split the coalition.

WILSON'S POLITICAL AIMS

When the US went to war, Wilson had spent three years handling foreign relations with warring powers. This didn't dampen his idealism regarding what could be achieved as he tried to create a new international system. In his April 2, 1917 war speech, Wilson gave America's political aims as: "The world must be made safe for democracy. Its peace must be planted upon the tested foundations of political liberty.... We desire no conquest, no dominion. We seek no indemnities for ourselves, no material compensation for the sacrifices we shall freely make."[40]

Wilson's democracy aim must be seen as one of history's most ambitious. Why? *Because it applied to the world.* Pursuit of this aim would complicate achievement of others, but it marked a dynamic change. The US went to war in 1898 seeking Cuba's independence. It now fought to make the world "safe for democracy." Wilson abandoned a traditional war aim: territorial expansion. The US is often accused of fighting wars for expansion or empire after this, but it's never the truth. The US fought to defend other regimes and overthrow them, but not for its own territorial or imperial aggrandizement. Only after the Second World War would other major powers – and only other liberal democracies – make the shift Wilson inaugurated.

Wilson didn't consult his Entente partners before making his announcement. He believed doing so would make them suspicious and hinder coordinating against Germany. He wrote House: *"England and France have not the same views with regard to peace that we have* by any means. When the war is over we can force them to our way of thinking because by that time they will, among other things, be financially in our hands."[41] Wilson understood that other states had their own political aims but drastically overestimated the power of the financial lever – particularly *after* the war when the situation wouldn't be dire. Many plead the strength of financial leverage over opponents, but something that might work with a small, weak state lacks potency against great powers with vast resources, enormous standing military forces, and central banks that can create internationally accepted currency.

COALITION WARFARE AND US GRAND STRATEGY

When the US entered the war, it became part of a powerful coalition arrayed against the Central Powers. It was a junior partner militarily (though didn't see itself so) and in the creation of grand strategy. The US depended upon its allies for nearly all of its heavy weapons and combat aircraft and much other equipment. American forces received British and French training and were reliant upon British shipping and French and British logistical support. At the same time, America's partners depended upon US money and material.[42]

Coalitions bring with them advantages: increased strength and capabilities, resource- and burden-sharing, propaganda and public opinion windfalls. They also bring problems. One can be political aims that are sometimes contradictory and perhaps even injurious to the interests of allies. Wilson used America's armed forces as a tool for achieving his political aims and gave his aims precedent over those of partner nations. Moreover, in comparison to Britain and France, Wilson believed achievement of his political aims would "further the interests of humankind, not the interests of a particular country." Moreover, "America's military involvement was designed to drive Germany's 'military masters' from power and to impose Wilson's liberal peace program on victors and vanquished alike."[43] London, Paris, and Rome viewed things differently.

The US declared war on April 6, 1917. Pershing was named commander of the American Expeditionary Force (AEF) and quickly dispatched 12,000 troops to work with the French. The American general staff insisted the US not fight in Europe until it could do so as an independent force. Pershing's orders gave him the leeway to cooperate with the "associated" powers as he thought best, awarding him more freedom to use his force than perhaps any previous US commander. But he was also instructed that "the forces of the United States are a separate and distinct component of the combined forces, the identity of which must be preserved." Pershing had no problem with his orders. He wanted to build an enormous American army and play a decisive role in the war; his superiors agreed. Secretary of War Baker convinced Wilson to support committing a large US force, and Wilson realized he couldn't control the peacemaking process without it. In July, Pershing dispatched the "General Organization Project." It outlined a 20-division, 1-million-man army to be created by 1918 and urged formation of a 3-million-man, 30-division force within two years.[44]

Pershing quickly learned that one of the biggest obstacles to putting a massive US force in the field was a shortage of shipping. The Entente also needed to control the sea lines of communication (SLOCs) to bring these soldiers to the front, supply them, and keep Britain in the war. Doing this necessitated countering the submarine. The British laid minefields in key areas to catch transiting German submarines (but British mines were unreliable) and had a barrage barrier crossing the Straits of Dover. The most important counter was establishing a convoy system at the end of April 1917. The British had resisted instituting a complete convoy system, despite its success in some areas earlier in the war. London had many flawed reasons why: convoys were too slow, arming merchantmen was considered more effective, and Britain lacked sufficient escorts (an assessment based on inaccurate sailing numbers).[45]

An obvious solution to the escort problem was tapping the Americans. Wilson allowed the US navy to establish contacts with the British when it looked as though war was coming and Rear Admiral William Sims was dispatched to lead the effort. In London, Sims discovered that if elevated merchant vessel losses continued, Britain faced defeat in a few months. London pressed for dispatch of escorts and construction of merchant and antisubmarine warfare (ASW) ships. Wilson took little interest in land ventures but manifested greater attentiveness in naval issues. The decision to dispatch the first six destroyers for antisubmarine warfare occurred a week after the declaration of war. These reached the British base in Queenstown, Ireland, in April. There were thirty-five on hand by the end of August.[46]

Driven by heavy April losses, Britain's new convoy system launched in May. Sims became an enthusiastic supporter; his superiors weren't. The system soon proved itself and losses fell, but the number of destroyers became a limiting factor. And convoys didn't operate everywhere, such as in the Mediterranean. Britain's admiralty remained resistant and skeptical even as the system showed its value, a mental inflexibility delaying institution of convoys for vessels departing Britain. The most important contributions of the US navy were convoy protection and antisubmarine warfare.[47]

The merchant shipping shortage remained a key constraint on implementing American strategy. The US lacked sufficient tonnage to transport US troops and relied on British bottoms. Washington also failed to try to improve this situation during the first few months of the war, instead concentrating on building an army it couldn't move to the theater of war. The German submarine campaign worsened the problem. The Americans launched a merchant ship–building program, but bungled it, upsetting the British. Washington also poorly managed its existing merchant capacity. Only in the latter months of 1918 did US ship-building bear fruit.[48]

PART II: FROM GREAT POWER TO SUPERPOWER

THE WAR IN EUROPE: MILITARY STRATEGY

A critical strategy debate among the Western Allies occurred between Easterners and Westerners, meaning whether the coalition's military emphasis should be on the Western Front in France and Belgium or someplace else. The Easterners argued for action against Germany's allies such as Turkey or Bulgaria.[49] The Americans deployed some troops to Italy but remained die-hard Westerners.

Pershing believed the war would be won on the Western Front and wanted Allied forces concentrated there. He insisted in November 1917 "that the efforts of the Allies should continue as now in progress, and that every possible energy that America can exert should be put forth there, whether the role is to be offensive or defensive." Pershing chose a section of Lorraine for the site of America's ground war, pleasing the French. Pershing wanted to control his own logistics lines through France, and eventually would. But more important to him was an army capable of producing a decisive result, something Wilson supported because this would provide leverage at the peace table. But Pershing was far from having the instrument for this.[50]

The document guiding American military action was a September 25, 1917 assessment of the German defenses between Verdun and the Swiss border: "A Strategical Study on the Employment of the A.E.F. against the Imperial German Government." This gave as the AEF's primary task – political aim – the "'displacement' of the Imperial German Government," meaning regime change. Wilson's desire for democracy required this, but changing the government didn't guarantee a democratic replacement. Wilson, meanwhile, continued to talk of "peace without victory," thinking supporters of peace in Germany would overcome the militarists, while the army spoke of "peace through victory" via defeating the German army. The plan argued against assuming any section of the British line or of putting American forces at the juncture of the Allied armies because it was thought this would prevent the US from playing a decisive role. Only minor offensive operations were planned for 1918 – reducing the St. Mihiel salient the most important – while building US strength to deliver a heavy blow in Lorraine in 1919. The Americans believed seizing the German rail lines behind the Lorraine front would break German defenses in the south and compel a withdrawal to the Rhine and eastern Belgium. The added seizure of key German salt, coal, and iron sources, in an example of wishful thinking, would strike a near-fatal blow against the German economy.

Underpinning the plan were some assumptions for which the US had no evidence: Pershing believed American men and tactics were superior, and that little could be learned from Britain and France. He saw Americans as the best at "open warfare" and more aggressive, enabling the US to play "the leading role in the last phase" of war.[51]

Wilson worried American public opinion wouldn't stand casualties like the 620,000 suffered by the British and French during the July to November 1916 Battle of the Somme if this didn't bring the US closer to victory. The general staff, though, fully expected victory to require a heavy blood price. They hoped massing US forces would give the Allies the necessary superiority in numbers and told Wilson the war would last until enough Americans were in Europe to defeat Germany by delivering a "knock-out blow" to the German army.[52]

After the failure of France's April–May 1917 Nivelle Offensive, the British and French abandoned hopes for a breakthrough and adopted a strategy of "wearing down and exhausting the enemy's resistance" and hoped growing American strength would shift the balance. British Prime Minister Lloyd George became a proponent of peripheral moves. After the disastrous October–November 1917 Battle of Caporetto in Italy, Lloyd George pushed a plan to create an Allied supreme war council to advise on Allied strategy and unify their efforts. The Allies recognized Russia would probably soon leave the war, allowing Germany to shift troops west.[53]

Established at Rapallo, Italy, on November 17, 1917, the Supreme Allied War Council comprised the leaders of Britain, France, Italy, and the US, or their representatives. Meeting roughly monthly, eight times, over the war's last year, the council recommended strategy. Other inter-Allied groups provided support and discussed such things as finance, the blockade, and munitions production. There was also an Allied Naval Council, though Washington didn't send a political representative until after the onset of the first armistice negotiations. Bliss, the American military representative to the Supreme Council, was handicapped in his role because the administration kept him in the dark – intentionally – on its political views.[54]

Wilson's initial aloofness from inter-Allied consultation and refusal to properly inform Bliss marked an effort to maintain diplomatic independence. He excused this by insisting he was waiting until the US could make a significant military contribution. But Allied disasters, British and French pressure, and German attacks drove Wilson to abandon his plan to limit military and political consultations with his partners, and he dispatched

House to the October 1917 conference as head of a US mission with orders to formalize technical cooperation.[55]

Near the end of 1917, the Allied situation grew desperate, and the British and French pressed for amalgamation of US forces with theirs. Bliss warned Wilson that if the US stuck to its plan to build for a 1919 offensive, the war might be lost. Pershing was told to keep the American forces together but consider other options for their use. Pershing ordered a reassessment. His advisors argued for sticking with the plan.[56]

WILSON'S EVOLVING POLITICAL AIMS AND GRAND STRATEGY

Leaders and states pursuing idealistic purposes usually encounter roadblocks to securing their ends and change course, especially when these aims apply to other lands upon which they lack the ability or the will to impose the desired outcome.

In a December 4, 1917 speech, Wilson presented his vision of what obtaining victory required. German power first had to be completely crushed, or "if it be not utterly brought to an end, at least shut out from the friendly intercourse of the nations." After this, when Germany had leaders who "accept the common judgment of the nations as to what shall henceforth be the bases of law and of covenant for the life of the world," then peace would come. Though Wilson didn't clearly state this, what he demanded required regime change in Germany, meaning the end of German Imperial rule.[57]

In January 1918, Wilson announced his Fourteen Points. He did this unilaterally and made it clear that US aims differed from those of America's partners. He was convinced the statements of Russia's Bolshevik revolutionary rulers regarding making peace without indemnities or territorial annexations required him to act. In line with earlier statements, Wilson sought a world "fit and safe to live in" for "every peace-loving nation." Such a peace would come about by achieving what is largely a list of political aims. "For such arrangements and covenants we are willing to fight," Wilson said, "but only because we wish the right to prevail and desire a just and stable peace such as can be secured only by removing the chief provocations to war, which this program does remove." His points were: 1) open and public diplomacy and treaties of peace; 2) freedom of navigation at sea in peace and war; 3) equality of trade among nations; 4) the reduction of arms as far as possible; 5) open and fair resolution of colonial territorial claims; 6) evacuation of Russia; 7) evacuation and restoration of Belgium; 8) evacuation of French territory, including Alsace-Lorraine; 9) altering Italy's borders on the basis of nationality; 10) autonomy of Austria-Hungary's minorities; 11) evacuation of Romania, Montenegro, and Serbia, with the latter given sea access; 12) autonomy to minorities in the Turkish Empire and freedom of navigation through the Dardanelles; 13) an independent Poland with sea access; and 14) what became known as the League of Nations. The idea for a League was not a new one. Napoleonic-era Habsburg Foreign Minister Clemens von Metternich had suggested something similar.[58]

MILITARY STRATEGY CONTINUED

Early 1918 found the Allies pursuing a defensive strategy while awaiting the arrival of Americans *en masse*. The March 3, 1918 Treaty of Brest-Litovsk saw Russia leave the war and cede vast territory to Germany. Berlin shifted forces west. This increased Allied desires for American troops. The Brest-Litovsk Treaty, and the German spring offensive that kicked off on March 21, forced Wilson to consider that perhaps Berlin was as dangerous as London; he was soon worrying about the outcome if Germany exhausted the Allies. Any peace would be a German peace, and thus a bad one. Continuing the war would be up to America, a potential responsibility under which Wilson shuddered because it affected the entire world.[59]

Wilson mistakenly viewed Germany's March 1918 offensive as a response to his Fourteen Points. It not only surprised him but also seems to have shattered his rose-colored diplomatic glasses. He had assumed the Central Powers' peace factions would force negotiations on the basis of his aims, an example of misunderstanding the opponents and scriptwriting, meaning mapping a course for an enemy's reaction that ignores their agency. The German offensive ended discussion of a negotiated peace. In his next Congressional speech Wilson demanded "Force, Force to the utmost, Force without stint or limit." The German offensive and American criticism of his lack of leadership drove him to greater involvement in the war. He circumvented his cabinet (it spent much of its time on jokes and stories) and formed a war council to handle mobilization and work with America's partners.[60]

The German offensive shattered Britain's Fifth Army and led to French General (later Marshal) Ferdinand Foch's appointment as the Allied supreme commander, with limited powers. On March 26, he was given authority to coordinate Allied forces on the Western Front but had to consult the French and British army commanders, Marshall Philippe Pétain and Field Marshal Douglas Haig, before ordering movements. Foch got his authority extended, which the Americans supported. Washington also insisted American forces fall under Foch's command. The Supreme War Council's influence shrank as Foch assumed many of its functions.[61]

Britain and France tried delaying formation of an independent American army, partly because they believed it would be unable to function autonomously until 1919. Britain continually and unsuccessfully pushed amalgamation. In early 1918, Wilson came under sustained Congressional attack because of the slow rate of US mobilization. This made it politically impossible for Wilson to allow US troops to serve under the British as this would be seen as proof of the incompetence charge. Britain's desperate need for manpower in the face of the German offensive, and its demand American troops be brigaded with Britain's, strained Anglo-American relations because the US simply refused to abandon its role as an independent army. Pershing was willing to commit his units but only as a US force. American troops entered combat *en masse* at Catigny on May 28, 1918.[62]

In mid June 1918, Britain finally accepted that Pershing wouldn't bend on amalgamation. London, seeing no hope of victory in 1918, began fearing it might not be possible in 1919, and worried that if they didn't receive sufficient American reinforcements, their army might be ground down so much that it became second-rate, injuring Britain's position at any future peace table. London's strategic priority became warding off defeat in the West. A secondary element was acting on the periphery to make political gains in case the Germans couldn't be defeated on the Western Front. Something occupying Bliss from July to October was trying to prevent Allied strategy from shifting from a focus on the Western Front to areas such as Macedonia and the Middle East. Action here wouldn't defeat Germany's army but meet French and British aims.[63]

THE RUSSIA INTERLUDE

After the Bolsheviks took Russia out of the war in March 1918, Britain and France began pushing intervention in hopes of reconstituting an Eastern Front and destroying the Bolsheviks. The Americans resisted, believing the Allies should concentrate on the Western Front. Intervention became a divisive inter-Allied issue, but Wilson capitulated in June 1918. He supported a landing in Murmansk to keep the Germans from seizing the port and the materials the Allies had sent Russia. The occupation of Archangel followed. Wilson's agreement to participate "represented an attempt to restrict the scope of undesirable but unavoidable inter-Allied adventures." In July, Wilson bent again and joined the intervention in Siberia with Japan to protect war materials, give economic aid to Siberia, and rescue the Czech Legion. Originally raised by the Russians to fight the Central Powers, largely from prisoners of war, the Legion was trying to escape Russia via Vladivostok to fight on the Western Front. The Bolsheviks had cooperated at first, but the Czechs soon found they had to seize the Trans-Siberian Railroad and fight their way out. Meanwhile, Wilson angered his Allies with a July 17, 1918 note insisting the US wasn't interfering in Russia's internal affairs while implying he was protecting Russia from both the Germans and the Allies.[64]

THE WAR IN EUROPE: THE FINAL PHASE

In July 1918, Pershing's superiors told him they expected him to defeat the Germans. He asked Foch for tasks and objectives for the American army and pushed the War Department to ensure he had 100 US divisions by July 1919. Late July 1918 saw Foch's strategy of continuous offensive pressure against the Germans, one characterized by short, quick attacks. These would restore some of France's industrial potential and alleviate communications problems by securing key rail lines extending from Paris. The attacks would also use up Germany's reserves while laying the groundwork for a future war of movement. The three national forces would act essentially independently but as parts of a larger, unified strategy. After some angry back and forth with Foch, on September 2 it was agreed the Americans would launch their St. Mihiel offensive and then take over a 60-mile stretch of front. The American attack was serendipitously timed, falling just as the Germans began retreating. America's Meuse–Argonne attack followed shortly after. On November 1, American troops broke through the German lines and made their biggest advances of the war. But the army was in many ways still in children's shoes as it depended upon its allies for logistical, artillery, and air support. Pershing looked toward the prospect of an American victory in 1919.[65]

September 1918 saw the position of Germany and the other Central Powers begin collapsing. The Allied victory over Bulgaria in Macedonia proved the final blow, convincing German military leaders to seek an armistice. The Germans tried to injure the Allied coalition by approaching the Americans and asking for an armistice on the basis of Wilson's Fourteen Points on the night of October 4/5, 1918. The Austrians had sent their own note on September 16. The direct approaches to the Americans produced anger among British, French, and Italian leaders. Driving Berlin's urgency was the growing collapse of its army. A new civilian government was formed under moderate Prince Max of Baden, a change to the governing system made to meet Allied demands. Wilson gave an initial noncommittal reply to Berlin without consulting Britain or France. Germany grasped the straw, though Wilson's second note demonstrated more concern for Allied views. Berlin was asked to accept his peace plan spelled out in the Fourteen Points and subsequent speeches, and to limit any further discussion to the "practical details of their application." Wilson also imposed stiff conditions for agreeing to an armistice: Germany's withdrawal from all conquered territory.[66]

One can wait too long to negotiate. By the time Berlin decided it could stomach a negotiated settlement, Germany's position had deteriorated to the point that it possessed no leverage. Baden dispatched a second note to Wilson on October 12 accepting the Fourteen Points in principle, the details to be decided at a peace conference. Turkey "sued for peace on the basis of the Fourteen Points" the same day. Wilson responded that the Allies would only accept an armistice if they had guarantees Germany couldn't restart the fighting. He reminded Baden that America had entered the war to break autocratic authority and wouldn't stop until it achieved this. Wilson wanted the departure of Kaiser Wilhelm and other key "reactionary leaders."[67]

Baden agreed. Democratic reforms expanding suffrage and an empowered German parliament followed. The British, meanwhile, worried Germany merely wanted a breathing space and asked Wilson to consult with his allies before making any other commitments. Wilson told Baden on October 23 that he would talk with his partners. If they agreed, the armistice would be granted. He also threatened to pursue unconditional surrender if he had to deal with a militarist government. The Austrians had also agreed to negotiate an armistice based on the Fourteen Points, with modifications regarding minority nationalities.[68]

Wilson wanted a moderate armistice ensuring fighting didn't restart and wasn't too humiliating for Germany. Britain wanted peace because it had reached its manpower limits and sought a postwar balance of power on the continent, a traditional British aim. Foch also wanted a military situation preventing Germany from resuming the war. This included German abandonment of Alsace-Lorraine, Allied bridgeheads over the Rhine, and the handing over of large stocks of military equipment and railroad rolling stock. Pershing argued for unconditional surrender as accepting an armistice too early might lose the Allies the chance to create a lasting peace. But the British and French, who had paid enormous costs in blood and treasure, worried that if they didn't take an armistice when offered, the Allies risked Bolshevik revolutions in Germany and Austria-Hungary, the

Germans rebuilding over the winter, and the wrath of their own citizens who had sacrificed so heavily. Worse, America might prove the vehicle of victory in 1919, ensuring Britain and France couldn't achieve their aims.[69]

During inter-Allied negotiations marred by infighting between the civilian and military leaders, House discovered "the Entente leaders hoped to by-pass the Fourteen Points." House thought US leverage would markedly decrease with the signing of an armistice and fought to get Allied agreement on the Fourteen Points beforehand. He said that if they weren't accepted, it would mean rejection of the negotiations Wilson had already conducted with the Central Powers (which were based on the Fourteen Points). Georges Clemenceau asked if this could lead to the US making a separate peace. "It might," House replied, essentially threatening to take the US out of the war. This had the desired effect, though House bent in regard to Lloyd George's desire to keep his ability to act in regard to freedom of the seas. Wilson disliked this but agreed. Clemenceau also managed to modify point eight to open the issue of reparations. In the end, the primary requirements of Wilson and Foch shaped the armistice proposal. Wilson won approval for negotiations based on his Fourteen Points, while Foch secured his territorial and armaments handovers, terms severe enough to stop Germany renewing the struggle. This gave the Allies greater freedom to construct peace terms. Germany announced Kaiser Wilhelm's abdication on November 9, ending German autocracy. When offered the armistice terms, in a surprise to the Allies, the Germans accepted. The armistice began on November 11, 1918.[70]

MAKING THE WORLD SAFE FOR TYRANNY: LOSING THE PEACE

Ideally, one wants to construct a peace that will last. Foch described what the victorious Entente powers achieved with the Versailles Treaty: "This is not a peace. It is an armistice for 20 years."[71] Despite the acceptance of Wilson's Fourteen Points as the armistice basis, the Allies agreed neither on their political aims nor the accompanying issue of what peace should look like. There are, of course, many things to consider when ending a war. But the biggest issues the combatants must address are an intertwined trio: 1) what to demand politically; 2) how far to go militarily; and 3) who will maintain the peace and how.

THE POLITICAL AIM

When the war began, Wilson wanted to delay discussion of peace terms until after its end, but as conditions evolved, he was forced to change tack. Wilson began preparing and established a team of experts under House to compile data. Moreover, Wilson "was determined to sustain his capacity to ensure an enlightened peace. If necessary, he would dictate a just settlement."[72] As we have seen, Wilson sought democracy abroad and insisted upon numerous things such as no territorial expansion or indemnities.

America's key allies possessed their own definitions of "just." Lloyd George sought territorial and economic gains to increase Britain's security and won his December 1918 election by promising a harsh peace with a heavy German indemnity. This limited his negotiating options. The French, led by Clemenceau, believed German power would revive and that France would again need British and American help to survive. Clemenceau sought to weaken Germany as much as possible but not at the expense of losing the support of London and Washington. Coalition partners should iron out the differences in their political aims before the time for peacemaking arrives.[73] Doing so removes grounds for conflict among allies; not doing so can guarantee disagreement while threatening construction of a lasting peace.

USING MILITARILY POWER

Wilson believed obtaining his aims required "victory over the Central Powers and the maintenance of American diplomatic independence." At the end of the war, the US had 2 million troops in Europe and 29 of the 42 US divisions had seen action. Pershing, as we saw above, pushed for continuing the war and unconditional surrender. He knew the US would only get stronger. His view angered his Washington masters. Wilson – contradictorily – wired House: "Too much success or security on the part of the Allies will make a genuine peace settlement exceedingly difficult if not impossible."[74]

Lloyd George was inclined to deliver his "knock-out blow." He argued for invading Germany and then dictating terms. He believed they had to punish the Germans as the Germans had France. He received little support. Field Marshal Haig argued Germany wasn't finished and could continue fighting into 1919. He also worried about the declining state of his own forces. He knew he couldn't replace his losses and that if the war continued, the Americans would be the dominant force on the battlefield and thus at the peace table. Stopping now meant the difference between a British peace and an American one.[75]

The French wanted to deal Germany a heavy blow and make it feel the war as France had at German hands in 1871. Military commanders like

Pétain wanted to push into Lorraine, others wanted to march into Germany itself, believing the Germans would never admit defeat otherwise. They couldn't get this but required Germany to retreat to the prewar border, permit Allied bridgeheads over the Rhine, and hand over tens of thousands of machineguns, mortars, and artillery pieces, as well as 1,700 aircraft, dozens of warships, and all of its submarines.[76]

But by stopping before Allied troops marched into Germany, the Allies, as Pétain feared, failed to make it clear to the Germans that they had been defeated. After the war, German Socialist Chancellor Friedrich Ebert greeted returning troops who marched through Berlin's Brandenburg Gate by remarking that no one had defeated them on the battlefield. The Germans weren't made to accept that their military forces had been beaten, as had their nation.[77] Defeat must be made clear to prevent the rise of falsehoods that undermine the peace. The Nazi "stab in the back" myth became perhaps the best-known example of this.

MAINTAINING THE PEACE

Wilson reached Paris for the negotiations that produced the Versailles Treaty in a reduced political position. Before departing Washington, he had tried to sell his postwar vision for a League of Nations over the heads of his Republican opponents by appealing directly to the people in the 1918 elections. The Republicans carried the House and the Senate. Wilson's advisors "urged him to send a bipartisan American team to the peace conference in Paris. Wilson refused." Germany's acceptance of an armistice meant he lacked military leverage, and he overestimated the influence of Allied war debt upon the United States. Moreover, Wilson wanted collective security via his League so deeply he eventually compromised on the covenant's structure, hoping to change it later. Wilson was surprised to learn the American people wanted a harsh settlement. He was trying to make peace in a political and emotional vacuum, one not bounded by the reality of human passions or awareness of the war's effects and costs upon his "Associated" powers.[78]

Wilson's coterie of experts known as "The Inquiry" accompanied him to Paris with the intention of doing "the right thing" in the peace. But Wilson discovered "that what was politically possible could not be determined by experts." Moreover, the failure of the Allied powers to produce a coherent vision of the peace meant the leaders wrangled over every detail piecemeal and presented the result at the end. The final product surprised even Lloyd George, especially the total demanded for reparations: approximately $33 billion in 1919 dollars, roughly equivalent to $6 trillion in 2021. This overwhelmed the perceived reasonableness of the individual parts.[79]

Wilson, Clemenceau, and Lloyd George did agree the peace would hold only if the wartime alliance continued. Wilson believed "the American sphere of responsibility" had to extend everywhere to ensure US security. Convincing others was the rub as Americans didn't agree. To Wilson the League of Nations, the Covenant for which was included in the Treaty of Versailles, was a tool for securing the peace. He believed the combined power of its members would usually constrain future bad actors. But he also realized that force had to underpin the League, or it lacked credibility: members would be bound to act against aggression. Among Clemenceau's security quests was the separation of the Rhineland from Germany, which Lloyd George and Wilson resisted. Clemenceau was convinced to drop this through treaties guaranteeing the US and Great Britain would fight alongside France against any future German invasion. The catch: both Britain *and* the US had to ratify the Versailles Treaty.[80]

When the long negotiations were finally completed, the Allies gave Germany little choice but to sign. This was neither shocking nor politically unusual. The Germans had imposed treaties on France in 1871, Romania in 1916, and Russia in 1918. The Germans signed (unhappily) and immediately declared it illegitimate because they had agreed to an armistice based on the Fourteen Points and not what they signed. The "War Guilt" clause in which Germany assumed blame for the war, and which enabled the Allied reparations demands, galled the Germans.[81]

In securing Senate approval for the treaty, Wilson faced opposition from both parties regarding its terms, the toughest being "disheartened Democrats." Membership in the League was the most contentious plank, even more so than Wilson's planned military alliance with France and Britain, which went against the traditions of protecting US sovereignty and non-entanglement with European powers. Some Senators disliked the collective security obligations in Article Ten of the League Covenant. This could drag the US into wars where it had no interests. More critically, it was seen as infringing Congress's constitutional power to declare war. The situation was worsened by the antagonism between Wilson and Senate leader Republican Henry Cabot Lodge, a predicament Wilson fed by his approach. Wilson believed League membership the best means of getting Americans to abandon their traditional resistance to foreign entanglements and insisted the Senate pass the treaty as it was.[82]

Wilson's opponents are sometimes derided as "isolationists." This is wrong. League membership raised sovereignty issues and had security implications. Wilson admitted to some Republican senators that joining the League meant the US "would willingly relinquish some of its sovereignty." Republican Senator Root explained the opposition on the security front: "If it is necessary for the security of western Europe that we should agree to the support of France if attacked, then let us agree to do that particular thing plainly.... But let us not wrap up such a purpose in a vague universal obligation." The opposition supported the alliance to preserve Europe's balance of power – hardly the response of "isolationists" – but balked at guaranteeing the world. League membership could follow, but not in a form where the US assumed nebulous security guarantees that may or may not also mean unwanted additional defense expenditures. Senators Root and Lodge offered a solution. They condensed fifty reservations into a perhaps not coincidental fourteen amendments to the treaty. Most revolved around preserving Congress' traditional constitutional responsibilities and powers. Senate opposition included a group known as the "irreconcilables" who were against League membership. They believed in non-entanglement, not isolationism. Republican Senator Robert Borah, for example, opposed League membership because it would mean an alliance with France and Britain.[83]

Overall, "about 80 percent of the Senate and a clear majority of the American people were prepared to accept the League in some form." Wilson, though, refused *any* changes, and tried to go over the heads of the Senate to the American people via a national speaking tour. The exhausted president had a stroke on October 2, 1919, ending his active campaign for the treaty and the League. On November 19, 1919, the Senate voted on a version of the treaty including Lodge's reservations. Wilson told Democrats to vote against it because of Lodge's amendments and it failed to pass. A second vote on March 19, 1920 had a majority but not the two-thirds required for ratification. Wilson's refusal to countenance any change meant the treaty and the League went down to defeat, and not just from a lack of Republican votes. Wilson believed the treaty would be ratified after the 1920 elections, but his party realized public opinion had turned against it. American rejection meant France didn't receive its security agreements from Britain or the United States. It also meant the US wouldn't help enforce the peace.[84]

The Versailles Treaty still went into effect – without a US signature. The settlement had myriad problems. The Italians disliked the terms because they didn't receive the territory promised them for entering the war. Self-determination was unworkable in places with intermingled populations such as the Balkans, was not applied to German-speaking Austria, and not even considered in the former Ottoman lands in the Middle East that became *de facto* British and French colonies under the League of Nations mandate system. In the end, Germany paid less in reparations than France after its defeat in the 1870–71 Franco-Prussian War.[85]

Wilson's "temporizing on Asia" added another layer of difficulty during the 1919 peace negotiations. Asian leaders such as Vietnam's Ho Chi Minh interpreted Wilson's endorsement of national self-determination as also applying to them. Wilson, though, was concerned with Europe. Wilson angered Japan by allowing rejection of an antiracism clause. Wilson then bent to Japanese territorial demands, partially to keep them from leaving the conference. He believed the concessions, which included Japan retaining Shandong, China, worth helping ensure the League's creation, a means of resolving future problems through the combined efforts of all powers. Wilson repudiated the Open Door by abandoning insistence on Chinese territorial integrity and the balancing of great-power interests in China.[86]

John Maynard Keynes famously criticized the Versailles Treaty in *The Economic Consequences of the Peace*, particularly on two fronts. First, he said the reparations demands were too high, unnecessarily included pensions, and had not been part of Wilson's Fourteen Points upon which the Germans had agreed to an armistice. Second, he insisted Germany couldn't pay the figure demanded because it lacked the ability to make the necessary transfer payments. This could only be done by selling assets such as its merchant marine (which the Allies had already taken) or significantly increasing its exports (which competitors would meet with tariffs) or gutting its imports (which the need for recovery made almost impossible). He also insisted reparations would fuel economic dislocation by robbing Germany of its ability to make payments abroad, something it had done in abundance before the war. Moreover, Germany's ability to pay had been injured by the war's effects, its loss of territory and population, and the massive devaluation of its currency. French economist Étienne Mantoux rebutted Keynes' argument in *The Carthaginian Peace; or The Economic Consequences of Mr. Keynes*. Mantoux argued that the speedy recovery of the German economy after the war, which eventually fed Hitler's rearmament, demonstrated not a lack of ability to pay but of will.[87]

In the end, the US left its former "associated" powers to enforce the treaty on their own. This proved exceedingly difficult, particularly because Germany refused to keep its terms. Most of the twenty-seven signatory nations quickly lost interest in enforcement. Only Belgium, Italy, and France took part in the 1923 punitive implementation by marching troops into Germany's Ruhr, where the Americans had participated as part of the postwar occupation force. Geography can affect the enforcement of peace terms just as it does a war's waging because of the proximity of the defeated to the victors. Distance and the Atlantic Ocean allowed the US to ignore a revisionist and revanchist Germany for a very long time; France had no such luxury.[88] The Versailles Treaty didn't cause the Second World War, but it failed to properly end the first one.

CONCLUSION

One of the great problems with Wilson was his establishment of ambitious, often idealistic political aims demanding heavy commitments while thinking these could be achieved "without commensurate cost or expenditure on the part of the United States." Failing to provide sufficient means for achieving the political aim is a prominent factor in American foreign relations and war making. Wilson's ambitions should have taught American leaders "the importance of selecting realistic war aims, developing a practical strategy for achieving them, and paying close attention to the execution of that strategy during the final stages of the conflict."[89]

The US made a dramatic contribution to the war, but it wasn't as decisive militarily as some insist. The British and French had stopped Germany's 1918 offensive *before* the Americans assumed control of significant portions of the front in France. One must applaud Pershing, Bliss, and other American leaders for creating an enormous army from scratch and doing so six months earlier than expected. Bernard Baruch and the War Industries Board helped make this possible by coordinating various government agencies, boards, and private businesses, and oversaw the production of vast amounts of material and supplies for US forces and the Allies. The army, though, wasn't a well-oiled machine. It suffered every possible command-and-control and logistical snarl in ways that betrayed its newness, and depended upon France and Britain for heavy weapons and aircraft.[90] Wilson failed to ensure the nation was prepared for the war and to exert oversight of American preparations.

Wilson's America wasn't a good ally. It also wasn't a good friend to its neighbors in Latin America. Wilson always knew best. And perfection became the enemy of the attainable. Wilson left us what is today nebulously referred to as Wilsonianism. The definition is disputed, but its core is seeking democracy abroad in an idealistic manner that insufficiently considers whether or not it is possible, coupled with a lack of realism in regard to the costs and burdens it entails. This was Wilson's lasting effect.

8

THE INTERWAR INTERLUDE, 1921–1939

INTRODUCTION

Historian John Rhea Dulles titled a chapter on the US in its post–First World War years "The Great Retreat." The opposite is the case. The US neither withdrew from the world nor became "isolationist." It entered its most intense period of peacetime international involvement yet. American political feuds circled – as always – around how the US used its power to relate to the world and for what purposes.[1] But the Great Depression brought new, even revolutionary uses of American power, as did a global war.

ASSESSMENT

Economically, America in the 1920s was the world's most powerful nation, but its leaders had no desire to develop corresponding military power. In 1920, the US had 106 million people; adding overseas possessions made this 118 million. More Americans now resided in urban than rural areas. Technological change accelerated at a quickening pace. Americans enjoyed a standard of living beyond that of any other nation, and the advent of films, particularly "talkies," marked the beginning of the export of American culture, giving the nation influence beyond its diplomatic, economic, and military power.[2]

The push for women's suffrage succeeded in 1920, while the campaign for equal rights for African-Americans intensified. From 350,000 to 400,000 Blacks had served in the armed forces in a war for democracy and self-determination yet endured segregation. Many were no longer willing to tolerate racial violence, including a lynching plague in an era where for a time the Ku Klux Klan became a political force. Prohibition's launch on January 16, 1920 marked a cultural and political watershed as a coalition dominated by Progressives and religious groups helped outlaw the sale and manufacture of alcoholic beverages. A 1918–20 global influenza pandemic killed millions, and America suffered its first Red Scare, a reaction caused by the emergence of antidemocratic left-wing groups in the US, including the Communist Party. Strikes, violent demonstrations, and bombings increased fears. The Red Scare culminated with nationwide raids by the FBI and police on January 2, 1920, producing 5,000 arrests and the deportation of 600 Communist Party members.[3]

Technically, the US remained at war with Germany and Austria-Hungary. Wilson's successor, Warren G. Harding, asked Congress to declare the conflict ended, and signed the declaration on July 2, 1921. Subsequent treaties with Germany, Austria, and Hungary followed, and America was officially at peace in August 1922. The US had $24 billion in debt from the war, a staggering sum for the time; its annual interest payments in the 1920s comprised the government's largest single expenditure. This, veterans' benefits, and defense spending constituted nearly the entire budget.[4]

THE RETURN OF REPUBLICAN PRESIDENTIAL DOMINANCE, 1921-33

Three Republican presidents followed Wilson: Warren Harding, Calvin Coolidge, and Herbert Hoover. The 1920 election gave Harding and the Republicans majorities in both houses of Congress. Republican administrations in the 1920s wanted to shrink Federal spending, including on defense. Republican foreign relations rested heavily on experts outside government in industry, finance, and academia.[5]

THE HARDING AND COOLIDGE ADMINISTRATIONS: POLITICAL AIMS AND A GRAND STRATEGY OF NORMALCY (SORT OF)

For Harding and Coolidge, sovereignty and security remained key. In his March 4, 1921, inaugural Harding, though not using the term, expressed his intention to maintain the sovereignty bequeathed by the nation's forefathers through "the resumption of our onward, normal way." From this came the phrase "a return to normalcy," meaning a version of pre–First World War America. The US would guard its interests, and the planks of the grand strategy for doing so hearkened to George Washington in one important respect – avoiding entanglement in Europe's affairs. This included eschewing foreign military alliances, reducing wartime taxes, retrenching government spending, and maintaining tariff protection for US industry. But this didn't mean disengaging from the world. Harding sought international disarmament and arms limitations agreements to reduce the costs nations incurred purchasing weapons.[6] This required engagement.

Harding died in 1923 and was succeeded by Calvin Coolidge. Coolidge also looked first to America's interests while realizing the nation had obligations to other countries. The administration defined security as peace and stability, and sought "peace based on that mutual respect that arises from mutual regard for international rights and the discharge of international obligations." Coolidge insisted the purpose "of government is to keep open the opportunity for a more abundant life. Peace and prosperity are not finalities; they are only methods."[7]

While Congress reasserted influence over foreign affairs, the era's laissez-faire approach to economics, particularly under Harding and Coolidge, applied to foreign relations, and they generally left these issues in the hands of their secretaries of state. Harding and Coolidge were fortunate to have Charles Evans Hughes, "one of the ablest ever to hold the post." A brilliant law career catapulted Hughes into New York's governorship, other distinguished positions, and an unsuccessful presidential run. As secretary of state, he supplanted Wilsonian passion in foreign affairs with reason and sought the "maximum of security with a minimum of commitment."[8]

Hughes insisted democracies should act honestly and in good faith. Those who demanded "justice and security" from others must first grant it themselves. He wanted foreign relations conducted as openly as possible, but diplomats should retain the freedom to negotiate privately and in secret as it was impractical to resolve issues otherwise. He believed in acting in America's interests and "identified American interests with the peace, prosperity, and well-being of peoples in other parts of the world." Hughes allowed a generally free flow of information to the press and made it a strict rule to never lie to reporters. He and the Republicans' 1924 Rogers Act helped professionalize the State Department. Wilson had stuffed it "with incompetent party hacks."[9]

Both Harding and Coolidge placed a primacy on domestic issues, "namely, to support business and economic growth by keeping taxes low" and "spending, government regulation and federal debt to a minimum." Republicans and US business leaders agreed upon a *de facto* grand strategy that included "high tariffs, a search for exports, arms limitations, strategic non-entanglement, debt repayment, and the use of surrogate diplomats from the private sector to promote international cooperation on financial matters. This ... permitted a regime of low taxes, balanced budgets and limited government interference at home."[10]

ECONOMIC STRATEGY

Harding faced an economic crisis when he assumed office. The economy suffered postwar unemployment and some inflation, and a brief depression occurred in late 1920 and early 1921, one driven by recalibration of the economy after the war and marked by unemployment and the collapse of agricultural prices. America's agricultural crisis derived from farmers increasing wartime production while taking on debt to expand. Demand dropped when the war ended as foreign producers rejoined the global market; a massive agricultural glut ensued. Falling prices combined with deflation to ruin many farmers. Bank failures followed. Harding faced pressure for an "emergency tariff" and tax cuts. He called Congress into special session and had the House tackle the tariff and the Senate the tax cuts. Harding believed that since US industries faced higher production costs, they should be protected by tariffs, which would also safeguard America's standard of living. A May 1921 emergency tariff law protected farmers and industries fearing European dumping; it was a six-month measure to buy time for Congressional action. The Republicans held Congress in the 1922 elections but suffered stunning polling losses before the economic revival began in 1922.[11]

Both parties and the president supported protectionism, and the Fordney–McCumber Tariff, "one of the highest in American history," became law in September 1922. It fixed some rates but gave the president authority to raise or lower others by up to 50 percent. Harding and Coolidge availed themselves of this power thirty-seven times, upping tariffs in all but five examples. Relatedly, Secretary of State Hughes established the practice of unconditional most-favored-nation trade treaties, ending country-specific most-favored-nation treaties with different terms for each nation. Hughes also helped open Middle Eastern oil concessions to US companies.[12]

When Coolidge succeeded Harding in 1923, he insisted he was continuing his predecessor's course while turning out corrupt hangers-on. Coolidge kept Harding's cabinet, including Hughes. He also retained Herbert Hoover, who dominated economic decision-making as secretary of commerce, which he grew in importance as a governance organ. Hoover worked closely with business and sought to increase American trade, detailing agents abroad to do this while expanding Commerce's business support by providing information on foreign markets.[13]

Coolidge had a particular interest in economic matters and preferred to deal with these. His best-known remark is from a 1924 speech: "the chief business of the American people is business." Coolidge thought cutting taxes critical as "Lower taxes would bring higher national income and produce more revenue for the treasury." To Coolidge, reducing the public debt allowed savings in interest and principal payments, thus permitting further tax reductions. But Coolidge insisted that tax revenue remain high enough to balance the budget. He noted in his December 1928 Congressional address that cutting taxes and government spending dramatically had put more money in the hands of the taxpayer and the economy soared as a result. He maintained a protectionist tariff and kept regulations "thin to the point of invisibility," regarding them as interference "with what he thought should be a free market." During the 1920s, America's economy grew 42 percent.[14]

DIPLOMATIC STRATEGY

America's involvement abroad took many forms. Hughes believed in the utility of international organizations and thought such groups could help great powers act but not ensure it. He supported League membership, though this was politically impossible, and US participation in international organizations designed to maintain peace. Harding supported American membership in multinational organizations and posted a US observer to the League. Intended as a tool for resolving peacefully international disputes, the League proved more symbolic than successful. There were numerous related organizations to which the US belonged that had more effect such as the International Labor Organization (ILO) and the League's Health Organization, a forerunner of the World Health Organization. Lobbying groups began exerting influence and proved critical in the international push for disarmament and outlawing war.[15]

LATIN AMERICA AND THE CARIBBEAN

The Republican administrations of the 1920s disliked Wilson's wars in Latin America and the Caribbean, the examples of military rule they inherited, and the Roosevelt Corollary, and abandoned "gunboat diplomacy." Harding criticized American actions in the West Indies as "bayonet rule" and deemed it hypocritical to try to impose "democratic values" on Caribbean and Latin American nations by force. Harding and Hughes wanted increased trade and political support from Latin American and Caribbean states and tried to gain this by offering counsel instead of intervention. Hughes' diplomacy marked the beginning of what became known as the Good Neighbor

Policy. This continuity was partly due to Sumner Welles, who ran the Latin American Division of the State Department under Hughes' tenure and was an undersecretary of state for Franklin Delano Roosevelt.[16]

Regional stability contributed to American security, and Hughes sought this through maintaining peace. He said in December 1922: "The interest of the United States is found in the peace of this Hemisphere and in the conservation of your interests." Two ideas drove America's Latin American and Caribbean strategy: the Monroe Doctrine and Pan-Americanism. Hughes thought foreign powers should be kept out of the Western Hemisphere but believed the Monroe Doctrine suffered from "extravagant utterances and pretensions." Hughes remolded it into part of a strategy of self-defense, especially against threats from Old World states. He urged other Western Hemisphere nations to adopt a similar approach and promised respect for regional territorial integrity. He accepted two modifications: that it applied to actions by all powers, even if states voluntarily changed their sovereignty. Hughes refused to abandon the US right to intervene, insisting upon its necessity in order to protect US citizens and property, but he sought to restrict this to the area around the Panama Canal, and to only when no other option remained. He would not make the Monroe Doctrine multilateral as this could tie American hands in unforeseen ways in the future. If the US did intervene, it should explain what it would and wouldn't do. Some have branded this Hughes's Caribbean Doctrine. Hughes made this shift in US strategy while emphasizing Pan-Americanism, meaning that the US and the other Western Hemisphere nations had all rebelled against tyrannical overlords. He extended some of his arguments to Russian and Chinese territorial integrity and said in these realms the US was "pursuing under different conditions the same aims of independence, security, and peace which determined the declaration of Monroe."[17]

In December 1922, State Department representative Welles negotiated what became the 1923 General Treaty of Peace and Amity with the Latin American states. This committed the signatories to non-interference in rebellions in other states and honoring territorial integrity. It also "stipulated nonrecognition of coup d'état governments unless legitimized by a free election." Military and civilian officials, and their relatives in power within six months before, were excluded from presidential office. Some argued this had the unintended effect of keeping out popular figures if a victor won through a fraudulent election. The later collapse of this system made the US more willing to accept totalitarian figures who kept order.[18]

Hughes believed US military actions in the region were the greatest obstacles to better US relations and sought to end American military occupations as quickly as internal political stability and the maintenance of security for foreigners allowed. Withdrawing the Marines from Cuba in 1922 was the first move. Hughes said, "Our interest is in having prosperous, peaceful, and law-abiding neighbors with whom we can cooperate to mutual advantage."[19]

Hoover, as Commerce Department chief, worked to improve US relations with Latin America because of the region's importance as a market for US goods and loans. He eventually abandoned Washington's role in assessing US loans to the region's governments but retained an interest in US investment. American investment streamed into Latin America, partly because of the great decline in European funds. The US worked through private financial experts and used loans to drive reforms to increase Latin American political and economic stability. This was done first in conjunction with the State Department in Bolivia, but protests in that nation forced a quieter approach in which the region's nations sought financial advice and help that produced the placement of private financial advisory missions. US investment – with State Department support – flowed to nations with such arrangements.[20]

MEXICO

The December 1920 election of General Álvaro Obregón as president didn't resolve the tensions between the US and Mexico as Wilson refused recognition. Under Harding, Hughes demanded payment for damages and expropriations and a promise to protect US lives and property before granting recognition. Harding eventually accepted a conference and negotiated via a banker an agreement with Obregón to avoid nationalization of American property, especially the oil industry, in return for loans and recognition. A new revolution in 1925 rekindled tensions because of Mexican efforts to create an anti-American government in Nicaragua and American trade and investment interests in Mexico. There was talk of war. Ambassador to Mexico Dwight Morrow reported that Coolidge told him: "My only instructions are to keep us out of war with Mexico." Secretary of State Frank B. Kellogg, Hughes' successor, wisely gave Morrow a free hand and his skilled negotiations ensured peace. The tensions produced the short-lived and quickly forgotten Coolidge Doctrine: "The person and property of a citizen are a part of the general domain of the Nation, even when abroad."[21]

THE INTERWAR INTERLUDE, 1921–1939

THE DOMINICAN REPUBLIC

In 1922, Hughes dispatched Welles to negotiate an end to American military governorship of the Dominican Republic and secure US withdrawal. The US left behind a provisional president chosen by the various political factions and a national guard for security but retained administrative control over customs duties. The Americans had little faith the Dominican Republic's internal political strife would end.[22] US forces departed in 1924.

HAITI

The journalists and their respective organs that supported Wilson's invasion of Haiti ignored the hapless nation during the Great War and turned against the American occupation after Versailles. American forces faced constant attacks by bandits and guerrillas up to 1921. A Senate investigation urged reform of the US administration and not withdrawal. Little changed beyond some reorganization of state finances as the US continued to control Haiti via the island's elite while Jim Crow racial laws remained in place. But American racism was bifurcated in that the occupiers aimed to improve the lot of the average Haitian, who was Black, poor, uneducated, and bereft of opportunity. From 1926 to 1929, earnest efforts were made to shift leadership positions in the constabulary to Haitian officers and "Haitianization" began in 1927. A military school was reestablished in November 1928 to train officers. Meanwhile, the Americans built roads and infrastructure to tie the country together and support governance.[23]

When president, in reply to foreign and domestic pressure, Hoover decided upon withdrawal. In February 1930, he instructed a review commission to determine how. Hoover considered the "goodwill created in Latin America by this change" "more important than any obligations ... we may have to Haiti." Hoover accepted the commission's recommendations for elections and the phased reduction of US troops through 1936. The Roosevelt administration withdrew the last American forces in August 1934, but Haiti remained a US "financial protectorate." Its debts were retired after the Second World War.[24]

HONDURAS

There was a revolution in Honduras in 1923–24 after a disputed election. American Marines landed to defend Americans and US property. Hughes dispatched Welles, who arranged a deal for a provisional president. This fell apart quickly, and fighting resumed, but a new US ambassador and leaders of neighboring states brokered an agreement for another president. Welles believed the fruit companies were to blame for much of the problem. American companies had supported different factions, which had endangered their property. They also acted in their interests and not necessarily those of the United States.[25]

THE SOVIET UNION

The Wilson administration had adopted non-recognition of Bolshevik Russia in August 1920, a position the Republicans maintained in an effort to isolate the regime. The US refusal to recognize what became the Union of Soviet Socialist Republics arose from Moscow's call for the overthrow of the US government and its subversion efforts in the US via organizations such as the Communist International, or Comintern. Hughes saw granting recognition under such circumstances as providing the enemy a base. Americans were very anti-Communist, an attitude fed by Moscow's actions.[26] Something often forgotten in discussions of the Soviet Union is that its leaders sought world revolution. This meant the overthrow of every other government and the destruction of their social and economic systems.

Not all US leaders felt as Hughes, including in his own party. The Congressional Peace Progressives, generally midwestern Republicans often incorrectly derided as "isolationists," proved a powerful Congressional bloc. They were antimilitarist, anti-imperialist, anti-interventionist, and anti–big business in regard to its sway over US foreign affairs. Led by Senator William Borah, they supported Soviet recognition because they believed economic engagement would reform the Communists when they saw capitalism's abundance. Subsequent American industrial investment in the Soviet Union, though, was driven by a quest for profits, generally forlorn. American experts and companies such as Ford and General Electric proved pivotal to Soviet dictator Josef Stalin's first five-year plan inaugurated in 1928.[27] Both failed approaches ignored that governments are driven by interests, political aims, and ideology. Later US leaders repeated this economic engagement error with Communist China.

None of this stopped America from feeding the starving Soviet people. The Soviets appealed for aid in 1921 and Hoover and the Harding administration helped via the non-governmental American Relief Administration. Hoover believed feeding the people countered Bolshevism. Around 10 million people were helped by mid 1923. Hoover convinced Congress aid would weaken the Soviet regime, but later said this might "have helped to set the Soviet Government up in business." American aid didn't stop

Moscow from later denouncing the efforts as espionage. An American diplomatic and economic approach based on illusion and wishful thinking helped preserve and industrialize a totalitarian regime.[28] It wasn't the last time.

THE WASHINGTON TREATIES

The end of the First World War marked a golden age of disarmament treaties lasting until the Second World War, an indicator of their cumulative success. International armaments reduction was a plank of Republican economic and diplomatic strategies. In theory, such agreements lowered defense spending, thus enabling lower taxes while creating a more stable and peaceful international environment amenable to business. The US also needed the 1922 agreements on naval limitations because Congress wouldn't vote enough funds to build the forces necessary to defend the US, its possessions, and sea lanes.[29]

Republican Senator Borah provided the catalyst for naval disarmament. A Peace Progressive, he believed disarmament the road to peace. Harding capitalized on Borah's Senate resolution calling for naval reduction to push what became the Washington Naval Conference. Britain saw a way to free up funding for postwar rebuilding. Japan saw a means of reducing strained relations with Washington. Talks that brought in France and Italy followed in Washington from 1921 to 1922.[30]

Hughes ran the conference and was told by the navy General Board the US required a fleet equal to that of Japan and Great Britain – combined – because of the Anglo-Japanese Alliance. Without this, the US needed parity with Britain and a fleet twice that of Japan. Hughes sought to end this alliance and secure an international agreement regarding China like Hay's Open Door. Hughes believed an agreement on China would reduce tensions with Japan, secure the Philippines, and ensure any naval limits, and saw the Washington Treaties as a means of defusing tensions in Asia. Britain convinced Hughes the Open Door's ambiguity made it useless and suggested a deal on Chinese trade and territorial integrity. Negotiations with Japan were eased by US cryptologists having broken Japan's diplomatic code.[31]

The four Washington Naval Treaties of 1922 limited the size and number of capital ships and heavily influenced the future US navy. The treaties established, respectively, a 5-5-3 ratio in tonnage (500,000-500,000-315,000) for British, American, and Japanese capital ships over 10,000 tons armed with 8-inch or larger guns. The lower figure angered many Japanese leaders (though not their diplomats). The French and Italians agreed to 175,000 tons. The Anglo-Japanese Alliance was abrogated. American fortification of certain islands was forbidden. A version of the Open Door in regard to China was fixed via the Nine Power Treaty, which returned Shandong and some extraterritorial privileges. Washington believed the agreements could deter Japan and resolve strategic challenges in Asia, while Tokyo saw a tool for restricting US strength. But American leaders failed to realize that international agreements the US entered needed the backing of US power. The accords marked the first time great powers "voluntarily surrendered their freedom to arm as they pleased." Harding, though, misjudged their value: "The four-power pact … abolishes every probability of war on the Pacific."[32]

ASIA

Underlying American faith in "the Washington Treaty System was an assumption that America's enormous financial and industrial power at the end of the First World War would increase both Chinese and Japanese dependence on American capitalism." Thomas J. Lamont, the head of J. P. Morgan bank and a veteran of Wilson's Versailles delegation, was directed to renew a Wilsonian version of Dollar Diplomacy in regard to loans in Manchuria. Later, Lamont filled a standard Republican role during this period of the international banker as diplomat. He believed Japan's dependence upon the US for trade and foreign reserves could bind Tokyo to Washington. By the end of the 1920s, Japan was America's fourth largest export market, a relationship Lamont insisted would lead to regional stability and cooperation with Japan. He said in 1927 that the US and Japan wouldn't go to war "over Japanese interests on the mainland of Asia."[33]

Hughes sought stability in China via the Washington Treaties and reaffirmation of the Open Door. He said in 1923: "We are seeking to establish a Pax Americana maintained not by arms but by mutual respect and good will and the tranquilizing process of reason." The tools were loans and trade. The State Department pushed loans "to promote economic development in China, thereby helping to protect its sovereignty as well as expand US trade." But US bankers had already extended millions in loans to a nation now undergoing a civil war. They preferred lending to Japan because it was more stable.[34]

The US was slow to understand China's rising nationalism, but by the time Chiang Kai-Shek's Nationalists gained the upper hand – for a time – Secretary of State Kellogg realized the Western treaty concessions were outdated and needed changing, and that it was now impossible to "parcel out China in concessions or by spheres of commercial influence by armed force." The US became the first state to abandon parts of the unequal treaties imposed upon China and granted it most-favored-nation trade status beginning in 1933.[35]

WAR DEBT AND THE DAWES PLAN

Republicans grasped the war's effects on Europe, but also understood the domestic political limitations on America helping relieve them. In Central and Western Europe, Hughes and Hoover wanted a Europe that could pay its war debts and buy US goods. The strategy was "to promote a liberal, integrated region characterized by peaceful economic growth, political stability, convertible currencies, open trading arrangements, great-power reconciliation and arms reductions." But Republican administrations lacked diplomatic, military, or economic leverage and failed to utilize relevant tools such as "security guarantees, strategic commitments, direct foreign aid, reduced tariff barriers, debt cancellation or formal political involvement." The supposed "soft power" of the popularity of US cars, soft drinks, and films provided no leverage. Washington's strongest tool was US bankers because European governments needed American loans to fund recovery and meet their war debts. Europe's postwar financial situation "depended on the continual flow of payments from Germany to the west."[36]

The severe international indebtedness from the war saw America become a creditor nation and New York supplant London as the globe's financial capital. The Allies had $27 billion in debt, including $10 billion to Washington. The Germans owed the Allies $33 billion for reparations; Berlin said this was too much for it to pay. Paris insisted upon payment in full, as did London, which tied what Berlin owed to the Allies to its own debt to America. The Allies, particularly France, contended they couldn't grant Berlin debt relief without receiving it themselves. France believed this request fair as it had paid a high blood price. Berlin's refusal to pay provoked French and Belgian occupation of Germany's Ruhr industrial region in January 1923. Germany replied with a campaign of passive resistance financed by printing money. The resulting hyperinflation savaged Germany's economy. As the crisis lengthened, Berlin feared Paris separating the Rhineland from Germany and capitulated.[37]

The events frightened Washington and Hughes renewed an offer to convene an expert panel on the debt. Chicago banker Charles G. Dawes created the Dawes Plan. The reparations total shrank, and a schedule of payments was constructed with amounts increasing as the German economy grew. Recipients of reparations were required to buy German goods, which helped Berlin's economy, while Germany received a $200 million loan and made economic reforms. The Coolidge administration soon allowed Allied debt payments based upon ability to pay and canceled 75 percent of Italy's debt to sway Italian-American voters.[38]

THE LOCARNO AGREEMENTS

The Locarno Conference of 1925 arose as a political adjunct to the Dawes Plan. The economic reintegration of Germany into Europe weakened France's strategic position and worried Paris, something Washington tried to address. Locarno's origins lay in a speech by the US ambassador to London. Alarmed by Germany's political instability, he warned that Washington might stop granting loans to European nations if something wasn't done. A reluctant Coolidge followed his ambassador's lead and international discussions produced the Locarno Treaties. These guaranteed the borders of Western Europe, promised continued demilitarization of the Rhineland, and extracted promises from France, Belgium, and Germany to not attack one another. This marked the first Washington-led effort to address a European problem.[39]

THE KELLOGG–BRIAND PACT

Hughes resigned after Coolidge's reelection and recommended Frank B. Kellogg as his successor. A dogged worker raised on a Minnesota farm, Kellogg had a successful law career that led him into Republican politics and the secretary's seat. His temper and tendency to get lost in detail hindered his effectiveness. Coolidge had scant interest in foreign affairs, which gave Kellogg freedom to act barring rare presidential tuning, but he faced a Congress determined to reassert influence over foreign relations. Kellogg, in contrast to Coolidge, and in Hughes' mold, interacted freely with the press, and tried to influence key media outlets such as the Hearst syndicate to support the administration, while sometimes dressing down critical newspapers.[40]

In the wake of Charles Lindbergh's May 1927 flight across the Atlantic, French Foreign Minister Aristide Briand tried to drag the US into a security agreement by issuing a public letter to the American people calling for outlawing war through a bilateral treaty, one he believed would link the US to France and thus deter Germany. Bowing to peace movement pressure, the Coolidge administration shelved its anger at Briand and responded favorably. But at the suggestion of Senator Borah, Coolidge raised the stakes by pushing for a multilateral deal. Though initially reluctant to be involved, Kellogg became dedicated to it and received the Nobel Peace Prize. In 1928, after tortuous negotiations, fifteen nations (including the European great powers) signed the Kellogg–Briand Pact outlawing war as a national political instrument. No one expected it to work; its lack of enforcement planks ensured this.[41]

THE YOUNG PLAN

The reparations issue reappeared during the Hoover administration as Berlin continued pushing reductions. In 1930, businessman and advisor to several presidents Owen D. Young was dispatched to negotiate. The Young Plan gradually reduced German reparations payments while ensuring the Allies received enough money to cover war debts. The agreement established the Bank for International Settlements, which Young saw as an economic extension of Kellogg–Briand. The Depression undermined the scheme because it relied upon German economic growth and foreign loans; both disappeared. Hoover negotiated a moratorium on payments of German reparations and Allied war debt.[42] Hitler abrogated the Versailles Treaty in 1936 and ended reparations payments.

THE LAST BANANA WAR: NICARAGUA, 1927-33

After the American withdrawal in 1912, a detachment of 100 Marines remained in Nicaragua as legation support. They also served as a barrier to revolution against the government and on one occasion the threat of their returning fire at the city ended a coup attempt. But they departed Nicaragua on August 3, 1925. Political violence erupted three weeks later.[43]

In March 1926, after an irregular election and a complex mix of violence, impeachment, and threats of exile, Emiliano Chamorro became leader. Revolt erupted immediately, and in a familiar spot: the largely American Bluefields settlement. The commander of the *Cleveland* landed Marines in Bluefields in May. The US aims were to secure "order and protection of American citizens and their property" and protect and keep the customs house, the government's source of revenue, from the rebels. The State Department representative, Lawrence Dennis, plunged America deeper into the Nicaraguan political quagmire by demanding Chamorro resign and advising the rebel opposition.[44]

The Mexican government began arming the rebels while American Admiral Julian Latimer increased the number of Marines in Bluefields and landed in Corinto on Nicaragua's Pacific coast. The US disliked Mexico's involvement but detested Chamorro more because he violated the 1923 Central American Conference treaties guaranteeing respect for legal presidential succession. Senator Borah and others accused the Coolidge administration of acting to support US business interests. But Latimer, in establishing numerous neutral zones to protect US citizens and foreigners seeking to escape the violence, acted in the traditional manner of naval commanders abroad. These enclaves, though, were *de facto* support for a government losing its war.[45]

The Americans arranged a conference in October 1926. Chamorro, knowing he would never get US recognition, resigned. In November, Nicaragua's assembly named former president Adolfo Díaz chief executive. Díaz, like many Latin American leaders of the era, excelled at manipulating American politicians and diplomats by playing on their fears of instability, and capitalized on American fear of interference from Mexico's leftist government. This, and the threat to US citizens, won him US support.[46]

When it became increasingly likely Díaz would be overthrown, Washington dispatched Henry Stimson to Nicaragua on a peace mission. Kellogg sent Stimson to thwart departmental demands for a larger US intervention. In a manner speaking highly of Stimson's intelligence and skill, he secured the Peace of Tipitapa in 1927; it included agreement for a 1928 election Americans would oversee. An uneasy peace – maintained by Marines – fell upon Nicaragua.[47]

But General Augusto C. Sandino refused to support the deal and relaunched the civil war. He proved a skilled leader, particularly in his ability to publicize his cause abroad and win sympathy and support. From his time in revolutionary Tampico, Mexico, Sandino was steeped in the idea of justice for those he deemed victims of American "capitalists." Initially, the Marines made a half-hearted effort against "the bandit" Sandino, whose forces were the most important of several rebel groups. They were disabused of their underestimation by a significant attack Sandino launched against the Marine garrison of Ocotal. Marine General Logan Feland soon discovered deep support for Sandino and recommended a strategy of denying to Sandino areas to assemble, sources of supply and material, and places to recruit. Publicly, the State Department minimized the Sandino threat as the US press criticized American actions. Privately, Feland asked for more Marines.[48]

By summer, Sandino switched to a guerrilla strategy and avoided fighting significant enemy detachments. By November, he massed in the rugged

El Chipote on Nicaragua's Pacific coast near Managua. In December 1927, the Americans mounted a two-pronged offensive to try to destroy Sandino's force but underestimated their opponent. Sandino ambushed both US columns, temporarily trapping one detachment. The Marines took El Chipote in January, but Sandino and his forces escaped. The Marines garrisoned the towns in Nueva Segovia on the Honduran border, but this gave them fewer men for patrols. Sandino, meanwhile, received external support – financial mostly – from groups in Mexico and the US and left-wing organizations elsewhere. In the spring of 1928, the Americans increased their troop numbers to 3,700 and had cruisers patrolling the coast. The new strategy was to push Sandino from Nueva Segovia, forcing him to move the war to the eastern lowlands. Sandino now attacked only US forces and businesses, particularly mines. An amnesty offered the rebels produced little.[49]

At the Sixth Pan-American Conference in January 1928, Latin American unhappiness with the US war infected the meetings. The US had generally controlled the agenda and kept inconvenient issues from being discussed, but not this time. Hughes handled the criticism effectively, largely through accommodation, and thwarted Argentina's effort to ban intervention.[50]

As promised before Sandino's revolt, Washington sent a US army-led electoral commission under Frank McCoy to oversee the 1928 balloting and aid electoral reform. The arrival of McCoy's commission marked the first involvement of the army in the region since the Veracruz landing and resulted from the administration's unhappiness with the Marine and navy failure to capture Sandino. The commission placed officials at polling stations, usually military officers. The 1928 and 1932 elections proved among the most honest in the region's history and the Liberal Party won clear victories.[51]

After the 1928 election, Stimson prepared to draw down US troops and train Nicaragua's constabulary. US numbers peaked at around 5,000 in early 1929, most pursuing Sandino and his forces. There were only 1,800 by the end of the year. Political suspicion and infighting, combined with the Nicaraguan practice of political leaders using the military for their own ends, hindered the creation of an effective, non-partisan constabulary. The National Guard was organized along military lines but acted more as a police force that also hunted bandits. The war waged in Nicaragua didn't include American political control like Wilson extended over Haiti and the Dominican Republic. Stimson believed his middle path the best because it allowed implementation of potentially lasting reforms in elections, governance, and security without the responsibility of governing the country because this remained in the hands of its inhabitants.[52]

Sandino left Nicaragua for Mexico in mid 1929. His supporters continued the war, which became a stalemate. The Sandinistas enjoyed the ability to disappear into the Nicaraguan wilderness and sanctuary in Honduras. This made it nearly impossible to completely defeat them without committing enough troops to secure contested areas and the frontier. The US had to hold the key population centers and prove to the people it was in their interest to cooperate. Sandino returned in May 1930 and launched a summer campaign beginning in June. The Marines relentlessly pursued but failed to capture him and never eliminated the guerrillas.[53]

The arrival of the Great Depression ensured American withdrawal. Stimson informed the military leaders in February 1931. In April, he announced the US couldn't provide protection for American citizens in Nicaragua any longer and declared the US would withdraw its forces after the 1932 Nicaraguan elections. Hoover, though, kept the Marines in Nicaragua until January 2, 1933, "because a democratically elected government had asked that they stay to assure the free election of its successor." The US terminated its six-year involvement by declaring the mission successful, having left the foundations of a democratic government and a nonpolitical National Guard to ensure future free elections. General Anastasio Somoza, the National Guard commander, soon took over Nicaragua, ruling until assassinated in 1956.[54]

POSTWAR MILITARY ORGANIZATION AND STRATEGIC PLANNING

At the end of the Great War, the US faced the problem of demobilizing its army, something for which it had no plans. Of the nearly 2 million troops in Europe at the time of the armistice, only 40,000 remained in August 1919. Wilson had no plan for returning to a peacetime economy and told Congress Americans were capable of doing this without the government. Foreign relations remained his priority.[55]

Harding inherited a 15,000-man US occupation force in Germany's Rhineland. He promised its removal when campaigning but retreated from this because leaving it increased European stability. But Congress wanted American forces out and passed a resolution to this effect. Harding withdrew them in 1923 when the French occupied the Rhineland. The active army remained small, 140,000, but the officer corps was twice the size it had been before the war and the army now had armor and air elements. In 1918, the US navy was the world's largest. But the Republican administrations were not interested in supremacy and sought parity with Britain in naval power and disarmament in general, suffering Democratic Party criticism as a result. By the advent of his administration, even the exceedingly budget-conscious Coolidge believed America's postwar military drawdown had gone too far. He urged strengthening the army and navy, saying in 1923: "We want no more competitive armaments. We want no more war. But we want no weakness that invites imposition. A people who neglect their national defense are putting in jeopardy their national honor."[56]

The various international treaties affected American military planning and development. The Washington Treaties forced the navy to develop technologies such as ocean-going drydocks and underway replenishment as a substitute for bases. The agreements influenced the decision to build large instead of small aircraft carriers as the treaties allowed conversion of two battlecruisers. They also pushed the Marines to look for another role – what became amphibious operations – as they no longer needed to defend forward bases. A US decision to build fifteen cruisers led to London accepting parity with the US here and the 1930 London Naval Conference, a final cooperative arms limitation effort.[57]

The Joint Army and Navy Board was reorganized and expanded in July 1919, gaining the authority to truly function as a joint planning organization and present guidance to the secretaries of the navy and war. Supporting it was a Joint Planning Committee with similar authority. In 1922, the War Plans division composed Plan BLUE, a mobilization plan. Another followed in 1928. The army and navy began writing plans to fight Japan in 1907, and War Plan ORANGE remained perhaps the most important of the Color Plans. By the time America entered the First World War, ORANGE had become a blueprint for gaining control of the Western Pacific. The original ORANGE assumed a political aim of defense of the Open Door. But within a decade, as Edward Miller wrote, "US strategists had retreated from seeing their nation as the firm guarantor of China to a nebulous restraining force that Japan would assail someday to unblock its ambitions." In 1924, ORANGE was changed to begin with the seizure of key islands. The 1928 version called for using economic instruments of power against Japan during any war by keeping it from credit or material from neutral nations as part of a strategy of exhaustion. By 1935, its main operational thrust had shifted from an offensive departing Hawaii for the Philippines to an advance via the Marshall Islands. Neither army nor navy planners believed they could hold Manila in a war against Japan.[58]

PART II: FROM GREAT POWER TO SUPERPOWER

THE HERBERT HOOVER ADMINISTRATION, 1929–33

In his December 1929 State of the Union Address, Herbert Hoover said that "To promote peace is our long-established policy," something seen in the administration's helping resolve the Chile–Peru and Bolivia–Paraguay disputes, allowing the Mexican government to have US arms to put down an insurrection, and the reduction of Marine numbers in Nicaragua and Haiti. Hoover's experience with the First World War stiffened his Quaker antimilitarism, and "he saw his presidency as an opportunity to encourage representative democracy and peace as the bases of international relations." This underpinned reluctance to deploy US troops abroad – except for self-defense.[59]

Hoover called for more naval arms limitations and in December 1929 criticized US defense spending, noting that "While the remuneration paid to our soldiers and sailors is justly at a higher rate than that of any other country in the world, and while the cost of subsistence is higher, yet the total of our expenditures is in excess of those of the most highly militarized nations of the world." He also noted the growth of the regular and reserve army and navy forces. Combined, these totaled "about 299,000 in 1914, about 672,000 in 1924, and about 728,000 in 1929."[60]

Hoover continued the economic strategy of Harding and Coolidge and had a vision of a liberal democracy ensuring Americans had equality of economic opportunity. To do this, the government would keep taxes low, restrain its spending (including on defense), maintain high tariffs to protect American business and agriculture, limit immigration to protect the pay of American workers, and impose only government regulation necessary to prevent business abuses and exploitation. This would unleash Americans to prosper individually and as a nation. Hoover wrote: "Liberalism is a force truly of the spirit, a force proceeding from the deep realization that economic freedom cannot be sacrificed if political freedom is to be preserved." These approaches fed economic success, and by 1929 the US had become the world's largest exporter, a rise fueled by American industrial innovation and the trimming of anti-trust rules.[61]

DIPLOMATIC STRATEGY

Hoover came into the presidency with the most international experience of any US president since John Quincy Adams. Hoover was a self-made man, having become wealthy in mining and engineering. He became well-known during the First World War running the non-governmental Commission for

Relief in Belgium and led a similar postwar effort in Central and Eastern Europe before becoming Harding's secretary of commerce. Hoover and his secretary of state, Stimson, believed in the strength of moral force in foreign affairs, but Hoover made the critical foreign policy decisions and had some views of a Wilsonian tenor. He believed in the connected nature of international relations and said in March 1929: "The United States fully accepts the profound truth that our own progress, prosperity, and peace are interlocked with the progress, prosperity, and peace of all humanity." After Japan's 1931 invasion of China and seizure of Manchuria, Stimson tried to counter Japan's threat to world order through "moral sanctions," meaning he would turn world opinion against Japan by painting a picture of its immoral behavior. The US also refused to recognize any territorial changes that altered American treaty rights. This became known as the Stimson Doctrine. Japan ignored it. Britain and France issued tepid critiques of Tokyo four months later.[62]

LATIN AMERICA AND THE CARIBBEAN

A wave of nationalism swept the Caribbean in the late 1920s and regional leaders challenged US leadership. Hoover believed that if the US didn't change its behavior, it couldn't win the respect of Latin America's states. He accelerated the trends of his Republican predecessors, fathering the Good Neighbor Policy, the primary plank of which became removing US troops. Hoover said in 1928: "True democracy is not and cannot be imperialistic." Stimson believed the US had to protect US citizens and their property from the region's habitual disorders and revolutions, but also thought free elections overseen by the US provided the solution to many Latin American problems by ensuring leaders had the popular support to govern. Honest elections, combined with a national guard to police bandits and revolutionaries, would ensure US "gunboat diplomacy" and interventions became unnecessary.[63] The administration sought democracy abroad but would not force it.

Hoover altered US diplomatic strategy for Latin America. He possessed some understanding of the growing importance of public relations in diplomacy, particularly radio and magazines, and spent an unprecedented seven weeks between his election and inauguration touring ten Latin American states. He renounced any territorial ambitions, used the term "good neighbor" in several speeches, and stressed disinterest in intervention. The war in Nicaragua and the regional condemnation of it helped drive Hoover's strategy. Stimson's 1930 Clark Memorandum officially severed the Roosevelt Corollary from the Monroe Doctrine, marking the official adoption of non-intervention (the US maintained the right to intervene in matters of self-preservation). Hoover failed to publicize this; it went almost unnoticed. In April 1931, Hoover abrogated Coolidge's insistence on the right to protect American citizens and property wherever they were, a decisive step away from this interpretation of the Monroe Doctrine. But Hoover soon faced the effects of the Great Depression as the area's export-based economies suffered heavily, and the region's shift toward governments favoring totalitarianism. Latin American agreement on non-recognition of governments that had illegally seized power died. Hoover saw the Caribbean states as raw material sources and battled the State Department over America's use of loans to their governments, differentiating between good loans (those generating social services) and bad (those for arms). Overall, Hoover bettered US relations in the hemisphere.[64]

ECONOMIC STRATEGY AND THE GREAT DEPRESSION

Hoover believed as others of the Progressive Era that limited government action could manage social change and that government could help individuals combine communally for national advancement. But in Hoover's view, the people led, and government didn't dictate as this was the path to tyranny. Hoover commissioned a monumental government study for the next stage of US development, but the onset of the Great Depression destroyed his plans. Hoover also believed government shouldn't sit when facing severe economic problems.[65]

Several factors fed the stock market boom. The decade's economic growth gave companies more cash, which they often invested in the market, as did banks, which lent vast sums for speculation, more than for real estate and other businesses. Individual investors moved into the market, but not even 2.5 percent of Americans owned shares. The common practice of buying stocks on margin, sometimes for only 10 percent of the share price, fueled speculation, as did the government's cheap money approach. This was a response to Britain's return to its prewar gold standard that fixed the pound's exchange value unrealistically high. Gold fled London for America and destabilized financial markets. Low US interest rates were to stem this and stabilize international markets, but they also fed speculation in the US by lowering borrowing costs. Credit became tighter in 1928, but stock prices still nearly doubled.[66]

But in late September 1929, and then more harshly in October, stock prices fell. The speculative bubble had popped. No one quite knows why.

Selling on October 29, 1929 – Black Friday – reached a pace not matched for thirty-nine years. The slide continued three weeks. By mid November, the market had lost about one-third of its September value. A common misconception is that the crash caused the Depression. Stock prices recaptured 20 percent of their fall by April 1930 to reach early 1929 levels. Moreover, unlike during similar drops, there were no failures of major banks or businesses. The market's fall "reduced private wealth by about 10 percent" and increased consumer indebtedness and uncertainty, which reduced consumption, but this wasn't enough to cause the Depression.[67]

Hoover tried to prevent spillover from the crash into the rest of the economy, particularly the banks, as failures were common after crashes. He met for two weeks with industry and banking leaders and extracted promises to keep wages steady to maintain consumer purchasing power. The Federal Reserve cut rates to most banks and Hoover pushed businesses, state and local governments, and the Federal government into infrastructure spending, nearly doubling Federal public works outlays over the next three years. But the economy continued shrinking, and businesses began to fail or cut back construction. The Gross National Product (GNP) declined 12.6 percent from 1929 to 1930. Governments were small in Hoover's time and their outlays had negligible effect. Federal spending in 1929 was only around 3 percent of GNP. Total state and local expenditures were five times Washington's.[68]

At the end of 1930, banks began to fail. The experts don't agree why. US banks had always been weak and the banking system chaotic. Most were local and not part of corporate firms and thus less capable of enduring losses and downturns. Only around one-third belonged to the Federal Reserve system and thus had access to liquidity, which often proved an inadequate form of salvation. The panic began in Louisville, Kentucky, when depositors began demanding their funds. The fire quickly spread. Pressed banks sold assets and called in loans. New York's enormous Bank of the United States (its business name) failed in December 1930, damaging physically its 286,000 depositors and psychologically the nation because of its moniker. The Federal Reserve's inability to find firms to rescue it weakened confidence in the agency.[69]

Actions in Europe and the US, particularly the Federal Reserve in the fall of 1931, converted an economic downturn in line with past American experience into the Great Depression. Austria's biggest bank, Credit Anstalt, collapsed in May. A run on the schilling was followed by one on the German mark. Fear leapt to the British pound and forced Britain off the gold standard. Germany and Britain devalued their currencies, and the selling of dollars began in earnest. Foreign investors, mostly European, began pulling gold and currency from US banks. Americans joined the flood, worsening the liquidity crisis already pummeling the banks. Britain's abandonment of the gold standard – meaning their refusal to make payments in gold to foreigners, something done to prevent currency deflation – fed the liquidity crisis by freezing many international payments. The US remained on the gold standard to prevent specie flight and help the dollar retain its value. Hoover and others, in line with the era's thinking, believed they had to stay on the gold standard to support the currency's value, which deepened the depression. Worse was that the Federal Reserve tightened by raising rates and shrinking the money supply. The banks needed liquidity – cash – to stay open. Moreover, "the Fed believed that it could restrict credit to Wall Street without harming the rest of the economy, it was mistaken." Tightening constrained credit and pushed down industrial production, which had stopped falling.[70]

Hoover then pushed to balance the federal budget via tax increases. His administration had deficit spent to the tune of $2.7 billion for 1932, something Franklin Roosevelt used as a bludgeon in the presidential election. In Hoover's view, balancing the budget would reassure foreign investors about the stability of the American economy and dampen their withdrawals. The government would be competing no longer with businesses for loans as its revenue would come from taxes. This would make more money available for business investment, and at lower rates, thus helping solve the liquidity problem caused by Fed tightening and bank runs. The low rates would also support the value of bonds banks held, lessening their need to sell them for their support. The Revenue Act of 1932 raised taxes on everyone with the aim of doubling revenue and set the tax floor for the next decade. Subsequent legislation further raised rates. Balanced budgets were the economic orthodoxy of both parties.[71] Raising taxes lessened spending. This worked against growth.

By the end of 1931, even Hoover was willing to experiment with government intervention in an effort to end the crisis. The 1933 Glass–Steagall Act allowed the Federal Reserve to issue more notes and sell more gold. The 1932 Reconstruction Finance Corporation (RFC) was established to provide emergency government loans to railroads, banks, and other entities.[72]

The Depression worsened America's postwar agricultural crisis. Immediately upon taking office in 1929, Hoover had called Congress into special session to deal with the desperate agricultural situation. Postwar overproduction meant prices for agricultural commodities plummeted, sometimes as much as one-third, and didn't recover until 1939. Coolidge had vetoed two government bills aimed at limited Federal control of the agricultural commodities market. Hoover quickly passed the Agricultural Marketing Act of 1929 creating the Federal Farm Board to buy surpluses to stabilize prices. The Great Depression overwhelmed its budget and storage capability.[73]

Hoover's special Congressional session also produced the June 1931 Smoot–Hawley Tariff. Hoover believed the rates needed revising because of economic changes and supported Smoot–Hawley to protect farmers and industry from foreign competition from nations with lower production costs and lower standards of living for their farmers and workers. The 1922 Fordney–McCumber Tariff Act had set key tariff rates very high, an average of 13.83 percent, and the platforms of both parties in the 1928 election demanded higher rates. Smoot–Hawley set rates at an average of 16 percent but excluded from duties over 60 percent of imported goods. It increased the number of items subject to duty by 27 percent but nearly 94 percent of the increases fell on agricultural products. Hoover accepted it because it raised agricultural tariffs, helping US farmers, while shifting control of rates from Congress to a bipartisan Tariff Commission with the authority to adjust duties by up to 50 percent, making it possible for Hoover to influence rates.[74]

Smoot–Hawley was not a cause of the Great Depression but a symptom of the era's protectionism. Tariff rates were already so high that if it could have caused a depression it would have already done so. It also didn't set the highest tariff rates in US history as is sometimes claimed. It moved tariffs closer to pre–First World War levels and nineteenth-century averages. Tariffs reduce demand for foreign goods, hopefully enabling internal demand. US "exports were 7 percent of GNP in 1929. They fell by 1.4 percent of 1929 GNP in the next two years." But this cannot be blamed completely on foreign retaliation for Smoot–Hawley (which came from twenty-five governments by 1932) because the global economy was contracting. Moreover, there was some offsetting growth in domestic demand because of the tariff. Between 1929 and 1931, US GNP dropped by more than 15 percent. This was not the fault of Smoot–Hawley.[75]

Over 10 million Americans were unemployed in early 1932, one-fifth of the workforce. Employed workers had shorter hours and smaller paychecks. Half of these worked part-time. Hoover had won the election in a landslide but lost his reelection bid on the receiving end of a greater one.[76]

CONCLUSION

The US became more dependent upon imports as the world's economies grew increasingly interconnected. America's astronomical economic growth saw the US become the globe's leading consumer of key raw materials such as rubber and oil. An economic boom followed the recession of 1919–21 and the US became the leading exporter by 1929 as the value of these goods jumped from 1922's $3.8 billion to 1929's $5.1 billion. Automobiles were 10 percent of this. The 1922 Fordney–McCumber tariff had imposed high import rates, but imports still rose from $3.1 billion to $4.4 billion between 1922 and 1929. The multinational corporation also became an economic fixture for the first time as US investment abroad sky-rocketed and the US became a creditor nation.[77] Despite the economic rocket that was the 1920s US economy, the Hoover administration proved unable to pull the US from the Great Depression.

American isolationism is a myth. Domestic economic concerns remained the critical issues for the US, but the Republican administrations achieved much abroad in ending unequal treaties with China, securing international arms control agreements, and ending American military occupations in Latin America. Generally, the Republican administrations acted pragmatically and relied heavily on diplomacy.[78] The US was fortunate to have skilled representatives from both parties working seriously. This was a stark contrast to the reliance upon military force of the Wilson years.

But not all was success, and a bit of Wilsonian utopianism had remained. The US couldn't control the other actors involved, and when Hoover left office in 1933, it was clear both the 1922 naval agreements and Locarno were finished. Outside of Latin America, Republican diplomatic strategy generally failed to secure the political aims. Moreover,

> Republican foreign policy leaders at the time declared and apparently believed that the United States would successfully promote a more democratic, prosperous and peaceful world order simply through the combined efforts of international law, arms negotiations, commercial exchange and public opinion. This was no strategy of offshore balancing; on the contrary, it was an attempt to transcend and escape international power politics all together.

As was too often usual, the US never committed the economic and financial means necessary to achieve its aims.[79] Indeed, achieving peace and security abroad was not possible without committing to other nations via military alliances. This wasn't politically possible.

The US erred in believing economic prosperity and economic tools of grand strategy are sufficient on their own to achieve political aims in an increasingly complex world with aggressive, revisionist powers. Economic tools – when effectively used – play important roles in helping the nation achieve its political aims. But the economic cart shouldn't try to pull the political horse. As always, the political trumps all. Analyst Colin Dueck writes, "In sum, the Republican foreign policy approach from 1921 to 1933 was essentially dovish, anti-interventionist, and libertarian in its underlying assumptions – resistant to the use of force, and optimistic about the pacifying effects of economic interdependence – while simultaneously nationalistic in its jealous guarding of US national sovereignty."[80]

◆

THE FRANKLIN DELANO ROOSEVELT ADMINISTRATION, 1933-39

Only Lincoln faced a more desperate situation upon his inauguration than Franklin Delano Roosevelt. In his address, delivered five days after Adolf Hitler became Germany's chancellor, Roosevelt analogized America's crisis with a war. The nation faced a banking catastrophe. More than 5,000 failed between the 1929 crash and March 1933, destroying $7 billion in depositor balances. Governors in thirty-two states had ordered banks closed. The New York Stock Exchange and Chicago Board of Trade had suspended trading. And 13 million of 125 million Americans were unemployed. The day after his inauguration, on March 5, 1933, Roosevelt tackled the bank crisis. He called an emergency session of Congress for March 9, suspended transactions using gold, and declared a five-day bank holiday. Intense meetings with Republicans hammered out the bipartisan Emergency Banking Act that reopened the banks and expanded the Federal Reserve's power to issue currency. On March 12, Roosevelt broadcast the first of what became known as his fireside chats. He explained what was happening and told people the banks were safer than keeping money in their mattresses. The banks reopened – calmly – the next day. Roosevelt became immensely popular, and he set out to maintain and use this support. Radio proved key.[81]

THE ASSESSMENT

The assessment of a problem – including its causes and any threats – usually influences how one addresses it, or at least it should. Roosevelt's advisors, particularly the academics, believed as did Roosevelt that the Depression's origins were domestic, thus the solutions were domestic, a logical fallacy as *A* does not necessarily prove *B*. Roosevelt believed the causes lay "in structural deficiencies and institutional inadequacies." The administration's members were Progressives who believed the existence of powerful businesses demanded more powerful government to regulate the economy and make its arms lift together in a master plan. Some wanted complete economic reorganization by Federal hand.[82]

ROOSEVELT'S AIMS

Underpinning Roosevelt's aims were near-revolutionary sentiment and political parochialism. Three things mattered: "social reform, political realignment, and economic recovery." Until the embers that produced the Second World War began smoldering, Roosevelt pursued economic growth for its own sake, and generally failed. He altered the traditional aim of security for the nation to economic security, something partly defined by his desire to create a better life for all Americans. Roosevelt believed government should "achieve the subordination of private interests to collective interests" and "substitute co-operation for the mad scramble of selfish individualism." This required "the restoration of hope that America's economic and governmental machinery could work."[83]

Parochially, Roosevelt sought to replace the Republican Party's national political domination with that of his Democratic Party. The Depression – and Hoover's failure – provided opportunity. This aim would be achieved by expanding the Democratic Party's geographic reach and altering its demographics. Roosevelt's obstacles included Southern Congressional Democrats who opposed his more radical ideas, forcing him to proceed cautiously. Roosevelt later moved the South toward industrialization and modernization.[84]

ROOSEVELT'S GRAND STRATEGY: THE NEW DEAL

Franklin, Theodore Roosevelt's distant cousin, was a lawyer, former New York state senator and governor, and assistant secretary of the navy under Wilson. Roosevelt possessed great personal charm but was a "notoriously sloppy administrator who knowingly appointed conflicting personalities to competitive positions." He blurred lines of authority and created "multiple agencies with overlapping responsibilities" and watched as they fought. This ensured all major decisions were pushed to the top and that Roosevelt could hide his true aims until he felt it time to reveal them.[85] He intended to use government power to create economic security and stability by addressing things he considered economic imbalances such as the income gap between agricultural and industrial workers. Growing the state was the primary tool. Roosevelt launched an aggressive legislative agenda, particularly during his first 100 days, targeting what the administration saw as the Depression's effects and causes.[86]

ROOSEVELT'S ECONOMIC STRATEGY: AMERICA FIRST

Roosevelt was an economic nationalist placing US economic well-being over that of other nations. In his inaugural address he stated: "Our international trade relations, though vastly important, are in point of time and necessity secondary to the establishment of a sound national economy." He insisted America's "greatest primary task is to put people to work." One way was bringing into government employment people to do "greatly needed projects to stimulate and reorganize the use of our natural resources." He retreated from a commitment to return to the gold standard, imploding the 1933 London Economic Conference dedicated to currency stabilization and destroying "any further prospect of international cooperation in the fight against the global depression." The home market mattered more, and Roosevelt believed he needed inflation to resolve *America*'s depression. Remaining on the gold standard wouldn't allow this. Roosevelt decided "the United States was not to be pushed around," rejected the internationalist program, and searched for domestic economic solutions. He also wanted a protective tariff to prevent dumping of cheap foreign goods.[87]

Farmers composed 30 percent of the 1933 workforce. The New Dealers thought that since the Great Depression began with agriculture, recovery should begin here. They believed in a closed economy in which its size and lack of dependence upon foreign trade made it self-contained. If they could raise consumer demand by lifting agricultural incomes, this would solve all problems. Thus, they would increase purchasing power by putting money into farmers' hands. But "agriculture" was not just small farmers. This included ranchers, orchard owners, milk producers, and a myriad others; there was no single solution. The sector suffered income drops of nearly 60 percent in the four years before 1933 and had been in depression for a decade. The crisis was worsened because while manufacturers cut output 42 percent, farmers increased production to compensate for lower prices.[88]

Two primary programs supported the farmers: the Agricultural Adjustment Act (AAA) and the National Recovery Administration (NRA). The AAA's Domestic Allotment Program paid farmers to leave land fallow or grow crops with no existing surplus. Almost 4,000 commodities had production quotas by 1934. The government paid farmers to plow under cotton and kill excess hogs. Cotton prices rose. Droughts in wheat- and corn-growing areas pushed up the prices for these commodities. From 1932 to 1936, agricultural incomes rose 50 percent, but this was due largely to several billion dollars in government payments. The AAA cotton-planting quotas hurt sharecroppers, who were disproportionately African-Americans in the South as lands they farmed were generally those taken out of production. The AAA included a tariff on agricultural imports to raise farm prices. The New Deal farm programs and subsidies "made the agricultural sector a virtual ward of the state." Large, commercial farmers benefited most.[89]

The National Industrial Recovery Act (NIRA) created the NRA and the Public Works Administration (PWA) to regulate and reform US industry. The NIRA governed working hours and minimum wages, and granted workers collective bargaining rights. The NRA controlled production in entire industries to raise wages and prices. Modeled on the 1917–18 War Industries Board, it assumed that since overproduction was the problem, creating scarcity was the solution. The NRA soon had 4,500 employees who wrote 13,000 pages of rules in only two years. This produced massive regulation of an economy already facing collapse, mass layoffs in some industries, and government support for monopoly practices. Business and labor revolted. The Supreme Court unanimously declared the NRA unconstitutional in May 1935. The PWA did public construction work; Roosevelt remained skeptical it would create many jobs.[90]

Farm belt anger and unrest led Roosevelt to push inflation by following a Cornell University professor's theory that buying gold "would spur inflation and thereby both reduce debt burdens and raise commodity prices." The October 1933 to January 1934 program, which had Roosevelt setting the government's daily gold purchase price, drove down the dollar's value by 40 percent while failing to create exports. Commodity prices continued to decline. This debacle's only achievement was perhaps quieting the agricultural community long enough for the Farm Credit Administration to begin saving farms from foreclosure and the AAA to begin supplying loans and benefit funds.[91]

Providing relief in the form of direct payments was part of the economic strategy. The Federal Emergency Relief Administration (FERA) gave states funds for unemployment payments. Roosevelt saw in government organization of relief payments a means of breaking corrupt political organizations such as the Democratic Party's Tammany machine, which held on to supporters by providing relief. Federal payments would shift their loyalty to political leaders in Washington. Roosevelt ensured FERA money flowed more heavily to swing voting states than the Democratic-controlled South "to win votes and cultivate political loyalty."[92]

Job creation, often through public works, formed another plank. The Civilian Conservation Corps (CCC) bill reached Congress in March 1933 and employed more than 3 million young men who did forest and flood control, and developed places like national parks. The Tennessee Valley

Authority (TVA) was created in May 1933, the first step in Roosevelt's hoped-for development of America's inland waterways. This furthered rural electrification, fed spin-off industries, created jobs, helped modernize the South, and grew Roosevelt's political coalition by attracting southern Democrats and progressive Republicans.[93]

The final bill of the "100 Days" was the Glass–Steagall Banking Act. It separated commercial and investment banking, and secured bank deposits via what became the Federal Deposit Insurance Corporation (FDIC). The Home Owners Loan Corporation (HOLC), Federal Housing Administration (FHA), and the Federal National Mortgage Association (Fannie Mae) helped Americans buy homes by establishing appraisal systems and mortgage insurance.[94]

Roosevelt lauded protectionism but Secretary of State Cordell Hull was "a relentless advocate of free trade." An internationalist and veteran of two decades in the House and Senate, Hull fervently believed America's protective tariff was "the largest single underlying cause of the present panic." To Hull, free trade meant peace, "high tariffs, trade barriers, and unfair economic competition" war. The 1934 Reciprocal Trade Agreements Program (RTAP) removed tariff control from Congress for three years (this was habitually renewed through 1945), permitting the president to raise or lower tariffs up to 50 percent. Hull's staffers mostly regarded it as a means of lowering US tariffs. Young, inexperienced academic appointees abandoned reciprocity and began picking American economic winners and losers without considering whether sacrificed industries were necessary to American security. The results: *decreased* US exports and *increased* foreign imports as Washington granted trade concessions to all but one major trading partner, all of which restricted US imports. The administration insisted the RTAP "strengthened world peace." The logic of this can be measured by the number of wars since. The RTAP inaugurated a shift that saw import duties fall "from 46 percent in 1934 to 12 percent in 1962."[95]

The administration repeated an error of Hoover's: increasing taxes in an economic downturn, though not initially significantly. The NIRA produced an increase of 2 percent on the business rate. The Revenue Act of 1934 covered the deficit caused by Depression-related spending and lowered rates for those earning under $20,000 per annum by a few tenths of 1 percent while raising rates a few tenths for those earning from $20,000 to $1 million.[96]

The administration can be congratulated for stopping a banking crisis, providing needed relief, and giving people hope. But its actions didn't resolve America's economic crisis. At the beginning of 1935, 10 million

Americans, 20 percent of the labor force, remained unemployed. Even Liberals began doubting the New Deal.[97]

THE EVOLVING ECONOMIC STRATEGY

Roosevelt benefited from being seen to act, and the continuing crisis provided the opening to remake the country, particularly in regard to labor laws and social legislation. Harry Hopkins, a Progressive, former social worker, future secretary of commerce, and key advisor, was among those who developed the reform agenda after the 1934 elections. Roosevelt said in June 1934 that since the Constitution established the government to promote the nation's "general welfare," it was the government's duty "to provide for that security upon which welfare depends." Economic security for Americans remained his aim. This included "decent homes," "productive work," and "security against the hazards and vicissitudes of life." Achieving this required reordering American life. Roosevelt would provide economic security via regulation and central planning, fulfilling the Progressive dream of bringing order to America's chaotic society.[98]

The 1935 Emergency Relief Appropriation Act authorized $4 billion in new spending while shifting $880 million to work relief (meaning jobs) and public works. Roosevelt and the act's other authors thought they were addressing the economy's structural inability to provide employment for all who wanted it. The Rural Electrification Administration (REA), the Farm Security Administration, and the Works Progress Administration (WPA) followed. Roosevelt ensured WPA money flowed to local political bosses – Democrats and progressive Republicans – to expand his political coalition.[99]

The 1935 Social Security Act was "the most important single piece of social legislation" in American history and funded old-age pensions and unemployment insurance. The Depression destroyed many state- and privately funded employment insurance and retirement programs. Unemployment insurance was structured at the state level because of legal concerns and Roosevelt's desire to leave as much in state hands as possible. The first Social Security check was dispatched in January 1940.[100]

THE RESULTS OF THE NEW DEAL

Most New Deal legislation was law by August 1935. Roosevelt was reelected in a historical landslide in 1936, winning 523 of 531 electoral college votes. Roosevelt's Democratic Party secured overwhelming majorities in the

House and Senate and most governorships. Roosevelt fought to protect his New Deal and the opportunity of enacting further change before recovery made this more difficult. He had three targets: the Supreme Court (which overturned some of his legislation), Congress, and opposition within his own party. His failed attack on the Supreme Court, characterized by the effort to "pack" the court by adding new judges, proved politically disastrous.[101]

The New Deal altered the relationship between Americans and their government as Washington assumed a greater role in their lives. The Federal government's share of GNP went from 4 percent in 1930 to 9 percent in 1936. The WPA soon employed 7 percent of US workers. Bank insurance saved the deposits of millions while the HOLC helped 4 million keep their property. GNP went from $73 billion in 1933 to $88 billion in 1935, but it had been $104 billion in 1929. In 1936, GNP passed the 1929 number for a short time. Between 1933 and 1937, unemployment fell from 13 to 7 million. The unemployment rate was still 14 percent. One of the major drags on recovery was the increase in corporate taxes, especially 1936's undistributed profits tax. The administration mistakenly believed this would drive firms to reinvest or pay dividends with money they were supposedly hoarding.[102]

By August 1937, a Depression within the Depression had hit hard. Industrial production declined almost 40 percent. Unemployment jumped 2 million during 1937 to 1938, reaching 19 percent. The causes of the downturn are debated. The typical contraction of a business cycle after expansion was perhaps part of it. The uncertainty and fear caused by the administration's tax increases and antibusiness actions and rhetoric contributed by creating business reluctance to invest. Roosevelt and other New Dealers – without evidence – saw a conspiracy on the part of business. Other New Dealers concluded that since government deficits from 1933 to 1937 had brought about recovery, reducing these deficits had caused the recession. This meant the government had to spend.[103]

Economist John Maynard Keynes urged Roosevelt to stop attacks on business to encourage investment while "priming the pump" via increased Federal spending. He argued in what became the heart of Keynesian economics that this would produce recovery and sustained growth. Roosevelt replied in 1938 by asking for $3 billion in emergency spending, not a substantial amount in a $100 billion economy, and launching investigations of monopolies featuring anti-trust suits intended to teach the business community that government held the reins of power. The economy limped along, only reaching the 1937 production levels in 1941 "when the threat of war, not enlightened New Deal policies, compelled government expenditures at levels previously unimagined."[104]

The New Deal failed to produce economic recovery.[105] It also failed to produce economic security because this is not possible without an economy producing jobs. The demands of war abroad soon helped do so.

DIPLOMATIC STRATEGY

To Roosevelt, foreign relations were secondary to rebuilding the American economy. He wanted to keep overseas events from interfering in reestablishing Americans' faith in their government. He recognized America's global interdependence, but took a Hoover administration idea normally associated with Latin America and insisted he would apply it to the world: "In the field of world policy I would dedicate this Nation to the policy of the good neighbor – the neighbor who resolutely respects himself and, because he does so, respects the rights of others – the neighbor who respects his obligations and respects the sanctity of his agreements in and with a world of neighbors."[106]

LATIN AMERICA

The December 1933 Montevideo Pan-American Conference provided the platform for formally announcing the Good Neighbor Policy for Latin America. Roosevelt kept Hoover's commitment to evacuate Haiti, repudiated the Roosevelt Corollary to the Monroe Doctrine, and killed the Platt Amendment allowing US intervention in Cuba. Roosevelt promised no interventions to protect US investments and retreated from non-recognition of Latin American governments coming to power by non-democratic means. His actions were applauded in the region. By the beginning of 1936, Roosevelt felt war was coming and Germany would start it and began trying to unite the Western Hemisphere.[107]

EUROPE

In his first two years in office, Roosevelt faced not "intense isolationism" but "a general indifference" to "expanded American ties abroad." Many Americans saw US involvement from 1917 to 1918 in the "European War" as a pointless endeavor costing 50,000 American lives for no benefit. Many from both parties saw foreign entanglement as not in the US interest and didn't believe the crises in Europe and Asia threatened US security. Roosevelt extended diplomatic recognition to the Soviet Union in 1933 in an unsuccessful attempt to expand US trade and "strengthen Soviet resistance to possible future Japanese expansionism in China." Stalin's killing millions of his own people, particularly in a self-induced Ukrainian famine, didn't hinder recognition. Benito Mussolini's Italy prepared for war with Ethiopia while Hitler abrogated the Versailles Treaty's armament clauses, revealed Germany's new air force, and announced plans to build a large army.[108]

Many in Congress and the populace supported abandoning America's traditional neutrality, but there was no consensus on what this might mean. Roosevelt was in the collective security camp but his effort to prevent a strict Senate neutrality law backfired. The August 1935 Neutrality Act, the first of five such laws, was intended as a temporary reaction to the 1935 Italo-Ethiopian War and required the president to declare a state of war existed and embargo sales of war material. The US refused to sell belligerents war material and Roosevelt attempted a "moral embargo" discouraging businesses from increasing trade with Italy which failed as quickly as Hoover's. Roosevelt secured in May 1937's Neutrality Act a "cash and carry" provision for belligerents buying raw materials because it favored Britain.[109]

After the Spanish Civil War began in July 1936, the US continued its strategy of non-interference abroad. But Roosevelt feared the war's spread, and worked with Britain and France to prevent this by supporting their diplomatic strategy of non-intervention. Like Britain, he was willing to accept a victory by Francisco Franco's Fascists if it prevented a wider war. Congressional action in January and May 1937 brought Spain under the Neutrality Act restrictions. In early 1938, Roosevelt faced pressure from groups noting non-intervention had failed and wanting repeal of the arms embargo because it was *de facto* aid to Franco, who was supported by Germany and Italy.[110]

ASIA

In July 1937, Japan invaded China. In October, Roosevelt suggested a strategy of "quarantine" by a concert of "peace-loving nations" against aggressor states. The malformed idea involved interested governments dropping "ordinary communications" and lacked a military threat or sanctions. The administration joined the signatories of the 1922 Washington Nine-Power Treaty in guaranteeing Chinese territorial integrity and political independence, and condemning Japanese aggression, and became a party to talks on ending the Sino-Japanese War, which affected the US directly in December 1937 when Japan attacked the American China gunboat *Panay*.

Roosevelt responded harshly, and Japan's apology, restitution, and promises to respect American rights in China defused the situation. The attack proved a catalyst for altering US grand strategy toward Japan. Roosevelt began considering embargos and sanctions to keep the US out of a war. He also aimed "to show aggressors that the United States was not indifferent to their actions." His hands remained tied by economic woes and a public desiring peace.[111]

MUNICH AND AFTER

In September 1938, Britain, France, Germany, and Italy signed the Munich Agreement. This awarded Nazi Germany Czechoslovakia's ethnically German Sudetenland and became the hallmark of British Prime Minister Neville Chamberlain's diplomatic strategy of appeasement. Roosevelt concluded Hitler could be neither appeased nor trusted and that a vulnerable US had to rearm. He announced $300 million in additional defense spending, especially on aircraft, and that American security demanded helping Britain and France, particularly with airpower. His military leaders wanted a balanced build-up. Civilian critics believed France should build its own planes. Roosevelt thought planes, not runways and barracks, could influence Hitler, but bent to the military's argument that the aircraft would be quickly obsolete and useless without support infrastructure and pilots. Half of the money went to training aircraft, which gave America the capacity to prepare large numbers of pilots and quickly expand its forces when war came. But Roosevelt also decided France was America's first line of defense. French purchases expanded America's aircraft industry.[112]

Germany's occupation of the remainder of Czechoslovakia in March 1939, and Britain's subsequent guarantee of Polish independence, coincided with a shift in US opinion and a hardening of will. Roosevelt pushed for changes in the neutrality laws, seeing supporting Britain and France as the most effective way of deterring Germany, but Congress opposed ending the arms embargo. Simultaneously, Roosevelt dispatched public messages to Hitler and Mussolini asking for pledges to not attack thirty-one different nations for at least a decade in exchange for a trade and disarmament conference. Both ridiculed him. Meanwhile, Roosevelt moved the US to a strategy of hemisphere defense.[113]

Roosevelt's attempts at international cooperation on disarmament failed, but he demonstrated commitment by shrinking America's 140,000-man army. In the decade before December 1941, "the percentage of federal expenditures devoted to military purposes fell lower than ever before."

Roosevelt cut the army but supported ship-building to make the navy Japan's equal and create jobs. Tokyo's March 1933 withdrawal from the League and abrogation of naval building limits encouraged this, and the US tripled funding for ship construction. Senator Carl S. Vinson proved decisive in preparing the navy. Roosevelt backed the 1934 Vinson–Trammell naval construction bill to meet the 1922 and 1930 treaty limits. Japan's abandonment of the 1935–36 London naval talks drove Roosevelt to seek the nation's largest peacetime increase in naval spending. Vinson's 1938 bill dramatically expanded the fleet. Events in Europe and Asia drove its supplement by the 1940 Two-Ocean Navy Act. Vinson's fourth naval law followed after France's July 1940 fall to Germany. Roosevelt, though, didn't want naval building to cause tensions with Tokyo and instituted a diplomatic strategy of "inaction and nonprovocation" toward Japan.[114]

CONCLUSION

The 1930s marred the nation with a decade of bipartisan economic failure. But revival was coming, partially because a warring world demanded US material. Roosevelt began leading a reluctant America to oppose some of history's greatest threats and was fortunate in having abundant, untapped American strength and innumerable individuals with the skills, intelligence, and courage who ensured America's survival and that it emerged stronger from the war it was about to face. Roosevelt also knew what he wanted to achieve.

9

MOVING ASTRIDE THE WORLD: THE SECOND WORLD WAR, 1939–1945

AMERICA'S ROAD TO WAR

On September 1, 1939, Hitler launched the Second World War by invading Poland. Britain and France declared war two days later. The Germans scored many early victories, exploiting a military built to fight quick wars against single opponents, its striking power concentrated in armored, mechanized units supported by aircraft. The Germans moved more quickly than their opponents as fast-moving armored forces cut enemy armies into pockets and were reduced by infantry, something known later as Blitzkrieg. Germany quickly conquered Poland, assisted by a Soviet invasion beginning on September 17, 1939, as Soviet dictator Josef Stalin began seizing the areas of Eastern Europe allotted him under the August Soviet–German Molotov–Ribbentrop Pact. The Germans conquered Norway and Denmark in April 1940. May 10, 1940, saw the Nazi campaign in the west. Italy entered the war as a German ally, and the fall of France, Holland, and Belgium in six weeks was followed by the establishment of the Vichy French collaborationist regime. A campaign in North Africa followed. The conquest of Yugoslavia and Greece began in April 1941. On June 22, 1941, Germany invaded the Soviet Union. Hitler had always aimed to acquire *Lebensraum* – living space – and self-sufficiency in agricultural and raw material resources in Eastern Europe and the Soviet Union, murdering the peoples the Nazis considered inferior, particularly Jews and Slavs. By December 1941, Hitler dominated Europe from the Pyrenees to Moscow. (See Map 9.1a.)

When the war began, Roosevelt told his cabinet to get ready to address the problems a war might bring but not prepare for war because he intended to keep the US out of it. He declared neutrality as the 1937 Neutrality Act and international law required. But Roosevelt's was not a disinterested neutrality. He believed it in America's interest to aid France and Britain (as did a slight American majority) and a moral issue. Preserving American values and the nation's way of life required Germany's defeat.[1]

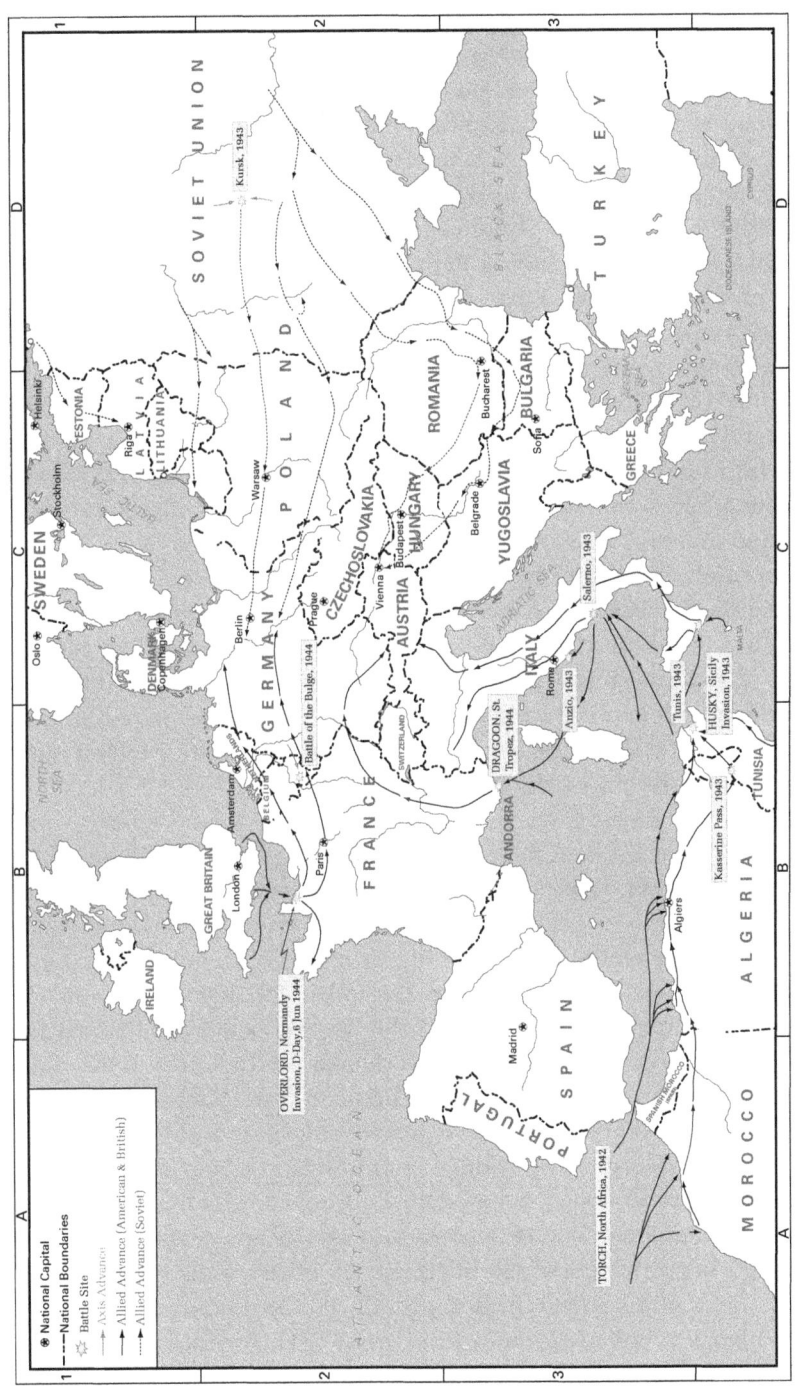

Map 9.1a Major operations in Europe, 1939-45

PART II: FROM GREAT POWER TO SUPERPOWER

To ensure America's security and contribute to Germany's defeat, Roosevelt moved on many fronts. Smart enough to act in a bipartisan manner, he secured neutrality law alterations in October 1939 allowing belligerents to purchase arms and material on a cash-and-carry basis. French and British debacles increased US support for aid and Roosevelt dispatched surplus equipment. When Italy entered the war on June 10, 1940 Roosevelt intensified assistance and American military preparations. He created a bipartisan cabinet by including Republicans: Henry Stimson became secretary of war and Frank Knox secretary of the navy. Britain's desperate need to guard its sea lanes produced a trade of fifty American destroyers for ninety-nine-year leases of British bases. Roosevelt secured the first US peacetime conscription law in late 1940, but Americans still overwhelmingly wanted to stay out of the war. This didn't stop Roosevelt from bending the Constitution to authorize Federal Bureau of Investigations (FBI) agents combating Nazi subversion to illegally use "investigations of political opponents and unlawful wiretappings and mail-openings."[2]

Roosevelt also began building the army. On May 10, 1940, the date marking the German offensive that saw the fall of France, the US army had only 5 deployable divisions – 80,000 men. The Germans had 140 divisions – 2 million men – in Western Europe. Roosevelt asked for $1.18 billion in additional defense spending. On May 16, he proposed building an air force with 50,000 planes. Congress appropriated $1.7 billion more, and increased the army from 280,000 to 375,000.[3]

British purchases of war supplies helped expand the US military industrial base. But as the war continued, London began seeing the end of its financial resources. Roosevelt came up with a way around the neutrality laws: Lend-Lease. The US would provide what Britain needed, and Britain could return the material after the war or make payment in kind, removing London's need for dollars. On December 29, 1940, Roosevelt told Americans he wanted to make the US the "arsenal of democracy," arguing that one of the best ways to keep out of the war was to send as much aid as possible to states resisting aggression. The Lend-Lease bill passed in March 1941. Roosevelt had the freedom to provide aid where and how he wanted and the power to order the production or purchase of war material.[4]

By May 1941, Roosevelt believed the US would have to enter the war but didn't intend to shoot first. He wanted to avoid wartime divisions by uniting the people beforehand and saw the actions of others abroad as the means. And he held an advantage in dealing with the Axis powers: the US had cracked Japan's diplomatic code. From April 1941, American cryptologists supplied information on Japan and Japanese views of German intentions.[5]

Roosevelt realized defeating the Nazis necessitated Allied control of the seas. Achieving this required defeating the German submarine offensive against British merchant shipping. After agreeing to protect Greenland, Roosevelt occupied Iceland in July 1941 to thwart a feared German attack and free up British shipping as well as troops occupying the Danish possession. Roosevelt extended aid to Moscow after the German invasion and made it eligible for Lend-Lease, moves influenced by the awareness among Secretary of War Stimson, Army Chief of Staff George C. Marshall, and Chief of Naval Operations Harold Stark of the importance of the Soviet front to Germany's eventual defeat.[6]

DIPLOMATIC AND ECONOMIC STRATEGY: JAPAN

In November 1938, Japan publicly repudiated the Open Door, declaring it would create its Greater Southeast Asia Co-Prosperity Sphere. The US objected. Roosevelt approved a $25 million loan to China, told Tokyo the US wouldn't leave China, and reinforced Hawaii and the Philippines. Roosevelt was inclined to a hard line against Japan but sailed a middle tack between advisors urging conciliation or strong economic sanctions by telling Tokyo Washington's refusal to impose sanctions was temporary. Roosevelt sought to prevent a US war in the Pacific, but the differing views on China between the US and Japan were insurmountable.[7]

The 1940 German victories in Europe convinced Roosevelt to renew efforts to reach a settlement with Japan. The victories emboldened Tokyo, which pressured Britain into closing the Burma Road supply route to China. Roosevelt balked at an Anglo-American plan to embargo all US oil exports to Germany and Japan but approved one on sales to Japan of high-octane aviation fuel, lubricants, and high-grade scrap metal. Anything more was considered pushing Japan too far. Tokyo objected, applied more pressure against the British, Dutch, and French colonies in Asia, then occupied parts of French Indochina in September 1940. The administration embargoed sales of iron and steel scrap, a move also designed to prevent shortages for US industry. On September 27, 1940, Tokyo joined the Axis by signing the Tripartite Pact with Germany and Italy, an alliance directed at the United States.[8]

American leaders began searching for ways to deter Japan to meet the greater German danger. They believed Tokyo wouldn't act unless German victory in Europe seemed inevitable and thought supporting Britain, while enabling a US Pacific defense, the best route to deterring Japan. Roosevelt sought peace in the Pacific through a combination of diplomacy, supporting China with loans, planes, volunteer pilots, Lend-Lease, shows of American strength, and negotiations with Japan. The administration hoped aid would deter Japanese attacks on British, Dutch, and French possessions. Protecting the Pacific would also aid Britain's war effort as London drew supplies from the region. The US replied to Japan's July 1941 occupation of all of French Indochina with further trade restrictions and freezing Tokyo's assets. Roosevelt told his advisors he wouldn't support a complete oil embargo because this would provoke a war but failed to clearly relay his views. This, and a fuzzy prohibition order, produced a *de facto* oil embargo on Japan and the suspension of trade in August. Roosevelt didn't notice until September and felt repeal would be taken as weakness. Holland and Britain followed suit. Japan, lacking dollars for purchasing war materials, was effectively under economic blockade. Roosevelt believed Tokyo's dependence on US trade would see them compromise.[9]

By late October 1941, Roosevelt believed Japan likely to move against the Soviets, but thought attacks on the US and Britain possible. American commanders in the Philippines and Hawaii were told to avoid provocations. If war came, the administration wanted the fault clear to Americans. Roosevelt continued negotiations, hoping to avoid or at least delay war in the Pacific, but Japan had already decided for war. The Americans demanded – most importantly – Japan's withdrawal from China. Tokyo refused.[10]

MILITARY PLANNING AND STRATEGY

Domestic political opposition constrained Roosevelt's preparations for war. The administration began mobilizing the government in April 1940, avoiding the First World War error of waiting until war was declared. It established bodies to purchase strategic materials such as rubber, the Office of Emergency Management, and the Selective Service System. Others followed after the attack on Pearl Harbor, including the War Labor Board and the War Production Board.[11]

Generally, the US pursued a strategy of disengagement and non-involvement beyond the Western Hemisphere. American defense priorities were the Continental US, Alaska, Hawaii, the Panama Canal, and the Philippines, and protecting American rights and interests in China. In the decades between the world wars, the US lacked the military power to do what it planned. This was particularly true with the ORANGE war plan against Japan. Moreover, as historian George Baer makes clear, the US had plans but no strategy. Plans are tools by which nations execute strategy.[12]

The results of September 1938's Munich Conference drove a reassessment. In November, the Joint Board directed examination of options in the face of simultaneous German, Italian, and Japanese attacks, the first time American planners studied a two-ocean war in conjunction with and against a coalition. The April 1939 report advocated a Pacific defensive, but its first priority was defense of the US position in the Western Hemisphere, especially the Panama Canal, the Caribbean, and the Atlantic approaches. Controlling these allowed navy operations in either ocean. American planners realized that "Not only must strategy be linked to policy [political aims], but it must also take cognizance of such intangibles as tradition, the spirit of the nations, and 'emotionalized public opinion'." In June 1939, the Joint Board authorized the five RAINBOW plans. Mid 1940 saw approval of RAINBOW 5's shifting Pacific strategy to a defensive one as Europe had grown in importance. The US would hold the area within an Alaska–Hawaii–Panama triangle and accept losing the Philippines, Wake, and Guam.[13]

November 1940 found Roosevelt receiving Admiral Stark's Plan DOG. Stark believed Britain's survival key to American security and that victory in Europe necessitated large-scale US participation and the concentration of US forces in the Atlantic, leaving few resources for war with Japan. The US would fight defensively in the Pacific with its fleet based in Hawaii. Roosevelt's primary concern was Britain's safety and the American–British Conversations (ABC) of early 1941 produced agreement Germany was the most dangerous foe, and that the Allies had to keep open the Atlantic sea lanes to Britain and deter Japan. The talks provided the basis of Allied strategy: Germany First. If Japan entered the war, the Allies would defend the Pacific and concentrate on Germany's destruction.[14]

ECONOMIC STRATEGY

The European conflagration helped end America's Great Depression. There was increased US defense spending, especially for naval and merchant ships. The prospect of profits spurred private investment. And the US expanded its money supply 11 percent annually as European gold flooded in.[15] The US also benefited from foreign spending.

Trade became a national security tool. Roosevelt's 1940 request for the RTAP's renewal insisted reciprocity was "an indispensable part of the foundation of any stable and durable peace." Between 1939 and 1941, the US signed numerous trade agreements featuring American tariff reduction in Latin America and with Turkey, Iceland, and Iran to economically link them with the US and either draw them away from the Axis or secure wartime cooperation.[16]

In July 1941, Roosevelt bent to the appeals of US mobilization planners and ordered an analysis of equipment and munitions requirements for defeating the Axis. The initial useless military estimates were reworked by Stacy May, a government economist. May, not Albert Wedemeyer, developed what became known as the Victory Program that provided the war's industrial strategy. Military leaders insisted they couldn't supply the economists with requirements for various proposed wartime circumstances, because they didn't know where they would be fighting or what kind of war it would be. May, from his post at the Supplies Production and Allocation Board, drafted his own parameters by assuming an army of 2 million by 1942's end as a basis, and also assessed Britain's. The result was the December 1941 Anglo-American Consolidated Statement delivered three days before the Pearl Harbor attack. It concluded America couldn't produce the needed war materials before 1944. Even before entering the war, "a small number of key economists and statisticians within the war planning boards already knew exactly how much of the military and other material called for by the current Victory Plan estimates the economy of the United States could produce and when it would be available." Moreover, these revelations made any landing in Western Europe before 1944 unfeasible. Army Chief of Staff Marshall was only informed in January 1943, right before the Casablanca Conference, that he wouldn't have the army he needed to invade Western Europe until 1944.[17]

After entering the war, the US increased income taxes and "the marginal rate went from 0.04 in 1939 to 0.29 in 1944." Tax increases and an excess profits tax provided 49 percent of wartime funding. Borrowing supplied another 28 percent. Deficit fears disappeared as "a debt of any size was preferable to losing the war." The remaining cost was covered by creating money. Price and wage controls allowed the government to funnel resources toward war production and pay less for it while postponing inflation, which peaked about one year after the war's end. Initially, the government hoped price controls on strategic items such as rubber and steel would keep all prices in check. This failed and consumer inflation averaged 12 percent annually during the war. The government introduced a new system in April 1943 to control almost all prices and wages.[18] Inflation also functioned as a war finance measure because the government paid its debts and bonds with inflated and thus less costly money.

Roosevelt depended heavily upon businessmen, particularly for innovative war production. The government often built plants and purchased machine tools, leasing everything to the manufacturer. Roosevelt's desire to make the US the "arsenal of democracy" was fulfilled by staggering US production. For example, in 1942, the US built 47,836 planes, and over 85,000 in 1943. Germany built 24,807 that year, Russia, 35,000.[19]

DIPLOMATIC STRATEGY AND THE EVOLVING POLITICAL AIMS

Roosevelt saw the interconnectedness of the world's disorders and wrote in January 1941 that "hostilities in Europe, in Africa, and in Asia [were] all parts of a single world conflict and [therefore] our strategy of self-defense must be a global strategy." The Atlantic Conference between FDR and Winston Churchill in Newfoundland in early August 1941 proved the first of many conferences producing Allied aims and much of grand strategy. The resulting Atlantic Charter wasn't a treaty because it was never sent to the Senate for ratification, but it committed the US to cooperating with a foreign power in pursuit of specific political aims. The pair agreed "to seek no aggrandizement, territorial or other," no coerced territorial changes, to free oppressed peoples so they could choose their own governments, open trade, better standards of living, and freedom of the seas. The sixth plank says: "after the final destruction of the Nazi tyranny" (which was indispensable for achieving the other aims), the leaders hoped for a peace allowing all to live safely. These were ambitious aims, especially since the US wasn't at war with Germany.[20]

The announcement of the Atlantic Charter did nothing to shift US public opinion toward entering the struggle. Roosevelt now tried to provoke an "incident" "that could lead to war." The US navy began escorting British convoys between the US and Iceland on September 1. American warships had orders to attack German submarines encountered. Roosevelt didn't announce convoying to the American people until after the US destroyer *Greer* cooperated with a British plane to attack a German U-boat and was fired upon. Roosevelt falsely painted this as German aggression, but he was waging an undeclared war against Germany in the North Atlantic, one the US public heavily supported. Contradictorily, this same public didn't back official, constitutional, entry into the war. Roosevelt, though, was trying to shift it by "devious means."[21]

AMERICA'S WAR

On December 7, 1941, Japanese carrier-based aircraft attacked American forces in Hawaii, bringing the United States into the Second World War. Even after the attack, Roosevelt remained focused on unifying public support as American public opinion remained split on involvement in a European war. Roosevelt asked Congress for only a declaration of war on Japan, knowing from intelligence reports that Hitler would likely declare war on the United States.[22] This happened on December 11.

GLOBAL WAR: THE POLITICAL AIMS

Roosevelt fixed the nation's political purposes in his January 6, 1942, State of the Union Address. "Our own objectives are clear;" he insisted, "the objective of smashing the militarism imposed by war lords upon their enslaved peoples, the objective of liberating the subjugated Nations – the objective of establishing and securing freedom of speech, freedom of religion, freedom from want, and freedom from fear everywhere in the world." This provided solid aims: smashing militarism (meaning destroying Nazi Germany, Fascist Italy, and Imperial Japan), and freeing "subjugated Nations." These are political goals towards which the state's elements of national power can be rationally directed. Critically, Roosevelt provided a vision of how victory looked and what it meant, and reminded Americans of the failures of 1918: "We shall not stop short of these objectives – nor shall we be satisfied merely to gain them and then call it a day ... this time we are determined not only to win the war, but also to maintain the security of the peace that will follow."[23] Roosevelt provided a clear, unlimited political aim for which to fight and against which to direct the nation's power – regime change – and wisely considered the imperative of winning the war *and* securing the peace.

The Arcadia Conference formalized the Allied alliance on January 1, 1942, via the Declaration of the United Nations. The twenty-six nations then at war with the Axis (eventually forty-five) pledged no separate peace. America committed to the Germany First strategy. Both Churchill and Stalin eventually sought the unlimited political aims of regime change against the Axis powers but had other purposes as well. Churchill wanted a return to the status quo antebellum. Stalin sought recognition of the territorial agreements he had made with Hitler, a postwar order that kept Germany weak and divided, and a Europe split into spheres of influence between Britain and the Soviet Union. The British wanted to maintain their colonies and trade protections while America wanted free trade.[24]

America's military command was reorganized in January 1942 when the Joint Chiefs of Staff (JCS) replaced the Joint Army and Navy Board. Its head, General George C. Marshall, "the finest organizational strategist in American military history," proved instrumental in delivering Allied success. In March 1942, the world was divided into three operational spheres for

Anglo-American forces. The US would run the Pacific Ocean war. Britain would control the area stretching from Singapore to the Mediterranean. The Atlantic Ocean and European theaters fell under the Anglo-American combined chiefs of staff. In November 1942, Marshall established the Joint Strategic Survey Committee (JSSC) to furnish strategic guidance for operational planning and to liaise with the State Department.[25]

THE UNITED STATES AND ALLIED GRAND STRATEGY: THE SECOND WORLD WAR

One cannot separate American grand strategy in the Second World War from that of its allies. America waged a coalition struggle against another coalition, with the Anglo-American elements in the European Theater of Operations (ETO) exerting a dominant influence upon Washington. Generally, the British and Americans worked well together, despite their prejudices, and this alliance proved one of history's most effective.

ASSESSMENT AND THE ENVIRONMENT OF STRATEGY MAKING

The Allies faced a global war against many dangerous enemies threatening one power more than others. For example, the Soviet Union was endangered by Germany (not Japan) and wanted immediate action by the Western powers to alleviate this. The US and Britain, though, couldn't ignore Japan. This was particularly true for Washington as a Japanese attack brought it into the war. The Allies resolved disagreements over political aims and strategy at conferences. Nine proved key: Arcadia, Casablanca, Trident, Quebec, Moscow, Cairo, Tehran, Yalta, and Potsdam.

Roosevelt exerted influence on Allied grand strategy through three means: 1) close advisors enabling him to circumvent the clumsy US bureaucracy, especially the Department of State; 2) conferences with Allied leaders; and 3) the possession and elaboration of a clear vision drawn from an understanding of the American people and "the need to temper that vision" with the reality of "balance-of-power" politics. Because much of grand strategy came from Roosevelt, this caused confusion regarding execution as his advisors often failed to mix the realistic and idealistic as Roosevelt. Compounding this was that his advisors stretched ideologically from Soviet-sympathizing Henry A. Wallace, vice president from 1941 to 1945, to conservatives such as Republican Secretary of War Stimson with no faith in liberal internationalism. Roosevelt also refused to address key postwar political issues with Allies. This avoided wartime problems but undermined longer-term planning.[26]

PART II: FROM GREAT POWER TO SUPERPOWER

STRATEGY AND STRATEGIC IMPERATIVES

There were certain imperatives considered indispensable for the execution of American grand strategy and the achievement of Washington's aims. The US needed both Great Britain and the Soviet Union to survive. Britain's geographic position and help were necessary to destroy German military resistance. It was also a key postwar pillar. If the Soviets failed to maintain their gigantic front, breaking the German military could prove impossible.[27]

GERMANY FIRST

The US chose the Germany First strategy, "the most important single strategic concept of the war," because its leaders believed it in America's interest. Both Washington and London saw Germany as their most dangerous foe and thought its defeat meant the rapid demise of its partners. They agreed in December 1941 that the main facets of their strategy would be: manufacturing the armaments outlined in the Victory Program (which necessitated protecting key industrial areas), guarding critical communication routes, "Closing and tightening the ring around Germany," "Wearing down and undermining German resistance by air bombardment, blockade, subversive activities, and propaganda," "continuous offensive action against Germany," and only holding needed Pacific positions.[28]

Defeating Germany required breaking Nazi military forces, overthrowing Hitler's regime, and occupying Germany itself. To do this, the US and Britain had to bring to bear their combined military might. This required controlling the sea lanes, especially across the Atlantic, dominating the air over Europe, and putting large land forces onto the continent. How to do these things, and particularly the issue of the timing of the Second Front in Europe (the Soviet or Eastern Front being the other) dominated Allied European strategy debates. But the US couldn't ignore the Pacific theater. To American leaders, particularly military heads, this meant the war in Europe needed to be waged as quickly as possible to enable America to turn against Japan. Marshall insisted "a democracy cannot fight a seven year war."[29] History later proved him incorrect, but he thought this true at the time.

Washington and London disagreed upon *how* to fight the Germans. Britain feared German strength and argued for a strategy of fighting Germany on its periphery (allowing London to escape the First World War death toll), with a bombing campaign, blockade, propaganda, aiding the Soviets, and feeding subversion in occupied Europe, all designed to undermine Germany's will and ability to fight. The final blow – a cross-channel offensive – would be launched after Germany was weakened and near collapse.[30]

American military leaders wanted to mass forces in Britain for an invasion of the German-controlled continent in 1942. Mass and concentration underpinned their view. Putting US forces into Europe as soon as possible was also the best way to block Soviet expansion, and an army on the continent ensured a voice in the peace and the postwar settlement. Absence could cede this to the Soviets. Marshall charged Dwight Eisenhower with developing the plan to defeat Germany delivered on April 1, 1942. It had three major parts: BOLERO, massing men and material in Britain for an invasion; ROUNDUP, a 1943 landing; and SLEDGEHAMMER, a small 1942 landing to be mounted only if the Soviets or Germans appeared near collapse. The Americans liked BOLERO. It furnished a focal point for mobilization and met Moscow's demand for a Second Front while quickly taking the fight to the enemy. Roosevelt approved. Believing they had Britain's agreement, Marshall and the JCS began preparing for SLEDGEHAMMER and its possible 1942 launch.[31]

Dwight David "Ike" Eisenhower was critically important in the design and execution of Allied grand strategy. He was deputy chief of American war planning early in the war. A West Point graduate and professional soldier, the well-read Eisenhower had survived Clausewitz's *On War* three times. Marshall respected Ike's intelligence and his imagination when tackling big problems and ideas. Roosevelt, when asked why he had chosen Eisenhower to command in Europe, said: "He is a natural leader who can convince other men to follow him, and this is what we need in his position more than any other quality." Ike later set up the Supreme Headquarters Allied Expeditionary Forces (SHAEF) in January 1944.[32]

British consent for the American approach proved short-lived. Germany's June 1942 capture of Tobruk in North Africa frightened London, as did a risky European landing for which it would have to provide most of the troops. Fearing disaster, London retreated from its commitment to a 1942 European invasion. The British argued North Africa was a better place to fight. Winning control here would free the Mediterranean for convoy traffic, saving the stretched Allies the equivalent of 200 ships monthly. Roosevelt decided in July 1942 that the US would invade North Africa. The JCS hated the change, particularly Marshall and the navy's new chief of naval operations, Admiral Ernest King. They argued for shifting the focus to Japan. Roosevelt ordered coordination with the British, insisting it was "of the highest importance that US ground troops be brought into action against the enemy [in Europe] in 1942." Roosevelt reminded Marshall and King that defeating Japan wouldn't affect Germany, while America focusing on Asia in 1942 and 1943 might seal German control of Europe and Africa. He told them to keep in mind three things: "speed of decision on plans, unity of plans, attack combined with defense, but not defense alone." Marshall later admitted SLEDGEHAMMER could have been disastrous.[33]

Roosevelt chose his course for several reasons. He saw it as politically necessary to be involved in the ETO in 1942. The Soviets appeared to be holding Germany at Stalingrad and along the Volga River; this meant the need to do something risky had subsided. The Solomon Islands campaign against Japan was then ongoing and the issue remained in doubt. Failure here would lead Americans to question why the US had troops sitting in Britain while forces in the Pacific were being driven into the sea. Roosevelt realized Americans needed to see their government mounting significant military operations each year, which would provide justification for the Germany First strategy. He believed defeating Japan would have little effect on the war in Europe, but Germany's demise would free the Allies to focus on Japan. Fighting in North Africa was the best option available for acting in the ETO in 1942. If successful, this force could combine with a British drive from Egypt to clear North Africa and open the possibility of attacking Italy. It could also be launched while the Allies continued to prepare for a 1943 Europe landing.[34]

The Anglo-American forces launched Operation TORCH. The Allies achieved complete surprise and the Americans landed their green, poorly trained, equipped, and led forces in French Algeria and Morocco on November 8, 1942. The Americans benefited from an initial slothful German response but faced surprising opposition from the collaborationist Vichy French forces they had expected to surrender. The Vichy soon cut a deal to change sides, quickening Morocco's and Algeria's fall. Two weeks before TORCH, on October 23, 1942, Bernard Montgomery's Eighth Army launched the offensive producing the British victory at El Alamein and broke open the Axis defenses in Egypt.[35]

The Allies hoped to clear North Africa by 1942's end, making it possible to land in Europe in 1943. But Tunisia's Vichy leaders refused to fold, easing German movement of reinforcements. Hitler, worried about Italy's collapse, moved units from the Eastern Front to Tunisia, and 178,000 Axis troops flowed into North Africa. Hitler planned to hold Tunis and mount an operation aimed at Casablanca. Realizing Tunis wouldn't fall quickly made it clear to British and American military leaders there wouldn't be a Second Front in 1943. Marshall worried the extension of North Africa operations might push a Europe landing past 1944.[36]

The Allies liberated North Africa in May 1943 and derived many benefits from their campaign. They gained a French army as the former Vichy troops became the core of a Free French force. They learned indispensable tactical and operational lessons. Their operations hindered Germany sending forces to relieve Stalingrad and consumed air transport capacity that could have helped supply the besieged Germans. The Allied campaign was far from brilliant. Montgomery, because of his slowness, missed many opportunities to trap Axis forces in his advance from Egypt to Tunisia. The Americans suffered a bitter defeat at Kasserine Pass, betraying US inexperience. The firing of numerous failed commanders opened doors for the rise of those who became among the most important US generals: Omar Bradley and George S. Patton.[37]

The initiative in the war now shifted to the Allies. The US and Britain had cleared North Africa. The Soviets had recaptured Stalingrad and the Nazis were in retreat. The US Solomon Islands campaign in the Pacific had succeeded (more on this shortly). But what next?

THE CASABLANCA CONFERENCE

Roosevelt held his first meeting to decide the step after TORCH on November 25, 1942. The Americans lacked a coherent strategy at this point. This was ironed out with Britain at the January 1943 Casablanca Conference. Historian James Lacey noted a pair of related historical myths: that Marshall went to Casablanca opposed to further Mediterranean operations, and that Britain won the briefing fight by being better prepared. American military leaders already knew it was too late to mount a 1943 cross-channel attack. Instead, they aimed for British agreement to invade Europe. The date could be fixed later.[38]

The Americans realized a France invasion force would have to be twice that originally envisioned to stack the deck for success. Both allies thought more training indispensable, and Marshall concurred with London's observation that Europe's railroad system would allow the Nazis to throw as many as seven divisions a day against a landing. TORCH's difficulties dampened US optimism toward landing against a tough opponent, and the material and munitions needed for OVERLORD wouldn't be available until 1944. The conference decided upon a 1944 invasion but not when. The debate on ground forces centered around how to use them in the Mediterranean.[39]

The American and British leaders agreed the most important tasks for 1943 were defeating the U-boat, increasing Lend-Lease aid to the Soviet Union and China, limited offensive operations in the Pacific, a small offensive in Burma, and the Combined Bomber Offensive. The massive resources bombing required helped convince the US to limit its army to eighty-nine divisions. The Allies also agreed, in Churchill's words, "to strike into the underbelly of the Axis" by invading Sicily as a step toward knocking Italy out of the war. Marshall supported HUSKY – the Sicily invasion – because the troops were there to do it. There was only one US division in Britain at the time of Casablanca.[40]

Roosevelt famously announced the aim of unconditional surrender of the Axis at Casablanca, something agreed to beforehand by the State Department. This wasn't a change in aims as it didn't differ from the original. American leaders didn't want to repeat what they viewed as Wilson's key error: failing to require a formal German surrender. This had allowed Germans to pretend they hadn't lost the war. Roosevelt also intended unconditional surrender to boost Allied morale, soothe an unhappy Stalin (who would soon be told there would be no Second Front in 1943), and reassure China's Chiang Kai-Shek. Considering their enemies, Britain's leaders viewed unconditional surrender as the only option for securing peace.[41]

The Americans and British reviewed their strategic plans at the May 1943 Washington Trident Conference. The US convinced Britain to agree to a date for the invasion of France: May 1, 1944. When informed of a delay of yet one more year, the angry Soviets temporarily pulled their ambassadors from London and Washington. Roosevelt backed his military leaders on the Second Front, agreeing that Allied strength should be concentrated and not dispersed in the Mediterranean, and the Americans insisted that any additional operations Britain wanted in the Mediterranean not delay an invasion of France. The Americans feared postponement would result in a separate Soviet–German peace that left the Nazis ruling most of Europe and the US to fight Japan alone. If Britain wouldn't commit to a 1944 landing, the US would concentrate on fighting Japan. Britain won consideration of an operation in the Mediterranean after Sicily fell, but the differences of opinion regarding what to do next were so intense it was decided to postpone any decision until after HUSKY and then allow Eisenhower to make the call.[42]

THE INVASIONS OF SICILY AND ITALY

The operational objective of HUSKY was to capture Sicily. The Allies lacked the intelligence dominance they possessed in Africa, but Britain launched a successful deception operation centered around dumping a corpse off the Spanish coast with fake invasion plans. This convinced the Germans the next Allied targets were Sardinia and Greece and they diverted forces that might have been in Sicily. The Allies, though, didn't sufficiently capitalize on the gains because of poor execution. The Anglo-American force landed on July 9, 1943, but Montgomery's unnecessary splitting of his forces slowed the Allied advance, and despite controlling both the sea and the air, the Allies failed to prevent the evacuation of most of the defending Germans. But HUSKY did as hoped. It fully opened the Mediterranean to Allied shipping, diverted Nazi forces from the East as Hitler halted the Battle of Kursk to shift reinforcements to the Mediterranean, and shook the Italian regime so violently the Germans recognized they needed more forces to hold the peninsula. The Allies gained air control over the Mediterranean and a springboard for invading Italy.[43]

In July, Eisenhower approved the invasion of Italy, a decision influenced by the air commanders who had objected but now insisted they needed Italian bases to increase pressure on Germany. Eisenhower adopted a British plan for landing at Salerno and crossing the Straits of Messina simultaneously. Tunisia's fall had seen Hitler begin planning for Italy's defection, which soon came. The Italians arrested Mussolini at the end of July, and a government under Marshal Pietro Badoglio negotiated Italy's surrender to the Allies on September 3, the same day the Allies invaded. The Germans rushed in to hold key points. The two Allied invasion prongs were supposed to support one another, but both commanders bungled their operations. US General Mark Clark's Anglo-American force fought its way out of their Salerno beachhead, plagued by the commander's inexperience and German reinforcements, while Montgomery crossed the Straits and sat. Naples eventually fell on October 1.[44]

As the campaign ground on in Italy, the invasion of France remained a sticking point. In November–December 1943, Roosevelt, Churchill, and Stalin met at Tehran, the first meeting of the "Big Three." Churchill tried to delay OVERLORD, the invasion of France, for further operations in the Aegean and Mediterranean. Roosevelt said they should put it to Stalin and decide together. Stalin wanted OVERLORD and ANVIL, the planned simultaneous landing in southern France (ANVIL was later delayed because of insufficient shipping). The British, who consistently supported other Mediterranean operations, opposed ANVIL. Stalin also promised to enter the war against Japan after Germany was defeated and to launch an offensive coinciding with OVERLORD. Roosevelt and Churchill agreed Stalin could keep the territory he received in the 1939 Molotov–Ribbentrop Pact. Poland would be compensated with territory from Germany, and Moscow would also get part of East Prussia.[45]

The endorsement of Roosevelt, Stalin's desire, previous British agreement, and the approval of the initial operational plan for OVERLORD at the Quadrant Conference in Quebec in August 1943 didn't dampen British opposition. Throughout the first half of 1944, Churchill pushed for a landing in the Adriatic and an advance through the Ljubljana Gap to Vienna. The Americans insisted upon staying the course. Part of British reluctance was fear of First World War-like losses, ones it couldn't replace, and which London couldn't politically endure. In the end, the British labored heavily to make OVERLORD work.[46]

ALLIED GRAND STRATEGY: THE PATH TO NORMANDY

On June 6, 1944, the Allies invaded France, securing a foothold for striking at the Reich's heart. The Allies took innumerable actions to put their force ashore and then supply and support it as it fought its way across Europe against a skilled and more experienced opponent. Two key achievements enabling the Normandy invasion were winning control of the sea, particularly the sea lines of communication (SLOCs), and control of the air.

NAVAL STRATEGY: WINNING CONTROL OF THE SEA

In the 1930s, the German navy, headed by Grand Admiral Erich Raeder, composed the Z Plan for constructing a large navy. He envisaged surface units forcing Britain to concentrate the bulk of its navy in the North Sea while other German naval elements raided British commerce. But the plan assumed Germany wouldn't be at war until 1946 or later. Admiral Karl Dönitz, head of the German submarine force and later Raeder's successor, believed he could strangle Britain through commerce raiding because London depended upon seaborne imports, particularly food and oil. Dönitz hoped to sink enough shipping to force Britain's surrender. He believed he needed 300 submarines to achieve this but only had 57 when the war began. Even though Germany could deploy only 10–15 submarines in the war zone at a time, in the first 15 months of the war these inflicted grievous losses, sinking 1,939 merchant ships displacing 7,050,000 tons. The Germans banked on attrition, hoping that sinking 400–500,000 tons monthly would drive Britain from the war.[47]

In early 1942, Dönitz went for the easy pickings: American ships on the Atlantic coast. German submarines sank 2.34 million tons of shipping over the next six months, a massacre resulting from US unpreparedness, a failure to adopt the proven British convoy system, the refusal of the army air corps and US navy to cooperate in antisubmarine patrols, and King's insistence convoys possess offensive capability against U-boats. As the navy lacked the ships for this, it didn't convoy. The army only began cooperating via aerial escorts and patrols after losses endangered its ability to accumulate men and equipment in combat theaters.[48]

King and other US military leaders had planned to fight a global, offensive war and King insisted upon an offensive in both theaters – simultaneously. But American offensive action required sea control because the US could do nothing if it couldn't project power. Securing sea control required defeating the U-boats. The Allies developed new technology to help find and kill submarines such as radio-direction finding, radar, and special weapons. Long-ranged aircraft bearing these proved particularly effective. British penetration of the German submarine code Enigma in December 1942 allowed the Allies to reroute convoys and kill German submarines. Small, escort aircraft carriers gave convoys continuous air cover while robbing the U-boat of its ability to hunt on the surface. Admiral Sir Max Horton, a veteran submarine commander and commander in chief of the Western Approaches, acquired new technology and more equipment, developed new methods, and integrated Allied efforts. By the late spring of 1943, the Allies were strong enough to send convoys into the teeth of the German submarines and kill them.[49]

Allied industrial superiority was also critical. King said in June 1942 that the war couldn't be won without first defeating the U-boats, and having enough escort vessels was a key. But the Combined Chiefs didn't give them production priority until January 1943. The Allies didn't make this mistake with merchant shipping. The Ships-for-Victory program built prefabricated cargo vessels – Liberty ships. US Maritime Commission yards built 5,777 vessels between 1939 and 1945, including 2,708 Liberty ships, "the greatest shipbuilding program in history."[50]

Allied merchant ship construction outpaced monthly losses to submarines beginning in July 1942, except for December 1942. U-boat losses rose steadily throughout 1943, averaging more than one a day by May, a month in which the Germans lost perhaps half their submarine force. Dönitz withdrew his submarines from the Atlantic to reequip and reorganize. By June, convoy losses had fallen dramatically, and the Allies had turned the corner in the Battle of the Atlantic. On October 25, 1943, King said the U-boats had been reduced "from a menace to a problem." During the war, the Germans sank 2,603 merchant ships, including 757 American vessels, killing over 6,000 merchant sailors; 25,000 of their British comrades died. U-boats also sank 145 warships. The Germans lost 681 submarines and 70 percent of the crew who served, 28,000 of 40,900 men. The Germans developed advanced submarines near the end of the war, but the most important effect of this was preventing Germany from building thousands of additional armored vehicles.[51]

AIR STRATEGY: WINNING CONTROL OF THE SKY

To successfully invade the continent – and keep the armies supplied and reinforced afterward – the Allies had to win control of the air. Doing this necessitated defeating the *Luftwaffe*, the German air force. This occurred – unexpectedly – via the Combined Bomber Offensive, an around-the-clock strategic bombing campaign.

Prewar strategic bombing theory insisted upon its decisiveness. The most rabid devotees believed bombing alone could bring down an enemy. Reality intervened. The ideas of three figures underpinned Allied airpower thought: Giulio Douhet, William "Billy" Mitchell, and Hugh Trenchard. Douhet, an Italian theorist and professional officer, authored *Command of the Air* in 1921. To Douhet, controlling the air was all-important. He argued there was now no difference between civilians and combatants, that a ground offensive succeeding was no longer possible (an assessment based on the First World War), and that the speed and capabilities of aircraft made it impossible to defend against them. Because of this, success in war necessitated immediate, massive, air attacks against civilian targets using incendiaries, explosives, and poison gas to quickly break the enemy's morale. This required an independent air force with heavy bombers. Similarly, army Brigadier General William "Billy" Mitchell fervently believed that airpower would dominate future warfare and fought during the 1920s for an independent American air arm. Air Chief Marshal Sir Hugh Trenchard's ideas underpinned British thinking. He advocated an independent air force and saw this as a way to avoid the First World War's slaughter. Similar to Douhet, he saw airpower returning decisiveness to war by striking directly at the sources of the enemy's strength – his material and morale – not its supposed manifestations – his military forces. Particularly important was attacking enemy civilians to destroy morale. The bomber was the key to quickly inflicting a fatal blow and a fleet of them was a deterrent. Some believed the bomber's speed would ensure it reached its target – "the bomber would always get through" – making air attacks unstoppable. Briefly, some bombers were faster than fighters, and radar didn't yet exist. Fortunately for the world, Britain developed a rounded force emphasizing defense based upon fighters and radar.[52]

During the 1930s, many US army air corps officers came to believe that the development of airpower presented a new way of defeating an enemy. It could strike directly at the industrial capacity necessary for supporting modern military machines without having to first defeat the enemy's air force. There was also no longer any distinction made between the military forces and the civilians whose labor supported them. The resulting doctrine emphasized pinpoint, daylight bombing of industrial targets to cripple specific industries and thus the enemy's ability to wage war.[53] Here is a common conceit in political and military thinking about war: we will not have to fight the enemy. This fails to ask: what if the enemy disagrees?

When the war began, Britain not only lacked the bombers to do what air enthusiasts insisted, Bomber Command realized striking Germany was suicidal and Britain's political leaders worried about retaliation against civilians at home. The military debacles of 1940 brought Churchill to power, and he saw in Bomber Command a means of hitting Germany that might relieve pressure on France. After the Germans bombed Rotterdam in May 1940, Churchill ordered attacks on German industry. The initial raids, mounted in daylight, suffered heavy casualties. Britain switched to night bombing, but this increased the inaccuracy. The intensity of bombing grew after France's surrender as Churchill saw a way to attack Germany. Both Churchill and Roosevelt became enthusiastic supporters of strategic bombing and their insistence made it a primary plank of Allied strategy.[54]

But was the bombing effective – meaning, did it injure the enemy's will or ability to fight the war at an acceptable cost? In theory, Britain was targeting industry. But a summer 1941 British study concluded that 20 percent of British bomber attacks on Germany hit within *75 square miles* of the target. Inaccuracy forced Britain to adopt area bombing. This intensified when Air Marshal Arthur Harris took over Royal Air Force (RAF) Bomber Command in February 1942. Harris didn't believe German morale could be broken via bombing but inherited this direction. He thought bombing could crush Germany's material ability to wage the war by destroying cities and forcing the *Luftwaffe* into combat. The British would bomb factories, infrastructure, support facilities for industry, and workers' housing. The civilian workforce became a military target.[55]

Operation POINTBLANK was the American bomber offensive. Roosevelt saw here a possible war-winning tool and a means of breaking German morale by bombing every town. In January 1943, as a result of a Casablanca Conference decision, the Allied combined chiefs of staff ordered "the progressive destruction and dislocation of the German military, industrial and economic system and the undermining of the morale of the German people to a point where their capacity for armed resistance is fatally weakened." Germany's aircraft manufacturing became the top target. Bearing production, which fed all German industry, was second. Its destruction would create industrial bottlenecks, particularly for aircraft production, an objective considered achievable because of the industry's concentration in a few areas, 42 percent in Schweinfurt.[56]

American airpower theorists believed unescorted heavy bombers with strong defensive armament flying at high altitude could attack Germany with acceptable losses. American estimates about the vulnerability of bearing production proved as mistaken as assumptions regarding bombing effectiveness and bomber survivability. Losses sometimes reached 28 percent. Combined bomber loss and damage rates in October 1943 hit 52 percent. Continuously replacing such casualties would have required a new bomber force every three months. The solution was long-range escort fighters. P-47s and P-51s were soon protecting the bombers. By April 1944, low-level fighter sweeps were launched into Germany, sometimes alongside bombing missions, specifically targeting the *Luftwaffe*.[57]

Airpower also attacked the critical vulnerability of the German war machine: oil. The Nazis suffered shortages of petroleum as early as 1940, but barring the 1943 raid on Ploesti, Romania, the Allies failed to target this. This changed in May 1944 when bombers began hitting German synthetic oil production and Romania after ULTRA intercepts from Britain's codebreaking efforts revealed a petroleum shortage. May raids cut German oil production by half. After a two-week pause to support the Normandy landing, the Allies resumed hitting Germany's petroleum industry. The effects rippled throughout Germany's war effort. Fuel shortages began robbing German ground units of mobility. Shortages hampered pilot training, making it harder to replace casualties. The German air force began suffering heavy losses of fighter aircraft and pilots at the end of 1943. By the spring of 1944, Germany monthly lost half its fighters and 25 percent of its pilots, robbing the German army of air cover and support.[58]

In September 1944, Air Marshal Tedder suggested a campaign against Germany's transportation system, insisting this could bring German industry to a standstill. He hoped to break the railroad network, halting the movement of finished goods and raw material. The Allies began hitting railroad marshalling yards and hubs in city centers, as well as the canal system. The effects were dramatic. German industry couldn't move sufficient raw materials to its factories or quickly replenish the fighting fronts. By early 1945, Germany's war economy was coming apart.[59]

Long-range escort fighters made American bombing effective, but this didn't mean bombing could destroy German industry. This was never possible and represents an example of the wishful thinking habitually afflicting airpower theorists. German industrial production continued to increase even at the height of the bombing. But this mattered not, because the bombing forced the Germans to fight and all but destroyed the German air force by mid 1944 via the simplest and most direct method: attrition. The Allied ability to read most *Luftwaffe* codes greatly helped.[60] Too much airpower theory ignores the bitter reality that achieving one's aims in a war requires killing the enemy.

The bombing campaign had other unintended effects. It forced the Germans to devote perhaps 2 million personnel and much valuable armaments to ground-based air defense. Destruction of war material by bombing, and the diversion of equipment to oppose it, robbed the German combat forces of weapons and equipment. Bombing didn't break German morale, but it exhausted, depressed, and harried the people while driving absenteeism to as much as 25 percent. This wrecked production plans.[61]

The bomber offensive had a high cost: 140,000 Allied airmen were killed during the war; 21,000 bombers were lost. Bombing didn't win the war as some airpower enthusiasts insisted. German war production rose as the bombing intensified, but it would have risen at higher rates without it. Economist John Kenneth Galbraith, who helped run the postwar Strategic Bombing Survey, concluded bombing had failed because it did not "reduce German munitions production or German morale." He agreed bombing of synthetic oil plants and rail lines had an effect, but this came late. Galbraith's conclusions fed his later opposition to US bombing in Vietnam.[62]

OPERATION OVERLORD – THE CROSS-CHANNEL INVASION

Having gained control of the sea and broken the *Luftwaffe*, the Western Allies landed in France on June 6, 1944. Eisenhower had orders to "enter the continent of Europe, and, in conjunction with the other United Nations, undertake operations aimed at the heart of Germany and the destruction of her armed forces." He wrote Montgomery: "My purpose is to destroy the enemy's armed forces and his power to resist."[63] It is tempting to see success as inevitable. It didn't appear so at the time. And the stakes were high. Failure meant military and political disaster. Could Churchill's government have survived? What would be the political cost in the US? How would Stalin have reacted to Allied failure and further delay of a Second Front?

What if the Soviets defeated Germany before American forces arrived, leaving Stalin dominant in Europe?

An instructive way to examine the invasion is to look at the risks and the rewards. To US military leaders, this was the war's key operation. They deemed a successful continental invasion necessary for victory and consistently pressed for a strategy of concentration to aim overwhelming force at the enemy's heart. The Allies needed to stack the deck in their favor by mitigating or removing as many risks as possible. Planning was the first step. British Lieutenant General Sir Frederick Morgan, known as COSSAC (Chief of Staff to the Supreme Allied Commander), led this. He brought to the post experience in North Africa and benefited from the input of innumerable British and American officers. At the May 1943 Trident Conference, it was agreed Morgan should plan for a May 1, 1944, invasion. Initially, COSSAC proposed landing three divisions supported by one airborne division. Eisenhower vetoed COSSAC's first plan. He wanted a much greater force in the first wave. The constraining factor was the projected number of available LSTs (Landing Ship Tank), a British-designed but largely US-built vessel critical for putting troops and equipment ashore. Many were allotted for the US Pacific campaign. Negotiations at the Cairo and Tehran Conferences in November and December 1943, respectively, saw British and American agreement to give OVERLORD first call on resources.[64]

One of COSSAC's key decisions was choosing a landing site. The range of land-based aircraft drove this and narrowed the suitable areas to the Pas de Calais or the Normandy region stretching from the Seine's mouth to the Cotentin Peninsula. Calais was the closest point to Britain, and on the direct line to Germany, but also where the Germans expected an attack and were the best prepared. To the planners, Normandy was the only real choice.[65]

The Allies had staggering logistical demands, not only for the landing but also the follow-on operations. For example, they intended to land 300,500 gallons of drinking water in the first three days, just one in a list of items ranging from bridging equipment to sulfa pills. Allied planning initially assumed the immediate demand to capture a port. A failed raid on Dieppe, France, in 1942 convinced them this would be too tough, and taught them the bulk of their men and material would have to enter across the beach. Moreover, the location chosen lacked a port. With nearly unlimited industrial capacity, the Allies simply brought a port with them. They built two artificial harbors known as Mulberries, something conceived by Churchill, installed them on Normandy's beaches and sank blockships.[66]

Additionally, the Allies savaged France's rail system via air attacks to wreck Germany's ability to put reinforcements against the invasion and also used attacks by the French Resistance. They mounted an enormous deception campaign – FORTITUDE NORTH and FORTITUDE SOUTH – that included fake armies, false radio traffic, and dummy tanks and planes. The Nazis kept twelve divisions in Norway and five in Denmark, and believed Calais the Allied target. The Allies reinforced what Germany thought would occur, something the Allies knew from intelligence. Hitler expected diversionary landings in the Normandy–Cotentin Peninsula and Brittany while the main assault went in at the Pas de Calais. He held critical units in Calais until July 25.[67]

Timing also mattered. The weather, moon, and tide parameters meant the Allies had to land in early May or during short windows in the first and third weeks of June. Dawn was considered the perfect landing time. This let the fleet approach in the dark and gave the invading force a full day to get ashore. A full moon was bad for the invading fleet, but it needed a partial one to drop paratroopers. Eisenhower chose June 5, but the weather forced a delay. Alerted to a break in the weather on the 6th, Eisenhower gave the order to go. He briefed reporters on the afternoon of June 5. In an impressive example of moral courage, and as was his practice before ordering major operations, Eisenhower wrote a note announcing failure and taking full responsibility.[68]

The final OVERLORD plan called for the Allies to land a division on each of five beaches: Gold, Sword, Juno, Utah, and Omaha. Three airborne divisions would be dropped on the flanks as blocking forces. The Allies planned to land 150,000 men on D-Day. This required 7,000 ships and other craft. Around 11,500 aircraft supported the landing. After getting off the beaches, Montgomery was to capture Caen on the first day, while the Americans took the Cotentin Peninsula and its ports, then Cherbourg and other ports south.[69]

THE GERMAN DEFENSE

To Germany, the stakes were high. To Hitler, France became the decisive theater, but Soviet pressure limited his options. In May 1944, Germany had 1,900,000 men in the West, 950,000 in the army. The commanders differed on how to defend France, but all agreed it critical to meet the enemy at the water in some measure. The Nazis constructed fortifications along 2,600 kilometers of coastline, concentrating on likely landing zones. The strongest defenses were at the Pas de Calais. Some magical thinking underpinned German planning: willpower would overcome the obstacles confronting them.[70]

PART II: FROM GREAT POWER TO SUPERPOWER

THE WESTERN EUROPEAN CAMPAIGN

The invasion began on June 6. After heavy fighting on a few beaches, the Allies began moving inland. By the end of the day, the Allies had over 155,000 men ashore. In two weeks, they landed 20 divisions, over 500,000 troops. In July, this number was 1 million, and 190,000 vehicles. The Germans responded slowly, then contained the Allies. The Allied timetable fell apart. An attritional slugging match ensued, and the Allied commanders began looking for ways to break out and exploit their mobility.[71]

Operation COBRA was the reply. Planned by Bradley, it began with a massive air bombardment of German forces on July 25, 1944. The air attacks killed a lot of Americans but shattered many German units. A two-pronged American and British offensive followed. The US swung the larger arm in the south. On July 30, US forces captured Avranches on the hills overlooking the Bay of Mont St. Michel, a geographic linchpin. On August 1, two corps of General George Patton's Third Army poured into open country. Hitler ordered a heavy German counterattack against Avranches to close the gap. The blow fell on the night of August 6–7, but decoded ULTRA intercepts told the Americans it was coming. US forces blunted the attack while continuing their end run. On August 11, the Germans began retreating. On the 16th, Hitler authorized a general withdrawal, but the Allies were advancing faster than the Germans could retreat. But they missed the chance to trap 100,000 Germans in the Falaise Pocket because Bradley halted Patton's force swinging from the south, and Montgomery failed to advance aggressively. Probably 20,000 Germans escaped.[72]

The Soviets dealt the Germans even heavier blows. Stalin had agreed in Tehran to launch an offensive coinciding with the invasion. Operation BAGRATION began on June 22, 1944, the anniversary of the German invasion, and crushed German Army Group Center. BAGRATION and subsidiary operations inflicted over half a million casualties, advanced nearly 200 miles, and unhinged Germany's front. The Soviets suffered over 1 million casualties, including more than 243,000 dead. As 1944 unfolded, the Soviets pushed into Poland, Eastern Europe, and Germany itself.[73]

Shortly after the invasion, Eisenhower pushed the southern France landing. The British argued for further operations in Italy and a drive into Hungary. Eisenhower believed the Allies could support only one primary continental theater and this should be in France. He also needed French ports for supply and the attack would open an invasion route into Germany's industrial Ruhr. Critically, the US needed ports to pour in over forty divisions waiting in America. This alone should have swayed

Britain, but it took Roosevelt's intervention. DRAGOON (formerly ANVIL) launched on August 15.[74]

The Allies still faced dramatic obstacles finishing the Germans. In August 1944, the big problem was logistical. Before the invasion, the Allies planned by September 4, the nineteenth day after the landing (D+90), to be supporting twelve divisions. In August, sixteen American divisions were fighting beyond the Seine. By D+98, Allied forces were where the planners had expected to be on D+350. The Allies had also suffered tremendous casualties. America could make good its losses; Britain was breaking up units for replacements.[75]

Meanwhile, the Allies pushed across France, into Belgium and Holland, and to the German frontier. British forces took Antwerp, one of the world's great harbors, on September 4, capturing the port facilities almost intact and potentially answering the Allied logistical problem. To make Antwerp useful, the Allies had to clear the Scheldt estuary, but they also had the chance to trap a large German force on the bordering Beveland Isthmus. Montgomery ordered a three-day halt when a short march would have isolated Beveland. The Germans then evacuated 86,000 men while leaving enough forces to hold Walcheren and control the Scheldt's mouth. The Allies missed another opportunity.[76]

Once the Allies pushed deep into France, a debate emerged over how to continue the offensive and win the war. The original post-invasion plan called for a broad-front advance driving the Germans to their border by May 1945 with two primary axes: the main, northern one moving from Amiens toward the Ruhr, supported by a southern push toward the Ardennes Forest on France's frontier. A single thrust was judged too risky because it would give Germany the opportunity to concentrate against it. But after Antwerp's liberation on September 4, Montgomery suggested to Eisenhower a change of strategy: "I consider we have now reached a stage where one really powerful and full-blooded thrust towards Berlin is likely to get there and thus end the German war." He argued the Allies lacked the resources to continue the two-pronged broad-front strategy and thus their assets should be devoted to a single thrust. This would need all available resources. Acting otherwise, Montgomery insisted, "will prolong the war." Eisenhower rejected the change, branding it "crazy" in his diary. He also rebuffed a single drive into central Germany proposed by Bradley.[77]

Montgomery's idea would have forced the Allies to assume unnecessary risks. Relieved from pressure in other areas of the Western Front, the Germans could have concentrated against the flanks of Montgomery's offensive to try and cut off and kill it. A disaster could have proven fatal to Britain's ability to significantly contribute to the European land campaign and possibly toppled Churchill's government. Even if the offensive took Berlin, something exceedingly unlikely, it wouldn't have ended the war. Berlin was not the German center of gravity – its source of strength – that was the German army. Anything less than destroying this would not bring peace.

One result of Montgomery's request was the decision to give him the lead in the Allied offensive. Montgomery wanted to drop three airborne divisions at key river crossings in Holland along a 65-mile corridor to seize the bridges. A quick-moving column would relieve them, success would catapult the Allies over the Rhine River and onto the North German plain. Operation MARKET GARDEN was history's largest airborne assault. Two US airborne divisions seized their bridges, and the relief force reached them, but the British paratroopers were dropped too far from their target and plagued by problems, including the British commander ignoring the two streams of intelligence confirming the presence of two German SS armored divisions in the British drop zone. The Allies suffered more casualties in this operation than at D-Day and failed to cross the Rhine. The opportunity costs included extending the time needed to clear the Scheldt and reopen Antwerp's port.[78]

In December 1944, under Hitler's direction, Germany launched its final offensive in the West through the Ardennes Forest, hoping to split the US and British armies, take Antwerp, sever the Allies' supply lines, and destroy four Allied armies. The Germans thought this might split the alliance or at least allow Berlin to shift forces eastward, and perhaps even collapse America's home front. A lack of rationality entombed the plan as the fuel-starved Germans had to capture Allied fuel stocks to reach the intended operational objectives. Despite initial surprise, what is called the Battle of the Bulge (because of the lump produced in the Allied lines) became a devastating German defeat. The Allies, though, missed another chance to destroy a large German force by failing to sever the bulge at its base. The crisis also forced the Americans to commit the units they held in reserve and drove concerns they had raised insufficient ground forces by limiting the army's size to build larger air and naval forces and maintain high levels of war production.[79]

After the Battle of the Bulge, Eisenhower decided the Allies would continue the broad drive to the Rhine. The main thrust was under Montgomery in the north; the Americans advanced in the south. In early March, US forces captured a bridge over the Rhine at Remagen. They pushed to the other side but failed to exploit the opportunity sufficiently. Other crossings followed. The Germans remained resilient defenders, but Allied strength was overwhelming, and the Western Allies pocketed enormous German armies, capturing the Ruhr industrial heartland as the Soviets overran Germany

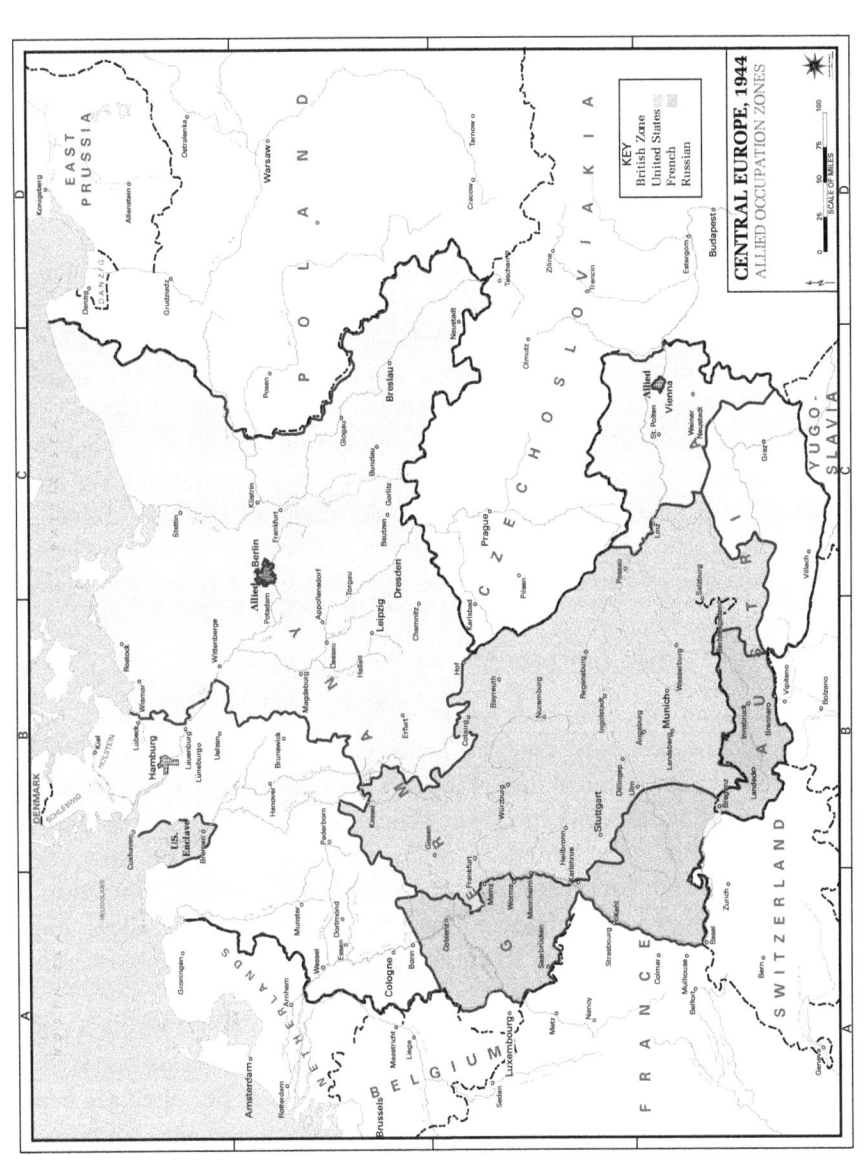

Map 9.1b Central Europe, 1944: Allied Occupation Zones

from the east and fought a bloody battle for Berlin. Eisenhower decided advancing to Berlin was not worth the cost in blood, especially since the February 1945 Yalta Conference put the German capital in the Soviet occupation zone. (See Map 9.1b.) With its armies defeated and destroyed, Hitler dead by his own hand, and the country occupied, Germany surrendered unconditionally on May 5, 1945. Roosevelt, who had died in April, didn't live to see achievement of his political aim.[80]

THE PACIFIC WAR

On December 7, 1941, at 7:50am, 214 Japanese aircraft appeared over Hawaii. They attacked Wheeler, Kaneohe, Ewa, and Hickam airbases, and – most spectacularly – Pearl Harbor. A second wave of 170 aircraft struck about an hour later. Together, they sank five battleships, two light cruisers, and the old target battleship *Utah*, damaged other ships, and destroyed most US aircraft in Hawaii. They also killed 3,000 Americans. The surprise attack, one launched before issuing a declaration of war, enraged and shocked Americans. For the next six months, Japan inflicted defeat after defeat on the US, Great Britain, and Holland. Tactical success at Pearl Harbor had a larger, unintended effect: it was the first step toward the destruction of the Japanese Empire.

THE ORIGINS OF THE PACIFIC WAR

The world economic crisis that began in 1929 provided an impetus for Japanese ultra-nationalists; they saw continental expansion as answering Japan's woes. In 1931, in defiance of Japan's political leaders, the army provoked a successful war with China over Manchuria. By 1936, the army dominated Japanese politics. Army leaders insisted Japan needed to conquer China to secure its resources and space for Japan's growing population. The army saw in the war a boon to Japanese pride, a tool for alleviating Depression-generated societal discontent, and a means for military and civilian elites to consolidate power.[81]

In July 1937, the Japanese invaded China. The ongoing Chinese Civil War convinced Tokyo the war would be short, but the Chinese proved resilient. The struggle became an attritional stalemate that poisoned Japan's relations with the United States, a chief supplier of the raw materials Japan needed to conquer China. Japan looked south. Its planning board managing the economy decided the nation had sufficient resources to wage a quick, decisive war to secure needed raw materials. A southward offensive would also break the stalemate in China by cutting Britain's Burma Road, the primary supply line to the Nationalist Chinese.[82] The Japanese launched a war against the US and Britain – two of the most powerful nations in the world – to fix a disastrous strategic situation created by earlier mistakes.

Most Japanese leaders believed war with America would last only a few months. America and democracy were degenerate and unable and unwilling to prosecute a long, bloody war. Japan's version of *Blitzkrieg* carried out across the Pacific would shatter American morale and enable Japan to achieve its limited political aims. Plus, it would take America more than a year to mobilize economically. By the time Washington shifted naval reinforcements to the Pacific, Japan would have a defensive perimeter to repel any US attacks. Tokyo expected this to take six months and thought little about what to do *after* or if their assessment proved mistaken. The Japanese believed Washington would negotiate instead of fight and expected to secure a settlement via a neutral party after seizing what they wanted but never made an official effort to do this. They understood America's industrial potential, but most considered the risk acceptable.[83]

Why did Japan choose December 1941 to go to war? When the US froze Japan's assets in July 1941, the British and Dutch followed, as did an oil embargo. Japan lacked the dollars it needed to purchase raw materials and was effectively under economic blockade. Both the army and navy considered delaying past December potentially "disastrous" because by March 1942 the arrival of American reinforcements in the Philippines and growing US naval superiority would make Japan's operations too dangerous and perhaps impossible. The British also would be better prepared in Malaya. The tides in December and January most suited amphibious operations, December's weather the most favorable, and the season provided time to finish operations in Malaya by spring. The Japanese would then be free to meet any potential Soviet attack in Manchuria.[84]

The Japanese struck very hard, attacking US, British, and Dutch possessions throughout the Pacific. In the first half of 1942, they quickly achieved most of their military objectives, established their defensive perimeter, and left the Allies reeling.[85] But Tokyo failed to break America's will or ability to fight and was now entangled with a nation possessing ten times its economic power and a determination to use it.

AMERICAN STRATEGY IN THE PACIFIC WAR

From Washington's perspective, this was the wrong war; Germany was the bigger threat. In line with prewar plans, the navy initially implemented a strategic defensive in the Pacific to hold an Alaska–Hawaii–Panama

PART II: FROM GREAT POWER TO SUPERPOWER

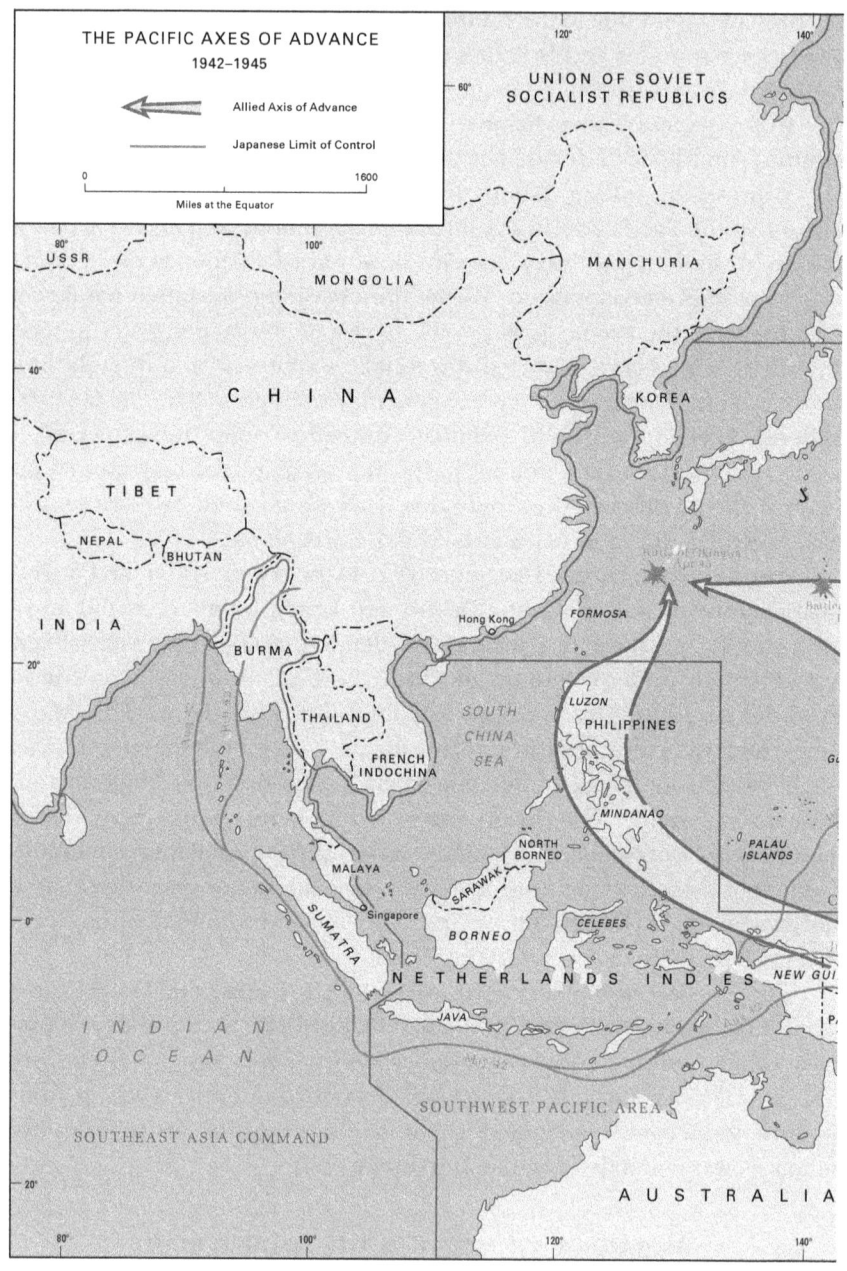

Maps 9.2a, 9.2b Pacific axes of advance, 1942–45

ASTRIDE THE WORLD: THE SECOND WORLD WAR, 1939–1945

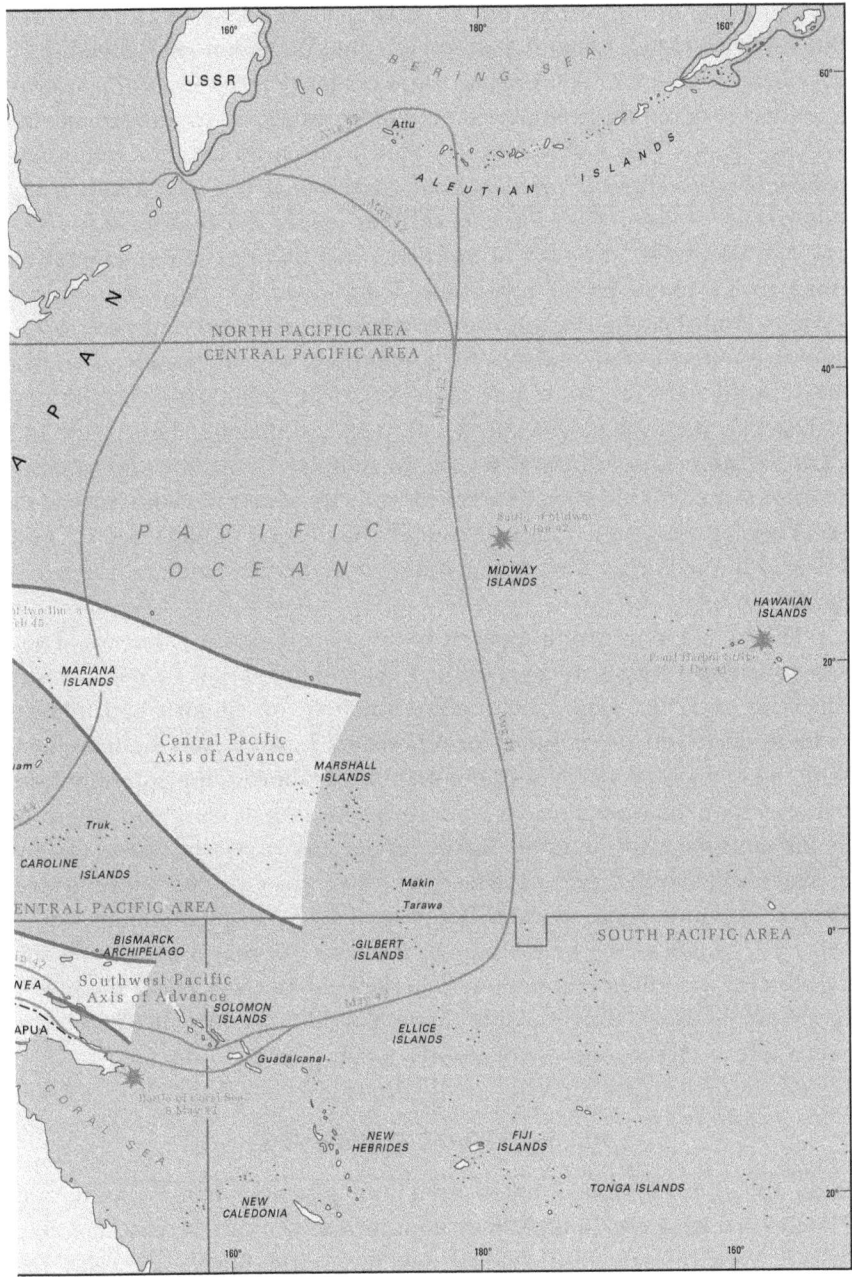

Maps 9.2a, 9.2b (cont.)

arc and maintain the supply line to Australia. (See Maps 9.2a and 9.2b.) But America didn't remain passive. On the afternoon of December 7, navy head Stark cast over America's prewar legal and doctrinal proscriptions and ordered the commencement of unrestricted air and submarine warfare against Japan. But America wasn't prepared for a German-style commerce war. Prewar international agreements had forbidden using submarines in Germany's First World War manner. The Americans also saw submarines as "the eyes of the fleet" and hadn't trained submarine commanders to display the aggression demanded for a commerce-raiding strategy. Poor leadership, improperly trained crews, and defective torpedoes prevented US submarines from exerting their influence early. But these problems were overcome, and American submarines waged one of history's most successful *guerres de course* campaigns. They sank 142 Japanese merchantmen the first year. By summer 1943, they were sinking about one a day. This form of attrition strategy benefited from America's breaking Japan's water transport codes.[86] By the end of 1944, the US had 156 subs in the Pacific. Commerce raiding was the first plank of America's Pacific strategy.

The Japanese were unprepared to meet a submarine offensive. They also saw submarines as the eyes of the fleet and failed to use theirs against American merchantmen. They underestimated the enemy's capabilities, thinking such duty too arduous for Americans. Japan lacked the merchant shipping to maintain its hemisphere-spanning seaborne empire, few prewar schemes for expansion, and no plans for protecting its merchant shipping or for antisubmarine warfare. Tokyo lacked escort vessels, was unwilling to assign ships to this, and possessed no true convoy system before March 1944. By this time, it was too late. The postwar US Strategic Bombing Survey observed: "Japan's merchant shipping fleet was not only a key link in the logistical support of her armed forces in the field, but also a vital link in her economic structure. It was the sole element of this basic structure which was vulnerable to direct attack throughout a major portion of the war."[87]

ALLIED STRATEGY EVOLVES

In the spring of 1942, the Allies focused upon guarding their flanks in Asia. The western flank was India, China, and Burma. The eastern was Australia. Britain bore primary responsibility for India and Burma, America for the east. Washington took operational control of the Pacific theater and though Germany First was the grand strategy, the need to guard the SLOCs to Australia resulted in large forces being sent to the Pacific in 1942.[88]

A factor dominating American strategic decision-making was the battle for resources. For example, as a part of his Pacific strategy, Admiral King wanted airfields for land-based air cover. He quickly stepped beyond the initial strategy of hemisphere defense and securing the route to Australia, raising the ire of Eisenhower and the army. Ike feared that committing too much in the Pacific would slow preparations for a cross-channel invasion. The JCS restrained King somewhat by refusing much of what he wanted.[89]

In March 1942, King gave Roosevelt a plan for a Pacific war. They would hold Hawaii and support the Australasian area, then mount an early advance northward from the New Hebrides islands (now Vanuatu, southeast of the Solomon Islands), which King insisted – correctly – would force the Japanese to reduce their pressure on other areas. King's plan painted a picture of the war in the South Pacific until mid 1944, and he tied to this hit-and-run carrier raids that kept the Japanese off-balance and unsure of US intentions. His strategy was essentially a strategic defensive with operational offensive strikes. Critically, the aircraft carrier assumed a new role. Before the war, battleships were considered the backbone of the fleet.[90] This remained a fixture in Japanese thinking even after they revolutionized naval warfare at Pearl Harbor. The Americans, their battleships on Pearl Harbor's floor, were forced to change. The aircraft carrier became the pivotal weapon of the Pacific War.

JAPAN REASSESSES

In the wake of their initial successes, Japan perceived American weakness in the Pacific and began examining expansion of its defensive perimeter. Japan's Admiral Isoroku Yamamoto, the godfather of the Pearl Harbor attack, wanted to destroy the unexpectedly absent US carriers by drawing them into a fight. But doing this around Hawaii was too dangerous as it now hosted much land-based airpower. He needed to seize something for which the US would fight. He chose Midway Island. Its capture would make US operations from Pearl Harbor more difficult, provide Japan a base for a future attack on Hawaii, and stop the Americans from using it for attacks against Wake Island.[91]

Yamamoto's plan faced resistance. His prestige carried the day, but there was a cost. To get support for his Midway operation, Yamamoto had to agree to an Aleutians push – *simultaneously* – and a *prior* offensive in the South Pacific. This would dissipate Japanese strength rather than concentrate it at what Yamamoto considered the decisive point. Taking the Aleutians would extend the defensive perimeter and injure America's ability to attack Japan.

It would cut the SLOCs between the US and the Soviet Union while protecting Midway's northern flank. The traditional view of this as a diversion is mistaken. It was an additional operation. The result: the Imperial Navy Operational Plans for Stage Two of the Great East Asia War. Naval forces would take Midway, the army refusing to supply troops. The plan went to the emperor on April 16, 1942. Two days later, a group of B-25 medium bombers commanded by Jimmy Doolittle took off from the US carrier *Hornet* and bombed Japan on a one-way trip. This shocked and shamed Japan's military leaders. In an about-face, the army threw its support behind Yamamoto's Midway attack *and* his follow-on plan to invade Hawaii.[92]

THE 1942 JAPANESE OFFENSIVES

Japan launched what is sometimes called the MORYALMI Plan, an acronym derived from abbreviations for the objectives of its operational prongs. The first were MO (Port Moresby in New Guinea and Tulagi in the Solomon Islands) and RY (the phosphate-rich island of Nauru). Attacks on AL (the Aleutians) and MI (Midway Island), which together used nearly the entire navy, would follow. Linked to the latter was a plan to complete the destruction of the US fleet, particularly its carriers. Follow-on attacks against Samoa and the New Hebrides were to cut Australia's SLOCs with America. The Japanese intended to build a perimeter stretching from the Aleutians in the north to Midway, then south to Fiji, Samoa, and New Caledonia.[93]

When the Japanese launched against Port Moresby, America countered, resulting in the Battle of the Coral Sea, the first sea battle in history where the warships never saw one another as it was fought by carrier aviation. Tactically, the battle was a draw. But it produced American operational and strategic success because it stopped the Japanese invasion. A key to US success, and why the battle occurred, was US cryptologists breaking Japan's JN-25 naval code. Moreover, the American commander, Chester W. Nimitz, was doing as King wanted: holding the South Pacific.[94]

The battle cost Yamamoto forces he planned to use against Midway. Two Japanese carriers were temporarily out of action and valuable aircraft and aircrew lost. Moreover, when launching the Midway and Aleutians operations Japan divided its navy. The Aleutian force included two light but slow carriers. A light carrier accompanied Yamamoto's battleship force trailing the main carrier battle group, while another fleet carrier protected the Midway invasion force. Yamamoto's plan assumed a decisive battle with the American fleet. A picket line of submarines between Hawaii and Midway was to spot and attack the US fleet (it didn't). Carrier air would soften up the Americans. Yamamoto's battleships – which Japan saw as the decisive arm – would finish the job.[95]

The Americans' information advantage meant they knew the enemy were coming and could meet them when and where they wished. The US commanders decided they possessed enough advantages to mitigate the risks and sprung a trap on the Japanese. Japan's defeat at Midway cost it heavily: 4 carriers, 1 heavy cruiser, 253 planes, and the best of its naval aviators. Little of this could be replaced. Japan never again possessed the offensive power it had before the battle. The Americans never again fought a defensive campaign. Production figures reveal one reason Japan's defeat was so devastating. From 1939 to 1945, Japan produced 45,000 combat aircraft, the US built 197,000. During the war, the US navy commissioned 18 large aircraft carriers, 9 light, and 110 small escort carriers. Japan produced 13.[96] Even while fighting in Europe, the Americans could replace their losses and grow stronger. The war was attritional, something unfavorable to industrially weaker Japan.

THE AMERICAN COUNTEROFFENSIVE

The Japanese, once ascendant in the Pacific, now, at best, had parity. They fell back on their defensive barrier, one now stretching 14,200 miles, an area impossible to defend without controlling the sea and the air. The Americans determined where and when they would strike and could mass at a chosen point and puncture it. Moreover, it remained virtually impossible for Japan to force the Americans into a decisive sea battle.[97]

The Pacific theater was reorganized into two commands on March 31, 1942, a move decisively shaping strategy. General Douglas MacArthur led one command. He had become a hero during the defense of the Philippines and was ordered to leave the islands by Roosevelt before its May 1942 surrender. Some Republican politicians pushed to have him named the supreme commander. King didn't want an army officer commanding navy ships. MacArthur was also senior to all other general and flag officers, none of whom wanted him back in Washington. As a compromise, King proposed two commands. MacArthur ran the Southwest Pacific Area and Admiral Chester Nimitz the Pacific Ocean Area. They received orders from their respective service heads in Washington, Marshall and King. Pacific strategy was composed by a staff drawn from both services, but this command arrangement produced dissension and duplication.[98]

The May 1942 Japanese invasion of the Solomons prior to the Battle of Midway threatened the SLOCs to Australia. Initial navy plans called for offensive sea control that began in the Solomons and aimed to halt Japan's advance and prevent it securing a position in New Guinea as a springboard to Australia. MacArthur urged a quick strike at the critical Japanese base at Rabaul, New Britain, northwest of the Solomons. He also wanted Australia to be the keystone of America's Pacific strategy because of its utility as a base. King had been pushing for offensive operations in the Pacific since March 1942, and the navy suggested a slower, more deliberate approach via the Solomons and New Guinea. MacArthur agreed but insisted upon command since it was his area. This produced a firestorm between the services, one resolved by moving the command line eastward and placing the Solomons operations under navy command. Its forces (which included the Marines) were to move up the Solomons while MacArthur's pushed along New Guinea's coast. They would link to take Rabaul. But then the US discovered the Japanese building an airbase on Guadalcanal. The struggle for airfields became key in the early war.[99]

Operation WATCHTOWER commenced on August 7, 1942, when the Americans landed on Guadalcanal. The American counteroffensive had begun. It was a risky operation mounted with few advantages at the end of a long logistical tether, but the enemy suffered similar difficulties. The Japanese decided they had to hold this important part of their defensive perimeter. The fight for Guadalcanal became a turning point. After bloody fighting, the Americans won control of the air and sea around the island and could also commit more men and material. Afterward, Japan remained largely on the defensive.[100] Attrition – on land, at sea, and in the air – became the order of the day.

THE AXIS AND ALLIES REASSESS

On December 31, 1942, the Japanese decided to evacuate Guadalcanal by February 1943, draw a new defensive line north of New Georgia and the Isabella Islands near the northern end of the Solomons chain, and try again to take Port Moresby. They foresaw a fight for the area, island for island, and hoped defeating MacArthur's forces in New Guinea would result in the US abandoning its drive in the South Pacific. Moreover, Hideki Tōjō, the general heading Japan's government, planned a new offensive in China to break the Nationalists, believing this would remove any American and British reason to continue; a negotiated peace would follow.[101] Simultaneously, they would push against India, contributing to the development of what became known as the CBI (China–Burma–India) theater.

Decisions at the January 1943 Casablanca Conference affected Pacific strategy. The US and Britain promised China more aid and a link to the Burma Road, which Japan had cut. The emphasis on defeating the U-boats meant production of antisubmarine craft delayed amphibious vessel construction. But the percentage of Allied resources for the Pacific theater increased from 15 percent to 30. Marshall supported the Germany First strategy, but also backed King's push for Pacific offensive action, partly because he feared that if the US met with a Pacific disaster, it could lead to calls for ignoring the ETO until the Pacific theater was sorted. Guadalcanal had been a close-run thing – too close for Marshall – and he thought this a dangerous way for the Allies to fight. The Pacific operational objectives became Rabaul and areas for bases in the Marshall and Caroline Islands. US forces were to "maintain and extend unremitting pressure against Japan with the purpose of continually reducing her military power and attaining positions from which her ultimate surrender can be forced." But none of this could be allowed to injure the war against Germany. The British preferred delaying offensive action in the Pacific but agreed to continued operations in the Southwest Pacific, the launch of King's Central Pacific offensive, and an Allied thrust against Japanese-held Burma.[102]

AMERICA'S CHANGING WAR

US Pacific plans changed as Allied capabilities grew and the strategic situation evolved. Operational objectives once deemed indispensable later disappeared from planners' maps. The twin American commands produced army- and navy-controlled areas, laying the foundation for the Dual-Pronged Strategy. MacArthur's army prong, based in Australia, continued northwest through New Guinea toward the Philippines to cut Japan's communications with the East Indies and eliminate its access to the area's raw materials. Nimitz's navy–Marine arm was anchored at Hawaii and acquired two main objectives: the Marianas Islands, considered key for Japan's supply network in the central Pacific, and Formosa (now Taiwan) and the Chinese coast. King supported the Central Pacific drive because it could allow the US to bring the Japanese navy to battle while interfering with Tokyo's communications, help America hold the initiative while keeping Japan off balance, and permit seizing islands useful as air bases for attacks against Japan.[103]

This two-pronged strategy has been criticized for leaving the Americans vulnerable to Japanese counterattacks. Others consider it a bad example of interservice rivalry and an immense waste of resources. Army air corps General "Hap" Arnold said "we continued operating in our inefficient way, with first three, then two commands ... both working towards the same end – the defeat of Japan, with overlapping lines of communication, overlapping air operations, and overlapping sea operations, and, finally, overlapping land Army operations."[104] Defenders argue it made use of America's vast military resources and kept the Japanese off balance and guessing while supplying pressure at multiple points.

In April 1943, JCS planners finished America's first wartime plan against Japan. It called for Japan's complete defeat to achieve the aim of unconditional surrender, recognized the possibility of invading Japan itself, and the necessity of blockading and bombing it. The planners saw advantages in mounting both prongs and laid out future moves in five phases: 1) forces under Nimitz and MacArthur advancing across the Pacific, the Central Pacific being the main thrust; 2) the liberation of the Philippines; 3) a push to the Chinese coast; 4) the liberation of Hong Kong; and 5) the strategic bombing of Japan. In May 1943, the new Joint Plans Committee added a sixth: the invasion of Japan. This became the Strategic Plan for the Defeat of Japan.[105]

At the May 1943 Trident Conference held in the wake of US victories at Midway and Guadalcanal, the Allies decided the new Pacific operational objectives. The Allied bombing campaign would expand by establishing bases for US bombers in China. Meanwhile, the Americans would recapture the Aleutians, take the Marshall, Caroline, and Solomon Islands, and the Bismarck Archipelago, and clear the Japanese from New Guinea, all while increasing attacks against Japan's communication lines. The increasing availability of material and shipping made the British more supportive of America's Pacific operations. At the August 1943 Quadrant Conference in Quebec, the operational objectives became taking part of the Eastern Carolines, Truk, the Palaus, Guam, and the Marianas.[106]

At the August 1943 Quebec Conference, it was agreed the military would compose a plan for the defeat of Japan within a year of Germany's fall. The November and December 1943 Allied conferences in Cairo and Tehran reduced China to a secondary place in Pacific strategy by shrinking Allied actions in the China–Burma–India theater. The Soviets committed at Tehran to entering the war against Japan three months after Germany's fall. This fed King's desire for Marianas' bases to help ensure Japan's defeat without Soviet help. Roosevelt had sought Moscow's support against Japan within a day of the Pearl Harbor attack – unsuccessfully. He needed the

Soviets to help fulfill his postwar security visions and believed that if he gave Stalin what he could while asking for nothing, the dictator would help establish "a world of democracy and peace."[107]

During November 1943's Cairo Sextant Conference, the Allies settled on the Overall Plan for the Defeat of Japan. Its elements were Nimitz taking the Marshalls in January 1944, the Carolines and Truk in July, and the Marianas in October, and MacArthur continuing the New Guinea advance. The JCS gave no priority to either prong. Both would continue but the Central Pacific path was thought easier and more likely to provoke a battle to destroy the Japanese fleet.[108]

We now have the foundational elements of US strategy against Japan: 1) an advance through the Southwest Pacific; 2) an advance through the Central Pacific; 3) the submarine offensive against Japan's shipping; and 4) a future air offensive directed at the Japanese home islands. Tied to this was King's idea of constant pressure on the Japanese and his desire to destroy its navy and win sea control. A number of factors enabled the strategy. American logistical ability was one. At sea resupply was critical to the Central Pacific drive. Tōjō thought it one of the keys to US victory. Marine Corps amphibious doctrine was another, as was America's ability to supply the needed ships, weapons, and troops. By the end of 1943, the US virtually controlled the air. Japanese Admiral Osami Nagano told postwar interrogators: "If I were to give you one factor as the leading one that led to your victory, I would give you the air force.'"[109]

THE DUAL-PRONGED OFFENSIVE

MacArthur's July 1942 instructions from the JCS designated Rabaul, New Britain, and Kavieng, New Ireland, as his operational objectives. His command's April 1943 Elkton III Plan was a mini two-pronged offensive, with one branch running along the north coast of New Guinea and the second through the Solomons. It became known as CARTWHEEL and originally included thirteen operations. MacArthur initially tried to clear everything Japan controlled and paid a price for it. But he switched his approach in June 1943. The US would now take only the spots it needed. "Leapfrogging" was how MacArthur described it. What enabled the change was growing US engineering and logistical capability, and the innovative use of airpower by MacArthur's army air corps commander, General George Kenny. The US no longer had to fight for every airfield. It could take a suitable place, build an airfield there, and project an air umbrella over the next target. Tokyo had left its southernmost troops as blocking units, intending them to fight to the death, but MacArthur attacked its strategy.[110] MacArthur's advance, though, especially in its early stages, gave Japan opportunities to strike at weaker US forces. CARTWHEEL continued until 1944, producing Rabaul's isolation and setting the stage for a jump to the Philippines.

JAPAN REASSESSES – AGAIN

In September 1943, Japan's latest strategy called for holding a new defensive line: the Absolute National Defense Sphere. It stretched from Burma to the Malay Barrier, through western New Guinea, up to the Caroline and Marshall Islands, to the Kuriles in the north. The Japanese lacked the forces to hold it.[111]

THE CENTRAL PACIFIC DRIVE

US commanders soon found it impossible to land in the Marshalls without taking units from Nimitz and MacArthur. They compromised by having Nimitz first take the Gilberts because this required fewer forces. MacArthur was dead-set against a Central Pacific advance, insisting his South Pacific route was more efficient. He lost the argument. The May 1943 Trident Conference authorized support for both prongs and an attack from the west to support the MacArthur–Nimitz offensives. King's cause was helped by the army air corps wanting bases for B-29s to attack Japan. Saipan and Tinian in the Marianas could supply these. King also saw the Marianas as a springboard to the Philippines and then to the Chinese coast, and a base from which submarines could cut Japan's supply lines, particularly to Truk.[112]

On November 20, 1943, the US Marines landed on Tarawa in the Gilbert Islands, the first target of King's Central Pacific drive. King believed both prongs should be part of the strategy and strong enough to support one another "to whipsaw [the] enemy rather than enable him to concentrate in [the] Solomons or attack on [the] Jaluit-Gilbert-Samoa line or on [the] Midway-Pearl Line." King also thought it necessary to mount the Central Pacific drive before London retreated from its Quadrant Conference commitment to more resources in the Pacific. This led to his launching the Tarawa assault in November 1943 instead of waiting for December and the higher tides that would have allowed landing craft to come closer to the beaches and thus reduce the casualties suffered in the landing. The Japanese had 5,000 defenders; only 400 were combat troops.[113] The battle was particularly bloody.

Nimitz, after hard arguing with his subordinate commanders, pushed through an attack on Kwajalein in the Marshalls at the end of January because ULTRA information showed it was lightly defended. The navy wouldn't try to take everything, just sites necessary for future bases and to isolate Japanese positions. The services learned from Tarawa and did a better job in the Marshalls. Nimitz's carriers struck hard at Japanese air bases. Army planes flying from Tarawa and Makin did the same. Things went so well that Nimitz pushed up his timetable and took Eniwetok in the Marshalls in February.[114] Truk was now isolated; taking it became unnecessary.

In March 1944 MacArthur's forces took the Admiralty Islands, above the Solomons. Success here inspired MacArthur to leapfrog numerous Japanese bastions. Washington ordered him to be ready to invade Mindanao in the Philippines in November 1944. By this time, the navy was copying a Japanese practice: massing carriers in large formations. Task Force 50 alone deployed more carriers than Japan possessed. The US had more and better ships and planes. The Japanese navy still sought a decisive battle with the US fleet, but attrition in the air was destroying its offensive capability. Despite this, the Japanese planned in 1944 to strike new blows in China and India.[115]

The January and February 1944 seizure of the Marshalls forced Japan's abandonment of Truk and further contraction of its defensive perimeter. Tokyo designated Saipan in the northern Marianas the site beyond which the Americans couldn't be allowed to go. The Japanese considered Biak, off New Guinea's north coast, the next likely US target and planned to meet the Americans here. But as they planned their riposte, MacArthur's forces took Biak in May 1944. The stunned Japanese had been expecting a Central Pacific attack. The dual-pronged approach paid dividends. US airpower smashed three counterattacks and Japan then put in motion a long-harbored scheme for forcing a decisive engagement with the United States.[116]

King and Nimitz also wanted a decisive battle and knew Japan had to fight for the Marianas. On June 15, 1944, the Americans invaded Saipan using over 500 ships. This occurred at the same time as the Normandy offensive, a great indication of US strength. Admiral Soemu Toyoda tried to trap the US fleet between the Japanese I Mobile Fleet and land-based aircraft. In the resulting Battle of the Philippine Sea, US carrier airpower destroyed the attacking Japanese air units and counterattacked Toyoda's fleet. The Great Marianas Turkey Shoot, as the air battle came to be called, decimated Japan's naval air units and sank three irreplaceable carriers. Japanese carrier aviation essentially ceased to exist.[117]

PART II: FROM GREAT POWER TO SUPERPOWER

AIRPOWER STRATEGY

In April 1944, Japan launched its Ichigō offensives in China to stop American bombing raids on Japanese supply lines and seize the air bases. Roosevelt, despite Marshall's protests, had ordered an air campaign from here in 1943, one he also hoped would boost Chinese morale. Japan made significant gains and disrupted the bombing but didn't improve its strategic situation. The AAF began bombing Japan from the Marianas in November 1944 to destroy Japan's major industrial areas. These high-altitude conventional missions using high explosives failed to have the effect doctrine insisted. In February 1945, under General Curtis LeMay, the AAF began targeting civilians in urban areas with incendiaries as an alternative. Numerous Japanese cities were burned to the ground and the raids killed far more people than the atomic bombs, usually 80–100,000 per attack. In April 1945, LeMay brought back conventional bombing and began striking Japan's petroleum industry.[118]

THE NEXT STEPS

US military leaders debated whether or not to aim next at Luzon in the Philippines or Formosa. The JCS picked Luzon after much debate, having earlier chosen Mindanao. Leyte would be seized first as a base. Logistical considerations, Japanese strength in Formosa, and other commitments drove the decision. Meanwhile, Japan again shrank its perimeter. The Philippines was now the front line. If Tokyo lost the islands, it lost control of the SLOCs to its oil supply south of the Philippines. Without oil, neither its navy nor air force moved. Japan decided yet again to try to force a decisive battle against the US navy. Admiral Toyoda explained why:

> Since without the participation of our Combined Fleet there was little possibility of our land forces in the Philippines having any chance against MacArthur, it was decided to send the whole fleet.... Should we lose in the Philippines operations, even though the fleet should be left, the shipping to the south would be completely cut off so that the Fleet, if it should come back to Japanese waters, could not obtain its fuel supply. If it should remain in southern waters, it could not receive supplies of ammunition and arms. There would be no sense in saving the Fleet at the expense of ... the Philippines.[119]

The Japanese fleet sortied in October 1944 to oppose the Leyte Gulf landings. One of the largest naval actions in history followed as Japan launched a complex, multi-pronged attack. It ended in disaster for Tokyo and produced one of the most controversial events of the war. Admiral William F. "Bull" Halsey pursued and largely destroyed Admiral Jisaburō

Ozawa's Japanese carrier force, which was a decoy dispatched to draw the main American forces away from the invasion fleet. This left the light units supporting the Leyte landing vulnerable to Japanese surface units. Tough and sacrificial resistance from the US navy vessels protecting the invasion fleet thwarted the Japanese, who could have destroyed the inferior American force by simply pressing their attack.[120]

The battle saw the introduction of a new Japanese weapon – the *kamikaze*. Vice Admiral Onishi Takijiro concluded the Americans so outclassed Japan that air attacks could succeed only by crash-diving into American ships. The later Battle of Okinawa became particularly famous for the severity of these attacks, which sank 26 ships and damaged 164 more. Overall, at Okinawa Japan sank 36 American ships and damaged 368. The US lost 4,907 sailors, more than in any other operation of the war.[121]

Japan had 300,000 soldiers and sailors defending the Philippines. MacArthur's forces landed on Leyte on October 20, 1944, took the island, and moved against Luzon in January 1945. They faced skilled and stubborn resistance and, in Manila, the only significant city fighting for US Pacific forces. Combat on Luzon continued until the war's end.[122]

THE CENTRAL PACIFIC DRIVE CONTINUES

In October 1944, King met with his Pacific commanders. He still wanted to push to Formosa, but Nimitz convinced him it was more useful for besieging Japan to take Iwo Jima and Okinawa. King bent. The JCS approved as both the army and the navy supported taking Iwo Jima. This helped seal the blockade of Japan while providing an emergency airfield for bombers and a home for fighter escorts. Moreover, the navy no longer needed bases in China as it had thought, and the 1944 Japanese offensive had revealed the weakness of the Nationalist Chinese (Japan deployed 1.7 million troops in Manchuria and China). The Marines landed on Iwo Jima on February 19, 1945, beginning one of the bloodiest battles of the war for the Americans: 6,000 Marines died here. The invasion of Okinawa followed on April 1, 1945. It was a stepping stone to Japan and a useful base. The particularly bloody battle lasted until July and cost Japan 110,000 troops. US killed, missing, and casualties at sea numbered 12,520.[123]

ENDING THE WAR

By late 1945, Japan was under blockade. Allied submarines, aircraft, and aerial mining had sunk most of its merchant fleet. Coastal shipping traffic that moved food and everything else neared collapse. But American military leaders disagreed upon how to finally secure the political aim of unconditional surrender. Marshall feared American war weariness if the conflict went on too long and believed invasion the quickest and surest route to victory. King believed the casualties would be too great and advocated bombing and blockade. King, though, knew he could not win this argument and agreed to preparing an invasion while insisting he would reexamine its necessity in August or September 1945, believing that then the situation would favor his view.[124]

The invasion plan – Operation DOWNFALL – had two phases. Operation OLYMPIC was to seize southern Kyushu and build a base area to support the main effort against the Tokyo region, Operation CORONET. As there was no history of a Japanese government ever surrendering, US planners feared having to kill every Japanese combatant to end the war. They also worried there would be no recognized Japanese authority with which to make peace. But in the eyes of US planners, an invasion seemed the only path for securing the political aim as MAGIC intercepts revealed Tokyo wouldn't accept unconditional surrender, even a version retaining the emperor, something Japan accepted after the atomic bombs.[125]

In April 1945, the new Japanese government wanted peace. The foreign minister, Shigenori Togo, the navy minister, and the emperor were also ready to end the war. The army still wanted to fight. American morale was considered weak, and the Japanese believed they could kill enough Americans to raise the cost beyond what the Americans were willing to pay, convincing the invaders to modify their peace terms. The imperial dynasty would continue, the military would keep its place in Japanese society, and there would be no Allied army of occupation. The plan was called *Ketsu Go*, or Operation DECISIVE. Even if the first landing succeeded, the Japanese believed the cost of further action would break the will of America's political leaders. But the Japanese knew that even success meant "millions of Japanese would die of starvation in 1946." A connected diplomatic strategy was attempting to have Moscow mediate between Tokyo and Washington, but Stalin had committed at Yalta to entering the war and strung along Japan.[126]

Japanese planners knew the likely American landing sites because of the range of US warplanes operating from Okinawa and Iwo Jima. The need for land-based air cover dictated landings on Kyushu or Shikoku, and southern Kyushu had suitable beaches. The Japanese brought in troops from Manchuria and raised new units, planning to have 2,903,000 troops to defend Japan, and to mobilize men from 15 to 60 and women from 17 to 40. The women would be expected to fight, and suicide attacks held a prominent place in Japanese thinking. The Americans knew from MAGIC that Japan had 14 divisions in Kyushu in August and possessed over 10,000 planes, half *kamikazes*. As it became clear what they faced on Kyushu, American planners began considering attacking Honshu instead. The intelligence made it unlikely OLYMPIC would ever launch "because it had become unthinkable."[127]

On July 22, 1945, Emperor Hirohito shocked his Supreme War Council by telling them to end the war. After the Allies' Potsdam Conference ended on August 2, the Allies again demanded Japan's unconditional surrender and President Harry S. Truman gave Tokyo time to reply. Nothing came. The first atomic bomb fell on August 6, on Hiroshima. The US hoped to create the impression that large numbers would follow. The Soviet Union declared war on August 8, a week earlier than Stalin had originally intended, and launched a devastating offensive against Japanese forces in Manchuria. This shattered Japan's plan for negotiating an end to the war. The Americans dropped a second atomic bomb, on Nagasaki, on August 9.[128]

The atomic bombs and the Soviet attack provoked infighting in the Japanese government regarding a response. They settled upon an announcement to the Allies in which Japan accepted the terms of the Potsdam agreement (which implied Japan could pick its future government and thus retain the emperor) as long as this included a clause that didn't "prejudice the prerogatives of His Majesty as Sovereign Ruler." This was essentially a demand that the emperor remain and have power to rebuff any postwar reforms.[129]

The Americans rejected the offer, but Truman authorized a reply stating that once Japan surrendered, "the authority of the Emperor and the Japanese Government to rule the state shall be subject to the Supreme Commander of the Allied powers." The US also included a British suggestion that someone could sign for the emperor. Truman ordered no more atomic attacks but continued conventional bombing to apply pressure. The emperor accepted the terms on August 15. Some in the Japanese military didn't and launched a coup attempt that failed. A few senior officers outside of Japan refused to surrender and the emperor had to broadcast twice the command to end the war. Hirohito gave three reasons for his decision. He had no confidence in the Imperial Army or its defense strategy, feared Japan's civic collapse under bombing and blockade and the subsequent destruction of the imperial system, and the atomic bomb. Hirohito's admission that the bomb helped drive his decision demonstrates the effectiveness of the weapon and vindicates its use as it helped end a war killing daily thousands of people throughout Asia. US occupation forces began landing in Japan on August 21. The Japanese signed the terms of unconditional surrender on the battleship *Missouri* in Tokyo Bay on September 2, 1945.[130]

SECURING THE PEACE: BUILDING THE POSTWAR ORDER

Roosevelt died on April 12, 1945. Harry S. Truman succeeded him but had been told nothing of Roosevelt's postwar plans. This was a failing on Roosevelt's part, but his death didn't stop the prosecution of the war or impede the achievement of the nation's aims. The US now faced the challenge of securing the peace. When examining how the US ended the Second World War, particularly in comparison to later wars, one must give high marks to US military and political leaders. There are many reasons for this. The political aim, unconditional surrender – an unlimited aim because it demanded the end of the ruling regimes of Germany, Italy, and Japan – provided a firm foundation for Allied agreement upon what was necessary for ending the struggle. The Allies also devoted as much military strength as necessary for as long as needed to achieve the aim. Unconditional surrender and possession of large military forces allowed the Allies to impose a peace they hoped ensured never having to fight another such war. They also secured formal acts of surrender.[131] This helped the Allies avoid one of their First World War errors: failing to ensure the defeated peoples knew their nations had lost.

The August 1941 Atlantic Charter provides a picture of Roosevelt's postwar vision. It committed the US and Britain to no territorial acquisition, freeing conquered peoples and allowing them to choose their own forms of government, free trade, freedom of the seas, improving living standards, and a peace that permitted all to live in safety. Roosevelt's administration believed the achievement of these aims demanded: 1) defeating the Axis powers; 2) ensuring the US remained involved in the world by including it in international organizations such as the United Nations and the World Bank; 3) convincing Britain to decolonize and open its imperial lands to trade; and 4) gaining Soviet cooperation by addressing its security fears and convincing it to behave like a normal state. The US did the first and the second, but numbers three and four were not achievable by American will and actions alone. US leaders ignored the nature, interests, and political aims of the states concerned, especially those of Britain. To preserve and protect its empire was part of why London was fighting the war.[132] The final point betrays poor understanding of Stalin, his imperial ambitions, and the Soviet system.

The Roosevelt administration took an institutional approach to securing the postwar world, particularly for political and economic structures. Before the Casablanca Conference, Roosevelt privately outlined some of his postwar vision, suggesting a world run by the Four Policemen: the US, Britain, the Soviet Union, and China. They would prevent future Japanese or German aggression and any subsequent world war. Roosevelt also wanted to remake Germany. He was determined to destroy Nazism and Prussian militarism and ensure no ground for regrowth, and was just as determined to root out Japanese militarists. When the occupation of Japan began, diplomat Dean Acheson stated its goal was the remaking of the nation's economic and social system so that it would no longer have the will to go to war. Former American ambassador to Tokyo Joseph Grew was instrumental in arguing for keeping the emperor in power, ensuring the peace was not punitive, and reintegrating a peaceful Japan into the regional community. Generally, though, Roosevelt insisted upon not discussing postwar issues until after the war. He wisely kept a firm hand on the political aim, ignoring requests even from Eisenhower to weaken the demand for unconditional surrender. But he refused to address key postwar political issues with Allies and wouldn't make decisions on the postwar situation until he had no choice. This avoided wartime problems but undermined longer-term planning and left Truman with no plans.[133]

But even as talented a politician and stateman as Roosevelt couldn't avoid or delay all such decisions, especially since he had allies. He allowed the late 1943 creation of the European Advisory Commission, which in theory was to put the Allies on the same page regarding war termination and Germany's postwar fate. The British took it seriously. Roosevelt didn't. It did secure agreement on the postwar occupation zones. Germany and Berlin were divided initially between the US, Britain, and the Soviet Union; a place for France was cut from the American and British zones at Yalta.[134]

The administration's postwar vision included free trade and the establishment of an international security system. The free-trade plank was driven by the assumption that this would – in Secretary of State Hull's view – remove jealousies regarding living standards between states by raising all living standards, thus "eliminating the economic dissatisfaction that breeds war." Hull worked from a false assumption regarding the causes of wars; he ignored the true reason: politics. The United Nations was intended to provide collective security and curb aggressive states.[135]

On January 2, 1942, twenty-six nations that Roosevelt called the united nations agreed to fight the Axis "in the name of life, liberty, independence, religious freedom, and justice." A few days before, Hull began designing what became the United Nations (UN). Roosevelt, a vastly superior politician to Wilson, ensured he had Republican support and participation for constructing his postwar world and the United Nations. With the UN, "its American founders honestly seem to have expected it to provide a solution to the dilemmas of international anarchy at no cost to anyone's interests."[136]

Other new institutions and practices were intended to help produce a stable, postwar, capitalist economic system. The July 1944 Bretton Woods Conference recast the global monetary system. It favored the US as international exchange rates were based upon the dollar, which was still anchored in gold, and the dollar became the global reserve currency. What became known as the World Bank (which made long-term investments) and the International Monetary Fund (IMF, which managed exchange rates, payments between states, and lent to nations running deficits) were created, as was the International Trade Organization. The US provided the bulk of the financing for the World Bank and the IMF. This system underpinned global finance until the late 1960s.[137]

Agreements at Yalta and Potsdam also helped shape the postwar order. At Yalta, in February 1945, the Allies agreed to four occupation zones in Germany, democratic elections in Europe, and the UN's structures. American officials such as Harry Hopkins left Yalta believing they had laid the foundations of a solid peace. The feeling was short-lived as Stalin began imposing Communist governments on Eastern Europe. Roosevelt traded away concessions Stalin wanted in Manchuria for Soviet help against Japan and thinly worded promises of Moscow's support for China's Nationalist regime. This placed the Soviets in control of Manchuria, which made them attractive to Mao Tse-Tung's Communists. American diplomat George Kennan warned in March 1945 against counting on Stalin's promises as a means of achieving US aims in China. He proved correct. States shouldn't depend upon what they cannot control for achieving their aims or implementing strategy. At the July–August 1945 Potsdam Conference, the Allies agreed upon reparations from Germany for the Soviets, and the expulsion of ethnic Germans from areas of Germany awarded Poland. Stalin never allowed the free elections he promised for Eastern Europe.[138]

Roosevelt planned to keep peace in Asia by using Pacific air and naval bases to watch and contain Japan. The US didn't anticipate a long-term occupation of Japan but intended to control what are now called the First and Second Island Chains running Japan–Taiwan–Philippines and Japan–Guam–the South Pacific, respectively. The services wanted never again to fight their way across the Pacific through these islands. They also realized the strength of land-based airpower and its projection capability. The General

Board began planning in 1943 for where the US would have postwar bases and for control of the former German islands the Japanese acquired after the First World War. Roosevelt insisted upon UN trusteeship, with US control, so that the US annexed nothing. Roosevelt knew he couldn't push the British and French to release their colonies if the US acquired its own.[139]

CONCLUSION

Roosevelt failed to cure the Great Depression but proved more successful at preparing the nation for war than any of his predecessors and did so against opposition that was often bipartisan and included members of his own administration. He worked with his coalition partners to help direct the wielding of American power to bring down two of history's most dangerous and murderous regimes. The US proved a generally good ally, sacrificing much, especially materially, for its partners. The administration didn't secure the basic freedoms of the Atlantic Charter for everyone, but it did so for hundreds of millions. Roosevelt focused clearly upon the destruction of US enemies and drove the elements of national power toward this.

The Americans proved solid strategists. They certainly made mistakes, but their successes were far more numerous. They planned and prepared, reassessed, and threw out what events made obsolete. They bought into bad theory at times, particularly on airpower, a constant American failing, but they adjusted. Leaders such as Marshall, Eisenhower, and King proved skilled at picking subordinates and empowering them to do their jobs. Eisenhower's role as the coordinator and interlocutor between the military and political leaders of several nations helped the machine of politics and war run as smoothly as one could have hoped.

The Second World War and its execution provides many lessons for grand strategy and strategists. But it was also an aberration in the American military experience. The United States hasn't fought a war of this magnitude since, but none know what the future brings. And as the Truman administration discovered, despite victory, unexpected challenges arise.

10

THE HOT PEACE AND THE KOREAN WAR, 1945–1953

INTRODUCTION

After the Second World War, the West mistakenly branded the rivalry with the Soviet Union and the Communist world the "Cold War." George Orwell used the term in October 1945. Bernard Baruch, a Wall Street veteran and advisor to Democratic presidents since Wilson, said in April 1947 that "We are today in the midst of a cold war." Journalist Walter Lippmann ran with it, publishing *The Cold War*.[1] But it wasn't a war.[2] It was rivalry. Traditional great-power competition that has never disappeared. Wars occurred amidst the contest, but the "Cold War" was not a war.

This unforced logic error helped corrupt America's ability to correctly and rationally assess and address challenges. Branding a thing something it isn't affects the difficulty of tackling it, perhaps even dangerously so, because the solutions can be constructed on a shaky foundation. This is not to say that the US got the "Cold War" wrong. The US and its allies did much well, and the West emerged victorious from the competition. But could things have been done better if the situation had not been intellectually half-framed as a military struggle when the contest was political and military means were but one tool for waging it? Clausewitz rightly advised us to understand the nature of the war. But understanding the nature of the competition when there is no war is also important.

A SHATTERED WORLD

One can't stress enough the uniqueness and enormity of the situation facing President Harry S. Truman and his advisors. Vast tracts of the world lay in ruins. Perhaps 60 million people had died in the war. Millions were refugees or displaced. The global economic system was in turmoil, much of it in collapse. Germany, Japan, and Italy, three great powers in 1939, were now occupied. France, defeated but reborn, remained troubled. Victorious Britain was financially devastated. European colonial power was broken and discredited, especially in Asia, and facing nationalist challenges that tested, then overwhelmed. Two powers in some respects on the international political fringes before 1939 – the USSR and the United States – fought as allies and emerged as victors with rival postwar visions. American leaders feared economic devastation fueling a sequel post–First World War totalitarian attraction. Thrown into this toxic pit of political, military, economic, and social uncertainty was a new creature – the atomic bomb – which upset traditional attitudes toward diplomacy and strategy.

America's place was a new one. For the first time, the US sat astride the global stage as the dominant power. At the war's close, it possessed staggering military strength. Over 12 million Americans served in uniform during the war and the US had forces from the Arctic to Brazil, from North Africa to China. The war had helped lift the American economy from its post-1929 lost decade, and the broken postwar order meant demand for the goods of the world's most powerful, productive – and undamaged – economy. At home, the US faced a myriad challenges. Millions of veterans were eager to take up lives they considered interrupted. Some US leaders feared the economic impact of the war's end and the return of prewar problems. The modern civil rights movement began challenging American inequality. American leaders were largely unprepared. And it's difficult to see how anyone could have been. Key military leaders such as Marshall and Eisenhower contributed greatly to the construction and successful execution of American grand strategy during the war, invaluable experience. The US, though, was no longer at war, despite the fact that to many it soon felt like it. A different situation demanded different answers.

THE ROOTS OF THE HOT PEACE

US officials didn't think tension between the US and the Soviet Union inevitable. Many hoped to continue the wartime alliance to ensure American security and the world's. Roosevelt's envisioned Four Policemen – the US, Great Britain, the Soviet Union, and China, imposing order – died at the Potsdam Conference in July–August 1945, killed largely by Stalin's unwillingness to allow free elections in Eastern Europe, his unilateral imposition of Communism there, and his fait accompli on setting Poland's borders.[3]

There exist many arguments about the Cold War's origins, but there's nothing the West or the US could have done to avoid rivalry with Stalin's Soviet empire. Stalin viewed civility as weakness, dishonesty, or attempted manipulation. And saw strength as a threat. Stalin had his own interests and aims, something often forgotten in critiques of Western actions, and believed the Marxist–Leninist teachings on the necessity and historic inevitability of world revolution to overthrow the governmental, economic, and social systems of the world. He combined this with a hearty dose of Russian imperialism. Revolutionary ideology and imperial expansion governed Soviet foreign relations. Roosevelt correctly understood that Stalin pulled the levers of power and was right to focus here, but even FDR's vaunted charm couldn't alter Stalin's behavior.[4]

Truman also wanted to get along with Stalin and was pushed by American military leaders to do so because they wanted Soviet help against Japan. US leaders generally desired postwar cooperation with the Soviets but also protected US interests and distrusted the Kremlin. Truman took a harder line against Soviet intransigence and Moscow's failure to keep its wartime promises; he mistakenly believed he was following Roosevelt's approach.[5]

A PERSISTENT MYTH

Republican Senator Arthur Vandenberg coined the phrase "politics stops at the water's edge" during the early Cold War as he worked in a bipartisan manner with Democratic president Truman. This depicted his vision of how the nation's foreign business should be done. The leaders of America's political parties do come together, particularly in a crisis, but political rivalries remain. The early Cold War was no exception, and the cooperative relationship between Vandenberg and Truman was "an aberration even in the years when it took place." Truman's secretary of state, Dean Acheson, called bipartisanship a "magnificent fraud" and said the administration built support for its actions by arguing that anyone who didn't agree "politics stops at the seaboard" was "a son of a bitch and a crook and not a true patriot." "Politics is a blood sport" accurately depicts the relationship. Democrats were drubbed in the 1946 elections, with the Republicans winning control of the House and Senate, which they hadn't held since 1932. Truman repaid Vandenberg for his foreign relations support by attacking the "do-nothing" Republican Congress during his 1948 reelection campaign. The Democrats took Congress in 1948. Foreign affairs disasters in Asia opened avenues for Republican attacks. The conservative wing of the Republican Party under Robert Taft was particularly upset over Truman's handling of China, America's expensive and growing military relationships, and revelations of Communist spying in the US.[6]

THE LACK OF A POLITICAL AIM

There seems to have been no clear delineation of political aims in the war's immediate aftermath, something understandable as the US was still trying to secure the peace from history's worst catastrophe. The tasks at hand were monumental; no one needed new ones. The strategy-making apparatus of the US also broke down. Many key civilian and military leaders left government service. Military leaders in the Pentagon (which was completed during the war) sought direction regarding postwar political aims and defense priorities but couldn't decipher the desires of their civilian masters. By mid September 1945, they had created their own, which was essentially achieving US security by defending the US, the Philippines, and the Western Hemisphere. But they also wanted forces enough to keep America's UN commitments and implement a strategy of "active defense" resting on overseas bases and intensive intelligence-gathering to avoid another Pearl Harbor. Marshall found the plan's expectations regarding Moscow too pessimistic and demanded revisions. It became quickly clear it wasn't pessimistic enough.[7]

ASSESSMENT, STRATEGY, REASSESSMENT

Truman and his advisors soon discovered the war had left Britain weaker than they realized, Europe and Japan more financially and economically shattered, revolutionary and nationalistic sentiments more potent, and the Soviets more aggressive. But in addition to no clear political aims there existed neither strategy for dealing with Moscow nor any general understanding of the Soviet Union itself, which had been a closed society before the war and remained so. US leaders worked from the false assumption that continued cooperation depended upon Western actions; the opposite was the case.[8]

With the arrival of Truman in the White House, and his appointment of James F. Byrnes as secretary of state, the US pursued a short-lived *quid pro quo* strategy based on the assumption that the Soviet Union was susceptible to outside pressures. Truman and his administration labored under two mistaken beliefs: that the Soviets needed US help, especially economically, and that the atomic bomb would give the US the upper hand. Moscow didn't want economic aid enough to make concessions, and use of the atomic bomb as a tool for applying diplomatic and military pressure was not politically expedient. Truman took a hard line toward the Soviets initially, pushing them to honor their agreements, but then pulled back, wondering if he had pressed too hard.[9] US leaders commonly make the mistake of placing their faith in economics and technology. The first is an especially poor foundation for reasoning when dealing with totalitarian states willing to kill millions of their own citizens. And the supposed leverage of groundbreaking technologies never pans out. For example, the Bomb didn't deter China from going to war with the US in Korea in 1950 or keep the Soviets from helping them. The US lacked any means of attracting or compelling the Soviet Union to act like a Western democracy.

Stalin's anti-Western February 9, 1946 speech and Soviet espionage sparked a Washington query to America's Moscow embassy regarding Soviet actions. On February 22, 1946, George F. Kennan, a Moscow State Department official, replied with what became a key building block for America's Cold War grand strategy – "the long telegram" – an assessment of and explanation for Soviet behavior. Kennan argued that Soviet leaders couldn't be won over because of their mistrust of the West, which meant US actions couldn't influence Moscow. Kennan pointed out that the Soviets saw foreign relations differently. The Kremlin's leaders could govern only by repression and required an outside threat to maintain the Soviet system and their own legitimacy, a role the US and the United Kingdom would be made to fill. There was no possibility of permanently resolving differences with a government conducting business so. Soviet foreign relations were driven by a mixture of Communist ideological zeal and traditional Russian expansionism. And since the Soviet system was built on suspicion, Kennan concluded the only way to win Soviet trust was complete disarmament. This was, of course, inconceivable. "In summary," he wrote, "we have here a political force committed fanatically to the belief that with [the] US there can be no permanent *modus vivendi*, that it is desirable and necessary that the internal harmony of our society be disrupted, our traditional way of life be destroyed, the international authority of our state be broken, if Soviet power is to be secure."[10] The threat to the US was existential.

It is rare that one document affects a profound shift in a nation's foreign relations; Kennan's "long telegram" did. It hit Washington when its puzzled leaders were receptive to clear analysis of a growing danger few understood. The result was a new, albeit short-lived, US strategy for dealing with the Soviet Union: Patience and Firmness – especially firmness. The US would no longer avoid discussions of problems with Moscow but instead clearly address them. The US also chose to resist additional Soviet expansion. To do this, Washington would rebuild its military strength and give allies military and economic help. Continuing negotiations with the Soviets would serve to achieve Moscow's agreement or win domestic and foreign support for the US by making public Soviet obstinacy. American leaders hoped Stalin, seeing the West's firm resolve, would prefer patience and moderate his behavior.[11]

A POLITICAL AIM: THE TRUMAN DOCTRINE

In late 1944, British troops landed in Greece and became involved fighting the Germans as well as Communist guerillas seeking to control the country who were later Soviet- and Communist Bloc–supported. But in February 1947, London told Washington it could no longer shoulder the burden in Greece and Turkey (the latter was under Soviet pressure). Truman decided the US had to become involved but believed he would face bipartisan resistance. Then Undersecretary of State Dean Acheson suggested that "Truman offer a bold global vision to sell this specific assistance." Talks with Republican Senators Vandenberg and Taft led to Truman's March 12, 1947 address to Congress in which he outlined what became known as the Truman Doctrine. Truman said: "One of the primary objectives of the foreign policy of the United States is the creation of conditions in which we and other nations will be able to work out a way of life free from coercion." Truman sought security for the United States. Freedom (i.e. democracy) in other lands would help ensure this, and, he said, one reason the US helped found the UN was "to make possible lasting freedom and independence for all its members." To do this, the United States needed "to support free peoples who are resisting attempted subjugation by armed minorities or by outside pressures." Truman asked for economic and military aid for Greece; these became core planks of American grand strategy. Pressure and pleading from numerous states produced growing US commitments of military and economic aid while spreading Washington's military footprint. Congress combined the majority of economic and military aid efforts under the Mutual Security Program of October 1951.[12]

The Truman Doctrine was a watershed in US grand strategy. Even though Truman never mentioned the Soviet Union or Communism (he did say "totalitarian"), he announced America's determination to resist Communism's spread and assist others to do the same, a precedent his successors followed. His speech suggested a broad, potentially global commitment using economic and military aid and possibly even military force, an issue Acheson quickly defused by insisting this would be done only where the US could act effectively. Even a lesser commitment would have stressed America's military as the US had followed its traditional practice of gutting its armed forces after a war. Between 1945 and 1946, army strength (including the air forces) went from 8,267,000 to 1,891,000, navy numbers fell to 983,000 from 3,380,000, and the Marine Corps dropped to 155,000 from 471,000. By 1948 the numbers were: army, 554,000; air forces, 387,000; navy, 419,000; and the Marine Corps 84,000. The United States, if pressed to act, could find itself with insufficient means for meeting its commitments.[13]

CRAFTING A GRAND STRATEGY

In April 1947, Truman began trying to bring organization to American grand strategy formulation and implementation by naming George Marshall secretary of state. Marshall set up the Policy and Planning Staff in May 1947 to bring together various government strands, do long-range planning, and develop a grand strategy. He made Kennan its first head. Kennan realized the US needed a peacetime grand strategy equal to one for wartime.[14]

Shortly after this, Kennan published "The Sources of Soviet Conduct" in *Foreign Affairs* magazine under the pseudonym X (the author's identity quickly became known). Here the world first heard the term "containment." Kennan adapted this from his "long telegram," retaining his assessment of the Soviet Union as being ideologically driven by Marxist–Leninist ideas and utterly suspicious of the West, making it all but impossible for the US to deal with Moscow in a normal manner. With his suggestion of containment Kennan provided a grand strategy for countering "Russian expansive tendencies." His recommendation was to "confront the Russians with unalterable counter-force at every point where they show signs of encroaching upon the interests of a peaceful and stable world." In Kennan's view, this meant more than military force. He realized the necessity of military strength but knew the value of diplomatic, informational, and economic tools in containing the Soviet Union to the areas it already controlled. Kennan also provided the political aims his grand strategy was supposed to achieve. I have italicized the key part:

> the United States has it in its power to increase enormously the strains under which Soviet policy must operate, to force upon the Kremlin a far greater degree of moderation and circumspection than it has had to observe in recent years, *and in this way to promote tendencies which must eventually find their outlet in either the break-up or the gradual mellowing of Soviet power.*[15]

It is easy to see the attraction of containment as a grand strategy, particularly after examining America's alternative courses of action. One suggested in numerous American political and military circles was waging a preventive (or preemptive) war against the Soviet Union. The Soviet

THE HOT PEACE AND THE KOREAN WAR, 1945–1953

pursuit of atomic weapons and American fear of what such a regime might do with them drove this. Truman – and most Americans – considered this irrational. Another option was the US disentangling itself from the reorganization of the postwar international order. This had no appeal because of the example of Wilson winning the war and losing the peace.[16] The memory of Munich made inaction unappealing.

How, though, does one implement containment? Kennan's ideas constantly evolved, and his views didn't always coincide with the actions of Truman and his successors. The administration used the various elements of national power, something with which Kennan agreed. Economic strategy played a large role as US leaders believed economic stability furthered a peaceful, international political environment.[17]

Truman saw Western Europe as "the decisive theater" and US leaders feared its economic distress made its states susceptible to Communism. In a June 5, 1947 speech, now Secretary of State Marshall put forward what became the European Recovery Act, better known as the Marshall Plan. The US would lend the European states money to help them rebuild. This would relieve suffering, revitalize their economies, help the US economy, and create a bulwark against the spread of Communism, which might find fertile ground in ravaged Europe. Revitalizing the western German economy was critical for European recovery and preventing a German drift toward Moscow. Truman secured $17.8 billion for the program in 1948, The receiving states were required to "liberalize their economies, reducing barriers to trade and investment" (which they proved unwilling to do), develop an integrated and cooperative "approach to economic and political problems," and "accept the economic and political rehabilitation of Germany." The final, unspoken element was their alignment with Washington in the Cold War. Linked to this was the revitalization of Asia's most important industrial area – Japan. The treatment of Japan shifted in 1948 as the US sought to create a stable, anti-Communist government and produce economic growth. A strong, stable Japan was necessary to counter to the Soviets in Asia while restoring the global power balance. Other areas were important, particularly for raw materials, but these two mattered most.[18]

There is debate about the effects of Marshall Plan aid, especially since 80 percent of the capital fueling postwar investment was European. Some think its most important accomplishment was Western European integration. US leaders believed in 1947–48 in the emergence of a European "third force," meaning a Europe strong enough to oppose Soviet or US actions. The US was also confident of resolving any differences with a democratic

Europe. Most Americans couldn't foresee an America bearing the primary defense burden over the long term.[19]

The administration tried to drive a wedge between Moscow and its satellites by offering Marshall Plan aid to Eastern Bloc states. This created strained relationships as expected, but not what followed. Stalin refused to watch the US secure Western Europe and attacked US strategy by feeding protests in France and Italy while moving to consolidate Soviet control. This culminated in a Communist coup in Czechoslovakia in February 1948.[20]

In November 1948, the Truman administration adopted NSC 20/4, the first comprehensive strategy study that became a frame for US grand strategy. This recognized that "Communist ideology and Soviet behavior clearly demonstrate that the ultimate objective of the leaders of the USSR is the domination of the world." It analyzed the threat the Soviet Union presented to the United States, its authors concluding Moscow could severely injure the US and also threaten it via political subversion, but smaller states around Moscow's periphery were in danger. It provided American political aims against the Soviet Union for peacetime and in the event of war. Interestingly, these were the same: "To reduce the power and influence of the USSR to limits which no longer constitute a threat to the peace, national independence and stability of the world family of nations," and "To bring about a basic change in the conduct of international relations by the government in power in Russia, to conform with the purposes and principles set forth in the UN charter." A big part of the strategy it recommended for achieving this was informational and focused on what we now call strategic communication as the US worked to undermine support for the USSR in foreign states and in the Soviet Union itself. The US needed to build its strength at home, militarily, industrially, and informationally while protecting itself from Soviet espionage, and strengthen the military, political, and economic abilities of other nations to resist the Soviets, all while placing as much stress as possible upon Moscow, its allies, and their alliance relationships. NSC 20/4 led to 1949's OFFTACKLE, a plan for a defensive war in Europe, the emergency war plan until 1951.[21]

ECONOMIC STRATEGY: AID AND TRADE

The Truman administration institutionalized foreign aid as a plank of American grand strategy. Domestically, on January 5, 1949 Truman announced pursuit of what he called the Fair Deal. This emphasized domestic spending over defense and included such things as health insurance, a higher minimum wage, and higher Social Security payments. Truman now essentially promised "to extend the New Deal" and his own domestic agenda, the Fair Deal, "to the world." Within three years, 34 nations were receiving $155.6 million in annual aid. Some critics claimed this was subsidizing socialism. One assumption was that economic development would produce democracy.[22]

American economic strategy had three planks: aiding the recovery of Western Europe to make it strong enough to help resist the Soviets; integrating Germany, Japan, and Italy into the Western economic system to anchor them to the West economically and militarily; and denying the Soviet Bloc Western technology. The primary tool was reconstruction aid (non-military aid between 1946 and 1953 was $33 billion). Trade was used to establish thriving, self-supporting economic systems abroad even if US producers suffered. Washington sought to increase the exports of allies to lower reconstruction costs, which meant opening America's market. This remained the approach from Truman to Eisenhower.[23]

Opening America's market forced a shift on tariffs. Though Truman promised Senator Vandenberg during the 1947 negotiations for renewing the Reciprocal Trade Agreements Program (RTAP) that American domestic producers would be protected, this didn't happen. Other nations surrendered almost nothing, protecting their producers while the US sometimes lowered tariffs 50 percent. State Department officials secured unilateral reductions even when they knew it would injure US producers. The promotion of foreign imports continued, sometimes aided by taxpayer funds. By the 1950s, active discrimination against US imports was a standard international practice. US efforts to encourage Western European economic union also wounded US exports. During the Cold War, "the US government sacrificed thousands of domestic jobs to create employment and prosperity elsewhere in the noncommunist world."[24]

The US considered funding economic recovery more important than immediately strengthening military power. Few informed observers expected an immediate Soviet attack. Economic investment was seen as producing more benefits and accomplishing more politically than the expansion of military forces. Key officials believed it possible to take a "calculated risk" on economic development.[25]

Aid produced pro-US political alignment, but Europe was not as eager to integrate economically and politically as Washington hoped. Reintegrating Germany was sour medicine, particularly in France. But revitalizing Europe required revitalizing western Germany. Paris demanded a US military alliance, something that by early 1948 other European states also pursued. Washington hoped more aid and combined staff relationships would suffice, but only a military accord would give Europeans the confidence to defend themselves and reassure Paris.[26]

DIPLOMATIC AND MILITARY STRATEGY

To the Truman administration a means of restoring stability and the balance of power was forming alliances and strengthening militarily friendly states. This provided the roots of US involvement in the North Atlantic Treaty Organization (NATO). The 1948 Communist coup in Czechoslovakia and the Berlin Blockade proved key catalysts. The coup proved the final straw for many, and in April 1948 several countries formed a defensive alliance, the Pact of Brussels. But Western Europe lacked the strength to repel a Soviet attack. The United States provided this, and NATO began in 1949. It was America's first peacetime military alliance, a defensive one designed to deter a Soviet attack. The Truman administration eventually signed alliances with forty-one different nations included in NATO, the 1947 Rio Treaty, and the 1951 ANZUS Treaty.[27]

The US began militarily supporting nations all over the world. What began as ad hoc measures to supply allies and friendly states with military aid became diplomatic and military tools of containment. The 1949 Mutual Defense Assistance Act formalized this and fathered similar bills. The US provided Nationalist China over $3 billion in military and economic aid between 1945 and 1949. To Truman, foreign aid would help countries become strong enough to defend themselves, lessening the need for US forces and permitting even further cuts in US defense spending.[28] Alliances fit well into the new American grand strategy but marked a sea-change. Non-entanglement as a tenet of American foreign relations was dead. Killed by Pearl Harbor and buried by Moscow.

Following close on the heels of the creation of NATO was the spring 1948 decision to allow the formation of a German government in the western Allied occupation zones to further economic recovery. Stalin responded in June 1948 by trying to force the Western Allies out of Berlin. He closed the road and rail routes but not the air corridors. The US and its allies launched the Berlin Airlift to supply the city. After nearly a year, Stalin reopened the land routes. The blockade hastened the creation of a West German state, which took place on May 21, 1949. Five months later, the Soviets officially formed a Communist regime in their German sector. The Soviet threat combined with European needs and fears to kill the US hope of developing Europe as a third force. Washington also seized the chance offered by Tito's defection from the Communist Bloc and began giving Yugoslavia aid. Kennan believed it was time for the US to emphasize offensive over defensive moves. Yugoslavia provided an opportunity.[29]

MEETING THE COMMUNIST CHALLENGE

The US was in many respects dragged into its post–Cold War role as nations approached Washington for military and security ties. Saudi Arabia wanted both, while Turkey sought an alliance. To Truman, the US had little choice. Refusing aid to weak and politically divided states such as Greece and Turkey risked their falling into Moscow's orbit.[30]

China was one of these. Ambassador to Moscow Averell Harriman inked an agreement with Stalin on August 14, 1945 in which the Soviets recognized Chiang Kai-Shek's Nationalist government and committed to giving the Nationalists the areas of Manchuria occupied by the Red Army in the war's last days. Stalin instead gave control to Mao Tse-Tung's Communists and stripped Manchurian industry and shipped it to the Soviet Union. Truman told the Japanese to surrender only to Nationalist forces and began transporting Chiang's troops to Manchuria. In mid September, 50,000 Marines landed in China to secure key ports and other areas and give the Nationalists time to take control.[31]

Truman hoped to establish a united, independent, and democratic China. Others had different aims. Truman asked Marshall to go to China in December 1945, and he brokered an odd ceasefire that came into effect in January 1946. It ended attacks on communications but didn't inhibit moving troops to reestablish Chinese control over Manchuria, which meant it didn't end the fighting because Manchuria was too great a prize. Marshall kept peace talks stumbling along as the war over Manchuria intensified. Mao's attacks in Manchuria were countered by Chiang's offensive. Marshall's mission failed because the "Nationalists would make no real concessions, and the Communists only pretended to do so." Truman and Marshall embargoed arms sales to Chiang until 1947 to try to force him to negotiate a settlement. Truman wavered between State Department recommendations to abandon Chiang and warnings from Secretary of Defense James Forrestal and others that insufficient aid to Nationalist China would see a Communist victory. Truman dispatched someone to investigate.[32]

In late 1947, as the civil war turned against the Nationalists, the JCS recommended a massive military and economic aid program to support Chiang. Kennan disagreed, believing a Communist victory wouldn't be catastrophic because of China's lack of development, the fact that the Soviets couldn't control China, and because the Nationalists were too incompetent to make good use of it. Secretary of State Marshall supported giving Chiang weapons and supplies (which the US had begun dispatching again earlier in 1947) but proved instrumental in November 1947 in preventing attachment of American military advisors.[33]

Mao's late 1948 offensive broke the Nationalist forces, though they inflicted perhaps 1 million casualties on the Communists. Mao declared victory on October 1, 1949. Dean Acheson's State Department saw this coming and concluded in January 1949 that the US wouldn't intervene but would try to divide Moscow and Beijing. The administration proved mistaken that there was no hope of a Sino-Soviet alliance and made no progress in separating the Red giants because this would have required softening US relations with Communist China. Neither the domestic political situation nor the hatred of Communism shared by Truman and Acheson permitted this. Mao also was uninterested in American overtures. America's aims in regard to China and its strategy "remained incoherent in the extreme."[34]

What if the US had continued arming Chiang and provided military advisors as it did in Greece and other places? America's temporary arms embargo starved the Nationalists of ammunition, and it's possible that American advisors and increases in equipment might have prevented Mao from consolidating his hold on China. A different outcome, even one that produced Chinese partition, would have affected the Korean and Vietnam Wars, which Communist China made possible. But it is equally plausible that Chiang's refusal to reform and endemic Nationalist corruption and mismanagement surrendered every advantage to a dedicated Communist rival that excelled at capitalizing on the enemy's mistakes.[35] Advising corrupt regimes rarely succeeds.

Mao's 1949 victory proved politically disastrous for Truman. His popularity had been slipping since the 1948 election, and the strong China lobby blamed Truman for "losing" China to Communism and pilloried his administration as "soft on Communism." The guilty convictions of Soviet agents Alger Hiss, Klaus Fuchs, and Julius and Ethel Rosenberg gave a sheen of credibility to Senator Joseph McCarthy's charges of Communist infiltration in the government, but his demagoguery and sweeping allegations, such as those leveled at Acheson for "harboring" Communists at the State Department, made more difficult the hunt for Moscow's legion of actual agents. The government's Venona project discovered 349 Americans working as Soviet spies, half of whom couldn't be identified.[36]

By the time of the Korean War, the Truman administration's approach to China "confused even the most subtle European diplomats." The US wouldn't recognize Communist China nor abandon the Nationalists ruling

Taiwan, a government the administration denounced and about which it remained undecided about protecting. On June 27, 1950, two days after the beginning of the Korean War, Truman deployed the Seventh Fleet to the Taiwan Strait, the State Department arguing that this neutralized the Strait and prevented Nationalist attacks upon the Communists.[37] Mao considered it US intervention in China's civil war.

Additionally, Washington began taking an interest in the Middle East because of its oil, largely to deny it to the Soviets. The fact Moscow hadn't yet evacuated Iranian Azerbaijan (the Allies occupied Iran during the war and also used it as a Lend-Lease corridor) helped produce Truman's September 1945 decision to construct an air base at Dhahran, Saudi Arabia. Truman inked a defensive pact with Riyadh in 1947. As it became clear Middle Eastern oil was instrumental to the Marshall Plan, North Africa and the Middle East became arenas of US interest, but the US largely counted upon Great Britain and France to keep this region secure.[38]

The US also became involved in Southeast Asia, particularly in what became Vietnam. The French returned to their possessions at the end of the Second World War and immediately found themselves in a war against a Communist insurgency led by Ho Chi Minh. The Truman administration began providing France military and economic aid after the outbreak of the Korean War to stop the spread of Communism and support France, whose help was needed for NATO and Europe's defense. By 1954, the US was paying 80 percent of the cost of France's Indochina war.[39]

A 1952 document expressed America's aim in Southeast Asia and encapsulated the strategy: "To prevent the countries of Southeast Asia from passing into the communist orbit, and to assist them to develop will and ability to resist communism from within and without and to contribute to the strengthening of the free world." A Communist takeover of Southeast Asia was deemed detrimental to America's short- and long-term "security interests" and expressed in terms that could have come from NSC 68 (examined shortly): "The loss of any of the countries of Southeast Asia to communist aggression would have critical psychological, political, and economic consequences." Moreover, losing any part of Southeast Asia was deemed to lead almost inevitably to the loss of the rest of the region, an expression of what was later called the Domino Theory, a concept originating as a reason for supporting Greece. Losing Southeast Asia would also threaten America's strategic position in Asia, particularly in regard to the "offshore island chain."[40]

A 1952 State Department analysis identified two choices in regard to Indochina: abandoning it to Communism or continuing financial support for a situation that might evolve and demand the expenditure of American lives "in a hopeless cause" that alienated "vital segments of Asian public opinion." Truman and Acheson picked the latter, though one is loath to judge them too harshly. Politically, doing anything else would have been difficult. The US pressured France to shift power in Indochina to the inhabitants, but Ho Chi Minh's obvious Communism led the administration to conclude it had no choice but to support France.[41]

MILITARY STRATEGY AND PLANNING

The JCS, which had been created during the war, had no official, legal standing and operated in a political vacuum during the early Cold War, because it had received neither political aims nor any guidance on how the administration would deal with Moscow. The growing tensions were clear, as was Soviet aggressiveness. But American political leaders were interested in demobilization and cutting spending. The JCS composed its first plans for war with Moscow in late 1945, but in the initial postwar years, US leaders didn't fear an immediate war. The Soviets had paid a high price during the Second World War and lacked modern air and naval forces, and a 1945 assessment projected Moscow needed five years to develop an atomic bomb, a figure later raised to ten. The CIA's 1947 assessment said Moscow would build military power while trying to increase its influence through means other than war.[42]

The National Security Act of 1947 reorganized and established what became America's national security apparatus. It combined the Navy and Army Departments and placed them under a new secretary of defense. The JCS became "the principal military advisors to the President and the Secretary of Defense," tasked "to prepare war, mobilization, and logistics plans and provide strategic direction of the armed forces in time of war." New security arms included the Central Intelligence Agency (CIA) and the National Security Council (NSC). The latter was partially a reaction to America's greater postwar commitments abroad. Its members included the president, the secretaries of state and defense, the navy, army, and air force chiefs, and the chair of the National Security Resources Board. The committee was to examine security issues and advise the president in regard to political aims as well as strategy, especially military strategy.[43]

There was widespread dissension and fighting among the top military brass as they battled to preserve service roles, seize shares of a shrinking defense budget, and develop forces capable of delivering atomic weapons. Attempts by the army and the newly independent air force to drastically cut the navy's air arm and shrink the carrier force produced the 1949 "Revolt of the Admirals." The air force fought against naval aviation while the navy fought against the B-36 bomber program. Bitter infighting contributed to the firing of the chief of naval operations and the suicide of Defense Secretary Forestal. It severely damaged military preparedness while proving the need for more reform, which followed in 1949. The secretary of defense had lacked real power or staff. This was fixed by making Defense a federal department equivalent to State or Agriculture. The office of Chairman of the JCS was created, and Truman recalled Eisenhower to fill this post in 1949. Ike was appalled by the military's terrible state and the effects of Truman's incessant gutting while simultaneously increasing overseas commitments. He found a disturbing absence of readiness and observed: "We are repeating our history of decades."[44]

America was not alone in neglecting its military forces: the West had essentially disarmed. Even with the US joining NATO, in 1949 the West deployed only ten divisions in Germany. Planners said it would require eighteen to even mount a fighting retreat against a Red Army invasion. The administration partially saw NATO membership as another cost-cutting measure. One reason Truman enthusiastically embraced it was that rearming Europe and ending the occupation of Germany would allow the withdrawal of approximately 100,000 US troops. Providing the $1 billion needed to arm NATO saved money by allowing future military budget cuts.[45]

Article 5 of the NATO Treaty committed signatories to supporting attacked members. The new alliance constructed strategy predicated upon an assessment that NATO was militarily inferior to the Soviets but had American atomic weapons. Defence Committee (DC) 13 was the basis of NATO planning and its forces were supposed to be ready in 1954. It called for 2,324 warships supported by 3,246 naval aircraft, 8,004 combat aircraft, and 90 NATO divisions. DC 13 was adopted – appropriately – on April 1, 1950, before the beginning of the Korean War. No NATO member proved willing to build the needed forces. The Korean War, though, raised European fears they were next. Eisenhower was appointed Supreme Allied Commander Europe (SACEUR) in December 1950 and established the Supreme Headquarters Allied Powers Europe (SHAPE).[46]

NATO plans discussed political aims and strategy for the alliance if at peace or if forced to go to war. In peacetime, NATO sought to prevent a war and convince the Soviets to not attack via "the development of an adequate military strength and a close coordination of the political, economic and psychological efforts of member nations." If attacked, NATO nations would fight a defensive war, concentrating on the protection of Europe as its loss could be fatal to all the alliance members. The war's political aims would be determined jointly by the NATO powers. The alliance would seek "to destroy by a strategic offensive in Western Eurasia the will and capabilities of the USSR and her satellites to wage war" while standing on the defensive in Asia. NATO published slightly altered plans in December 1951 that included holding the Soviets as far east as possible and working with Middle Eastern partners.[47]

The US – in theory – could depend upon its atomic arsenal for defense. But it lacked the technicians and industrial capacity to make this work as demobilization hit here as well. In 1947, the US had thirteen bombs, and fifty in 1948. The Strategic Air Command was established in March 1946 to deliver the bombs, but in 1948 it had only thirty-two planes that could carry these weapons, only twelve crews trained to drop them, and another eighteen preparing. Truman tried to establish international control over atomic weapons, but when reality smashed this plan, he signed NSC 30 in September 1948. This restricted the authority to order the use of atomic weapons to the president.[48]

Two views on using atomic weapons emerged by 1947. Army and navy leaders held they were important elements of American military strength. Many air force leaders saw a war-winning weapon for breaking the enemy's ability and will to resist. This was despite the fact that early analysis of an atomic attack on the Soviet Union concluded it wouldn't force Moscow's surrender even if American disarmament hadn't ensured it lacked the required planes and bombs. By 1948, the view dominating American strategic circles was that a Soviet war would be for global domination and atomic weapons could counter Moscow's conventional advantage.[49]

For Asia in 1948–49, the US concluded that if it controlled key islands around the perimeter of Asia (Japan, Okinawa, the Aleutians, and the Philippines) the US could guard its interests in the region and hold the sea lines of communication to Japan, the region's only industrial power, while not being entangled on the mainland. This defensive perimeter was the subject of Acheson's famous January 1950 Press Club speech and part of the US effort to pivot away from the Nationalist Chinese.[50]

US military strength continued to decline, and active-duty military personnel in mid 1949 numbered 1,591,232. When President Truman fixed a 1950 military budget at $14.4 billion, the JCS warned this would force even more cuts. Truman refused to bend. Shrinking budgets pushed the services to rely more upon atomic weapons because they were cheaper. But the situation in Europe was forcing the JCS to think about defending Europe conventionally, something heretofore thought impossible. Overall, the Truman administration consistently failed to provide sufficient military means to implement the grand strategy upon which it had embarked. Secretary of State Acheson confessed that "Mr. Truman's period of retrenchment in 1948 and 1949 ... put means out of relation with ends." The administration continuously added commitments but didn't ensure it had the military capability to fulfill them. Domestic political concerns explain why.[51]

REASSESSMENT: NSC 68

In 1949, two events convinced Truman to authorize a study to produce a coherent US grand strategy: the "loss" of China with the victory of Mao's Communists over Chiang Kai-Shek's Nationalists, and the Soviet Union's explosion of its first atomic bomb. NSC 68 was drafted by a team headed by Paul Nitze, who succeeded Kennan as head of the policy and planning staff in 1949; Kennan was consulted.[52]

NSC 68 is an oddly structured and difficult tract. It takes as its aims those in NSC 20/4. This is mentioned early but only discussed in detail near the conclusion. These aims were essentially to shrink the Soviet Union's power so that it was no longer a threat to other nations and convince it to behave as other states. But the Cold War had worsened since NSC 20/4's November 1948 promulgation and grew darker because of the possible development of hydrogen weapons and Moscow detonating an atomic bomb. Because of this, NSC 68 insisted, American strategy needed to change. America's political aims against the Soviet Union were limited, meaning America did not seek the overthrow of the Soviet regime. It sought its moderation. The struggle between the US and the Soviet Union is generally depicted as existential, and indeed it was for the United States, which also sought the preservation of its own system, another limited aim. The Soviets sought the destruction of the US government, an unlimited aim. Neither could hope to achieve their aims without the application of enormous means.[53]

NSC 68 suggested two strategies: "attempting to develop a healthy international community" and containment. The first the US was doing via the UN, development aid to Europe, and other actions. Containment "seeks by all means short of war" to halt Soviet expansion, "expose the falsities of Soviet pretensions," and "induce a retraction of the Kremlin's control and influence." This would, in line with Kennan's original assumption, "foster the seeds of destruction within the Soviet system" and bring Moscow "at least to the point of modifying its behavior to conform to generally accepted international standards." All elements of national power were critical for doing this, but military power was considered the most important – and indispensable. The US should negotiate with the Soviets while applying pressure, being careful to not injure Soviet prestige and giving Moscow windows to retreat. The US had failed to do this thus far or to build sufficient military power. NSC 68 urged developing the capability to implement its strategy to achieve the desired aims. Allies were important and necessary, and if the US demonstrated strength, they would be encouraged to do so as well. Together, they could build military forces strong enough to "probably" deter Soviet aggression or at least blunt any offensive. But the clock was ticking, and the US didn't have unlimited time to address the crisis it faced. In its analysis of different options, NSC 68 mentioned the possibility of "rolling back the Kremlin's drive." This suggested the prospect of reclaiming areas previously lost to Communism and became known as "rollback."[54]

NSC 68's last page says: "the cold war is in fact a real war in which the survival of the free world is as stake." The authors were correct on the stakes but incorrect to call the competition between the US and the Soviet Union a war. It was international rivalry and competition, executed at times with subversion, but it was not a war because it lacked the prime characteristic: violence purposely directed at an opponent for a political aim where one is trying to impose one's will upon the opponent.[55] Understanding the distinction is critical because one can do things when at war – particularly with military power – that one cannot do when at peace. This confusion has undermined American strategic thinking ever since.

Truman agreed with NSC 68's contentions but disliked this requiring perhaps tripling the defense budget. But then North Korea invaded South Korea. Truman approved NSC 68 in September 1950 and the US embarked upon the defense build-up he never wanted.[56]

THE KOREAN WAR, 1950–53

On Sunday, June 25, 1950, Soviet-backed North Korea invaded US-supported South Korea. (See Map 10.1.) The North had a clear and unlimited political aim: the conquest of South Korea. Japan had acquired Korea during its victorious 1904–05 war with Russia. When Soviet forces swept into Manchuria and Korea in the closing days of the Second World War, the Pentagon feared Soviet occupation of the entire peninsula and dispatched US troops. American forces landed in November 1945 with the aim of creating an independent democracy on the peninsula. A pair of US army colonels, one named Dean Rusk, created two occupation zones by drawing a line on a map at roughly the peninsula's halfway point. The Soviets agreed. The US garrisoned the South, the Soviets the North. But Stalin sought to keep Korea from American or Japanese control.[57]

THE HOT PEACE AND THE KOREAN WAR, 1945–1953

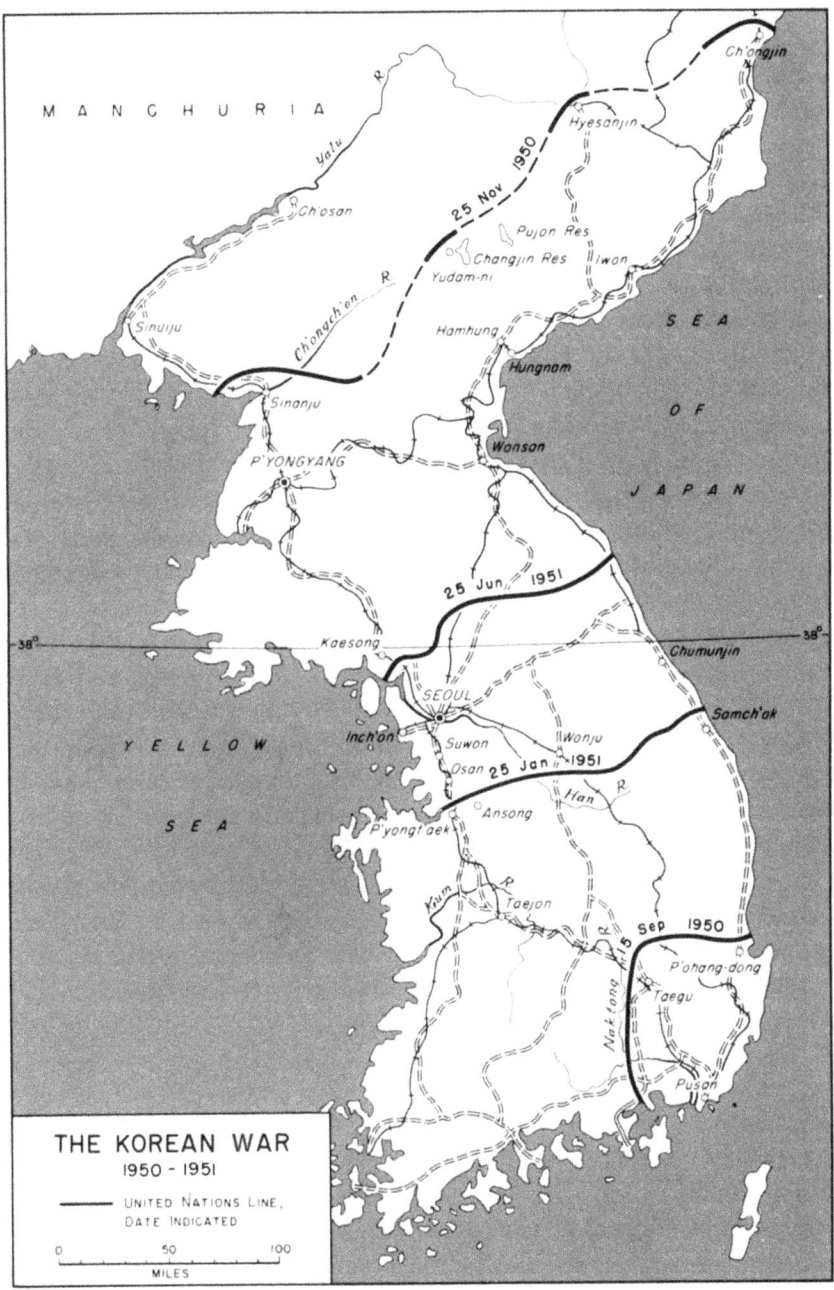

Map 10.1 The Korean War, 1950–51

After the war, neither US military nor civilian officials wanted to garrison Korea, and some military leaders pressed to withdraw US forces for use in Europe, even if the South fell to Communism as expected. But the administration wanted to balance US prestige in the area against "a precipitous withdrawal" and, as part of its effort to offload Korea onto the UN, backed free elections in May 1948. The South elected 73-year-old nationalist Syngman Rhee and established the Republic of Korea (ROK). The US began building a South Korean constabulary. The North boycotted the elections, established a Stalinist Communist regime in the North under 36-year-old Kim Il Sung, a veteran of the Chinese Communist guerrilla war against Japan and the Soviet army picked by Stalin. Both Korean leaders declared their intention to unite the peninsula, but the North acted, launching a guerrilla campaign in 1948 that cost 30,000 lives. Some argue this marked the war's beginning.[58]

The North prepared thoroughly. Conscription was introduced and about 10,000 Koreans went to the Soviet Union for specialist military training. Mao transferred two divisions of ethnic Koreans. Soviet weapons and equipment, a 1949 arms pact, and a military advisory mission of 1,000 that planned the invasion helped Pyongyang build a force of 100,000 (at least one-third had combat experience). The North had modern tanks and artillery, some aircraft and naval vessels, and 50,000 constabulary troops. For South Korea, Truman's political troubles, the desire to contain government spending, and US discontent with Rhee conspired to limit American aid. Europe and the Middle East were vital; South Korea wasn't. In August 1948, the Korean constabulary became the Republic of Korea (ROK) army, and a US military advisory group trained it. By June 1949, the ROK army had 100,000 men and the constabulary 53,000. But the army was inadequately trained, inexperienced, and armed only to conduct counter-guerrilla operations. It had no tanks, little artillery, inadequate transportation, and insufficient ammunition.[59]

THE COMMUNIST DECISION FOR WAR

Initially, Stalin didn't want war in Korea. But as the Cold War heated up, and after signing an alliance with Mao's China, Stalin changed his mind. He feared America rearming Japan, making South Korea a staging point that needed liquidating. Stalin thought the risk low because America wouldn't defend it, a view fed by Moscow breaking the atomic monopoly in 1949, America withdrawing its troops from South Korea, Acheson delineating an American defense perimeter absent Korea in a January 12, 1950 Press Club speech, and Stalin's exceptional intelligence sources reporting scant hope of US help.[60]

Stalin told Kim during March and April 1950 meetings that Mao's victory and growing Soviet atomic strength meant he could now attack. But he demanded Kim provide assurances of no US intervention and of Mao's support. Mao agreed and Kim insisted America wouldn't intervene because it hadn't in China, which was more important. Stalin feared US intervention and what might result but was convinced by Kim's promise to capture South Korea's capital of Seoul within three days after launching a surprise attack supported by a southern uprising numbering 200,000. A quick conquest would follow, presenting the Americans a fait accompli. Stalin bit but told Kim: "If you should get kicked in the teeth, I shall not lift a finger. You have to ask Mao for all the help." Kim told Mao the war would be over in a month and that America couldn't respond by then.[61]

THE KOREAN WAR: THE FIRST PHASE

The invasion began at 4am on June 25, 1950. Kim Il Sung "ordered his army to secure victory in eight weeks." The plan assumed collapse of South Korea's government within one week, perhaps less, and that seizing Seoul was pivotal. If this didn't deliver victory, four prongs of the North Korean People's Army would drive southward. Kim hoped to be in the critical port of Pusan anchoring Korea's southeast corner on August 15 and had an excellent intelligence picture of the South from his perhaps 5,000 spies.[62]

The North achieved complete surprise. The four prongs advanced, and Seoul fell within four days, but there was no uprising. Unexpectedly, the US quickly responded with air attacks and piecemeal commitment of poorly trained and equipped troops from Japan. The offensive could have continued exploiting the main axis of advance down the Seoul–Taejon railway line, but a ten-day pause followed as the North Korean army was redeployed. Without this, South Korea probably would have fallen. Stopping gave the US time to commit troops and stiffen the South.[63]

THE US DECISION TO INTERVENE: THE POLITICAL AIM AND THE PROBLEM OF INTERESTS

The invasion surprised Washington. State Department officials saw a Soviet move. Before consulting Congress or going to the United Nations, Truman authorized air and naval support and ordered Douglas MacArthur, who commanded the occupation forces in Japan, to throw the North Koreans from the South. Truman was determined to use the UN to establish an international and domestic political foundation for the war; this became a key part of American diplomatic strategy. He put the idea of collective security to the test and, only a little more than seventy-two hours after the invasion, had gathered an international coalition and secured support for intervention from the UN Security Council. The UN called for an end to the fighting and North Korea's withdrawal, and urged its members to assist "the Republic of Korea as may be necessary to repel the armed attack and to restore international peace in the area."[64]

UN support was made possible by the Soviets boycotting the Security Council to protest Communist China not being allowed to assume China's Nationalist-held seat. Security Council members can veto any proposal, but the Soviet representative was absent. The US's political aim of restoring South Korea became the UN's aim. Other reasons have been advanced for the Soviet absence: Stalin ensured this to keep the Chinese Communists from securing the seat, and also didn't want a confrontation with Truman arising from a Soviet veto.[65]

Before the invasion, the administration would have insisted it wasn't in America's interests to fight in Korea. One reason America withdrew its troops was fear Rhee would attack the North and drag America into a war.[66] The US decision to fight here illustrates the difficulty in determining interests: sometimes a new threat arises and makes acting in a previously unthinkable realm a necessity.

The administration had many reasons for intervening. Truman and others saw the ghost of appeasement at Munich and believed that if the West failed to act against totalitarianism on the march, the Soviets would perceive weakness – and opportunity. Truman told the leaders of both parties it was critical to stop the Soviets and advised US allies success in South Korea would make the Soviets less likely to try something similar. Some Western leaders saw the invasion as part of a larger Soviet plan, or possibly a diversion. JCS chair Bradley branded it a "softening-up operation," while others worried about committing troops in a peripheral place like Korea because the Soviets might move against Europe or Iran.[67] Not a few feared the beginning of a Third World War. Inaction would undermine American credibility. The stakes were too high to stand aside.

ARE WE AT WAR?

None of this settled the American debate on entering the conflict. Chief among the issues was whether to declare war. This was so contentious it marks the beginning of the preface to then army Chief of Staff J. Lawton Collins' memoir: "The Korean War was the first large-scale war in American history that began and ended without a declaration of war by the Congress of the United States." By not seeking Congressional approval, Truman left an opening for critics, who by June 27, 1950 charged he was ignoring the Constitution.[68]

Truman bypassed Congress and broke with US tradition and arguably law because he knew he had the support of the American people. He would have won a Congressional vote but feared a prolonged debate. Truman argued that since the US Senate had approved the UN Charter, it had transferred its war-making authority, in certain circumstances, to the UN Security Council, which had voted to use force. This argument was disingenuous. Congress and Truman had addressed it via 1945's United Nations Participation Act, which said the US could only send troops to back UN actions if Congress approved, something to which Acheson had testified before Congress.[69] The UN Charter doesn't supplant the US Constitution in American law.

Now Secretary of State Acheson worried about the conservative Taft wing of the Republican Party using Korea as a bludgeon against the administration's handling of defense matters and Asia. Taft insisted Truman had done the right thing in the wrong way by intervening without a Congressional resolution. Acheson condemned criticism as partisan politics and justified Truman's war with a memorandum listing eighty-five pre-1941 incidents where a president initiated military action on his own authority. He insisted Congressional debate would have generated unnecessary criticism and undermined the morale of US troops fighting a desperate rearguard defense. These were *ex post facto* justifications of actions he endorsed while ignoring that the desperation partly resulted from his administration's failure to prepare militarily. Constitutional scholars rebuffed Acheson's document. One branded it a "lengthy list of fights with pirates and bandits."[70]

The issue resurfaced in the 1951 MacArthur Senate hearings. When asked whether or not it would have been preferable to request a declaration of war, Acheson insisted there was no time and added: "I do not believe the President would have gone to Congress for the purpose of asking for a declaration of war against anybody, because this was an action of the United Nations to repel an aggression and was not a question of war against any other country."[71] If America wasn't at war against North Korea (and, at the time of his testimony, China as well), what was it doing in Korea? Moreover, Acheson helped change America's political aims, producing the American invasion of North Korea feeding China's entry decision.

Acheson's words illuminate a problem plaguing America since: American leaders refusing to admit when the nation is at war. At a June 29,

1950 press conference, four days after the North Korean invasion, a reporter queried the president: "Everybody is asking in this country, are we or are we not at war?" Truman replied: "We are not at war" and explained when pressed that "the members of the United Nations are going to the relief of the Korean Republic to suppress a bandit raid." A second journalist asked: "Mr. President, would it be correct, against your explanation, to call this a police action under the United Nations?" "Yes," Truman replied. "That is what it amounts to." Truman branded the Korean War a police action, approved this as an official term, "and used it throughout the summer of 1950." In his memoir Truman resisted calling the Korean War a war, referring to it as an "action," "situation," or "affair."[72] This is neither intellectually honest nor politically wise. Also, if you aren't at war, does winning it or ending it matter?

Procuring a supporting Congressional resolution or a declaration of war wouldn't have silenced criticism but would have shackled it. Some of those approving it would find it politically difficult to refuse funding or publicly turn against it. Under US law, if the nation is attacked, it is at war and no declaration is necessary. But this wasn't the case. The administration simply ignored the constitutional requirement for Congress to declare war. The oddest thing was that Truman could have easily secured a declaration. Taft and some other conservatives are falsely accused of being isolationists, but as the *Washington Post* pointed out in 1950, these so-called isolationists were deadly serious about resisting Stalinism and possessed an anti-Communism "the antithesis of isolationism." Truman and Acheson were correct that their political opponents would have ensured a contentious debate, but this happened anyway. What is easily forgotten from our distant perch is the bitterness of the political and strategic debates of 1945–50, particularly over China's fall to Communism. It is understandable Truman and Acheson wanted to avoid a revisiting. But they launched America's practice of refusing to call a war a war and gave Congress an out.[73]

THE INSTRUMENTS OF WAR: THE POOR STATE OF US FORCES

Early in the morning of June 30, 1950, the administration approved movement of two divisions to Korea and a naval blockade. By dusk on July 1, advance American elements were in Korea. The troops were from MacArthur's Eighth Army garrisoning Japan. Its 108,000 men made up one-fifth of the army's 591,000 complement. This force was understrength, insufficiently trained, and so short of equipment it scavenged vehicles and tanks from depots and museums. Much of the blame for this lies with

Truman and Secretary of Defense Louis Johnson. But MacArthur, who would be appointed UN commander, also bears responsibility as it was his command, as do his superiors in the Pentagon and the members of Congress responsible for oversight. The first troops dispatched were the 406 men of Task Force Smith, which North Korean forces overran on July 5. US leaders underestimated the North and assumed American forces would quickly take matters in hand.[74]

The US immediately committed its airpower, savaging North Korean units and logistics. In July 1950, after winning air superiority, the United States Air Force (USAF) began a strategic bombing campaign against North Korea, but its leaders chafed at being limited to precision bombing against military targets. Here, as in Vietnam, the administration feared the effects of bombing on third parties and imposed constraints by restricting air attacks along the Chinese and Soviet borders, including against the Yalu River hydroelectric plants.[75] Constraints later lessened but never disappeared.

General Walton Walker assumed operational command on July 17, 1950. He had little choice but to fight a delaying action and concluded he must hold an area around the port city of Pusan or lose any ability to maneuver or counterattack. On July 29, he issued his "Stand or Die" order: "There will be no Dunkirk....We must fight until the end.... If some of us must die, we will die fighting together.... I want everybody to understand we are going to hold this line. We are going to win." By August 1, Walker secured the Pusan Perimeter, a 100- by 50-mile pocket.[76]

THE SECOND PHASE

The administration consistently proved reluctant to commit additional forces to Korea, partly because America had essentially disarmed, and partly because doing so "forced the JCS to move along the road to wartime mobilization," which wasn't "a trip the chiefs wanted to make because Harry Truman and [Secretary of Defense] Louis Johnson were not ready to admit that the United States was at war." MacArthur was asked on July 13, 1950 what he needed to achieve the aim. He said eight divisions and additional support forces, four more divisions than he possessed. The JCS couldn't immediately dispatch this but began sending smaller units. By stripping garrisons around the world and mobilizing reserves, MacArthur had his eight divisions by September.[77] He already knew what to do with them.

MacArthur began considering an amphibious landing even before American troops entered the fight. It became Operation CHROMITE, and

MacArthur eventually chose Inchon on South Korea's western coast for the landing. It had an excellent harbor and was near the capital, Seoul, which controlled the road and rail routes into South Korea and became the operational objective. But Inchon had dangers. Invaders had to transit a narrow channel, seize the island fortress of Wolmi-do, then assault a city protected by a seawall. The 30-foot tides and enormous mudflats made it impossible to reinforce the landing until the next high tide. To mitigate the risks, MacArthur banked upon surprise and wanted to attack before North Korea had time to strengthen its forces. The potential rewards were great. A successful landing combined with a breakout from Pusan would destroy the North Korean army – the enemy's center of gravity (its source of strength) – and make it possible to win the war. MacArthur overcame resistance from the JCS and the commanders leading the assault, but doubts remained. Assembling the personnel and material required Herculean efforts and taking risks, including weakening Pusan's defense to strengthen the invasion force. The US global reserve consisted of the 82nd Airborne Division.[78]

Operation CHROMITE went ahead on September 15, 1950. It achieved complete surprise but shouldn't have. Kim ignored warnings from Beijing and his Soviet advisors about a possible landing, Inchon being the most likely of a half-dozen sites. Within six hours, the Marines held the port. By dawn the next day, MacArthur's forces cleared the city. On the 16th, the Pusan offensive began. After less than a week, the Korean People's Army (KPA) came apart under the weight of UN attacks and the severing of its lines of supply and communication. The two UN forces linked up on September 26. MacArthur's gambit delivered the KPA's defeat and the liberation of South Korea. But weak operational planning saw much of the broken enemy force escaping northward.[79] The success of MacArthur's plan laid the foundation for victory in Korea at a fairly low cost. America's political leaders simply needed to realize how lucky they had been.

CHANGING THE POLITICAL AIM

US and ROK forces reached the 38th parallel in the closing days of September. Most of the KPA fled north, though elements remained behind as guerrillas. The US and UN had achieved the aim of the restoration of South Korea. MacArthur and his forces had won what seemed a lost war. But on September 9, 1950, *before* US forces landed at Inchon on September 15, the Truman administration changed its political purpose: it would now unify Korea.[80] This decision was one of the most important of the war and in the history of American grand strategy as it threw away a hard-won victory.

Interestingly, the literature on Korea is overrun with examples blaming MacArthur for a decision resting with Truman and the State Department, especially Acheson, who pushed hard for the invasion.[81] Numerous primary and secondary sources are clear this decision wasn't MacArthur's.[82]

There was intense State Department debate on whether or not the US political aim should change to unification of Korea under the auspices of the UN. John M. Allison, the director of the State Department Office of Northeast Asian Affairs, pushed for this as early as July 1, 1950, and was willing to risk global war. Dean Rusk, his superior, coauthor of the 38th parallel, and future secretary of state under John F. Kennedy and Lyndon Johnson, agreed. Acheson dispatched a draft statement on the necessity of liberating Korea on August 1, 1950. Kennan urged Acheson to ignore those advising invading North Korea because of the risk of war with the Soviet Union and China. Kennan said the US could expect the Communists to act to save North Korea just as the US had South Korea.[83]

The decision to cross the 38th was driven partly by fears of what would happen if the US didn't. A July 31, 1950 Department of Defense memorandum insisted that "a return to the status quo ante bellum would not promise security." Some in the Department of Defense saw an opportunity to "roll back" Communism while Truman conducted a public campaign to win support for the move. To others, only unification could prevent a future North Korean attack. Truman declared unification of Korea the political aim on September 1, 1950. September 9's NSC 81/1 made it official. The US decided to reunite Korea under the South's government, using three prewar UN General Assembly resolutions as the underpinning. The US sought UN approval, which followed on October 7. Now Secretary of Defense Marshall sent MacArthur orders to advance north of the 38th on September 27.[84]

Truman moved America and the UN from fighting a war for a limited aim to waging one for an unlimited political aim because achieving his purpose required the destruction of the North Korean regime. He changed the political aim; thus he changed the nature of the war. This was done with shallow consideration of the effects. Critically important decisions demand deep analysis. Changing the aim alters what the war is about for you, the enemy, your allies, and potential third-party actors that may now consider their interests threatened. Whether you think altering the aim threatens the interests of others is irrelevant if they see it as doing so.

Changing the political aim can also alter the ends–ways–means relationship, especially when moving from a defensive, limited aim to an unlimited one. If the aim changes, the mission changes; if the mission changes, the needed strategy likely changes, as do the force requirements. A complete reassessment is now necessary. Some US leaders envisaged worst-case scenarios such as Chinese or Soviet intervention but didn't take this seriously even though the administration feared it could bring about a Third World War. Truman later insisted that everything he did in Korea was to prevent a Third World War.[85] If true, why did he invade a Soviet client state?

The JCS feared that if the military pressure ceased, the North Koreans would regroup and told MacArthur his military objective was to destroy the North Korean armed forces. He was to keep at this as long as there was no entry by or threat of entry from Chinese or Soviet forces. He couldn't enter Chinese or Soviet territory and was ordered to use only Korean troops in the areas around the Chinese border. Later, Marshall told him to feel unhampered tactically in his operations north of the 38th parallel. As more reinforcements arrived, MacArthur's strength reached 300,000.[86]

ROK units crossed the 38th parallel on October 1. American forces followed on October 7. ROK elements reached Wonsan by the 11th, where the Marines later landed and composed most of the UN east wing. The Eighth Army was the larger force and formed the left or western wing of an advance spreading across the widening peninsula. All advanced against sporadic resistance. Pyongyang fell to ROK troops on October 20. They filled their canteens in the Yalu five days later. Tenth Corps, the right or western UN wing, continued to the Yalu and the Chinese border. In places, North Korean resistance stiffened.[87]

Before the Americans crossed into North Korea, the Chinese warned they would intervene if non-Korean troops came north. The State Department received a number of messages on October 3, 1950 relaying this. Similar information came from Moscow, New Delhi, and Stockholm, including via India's Beijing ambassador, K. M. Panikkar, and China's foreign minister, Chou Enlai. Nitze, director of the Policy and Planning Staff, also saw China's Panikkar warning. But Panikkar, Truman wrote, had no credibility in Washington because he had "played the game of the Chinese Communists fairly regularly." Truman raised the possibility of Chinese intervention with MacArthur on Wake Island on October 15. Like nearly every American leader, MacArthur saw China as lacking an interest in intervening and the capability. American leaders spent little time analyzing China's possible reaction and were more concerned with Moscow. The US failed to prepare militarily to counter either. The consensus was that China wouldn't intervene from fear of the results of war with the United States. Army Chief of Staff Collins wrote: "the Central Intelligence Agency had plenty of company; everybody was wrong."[88]

THE OTHER SIDE OF THE WALL: CHINA ENTERS THE WAR

The landings at Inchon destroyed Kim's plans and those of his Communist big brothers. Kim told Stalin on October 1, 1950 that he needed assistance the moment UN troops crossed the 38th. Barring that, he wanted help organizing "international volunteer units in China and other people's democracies." Stalin had already decided he wasn't dispatching troops as that would provoke confrontation with Washington and passed the buck to China. Mao worried about America declaring war. Stalin assured him the Sino-Soviet alliance would keep America from that and included a bluff, telling Mao that even if the Third World War did break out, "let it happen now, and not in a few years," when it was assumed Japan would be rearmed and the Western powers stronger. The Chinese debated hotly, then joined the fight. Mao believed China had to demonstrate solidarity with the world Communist movement and protect the revolution. If China did nothing, the US might "run wild" all over Asia and perhaps invade China. Mao feared Western forces dominating Korea and being on the Yalu on Manchuria's border, China's most industrially developed region. Aiding Mao's decision was the February 1950 Soviet–Chinese Treaty of Friendship, Alliance, and Mutual Assistance.[89]

Mao intended to take the entire peninsula and "solve" the Korea problem, writing "we shall aim at resolving the conflict, that is, to eliminate the US troops within Korea or to drive them and other countries' aggressive forces out." Mao pursued an unlimited aim against South Korea as he intended to destroy it but had limited aims against Seoul's coalition partners as he sought their expulsion. Chinese troops – 260,000 – began crossing into North Korea on the night of October 19, 1950. Mao planned to attack ROK forces and isolated US units, then hold the mountainous regions of North Korea while increasing and reequipping his forces. If the US didn't advance past this area, in six months or so a settlement would occur. Mao expected "puppet" ROK troops to fold quickly but anticipated more difficulty defeating the Americans. Mao believed the path to victory was killing large numbers of US troops to raise the cost beyond what Washington was willing to pay, thus securing negotiations.[90]

US and South Korean soldiers faced their first Chinese troops on October 25. The South Korean II Corps collapsed; two US divisions were mauled. The Chinese stopped attacking on the night of November 6–7 and dropped from view. MacArthur postponed his November 15 offensive intended to reach the Yalu and unify Korea to the 24th. The JCS and Acheson approved. The administration tried to reassure China it wouldn't cross the Yalu. MacArthur's offensive attacked China's strategy, robbing them of their anticipated breathing space. Mao instead launched phase two of his offensive on November 25. China now had 450,000 troops in North Korea facing 220,000 coalition forces. US intelligence estimates placed Chinese strength at 15–20,000. Mao's attack lasted until December 24, inflicting a horrendous defeat upon the enemy. Winter temperatures dropped to –30 Fahrenheit. Broken UN units ran a gauntlet of ambushes and escaped south. Walker ordered them to reestablish north of Seoul. One of the few shining examples of American military behavior came from the US Marines who, with some army and British units, conducted a fighting retreat from the Chosin (Chongjin) Reservoir and were evacuated by sea from Hungnam with the surviving elements of X Corps and 100,000 refugees. The Chinese facing them suffered 40,000 casualties from combat and cold.[91]

WASHINGTON SEARCHES FOR A RESPONSE

A November 28, 1950 MacArthur cable began: "We face an entirely new war." When China entered the war, its nature changed. American political and military figures began considering ways to increase the amount of force being used and expand the war's geographic boundaries. The war also began straining America's relations with its allies. On November 30, Truman said at a press conference that using atomic weapons was on the table. Overwhelming international criticism induced White House "clarifications." British Prime Minister Clement Attlee immediately flew to Washington. He worried the US was being distracted from strengthening NATO and Truman promised to consult the British about using atomic weapons, which London opposed. Local commanders saw no suitable targets, while American military leaders saw the war as a Soviet feint and wanted the weapons saved in case the Soviets moved in Europe. It is important to note that before the advent of hydrogen weaponry and intercontinental ballistic missiles (ICBMs), many saw atomic devices simply as larger bombs.[92]

In the first week of December 1950, MacArthur believed that if China's offensive continued, the constraints against air and naval attacks against China weren't removed, and no reinforcements arrived, UN forces would have to abandon the peninsula. But MacArthur said they could hold if he could launch a naval blockade of China, bomb it, beef up the UN forces in Korea with Chinese Nationalist units, "and possibly use atomic bombs." On the 19th, MacArthur again asked for reinforcements. JCS chair Bradley,

Secretary of Defense Marshall, Acheson, and Britain all opposed this as it would divert troops from Europe. Korea was a distraction from the more important *potential* area of conflict. The administration instead ordered four divisions to Europe to meet its NATO commitment, a decision not announced formally until February 1951. MacArthur remarked that after the Chinese intervention "I could obtain only a trickle of soldiers from Washington, under the plea that they were needed in Germany where there was no war." Later, more than one US military leader expressed distaste over America's allocation of its military means.[93] American and British leaders took council of their fears and failed to commit sufficient forces to the war they were fighting from worry about a war that never occurred.

The administration limited air attacks near North Korea's border with the Soviet Union and China from the war's early days. But Chinese entry meant constraints on airpower began falling away. In November 1950, the administration temporarily blocked a MacArthur request to bomb certain Yalu bridges but soon allowed strikes on their Korean ends, though not against powerplants and dams. MacArthur removed the constraint on attacking only military targets and the US began dropping incendiaries on cities. The administration didn't protest. MacArthur sought to expand the use of airpower into China itself, believing that since China had forced war upon America, the US should respond appropriately. Other leaders also advocated military action against China. MacArthur never wanted to put US troops into China but did want to bomb Manchuria and blockade China's coast.[94]

Self-imposed geographical constraints dictated where and sometimes how US forces were allowed to fight. Wars are always fought under constraints. The question is whether or not these are wise. The administration restricted combat operations to the peninsula and its surrounding waters because it feared expanding the war into China or the Soviet Union would cause a Third World War. Truman retained this constraint after China's entry even though it provided Beijing untouchable airfields and supply bases. Many disagreed then and later. One can argue Truman should have imposed *more* constraints on the use of airpower. It's difficult to see how incendiary raids against North Korean cities helped the UN along the road to victory. Later, when the US negotiated with Mao's representatives, bombing *North Korean* civilians did nothing to pressure the *Chinese* and possibly hindered securing a settlement as China and North Korea publicly vowed to never yield to such a blatant, tactical use of force.[95]

It slowly dawned on Truman and his advisors that the US would have to increase its military and economic strength to fulfill its NATO commitments and possibly fight a "major war" with China. On November 22, 1950, the administration ordered the army's expansion to eighteen divisions by June 30, 1954. On December 5, this plan was accelerated to June 1952 and included air force and navy expansion. Truman announced a state of national emergency on December 15, 1950 and directed two National Guard divisions to report in January 1951. Meanwhile, the JCS argued the Korean War was draining US military and economic resources and benefiting Beijing and Moscow. In the event of another world war, primarily against the Soviets, the Chiefs deemed Korea "strategically unimportant."[96] Why, then, did US military leaders push for invading North Korea if it was "strategically unimportant" in the event America received its worst-case result?

By mid December, the Chinese had driven the UN forces to the 38th parallel. China's third-phase offensive ran December 31, 1950 to January 8, 1951. Mathew B. Ridgway, an experienced Second World War combat commander, became UN commander on December 29, Walker having perished in a jeep accident. MacArthur thought the best they could hope for was to inflict "a broadening defeat" upon the enemy and keep South Korea. MacArthur told Ridgway "We are now operating in a mission vacuum while diplomacy attempts to feel its way," and ordered Ridgway to hold "as far north as possible" and keep Seoul "for political and psychological reasons but not allow it to become a fixed position." Ridgway tried to hold north of Seoul and counterattack, but Chinese pressure and the state of the UN units forced him to withdraw. By January 15, 1951, the battle lines lay south of Seoul and the Chinese had run out of steam.[97]

The JCS ordered MacArthur to hold several points north of the old Pusan Perimeter and "to damage the enemy as much as possible, subject to the primary consideration of the safety of his troops and his continuing responsibility for the defense of Japan." If Chinese pressure necessitated withdrawing troops from Korea, the JCS would make this decision. MacArthur replied on January 10, 1951 that "the two courses of action were incompatible in that they could not be carried out simultaneously." Collins, MacArthur's superior, described the dilemma facing his subordinate and believed MacArthur wanted "a spelling-out of the continuing political objectives that should govern the decision whether the United Nations forces should remain in Korea and under what conditions." Collins noted the key problem: the military leaders kept trying to get the State Department to detail the political aims now that China had intervened, but the diplomats would only respond by asking for delineation of military capabilities. The JCS stuck to their December 30, 1950 directive that it was "in the national interest to hold as long as possible so as to permit diplomatic and military consultations with other United Nations members, to maintain United States prestige throughout the world, and to sustain confidence in the United Nations and, among our allies, in NATO."[98]

As the UN forces continued their retreat and approached the 38th parallel, Collins noted that State still refused to deliver a political aim for the war in Korea "until military capabilities there were established," while the JCS wanted a political decision so they could determine the required military courses of action. Collins eloquently described the problem:

> The State Department representatives were laboring under the same basic difficulty as the Chiefs: the lack of a clear United States or United Nations *policy* [political aim] with respect to Korea in the light of the existing circumstances. Such a policy could only be determined by the National Security Council for the United States – and, for all practical purposes, for the United Nations – and by the heads of state of the nations actively participating in the war. On the other hand, the National Security Council needed recommendations from the State Department staff and the JCS to assist it in determining the basic policy. This was what the State-JCS discussions were struggling to provide. But under our American philosophy that the military should be subservient to civilian control – to which the JSC fully subscribed.

The confusion over the political aim continued through the winter and early spring of 1951.[99] Truman and Acheson failed by not addressing this.

Ridgway rehabilitated his army and launched a counteroffensive on January 25, 1951, and recaptured Inchon in early February. The Chinese responded with their fourth-phase campaign from January 25 to April 21. The recovery of UN forces surprised them. The coalition fought a series of defensive actions and launched counterattacks in which the Chinese suffered grievously. The primary Communist blow began on the night February 11–12. Ridgway's forces broke it. By mid February, the Communists were retreating. Another UN offensive beginning on March 7 recaptured Seoul and put UN troops on the 38th parallel. Further success followed in March and April.[100]

As Ridgway pushed back the Chinese, MacArthur laid the foundation for his own dismissal. Truman was eager to be done with Korea and decided to announce his willingness to negotiate. The JCS told MacArthur this would come on March 20, 1951, and asked what parameters he would need to fight north of the 38th. MacArthur responded by issuing his own offer to negotiate that resembled an ultimatum. Truman canceled his proposal and hoped continued military pressure would suffice to convince the enemy to seek an armistice.[101]

A rightly angry Truman was debating firing MacArthur when the general committed another of many insubordinate acts. Republican House leader Joseph W. Martin had asked MacArthur's opinion about several war-related issues. MacArthur criticized the administration in a letter Martin read on the House floor. Truman relieved MacArthur on April 11. Ridgway replaced him on April 14. General James A. Van Fleet assumed Ridgway's post. A political firestorm for Truman ensued, as did a series of Congressional hearings and investigations into the conduct of the war. Truman was supported in his decision by the JCS, including their head, Bradley, and Secretary of Defense and retired general Marshall.[102]

Truman rightly fired MacArthur for insubordination and probably should have done it sooner. But something forgotten here is MacArthur's accurate complaint in the wake of China's intervention that he hadn't received clear political guidance from his superiors regarding what he was supposed to achieve in Korea now that the war included China. MacArthur said in a Congressional hearing: "I felt that the position I was in, the military position, was untenable without having some directive, some mission which was more realistic than that which existed at the time; and I felt, in all conscience, I could not go on ordering men to their deaths by the thousands, in such a complete vacuum of policy decisions."[103] None of this, though, excuses MacArthur's behavior. He had numerous official channels through which to voice complaints.

When Ridgway replaced MacArthur, he faced the same problems: a lack of clear political direction, and confused and contradictory military constraints, particularly on deploying troops above the 38th, that made it impossible for Ridgway to do what his orders said. For example, he was ordered to destroy the Chinese and North Korean armies but couldn't advance into North Korea beyond the Kansas–Wyoming Line, a defensive line slightly north of the 38th parallel, without Washington's approval. Also, since he couldn't withdraw troops from Korea without permission, his orders defining his primary mission as the defense of Japan robbed him of the authority to dispatch forces there if needed.[104]

Meanwhile, the MacArthur hearings in Congress focused attention on the war. On May 17, 1951, Truman approved NSC 48/5. The US political aim became reestablishing peace based on the prewar frontiers. Ridgway, after much wrangling, now received orders he could fulfill. On May 31, 1951, he was instructed to terminate the war at the 38th parallel. On June 1, he was ordered to: "Inflict maximum personnel and materiel losses on the forces of North Korea and Communist China operating within the geographic boundaries of Korea and waters adjacent thereto, in order to create conditions favorable to a settlement of the Korean conflict." The JCS still forbid any significant advance beyond the Kansas–Wyoming line, but Ridgway now knew what he was supposed to do. Collins wrote that after the change in political aim, "The purpose of US and UN forces from this point was to put enough pressure on the enemy and kill enough of them to make them sign an agreement that would end the war." The strategy became attrition. The Communists by this point were implementing the same strategy. But here is an example where technological superiority, especially at the tactical level, gave the US a leg-up in a situation where attrition might seem counterintuitive: the US had a much greater ability to kill the enemy.[105] To make this work, though, the US had to be willing to act when the opportunity came, and risk its own forces.

All of this demonstrates terrible problems with the administration's creation of political aims and strategy. It only made the key decision to determine the purpose of its war in Korea – the political aim – "after General MacArthur, the Joint Chiefs of Staff, and the senatorial investigating committee investigating General MacArthur's dismissal had attempted to discover what we were trying to accomplish in the war."[106]

THE DECISIVE MOMENT?

Mao still aimed to remove the Americans from the peninsula and developed a new strategy in February and March 1951: "Rotational Warfare." The Chinese would continually rotate troops in and out of Korea while trying to inflict enough casualties to break America's will to fight – a form of attrition. He poured troops into Korea. These numbered 950,000 by mid April. The North Koreans fielded 350,000. The UN had 340,000, including 150,000 Americans. Mao launched a fifth offensive from April 22 to June 10, 1951. It proved disastrous for the Chinese, who suffered 105,000 casualties and inflicted about 40,000. Many of these resulted from Ridgway spotting China's overextension and attacking across the entire front on May 19. The UN forces began capturing thousands of prisoners and large amounts of equipment.[107]

The US now had an opportunity. The Communist forces were exhausted and suffering immense logistical difficulties. Breaking them would give the US leverage and increase the chances of securing an armistice or perhaps even a peace treaty. But there would be costs. Van Fleet, who now ran the ground war, believed that from May 22 to June 10, 1951 the UN had the opportunity to crush the Chinese. He thought a land offensive, combined with an amphibious invasion at Tongchon behind the

Communist lines south of Wonsan on the peninsula's eastern shore, would allow encirclement and destruction of retreating Chinese forces and establishment of a defensive line across the peninsula's narrowest part, roughly from Pyongyang to Wonsan. "We had him beaten and could have destroyed his armies," Van Fleet later wrote. But the US failed to act, squandering an advantage. After June 10, Van Fleet thought the Chinese too well dug in. Ridgway refused to give Van Fleet his leash because the operations would have meant a US attack beyond the Kansas–Wyoming line (removing this constraint necessitated discussion with many Federal branches and foreign governments), rumors of a ceasefire were in the wind, and he considered the key UN forces exhausted and in need of rest.[108]

The Chinese were ripe for destruction. At the end of May and in early June 1951, their eroding military position frightened them, and they feared being pushed back to the Pyongyang–Wonsan line. Mao wanted a two-month pause (June and July) to prepare for renewed offensive operations in August. Mao wrote Kim: "If the enemy does not make large-scale amphibious landings in our rear, then our goal can be achieved. If the enemy does not send new reinforcements and does not make an amphibious landing, then in August we will be significantly stronger than now." By June 1951, China decided it couldn't win the war but could deny the Americans victory by protracting the conflict via limited attacks and a ceasefire. Talks between Kim, Mao, and Stalin ensued during the first two weeks of June and Stalin gave his permission to seek an armistice. By this time, the US had stopped advancing and made clear it wanted talks. Americans would have benefited from heeding Sun Tzu's advice to be suspicious of your enemy's desire to negotiate.[109]

Should the US have tried to defeat the Chinese force in the hopes this would lead to negotiating an acceptable peace? The US didn't take the chance and the UN forces instead began slowly and methodically pushing back the Communists. China asked for armistice talks and US pressure subsided. Mao used the breather to dig in and reconstitute his forces. Criticism of the decision to halt and negotiate has been intense: Henry Kissinger, Bernard Brodie, Raymond Aron – all insist it was a mistake.[110] The war continued for two more years.

THE ARMISTICE NEGOTIATIONS

Truman first announced his desire to negotiate in an April 11, 1951 radio address to the American people. Kennan met with the Soviet UN representative, Jacob Malik, on May 31 and again on June 5, and Ridgway was told negotiations were in the offing. The first public call for an armistice came from Malik on June 23. A statement from Soviet Deputy Foreign Minister Andrei Gromyko followed on June 27. The UN ruled the US could negotiate an armistice. An agreement was also made to negotiate via the military commanders, a task they undertook only because Truman made them. Ridgway was instructed "that the chief interest of the United States was to end the fighting and to obtain assurances that it would not be renewed." He was to stick to military matters aimed at doing this, not political issues pertaining to Korea's fate (this is an important distinction). Ridgway broadcast on June 30 that the US had received word of interest in an armistice and was willing to talk. The July 1 reply led to talks beginning at Kaesong on July 8.[111]

South Korean President Rhee resisted: he wanted unification. Van Fleet said of Rhee: "When the truce talks began in July of 1951, he warned they were a trick to save a defeated enemy. That has turned out to be precisely true." The head of the UN armistice delegation, American Vice Admiral C. Turner Joy, believed this was demonstrated on July 12, 1951, when Ridgway forbade the UN delegates to return to the talks at Kaesong until the Communists agreed to honor their commitment to remove troops from the meeting area and stop interfering with delegates' movements. Joy wrote: "Their urgent need for a breathing spell left the Communists no choice except that of acceding to General Ridgway's just demands."[112]

Both sides used military action to influence negotiations and the enemy's behavior, sometimes successfully. Large-scale attacks subsided when the negotiations began, but Ridgway increased air and naval interdiction against Communist supply lines and communications and launched heavy bombing raids against Pyongyang, all intended to injure the enemy's ability to grow stronger. After a number of incidents at the negotiation site, the talks were suspended on August 22. Ridgway refused to allow their renewal until they were moved to a new location – Panmunjom – which would prevent Communist interference or manipulation.[113]

Between the suspension of the talks on August 22 and their recommencing on October 25, the fighting continued. American attacks improved their defensive positions and, in Ridgway's opinion, encouraged the Communists to return to the table. They also provoked anger in the US because of the casualties. But American negotiators found the UN autumn 1951 offensive an effective negotiating tool. In the midst of this, the Communists suddenly became cooperative. Admiral Joy wrote later: "I am convinced beyond any doubt that had our powerful offensive during the autumn of 1951 continued, we would have had an armistice in Korea a year earlier than we did."

The primary lesson of Joy's account of leading the negotiators is that military pressure should be maintained until an agreement is reached. Ridgway told Van Fleet to go on the defensive when the talks resumed. Operation STRANGLE, the ongoing air interdiction effort, continued, and the coalition launched Operation RATKILLER, which lasted until January 1952 and killed or captured nearly 20,000 bandits and guerrillas in South Korea.[114] The war evolved into a stalemate characterized by small offensives and trench warfare reminiscent of the First World War.

Public support also began to wane. This affects the duration of a war and sometimes how it is waged. Like their 1960s successors, Truman's officials worried the public leaned toward overreaction and might be uncontrollable. This restrained the administration's rhetoric, but it also needed to mobilize support, which it initially enjoyed. In a July 1950 poll, 77 percent of Americans said the US should keep fighting in Korea, 12 percent said stop and leave, while 11 percent held no opinion. But support dropped steadily. After MacArthur's firing, Truman's approval rating never topped 33 percent, and approval for the war never rose above 50 percent. By April 1951, 51 percent of Americans felt the war a mistake, 35 percent didn't, and 14 percent had no opinion. A bribery and corruption scandal among Truman administration cronies drove his approval rating to 23 percent in December 1951. Support among allies also fell. Truman's public approval was less than 30 percent when he decided to not run for reelection. The war became a key reason for the 1952 Republican electoral victory.[115]

The Communists may have agreed to the October 25, 1951 resumption of armistice talks but both Stalin and Mao saw benefit in continuing the war. To Stalin, it was a cheap distraction that allowed the gathering of intelligence about the US while keeping its military tied down and enabling him to keep China on a tight leash. Mao found it useful for foreign prestige and to get developmental aid from Moscow to modernize civilian and military structures. China also saw the possibility of the US–South Korea alliance collapsing over Rhee's desire to unify Korea.[116]

On the US side, the negotiations were injured by "the lack of firm instructions from Washington." Joy and his team didn't have final decision-making authority. They suffered from the vacillation of superiors far away who themselves faced domestic pressure to end an increasingly unpopular war. The Communists had no such burdens and could stall for concessions. Additionally, the talks were decisively influenced by the constraints placed upon the use of force. The UN negotiators never worked from a position of strength.[117]

The biggest sticking point to agreement surrounded the repatriation of prisoners of war. The US refused to force any Korean or Chinese prisoners it held to return to Communist lands. China branded this insulting. A full exchange of prisoners meant equal standing and Beijing didn't see itself as a defeated power – with good reason: it had fought the US to a draw. "This negotiation is not one between winners and losers," the head of the Chinese negotiating team told his people in November 1951. But the prisoners were sometimes South Koreans dragooned into the North Korean army or former Chinese Nationalist soldiers. Many didn't want to return to a totalitarian state, and Truman and Acheson refused to make them. Acheson had opposed the forced repatriation of former Soviet citizens who had served the Germans during the Second World War and knew imprisonment and execution awaited. Many US military commanders and negotiators were unhappy with this decision as it prolonged the war and thus the fighting and dying. Ridgway supported forced repatriation if this was the only thing preventing peace. Joy believed Truman's decision placed the security of enemy POWs over that of US and UN prisoners, saying: "Since we were not allowed to achieve a victory, I wanted the war halted."[118]

After seemingly endless negotiations, on April 28, 1952 Joy gave the Communists the UN's final terms and left to take up a new post. The armistice talks went on until being suspended on October 8, 1952. They resumed on April 6, 1953. The agreement eventually signed on July 27, 1953 – fifteen months after the April 1952 agreement – was substantially the same, barring its prisoner provisions.[119]

THE WAR CONTINUES

On May 12, General Mark W. Clark replaced Ridgway. The war had settled into something akin to the First World War in France, but the American use of airpower increased. In May 1952, the air war shifted to a pressure strategy targeting Communist material strength and infrastructure to "pressure" the enemy into a deal. Attacks on the rail system continued but electrical power generation, particularly hydroelectric power, including the Yalu plants, were prioritized, beginning on June 23. Attacks on airfields, communication centers, war industry, and cities, including Pyongyang, were added, or increased. The city raids provoked international criticism. US assessments showed most urban areas had suffered from 40 to 90 percent destruction.[120] It is difficult to see how bombing *North Korea* could convince *China* to come to terms.

By summer 1952, the front stretched for 120 miles. China didn't think a decisive victory possible but began offensive operations in September 1952. Van Fleet, who was still the operational commander, suggested an attack to strengthen the UN line by taking the hills in the Iron Triangle, an area slightly left of the center of the peninsula near the 38th parallel. He predicted fewer than 200 killed and Clark approved. The attack produced 9,000 casualties. Clark resisted subsequent offensive operations, saying later: "I couldn't see the wisdom of paying lives for pieces of ground in Korea unless we were going all out to win the war."[121]

But Clark wanted to win. On October 16, 1952, after armistice talks collapsed, he proposed a plan resembling earlier proposals: OPLAN 8-52. Pyongyang would be seized in a two-pronged attack followed by an amphibious landing at Wonsan and airborne landings behind the Communist lines, a naval blockade of China, and even naval and air attacks. A subsequent push to the narrow waist of Korea was intended to destroy the Communist forces. Clark intended to win the war or secure an armistice.[122] Approval wasn't forthcoming.

EISENHOWER TAKES COMMAND

On January 20, 1953, Dwight Eisenhower was inaugurated president. Ike had been skeptical of the Truman administration's handling of Korea from the beginning. In 1950, after meetings at the Pentagon with many of his old subordinates, he feared Truman didn't understand the scale of the conflict and that army leaders had failed to make its difficulties clear to their president. He also found disconcerting talk around Washington about a so-called "limited conflict," remarks apparently directed at the level of means used for fighting. Eisenhower wrote: "My whole contention was that an appeal to force cannot, by its nature, be a partial one."[123]

Eisenhower's election frightened the Chinese, particularly his promise to bring peace to Korea through "deeds" instead of "words." During his campaign, Eisenhower promised that if elected, he would visit Korea. He did so on December 5–8, 1952. On his trip home, Ike decided more had to be done to force the enemy to make an agreement, including using or threatening to use atomic weapons as this offered the hope of being less costly in lives by forcing a quick armistice. After his inauguration, Clark was told to revise OPLAN 8-52 to include atomic weapons while the administration told the Communists the war could intensify unless an armistice was signed.[124]

Discussions regarding atomic weapons use in Korea were not unusual. On June 28, 1950, then General Eisenhower suggested this. On July 9, 1950,

JCS chair Bradley, when responding to a request from MacArthur for more support, suggested the JCS consider using atomic weapons. Both the army and air force studied their use in Korea and found them tactically unsuitable. The army also doubted the political utility, and neither service thought their use of much psychological value. The army did think they might be valuable in an emergency.[125]

Stalin died on March 5, 1953. The new Soviet chiefs feared the war's expansion and told Kim they wanted a negotiated settlement. Kim and Mao agreed. Mao realized his military assistance from Moscow was in peril if he delayed but launched one last offensive from April to July 1953 to punish the enemy. The war might have soon ended without Stalin's death as he had decided to make the necessary concessions before his March 1, 1953 stroke.[126]

The armistice talks resumed on April 26, 1953, after China suggested a neutral nation ensure prisoners were allowed to decide their fate. A few weeks before, an Eisenhower administration reassessment of alternative courses of action for ending the war led to April 1953's NSC 147. It presented options under two broad categories: maintaining or removing the constraints on military action. Alternative uses of force included previous suggestions such as raising China's cost beyond what it could bear via air attacks and a naval blockade, and an offensive to seize the narrow waist of Korea that inflicted massive damage on the Communist forces. A last option combined these with the destruction of Communist armies in Korea and the political aim of establishing a unified, non-Communist Korea. It also considered using atomic weapons. At a May 13, 1953 NSC meeting, Eisenhower suggested something in line with the administration's ongoing Project Solarium reassessment: it might be cheaper to use atomic weapons in Korea, something he knew would have political costs. He also said that expanding the war to China would be politically dangerous to the US because most Europeans feared a global war more than Communist expansion. He knew Europeans were instrumental to US defense and thus had to consider their views.[127]

On May 19, 1953, the JCS recommended pursuing a combination of actions from NSC 147 and the next day briefed Eisenhower on Clark's revised OPLAN 8-52. It urged a surprise, massive use of force including strategic bombing, atomic weapons, air and naval attacks against China, an offensive to seize Korea up to its waist, and preparations for follow-on operations. May 1954 was a possible launch date. The administration decided that if it became clear the enemy wouldn't sign an armistice, the US would expand the war into China via an attack including atomic weapons.[128]

As negotiations and the administration's internal debate continued, the US ratcheted up pressure on the Communists from the air. In May 1953, UN forces began hitting the dams of North Korean reservoirs to attack the North's food supply. This was driven by the ultimately futile belief it would destroy rice production and result in farmers blaming the North Korean government for the war.[129] Too often, particularly in the use of airpower, American strategists assume attacks will produce a result that depends upon the reactions of people the strategists do not understand and cannot control.

At the ongoing armistice negotiations, China's prisoner repatriation proposal produced bickering and maneuvering. For once, the US followed the Communist practice of taking a proffered concession and demanding more. Realizing the error, the administration backtracked while, as we have seen, deciding to expand the war if the talks made no progress. On May 22, 1953, Clark received the final US armistice proposal and instructions to tell the enemy this was indeed the last offer. He was also authorized to end the truce talks and fight the war in new ways, including heavier bombing of the North Korean dikes critical to prevent flooding. The final UN offer was made on May 27. Meanwhile, Secretary of State John Foster Dulles delivered an ultimatum via Indian Prime Minister Jawaharlal Nehru that included a threat to use atomic weapons. Nehru said he never forwarded Dulles' atomic menace, and there is no indication that this influenced China's decision to sign the ceasefire. Ike never thought it did.[130]

The UN promise to break off talks combined with China's desire to end the war to produce agreement on an armistice line and construction of a neutral-nation prisoner repatriation commission. The Communists accepted the POW plan on June 4, 1953, but Rhee didn't want to stop the war because he sought a unified peninsula under the South Korean flag. He tried to sabotage the negotiations by unilaterally releasing 27,000 prisoners resisting repatriation. Rhee threatened to continue the war alone; the US threatened to let him. Warnings of abandonment, promises of a security pact, and – after he accepted the armistice – future economic aid pushed Rhee into line. Mao ordered attacks on ROK troops to apply pressure. Rhee agreed to "support" the armistice but refused to sign it.[131]

The terms were decided by July 12; it was signed on July 27, 1953. The UN suffered 45 percent of its casualties after negotiations began in 1951 – 124,000, including 9,000 US dead. Clark bitterly noted: "I believe that the Armistice, by and large, was a fair one – considering that we lacked the determination to win the war."[132]

SOME EFFECTS AND CONCLUSIONS

When a nation is trying to end a war there are three key, interrelated factors to consider: what to ask for politically, how far to go militarily, and who will enforce the peace and how. The US changed its political aim – twice – dithering for months before reverting to its initial limited aim. But then failed to apply sufficient force to convince the enemy to make peace while agreeing to talk when the enemy needed a pause. The US then spent two years applying insufficient means (the ground war) or ineffective means (the air war) in the hope of securing an armistice. One was finally obtained, partially by the promise of the continued presence of US forces. No peace treaty was concluded.

In his April 1951 address to Congress, MacArthur uttered the well-known phrase: "In war there is no substitute for victory." Overlooked is the previous sentence: "War's very object is victory, not prolonged indecision."[133] In the case of Truman's war in Korea, MacArthur was wrong. America got "prolonged indecision." This also depicts too many American wars, and often for the same reasons: refusing to acknowledge the nation is at war, a lack of military preparedness, not understanding the importance and effects of the political aim, shoddy analysis and assessment, underestimating the enemy, and refusing to supply the means needed to achieve the war's political aim. These are the most devastating flaws in American warfighting.

One thing the Truman administration got right in regard to the Korean War, at least partially, was to pay for it. The fiscally conservative Truman insisted on covering its costs via taxes as much as possible, including an excess profits tax and various other increases. But Truman also instituted wage and price controls that led to a 1952 confrontation with some steel manufacturers. Truman seized the mills, found himself blocked by the courts, and then had to endure a strike by steel workers that helped cause an ammunition shortage.[134]

The North Korean invasion frightened America's European allies, who now feared a Soviet invasion. America wanted the Europeans to bear the main burden of defending themselves and tried to convince its allies of the necessity of German assistance. The glacial pace of European rearmament undermined the first, French resistance slowed the second, which meant America sent troops to Europe on a scale it had hoped to avoid. The poor performance of US military forces in Korea injured American military credibility in Germany.[135] And as we will see, the civil–military relations breakdown due to MacArthur contributed to problems between the military and civilian leaders during the Vietnam War.

PART II: FROM GREAT POWER TO SUPERPOWER

The Cold War, the Communist victory in China, and the Korean War drove changes in US plans for Japan. Economic revitalization and political stability began supplanting democratization and the dismantling of Japanese business cartels as the main planks of US Japan strategy. The US returned to Japan its sovereignty and made a peace treaty earlier than intended. Japanese leaders accepted US bases but resisted efforts to rearm Japan and agreed only to a 50,000-man "police reserve force." As in Europe, the US carried the defense burden.[136]

The Korean War became known as America's first "limited war" and proved one catalyst for "limited war theory." This was a flawed, means-based analytical approach that often confused peace and war and created bad theory from false pictures of events. For example, Harvard economist Thomas Schelling, one of the best-known writers on "limited war," likened the Korean War to a "negotiation" over the fate of that country. North Korea sought to annex South Korea using military force – violence – to achieve a particular political aim. The US and UN used military force – more violence – to keep this from happening. To say this was anything other than a war obscures the nature of the problem and removes "war" from writing about war.[137]

The manner in which the US constrained use of military means in the Korean War presents a mixed picture. The desire to support NATO commitments is understandable, but this injured the American ability to support allies in Asia and fight the war it had decided to fight and then expand. Truman simply refused to commit what was necessary to quickly achieve the aims he decided to pursue and, in the end, to win. America and its UN allies paid in blood for this because the war continued longer than it should have. As a war goes on, its costs and risks rise.

Who won the Korean War? Victory in a war – not in battle – is defined by the achievement of the political aim sought. All the powers involved were frustrated in Korea. China, the US, and North and South Korea all wanted control of the peninsula at some point. All were ultimately denied. Some judge Stalin the winner as the war cost the Soviets little. But Moscow got militarization of the Cold War, American and European rearmament, and West Germany rearmed as a NATO ally because of a war Stalin approved and that would have been all but impossible without his support. China kept the West from its border. The US eventually secured South Korean independence, a boon to South Koreans. One could judge these effects as victory, but certainly not ones wisely achieved. The Korean people lost the most.

ASSESSING THE TRUMAN ADMINISTRATION, 1945–53

Truman had no preparation for constructing grand strategy. If America's leaders had any formal geopolitical education, it focused upon the teachings of Halford J. Mackinder and Nicholas John Spykman. Both essentially saw the world as being a "Eurasian Heartland with peripheral Rimlands" and worried that the US could find itself isolated geographically, something that seems far-fetched considering its size, power, and attractiveness as a market. One author gives us a particularly harsh judgment of Truman: "He had little or no grasp of grand strategy or military power. Worse, he did not concede that weakness. On the contrary, he fancied that with one or two exceptions he knew more about the military and grand strategy than all his generals and admirals put together."[138]

Truman seems to have been unable to tell the difference between the political aim sought and the strategy for achieving it, while simultaneously disagreeing with nearly every commentator since about the key component of his administration's grand strategy. Truman wrote in his 1955 memoir: "Our foreign policy was mistakenly called by some a policy of containment. This is not true. Our purpose was much broader. We were working for a united, free, and prosperous world."[139] One hardly knows where to begin with such a statement. Truman mixes an expressed political aim – "a united, free, and prosperous world" – with the grand strategy for achieving it – "containment" – something that is not unusual. Far more interesting is his insistence that his administration – the one in which Kennan coined the term "containment" – was doing no such thing. This is perhaps the most important thing one needs to know about Truman and grand strategy.

11

THE HOT PEACE: THE EISENHOWER, KENNEDY, AND JOHNSON YEARS, 1953–1969

THE DWIGHT EISENHOWER ADMINISTRATION, 1953–61

The United States emerged fully into its new global role in the 1950s. It had military forces stationed across the world, supported by what was for Americans the novel practice of peacetime conscription. The military and its support system expanded so dramatically Eisenhower famously warned in his January 1961 farewell address of the dangers of an entrenched "military-industrial complex." The nation's civilian arms also grew. The State Department now had 20,000 employees, a fourfold increase from before the Second World War. The US soon had military alliances or support agreements with forty-two nations, spent $5 billion annually on foreign aid, and spied on the Soviet Union via numerous intelligence agencies.[1] The founders would have called this anathema, but they would have recognized the political aim this was supposed to deliver: the security of the United States.

Before becoming president, Eisenhower developed solid views of the Soviet Union and how to counter its threat to America and the Free World, ideas shaped by his postwar positions as JCS chair and SACEUR at NATO. He saw a militarily strong Soviet system afflicted by internal weakness with leaders who understood only force, views not unlike Kennan's. Eisenhower believed only America could provide the leadership to counter Moscow and needed to apply "the full influence deriving from our financial, economic, political and military power." Europe remained the primary front as American security depended upon maintaining Europe's freedom and security. NATO was a key tool. American assistance would build this strength, but each ally should provide its core defense. Eisenhower valued economic power and understood how this supported both the ability of a nation to defend itself and underpinned its national morale. Human rights and cultural issues also couldn't be ignored. The security of the US depended upon wise consideration and use of all of this.[2]

Eisenhower agreed with NSC 68's assessment that the global balance of power was so fine America could surrender nothing else to Communism, but with little else in it. He considered Truman's containment strategy "incoherent and immorally passive." It surrendered the initiative and allowed too many people to fall under Communism's yoke. Moreover, Ike saw the military's growth under Truman as economically dangerous and potentially undermining US strategy by detrimentally altering American society. He feared this driving inflation or more government economic control and intervention, and the necessary high taxes threatened public support and the economy. Ike thought money better spent on domestic improvements.[3] He, with Secretary of State John Foster Dulles, shifted American grand strategy.

REASSESSMENT: THE SOLARIUM PROJECT

In late spring 1953, the administration launched the Solarium Project, so named because of its first meeting in the White House solarium. Part of a general reassessment, it examined strategic options with the intent of developing a new grand strategy for dealing with the Soviet Union and the Communist threat. The three teams considered different visions, and the June 1, 1953 instruction pointed out the diversity of American political aims and that some aims possessed more value than others. The team chaired by Kennan won out.[4] The grand strategy that emerged was the New Look.

THE POLITICAL AIMS AND THE NEW LOOK

The reassessment produced NSC 162/2 in October 1953, a document intended to help America "meet the Soviet threat to US security." NSC 162/2 retained Kennan's analysis of Soviet revolutionary motives and aims, and discussed Moscow's growing atomic and nuclear strength, unrest among subject peoples in the USSR and Eastern Bloc, and the solidification of Communist control of China. It didn't expect the Soviets to go to war in the near term but noted Moscow would continue subversion against the West and take advantage of nascent nationalist movements. Some in the administration, especially Secretary of State Dulles, ascribed to Moscow a coherent and well-executed program of expansion that was nonexistent. Others, like Eisenhower, sometimes mistakenly saw Moscow behind international events when it wasn't. The aim in January 1955's NSC 5501 was "to preserve the security of the United States, and its fundamental values and institutions." December 1953's NSC 174 established a long-range political aim of Soviet Bloc states having the right to choose their own governments.

The US would encourage dissent but not push Moscow to go to war over this or encourage subject peoples to rise prematurely.[5]

The New Look, the administration's version of containment, sought to integrate the elements of national power to make America secure, and do so more effectively and efficiently at lower cost. It can be described as a grand strategy of deterrence because it sought to deliver security by deterring the Soviets from attacking the US and its allies. Deterrence, like all strategies, entails assuming risk, but it's difficult to mitigate risks with this approach, because the deterring power lacks explicit influence over opponents and can't disarm them. It is also difficult to determine the effects of actions upon opponents, particularly totalitarians.[6]

MILITARY STRATEGY

The most important military challenge facing Eisenhower was the Korean War, but this was only part of the picture. Eisenhower understood the difference between wartime and peacetime strategies, distinctions rooted in the political aims and the methods used to pursue them. Using military *power* in peacetime to deter an enemy, the essence of Cold War military strategy, was starkly different from using military *force* in wartime.[7]

Eisenhower's military strategy was built around US atomic and then nuclear weapons. He wasn't as convinced as many others that atomic weapons inaugurated a revolutionary change in warfighting. Dulles spoke of removing the employment taboo while Ike considered them just another weapon, a valuable addition to the conventional forces the US still needed. American atomic superiority compensated for Soviet material and manpower advantages. If the Soviets attacked, Eisenhower would have dispatched the Strategic Air Command bomber forces with their atomic payloads. Dulles' famous January 12, 1954 speech, an element of the administration's informational strategy for selling the New Look, discussed as part of collective security efforts the US intention to back local forces with "massive retaliatory power." "Massive retaliation" became a moniker for part of the administration's strategy. Being able to react in this manner, the administration believed, would allow regaining the initiative in the struggle with the Soviets while lowering costs as atomic and nuclear weapons were cheaper than large conventional forces, providing "a maximum deterrent at a bearable cost."[8]

Today, this emphasis on atomic weapons seems irrational. But in 1953 and 1954, one could consider using them in a war with the Soviets in which the nation survived, albeit in an injured state. New technology changed this.

Hydrogen weapons, first tested in 1952, possessed many times the destructive power and toxic fallout of their atomic predecessors.[9] But the development of Intercontinental Ballistic Missiles (ICBMs) in 1957 combined almost assured delivery with exponential explosive power, converting city killers into potential civilization killers. Defense writers expounding upon the complete deterrent power of such weapons also proved wrong, something that should have been apparent as early as 1951 when China entered the Korean War. America's nuclear weapons failed to deter the North Vietnamese and a myriad non-nuclear US enemies. But an attack by a dangerous superpower with the ability to destroy the United States would have produced a brutal American response.

Building a military strategy emphasizing atomic weapons meant restructuring the armed forces. Cuts fell hard on the army. Tactical atomic weapons were added; the strategic arsenal expanded. Bombers such as the B-52 entered service, and the nuclear triad arrived with the development of Minuteman (land-based) and Polaris (submarine-based) missiles. The US maintained conventional land forces, but the air force and navy dominated. It was believed any war with the Soviets would quickly produce a nuclear exchange. If it continued, America would create additional conventional forces. In conflicts not including the Soviets, the nations involved were expected to field most of the military units. Moreover, Eisenhower believed nuclear weapons made transporting large numbers of troops overseas likely impossible and, in a war with the Soviets, US troops would be needed at home to handle the aftermath. Civil defense became part of the American cultural fabric through "duck and cover drills" at schools. This marked a shift for Americans as they were now in the crosshairs of a potential enemy attack. There was a deterrence aspect in all of this as well. Eisenhower believed making a nuclear exchange the only American option in a war with Moscow the best way to insure it didn't happen.[10]

Ike supported international organizations, including the UN, and used alliances (a component of his deterrence strategy) to try to block the growth of Soviet influence. Alliances permitted Washington to cut defense. Eisenhower didn't want to burden America with the cost and responsibility of protecting every area threatened by Communism. Regional states could provide the ground forces while the US supplied naval, air, and, if necessary, atomic and nuclear backing. Eisenhower feared America's allies allowing Washington to shoulder the heaviest burden, which happened. He had little luck convincing the Europeans to sufficiently fund their own defense.[11] This problem remains.

PART II: FROM GREAT POWER TO SUPERPOWER

Ike built upon Truman's legacy to construct a barrier of states around the Soviet Union and China. The administration strengthened NATO by deploying tactical (battlefield) nuclear weapons to Western Europe in 1953. The Soviet manpower advantage was countered by the threat of immediate use if conflict erupted. Renewed fighting in Korea or a Chinese assault on Formosa (now Taiwan) were other likely atomic triggers. In 1954, the administration created the Southeast Asia Treaty Organization (SEATO) and in 1959 a regional alliance, the Central Treaty Organization (CENTO). CENTO evolved from the 1955 Baghdad Pact alliance after Iraq's 1959 exit and included Great Britain, Iran, Iraq, Pakistan, and Turkey. The US joined as an associate member in 1959, but the member states were connected to Washington by military aid and advisors. CENTO failed to defuse regional tensions, and critics argued it fed them, as some members found it intrusive.[12] It dissolved in 1979.

Moscow launching the first artificial satellite, Sputnik, in October 1957 shocked Americans and US strategic thinking. The technology for putting a satellite into space could produce missiles able to strike America from Soviet soil within thirty minutes. Americans now worried the USSR could build ICBMs earlier than believed possible. Democrats attacked Eisenhower by claiming the US had fallen behind the Soviets in missile production, a falsehood fed by the flawed Congressional Gaither Committee Report overestimating Soviet industrial capabilities. A supposed "missile gap" between the US and Moscow became an election stumping point. Senator Lyndon Johnson seized on it, held hearings to burnish his presidential credentials, and the Democrats won solid control of Congress in 1958. Eisenhower's efforts to defuse the issue failed, and he refused to release the intelligence information proving his political opponents wrong. Eisenhower also declined an expensive, crash-course expansion of US nuclear forces, especially since Soviet ICBM development was proceeding slowly. Eisenhower believed firmly in a concept later known as "sufficiency," the idea that increasing the number of weapons beyond a certain point has no purpose. America's successful January 31, 1958 satellite launch, combined with Eisenhower's calls to increase defense spending, helped his case. Subsequent increased military spending to offset this apparent Soviet leap forward produced unbalanced budgets for four years.[13]

Depending upon atomic and nuclear weapons didn't pass without criticism. There is doubt this led to regaining the initiative, and it could have restricted the administration's options in a crisis because it had insufficient conventional means. "Massive retaliation" was rapidly losing support by the end of the 1950s. This began early. Even Dulles questioned America's ability to deal with wars not justifying attacking the Soviet Union.[14]

DIPLOMATIC STRATEGY

Eisenhower was open to talks with Moscow and saw negotiations as a tool for resolving situations he thought couldn't safely continue. Eisenhower could negotiate without the charges of appeasement that might dog Democrats because Republicans were seen as stronger against Communism. Stalin's death created the opportunity. Ike extended the olive branch via an April 1953 speech, which Moscow's suspicions didn't initially allow it to grasp. Stalin had designated no successor, and Nikita Khrushchev emerged as leader after a power struggle. He launched de-Stalinization with a speech denouncing Stalin's crimes but sought the traditional Soviet aims of world revolution and expansion, while simultaneously desiring "peaceful coexistence" with the West to lessen tensions. Stuck between two poles, the Soviet leader increased global tensions with his actions abroad, while his efforts to reach an understanding with the West alienated Beijing. Khrushchev replaced Stalin's murderousness with caprice and a willingness to take risks abroad, while also negotiating. Eisenhower's five foreign minister meetings and three summits legitimized negotiations with Moscow but achieved little.[15]

Eisenhower balked at negotiations with China unless it abandoned aggressive behavior, though there were informal contacts. Amidst Chinese threats to invade Formosa, Eisenhower penned a mutual defense treaty with its Nationalist government in December 1954. The January 1955 Formosa resolution granted the president authority to defend Formosa without consulting Congress, a response to Chinese attacks on Quemoy and Matsu Islands that almost produced war between the US and China. In what became known as the Taiwan Straits Crisis, the public discussion included using atomic weapons in response to Beijing's attacks. The Communists kept 400,000 troops across the straits from Formosa, and as long as the face-off continued, Beijing demanded Soviet support. Moscow's refusal to back China during the 1955 and 1958 Matsu–Quemoy Crises fed Mao's discontent with Moscow. Ike supported the Nationalists to nurture this. The crises produced a neologism describing aspects of the administration's diplomatic strategy: "brinksmanship": in a 1956 interview, Dulles rattled on about how in dealing with other states one needed the courage to "go to the brink" to achieve success.[16]

A criticism of Eisenhower's New Look was that it didn't address revolutionary, nationalist, and independence movements emerging in the 1950s, particularly as European decolonization accelerated. Washington worried about decolonization's effects on its European allies, but Eisenhower wanted to be on the side of the independence movements and privately pushed the Europeans to free their colonies while receiving warnings from his advisors about the dangers of "premature independence." But the US feared Communism's expansion and worried about the new non-aligned movement (a loose-knit grouping of states siding with neither Washington nor Moscow). This invariably drove Washington to lean toward the Europeans. The administration hoped to channel national liberation movements away from Communism and opposed growing Third World Communism. Aid to indigenous forces – economic and military – was coupled with bilateral security pacts and advisors. Eisenhower believed doing more opened Washington to charges of imperialism.[17]

One danger of having allies is being dragged into their problems. In 1952, rebel Egyptian army officers led by Gemal Abdel Nasser turned Egypt into Pan-Arabism's center. Nasser wanted to end European control in the Middle East, especially British influence in Egypt, and was willing to work with the Communists to do it. In 1956, Nasser nationalized the Suez Canal, which became a pretext for an Anglo-French invasion. The real catalysts were Nasser buying arms from the Czechs (a Soviet client), French fear of Egyptian support for Algeria's rebels, and having the Soviets build the Aswan Dam. The British and French invaded to overthrow Nasser and recruited Israel to help. The badly planned and executed invasion caused an international crisis. Khrushchev threatened nuclear retaliation and to dispatch Soviet forces. A surprised Eisenhower demanded the invaders withdraw, injuring relations with Britain and France. The war exacerbated Ike's difficulties dealing with the 1956 Soviet invasion of Hungary.[18]

The aftermath saw the administration abandon hopes of negotiating peace between Israel and its neighbors. It began supplying military and economic aid to Arab states such as Jordan and Saudi Arabia and received Congressional approval for what is sometimes termed the Eisenhower Doctrine: the freedom to commit US troops to aid any nation threatened by Communism. The administration used this to intervene in Lebanon, which was threatened by the pro-Soviet, Pan-Arabism of the united Egyptian–Syrian state. The Soviets had threatened to send "volunteers" to support pro-Nasser rebels in Lebanon. Beirut's pro-Western government pled for help on July 14, 1958, and Washington, London, and Paris answered. US Sixth Fleet Marines landed on July 15 and the Soviet threat evaporated. Eisenhower called the Soviet bluff and the Marines departed on August 21.[19]

Washington tried to prevent the Communists from securing any foothold in the Southern Hemisphere. Guatemala's leftist President Jacobo Arbenz sparked fear in Washington when he legalized the Communist Party, began cooperating with it, and threatened to nationalize the assets of US companies, including expropriating unused lands. Weapons from Czechoslovakia catalyzed a 1954 US-backed coup.[20]

INFORMATION STRATEGY

The term "information strategy" encompasses what the administration inexactly termed "psychological warfare" (there was no war) and other actions supporting its deterrence strategy. Eisenhower and Dulles believed declarations of strength and determination with a firm face worried the Soviets. Information operations included sending printed material and radio broadcasts into the Communist world that often played on the appeal of the US system by publicizing differences between democratic freedom and Communist totalitarianism. Moscow tried driving wedges between the US and its allies; Washington reciprocated toward Moscow's control over its European satellites. This effort's credibility was destroyed by Eisenhower's refusal to respond militarily during the 1956 anti-Soviet Hungarian uprising. Democrats used the revolt and lack of US response to criticize the New Look. The popular Eisenhower easily won reelection, but his Republican Party lost control of both houses of Congress.[21]

The administration also launched covert operations that couldn't be directly attributed to Washington. "Subversion" is an apt descriptor. Eisenhower thought the seriousness of the international situation necessitated measures that previously wouldn't have been entertained. Some find this a moral shift. The opportunities here against the Soviet Bloc were few, considering Moscow's grip. But the world had become an arena. The administration inherited the basic tools for covert action and developed them. Most of the operations fell under the auspices of the Central Intelligence Agency (CIA) created in 1948. It was involved in attempts to overthrow a number of foreign governments from 1953 to 1961. It succeeded in Iran in 1953 and Guatemala in 1954, but failed in Syria in 1956–57, Indonesia in 1958, and Cuba in 1960–61. It engaged in intelligence gathering, spreading propaganda abroad, plotting assassinations of hostile leaders (Cuba's Fidel Castro, for example, who came to power in January 1959), and other activities the US had hitherto only seriously engaged in during wartime.[22]

ECONOMIC STRATEGY

The administration's economic strategy possessed domestic and foreign arms. Domestically, Eisenhower believed low taxes, low inflation, and a balanced budget would unleash America's talent to produce prosperity. The US was helped by Eisenhower's fiscal restraint. There was a short recession in 1958, but from 1952 to 1958 America enjoyed an economic boom as GDP grew nearly 4 percent annually. Median family income gained 30 percent in purchasing power in the 1950s; inflation was virtually nonexistent.[23] Prosperity was important for building the economic base critical for defense in a protracted struggle against the Communist world. Economic problems undermined civilian morale and thus support for government and its actions.

Overseas, the administration continued using lower American tariffs to raise living standards abroad, something assumed to combat Communist influence. Not everyone agreed with this approach, and former President Hoover was among the Republicans warning it would destroy the American textile, pottery, rubber products, and ceramics industries. Tariff concessions were granted to Japan during the negotiations for the peace treaty to secure Tokyo's military and political cooperation and tie Japan to the West. The concessions on Japanese textiles produced appeals from American companies. Enough concern arose over US trade practices that the Senate refused Eisenhower's 1958 request to renew the Reciprocal Trade Agreements Program (RTAP). Foreign development aid was used to help states resist Soviet encroachment and prevent the creation of leftist governments. In 1954, 95 percent of these funds were for military support; this dropped to 50 percent by 1960.[24]

VIETNAM AND INDOCHINA

Many of the strands of grand strategy came together in Indochina, especially Vietnam. Asking whether or not becoming involved here was in America's interest is important. On a purely material basis, whether this means natural resources or access to bases, Vietnam offered nothing significant to America. Eisenhower thought it was in the nation's interest to oppose the expansion of Communism and decided to do so in Indochina. Eisenhower believed in the Domino Theory: if a state fell to Communism, others in the region would follow. He made the phrase famous in April 1954, but it originated in relation to Greece's post–Second World War Communist insurgency. But Eisenhower had limits: no US troops.[25]

The French defeat at Den Bien Phu in May 1954 was followed by the Geneva Accords partitioning Vietnam along the 17th parallel into a Communist north under Ho Chi Minh and a non-Communist south under Ngo Dinh Diem while creating Laos and Cambodia. Vietnamese Communists held a commanding military position in Vietnam, but China pressured them to accept partition because they thought it would keep the US out and Vietnam divided. The Soviets backed partition to show France that Moscow wasn't dangerous and to discourage Paris from joining the European Defence Community. Ho needed outside support and put his ambitions on hold. The partition was intended as temporary until elections were held, but neither Diem nor the US signed the accords or felt the need to have elections that meant surrendering South Vietnam. To keep the South from Communism, the administration became its patron and embarked upon a grand strategy of nation building, emphasizing the construction of a South Vietnamese army on the hollow, Vietnamese force France had begun. A Military Assistance Advisory Group (MAAG) arrived in early 1956. Washington funded the Michigan State University Vietnam Advisory Group to guide economic development. The CIA's Edward Lansdale advised on counterinsurgency.[26]

Diem, a Vietnamese nationalist, became head of South Vietnam in June 1954. Former Emperor Bao Dai chose him as his titular successor largely because he knew Diem had the support of many US figures and Bao needed a rich patron. Devoutly Catholic, Diem spent a number of years in exile in the US, sometimes in religious communities. Personally incorruptible, he was autocratic, aloof, patriotic, and elitist. His survival was almost miraculous. He overcame military coups, opposition from religious sects, and virtual civil war against a bandit army. American money helped. August 1954's NSC 5429/2 saw the US paying for South Vietnam's government. By the end of the Eisenhower administration in 1961, the US had given Vietnam $7 billion in military and economic aid. South Vietnam was not unusual. France's defeat drove the establishment of SEATO and intensification of the application of various economic, diplomatic, and military planks of the grand strategy of containment to protect Japan and other nations in Asia.[27]

THE NEW SECURITY STRATEGY

In August 1959, the Eisenhower administration completed NSC 5906/1, a forerunner of the modern *National Security Strategy*. The idea for a single document encapsulating American political aims and grand strategy resurfaced during the Kennedy and Johnson administrations but wasn't adopted.

Though NSC 5906/1 suffers from a lack of consistency in its use of terminology, it is a grand strategy document in the best sense of the word. It gave the nation's "basic objective" as being "to preserve and enhance the security of the United States and its fundamental values and institutions." Its assessment identified the Soviet and Chinese Communist regimes as the greatest threats. The growing Soviet nuclear arsenal was viewed as the worst element of this danger, a factor emboldening the Soviets to act more aggressively. Though it sometimes used different terms, the document addressed diplomatic, informational, military, and economic strategies that the US should pursue. Diplomatically, while continuing "to provide leadership for the Free World," the US would maintain its alliances and friendships while expanding them through various means such as economic and military aid, building relationships, supporting decolonization, and helping thwart Communist subversion. The US would negotiate with the Soviets, seeking to halt nuclear weapons proliferation. Informationally, America would publicize the advantages of Western freedoms while overtly and covertly trying to undermine the influence and efforts of the Communist powers in their own spheres abroad. Militarily, in peacetime, deterrence based upon nuclear weapons remained the strategy, but the US and its allies needed to maintain the ability to successfully fight any war the Communists launched. Economically, the administration sought to strengthen the economies of America and its allies. Spurring growth at home and keeping inflation and Federal spending at bay were considered key. Free trade was viewed as strengthening the US and its allies and partners. The US would invest in developing the decolonizing world to thwart Communist influence and encourage its allies to do the same while supplying aid and loans where appropriate.[28]

CONCLUSION

Eisenhower's grand strategy was intended to deliver security while deterring Communist expansion, especially by the Soviet Union. Khrushchev considered Dulles a "worthy adversary" and admitted that it "kept us on our toes to match wits with him." The deterrence strategy as structured could only possibly work against the Soviet Union and nations they controlled and, as the Taiwan Straits Crisis perhaps proved, for China.[29] It didn't stop the revolution in Cuba that brought Castro to power or the slide of Egypt into the Soviet camp. But it's difficult to see how any administration could have prevented these events without going to war.

Eisenhower hoped to put the government on a better economic footing. Defense spending didn't decrease despite Eisenhower's best efforts. From fiscal year 1956's $42.5 billion it climbed to $49.6 billion in 1961. But defense spending as a percentage of the Federal budget and GDP declined as America's economy grew rapidly. The administration developed or built the forces that undergirded America's strategic nuclear capability for decades. The US was militarily stronger vis-à-vis the Soviets when Eisenhower left office.[30]

There were problems with the administration's military strategy. It relied heavily upon allies and friendly states for conventional forces. One danger here is the possibility of allies dictating your options because you lack the ability to do what you think needs doing. The administration rested upon atomic and then nuclear weapons. As these became more powerful, and the Soviet arsenal expanded, Dulles began doubting the efficacy of this. He began trying to shift the deterrence emphasis from dependence upon these weapons but met resistance from Eisenhower. Ike believed the way to avoid nuclear Armageddon was to make it clear that if the guns began firing this was the only possible result because the US had no other choice.[31]

Also popular was the assumption that using atomic or nuclear weapons might not unleash a larger nuclear exchange. This would have been a dangerous die to roll. One cannot control the actions of other states, especially great powers, and one never knows the enemy's mind. A massive literature developed beginning in the late 1950s on so-called "limited nuclear war." These works universally suffer from a means-based definition of "limited war" that ignores the aims being sought. They also assume the enemy inherently will agree to some kind of "limits" on the use of such weapons. This delusion ignored the tendency of war's violence to escalate toward the extreme (which here means rows of mushroom clouds) while ignoring Soviet political aims and strategic thinking. Moscow believed that *any* use of atomic or nuclear weapons – even so-called tactical ones – meant they had the right to reply in any manner against any target. Later Cold War Soviet war plans called for immediate nuclear strikes on NATO forces in Western Europe. The theory surrounding "limited nuclear war" was untethered from the historic behavior of peoples and states.[32]

THE JOHN F. KENNEDY AND LYNDON B. JOHNSON ADMINISTRATIONS, 1961–69

With the arrival of the new John F. Kennedy administration, strategy changed. Kennedy's advisors – the most important for our purposes being Secretary of State Dean Rusk and Secretary of Defense Robert

McNamara – also became Lyndon Johnson's team. They were, in the words of journalist David Halberstam, "the best and the brightest." They had intelligence and credentials (usually Ivy League) but suffered from inexperience and wishful thinking. To most observers, they lacked judgment as well as knowledge "of the world beyond America's shores." Questioning ingrained assumptions would have served them well.[33]

THE ASSESSMENT

Kennedy insisted America's interests were "best served by preserving and protecting a world of diversity in which no one power or no one combination of powers can threaten the security of the United States." The key idea was that American security would be assured as long as "neither Russia nor China could control Europe and Asia." Supporting the independence of other states was necessary, but Eisenhower had failed to provide the means. The administration agreed with its predecessor that America should try to guide the changes in the developing world and (mistakenly) that Communism was a monolithic force. Both administrations also didn't insist nations receiving support be democracies, though they preferred and hoped for this. It was more important to keep them from Communism because the larger the number of nations in this circle, the more difficult and inhospitable the global environment for America.[34]

To meet the Communist threat, it was necessary to expand America's military means. Conventional means had to increase to avoid having to rely heavily upon nuclear deterrence and provide options. Kennedy also wanted more financial resources and believed Eisenhower worried too much about balancing the budget. Growing the economy would allow more money for defense and other programs. Kennedy wanted the US to have the option to respond diplomatically, economically, and in a broad range of military circumstances.[35]

A confluence of factors altered the nature of the global competition between the US and the Communist world. Accelerating decolonization produced a continuous flow of newly independent states, each a potential competitive arena. It also changed the UN's shape. The emerging Sino-Soviet split proved important as China entered the global competition for influence.[36] Kennan's prediction of fragmentation in the Communist world proved prescient. Moreover, a bipolar world never existed. At best it was tripolar, with China forming a leg, but even this is simplistic and ignores the agency of the globe's states and the existence of the non-aligned movement born at the 1955 Bandung Conference.

THE IDEAS

Part of the administration's intellectual foundations was "modernization theory," a concept formulated by Kennedy's deputy national security advisor and Johnson's last national security advisor, Walt Rostow. Rostow's modernization theory taught that since US methods were undoubtedly the best and most successful in the world, problems in emerging nations (including those suffering Communist insurgencies) could be solved by implementing US practices. To Rostow, the nation and its particular situation or characteristics were irrelevant. It was based upon the false assumption that the US always had the better way, and *de facto* assumed *all* states were the same. Modernization theory underpinned some administration foreign aid programs and was important for Kennedy's Vietnam War strategy.[37]

Another influence were the era's so-called "limited war" theories. Though "limited war" is affixed sometimes to the European wars of the eighteenth century, different thinking on this arose because of the revolutionary destructive effects of atomic and nuclear weapons. "Limited war" writing sought to fill a perceived but nonexistent military theory gap. The new theorists failed to distinguish between the political aims sought and the means used, and built a theory upon the constraining of means, a subjective basis that doesn't provide a foundation for analysis. Clausewitz's insistence upon beginning with the political aim provides a firm, objective starting point. The means used – and this includes nuclear weapons – are critical factors contributing to the nature of the war or international competition, but the means neither define the contest nor tell us what it is about.[38]

The administration's national security *Foreign Relations* documents discuss "limited war" with a lack of clarity mirroring the literature. Administration figures generally saw so-called "limited wars" as ones lacking Soviet involvement or perhaps even Chinese, and "small wars" as dominated by an insurgency or guerrilla activity, which ignores the massive scale of the Chinese Civil War that birthed modern thinking on guerrilla struggle. The discussions generally center on the use of various military and non-military means without any statement of political aims, and little or no discussion of whether or not using these means can deliver an aim. This flawed, means-based analysis underpins the construction of the Kennedy administration's strategy, and Lyndon Johnson's as well.[39]

THE POLITICAL AIM AND THE GRAND STRATEGY

The administration reviewed past recommendations on military strategy and force needs, including how to use nuclear weapons. National Security

Advisor McGeorge Bundy's initial direction here lacks a political aim. The administration also undertook revision of the Eisenhower administration's 1959 Basic National Security Policy. The task of drafting the report fell to Rostow, then deputy special assistant to Bundy on the NSC staff. The grand strategy that emerged was branded Flexible Response, a term derived from General Maxwell Taylor's book that inspired it: *The Uncertain Trumpet.* There is, though, no defining document. The best account of what the administration thought it was doing is Rostow's Basic National Security Policy, though the administration never officially approved the 285-page text.[40] Neither the Kennedy nor Johnson administrations seem to have created anything that can be construed as a national security strategy.

Kennedy sought security against Communism and famously said America would "pay any price, bear any burden, meet any hardship, support any friend, oppose any foe, in order to assure the survival and success of liberty." An early draft of Rostow's Basic National Security Policy clearly mentions the pursuit of security, but in an international sense: "Our basic national purpose is to help in the creation of a world environment in which a nation with values and purposes such as ours can flourish."[41]

The administration's version of containment strategy, like Eisenhower's, was essentially deterrence. Kennedy made this clear on March 28, 1961: "To deter all wars, general or limited, nuclear or conventional, large or small – to convince all potential aggressors that any attack would be futile – to provide backing for the diplomatic settlement of disputes – to insure the adequacy of our bargaining power for an end to the arms race." The Johnson administration followed the same path.[42]

MILITARY STRATEGY

The Kennedy administration initially sought massive expansion of conventional and nuclear forces to defend the US, its allies, and vital areas. It would enhance US civil defense capabilities while helping foreign nations combat subversion. But within two years, the administration retreated from some of its early intentions, particularly in regard to civil defense and nuclear capabilities. McNamara began insisting in 1963 that America and its allies were not as outnumbered by the Soviets as once believed. He also discovered that giving the services essentially free rein to request funding and capabilities meant it never stopped. McNamara began restricting their tasks to drive down costs.[43]

Kennedy hoped to provide more money for defense, and more efficient expenditure. Part of this was accomplished by McNamara's implementation of the Planning-Programming-Budgeting System (PPBS). This pushed coherent planning and implementation procedures for defense needs and covered everything from force mixture ratios to standardizing military belt buckles. The administration took a special interest in strengthening the nation's unconventional or irregular warfare military capabilities to meet the threat of "wars of national liberation," which were generally pursued by mounting insurgencies against established governments. This included Special Forces such as the army's Green Berets, and training and education on the subject at the nation's military colleges and the State Department's foreign service school.[44]

The Kennedy team believed in the *political* necessity of calling for increased conventional forces to deter Soviet attack but didn't consider this a *strategic* necessity. The mobilization of reserve and National Guard forces temporarily grew the army after Khrushchev's blustering at the June 1961 Vienna Conference, and the army was soon expanded to sixteen divisions to give it the ability to simultaneously fight two wars and handle another crisis (two-and-a-half wars). But McNamara budgeted no additional funds to build conventional units to send to Europe. Moreover, Kennedy threatened to withdraw troops from Europe on several occasions because of America's injurious balance of payments deficit, meaning the value of US imports exceeded exports, forcing the government to borrow abroad. The administration also pushed for stronger NATO forces. Kennedy complained in 1963 that the US couldn't "continue to pay for the military protection of Europe while the NATO states are not paying for their fair share." The administration opposed an independent European NATO nuclear force, but privately offered Britain and France nuclear technology, including Polaris missiles and nuclear weapons. This was done privately because Washington didn't want Germany to expect similar access or to acquire nuclear weapons. By 1962, Kennedy saw only one significant need for US troops in Europe: reopening a route to Berlin if Moscow closed it. They weren't needed to defend Western Europe because any Soviet attack faced immediate nuclear counterattack. But he understood that reducing the number of US troops meant that if war came, the use of nuclear weapons would occur even sooner. Kennedy removed some troops after Germany committed to remaining a non-nuclear state. This reduced tensions with Moscow while helping address balance of payments problems.[45]

Kennedy had campaigned on the existence of a missile gap, one he found didn't exist upon taking office. Admitting this publicly was deemed politically unwise, and the administration stuck to its plan to expand the nation's nuclear weapons arsenal beyond what even Eisenhower had planned. Gaining a decisive superiority in such weapons was seen as deterring Moscow. But how to use such weapons? There is an extensive theoretical literature speculating upon this. Game theory might be popular among Thomas Schelling's disciples and a narrow coterie of academics, but these ideas played no role in shaping US nuclear strategy. Schelling's offense "was to transform strategy once again into tactics writ large – not military tactics this time, but bargaining tactics, the problem of war and peace, was reduced to the problem of behavior during times of crisis and after the outbreak of hostilities." Such work suffered from being "apolitical in substance" and "ahistorical in method." Discussion and analysis of nuclear strategy generally occurs bereft of political aims.[46]

The Kennedy administration abandoned massive retaliation as a nuclear strategy, but US war plans for using nuclear weapons changed little. McNamara never considered realistic a counterforce for a second strike and even used a speech to try to convince the Soviets to *increase* their nuclear forces because if they were stronger, they would not feel threatened and thus not need to attack first. The administration's nuclear strategy became Mutual Assured Destruction, known by history's most appropriate acronym: MAD. The best way to protect one's population was to leave it undefended while possessing the ability to destroy the attacker's population.[47]

DIPLOMATIC STRATEGY

Kennedy sought to expand Eisenhower's negotiation effort with Moscow but faced the same problem: Khrushchev. Soviet behavior swung from trying to resolve differences to hostility more often during Kennedy's tenure than any previous time. Khrushchev, who decided Kennedy was weak, pursued a strategy of brinksmanship often centering upon bluster and threats of nuclear immolation. Khrushchev simultaneously called for "peaceful coexistence" with the West and revolution in the Third World, while provoking international crises in Berlin or Cuba. Kennedy refused to be intimidated into discussions or to be seen as negotiating from a position of weakness. His willingness to talk eventually produced results: a limited nuclear test-ban treaty, the hotline between Washington and Moscow, and sales of US wheat to the Soviet Union, though these derived more from a shift in Moscow's attitude, particularly after the two states came to the brink of war during the Cuban Missile Crisis.[48]

The Kennedy administration supported a unified Europe capable of defending itself and thus lessening Washington's defense burden. It was not happy with SEATO or CENTO as they lacked the strength to protect themselves and thus had little choice but to turn to the United States even when facing insurrections. The administration sought relationships built less on defense while trying to convince the Asian members of such organizations to devote their military efforts to thwarting Communist insurgencies. Non-military tools of grand strategy were seen as equally important.[49]

Under Kennedy, Africa became a point of American focus for the first time as part of the administration's anticolonialism push. Kennedy's support for African-American civil rights was partially aimed at African eyes. The Johnson administration was more aggressive here as decolonization heated up. The former European colonies were seen as adolescents needing protection from Communism and help growing up, which Washington could provide. But Cold War security concerns often trumped support for African independence movements. The African states sometimes saw US actions as counter to their own interests, while America's civil rights movement highlighted discrimination against Black Americans. The shift leftward politically of many Third World independence movements, a radicalization partially fueled by the Algerian War (1954–62), also created tensions. The shape of the UN, which the US had traditionally used to keep a focus on Communist evils, became more independent-minded with the entry of numerous new nations and the growth of the non-aligned movement. In 1964, the US used mercenaries and the CIA to help defeat a Cuba-assisted Communist insurgency in Congo.[50]

In the Middle East, Kennedy sympathized with Arab nationalists and tried to not show favoritism between the Arab states and Israel. He particularly sought to keep Egypt from Soviet influence, which proved impossible because of Nasser's adventurism in places such as Yemen and support in America for Israel. The tight US–Israeli relationship started under Kennedy as the US began granting Israel access to US weapons and committed to helping the small state if it was attacked. Johnson worried about Israel's nuclear ambitions but supplied military hardware to counter Moscow's arming Arab states, believing this would curb Israel's nuclear pursuits.[51]

Kennedy consciously tried to model his approach to Latin America along the lines of the Good Neighbor Policy and established in 1961 a kind of Marshall Plan for the region, the Alliance for Progress. It supported democratic and economic development and reforms, but never succeeded in producing the annualized 2.5 percent economic growth planned as it suffered from mismanagement and ignored regional, cultural, and economic realities. It ended in 1973. Washington doubled regional military aid to $77 million annually. But Cuba's revolution changed things, and the administration did all it could to prevent establishment of additional Latin

American Communist regimes. It looked the other way as local military forces overthrew a leftist regime in Argentina in 1962 and in the Dominican Republic in September 1963, and helped prevent the election of a Marxist ruler for newly independent Guyana.[52]

INFORMATIONAL STRATEGY

The Kennedy administration wanted to use US resources to help countries make Communism less attractive to their inhabitants while strengthening internal resistance to Communism. The most famous program for this was the Peace Corps, which sent US volunteers to support the development of Third World countries. Others included the aforementioned Alliance for Progress, the Agency for International Development (later USAID), and Food for Peace, which dispersed surplus US agricultural produce. These were parts of Third World nation-building strategies the administration launched in areas suffering insurgencies; modernization theory played a part. Economic and social reform could – theoretically – alter these states, put them on better paths, and make them more resistant to Communism.[53]

ECONOMIC STRATEGY

The economy was contracting when Kennedy took office, and unemployment was 6.6 percent. The administration wanted to stimulate employment. It believed this would mean higher inflation, but it was seen as more helpful to the middle and working classes and thus worth additional inflation. The administration increased domestic and military spending, which Kennedy initially wanted to finance with a tax increase, but he was advised this would hurt any economic recovery. Despite rhetoric about ignoring self-imposed fiscal constraints, Kennedy was in many ways fiscally cautious. He feared being seen as irresponsible here and was reluctant to launch deep deficit spending. This changed during his last two years as president. Kennedy was convinced the way to expand employment was a dramatic tax cut, even if it produced a deficit, but he ensured this remained lower than the highest one under Eisenhower to dampen criticism. Kennedy and Johnson also tried to reduce government spending, including military spending, to stop conservative criticism.[54] The Vietnam War ended this.

The tax cuts were not passed until February 1964, by which time Johnson was president. This "was the most important piece of tax legislation since World War II" and lowered corporate and personal rates. The individual rates, ranging from 20 to 91 percent, dropped to 14 to 70 percent.

The next three years saw unemployment fall. Meanwhile, beginning in 1961, the Federal Reserve ceaselessly expanded the money supply until the end of the decade, partly to help pay for the war in Vietnam. The tax cuts helped accelerate economic growth and the Kennedy–Johnson team bet – successfully – that "even at reduced tax rates, federal revenues would begin to expand." They expected growth of 4 to 4.5 percent GNP per annum until the end of the decade and large budget surpluses.[55]

MEETING THE COMMUNIST CHALLENGE

Kennedy inherited a CIA plan to overthrow Castro's Communist regime. It called for landing a Cuban exile force at Trinidad on the south coast. It would be supported by an assumed uprising. If this didn't happen, the exiles, who received no training in this, were to wage a guerrilla war from the safety of the Escambray Mountains. The JCS reviewed the CIA plan but hesitated to critique it because it was considered improper to do this to the plans of other agencies when you weren't responsible. The Chiefs told Kennedy it had a "fair chance" of success while privately saying 30 percent. Kennedy ordered them to reexamine it. They concluded it couldn't work but buried this in their report's annexes. Kennedy's civilian advisors – McNamara, Rusk, and Bundy – also failed to tell Kennedy their doubts.[56]

Fears of political fallout in Latin America from too obvious American involvement drove Kennedy to give the CIA four days to plan a smaller operation. The landing would be made at night 80 miles west at the Bay of Pigs, which lacked a nearby mountain refuge. Kennedy approved it after a 20-minute discussion. Amateurish planning was compounded by an impoverished assessment as the Americans misread Castro's internal support and military preparation. Even after multiple newspapers revealed an impending invasion, Kennedy authorized the attack, which began on April 17, 1961. The debacle saw most of the 1,200-man force killed or imprisoned. This injured Kennedy politically and created a lasting mistrust toward the Chiefs from Kennedy and McNamara. Kennedy took public responsibility for the catastrophe, which helped him overcome the incident politically. But he felt the CIA and the JCS had served him poorly.[57]

The administration remained determined to get rid of Castro and launched Operation MONGOOSE to destabilize his regime. The administration believed a blockade and subversion would produce rebellion. Robert Kennedy, the president's brother and attorney general, ran it. In August 1961, Castro's regime secretly approached the Kennedy administration about coming to terms, promising not to make an alliance with the Soviets.

Kennedy, worried about conservative criticism, balked. On September 4, Castro asked Khrushchev for military equipment, and MONGOOSE sabotage operations frightened Castro into pushing harder for Khrushchev's help. Kennedy remarked to a Soviet reporter that the US resented a hostile power so close to its shores, compared the 1956 events in Hungary with Cuba, and made Eisenhower's partial embargo against Cuba complete to cripple its economy. This convinced Moscow and Havana an invasion was near.[58]

The June 1961 Vienna summit increased tensions. Khrushchev was angry over the situation in West Berlin and browbeat Kennedy. The Soviets saw West Berlin as a bleeding capitalist sore on the socialist body, one draining East Germany of its youngest and best educated while costing Moscow vast sums for subsidies. Kennedy replied with a speech promising to defend Western rights in Berlin. This increased the strains. Khrushchev attacked the speech and in August 1961 began encircling West Berlin with a wall that became perhaps the most powerful symbol of the Cold War.[59]

The Bay of Pigs debacle, and the refusal to help the landing force, convinced Khrushchev of Kennedy's weakness. Khrushchev saw in Cuba a way to counter America's nuclear strike superiority by doubling the number of Soviet nuclear weapons that could reach America by installing Medium Range Ballistic Missiles (MRBMs). A Soviet military presence would also prevent a US invasion. Political pressure for Kennedy to act against this new threat mounted quickly. Against the advice of his military leaders – who pushed *extremely* hard for an invasion – Kennedy established a quarantine of Cuba. It wasn't branded a blockade because that is an act of war under international law. Kennedy promised harsher measures for any Soviet breach while preparing to invade Cuba, if necessary.[60]

The crisis was defused on October 28, 1962, by Kennedy's secret deal with Khrushchev. The US would publicly promise to not invade Cuba while secretly removing missiles from Turkey. The Soviets agreed to take their missiles from Cuba. Kennedy took the deal over the resistance of most of his close advisors. Critically, during the crisis Khrushchev dispatched orders to the Soviet personnel in Cuba forbidding them from launching the now operational missiles without instructions from Moscow.[61]

The administration now trusted even less the judgment of its military leaders. Undersecretary of Defense Cyrus Vance noted that its members came to believe that the gradual application of force could bring about negotiations, a lesson applied to Vietnam.[62] Among the many problems with Vance's statement is that the administration hadn't used force. It had used military *power* but not military *force*. As dangerous as it was, the Cuban

Missile Crisis was not a war. Vietnam was. Taking a lesson derived from an international, peacetime standoff (albeit one of the most dangerous in history) and applying it to an actual war sours the critical analysis. This is a failure to distinguish between peace and war.

The Cuban Missile Crisis was probably the closest the world has yet come to the outbreak of a conflict including a nuclear exchange. This prospect laid the foundation for pursuit of less tense relations. The Soviets wanted more stability and predictability in both their leader and the world and forced out Khrushchev on October 14, 1964. Moscow, though, embarked upon a massive nuclear missile–building program to ensure it would never again be militarily weaker than America.[63]

THE LYNDON JOHNSON ADMINISTRATION

Lyndon Johnson became president after Kennedy's November 22, 1963 assassination. The Vietnam War and how it was waged became the defining issue of his administration and is discussed in the next chapter. It was not what Johnson wanted or intended. He loved the legislative process and had little interest in foreign relations and none in fighting a war. His concern was social reform. A veteran New Dealer from Texas, a former congressman, and a dynamic and masterful Senate majority leader, he combined a love of rough-and-tumble politics, where winning elections was more important than doing so legally, with a sincere desire to better the lot of the poor and African-Americans.[64]

THE SOVIET UNION AND THE COMMUNIST CHALLENGE

The rivalry with the Soviet Union remained a critical concern and the administration continued Kennedy's Flexible Response containment strategy. The situation Johnson faced with the Soviet Union was far less tense. Khrushchev's replacement, Leonid Brezhnev, was one reason. The growing Sino-Soviet split was another. The Soviets wanted less tension with the US but remained dedicated to the Cold War contest, while China emerged as a heavier Cold War player and began competing with the Soviets to sponsor Third World revolutionaries and exploded its own atomic bomb in 1964. But Mao's Great Cultural Revolution caused upheaval and famine and killed 500,000 people. The famines of 1959–61 created by Mao's Great Leap Forward killed at least 20 million.[65]

The Soviet interest in better relations found a receptive ear in Johnson. He said in his January 1967 State of the Union Address that "Our objective is not to continue the cold war, but to end it." In an October 7, 1966 speech, Johnson dropped the requirement for German unification before having better relations with Moscow, announced a shift to "peaceful engagement," and supported enormous increases in exchanges with Moscow and the Eastern Bloc. In July 1968, the administration inked a Nuclear Non-Proliferation Treaty with Moscow and Britain. The war in Vietnam didn't prevent improvement in relations because Johnson made clear he didn't intend to take the war beyond South Vietnam, though better relations and increased trade never translated into Soviet help in negotiating an end to the war, as Johnson hoped. Johnson even asked Congress to grant the Soviet Union most-favored-nation trade status. It refused because of the extensive aid Moscow and the Eastern Bloc provided North Vietnam.[66]

In 1968, Brezhnev crushed the Czechoslovakian reform movement, the Prague Spring. He marked the birth of the Brezhnev Doctrine by declaring the Soviet Union had the right and duty to intervene in Communist states where socialism was endangered. The administration canceled a planned summit but reacted cautiously to ensure they weren't encouraging the Czechs; memories of 1956 were still fresh. Caution from both sides defused tensions.[67]

DIPLOMATIC STRATEGY

In Latin America, US strategy shifted from favoring reform to supporting stability – what is sometimes called the Mann Doctrine. Johnson sought to prevent another Cuba as security above all other things drove American involvement in Latin America. The administration convinced the Organization of American States to cut trade and diplomatic ties with Cuba and told Brazilian military officers Washington would support the 1964 coup against Brazil's leftist government because it feared the country moving to Communism. Johnson defused Panamanian protests against the US and renegotiated the terms for control of the Canal. He intervened militarily in the Dominican Republic in 1965 when a rebellion against the leader Kennedy had supported evolved into a civil war. The public reason was to save American lives. The real reason was to ensure the Dominican Republic didn't go Communist. The first Marines landed in late April, and there were 24,000 troops in the country by mid May. US fears proved exaggerated, and Johnson later regretted his decision.[68] The Americans departed in September 1966.

When the Six Day War erupted in 1967, Israel's successes against Moscow's Egyptian and Syrian clients were followed by Soviet threats delivered to Washington promising drastic action. Johnson dispatched the Sixth Fleet and told the Israelis to accept an immediate ceasefire. Israel stopped on June 11 and the crisis subsided. In the war's aftermath, US grand strategy in the Middle East shifted to what is known as the Three Pillars Approach. Israel, Iran, and Saudi Arabia became the pillars, and the US began arming Iran.[69]

MILITARY STRATEGY

The Johnson administration remained committed to NATO but struggled to convince its members to develop a broad range of military responses. Underpinning this push was the necessity of addressing sources of allied tension. In 1966, the French withdrew from NATO's unified command structure and the Germans abrogated the payment terms agreed upon to address the balance of payments issue. McNamara threatened to withdraw two divisions – unless the Germans dealt with the payments problem. The concerns about reductions were more political than strategic. The US troop commitment was important for integrating Germany into Europe, and in 1963 Germany pledged to not develop nuclear weapons "so long as the United States guaranteed its security." The political arguments won out. This, combined with Vietnam's demands, led to US troop withdrawals from Europe.[70]

Another source of tension between the US and its allies was the Vietnam War. The US insisted it was necessary for Western Europe's protection. Japan was against America's involvement and feared being drawn in. But many Pacific nations supported America's war. Australia and New Zealand dispatched small contingents of troops while South Korea deployed as many as 50,000. Taiwan provided basing, and its links with the US strengthened. Singapore's prime minister, Lee Kuan Yew, believed his country would have fallen to Communism but for the US commitment to South Vietnam, while the American escalation in 1965 encouraged a 1967 countercoup in Indonesia against Sukarno's autocratic and revolutionary regime.[71]

ECONOMIC STRATEGY

Kennedy pursued social legislation generally lumped under his reference to a "New Frontier" but had little success. Johnson seized upon Kennedy's death to push bills related to Kennedy's two major domestic planks: civil rights and tax cuts. Johnson secured passage of a number of historic bills breaking many forms of institutional discrimination against African-Americans, particularly in the segregated South. These included the Civil

Rights Act of 1964 and the Voting Rights Act of 1965. But Johnson continued Kennedy's practice of having the FBI spy on civil rights activists such as Martin Luther King Jr. The tax cuts became law in February 1964. The booming economy and Johnson's own desire to emulate the New Deal enabled the new president to try to build his Great Society.[72]

Johnson launched a social experiment, elements of which became known as the "war on poverty," based upon the assumption the poor needed a leg up and the government could provide it. The intention was to give people the ability to help themselves, especially through education and training programs directed at youth, but it also included direct welfare payments to the neediest. But the government didn't seriously study whether any of its new schemes would work. The 1964 anti–poverty bill funded (insufficiently) a litany of programs that generally failed to help the poor. The next year saw aid to primary and secondary schools and the establishment of Medicare and Medicaid, all fronts in Johnson's "war on poverty."[73]

Johnson established these various social programs without raising taxes, and their costs became far more than originally estimated. The economy was also not growing as quickly as projected "and although inflation drove up tax revenues, they tended not to increase as rapidly as expenditures. The result, evident by the early 1970s, was a situation in which nondefense programs had begun to compete with, and increasingly to squeeze out, defense spending."[74]

In Johnson's second term, the economic effects of the Vietnam War began undoing the economic success of the Kennedy administration and early Johnson years. The war's cost for 1967 was expected to run to $67 billion. Johnson was advised to raise taxes across the board to pay for the war and also tamp down inflation. He refused, believing this politically injurious; it might hurt support for both the war and his domestic agenda. He instead approved some not so obvious measures such as rises in excise taxes.[75]

Even though the Federal Reserve tightened the money supply, inflation continued, and Johnson eventually passed "the single largest tax increase since World War II." It was branded a "surtax," meaning a temporary increase. He could have easily gotten Congress to pass a tax dedicated to paying for the war but feared the political repercussions of admitting he had taken the country to war. Moreover, this might hurt funding for his Great Society programs because, if America were at war, this could make it harder to win support for social spending. The inflation America suffered was caused by both domestic and military spending, but that for the military mattered more. The war also caused a balance of payments problem because money flowed out to fund it. America's postwar economic boom ended in 1968.[76]

ASSESSING THE KENNEDY AND JOHNSON ADMINISTRATIONS

Both the Kennedy and Johnson administrations labored under the weakness of lacking sufficiently clear political aims. But this did not prevent them from constructing and implementing variations of containment strategy, and Kennedy did so against one of Moscow's most volatile and unpredictable leaders.

Both administrations placed enormous faith in unproven theoretical ideas. In the foreign affairs and military realms these included modernization theory, limited war, bargaining, and signaling (about which we will learn more shortly). These provided poor foundations for analysis, undermined American strategic thinking, and proved destructive in Vietnam. Johnson followed a similar course in social reform by not thoroughly studying the causes of poverty and the proposed solutions before implementing programs that failed to deliver what their proponents promised. Kennedy and Johnson successfully met the challenge the Soviet Union offered in the realm of peaceful but often intense competition. The more difficult test was in Vietnam.

12

THE VIETNAM WAR, 1961–1969

INTRODUCTION

The American war in Vietnam was Wilsonian. American leaders believed they could make Vietnam a better place, saving the South Vietnamese from Communism and themselves. Wilson believed in management by a government of elite technocrats, one *exactly* like Kennedy's team. To them, the war was a problem to be managed. *They* would manage it. And everything would be fine. But war is not a management exercise where one can apply lessons from a Harvard Business School case study. Wars are a "serious, bloody business" driven by desires to achieve political aims – often by *any* means necessary. Assuming anything less courts disaster.

NORTH VIETNAMESE POLITICAL AIMS AND GRAND STRATEGY

Something overlooked is that North Vietnam's political aims and the planks of its grand strategy were in place *before* America escalated its involvement. The North's early leader was Ho Chi Minh, "an apparent nationalist who was in reality pursuing the interests of the Communist International." But unknown to American observers, Ho was shunted aside in 1960 and replaced by Le Duan. The North Vietnamese had clear political aims. A captured 1952 Communist Party document noted: "The ultimate aim of the Vietnamese Communist leadership is to install Communist regimes in the whole of Vietnam, in Laos, and in Cambodia."[1] The North had imperial aims not unlike those of the French against whom they had fought. Conquering South Vietnam was the next step. And the most important.

Hanoi's grand strategy was North Vietnamese Revolutionary Warfare. It generally followed the three phases laid out by Mao Tse-Tung in his 1938 *On Protracted War*. Mao's phase one was the strategic defensive, or the "organization, consolidation, and preservation" phase. The much weaker Communists acted on the strategic defensive, building their party organizations and winning support via popular measures such as land reform while using terror to undermine support for the government. Peasant support was critical for recruits, supplies, information, and sanctuary. Mao said, "the guerrilla must be in the population as little fishes in the ocean." Phase two was the strategic stalemate, the "progressive expansion," or "equilibrium" phase. One moved to phase two when roughly equal to the enemy. The guerrillas established bases, increased recruiting, began training regular forces, and established an alternative government. Phase three was the strategic offensive, "decision," or "destruction of the enemy" stage. The guerrillas were strong enough to fight conventionally and win. Much of their force became a regular army, but guerrilla warfare might continue. This phase would be shorter and ideally unnecessary. Mao believed his strategy particularly dangerous to countries with legislative governments because they were less able to endure extended financial and psychological burdens. North Vietnam added a planned "General Uprising."[2]

Building on Mao's ideas, the North constructed an integrated military and political grand strategy based upon the concept of struggle, or *dau tranh*. The North would use all elements of national power to destroy South Vietnam's regime. Political struggle would indoctrinate the peasants, destabilize the government, and weaken the South Vietnamese Army (ARVN) while diplomacy won support abroad. Political struggle included terrorism against "class enemies" and supporters of South Vietnam. Epitomizing this was the "Extermination of Traitors Campaign." Between 1957 and 1972, the Communists murdered 36,000 teachers, officials, and others, and kidnapped 58,000. The military struggle was carried on by North Vietnamese military forces and the Viet Cong (VC).[3] Local VC served part-time in their villages. VC Regional Forces, identified by their black outfits, were full-time soldiers indigenous to their service areas. Main Force VC were full-time soldiers organized into light infantry units, sometimes division-strength.

Diem consolidated his power and launched an effective campaign of suppression against Communist elements, but his autocratic tendencies, preference for nepotism over competence in military and political appointments, and the nation's eventual endemic corruption undermined his rule. In January 1959, the North launched its war of conquest. It activated a cadre left behind in 1954, launched an insurgency, and established the Central Office of South Vietnam (COSVN) in Cambodia to run their war in the south. In May 1959, Hanoi began building through Laos the Ho Chi Minh Trail. It became a 12,500-mile-long highway with 5,000 kilometers of fuel pipelines. By 1975, it had twenty-five branches into South Vietnam. At its height, 50,000 transport workers, 50,000 North Vietnamese Army (NVA) engineers, and 12,000 NVA troops ran and guarded it. Some 2 million people traveled it during the war. In 1960, Hanoi created the National Liberation Front (NLF) to mask Communist control of the insurgency.[4]

THE KENNEDY ADMINISTRATION

Kennedy was cautious toward South Vietnam. He was reluctant to commit too deeply yet believed it couldn't be abandoned for political reasons. He feared being portrayed at home as soft on Communism and abroad as weak. He expanded America's role while trying to keep it restrained. This failed to improve the situation while laying the foundation for Washington to take over the war.[5]

THE POLITICAL AIM AND THE GRAND STRATEGY

On May 11, 1961, after a reassessment, Kennedy approved this aim: "To prevent Communist domination of South VietNam [sic] and to create in that country a viable and increasingly democratic society."[6] The administration continued Eisenhower's nation-building strategy while helping South Vietnam implement a counterinsurgency strategy. In a conflict involving an insurrection or insurgency, there are three key issues: support of the people, sanctuary, and outside support. The administration – and Diem – attempted to address all three – and failed. "Pacification" is used interchangeably with "counterinsurgency" in Vietnam discussion. Pacification involves separating the population from the insurgents, winning their compliance, if not loyalty, and the reestablishment of governmental control. It usually requires a mixture of military and non-military means, is manpower-intensive, and takes a long time.

A January 1961 plan identified *key* problems facing South Vietnam: it suffered from internal subversion and the threat of conventional invasion. It proposed extensive economic, political, governmental, and military development. The US eventually implemented an alphabet soup of programs. In late November 1961, the US and Vietnam produced a two-pronged war plan. The first prong was an ARVN offensive against the Communist guerillas. Key to implementation was the Military Assistance Command, Vietnam (MACV) created on February 8, 1962. Kennedy refused US military requests for combat troops, but the ARVN was expanded via PROJECT BEEFUP, and he rapidly increased the number of advisors from 948 in November 1961 to 16,732 by October 1963. They were soon fighting alongside the ARVN. The administration hid the number of advisors and lied about their engaging in combat operations. Unnecessary presidential deception about the war continued until its end and helped discredit the conflict and the American government in the public's eyes. Late 1962 saw the arrival of press criticism of American involvement, which seemed deeper than the government admitted, and stories on Diem regime corruption and incompetence.[7]

The second prong was the Strategic Hamlet Program launched in March 1962. South Vietnam had already failed implementing a similar rural population security project, the 1959–60 Agroville Program. The sequel was influenced by Sir Robert Thompson, who had helped break Malaysia's Communist insurgency. Rural citizens were brought into fortified villages, isolating them from the guerillas and thereby starving the insurgents into submission. The program showed some success, fed optimism in the administration, and worried Hanoi enough to focus attacks on the hamlets. Failure came from mismanagement, the absence of land reform, alienating peasants by forcing them from lands where they had ancestral religious ties, not including Thompson's security elements (such as linking the hamlets to troops), refusing to give residents power, and a key official being a Communist agent. To Diem, the program was for population control and extracting aid from Washington.[8]

Hanoi reacted to Kennedy's growing support for Saigon by escalating the war. In 1961, 5,000 NVA troops (mostly former Southerners) moved south to support the 25,000-strong People's Liberation Army Forces (PLAF), generally known as Main Force VC, already in the South, and the 80,000 Communist guerrillas. Le Duan planned to send another 30–40,000 NVA soldiers by the end of 1963. The ARVN numbered 285,000 and was supported by 3,000 US troops. The North divided the South into three zones and pursued different forms of struggle in each: "military in the mountains; equal parts military and political in the plains; and political in the cities." The "armed struggle" moved to the offensive to try to destroy the South's military. Le Duan's problem was how to put enough military and political pressure on Diem to destroy his regime "without provoking full-scale US military intervention."[9]

THE DIPLOMATIC STRATEGY

Kennedy faced other, related challenges in Southeast Asia. Eisenhower warned Kennedy about the low-level civil war in Laos where Communists sought to overthrow the Laotian government. Kennedy was taken aback by the military suggesting intervention – which included using nuclear weapons – that might lead to war with China. Kennedy elected to try to neutralize Laos, thus denying the Communists sanctuary and a critical supply route.

The July 1962 Declaration of the Neutrality of Laos established a multi-party coalition government. All foreign troops were to depart within forty-five days. North Vietnam withdrew 40 men but left 5,000–7,000. Kennedy looked the other way. Laos became Hanoi's transit and supply line, one the US never closed. Spring 1961 saw the CIA begin arming what was eventually 9,000 Hmong tribesmen to attack the Ho Chi Minh Trail. Laos became a Communist sanctuary, making it nearly impossible to counter the key threat to pacification and nation building: Communist infiltration.[10]

THE DECISIVE ACT?

By August 1963, many top American officials believed Diem couldn't defeat the VC and had to go. Diem resisted American pressure and insisted on running his country his way. The Americans disliked his autocratic tendencies and repressive actions, particularly of his brother, Ngo Dình Nhu, who helped run the government. NSC head James Forestal pushed a recommendation for Diem's overthrow that Kennedy approved but later regretted. A group of South Vietnamese generals murdered Diem and his brother on November 1, 1963. The Kennedy administration added incompetence to criminality by failing to determine a successor beforehand – something Kennedy raised earlier.[11] He was assassinated two weeks later.

The Americans hoped replacing Diem would bring stability; it produced chaos. South Vietnam's government suffered six additional coups over the next eighteen months.[12] Some judge this *the* decisive American action, making the war unwinnable. This is difficult to prove but carries weight. The US needed to establish a firm government supported by the people to give South Vietnam a chance to stand on its own. Diem, despite his flaws, provided something around which to build. The subsequent revolving door of generals increased this challenge.

The North saw opportunity. Le Duan believed Vietnam didn't need to advance through Mao's three stages and abandoned protracted war. He gathered conventional forces in South Vietnam's Central Highlands, the north central region of the South, and near Saigon, increased the regular army to 300,000, and dispatched regiments south. The 1964 General Offensive–General Uprising sought a quick victory via a military offensive combined with political activities (information operations) to fuel an uprising.[13] Saigon suffered an onslaught from the North made possible by military, financial, and advisory support from China, the Soviet Union, and the Communist Bloc. (See Figure 12.1.) The Cold War context mattered as both sides saw more at stake than just South Vietnam's fate.

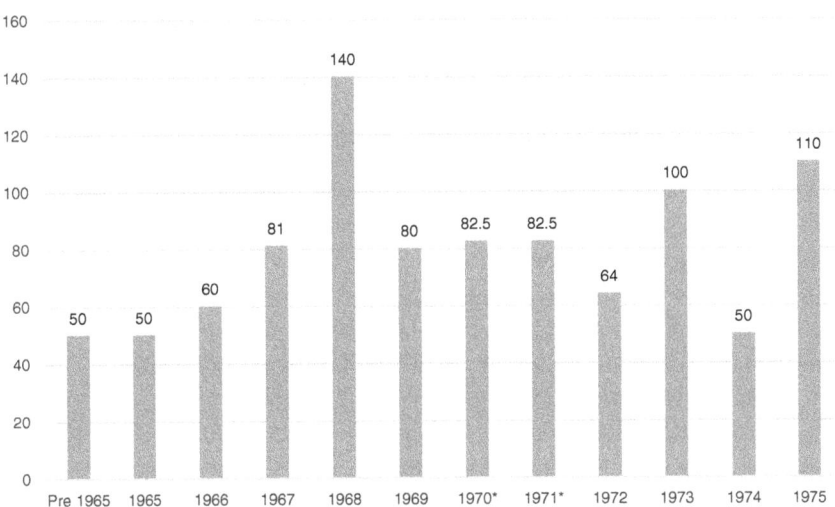

12.1 North Vietnamese Army infiltration into South Vietnam, 1965–75 (in thousands)

THE LYNDON JOHNSON ADMINISTRATION AND THE VIETNAM WAR

Upon becoming president in 1963, Johnson wanted and promised continuity. This included reaffirming US support for South Vietnam four days after Kennedy's death. His administration sought to stave off what they saw as the threat of Chinese Communist expansion into Southeast Asia long enough for regional states to learn to defend themselves. Protecting South Vietnam was also seen as deterring China. Johnson took great interest in Vietnam and had done so as vice president. He considered it the nation's most important military concern and directed key subordinates to put their best people in Saigon, but he didn't want to commit large forces from fear of upsetting his domestic legislative agenda. The initial Johnson administration strategy in South Vietnam was essentially "to do more of the same and do it more efficiently."[14]

In early 1964, South Vietnam became increasingly unstable. The counterinsurgency strategy had failed, and the JCS wanted a conventional approach. Johnson didn't want a war in Vietnam – he knew Americans would find it unpopular – but believed failing to resist Communist expansion encouraged them to act. He feared Saigon's fall but wouldn't countenance a war before the November election. The US expanded and improved the ARVN and formed guerrillas to operate in North Vietnam and Laos. In a May 27, 1964 meeting, Johnson expressed fear the US was stepping into another Korean War, adding, "I don't see what we can hope to get out of there with, once we're committed ... I don't think it's worth fighting for."[15]

THE GULF OF TONKIN RESOLUTION

On August 2, 1964, the destroyer *Maddox* was attacked by North Vietnamese patrol boats. On the night of August 4, *Maddox* and *Turner Joy* reported another attack, one that never happened. Poor radar and sonar readings were misinterpreted in bad weather. Johnson found the first attack surprising and elected to not retaliate. But notice of the second attack convinced him the North needed to be punished, and bombing followed.[16]

Johnson also saw political opportunity. He already had a draft resolution authorizing US action in Vietnam composed by McNamara, Bundy, and Rusk, and used the crisis to get Congress to pass the Gulf of Tonkin Resolution on August 7. This thwarted criticism from the political right going into the presidential election as Johnson wanted to avoid what he saw as Truman's mistake of not having Congressional approval before fighting in Korea. He also wanted to ensure Congress was responsible. There were only two negative votes. Johnson considered a declaration of war too provocative in the Cold War setting and feared it being taken as a threat to destroy North Vietnam, one provoking Soviet or Chinese intervention (the ghost of Korea hung over Vietnam), leading to a Third World War.[17] To Johnson, the Resolution provided political cover while reducing the risk of intervention by third parties.

The Gulf of Tonkin incident also undermined how the US trains its strategic thinker. At the time, economist Thomas Schelling was a Department of Defense consultant; his ideas influenced key officials. In 1966, Schelling published *Arms and Influence*, which "made Johnson's Tonkin Gulf reprisal a centerpiece example of rational signaling."[18] A book based partially upon a flawed historical picture that pushes signaling ideas discredited by their failure when applied during the Vietnam War (which we see shortly) is a standard strategic studies text.

THE JOHNSON ADMINISTRATION'S VIETNAM WAR

In his major Vietnam decisions, Johnson often followed the advice of advisors. This was a mistake. His instincts proved better than those of the "Best and Brightest." For example, Johnson feared the US couldn't find a way out once it was in and believed the bombing campaign he eventually authorized and controlled wouldn't work.[19] Kennedy, when pressed by his advisors to invade Cuba during the Cuban Missile Crisis and drastically escalate the US commitment to Vietnam, had followed his own mind. When he didn't and authorized Diem's assassination, he regretted it.

Robert Strange McNamara was Kennedy's Vietnam point man and thus became Johnson's. He was an experienced manager but knew nothing about Vietnam; few Americans did. Schooled in statistics, head of Ford Motor Company, and a Second World War veteran, he emphasized quantitative analysis and judged the quality of information based upon the numbers behind it. He failed to grasp the dominance in war of intangibles such as leadership and courage, and told a journalist: "Every quantitative measurement we have shows that we're winning this war." Statistical analysis is valuable, but these tend toward tactical, logistical, and industrial matters. The formation of strategy and its even more difficult execution demands dealing with innumerable abstract and often unmeasurable factors, the most important being the human will. Gauging this requires placing yourself as much as possible in an opponent's shoes. Studying their history, religion, language, culture, and economy provides glimpses but aren't sufficient because you must also understand what they want to achieve or prevent, and *why*. To historian and analyst Bernard Brodie, the Vietnam War proved "the nearly total irrelevance of 'cost-effectiveness' analysis, which some people in Washington and elsewhere have assumed to be coterminous with the whole realm of strategy." McNamara's methods might work for buying stuff, but not for making strategy.[20]

Once America began fighting the war in earnest and the problems multiplied, administration foibles increased the friction. Johnson's insistence upon consensus between his civilian and military leaders stifled debate. Civil–military relations in the administration were poor because of Johnson's mistrust and "MacArthur Syndrome": both military and civilian leaders worried about a repetition of the Korean War's MacArthur–Truman controversy. Johnson, in a February 1966 meeting with General William Westmoreland, told him: "I hope you don't pull a MacArthur on me." The JCS, fearful of being construed as challenging civilian authority, suppressed debate and delivered unified proposals.[21]

THE POLITICAL AIM

McNamara clearly articulated America's political aim in South Vietnam in a March 16, 1964 document that became National Security Action

Memorandum (NSAM) 288. "We seek an independent non-Communist South Vietnam," it noted.

> We do not require that it serve as a Western base or as a member of a Western Alliance. South Vietnam must be free, however, to accept outside assistance as required to maintain its security. This assistance should be able to take the form not only of economic and social measures but also police and military help to root out and control insurgent elements.

McNamara also explained the object's value, insisting if Washington couldn't "achieve this objective in South Vietnam, almost all of Southeast Asia will probably fall under Communist dominance (all of Vietnam, Laos, and Cambodia)." Other states in the region would then become susceptible to Communist influence or domination, thus threatening America's allies in the hemisphere. On December 7, 1964 (an inauspicious choice), the administration linked the American effort in South Vietnam with a regional struggle for the security of the nations of Southeast Asia.[22]

The Chiefs consistently referred to NSAM 288 as the document delineating the political aim. Unfortunately, the administration's civilian and military leaders failed to ensure general officers fighting the war understood the aim – "a stable and independent South Vietnam" – and thus *why* they were in Vietnam. Postwar interviews revealed 70 percent were unclear on this.[23] The US pursued limited political aims, as it sought preservation of South Vietnam and Laos and not the overthrow of North Vietnam's regime.

PREPARATION AND THE DECISION TO INTERVENE

In mid 1964, MACV noted that in six coastal areas VC attacks were preventing pacification's progress. By the second half of 1964 "American strategy had failed to do anything to halt, much less reverse, the spread of the Viet Cong in the countryside." American civilian and military leaders urged action against the North. In November 1964, Westmoreland said pacification had little chance of succeeding as long as the North's support and guidance of the VC continued, and noted the impossibility of closing South Vietnam's borders to a North dedicated to piercing them. Only military force and psychological pressure could convince the North to stop.[24]

Undersecretary of State George Ball was the only dissenter among Johnson's key advisors on military escalation. In early October 1964, he questioned bombing by pointing to a September 1964 Pentagon war game indicating that destruction of the North's ninety-four industrial sites wouldn't significantly injure its ability to supply the VC. He said escalation was something Washington's allies in Europe and Asia didn't want, and he didn't believe military intervention would deliver NSAM 288's aim. He advised telling Saigon it was responsible for establishing a good government that could defend itself or negotiate its neutrality. He felt international talks the best course of action.[25]

During his 1964 election campaign, Johnson insisted Americans wouldn't fight in Asia while planning to do so. The day before the election, he authorized a working group to examine future courses of action in Vietnam. It recommended retaliation for VC attacks on Americans and, if Saigon's government made acceptable progress, airstrikes and troop increases in South Vietnam and Thailand within thirty days. This set the escalation stage. Johnson had just been reelected in a landslide and increased his House and Senate majorities.[26]

The South's third coup occurred on December 19, and Ambassador Maxwell Taylor concluded that meeting Johnson's aforementioned requirement for a stable government was impossible. He recommended bombing, and Johnson decided he had to act. Johnson feared a North Vietnamese victory provoking a divisive debate destroying his presidency and hope of securing his domestic agenda while injuring America's democracy. He might be blamed for "losing" South Vietnam the way Truman was blamed for "losing" China.[27] For Johnson, the value of the object – an independent, non-Communist South Vietnam – was high enough to justify war, but the North Vietnamese valued South Vietnam more.

THE ASSESSMENT

At the end of 1964, Johnson was told achieving stability in South Vietnam required dramatically increasing America's military commitment. South Vietnam was coming apart and many American military leaders believed the ARVN bordered on collapse. The greatest problem was not Saigon's corruption and incompetence, but Hanoi's war of conquest. This dramatically increased the difficulty of governing while discrediting the government – which was the point as Communist insurgents established a shadow administration in areas they controlled. Counterinsurgency theorist Bernard Fall wrote in regard to Vietnam: "When a country is being subverted it is not being outfought; it is being out-administered."[28]

Westmoreland realized in 1965 that North Vietnam had changed its strategy. The Communists added conventional invasion to subversion and guerrilla war. Westmoreland correctly assessed the threat as VC guerrillas and the NVA. A different threat necessitates a different response.

The American counterinsurgency strategy was now dead. But an accurate assessment doesn't necessarily translate into victory, especially as the Americans underestimated their opponent.[29]

THE AIR STRATEGY: SIGNALING, BARGAINING, AND FAILURE

A consistent criticism leveled at Johnson's administration is that it never matched the means to the end being sought, and that the constraints it placed upon the use of these means doomed the US effort. The answer to this is not simple and addressing it properly requires separating the air war from the ground war while remembering their interconnectedness.

Johnson has been pilloried ceaselessly for most of his actions related to the Vietnam War. Often this criticism is justified. US presidents are responsible for what happens during their tenures. But what is often ignored are the theoretical concepts driving the advisors who guided Johnson toward his decisions, thus shaping aims and strategies. Rostow's flawed modernization theory was one. As we've seen, it assumed American methods were the best and thus the answer. But Schelling's so-called "limited war" ideas underpinned the airpower strategy. McNamara and the administration bought into Schelling's theory, insisting force was an element of signaling that demonstrated resolve. This would either deter an enemy or convince him to negotiate a settlement. To the administration, this offered a way to fight on the cheap without risking war with Beijing or Moscow, but it dramatically underestimated how much pain North Vietnam was willing to endure.[30]

Johnson and his advisors concluded a bombing campaign was the solution. The military wanted a heavy offensive against military, industrial, and infrastructure sites, and the mining of Haiphong Harbor. This would force Hanoi to quit or face destruction. Rostow, director of policy and planning and later national security advisor, expressed a concern that "too much thought is being given to the actual damage we do in the North, not enough to the signal we wish to send." He believed Washington should use as little force as possible, and this should be done to signal and as a deterrence.[31] He made the logic error of believing he could deter an enemy already fighting.

Johnson's national security advisor, McGeorge Bundy, wanted "a gradual escalation strategy." His assistant, John McNaughton, was unsure what type of campaign would suffice, but wanted to ensure the enemy received the proper signals and approached his old Harvard colleague Schelling for ideas. Seeing war as a form of bargaining, Schelling urged bombing and insisted it would succeed in a matter of weeks. In addition to ignoring the actual manner in which states conduct their relations, the great problem with signaling is that the enemy might misunderstand what you're trying to signal.[32]

After the November 1, 1964 Communist attack on the US air base at Bien Hoa, the US examined three approaches to bombing and chose Rostow's "graduated response." This became ROLLING THUNDER. McNamara and other Defense civilians saw this as "a complicated game of signals with the North, as much psychological as military." The JCS never accepted a signaling strategy as feasible. A February 7, 1965, VC attack on the US airbase at Pleiku proved bombing's catalyst. Johnson launched a retaliatory air attack and on February 13 ordered "a program of measured and limited air action." Johnson tightly controlled targeting and the intensity. ROLLING THUNDER lasted from March 2, 1965 to October 31, 1968. Its primary military objectives were forcing the North Vietnamese to stop feeding men and material into the South and convincing the North Vietnamese to enter peace negotiations. Admiral Ulysses S. Grant Sharp Jr., head of US Indo-Pacific Command and thus the commander, believed it would strengthen South Vietnam's morale and political structures. The strategy, which emphasized the idea of "graduated pressure," was to pressure Saigon by threatening to destroy its industrial base. The level of force used would be controlled, because using too much would destroy the hostage, that is, North Vietnam's industry. The bombing would escalate gradually, convincing Hanoi of America's willingness to go farther and – in Taylor's words – "convey signals" that their destruction was nigh. Diplomacy would be tied to the bombing, which to the civilians necessitated keeping the military on a tight leash. One of the strategy's great flaws was that North Vietnam had fewer than thirty industrial sites.[33]

There was scant confidence – beyond Rostow – that ROLLING THUNDER would work. Johnson didn't believe airpower could deliver victory. McNamara's Defense Department concluded Rostow's approach was unlikely to succeed because North Vietnam's economy was 88 percent agricultural, the country wasn't dependent upon maritime trade, and the bombing didn't address the insurgency, while saying this might be the best available option.[34]

ROLLING THUNDER's first phase ran from March to August 1965. The bombing attacks were designed to "roll" progressively north. The March attacks struck targets south of the 19th parallel. In May 1965, ROLLING THUNDER hit targets up to the 20th parallel. In July, the US attacked a few targets above the 20th. The second phase lasted from August

1965 through May 1967. Its main purpose was interdiction against North Vietnamese troops and supplies moving south and included attacks on the Ho Chi Minh Trail in Laos. As the campaign lengthened, the target list expanded to petroleum-related industry and electrical power generation, a result of Johnson gradually removing constraints, a normal occurrence when a strategy proves ineffective.[35]

May 1967 through March 1968 marked phase three. Since the bombing had failed, and feeling pressure from public opinion and Congress, Johnson removed more constraints, and the US began hitting industrial and transportation sites while maintaining the intensity. The bombing still failed to deliver, and it was no longer possible to increase the theoretical pressure because the hostage – the industrial sites – had been destroyed. April to November 1968 brought the final phase. The US gradually reduced the bombing and Johnson bowed to a US public turning against it. After November 1968, he halted bombing of the North, except for interdiction raids along the border.[36]

The administration coordinated diplomacy with the bombing. In June 1964, through Blair Seaborn, a Canadian official, the US promised escalation and destruction unless Hanoi stopped supporting the VC. It was a hollow threat. Bombing North Vietnam couldn't destroy the North's ability to fight because most of its military equipment came from its Communist brethren. The Americans fell victim to "mirror imaging": assuming the enemy saw things the same way and had the same priorities, specifically, that the North valued economic growth above all else, just like Rostow. The administration also paused ROLLING THUNDER eight times. For example, McNamara suggested the US stop bombing over Christmas 1965 to open the door for negotiations. Johnson agreed, even though he expected nothing. The bombing ceased for thirty-seven days, beginning on December 24. Johnson proved correct. Neither Sharp nor Westmoreland were aware of the plan for a pause.[37]

ROLLING THUNDER produced the opposite of what was intended. Ambassador Taylor mistakenly believed bombing had helped end the Korean War and thus could do the same in Vietnam. He termed ROLLING THUNDER "a strategy of gradualism" because of "the piecemeal employment of military forces at slowly mounting levels of intensity," a strategy he later admitted was wrong: "Designed to limit the dangers of expanded war, it ended by assuring a prolonged war which carried with it dangers of expansion. The restrained use of airpower suggested to the enemy a lack of decisiveness." As ROLLING THUNDER heated up, Alexei Kosygin was among Soviet diplomats fearing escalation in Vietnam and Johnson's simultaneous intervention in the Dominican Republic could fuel action against Cuba and produce a war between Moscow and the West.[38]

In addition to being incapable of delivering the military objectives, ROLLING THUNDER could not achieve Washington's political aim because it couldn't decisively affect North Vietnam's will or material ability to fight. It was also costly. By early 1968, America lost over 900 aircraft and over 1,000 aircrew, half killed. It cost $10 to inflict $1 worth of damage. Between 1965 and 1968, the North received from abroad "approximately $600 million in economic aid and $1 billion in military assistance," while the bombing inflicted $370 million in damage. The US couldn't stop the supply flow or infiltration because – as Ridgway pointed out – air interdiction wasn't as effective as people hoped. Air war commander Sharp wrote: "I had made the point many times that air attacks on lines of communication have never been able to stop infiltration, only hinder it. The primary objectives of using airpower should not be to try to stop infiltration, but rather to destroy the sources of the material being infiltrated."[39] Airpower and signaling theories failed the test of reality.

MILITARY STRATEGY: THE GROUND WAR

After America's initial, pre-ROLLING THUNDER air attacks, the VC attacked US airbases in South Vietnam. Westmoreland requested a pair of Marine battalions to guard the Da Nang airfield on February 22, 1965 before ROLLING THUNDER's first raid. Many administration figures supported the bombing campaign because they believed it meant the US wouldn't have to commit troops, but no one considered the necessary logistical and security measures. Realizing this, McNamara said later, "might have influenced our decisions with respect to the initial deployments." Taylor argued against Westmoreland's troop request, fearful of opening a floodgate impossible to close. Johnson feared losing planes if he didn't act. The Marines landed in Da Nang Bay on March 8, 1965. The commitment of the first combat troops marked a shift from civilian to military dominance over the ground war.[40]

The mission of the Marines was "to occupy and defend critical terrain features in order to secure the airfield and, as directed, communications facilities, US supporting installations, port facilities, landing beaches and other US installations against attack." Moreover, "The US Marine Forces will not, repeat will not, engage in day to day actions against the Viet Cong." This, of course, assumed Viet Cong cooperation. National Security Advisor Bundy wrote in January 1965 that dispatching ground forces was another way to "signal" to the enemy.[41]

A week later, Westmoreland asked for another battalion to protect another air base, and army Chief of Staff Harold Johnson urged heavier bombing and deploying an army division to the Central Highlands. The Chiefs asked for two divisions on March 20. All of this shocked the civilian leaders. In only the first month of ROLLING THUNDER, military commanders had dispatched three troop requests. This became a constant.[42]

A presidential review beginning on April 1, 1965 produced NSAM 328. It approved dispatching 18–20,000 army troops (one division) and dozens of actions requested by Taylor, the CIA, and army. At McNamara's April 20, 1965 Honolulu conference with his military leaders, he agreed to raise US troop strength from 33,000 advisors to 82,000 combat troops. Johnson publicly soft-pedaled the increase. He wanted nothing to upset the Senate's completion of the Voting Rights Act.[43]

The Marines' mission shifted from base defense to implementing an enclave strategy designed by Taylor. US troops would hold five key coastal cities and could sortie up to 50 miles to conduct counterinsurgency operations or assist ARVN forces. To Taylor, deploying forces in this manner meant they could be quickly withdrawn. It was also cheap and low risk. Johnson agreed. It was also short-lived: mid April to mid June. Both Westmoreland and the JCS objected to putting troops in populated areas, believing it would antagonize the Vietnamese, repeat France's error of leaving other areas to the VC, abandon a hard-pressed South Vietnamese Army, and surrender the initiative because it was defensive. But the enclave strategy had a more serious problem: it was built on the assumption that ROLLING THUNDER would force the Communists to negotiate, which wasn't happening.[44]

South Vietnam, though, was collapsing. On June 7, 1965, Westmoreland dispatched the most disturbing cable McNamara said he received when secretary of defense. The ARVN was breaking under Communist attacks, Westmoreland said, and the government "cannot stand up to this kind of pressure without reinforcements." He wanted US troop strength increased to 175,000 so he could wage an offensive instead of defensive war. Johnson resisted, telling McNamara: "I'm very depressed about it because I see no program from either Defense or State that gives me much hope of doing anything except just praying and gasping to hold on and hope they'll quit. I don't believe they're ever going to quit. And I don't see any plan for victory – militarily or diplomatically." But the VC killing 1,000 ARVN soldiers in a single battle convinced McNamara to support Westmoreland's request and he sent 100,000 more troops by 1966's end.[45]

THE VIETNAM WAR, 1961–1969

Johnson concluded he had to escalate because failure would destroy American credibility and his chance to pass his Great Society legislation. Advisors George Ball and Clark Clifford argued against escalation. Every other important civilian and military leader supported it, as did the "Wise Men," a group of senior former military and civilian leaders including Dean Acheson and Omar Bradley.[46] Leaders should always be wary of taking advice to act – especially involving the use of military force – from people who aren't responsible for the results.

WESTMORELAND'S STRATEGY

America's ground war strategy is usually simplistically branded attrition. This was the dominant aspect, but it actually had three planks: attrition, pacification (or counterinsurgency), coupled with "rural construction," and training South Vietnamese forces, particularly the ARVN. Westmoreland noted on January 7, 1966: "It is abundantly clear that all political, military, economic, and security (police) programs must be completely integrated in order to attain any kind of success in a country ... greatly weakened by prolonged conflict and is under increasing pressure by large military and subversive forces." Westmoreland intended his strategy to address the new primary threats to South Vietnam: the NVA and Main Force VC. Defeating the North's ground troops was necessary to provide security for the South's population. Westmoreland thought it "would entail a protracted war of attrition."[47] Attrition is generally associated with the wearing down of the enemy's military forces with the intent that their forces will be destroyed or their ability or will to resist will collapse.

The administration imposed constraints on the ground war. The Chinese intervention in Korea haunted Johnson and he feared a repeat, a worry backed by a 1965 CIA paper arguing China would support Hanoi militarily against a US invasion. This was true. China had troops in North Vietnam until 1970, and promised help if America invaded. Some administration members even wondered if intervention in South Vietnam would provoke Chinese or Soviet entry. The result was the restriction of US ground forces to fighting in South Vietnam. This meant Laos, Cambodia, and North Vietnam became sanctuaries while Hanoi developed supply and infiltration routes through Laos and Cambodia, and a Cambodian base area (COSVN) within striking distance of much of South Vietnam, including the capital, Saigon.[48]

On June 26, 1965, Westmoreland's Washington masters gave him permission to put troops into South Vietnam wherever he believed necessary.

At the beginning of 1965, there were 23,000; at the start of 1966, 184,000. In July, Westmoreland presented his three-phase war plan. By the end of 1965, he would deploy enough troops to keep South Vietnam from collapsing (forty-four battalions). Next, the US and its allies would go on the offensive in the most important areas, destroying enemy units and doing pacification. He offered no time limit. Finally, if the enemy were still a problem, he would spend a year to a year and a half after the completion of phase two to destroy the NVA and VC forces and their base areas. Westmoreland refused creation of a combined US–South Vietnam command, believing this would feed Communist propaganda accusing the South of being an American puppet and make it more difficult to hand over responsibilities when US forces departed. Westmoreland's superiors supported his approach, believing the general should be allowed to run his war. McNamara explained to Johnson that Westmoreland's strategy would wear down the enemy and bring them to agree "to terms favorable to South Vietnam and the United States," and show Hanoi it couldn't win.[49]

Westmoreland formally presented his strategy to Johnson and administration officials at a February 1966 Honolulu conference. He said the war would be long and require a number of campaigns. Strategy was encapsulated in a 1966 directive instructing him, among other things, to "Attrit" "Viet Cong and North Vietnamese forces at a rate as high as their capability to put men into the field" by the end of 1966, while shrinking the VC base areas, increasing pacified areas, and defending his bases. This was in effect until August 1969.[50]

What mattered most to Westmoreland in 1965 was countering the North's offensive into South Vietnam's Central Highlands as this threatened to cut the country in half. He used most of his initial troops to build his logistical foundation and protect the bases needed for follow-on forces. Support for pacification was not part of phase one. The twenty-four battalions in the second phase would give him the strength to take the offensive and "resume and expand pacification operations" in key areas. Half of US troops in Vietnam in January 1966 were protecting bases.[51]

From the first large-scale commitment of US troops in 1965 until January 1968, Westmoreland implemented attrition via "search and destroy" operations, defining these as "an operation to find the enemy and to eliminate his base camps and logistic installations." He believed he could inflict enough casualties on the enemy to drive them past a "crossover point" where they were losing more men than they could replace. A controversial and easily manipulated and bungled "body count" of enemy killed was a measure for evaluating this. Search and destroy missions against Main Force units could, in theory, be directed at less populated areas. Pacification was the ARVN's job, and Westmoreland paid less attention to this and developing South Vietnamese forces, which were supposed to be dealing with the guerillas by conducting pacification. Westmoreland argued that he didn't have the troops to do both pacification and search and destroy.[52] In 1965, this was the case.

Westmoreland's strategy had its first significant test in the Battle of Ia Drang, fought in Pleiku province near the Cambodian border November 14–18, 1965. The North Vietnamese Army mounted an offensive against South Vietnam and overran some Special Forces camps doing pacification. The North was trying to drive to the sea, cut the nation in half, and defeat an American force. US units helicoptered into an NVA base area to enact "destroy." A bloody fight ensued. The remnants of the two NVA regiments withdrew. The estimated 12 to 1 kill ratio in America's favor validated attrition in Westmoreland's eyes.[53]

The first half of 1966 saw Westmoreland's troops fighting in the coastal plains to protect the population. US forces were to sweep through and eliminate large enemy forces. The ARVN would come behind and destroy the VC infrastructure and guerrillas, and provide population security. Numerous operations followed over the next two years as American strength increased. The South lacked the ability to secure areas afterward or instead copied the Americans. The US would win battles while repeatedly clearing the same areas and leaving, allowing the enemy to return. Because the operations took place in populated areas, they created tens of thousands of refugees and evacuees.[54]

Despite these problems, Westmoreland had some success. Between early 1967 and March 1969, the Viet Cong was heavily mauled (the North's failed Tet offensive contributed greatly to this) and the US made much progress toward pacification. Moreover, Westmoreland succeeded in propping up South Vietnam and forcing the North Vietnamese over to the defensive and to operate from their bases in Cambodia and Laos.[55]

But Westmoreland's strategy, and American strategy in general, failed to address the three core issues in a war with an insurgency: securing support from the people, eliminating sanctuary, and preventing the enemy from receiving outside support. Political and geographical constraints meant it couldn't address the third. Westmoreland's operational approach helped undermine the US grasp on the first two by doubling the number of refugees in South Vietnam. Particularly problematic were "free fire zones," which involved forcibly evacuating an area, designating any person remaining an enemy combatant, and pounding any target with artillery.

But people sometimes refused to leave or returned too early. Injudicious use of firepower alienated people it was meant to protect and win over, and caused needless civilian casualties while providing the enemy recruits and a propaganda tool.[56]

The logic behind the attrition strategy was also flawed. It was arguably impossible to determine the "crossover point" at which the North could no longer replace its losses or, because of sanctuary, inflict sufficient casualties unless Hanoi cooperated, which it did in some respects by meeting escalation with escalation. The North possessed abundant manpower as 200,000 men became eligible for the draft annually. The NVA numbered 700,000 by the end of 1966; 230,000 were in South Vietnam. Main Force VC numbered 80,000, supported by 174,000 irregulars, South Vietnamese sympathizers, and Viet Cong conscripts. China dispatched more than 320,000 troops from 1965 to 1968; 130,000 were in North Vietnam in 1968. This allowed Hanoi to send more forces south.[57] The North could also choose when to decrease its commitment, which it did after defeat of its 1968–69 Tet Offensive.

The problem of external sanctuary in Laos, Cambodia, and North Vietnam was never resolved, but Westmoreland tried to tackle it after a reassessment. On March 18, 1967, he requested 200,000 more troops. Westmoreland had 470,000 but believed he lacked enough to "secure his base areas, maintain the initiative in the field, and expand security in populated areas," especially as infiltration continued. Westmoreland wanted to stop this, isolate the area of operations, and remove the enemy sanctuaries, thus putting the US in a position to force the North to make peace. Cutting the Ho Chi Minh Trail in Laos was a first step. More troops would enable this, a quicker defeat of the enemy, and the removal of sanctuaries inside South Vietnam. The JCS backed Westmoreland's plan, but with additions: intensified bombing, particularly of the North's lines of supply, mining of ports such as Hanoi's Haiphong Harbor, operations in Cambodia, and "a possible invasion of North Vietnam."[58]

A sharp internal debate on the direction and execution of the war ensued. Military leaders pushed escalation of military force and expansion beyond South Vietnam. McNamara urged the opposite via deescalating bombing and abandoning the political aim of an independent, non-Communist South Vietnam for a confused statement of American "commitment" that would end if "the country ceases to help itself," all while pursuing a negotiated settlement. Johnson charted a middle path. He refused to mobilize the reserves required to meet Westmoreland's request as that would cause domestic political uproar but gave Westmoreland another 55,000 troops and allowed some increased bombing. He refused the mining of Haiphong or any expansion of the ground war. American troop strength peaked at 549,500 in January 1969. In August 1966, Marine Commandant General Wallace Greene said he believed it would take 750,00 troops five years to win the war with America's strategy.[59]

Should Johnson have broadened the war? He wisely avoided invading North Vietnam, something the memory of Truman's invasion of North Korea made impossible. Operations into Laos and Cambodia probably wouldn't have required greater means than America committed and may have demanded fewer. The Kennedy administration considered effectively partitioning Laos by inserting 150,000 American troops to support the non-Communist forces controlling southern Laos.[60] This would have changed the nature of the war in Southeast Asia by severing the Ho Chi Minh Trail and stopping most Communist infiltration, thus lowering US force requirements. It would deny the insurgency external sanctuary and support, buying time for South Vietnam to destroy it behind a US screen, possibly producing a Korea-like situation. Blocking infiltration would also remove the primary factor in Cambodia's destabilization and destruction: North Vietnam. Hanoi could still supply its forces in South Vietnam via Sihanoukville, until the US blockade. But invading Laos raises other questions: is it worth the political costs of its *de facto* partitioning? And does it risk Beijing's involvement because Laos abuts China?

THE PACIFICATION STRATEGY: COUNTERINSURGENCY AND NATION BUILDING

In Vietnam, pacification acquired the moniker "the other war." Westmoreland's MACV defined pacification as "the military, political, economic, and social process of establishing or re-establishing local government responsive to and involving the participation of the people." After the February 1966 Honolulu conference, Westmoreland put more emphasis on pacification and development. As his force grew, the US became more involved in pacification via civil affairs teams and furnishing security and advisors. Civil affairs teams did innumerable tasks such as providing medical care and refugee relief while doing development. The VC and poor South Vietnamese (SVN) follow-up often undermined these efforts.[61]

Pacification was always part of American and South Vietnamese strategy. In March 1964, the South Vietnamese government announced the *Chien Tang* (Victory) National Pacification Plan, an integrated social, economic, and government reform program based upon Britain's Malaya experience. It was destroyed by governmental instability after Diem's assassination but poured a foundation for uniting military and political functions. In January 1966, Major General Nguyen Duc Thang, an industrious and effective leader, combined several development programs to create the Revolutionary Development Cadre (RD). A tool for building government support, these self-sacrificing teams of twenty-nine 20-somethings were a combination security team and nation-building task force assigned to a hamlet. They endured VC attacks, constant drains on their personnel from other government arms, and Saigon's corruption and failure to provide population security. South Vietnam's *Chieu Hoi* program focused on turning VC members and produced over 20,000 "ralliers" in 1966 alone. Saigon created numerous police and militia security forces. The Civil Guard and Self-Defense Corps became the Regional Forces/Popular Forces (RF/PF) in 1964, numbered over 300,000 in 1966, and were integrated into the armed forces. Corruption and personnel issues plagued both. In 1966, 5,000 US military advisors scattered among every command provided training.[62]

Johnson and his advisors realized in 1966 that the "other war" was receiving insufficient emphasis. Johnson appointed Republican Henry Cabot Lodge Jr. as ambassador to South Vietnam in an ultimately failed coordination effort. Johnson extracted promises in January 1966 that Saigon would push a South Vietnamese version of the Great Society including rural development, local elections, and increased security for pacification efforts. But the expected level of coordination didn't happen. Robert W. "Blowtorch Bob" Komer then became the president's special assistant for managing pacification, with broad authority and direct presidential access. Saigon was now pushed to provide more security for the RD teams and agreed to devote half of its 100 ARVN battalions. They launched clear-and-hold operations and devoted more time to training the RF/PFs, something made possible by US forces taking over the war. ARVN officers disliked this as much as their American counterparts.[63]

Komer borrowed ideas from the army's 1966 study, "The Program for the Pacification and Long Term Development in Vietnam" (PROVN). Among its observations was that poor interagency cooperation hindered pacification. In March 1967, Johnson consolidated pacification operations under a new organization headed by Komer, Civil Operations and Revolutionary Development Support (CORDS). Komer became Westmoreland's deputy for both civilian and military pacification. He built upon existing efforts with Operation TAKEOFF. It improved pacification planning for 1968; accelerated *Chieu Hoi*; pushed more and better ARVN pacification support; expanded RD teams; improved refugee management and police forces; and did land reform. Attacking the VC Infrastructure

(VCI) – the leadership – took prominence. The major tool was the Phoenix Program, which killed or arrested its affiliates. Komer also introduced the Hamlet Evaluation System (HES) to measure pacification's effectiveness.[64]

American military pacification efforts included the Marine Combined Action Platoons (CAPs) program that placed fifteen Marines in the hamlets that together formed a Vietnamese village to train and fight alongside thirty-four PF militiamen. Launched in 1965, by 1967 there were seventy-nine CAPs. Some tout this as a potent pacification tool because it addressed a key American failure by providing direct population security. It was also a potential basis for an oil-spot counterinsurgency strategy that spread control using a minimum of manpower. Komer and General Thang both believed CAPs suffered from a lack of mobility and created dependency among the villagers. CAPs proved unable to identify VCI, couldn't stop enemy forces from breaking pacification programs, and few Americans had needed language skills. Some Marines believed them unworkable because the local VC infrastructure had existed for twenty years (but this could occur nearly anywhere). In one village with a CAP from 1966 to 1967, support for the Communists never dropped below 80 percent. This fell to around 50 percent during later operations by the 101st Airborne Division, about what it had been before CAP was implemented. Some CAP advocates take a tactical application and try to make a strategy out of it while ignoring the conventional aspects of the Communist war. But CAPs did try to tackle the critical problem of population security, and one wonders about the result if done on a large scale by properly trained ARVN units. CORDS developed something similar, Mobile Advisory Teams (MATs) (354 eventually), with five US and two South Vietnamese personnel that moved from village to village training the RF/PFs. Westmoreland rejected CAPs as foundation for a strategy "from the need to confront multiple dangers to the stability of South Vietnam."[65]

Innumerable problems plagued pacification. The Communists consistently attacked it, which the US couldn't prevent because it couldn't control infiltration. American units rarely remained long in infected areas, but a continuous troop presence was necessary, particularly where the VC had multigenerational links dating to the 1930s. Major US and ARVN operations disrupted pacification operations and created refugees. Nguyen Van Thieu, who from 1965 headed a military government and became president in 1967, refused to remove corrupt military commanders, fearing this would injure national unity. This wounded government effectiveness and credibility. Compounding this was Saigon's consistent failure to provide security. Historian Richard Hunt observed: "The key ingredient of successful pacification was an indigenous government that ably served and protected its citizens." Frustrated by corruption and Saigon's inefficiency, General Thang resigned from the joint general staff in January 1968. This knocked the legs from the pacification plank of Westmoreland's strategy, as it depended upon the ARVN.[66]

Pacification strategy rested on several weak reeds. The US assumed an outside force could build support for a *domestic* government. Even when US troops provided security for the population, this didn't necessarily translate into breaking their links with the Communists or support for Saigon. The US merely demonstrated – temporarily – that it was stronger. The village might be secured, but that differed from government control. If the host government cannot or will not clean its house and prove able to win the support of the people, the chances of an external power succeeding are greatly decreased. The Americans didn't understand that material improvement lacked the same appeal as a social and political revolution promising to overturn a status quo many disliked.[67] American development – based on Rostow's modernization theory – reduces people to creatures driven by material desire. The Communists proved ideas could attract, and where the idea was insufficient, violence did the job.

NAVAL STRATEGY

In 1960, at Chief of Naval Operations (CNO) Arleigh Burke's prodding, the US navy began examining using naval forces for counterinsurgency. The suggestions included coastal and river patrols and deploying units such as Seabee construction detachments and Special Forces. The navy's involvement deepened between 1962 and 1964 as it trained and supported the South Vietnamese navy, something it had been doing since 1950. Its most important role was logistics and transport. It is 7,000 miles from the US to South Vietnam and around 95 percent of supplies came by sea. It played a heavy part in air support and bombing, inserted Marines and Special Forces, and fought Communist coastal infiltration and supply efforts. Operation MARKET TIME, launched in March 1965, and later SEA DRAGON, forced the Communists to shift more of their sea supply effort to Sihanoukville, Cambodia. After the 1968 Tet offensive, CNO Elmo Zumwalt launched SEA LORDS, a systematic "brown water" interdiction operation for the Mekong Delta, and later GARDEN TIME to regain control of the South's major rivers.[68]

INFORMATIONAL STRATEGY

American public opinion initially supported the Vietnam War. But Johnson wanted to fight the war in "cold blood," fearing if he did too much to rally

Americans, they might push for a bigger war than he wanted. Johnson's January 10, 1967 State of the Union Address provides a picture of this:

> Whether we can fight a war of limited objectives over a period of time, and keep alive the hope of independence and stability for people other than ourselves; whether we can continue to act with restraint when the temptation to 'get it over with' is inviting but dangerous; whether we can accept the necessity of choosing 'a great evil in order to ward off a greater'; whether we can do these without arousing the hatreds and passions that are ordinarily loosed in time of war – on all these questions so much turns.[69]

Passion, though, as Clausewitz tells us, is a part of war. North Vietnam had no shortage of this.

Johnson tried to wage the war while doing nothing to maintain public support. Secretary of State Rusk said: "we never made any effort to create a war psychology in the United States.... We tried to do in cold blood perhaps what can only be done in hot blood, when sacrifices of this order are involved." This is dangerous when you are dispatching hundreds of thousands of draftees to fight a foreign war in which they often see no value. The Johnson administration eventually realized its error and in 1967 began trying to build support. It was probably too late, especially when the American public saw the Tet Offensive break across South Vietnam in 1968 – just after Westmoreland testified before Congress that the war neared its end. Johnson "failed to communicate his goals to the nation, and often appeared devious and deceitful. He suppressed internal dissent within his administration, he misled Congress and then sought to stifle legislative criticism, and he assaulted his public critics, denouncing them as 'nervous Nellies.'" This failure meant the media had a larger than expected effect on public opinion.[70]

There is also the value of the object (aim) in the eyes of the people and the war's ongoing blood cost. The higher the casualties in relation to the value of the object, the more quickly the people abandon the war. In theory, if the cause has some value to the public, and the casualties and financial costs continue to fall only upon a small percentage of the populace, the war could be prosecuted nearly indefinitely. This, of course, brings with it its own problems. Sun Tzu argued vociferously against a protracted war.[71]

THE RESULTS

By 1967, the government of South Vietnam stabilized when Thieu became president. Westmoreland's campaign had forced the NVA to the defensive.

But the South Vietnamese countryside was in disorder and perhaps one-fifth of the rural population were refugees.[72] Many in the US thought America was winning the war. But it was a stalemate where both sides were implementing attrition.

The North matched American escalation and fought an aggressive war. Some older sources say the North dropped to Mao's phase two but that wasn't the case. Le Duan insisted Main Force operations be the primary thrust, but Hanoi also conducted guerrilla operations, which increasing casualties forced. The failure of the attrition strategy and ROLLING THUNDER, and American and South Vietnamese military losses and political problems influenced Hanoi to attempt a knockout blow aligned with 1968's presidential election. Le Duan prepared another General Offensive–General Uprising. Main Force units would tie down US troops away from urban areas. Large-scale attacks would follow against the cities and towns of South Vietnam. This would produce mass uprisings and the Saigon regime would fall.[73]

The Tet Offensive occurred in five phases. (See Map 12.1.) Phase one was the largest and most important, and took advantage of the traditional Lunar New Year Truce, beginning on January 30–31, 1968. Approximately 84,000 VC and NVA troops launched attacks throughout South Vietnam, hitting 36 of the 44 provincial capitals, Saigon, and numerous other hamlets and cities. This was not a surprise; Westmoreland had been expecting something. But the intensity stunned both Washington and Saigon. The "General Uprising" never occurred, and after the initial surprise, US and ARVN units mauled the Communists, who lost around 60 percent of the force engaged, perhaps 50,000 soldiers, by March 31, 1968.[74]

Phase two lasted from May 4 to August 17, 1968. Phase three ran from August 17 through September 30, and was timed to coincide with the US presidential race and negotiations that had begun between Washington and Hanoi. Since it was now clear Tet wouldn't deliver its aims, North Vietnamese strategy became "talking while fighting." But General Vo Nguyen Giap and others wanted less emphasis on "fighting." Le Duan won the debate, and the attacks continued. Phase four ran from February 22 through March 30, 1969, and Phase five from May 11 through June 25, 1969. Tet nearly destroyed the Communist infrastructure in South Vietnam. It also soured relations with Beijing. Mao withdrew his troops. He believed Hanoi was following Soviet strategy and disliked it entering into talks after the failure of Tet's first wave. It took the North three years to recover militarily from Tet.[75]

THE VIETNAM WAR, 1961–1969

Map 12.1 North and South Vietnam

Tactically and operationally, Tet was a great victory for the US and South Vietnam. Strategically, it was disastrous. It exposed the administration's dishonesty and discredited military contentions that the war was almost won. It fed American disillusionment, including Johnson's, fueled antiwar feeling, and injured pacification. Of the 5,000 RF/PF posts, around

500 were destroyed. Over 6,500 territorial troops were killed, and many RD cadres lost. About half the security forces involved in pacification had to help defend South Vietnam's cities. American observers feared this weakened pacification by showing the people the government couldn't protect them. But many VC units were decimated, and its reputation suffered because it failed to hold any cities.[76]

THE JOHNSON ADMINISTRATION REASSESSES

At the end of February 1968, pressed by army Chief of Staff Earle Wheeler, Westmoreland asked for 206,000 troops, only half for Vietnam. This would force Johnson to mobilize reserves, which Wheeler viewed as a way of strengthening the global US force strained by Vietnam. Wheeler told a February 28 cabinet meeting that the troops would be needed to help the ARVN retake the countryside from the VC. Westmoreland, though, wanted the reinforcements for pacification operations and an offensive against the weakened enemy and his sanctuary and base areas in South Vietnam and, if permitted, also Laos and Cambodia.[77]

A shocked Johnson ordered a review headed by his new secretary of defense, Clark Clifford. He instructed Clifford to give him "the lesser of evils." Clifford met with the JCS on March 1 and asked if these troops would be enough to finish the job; if not, how many more would be needed. The Chiefs could answer neither question. Then a frightening conversation ensued:

CLIFFORD: What is the plan for victory?
JCS: There is no plan.
CLIFFORD: Why not?
JCS: Because American forces operate under three major restrictions; the president has forbidden them to invade the North ... he has forbidden the mining of Haiphong harbor ... he has forbidden pursuing the enemy into Laos and Cambodia.

An appalled Clifford refused the request as he could see no limit and urged a change in strategy to one that protected the population, the US forces acting as the shield behind which the South could develop militarily and governmentally and assume a larger burden.[78] This was much of what the US had been doing.

As part of his reassessment, Johnson again met with the "Wise Men," a mixture of civilian and military dignitaries led by Acheson. Their opinions were split, but many in the foreign relations community had turned against the war. The group told Johnson that the war couldn't be won.

The defection of these former hawks shocked the president and he said privately: "the Establishment bastards have bailed on me." Nevertheless, Johnson took their advice for finding a way out. On March 31, 1968, he announced he was limiting ROLLING THUNDER and seeking negotiations with Hanoi. And shocked America by withdrawing his presidential candidacy.[79]

Hanoi agreed to talks that began in Paris in May 1968. The Communists proved intransigent, insisting upon a bombing halt while Washington wanted to see North Vietnamese "restraint." A compromise was reached in which the US stopped bombing "with the expectation North Vietnam would curtail military activities." Johnson halted bombing of North Vietnam on October 31, 1968 (attacks continued in Laos). He hoped this would produce "serious negotiations" while helping his vice president, Hubert Humphrey, in his presidential race against Richard Nixon. Johnson also ordered continued military pressure on the ground to "keep the enemy on the run." To Hanoi, the bombing halt was a victory; Saigon's stunned leaders agreed. Nixon tried to secretly torpedo Johnson's talks, sending word to Thieu that if Saigon balked at negotiations, a Nixon presidency would take a hard stand against the Communists. The South announced it wouldn't participate. Upon discovering the gambit, Johnson said, "It's despicable, and if it were made public it would rock the nation." Some considered the move treasonous, but Johnson did nothing and left it to Humphrey. He declined action to avoid injuring attempts to get Thieu to negotiate and stirring further internal American discord. Raising it, though, could have produced retaliatory charges regarding Johnson's election fixing.[80] Nixon's interference had no effect. Hanoi had no intention of making peace.

MILITARY REASSESSMENT

On March 23, 1968, Westmoreland was promoted to army chief of staff. Creighton Abrams, Westmoreland's deputy, replaced him on July 3. Abrams proved more aggressive than Westmoreland. He urged American troops to pursue, defeat, and destroy the enemy, and wanted hamlet militia to intensify patrols and "night ambushes." But the enemy forces, bloodied by Tet, increasingly avoided action or withdrew to Cambodian sanctuaries. Abrams, like Westmoreland, operated under constraints. Clifford told him to reduce his casualties to dampen criticism and forbid US troops to enter Cambodia or Laos. North Vietnam remained off-limits. Abrams pushed aggressive patrolling of rural regions during the summer of 1968 "to provide a shield behind which the GVN [Government of Vietnam] could regain its political footing after Tet."[81]

The destruction of much of the VCI gave room for pacification to make gains, but the VC remained dangerous and more effective politically than South Vietnam's government. In November 1968, Komer launched the Accelerated Pacification Campaign, seeking to extend control to 1,000 hamlets. His plan, in which he expected the South to lead, included spoiling attacks against large enemy formations, Phoenix operations, expanded RD efforts, *Chieu Hoi*, arming 200,000 members of a People's Self-Defense Force (PSDF), and an information campaign trumpeting government accomplishments. Thieu authorized it on November 1. It was to be completed by February 1969, and after the expected, upcoming Tet 1969 attacks, normal operations would then resume. Abrams reluctantly agreed. It was implemented by Komer's successor, William Colby, who saw it as a means of attacking the VCI. Abrams hoped it would convince American critics "the war was winnable and pacification succeeding" and impress the new Nixon administration. He believed that if Accelerated Pacification succeeded, South Vietnamese development and reform would be possible.[82]

The campaign brought over 1,000 hamlets to "relatively secure" status, bringing 1.7 million more people under Saigon's control. *Chieu Hoi* brought in 8,500 defectors; Phoenix killed or captured perhaps 7,000 VCI, possibly more. The PSDF grew dramatically, and extended elected and appointed government control to 730 additional hamlets. The weakened VC responded largely via propaganda and terrorism. February 1969's Tet attacks failed to roll back the South's gains. More US troops were committed to pacification and ARVN improvements, and the expansion of RF/PF units made progress. But securing areas didn't mean the creation of support for the government of South Vietnam. It also couldn't counter war-weariness.[83]

In October 1968, Abrams declared there was "one war," stressed to his commanders the importance of pacification, and said the "order of the day is to intensify your offensive against infrastructure, guerrillas, and local force units." He placed particular emphasis on destroying the VCI.[84] Abrams' approach became a plank of the Nixon administration's grand strategy for its Vietnam War.

CONCLUSION

Something stunning about the development and implementation of grand strategy in the Kennedy–Johnson years was the ease with which American leaders adopted unproven and indeed unproveable ideas. By relying upon modernization theory and so-called "limited war," the US had a bankrupt intellectual approach underpinning elements of its Vietnam War. America's involvement was also a manifestation of the Wilsonian strand of Progressive idealism driving US actions abroad we will see again. American power is abundant and can be overwhelming, but it is not always capable of solving problems beyond America's shores.

US grand strategy for the Vietnam War from 1961 to 1969 suffered under shoddy theories, broken metrics, overconfidence, and a shallow understanding of the enemy. Once the US decided to fight this war, it needed to conduct a deep assessment of North Vietnam to identify its center of gravity – its main source of strength. It then needed to target this in an effort to force Hanoi to make an agreement. But what was North Vietnam's center of gravity? And could the US bend Hanoi to its will? Determining these answers was now Nixon's job.

13

DÉTENTE AND DEFEAT: NIXON, FORD, AND VIETNAM, 1969-1977

INTRODUCTION

Continuity marked the 1969 to 1977 period encompassing the Republican administrations of Richard Nixon and Gerald Ford, because of Henry Kissinger's sometimes double-hatted roles as national security advisor from 1969 to 1975 and secretary of state from 1973 to 1977. The Nixon–Kissinger duo brought ambition to American grand strategy, an ability to look past current obstacles and long term, and the belief (especially by Kissinger, who had studied Metternich, Castlereagh, and Bismarck) that statesmen should grasp the situation and shape it to the nation's interests and ends. Both adamantly believed new thinking was required, and thus new courses, but in addition to foreign challenges – the Vietnam War the most pressing – faced the challenge of leading the bureaucracy and public in directions that were sometimes alien and perhaps revolutionary.[1]

The administration faced an international situation greatly changed from what Johnson encountered upon his 1963 inauguration. The Soviets would soon reach nuclear parity. China entered the nuclear age in 1964 and stepped toward global power. Beijing and Moscow had split, presenting both danger and opportunity. Decolonization expanded the ideological battlefield. American economic and diplomatic strength vis-à-vis other nations suffered relative decline with the rise of Japan, the Federal Republic of Germany, and regional powers such as China and Brazil. The Soviet threat remained paramount.[2]

THE ASSESSMENT

The US needed to recover flexibility in order to meet a myriad new challenges. Kissinger wrote: "It is beyond the physical and psychological capacity of the US to make itself responsible for every part of the world." But America had the anchor of Vietnam, a peripheral interest, strapped to its back. Nixon wanted, in a manner not dissimilar to Eisenhower, for states to act more on their own behalf, and no repetition of Vietnam. Kissinger believed America needed to reassess its interests, shed idealistic illusions, and accept the reality of the diversity of rule among states. The administration didn't buy that economic development and movement toward democracy necessarily increased US security. Economic and political reform were as apt to feed instability, and states with open economies and democratic governments didn't necessarily act in America's interests. One could find common interests, particularly in the security realm, with differently governed states. A more politically pluralistic world was emerging where America didn't play the overweening role and could reduce its global burdens. If handled properly, increased stability could result. This required changing how America determined threats. Ideology – specifically Communism – was no longer the basis. The threat to US interests mattered.[3]

THE POLITICAL AIM

Kissinger's First Annual Report to Congress (1970) discussed elements of the administration's grand strategy but lacked a clear political aim. But one section, "The Framework for a Durable Peace," points in that direction, as do Nixon's remarks in his inaugural address, especially this: "Let us take as our goal: where peace is unknown, make it welcome; where peace is fragile, make it strong; where peace is temporary, make it permanent." The Nixon administration sought the security of the United States. Peace – for the US and others – would deliver this.[4]

It is perhaps iconoclastic to express Nixon's political aim so, and there were undoubtedly underlying political motivations to play to an American public that wanted peace – especially in Vietnam. But it's important to understand that the country *needed* peace. Discontent over the Vietnam War was the great driver of internal troubles, but there were others. Tragedy and chaos marked 1968: the Tet Offensive, the assassinations of Martin Luther King Jr. and Robert Kennedy, riots at the Democratic National Convention and elsewhere. The economy was slowing, inflation and unemployment increasing, and extremism was on rise as radical groups, particularly among the New Left, launched hundreds of bombing attempts; scores succeeded. A polarized nation seemed to be coming apart and in decline.[5]

But, as mentioned above, Americans most wanted peace in Vietnam. Nixon sought to give it to them. And he also wanted more. Kissinger wrote: "Peace must be far more than the absence of war. Peace must provide a durable structure of international relationships which inhibits or removes the causes of war." Nixon and Kissinger are generally referred to as foreign policy "realists." Indeed, this was how they saw themselves.[6] But they had a Wilsonian aim.

THE GRAND STRATEGY

To implement the envisaged turnaround, Nixon and Kissinger needed to control the process of strategy creation and implementation. This meant stiff-arming the bureaucracy and cabinet officers away from planning and implementation. Kissinger, as NSC head, supplanted the secretary of state as the president's principal advisor (and chair) at key meetings. The NSC became chief evaluator and gatekeeper of ideas, and retained power to push its own while directly advising the president.[7]

Nixon believed a balance of power between the United States, Japan, China, Europe, and the Soviet Union meant a more stable world. This was more in line with US interests as the supposed bipolarity removed flexibility, though managing multipolarity was more difficult. This didn't mean each area required commensurate military power. Economic power made Europe and Japan key players. Kissinger preferred stability, and shaping events rather than reacting, seeing this as the essence of statesmanship.[8] An advantage of this approach was that geopolitical bipolarity didn't exist to the extent believed.

The US couldn't be effective everywhere, and the administration hoped to reduce tensions while shrinking American costs and responsibilities. This would thwart critics, keep America involved in the world, and lessen Vietnam's ill-effects on the body politic. In July 1969, on the island of Guam, Nixon launched what became known as the Nixon Doctrine after grasping a press description and making it his own. The United States would continue to support its friends and allies, but it wouldn't make all the decisions and plans, nor bear all the burdens. States were expected to carry the load for their own defense. "Our interests," Kissinger wrote later, "must shape our commitments rather than the other way around."[9]

Nixon's announcement surprised Kissinger, and the creation, development, and implementation of the Nixon Doctrine was ad hoc. Kissinger tasked Winston Lord with giving it flesh, and the administration started building grand strategy around it. It planned to decrease US forces in Asia, and not just in Vietnam. South Korea, Thailand, and Japan also made the list. As it reduced troop numbers in Asia, the administration balked at Congressional efforts to shrink US NATO forces. Europe remained the priority. Washington would contribute to European order while reducing its costs. In the Third World, the Nixon and Ford administrations sought to build up regional powers to carry the anti-Communist struggle via economic aid, military sales, and political backing. Of the key states – Israel, Brazil, Indonesia, South Africa, Iran – only the first was a democracy.[10]

POLITICAL AIMS AND STRATEGY: THE SOVIET UNION AND CHINA

The Nixon administration pursued a version of containment strategy called détente. A common term in diplomacy denoting easing of tensions between states, it was used in regard to the East–West relationship in the 1960s by France's Charles De Gaulle and NATO. It was first attached to the Nixon administration in 1969, a moniker it initially tried to avoid. To Kissinger, détente meant "habits of mutual restraint, coexistence, and, ultimately, cooperation." The aim was to end the Cold War by convincing Moscow to alter its view of the international system and become a member of the community. The grand strategy of détente would be built around "a new combination of pressures and inducements that would, if successful, convince Kremlin leaders that it was in their country's interest to be 'contained.'"[11]

The new system required reaching an understanding with Moscow. Kissinger insisted negotiations would be informed by the ideological reality of America's Communist opponents, free of illusion, and both prod and attract the Soviets to convince them of cooperation's value. Through "carrots and sticks" and "linkage," Moscow would see there was only so far strength and ideology could take it, and become a superpower not bent on destabilizing the international system. The US would resist Soviet actions, making it clear Moscow couldn't do as it wished while demonstrating that good behavior won what it desired and needed. But if the Soviets wanted something, the US would link this to other and often broader issues.[12]

The administration forged some agreements with Moscow. The 1972 summit produced the "Basic Principles of Relations," in which both parties agreed to restraint in dealing with international conflicts, and the "Agreement on the Prevention of Nuclear War," calling for consultation when events threatened relations between the two. Some read this to mean China. None of this mattered. To Moscow, détente was another way to pursue world revolution; the "class struggle" hadn't ended. And even if Moscow had wanted a peaceful Third World, it couldn't control its clients. Egypt's Anwar Sadat launched the 1973 Arab–Israeli War for his own reasons, and Castro did as he wished in Angola.[13]

Both Nixon and Kissinger believed a stable global system impossible with China semi-isolated. Opening this door also pressured Moscow.

PART II: FROM GREAT POWER TO SUPERPOWER

Nixon pushed Kissinger toward exploring an opening in February 1969 and guided the ship of state on this course despite initial skepticism from Kissinger and the bureaucracy. The spring 1969 Sino-Soviet border war made the fissures between the Communist giants apparent, especially when Moscow asked for Washington's view if Moscow preemptively obliterated Beijing's nuclear capability. Nixon thought it not in America's interest to have China defeated in the war that would follow. This could upset the balance of power by removing a state that could help the US balance Moscow. By July 1969, Kissinger was urging better relations with both Communist giants.[14]

In July 1971, Kissinger made a secret trip to China. Nixon met with Mao in February 1972. Nixon's outreach created a staggering geostrategic change. It stunned enemies and friends, some of whom were informed only shortly before its announcement. Shocked Asian friends (except Taiwan) soon saw advantages, while Taipei saw its UN positions given to Beijing and Washington alter its diplomatic but not military relationship with them. The administration hoped rapprochement with China would aid its Asian and global rebalancing, reducing defense responsibilities and costs while creating problems for the Soviets and making them open to negotiating. It had the desired effect on Moscow, and the administration quickly concluded the Strategic Arms Limitation Treaty (SALT), the Anti-Ballistic Missile Treaty (ABM), an agreement on Berlin's status, and another committing both to "peaceful coexistence." And the Soviets didn't protest Nixon's bombing of North Vietnam after Hanoi launched its 1972 Easter Offensive against South Vietnam. Nixon hoped also for Beijing's help with Hanoi. The opening did most of what Nixon wanted. The US lowered its Asia troop numbers and increased support for Europe. The Soviets felt more pressure to support détente, though encouragement for Hanoi to abandon its quest for South Vietnam from Moscow or Beijing wasn't immediately forthcoming. The audacity of Nixon's act regained the initiative for Washington.[15]

The weakness of the Nixon–Kissinger approach was a failure to appreciate Moscow and Beijing pursued their aims regardless of US actions. Kissinger wrote of the Soviets: "It is up to us to define the limits of Soviet aims." And later of Beijing: "The leaders of China were beyond ideology in their dealings with us."[16] This wasn't the case. Kennan's original assessment that the US could not significantly alter Soviet behavior remained true and applied equally to Communist China. This also marked the beginning of an era of misconceptions regarding American ability to alter China via engagement.

DIPLOMATIC STRATEGY: BEYOND CONTAINMENT

Tolerance of different governmental systems didn't apply to allowing Marxist or Communist regimes to bloom. In Latin America, the Nixon administration backed the overthrow of Brazil's left-wing regime by the military in 1971, and the successful coup against Chile's Salvador Allende in 1973. In the Middle East, the Nixon Doctrine's emphasis on other states doing more saw the administration delegate responsibility. Kissinger created the "twin pillars" strategy, counting upon Iran and Saudi Arabia to balance growing Soviet influence in Iraq and Egypt. The West's position was weakened by Britain's 1968 decision to remove its military forces east of Suez, which was completed in 1971. Kissinger and Nixon convinced Iran's shah to take up the security mantle and help stabilize the Persian Gulf, and opened the arms stores in return.[17]

Kissinger used the 1973 Arab–Israeli War to convince Israel to be more malleable since they couldn't defend themselves without US help and persuade Arab states peace could come only through America. During the war, Kissinger took what he deemed reckless actions aimed at Moscow because he believed this "the safest course." Kissinger said later: "Our general strategy is to make a lot of moves, all at the same time, to give the other side a lot of decisions to make. And then, if we move military forces, to maneuver very dangerously, so that the other side doesn't think it is riskless to challenge." These moves included putting US nuclear forces on alert. By 1975, Kissinger launched a process that eventually bore fruit while sidelining Moscow as he shifted the US from a pro-Israeli position to a more balanced one, garnering friends for Washington in the Arab world.[18]

None of this prevented the Arab oil embargo. Angered by US support for Israel, Middle East oil producers embargoed oil sales and hiked prices at the shah's instigation. Saudi Arabia and Iran, two pillars of American Middle East strategy, drove a stake into an already weakened American economy. The devastation was so great Kissinger examined seizing Saudi oil fields. Riyadh was eventually convinced to relent, partially because the US agreed to sell it modern weapons. But the price drop broke Iran's finances, caused unemployment, and fed unrest.[19]

In Asia, the administration learned the political costs of relations with dictators and looking the other way. The Pakistani government killed hundreds of thousands of its citizens in East Pakistan (now Bangladesh) when it revolted in 1971. Kissinger insisted upon siding with Pakistan because India tilted Soviet and Pakistan was the conduit to Beijing, and worked to prevent

India from winning the war that followed. This blew up in the administration's face after publication of incriminating leaked documents. India was more non-aligned than pro-Moscow, a misreading that helped prevent a warming of US–Indian relations until the Reagan administration.[20]

The Gerald Ford administration faced the effects of South Vietnam's fall and the Nixon Doctrine on Asia strategy. An effort to restore post-Vietnam credibility saw the ill-fated May 1975 rescue operation of the crew of the *Mayaguez*, which had been seized by Cambodia's Khmer Rouge. Unknown to Ford, the crew had been released before the US attack. The administration conducted a massive evacuation from South Vietnam in 1975 and rescued thousands of refugees fleeing Communism's victory. US forces left Thailand in 1976; SEATO dissolved in 1977.[21]

Realizing it needed a new approach in Asia, the Ford administration reassessed. On December 7, 1975, Ford announced the New Pacific Doctrine. He declared "dedication to America's bipartisan policy of pursuing peace through strength and dedication to a new future of interdependence and cooperation with all peoples of the Pacific." The administration sought security in the Pacific through a regional balance of power, stability, the maintenance of state sovereignty, reaffirmation of ties to America's Asian allies and partners such as Japan and Korea, normalization of relations with China, and increased economic cooperation.[22]

Kissinger and Nixon valued stability over human rights and found the growing global human rights push moralistic and naïve, and were skeptical of America's ability to promote human rights or democracy abroad. The Nixon–Kissinger–Ford diplomatic strategy faced criticism from left and right that it lacked morality because it seemed to accept Communist mass murder in China, Cambodia, and the Soviet Union, and Pakistani massacres in Bangladesh. Kissinger's defense included a July 1975 speech arguing the necessity of a pragmatic approach for delivering American security, but said "security is a means, not an end" because "the purpose of security is to safeguard the values of our free society."[23] But security is an aim, not a means. Nations act to achieve security.

The 1975 Helsinki Final Act between Moscow, Washington, and their respective allies addressed trade and security, and recognized Eastern Europe's borders. This provoked attacks on Ford from conservatives, including Ronald Reagan, because it approved Moscow's Second World War expansion, and cost Kissinger his national security advisor post. The agreement had human rights provisions Soviet dissidents exploited, but it couldn't protect them.[24]

INFORMATIONAL STRATEGY

The Nixon administration waged a two-front information campaign. Internationally, it sought to produce uncertainty in the minds of opponents regarding what the US would do. This was a deterrence tool as it made foes uncertain how far they could push and how much they could risk. Domestically, the administration attacked internal government subversion and obstacles, both real and imagined. Nixon and Kissinger feared leaks undermining negotiations and sought to isolate the bureaucracy from strategy formation, thwart resistance from career Democrats, and escape the paralysis inflicted on strategy's creation and execution by slow-moving and unimaginative bureaucracies. Congress had oversight but needed to be kept from the diplomacy and the details; it lacked the flexibility to achieve results.[25]

Nixon thought solid actions and success would produce acceptance for his strategy. He soon realized his error and the need for a public relations campaign to maintain support, something made clear by political opposition and press criticism from the left. When Kissinger came around to the necessity of this, he soon spent perhaps one-third of his time with the press. The administration published extensive, declassified annual reports of its grand strategic efforts that received plaudits from the likes of Kennan but had no noticeable effect on public opinion.[26]

The administration was racked by infighting and spying between departments, activities partially provoked by Nixon and Kissinger trying to control as much as possible while keeping others (such as the State Department) out of the loop because they feared leaks or mistrusted them. The JCS resorted to having a sailor bring them stolen White House documents to keep abreast of matters. In May 1969, when news broke of the secret bombing in Cambodia, Kissinger ordered the bugging of a trio of his NSC staffers in an unsuccessful effort to find the leak. The arrest of five men during a break-in at the Democratic National Headquarters at the Watergate Hotel and the Nixon cover-up that followed launched the domestic crisis that destroyed Nixon's presidency and forced his August 1974 resignation.[27]

ECONOMIC STRATEGY

In 1970, the US was the dominant economic power, but its percentage of global GDP had fallen from 27.3 to 22.4 percent. European and Asian Second World War recovery and economic growth accounted for much of this. Post-Vietnam inflation resulted from "war economics" – fiscal and monetary stimulus coupled with price and wage controls – and other factors: higher food and oil prices, continuous expansion of the money supply to reduce unemployment, and falling productivity growth rates.[28]

America was also no longer the world's largest oil producer. Global demand for crude skyrocketed in the two prior decades, but the US couldn't dramatically expand production in an emergency. Simultaneously, the Organization of Petroleum Exporting Countries (OPEC) arose. Two members, Libya and Iran, helped increase prices by 45 percent between 1970 and 1973. The October 1973 Arab–Israeli War saw Arab producers cut production and embargo oil sales to America as OPEC quadrupled prices. This injured economic growth and fed inflation and unemployment. The US unemployment rate doubled to 9 percent while GNP shrank 6 percent from 1973 to 1975. US inflation hit 13.5 percent by 1979.[29]

The Vietnam War's costs also caused problems, and America had difficulty paying for its global commitments. In 1971, inflation was 5.9 percent, unemployment over 6 percent, and the US had a trade deficit for the first time. Nixon converted to Keynesian economics and embarked upon severe government intervention in the economy. In August 1971, he launched his New Economic Policy (Lenin used the same name in 1921). Sold as temporary measures to get the economy going, he first tried to stop inflation by imposing a ninety-day wage and price freeze. To attack the trade deficit and help American business, he imposed a 10 percent surcharge on imports (a tariff). He cut government spending and increased taxes. Most significantly, he ended the dollar's convertibility into gold. Its value fell dramatically against major currencies. This helped the US balance of payments problem resulting from the decrease in the US share of the global export market and was intended to aid American business by lowering export costs. It killed the fixed currency exchange rates established at Bretton Woods and generally floating rates followed. The US, though, no longer bore the burden of propping up the global economy. Additionally, the dollar's lower relative value made US exports more attractive, all while the dollar remained the world's reserve currency. American exports received a short-term boost, the balance of payments deficit shrank, and inflation fell slightly, but none of this helped very much.[30]

Kissinger believed tying Moscow economically to the world economy would "foster a degree of interdependence that adds an element of stability to the political equation." Enmeshing it in the Western economic system would create a link that could be cut when needed, supposedly making it harder for Moscow act against the West. Congress thwarted Kissinger's most-favored-nation agreement with an amendment preventing its extension to "non-market economies" forbidding emigration, a salvo aimed at

Moscow's mistreatment of Jews and dissidents.[31] Economic strategies rarely deliver leverage, particularly against totalitarian states, as nations often act in support of their political aims even at the cost of economic pain.

MILITARY STRATEGY

Kissinger believed approaching Soviet nuclear weapons parity, and the near-impossibility of their use, had reduced their importance, and noted they had exerted no effect on any crisis since 1962. Kissinger applied the idea of "sufficiency" in nuclear arms to other elements of defense as US increases in military power were only met by similar Soviet efforts. The Johnson administration had already felt the economic impact of this, and it was judged in America's interests to convince the Soviets to see this as well. Kissinger wanted the SALT agreement in order to avoid additional nuclear weapons costs.[32]

On other fronts, Kissinger neglected NATO during most of his tenure. It regained his attention in 1974 and 1975 when it seemed Communist parties might join coalition governments in Portugal, France, and Italy via election victories. NATO's peacetime strategy remained deterrence of a Warsaw Pact attack. It was to maintain enough conventional forces to hold the Warsaw Pact for ninety days without losing much territory. To do this, America's NATO allies needed to improve their conventional capabilities, and Nixon pushed them to fulfill their commitments under the European Defense Improvement Program by spending an additional $2 billion across the next decade. America's peacetime nuclear strategy remained deterrence. In the event of war, the US would seek to end it as quickly as possible "on terms acceptable to the United States and its allies."[33]

American military power declined during the Nixon–Ford years, partially because Nixon abandoned the standard established under Kennedy of being able to simultaneously fight two-and-a-half wars for a one-and-a-half war requirement. Congress was the primary driver of military retrenchment, but others included disillusionment, the post-Vietnam drawdown, and the increased per soldier cost of the all-volunteer army after Nixon ended the draft in January 1973. Meanwhile, the Soviets modernized and expanded.[34]

THE NIXON ADMINISTRATION AND THE VIETNAM WAR

To Nixon, US participation in the Vietnam War had been in America's interest, particularly as an element of the Cold War and containment. He was urged to withdraw but couldn't abandon 17 million people to

Communist tyranny. Departing would feed Communist aggression and devastate "peace and freedom in all of Asia." Globally, losing the South would injure America's ability to regain its leadership position and build a US-led system. The adminsitration wanted peace in Vietnam, but on terms serving American interests, and needed to end the war to address "the domestic and international crises facing the United States." Nixon thought Johnson's use of force ineffective and believed he could do better. He and Kissinger agreed Hanoi had a breaking point and an end could be negotiated.[35]

REASSESSMENT

Nixon saw the war as part China's effort to spread Communism. He realized Hanoi hadn't abandoned its aims and that America was failing to attrite the North's forces faster than they could be replaced. He assumed Hanoi wanted simultaneously "to negotiate a mutual withdrawal and a political settlement" and understood the North would do everything to weaken American public opinion and will while trying to overthrow Saigon's government. Nixon told the NSC to look for new approaches. Kissinger had a thinktank, RAND, do a reassessment between the election and inauguration. Finding no consensus, Daniel Ellsberg, one of the team's leaders (who later leaked the classified Defense Department volumes on the war known as the *Pentagon Papers*), suggested deeper collecting of opinion from government agencies. Kissinger liked the idea. It would tell him how the war was viewed while burying the bureaucracy in work.[36]

Kissinger launched the reassessment via a series of questions in National Security Study Memoranda (NSSM) 1. The result provided little clarity beyond that US withdrawal necessitated improving the ARVN and a government that removed corruption and was supported by the people. Neither the government nor the ARVN were thought capable of standing without US support.[37] The summary report included an inadvertent indictment of US strategy:

> The enemy have suffered some reverse but they have not changed their essential objectives and they have sufficient strength to pursue these objectives. We are not attriting enemy forces faster than they can recruit or infiltrate. Soviet and Chinese supplies have enabled the enemy to carry on despite our operations.[38]

The problem, of course, was what to do next.

THE POLITICAL AIM

There is confusion regarding Nixon's political aim in South Vietnam, because of controversial statements and the seeming absence of a specific document. Nixon's aim was that of Kennedy and Johnson: maintaining an independent, non-Communist South Vietnam. Nixon said in a June 8, 1969 speech that "no action will be taken that endangers the attainment of our objective, the right of self-determination for the people of South Vietnam." But Nixon also sought what he called an "honorable peace," a term he used in a May 5, 1968 campaign speech and a message to Hanoi shortly before his inauguration. To Nixon, this meant an independent South Vietnam.[39]

Preserving South Vietnam safeguarded American credibility. But as the war went on, it became clear America's strategy wasn't succeeding, the meaning of preserving South Vietnam changed, and Nixon and Kissinger accepted "the decent-interval solution," which meant an American exit not guaranteeing the Saigon government's survival. Nixon said in 1971: "our policy is, is to win the war.... And winning the war simply means ... letting South Vietnam survive. That's all." Only at the finish, in a January 23, 1973 speech announcing the war's end, did Nixon use the term "peace with honor."[40]

NIXON AND GRAND STRATEGY IN VIETNAM

Before his inauguration, Nixon had thought much about the war. He was aware of the necessity of applying the elements of national power to the struggle and said in 1968: "The only course is to increase pressure on all sides – militarily, diplomatically, economically." He also noted the necessity of public support. Nixon said he didn't have a plan for the war (he is accused of the opposite) and denied ever saying he had a "secret plan." What he did admit to having were some "strategic ideas": diplomacy with the Soviets, China, and North Vietnam, backed by the threat of escalation via the "Madman Theory" (more shortly), US troop withdrawals, more emphasis on pacification, and turning over the war to the South. This last was seen as a way to prop up domestic support, as were discussions on altering the draft.[41]

Before the final NSSM reassessment report appeared on March 26, Nixon and Kissinger had decided what to do in Vietnam.[42] Nixon didn't see the possibility of an immediate political settlement and offered an outline for his administration's grand strategy on January 25, 1969:

> The mix of actions should be something like this. We talk hard in private but with an obvious peaceful public stance, seeking to gain time, initially

giving the South Vietnamese a chance to strengthen the regime and add to the pacification effort while punishing the Viet Cong (VC). Within three or four months bring home a few troops unilaterally as a separate and distinct action from the Paris negotiations, and as a ploy for more time domestically, while we continue to press at the negotiating table for a military settlement.[43]

To Nixon, the key elements were diplomacy and force. Nixon wanted a negotiated settlement and believed "his diplomatic-military strategy would provide him with the bargaining leverage he needed to pry a negotiated settlement out of Hanoi and Moscow within his first year in office."[44]

Nixon's strategy of secret talks, withdrawing US troops, and providing population security was leaked to the *New York Times*, which published an article about it on April 6, 1969. This and similar stories revealing unilateral withdrawal of US forces frightened Thieu. The leaker was Nixon's secretary of defense, Melvin Laird, who acted to counter Kissinger pushing for escalation and against withdrawal. Laird also leaked to Congress to publicly put a presidential stamp on Vietnamization (more shortly) "before Nixon agreed to its implementation."[45]

DIPLOMATIC STRATEGY

Nixon's diplomatic strategy had three fronts: Hanoi, Moscow, and Beijing, Hanoi being the most important. But diplomacy didn't stand alone. Nixon said: "I was convinced that unless we backed up our diplomatic efforts with strong military pressure, the North Vietnamese would continue their strategy of talking and fighting until we tired of the struggle and caved." Nixon didn't think Hanoi would seriously negotiate unless facing overwhelming force and believed he needed six months of military action against the Communists. Both he and Kissinger thought military pressure had to be maintained or the negotiations would drag on like in the Korean War. Kissinger felt the North "could only be brought to compromise by being confronted by insuperable obstacles on the ground." Negotiations would gain time to pummel the enemy.[46]

Nixon called his negotiations approach his "Madman Theory," to him a form of psychological (information) warfare. Enemies would be convinced of his willingness to use overwhelming, even unnecessary, force, including nuclear weapons. Nixon mistakenly believed Eisenhower's threat to use atomic weapons had helped end the Korean War and thought convincing the North he was "unpredictable and capable of the bloodiest brutality" would push them to negotiate. In March 1969, Nixon sent Ho Chi Minh a letter relaying a preference for peace while threatening renewed bombing on November 1 – if negotiations weren't fruitful. Nixon believed secret talks the most productive. The first occurred in March 1969. Hanoi produced its demands, standard since March 1965 and which remained essentially unchanged until October 1972: establishment of a new government in South Vietnam that made Communist control inevitable and a unilateral US troop withdrawal. American demands were based on Johnson's 1966 Manila note calling for mutual withdrawal of foreign troops from South Vietnam, with a small US force remaining until the North recognized the South. Nixon believed he needed more leverage. Outreach to China become a part. Kissinger linked Soviet help with resolution of other issues and told Moscow America would compromise while passing along threats of "other alternatives."[47]

MILITARY STRATEGY: PART I

The North launched a small continuation of Tet on February 22, 1969. Nixon replied with Operation MENU, the "secret" bombing of North Vietnamese bases in Cambodia. American planes began hitting North Vietnamese sites in Cambodia on March 18. Army leaders saw this as a way to destroy COSVN bases and break up offensive preparations, but to Kissinger and Nixon it was psychological warfare, part of the "Madman Theory," and something to influence negotiations. Nixon also ratcheted up bombing of Communist targets in Laos and South Vietnam. The Johnson-era restrictions on bombing North Vietnam remained for now, but Nixon began planning a massive blow – DUCK HOOK – to demonstrate seriousness if his November 1 deadline passed unmet.[48] One wonders how bombing *Cambodia* and *Laos* – even Hanoi's forces there – could force *North Vietnam* to the negotiating table.

Secretary of Defense Laird believed only withdrawing troops could assuage public pressure against the war. Congressional criticism was also growing. Laird told Thieu what was coming, and that Saigon needed to carry more weight. The Johnson administration had raised the idea of Saigon taking over the war but never built a program. Laird saw here the only way to save South Vietnam.[49] He said:

> Consideration should be given to border area operations that will at least temporarily diminish the advantage to the enemy of our self-imposed geographical restrictions. Unless we are willing to expand greatly the geographic confines of the conflict, however, the availability of sanctuary areas for the enemy will continue to contribute to the impossibility of a final military solution.[50]

He also identified another fundamental issue: "The basic problem remains that of achieving permanent South Vietnamese governmental control over the country." To accomplish this, the US needed to accelerate the modernization program and reequip the ARVN so it could take over the war. He recommended removing 50–70,000 troops by 1969's end.[51]

But troop withdrawals could injure Vietnamization and undermine America's negotiating position. Le Duc Tho, North Vietnam's negotiator, told Kissinger in February 1970 that the Communists understood "US strategy was to withdraw enough forces to make the war bearable for the American people while simultaneously strengthening the Saigon forces so that they could stand on their own." He then noted: "Before, there were over a million US and puppet troops, and you failed. How can you succeed when you let the puppet troops do the fighting? Now, with only US support, how can you win?"[52]

But Nixon believed public and domestic political pressure wouldn't permit delaying troop withdrawals. He tried to buy time with a May 14, 1969 speech, but it occurred during the bloody Battle of Hamburger Hill. By May 21, Nixon decided to Vietnamize the war and chose 25,000 as the number for the first withdrawal. He met with Thieu on June 8 and announced the decision, privately telling him he hoped to end the war by the 1970 Congressional elections. Nixon's drawdown, which began in mid 1969, mirrored the 1965–68 build-up rates.[53]

VIETNAMIZATION

Turning over the fighting to the South needed several years, and both Nixon and Kissinger doubted they had time. Laird disagreed, developed a plan, and sent it to Nixon. Nixon was reluctant to approve it but was convinced to do so by the Senate Foreign Relations Committee's J. William Fulbright, who told him the American people had elected him to end the war. Rather than calling it "de-Americanizing" the war, Laird suggested "Vietnamizing," which quickly became "Vietnamization." "Nixon praised Laird's political subterfuge" and approved the plan in March 1969. It had two parts: expanding Saigon's control over the countryside and making the ARVN capable of fighting on its own. This would lower US costs. Nixon ordered the first withdrawal for July 1, 1969. Kissinger wrote in July 1970: "Vietnamization is designed to induce the enemy to negotiate by posing the prospect of a gradual American disengagement that maintains our domestic support while successively strengthening the South Vietnamese forces." But "The basic problem has been that to date the enemy has been able to calculate that we have greater problems than they do, that protracted struggle is preferable to real negotiations to accomplish their objectives." Kissinger had no new idea and suggested staying the course.[54]

MILITARY STRATEGY: PART II

The most convenient though perhaps not the most accurate descriptor of US military strategy came from Westmoreland's replacement, Abrams. Taking a phrase from the US ambassador to Saigon, Ellsworth Bunker, Abrams said in October 1968 that the North realized "that this is just one, repeat one, war. He knows there's no such thing as a war of big battalions, a war of pacification, or a war of territorial security. Friendly forces have got to recognize and understand the one war concept and carry the battle to the enemy, simultaneously, in all the areas of conflict." Abrams launched his One War strategy in September 1968. Westmoreland had drafted this new approach in January 1968, but Tet prevented the shift.[55]

The debate over whether or not US strategy changed during Abrams' tenure misses key points. The confusion results from failing to distinguish strategy from operations. The operational elements of the war remained consistent. The US still mounted large sweeps (search-and-destroy *operations*) intended to injure the enemy, and continued pacification and training. But the US no longer attempted attrition. Abrams' approach belied the simplicity of single-word branding. His was a defensive strategy supported by operational offensives, counterinsurgency, and nation building. Abrams counted on keeping the enemy off-balance and relied on airpower to do so. By March 1969, the US was dropping 130,000 tons of bombs a month on Laotian and South Vietnamese targets. But military leaders realized the necessity of countering Communist forces. Nixon gave the military the leeway "to apply maximum military pressure against the enemy within South Vietnam." Numerous large ground operations followed, some of which created badly managed refugee problems.[56]

On July 7, 1969, Laird secured a promise for more troop withdrawals and a mission change for MACV from defeating the Communist forces and driving them from South Vietnam, to helping the South Vietnamese government by improving its military forces, supporting pacification, and stopping the influx of enemy supplies. But Kissinger wanted intensified military action to force an end to the war within six months. Both he and Nixon wanted to "go for broke," and Nixon said he "would attempt to end the war one way or the other – either by negotiated agreement or by an increased use of force."[57]

Nixon approved Laird's change but tried to revoke it before its August 15 implementation date, "but Laird unilaterally issued the formal order and then publicly announced this change." He "reiterated that Vietnamization was the Defense Department's 'top priority.' And that the US forces were moving towards a supportive role in South Vietnam." Laird gave MACV four tasks for 1970: making Vietnamization succeed, lowering US casualties, drawing down US forces, and "stimulating" negotiations. In the 1971 Combined Campaign Plan, the role of US forces shifted from combat operations to support for the South Vietnamese.[58]

Meanwhile, Kissinger worked with Wheeler on DUCK HOOK, "an intense air and naval offensive to decimate North Vietnam," force them to negotiate, and more quickly end the war. But Ho Chi Minh's death, growing dissent at home, and improvements in South Vietnam produced DUCK HOOK's cancellation and Nixon's formal shift to Vietnamization on October 11, 1969. He used a scheduled November 3 address now known as his "Silent Majority Speech" to build support for Vietnamization, describing it as "a plan that will bring the war to an end regardless of what happens on the negotiating front." This speech was part of the administration's information strategy as Nixon argued for public support of his efforts to end the war. It didn't increase.[59]

NATION BUILDING: ARMY AND GOVERNMENT

MACV's focus shifted to development and training of South Vietnamese forces. It's forgotten that Saigon's regular and militia forces did much of the fighting. On June 20, 1968, South Vietnam promulgated a "general mobilization law" to add 250,000 men to the military. The ARVN expanded by 60 percent from 1967 to 1970, but its performance continued to be evaluated by the body-count metric. This rapid expansion was plagued by a shortage of capable officers, and desertion rates rose in 1970 from the prior year as the nation was being torn apart socially, economically, and physically, experiencing a social and political revolution in the midst of the war. ARVN soldiers often lacked national consciousness and an awareness of why they were fighting despite a training and indoctrination program ongoing since 1965. Some South Vietnamese fought quite professionally during Tet, as did many militia units, and sometimes even civilians. The difficulty was getting all ARVN units to this level. Abrams pushed combined operations with US forces to speed the ARVN's development, and military aid went from $1.2 billion in 1968 to $3.3 billion in 1973 as the US rearmed South Vietnam.[60]

The development of a part-time People's Self-Defense Force (PSDF), a local militia, followed the 1968 general mobilization law. It went from 1.4 million to 3.9 million between June 1969 and September 1972, and drew in men aged 16–17 and 39–50. RF/PF strength expanded from 320,000 to 500,000 from 1967 to the end of 1972. The Revolutionary Development Cadre (known in English as the Rural Development Cadre) had 50,000 personnel in 1968 and the National Police 80,000. RF/PF performance was mixed during the 1972 Easter Offensive and suffered desertion. The ARVN was best suited for pacification but the RF/PFs carried much of the weight, often too much, as militia can rarely stand against regular forces or serious insurgents. The US spent little on non-ARVN forces; perhaps only 2 percent of American funds went for RF/PF forces and police. Total US and South Vietnamese pacification funding for 1968 was $1 billion.[61]

Perhaps Abrams' biggest challenge remained building a functioning South Vietnamese government supported by its people and doing so in a state where the government meant little to most of the populace. The South needed good local and regional leaders to help build backing, but Saigon put South Vietnamese generals in what were civilian positions, winning only criticism and charges of corruption as too many used the positions to line their pockets. Political development also remained susceptible to North Vietnamese attacks. By 1970, 98 percent of hamlets had elected leaders. But the 1972 Easter Offensive saw this ended to counter Communist influence. Thieu held a presidential election without an opponent in October 1971, despite US insistence he have one. Thieu thought the country couldn't tolerate the uncertainty of who was in charge in the midst of the war. Rampant inflation also injured the government's credibility.[62]

South Vietnamese nationalism grew in the late 1960s, but American observers "questioned whether a combination of national pride, loyalty to the government and plain endurance would be enough for South Vietnam to survive on its own." A key failing of US nation building was that American leaders didn't understand that "Building state structures – the organizational bureaucracy of the state, its economy, its security forces – was not the same as nation building." South Vietnam's leaders failed to build support for the government in rural areas. As one US army officer observed in 1970, America provided material benefits while the Communists sought "to capture men's minds" – a crushing indictment of modernization theory. The Nixon administration continued the Kennedy–Johnson mistake of assuming US-provided material benefits could weaken North Vietnamese influence while strengthening South Vietnam. This proved staggeringly incorrect. Most South Vietnamese were willing to support whichever side was winning.[63]

THE PACIFICATION STRATEGY

In July 1968, Abrams created the Long-Range Planning Task Group (LORAPL). Its November 1968 report urged "population security, CORDS support of pacification, and national development." It became the basis of Abrams' March 1969 strategic plan. This gave as the political aim a "free, independent and viable nation of South Vietnam that is not hostile to the United States, functioning in a secure environment both internally and regionally." The primary tasks of the US and ARVN were pacification and population security.[64]

CORDS chief William E. Colby, a veteran of the Office of Strategic Services (OSS) and the CIA, changed little when he replaced Komer. The pacification campaign plan for 1969 focused on the village rather than hamlet level (a number of hamlets formed a village) and rested upon a previously established trio of "mutually supporting principles" that Colby called the "three selfs": "self-defense, self-government, and self-help." The territorial forces were to bring increasing numbers of people under government control while economic development continued. They would attack the VCI while "building democracy" and increasing security. But whenever a hamlet showed signs of being pacified, the VC would increase assassinations.[65]

The South continued many older pacification programs and launched others. *Chieu Hoi* convinced 200,000 VC to defect and serve the South by 1972. The North found it dangerous, but the South didn't eagerly support it because it distrusted defectors. Thieu continued trying to expand support for the Saigon government via creating local village governments and efforts such as 1970's Land for the Tiller program, which gave 2.5 million acres of property to landless peasants. Many farmers loved the program, others found it corrupt. Some believe it did little to shift the people away from the North. Others see the opposite. In Long An province, it did more to bring people to the government's side than anything else. In 1970, Abrams told allied forces to participate in rather than just support pacification operations. Abrams remained focused on pacification's security plank and followed Westmoreland's sequence: security, population control, development. The pacification strategy included clearing and holding. The holding elements were the RF/PFs. But the VC often returned after the regulars departed.[66]

Pacification faced the same continuing threats. The war disrupted it while destroying the countryside's social structures. VC and NVA combat operations often wrecked pacification efforts. US and ARVN operations could do the same, but with artillery and airstrikes. The poor behavior of some ARVN units (and on rare occasions American ones) fed disillusionment with Saigon among South Vietnamese who already lacked faith in the ARVN because it failed to protect them from the Vietcong. It also often took a long time to get programs running.[67]

But what did pacification achieve? Judging its effects is difficult. It removed areas from VC control and the Communists believed 1969 the worst year they faced. But the slowly growing rural middle class also turned people from Communism. The country was enduring great social change, much of it a result of the US presence and the war, but neither side understood nor could use this. Small VC attacks increased from 1968 to 1972, particularly against RF/PF units, while battalion-sized attacks nearly disappeared. Internal US and South Vietnamese indicators said pacification was working and people were becoming more supportive of the government. This, though, isn't decisive evidence of effectiveness. The best proof perhaps is that Hanoi's 1970–71 Nineteenth Party Plenum concluded pacification was working, which influenced the decision to launch the 1972 Easter Offensive.[68]

But pacification failed to build bonds between the people and the government. And the South and America failed in the most critical task: providing security. Regarding CORDS' labors, "it appeared doubtful that the program had helped establish a strong political community." Moreover, it couldn't overcome poor execution, "ubiquitous corruption, and the failure of the South Vietnamese government to build a broad, self-sustaining political base."[69] It's difficult to see how *American* effort could build credibility for a *South Vietnamese* government.

INVADING CAMBODIA

The longer Nixon was in office, the more constraints upon military force disappeared. Nixon first allowed bombing of Communist Cambodia bases. Next was attacking them, with ground forces, something American military leaders had pushed since at least 1964. In January 1969, even before taking office, Nixon considered this. Abrams suggested hitting COSVN in Cambodia to destroy it and break up any offensive planning. Nixon, concerned about the enemy taking the initiative, agreed.[70]

Technically, Cambodia was neutralized by the 1954 Geneva Accords, but Prince Norodom Sihanouk had struggled unsuccessfully against North Vietnamese infiltration. This overwhelmed some of the western provinces, where the Communists expanded the Ho Chi Minh Trail and established

COSVN. By 1970, US intelligence reported that 80 percent of supplies supporting Communist operations in the southern areas of South Vietnam and eastern Cambodia came through the Cambodian port of Sihanoukville. Nixon wanted Cambodia to remain neutral, but this changed when the Cambodian National Assembly deposed the king in March 1970. His replacement, General Lon Nol, asked for assistance from the United States.[71]

Lon wanted the Communists out and Nixon saw an opportunity. Many of Nixon's senior military advisors urged intervention on Cambodia's behalf. Secretary of State William P. Rogers and Secretary of Defense Laird argued against it because it would destroy the election chances of Republican candidates. Nixon and Kissinger decided the US needed to hit the North Vietnamese base areas in Cambodia to improve Vietnamization's chances and pressure Hanoi to come to terms. Abrams wanted to destroy the sanctuary areas to protect his forces and Vietnamization, and prevent the stockpiling of supplies for another Communist offensive. The US didn't include the ARVN in its early planning from fear of leaks, and Nixon restricted the duration to June 30 and the limit of the advance to 30 kilometers.[72]

ARVN forces attacked the Parrot's Beak, an area of Cambodia protruding into South Vietnam, on April 29, 1970. The Communists suffered damage but were just as aware of the timetable and generally gave ground. The offensive also pulled troops from pacification. US and ARVN forces attacked a second salient, the Fishhook, on May 1. The 31,000 US and 19,000 ARVN troops were supported by air units as naval forces blockaded Sihanoukville. The operation destroyed some enemy forces and material but failed to eliminate COSVN, the base areas, or have a lasting effect on the North's sanctuary, while Hanoi grew more obstreperous in negotiations. Hanoi's occupation and subversion, internal civil war fed by North Vietnam and China, and American bombing and invasion ripped Cambodia apart. Nixon's August 1970 Southeast Asia strategy resulted in military and economic aid for Cambodia.[73]

Domestically, because of the invasion, Nixon faced heavy criticism from Democratic and Republican lawmakers. US public opinion was split, but not on university campuses. The incursion fed the American antiwar movement, including its most tragic event in May 1970, when four students at Ohio's Kent State University were killed by National Guard troops. Follow-on protests erupted at universities across the country.[74]

The administration also endured resentment and criticism from the intellectuals who had supported the war and made it possible, but then turned against it when it became harder than anticipated and politically unfashionable to support. Shortly after the April 1970 invasion, a band of

Kissinger's former Harvard colleagues, including Schelling, one of the war's key early architects, "met with him to protest American policy" in Vietnam. They pressured the secretary of state to resign, telling him "they had lost confidence in the diplomacy of the United States and would no longer consult for their country."[75]

Congress began reasserting influence over foreign relations. It had initially given Nixon time, even though opposition Democrats controlled both houses, but the honeymoon was over by early 1970. Much of Congress now opposed the war and launched an offensive against Nixon. Republican Senator Mark Hatfield and Democratic Senator George McGovern tried but failed to attach to a bill an amendment ending the war by June 1971. This undermined Kissinger's negotiations. The first Cooper–Church amendment passed in December 1969; it restricted use of US forces in Thailand and Laos. The second, passed in December 1970, forbade using the US ground forces outside South Vietnam. Congress removed all funding for operations in Cambodia in January 1971 and repealed the Gulf of Tonkin Resolution. Congress became a constraint on the war's execution.[76]

LAOS

In 1969, Nixon intensified America's war in Laos to tie down Communist units and keep them from injuring Vietnamization. He increased bombing of the Ho Chi Minh Trail and built up Hmong forces that fought alongside Royal Lao and Thai troops. Hanoi directed the 40,000 North Vietnamese troops in Laos to help the Pathet Lao, the Laotian Communists. Of these, 25,000 maintained the Ho Chi Minh Trail. A Hmong-led offensive took the Plain of Jars in Laos' north. Hanoi responded with a counteroffensive in February 1969 that threatened the Hmong's nearby primary base at Long Tieng. Nixon supported the anti-Communist forces with massive B-52 strikes and the Communist drive was stopped.[77]

South Vietnam launched its own offensive into Laos, Lam Son 719, the brainchild of Ambassador Bunker, Abrams, and Thieu. Nixon approved Abrams' plan for an ARVN force to enter Laos, cut the Ho Chi Minh Trail, and destroy the main Communist logistics center at Tchepone and its lines of communication, eliminating or at least dramatically reducing the Communist ability to mount operations into South Vietnam and Cambodia for "the indefinite future." If this went well, the ARVN would then attack nearby Communist base areas. Success would damage infiltration efforts, buy time for Vietnamization, ease America's withdrawal, and help Lon Nol's Cambodian regime survive by injuring the flow of materials to North

Vietnamese forces in his country. Nixon saw the offensive as a way to hurt the North while helping create a South Vietnam that could stand on its own. Kissinger had high hopes, seeing even a possible path for ending the war. Laird approved because he thought it would show Vietnamization's progress. Congressional restrictions prevented US troop participation, but American airpower supported Saigon.[78]

The offensive – intended to last three months – began on February 12, 1971, as 17,000 ARVN forces attacked 22,000 primarily NVA logistics troops. But Hanoi, alerted by South Vietnamese leaks, brought 60,000 troops to bear. Several weeks of fighting ensued. On February 28, Thieu changed the plan and decided that taking the Tchepone supply area, holding it, and departing would suffice. He told his commander: "You go in there long enough to take a piss and then leave quickly." The South took Tchepone on March 7 and began withdrawing the next day. Nixon and Kissinger blamed Abrams for the failure. The North applauded their victory and saw Lam Son 719 as proof Vietnamization had failed. In the operation's wake, Nixon remarked to Kissinger that "Winning the war simply means ... letting South Vietnam survive. That's all."[79]

REASSESSMENT AND RECALIBRATION

By the end of 1970, his initial strategy of military pressure and negotiations was dead. Nixon had hoped to end the war within a year but spent his first four presidential seasons trying to negotiate a settlement. He partially understood why this had failed: "Hanoi was playing a game – it had obtained a bombing halt from us in return for entering into talks but had no intention of reaching a political settlement. While we wanted negotiations, it wanted South Vietnam, and looked on the talks as a screen behind which it could carry on the war without being bombed."[80]

The troop withdrawal continued. US strength peaked at 549,500 in January 1969. On June 8, 1969, Nixon made his first withdrawal announcement: 25,000 troops. On September 1, 1969, to build public support, Nixon announced the withdrawal of 35,000 soldiers. On April 15, 1970, he declared the withdrawal of 50,000. On April 20, he proclaimed removal of another 150,000 by the next year, though he intended early 1971 to mark their departure. On November 12, 1971, Nixon announced the withdrawal of 45,000 troops and cessation of American participation in offensive ground operations. The campaign plan for 1972 had US forces shifting to supporting ARVN population security efforts. As it became increasingly clear that the North was preparing a massive offensive for 1972, the US began bombing concentration points in Laos and Cambodia. The troop withdrawal, though, was weakening discipline in an army already suffering the effects of a troubled home front and the reality that the US was leaving. Departure doesn't motivate sacrifice.[81]

The administration's efforts to get the Soviets to apply pressure on Hanoi accomplished nothing for two years; Soviet aid to Hanoi *increased*. Military pressure and negotiations also failed. Nixon and Kissinger began redefining "victory." On October 7, 1970, Nixon offered a ceasefire in place, but had no faith something would come of this; Hanoi condemned his speech. But Nixon had opened a door. On May 31, 1971, Kissinger offered the North "a ceasefire in place and the withdrawal of US troops in exchange for a return of US POWs." The agreements reached in October 1972 and January 1973 differed little from this. Immediately after, the administration embarked upon "triangular diplomacy," an effort characterized by its outreach to China and talks with the Soviet Union.[82]

Kissinger's first secret trip to China took place July 9–11, 1971. Bringing China into the new global balance of power system the administration hoped to create was only part of the purpose. Vietnam was also important, and Kissinger wrote on his briefing book: "We want a decent interval." During his conversations with Chinese Premier Zhou Enlai, Kissinger said in regard to South Vietnam, "if it is overthrown after we withdraw, we will not intervene." He also mentioned that the US could accept an eighteen-month time limit on the ceasefire and told Zhou: "What we require is a transition period between the military withdrawal and the political evolution.... If after complete American withdrawal, the Indochinese people change their government, the US will not interfere." But Mao refused to pressure Hanoi to come to terms.[83]

The administration kept trying. During his April 1972 trip to Moscow, shortly after Saigon launched its Easter Offensive, Kissinger told Brezhnev Washington had "two principal objectives. One is to bring about an honorable withdrawal of all our forces; secondly, to put a time frame between our withdrawal and the political process which would then start." In a May 27, 1972 meeting, Kissinger told Foreign Minister Gromyko he could tell Hanoi that after making a deal it would have "great possibilities" within a year. "We are prepared to leave so that a communist victory is not excluded, though not guaranteed." In a heated exchange with China's Zhou Enlai in June 1972, Kissinger said:

> It should be self-evident that in the second term we would not be looking for excuses to re-enter Indochina. But still, it is important that there is a *reasonable*

interval between the agreement on the ceasefire, and a reasonable opportunity for political negotiation ... the outcome of my logic is that *we are putting a time interval between the military outcome and the political outcome.*[84]

THE 1972 EASTER OFFENSIVE

The North now sought to end the war on its terms. Victory in Laos convinced Hanoi Vietnamization had failed, Saigon could be easily finished, and enough US troops had left to ensure Northern battlefield superiority. They feared Nixon's diplomatic successes in Beijing and Moscow ending the support received, and judged pacification as working, particularly in the Tri-Thien region in northern South Vietnam. The North believed victory in the South would allow them to resist pressure from Beijing and Moscow, while breaking the ARVN meant Washington had "to settle on Hanoi's terms." They prepared a multi-pronged conventional military invasion from North Vietnam, Laos, and Cambodia, and believed they could provoke city uprisings by having more units fight there. On March 20, 1972, the Easter Offensive began. The biggest blows fell in the Mekong Delta and northern South Vietnam. Soviet equipment and Chinese support enabled this. The North scored much success in the first month and a half, but the ARVN was throwing them back by late summer, backed by US air support and advisors. The US still had 95,000 personnel in South Vietnam but only 6,000 combat troops.[85]

One of the South's many problems was that, from 1968 to 1972, the ARVN had generally been doing counterinsurgency, not preparing to fight a conventional war. This meant the South made great leaps toward succeeding at pacification but not developed the skills for countering a conventional North Vietnamese invasion. The ARVN forces were also spread thin after the US withdrawal because they had assumed the war's burden. The South's strategic situation was worsened by its geographical disadvantage. The North could attack across its border as well as from Laos and Cambodia.[86] The ARVN forces needed to be larger, because the North could gain superiority where it chose.

Nixon countered the North's offensive. Diplomatically, the administration complained to Beijing through backchannels while raising this publicly with Moscow. Kissinger left for Moscow on April 20, 1972 to lay the groundwork for the upcoming Nixon–Brezhnev summit, but more importantly to get Moscow to put the thumb on North Vietnam to stop its offensive. He relayed that Nixon would do what was needed to stop the attack, even if this injured relations with Moscow. Brezhnev passed along Kissinger's words and received insolent replies from Hanoi.[87]

Nixon's diplomatic strategy prior to the Easter Offensive made it possible for him to remove the self-imposed constraints on bombing North Vietnam and mining Haiphong Harbor. Nixon launched FREEDOM TRAIN on March 31, a small bombing offensive against North Vietnamese military targets south of the 18th parallel. More followed. Nixon said in April 1972: "the bastards have never been bombed like they're going to be bombed this time." Air and sea attacks hit targets around Hanoi on April 16 and 17, and B-52s began striking targets in the North for the first time in Nixon's administration. On May 10, he launched Operation LINEBACKER. It hit areas north of the 20th parallel, including around Hanoi, concentrating on the North's railways and logistical systems to slow the North's offensive, and mined Haiphong Harbor. He also offered the North terms. LINEBACKER's effectiveness was hindered by the NVA's prepositioning of supplies in Laos and Cambodia. This bought the North time to shift its network from the now destroyed railroads to road transport. Shortages never affected their operations. LINEBACKER failed at interdiction but succeeded in pummeling NVA forces and supporting the ARVN. The North's offensive broke. A successful ARVN counteroffensive followed – one supported by mass US airpower that inflicted heavy losses upon the North.[88]

The ARVN's performance was mixed. Some units folded under NVA assaults. Others fought well and inflicted heavy casualties. Elite units such as the Marines and Airborne divisions performed exceptionally well and were key to the recapture of Quang Tri City. But Abrams believed the ARVN machine was held together by US advisors. After the 1972 Easter Offensive, the South Vietnamese began putting soldiers in the villages to work with the RF/PF forces as the US Marines had done, resulting in a great boost in security.[89]

ENDING AMERICA'S WAR

As we have seen, there are three key, intertwined issues to keep in mind when trying to end a war: what to ask for politically; what to do militarily; and how to secure the peace. Washington faced the unique problems caused by waging a war for limited political aims, especially one that was unpopular domestically. Washington's leverage was also decreasing as US troops withdrew. The last ground unit departed on August 23, 1972.[90] Advisors remained.

Wars for limited aims are almost always ended by talks. America faced tough and skilled negotiators. Since the Bolshevik Revolution, the Communists had used negotiations as a propaganda tool and weapon, one intertwined with combat. In 1965, a North Vietnamese general explained Hanoi's approach: "Fighting while negotiating is aimed at opening another front, at making the puppet army more disintegrated, at stimulating and developing the enemy's contradictions and thereby depriving him of propaganda weapons, isolating him further, and making those who misunderstand the Americans clearly see their nature." Throughout the long, often secret negotiations, Hanoi wasn't interested in compromising. Since the American forces were leaving, why should it? Fueling its resilience was America's antiwar movement and Congressional controversy. The North Vietnamese delayed the resumption of secret negotiations until they launched their spring offensive. Kissinger called it "very smart, tough bargaining on their part."[91]

By June 1972 it was clear to the North its offensive had problems. They approached the Americans, and renewed negotiations were scheduled for July. In August, Le Duan reassessed and concluded Hanoi was losing the war in the countryside. When the ARVN recaptured Quang Tri City in September, Le Duan decided Hanoi's main focus had to be negotiations to secure America's exit. The same month, Nixon intensified bombing and began hitting targets north of the 20th parallel, having decided he could end the war by bombing North Vietnam into submission. The North replied by dropping some of its demands. Eventually, because of progress in the talks, Nixon agreed to stop the bombing above the 20th parallel, though he refused a complete halt before an agreement was signed.[92]

Le Duc Tho told Kissinger on October 8, 1972 that Hanoi would discuss a ceasefire based on the terms Nixon proposed in May: US forces would withdraw, Hanoi would release POWs it held, and North Vietnamese forces could remain in the South. A deal was hammered out by October 18. The negotiations had been conducted without Thieu, who refused to accept the accord. His people also discovered a clandestine North Vietnamese effort to change the wording in the Vietnamese version of the treaty. The big sticking point for Thieu was allowing the North to keep its units in place in South Vietnam, *de facto* surrendering large parts of the nation while leaving the enemy a strong position for a later campaign. Thieu saw signing the October agreement as national suicide. Kissinger told Hanoi of Thieu's refusal. The North, thinking it had been tricked, struck back on October 26 by releasing the terms of the agreement. Hanoi also refused to meet with Kissinger, but pressure from Moscow and Beijing, which Kissinger requested, saw Hanoi ask for an October 31 meeting. They insisted the US sign the agreement as negotiated.[93] Negotiations about negotiations ensued.

DÉTENTE AND DEFEAT: NIXON, FORD, VIETNAM, 1969–1977

In late 1972, Nixon faced several ticking clocks. American public opinion wanted the US out. Nixon won his 1972 presidential reelection in a forty-nine-state landslide, but the Democrats controlled both houses of Congress and had turned against the war its leaders had made. Congress would certainly end American involvement when it sat in January 1973 and Nixon feared it would sever aid to South Vietnam. He had to end the war before it convened. Intermittent negotiations with the North began anew on November 20, 1972. Hanoi now wanted to preserve its units for its future fight against South Vietnam by ending US bombing. Hanoi was also under pressure from Moscow and Beijing to settle, though its Communist big brothers still supplied Hanoi, partially as a means of jockeying for influence. But the US was trying to address some of Saigon's concerns.[94]

The talks broke down in mid December. Nixon concluded bombing could force a deal. The result was LINEBACKER II, or the Christmas Bombings, which began on December 18, 1972. Nixon intended to show *both* North and South Vietnam he was serious about forcing a peace. The North asked the US to stop through the Soviets and agreed to resume talks, which began on January 8, 1973. Both Moscow and Beijing encouraged Hanoi to negotiate. The accord was signed on January 17, 1973. Nixon pressured a reluctant Thieu, even threatening a unilateral US withdrawal. Kissinger told Nixon: "I think that Thieu is right, that our terms will eventually destroy him." Nixon combined the carrot of aid and a future US return in the face of any North Vietnamese offensive, with a threat to cut a deal with the North that didn't include Saigon. Thieu agreed to sign, but only after promises of aid and being told Congress would probably no longer provide support if he balked. State Department official John Negroponte said: "We bombed the North Vietnamese into accepting our concessions."[95]

Nixon gave a television address on January 23, 1973 to announce "an agreement to end the war and bring peace with honor in Vietnam and in Southeast Asia." The formal agreement was signed on the 27th; a ceasefire began at midnight Greenwich Mean Time. The terms allowed Communist forces to stay in place, freed prisoners, committed Washington to withdrawing its troops within sixty days, and required the removal of foreign forces from Laos and Cambodia. Nixon also said in his speech that "The people of South Vietnam have been guaranteed the right to determine their own future, without outside interference."[96] This proved exceedingly untrue.

It is often argued that during the Vietnam War the US simply ran out of time because the support of the American people collapsed. This is overly simplistic. There was indeed significant opposition to the war in Vietnam, but what is forgotten is that Nixon was reelected in a landslide in 1972 despite the fact that the US had been fighting in Vietnam in a dramatic fashion since 1965 and Nixon had failed to extricate the country from the war. In theory, if the political leadership had been willing, the US could have maintained a low level of military involvement in Vietnam where the American effort stood on the backs of US airpower and advisory forces, as it did in 1972–73. The fact that the draft was abandoned in 1973 and the US began relying upon a volunteer force theoretically makes this possible – if the casualties were not too high, and South Vietnamese forces continued improving, and many other "ifs" fell into place. But the political classes of both parties had tired of the war and didn't think it worth the costs. This was the deciding factor.[97]

FAILING TO SECURE THE PEACE: THE FALL OF SOUTH VIETNAM, 1973–75

Nixon extricated the US from Vietnam, but how would the peace be secured? US military aid and, if necessary, intervention were to do this. They didn't. The Watergate scandal destroyed Nixon's presidency. He resigned on August 8, 1974. Gerald Ford succeeded him. Drastic cuts in aid promised Thieu by a Democratic Party–controlled Congress eager to be done with Vietnam followed. This left South Vietnam unable to properly supply and equip its forces against a North Vietnam being rearmed by the Soviets and Chinese. The oil crisis that began in 1973 pummeled South Vietnam's economy. Heavy inflation followed, which destroyed wages and created unemployment and demoralization. When the Communists violated the 1973 accord by launching their 1975 offensive (which began in December 1974), the US failed to keep its promise to intervene in support of South Vietnam. Even if Ford had wanted to, he couldn't have done so as Congress had passed the Case–Church Amendment in June 1973: American military action in Vietnam, Laos, and Cambodia now needed Congressional approval. The War Powers Resolution followed. This required the president to notify Congress within forty-eight hours of the commencement of military action and to seek Congressional consent for continuance within sixty days.[98] Saigon fell to the conventional forces of the North Vietnamese Army (not VC guerrillas) on April 30, 1975.

The North Vietnamese suffered 3.5 million killed. The US had 47,364 killed in action, another 10,797 deaths from accidents and disease, and 313,616 wounded. South Vietnam had more than 200,000 killed in action, and of the 17 million South Vietnamese probably over 2 million became casualties in some way. The US involvement in Vietnam gave Indonesia and

Thailand a window to secure their nations against Communism. But US involvement in Cambodia and Laos added to the destabilization of these unfortunate states begun by Communist North Vietnam.[99]

Something that seems to have escaped both the Johnson and Nixon administrations in regard to negotiating with Hanoi was an understanding of the immense value it placed upon achieving its most important political aim: the unification of an independent Vietnam. Some of North Vietnam's key leaders, such as Ho Chi Minh (who died in 1969), spent fifty years working and fighting for this. This isn't to say they had no breaking point – everyone does. Perhaps the only thing that could make Hanoi abandon its quest for Vietnamese unification was the possibility of the destruction of their North Vietnamese regime. Nixon discovered this, arguably accidentally, with the LINEBACKER II bombing, which shook the regime's foundations and helped convince it to make a deal.

The North erred in not making an agreement sooner, particularly after Kissinger consented to Northern troops remaining in South Vietnam and a ceasefire line based upon what North Vietnam controlled. Hanoi had no intention of keeping any agreement that didn't give it South Vietnam and could destroy the Saigon government once America withdrew – which happened. The North could have achieved this sooner at less cost but feared a repeat of 1954.

One of the common arguments in regard to Vietnam made by Laird and others is that the US "grabbed defeat from the jaws of victory" by failing to uphold its commitments to arm and supply Vietnam as well as provide support in the event of a North Vietnamese attack.[100] It is irrefutable that Washington didn't provide its promised support. The Democratic Party–controlled Congress cut funding, and Republican President Ford failed to militarily support South Vietnam in 1975 and to ask Congress to allow it. But claiming that this and other factors contributed to turning a US victory into a defeat is to misunderstand the situation.

To be victorious is to achieve one's political aims. Nixon initially sought an independent, non-Communist South Vietnam, like his predecessors. Attached to this was a caveat: "South Vietnam must be free, however, to accept outside assistance as required to maintain its security." The accord ending the war specifically excluded this. Later, Nixon just wanted out. The US did leave an independent, non-Communist South Vietnam, but this was a South Vietnam inhabiting such a disastrous strategic position that almost any nation would have found it impossible to survive. Huge tracts of South Vietnam's territory – perhaps 50 percent – were held by an enemy being rapidly rearmed by other Communist powers; much of this territory

North Vietnam didn't control before America's 1965 escalation. Hanoi also maintained its ability to attack from Laos and Cambodia, in violation of the agreement.[101] Even if South Vietnam hadn't suffered self-inflicted wounds, if would've had a difficult time surviving.

The feelings and beliefs of both Nixon and Kissinger on the ending of the war were complex. Both believed South Vietnam's fall likely, though didn't think it written in the stars. But, in the words of one historian, "Without a stable and effective South Vietnamese government, no amount of US help would win the war."[102] The North Vietnamese also had the best things any warring state could hope for: one opponent unwilling to do what was necessary to survive, and another that consistently overestimated its ability to shape events.

The US left Vietnam in defeat. There is no other way to interpret this.

CONCLUSIONS

The Nixon administration sought security above all else. It certainly supported and preferred the development of democracy abroad, but it didn't seek its expansion. Nixon and Kissinger considered themselves "realists." But the grand strategy they constructed was rarely based upon realistic assessments of the motivations of America's enemies, opponents, or friends. They consistently failed to properly consider the political aims of Washington's rivals, the value they placed upon these aims, how this would affect their actions, and how American actions and desires had little chance of altering the behavior of its most important foes. Détente failed to convince Moscow to abandon its aims. China opened to the US and the world, a decision it made to serve its interests, not America's. North Vietnam remained ruthlessly fixed upon the achievement of its aims. Nixon and Kissinger sought to improve American security and create a balance of power in the world. The first can be done; the second was beyond Washington's ability, because it couldn't control the actions of other nations, particularly great powers. There were limits to American power – as always.

14

FOR WANT OF A VISION: THE CARTER YEARS, 1977–1981

INTRODUCTION

James "Jimmy" Earl Carter Jr., Georgia's former governor, brought no foreign relations experience to the presidency. Carter inherited a United States perceived by many as in decline, an assessment he didn't share. Carter saw no threat of Soviet expansion, thought Washington could move beyond containment, and believed that in implementing this strategy America had erred by adopting some of the worst practices of its enemies, such as embracing dictators. He intended a more optimistic diplomatic strategy built upon "constant decency." But Brezhnev's Soviet Union felt empowered by America's Vietnam defeat and launched a Third World offensive, while America's foreign affairs cognoscenti saw almost no situation abroad meriting America's use of force.[1]

Foreign relations advice in the Carter administration came primarily from Secretary of State Cyrus Vance and National Security Advisor Zbigniew Brzezinski. Vance, a lawyer and veteran of the Kennedy and Johnson administrations, focused primarily on furthering détente, including SALT II. Better relations with Moscow would allow defense cuts. He wanted more interest in relations with America's southern neighbors and thought "practical self-interest" dictated Washington concerning itself with "human rights, economic development, energy, population growth, environmental damage, food, nuclear proliferation, and arms transfers."[2]

Brzezinski, a Polish emigrant with a Harvard PhD, had a long record of publications on security issues and the Soviet Union and wanted the NSC staff to function as a kind of "think tank" to aid presidential decision-making. He had seen the Nazis and Soviets destroy his native Poland, and believed Soviet power and aggression the primary obstacles to global stability. Brzezinski criticized Kissinger's diplomatic strategy as having neglected Washington's allies while benefiting its enemies. He didn't believe the Soviet Union's existence permanent and had long harbored the "ambition" to formulate "a coherent strategy for the United States, so that we could eventually dismantle the Soviet Union," a vision Carter didn't share. Brzezinski disdained Wilsonian moralism. Carter did not.[3]

Vance was the negotiator who handled the daily foreign relations issues. Brzezinski was the administration's strategist managing the president's major moves, especially new ones. Soviet Third World aggression strengthened his position. Tensions between Vance and Brzezinski arose, but there were many things on which they agreed. Leaks to the press by their subordinates, particularly Vance's assistants, fed their disputes. Carter made the decisions – not Brzezinski or Vance – but had difficulty establishing diplomatic priorities and choosing a course when Vance and Brzezinski presented different options. He saw the State Department as did Nixon – a bureaucracy nearly incapable of providing good ideas but exceedingly good at leaking to the press – and kept his decision to normalize relations with China from Vance, because he didn't want it leaked, a threat Vance admitted was real.[4]

POLITICAL AIMS AND GRAND STRATEGY

Carter "lacked a well-developed strategic vision." He wrote in his memoir that he "focused on those concerns that embodied" his "most important values – human rights, environmental quality, nuclear arms control, and the search for justice and peace."[5] But he failed to reveal any initial political aims or grand strategy.

Before the inauguration, Carter told Brzezinski to "outline our objectives." In January 1977, Brzezinski, with the help of political scientist Samuel Huntington and military advisor William Odom, composed a list of ten items Brzezinski called the administration's "foreign policy agenda." Much of it was directed at thwarting Soviet influence. Brzezinski recommended that the administration: 1) increase cooperation with Europe and Japan; 2) increase political and economic cooperation with the "new regional poles" – India and Indonesia in Asia, Brazil and Venezuela in Latin America, Nigeria in Africa, Saudi Arabia and Iran in the Middle East; 3) improve North–South relations and address the Panama Canal; 4) finish the SALT II talks and negotiate further strategic arms reductions; 5) normalize relations with China; 6) secure an Arab–Israeli peace to prevent regional radicalization and a shift toward Moscow; 7) push South Africa and Rhodesia (later Zimbabwe) to become biracial democracies, thus preventing Soviet involvement; 8) limit global arms sales (including American) and push non-proliferation treaties; 9) stress human rights and push other nations to emphasize this; and 10) keep defense strength sufficient to "dissuade the Soviet Union from committing hostile acts."[6]

Brzezinski wrote of the list: "It has been said that the Carter Administration had no central strategy. I believe this to be incorrect. A review of the ten goals in the light of the four-year experience of the Carter administration suggests that by and large it did have a defined philosophical perspective and certain basic priorities."[7] In addition to dodging the criticism *he* raised, thus yielding the point, Brzezinski's statement, combined with an examination of the list, reveals that he didn't understand that he delivered a mixture of political aims and diplomatic and military strategies. Points 5 through 7 are political aims: normalization of relations with China, Arab–Israeli peace, democracy in South Africa and Zimbabwe. The rest, barring number 10's emphasis on military strength, are elements of diplomatic strategy. The administration implemented or achieved all but numbers 4 (SALT II), 7 (biracial states in South Africa and Zimbabwe), and 8 (reducing arms sales).

Carter's inaugural address and his unusual follow-on message directed at a global audience provide clues to the new president's thinking. He stressed support for "freedom abroad" and said: "Because we are free, we can never be indifferent to the fate of freedom elsewhere. Our moral sense dictates a clear-cut preference for those societies which share with us an abiding respect for individual human rights." He also mentioned the aim of eliminating nuclear weapons, but this is a means of improving security, and unrealistic. In the second address he said: "The United States will meet its obligation to help create a stable, just, and peaceful world order" and "We will not seek to dominate nor dictate to others."[8]

In his January 1978 State of the Union Address – a year into the administration – Carter laid out what can be interpreted as the administration's key political aims and components of the administration's grand strategy. These were framed as elements of foreign relations intended to "serve the interests of every American." He said: "The first and prime concern is and will remain the security of our country." Achieving this required a strong national will, a strong military, alliances, and agreements with "potential adversaries," including arms limitations, and ending nuclear proliferation. His second aim was "a world at peace." This would be achieved through diplomacy, particularly in the Middle East. He wanted "world economic growth and stability." The administration was working to achieve this by stabilizing the global price of oil, pushing energy conservation, and protecting the dollar's value.[9] The problem with this line of thinking is that economic growth and stability, though certainly desirable, shouldn't be pursued as ends in themselves. They are elements of economic strategy supporting the achievement of political aims.

Carter went on to say: "We are trying to develop a more just international system. And in this spirit, we are supporting the struggle for human development in Africa, in Asia, and in Latin America." He added: "the purposes of our own Nation's policy: to ensure economic justice, to advance human rights, to resolve conflicts without violence, and to proclaim in our great democracy our constant faith in the liberty and dignity of human beings everywhere." This statement confuses the end (the purpose) with the means for getting there. The four things mentioned are parts of a strategy for achieving an aim, which seems to have been expansion of democracy abroad. Carter said in June 1978: "We are particularly dedicated to genuine self-determination and majority rule in those areas of the world where these goals have not yet been attained."[10]

This raises complicated, perhaps unresolvable, issues around the question of how dependent US security is upon the political and economic situations in other parts of the world. The answer: it depends. America's global interconnectedness means there is nearly always some bearing upon the nation's ability to achieve security exerted by events abroad. But the relative importance of these occurrences is always in flux, with different regions assuming greater importance at different times. Judging the shift can be difficult, especially before a crisis strikes and forces readjustment. The equally complicated related issues include judging the level of danger, whether or not the US can address this at acceptable cost and risk, whether and how it is in US interests to do so, and what the effects of addressing it might be, many of which will never occur to even the most brilliant statesmen and soldiers tasked to deduce them. None of this is easy.

The Carter administration is often accused of weakness and indecision because of Carter himself, a criticism with bite because of his tendency to micromanage.[11] If Carter had established clear political aims, this would have provided purpose and guidance to the government's arms. The respective leaders could then ask whether or not the actions of their branches were contributing to the achievement of these aims. This is hardly a perfect system – there isn't one – but it can reduce drift while lessening the appearance of indecisiveness.

THE ASSESSMENT

"Being confident of our own future," Carter said in a May 1977 speech, "we are now free of that inordinate fear of Communism which once led us to embrace any dictator who joined us in our fear." He went on to note that American diplomatic strategy during the Cold War had been "guided by two principles: a belief that Soviet expansion must be contained, and the corresponding belief in the importance of an almost exclusive alliance among non-Communist nations on both sides of the Atlantic." In Carter's mind, this was no longer the case. "That system could not last forever unchanged. Historical trends have weakened its foundation. The unifying threat of conflict with the Soviet Union has become less intensive, even though the competition has become more extensive." More important were "the new global questions of justice, equity and human rights." This new approach, he said, "is designed to serve mankind."[12]

Carter attempted to change the basis of American political aims and grand strategy from national interests to human rights. A danger in doing this is that other nations are basing their aims and strategies on what they perceive as their national interests, and not necessarily from malice. Failing to do this can undermine or even destroy the ability of the state to protect its people. If the state fails here, it might not survive to err so again, a fact applying equally to the state's leaders. Additionally, before his inauguration, after extensive interviews with members of Congress and discussions with his cabinet members, Carter decided to act early on some key issues mentioned above: Middle East peace, the Panama Canal, normalizing relations with China, and SALT II.[13]

Criticism that the US was now the "Number 2" power, having fallen behind the Soviet Union, led Brzezinski to propose to Carter a general interagency reassessment. The result was the Team B study headed by political scientist Samuel Huntington that produced Presidential Review Memorandum (PRM) 10, Comprehensive Net Assessment and Military Force Review. Its model was NSC 68, and it compared the US and the Soviet Union in important areas such as economics and alliances. Completed in June 1977, it argued for using access to US technology as part of the economic strategy for dealing with the Soviet Union and that the Middle East was the most likely area of US military involvement; Washington thus needed better capability for deploying forces there. PRM 10 led to August 1977's Presidential Directive (PD) 18, US National Strategy, discussed below.[14]

GRAND STRATEGY – PART I

In May 1977, Carter laid out five principles of a new diplomatic strategy: an emphasis on human rights, increased cooperation among "industrial democracies," better relations with Moscow and Beijing (underpinned by a "strong defense"), increased help to developing nations, and the encouragement of "all countries to rise above narrow national interests and work together to solve such formidable global problems as the threat of nuclear war, racial hatred, the arms race, environmental damage, hunger and disease."[15]

In August, the administration completed the new US National Strategy, PD/NSC 18. It has no clear political aims, though the military strategy portions remain redacted. It insisted relations with the Soviet Union presented opportunities for cooperation and competition "with the attendant risk of conflict as well as the opportunity for stabilizing US-Soviet relations." The US, though, possessed great advantages over the Soviets that could be exploited. Because of this, "US national strategy will be to take advantage of our relative advantages in economic strength, technological superiority and popular political support to: Counterbalance, together with allies and friends," and by using military, diplomatic, and economic strength, "Soviet military power and adverse influence in key areas, particularly Europe, the Middle East, and East Asia." Political competition with the Soviets would consist of supporting "human rights and national independence." Shades of détente remained as the US would seek Soviet help "resolving regional conflicts" and lowering tensions that might provoke superpower conflict, while security would be improved via negotiations and disarmament agreements. Finally, the US would try to involve the Soviets "constructively in global activities, such as economic and social developments and peaceful non-strategic trade." To implement this strategy, the US needed to maintain the current military balance, which meant meeting a previous commitment to raise defense spending 3 percent annually, something America's allies were also expected to do (Carter instead initially cut defense). The majority of US military forces would be aimed at reinforcing Europe. In Asia, force levels would remain the same to provide an effective deterrent, except for the withdrawal of forces from South Korea.[16]

INFORMATIONAL STRATEGY

The cornerstone of the Carter administration's strategy was human rights. But this tool of informational and diplomatic strategy was treated as an end in itself and not directed at achieving a particular aim or defense of a current position. Vice President Walter Mondale affirmed, for example, that the administration was "for human rights not because we are against

Communism, but because we believe in human rights." NSC staffer Jessica Tuchman pinpointed the problem for her boss, Brzezinski:

> *What are we really after?* Is it to change totalitarian systems to democracies? To improve the social and economic welfare of the billions of impoverished people of the world? To increase domestic support for foreign policy in general? To make ourselves feel good? etc. These are not simple questions, but I suspect that a careful effort to analyze them would dictate quite different policy choices for the short term as well as the long.[17]

The administration's February 1978 directive on human rights, NSC 30, failed to resolve the problem of a strategy directed at no clear aim that Tuchman identified. It stated: "It shall be a major objective of US foreign policy to promote the observance of human rights throughout the world." It did at least delineate what the administration meant by "human rights":

> 1. It shall be the objective of the US human rights policy to reduce worldwide governmental violations of the integrity of the person (e.g., torture; cruel, inhuman or degrading treatment; arbitrary arrest or imprisonment; lengthy detention without trial, and assassination) and, to enhance civil and political liberties (e.g., freedom of speech, of religion, of assembly, of movement and of the press; and the right to basic judicial protections). It will also be a continuing US objective to promote basic economic and social rights (e.g., adequate food, education, shelter and health).[18]

But again, this was pursuit of human rights issues with no aim in mind. The next administration did this differently.

Another problem was implementation. The administration often singled out America's allies and partners for harsher treatment than its adversaries. A nation's human rights record became the litmus test for receipt of foreign assistance. One administration human rights official branded some long-term allies "retrogressive fascists" and pushed for the US to end aid to twenty-eight different nations.[19]

MILITARY STRATEGY

Carter initially retrenched militarily. His secretary of defense was Harold Brown, an experienced Department of Defense veteran. Among the least ideological of Carter's appointments, his views generally aligned with Brzezinski's. He believed Europe the most important US strategic concern and struggled to manage a shrinking defense budget while hoping increased Japanese defense spending would take up some of the slack in Asia. Carter's initial decision to cut defense by $6 billion and remove nuclear weapons and some troops from South Korea painted an image of weakness the administration never overcame. Retrenchment meant canceling the B-1 bomber and the neutron bomb, and reductions in ship construction. The parallel gutting of the CIA's operational capabilities and the Special Operations community reduced American options for responding abroad. Nuclear strategy remained based upon MAD, but Carter intended SALT II to allow dramatic reductions in the numbers of nuclear weapons, which didn't happen. NATO remained a defense pillar. Carter strengthened it in May 1978 via the Long Term Defense Program. NATO members committed to annual 3 percent defense increases until 1985. This shift fed new army weapons programs that developed the M-1 Abrams tank, the Bradley infantry fighting vehicle, advanced helicopters, a host of improved munitions, better NATO interoperability, and the stockpiling of equipment and munitions for the six army divisions posted to Europe to fight a war NATO planners projected would last only thirty days.[20]

The navy's part was based upon planning for one-and-a-half wars and the Single Integrated Operation Plan (SIOP). The major enemy remained the Soviet Union and its Warsaw Pact. If this war erupted, the navy was to swing its Pacific forces to the European theater under the NATO plan. But navy leaders, facing a growing and now global Soviet naval presence, believed this would mean abandoning the Pacific, with disastrous consequences. The navy also saw opportunities as Soviet Pacific forces were vulnerable. Its planning began shifting from a largely defensive Pacific bent to offensive action against the region's growing Soviet naval forces, and strikes on bases to tie down forces that could be shifted against NATO. The navy's leaders pushed offensive sea control.[21]

THE SOVIET UNION

Administration members disagreed upon how to deal with the Soviets. Brzezinski wanted a harder line from the beginning. Carter didn't. In May 1977, Carter stressed support for détente, but in all parts of the world, something resembling Kissinger's linkage, and expressed hope Moscow would cooperate to improve situations in Africa and the Middle East and be convinced they couldn't impose their system on others "through direct military intervention or through the use of a client state's military force – as with the Cuban intervention in Angola."[22]

Brzezinski was skeptical of détente, concluding by 1974 that only Moscow benefited, both economically and in improving its global strategic position.

The US was constraining itself internationally while the Soviets used détente to stabilize relations with Washington and mount a Third World offensive. Moscow's primary tools were propaganda and weapons. Brzezinski believed unless America made détente "reciprocal and global," it would soon face a more aggressive Soviet Union undermining US leadership and condemnation from allies and the American public. Brzezinski urged reversing the trend by strengthening alliances, resisting Soviet and Cuban actions in West Africa, the Horn of Africa, the Near East, and other places, and growing the relationship with China, including militarily.[23]

Brzezinski and Vance clashed on détente. Vance believed in détente and interpreted Soviet Third World activity as opportunism, believing Moscow was often simply reacting to American moves. He thought the SALT agreements, along with détente, would help stabilize the relationship between the superpowers. Carter proved indecisive and didn't choose between them.[24] His administration's version of containment became a mixture of both.

A human rights–based approach, which Vance didn't want, underpinned the strategy toward Moscow. Carter launched his human rights push when Vance was trying to finalize SALT II. Carter supported the cause of Soviet dissidents by criticizing Moscow for violations of the 1975 Helsinki Accords, which, among other things, included non-treaty human rights agreements. He believed he could do so while making progress on other issues. The Soviets interpreted Carter's approach as "linking détente to the domestic situation in the Soviet Union." Nevertheless, the SALT II negotiations plodded along, which Brzezinski pushed Carter to support. But in June 1979, Carter withdrew the treaty from the Senate ratification process after the Soviet invasion of Afghanistan and a domestic political flap over the supposed "discovery" of a Soviet combat brigade that had been in Cuba since the 1962 missile crisis.[25]

Brzezinski saw in the minority nationalities in the Soviet Union and Soviet Bloc tools to use against Moscow and supported "actions intended to harass and destabilize the Soviet bloc." Many of these centered on information operations, and he pushed a propaganda campaign aimed at Soviet nationalities using radio broadcasts by the Voice of America (VOA) and others. He had dissident literature clandestinely distributed in the Soviet Union, but other efforts to stir the Soviet internal pot were resisted by the State Department and the CIA. Brzezinski saw human rights as a way of exploiting internal Soviet contradictions. The advent of satellite technology and other new modes of communication eased discovery and highlighting of human rights abuses. The year 1977 saw efforts to feed the separation impulse, particularly in Poland. The administration imposed sanctions to prevent Soviet high-technology purchases in 1978, a reaction to Moscow's persecution of dissidents and the dismay in Europe from Moscow's deployment of SS20 missiles.[26]

CHINA AND ASIA

Before his inauguration, Carter decided to seek normalization of relations with China. Like Nixon, he had to move cautiously and, also like Nixon, negotiated without the State Department (though he used Vance) and generally kept this from Congress. Normalization meant looking the other way in regard to China's human rights record, and the murderousness of its ally, Cambodia.[27]

Vance and Brzezinski argued over the China approach. Vance wanted to balance it with the relationship with the Soviets, while Brzezinski wanted better relations with China for leverage against Moscow. Carter chose a middle path. When Vance got nowhere in his August 1977 negotiations, Brzezinski convinced Carter to give him the portfolio and more leeway in the talks. Normalization of relations followed in December 1978. For Chinese leader Deng Xiaoping, this was a pivotal moment. It enabled him to consolidate his power and opened the door to economic reforms that transformed China. Beijing benefited from Carter waiving an amendment of the 1974 Trade Act forbidding the extension of normal trade privileges to "any nonmarket economy that denied its citizens the right to emigrate." Vance wanted to grant trade rights equally to Moscow. Carter refused.[28] It is interesting to speculate on the fate of a Soviet regime enjoying full access to America's economy.

The new situation shocked Moscow because Carter had told them he would keep them informed regarding relations with China. It also shocked Congress because none of its leaders were told. Many were angry the deal required America canceling its defense treaty with Taiwan while not securing a Beijing promise to forgo attacking it. Carter had to sign a Congressional amendment to the Taiwan Relations Act stating Washington would sell Taiwan defense material. The debacle damaged relations with Beijing and Taipei.[29]

Carter's administration worried many Asian leaders, fears sparked by Carter's campaign promise to pull US forces from Korea and administration members from the human rights lobby criticizing American allies. The administration began reshaping America's strategic alliances based upon the assumption that neither Congress nor the American public would tolerate supporting non-democratic regimes. Relations with allies and partners such as South Korea, the Philippines, and Taiwan would now be based upon their human rights records. In January 1977, Carter announced the withdrawal of US troops from South Korea and soon made aid to Manila and Seoul contingent upon human rights reforms. The administration tried to assuage shellshocked Asian partners by telling them this didn't matter because the opening to China made Asia safer. Japan proved particularly antagonistic. Carter remained adamant despite growing opposition from inside his administration and Congress. He only relented when the House Armed Services Committee asked him to delay the withdrawals until it could study recent intelligence revelations on the increased numbers of North Korean forces, and the move threatening Congressional support for SALT II. Carter retreated on withdrawal from South Korea and cutting aid to Ferdinand Marcos' Philippines regime partially because it became clear Moscow was building forces for a front against the US in Asia. The acrimony damaged US relations in Asia.[30]

The administration also warred internally over pushing Japan to spend more on defense. Vance supported this while his successor, Edmund Muskie, refused to raise the issue with Tokyo. Trade issues also caused tensions between the two powers. The Japanese, meanwhile, complained about the absence of any US strategy for Asia while simultaneously refusing to take much responsibility for their defense.[31]

THE MIDDLE EAST

Carter said in May 1977 that he was trying to bring peace to the Middle East – which is an aim – and made a serious effort to do so. February 1977 saw Vance dispatched to the region, followed by Washington visits from Middle East leaders between March and May. The idea of a general settlement was soon found impossible, and the administration decided to build on Egyptian leader Anwar Sadat's public outreach to Israel. Achieving peace between Egypt and Israel was seen as a platform for solving other issues. The Camp David Accords, signed on September 17, 1978, validated a team effort. Vance "was largely responsible" and deserving of applause. Brzezinski helped secure the signing of the March 1979 Egypt–Israel peace treaty.[32]

In the greater Middle East, the administration continued the "twin pillars" approach focused upon Iran and Saudi Arabia to counter Soviet influence in Iraq and Egypt. Neither Tehran nor Riyadh were good allies. Iran had exploited the 1973 Arab oil embargo, which Riyadh supported, to further drive up oil prices, and then called for the embargo to end.

The shah's growing military power unnerved some American allies, such as Saudi Arabia. The shah pursued his own aims, and one of these may have been regional dominance. The administration differed here from its predecessor by linking weapons and backing to democratization but failed to make clear its support for the shah as Iran became increasingly unstable.[33]

THE THIRD WORLD

In January 1977, immediately after his inauguration, Carter tasked the Policy Review Committee to examine "relations between the developed and developing nations." The order directed the creation of studies on economic issues, technology, and migration, and ordered analysis based upon US interests for action options in these arenas. The document provided no political aims that its recommendations were to achieve.[34]

Brzezinski believed the Third World saw America as a reactionary state because of its support of dictators. He backed the shift to human rights as the core of the administration's diplomatic strategy to repair Washington's image. Stressing freedom and human rights also countered Soviet propaganda on equality and class struggle. Better relations and economic development could help here, but the administration failed to secure Congressional funding for economic improvement and abandoned this to concentrate on enhancing diplomatic relations.[35]

The administration's Latin America relations suffered from a lack of clear political aims and an ambiguous approach. Deputy Secretary of State Warren Christopher, who oversaw Latin American relations, said: "The best overall policy may be a non-policy." In May 1977, Carter said he wanted improved Latin American relations but insisted: "We do not need another slogan." Carter believed pushing human rights reforms would move Latin American states toward democracy while eliminating the tensions and oppression producing revolutions. But linking human rights requirements to US military aid lessened American influence as several nations broke defense ties rather than make reforms. The administration successfully transferred sovereignty over the Canal to Panama, securing ratification in March 1978. Carter believed this an act of justice.[36]

Carter limited military aid and arms sales to Nicaraguan strongman Anastasio Somoza to push him toward elections and democratic changes. Carter couldn't convince Somoza to step down and refused to force him out. But American pressure weakened him, opening the door for Nicaraguan moderates to unite with the Communist-backed Sandinistas. Somoza was overthrown in 1979, and Nicaragua soon had the radical regime the administration feared. Deputy Secretary of State Christopher believed human rights "was perhaps the principal engine that brought about the downfall of Somoza." Nicaragua's new strongman, Daniel Ortega, demonstrated his gratitude for Carter's request that Congress give Nicaragua $75 million in aid by allying with the Soviet Union and Cuba, establishing single-party rule, and supporting an insurgency in El Salvador.[37]

The administration pushed South Africa and Rhodesia (Zimbabwe) toward majority Black rule. Carter had little success against South African Apartheid, but US pressure helped Robert Mugabe win the election that brought him to power in Zimbabwe.[38] He ruled from 1980 until being overthrown in 2017, a dictatorship marked by violence, corruption, and decimation of the nation's freedoms and economy.

ECONOMIC STRATEGY

The 1970s marked the birth of an intensified era of global economic integration as world trade and the growth of multinational corporations and global lending increased spectacularly over the next two decades. Carter supported free trade and insisted that "Most nations share our faith that in the long run, expanded and equitable trade will best help developing countries to help themselves."[39] This was not always the case. Other nations acted in their own interest when regulating trade.

Carter addressed the nation's economic woes in his January 1978 State of the Union Address. He insisted that "We here in Washington must move away from crisis management, and we must establish clear goals for the future – immediate and the distant future – which will let us work together and not in conflict." Yet Carter failed to provide an aim, a consistent failing. He delivered proposals for addressing the symptoms of the administration's two biggest inherited economic challenges: inflation and the energy crisis. He asked for voluntary wage and price controls in an effort to restrain inflation and committed to reducing government regulations because they pushed up prices. On energy, he said the US needed to pump more oil and reduce waste.[40]

In 1978, the Carter administration helped stop a dangerous slide in the dollar's value by raising the Federal Reserve's discount rate and thus constraining borrowing. But this also fed economic contraction. In 1979, Carter appointed Paul Volcker Federal Reserve Chairman. To tackle inflation, Volcker began raising interest rates. These soon approached 20 percent and led to high unemployment and recession. The next administration continued Volcker's approach, bringing inflation under control.[41]

Carter saw the energy crisis as a national security issue for America and its allies, and spent nearly four years trying to address it. In July 1979, Carter laid out responses to the energy challenge in his "Crisis of Confidence" speech. He said the greatest threat to American democracy was a lack of confidence in the American system and proposed to help solve the energy *shortage* by *reducing* oil imports via fixed quotas to ensure America never imported more oil than it had in 1977. Dependence upon foreign oil would be reduced by solar, more coal, alcohol-based fuels, conservation, and increased use of public transport. A "windfall profits" tax on oil companies was also passed. Oil imports and consumption decreased. He also established the Department of Energy. Branded the president's "Malaise Speech," it was not helpful to Carter's presidency. The stresses of the oil crisis drove innovation as America began shifting from an industrial-dominated economy to one driven by technological advances and the service industry.[42]

Despite its problems and growing international competition, the US was attractive to overseas investors. Selling its treasuries abroad meant foreign wealth financed government spending while permitting "Washington the luxury of living beyond its means." Carter, though, was generally fiscally conservative and didn't like deficit spending.[43]

A FATEFUL YEAR: 1979

In 1978, "the administration was too absorbed by various urgent dossiers to be able to implement any sort of grand geopolitical vision." The next year was worse, proving the administration's *annus horribilis*. In Iran, as opposition to the shah mounted, the US sent mixed signals. Brzezinski said, "US assurances of support were watered down by simultaneous reminders of the need to do more about progress toward genuine democracy." The confused US reaction fed the shah's indecision and contributed to his fall. At the same time, American support allowed the shah's political opponents to depict him as an American puppet and undermine his legitimacy. After the shah's January 1979 abdication, Carter dropped his support, which won no plaudits from Iran's replacement despot, Ayatollah Ruhollah Khomeini. Carter still believed Iran could provide stability in the region and that neither he nor the Iranians wanted a Communist Iran. Brzezinski's efforts to negotiate came to naught.[44]

Dreams of conciliating Iran soon ended. Carter allowed the shah to enter the US for medical treatment and Iranian anti-Americanism boiled over. In November 1979, the Iranians seized the US embassy in Tehran and fifty-two Americans. The Carter administration replied with negotiations, then sanctions, the severing of relations, and finally a complex rescue attempt culminating in a tragic fiasco. Vance resigned when Carter ordered a rescue. Negotiations continued, and the hostages were freed on January 20, 1981, the last day of Carter's administration, in exchange for the unfreezing of $7.977 billion in Iranian assets. The inability and failure of the US to rescue the hostages convinced Pentagon officials to speed creation of a Rapid Deployment Force (RDF).[45]

The Iranian Revolution destroyed Iran's oil output, oil prices tripled, and the US became more involved in the region. Saudi Arabia, though not strong militarily, was anti-Communist, and became an attractive replacement for Iran in American regional strategic thinking. But Riyadh was reluctant to draw close to Washington, especially after the Camp David Accords, which shattered the anti-Israel Arab front and led Saudi Arabia and other Arab states to sever relations with Egypt. The shah's fall, and the failure of the US to protect his regime, hurt America's reputation and stunned some, such as Bahrain. Many of the Arab states disliked the shah and Iran, but they disliked Khomeini's Iran more as he threatened their regimes and promised to take his version of Shia Islam to the region and the world, eliminating US influence and the Gulf's Arab monarchs. Moscow was "Emboldened by previous political and strategic gains and by American failures." In November 1978, the Soviets "warned the United States against intervening in Iran." The Carter administration said it "had neither the desire nor the ability," a reply numerous regional officials and Americans saw as weak. It particularly angered the Saudis.[46]

A pro-Moscow Communist coup in the Afghan capital of Kabul in 1978, followed by the standard totalitarian repression and execution of political prisoners, provoked widespread resistance from the rebel Mujahideen. In July 1979, the administration approved non-lethal support in the form of money, supplies, radio propaganda, and other things. A conspiracy theory based upon misreading a 1998 article holds that Brzezinski and the Carter administration now proceeded to trick the Soviets into invading Afghanistan. Debunking the idea, Brzezinski said that when the Mujahideen started fighting the Soviet-controlled regime, the US:

> first started giving them money about six months before the Soviets went in. When we started to give them money, I told Carter that I think they'll go in, and they'll probably use that as an excuse in part, but that they're going in anyway, because they are taking over the regime. So we didn't suck them in but we knew what we were doing, namely we were in a sense engaging them in a preliminary skirmishing, prior to their more overt intervention.

We know from the Soviet side that Moscow invaded Afghanistan to protect its failing puppet.[47]

The invasion sparked fears of a Soviet Union again on the march. Brzezinski found the occupation of Afghanistan a particularly dangerous sign of a larger trend, telling Carter it was the seventh nation to fall to Communism since 1975. Contrary to Brzezinski's fears, the Soviets had no plan to push to the sea or to dominate the region after invading Afghanistan. Moscow sought only to prop up a client. Carter decided to make the invasion "as politically costly as possible" to Moscow. US arms and aid began flowing to the Mujahideen. But the damage to US prestige was done, and US credibility eroded further with the "perception of Soviet political and military gains in Angola, Ethiopia, South Yemen, and now Afghanistan, coupled with Washington's loss of Iran as an ally and the unending hostage crisis."[48]

THE CARTER ADMINISTRATION – PART 2: REASSESSMENT, POLITICAL AIMS, AND GRAND STRATEGY

The invasion of Afghanistan catalyzed an administration strategic awakening – particularly for Carter – regarding the Soviet danger to America and its interests. A trio of currents caused this: "the steady growth and increased projection of Soviet military power beyond its own borders; the overwhelming dependence of the Western democracies on oil supplies from the Middle East; and the press of social and religious and economic and political change in the many nations of the developing world, exemplified by the revolution in Iran." Carter's January 1980 State of the Union Address marked the change. He committed to working in the nation's interests and gave his political aim: "Peace – a peace that preserves freedom – remains America's first goal."[49] This had become a standard refrain in the speeches of US leaders, one Carter's successors repeated.

But by 1980, many doubted "whether the Carter administration had a coherent view of the international situation, a sense of global strategy, and consistent policies and objectives."[50] The administration had created an atmosphere of doubt at home and weakness abroad. Carter's failures led to his being labeled naïve. But in a somewhat disjointed manner, he laid out in January 1980 how the administration intended to use national power in pursuit of its aim. The administration developed a grand strategy that considered threats and interests and provided a coherence dramatically different from what came before.

Countering the Soviet offensive became most important. Before January 1980, the administration had already replied to Moscow's invasion of Afghanistan by enacting punitive economic measures such as severing access to US technology and agricultural goods while asking America's allies to act similarly. Washington boycotted the Moscow Olympics and called for a revival of Selective Service registration, the backbone of any potential future draft. In 1980, Carter called for annual 5 percent increases in defense spending over the next five years.[51]

The administration updated the National Strategy (PD 18) because of the "increased projection of Soviet power which threatens US vital interests in the Persian Gulf region." Middle East instability had increased because of Soviet actions in Afghanistan and the Horn of Africa, ongoing Arab–Israeli and Arab–Arab problems, the Iranian Revolution, and the Iran–Iraq War that Iraq's Saddam Hussein launched in September 1980. Washington feared this chaos providing doors for Moscow to exert control over the region's oil-producing states, thus threatening the US, Europe, NATO, and Japan. NATO remained the primary defense concern. The US developed plans for quickly deploying forces to the Middle East and pushed strengthening of Japan's defense forces and those of NATO and SEATO members. NATO nations particularly needed to meet their commitments and absorb some of the slack created by the shift of US forces to the Persian Gulf. France, Britain, and Australia were expected to also provide forces, while Germany and others furnished non-military support. Turkey and Pakistan – the two nations flanking the region – would be given military and economic aid. Washington strengthened its military forces in the southeastern US and areas south of this to counter Soviet and Cuban influence. The US "vigorously" pursued arms limitation talks with Moscow to lower defense costs and reduce the possibility of a nuclear exchange.[52]

In January 1980, the president announced what became known as the Carter Doctrine. This arose from fears of Soviet expansion into the Middle East brought about by the invasion of Afghanistan and the Iranian Revolution. Carter said: "An attempt by any outside force to gain control of the Persian Gulf region will be regarded as an assault on the vital interests of the United States of America, and such an assault will be repelled by any means necessary, including military force." The administration committed to building up forces in the Middle East and growing its ability to deploy there as a means of deterring Soviet intervention and protecting the Straits of Hormuz from the problems caused by the Iran–Iraq War while strengthening partner nations and getting America's allies to do more. Carter hoped to reduce the threat from radical groups by furthering the Arab–Israeli peace process. Brzezinski worked to create a regional security system via agreements with partners like Egypt, Somalia, Kenya, Oman, and others for bases and support. Brzezinski proved instrumental in the creation of the 100,000-person Rapid Deployment Joint Task Force intended to provide quick support to an attacked ally.[53]

The rise of Poland's Solidarity union movement provided the administration a way to pressure the Soviets. As strikes increased in Poland, Brzezinski wanted to prevent a repetition of the 1968 Soviet invasion of Czechoslovakia. When US intelligence began detecting signs of an invasion, Brzezinski convinced Carter to warn the Soviets against such a move while assuring them the US wouldn't take advantage of their troubles. Moscow blanched at invading Poland, worried about possible resistance and the economic fallout from Western sanctions that might result. It had the Polish government restore order.[54]

In addition to the Mideast peace process, Carter's diplomatic strategy included improving relations with Turkey, Pakistan, Ethiopia, Somalia, Djibouti, and the Middle Eastern states, thus blocking the growth of Soviet influence. The economic strategy included securing the availability of oil at a reasonable price, corralling aid from Western states for the region, and Saudi financing of regional security needs. Economic stability was considered critical. The CIA was to develop a regional intelligence program to supply needed information.[55]

As Soviet actions intensified, American public opinion shifted in support of a harder line, but the US lacked the military means and intelligence resources to mount a stronger challenge. The administration was constrained by its inability to demonstrate strength as well as "decisions made in fits and starts that did not satisfy the hawks but irritated the Soviet Union." The administration birthed a defense renaissance partially fueled by the view that the US was stronger than the Soviet Union, even more than appeared at the time, an understanding not shared by Nixon and Kissinger. The administration launched many weapons programs that bore fruit in the next administration.[56]

Despite resistance from Vance and his successor as secretary of state, Muskie, the US overhauled its nuclear strategy. Carter launched a study of nuclear strategy almost immediately after his inauguration. This produced PD 59, a better-constructed document than comparable administration texts. It lacks a political aim but makes clear US nuclear and conventional forces were for deterrence. The US would maintain sufficient forces to show an adversary that "no plausible outcome would represent a victory on any plausible definition of victory." The US also needed to be strong enough that in the event of an attack it would "preserve the possibility of bargaining effectively to terminate the war on acceptable terms that are as favorable as practical." In the event of war, use of nuclear and conventional forces would be coordinated to pursue "policy objectives" determined by the administration.[57]

This revision marked MAD's abandonment and was based on the belief that MAD no longer sufficed as the Soviets appeared prepared to fight a war where they only used a portion of their nuclear arsenal or used it in conjunction with conventional forces. The US adopted a "countervailing" or "counterforce strategy" related to the use of nuclear weapons. This meant the administration sought more flexibility in the intensity of nuclear weapons usage and in the targeting, which noted 50,000 potential sites. The US had to be able to destroy not just civilian targets, as MAD dictated, but also industrial, military, and political ones. It was assumed the strength of the deterrence would improve as it became clear the US could credibly use its weapons. All of this meant the US needed more warheads, particularly MIRV (Multiple Independently Targetable Reentry Vehicle) types on its ICBMs and SLBMS. ICBMs, strategic bombers, and nuclear submarines continued to form the nuclear triad. The Reagan administration kept this strategy.[58]

The Soviet global offensive had unintended effects that were not so clear in 1980. As Moscow's reach increased, its ability to sustain its worldwide position was beginning to decline. By the 1980s, the Soviets backed numerous Third World despots incapable of doing anything for their subjects, while facing potentially existential threats from insurgencies. The Soviet quest for superiority in arms taxed its inefficient economy and risked provoking an arms race with a stronger foe. Deployment of SS20 missiles to Europe rattled NATO, convinced its European members to take defense more seriously, and led to the deployment of US Pershing II and Tomahawk missiles to Europe. But no administration actions altered the public's view of Carter as weak and ineffective.[59]

The Soviet invasion of Afghanistan led Carter to pursue a military relationship with China. The US refused to sell advanced offensive weapons or engines for jet fighters but did agree to defensive weapons it concluded couldn't be used against America's regional maritime partners, such as anti-aircraft systems and anti-tank missiles. China replied by supplying arms and ammunition to the Mujahideen fighting the Soviets in Afghanistan. Help to China included supporting the Beijing-aligned genocidal Cambodian Khmer Rouge at the UN after Vietnam invaded the country on December 25, 1975. Carter preferred normalizing relations with Vietnam, but Brzezinski convinced him of China's greater importance. The Khmer Rouge regime was one of the most murderous in history, though

China holds first rank, and the support Carter rendered China and its allies destroys any argument for the administration's moral superiority. US leaders acted to increase Moscow's difficulties and saw no danger aiding a state as poor and backwards as China.[60]

SOME CONCLUSIONS

In 1980, the Carter administration's grand strategy gained coherence as a result of a clear-eyed reassessment on the part of Carter and his advisors as the president awakened to the reality of the Soviet threat. The administration, despite its early projections of weakness and naivety, had some notable successes. The Camp David Accords and the Egypt–Israel peace treaty are properly lauded. The administration largely succeeded in restoring US leadership in the Third World, particularly in regard to Latin America, Southern Africa, and the Middle East, but its actions helped antidemocratic regimes into power, such as the Sandinistas in Nicaragua. Carter was trapped by the 444-day Iran hostage crisis, and a failed rescue operation made the US appear weak.[61]

The administration's greatest failures were economic. Inflation, which Carter inherited, was 9 percent in 1978, averaged 11.8 percent in 1979, and remained above 13 percent in 1980. Unemployment went from an average of 6 percent in 1977 to May 1980's 7.8 percent. Carter never succeeded in solving the energy crisis, though this was probably beyond any president.[62] Making it more difficult to import oil was not the answer.

Debate continues over whether the administration's focus on human rights can be judged a success. It provided hope for many desperate dissidents. But the administration looked the other way in China and Cambodia, while bludgeoning US allies such as South Korea and the Philippines and clumsily undermining partners (albeit disreputable ones) ruling Nicaragua and Iran, thus helping ensure the establishment of regimes even more inimical to freedom and US interests. Carter's approach won few friends in the Third World. When he was introduced as the honorary chair of the 1993 conference on human rights in Vienna, "hundreds of Third World delegates mocked and heckled him until he abandoned the podium. To them he represented the worst sort of paternalistic American meddling."[63] Carter's most innovative move was taking up the mantle of human rights. The problem was that "human rights," like many elements of the administration's grand strategy, needed to be clearly directed at a positive aim.

15

WINNING THE HOT PEACE: REAGAN'S GREAT-POWER COMPETITION, 1981–1990

THE RONALD REAGAN ADMINISTRATION, 1981–89

At the end of the 1970s, many saw a US in decline. This proved staggeringly untrue. America was troubled. America had problems, economic ones the most pressing. Détente was dead. The Soviets were stronger militarily, particularly in the nuclear realm, and on the march. Afghanistan, Angola, Nicaragua, and South Yemen fell under Communism's sway. Many Westerners feared the tide was shifting toward Moscow; Soviet leaders thought so.[1] Imaginative leadership, clear political aims and serious pursuit of them, Soviet weaknesses, and other factors combined to disprove the doubters.

THE ASSESSMENT

Before taking office, Ronald Reagan understood these weaknesses and how to exploit them. He was famous as an actor and California's governor before his 1980 landslide presidential election victory. Reagan took up the leadership of a nation suffering "stagflation" – a vicious combination of high inflation and high unemployment. But Reagan possessed a powerful tool: an unbounded confidence in America and its people. Historian John Lewis Gaddis sums up Reagan's core views: "an unshakeable belief in democracy and capitalism, an abhorrence of communism, an impatience with compromise in what he regarded as a contest between good and evil, and – very significantly – a deep fear that the Cold War might end in a nuclear holocaust." Reagan disagreed with much of America's grand strategy toward the Soviet Union. He assailed Kissinger and rejected détente as a system seeking agreement for its own sake while not relying on American strength. It weakened America as it strengthened Moscow by allowing it access to Western technology, trade, and money, even as its global offensive undermined the free world. True peace and security were attainable only after creating a military deterrent strong enough to show Moscow it must negotiate arms reductions.[2]

Reagan regarded the Cold War struggle as one of freedom versus totalitarian evil, saw a Soviet people weary of a repressive regime, and viewed Communism as so contrary to human nature its survival could only be temporary. His administration's eventual grand strategy "drew heavily on Reagan's own ideas and involvement," and was based on the assessment America was far stronger economically and in the arena of ideas, while Moscow was weaker than it appeared. "I wondered how we as a nation could use these cracks in the Soviet system to accelerate the process of collapse," Reagan wrote. The US could leverage American power to outbuild and outpace Moscow. Then, from a position of strength, Reagan said, extend "the hand of friendship" and "invite them to join us in lowering the level of weapons on both sides." Meanwhile, many American intellectuals insisted the Soviet economy was strong.[3]

Reagan wrote in March 1980, "We must above all have a grand strategy; a plan for the dangerous decade ahead." On February 5, 1982, Reagan ordered a review to produce a new strategy. The resulting document, NSDD 32, mixed political aims and elements of grand strategy, and unsurprisingly identified the most dangerous threat as Moscow and its allies. The administration considered war with the Soviets unlikely because it thought Moscow understood the dangers, but unstable areas gave Moscow opportunities. The political, economic, and other problems made its authors fear the 1980s could be the most dangerous period for the US since the Second World War, but the American "response could result in a fundamentally different East-West relationship by the end of this decade." American security required "development and integration of a set of strategies, including diplomatic, informational, economic/political, and military components." Soviet strength, the loss of American strategic superiority, and natural resource demands meant Washington had no alternative but cooperation with allies and partners. This necessitated strengthening NATO and other allies, relying on regional partners, and maintaining the ability to support them militarily.[4]

The administration, though, got off to a bumpy start, plagued by chaos, infighting, and leaking that Reagan failed to contain and that never disappeared. Defense Secretary Caspar Weinberger, like the second secretary of state, George Shultz (Al Haig held this post the first eighteen months), constantly clashed over strategy toward the Soviet Union. But they agreed upon the foundations: increased American strength integrated with that of democratic allies to roll back Soviet influence. Weinberger wanted Washington to use its strengths while exploiting Moscow's weaknesses. This meant focusing on economics and technology and concentrating on technologically superior weapons. Weinberger believed in what he called economic warfare. It wasn't warfare (it lacked violence) but the weaponization of economics. The administration also had six national security advisors, plus one acting, which weakened the creation and execution of grand strategy.[5]

The administration's stumbling start bred accusations of an incoherent approach to foreign relations. But Reagan understood the course he was charting and why. He insisted in 1981 that he indeed had a diplomatic strategy, "I just don't happen to think that it's wise to always stand up and put in quotation marks in front of the world what your foreign policy is."[6]

THE POLITICAL AIMS

The administration failed to immediately formulate clear political aims, but Reagan had ideas about what he hoped to achieve before entering office: "We win, they lose." During his election campaign, Reagan responded to critics of his aggressive, anti-Soviet rhetoric by saying: "Our goal is a stable peace." Reagan said in his inaugural: "As for the enemies of freedom, those who are potential adversaries, they will be reminded that peace is the highest aspiration of the American people." Reagan also sought peace in Europe, which he hoped to achieve by negotiating with Moscow and maintaining Washington's NATO commitment. But, Reagan said, "The American concept of peace goes well beyond the absence of war. We foresee a flowering of economic growth and individual liberty in a world at peace."[7]

Reagan's thinking on possible US and Western achievements also moved on other lines. "The years ahead are great ones for this country," he said in November 1981, "for the cause of freedom and the spread of civilization. The West won't contain communism, it will transcend communism. It won't bother to dismiss or denounce it, it will dismiss it as some bizarre chapter in human history whose last pages are even now being written." A month later, Poland's Communist government cracked down on the Solidarity union movement. This proved a catalyst for Reagan declaring democracy abroad as a political aim in June 1982. He quoted Winston Churchill: "But what we have to consider here today while time remains is the permanent prevention of war and the establishment of conditions of freedom and democracy as rapidly as possible in all countries." Reagan then said: "this is precisely our mission today: to preserve freedom as well as peace." He added: "If the rest of this century is to witness the gradual growth of freedom and democratic ideals, we must take actions to assist the campaign for democracy."[8]

In September 1982, the administration delineated its political aims toward the Warsaw Pact nations: "I have determined that the primary long-term US goal in Eastern Europe is to loosen the Soviet hold on the region and thereby facilitate its eventual reintegration into the European community of nations." The US strategy was attacking the rival's alliances (as Sun Tzu advised) by encouraging liberal political and economic reforms and greater economic ties with the West. The US would support most-favored-nation trade status, trade credits, International Monetary Fund (IMF) membership, debt relief, and technology sales to liberalizing nations demonstrating independence from Moscow. This continued a practice of the previous twenty years of differentiating between Moscow and Warsaw Pact members – but Reagan intended to be more discriminating.[9]

The clearest delineation of the administration's key political aims (and of elements of its grand strategy, particularly toward the Soviet Union) appeared in January 1983's NSDD 75, "US Relations with the USSR." Like NSDD 32, this mixes grand strategy elements and political aims, but clearly relays the administration's intent: "To promote, within the narrow limits available to us, the process of change in the Soviet Union toward a more pluralistic political and economic system in which the power of the privileged ruling elite is gradually reduced." The Reagan administration sought to compel the "mellowing" of the Soviet regime Kennan suggested as an aim. Richard Pipes, one of NSDD 75's authors, said Washington's "goal was no longer to coexist with the Soviet Union but to change the Soviet system. At its root was the belief that we had it in our power to alter the Soviet system through the use of external pressure."[10]

GRAND STRATEGY AND THE GLOBAL COLD WAR

To produce Soviet "mellowing" and "rollback" of its empire, the US would – in the words of NSDD 75 – "contain and over time reverse Soviet expansionism by competing effectively on a sustained basis with the Soviet Union in all international arenas – particularly in the overall military balance and in geographical regions of priority concern to the United States." There were three primary thrusts: "external resistance to Soviet imperialism; internal pressure on the USSR to weaken the sources of Soviet imperialism; and negotiations to eliminate, on the basis of strict reciprocity, outstanding disagreements." This required carrots and sticks. The US would use elements of national power to show Moscow its malignant actions cost more than they gained while making clear good behavior won benefits.[11] Containment had to continue until the US rebuilt its strength; then rollback could begin.

The Reagan administration pushed democratic freedoms and fundamental rights to achieve the aim of democracy. Reagan said:

> The objective [strategy] I propose is quite simple to state: to foster the infrastructure of democracy, the system of a free press, unions, political parties, universities, which allows a people to choose their own way to develop their own culture, to reconcile their own differences through peaceful means. This is not cultural imperialism, it is providing the means for genuine self-determination and protection for diversity.[12]

But Reagan's freedom agenda differed from Wilson's: it wouldn't be imposed.

Connected to this is what became known – mistakenly – as the Reagan Doctrine: aiding groups fighting for their freedom against Communist tyranny. It is common to date this from Reagan's 1985 State of the Union speech, but Reagan didn't announce a Reagan Doctrine here: he merely emphasized what the administration had been doing. The term arose from a political commentator who insisted a few weeks later on April 1 (of all dates) that he had found a guiding principle. Reagan himself later used the term in a speech, but there was no conscious decision to create a Reagan Doctrine.[13]

The administration knew achieving its aims would take time and believed the US faced dangers from Moscow testing America's resolve, particularly in the next five to ten years. But to end détente and take advantage of Soviet weakness, Reagan had to act. One result was that the first two years of his presidency became some of the most dangerous of the Cold War.[14] The weakness, fragility, and paranoia of the Soviet Union created more hazard than Reagan or any in his administration realized.

ECONOMIC STRATEGY

The nation's dire economic situation made first addressing economic issues a political and security imperative. America's economic strategy had two major thrusts: strengthening itself and its allies while weakening Moscow and its clients. Balancing these proved difficult. America, Reagan said before the election, faced "three grave threats ... any one of which could destroy us ... a disintegrating economy, a weakened defense[,] and an energy policy based on the sharing of scarcity." Two were economic issues.[15]

Freeing America's people and economy to be as productive and innovative as possible necessitated retrenching government control over people's lives. The administration sought Federal spending cuts by freezing government hiring and began removing economic restrictions such as wage and price controls and oil production limits. It froze pending Federal regulations for 60 days and cut 23,000 pages from the Federal Register (which contains US government rules) its first year. Reagan also promised deficits wouldn't become "simple facts of life in this administration."[16] This proved easy to say.

The failure of Keynesian economics in the 1970s saw the birth (really rebirth) of supply-side economics stressing the rollback of state regulation and control (including taxes) to unleash the efficiencies of the free market and individual creativity. The resultant growth in the economy was to produce greater tax revenues than the higher rates. Market solutions (or a form of them) became the favored treatment for economic malaise in numerous nations around the globe from the US, to Chile, to Britain, to China.[17] Coolidge and Kennedy had acted similarly.

Reagan sought tax cuts and said: "I am reminded that every major tax cut in this century has strengthened the economy, generated renewed productivity and ended up yielding new revenues for the government by creating new investment, new jobs and more commerce among our people." Reagan worked hard to secure Congressional support and succeeded in August 1981. The top individual tax rate fell from 70 to 50 percent; all other rates declined, the average reduction being 23 percent. The total individual tax savings over five years was $750 billion.[18]

But Reagan miscalculated. He had wanted to end America's fiscal deficit habit but couldn't stop bipartisan Congressional spending. His grand strategy also necessitated dramatic defense spending increases. The national debt climbed from $914 billion in 1980 to $2.7 trillion in 1989. He was forced to surrender on some tax increases in 1982, including on corporations, but again secured income tax cuts in 1986 that lowered the upper rate to 28 percent while closing loopholes. The number of jobs increased by over 18 million from 1981 to 1989.[19]

One of the most dangerous monsters was inflation and Reagan took office with the nation suffering its historically worst long-term inflation; this produced crippling ripple-effects across the economy and people's lives. The administration broke inflation's back by supporting Federal Reserve Chairman Volcker's use of high interest rates. Inflation dropped to a manageable 3.5 percent within five years from its 1979 average of 11.3 percent. But this also produced a recession in late 1981 through early 1982 that pushed unemployment to 9.7 percent while injuring Reagan's popular support. But unemployment fell to 5.5 percent by 1988. The effect of any specific economic action is debatable, and the situation of every administration is different, but the best measure of success in the eyes of the American people was Reagan's 1984 reelection in one of America's greatest electoral college landslides, securing 525 of 538 electoral votes and winning 49 states.[20]

In Reagan's second term, he faced protectionist pressures from Congress in regard to Japan, partially because America was suffering the effects of extensive overseas competition. In 1985, for the first time in fifty years, trade became a critical political issue. Reagan was a free trader and believed protectionism often helped one industry or group at another's expense. He preferred altering Japan's trade behavior with negotiations fueled by Congressional pressure rather than retaliation. The administration secured a deal to reduce the dollar's value against Japan's yen and Germany's mark, making US exports cheaper.[21]

The weaponization of economics against the Soviets took two primary forms: altering Western economic relations with the Soviet Bloc, and denying Moscow and its allies Western money (loans or income) and technology, particularly for military purposes. This would pressure the Soviets to make structural changes. The US promoted trade that benefited both sides, but not if the West subsidized it, and only in non-strategic items such as grain. Implementing the economic strategy required the US to work closely with allies as it demanded a unified approach.[22]

In 1981, the administration tried to kill Moscow's Urengoy pipeline to bring natural gas to Europe. Reagan embargoed the sale of US equipment for the project on December 29. The Europeans filled the void. The administration then forbade sales of US equipment under license. The effort strained the alliance and Reagan backed away. The internal contretemps over the impact on European relations contributed to Haig's departure. The US later restricted exports of Soviet natural gas to Europe via a spring 1983 agreement with the International Energy Agency.[23]

Washington worked hard to sever Soviet access to foreign technology, trade, and money. It used the Coordinating Committee for Multilateral Export Controls (COCOM), which oversaw export of strategic items and technology to Communist states, and the 1979 Export Control Act to increasingly restrict American technology sales and transfers. Washington secured cooperation from allies and the three neutral states serving as the primary conduits (Austria, Sweden, and Switzerland) while waging a generally successful campaign against trans-shipment. The Soviets conducted extensive espionage to steal Western technology or simply purchased it. The US also ran a "technical disinformation campaign" against Moscow entailing the distribution and sale of flawed technical plans.[24]

Western governments and private finances supported Moscow's tottering economy. The administration pushed increased interest rates on loans to Moscow and trade credit reductions, and secured agreement from major European allies to not subsidize Soviet Bloc economies via trade or allow trade supporting military purposes, while the NSC worked to block new loans. Credit began drying up. By 1982, the Soviet Bloc had almost no private Western sources for long-term credit and had loan repayment problems. The Saudis were pushed to increase oil production to lower prices and injure Moscow's access to hard currency from oil exports.[25]

The economic success of the Reagan administration is clear. US economic growth from 1973 to 1981 averaged 2.3 percent annually. This outpaced all other large economies save Japan. US economic contraction from 1979 to 1982 was followed by an economic boom. The US economy grew *7.2 percent in 1984 alone and at 3–4 percent for the rest of the 1980s* while inflation dropped below 3 percent and stayed there until the end of the millennium. America's average GDP growth from 1973 to 2001 was 2.94 percent, a number superior to the average rates of Germany, Western Europe, and Japan.[26]

MILITARY STRATEGY

Foundational to Reagan's thinking was the necessity of American strength – particularly military strength. In November 1981, he committed to a five-year expansion of American conventional and nuclear weapons. He noted Moscow had an army twice the size of America's, 50,000 tanks, and a large navy, and had moved 750 new nuclear warheads to Europe while America removed 1,000. More deployable forces, expanded reserve forces, and increased security assistance were needed. Reagan benefited from bipartisan Congressional support and the defense budget between 1980 to 1988 grew from $155.2 billion to $319.8 billion.[27]

Defense Secretary Weinberger sought to exploit America's technological advantages in the defense build-up while denying this technology to Moscow. Militarily, the US would modernize its conventional and nuclear forces so the Soviets could see no possible benefit in starting a war while demonstrating America wouldn't tolerate being second militarily. NATO would be strengthened, while the US built forces to show any attack risked retaliation. Moreover, the "heart of US military strategy" remained deterring an "attack by the USSR and its allies against the US, its allies, or other important countries, and to defeat such an attack should deterrence fail." A diplomatic strategy to gain agreement from and create consensus among allies supported this.[28]

Because of Soviet military strength, war plans assumed conflict with Moscow wouldn't be confined to a single theater. Defending North America was most important; NATO and the relevant lines of communication were next. Following this was "ensuring access to the oil in Southwest Asia," then defending allies in the Pacific and "the lines of communication for the Indian and Pacific Oceans, and then the defense of other friendly nations in Latin America and Africa." The US would also block or thwart Soviet efforts to increase its influence.[29]

Defense guru Andrew Marshall's 1972 concept of a "cost-imposing strategy" exerted influence. Marshall suggested that particular defense outlays, especially where the US had technological advantages, could drive Moscow to incur injurious costs trying to keep up. This had some effect on the Ford and Carter administrations, but Reagan took the idea further, particularly in developing stealth technology and nuclear weapons. It became part of Pentagon planning in 1982. The Soviets faced the choice of falling behind or enduring the economic damage of keeping up. As we will see, the Strategic Defense Initiative proved the ultimate example of this.[30]

The navy developed the Maritime Strategy (it was not merely a naval strategy because it went beyond sea control). A greatly expanded navy would be a peacetime deterrent that could act globally. In the event of war, it would attack Soviet forces, the Soviet Union itself, and around its periphery, including in the Pacific. Its hallmarks were "power projection" and "offensive sea control" and to protract the war (while keeping it non-nuclear) because this played to America's strengths. The administration neither officially accepted the navy's approach nor integrated it into an overall military strategy. Secretary of the Navy John Lehman failed to secure his 600-ship navy, but it reached 574 in 1990.[31]

In the 1970s, the army and air force capitalized on America's technological edge to develop the concept of AirLandBattle to frustrate a Soviet attack in Europe without resorting to nuclear weapons. AirLandBattle planned for an immediate counteroffensive in Europe against a Soviet assault, one supported with airstrikes on enemy forces in the Warsaw Pact nations. Weinberger secured a NATO-wide high-technology focus and acceptance of AirLandBattle.[32]

Nuclear forces remained a key part of peacetime deterrence strategy by ensuring Moscow could expect an unbearable counterattack; the administration launched a modernization program. If deterrence failed, American planners believed the US "must be prepared to wage war successfully." US documents insisted the US nuclear force be capable of preventing a Soviet military victory and "force it to seek earliest termination of hostilities on terms favorable to the United States" even after suffering a first strike.[33]

Such thinking on wartime nuclear weapons usage frightened Reagan. A nuclear exchange was among his greatest fears, and he believed reliance on them increased their chances of use. He called MAD "the craziest thing I ever heard of" and had trouble seeing how living under a "balance of terror" was good for international stability. He rejected SALT II because it institutionalized large nuclear arsenals when he wanted reduction. Instead, he suggested eliminating from Europe intermediate-range nuclear missiles.[34]

Reagan broke the strategic-thought status quo in March 1983 by announcing the Strategic Defense Initiative (SDI), a program to develop an antiballistic missile defense system known colloquially as Star Wars. There were previous antimissile systems, and the 1972 Anti-Ballistic Missile (ABM) Treaty with Moscow had permitted some, which the US had abandoned. Reagan saw SDI as a means of lowering the threat of a nuclear exchange by making such weapons obsolete. Its development would force the Soviets to compete with the US in an area where they probably couldn't build enough missiles to drown an SDI system. Consideration began in October 1981. By 1985, it was a tool for arms reductions.[35]

Reagan's announcement of SDI stunned his staff and left Secretary of State Shultz and Secretary of Defense Weinberger scrambling. Reagan increased the shock by offering to share the technology with Moscow. SDI frightened Moscow. The Soviet organ *Izvestia* said: "They want to impose on us an even more ruinous arms race. They calculate that the Soviet Union will not last the race. It lacks the resources, it lacks the technical potential. They hope that our country's economy will be exhausted." Reagan would have nodded agreement. Moscow feared this countering its ICBM force, the world's largest, negating its key source of international power, and they lacked the technological and economic power to reply or build enough missiles to overwhelm it.[36]

Soviet dictator Yuri Andropov, a former KGB chief, denounced SDI as a scheme for trying to fight and win a nuclear war. Soviet leaders began fearing the US was preparing for conflict. In March 1983, Reagan delivered his "evil empire" speech. Two weeks later, SDI was announced. In September, the Soviets shot down a South Korean airliner that strayed into their airspace. October saw the American invasion of Grenada. American Pershing II missiles began arriving in West Germany in November. Meanwhile, throughout the fall, shoddy Soviet early warning systems delivered false signs of an American attack. NATO's planned ABLE-ARCHER 83 exercise further unbalanced Moscow. Andropov convinced himself the US intended to mount a nuclear first-strike and had his intelligence services searching for information on this, which they faked when they couldn't find it. Western intelligence on Soviet fears saw NATO scale back the exercise to lower tensions. The crisis was defused in time, but frightened Reagan. Shortly after, he received his first briefing on US plans for waging a war with nuclear weapons. This scared him even more, especially his realization that there were those on both sides who believed one could fight a war with these weapons and emerge victorious. The ABLE-ARCHER incident produced an epiphany for Reagan. Realizing the Soviets viewed America as a threat, he became more cautious.[37] Reagan had made a common error: failing to put himself as much as possible into the other side's shoes.

The administration tackled the growth of international terrorism because of attacks on Americans, terrorism's potential to weaken allies and partners, and possible Soviet sponsorship. It is common to simply brand groups as "terrorist," which is weak analytically because it lumps organizations by the means used while forgetting terrorism is a violence tool for achieving political aims, one states sometimes exploit. A solid definition is: "terrorism is the intentional use of, or threat to use, violence against civilians or against civilian targets, in order to attain political aims." January 1986 saw finalization of the National Program for Combatting Terrorism where the US announced its "unequivocal" and "firm opposition to terrorism in all its forms," domestic or international. Doing anything less, and bending to "terrorist demands," was seen as putting "more American citizens at risk." It also said: "States that practice terrorism or actively support it, will not be allowed to do so without consequence."[38]

The administration drafted its own approach to so-called Low-Intensity Conflict (the intensity is never low to those involved), which it defined as "political-military confrontation between contending states or groups below conventional war and above the routine, peaceful competition among states," a convoluted definition risking confusion between war and peace. The composers mistakenly based their definition on the means used, but their chosen characteristics describe most insurgencies: they are protracted, include subversion, and generally occur in the Third World. Such struggles were a threat because they could separate Washington from alliance and trade partners while weakening the Free World, particularly via the cumulative effects of numerous lost wars. The US would involve itself in such conflicts only after considering the following criteria: "strategic interests, freedom and democratic values, opposition to Soviet expansionism/adventurism, and the supported group's or government's depth of commitment to the struggle." The US would work internationally to reduce the causes of such wars and support democratic forces striving to free themselves against powers acting contrary to US interests, while countering Soviet-backed terrorism and violence. If the US decided to support militarily a resistance movement, it should avoid "Americanizing" the fight. It must also remember involvement here is usually long.[39]

DIPLOMATIC STRATEGY

Reagan's desire to win the Cold War competition with Moscow dominated his diplomacy. US moves involved countering Communist actions, raising the Soviet Union's costs, and direct negotiations, particularly on reducing armaments. NSDD 75 made clear a key American diplomatic task was countering globally the actions of Moscow and its allies. The US rebutted Soviet expansion in the Third World with arms sales, military assistance, the deployment of military forces, diplomacy, and government and free-market economic assistance. Washington opposed Soviet penetration of the Middle East by supporting the Arab–Israeli peace effort. It tried to limit Cuban involvement in Angola and southern Africa, resisted Moscow in Southwest Asia, and strengthened Beijing against Moscow.[40]

In the Soviet Empire, the US sought "wherever possible to encourage Soviet allies to distance themselves from Moscow in foreign policy and to move toward democratization domestically." The US worked "to loosen Moscow's hold" in Eastern Europe by promoting human rights and discriminating in trade in favor of nations demonstrating independence from Moscow or a liberalizing trend. Washington tried to undermine Soviet Third World alliances by encouraging democratic movements. Reagan used William J. Casey's CIA to help anti-Communist forces "roll back" Soviet influence and raise Moscow's costs in Afghanistan, Nicaragua, Angola, and Cambodia, and blunt Cuban destabilization operations in Latin America. Reagan used a version of the Communist strategy against them, though generally without US troops.[41]

Also important was negotiating with Moscow. Against the advice of some advisors, Reagan pushed for talks as early as April 1981. He coupled rearmament with calls for reductions and "favored the eventual elimination of nuclear weapons." George Shultz said of this seeming dichotomy: "Strength and realism can deter war, but only direct dialogue and negotiations can open the path toward a lasting peace."[42]

INFORMATION STRATEGY

The Reagan administration conducted extensive information operations against Moscow. Reagan himself played a key role via speeches and personal statements, and highlighted Soviet criminality, repression, and failures in contrast to the West's freedoms and free-market success. Reagan's rhetorical attacks inspired Eastern Bloc dissidents, exposed the Soviet system's contradictions, and forced Soviet leaders to take what they usually only gave. The Voice of America (VOA) conducted extensive print and audio campaigns showing the truth of the Soviet system, and VOA and Radio Free Europe broadcasts into the Soviet Bloc improved.[43]

Reagan's team initially dismissed using human rights issues against Moscow but changed course after realizing their potency and their demonstrating "what is ultimately at issue in our contest." The US used the Conference on Security and Cooperation in Europe, NATO, and presidential rhetoric to publicize Soviet human rights abuses and pressure Moscow to grant Eastern Bloc states more say in their affairs. Part of the information strategy was directed at ensuring Americans understood Washington needed time to produce results.[44]

The administration used covert action against the Soviets, and the CIA discovered ways to increase Moscow's difficulties, but it had to be rebuilt. It was suffering the effects of Cuba- and Vietnam-related failures, and investigations such as the Church Committee. CIA activities also produced unintended effects. The Saudis wanted to support Wahabis in Central Asia to undermine Soviet control and take the Afghan war to the Soviets. This proved not in America's long-term interests. Covert actions backed dissident movements such as Solidarity. The administration publicly warned Brezhnev of the diplomatic costs and damage to the East–West relationship of invading Poland. Secret US support kept Solidarity going (Reagan called it "the 1st major break in the Red Dike") and the administration developed close ties with Pope John Paul II.[45]

The Kremlin replied by trying to sabotage Reagan's reelection by disseminating propaganda branding him a war monger and other equally ineffective efforts.[46] Moscow was also offered American assistance here. In May 1983, US Senator Ted Kennedy, who had had a number of contacts with the Soviets, sent a message through former US senator John Tunney offering to assist Soviet dictator Andropov deal with Reagan. When offering to collude with a foreign power in an effort to thwart Reagan's actions, Kennedy made sure to mention that the Democratic Party could turn to him for its nominee for the 1984 election, and his intention of running in 1988. Andropov never acted on the note and died within eight months.[47]

THE GLOBAL STRUGGLE

The Cold War had been a global affair since its arrival, but Moscow's Brezhnev-era offensive carried it into new arenas via conquest and subversion. The Reagan administration both defended and attacked in the Third World, which required individual approaches to specific challenges.[48]

AFGHANISTAN

Reagan wanted Moscow's costs raised, and Afghanistan was a place to do so. But by 1983, CIA Director Casey saw more: a place to defeat Moscow. The biggest US covert operation was supporting the Mujahideen with material and arms (including Stinger missiles) via Pakistan's Inter-Services Intelligence agency (ISI). In January 1985, the US learned Moscow was going to mount a massive effort to try to win its Afghan War. The administration delineated a new tack in March 1985: "the removal of Soviet forces from Afghanistan and the restoration of its independent status." Forcing "the removal of Soviet troops" was how to achieve the aim, but the point comes through. The US grand strategy included diplomatic pressure for withdrawal.[49]

The war in Afghanistan produced unexpected effects. The Saudis interpreted the Soviet invasion as a move toward the Middle East. This made Riyadh open to lowering energy prices, which the administration wanted as part of its economic strategy to starve the Soviets of hard currency while aiding Western economic growth. The Saudis saw Soviet encirclement as Moscow had advisors in North and South Yemen, Syria, Iraq, and Ethiopia, and 100,000 troops in Afghanistan.[50]

THE GRENADA WAR, 1983

In 1979, a Marxist-Leninist coup led eventually to a dictatorship under Maurice Bishop in the Caribbean nation of Grenada. In early October 1983, the Reagan administration grew concerned that Grenada's Cuba ties made it a base for antidemocratic elements in other island nations. The region's sea lanes were critical to US economic and military security, and the administration decided the defense needs of Washington and other states required increased military and economic support for democratic forces. The US sought "in the Eastern Caribbean ... to promote economically viable, independent democratic governments friendly to the United States and free of Cuban and Soviet influence."[51]

But the situation in Grenada deteriorated. Bishop proved insufficiently radical for his opponents and resisted moving closer to Moscow. He was overthrown on October 13, 1983 and executed. Grenada's new rulers aligned themselves with Havana, raising the specter of Cuban and Soviet penetration. Washington also worried about the safety of Americans on the island. The Organization of Eastern Caribbean States unanimously agreed to join Washington in restoring Grenada's democratic government and asked the US and other states to help. The administration ordered an invasion. It had three aims: protect American citizens, restore democratic governance, and eliminate and keep out any future Cuban invaders.[52]

The hastily planned and organized war began on October 25, 1983. The initial force of 2,100 faced 600 Cuban engineering troops and the small Grenadine army. Concern over the safety of about 1,100 Americans, half medical students, influenced how the US fought. Poor intelligence and tightly restricted artillery and airpower constrained America's war. The enemy forces were defeated in six days. The 6,000 US troops helped reestablish a democratic government, which the now free Grenadines appreciated.[53] The US war here is sometimes mistakenly depicted as a "limited war" because of the small size of the forces used. But this war was fought for an unlimited political aim – regime change – that used a small force.

LATIN AMERICA

In Latin America, El Salvador and Nicaragua absorbed the administration's concerns. Nicaragua became a Communist state in 1979 under the Moscow-aligned dictatorship of Daniel Ortega and his Sandinista movement. The Sandinistas began supporting the Farabundo Martí National Liberation Front (FMLN) in El Salvador and accepted Cuban advisors. In 1981, the administration tried to get Nicaragua to drop its FMLN support in exchange for better relations. Ortega rebuffed the effort. El Salvador's government, which Carter had begun assisting against the Communist insurgents, looked as though it might fall. Reagan refused to allow El Salvador to "become another Cuba on the mainland." US military aid helped defeat the 1981 insurgent offensive, but the war continued. Millions in economic and military funds flowed alongside diplomatic support.[54]

In January 1982, the administration adopted the aim of defeating the Communist insurgency in El Salvador. The strategy included blocking Cuba, Nicaragua, and others from introducing troops, importing heavy weapons, arming insurgents, and feeding subversion. Accompanying this was an information campaign, and economic, military, and intelligence aid and assistance to El Salvador and Honduras, help defeating externally directed insurgencies, and tightening sanctions on Cuba. Trade with Nicaragua would continue – as long as it allowed private business – and Washington would help democratic forces there. February 1983 saw Washington establish the aim of "a stable, democratic government in El Salvador." The strategy included internal negotiations, increases in military aid and advisors, improving El Salvador's military, and economic support. The situation in Latin America worried the administration enough to establish a multi-agency Central America Working Group to provide information for the president's daily briefing.[55]

The US took a more active role against Ortega's regime in 1981 by training in Honduras an anti-Sandinista military force – the Contras – that eventually numbered 15,000. The administration sought "victory for the forces of democracy." The Contras weren't an existential threat to the Sandinistas (their economic mismanagement was more dangerous), but they created problems.[56]

Ortega's consolidation of power and export of violent revolution threatened US Central American interests. In July 1983, Washington increased support for democratic states in the region and those "on the road to democracy." In February 1984, the administration pushed "the advancement of democracy and implementation of a free and open electoral process in all countries of Central America" and used the standard tools of economic, humanitarian, military, and security assistance, and advice on democratization. It also countered subversion from Cuba, the Soviet Union, and Nicaragua to create an environment amenable to success. The administration pushed El Salvador to democratize and support "reforms against attacks from the violent left and the violent right." It sought international diplomatic support for El Salvador, pushed its government on land reform, and financed improvements to the judicial system while funding and training the military. The US held military maneuvers in Honduras and pressured Nicaragua with a coastal naval presence. Part of the response to Cuba's ideological imperialism in Nicaragua and Angola was to tighten the US embargo.[57]

In February 1987, Reagan clearly described what he sought in the region and US actions – "I expressed my determination to see democracy prevail in Central America" – and noted that

> It is already the policy [strategy] of the US Government to promote democracy throughout the Western Hemisphere. The recent rapid growth of democratic governments in Latin America indicates that this is also the preference

of the people of the region.... In 1980 there were four dictatorships and one democracy in Central America. Today ... only one dictatorship remains in the midst of four democracies. The Sandinista dictatorship in Nicaragua.[58]

Three months before, on November 3, 1986, the Iran-Contra Scandal broke. This was the Reagan administration's secret effort to sell weapons to Iran in exchange for Iran using its influence with Hezbollah to free eight US hostages it held in Lebanon. The profits funded the Contras, as did Saudi Arabia and others. This went against the administration's own embargo on arms, restrictions against negotiating with terrorists, a January 1984 designation of Iran as a terrorist-sponsor state because of its connections with the October 1983 bombing of the US Marines barracks in Lebanon, and December 1982's Boland Amendment forbidding use of Department of Defense and CIA funds for anti-Sandinista efforts. The operation occurred over the objections of Weinberger and Shultz, and could have cost Reagan his presidency or at least resulted in his impeachment, but no order from him was found. Some blamed the debacle on Reagan's sloppy control over subordinates.[59]

The scandal led to Congress ending the arms flow to the Contras, which Reagan believed meant lost leverage over Ortega. Costa Rica's president, Oscar Arias Sánchez, arranged a ceasefire in 1988 that led to 1990 elections Ortega lost. Soviet and US aid fueled Nicaragua's civil war, killing perhaps 30,000 and producing 100,000 refugees. The administration saved El Salvador from Communism, but its people suffered at the hands of the left and right. Perhaps 70,000 died.[60]

The push for democracy intensified, particularly in Latin America, as the administration lengthened, and the pressures of the Cold War began falling away. Strategy shifted from defending Cold War allies with dictatorial regimes such as Chile and Paraguay, to using diplomatic levers to drive them toward democracy or make it clear to governments about to backslide (such as Peru) the costs of authoritarianism would be high. "I have a vision of a democratic Western Hemisphere," Reagan said in 1987. The administration's efforts directly affected democratic transitions in Argentina, Bolivia, Chile, Guatemala, Haiti, Honduras, and Paraguay.[61]

THE MIDDLE EAST

The administration sought to prevent Soviet dominance of the Middle East and South Asia while maintaining access to oil for the US and its allies. Washington supported Israel, pushed the Arab–Israeli peace process, aided local economic and defense improvements, and intended to defend these areas as far forward as possible. US leaders, particularly Weinberger, didn't want Moscow gaining a foothold in the Persian Gulf. Its presence endangered the West's access to the region's oil, without which it couldn't survive. Cooperation with NATO allies, Japan, various Arab states, Pakistan, and India was considered pivotal.[62]

THE PERSIAN GULF

Reagan said in October 1981 that the US wouldn't tolerate "Saudi Arabia threatened to the point that the flow of oil could be shut down." This occurred during the 1980–88 Iran–Iraq War, which began in September 1980 when Saddam Hussein's Iraq invaded Ayatollah Khomeini's Iran. The conflict quickly spilled into the Persian Gulf as both states depended upon oil revenue. Iraq adjusted by shipping oil overland via pipelines and importing goods through United Arab Emirates (UAE) ports. The Iranians attacked ships in the Gulf going to the UAE, Kuwait, and Gulf Cooperation Council (GCC) members supporting Saddam. June 1, 1984's UN Resolution 552 condemned the Iranian attacks and insisted upon non-interference with non-combatant shipping. Iran replied by deeming much of the Gulf "free-fire zones" and stepping up attacks.[63]

Iran was now a regional threat, and by 1982 Washington was providing satellite imagery on Iran to Iraq and allowing Kuwait and Jordan to send Baghdad US weapons. This support increased as the war dragged on, and high-level US officials like Middle East envoy Donald Rumsfeld met frequently with Saddam. The US restored diplomatic relations with Iraq in 1984, launched Operation STAUNCH to prevent arms sales to Iran in 1983, and tightened Iran sanctions in 1984.[64]

The US aimed to keep open the Straits of Hormuz because of the economic and psychological effects if the oil stopped flowing. Reagan ordered that "US military forces will attempt to deter and, if that fails, to defeat any hostile efforts to close the strait to international shipping." In January 1983, Washington upgraded Carter's Rapid Deployment Force by making it Central Command. Weapons sales to Riyadh followed, partially to convince it to drop oil prices and injure Tehran and Moscow. It did so in August 1985.[65]

Iran's attacks produced Kuwaiti inquiries in Washington and Moscow in September 1986 about protecting its tankers. Washington saw Iran's action as part of its effort to dominate the Gulf and offered to reflag Kuwaiti tankers on March 17, 1987. The administration justified the reflagging and escort effort to Congress as a means of preventing Soviet regional encroachment and protecting commercial freedom, especially in oil, and cited the Carter Doctrine. Operation EARNEST WILL launched on July 22, 1987. The Iranians responded by laying mines and attacking neutral vessels. What followed were tit-for-tat mine and missile strikes as the US retaliated for Iranian actions. This culminated in April 1988's Operation PRAYING MANTIS. The US sank several Iranian ships and destroyed two oil platforms, and then sank an Iranian frigate after being fired upon. The Iranians refused to alter their behavior until after the accidental downing of an Iranian airliner in July 1988 by the USS *Vincennes*. The Iranians, meanwhile, had suffered defeats at Iraq's hand and agreed in late July to negotiate an end to the Iran–Iraq War.[66]

Political scientist John Mearsheimer insists the administration's actions in the Gulf demonstrate successful execution of an "offshore balancing" strategy because its forces remained "offshore," relied on others to carry the security burden, didn't rely on permanent bases, intervened when necessary, and then departed. First, this analysis arises from bad theory: it takes tactical basing and deployments and makes them requirements for a strategy. Second, this contention doesn't match the historical record. The administration made no effort to "balance" Iraq and Iran. It aided the Iraqis because they were fighting Iran. Mearsheimer also mistakenly brands the Carter-created Rapid Reaction Force as being directed at a regional power becoming a threat. It was created to counter any Soviet move. The US also never left. The Reagan administration used military presence in an effort to get what it wanted. When this failed, it used force.[67] Reagan fought an undeclared war for limited political aims against Iran.

LEBANON, 1982–83

Perhaps the administration's biggest blunder occurred in Lebanon. The chaos from the civil war erupting here in 1975 provided a vacuum filled by Hezbollah, a militant Lebanese Shia organization. The Israelis responded in spring 1982 by invading, eventually pushing to Beirut. A Reagan representative negotiated a ceasefire and the commitment of a multinational US, French, and Italian force to help resolve the nation's civil war and oversee the departure of Palestine Liberation Organization (PLO) leaders. This took two weeks, and the troops left in early September 1982. Weinberger opposed involvement and, when it occurred, urged quick departure from the fractious nation where the US had no firm military associate.[68]

In revenge for the assassination of the Phalangist president Bashir Gemayel, his supporters massacred between 700 and 2,000 Palestinians in refugee camps. The killings upset the administration and Multinational Force II followed. American Marines arrived at the end of September 1982, less than a month after the earlier departure. British, French, and Italian forces joined them. Weinberger was among those opposing this intervention as well. The administration supported reestablishment of Lebanon's government and removal of foreign troops, but US military forces had an unclear mission and peacetime rules of engagement. It was thought their deployment would be about sixty days, but this became extended as the US tried to negotiate peace between Israel, Lebanon, and other warring parties. A truck bomb detonated at the US embassy on April 18, 1983, killed sixty-three people, including seventeen Americans. The battleship *New Jersey* was dispatched to strengthen the military presence and support an expanded protection mission that changed nothing. It did enable September 26's "ceasefire and reconciliation" negotiations.[69]

On September 10, 1983, the administration completed NSDD 103, Strategy for Lebanon. It said: "Our objectives in Lebanon remain: (a) to restore the sovereignty of the Government of Lebanon throughout its territory, (b) obtaining the complete withdrawal of all foreign forces, and (c) ensuring the security of Lebanon's borders, especially the northern border of Israel." US forces were to deter an attack on the Lebanese government and coordinate with the Multinational Force in defense and humanitarian relief and quicken their training of Lebanese government forces. Then, on October 23, 1983, Iranian-backed jihadists set off a truck bomb at the Americans' Beirut airport barracks, killing 241 people – most Marines. Defense and the JCS wanted the troops out. Reagan resisted. Further fragmentation of Lebanon's government and the arrival of an election year produced a February 1984 order for "redeployment" of US troops to ships off Lebanon's coast.[70]

One result of this debacle was the Weinberger Doctrine. Secretary of Defense Weinberger developed six tests for committing US troops: it must be a "vital" US interest; Washington must commit sufficient forces and intend to win; the US should have clear political aims and military objectives, know how its forces can accomplish them, and commit sufficient strength; the relationship between the political aim and forces dispatched must be constantly reassessed and altered as needed to win, and if the US wasn't going to win, it shouldn't go; the commitment must be supported by Congress and the American people; and sending combat troops "should be the last resort." To support his insistence upon clear political aims and understanding how to achieve them, Weinberger quoted Clausewitz: "no one starts a war – or rather, no one in his senses ought to do so – without first being clear in his mind what he intends to achieve by that war, and how he intends to conduct it."[71] This approach was not institutionalized.

General Colin Powell, Reagan's final national security advisor, expressed things similarly in the Powell Doctrine or the Powell Corollary. He was reluctant to use military force because of America's Vietnam War experience and his own. He wrote in 1995: "War should be the politics of last resort. And when we go to war, we should have a purpose that our people understand and support; we should mobilize the country's resources to fulfill that mission and then go in to win."[72]

LIBYA

Moammar Qaddafi, who seized control of Libya in a 1969 coup, was an erratic leader who alienated his neighbors. In August 1981, the US navy was dispatched to challenge Qaddafi's creative opinion of what represented a nation's waters. The contretemps saw the navy down two Libyan fighters. The bigger problem was Qaddafi's using terrorism. His being linked to a pair of December 1985 attacks produced January 1986's decision to try to sever Libya from Western money and trade.[73]

Libya's continuing attacks and support for terrorism led to US air patrols of Libya's coast in January 1986. The Americans destroyed a Libyan naval assault against a US carrier task force in April. Libya replied by blowing up a West Berlin disco filled with American soldiers. Reagan then launched what in the nineteenth century would have been termed a punitive war against Libya. It was also a short war for limited aims. The official instruction read: "The objective of our action is to inflict serious damage to the infrastructure that Qaddafi uses to provide direction and support for global terrorism." An April 15 attack on military and political targets followed.[74]

The administration noted restraint by Qaddafi afterward, but he relapsed. Washington wanted to prevent further assaults but also began exploring ways "to enhance the chances of a positive change of leadership" that didn't benefit Moscow. The administration blocked trade with Libya, eliminating as much as possible its oil exports to Western Europe, gathered international pressure, especially from Europe, and kept military forces nearby, just in case.[75]

CHINA AND ASIA

Reagan supported Taiwan and disliked Carter's approach to China and the terms of normalization with Beijing, which he tried unsuccessfully to alter. He sought friendly relations with Beijing but insisted on conducting affairs with Taipei according to the Taiwan Relations Act. But China strategy was confused, partly because Secretary of State Haig wanted China as the heart of Asia strategy and a weight against Moscow. Reagan was more realistic about the so-called China Card as a counter to Moscow. The difference contributed to Haig's resignation.[76]

On August 17, 1982, Washington and Beijing inked the Third Communique as a basis for US relations with Beijing and Taipei. Washington committed to reducing and eventually eliminating arms sales to Taiwan but linked this to China's promise to seek "peaceful resolution of the Taiwan question" and efforts by both to resolve differences. Washington gave Taiwan the Six Assurances promising, among other things, to abide by the Taiwan Relations Act and not force Taipei to accept a deal offered by Beijing.[77]

In September 1983, Reagan told his team to "continue to do things which will encourage Chinese efforts to moderate the Communist system and expand their opening to the West." The administration sought to keep China outside Moscow's orbit and "encourage China's efforts to modify and liberalize its totalitarian system, introduce incentives and market forces in its economy, and continue expanding its ties with the major industrialized democracies." It also sought to help China modernize on the assumption it would be a "force for peace, both in Asia and in the world, if the two objectives above are realized."[78]

Shultz believed the core of America's Asian strategy should be Japan. He wisely pointed out that China's *rapprochement* with America was for its own self-interest and potentially transitory. Japan, though, was more important economically and was a democracy. Shultz supported engaging China but possessed few illusions. To him, engagement should rest on democratic values and commitment to alliance partners. This was the best way of pushing China in a more modern, open direction. In 1987, Shultz privately urged Beijing to move on democratization and human rights. In 1988, Deng Xiaoping told Shultz China would make slow political reforms. Shultz remarked in 2014: "Of course, that has not happened."[79]

Reagan implemented an engagement strategy that assumed economic integration would induce political change. This often fails because leaders forget the political aims and ideology of the regime engaged and assume economic issues trump political ones. Engagement is a useful strategy with a non-democracy – linked with reform and a push toward democracy. But engaging an authoritarian state can mean supporting development of a rival that can become a threat to your interests or those of allies and partners. Totalitarian and authoritarian states with strong ideological bases are particularly resistant to outside actions.

Elsewhere in Asia, the administration wanted Japan to do more for its own defense and was fortunate Tokyo supported greater defense coordination. The administration quietly supported India's emergence as a regional power by 1982; this became part of strategy by 1984. The Soviet presence in Afghanistan and the shah's overthrow in Iran increased the importance of India and Pakistan. Better relations with both, accompanied by improved Sino-Indian relations, was considered a path for weakening Soviet regional influence and control in Afghanistan. The administration wanted to prevent any future India–Pakistan war because this could produce opportunities for Moscow, but mistakenly believed aiding Pakistan gave it "a sense of security and an incentive to forgo a nuclear weapons program."[80] US officials consistently overestimate the effects of US aid and support.

Like other administrations, Reagan's supported some authoritarian, anti-Communist rulers in Asia. Philippines' strongman Ferdinand Marcos faced deep opposition to his corrupt rule. The administration disliked him but feared a Communist takeover if he fell, and Reagan didn't want to abandon an ally as Carter had the shah. But Marcos' rigging of the 1986 presidential election provoked massive protests and proved the catalyst for Reagan shifting US support to his opponent, Cory Aquino. Marcos went into exile on an American helicopter. The next year, Washington began supporting democratization forces in South Korea, a nation racked by protests against the regime. Seoul was told it risked losing US support if it didn't permit free elections. Held on June 26, 1987, they marked the birth of South Korean democracy. Taiwan also soon moved into the democratic fold.[81] Reagan helped create a more democratic Asia.

AFRICA

In September 1985, the administration made it clear that Pretoria's relationship with Washington depended upon ending apartheid and moving toward democracy. This was also seen as defusing a potentially revolutionary situation and removing an opening for Moscow. As did others, the US applied sanctions and diplomatic pressure. Washington also wanted Soviet and Cuban influence removed from southern Africa. In Angola, it sought to end the war via reconciliation among the warring groups and tried to end the fighting in Namibia. The US and South Africa supplied UNITA rebels in Angola, though Pretoria did more. Washington secured withdrawal of Cuban forces from Angola and Namibia's independence.[82]

PART II: FROM GREAT POWER TO SUPERPOWER

1985: CHANGE AND REASSESSMENT

One of Reagan's great strokes of luck was Mikhail Gorbachev's March 1985 appointment as general secretary of the Soviet Communist Party. Reagan had softened his rhetoric by the end of 1983 and added efforts to conciliate and reassure the Soviets. This more moderate approach and tone left the administration in a position to benefit from Gorbachev's ascension. Gorbachev proved a different Soviet leader but wanted space for reform. Reagan was willing to give him this but wanted Kremlin actions to change.[83]

The administration realized that even though it had accomplished much, it needed to "further develop" its "strategy of peace for the future." In September 1986, a new Basic National Security Strategy – NSDD 238 – replaced NSDD 32. This, and its related papers, formed the new foundation for American grand strategy. NSDD 238 suffers from the standard mixing of political aims and the elements of strategy used to obtain them. It declares that: "The primary objective of US foreign and security policy is to protect the integrity of our democratic institutions and promote a peaceful global environment in which they can thrive." This isn't as clear as one would like, but the first half can be read as security for the United States. The second half mixes the end – "a peaceful global environment" – with the way of achieving it – by promoting peace. It identified the Soviets and their actions as the primary threat but didn't see war with Moscow on the immediate horizon. It considered Gorbachev's arrival and worried his "more vigorous and dynamic" nature might produce "creative and energized" actions "inimical to US interests."[84]

NSDD 238 is rare in that it has a section titled "grand strategy." It reads: "This grand strategy requires the development and integration of a set of strategies to achieve our national objectives, including political, diplomatic, military, informational, economic, intelligence, and arms control components." Additionally: "The grand strategy of the United States is to avoid nuclear war while preventing a single hostile power or coalition of powers from dominating the Eurasian land-mass or other strategic regions from which threats to US interests might arise."[85]

A section titled "Global Objectives" largely addresses ways and expands on the administration's grand strategy elements. Deterring a Soviet military attack against the US and its allies remains at the core. The other elements are familiar: strengthening and growing alliances, allies, and partners; promoting democracy, using "diplomatic, political, economic, and information efforts"; and blocking Soviet moves, weakening Moscow's relations with its allies, and forcing it to bear its economic ineptitude while denying it Western technology. The US would also continue "To contain and reverse the expansion of

Soviet control and military presence throughout the world, and to increase the costs to the Soviet Union and other countries that support proxy, terrorist, and subversive forces." Additionally, the US would provide economic and military aid, "assist democratic and nationalist movements where possible in the struggle against totalitarian regimes," and recruit help. The US would use diplomacy and pursue arms reductions to lessen the nuclear danger while building its own defenses, including those against nuclear weapons. Economically, among other things, the US would ensure access to sea routes and trade, while pushing to remove trade and financial barriers to the free market, and isolate radical regimes hostile to US interests. Some regional concerns would be met by supporting partners and countering the Soviets and their proxies. In the Middle East, though, Washington "remains committed to securing Western access to oil resources and maintaining freedom of commerce in the Persian Gulf. We will maintain a strong naval presence in the region, and seek to develop a land presence to the extent regional sensitivities and local political constraints will permit."[86]

NSDD 238 distinguished between US strategy in war and peace. In wartime: "If deterrence fails, we must have the capability to counter aggression, to control escalation, and to prevail." It also shows the influence of the Weinberger Doctrine:

> In a conflict not involving the Soviet Union, the United States will rely primarily on indigenous forces to protect their [sic] own interests. Commitment of US combat forces will be made only when other means are not considered viable. Such commitment is appropriate only if political objectives are established, our political will is clear, and appropriate military capabilities are available. If US combat forces are committed, the United States will seek to limit the scope of the conflict, avoid involvement of the Soviet Union, and ensure that US objectives are met as quickly as possible.[87]

Moreover:

> In global war [redacted] our overall objectives are to limit damage to the United States and its allies, control the scope and intensity of the conflict, and terminate hostilities on terms favorable to the United States and its allies. This requires defeating the geopolitical objectives of our enemies, preserving the territorial integrity and political independence of our allies, and emerging from the conflict with a global political orientation favorable to the United States and in which the long term threat from the Soviet Union is reduced and the prospects for lasting peace enhanced. In implementing these objectives [this strategy], we will seek to prosecute the war as far forward and as close as possible to the sources of greatest threat.[88]

The regional objectives are redacted.[89]

Problems in executing the war in Grenada combined with the Beirut tragedy to produce Congressional reform: the 1986 Goldwater–Nichols Defense Reorganization Act. It made the JCS chair the president's chief military advisor with the right – through the defense secretary – of presenting the president his or her views while removing the requirement to present dissenting service-chief opinions. Goldwater–Nichols introduced "jointness" into the military lexicon by giving more authority to the heads of US commands over the service branches in their areas. Training and education for joint – meaning cooperative – operations among the services became required.[90]

Goldwater–Nichols required the president to submit to Congress a National Security Strategy (NSS) alongside the annual defense budget. It was to discuss "interests, goals, and objectives … vital to the national security of the United States" and describe how the various elements of national power would be used to deter aggression and secure the nation, both in the short and long term, examine the nation's capability in doing this, and provide Congress the information it needed on national security issues. The president was essentially tasked with delivering a grand strategy.[91]

The first National Security Strategy (1987), like the Basic National Security Strategy, suffers from mixing of the political aims being sought and the strategies for achieving them. It begins with a statement of US interests and moves to national objectives. The two sections are best considered together because they mix interests, aims, and elements of strategy. Expanding democracy and political and economic freedoms are declared in America's interests. The first "interest" listed was really a political aim: "The survival of the United States as a free and independent nation, with its fundamental values and institutions intact." The clearly expressed political aims include: "To maintain the security of our nation and our allies," and "To defend and advance the cause of democracy, freedom, and human rights throughout the world." The elements of grand strategy – conveyed throughout – are repeated from previous strategy documents.[92]

The administration quickly followed with its 1988 *NSS* issued as part of an effort to overcome Congressional resistance to funding the administration's grand strategy. It differs little from its predecessor barring including items from NSDD 238. It noted the danger to US interests of hostile domination of Eurasia; containment, in various forms, was the answer to this. It included:

two additional emphases worth noting. The first is realism. We have sought to deal with the world as it is, not as we might wish it to be. A strategy without illusions, based on observable facts.... At the same time, we have emphasized our willingness ... to engage our adversaries ... in negotiations aimed at finding areas of common interest.[93]

THE FINAL SOVIET OFFENSIVE

Gorbachev proved a remarkable change from his sclerotic predecessors. He realized Moscow faced numerous problems – the war in Afghanistan, a declining international position, and severe economic strains – and feared America verged on creating SDI. And Reagan's grand strategy had worsened a weakening Soviet position. Gorbachev knew Moscow needed reforms, but he and other Soviet leaders were initially unwilling to alter Soviet actions, particularly abroad. Gorbachev believed he could turn around their position and launched a campaign to do so. He intensified military and diplomatic efforts in Afghanistan and pressured Pakistan. Moscow's war costs rose 30 percent and CIA-backed Mujahideen expanded attacks into the Soviet Union. Gorbachev increased economic aid to Nicaragua 40 percent, funneled weapons through Cuba, supported El Salvador's FMLN, and insisted Moscow hold its gains in Africa.[94]

Gorbachev's actions validated Reagan's decision to continue applying pressure, which he did while extending the negotiations olive branch. Reagan suggested a summit right after Gorbachev came to power. Gorbachev and Reagan held five summits from 1985 to 1988. Critical to Reagan was establishing trust. On negotiations he said: "You shouldn't back your adversary into a corner, embarrass him, or humiliate him; and sometimes the easiest way to get some things done is for the top people to do them alone and in private." Reagan believed personal diplomacy with a Soviet leader could pay dividends. This proved correct when Reagan and Gorbachev first met in Geneva in November 1985. They disagreed on many things but quickly developed a rapport.[95]

Washington implemented a form of linkage in its diplomacy by raising various issues. For example, the administration wanted human rights changes before discussing increased trade. Reagan realized he could wait until the Soviets started giving Washington what it wanted. The US continued increasing the strain to give negotiations a better chance, which included aid to Angola and more pressure in Afghanistan. Reagan was careful to not push the Soviets into a corner or make threats. But he continued the information offensive with his June 1987 Berlin speech, famously saying: "Mr. Gorbachev, tear down this wall!"[96]

PART II: FROM GREAT POWER TO SUPERPOWER

The Reykjavik Summit in October 1986 proved pivotal. Gorbachev stunned the Americans by suggesting a 50 percent reduction in nuclear weapons; further talks raised the offer to eliminating all nuclear weapons, though agreement foundered on Gorbachev's caveat of Washington dropping SDI. The summit's result was both leaders realizing they could do business. By 1987, Gorbachev concluded Moscow had no choice but to reach an understanding. The December 1987 Intermediate Nuclear Forces (INF) treaty eliminated an entire class of Soviet and American IRBMs. Agreements for deep cuts in strategic bombers, SLBMs, and ICBMs followed.[97]

The value of having Gorbachev in power proved immense. By the end of 1987, the Soviet contraction began. Moscow approached Washington for help ending the wars in Angola and Namibia. The Soviets stopped sending arms to Nicaragua and reduced support for the FMLN after telling both to make peace. Soviet troops began withdrawing from Afghanistan in May 1988. But Washington continued aiding the Mujahideen fighting Afghanistan's Communist regime. In December 1988, Gorbachev announced he was unilaterally withdrawing 500,000 soldiers from the Eastern Bloc. When the Communist regimes in Eastern Europe began to collapse, Gorbachev didn't defend them. Reagan publicly praised Gorbachev's reform efforts.[98]

───◆───

THE GEORGE H. W. BUSH ADMINISTRATION, 1989–91: PART I

The George Herbert Walker Bush administration was in many ways a continuation of Reagan's. Bush, Reagan's vice president, brought to the presidency enormous government experience, beginning with his service as a decorated navy pilot in the Second World War. He served in Congress, as UN ambassador, Washington's representative to Beijing, and CIA director. But Bush differed from Reagan and said of himself that he lacked "the vision thing." Too much has been made of this. He and the talented and experienced legion that served him proved exceedingly capable of securing benefits for America and the rest of the free world. And they did so at a time – in the words of Secretary of State James Baker – "when long-held beliefs about grand strategy were being turned upside down."[99]

THE ASSESSMENT

The Bush 41 administration was initially concerned primarily with ending the Cold War. Bush ordered completion by March 15, 1989 of an NSC review of the relationship with Moscow, the formulation of long-term aims to the century's end, and reviews of US relations with Eastern and Western European states, the latter to address the future of NATO. Secretary of State Baker and National Security Advisor Brent Scowcroft worked well together and were Bush's most important advisors. Bush and his administration thought America's global responsibilities continued even though the Cold War had ended. Bush believed "America had a distinctive moral calling to advance human freedom and well-being and that this responsibility required a self-confident, assertive foreign policy." Successful planks of post–Second World War grand strategy would be kept, such as maintaining Washington's alliances, keeping "favorable geopolitical balances in key regions," and continuing to lead in international organizations while working "to shape a global environment ideologically and economically congenial to the United States."[100]

THE POLITICAL AIMS AND THE GRAND STRATEGY

Bush's speeches betray the standard definitional weakness regarding the aims sought and the means and methods of achieving them, but these come through. In May 1989, Bush said he wanted: "a growing community of democracies anchoring international peace and stability, and a dynamic free-market system generating prosperity and progress on a global scale." He added: "our goals must also include security and stability ... and an end to regional conflicts." And also said: "I see a Western Hemisphere of democratic, prosperous nations."[101]

Achieving these aims in an international environment undergoing its greatest upheaval since 1945 required a new approach, and the administration's review influenced this. Bush noted in May 1989 that "The grand strategy of the West during the postwar period has been based on the concept of containment," but the US now has the "opportunity to move beyond containment." Though he depicted "containment" as an aim instead of a strategy (a common tick), he insisted the way to achieve America's political purposes was "the integration of the Soviet Union into the community of nations." Bush noted the difficulty, urged caution, and detailed the necessity of remaining strong militarily "to deter war," "defend ourselves and our allies," "convince the Soviet Union that there can be no reward in pursuing expansionism," and show Moscow "that reward lies in the pursuit of peace."[102] Some works inaccurately argue US military strength was for securing "hegemony" without making clear whether "hegemony" was an aim or a strategy, but Bush clearly stated strength was for deterrence.

To achieve peace, security, and democracy, the Western nations "must encourage the evolution of the Soviet Union toward an open society."

Securing America's aims required the Soviets to continue reducing their forces in Europe, allow self-determination in Central and Eastern Europe, work to resolve disputes with the West, "achieve a lasting political pluralism and respect for human rights," and unite with the West to address global issues. Successful strategic arms reduction talks, it was hoped, would lessen the chances of a nuclear exchange. The administration's interests, aims, and strategy were articulated in more developed form in the March 1990 *National Security Strategy*, though this mixes interests, aims, and strategy planks.[103]

THE COLLAPSE OF THE COMMUNIST BLOC, 1989

While the administration reassessed and crafted a new grand strategy, events overtook them. Gorbachev's willingness to stand aside proved critical. In summer 1989, Hungary's premier ordered its border fence with Austria removed. East Germany protested to Moscow. Moscow said it could do nothing. Economic problems led Polish leaders to offer elections to a new bicameral legislature in June 1989. Solidarity swept the vote. Moscow said it was Warsaw's concern. East Germans began fleeing via Hungary. Gorbachev came to the German Democratic Republic to celebrate its fortieth anniversary and was met by cheering crowds asking for help. In October, antigovernment protests culminated in the leaders resigning. The next month, a botched government press interview meant to open travel to the West for East Germans came across as freedom to exit. Crowds were soon dancing on the Berlin Wall.[104]

The floodgates of freedom opened. On November 10, Bulgaria's Communist leader resigned. The Bulgarian Communist Party began negotiating with the opposition and promised free elections. On November 17, protests broke out in Prague. By the end of the year, playwright and democracy advocate Vaclav Havel was president. On December 17, 1989, Romania's dictator, Nicolae Ceausescu, ordered his security forces to fire on demonstrators in Timisoara, killing ninety-seven. Ceausescu called for a rally of supporters in Bucharest for December 17; he got the opposite. He fled. He and his wife were captured, tried, and executed by a firing squad so eager to shoot them the guards barely had time to get out of the way.[105]

DIPLOMATIC STRATEGY

The 1990 *NSS* recognized the staggering historical changes connected with the Cold War's end and Moscow's retrenchment. It reiterated the necessity of moving beyond containment "to seek the integration of the Soviet Union into the international system as a constructive partner" while envisioning a "Europe whole and free."[106] It reveals an administration seeking democracy abroad and using its elements of national power to achieve this. Diplomacy was the primary tool.

THE SOVIET UNION AND THE END OF THE COLD WAR

Bush and his key advisors initially didn't trust Gorbachev and worried he sought the Soviet Union's revival to better compete with the West. Gorbachev allowing the end of Communist regimes in Poland and Hungary in summer of 1989 shocked them. The fall of the East German government and the Berlin Wall shortly followed. China's June 4, 1989 Tiananmen Square massacre of protesters fed Bush's cautiousness. He wanted no violence and made a point of not trying to drive the changing situation too fast or "poke a stick in the eye of Mr. Gorbachev." Encouraged by the changes, the administration continued promoting democratic and free-market values in the Soviet Union and began trying to integrate it with the rest of the world. But the Soviets would have to earn this by demilitarizing their foreign relations, ending efforts to overthrow other governments, and permitting Central and Eastern European self-determination. But the US could only do this from a position of strength. It had to maintain sufficient military power to provide a deterrence. The administration, meanwhile, pursued arms control agreements with Moscow, searched for ways to cooperate on resolving international problems, and broadened trade in non-strategic items.[107]

Bush moved prudently and began trying to construct a Europe including former Warsaw Pact nations. The dramatic changes produced new political aims, including reunification of Germany within NATO. The administration was not responsible for reunification but helped shepherd it through deft diplomacy in which it didn't hesitate to exert leverage (usually gently) over Washington's allies and a weakening Soviet Union. Bush saw here a way to consolidate the West's Cold War victory. Scowcroft agreed, seeing German reunification under the West as a move that would "rip the heart out of the Soviet security system." It would also help spread democracy and democratic values to the Eastern Bloc. But it had to be a Germany in NATO and not neutralized – that would be a Western defeat. NATO tied the US to Europe, and Bush considered a continuing US troop presence in Germany critical to European stability and security.[108]

Soviet leaders realized East Germans wanted reunification and knew opposing it would discredit Moscow's claims to now support democracy and self-determination. But they weren't keen on a united Germany – Russia's traditional enemy – in NATO. Extensive negotiations ensued. The Bush administration balanced the complex factors, including, most importantly, gaining Soviet acquiescence, as Moscow still had 400,000 troops in East Germany. The West made a number of concessions, such as promising to not move NATO forces eastward (which brought future controversy), limiting the size of the German army, and telling Gorbachev NATO wouldn't expand. Kohl giving Moscow 12 billion marks in loans and subsidies helped.[109]

In the Western Hemisphere and Latin America, Reagan's push for democracy continued. The 1990 *NSS* insisted upon the possibility of the Western Hemisphere becoming "history's first entirely democratic hemisphere." Bush sought democracy in Nicaragua through diplomacy, pushing to remove Soviet backing while continuing to support resistance and internal opposition. Better relations with Cuba, though, hinged upon liberalization that wasn't forthcoming. The US also pressed for democracy in Haiti.[110]

ECONOMIC STRATEGY

During his campaign, Bush said: "Read my lips: No new taxes," but didn't keep the promise. His modest tax increases added $500 billion in annual revenue, but he did nothing to staunch growing Federal spending, much of it driven by entitlements such as Social Security. US deficits and debt continued to climb. Bush supported free trade and negotiated the North American Free Trade Act (NAFTA) in 1992, which eliminated many tariff barriers between the US, Mexico, and Canada, but didn't win Congressional approval before leaving office.[111]

MILITARY STRATEGY

Military strategy intertwined diplomatic strategy. Deterrence, forward defense, alliances, and the ability to project power abroad remained key. Defense spending fell from $299 to $282 billion. Bush hoped for arms reductions and renegotiated the Strategic Arms Reduction Treaty (START) with Moscow, committing both nations to reducing their nuclear warheads from 13,000 in 1990 to 7,000 in 1995. Talks with Gorbachev produced removal of almost all US overseas nuclear weapons.[112]

Even before the Soviet Union fell, the administration saw in the collapse of Soviet power an opening for consolidating the US position in

Europe and planned assuming Moscow remained Europe's greatest military power. NATO remained a pillar of American strategy, but by March 1990 Washington saw here a tool for organizing Eastern Europe. NATO's form became an increasingly important issue. The administration gave Moscow repeated informal assurances in 1990 that NATO wouldn't expand and "indicated that Europe's post–Cold War order would be acceptable to both Washington and Moscow" and "include the Soviet Union." By late 1990, the administration decided against immediate NATO expansion, but was careful to not relay the impression that NATO would always remain a closed shop.[113]

THE PANAMA WAR, 1989–90

General Manuel Noriega had been Panama's *de facto* ruler since 1983. He had been useful to the US during the Cold War because of his anti-Communism and received substantial economic and military assistance, some of which flowed to the Contras. He had a deep relationship with the CIA and other intelligence agencies, including Cuba's. But his corruption, brutality, and drug-trafficking won him no support abroad, and a US court indicted him for drug-trafficking in February 1988. In May 1989, he illegally invalidated Panama's presidential election. When it became clear Noriega wouldn't allow the elected government to sit, Washington's political aim became removing him and installing the democratic victors. To force out Noriega, the administration withheld diplomatic recognition, called on other states to do the same, and applied economic pressure by freezing Panamanian government assets and suspending Canal payments.[114]

Bush also tried to negotiate a resolution. But Noriega declared Panama was at war with the US and backed attacks on US service members in Panama City that left one dead. On December 20, 1989, 27,000 US troops, half from the Canal Zone, invaded Panama in Operation JUST CAUSE. The US applied overwhelming force, defeating Noriega's forces in eight days. In all, 23 Americans were killed and another 394 wounded. Bush withdrew US forces as quickly as possible, leaving the May election victors in power.[115]

ASIA AND CHINA

The Bush administration sought stability in South Asia "as a bulwark against Soviet influence and expansion." This was seen as particularly important in the relationship between Pakistan and India. Pakistan received pride of place because the US needed it to achieve its political aims in Afghanistan. Like its predecessor, the Bush administration mistakenly believed a security relationship with Pakistan would help dissuade it from developing nuclear weapons.[116]

In Afghanistan, in 1989 the US achieved its aim of forcing out the Soviets and now sought a government in Kabul representing the nation's people. The US tried to work with Pakistan to secure a peaceful transition of power, hoping to prevent a civil war or emergence of a pro-Iranian, pro-Soviet, or "messianic-Islamic" government. Mohammed Najibullah's Communist regime faced a civil war against a loose coalition of jihadist groups, but now without Red Army support. On September 13, 1991, the Bush administration and Moscow signed an agreement in which both would stop arming Afghanistan's factions by January 1, 1992.[117]

The civil war continued, but neither the US nor Russia cared. Najibullah's government was overthrown on April 15, 1992 by what became known in the West as the Northern Alliance. Opposing them was a coalition dominated by Afghanistan's majority Pashtun and supported by Pakistan. In February 1993, State Department official Peter Tomsen warned the US was in danger of throwing away its contacts and gains in Afghanistan and believed minimal investment "could significantly contribute to the favorable moderate outcome."[118] The US had no plan for what to do after succeeding.

The most important event in China–US relations was Beijing's massacre of pro-democracy supporters in Tiananmen Square on June 4, 1989. The Communists killed perhaps 3,000 people, wounded 10,000, and arrested scores. The Bush administration did little beyond imposing sanctions and suspending arms sales to Beijing. The administration worried about regional effects if China destabilized, and Bush believed commercial engagement would pull China toward democracy. He dispatched Baker on a secret mission to Beijing to make it clear that relations with Washington were not in danger. Some critics describe Bush's handling of China as "appeasement."[119]

The end of the Cold War, though, altered China's strategic importance to Washington as it was no longer needed as a counterweight to Moscow. Simultaneously, China's Communist leaders looked fearfully at the Soviet Union's demise and became increasingly resistant to any US intervention in China's internal affairs. The 1990 *NSS* "strongly deplored the repression in China" but insisted maintaining ties was "crucial to China's prospects for regaining the path of economic reform and political liberalization."[120] The strategy of engagement based upon the unsubstantiated idea that this would ensure China's transition to democracy continued – unexamined.

THE MIDDLE EAST

The Persian Gulf remained important because of the oil flow and key regional states, the defense of which Washington supported. Both the Reagan and Bush administrations saw Saddam as the only obstacle to Iranian seizure of the Middle East, and both hoped to convince him to moderate his behavior. Bush sought normalization of relations with Iraq and adopted a diplomatic strategy of "constructive engagement," something driven by Iraq's emergence as the region's most powerful state after 1988. Bush hoped to make Iraq a productive member of the world community, and used economic and political inducements to try to alter Saddam's behavior, but it was clear by April 1990 that this had failed, and the administration suspended a $1 billion agricultural credit program. February 1989 saw Washington's first serious warning that Saddam was trying to develop nuclear weapons. America's line toughed between February and August 1990 but remained conciliatory. Bush was open to normalizing relations with Iran, but only after Tehran released the American hostages it held, and ended terrorist activities and subversion against its neighbors.[121]

THE COLLAPSE OF THE SOVIET UNION

The Bush administration had worried about a Soviet revival, but soon found itself fearing its collapse. The administration supported Gorbachev and Moscow to slow the fall, but Soviet subjects saw no improvement in their lives. Command economy inefficiencies, single-minded dedication to defense spending, and collapse of the global oil price powered the Soviet demise. Gorbachev hadn't considered a replacement and hoped economic reform would dampen secession. But the subject peoples pushed for the same freedoms now enjoyed by Eastern Europe. In January 1991, Soviet troops in Lithuania fired on demonstrators. On February 19, Lithuania voted for independence. Latvia and Estonia followed.[122]

In June 1991, Boris Yeltsin was elected president of the Soviet State of Russia. He was determined to abolish the Communist Party, bring down the Soviet Union, and make Russia an independent, democratic, capitalist state. Others disagreed. On August 18, Gorbachev was placed under arrest by a group attempting a coup. Yeltsin publicly resisted the rebellion by standing on a tank outside the Russian Politburo. Yeltsin abolished the Communist Party, confiscated its property, and recognized the independence of the Baltic States. Armenia, Kazakhstan, and Ukraine then declared independence. On December 25, 1991, Gorbachev signed the decree abolishing the Soviet Union. The USSR breathed its last on December 26, 1991, when its deputies voted it out of existence. Gorbachev said: "An end has been put to the 'Cold War,' the arms race, and the insane militarization of our country, which crippled our economy, distorted our thinking and undermined our morals. The threat of a world war is no more."[123]

President Bush said in a January 1991 speech: "The end of the Cold War has been a victory for all humanity. A year and a half ago ... I said that our goal was a Europe whole and free. Tonight, Germany is united. Europe has become whole and free, and America's leadership was instrumental in making it possible."[124] But no one had a plan for what came after.

CONCLUSION

One cannot stress too much the historical significance of the Cold War ending on American terms. The world was profoundly different afterward, and removal of the constant threat of a thermonuclear exchange between two heavily armed superpowers was one of the greatest benefits. There is some nostalgia for the supposed stability of the Cold War world and the presumed bipolar geopolitical environment. The rivalry between Washington and Moscow provided two ideological poles around which states could revolve, but there was never anything so simple as bipolarity. States changed sides (Yugoslavia, for example) and pursued their own aims independent of the superpowers, which proved tinder for potentially greater explosions because of the Cold War. Cuba, Vietnam, the Arab–Israeli Wars, and the 1956 Suez Crisis provide examples.[125] China came to form its own pole. The non-aligned movement another. But every state pursued its own aims.

But why did the US emerge triumphant? Part of it was Soviet weakness: its failed statist system no longer had any appeal. Historian Hal Brands accurately observed that "Reagan's grand strategy did not cause this crisis of Soviet power, but it did allow the United States to exploit its geopolitical effects."[126] Reagan clearly established winning the Cold War and spreading democracy as purposes and used American power intensely in their pursuit, bringing decisive pressure to bear on an already shaky system. Reagan was also lucky to have Gorbachev as a partner in the creation of a more democratic world.

And that was what the Reagan–Bush grand strategy left behind. A great expansion in global democracies began after 1975. The number doubled between 1975 and 1990 and reached 120 by 1999, when roughly two-thirds of the world's nations were electoral democracies. The march of democracy Reagan and Bush encouraged – especially Reagan – helped bring freedom to millions. This continued after Bush. Between 1982 and 2002, thirty-two democracies emerged. When Bush left office, only two Western Hemisphere nations – Guyana and Cuba – suffered authoritarianism.[127]

PART III

THE POST–COLD WAR WORLD

16

THE GULF WAR, OR FIRST IRAQ WAR, 1990–1991

INTRODUCTION

In an August 2, 1990 speech, George H. W. Bush mentioned trimming US military forces by as much as 25 percent but stressed the need to retain enough strength to keep commitments and meet existing threats. Saddam Hussein's Iraq invaded Kuwait the same day. Saddam had particularly bad timing. The Cold War had ended. Both Washington and Moscow supported action against him, as did the UN.[1] And the US was at the end of a military build-up ongoing since 1980.

THE FIRST IRAQ WAR, 1990–91

Iraq had a history of border disputes with both Iran and Kuwait dating from Iraq's 1932 independence and mixed these with challenges to Kuwait's sovereignty. The 1980–88 Iran–Iraq War broke Iraq's economy. Saddam faced $80 billion in foreign debt and perhaps $230 billion in rebuilding costs. He needed a debt moratorium and $30 billion. In February 1990, he began making threats: "Let the Gulf regimes know that if they do not give this money to me, I will know how to get it." He pushed other states – particularly Kuwait and the UAE – to increase oil prices and keep their OPEC quotas, and branded quota violations acts of war. Kuwait refused to decrease production, forgive loans made during the war, provide more financial grants, or make a $10 billion "contribution" demanded in June 1990. In July 1990, Kuwait and the UAE bowed to Arab pressure to obey the quotas. Saddam didn't believe either would keep its word.[2]

On July 17, Saddam threatened Kuwait. Washington said it would defend its friends and interests in the region. Saddam took this as a threat. A meeting with America's ambassador to Baghdad, April Glaspie, followed. Saddam menaced the US with terrorist attacks. Glaspie tried conciliation but failed to make clear how serious America took the situation. Saddam assured Glaspie he wouldn't attack Kuwait, and she told Washington she believed his statements about desiring a peaceful settlement. US intelligence assessments initially decided the 100,000 Iraqi troops massed on Kuwait's border were for intimidation. Bush cautioned Iraq about using force against Kuwait. On July 30, the Defense Intelligence Agency concluded Saddam meant war. Saddam didn't believe the US would react. On July 27, despite the administration's objections, the Senate voted sanctions against Iraq. Saddam invaded on August 2, aiming to add Kuwait's wealth to Iraq's and enable the reconstruction he had promised his people. He would "liberate" Kuwait, make Iraq a leading power in the Arab world, and ensure his position and survival.[3]

THE ASSESSMENT

Bush immediately decided to oppose the invasion. He saw a threat to the new post–Cold War "New World Order" he was trying to create and said: "The acquisition of territory by force is unacceptable." Saddam had also committed an act of unprovoked aggression in an area where the US had vital interests as it imported almost half its oil from the Middle East. Countering Saddam's attack was deemed more important than Kuwait itself. Letting it pass would send the wrong message to dictators. Britain's prime minister, Margaret Thatcher, encouraged Bush to act, and both drew comparisons with Hitler's 1930s aggression and democratic appeasement.[4]

Bush saw in his actions the establishment of an international precedent for dealing with such matters via the United Nations. National Security Advisor Scowcroft described it thus: "Use the United Nations, don't go farther than the mandate of the United Nations, operate in a way that you earned the trust of the smaller countries." The administration also had a window for its approach. The Cold War's end meant the Soviet Union was no longer an automatic veto, while Beijing wanted to keep its head down because of the international outcry against its 1989 Tiananmen Square massacre of pro-democracy protesters.[5]

By August 3, more Iraqi troops were moving to the Saudi border. Bush worried they would invade and began trying to convince Riyadh to invite US help. He told JCS chair Powell to examine the options offered by Central Command (CENTCOM) commander General Norman Schwarzkopf. Riyadh feared an invasion because the 140,000 Iraqi troops on the border were more than enough to hold down Kuwait but was unsure it could depend upon America. The US demonstrated its seriousness by saying it intended to send 100–200,000 troops. The Saudis agreed; the force deployment orders went out on August 6.[6]

THE GULF WAR, OR FIRST IRAQ WAR, 1990–1991

Bush said,

> The stakes are high. Iraq is already a rich and powerful country that possesses the world's second largest reserves of oil and over a million men under arms. It's the fourth largest military in the world. Our country now imports nearly half the oil it consumes and could face a major threat to its economic independence. Much of the world is even more dependent upon imported oil and is even more vulnerable to Iraqi threats.

Moreover, Saddam now controlled over 20 percent of the world's oil supply, and with this came the military and economic power "to intimidate and coerce its neighbors – neighbors who control the lion's share of the world's remaining oil reserves. We cannot permit a resource so vital to be dominated by one so ruthless."[7]

POLITICAL AIMS AND GRAND STRATEGY: PEACETIME

Bush made clear he would accept nothing less than the restoration of Kuwait's sovereignty and would have been happy to secure this without a war. He delineated the administration's four political aims in an August 8, 1990 speech and documents that followed: "the immediate, complete, and unconditional withdrawal of all Iraqi forces from Kuwait"; "the restoration of Kuwait's legitimate government"; "a commitment to the security and stability of the Persian Gulf"; and "the protection of the lives of American citizens abroad." To achieve these aims, Secretary of State Baker said in September 1990: "Our strategy is to lead a global alliance ... to isolate Iraq politically, economically, and militarily."[8]

Diplomatically, the administration proved exceptionally successful at the UN. Bush had Thatcher's able cooperation. She remarked on August 5, 1990 that "Iraq's invasion of Kuwait defies every principle for which the United Nations stands. If we let it succeed, no small country can ever feel safe again. The law of the jungle would take over from the rule of law." On August 2, 1990, UN Resolution 660 condemned Iraq's invasion and demanded immediate withdrawal; it received no dissenting vote. On August 6, the UN passed Resolution 661, which embargoed all trade with Iraq and Kuwait except humanitarian and medical supplies. Security Council Resolution 665 passed on August 20, 1990, giving teeth to enforcement of a maritime embargo. Bush backed the UN resolutions while trying to resolve the situation peacefully and secured GCC and Arab League support. Bush froze Iraqi and Kuwaiti assets in the US and urged oil producers to pump more to counter economic effects. The success rate of sanctions didn't inspire confidence, and both Bush and Thatcher had little hope this would deliver the political aim.[9] How much the nation suffering sanctions desires membership in the international community helps determine whether they work.

Militarily, the US launched DESERT SHIELD on August 7. At the request of Kuwaiti and Saudi rulers, the administration sent forces to the Gulf "to deter and, if necessary, defend Saudi Arabia and other friendly states" and help enforce UN sanctions. Washington sought allies and tried to placate the Soviets, inviting them to join the coalition. Thirty-five nations eventually contributed troops. The largest contingents came from: America: 532,000; Saudi Arabia: 110,000; Great Britain: 42,000; UAE: 40,000; Egypt: 40,000; France: 20,000; Turkey: 120,000 on its border; and Syria: 50,000 on its border and another 2,000 in Saudi Arabia.[10]

Coalition burden-sharing included money. The administration sought foreign financial support to head off Congressional criticism Washington was bearing the costs. Nations such as Germany, Japan, Kuwait, Saudi Arabia, and South Korea provided $48 billion to help cover US costs of around $62 billion, and $6 billion in material and economic relief to nations hurt by the embargo. This was the first time since its War for Independence that America relied upon foreign financing for a war. The US got Saudi Arabia to increase oil production to help keep prices from rising and reduce chances of a US recession.[11]

Saddam refused to budge. On November 29, 1990, Bush secured passage of UN Resolution 678. This gave Iraq until January 15, 1991 to evacuate Kuwait. If it didn't, the member states were authorized to do everything necessary to bring this about. Bush now offered Saddam a final chance to negotiate. Saddam saw this as weakness, but it led to a January 9 Geneva meeting between Baker and Saddam's foreign minister, Tariq Aziz. Nothing came of this, but Baker delivered a letter from Bush making it clear that if Saddam used weapons of mass destruction (WMD) or destroyed Kuwait's oil fields or related infrastructure, Iraq would "pay a terrible price." Baker also told Aziz: "If there is any use of weapons like that, our objective won't be the liberation of Kuwait, but the elimination of the current Iraq [sic] regime and anyone responsible for using those weapons would be held accountable."[12]

Bush never considered a declaration of war. Congressional sanction for military action was considered most important politically. There was, of course, political opposition. Democratic Senator Sam Nunn's televised Senate Hearings convinced many in Iraq the US wouldn't attack. Bush believed the hearings were stacked against him, but the House of

Representatives voted 250 to 183 to approve military action, the Senate 52 to 47. Bush later said: "even had Congress not passed the resolutions I would have acted and ordered our troops into combat. I know it would have caused an outcry, but it was the right thing to do. I was comfortable in my own mind that I had the constitutional authority."[13] It is difficult to see how he was correct on constitutional grounds as Iraq hadn't attacked the United States.

THE POLITICAL AIM: WARTIME

The administration's political aims in the event of war were formalized in NSD 54 and resembled those in Bush's August 8, 1990 speech, but now the administration planned to achieve them using force. The aims were the "withdrawal of all Iraqi forces from Kuwait," restoration of Kuwait's government, protecting "the lives of American citizens abroad," and promoting "the security and the stability of the Persian Gulf."[14]

It is important to note that Washington had limited political aims. It didn't seek Saddam's overthrow, something made clear publicly. This was discussed but not considered acceptable. It was outside the parameters of the UN resolution, could shatter the coalition, and embroil the US in an occupation and nation building. The administration wanted to weaken Saddam enough to keep him from threatening his neighbors while leaving him strong enough to balance against Iran, but also believed defeat might lead to his military overthrowing him.[15]

NSD 54 had caveats in regard to its political aims: "Should Iraq resort to using chemical, biological, or nuclear weapons, be found supporting terrorist acts against US or coalition partners anywhere in the world, or destroy Kuwait's oil fields, it shall become an explicit objective of the United States to replace the current leadership of Iraq." But the primary purpose was Kuwait's liberation.[16] The US didn't exercise its self-declared option when Iraq began destroying Kuwait's oil fields.

This same document provided military guidance and objectives. These included protecting "Saudi Arabia and the other GCC states against attack"; stopping Iraq from attacking its neighbors with ballistic missiles; destroying Iraq's nuclear, chemical, and biological weapons; demolishing "Iraq's command, control, and communications capabilities"; eliminating "the Republican Guards [sic] as an effective fighting force"; and mounting military operations "designed to drive Iraq's forces from Kuwait, break the will of Iraqi forces, discourage Iraqi use of chemical, biological or nuclear weapons, encourage defection of Iraqi forces, and weaken Iraqi popular support for the current government." Military operations would cease only when Bush "determined that the objectives ... have been met." The US would also work with partners and try to keep Israel from becoming involved.[17]

CONSTRUCTING STRATEGY

The US supplied the majority of the military forces and thus dominated coalition strategy making. In some respects, it was a maritime war. Nearly 500,000 troops went by air, but most equipment and supplies – 3.4 million tons, and 6.1 million tons of fuel – went by sea. The quality of Saudi ports made this possible. The US had to take ships out of its ready-reserve, many of Second World War vintage. Only 5 percent of cargo went by air. The eventual deployment included four US aircraft carriers and over 1,200 aircraft. Iraqi forces numbered 400–450,000 in 36 divisions, and had perhaps 4,000 tanks and 3,000 artillery pieces. The prewar embargo shifted to a naval blockade of Iraq.[18]

JCS chair Powell and Secretary of State Baker were unenthusiastic about military action, and the planning didn't occur without tension. In an August 2, 1990 meeting that included Secretary of Defense Dick Cheney, Undersecretary of Defense for Policy Paul Wolfowitz, and JCS chair Powell there was a back-and-forth discussion about how the US should respond. Powell, fearing the American public wouldn't support it, was reluctant to use military force over the fate of Kuwait. As the conversation extended, Cheney pressed Powell about military options. Powell insisted his civilian leaders first provide the political aims they wanted achieved. Growing irritated, Cheney exploded at Powell, growling, "I want some options, General." "Yes, Mr. Secretary," Powell replied, and the meeting ended.[19] Powell's critics argue that he worked to discourage the war and was out of bounds, but his insistence upon his political masters deciding what they wanted before taking the country to war was correct. He asked *the* fundamental question. Military leaders cannot plan properly if they don't know the political aim they are expected to deliver.

THE AIRPOWER STRATEGY

The foundations for the air strategy came from USAF Colonel John Warden, who led the air force Pentagon planning group CHECKMATE. Its development was marked by the American tendency to grasp bad theory and the normal overpromising on what airpower can deliver. In prewar writings, Warden expropriated Clausewitz's term "center of gravity" – which means a strategic source of power – but not the concept, as Warden largely focused on operational and tactical factors. Of the five centers of gravity Clausewitz provides – army, capital city, allies, leader, public opinion – the enemy's army was judged usually the most important. Warden's centers of gravity were logistics, geography, personnel (specifically pilots), and command and control.[20]

Warden framed his plan by depicting the enemy state as a dartboard. The first ring, or center, was the decision-making hub of command, control, and communications. Enough damage to this could supposedly bring down the enemy. The second ring was military and economic production, which included things such as factories and the electrical grid that were required to keep the war going. The third ring was the transportation net. Destroying this would paralyze the enemy. The fourth ring was the population and food supply. It was politically unacceptable to attack this because of the moral outrage generated. The fifth ring was the enemy's military forces. Warden considered this the least important even though it existed to protect the inner core and threaten the enemy. He encapsulated his theory in a 1995 article in which he says: "As strategists and operational artists, we must rid ourselves of the idea that the central feature of war is the clash of military forces."[21] But war is inherently a violent clash of forces.

Warden constructed an air attack plan based upon his concepts named INSTANT THUNDER to contrast with the Vietnam War's ROLLING THUNDER. Its stated political aims were convincing Saddam to leave Kuwait and ask for peace, while creating conditions for his overthrow if he didn't. This would be achieved by simultaneously hitting Saddam's command and control and instruments and symbols of power in and around Baghdad – marked by eighty-four key targets – as well as the second and third rings. The military objective was destruction of the infrastructure needed to fight the war, while making it impossible for Saddam to run the country and creating a rift between him and the people. This would take six days.[22]

Warden briefed his plan to Schwarzkopf, who liked it and told him to brief Powell, which happened on August 11. Powell generally approved but then asked the important question: What happens after day six? One air force general in attendance said Saddam's regime would no longer be able to keep doing what it was doing. Another refused to offer guarantees about what might occur. Powell wouldn't tell the president victory could be achieved with airpower alone, knowing any campaign would require ground troops. He also saw the flaw in Warden's plan: it did not include attacks on Iraq's ground forces. This was important because achieving the political aim of long-term security in the region, as well as allowing the US to leave, required hammering Iraq's army. Powell said: "I won't be happy until I see his tanks destroyed. I want to leave their tanks as smoking kilometer fence posts all the way back to Baghdad." Powell approved intensified planning including all of the services.[23]

Warden was pushed out of the planning by skeptical air force Lieutenant General Buster Glosson. INSTANT THUNDER became OFFENSIVE CAMPAIGN PLAN 1. Glosson gave fourteen to twenty-one days for execution – if the weather was good. If this proved insufficient, another seven to ten days of attacks on Iraqi forces would follow. The air campaign might last a month and aimed at "decapitating" the regime, which meant eliminating command-and-control capability. At the end of this Iraq would quit or its forces be so broken the army could run over them. This was his "worst case" scenario. Powell told Bush he didn't think Iraq would leave Kuwait just because of an air campaign. The air plan continuously evolved over the next five months. It still called for striking key targets as Warden advised, but included the destruction of Iraq's air defense systems, strikes on bridges and chemical, biological, and nuclear weapons development facilities, an intensive interdiction campaign against the Iraqi army's logistics, and attacks on the enemy forces.[24]

THE GROUND STRATEGY

CENTCOM possessed only defensive plans for war with Iraq. Schwarzkopf established a CENTCOM planning cell in Saudi Arabia in September – an army team that included no one from the United States Marine Corps (USMC) and whose members were soon dubbed the Jedi Knights. Schwarzkopf told them the operational objective was the junction of the highways north of Kuwait City connecting it to Basra, Iraq, and said their plan should involve not moving through Kuwait City itself. The planners developed three courses of action: a direct attack on the Iraqi forces in Kuwait and two versions of an attack farther west. They decided the western attacks were impractical because of the logistical requirements, which left the planners arguing for a direct assault on Iraqi forces – a risky one – because the coalition was outnumbered. They believed the force needed more strength, specifically another corps.[25]

Schwarzkopf was told to have the plan briefed in Washington. He thought it unready and marked his concern by including a slide saying they needed another corps. When it was briefed on October 11, National Security Advisor Scowcroft asked, after Glosson finished his presentation, why the army was hitting the Iraqis in the teeth and not their western flank. Powell replied that they lacked the logistical and ground forces to do this. Bush asked what it would take to make the assault from the west. Another corps, Powell said. The plan was rejected, and the army was sent back to the planning board. Dissatisfaction here encouraged administration figures to study how to fight the war. Parallel lines of planning followed in Cheney's Defense Department, the Pentagon under Powell, and in Iraq by the Jedi. This created unnecessary civil–military and intra-military friction but eventually resulted in a plan for a ground offensive consisting primarily of two offensive prongs: one launched into Kuwait, and another across the western desert of southern Iraq.[26]

Meanwhile, at an October 31 NSC meeting, Powell asked for essentially a doubling of the US forces to meet Schwarzkopf's requirements. Bush quickly agreed, wanting to provide the forces the military insisted it needed. Powell, for his part, wanted to apply overwhelming force to win the war quickly.[27] Bush's swift agreement contrasts with the reluctance of Truman and Johnson to meet the troop requests. The US had leaders willing to ensure sufficient force for the task, but also benefited from the Cold War's end, having no other threat, no danger of third-party intervention, and no geographic constraints upon operations against the enemy.

THE MILITARY STRATEGY

The military strategy can be described as overwhelming force, perhaps even annihilation – meaning annihilation of the enemy forces, not the enemy or the regime. On November 14, Schwarzkopf outlined the four stages of DESERT STORM. (See Maps 16.1a and 16.1b.) Bombing of strategic targets, followed by gaining control of the air over Kuwait, then air attacks on Iraqi military units and equipment, and a ground campaign. Before launching the ground offensive, the coalition would extend its forces westward in Saudi Arabia, opening an area the size of Pennsylvania for combat that included parts of southern Iraq and all of Kuwait.[28]

The ground assault had four prongs. On the east (or right) of the front, two Marine divisions and a Saudi force would attack into Kuwait, "tying up Saddam's forces and eventually encircling Kuwait City." To its left, an Arab force would attack parallel to the Marine–Saudi units to cut Iraqi supply lines by seizing the highway intersections northwest of Kuwait City, and then take the city itself. A Marine amphibious force in the Gulf would feint an amphibious landing as part of a deception operation to keep Iraqi attention on the south and east instead of the western desert. Iraq kept seven

PART III: THE POST-COLD WAR WORLD

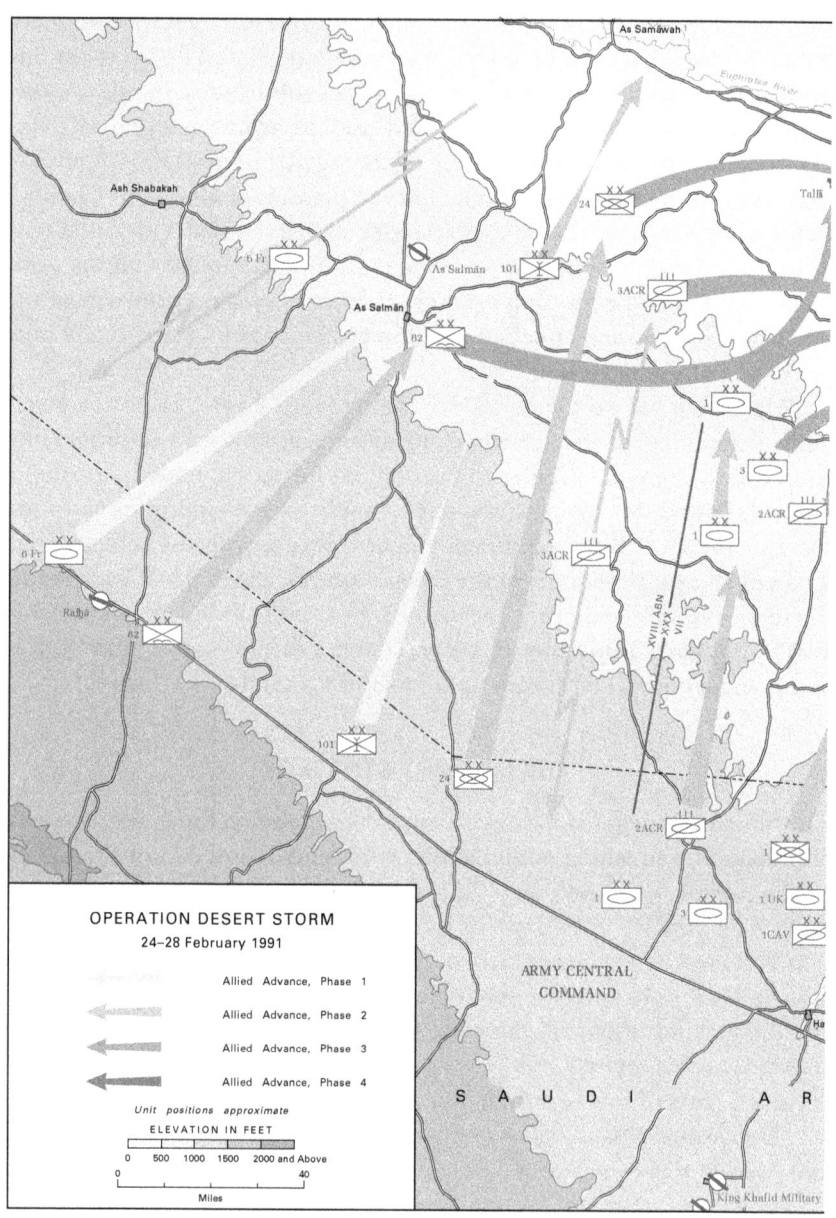

Maps 16.1a, 16.1b Operation DESERT STORM, 1991

THE GULF WAR, OR FIRST IRAQ WAR, 1990–1991

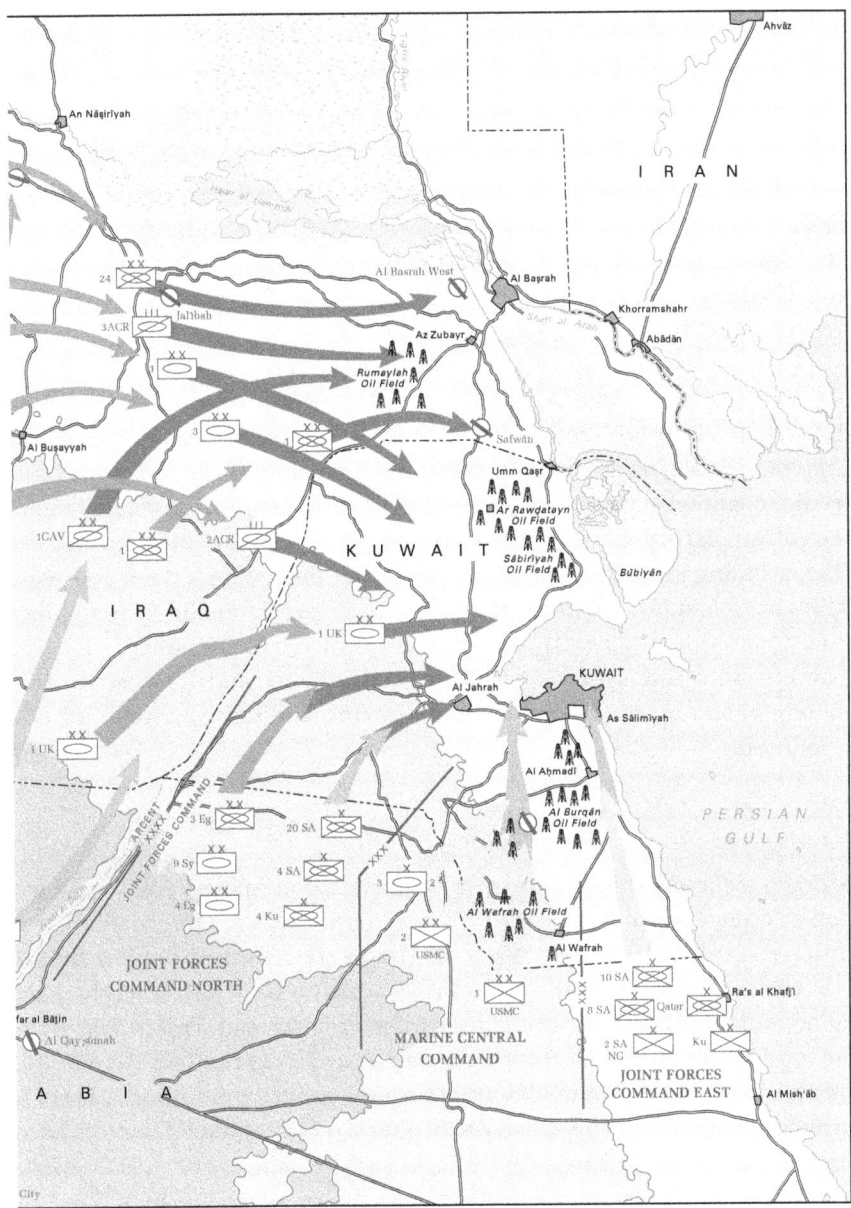

Maps 16.1a, 16.1b (cont.)

divisions on the coast. At the far western end (or left) of the front, 350 miles from the Gulf, was the XVIII Airborne Corps. It would advance at the same time as the Marines, rushing to the Euphrates to cut the Republican Guard's retreat route and Iraq's Highway 8. After this, it could turn eastward to help attack the main Iraqi force. The Marine offensive was intended to help its advance by distracting the Iraqis. To the army it also served as a fixing attack, but the Marines intended to capture Kuwait City within three days. Marine planners had joined the Jedis in early November, but Schwarzkopf also allowed the Marines to make their own plans. This produced a disconnect the consequences of which we see later.[29]

Between the Marines and XVIII Corps was VII Corps, the main striking body. It was tasked with destroying the Republican Guard. These forces didn't move into position until after the air campaign began in order to keep the Iraqis guessing and prevent Saddam from shifting forces to counter the coalition plan. On day two of the land offensive, the "Left Hook" was to launch from the west and cross the desert into Kuwait and southern Iraq, avoiding most Iraqi forces and attacking the enemy's flank and rear. This prong had two operational objectives: seizing Basra and its road junctions to sever the Iraqi escape route, and destroying the Republican Guard. The offensive intended to ruin the Iraqi military and liberate Kuwait, thereby achieving the coalition's political aims and satisfying relevant UN resolutions.[30]

SADDAM'S GRAND STRATEGY

Saddam believed this would be a long war, determined Iraqi strategy, and micromanaged. Knowing his navy was no match for the coalition, he ordered it to not take part. At sea, the Iraqis concentrated on area denial via coastal minefields and set hundreds adrift in the Gulf, severely damaging and almost sinking the US warships *Princeton* and *Tripoli*. The Iraqi air force generally hid, and Saddam sent some aircraft to Iran despite the bitter enmity between the two. Iraqi air defense centered upon a French ground-based system – KARI (*Irak* in French, backwards). It would have proved dangerous to anyone but the Americans, who simply tore it apart. The ground forces adopted a "Pufferfish Defense," which meant bulking up to make the enemy believe you were too big to attack, and Saddam ordered thirty-five more divisions created. He planned a strategy of attrition, fighting defensively to inflict enough casualties on the Americans to make them quit as Iraq had done against Iran. Forces dug in along the Saudi border were supported by an armored reserve for counterattacks. Saddam pumped oil into the Gulf to impede shipping and used propaganda to try to split the coalition. Interestingly, by November 1990 the Iraqis developed a remarkably accurate assessment of coalition strategy, predicting its dependence upon airpower, much of the targeting, its "use the indirect approach to achieve a rapid decision and avoid a large number of losses," attacking from an unexpected direction, and a fixing attack. It erred only in predicting airborne and amphibious attacks.[31] One can correctly assess the opponent and still suffer defeat.

THE WAR BEGINS

On January 16, 1991, Bush told the nation the war had begun. Press reports incessantly echoed Iraq having a battle-hardened army, the fourth largest in the world, and an "elite Republican Guard." Many expected high casualties. Estimates ranged from 500 to 15,000. Part of this was fear of Iraqi WMD use. Between 1988 and 1990, Iraq intensified WMD development, including on nuclear weapons, and used chemical weapons in the Iran–Iraq War and against Iraq's Kurds. American intelligence estimates reported preparations for their use. Bush's threat deterred Saddam, and Iraq instead dispersed its stocks to protect them from air attacks. After the war, defecting Iraqi nuclear scientists revealed that efforts to develop a bomb by the end of 1991 were nearing success.[32]

THE AIR CAMPAIGN

In the first 24 hours of the air campaign, over 400 coalition aircraft flew more than 1,300 sorties; 2–3,000 sorties daily became the average. The coalition tried to minimize civilian casualties and limited strikes in Baghdad to F-117 Stealth fighters and cruise missiles but couldn't stop tragedies such as the bombing of an Iraqi shelter filled with civilians. This produced a rare White House constraint on airpower as most sites in downtown Baghdad were removed from target lists. The airstrikes produced a "cumulative effect" on the Iraqi army. By the first week in February, its morale was cracking. Saddam apparently didn't realize this. Frontline units were soon suffering supply difficulties and not receiving needed food and water. Saddam fed national disillusionment by ordering air defense forces to conserve ammunition for the expected long war. Reducing resistance hurt civilian and military morale while increasing the bombing's effectiveness. After the bombing began, the Soviets offered to approach Saddam for a commitment to withdraw from Kuwait if the attacks ceased. Bush refused, and later explained why: "I have in mind the bombing pauses that Johnson and Nixon were pressured into calling during the Vietnam War. Instead of bringing peace, they gave the enemy a chance to regroup. I was determined not to repeat the mistake."[33]

The coalition air campaign lasted forty-three days, from January 17 to February 28, 1991. It didn't deliver what its starkest advocates desired and continued longer than they promised would be needed. But it laid the foundation for coalition military success. It destroyed much of Iraq's key infrastructure, electrical grid, command and control, and intelligence facilities; damaged or destroyed enormous numbers of bridges; and stopped oil refining. It pummeled Iraq's known nuclear, chemical, and biological weapons facilities, and SCUD short-range ballistic missile production, and rendered from 30 to 50 percent of Iraq's ground forces ineffective. Coalition aircraft flew 109,876 sorties, 49,345 of them combat, and dropped more than 90,000 tons of ordnance.[34]

SADDAM REASSESSES

Saddam concluded his strategy to raise the war's costs wasn't working and decided to take the fight to the enemy to inflict casualties and force them to come to terms. This led to an attack against the Saudi border town of al-Khafji beginning on January 29, 1991. The Iraqis suffered a stunning defeat by January 31. Afterward, Saddam should have realized how outmatched he was. The US should have learned the Iraqis weren't as good as many believed. Some think the battle's results should have driven reassessment of the ground war plan.[35] The US overestimated its enemy but didn't repeat its Korean and Vietnam War errors of underestimation.

Saddam made another effort to change the nature of the war: he launched SCUDs at Israel in an effort to trigger an Israeli attack against Iraq – an Arab state – hoping to shatter the coalition. This was perhaps Saddam's wisest strategic move. It cost him little, one more enemy hardly mattered, but if it worked, the payoff could be substantial. The Americans had to sit on the Israelis diplomatically while supplying them with Patriot missile defense batteries to keep them from attacking Iraq. The coalition also devoted Special Operations forces and aircraft to hunting Iraq's mobile SCUD force.[36]

THE GROUND CAMPAIGN

When the air war began, Iraqi troops began destroying the Kuwaiti oil fields at al-Wafrah and al-Burqun, and there were probably 140 wells burning by

February 22, 1991. Bush told Schwarzkopf to launch the ground campaign when he chose after February 21. It began on February 24. Of the fifty-one Iraqi divisions facing the coalition, all but seventeen were dug in behind sand berms and trenches filled with sometimes burning oil. But the Iraqi units had been badly depleted by desertions and casualties. The original maybe 500,000-man force was now perhaps 300,000. The coalition forces numbered around 575,000.[37]

The First Marine Expeditionary Force anchoring the coalition's right immediately cut through the Iraqi defensive positions and began taking hordes of prisoners (over 10,000 the first day). Schwarzkopf had planned to give the Marines twenty-four hours to breech the Iraqi defenses before launching the western arm. But at noon on the first day of the attack, he received word the Iraqis had blown up Kuwait City's desalinization plant, its only fresh-water source; this meant they planned to withdraw. Schwarzkopf accelerated the main offensive and ordered all forces to advance at three o'clock on the afternoon of the 24th. By the next morning, XVIII Airborne Corps – which had jumped off with the Marines – had made stunning progress. VII Corps, commanded by the cautious Frederick Franks, halted that night, sticking to the original plan instead of adjusting to events. The Marines and Saudis had meanwhile advanced on Kuwait City; the pan-Arab force tasked with liberating the capital lagged behind.[38]

On February 25, the Iraqis hurriedly composed a withdrawal plan. The next day, Saddam broadcast a speech via radio insisting withdrawal was a victory and later branded it a "retreat battle." Saddam's forces were told to retreat into Iraq and prepare to fight in various cities, raising the population to help them. This was the only withdrawal order most units received. It fueled a panic already underway.[39]

The coalition picked up the broadcast at around 2am on February 26. Schwarzkopf applied more pressure on Franks to move and allowed XVIII Corps' 24th Division to push to the Euphrates without waiting for the rest of the army. On February 26, after destroying one Iraqi armored division that morning, elements of VII Corps hit the Tawakalna Division of the Republican Guard at 73 Easting. The battle continued all night, but the result was never in doubt. The next day, US forces fought the largest tank battle of the war at Medina Ridge, destroying over seventy Iraqi tanks and hundreds of other vehicles while suffering only four tanks damaged.[40]

The Iraqi forces in Kuwait were now in full retreat toward Basra. The Marines encircled Kuwait City and, on February 26, took Kuwait International Airport and fought their way onto Mutla Ridge, giving them control over the highways in and out of Kuwait City. The Iraqis had already begun a headlong retreat. Coalition aircraft and armor destroyed over 2,000 vehicles. Journalists dubbed the route the "Highway of Death."[41]

The coalition advance was staggeringly successful, but its primary operational objectives hadn't been achieved: Basra wasn't in coalition hands and the Republican Guard, though wounded, still lived. Not seizing Basra meant the Iraqi retreat route remained open.[42] The offensive resembled a mirror image of Germany's 1914 Schlieffen Plan offensive designed to swing a German army behind Paris and quickly knock out France before Russia could fully mobilize. The first prong – dominated by the Marines – was to drive into Kuwait City. The US, though, inadvertently repeated a form of Germany's 1914 mistake. When the German arm swung through Belgium, the French launched their own offensive. Troops on the Franco-German frontier stopped the French attack and then, instead of remaining a fixing force, counterattacked, and helped push the French into a retreat that helped it escape encirclement. In Kuwait, the supposed Marine fixing attack (which the Marines never saw this way) cut through Iraqi defenses and became a piston pushing them from the coalition's bag.

ENDING THE WAR

One of the most difficult parts of waging a war for a limited political aim is ending it. An important reason for this is that the victor is rarely in a position to impose an agreement upon the enemy. As you recall, there are three intertwined things to keep in mind when trying to end a war: what to ask for politically; how far to go militarily; and who will enforce the peace and how.

A number of administration figures realized early they needed a plan for the war's conclusion. Bush wrote: "We've got to find a clean end, and I keep saying, how do we end this thing?... How do we quit? How do we get them to lay down their arms? How do we safeguard civilians? And how do we get on with our role with credibility, hoping to bring security to the Gulf?" Powell had read Iklé's *Every War Must End* and was sufficiently impressed by his ideas, particularly his discussion of how little thought leaders give to ending wars, to give photocopied pieces of the book to Cheney, Scowcroft, and members of the JCS. State Department representatives discussed ending the war with their opposite numbers in Britain and Schwarzkopf's staff included an expert in war termination. Bush's Special Assistant prepared three different drafts of a war termination memo, none of which Bush liked. Despite all of this, the administration failed to prepare for what it knew was coming.[43]

On February 25, 1991, at 9pm Eastern Standard Time, Bush made a speech in which he included ceasefire terms: Iraqi compliance with relevant UN resolutions; restitution for damages caused; the release of all POWs and detainees; and that the Iraqis meet with Schwarzkopf within the next forty-eight hours. Meanwhile, the coalition forces kept up the military pressure. On February 27, Schwarzkopf gave what became known as "The Mother of All Briefings." He discussed the ground war and announced the coalition had accomplished its mission.[44]

Powell and Schwarzkopf had begun thinking the end was near and discussed this on February 27. The Iraqis were in full retreat and the media had begun talking about the "Highway of Death." Scowcroft and other officials worried about the international impression. After four days of the ground war, though, Schwarzkopf said he needed a fifth to ensure Iraq's military was so degraded Saddam could no longer threaten his neighbors. When Powell briefed Bush, he reported the Iraqi army was broken and fleeing, and said he would probably bring a recommendation to stop the fighting tomorrow. Bush surprised Powell by asking him that if this were so, could not they end the war immediately? Conversations between Powell and Schwarzkopf and Schwarzkopf and his commanders followed. No one objected. The JCS supported the president. Bush ordered a halt, producing a discussion of timing. White House Chief of Staff John Sununu suggested midnight Washington time because this would make it "the Hundred-Hour War." This would be Thursday, February 28, 8am Riyadh time, which gave Schwarzkopf almost the day he had wanted. And calling it "the Hundred-Hour War" had a nice ring. Scowcroft later called this "probably too cute by half."[45] Many observers note this ignores the previous six weeks of bombing.

The bigger issue was the decision's unilateral nature, meaning the enemy wasn't involved. President Bush wrote: "I decided it was our choice, not Saddam's; we would declare an end once I was sure we had met all our military objectives and fulfilled the UN resolutions." The US, Powell said, branded it a "suspension of hostilities" "to make clear that this was not a cease-fire negotiated with the Iraqis, but a halt taken on our own initiative."[46]

On February 28, the very day of the ceasefire, Saddam said Bush's unilateral decision demonstrated Iraq had won because when Bush acted, the Iraqi army was still fighting. The coalition quitting because it was taking casualties found its way into Iraq's official history. Bush's reaction is worth recounting in full:

> It's now early Thursday morning on the 28th. Still no feeling of euphoria. I think I know why it is. After my speech last night, Baghdad radio started

broadcasting that we've been forced to capitulate. I see on the television that public opinion in Jordan and in the streets of Baghdad is that they have won. It is such a canard, so little, but it's what concerns me. It hasn't been a clean end – there is no battleship *Missouri* surrender. This is what's missing to make this akin to WWII, to separate Kuwait from Korea and Vietnam.[47]

Moreover, after the decision to stop the war was made, Schwarzkopf informed Powell that if they halted, some of the Republican Guard units might escape. Powell wrote: "I told him to keep hitting them, and I would get back to him. I passed Norm's report to the President and the others. Although we were all taken slightly aback, no one felt that what we had heard changed the basic equation." They believed they would have to absorb criticism for not extending the war, but Bush stuck to his decision. One of the administration's political aims was increasing security and stability in the Persian Gulf. To Powell, accomplishing this required the Republican Guard's destruction. The operational – or military – objectives of the US in the conflict thus included its devastation. But the US unilaterally stopped the fighting before accomplishing this. Another day of combat with this in mind could have seen its destruction. The administration also didn't destroy Saddam's ability to threaten his neighbors and the US had to surge troops into the region twice in the next decade.[48]

When it came time to negotiate a ceasefire, Schwarzkopf and Powell discussed having talks on the battleship *Missouri*. "I wanted to make it obvious that this meeting was a surrender ceremony in everything but name," Schwarzkopf wrote later. But this they ruled out because they had too little time to prepare and gather the delegates. Instead, Schwarzkopf chose the Iraqi air base at Jalibah, 95 miles inside Iraq. Having it on Iraq's ground symbolized its defeat and it was easy for the Iraqi delegates to reach. But the site proved too dangerous because of unexploded ordnance. Schwarzkopf then chose Iraq's Safwan airfield near the Kuwait border. He had ordered the nearby crossroads taken the day before, and was told it was done, but then discovered this wasn't true. He ordered VII Corps to seize it.[49]

The Iraqi delegation had problems getting through areas already controlled by a growing anti-Saddam rebellion and had to be escorted by Republican Guard tanks. Saddam instructed them to go to the negotiations "with the feeling and spirit of the victorious." The Iraqis were represented by a pair of three-star generals Schwarzkopf had never heard of. Washington had concerns about Iraq's representatives but decided that if Lieutenant General Sultan Hashid Ahmad led them and held sufficient governmental authority, he was acceptable.[50]

THE GULF WAR, OR FIRST IRAQ WAR, 1990-1991

Earlier, Powell had had Schwarzkopf work up ceasefire terms. He sent these to Powell, and they were reviewed by Defense, State, and the White House. Approval and transmission to the Iraqis via Moscow followed. The terms included the return of POWs and the remains of those killed in action; the location of WMD sites; a demarcation line between the forces so there were no accidents; a Saudi request for confirmation of Kuwaiti and Saudi sovereignty; and other issues, such as the return of around 3,000 Kuwaiti men the Iraqis had taken hostage.[51]

The meeting began at 11am, March 3, 1991. The Iraqis accepted the US terms and a version of what the Saudis wanted. The ceasefire line was the only initial sticking point. This was inside Iraq, and the Iraqi generals only bent after being assured it was temporary and didn't mean a border change. At the end, Schwarzkopf asked if the Iraqis had any matters to raise. They asked to fly helicopters to move their officials inside Iraq. Schwarzkopf wrote in his memoirs: "It appeared to me a legitimate request. And given that the Iraqis had agreed to all our requests, I didn't feel it was unreasonable to grant one of theirs." (One isn't obligated to grant an enemy's request.) Ahmad asked if this included armed helicopters; Schwarzkopf said it did. This was the day's most controversial issue. Schwarzkopf revealed why: "In the following weeks, we discovered what the son of a bitch had really had in mind: using helicopter gunships to suppress rebellions in Basra and other cities." Schwarzkopf and others later argued that the twenty to twenty-four intact divisions Saddam possessed in Iraq were more important.[52]

The administration's failure to plan for ending the war now began causing problems. Schwarzkopf received little guidance from his political superiors before he went into the ceasefire meetings and made little effort to obtain any. Schwarzkopf described his approach: "If need be, I would go to Safwan and wing it. For one thing, the talks would be limited to military matters, and I understood what needed to be done; for another, our side had *won*, so we were in a position to dictate terms."[53]

The US had "won" – on the battlefield. But the war wasn't over. Negotiations are a part of the struggle, not detached from it. Going in unprepared is unhelpful and dictating terms is not so easy if you're unwilling to continue using force or the enemy leaders are insensitive to the effects of refusing to agree upon their people and nation. Clausewitz's caution comes to mind: "To bring a war, or one of its campaigns, to a successful close requires a thorough grasp of national policy [political aims]. On that level strategy and policy [political aims] coalesce: the commander-in-chief is simultaneously a statesman."[54] Ending the fighting, and ending the war itself, are simultaneously political *and* military issues.

PART III: THE POST-COLD WAR WORLD

A CHANGING POLITICAL AIM?

Bush – unintentionally – added another layer of confusion to the problem of ending the war. The primary US political aim was Kuwait's liberation. This mattered most.[55] US leaders didn't repeat the Korean War mistake of changing the political aim without sufficiently considering the effects, but their thoughts and actions began moving from a limited political aim – liberating Kuwait – to an unlimited one of overthrowing Saddam.

After the war, Secretary of State Baker said in regard to removing Saddam and thus changing the regime that the administration was "careful not to embrace it as a war aim or political aim." But the coalition bombed targets in the hope he was there, which is understandable, as his death would have probably immediately ended the war. National Security Advisor Scowcroft worried that if Saddam fell the US would be stuck with a massive nation-building effort and Iraq would end up being ruled by "another, perhaps less problematic, strongman."[56]

On February 15, 1991, before the Iraqis agreed to a ceasefire, even before the beginning of the coalition ground offensive, Bush said in a speech that another way to avoid bloodshed was for the Iraqis to overthrow Saddam. He said later he added this "impulsively." It sparked a press frenzy regarding whether or not the US had added another aim: overthrowing Saddam. Bush replied that it had not. But he repeated his call for Iraqis to rebel on March 1 when announcing the Safwan talks.[57]

This raises a key question: did the US political aim change? Scowcroft called the first mention of revolt an "impulsive ad lib" he believed resulted in Bush facing unfair charges he "had encouraged the Iraqi people to rise against Saddam and then failed to come to their aid when they did." A presidential speech is never routine, especially one concerning a war. Repeating the call as Bush did arguably demonstrates a deeper commitment to or consideration of the idea. Scowcroft went on to say: "It is true that we hoped Saddam would be toppled. But we never thought that could be done by anyone outside the military and never tried to incite the general population." Deputy National Security Advisor Robert Gates said the administration thought "that the magnitude of the defeat was so overwhelming that the army would take out Saddam when the war was over." After the war, the administration temporarily insisted the US wouldn't agree to lifting economic sanctions as long as Saddam remained in power. This constituted a *de facto* change to a political aim of regime change.[58]

So, had the war's aim changed? Or had it become unclear? The fact that it is difficult to answer this question pushes toward a lack of clarity in political leaders' minds. As we have seen before, this is a problem. If you don't know what you want, how do you make a peace that will help you get it? Having a clearer vision of what they wanted the war's end to look like might not have prevented the problems encountered in its ending because this is difficult even for a combatant who has succeeded spectacularly on the battlefield. But it wouldn't have hurt.

CONTINUED MILITARY ACTION?

Should the US have continued the fighting? The question that immediately follows is: to what end? What do you want it to achieve? Driving to Baghdad and overthrowing Saddam wasn't an option the administration considered. The UN resolutions didn't support this, the coalition wouldn't have survived it, and the administration had no desire to engage in a massive nation-building effort they believed would follow. But continuing the fighting until Saddam's forces were further shattered was an option that would have helped make possible the Bush administration's desire for Saddam's overthrow but not guaranteed it. Further destruction of Saddam's forces could have helped achieve the aim of increasing security in the Gulf by weakening Saddam's ability to attack or threaten his neighbors.[59]

Some insist Bush should have continued the war until Iraq surrendered unconditionally. The events of the 2003 Iraq War show Saddam's agreement to an unconditional surrender unlikely under any imaginable circumstance. Some argue continuing the war would force Saddam to admit defeat and possibly sign the ceasefire himself. This is possible. But the administration feared it couldn't compel him to appear and would then be forced to abandon its demands. They were likely correct, but a push into southern Iraq combined with promises to halt as soon as Saddam signed a ceasefire – or better yet an actual peace treaty – or had someone sign it for him might have encouraged the Iraqi dictator to bend. The response of Bush and Scowcroft to such arguments was this: "Trying to eliminate Saddam, extending the ground war into an occupation of Iraq, would have violated our guideline about not changing objectives in midstream, engaging in 'mission creep,' and would have incurred incalculable human and political costs."[60]

Other critics suggest temporarily keeping forces in the areas of southern Iraq the US controlled. During the ceasefire negotiations at Safwan, the Iraqis raised their presence. Schwarzkopf promised their evacuation as soon as possible. He (and his superiors) could have used them as leverage as the Iraqis so obviously wanted them out. Removal was a bargaining chip for inducing Saddam to sign an agreement. The Iraqi resistance to a ceasefire line based upon where the forces stood because they feared it meant surrendering territory indicates the importance of territorial integrity in at least their eyes and probably in Saddam's. Additionally, Thatcher suggested before the war the seizure of the Rumaila oil field and holding it until the coalition recovered the cost of the war and Iraq met its other demands.[61]

LOSING THE PEACE?

The Iraqi rebellion against Saddam began on February 28, 1991 in a pair of Sunni towns about 60–70 kilometers from Basra, three days before the ceasefire's signing. It quickly spread. These revolts, particularly in the south, were fed by retreating soldiers. But Shia tied to Iran began calling for Islamist rule. This alienated many and allowed Saddam to begin rallying domestic support as Iraqis feared Islamist rule more than Saddam's. The retreating units attacked by the US were those most heavily involved in the uprising, and were the ones about which Saddam had been most concerned. The most loyal elements remained intact.[62] This gave Saddam the power to put down the revolts and stay in power.

In the north, the Kurds saw the southern unrest and also rose. Saddam's attacks upon them displaced 2 million people. Most fled to Turkey, which eventually limited how many it would take. Around 300,000 were trapped in the mountains of northern Iraq. The ensuing humanitarian nightmare convinced Bush to mount Operation PROVIDE COMFORT. The US and many of its NATO allies dispatched troops and relief supplies. Quickly following was the establishment of a no-fly zone for Iraqi aircraft in the north that remained in effect until 2003. There was another no-fly zone in the south beginning in 1992.[63]

The April 3, 1991 United Nations Security Council Resolution 687, referred to as "The Mother of All Resolutions" because it was the Security Council's lengthiest, formalized the ceasefire conditions. One could argue this was as close to a peace treaty as one could get. It added other sanctions and inspections, mandated Baghdad disclose all of its WMD and ballistic missiles to UN-supervised destruction, and ordered Iraq to pay for damages inflicted upon Kuwait, and the environmental damage done to the Gulf by pumping oil into the sea. All revenue Iraq derived from oil sales was to enter a fund to pay these damages; the remainder could be used for food or reconstruction. The "Oil for Food Program" evolved from this.[64]

After the war, the US implemented a containment strategy against Saddam with the aims being to prevent new Iraqi aggression and keep

Saddam from rebuilding his military capability. Containment had four primary elements: 1) disarmament via the UN program, particularly in regard to WMD and ballistic missiles; 2) UN monitoring; 3) the presence of US military forces; and 4) maintaining sanctions put in place during the war. None had expected sanctions would drive Saddam from Kuwait, but now expected them to alter his behavior. Over the long term, the sanctions system began breaking down through corruption in the UN-backed "Oil for Food Program" and the willingness of nations such as China to simply ignore them. Publicly, Saddam cheated at every opportunity and began rebuilding his chemical, biological, and nuclear programs.[65]

One only has so much time to enforce disarmament clauses and other terms because states start wriggling out of the provisions. The victors and the international community can also lose interest or become distracted by other events. United Nations Special Commission (UNSCOM) inspections in Iraq became less important in the face of the collapse of Yugoslavia and the wars there. The international community can block enforcement because members begin seeing the victor in a bad light. Washington and London were criticized for enforcing the no-fly zones.[66]

CONCLUSION

The Bush administration handled the ending of the First Iraq War poorly. Its worst mistakes were common ones: not having a plan for ending the war or for what came after, becoming unclear on the political aims, and not understanding the effects of this. But they did far more correct than wrong and avoided the mistake of providing insufficient force. They secured the primary political aim – the liberation of Kuwait – and did so at low cost in American blood: 148 Americans were killed in action, 145 died in accidents, and 65 coalition soldiers perished. The number of Iraqis killed is unclear. Estimates range from 25,000 to 50,000. American troops remained in Saudi Arabia afterward. The presence of "infidels" in the "land of the Prophet" enraged Islamists.[67]

Bush and his administration tackled the Gulf War while managing the Cold War's end.[68] Things went far from perfectly in either, but when comparing this administration to others – especially those of both parties that follow – one is consistently struck by the rationality and experience of the key figures and their ability to steer the US and indeed, the Western world, through so many unknown shoals.

17

THE NEW WORLD DISORDER: BUSH AND CLINTON, 1991–2001

THE GEORGE H. W. BUSH ADMINISTRATION: PART II

On September 11, 1990, President Bush gave a Congressional address sometimes branded his "New World Order" speech. It largely concerned Iraq's invasion of Kuwait, but he spoke of "a new era – freer from the threat of terror, stronger in the pursuit of justice, and more secure in the quest for peace. An era in which the nations of the world ... can prosper and live in harmony." What Bush and later commentators meant by a New World Order was unclear and Bush used the term in different ways. Crystalline was that the Soviet Union's unexpected collapse redrew the geopolitical landscape. This surprised American leaders as much as anyone. And no administration seems to have considered how to consolidate the victory (perhaps temporary) of democracy, political pluralism, freedom, and capitalism, over totalitarian, statist, control. Bush aimed to do so and extend the gains. Secretary of State Baker believed America had "a once-in-a-century opportunity to advance American interests *and* values throughout the world." The administration feared the result of inaction, worried about ethnic and nationalist tensions reawakening, and despotic regimes arising in successor states. Tying a reunified Germany to NATO was considered one way of defusing such problems. The US had to remain involved because the twentieth century's history gave no one confidence in the Europeans, who generally supported a greater US role. Washington allowed Europe more leeway, and NATO remained the foundation of transatlantic security.[1]

NEW AIMS AND A NEW GRAND STRATEGY

Bush's August 1991 letter in the *National Security Strategy* has the heading "A New World Order." It begins: "A new world order is not a fact; it is an aspiration – and an opportunity. We have within our grasp an extraordinary possibility that few generations have enjoyed – to build a new international system in accordance with our own values and ideals." The Soviet Union's demise and the Cold War's end birthed a new era. Bush saw in UN and international action during the Gulf War "a glimmer of a better future." America's role was guarding US interests and helping "create a new world in which our fundamental values not only survive but flourish." The US would work with other states but must also lead. Baker clarified matters in April 1992: "Our idea is to replace the dangerous period of the Cold War with a democratic peace."[2]

The era might be new, but much of American grand strategy wasn't. Engagement of China continued, as did pursuing arms control agreements with Moscow, blocking WMD proliferation, expanding and strengthening free-market economies, and free trade. Security for oil supplies was important. Deterrence and forward presence remained planks of military strategy, though the US military was expected to shrink by 25 percent by the mid 1990s. American leaders knew US military strength underpinned global security while providing diplomatic leverage, and Washington maintained forces in Europe and Asia to meet threats in the Middle East and Asia. The US would maintain its technological edge and, though the Soviet Union was gone, it might be replaced by a rising power-seeking hegemony. Only the US had the strength to maintain and grow the post–Second World War liberal order it had created.[3]

REASSESSMENT AND THE EVOLUTION OF GRAND STRATEGY

The Cold War's end necessitated reassessment. Wolfowitz's undersecretary of defense for policy office began drafting a new Defense Planning Guidance (DPG). This routine document addressing acquisition and budget issues for the next five years became a strategic thought-piece. The 1994–95 draft DPG was completed in February 1992. Illegally leaked to the *New York Times*, it caused a storm for the administration. The outrage partly derived from the inability of commentators to distinguish between political aims and strategy, something fed by the document's impoverished structure and it being a rough draft. Conspiracy mongering has trailed it, but reading it betrays little controversial, and it resembles the Bill Clinton administration's thinking. Much of the untethered reaction arose because it was an election year, and Clinton's campaign grasped it as a bludgeon.[4]

The DPG noted the Soviet collapse removed any immediate future threat from here. Potential dangers remained, and "Our strategy must now refocus on precluding the emergence of any potential future global competitor." But since the US faced no great-power threat, this could be done at lower costs, if the US were willing to "reconstitute" needed forces later.

Regional threats were most likely and would necessitate peacekeeping as the Cold War's demise lessened "pressure for US military involvement in every potential regional or local conflict." NATO remained indispensable, but any European security system undermining it should be prevented. The document doesn't clearly articulate any aims but urged strengthening democracy in East and Central Europe by encouraging membership in the European Economic Community and a deeper NATO relationship, thus protecting US interests while increasing stability. Washington also needed to maintain a strong military position and connections in Asia to "prevent emergence of a vacuum or a regional hegemon."[5]

This DPG birthed an insistence that Bush aimed at primacy, probably because of this statement: "Our strategy must now refocus on precluding the emergence of any potential future global competitor." Insisting the US ever sought primacy – whatever this means – is problematic as it lacks evidence and has fed conspiracy theories about "American Empire." This discussion also suffers from confusion between strategy and aims and a failure to identify any political aims. The administration sought a "democratic peace," not "primacy," which isn't an aim. Its military power was for deterrence. "International primacy," political scientist Samuel Huntington wrote, "means a state has more power than other actors."[6] This does not mean domination. Preventing emergence of a dominant power – which is what the DPG suggested – isn't the same as seeking to dominate, which is what for many "primacy" implies. Indeed, if the US had actually sought dominance – or control – it wouldn't have retrenched militarily. Moreover, the post-9/11 era demonstrated the absence of so-called American primacy (or hegemony, which sometimes is used interchangeably). The administration sought a democratic peace, believing this would make America most secure. This would be achieved primarily via engagement and deterrence underpinned by preeminent military power, support for basic freedoms, and free markets.

THE BUSH ADMINISTRATION'S FINAL ITERATION OF GRAND STRATEGY

The DPG provided a foundation for the administration's last strategy documents, including the 1993 *Regional Defense Strategy* (*RDS*). Its primary political aim was security for the United States, though the document's confused structure makes it difficult to decipher aims and strategy. It insisted that since there was no longer a global danger, America should focus upon regional threats. America and its allies and partners had secured a democratic "zone of peace," "a community of democratic nations bound together by a web of political, economic, and security ties." This should be preserved and enlarged, even to Russia, the Ukraine, and the former Warsaw Pact. Washington would seek to prevent domination of key regions by non-democratic powers. This would "help to preclude the emergence of a hostile power that could present a global security threat comparable to the one the Soviet Union presented in the past." The US wouldn't sit and allow a new global danger to emerge. Implementation required the US to counter threats, deter attacks, defeat attacks if deterrence failed, strengthen ties with allies, reduce the chances of conflict by removing instability, and ending conflicts quickly when they occurred. A collective response was preferred, but this wasn't always possible. The core military elements were nuclear deterrence and defense against such attacks, forward deployed deterrent forces, and maintaining the ability to respond quickly to a crisis and create new forces.[7]

We see the DPG's influence in the final Bush *NSS*. Published in January 1993 after Bush's election defeat, it was partially intended to burnish the Reagan–Bush successes. It had "one overriding goal: real peace," and hoped to have the same peace with former Warsaw Pact states it had with others. It encouraged Americans to "work together to lead the world toward the 21st Century, the Age of Democratic Peace." Moreover, via "a strategy of engagement and leadership" America could achieve aims that included "Open, democratic and representative political systems worldwide."[8]

THE NEW WORLD ORDER PROVES NOT SO ORDERLY: YUGOSLAVIA AND SOMALIA

Speculating about American power didn't equate to using it. The US held a rare spot, and many nations possessing such military and economic preeminence would've sought global domination instead of trying to act as its shepherd. But to the administration, perceived national interests still trumped all, something an unwillingness to intervene in the Balkans' funereal struggles showed.[9]

Croatia and Slovenia declared independence from Yugoslavia in June 1991. The Serbs refused to see so many ethnic Serbs subsumed into Croatia and went to war. Bosnia seceded nine months later. Serbia expanded the war in a particularly vicious manner, launching in April 1992 what became a three-year siege of Sarajevo. Bush thought the Europeans should handle this and focused on reelection. The Europeans watched. The UN worsened Bosnia's situation by imposing an arms embargo, robbing it of the chance to acquire the weapons Serbia already had. Serb efforts at genocide and the creation of 1.7 million Muslim refugees followed.[10]

In Somalia, when armed groups prevented relief organizations from feeding the starving, the administration told the UN it would provide troops for a multinational relief effort that became Operation RESTORE HOPE under US command. "Our mission has a limited objective," Bush said. "To open the supply routes, to get the food moving, and to prepare the way for a U.N. peacekeeping force to keep it moving. This operation is not open-ended. We will not stay one day longer than is absolutely necessary." The US intended to hand off to UN peacekeeping forces as soon as "a secure environment in the hardest hit parts of Somalia" was created to allow food deliveries. The first of 26,000 US troops landed on December 4, 1992. Violence in Mogadishu temporarily subsided, and the mission thwarted mass starvation. US troop numbers dropped to about 5,000 by the end of Bush's term.[11]

THE BILL CLINTON ADMINISTRATION AND GRAND STRATEGY, 1993–2001

A unique American event helped make possible William Jefferson Clinton's administration: a viable third-party presidential candidate. Texas businessman H. Ross Perot's campaign tapped growing worries about exporting American jobs, and he insisted these would flee to Mexico because of the North American Free Trade Agreement (NAFTA) Bush was negotiating. Perot's on-again, off-again campaign, Bush's stumbles (including recanting a pledge to not raise taxes), a short recession, and Clinton's political talent put the Arkansas governor in the White House.[12]

The "New Democrats" advising Clinton stressed internationalism, strong defense, and spreading democracy. Clinton criticized Bush during the campaign for being weak on foreign affairs: he hadn't deposed Saddam, was soft on China after Tiananmen, and failed to act in the Balkans despite a genocidal tragedy.[13] Once elected, Clinton failed to depose Saddam, was soft on China, and watched genocide unfold in the Balkans and Rwanda.

Clinton's grand strategy was shaped by National Security Advisor Anthony Lake and his assistant, Samuel "Sandy" Berger – two Carter administration veterans – and proposals from the Progressive Policy Institute (Clinton was a member) that insisted it offered a Third Way between liberal and conservative ideas. Lake viewed himself as a Neo-Wilsonian, those trying "to create a world that was neither naively liberal in the Wilsonian sense nor relentlessly realist in the conservative sense." In a December 1991 speech, Clinton made supporting democracy – the consolidation of gains and its further spread – a campaign plank. Security was a prominent aim and the speech's focus. Strengthening the economy also featured, though this is a tool for pursuing aims. Engagement and ensuring the US retained the military strength to deal with any threat were grand strategy elements. In his inaugural address, Clinton stressed the need for America to lead in the post–Cold War world it helped create.[14]

Former Clinton Chief of Staff Leon Panetta said the Clinton White House's first year "was undisciplined, almost chaotic." Plaguing the transition were inexperience, "a reluctance to confront difficult problems; a commitment to diversity that hindered decision making; and an inclusiveness that hampered an ability to say 'no.'" Clinton's lack of confidence in foreign relations and acting as commander-in-chief were weakening, as was belief that if Washington did less abroad others would do more. Clinton spent scant time on foreign affairs and had little interest in them, particularly in the beginning. He made clear he would concentrate on domestic priorities and gave slight time to his defense secretary and national security advisor. There was a near-total absence of foreign relations planning.[15]

THE ASSESSMENT

Outgoing Secretary of State Lawrence Eagleburger, writing in the wake of Bush administration experiences in the Balkans and Somalia, penned a twenty-two-page memo for Clinton's secretary of state, Warren Christopher, that became a Clinton team "must-read." Eagleburger believed America's greatest coming challenges derived from the effects of economic integration resulting from "globalization" and increasing fragmentation of states. Meeting these demanded "the broadest possible definition of security" and using all arms of national power. The economic challenges, if not properly addressed, would "undercut competitiveness ... devalue US leadership and, perhaps more importantly, threaten domestic support for strong international engagement." Political fragmentation abroad would "confront us with the dilemma of whether to take part in limited military interventions in situations which do not directly threaten our interests." Eagleburger feared that if democratizing nations failed to make the transition, they might fall into dangerous versions of nationalism or religious extremism such as Islamism. The US needed to maintain its position as a global leader because "For better or worse, people and governments still look to us to make sense of the changes swirling around them and show some initiative and purpose. No one else can do this." To meet these challenges, America must develop an approach to humanitarian intervention and be prepared for peacekeeping. Maintaining economic strength was important, because "our domestic economic shortcomings undercut our competitiveness. They devalue US leadership and, perhaps more importantly, threaten domestic support for strong international engagement."[16]

Political scientist Francis Fukuyama influenced administration thinking. He insisted in 1989 that we had reached "the end of history," meaning history was moving inevitably toward "the end point of mankind's ideological evolution and the universalization of Western liberal democracy as the final form of human government," for which there was no real competitor. The administration decided that since movement toward democracy was inevitable (Fukuyama's argument reminds one of Marxist determinism, something he mentions), Washington engaging with other states would enable it to "'enlarge' those processes." Eagleburger gave a better answer: "The collapse of Communism represents an [sic] historic triumph for democracy and free markets, but it has not ended history or brought us to the brink of ideological uniformity."[17]

The administration arrived divided over whether it needed a "doctrine," a situation exacerbated by Clinton's ambivalence. He said FDR and Truman had "powerful instincts about what had to be done, and they just made it up as they went along." The picture of them having a grand strategy was simply added later, creating a "huge myth that we always knew what we were doing during the Cold War." But Clinton saw such branding as a way to quickly convey complexity to the public. He complained in mid 1994 that he lacked this, saying: "a bunch of smart people haven't been able to come up with a new slogan." Deputy Secretary of State Strobe Talbot raised the issue with Kennan at an October 1994 dinner. Kennan cautioned against a "bumper sticker" because this could produce oversimplification as had "containment." Clinton laughed at the story and said: "that's why Kennan is a great diplomat and scholar and not a politician."[18]

"IT'S NOT ALWAYS THE ECONOMY, STUPID!": A "GRAND STRATEGY" OF ECONOMICS

Economic issues mattered most to Clinton, and he tried to redefine economics as security. National Security Advisor Lake told the staff at the first NSC meeting: "We are not going to trouble the president with foreign policy." In a February 17, 1993 speech before Congress, Clinton painted a picture of two decades of economic failure after a decade of spectacular growth. He criticized government debt accumulation, about which he was correct, and praised the private sector as the "real engine of economic growth" while insisting government could demand more from it (taxes) because it created the conditions under which it operated. As was the norm for his speeches, a list of proposals followed. In addition to tax increases, he called for spending cuts, health-care reform, defense cuts, and a tough crime bill. But economics reigned supreme.[19]

Clinton enthusiastically pursued economic globalization, believing "he had to convince Americans that foreign and domestic policies were inextricably linked in a globalizing world." Clinton wanted tighter coordination of foreign and domestic economic issues and created the National Economic Council – an economic NSC – in January 1993. Part of its task was pushing "a shift of priority and resources away from national security as traditionally defined, toward ... making America competitive in a fiercely competitive world." Clinton was a free trader, saying in January 1997: "In a truly open market, we can out-compete anyone, anywhere on Earth." (He inadvertently revealed the problem: "truly open.") The administration emphasized bilateral trade agreements and access to foreign markets as "96 percent of global consumers" were abroad. Clinton supported NAFTA, but opposition from trade unions and Democrats fearful of losing manufacturing jobs had prevented its approval under Bush. To Clinton, it meant exports, which meant jobs, while tying together the hemisphere's democracies. Clinton won NAFTA's approval in 1993 and promised it would create 200,000 US jobs by 1995.[20]

The effects of NAFTA are disputed and difficult to pin down as it is part of a complicated economic equation. One author says: "NAFTA had already created more than 100,000 American jobs by 1995, a figure that jumped to almost 310,000 by 1998." Another pointed out that it "accelerated the decline in apparel employment," delivering a *coup de grâce* to the American garment industry, and probably cost the US "labor-intensive assembly jobs." Its effect was clear at the ballot box. In November 1994, unskilled workers abandoned the Democratic Party, helping hand Republicans Congressional control "for the first time in forty years."[21]

At first glance, Clinton's strategy resembles Reagan's, but in the Reagan administration, the political trumped economics because it produced democracy and basic freedoms. Free markets can support political freedoms, but they don't produce them. Also, the Clinton administration pushed emerging democracies to open their markets to foreign investment without understanding the economic devastation wrought in these nations when they suffered economic or political problems and foreign investors fled.[22]

Clinton's initial economic strategy included lowering military spending $112 billion over five years and cuts to shrink the 1992–95 annual budget shortfalls. The deficit fell for the first time since Truman's presidency. Clinton raised taxes, but not enough to kill the Reagan–Bush economic boom. He kept government spending in line and his budgets began producing surpluses, which hasn't happened since. He benefited from fiscally responsible elements in both parties but relied on Democrats to raise taxes. Surpluses meant less Federal borrowing, which kept the government out of the bond market and helped produce lower loan interest rates; this fed investment and thus economic growth, and expansion increased Federal tax revenue. Overall, the economy boomed, yet "workers faced a decline in real wages, a rise in health care costs, and the prospect of continued outsourcing of jobs to developing nations."[23]

THE TWIN BLOWS: SOMALIA AND HAITI

Events drove daggers through Fukuyama's insistence the world had reached "the universalization of Western liberal democracy." Authoritarianism remained. Clinton inherited Operation RESTORE HOPE in Somalia, which originated in December 1992 as a UN humanitarian mission. Lake, Berger, and UN Ambassador Madeleine Albright backed humanitarian missions. Albright had developed Assertive Multilateralism, arguing that if the US lacked the resources or will to act on its own, it should do so with a coalition but lead. This didn't preclude unilateral action. Other advisors argued the US had no interests in Somalia and urged withdrawal.[24]

Clinton paid little attention to Somalia between January and October 1993. He held no meetings on it with his primary foreign affairs advisors but four on Haiti and eighteen on Bosnia. In a May 1993 speech, Clinton said Lieutenant General Robert B. Johnson had told him "mission accomplished," but the UN peacekeeping action, which included American troops, continued. Clinton could make this argument because in March 1993, pushed by Washington, UN Secretary General Boutros Boutros-Ghali morphed the peacekeeping operation into a UN nation-building exercise via Security Council Resolution 814. The US had by this time drawn down its forces to around 4,100. Somali warlord Mohammed Farah Aideed, fearing UN forces might aid his foes and take his weapons caches, decided he needed to strike. In early June, his Somali National Army attacked Pakistani peacekeepers. The UN ordered Aideed's arrest. The Clinton administration then changed its political aim. Albright revealed the administration would pursue the UN aim of restoring governmental control in Somalia, and not just any form – an "emerging democracy."[25]

A June 6, 1993 UN Security Council Resolution backed what was now a war against Aideed. Both Clinton and Lake believed the US had defeated Aideed after a successful June airstrike on his headquarters. But the violence increased. In August, four US soldiers were killed by an improvised explosive device (IED). Retired American admiral Johnathan T. Howe, the UN representative in Somalia, pushed Albright for sufficient troops and equipment to achieve the administration's aim, and Albright pushed the administration. Clinton's Defense Department resisted, claiming an unwillingness to "Americanize" the problem. The administration refused to send heavy forces but eventually dispatched a 400-man task force and Special Forces to capture Aideed. The Americans started taking casualties and, by mid September, political support from Congress was waning and African leaders were pressing for a political solution. On September 22, the US convinced the UN Security Council to adopt a strategy built on diplomatic and economic power that didn't mention Aideed. American leaders discovered there was no diplomatic solution, and Aideed kept mounting attacks. The US tried to grab him unsuccessfully on October 3 in Mogadishu but snagged more than two dozen of his aides. When trying to extract them, a Blackhawk helicopter was shot down. A battle made famous by the book and movie of the same name – *Black Hawk Down* – ensued. It killed eighteen Americans and wounded or injured seventy-three.[26]

"The administration went into freefall," and its situation worsened two days later when Secretary of State Warren Christopher and Defense Secretary Les Aspin came to Capitol Hill and instead of providing a plan of action requested guidance. Clinton reasserted control over foreign affairs. He abandoned the aim of capturing Aideed, resisted pressure to immediately withdraw, and maintained Congressional support for involvement. He ordered the evacuation of Somalia by March 31, 1994 but reinforced those already deployed by dispatching another 1,700 US troops. The decision to send more forces was easy, Lake said; doing otherwise "would have made it open season on Americans around the world. The potential message: Kill and humiliate our people and the United States will immediately retreat."[27]

In a September 27, 1993 UN speech Clinton said: "Together we must prepare U.N. peacekeeping for the 21st century. We need to begin by bringing the rigors of military and political analysis to every U.N. peace mission." This could be done by asking harder questions:

> Is there a real threat to international peace? Does the proposed mission have clear objectives? Can an end point be identified for those who will be asked

to participate? How much will the mission cost? From now on, the United Nations should address these and other hard questions for every proposed mission before we vote and before the mission begins.[28]

This would have been a solid template for the UN and the administration.

Clinton's speech revealed that neither he nor his administration realized they had converted a peacekeeping mission into a war. They also didn't understand the effects of adopting as political aims the creation of a new government in Somalia and the arrest of Aideed. Changing the purposes changed the mission. This meant the strategy should be reassessed and adjusted, and that the force requirements were almost certainly different. Albright said later, "the truth was we had not provided the means to achieve the goals we had set, and some brave Americans died."[29] Failing to understand they had taken America to war helped produce tragedy.

The Somalia War had follow-on effects partially resulting from "America's seeming hypersensitivity to casualties." A picture emerged of an America easily coerced by losses. Aideed said the Somalis knew they could drive out the Americans simply by killing some of them and letting public opinion force them to leave. This was among the events that convinced the Saudi-born Osama Bin Laden the US was weak.[30]

HAITI

In 1991, Raul Cedras' military coup overthrew Haiti's first democratically elected leader, Jean-Bertrand Aristide. Violent repression followed, as did UN sanctions that multiplied the population's desperation. Fleeing refugees and a humanitarian crisis ensued. In summer 1993, the UN made an agreement for Aristide to return by October 3, 1993. It included a 1,200-strong peacekeeping force to which the US would contribute. Defense Secretary Aspin and CIA Director James Woolsey feared for the security of these lightly armed units and opposed their deployment. Lake, Christopher, and Albright believed US credibility necessitated their dispatch. Bending to political pressure, Clinton elected to send troops to restore Haiti's democratic government. The navy's *Harlan County* reached Port-au-Prince on October 11, 1993. Greeting it was a raging crowd of Cedras supporters screaming "Somalia! Somalia!" Unable to safely dock and unload, the ship sat offshore for a few days until Clinton ordered it home. This was little more than a week after the Mogadishu battle and the administration feared more violence. Lake called the operation "a total fuckup." Its failure put the lie to US hegemony (and primacy) as America "did not even hold dominion in its own hemisphere."[31]

REASSESSMENT

The administration realized by June 1993 – before the twin debacles of Somalia and Haiti – that there was no coordination of its foreign and domestic strategies. Facing increased criticism he had no hand on foreign affairs, Clinton told his subordinates to craft a new strategy he could unveil in his September 1993 UN General Assembly speech. Key administration officials would give supporting talks. Together, these would inform the public and political elite, and focus the bureaucracy.[32]

National Security Advisor Lake ran among his team a Kennan Sweepstakes to find a concept with the textual simplicity of containment. One of his speech writers won with "democratic enlargement." This meant increasing the number of market-based democracies. America wouldn't be stopping a rival but growing its base of friends. Lake delivered the key speech on September 21, 1993. He addressed concepts from Fukuyama and Samuel Huntington's "Clash of Civilizations," insisting "the idea of freedom has universal appeal. Thus, we have arrived at neither the end of history nor a clash of civilizations, but a moment of immense democratic and entrepreneurial opportunity. We must not waste it." Lake described the situation confronting Washington and saw "America's core concepts – democracy and market economics" as "more broadly accepted than ever." The threats he saw were terrorism and economic problems but nothing creating the existential dread of the Soviet Union. To Lake, "democratic enlargement" provided the solution.[33]

THE POLITICAL AIMS AND THE GRAND STRATEGY

The administration's slowness developing a grand strategy resembled previous administrations. The supporting statements and documents suffer the standard confusion between political aims and strategy and the conceptual error of seeking economic growth as an end. Lake gave expanding democracy and the free market as political aims. These aligned with democratic peace theory, which saw democracies as less likely to fight one another. Spreading democracy, opening the world's economies, replacing command economies with free ones, would increase American prosperity and security. Clinton described the spread of democracy as a domino theory in reverse, and liked that democratic enlargement was intertwined with economic rebirth while seeking to ensure the US held its position as the globe's exporter. The best description of the political aims, grand strategy, and reasons for this approach appeared in Clinton's January 1994 State of the Union Address: "Ultimately, the best strategy to ensure our security and to build a durable peace is to support the advance of democracy elsewhere. Democracies don't attack each other, they make better trading partners and partners in diplomacy."[34]

Lake said (italics in the original) containment's successor "*must be a strategy of enlargement – enlargement of the world's free community of market democracies.*" For this to succeed, "a strategy of enlargement must provide distinctions and set priorities. It must combine our broad goals of fostering democracy and markets with our more traditional geostrategic interests. And it must suggest how best to expend our large but nonetheless limited national security resources: financial, diplomatic and military."[35]

To Lake, democratic enlargement had four planks. The first was strengthening democratic states, including the US, because they provided the core for democratic expansion. Second was aiding new democracies and helping other states make the transition, particularly in vital areas, most critically Russia, but also Central and Eastern Europe, Asia, Africa, and Latin America, while the administration tried to stop democratic reversal in Haiti, Guatemala, and Nigeria. Third, the US had to thwart and help change Backlash States. These authoritarian nations such as Iraq and Iran were hostile to democracy and free markets, brutalized their citizens, and sought WMD and dangerous missile technology. The US wouldn't impose democracy but steer them in this direction. This was particularly important for relations with China. Finally, "we need to pursue our humanitarian agenda not only by providing aid, but also by working to help democracy and market economics take root in regions of greatest humanitarian concern." This would build domestic support for enlargement while helping "stimulate democratic and market development in many areas of the world." Lake insisted America must remain engaged but missed making the case that engagement was necessary to implement other elements of strategy. When the US did act, it would do so in its interests, multilaterally, if possible, unilaterally if necessary.[36]

Lake referenced Wilson in his rollout speech and presented a "pragmatic Neo-Wilsonian" approach. He tried to get Christopher and Albright on the same page, but they had no interest in pushing a single concept to replace containment. To Christopher, the aim was "to ensure the security of our nation and ensure its economic prosperity as well – and to promote democratic values." He preferred engagement and branded "democratic enlargement" "a trade policy masquerading as a foreign policy." He believed the administration needed a new and firm approach to foreign affairs but advised Clinton to not seek a single term for describing it, insisting the situation was too diverse for this. Albright believed Lake's replacement quest useless and publicly touted her Assertive Multilateralism two days after Lake's speech. This proved short-lived. The administration was already retreating from multilateral action as it came to see the UN as a place destroying collective action that couldn't be counted upon to help keep order unless America was willing to act unilaterally. A bigger disconnect existed between Clinton and his national security advisor. Lake said Clinton "never actually got into it very much, which disappointed me." Clinton had no love for the "speech or the theme. And I would occasionally have to remind him or his speech writers that we needed to include democracy as a strategic goal."[37]

Despite the space between Clinton and his national security team, and between its branches, democratic enlargement underpinned the administration's first *National Security Strategy* (July 1994), but it had become engagement and enlargement, engagement meaning maintaining global involvement. Lake disliked the addition and branded "engagement" "rather wimpy, because of course we were going to be engaged." He thought it was included "just to make everyone happy." Above Clinton's signature appeared this political aim: "Protecting our nation's security – our people, our territory and our way of life." The administration saw democracy and free trade as intertwined and democratic states as more likely to cooperate and less likely to threaten American interests. The administration's "central goals" (mixing ends and strategy) were "To credibly sustain our security with military forces that are ready to fight…. To bolster America's economic revitalization" and "To promote democracy abroad." The administration sought security at home and democracy abroad via democratization efforts. The "three central components of" the "strategy of engagement and enlargement" were "efforts to enhance … security by maintaining a strong defense … and promoting cooperative security," opening "foreign markets" to stimulate "global economic growth," and "promotion of democracy abroad." The 1995 and 1996 *NSS*s differ little beyond listing administration accomplishments.[38]

DIPLOMATIC STRATEGY

The administration sought a democratic Western Hemisphere and promoted and defended democratic governments. Democracy promotion was institutionalized under the State Department's undersecretary for democracy and global affairs. There was an economic element: democratic nations were seen as healthy markets for US goods and – in the first such mention I've discovered – services, though American banks had long worked abroad. The administration sought free-trade agreements in the region and the protection and promotion of human rights, the defense of which was a prerequisite for economic aid.[39]

RWANDA

Beginning in April 1994, Rwanda's Hutu killed at least 800,000 Tutsi in 100 days. The administration held no meetings on this. The State Department was reluctant to brand the genocide "genocide" because international law would obligate the US to act. Bosnia and memories of Somalia held administration attention. Clinton later apologized for his inaction. At the time there was little criticism for standing aside. Few Americans wanted the US involved.[40]

CHINA

Clinton criticized Bush for being weak on dictatorships like China and normalizing relations with Beijing too soon after the Tiananmen Square massacre. His administration hoped to integrate China into the world market by dropping trade barriers and tried different approaches to link most-favored-nation approval to human rights reform. These failed. Clinton didn't raise China's humanitarian abuses with Beijing and said the "impulses of society and the nature of economic change," combined "with the availability of information from the outside world, to increase the sphere of liberty over time," were enough. China couldn't "hold back that."[41]

Republicans charged Clinton was ignoring Beijing's bad behavior and insisted "China was an adversary" not – as the administration claimed – "a strategic partner." One proof offered was China's effort "to influence the 1996 election by donating money to Democrats." But Republican opposition was shallow, and Clinton was given half the needed votes for granting China Permanent Normal Trade Relations in May 2000. This put Beijing on the road to World Trade Organization (WTO) membership, which it received on December 11, 2001. The Clinton team wanted to discover "whether true economic growth will create a larger middle class in China," and whether this would drive democratic reforms because the educated want a say in government.[42]

The administration stood against Chinese efforts to intimidate and threaten Taiwan and deployed a pair of aircraft carrier task forces in March 1996 to counter Chinese threats and missile tests. In 1997, Assistant National Security Advisor Berger delivered a speech defending the administration's approach to China in which he insisted China had abandoned "its dying ideology" and was embracing "the first stirrings of change."[43]

NORTH KOREA

In June 1994, North Korea announced it was removing reactor fuel rods to extract plutonium to make nuclear weapons. This provoked a crisis. Clinton worried that isolating a nuclear-armed North Korea would make it more dangerous. It could attack South Korea and sell the technology. The administration considered economic sanctions, but North Korea threatened war. By mid June 1994 the administration was preparing to move more military forces into the region and examining a preemptive strike on North Korea's nuclear plant. Jimmy Carter's visit to Pyongyang in the guise of a private citizen defused the crisis. Months of negotiations produced the Agreed Framework. North Korea promised to freeze nuclear weapons development, the US gave energy support, and technological and economic assistance, and eased sanctions. North Korea tested its first nuclear weapon on October 9, 2006.[44]

RUSSIA, EUROPE, AND NATO EXPANSION

Clinton sought a democratic, free-market Russia as a partner. But the administration feared Yeltsin's government was failing, made support contingent on reforms, provided $4.3 billion in financial assistance (Bush had acted similarly), and loosened export controls. The 1996 Russian elections gave the administration hope, but it failed to understand "trade compacts did not necessarily alter ... national characters or calculations of ... geostrategic interests." Western leaders also didn't comprehend the effects of the social changes engulfing Russia. Yeltsin concentrated on creating economic wealth and failed to build "the open society and democratic accountability that in the West went hand in hand with it." The money America poured in helped fuel "gangster capitalism." Abuse by Russian oligarchs, disorder, and corruption – all contributed to Vladimir Putin's 2000 election.[45] Fix the political problems first.

The administration used NATO expansion to solidify democratic growth and achieve further democratization in Europe, increase European unity and integration, and push economic reform. Some urged quick expansion before a strong Russia reemerged. The White House chose a slower approach where Russia was encouraged to work with NATO on security. Defense Secretary Aspin formally proposed NATO expansion at an October 21, 1993 NATO meeting. Christopher broached expansion and pushed NATO's Partnership for Peace. This was open to all former Warsaw Pact states and intended to assuage Russian fears. Yeltsin applauded it and discussed ways Eastern European states could work with NATO without injuring Russia and "a plan of action for Russia to join NATO." Clinton subsequently told Yeltsin NATO would expand, but this wouldn't be rushed, and Russia would be neither suddenly surprised nor excluded. But there was never any intention of allowing Russia to join.[46]

Moscow was surprised to learn in December 1994 of an expansion plan. An angry Yeltsin publicly warned of descent of a "cold peace." Clinton calmed tensions with reassurances Russia would be part of the Organization for Security and Cooperation in Europe (OSCE) and "the new NATO." But by May 1995 Yeltsin was warning Clinton that expansion meant humiliation for Russia. In an April 1996 meeting with Yeltsin Clinton said: "My objectives are first, an integrated, undivided Europe; and second, a cooperative equal partnership with a democratic, economically successful Russia which is influential in the world."[47]

Leaders of former Warsaw Pact nations pushed Clinton for NATO expansion. Poland, the Czech Republic, and Hungary joined in 1999. Critics worried expansion would "provoke resistance from a resurgent Russia," resulting in America carrying the weight of defending "militarily weak states near or adjacent to the Russian border." Kennan called it "the most fateful error of American policy in the entire post–Cold War era," "a badly conceived strategy," and worried "NATO enlargement would have an adverse effect on Russian democracy and lead to another Cold War due to Russian militarism."[48] The counterargument is that this ignores Russian agency. Moscow makes its own decisions.

HAITI – AGAIN

In late July 1994, with administration prodding, the UN Security Council unanimously passed a resolution authorizing the use of force to restore Aristide to power in Haiti. Clinton, though, remained reluctant to act, fed by polls showing most Americans against intervention. The American Left pressured Clinton to move on Haiti, the Right opposed intervention. The arguments of aides that this was about restoring democracy won out. But then Jimmy Carter proposed going to Haiti accompanied by Colin Powell and Senator Sam Nunn. Clinton reluctantly agreed while preparations for landing troops proceeded. Haiti's junta bent, upon learning an invasion was coming. Clinton officials branded Carter's "freelancing" "sanctimonious" but pocketed the gain. US troops landed unopposed in Haiti on September 19, 1994, in the "immaculate invasion." Twenty-eight other nations sent forces. Democracy was reestablished and Aristide back in power on October 17.[49]

THE BOSNIAN WAR

Muslim Bosnia-Herzegovina declared independence from Yugoslavia in 1992. Serbia invaded, occupied 70 percent of the country, and forced 750,000 Bosnians from their homes amidst mass murder and mass rape. During the Bush administration, NATO and the UN inserted a small force to protect Bosnian refugees that accomplished nothing. Clinton agreed to participation in supply flights and NATO's no-fly zone. Clinton and JCS chair Powell both felt America's allies should deal with their respective regional problems. Powell opposed airstrikes and said intervention required 300,000 troops. This ensured Clinton balked. Powell continually argued against dispatching troops before setting political aims. He wrote that in a National Security team meeting shortly after Clinton took office:

> The debate exploded at one session when Madeleine Albright, our ambassador to the UN, asked me in frustration, 'What's the point of having this superb military that you're always talking about if we can't use it?' I thought I would have an aneurysm.... I patiently explained that we had used our armed forces more than two dozen times in the preceding three years for war, peacekeeping, disaster relief, and humanitarian assistance. But in every one of those cases we had a clear goal and had matched our military commitment to the goal. As a result, we had been successful in every case. I told Ambassador Albright ... my advice would always be that the tough political goals had to be set first.[50]

Clinton faced increasing domestic and foreign criticism as the Balkan tragedy deepened. Strategy became Lift and Strike: lift the arms embargo on Bosnia and threaten Serbia with NATO airstrikes. The Europeans wanted leadership; this produced an image of weakness. They also disliked raising the arms embargo, fearing this would endanger their peacekeepers. The administration let the matter go and blamed the Europeans. The Somalia–Haiti twin debacles paralyzed Clinton when it came to acting abroad. Albright, for example, was told to kill a UN effort to send 5,500 troops to Rwanda. Clinton said America should lead but didn't want to act unilaterally, a view also expressed by Republican Senator Bob Dole. The administration used statements by European leaders that Balkan problems were a European affair to remain uninvolved. Albright said of their two-year

Bosnian muddle: "our goal was a negotiated solution, but we never applied the credible threat of force necessary to achieve it. Instead we employed a combination of half-measures and bluster that didn't work."[51]

By summer 1995, 300,000 people had died in Bosnia and there were over 1 million refugees. The international community had enacted sixty UN resolutions, negotiated a temporary ceasefire, and imposed economic sanctions, and NATO launched some airstrikes against the Serbs. The fighting continued. The ongoing crisis began injuring US–Europe relations and American credibility. The possible withdrawal of French and British peacekeepers (which would necessitate US help), combined with the murder at Srebrenica of 6,000 Muslim men and boys and Lake warning Clinton's reelection was endangered, catalyzed Clinton to act.[52]

The administration took charge and began telling the Europeans what to do. Many officials now saw the UN as a tool states used to do nothing. NATO became the chosen instrument and Clinton secured a NATO-backed bombing threat against Serbia if it continued attacks. When the Serbs shelled a market in Bosnia's capital Sarajevo on August 30, 1995, NATO launched Operation DELIBERATE FORCE. The seventeen-day air war drove Serb forces from their sieges of Bosnian cities. America simultaneously mounted a diplomatic effort to unify Bosnia. The bombing was effective, but more important was a Croatian military offensive (one made possible by US contractors) that threw the Serbs out of Croatia and parts of Bosnia.[53]

The Serbs decided to negotiate. A ceasefire began on October 5. The various representatives met in Dayton, Ohio, in early November. By November 21, Assistant Secretary of State Richard Holbrooke wrangled a settlement ending Serbia's wars with Croatia and Bosnia and securing an independent Bosnia. The peace would be enforced by NATO troops, including 17,000 Americans, something the administration accepted before going to war. Clinton said America had a responsibility to help secure the peace. "If we're not there," he said. "NATO will not be there" – a hard truth – "And America's commitment to leadership will be questioned if we refuse to participate in implementing a peace agreement we brokered." But the administration feared charges of mission creep like those arising from its Somali debacle. This produced narrow mission guidelines and a one-year withdrawal date even though most realized this was insufficient. The administration worried about the election-year effects of an open-ended commitment and wanted, in Berger's words, to "show success." But the self-imposed constraint complicated implementation. Clinton shifted to staying until the job was done.[54]

Holbrooke branded the approach to Bosnia "the greatest collective failure of the West since the 1930s" and railed against "a decision-making apparatus run by people incapable of making decisions."[55] The American involvement in Bosnia exposed a failure of US grand strategy: America had allowed its European allies to become dependent upon US leadership to act.

THE EFFECTS THUS FAR

Clinton mentioned after the Haiti fiasco that he believed his administration was missing a chance to define the post–Cold War world. The administration suffered intense criticism of its conduct of foreign affairs, often from its own party. Carter's Korea and Haiti successes made Clinton look weak and fed an image of a shaky and incompetent president. An influential critique came from former campaign advisor Michael Mandelbaum. His 1996 article "Foreign Policy as Social Work" stressed the failures in Somalia, Haiti, and Bosnia. The administration had changed the aim in Somalia from providing relief to, in Albright's words, "the restoration of a nation." In Bosnia and Haiti, the administration made things worse, then resorted to force, but only to "bolster the administration's political standing, which was suffering from the failure to resolve these problems." In Haiti, Clinton committed to restoring a democratic government, necessitating a long-term commitment it was unwilling to give. Mandelbaum said these interventions in peripheral areas weren't done in American interests but to export American values. The administration also didn't seek Congressional approval because it wouldn't get it. To many, Mandelbaum confirmed fears of Democratic Party weakness and ineptitude in military and diplomatic affairs.[56]

Clinton's key advisors changed in his second term (1997–2001). Albright became secretary of state. She rarely shied from advising the use of force against Saddam or Serbia's Slobodan Milošević. She once wrote "Freedom is America's purpose." Lake was replaced by Berger, who was later convicted of stealing administration documents from the National Archives. Clinton had gained some confidence in foreign affairs and told Albright he wanted a more "activist" approach. The term "indispensable nation" is usually associated with Albright, but Clinton (thanks to advisor Sidney Blumenthal) used the term extensively during his 1996 campaign and in his second inaugural address. It conveyed the reality that few international problems were resolved without the United States. Both Clinton and Albright used it to rally Americans to international action that might require sacrifice, and to push Clinton's free-trade agenda.[57]

PART III: THE POST-COLD WAR WORLD

THE NEW NATIONAL SECURITY STRATEGIES

May 1997 saw the arrival of *A National Security Strategy for a New Century*. It echoed its predecessors in many ways, including in its stated "core objectives" of security, economic strengthening, and promoting "democracy abroad." It stressed the importance of protecting US sovereignty, something largely absent since Hoover's administration. Engagement remained a strategy and was accompanied by democracy promotion, NATO expansion, and strengthening Asian alliances to achieve the aims above and "an undivided, democratic and peaceful Europe," while fostering Asian stability and creating US economic opportunity, which free trade assisted.[58]

The 1998 and 1999 national security strategies differ little from 1997's. *A National Security Strategy for a Global Age* (2000) had substantive changes, including the disappearance of sovereignty as an aim. The key aims remained security, increased US economic strength, and democracy abroad. Engagement provided the guts, supported – most importantly – by alliances, free trade, democracy promotion, and diplomacy. The concept of globalization (which in its simplest definition means growing international integration and interdependence) made it into the final *NSS* and had become an underpinning of the administration's foreign relations.[59]

MILITARY STRATEGY

The US spent nearly as much on defense as the rest of the world combined. The administration wanted to "remain the world's preeminent military power and its chief advocate for liberalizing the global economy." The 1993 "Bottom Up Review" shrank forces (the public expected a "peace dividend" after the Cold War). The administration worked to counter nuclear proliferation and pursued denuclearization of Belarus, Ukraine, and Kazakhstan, and secured nuclear material in parts of the former Soviet Union. The administration initially reduced emphasis on developing missile defense but became enthusiastic by the end.[60]

In January 1994, Clinton asked Congress to stop cutting the defense budget. The 1994 *National Security Strategy* said the US would use military force when its vital interests were threatened, even unilaterally. The US would seek the help of allies and consider:

> What types of US military capabilities should be brought to bear, and is the use of military force carefully matched to our political objectives? Do we have reasonable assurance of support from the American people and their elected

representatives? Do we have timelines and milestones that will reveal the extent of success or failure, and, in either case, do we have an exit strategy?[61]

This guidance doesn't seem to have reached decision-makers.

May 1997's *Quadrennial Defense Review* (*QDR*) built upon the 1997 *NSS*. It was mandated by legislation beginning in 1997 and was an assessment combined with a statement of US military strategy. The *QDR* stated America had traditionally sought "to maintain the sovereignty, political freedom, and independence of the United States." These aims could be achieved best in a stable, peaceful, international environment conducive to free trade with growing economies and respect for human rights and international norms. The US would lead in the world, working with (and strengthening) allies and nations of like values "and influencing those that can affect US national well-being." America would implement a strategy of engagement to enable preservation of "peace and stability in regions where the US has vital or important interests" while expanding "the community of free market democracies." The section on US interests includes "preventing the emergence of a hostile regional coalition or hegemon" but doesn't discuss trying to do so.[62]

At the time of the *QDR*, the US had 1.45 million people in its active forces with a budget of $250 billion. The *QDR* didn't anticipate a major "peer competitor" before 2015, but afterward Russia and China might emerge as such. Force would be used only in American interests and after determining "whether the associated costs and risks are commensurate with the US interests at stake." This "should also depend upon our ability to identify a clear mission, the desired end state of the situation, and the exit strategy for forces committed." (Securing victory – the political aim – is preferred over "exit strategy," which can imply defeat.) The basic US military strategy remained deterrence, which required maintaining US commitments, making it clear America would respond, and maintaining broadly capable forces, including nuclear ones. The US would maintain the capability to fight and win two "major theater wars nearly simultaneously" and exploit the Revolution in Military Affairs (RMA), which essentially meant technology. The RMA became yet another concept hypnotizing the security community – until the next war.[63]

By 1995, the military was training for Military Operations Other Than War (MOOTW), a short-lived concept that at least understood peace and war differed. In 1997, the US tried to capture some experience from its military deployments, now termed "complex contingency operations," which meant peacekeeping and humanitarian actions. It also tried to develop an interagency process for dealing with these and created a planning template that insisted upon understanding the political aim and having a plan to get out.[64]

TERRORISM AND AL QAEDA

The administration faced the growing problem of armed extremist organizations using terrorism. On February 26, 1993, a truck bomb exploded beneath the World Trade Center. The response was largely judicial. Later, a group named Al Qaeda was linked to the attack. The bomber was a nephew of Khalid Sheik Mohammad, who planned the 9/11 attacks. In June 1995, the administration completed a counterterrorism strategy. Washington sought to prevent attacks on its citizens and facilities through deterrence but reserved the right to unilateral and preemptive action. By 1996, it was trying to break groups using terrorism via rendition, having foreign nations send suspects to third countries without going through the legal system. Iran was named the primary state using terror.[65]

In May 1996, Osama Bin Laden returned to the Taliban-ruled part of Afghanistan from Sudan and established a relationship with Pakistan's Inter-Services Intelligence agency (ISI). Afghanistan soon hosted a system of training camps (partially Pakistani staffed) to supply Islamist foot soldiers in the fight against Ahmad Shad Masood's anti-Taliban Afghan United Front and fill Al Qaeda's ranks. By 1998, they were training jihadis from all over the world. The US outsourced Afghanistan to Pakistan and disengaged. Pakistan sought a government it controlled in Kabul, something successive US administrations didn't grasp. In August 1996, Bin Laden declared war on the United States. Al Qaeda cells attacked American embassies in Nairobi, Kenya, and Dar es Salaam, Tanzania. Clinton struck Al Qaeda's Khost, Afghanistan, training camp on August 20. The ISI relayed advance warning.[66]

Clinton secured two Security Council Resolutions sanctioning the Taliban that demanded Bin Laden's handover and ending support for international terrorism, and embargoed arms. Efforts to secure Pakistan's help convincing the Taliban to surrender Bin Laden foundered. Al Qaeda was placed on the State Department's list of terrorist organizations in October 1997. A three-year CIA effort from 1998 to 2001 to kill or capture Bin Laden followed, one largely conducted from Pakistan. This necessitated ISI support, foreordaining failure. Clinton's fear of US losses and "collateral damage" (a euphemism for civilian casualties) hindered efforts; he refused to take risks.[67]

THE MIDDLE EAST

The administration sought to increase American security and convince rogue regimes such as Iran and Iraq to change their ways. The Arab–Israeli peace process was part of an integrated regional approach to increase Iraqi and Iranian isolation. In September 1993, the administration secured the Oslo Accord, which transferred the Gaza Strip and the West Bank to Palestinian control, and in 1994 formalized an Israel–Jordan deal. Clinton fought for a new Camp David Accord. It died, Clinton said, on Yasser Arafat's intransigence.[68]

Between 1992 and 1998, the administration implemented a strategy of Dual Containment toward Iran and Iraq. It hoped to achieve moderation of Iran's behavior and a *rapprochement*. For Iraq, the administration wanted Saddam in "full compliance with all UN Resolutions." Lake said Dual Containment was a rejection of past efforts to build up either Iraq or Iran to counter the other. Instead, by working with US allies in the region, the US would try "to maintain a favorable balance without depending upon either." The administration couldn't get other nations onboard. China and Russia sold Iran nuclear reactors and arms. Washington's allies made business deals and extended loans. Saddam circumvented sanctions via smuggling and manipulating the Oil for Food program. The sanctions began building sympathy for Iraq, and critics painted the criminal as the victim, an image furthered by Iraqi propaganda.[69]

Iran's nefarious activities included international terrorism, WMD and missile development, trying to derail the Arab–Israeli peace talks (this hardly needed assistance), and efforts to destabilize other Middle East states. Lake and others tried to downplay the religious elements of Iran's regime, and said they had no objections to its Islamic government and didn't seek its overthrow. They weren't naïve regarding Iranian support for terrorism and were dead set against it developing nuclear weapons. The administration pressured friends, rivals, and enemies on trading with Iran as income from this supported terrorism. They believed they had about five years before Iran became what Iraq had been in the late 1980s.[70]

In 1994, under pressure from Congressional Republicans, Clinton authorized propaganda against Tehran. Two years later, the CIA launched covert operations to "change the nature of the Government." The administration abandoned Scowcroft's efforts to improve relations and in August 1996 ratcheted up pressure via sanctions, rejecting as "wrongheaded" a British–French belief in trade changing Tehran's behavior. The administration determined Iran, with Hezbollah's help, was responsible for the June 25,

1996 truck bombing of the Khobar Towers housing US air force personnel in Saudi Arabia. It began planning military retaliation, but the May 1997 election of Mohammad Khatami birthed optimism and Washington was prepared to move to engagement. The Iranians refused to meet halfway.[71]

When running for president, Clinton opened the door to normalizing relations with Saddam, but this appeared in the *New York Times* before his inauguration and he backed away within twenty-four hours, "a retreat that did little to inspire confidence in the incoming administration or its capacity to stand by stated principles or policies." Clinton took a path similar to his predecessor to avoid accusations of weakness and intended Dual Containment to help prevent Saddam from rebuilding the capacity to harm his neighbors. In 1996, Clinton intensified Bush-inherited support for internal actors trying to overthrow Saddam.[72]

The no-fly zones remained, and Clinton fought several punitive wars against Iraq. In June 1993, Clinton struck the secret police headquarters in Baghdad because of Saddam's plot to assassinate former President Bush during his April 1993 Kuwait visit. Baghdad was hit by cruise missiles twice in September 1996 after Saddam sent troops into the Kurdish provinces. Additionally, Operation VIGILANT WARRIOR, from October to December 1994, countered an Iraqi military build-up on Kuwait's border by deploying 50,000 troops and other forces to deter Saddam.[73]

As Iraq became more troublesome, the administration adopted regime change and establishing a democracy as political aims. The Republican Congress passed the Iraq Liberation Act in October 1998. Clinton had little interest in removing Saddam, but vetoing the legislation wasn't worth the political capital when he faced impeachment. The hope was to get rid of Saddam through internal revolt and the new law funded anti-Saddam groups. Containment Plus became the new strategy. Washington tightened the screws via tougher sanctions and no-fly zone enforcement.[74]

The sanctions pummeled Iraq's currency and economy, but instead of dividing the Security Council by exploiting the split over this, Saddam expelled UN weapons inspectors. Clinton responded with Operation DESERT FOX, another punitive war entailing a four-day air campaign lasting December 16–19, 1998. The US hit believed WMD-related targets in "the first major American military operation conducted against Iraq on the basis of erroneous intelligence." Iraq's WMD programs were secretly shuttered in late 1998. Unlike previous attacks, this was intended to shake Saddam's grip on power. The no-fly zones continued, and the US spent perhaps $1 billion annually containing Saddam. The strategy of trying to disarm Iraq via inspectors ended. This latest Iraq crisis arose when Congress was voting to impeach Clinton over perjuring himself for comments on his relationship with an intern 27 years his junior. Clinton provided ammunition to a Congress already disposed against him.[75]

In the wake of the strikes, and after reports the bombing wounded Saddam's grip, CENTCOM commander General Anthony Zinni conducted a wargame (DESERT CROSSING) that assumed Saddam fell and CENTCOM had to clean up. CENTCOM worked two scenarios. The first assumed new Iraqis rising to the top, the second Washington establishing the political structures and holding elections, which meant greater US costs and commitments. The participants concluded that "A change in regime does not guarantee stability," and that "Neighboring regimes will also be concerned with all catalyzing effect on their own pro-democracy movements. In a sense, a western-style democracy may not engender long-term stability without considerable stabilization, preparation, and long-term sustainment." The George W. Bush administration never studied DESERT CROSSING.[76]

THE KOSOVO WAR, 1999

Clinton later took more interest in foreign affairs and played a direct role in overseeing the March to May 1999 Kosovo War. He sought neither Congressional nor UN backing and fought it "in the face of an explicit congressional refusal to authorize it," though the Senate approved an air campaign. He feared Republican Congressional opposition and wanted to guard presidential prerogatives. The certainty of a Russian or Chinese veto made seeking UN approval pointless, while proceeding demonstrated the UN didn't determine NATO or US actions.[77]

The war occurred in response to Serbia's efforts since 1998 to ethnically cleanse Kosovo, a part of the former Yugoslavia that Belgrade controlled, of Muslim Kosovars. Resisting was the Kosovo Liberation Army, which sought an independent, Muslim-ruled state. Bush's team told Milošević it would take military action if Serbia attacked, a warning Clinton backed. NATO and the US drove both to negotiate in February 1999, but Serbia refused NATO peacekeepers, insisting this violated its sovereignty. The Serbs concentrated for an attack and Clinton dispatched Holbrooke with an ultimatum. Milošević assumed any response would be short, like DESERT FOX, and refused to bend.[78]

Clinton and his advisors "believed they were defending the principle that a country's government had to be held responsible for how it treated its own citizens." Clinton advisor Talbott argued that a government that "systematically and massively abuses its own citizens ... is subject to either being put out of business or having its authority suspended in that area of the country where it is running amok." From this arose "responsibility to protect." Those worried about a Kosovo "quagmire" or against using the military for "humanitarian" missions were attacked as "neo-isolationists." NATO launched its bombing campaign on March 24, 1999. Oddly, "it was emphatically stated, [this] was not a war, and none of the NATO leaders had any intention of waging one." Nonsensical thinking appeared elsewhere. US leaders, particularly at State, had pushed bombing as "an element of coercive diplomacy."[79] "Coercive diplomacy" is a ridiculous term. It implies state political violence against another state. This is war, not diplomacy, and another example of confusion about the differences. Unsurprisingly, the war didn't go as NATO hoped.

Clinton declared on March 22, 1999: "Our objective in Kosovo remains clear: to stop the killing and achieve a durable peace that restores Kosovars to self-government." Two days later, he argued action was imperative to halt ethnic cleansing and violence and failing to do so could produce a larger war. He also said: "If NATO is invited to do so, our troops should take part in that mission to keep the peace. But I do not intend to put our troops in Kosovo to fight a war." NATO intended, Clinton said, "to restore the peace," and "demonstrate the seriousness of NATO's purpose" to Serbia, "deter an even bloodier offensive against innocent civilians in Kosovo and, if necessary, to seriously damage the Serbian military's capacity to harm the people of Kosovo." The use of ground forces wasn't considered as all feared the domestic public-opinion effects. NATO believed two weeks of bombing alone would cause Milošević to break as he had in 1995. None understood the difference between Serbia seizing territory in another province of former Yugoslavia and defending a part of Serbia they considered among the most historically important. The value of the object was higher.[80]

The air offensive struck targets in Serbia and its Kosovo forces. Milošević used it as an excuse to mount a planned campaign of ethnic cleansing, killing about 10,000 people and displacing over 1.3 million. NATO chief General Wesley Clark found it difficult to fight the war because he had to discuss every action with the Pentagon and eighteen NATO allies. The administration's self-imposed constraints – no ground troops, and no air attacks from less than 15,000 feet – added to the tactical, operational, strategic, and political difficulties, helped ensure the war continued longer than necessary, and helped produce the tragedy Clinton had hoped to avoid. As the war dragged on with no end in view, some observers feared NATO's defeat.[81]

Worried and under criticism that it had misjudged the situation, the administration reassessed. Albright wrote: "We agreed among ourselves that Kosovo would have to become an international protectorate after the war, with Yugoslav sovereignty retained in name only." The intensified Serb violence in an effort to expel the entire population helped convince Washington and NATO the aim should be autonomy for Kosovo. NATO formalized the change on April 12, 1999 and reaffirmed it on April 23. The US and NATO aim of an independent Kosovo as a UN protectorate was obscured to keep all the powers onboard and win Russian and Serbian agreement. It would be implemented by a peacekeeping force working from an NSC plan developed seven months before in a rare example of American postwar planning.[82]

The war began turning in NATO's favor in May. Better weather increased bombing's effectiveness, NATO committed more forces, and the Kosovo Liberation Army increased attacks. By June, Serbia was suffering growing casualties and equipment losses, and its electrical and water infrastructure was being torn apart. Only when NATO began preparing to insert troops, and Russia had been convinced to help negotiate, did Milošević bend. The bombing lasted seventy-eight days.[83]

The administration resisted attempts to create from this any "doctrine" for conducting foreign affairs. Berger refused for a reason that also argues against the adoption of a blanket grand strategy: "They usually emerge from a particular set of circumstances and you get into trouble when you try to apply them to others."[84]

CONCLUSION

World opinion shifted against America because of its use of force against Iraq and Serbia. European leaders attacked America for failing to lead on Bosnia. Then pilloried Clinton for leading on Kosovo.[85] Clinton faced the Catch-22 of post–Cold War US leaders: American action is criticized; American inaction is criticized. American power is disliked while being misunderstood, especially by Europeans (until they are in trouble; then they love it). They fear America will use its power as Europeans traditionally used theirs – conquest, genocide, colonization, Third World exploitation – and often equate America's use of power with that of totalitarian states. But they ignore or don't understand the history of America's use of power, especially after the Second World War, and don't acknowledge the differences in purpose.

The administration's grand strategy pleased few. A rough ride from his Republican political opposition was expected, but many of Clinton's fiercest critics lived in his camp. Some liberals who criticized America for being too militaristic denounced Clinton for waiting to go to war with Serbia over Bosnia. When he did, Carter accused him of racism for not intervening in certain African nations. Leslie Gelb, Carter administration veteran and Council on Foreign Relations president, said the administration "confused trade policy with foreign policy," and that "A foreign economic policy is not a foreign policy and it is not a national security strategy."[86]

Democratic enlargement encompassed core neo-liberal and neo-Wilsonian ideas. It assumed the US could spread democracy and free trade, and that this would create a more peaceful, secure world, particularly for the US and its allies. A number of Asian nations branded enlargement "a form of imperialism" and touted "Asian values." Both Asian and European states resisted removing their trade protections, leaving free-trade America vulnerable. Overall, on expanding democracy abroad, one analyst wrote "that the best the policy [strategy] achieved was to maintain the equilibrium."[87]

Lake said, "there's a tendency for all of us, when we're going back and analyzing things, to impute more order to processes than in fact there is and to give more weight to strategy papers than they deserve." For much of his eight years, particularly in his first term, Clinton largely left foreign affairs and grand strategy creation to the administration's national security and diplomatic wings. He did what he wanted. They did what they wanted. Until disaster struck. When Clinton become involved, he was often too concerned with the domestic political effects of actions, something he might have overcome with more determined leadership. But Clinton had obstacles he couldn't overcome: the weaknesses of NATO or the UN as problem-solvers.[88]

The administration had successes, most famously in its negotiations between Israel and the Palestinians. Clinton emissary Senator George Mitchell helped negotiate the 1995 Good Friday Agreement that ended the "Troubles" in Northern Ireland. Clinton's greatest success was on the domestic economic front. He did many things right: the budget produced surpluses (and hasn't since) and the economy boomed. But the outsourcing of American jobs to "low-wage countries such as China" wasn't auspicious.[89]

But there was another issue: American administrations underpinned by Wilsonian or neo-Wilsonian ideas exhibit a greater predilection for using force abroad. The Clinton administration, for example, deployed US troops abroad eighty-four times in eight years.[90] It fought wars in Somalia, Bosnia, and Kosovo, and several against Iraq. There were more to come.

18

WILSONIAN REVOLUTIONARIES: THE BUSH ADMINISTRATION, 2001–2009

INTRODUCTION

George W. Bush, son of President George H. W. Bush, was governor of Texas and held high-level business positions before becoming president. His 2000 election victory was marred by Florida's inability to prove it could do an accurate recount, producing a Supreme Court ruling awarding Florida's twenty-five electoral votes to Bush. When campaigning, Bush insisted his guiding principle for using American power was whether or not it was in American interests. He branded the Clinton administration interventionist, decrying its involvement in Bosnia, Haiti, and Kosovo, disapproved of nation building, and was skeptical of multilateral organizations. He pushed for a harder line against North Korea and Russia, and insisted China wasn't a partner but a rival. Like Clinton, he had little interest in things abroad, telling his future national security advisor, Condoleezza Rice, "I don't have any ideas about foreign affairs."[1]

The administration seems to have had no significant political aims upon taking office. Bush maintained America's presence abroad, pushed more military spending and force modernization, and spoke often of freedom. He supported "free markets, free trade, and freedom from oppression," opposed nuclear proliferation, and wanted to cut taxes, and insisted "open trade" was "a force for freedom in China, a force for stability in Asia, and a force for prosperity in the United States." The administration withdrew from talks with North Korea and the 1997 Kyoto climate accord, provoking the standard false cries of "isolationism."[2]

THE "GLOBAL WAR ON TERROR"

When in Sudan, Bin Laden aimed at reestablishing the ancient Islamic caliphate. This required defeating the United States, which would be done by dragging it "into a war with Islam" across an area too large for Washington to handle. But in spring 1999, Bin Laden told Khaled Sheik Mohammed to unroll a plan Mohammed previously composed for attacking America with four highjacked airliners. Bin Laden believed the US was weak and could be destroyed. American failures in Vietnam, Lebanon, and Somalia proved this. Hit hard at key spots, America would unravel.[3]

On September 11, 2001, Al Qaeda operatives crashed hijacked airliners into both World Trade Center towers in New York City. A third plane was flown into the Pentagon. A fourth crashed in Pennsylvania after its passengers revolted. Nearly 3,000 Americans died.

ASSESSMENT, POLITICAL AIMS, AND GRAND STRATEGY

The 9/11 attacks shocked all Americans, not least those in the administration. In his first call to the vice president on September 11, Bush told Dick Cheney the nation was at war. Constitutionally it was, as the nation had been attacked. The CIA quickly concluded Al Qaeda was to blame. Passenger lists showed its members, and it was the only such organization with the capability. After 9/11, Cheney said, "all our assumptions about our own security had changed.... We were in a new era and needed an entirely new strategy to keep America secure."[4]

Just days after 9/11 some administration officials looked toward Iraq. On September 15, 2001, Deputy Secretary of Defense Wolfowitz suggested tackling Iraq because of its history of supporting terrorism. Secretary of State Powell disagreed, insisting the US "would lose the UN, the Islamic countries, and NATO. If we want to do Iraq, we should do it at a time of our choosing. But we should not do it now, because we don't have linkage to this event."[5]

In his September 20, 2001 national address, Bush mentioned terrorists in sixty countries and issued an ultimatum to the Taliban to hand over Al Qaeda's leaders, release foreign hostages, close terrorist training camps, and let America access them. He said: "Our war on terror begins with Al Qaeda, but it does not end there. It will not end until every terrorist group of global reach has been found, stopped and defeated." He promised to direct all of the resources at his disposal "to the disruption and to the defeat of the global terror network." He warned of a long struggle, and said: "Every nation, in every region, now has a decision to make. Either you are with us, or you are with the terrorists. From this day forward, any nation that continues to harbor or support terrorism will be regarded by the United States as a hostile regime." He asked every nation to join the world's fight for civilization and freedom.[6]

October 25's strategy document, "Defeating the Terrorist Threat to the United States," formalized the political aims. It mixes aims and strategy, but its intent comes through. The US purpose: "Eliminate terrorism as a threat to our way of life and to all nations that love freedom, including the elimination of all terrorist organizations, networks, finances, and their access to WMD." This would be achieved by attacking those responsible for the 9/11 attacks and their protectors. America would "defeat Al-Qaida and eliminate the threat from other terrorist groups that attack Americans or American interests," and "Convince, and if necessary compel, states and non-state entities to cease harboring, sponsoring, and providing safe-havens to such terrorists." The US would harness all elements of national power and work with allies and partners to destroy terrorist networks while holding accountable nations "that harbor or support terrorists." Particularly important was denying "terrorists and the countries that support them" access to WMD. Washington reserved the right to act alone. From this arose the Bush Doctrine. Bush described it as having four prongs: 1) refusing to recognize a distinction between terrorist groups and those sheltering them while holding both responsible; 2) fighting abroad before the enemy brought the war to America; 3) acting against threats before it was too late (preemption); and 4) advancing democracy, the Freedom Agenda.[7]

Some deem the administration's approach "astrategic" because it partly aimed at destroying a particular fighting approach. "Terrorist organizations" is valuable politically but weak analytically. Terrorism is a violence tool used by states and non-state groups pursuing political aims. Focusing on the act risks analysis becoming means-based and ignoring the political aims, producing emphasis on tactical uses of force while forgetting the political nature of the problem. The administration later compounded its difficulties with its "Long War" moniker.[8] This conflates several wars, hindering development of solid strategy for any.

On October 3, 2001, Secretary of Defense Donald Rumsfeld distributed a brief titled "Strategic Guidance for the Campaign against Terrorism." It's convoluted and confusing but provided direction for Defense Department thinking. It identified threats: entities utilizing terrorism, the states, groups, and organizations supporting them, and the possibility of their obtaining WMD. And delineated "Strategic Objectives," mixing political aims with strategy while doing so. Washington's political aims toward "terrorist organizations" that could hurt it were to "Disrupt, damage and destroy them" (the first two are strategies) by attacking "their leaders, forces, support personnel and networks of state and non-state supporters." The US would also prevent their securing WMD. The administration sought to convince terrorism-supporting states to stop by isolating them internationally and by being willing to "Disrupt, damage or destroy internal control mechanisms and the military capacity, including WMD" of any that continued. The aim against non-state groups and institutions: convince them to stop.[9]

There was also a Rumsfeldian potpourri of other "strategic objectives," including protecting America and its allies, thwarting and deterring attacks against them, defeating those deterred, creating an international environment hostile to the use of terrorism and supporting it to "Prevent or control the spreading or escalation of conflict," and encouraging revolts by those under the sway of "terrorist organizations." Rumsfeld envisioned using all elements of national power, preferably in partnership with other nations, in a struggle of "Extended Duration" on many fronts, "to break the determination of terrorist leaders, states and non-state actors that support terrorism." He warned his subordinates: "Prepare for sustained military campaign comprising multiple global, concurrent actions."[10]

THE AFGHAN WAR, 2001–08

Afghanistan, a large, mountainous, land-locked country the size of Texas, had about 24 million inhabitants in 2001. It is tribal, heavily factionalized, and one of the world's most inconvenient places to fight. The Taliban, a Wahabi Islamic group, took Kabul in September 1996 and consolidated its rule, except in the area controlled by Masood, the Panjshir Valley, north of Kabul (Bin Laden had Masood assassinated two days before 9/11). When Bin Laden fled from Sudan to Afghanistan in May 1996, he formed a close bond with Taliban leader Mullah Omar. Initially, the Bush administration continued acting in Afghanistan through Pakistan. In July 2001, intelligence reports noted a possible attack on America. By September 10, the administration was considering giving the Taliban an ultimatum to turn over Bin Laden. Refusal would produce support for the anti-Taliban Northern Alliance led by Masood (who was assassinated by Al Qaeda on September 9). Continued Taliban intransigence would lead to overthrowing the regime.[11] Events overtook them. (See Map 18.1.)

THE POLITICAL AIMS

Democratic Senator Robert C. Byrd asked Bush if he wanted a declaration of war. Bush declined, instead requesting a resolution supporting the use of force. The Authorization for Use of Military Force (AUMF) passed on September 18, 2001, with one negative vote. It gave the president authority to act against any nation, organization, or person involved in or that provided support for the September 11 attacks. On October 3, 2001, the

WILSONIAN REVOLUTIONARIES: THE BUSH ADMINISTRATION, 2001-2009

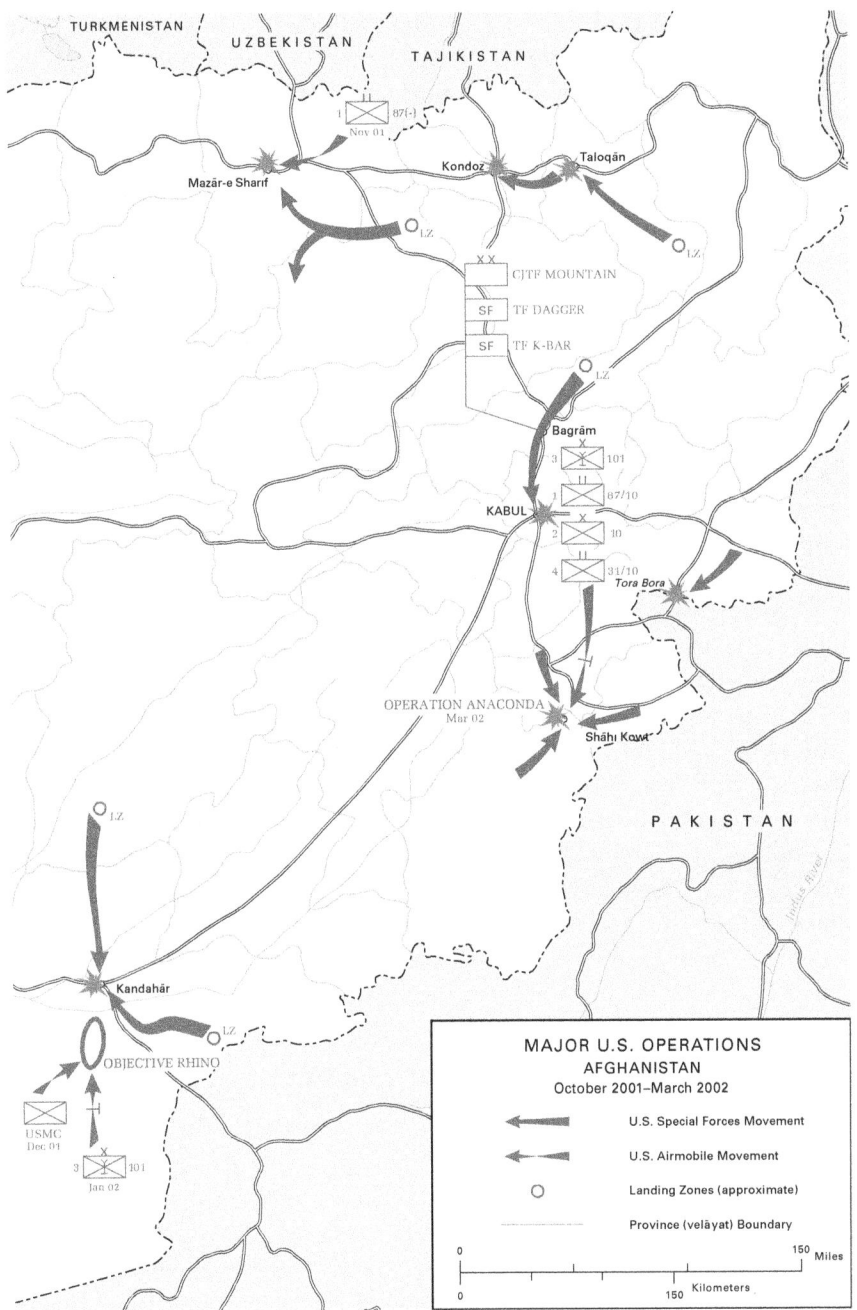

Map 18.1 Major US operations, Afghanistan, 2001–02

administration decided the Taliban had to go. The political aims Bush established were "removing the Taliban, denying sanctuary to al Qaeda, and helping a democratic government emerge." Washington also wanted Bin Laden. There was no plan for a replacement government, but the decision to launch a nation-building effort came later that day as the administration decided to bring in international organizations such as the UN.[12]

DIPLOMATIC STRATEGY

Powell called Pakistan's President Pervez Musharraf on September 13 and told him Islamabad had to stand with or against the United States. Musharraf did both. As demanded, he condemned the 9/11 attacks, committed to intelligence sharing, granted overflight rights, and officially denied Al Qaeda sanctuary. Pakistan received sanctions relief, was designated a "major non-NATO ally" in 2004, given $12.4 billion publicly, and billions covertly. Pakistan simultaneously pursued its own aims, and America was soon helping fund the war against itself via Islamabad.[13]

Washington built a coalition and secured a UN Security Council Resolution calling for states to sever links with groups using terrorism. NATO invoked Article 5, declaring the September 11 attack an assault on all member states. CENTCOM worked to build good relations with Arab nations, to put Afghans in the lead in the war, and to secure help from Pakistan, Uzbekistan, and other nations for basing and overflight rights, and to seal Afghanistan's frontiers to block escaping Al Qaeda members. The administration launched an information campaign to explain the struggle to the American people. The Treasury Department went after Al Qaeda's finances. The CIA received more authority to act covertly. And more was done to protect the homeland. On October 6, 2001, Bush dispatched to the Taliban a final warning to hand over Bin Laden.[14]

MILITARY PLANNING AND STRATEGY

The administration had no war plans for Afghanistan and knew nothing about its tribal system or Pakistan's Taliban and Al Qaeda connections. CENTCOM commander General Tommy Franks told Rumsfeld it would take two months to develop a war plan. Rumsfeld pushed Franks and CENTCOM to think flexibly and move quickly. The result combined CIA and military ideas. CIA and Special Operations Forces (SOF) would open the door for follow-on units. A three- to five-day air campaign concentrating on the north of Afganistan would target the Taliban and Al Qaeda while dropping relief supplies. CIA and SOF teams and American airpower would back a Northern Alliance attack on Mazar-e-Sharif, then move south on Kandahar. Meanwhile, more US troops would help finish Al Qaeda and Taliban forces. CENTCOM was ordered to use a small footprint from fear of looking like an occupier and repeating a Soviet error. Washington wanted Afghans to do most of the fighting and to cause minimum damage, to speed reconstruction and hand over to Afghan governance. The last step was stabilization and helping "the Afghan people build a free society." Bush said: "our strategy is to create chaos, to create a vacuum, to go after the bad guys moving." On September 26, 2001, a CIA Special Activities team touched down in northeastern Afghanistan's Panjshir Valley.[15]

The Taliban didn't respond to Bush's demands. He ordered the war's beginning on October 6. Air attacks began on October 7. The US struck fixed targets for five days and then began hitting "targets of opportunity." SOF teams entered Afghanistan on October 18 (Washington time, October 19 in Afghanistan) to support Northern Alliance forces near Mazar-e-Sharif, in the Kabul–Bagram area, and at Kunduz, the major Afghan cities. The attack on Mazar-e-Sharif began on November 5. It fell on November 10; many of the defeated troops changed sides. The Taliban position in northern Afghanistan disintegrated.[16]

Northern Alliance troops reached Kabul's outskirts on November 13. The Taliban surrendered the city within two hours and the inhabitants began looting. A two-week siege of 5,000 Taliban in Kunduz followed. It was Pakistan's base for operations against the Northern Alliance, and its defenders included "hundreds of ISI officers and soldiers from the Pakistani Frontier Corps aiding the Taliban" and Al Qaeda. Musharraf convinced the administration – which didn't understand the situation – to allow Pakistan to evacuate its people. Hundreds of ISI, AQ, Taliban, and others were flown out before Kunduz's November 26 surrender.[17]

Frustrated by delays, on October 10 Rumsfeld pressed the Chiefs for more military options; they pressed the combatant commanders. Vice Admiral Willy Moore, commander of Fifth Fleet in Bahrain, believed the Taliban wouldn't defend Kabul but flee to Kandahar and regather. He suggested opening another front. Marines began landing on November 26 at Camp RHINO, an air base 90 miles south of Kandahar captured by army rangers on October 19. They began hitting Kandahar's defenses, and Al Qaeda and Taliban fleeing to Pakistan.[18]

A second offensive prong aimed at Kandahar developed around Hamid Karzai, chief of the Popalzi tribe based in Kandahar province. Ordered out of Pakistan by the ISI, he returned on October 8 to raise insurgents.

The inhabitants of Tarinkot, about 70 miles from Kandahar, rebelled on November 15 and began helping Karzai and an American SOF team supporting him. Kandahar became the focus of the fighting, and Karzai convinced the strongest southern tribes to support a push on the city. Another Afghan force accompanied by US SOF pressured the Taliban in Kandahar. Mullah Omar fled to Pakistan on the night of December 6. Kandahar surrendered on December 7, 2001.[19]

After Kabul's fall, many Taliban and AQ fighters retreated to the Tora Bora Mountains' caves and fortified positions only 20 miles from Pakistan. A CIA team linked up with a warlord army under Hazrat Ali in Jalalabad on November 18 to help pin Bin Laden in Tora Bora until more troops arrived. American bombing helped push Al Qaeda forces into the caves, which Ali's men had no desire to assault. Another warlord soon arrived: Haji Mohammed Zaman Ghansjarik. His connections included Mohammed Younes Khalis, who invited Bin Laden to Afghanistan.[20]

On December 3, the CIA's team leader, Gary Berntsen, asked for 800 army troops, which could've deployed to Tora Bora within 48 hours. CIA Director George Tenet and Brigadier General Jim Mattis asked to insert blocking forces between Tora Bora and the Pakistani frontier. Mattis dispatched a plan for covering the several dozen possible escape routes from Tora Bora to CENTCOM, heard nothing, and then began making calls warning about losing Bin Laden. Two weeks passed. There were 4,000 deployable Marines in the theater and other US forces in Kandahar, Bagram, and 800 men of the army's 10th Mountain Division in Uzbekistan. Franks denied the requests, insisting it would take too long to deploy the troops and that Bin Laden would be gone. Franks asked for Musharraf's help, and Pakistani forces were on the border by December 9. Some Bush administration veterans consider failure to act here America's greatest Afgan War error.[21]

Afghan forces launched a sporadic assault on the cave complex on December 3. Three dozen SOF soldiers arrived three days later. Coalition forces took Tora Bora's peak on December 9, but Zaman, without American permission, negotiated a ceasefire on December 12. The Americans kept it for about two hours, then renewed bombing. Meanwhile, perhaps 800 Al Qaeda escaped to Pakistan. The ground attacks recommenced. The caves fell on December 17. Bin Laden escaped the night before. Khalis told the Afghans to let Bin Laden get away.[22]

Meanwhile, Al Qaeda forces gathered near Gardez in the Shah-i-Kot Valley. Operation ANACONDA was conducted March 2–10, 2002 by a mixture of Afghans and SOF (including Australian SAS), and troops from regular units. They fought and defeated probably 800 Al Qaeda and Taliban at altitudes of 8,000 feet and above. On May 1, 2003, Rumsfeld declared the end of "major combat activity" in Afghanistan. The same day, Bush declared "Mission Accomplished" in Iraq.[23] America's enemies didn't agree.

FAILING TO SECURE THE PEACE

In three months, using CIA paramilitary teams, Special Forces, airpower, and local proxies, the US overthrew the Taliban regime, defeating its force of perhaps 60,000, and destroyed Al Qaeda's base in Afghanistan at the cost of only 12 US lives. But this didn't translate into victory. The US failed to achieve its aim of killing or capturing Bin Laden while numerous Al Qaeda and Taliban leaders escaped. Around 5,000 Al Qaeda escaped to seed global jihadist groups; perhaps 2,000 had been at Tora Bora. Musharraf surrendered more than 200 Al Qaeda Arab fighters but not Bin Laden and Zawahiri. CIA officer Henry Crumpton had warned Bush that not sending enough troops and relying on the Afghans risked Bin Laden escaping. The aims of your proxies and allies are not necessarily yours, and even if they are, they're unlikely to value them the same.[24]

Committing sufficient forces to achieve the desired purposes could have stacked the deck in favor of also securing the aim of killing or capturing Bin Laden. Those arguing against using larger numbers of US troops based upon the Soviet war misunderstood Moscow's experience and actions. The problem wasn't troop numbers but terrorizing the population.[25] The US never intended to fight the same kind of war, nor to stay and impose a puppet regime. Washington instead repeated a mistake dating to the War of 1812: assuming a war could be fought successfully as it wished with a minimum commitment rather than how it should be: with sufficient troops and resources for achieving the political aims.

Others suggest the impossibility of stopping Bin Laden's escape from Tora Bora. One study insisted it would have required 3,000 troops to block the 106 border passes. But if this is correct, the US had the forces to try.[26] Putting them in position would have been tough, keeping them supplied difficult, with no guarantee of success, but there are never guarantees in war. The US should have made the utmost effort to block what it could while providing as much reconnaissance as possible. At Tora Bora, Franks failed to bring to bear sufficient forces to achieve the aim his president had ordered him to secure, and his superiors failed to make him. The American predilection for bad theoretical ideas helped insure this – transformation, the technological dominance of America's Revolution in Military Affairs

(RMA), a small footprint – these undermined American thinking, particularly Rumsfeld's.

The US also missed an opportunity to secure an end to its war against the Taliban. The Taliban leaders realized their rule was collapsing and negotiated a surrender deal with Karzai on December 5, 2001, one allowing the Taliban leader and his supporters to relinquish power and return to their home villages. It was an Afghan-style solution, but not one the administration could live with.[27]

The US set out to build a democratic Afghanistan, a vastly different aim from regime change and thus requiring a different commitment of forces and material. Achieving this aim meant nation building. Bush had criticized Clinton for this. "But after 911," Bush wrote, "I changed my mind." He decided it was in America's interest to rebuild Afghanistan because organizations using terrorism could live and grow in chaotic lands. The administration, though, lacked a strategy for it, possessed institutional distaste toward it, and was already shifting its attention to Iraq. At an NSC meeting on October 4, 2001, Bush asked who was going to run the country after the war and was met with silence. He told Powell to develop a plan for moving Afghanistan to democracy.[28]

A STRATEGY OF NATION BUILDING

With help from Powell and the UN, the December 2001 Bonn Conference produced a roadmap for a democratic Afghan government modeled on a 1963–73 predecessor with a grand council, or Loya Jirga. It also established the International Security Assistance Force (ISAF). NATO took command in fall 2002. In June 2002, a second Loya Jirga chose Karzai as the new government's head after intervention by Zalmay Khalilzad, an Afghan-American diplomat and Bush's Afghanistan point, enabling Karzai's opponents to brand him a US puppet. A Loya Jirga in January 2004 ratified a new constitution, and Karzai won Afghanistan's first free presidential election in October 2004.[29]

Nation building took a "lead nation" approach that failed. The April 2002 Group of 8 (G-8) meeting assigned America to build the Afghan National Army, Germany the police, and Italy the judicial system, while Britain did counternarcotics work, and Japan handled militia disarmament and reintegration. Germany bungled the police plank by failing to send enough trainers. America took over. Numerous, disjointed programs followed that trained at least thirteen different forces that usually failed even in basic law enforcement. A pivotal mistake was using police as "little soldiers" to support counterinsurgency operations against better-armed insurgents. The Italians failed to send a judicial team for a year. The British counternarcotics program accidentally subsidized opium production, which became Afghanistan's second-largest source of revenue after foreign aid and helped fund the insurgency. Japan funded disarmament and reintegration, but the lack of a negotiated peace ensured failure.[30]

The US began training a new Afghan army in May 2002. Lieutenant General Karl Eikenberry headed the Office of Military Cooperation–Afghanistan and led this effort from autumn 2002. He reformed the existing Ministry of Defense and enjoyed some success before departing in 2003. Two air force generals who knew nothing about building an army followed. In early 2005, Rumsfeld agreed to an Afghan plan to build a 70,000-man army but forced Kabul to find part of the money elsewhere.[31]

The US relied on warlords to provide security instead of the traditional village elders and council leaders, unaware of the influence these seniors exerted. This unintentionally undermined Karzai's authority while making it difficult to build links between local communities and the central government. Pragmatically, Karzai put warlords in positions of power, producing institutional corruption and drug-trafficking by government, military, and police officials. His failures weakened support from abroad and increased his dependence upon Washington. The Americans, meanwhile, alienated Afghans via civilian casualties from airstrikes, night raids, and US-controlled prisons inside Afghanistan.[32]

Afghanistan was captured by the international so-called *developmentistas*. Some were idealists, but others, including UN officials, saw a way to keep their bureaucracies funded. Billions of dollars flowed to bloated aid and relief organizations, enormous NGO salaries, contractors, corruption, high rents, and security forces. These groups injured government development by taking the most qualified Afghans and by refusing to move aid through government agencies, which could have built Kabul's credibility but instead fed waste and duplication. By 2008, $14.5 billion in aid had been spent, yet Karzai's government couldn't fund various educational and agricultural programs or pay decent salaries. The coalition dramatically expanded education at all levels, but half the children remained unschooled, and the system suffered every imaginable shortage.[33]

THE WAR'S NEXT PHASE, 2002–09

With the toppling of the Taliban government, the nature of the war changed. Both the Taliban and Al Qaeda found sanctuary in Pakistan.

The complicity of the Pakistani government and its weak control over its Freely Administered Tribal Areas (FATA) made this possible.[34] Washington moved from fighting for unlimited political aims such as Al Qaeda's destruction and overthrowing the Taliban regime, to seeking an unlimited aim against Al Qaeda and the limited aim of defending the new Afghan government. But Washington now faced an insurgency from enemies it had defeated but failed to destroy or bring to terms. As you will recall, the key things to consider here are sanctuary, foreign assistance, and support from the people.

Success demanded a larger force. Rumsfeld wanted a small one. This produced the light-footprint strategy, which US leaders saw as lessening chances of provoking large-scale resistance. Some 4,000 ISAF troops secured Kabul while 8,000 Americans deployed by 2002. The light footprint caused Karzai to doubt America's commitment, making him less willing to fix problems. Relying upon warlords to fill the security vacuum undermined Afghan support for the government. A small force could overthrow the Taliban regime and defeat Al Qaeda but couldn't secure or stabilize Afghanistan. Bush kept US numbers low to avoid America appearing as an occupier but later admitted this meant insufficient personnel to achieve the aims. To American military leaders, their job was fighting Al Qaeda. They didn't want to do nation building and believed they could work with Afghan forces, supported by US airpower, to provide security.[35]

But nation building was part of the strategy. British army Colonel Nick Carter developed Provincial Reconstruction Teams (PRTs) in summer 2002 to extend the government's reach. American then-Lieutenant General Dan McNeill saw a tool for keeping out the Taliban and secured Rumsfeld's support in September 2002. The first PRT was launched in Gardez, about 80 miles south of Kabul, in February 2003. NATO nations unwilling to fight formed PRTs, freeing US resources for combat and Iraq. The coalition suffered because some nations had very restrictive rules of engagement (ROE), including constraints such as avoiding casualties. American soldiers joked that ISAF meant "I Saw Americans Fight."[36]

In June 2003, the administration adopted a plan focused on creating government institutional capacity by appointing better officials, public- and private-sector economic development, particularly in rural areas (where Afghan wars were won), disarming militias, and attempting reconciliation with the Taliban. This became part of a strategy called "Accelerating Success." Strategy officially shifted from anti-terrorism to counterinsurgency and nation building while US troops were told they weren't doing counterinsurgency but hunting terrorists.[37]

In October 2003, Major General David Barno took command of US forces. He found disorganization and "no campaign plan." In November, Khalilzad became the US ambassador to Afghanistan. He and Barno understood the importance of military and civilian leaders cooperating and realized Afghanistan faced an insurgency. Barno created three regional commands and developed a "Counterinsurgency Strategy for Afghanistan." Military strategy went from focusing on killing the enemy to protecting Afghans in order to secure the 2004 and 2005 presidential and parliamentary elections. US airpower was restricted to combat support and interagency cooperation stressed. The coalition was to "Defeat terrorism and deny sanctuary," and "Enable the Afghan security structure," while backing reconstruction and governance development. Diplomatically, neighboring states, particularly Pakistan, were engaged. Informationally, the coalition would try to win the war of ideas. The 12,000 coalition forces grew to 20,000 US and 10,000 NATO.[38]

Barno secured the elections, but progress was short-lived. Insurgent activity – largely Taliban – increased. The Taliban and others intensified attacks, mounting a 2005 offensive on three fronts coordinated by Pakistan's ISI, recapturing many rural areas. In 2005 and 2006, the new Afghan army participated in a trio of operations, making a common counterinsurgent error: clearing an area and departing without providing population security. It was clear by 2006 America's strategy wasn't working. Afghanistan was suffering a toxic mix of poor governance, insurgency, corruption, drug-trafficking, smuggling, and its highest levels of violence since 2001. In 2006, British army General David Richards assumed the NATO command. He said later the coalition had been "trying to get a single coherent long-term approach – a proper strategy – but instead we got a lot of tactics." He told interviewers: "There was no coherent long-term strategy." In reply to a Rumsfeld query as to why the situation in southern Afghanistan was deteriorating, McNeill said it was because he had insufficient resources. Rumsfeld replied: "General, I don't agree."[39]

The Taliban enjoyed sanctuary in Pakistan and support from parts of Afghanistan's population. Taliban attacks on coalition forces tripled after Washington rebuffed a September 2006 Musharraf plan that would have handed much of southern Afghanistan to the Taliban. Assistance for the Taliban grew more brazen, including a Pakistani attack upon American and Afghan forces. The administration accepted Islamabad's claim it was the fault of one crazed Pakistani soldier. Bush approved pursuit of insurgents into Pakistan in 2006 but nothing came of it from fear of injuring US–Pakistan relations. The two agreed to American use of Predator drones in certain areas – if the US provided warning. Bush approved $750 million in aid for the tribal areas; the Pakistani military pocketed much of it. Musharraf's double-game bit him when some Islamist groups he supported fractured and turned against Pakistan. He survived two assassination attempts in 2007. The same year, Pakistan put 100,000 troops into the Northwest Frontier Province to counter the Pakistani Taliban. Musharraf resigned in 2008.[40]

In February 2007, McNeill returned to Afghanistan, this time as NATO commander. "I tried to get someone to define for me what winning meant," McNeill said, "nobody could." He also discovered "There was no NATO campaign plan." He had 25,000 US and 12,000 NATO troops, and 60,000 Afghan soldiers. McNeil wanted to take the fight to the Taliban via a counterinsurgency campaign. The army was experimenting with forces in small bases along the Pakistani border and tried to implement a form of "clear, hold, and build." This produced some of the war's most intense fighting, particularly in the Korengal Valley.[41]

Meanwhile, Britain's Helmand effort evolved into a counterinsurgency campaign needing troops it wouldn't receive. British and other NATO units cleared Sangin in Helmand in April 2007; then the main force withdrew. Afghan troops and police were supposed to hold the area but there weren't enough of them. The Taliban reasserted control a few weeks later and the British cleared it again. US and NATO troop levels reached 41,000 at 2007's end, but the Taliban held the initiative. In 2007, from its Pakistan sanctuary, Al Qaeda remained active in Afghanistan and globally. Between 2002 and 2006, excluding Iraq and Afghanistan, Al Qaeda and its affiliates mounted an average of ten overseas attacks annually. By mid 2008, things were clearly going poorly in Afghanistan. The Bush administration had consistently failed to commit the means to achieve its political aims.[42] It also never addressed Pakistani sanctuary and support.

In June 2008, Bush tasked his "war czar," the NSC's Lieutenant General Douglas Lute, with a strategy review. When concluded in November, it didn't deliver good news. The US had 38,000 troops in Afghanistan; NATO and other allies, 29,000, spread thinly throughout Afghanistan. The coalition efforts were uncoordinated, with each country fighting its own war. Both Lute and General David McKiernan agreed on the need for more troops and McKiernan requested 30,000. The report argued America needed to do three things to win: 1) ensure better governance and reduce corruption; 2) deal with the opium trade, which funded corruption and the Taliban; and 3) remove the enemy sanctuaries in Pakistan. The administration decided against releasing the report and elected to let the new administration choose its own path.[43]

CHANGING AIMS, EVOLVING GRAND STRATEGY

After 9/11, the administration looked for the root causes of external threats. Condoleezza Rice, Bush's first national security advisor and later secretary of state, said the administration realized American "policies to try and promote what we thought was stability in the Middle East had actually allowed, underneath, a very malignant, meaning cancerous, form of extremism to grow up underneath because people didn't have outlets for their political views." Democracy was seen as a cure for "transnational terrorism." The administration believed Washington needed to change tack.[44]

Bush said in January 2002 that assuring the security of the United States was his most important aim, but he mentioned others. "Revitalizing the economy" and "destroying terrorist camps" are really means of achieving political aims. But America had "a greater objective than eliminating threats and containing resentment. We seek a just and peaceful world beyond the war on terror." The September 2002 *National Security Strategy* echoed this: The US "will actively work to bring the hope of democracy, development, free markets, and free trade to every corner of the world." Creating democratic governments would establish long-term peace and stability as governments that respected the rights of their own people were more likely to act responsibly toward other states. To achieve the aim of democracy, Bush proposed the Freedom Agenda. Freedom, Bush said, "is not America's gift to the world. Freedom is God's gift to everybody in the world." He said in 2002: "The peoples of the Islamic nations want and deserve the same freedoms and opportunities as people in every nation." July 2008's "Institutionalizing the Freedom Agenda" declared it "the policy of the United States to seek and support the growth of democratic movements and institutions in every nation and culture with the ultimate goal of ending tyranny in the world."[45]

The September 2002 *NSS* laid out some of the grand strategy planks, including democratization and "economic openness." A military element was preemption, meaning the right to preemptively strike a threat to the nation's security. In discussing rogue nations securing WMD and supplying them to organizations like Al Qaeda, Bush said: "I will not wait on events while dangers gather.... The United States of America will not permit the world's most dangerous regimes to threaten us with the world's most destructive weapons." This was encapsulated in 2002's *NSS*: "America will act against such emerging threats before they are fully formed."[46]

Preemption was neither controversial internationally nor new for America. But critics insisted Bush was going beyond preemption and asserting the right to wage a preventive war. Theodore Roosevelt justified military action in Central America and the Caribbean as a form of preemption. And this was a common discussion in the early days of the Cold War. Another criticism was that in charting this course, America gave other states leeway to do the same.[47] It provides an excuse, but states act in their own interests.

Bush said in June 2002 that "America has no empire to extend or utopia to establish."[48] He was certainly correct about empire; America has wanted no more of that since seizing enough of Panama for a canal. But the administration's aim of creating a democratic globe could raise doubts about the second.

THE SECOND IRAQ WAR, 2003–09

Bush had no pre-election inclination for war with Iraq. But after September 11, he decided the risk of inaction – especially because of WMD – outweighed the benefits of inaction. He said later that Saddam's "capacity to create harm" and "all his terrible features" meant "Keeping Saddam in a box looked less and less feasible." The "Cheney Rule" supported this: "If there is a one-percent chance that Pakistani scientists are helping al-Qaeda build or develop nuclear weapons, we have to treat it as a certainty in terms of our response." Clausewitz advises us to focus upon what is most probable and not everything that is possible. Fear was the primary factor driving Bush to Iraq, but he believed success here would lead other nations to fall in behind the United States. But many of these didn't view terrorism as their worst danger. This created difficulties with allies and potential partners who thought US actions destabilizing.[49]

THE POLITICAL AIMS

The Freedom Agenda underpinned the political aims against Iraq. An August 12, 2002 meeting produced a confusing draft document titled "Iraq: Goals, Objectives, and Strategy." This evolved into an August 29 Bush directive noting the aims as overthrowing Saddam's regime and establishing a new, democratic Iraqi government that would no longer threaten its neighbors, develop WMD, or harbor terrorists. All elements of national power would be used, when possible, in conjunction with other states. Bush saw replacing Saddam's regime with a democracy as a catalyst for Middle East peace. It would remove Iraqi funding for Palestinian suicide bombers "and set in motion progress towards a truly democratic Palestinian state" while warning others to stop sponsoring terrorism.[50]

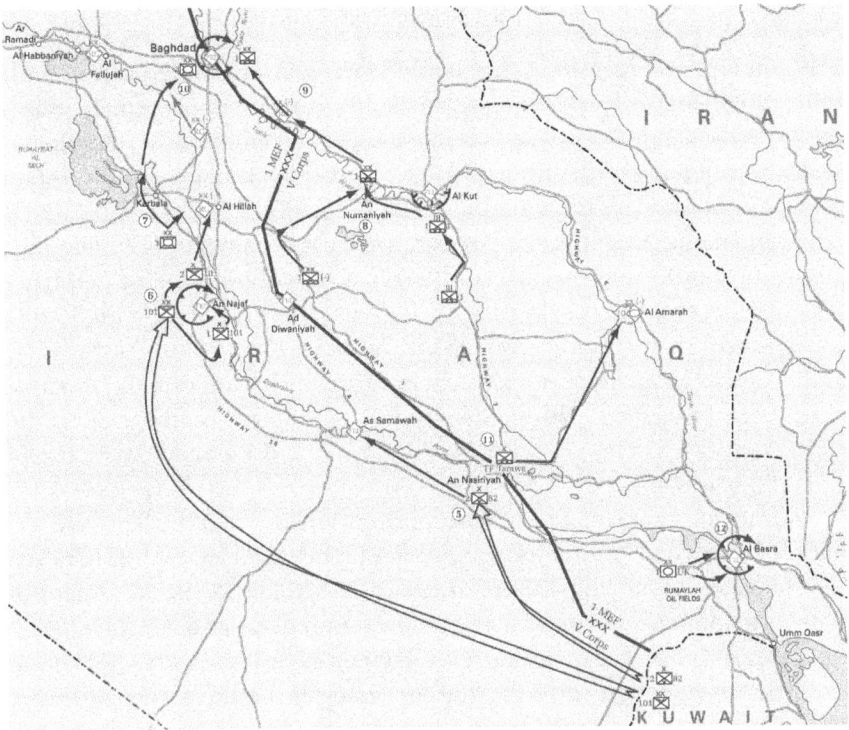

Map 18.2 Southern Iraq and vicinity, 2003

Bush made clear US purposes in Iraq, but there arose early a disconnect between what he and his White House thought they were doing in Iraq and the views of Rumsfeld's Defense Department. This continued through much of the war. Rumsfeld suggested Bush tone down his democracy rhetoric and wrote later: "Bringing democracy to Iraq had not been among the primary rationales." This, of course, ignores what Bush said and Rumsfeld's own discussions with administration officials. The military officers crafting the war plan were instructed to work from the following political aim: "A stable Iraq, with its territorial integrity intact and a broad-based government that renounces WMD development and use and no longer supports terrorism or threatens its neighbors."[51] This says nothing about establishing democracy.

There was another dangerous problem: the administration didn't realize it was seeking two political aims. Overthrowing the Iraqi regime is one aim. Building a democratic Iraq is another. The aims are different, thus the mission is different, thus the strategy must change, thus the force requirements are different, and so on. Everything flows from the political aim. Not understanding this opens the door to disaster.

PART III: THE POST-COLD WAR WORLD

ASSESSMENT

The intelligence regarding Saddam's WMD didn't change after 9/11. What did change was how dangerous the information appeared. To Bush, the "gravest danger" was the "crossroads of radicalism and technology." WMD combined with ballistic missiles allowed weak states and non-state groups to harm even large nations. The US had long relied upon deterrence and containment, strategies useful against certain nations that didn't apply here. Bush said the threat of retaliation had no hope of deterring "shadowy terrorist networks with no nation or citizens to defend," while containment could not succeed against "unbalanced dictators" with WMD and a delivery capability who might provide such weapons to "terrorist allies." The struggle, to Bush, had a moral component reminiscent of the Cold War: "We are in a conflict between good and evil, and America will call evil by its name."[52]

For the postwar situation, the administration assumed the best-case scenario of a welcome and quick formation of a new government. It believed the Iraqis would be happy to see the back of Saddam, keep the organs of state functioning, and cooperate. This meant no occupation. Powell didn't think Iraq a great threat and believed containment the approach. He told Bush that if they went to war, "You are going to be the proud owner of 25 million people. You will own all their hopes, aspirations, and problems. It's going to suck the oxygen out of everything. *This will become the first term.*"[53] Powell was incorrect: it became *both* terms.

DIPLOMATIC STRATEGY

The administration preferred acting multilaterally and built a "coalition of the willing." The informational arm of grand strategy intertwined this but was secondary.[54] There were two tacks taken for convincing other nations and the American people to support the war: links between Saddam and organizations using terrorism and Saddam's possession of WMD.

There were a number of contacts between representatives of the Iraqi regime and Al Qaeda after the 1990–91 Gulf War. Saddam developed a minor relationship with Bin Laden in 1994 and 1995 and agreed to broadcast anti-Saudi sermons into Saudi Arabia. Bush received intel reports in the summer of 2002 that Al Qaeda's Abu Musab Al Zarqawi was in Iraq, but his relationship with Saddam was unclear. Saddam gave Al Qaeda no known weapons or support.[55]

The "sure-thing" was Iraqi possession of WMD. Assistant Secretary of Defense Wolfowitz said: "For bureaucratic reasons we settled on one issue, weapons of mass destruction, because it was the one reason everyone could agree on." Belief in Saddam's continued possession of WMD was widespread and included Democrat Senator John Kerry and the intelligence agencies of Great Britain, China, Egypt, France, and Germany. The CIA's September 2002 National Intelligence Estimate insisted Iraq possessed chemical and biological weapons. In his September 12, 2002 UN speech, Bush said: "The overlap between states that sponsor terror and those that pursue WMD compels us to action." The final effort on this front was Powell's February 5, 2003 UN speech.[56]

The administration sought international and domestic support in the hope of frightening Saddam into changing. Because of Powell, instead of circumventing the UN, Bush sought a new resolution deeming Iraq in violation of prior UN declarations and "demanding new weapons inspections." On September 12, Bush detailed Saddam's crimes against the Iraqi people and other states, and noted Iraq was in violation of UN Resolutions 686, 687, 688, and 1373. The latter pair concerned supporting organizations using terrorism, which Saddam continued to do. On November 8, 2002, Bush secured a seventeenth resolution, 1441, deeming Iraq "in material breach" of the previous resolutions. Iraq was given thirty days to comply.[57]

Iraq responded by turning over reams of documents, allowing the return of inspectors, and insisting it no longer had WMD programs. This changed nothing. Saddam had used WMD many times against the Iranians and his own people, and UN weapons inspectors consistently found traces of the programs and infrastructure. But Saddam was laboring to show he had shed his WMD. No one believed him because of his history of serial deception and he didn't understand the change wrought by the 9/11 attacks. The US and Britain pushed for an eighteenth resolution essentially approving war. Both Russia and France threatened a veto, and Bush and Britain's prime minister, Tony Blair, abandoned this effort. On March 17, 2003, Bush demanded Saddam leave Iraq in two days.[58]

The Senate Foreign Relations Committee held hearings on July 31 and August 1, 2002. Congress approved military action against Iraq on October 11, 2002, with significant margins: 296 to 133 in the House, 77 to 23 in the Senate. Supportive votes came from prominent opposition Democrats such as Senators Joseph Biden, Hillary Clinton, John Kerry, and Harry Reid.

A *Who's Who* of America's commentariat voiced support, including Peter Beinart, Thomas Friedman, George Packer, and David Remnick, on the left, and Stephen Hayes, Robert Kagan, William Kristol, and George Will on the right.[59]

The administration worked hard to build a coalition and prepare the diplomatic ground. The German chancellor, Gerhard Schröder, and the French president, Jacques Chirac, published a joint statement opposing the war. French fears of American "hyperpower" were more acknowledgment of French weakness and corrupt business dealings with Iraq than concern over American strength. Some charged the war was "unilateral." The US bore the weight, but the administration assembled one of the largest coalitions in history – thirty-eight countries – sometimes using hundreds of billions of dollars in aid to grease the skids. The war was broadly supported – while it went well. Critics accused Bush of waging a "war of choice" instead of a "war of necessity." This argument is logically flawed. *All* wars are wars of choice. One chooses to fight. Or chooses not to.[60]

MILITARY STRATEGY: PLANNING

In November 2001, Bush ordered CENTCOM to plan for war against Iraq, a country of 25 million roughly the size of California. Rumsfeld instructed CENTCOM commander Franks to update existing plans on November 27 and a week later said to aim at achieving the following:

1. Iraq's regime enablers, leadership, and power base destroyed
2. Iraq's WMD capability eliminated
3. Iraq retaining sufficient forces to defend itself but no longer having the power to threaten neighbors
4. Iraq having an "acceptable provisional government in place"
5. Iraq's territorial integrity remaining intact.

Franks was then neck-deep in the Afghan War.[61]

The plan was built around the military's then four doctrinal phases. Phase I was building the coalition (which was done by Franks and the administration). Phase II was a "shaping operation," including deception and psychological efforts. Phase III was the military operation intended to "decapitate the Iraqi regime" and destroy its military forces. Phase IV was stability operations and transferring power to the new government. Numerous planning iterations followed, and Rumsfeld and Wolfowitz drove the planners to go smaller, get in faster, get out quickly, and justify every military unit. The Afghan War proved to Rumsfeld the reality of the RMA – technology trumped all – and the obsolescence of the military's thinking. This was also a liberation – not an occupation – one Iraqis would generally welcome. For much of the process, the planners assumed the ability to mount one invasion prong from Turkey, but Ankara balked, and the threat of attack from here became part of CENTCOM's deception scheme. The planners assumed Saddam had chemical weapons (and would use them when the coalition breached his "Red Line"), that the bulk of his army would not fight, and that it would be recalled to service to provide security. Ground and air attacks were to commence nearly simultaneously.[62] (See Map 18.2.)

In late summer 2002, McKiernan took over the Coalition Forces Land Component Command (CFLC). He guided creation of the final plan, naming it COBRA II (the original was the Allied breakout from Normandy). It included inserting Special Forces to destroy SCUDS and link up with anti-Saddam Shia and Kurdish groups. A bombing campaign would hit air defense systems and command, control, and communications to create confusion and prevent troops concentrating in Baghdad. Information operations would try to convince units to not fight. All of this was to ease defeat of key forces such as the Republican Guard. Iraq's southern cities would be bypassed, and the objective given the ground forces was "to isolate the regime and defeat the Iraqi Regular Army and Republican Guard forces." When reaching Baghdad, they would throw a cordon around the city, hit key regime centers, and break Saddam's defenses by pushing heavy columns through the city. The operation order for COBRA II was dispatched in October 2002. The Phase IV stability plan, ECLIPSE II, was based upon four precepts: 1) abundant Iraqi police and troops coming over; 2) other nations and NGOs helping and replacing US troops; 3) US forces securing the infrastructure; and 4) an Iraqi government arising quickly and being handed control. Execution would take five to seven months.[63]

By December 18, 2002 Bush, who was dissatisfied with the Iraqi response to the UN's questions on Saddam's weapons programs, concluded war was inevitable. Rumsfeld told Undersecretary of Defense Douglas Feith to launch a civilian office for postwar planning, something ordered earlier but canceled. Bush's January 20, 2003 order formalized this as the Office of Reconstruction and Humanitarian Assistance (ORHA) under former lieutenant general Jay Garner. Franks was happy to hand Phase IV to ORHA, which was always intended as temporary. CENTCOM postwar planning worked from the assumption that government civilian wings would carry the weight. Garner, who committed to serving only four months, planned to remove Saddam's closest followers, quickly put governance into Iraqi hands, and run the country using the existing ministries assisted by American advisors. The Iraqi army would be recalled to maintain order and rebuild. After a few months, to ensure no humanitarian crisis, a former American ambassador or governor would become the mission's face. Occupation and nation building were not part of the plan. On March 12, 2003, Bush approved.[64]

Garner convened officials to identify the challenges, pinpointing four possible causes of failure: 1) not defining the job of agencies such as ORHA; 2) the military not carrying the police role until replaced by Iraqis; 3) the absence of a decision regarding the size of the US force and whether it would do development or conduct operations; and 4) failing to quickly establish order and the rule of law, something "achievable only if funds and staff are made available *now*." The numerous planning efforts for Phase IV included six uncoordinated military efforts and one State. This was CENTCOM's job, but no one was in charge or oversaw it as it didn't interest Franks. The invasion units had no Phase IV plans at their level, and the only interagency meeting on postwar Iraq at the "operator" level occurred February 21–22, 2003.[65]

Franks' CENTCOM was responsible for the postwar situation, but the war plan passed to Rumsfeld on January 24 didn't address this. It also left open routes to Syria later used to create sanctuary for the insurgency. The planners raised with Franks their concerns that since they were breaking all the elements of control in Iraq, this would open operational space for terrorist and criminal organizations, partially because the plan lacked enough troops to seal Iraq's borders. Their concerns were brushed aside.[66]

The force level became a public controversy. On February 25, 2003, army Chief of Staff General Eric Shinseki testified before Congress that the postwar situation demanded more troops than conquering Iraq, "something on the order of several hundred thousand," an estimate based upon past postwar actions. Wolfowitz, Rumsfeld's assistant, pushed back, telling the House "it was hard to imagine" needing more troops to ensure postwar stability than to fight the war. The National Intelligence Council warned of potential conflict among Iraqi groups. An Army War College report said a successful postwar operation demanded large forces, extensive interagency planning, and years to implement, while US forces would face problems from Iraq's tribal, religious, and ethnic fractures. Leaving demanded creating a political system capable of standing alone, a heavy lift considering Iraq's problems.[67]

Oddly, on force size both Rumsfeld and Shinseki were correct. The US only needed a relatively small force to topple Saddam, but a far larger one to secure the country. Rumsfeld and Franks were happy with a light force and "determined to avoid anything resembling a large or protracted US commitment," and the army planned to drawdown to 30,000 troops by late summer 2003. The administration would quickly overthrow the regime, remove the leaders, leave in place the governing structures, the army, and the police, install a transitional government to move the Iraqis to democracy, and leave.[68]

OPERATION IRAQI FREEDOM

As historian George Baer tells us, a plan isn't a strategy. The strategy the plan was to implement can be described as decapitation as it was to eliminate the regime's control elements quickly: Franks' descriptor – "Speed kills – the enemy." The forces would move fast, bypassing major population centers, only stopping when hitting resistance. Franks and his commanders saw Baghdad as the Iraqi center of gravity, which Clausewitz defined as the "hub of all power and movement, upon which everything depends." Baghdad was also the operational objective. Its capture would topple the regime, an aim Franks made clear in his commander's intent. Rumsfeld stressed speed: the longer the war continued, the greater the chance of problems like humanitarian and refugee crises.[69]

Operation IRAQI FREEDOM began on March 19, 2003. The initial attack was "referred to with overcharged bravado" by branding it "Shock and Awe." Franks appropriated the catchphrase (and nothing else) from a study Rumsfeld provided. The invasion consisted of fewer than three US army Divisions, a reinforced Marine Division, and a British Division, about 145,000 troops, plus follow-on forces. There were around 360,000 US and Coalition military personnel in the Area of Operations (AOR). The Iraqis had 400,000 troops, 4,000 tanks and other armored vehicles, and tens of thousands of irregulars, Fedayeen Saddam, and others. Operationally, the campaign focused on destroying the Iraqi army, its ability to fight, and the regime's structures, which it did exceedingly well.[70]

The army's Third Infantry Division quickly advanced 90 miles to Nasiriyah, took the airfield and some bridges over the Euphrates, turned them over to the Marines, then advanced up the west bank of the Euphrates River to Karbala. After taking the oil fields in the south, the Marines moved north, crossed the Euphrates near Nasiriyah, and pushed further north between the Tigris and Euphrates. The British took Basra. Special Operations forces hunted SCUDS in the west and worked with the Kurds in the north.[71]

Iraqi leaders in the south were expected to surrender or defect with their troops, and the US dropped leaflets telling them to leave their weapons, go home, and wait to be recalled to provide security. The surrenders didn't happen. And Iraq unexpectedly used irregulars and suicide car bombs. The effectiveness of US forces and weapons, even in the March 24–27 sand- and rainstorm, quickly broke the Iraqi will to fight. On April 3, the Third Infantry Division took Saddam International Airport on Baghdad's western edge. The US launched two armored "Thunder Runs" through the city, on April 5 and 7, respectively.[72] The regime collapsed. Unexpectedly, so did order in Iraq.

On April 16, Franks told Rumsfeld Iraqi forces were defeated and it was time to switch to Phase IV (Stability Operations). He believed this would encourage commitment of foreign troops and allow the US to begin withdrawing. McKiernan would become head Combined Joint Task Force-Iraq for ninety days, during which time Garner was to work with McKiernan to transition control to a new government. The US used its troops to provide some security but was preparing to withdraw and halted units originally slated for the theater. Garner pushed ahead with restarting public services and helping form a new government.[73]

On May 1, 2003, President Bush announced an end to major combat operations from the deck of the carrier *Abraham Lincoln* under a banner reading "Mission Accomplished." "It was a big mistake," he said later.[74]

FAILING TO END THE WAR, FAILING TO SECURE THE PEACE, AND A DIFFERENT POLITICAL AIM

"With Saddam gone," Bush wrote, "our central objective became helping the Iraqis develop a democracy that could govern itself, sustain itself, defend itself, and serve as an ally in the war on terror." But no one understood that a different aim changed *everything*. The administration hadn't prepared for this, failed to secure the peace it had just won, and repeated mistakes made in Afghanistan. It didn't obtain a formal Iraqi surrender even though it held officials like Foreign Minister Tariq Aziz. Because it committed too few troops, it couldn't stop nationwide looting that injured American credibility. The small footprint meant the US couldn't control Iraq's borders. Many members of Saddam's Ba'ath Party, which was one of his tools for keeping power and running the country, fled to Syrian sanctuary, and jihadists infiltrated. The US lacked forces to build a new Iraqi army, units trained to deal with detainees, or enough troops to secure millions of tons of armaments US forces were reluctant to destroy because of the possible presence of WMD. There was no unity of command, thus no integration of military and civilian efforts.[75]

Washington also found a worse situation than expected. Looting injured the already wrecked infrastructure, and, Bush wrote, the "security vacuum was accompanied by a political vacuum. I decided to name an American administrator to provide order while we worked to develop a legitimate government." The administration told Garner his last day was April 30, 2003, and on May 6 announced former ambassador to the Netherlands L. Paul "Jerry" Bremer III's appointment as head of the Coalition Provisional Authority (CPA). Rumsfeld, an old friend, ensured Bremer got the post. He reported to Bush via the Pentagon. Bush gave Bremer nearly unlimited authority, including over US personnel. He had two weeks to prepare and read a RAND report on reconstructing Germany and Japan. Khalilzad, who had pulled together key Iraqi leaders to form an interim government, was shunted aside.[76]

Bremer's appointment proved critical. A democratic Iraq remained the aim. The grand strategy boiled down to quickly handing the Iraqis power and leaving. Bremer changed the grand strategy. There also arose dangerous disconnects between the Pentagon, the White House (especially in the NSC), and the military commanders on the ground regarding strategy.

Bremer killed quick transition to Iraqi rule. Feith and Wolfowitz at Defense discouraged this, but Bush told Bremer to examine the situation and do what he thought best. Bremer composed a 7-step, 540-day plan to create a democratic Iraq that became sovereign after free elections and the drafting of a constitution. He established an Iraqi Governing Council, but it couldn't stop US actions, and told them to accept an occupation. On May 22, 2003, UN Resolution 1483 designated the US and Great Britain occupying powers. The administration forced Bremer to shorten his plan and the US handed control to the Iraqi Interim Government in June 2004. It was succeeded in May 2005 by a transitional government, and a permanent one in May 2006.[77] But "liberation" became "occupation."

Rumsfeld's Pentagon told Bremer on May 9, 2003 – before he left for Iraq – to issue a de-Baathification order. Bremer issued CPA Order Number

1 on May 16, 2003 (Franks had outlawed the Baath Party on April 16). Feith's Office of Special Plans at the Pentagon authored the plan removing and excluding from the new government the top four Baath Party ranks. Garner and others warned Bremer this was extreme and would turn tens of thousands against America while making Iraq difficult to run and rebuild. Bremer went ahead. De-Baathification broke nearly every Iraqi administrative organ and threw tens of thousands out of work.[78]

CPA Order Number 2, issued on May 23, dissolved the Ministry of Defense and thus all military and intelligence branches. The idea came from Walter Slocombe, a Democrat and Clinton administration veteran recruited by Feith to work on building a new Iraqi army. The less extreme proposal approved by Bush on March 12 disbanded the Fedayeen Saddam and the Republican Guard, removed high-ranking regular army commanders, and vetted remaining officers for Baathist ties. But Slocombe suggested Bremer issue an order officially disbanding the Iraqi army. Slocombe wrote afterward: "Given our objective of replacing Hussein's regime, and not just its leader, it would have been a mistake, I think, to try to convert an army that was a principal tool of his oppressive system into the armed guardian of a new democracy." He developed this with Wolfowitz, Feith, and Bremer.[79]

On May 19, Bremer told Rumsfeld he was going to shortly issue the order and that it would put 400,000 people out of work. He also wrote: "The generally positive reaction to the earlier de-Ba'athifcation order of 16 May 03 leads me to believe this order will generate a good deal of public support, despite its impacting many more people." Bremer didn't consult the CIA, NSC, or State. Franks knew nothing about it, nor did JCS chair Peter Pace, McKiernan, or Garner. Bremer's conversations with Shia and Kurdish leaders convinced him that not disbanding the army would've caused a civil war. (The US disbanded the army and got a civil war.) Bremer wrote later. "I was following the chain of command established by the president [meaning his communications went through Rumsfeld]. It was not my responsibility to do inter-agency coordination." The defense of Slocombe, Bremer, and Rumsfeld was that the army dissolved itself. As Powell noted, the army had gone home but had not disbanded. The unit and command infrastructure remained.[80] This didn't cause the insurgency; but it helped.

The CPA plan for establishing a representative democratic government included building new police, a new, smaller army uninvolved in politics or internal security, restoring basic services like electricity, repairing and building schools, and transitioning to a market economy. The police went home during the invasion. When asked to return, 15,000 answered, but the CPA estimated Iraq needed 65–72,000. Additionally, Bremer began privatizing state-run industries to push Iraq to a free-market economy, alienating more people, especially in the middle class, and feeding unemployment. He also prevented the military from allowing local elections. Instead, people were appointed.[81]

Bremer changed American grand strategy after consulting Rumsfeld and a handful of Pentagon political appointees. The military commanders on the ground were caught unprepared as Rumsfeld and his Pentagon communicated neither with them nor the government's other arms. In July 2003 Rumsfeld told Bremer: "You are doing a good job, my friend! Keep at it."[82]

MILITARY STRATEGY

By the time Bremer went to Iraq, Rumsfeld had concluded the war was over and began bringing units home. A mid-April order stopped reinforcements while putting the US on the path to drop troop numbers to 30,000 by summer's end. In mid June 2003, Rumsfeld made Ricardo Sanchez the new commander in Iraq. Sanchez was promoted to become the army's youngest lieutenant general. General John Abizaid replaced Franks at CENTCOM. Sanchez and Bremer had different ideas about what was supposed to be happening in Iraq.[83]

Sanchez is accused of focusing on tiny details and of being in over his head because of his inexperience. He never issued a Commander's Intent (direction regarding what he wanted done). But Wolfowitz had signed an order that – in Bremer's words – "established that the military in Iraq should pay attention to my desires as 'commander's intent.'" Sanchez was starved of staff and pled unsuccessfully for the return of personnel Rumsfeld sent home. Sanchez got CENTCOM commander Abizaid to stop troop withdrawals but was given no reinforcements and told to work with what he had.[84]

By July 2003, it was clear to Abizaid and Bremer that they faced a growing insurgency. Syria, ruled by its own Baath Party, was a conduit for foreign fighters who found sanctuary in Iraq's Sunni triangle, a chunk of the Euphrates Valley north of Baghdad. US pressure on Syria to control the flow produced nothing. Meanwhile, the US was planning to replace some units with smaller foreign contingents. Abizaid told Rumsfeld this would leave insufficient forces in Iraq. Bush said the US troops would be replaced.[85]

Rumsfeld's Pentagon also failed to communicate the political purpose to its generals. Major General Jim Mattis wrote that when he received orders in late 2003 to take the First Marine Division to Iraq, "I had to read the newspapers to understand the end state desired by President Bush. It was called the 'Freedom Agenda.'" When deploying to Anbar province in 2004, Mattis wrote: "I had not [sic] specific policy guidance."[86] This echoed a Defense Department Vietnam War failure.

THE INSURGENCY BEGINS

In June 2003, the insurgency heated up, a fact many US leaders were slow to comprehend.[87] American and coalition forces had new threats and a new war. This meant US leaders needed to reassess everything they were doing, something demanding intellectual flexibility, creativity, and not a little courage. Achieving the political aim required eliminating the insurgency, something that demanded *more* forces and *much more* time than toppling Saddam's regime.

Iraq's insurgency was perhaps the most diverse in history. There were four main groups: 1) former regime elements – Baathists desiring a return to power; 2) nationalist groups wanting America out, some Sunni, some Shia; 3) religiously motivated elements seeking America's expulsion, Sunni and Shia; and 4) Al Qaeda in Iraq and similar jihadist organs. Criminal gangs and sectarianism added violent strands. The Sunnis, though a minority of the population, had been politically dominant under Saddam, and now feared a government led by the Shia majority. Iran began supporting insurgent and sectarian groups. By summer 2003, Shia leader Moqtada al-Sadr built an organization that looked like Hezbollah, was later advised by them, and had ties with Iran. In August 2003, the insurgency escalated. Attacks focused on non-US coalition elements to break it apart, though they also hit US forces. A truck bomb detonated outside UN headquarters in Baghdad on August 19, 2003. The UN withdrew. Other NGOs followed.[88]

In July, Sanchez and his staff developed their plan: defeating "internal armed threats," disarming the Iraqi militias, finding WMD caches, transferring security duties to Iraqis by February 2004, and withdrawing US forces in six months. There existed a stark disconnect between the Pentagon's civilian leaders such as Bremer and its military commanders. Bremer was busy constructing a multi-year plan to transition to Iraqi sovereignty after disbanding every major governmental arm; the army was packing to go. US troops focused on training Iraqi replacements, not providing security, while Bush and other leaders "worried we would create resentment by looking like occupiers." But Bremer had created an occupation. Troop levels fell from 192,000 to 109,000 in "the ten months following the invasion." Bush wrote later: "Cutting troop levels too quickly was the most important failure of execution in the war."[89]

But during the first year of the occupation, Sanchez didn't produce a plan addressing the insurgency and reconstruction, and the military failed to provide security. The various US divisions did as they would and there was poor military–CPA coordination, something worsened by a civilian–military culture clash and Sanchez and Bremer refusing to get along. Bremer tightly controlled CPA decision-making while repeating the Afghan War error of not running funds through the new government. The CPA instead awarded contracts to foreign companies, generating fewer Iraqi jobs. In May 2004, the Army Center for Lessons Learned revealed a consensus belief that there was no plan, and that if the CPA had one, it wasn't being relayed.[90]

A primary plank of American strategy was building an Iraqi army, something the US was slow to treat with sufficient seriousness. CPA Order Number 2 authorized a new, three-division army totaling 44,000. In May 2003, Major General Paul D. Eaton was made commander of the Coalition Military Assistance Training Team. His task was number five on the Pentagon's Iraq priorities list, his initial staff numbered six, he never received more than half the promised 250 personnel, and looting had destroyed the training infrastructure. In June 2003, the US began hiring contractors to do the training. It was clear by December that the program was failing, a point driven home in April 2004 when the first battalion deserted on its way to Fallujah after being attacked physically and verbally for going to fight its own people. In May 2004, Iraqi military and police training was placed under CENTCOM. Money and personnel began flowing and January 2005, the date for Iraqi elections, became the target for training twenty-seven Iraqi army battalions. Between 2003 and 2007, the US spent $19.2 billion on Iraqi security forces.[91]

In October 2003, the insurgency launched its Ramadan Offensive. Insurgent attacks focused on US forces and Shiite leaders allied to the Americans. US forces separated themselves from the Iraqi people and by the end of 2003 generally hunkered down in big bases. America was also in Iraq one year before seriously attempting to secure the borders. Meanwhile, the US missed an opportunity. In October 2003, an army intelligence cell learned many Sunni sheikhs in Anbar wanted to work with the US to maintain their positions. They offered to provide border security, keep the roads clear of IEDs, and wanted US help against the insurgents. But they needed arms. The intelligence group worked out a $3 million plan where the Sunnis policed their areas, the US providing the arms, vehicles, supplies, and salaries. Colonel Carol Stewart briefed staff working for Sanchez, Bremer, and the British commander, Major General Freddie Viggers. Nothing. She pitched the idea directly to Bremer. He said he didn't have the money. The fabric of society had been destroyed in these areas. The CPA missed a chance to help fix it.[92]

In December 2003, after Saddam's capture, through February 2004, Baathist insurgents began turning themselves in or asking for amnesty. The administration and the CPA weren't inclined to negotiate, and thus missed another opportunity. The US reduced its troop numbers in Iraq during the big unit rotation in the winter of 2003–04, partially because violence had fallen off after Saddam's capture. Experience and intelligence-gathering capacity departed with these units. In February 2004, US troop levels reached their lowest point between 2003 and 2004: 109,000. The same month, Abizaid said the big insurgent problem was Sunni groups aligned with Al Qaeda. He identified the insurgent strategy as attacking the new Iraqi force to destroy it before it could stand on its own. The US also captured a Zarqawi courier, who later gave up clues leading to Bin Laden, with a letter laying out Zarqawi's plan to spark a Sunni–Shia civil war in Iraq.[93]

In spring 2004, the insurgency intensified. On March 31, 2004, four American contractors were killed in Fallujah. Riots followed. Mattis developed a plan to restore control over Fallujah without a large attack but was overruled. Rumsfeld, Abizaid, and Bremer wanted a hammer. On April 3, 2004, Sanchez ordered apprehension of the murderers and elimination of insurgent sanctuary in Fallujah. Operation VIGILANT ASSAULT began on April 5, 2004. Bush halted it on April 9 after Bremer reported continuing could shatter the Iraqi Governing Council and prevent the US from transferring sovereignty in June. Fallujah became an insurgent safe haven, a magnet for foreign fighters, and proof they could defeat the United States.[94]

Fighting broke out all over Iraq in April 2004. Shiite militias under Sadr and others joined the war. Sadr's forces attacked army troops in Sadr City and other places. In mid June, Sadr agreed to a ceasefire, something he did habitually to protect his force. The new Iraqi army and police collapsed during the offensive, destroying a major plank of US strategy. US casualties were heavier than necessary because its forces were too small for the job. The administration reassessed its Iraqi army training plan and gave it to Lieutenant General David Petraeus in mid 2004.[95]

The violence revealed the "Coalition of the Willing" wasn't much of a coalition and not particularly willing. Al Qaeda strategists concluded one way to weaken America in Iraq was to strike its allies. They blew up two trains in Spain on March 11, 2004, before its general election. The anti-American Socialist Party won the ballot, as Al Qaeda hoped, and withdrew Spain's troops from Iraq in May. A stream of coalition members departed in 2004 and 2005.[96]

SUMMER 2004: THE CHANGING OF THE GUARD

On June 28, 2004, Bremer transferred power to Prime Minister Ayad Allawi. John Negroponte became ambassador. General George Casey Jr. replaced Sanchez on July 1. Casey and Negroponte were offered an opportunity to work with the Sunni tribes in Anbar but ignored it. Casey concluded from his Balkans experience that if the Americans did too much, the locals would be slow to take responsibility. He was uninterested in nation building and received little guidance from Bush or Rumsfeld. CENTCOM commander Abizaid, who believed the American presence a big part of the problem, thought ensuring January 2005's elections, protecting Iraqi leaders, building Iraq's security forces, and pushing them into the lead most important.[97]

Casey understood the aim was securing a democratic Iraq. He and Negroponte ordered a reassessment. The Red Cell planning team insisted the insurgency was worse than it appeared, its core being 8–12,000 Sunni and no more than 1,000 Islamists. Both leaders agreed and wrote a Joint Mission Statement influencing the first strategy for attacking the insurgency. Issued on August 5, 2004, "Operation Iraqi Freedom (Partnership: From Occupation to Constitutional Elections)" covered the next eighteen months. Casey saw the Iraqi government's legitimacy as the "theater center of gravity" and ordered implementation of a counterinsurgency strategy while training Iraqi forces and transitioning areas to their responsibility. Other planks included reconstruction and improving governance and security. But Casey, Abizaid, and Rumsfeld also assumed American troops were the problem, thus the plan called for consolidating US forces into nine bases. Counterinsurgency demands winning over the populace, which requires providing security. Concentrating forces abandons the population. Casey's plan also depended upon Iraqi forces that didn't yet exist.[98]

To secure the 2005 elections, America had to tamp down the insurgency in the Sunni triangle by clearing Fallujah, Samarra, and other cities. But the Sadrist Shia in Najaf, Sadr City, and other places reopened fighting in August 2004. Sadr again agreed to a ceasefire to avoid destruction and

Casey moved to clearing Sunni strongholds in October, Samarra first, then the Sunni and Al Qaeda stronghold of Fallujah on November 7, right after Bush's reelection. Some of the war's worst fighting followed. The city was retaken, but Al Qaeda leaders and other insurgents fled before the attack or escaped.[99]

In April 2005, Casey planned to hand the Iraqis the counterinsurgency (COIN) burden by November 30 of that year and province security by mid 2006. The US would help provide security in key cities but concentrate on Baghdad. Casey increased the number of advisors and trainers, and pushed Iraqis into the lead while transitioning control. He shrank the US footprint by consolidating bases. Casey assumed the insurgency wouldn't intensify, but proved mistaken about this and Iraqi ability to take up the slack.[100]

In July 2005, Khalilzad became US ambassador. Part of his job was convincing Sunnis to enter the electoral process. Casey gave him a brief titled "Securing Strategic Success." Its military objective was reducing the insurgency to the point Iraqi forces could handle it by securing Baghdad and the Sunni triangle areas around it, holding down areas to the capital's north and south, and blocking cross-border infiltration. The US would transition security responsibilities to Iraqi forces by 2006. But Khalilzad wanted a review. Casey agreed, and a new military–civilian Red Team evaluated US strategy based upon past experience with insurgencies. Casey's previous reviews in December 2004 and June 2005 concluded things were going well. The new Red Team argued the coalition wasn't gaining ground, Iraqi forces weren't progressing quickly enough, and Casey's transitioning timetable was unrealistic. Casey, one work observed, "had a plan for taking American troops out of Iraq but not for leaving a stable and democratic country in their wake."[101]

The review team developed a strategy for breaking the insurgency in one year and completely defeating it in three. It suggested an "ink-spot" strategy securing specific points and then spreading. But this required lots of troops, and Casey was trying to draw down. The worst problem the Red Team identified was disagreement on what US strategy was supposed to accomplish in Iraq. Khalilzad thought they were supposed to defeat the insurgency. Casey thought they were supposed to build an Iraqi security force sufficiently strong to take on the insurgency.[102]

Casey disliked the Red Team's conclusions, attacked their reasoning, and never let them present their slides. Khalilzad didn't want to directly oppose Casey, so he backdoored him by taking the Red Team brief to Washington. National Security Advisor Stephen Hadley told him to somehow push a copy of it into the military chain of command so it could assume ownership. A British member of the Red Team got a copy to British Prime Minister Blair, who raised it with Bush. But then it died. The result: "It would take another sixteen months before Casey's strategy of handing off to the Iraqis was formally rejected and for the concepts in the ink spot approach to return in the guise of the surge." The review and the command's June Campaign Progress Review combined to propel Casey to plan beyond 2005. The result was the Bridging Strategy, lasting until mid 2006 and described as "Al Qaeda out, Sunni in, ISF [Iraqi Security Forces] in the lead" because it focused on destroying Al Qaeda, bringing the Sunni into the governing process, and putting Iraqis in the fore.[103]

Casey's forces mounted numerous operations, particularly in summer and fall 2005, including efforts seal the border with Syria, the commitment of more troops to Anbar province, and Colonel H. R. McMaster's pacification of Tal Afar. In the fall, US forces cleared towns along the Euphrates Valley between Baghdad and the Syrian border. The idea was to clear and hold. The US did the clearing but lacked troops for holding. Iraqis were supposed to do much of this but were too few or not up to the job. By the end of 2005, the insurgency was perhaps stronger than at the beginning of the year. Casey began making new commanders learn COIN but ignored yet another chance to work with the Sunni, this time those near the Al Qaeda capital of al Qaim.[104]

THE ADMINISTRATION'S STRATEGY

Meanwhile, some at the State Department searched for a new strategy. Philip Zelikow, one of Secretary of State Rice's advisors, from studying the Vietnam War picked up the idea of "Clear and Hold" and concluded after touring Iraq that the war was a stalemate, and that American strategy should be "Clear, Hold, and Build." He discussed this with Lieutenant General Raymond Odierno, who liked it. Zelikow then put the idea in Rice's brief to Congress, the State Department hoping that if it said it enough times, the Pentagon might pick it up. Rumsfeld got a copy of Rice's brief beforehand but doesn't seem to have paid attention to it. When Rice presented Congress this strategy in October 2005, it shocked both Rumsfeld and Casey.[105]

The idea was developed further by another civilian, Peter Feaver, an academic in an NSC strategic-planning cell. He wrote *The National Strategy for Victory in Iraq* (which the administration published in November 2005), developing "Clear, Hold, and Build." The military would clear, hold, and build (assisted in holding and building by civilians and the international community), thus isolating the insurgents and winning over the Sunnis. Bush followed with a speech touting American success in Tal Afar and a public relations campaign to keep up public support. The strategy declared: "Iraq is the central front in the global war on terror. Failure in Iraq will embolden terrorists and expand their reach; success in Iraq will deal them a decisive and crippling blow."[106]

All of this demonstrates the continuous lack of clear communication and control regarding strategy in the administration. Casey wasn't told about this beforehand, and on a January 2006 Washington trip, wasn't asked to change strategy. Bush requested he remain in command until spring 2007. Casey agreed, went back to Iraq, and kept on as before. Casey's metric for success was how much of the country had been handed off to Iraqi forces. Casey continued the drawdown and consolidation of American forces, surrendering parts of Diyala and Baghdad to the insurgents. On April 28, 2006, he issued a new campaign plan: "Transition to Iraqi Self-Reliance." This was the same as the old plan. The point was getting out, not winning. Casey directed an intense fight against the insurgency but was failing to break it.[107]

THE IRAQ WAR TO THE JIHADISTS

Iraq wasn't just the central front in Bush's "war on terror," but the jihadists' as well, particularly Al Qaeda. In 2003, some jihadists insisted Iraq was the perfect place for a victory. They could bleed America to death economically and physically, creating a decisive turning point in the fight against the "Jewish–Crusader" alliance while securing a base for global jihad. Iraq became a magnet drawing the world's jihadists. Al Qaeda in Iraq and its leader Zarqawi led Iraq's descent into sectional strife. In January 2006, Zarqawi created the Mujahideen Shura Council to pull groups under Al Qaeda's umbrella. On February 22, 2006, as part of Zarqawi's plan to start a Sunni–Shia civil war, Al Qaeda operatives blew up the dome of the Al Askari Mosque in Samarra, one of the most important Shia sites. Even as sectarian violence increased, Casey refused to budge from concentration and drawdown. The Iraqi Interior Ministry, which included the police, was heavily infiltrated by Sadr supporters, and pursued ethnic cleansing against Sunnis. Iraq descended into a Sunni–Shia civil war.[108]

By spring 2006, Joint Special Operations Command had intensified its attacks against insurgents and Al Qaeda. It concentrated on western Anbar and the area south of Baghdad known as the "southern belts" or the "Triangle of Death." The raids produced valuable intel for deciphering

WILSONIAN REVOLUTIONARIES: THE BUSH ADMINISTRATION, 2001-2009

Zarqawi's network, tracking him, and having an air force F-16 drop large pieces of ordnance on the house where he was hiding. Analysis of the scene yielded intel for further raids and Al Qaeda's plan to control the belts – or villages – around Baghdad. Zarqawi's death and establishment of the new Iraqi government convinced Casey his strategy was working.[109]

Throughout 2006, Abizaid and Casey continued shifting responsibility to the Iraqis while reducing troop numbers and consolidating, but increased violence after the Samarra bombing made this impossible. Military leaders continued rejecting the dispatch of more troops, clinging to the belief that America's presence worsened things while allowing Iraqis to do less.[110] This played into the enemy's hands by reducing US military strength in relation to the enemy's and decreasing America's chances of success while increasing the opponent's effectiveness at no cost to them. US leaders consistently failed Clausewitz's supreme test for wartime leaders: understanding the nature of the war in which they were involved. They faced a significant, multi-headed insurgency. Defeating this demands large forces to eliminate or block sanctuaries, prevent outside assistance, and secure the population.

THE BUSH ADMINISTRATION REASSESSES

The aftermath of the Samarra bombing was a wake-up call for Bush. "For two and half years," he wrote, "I had supported the strategy of withdrawing our forces as the Iraqis stepped forward." He feared his commanders were failing. Bush decided an actual counterinsurgency strategy might be the answer, a view influenced by McMaster's success in Tal Afar and Petraeus' in Mosul. Bush also learned that commanders below Abizaid and Casey believed they needed more troops. By summer 2006, Bush worried the US would lose the war. Americans disapproved of his handling of it by nearly two to one. He understood the importance of keeping public support and "made a conscious decision to show resolve, not doubt, in public." Unlike many others, Bush believed America could still win.[111]

In August 2006, after Casey launched two Baghdad operations that failed to restore order, Bush concluded American strategy needed to change, as did his military commanders and defense secretary. But he delayed until after the midterm elections, fearing this would be seen as being made for political reasons. It would have been better to tackle the problem immediately. By this time, the US was conducting three different strategy reviews. The most important was pushed by Bush and run by Hadley and the NSC. This included Bush meeting with Iraq's president, Nouri al-Maliki, who promised to crack down on sectarian violence, even from his coreligionist Shia.

The JCS were doing a review in which Bush had them consider sending more troops. Zelikow headed another at the State Department. By late 2006, a consensus arose among Bush, his new secretary of defense, Robert Gates, Maliki, members of the bipartisan Iraq Study Group, and numerous others that exerting control over Baghdad was pivotal to winning the war. On December 13, Bush attended a Pentagon JCS meeting on Iraq strategy. Rumsfeld was there, as was his replacement, Gates, who had not yet been confirmed by the Senate. Bush asked about adding more troops. The Chiefs worried this would break the military from the strain on personnel and their families. Bush told them: "The surest way to break the military would be to lose in Iraq." Worse was their focus. Gates wrote: "I was struck in the meeting by the service chiefs' seeming detachment from the wars we were in and their focus on future contingencies and stress on the force. Not one uttered a single sentence on the need for us to win in Iraq."[112]

Bush and Gates decided the new commander in Iraq would be Petraeus. Casey was promoted to army chief of staff (as had been Westmoreland after Tet). Ryan Crocker became ambassador; he and Petraeus worked as a team. Bush decided to commit more troops in what became known as "the Surge." Discussions encompassed sending more forces to Anbar to support the Sunni or Anbar Awakening as Sunni tribes turned against Al Qaeda.[113]

On January 10, 2007, Bush announced a strategy change and dispatched an additional 20,000 troops (it became 30,000). Counterinsurgency, the "Clear, Hold, and Build" version, officially became strategy. This time it came from the president, and he had people at the Pentagon and in Iraq to implement it. Bush emphasized the importance of securing Baghdad and noted the US hadn't done so earlier because of a lack of troops and failing to enter the Shia enclaves birthing violence. The US had cleared areas of the city but not held them. Now, Iraqi and US troops would clear and hold. Bush told Maliki no sectarian differences would be tolerated, that "America's commitment to Iraq was not open-ended," and announced that to "establish its authority, the Iraqi government plans to take responsibility for security in all of Iraq's provinces by November." Bush sent 4,000 more troops to Anbar to act against Iranian and Syrian networks supporting insurgents. Reconstruction – Build – continued. To Bush, the Iraq War was part of a larger struggle developing in the Middle East, "the decisive ideological struggle of our time ... between the forces of freedom and extremism."[114]

Bush faced intense resistance to and reaction against his decision. Like Vietnam, the Iraq War had become hard. Opposition crossed political lines. Rice and Zelikow opposed it, as did Republican New Hampshire Senator

Bob Smith, but Democrats such as John Kerry dominated the ranks of freshly minted dissenters. Senators Hillary Clinton and Barack Obama were against it, positions, they later admitted to Bob Gates, adopted purely for narrow political reasons. The new Democratic Party–controlled Congress passed a resolution in February 2007 against Bush's "Surge." Democratic Senator Harry Reid (who had voted for the war) declared it lost and said: "We're going to pick up Senate seats as a result of this war." In May, Congress passed a defense bill (which Bush vetoed) mandating US withdrawal begin on October 1, 2007, and conclude in 180 days. The *New York Times* declared the war lost in July. Bush made the "Surge" decision against the advice of some military commanders and replaced them.[115] But why did Bush's defense secretary, Rumsfeld, and the chief American military leaders fail to see that more troops were needed in Iraq and resist this? Why, also, were they unable to see the importance of winning the war? The system for selecting and educating senior civilians and officers had serious flaws.

The additional 30,000 US troops were joined by forces from other nations. American strength in Iraq peaked at around 170,000 in November 2007. Petraeus assumed command in February 2007. He moved troops from bases outside the city into outposts in Baghdad and then to its Belts. Violence immediately declined. Petraeus and Crocker also launched a review. On April 20, 2007, McMaster's Joint Strategic Assessment Team (JSAT) emphasized moving sectarian groups toward reconciliation and ending the Iraqi government's feeding of sectarian violence. Population security became the military focus. Troops supported the Anbar tribes and insurgents were encouraged to switch sides. The training of Iraqi security forces intensified. The team aimed for "sustainable security" by early 2008.[116]

The "Surge" showed success by July. One reason was the Anbar Awakening, where Sunni tribes fought Al Qaeda. Its exact origins remain unclear, but it began when sheikhs allied to fight Al Qaeda in response to American efforts at outreach and building a police force. A formal Awakening document issued on September 14, 2006 called for cooperation with the Americans. US troops encouraged local leaders to reach out and helped spread the Awakening beyond Anbar.[117]

The strategy change and Sunni shift brought the near-destruction of Al Qaeda in Iraq, and Sadr's suppression. It had costs: 1,124 Americans were killed, 7,710 wounded; Iraqi military, police, and civilian losses numbered 24,000. But America established the security necessary for achieving political accommodation. At the end of May 2008, CIA Director General Michael Hayden mentioned the "Near strategic defeat of al-Qaida in Iraq." But the US failed to finish Al Qaeda at the moment it was morphing into

Islamic State. Bush and Maliki inked a Status of Forces Agreement (SOFA) in December 2008 fixing the US withdrawal for 2011's end.[118]

America made many mistakes. It assumed a rarity in war: all would be quick and easy. Tied with this was a failure to understand the nature of the war and adapt strategy to meet the reality and its aims. The traditional American refusal to commit sufficient military means nearly proved fatal. The opposite – overwhelming force – can sometimes trump other strategic sins and provide time to recover. The administration failed for too long to dominate the counterinsurgency trio: support of the people, controlling sanctuary, and controlling outside support. Iraqi failures were staggering: slowness to compromise politically, sectarian violence, ethnic cleansing, and extensive government corruption.

BEYOND AFGHANISTAN AND IRAQ

The administration's "Global War on Terror" reached many places. By June 2002, Americans were training forces in the Philippines, Yemen, and Georgia, while more than 90 states detained or arrested more than 2,400 terrorism suspects, and over 180 had given or offered support. CENTCOM conducted operations against Al Qaeda in Yemen made possible by a joint task force working from Djibouti cooperating with numerous governments in eastern Africa and the Arabian Peninsula.[119] Action in numerous other nations followed.

The Iraq War initially produced some of the international effects the Bush administration wanted. Libya's Qaddafi ended his chemical and nuclear weapons programs. The Cedar Revolution followed in Lebanon, as did minor reforms and elections in Kuwait and Egypt, and elections in the Palestinian territories. But elections could be a setback: Hamas won the 2006 Palestinian ballot. And Iraq's chaos discouraged democratization. There were also missed opportunities. After 9/11, Iran approached the administration. Saddam's quick fall made Tehran willing to discuss its support for Hamas and Hezbollah and its nuclear weapons program. The administration failed to grasp this opportunity, a reluctance partly resulting from the assumption Iran's regime verged on revolution. In April 2005, Iran began creating uranium gas. By August, it was enriching uranium.[120]

Bush extended the Freedom Agenda to Liberia by using US forces to encourage the departure of its dictator. Bush backed NATO expansion and withdrew from the ABM treaty with Russia to have the freedom to develop missile defense. A newly aggressive Russia occupied two provinces of Georgia in August 2008. Pyongyang detonated its first nuclear device in November 2006. UN sanctions followed. A deal was cut in which North Korea received aid and removal from the US list of terrorism sponsors in return for destroying its Yongbyon nuclear facility. This didn't stop North Korean nuclear development. Deterrence remained America's primary global strategy, but Washington insisted upon maintaining the ability to defeat any adversary.[121]

CHINA

The 2000s marked profound changes in America's economy from "import shock" as China entered global manufacturing and became the hub for labor-intensive assembly jobs. Chinese competition furthered American deindustrialization. Restricting imports wasn't considered a tool for managing trade, partially because of the rules of the World Trade Organization, which China joined in December 2001. China was open to foreign investment and thus suffered limited pushback from American politicians and business interests, except for unsuccessful efforts to counter Chinese currency manipulation. Washington pursued a strategy of dissuasion to convince China to not seek regional hegemony in order to preserve the Asian balance of power, action partly driven by the Defense Strategy Review concluding that growing Chinese military power was a threat. The planks of the strategy included increased engagement of China, strengthening regional alliances, and increasing the military capabilities of allies and partners. China concentrated on growing militarily and economically. The trade deficit with China went from $83 billion to $273 billion from 2001 to 2010, while US debt held by China rose from $78 billion to $1.1 trillion from 2001 to 2011.[122]

ECONOMIC STRATEGY

Bush consistently supported free trade, even after the 2008 global economic meltdown, believing this and open markets produced global economic growth and that "Economic freedom also reinforces political freedom." He helped pass the Central American Free Trade Agreement, secured fifteen free-trade accords, and used regional and bilateral trade deals to pressure other states to lower trade barriers and move toward Washington's free-trade orthodoxy.[123]

Bush pushed for lower taxes to increase incentives to invest and work, and reduced government regulation to encourage growth in the belief that free-market economies produced the most prosperity for the most people. One reason Bush pushed tax cuts early was an advisor warning the NASDAQ's explosion in value was probably a speculative bubble. This proved correct when the dot.com bubble burst and a recession began in March 2001. Bush saw the cuts as stimulus. The 9/11 attacks drove a short recession, but the economy quickly revived, and unemployment fell. Growth and spending remained high during Bush's tenure, and the economic recovery began after the tax cuts. Deficits increased and Clinton's surplus disappeared as military, discretionary, and social spending climbed. The deficit-to-GDP ratio increased, but the debt-to-GDP ratio declined because of economic growth.[124]

During the 2008 presidential campaign, the US was struck by its greatest economic crisis in eighty years. Between October 9, 2007 and March 2009 the stock market lost more than half its value. Investment firm Lehman Brothers collapsed in September 2008. Global shockwaves followed. The issuance of massive numbers of subprime (higher-risk) mortgages during a booming housing market fueled by easy credit was the primary cause. Investment banks bundled the loans and sold them as securities, often with fantasy AAA ratings. Banks and financial advising companies invested heavily. When rapid housing price increases stopped, the bubble burst.[125]

Bush staunched the economic bleeding through buying toxic assets, the September 2008 bailout of America's largest mortgage lenders, Fannie Mae and Freddie Mac (Bush's earlier efforts at reform here had been blocked by Democrats), and the October bailout of the banking system. Part of this was done via the Troubled Assets Relief Program (TARP). This allowed banks to open the flow of credit the crisis had constrained and ensured the administration didn't repeat a major Depression-era mistake of shrinking available credit. Bush propped up the auto industry with loans, allowing it to restructure, thus preventing its collapse.[126]

The effects of these economic actions are difficult to assess because of the confluence of factors: the bursting of the dot.com bubble, the recession that followed, tax cuts, spending for two wars, the expansion of entitlement and discretionary spending, and the 2008 economic meltdown. GDP growth averaged 2.1 percent annually, a number including the dramatic 2008 drop. It was 2.5 percent without this. The Clinton economy averaged 3.9 percent. The national debt reached $10 trillion. It was $5.6 trillion when Bush entered office.[127]

CONCLUSION

Bush's presidency was an anomaly for modern Republican presidents as for nearly the entire previous century Democratic leaders had generally led the US into wars or held power when America was attacked and felt it had no choice but to fight.[128] Military force became the dominant tool of the administration's grand strategy, backed by an overconfidence in what it could achieve combined with continuous failure to understand how to use it. This becomes clearer by listing the mistakes duplicated in Afghanistan and Iraq: failure to supply sufficient means; failure to negotiate an end to the war with the defeated side; failure to deal with looting in both capitals; failure to have plans for securing the peace; and failure to remove or address insurgent sanctuary. The Bush administration didn't understand the use of power – military, political, or otherwise. It eventually learned in Iraq, but almost too late. Firing subordinates who didn't perform could've helped.

Also disconcerting is the lack of debate from key administration figures about whether or not overthrowing Saddam's regime and democratizing Iraq was a good idea. One analyst notes: "The rationale for going to war was not deeply interrogated – indeed, it was never debated in an NSC meeting." The administration also made no effort to mitigate the enormous risk it assumed. Both the US and Iraq paid the price. The administration also launched its "global war on terror" without serious analysis by or resistance from most administration figures.[129]

One critic of the administration's approach to foreign affairs wrote that "values and ideals have trumped interests" and "risk taking has overcome prudence." It also trumped the basic components of logical strategic thinking. Analyst Colin Dueck wrote of the Bush administration: "To pursue a global grand strategy without providing the means – military, political, and economic – for it is to invite not only humiliation, but disaster."[130]

PART IV

RETREAT AND DEFEAT

19

RETRENCHMENT, ENGAGEMENT, AND WAR: THE OBAMA YEARS, 2009–2017

INTRODUCTION

Barack Obama faced the worst economic crisis of any president since Franklin Roosevelt as America's economic calamity became a global meltdown. The US suffered a 4.1 percent drop in GDP and "the steepest peak-to-trough recession in the post-World War II era." Housing prices plummeted by as much as 40 percent; unemployment reached 10 percent and remained high.[1]

ASSESSMENT

Obama believed US foreign actions too often damaging, especially during the Cold War. He saw "international politics as an expensive business" America wasn't "obliged to fund," and mistrusted and dismissed the views of the supposed bipartisan foreign affairs "Blob." Like presidents before him, he blamed his predecessor for foreign relations and economic troubles. This was partly true, especially regarding Iraq. The administration believed Obama's own "special story," combined with what they perceived as a humbler approach, would pay dividends. Obama traveled extensively in 2009. It produced little.[2]

THE POLITICAL AIMS

Obama intended his presidency to be as transformative as Reagan's, but in a Progressive way. The administration initially lacked clear political aims but wanted global nuclear disarmament (unachievable), to improve US relations with the Muslim world, to repair US relations and reputation injured by the 2003–11 Iraq War, an Iran deal, and a "reset" with Moscow. Obama told incoming CIA Director Leon Panetta his agency's most important task was killing or capturing Bin Laden. Susan Rice, Obama's UN ambassador and last national security advisor, said Obama sought "to renew America's global leadership."[3]

The 2010 and 2015 *National Security Strategies* lack clear aims while confusing aims with strategies, but one comes through in the 2010 *NSS*: "The United States supports the expansion of democracy and human rights abroad because governments that respect these values are more just, peaceful, and legitimate." Obama repudiated using force to impose democracy and said in May 2011 during the Arab Spring (discussed below): "it will be the policy of the United States to promote reform across the region, and to support transitions to democracy."[4]

A GRAND STRATEGY OF TACTICS

Middle East expert and administration veteran Vali Nasr said the administration lacked foreign relations vision and that tactical political decisions dominated decision-making. Obama had a "habit of funneling major foreign policy decisions through a small cabal of relatively inexperienced White House advisers whose turf was strictly politics." Their worry was "how any action in Afghanistan or the Middle East would play on the nightly news, or which talking point it would give the Republicans." Middle East and Afghanistan actions were "reshaped to accommodate partisan political concerns." White House "micromanagement" was common, particularly in military matters.[5]

A key grand strategy plank was retrenchment, which "looks for ways to reduce a country's international and military costs and commitments." Retrenchment is risky. It can indicate weakness or decline, injuring relations with allies and emboldening enemies. It's sometimes executed via accommodation or conciliation. Obama thought accommodating rivals could shift them from being adversaries and possibly make them friends. Retrenchment partially reflected American public opinion, and Obama's pragmatism aided implementation. But his approach rested upon two false assumptions: that America's adversaries wanted to be conciliated, and that it was possible to accommodate them. The administration also practiced engagement.[6]

Obama said he had no "grand strategy in" his "back pocket," but there was an early effort to create one. In July 2009, Chairman of the JCS Admiral Mike Mullen wanted strategic guidance that looked beyond military power. The result was August 2009's *National Strategic Narrative*. Its most important "strategic imperative for the twenty-first century" was sustainability and proposed a strategy "to achieve sustainable prosperity and security ... through the application of credible influence and strength, the pursuit of fair competition, acknowledgement of interdependencies and converging interests, and adaptation to complex, dynamic systems – all bounded by our national values." It was ignored in the first term. A revised and expanded version was reexamined after Obama's reelection and also rejected.[7]

"DON'T DO STUPID SHIT": AN OBAMA DOCTRINE?

The closest Jeffrey Goldberg's well-known "The Obama Doctrine" comes to identifying a grand strategy is: "Double down in those parts of the world where success is plausible, and limit America's exposure to the rest." Obama believed Washington possessed standard reactions – a "playbook" – that pushed the US into wars. America's entry into each war is unique. Ben Rhodes, who began as a campaign speechwriter and became deputy national security advisor for strategic communication, emerged in Obama's second term as the administration's most influential foreign relations voice. The administration didn't develop a doctrine, Rhodes said, because "The world was too complicated to sum up in a doctrine." In the spring of 2014, after meeting with prominent presidential historians, Obama concluded one of the most important things was avoiding a serious foreign relations mistake. He told reporters: "What's the Obama doctrine?" 'Don't do stupid shit.'" Hillary Clinton, Obama's first secretary of state, later criticized her former boss. "Great nations need organizing principles," she said. "'Don't do stupid stuff' is not an organizing principle."[8]

ECONOMIC STRATEGY

The global economic crisis dominated the administration's early days. Obama helped General Motors and other firms and convinced many G-20 nations to fund financial stimulus. Obama secured a $787 billion package largely of relief measures. It included infrastructure spending to create jobs but provided hundreds of millions of dollars securing loans to companies that failed, like Solyndra, an example of the administration effort to drive a shift to "green" energy. The money helped shore up the nation's safety net but failed to induce growth. One economist called it Keynesianism's greatest failure since the 1970s.[9]

Obama avoided the Great Depression error of generally raising income taxes during an economic downturn, passed a minor payroll tax deduction, and agreed to make the Bush tax cuts permanent. But he repeated Roosevelt's mistake of increasing the regulatory burden. Small business rules grew 38 percent by 2012, injuring a primary American job creator. Economic uncertainty and growing regulation saw large corporations hold the highest percentage of their wealth in half a century – $1.7 trillion – by July 2010. America possessing the world's highest developed-nation corporate tax rate – 35 percent – injured competitiveness and fed business "off shoring." The administration followed the free-trade consensus and wanted to double foreign trade by 2015. It inked the Transatlantic Trade and Investment Partnership (TTIP) and the Trans-Pacific Partnership (TPP), the latter part of the "pivot to Asia," examined shortly. The TPP died during the 2016 election campaign, denounced by both presidential candidates.[10]

In December 2007, the unemployment rate was 5 percent. It peaked at 10 percent in October 2009 during the recession. Unemployment was 4.8 percent when Obama left office. Respectively, GDP growth in Obama's first and second terms averaged 2.0 and 2.3 percent annually. The US average between 1947 and 2015 was 3.2 percent. Obama increased the national debt from $10.65 trillion to $19.95 trillion.[11] Congress, which approves spending, always assists here.

INFORMATION STRATEGY

Rhetoric and narrative were important to the administration. Informationally, Obama launched an outreach effort to the Muslim world exemplified by his 2009 Cairo speech, hoping to establish a new approach for Western cooperation. George W. Bush's 2003 Iraq War damaged US relations with some Muslim nations, but not as much as believed. The speech's good effects proved temporary. Critics from Obama's own party saw a disconnect between words, actions, and implementation. Former Carter national security advisor Zbigniew Brzezinski said: "I greatly admire his insights and understanding. I don't think he really has a policy that's implementing those insights and understandings. The rhetoric is always terribly imperative and categorical: 'You must do this,' 'He must do that,' 'This is unacceptable.'" "He doesn't strategize. He sermonizes."[12]

DIPLOMATIC STRATEGY

Obama harbored suspicions of the foreign affairs cognoscenti (understandably) but didn't doubt diplomacy's utility. Here, as in military matters, he gained a reputation for deliberateness. Critics branded it "dithering." With some unsolvable problems, Obama followed the bureaucratic practice of asking for another report. Defense Secretary Bob Gates, who worked for eight chief executives, valued Obama's approach: "I found it refreshing and reassuring." The administration was willing to deal with any regime regardless of its ideology – an asset – but often ignored competitors' ideological motivations and political aims. Obama planned to personally engage the leaders of Iraq, Syria, and Iran, saying: "Once it's clear that we are not intending to stay for ten years or twenty years, all these parties have an interest in figuring out: How do we adjust in a way that stabilizes the situation?" But these states defined their own interests and aims.[13]

CHINA AND THE PIVOT TO ASIA

Obama wanted more engagement in Asia, decided to treat China as the global power it was becoming, and saw here a potential partner. Attempts to accommodate China included Secretary of State Clinton stating publicly that human rights disagreements wouldn't affect other matters. The administration hoped a rising China would be a stabilizing force, but Beijing became increasingly aggressive after 2008, noticeably so by 2010, especially in the South China Sea where it alienated neighbors with disputes over islands and shoals.[14]

In October 2011, Clinton announced the "pivot to Asia," a shift in emphasis from Afghanistan and Iraq. The administration argued America was overcommitted in the Middle East but insufficiently in the Asia Pacific where economic connections were growing increasingly important. National Security Advisor Tom Donilon said: "our overarching objective is to sustain a stable security environment and a regional order rooted in economic openness, peaceful resolution of disputes, democratic governance, and political freedom." This arose from a vision of "a region where the rise of new powers occurs peacefully" and wasn't an effort "to contain any nation." The strategy rested upon reinforcing alliances, strengthening relations with emerging powers such as India, more involvement with regional organizations like the G-20 and the Association of Southeast Asian Nations (ASEAN), "pursuing a stable and constructive relationship with China," and growing economic integration. The administration planned to have 60 percent of the navy in the Pacific by 2020.[15]

Observers questioned whether Washington had the military power to support the pivot as it dispatched to Asia a larger percentage of a shrinking military. The administration's acceptance of China's 2013 self-declared East China Sea Air Defense Identification Zone (ADIZ), even though it violated international law, undermined its credibility among Pacific democracies and the pivot itself. In December 2013, China began building artificial landmasses on Spratly Islands reefs. Like everyone, the administration believed engagement could change China. Brookings Institution scholars wrote that

PART IV: RETREAT AND DEFEAT

Chinese officials believed Obama "places too much faith in the capacity of ideas to bend history, whereas the Chinese understand the greater importance of *real politik* [sic]."[16]

RUSSIA, EUROPE, AND NATO

Obama thought US–Russia relations were troubled because of Bush. Putin's war against Georgia in 2008 failed to shake this view. Obama's approach to Russia was marked by a March 2009 meeting when Clinton gave the Russian foreign minister, Sergey Lavrov, a red button she believed said in Russian "reset" but that read "overcharge." Putin disliked NATO expansion and particularly worried about US plans for missile defense in Europe to counter Iran, fearing a future counter to its ICBMs. Administration reassurances that this would go away if there was no Iranian missile threat had no effect. The administration tried conciliating Russia, and the White House insisted the "reset" worked but Putin cooperated only when in his interests. For example, the lower numbers of the New Strategic Arms Reduction Treaty (START) benefited Moscow because of the financial savings while validating what it was already doing.[17]

In February 2014, Russia invaded Ukraine's Crimea region and subsequently annexed it. November 2014 saw Putin extend his war into eastern Ukraine. Obama and America's European allies and partners responded with limited sanctions, non-lethal aid to Ukraine, deployments of NATO forces to states bordering Russia, and expelling Russia from the G-8. NSC advisor Rice said the US aim "was not just to punish Russia for its actions but to pressure it to withdraw its military from Ukraine and restore its sovereign border" (pressure is a strategy, withdrawal is an aim). Administration detachment from the reality of authoritarian state behavior was exemplified by Secretary of State Kerry's March 2014 comment that Russia was "engaging in activity that is completely contradictory to the standards that most of us are trying to operate by in the 21st century." Obama said Russia "was on the wrong side of history." On September 5, 2016, at the G-20 summit, Obama warned Putin about election interference and threatened punishment, but did nothing before the 2016 presidential election.[18]

Obama maintained America's NATO commitment but reduced America's European forces from 75,000 to 50,000. He believed America's allies should carry more of their defense burden and was aggrieved by NATO members not spending their promised 2 percent of GDP on defense. "Free riders aggravate me," Obama said, and successfully browbeat the British prime minister, David Cameron, to have Britain keep its word. NATO approached deterrence with renewed seriousness after Russia's Ukraine war and Islamic State's rise.[19]

THE ARAB SPRING AND THE MIDDLE EAST

The Arab Spring was sparked by the December 17, 2010 self-immolation of Tunisian vendor Mohamed Bouazizi to protest his arbitrary treatment by Tunisia's dictatorship. His shocking act provoked demonstrations that toppled Tunisia's government on January 14, 2011. When protests erupted against Egypt's Hosni Mubarak the same month, Obama ended thirty years of American support and pressured Mubarak to step down. American allies in the region were stunned, many wondering if Washington would treat them similarly in the face of protests. On May 19, 2011, Obama promised to support political reform, transitions to democracy, and human rights in the Middle East and North Africa. Obama backed the Islamist Muslim Brotherhood government of Mohamed Morsi that succeeded Mubarak. Its extremism and incompetence generated mass protests. Egypt's military overthrew it in July 2013.[20]

Obama bet on working with supposedly moderate Islamists and lost. Supporting Morsi injured relations with Saudi Arabia. The administration tried unsuccessfully to push the Saudis and Iranians toward détente. It addressed the Israeli–Palestinian hedgehog by focusing on halting Israeli settlement construction and encouraging the Palestinians to abandon violence, while misjudging its ability to stop settlement construction and reopen talks. Obama insisted Israeli leaders didn't understand what was in their own best interests.[21]

THE LIBYA WAR, 2011

The Arab Spring quickly reached Libya. On February 15, 2011, Qaddafi's troops fired on demonstrators. By the end of February, rebels controlled much of the country's east. The administration froze $30 billion in Libyan assets, imposed sanctions, and sealed a UN Security Council Resolution embargoing arms sales. On March 3, after discussions with Germany's Angela Merkel, Obama publicly called for Qaddafi to go.[22]

On March 12, the Arab League called for the imposition of a no-fly zone. Obama was trying to exit Iraq and Afghanistan and didn't want another war. Britain and France were vociferous about intervening, as were key administration members: Clinton, Rhodes, Rice, Samantha Powers, and Antony Blinken. Biden warned against it. Defense Secretary Gates asked: "Can I just finish the two wars we're already in before you go looking for new ones?" When it appeared Qaddafi might recapture Benghazi and a humanitarian disaster ensue, those wanting a US war triumphed.[23]

As a no-fly zone wouldn't prevent Gaddafi retaking Benghazi or killing its inhabitants, Obama secured a March UN Security Council Resolution allowing "'all necessary measures' to protect civilians on the ground." This was – Rhodes said – "a euphemism for war." Washington would lead in establishing a no-fly zone and dismantling Libya's air defenses but commit no troops, leaving that to Europe and the Arab League. In April, Clinton "helped NATO leaders craft a communique that made Gaddafi's ousting a formal political objective of the military action." The administration chose to fight a war against Libya, regime change being the aim. Obama insisted inaction would discredit the UN Security Council.[24]

Unlike Bush, Obama went to war without Congressional approval, refused to call it a war, and said the War Powers Act didn't apply. He insisted before his election: "the president does not have the power under the Constitution to unilaterally authorize a military attack in a situation that does not involve stopping an actual imminent threat to the nation." White House lawyers told Rhodes to not use "war" in Libya discussions; he substituted "kinetic military action." The Republican-controlled House admonished Obama with a nonbinding resolution supported by forty-five Democrats. Democratic Congressman Dennis Kucinich tried to pass a resolution to end the war.[25]

Obama's Libya war, hailed as a model, became a debacle. Obama took "a much more hands-on approach than he ever took to daily operations in Iraq or Afghanistan." The US-led Operation ODYSSEY DAWN commenced on March 19, 2011. NATO forces established air control over the major cities, struck Libyan air defenses and ground forces threatening civilians, and established a no-fly zone. NATO warships, nineteen American, imposed a blockade on March 23. The rebels went on the offensive after the initial air attacks. On March 31, NATO assumed command of what was now called Operation UNIFIED PROTECTOR. On August 22, the rebels took Tripoli. On October 20, they killed Qaddafi. The regime collapsed within three days. Obama achieved his political aim but had no plan for after. Libya sank into civil war and became a haven for groups using terrorism.[26]

The war injured the administration. In May 2011, an Obama advisor described their approach as "leading from behind," provoking ridicule. Worse, the war fed Putin's paranoia. Obama had convinced the Russians to not veto the UN resolution by portraying the intended actions "as limited and merely humanitarian." The war instead overthrew a Russian partner.

Tragedy and scandal followed. On September 11, 2012, Al Qaeda killed US Ambassador to Libya Christopher Stevens and three other Americans. The administration decided upon a "counternarrative" and dispatched UN Ambassador Rice. When Rice told her mother she was doing the Sunday morning news shows because Clinton was too exhausted, her mother said: "I smell a rat. This is not a good idea." On September 16, 2012, she pushed the administration's line: a video drove violent protests which "extremists" infiltrated. The House of Representatives investigation concluded the administration knew "in real time" it was a terrorist attack and covered it up because it was fifty-six days before the presidential election.[27] This kept Rice from becoming secretary of state. Always listen to your mother.

In Libya, Obama repeated the most grievous Bush administration mistakes: not understanding the effects of the political aim, abysmal preparation for after the war, and thinking the international community would step in after America disengaged. Later, Rice's NSC tried to help stabilize Libya and deal with the Islamic State threat there, but "Obama was content to leave a liberated and collapsing Libya well alone." Libya's civil war was soon exporting extremists.[28]

THE SYRIAN CIVIL WAR

The Obama administration initially pursued a strategy of accommodation and engagement with Bashar al-Assad's Syrian dictatorship, for what aim isn't clear. Assad was branded "a reformer" by Clinton and her successor, Kerry. In early 2011, the Arab Spring reached Syria, sparking a growing protest movement catalyzed by Assad's arrest and torture of a group of schoolchildren for painting anti-Assad remarks on a school wall. Further regime violence followed, then a multi-faction civil war. In August 2011, Obama declared "the time has come for President Assad to step aside," something echoed by European leaders. Obama believed Assad would soon follow Mubarak and increased economic sanctions while providing humanitarian assistance.[29]

On August 20, 2012, Obama declared Syrian chemical-weapon use a "red line" that if crossed would provoke US action. In August 2013, Assad unleashed these weapons on Syrian civilians. The administration began preparing punitive airstrikes that Secretary of State Kerry called "unbelievably small." Obama approached Congress for a vote but backed away in the face of certain defeat. Most US allies refused to support strikes. Obama grasped Putin's offer of a deal to remove Syria's chemical weapons, which failed to prevent Assad's later WMD attacks. By laying down a "red line" and not following through, Obama injured his credibility and, Kerry confessed, made the US appear weak. A Pacific nation diplomat told General Mattis: "I guess we're on our own with China." Ongoing negotiations with Syria's ally, Iran, influenced inaction, and the administration fed Syria's carnage by working with the Muslim Brotherhood and other Islamists rather than secular Syrian groups.[30] No free nation cared about Syria. The parallel to the 1930s Spanish Civil War is disturbing: the democracies looked away, authoritarians intervened, mass murder and refugees followed.

IRAN

Obama inherited a deteriorating situation with an Iranian regime believing nuclear weapons would give it a shield against America and protect it from any ideological compromise. Bush and the Europeans worked to prevent an Iranian bomb by emphasizing the possibility of negotiations while imposing economic sanctions. Bush refused to talk to Tehran until it abandoned its nuclear program. Obama followed suit, increasing sanctions while adding subversion via cyberattacks. He secured international sanctions where Bush failed.[31]

Obama wanted to remove Iran's nuclear weapons development as a tension point, thus allowing Washington to disentangle itself from the region. Outreach began two months after his inauguration. Tehran was uninterested until June 2009 demonstrations against Iran's corrupt presidential election shook the regime. The first talks in October 2009 produced nothing and the administration returned to pushing sanctions, securing Russian support by stepping back from supporting Georgia ("You sold us to the Russians," Georgian President Mikheil Saakashvili told Holbrooke), and retreating temporarily from talk of Russian democracy and freedom. Engagement produced a complicated October 2009 deal that Iran killed. Obama continued the pressure strategy, securing UN sanctions in June 2010.[32]

The administration believed from intelligence reports that Iran was on the path to having nuclear weapons, possibly even during Obama's tenure. This could be politically fatal domestically and had to be stopped or pushed beyond Obama's presidency. Halting it required a war, which was unacceptable. Delaying it required an agreement. The administration hoped a deal would postpone Iranian nuclear weapons development long enough for the regime to change. Iran didn't want to abandon its program, believing Qaddafi's doing so had doomed him. But it needed sanctions relief to steady the regime, which required a deal. The result was July 2015's Joint

Comprehensive Plan of Action (JCPOA). Iran dismantled parts of its program and allowed inspections, while keeping the keys to future weapons. This delayed Iran's development of nuclear weapons for, at best, fifteen years, which – in Obama's words – was long after he left office. Its terms were unverifiable and unenforceable, and Iran was clear all facilities weren't subject to inspections: "In the inked roadmap, no permission has been issued for the IAEA's [International Atomic Energy Agency] access to any military centers and the nuclear scientists." Obama approved the JCPOA by executive order on January 16, 2016. The Iranians received sanctions relief, $150 billion in previously frozen assets, and $1.7 billion in cash, principal and interest on a debt from the 1970s in exchange for returning four American captives. Secretary of State Kerry admitted knowing Iran would use some of the money for terrorism.[33]

OBAMA'S AFGHANISTAN AND IRAQ WARS

Obama initially rejected Bush's "Global War on Terror" epithet for the worse "overseas contingency operations." Obama concentrated "on defeating Al Qaeda in Afghanistan and Pakistan (as well as in Yemen and Somalia) and removing it as a threat to the United States and the emerging global order." But Obama erred in thinking terrorism a "tactic." His 2010 National Security Strategy said "this is not a global war against a tactic – terrorism or a religion – Islam. We are at war with a specific network, Al-Qa'ida and its terrorist affiliates."[34] Obama confused tactical destructive acts with a strategic use of violence in pursuit of political aims.

OBAMA'S AFGHAN WAR, 2009–17

Obama initially tackled the Afghan war "at least in part as an election year tactic, to protect himself against perennial accusations that Democrats are soft on national security issues." He called Afghanistan the "war of necessity" while Iraq was "the war of choice," a construct used to criticize actions. *All* wars are wars of choice. One chooses to fight or not.[35]

THE ASSESSMENT

Vice President Biden and Republican Senator Lindsey Graham traveled to Afghanistan before Obama's inauguration, discovering "confusion at all levels" regarding "strategy and objectives." The administration blamed "the spectacular failure of the Karzai government paired with wrongheaded military strategy, inadequate troop numbers for defeating an insurgency, and the Taliban's ability to find a safe haven and military and material support in Pakistan." Obama's NSC held its first Afghanistan meeting on January 23, 2009. Obama had Middle East expert and campaign advisor Bruce Riedel lead a 60-day review and addressed McKiernan's pending request for 30,000 troops (later pared to 17,000) made near the end of Bush's administration to blunt the Taliban's summer offensive and protect the elections. Obama approved it on February 16.[36]

After a February 13, 2009 NSC meeting, Washington and its coalition partners pushed Karzai to delay May elections mandated by the Afghan constitution until August, partly in the hope of getting someone other than Karzai. Secretary of Defense Gates, who Obama retained from the Bush administration, wrote: "No one, including me, was indelicate enough to mention that the new administration, dedicated to building 'the rule of law' in Afghanistan, had just decided to violate the Afghan constitution and connive with Karzai on keeping him in power illegally for several months." Obama special envoy Holbrooke worked hard to ensure Karzai's defeat but failed. Karzai's deals with warlords and fraud on a large scale won out. Gates wrote: "Our future dealings with Karzai, always hugely problematic, and his criticisms of us, are at least more understandable in the context of our clumsy and failed putsch."[37]

THE POLITICAL AIM, GRAND STRATEGY, AND REASSESSMENT

Obama announced a new grand strategy for the Afghan war on March 27, 2009. The political aim, derived from Riedel, was "to disrupt, dismantle and defeat al Qaeda in Pakistan and Afghanistan, and to prevent their return to either country in the future." "Defeat" is an aim, but "disrupt and dismantle" are things one does to achieve an aim, a mistake echoing Bush documents. (The July 2009 Strategic Implementation Plan (SIP) clarified the political aim to "defeat" the Taliban.) Obama identified "Al Qaeda and its extremist allies" (the Taliban) as the enemy and correctly linked Afghanistan and Pakistan. Obama said Pakistan needed to eliminate sanctuaries and "demonstrate its commitment to rooting out al Qaeda and the violent extremists within its borders." The diplomatic plank included trying to negotiate with the Taliban. Washington would push the Afghan government to crack down on corruption while continuing development supported by more civilians. Obama announced 4,000 more troops as trainers beyond the 17,000 recently approved. NATO would be asked for additional trainers. Riedel's report concluded: "A fully-resourced counterinsurgency campaign will enable us to regain the initiative and defend our vital interests." The new forces would take the war to the Taliban in the east and south of the country, train Afghans, and help secure the border and the August presidential election. The administration planned to build an Afghan army of 134,000 and police forces of 82,000. Afghans assuming security duties was the key to departure.[38]

Gates believed the new strategy needed a commander more attuned to counterinsurgency and counterterrorism. This became General Stanley McChrystal. When Gates told Obama and his advisors about asking McChrystal for a sixty-day review that would include recommendations for any possible troop increases "The room exploded." The vitriol revolved around the politics, especially Democratic resistance and potential Republican opportunism. Gates noted that "Not a word was mentioned about doing whatever it took to achieve the goals the president had so recently set." The administration's leaders didn't understand the military saw its job as achieving the aims the president ordered. Gates "reminded everyone that the troop increase approved in February had preceded the president's decision on strategy in March. McChrystal's assessment would describe the situation as he saw it and then describe how he would operationally implement the president's March strategy decisions, including the resources required."[39]

McChrystal found Afghanistan worse than he expected and concluded ISAF was waging five different campaigns. Fixing the command structure became part of his approach. He believed the insurgency was stronger than at any time since 2001 and that corruption was undermining the people's confidence. McChrystal proposed shifting from chasing insurgents to protecting the population (a core counterinsurgency plank) from the Taliban, American mistakes, and corrupt Afghan officials. He concluded the coalition needed to control 80 key districts of Afghanistan, some of which had to be retaken. An "ink spot" COIN strategy would be implemented, meaning the population in specific spots was secured, governance improved, and thus the government's credibility. The spots would then spread to join others. Implementation would be through "clear, hold, and build." McChrystal later added "sustain." He recommended growing the police to 160,000 and the army to 240,000, questioned the logic of sending troops to isolated valleys like the Korengal, and concluded Kandahar Province, which had the second most populous city, was the place to focus. Legitimate governance was considered a key to success, but security had to come first. McChrystal wanted a minimum of 40,000 more troops and wrote: "I never thought we would crush the Taliban in a conventional military sense; I calculated we didn't need to. I hoped to defeat it by making it irrelevant." Gates said he would try to get Pakistan to eliminate insurgent sanctuaries but lacked confidence in succeeding (he didn't tell McChrystal).[40]

An odd disconnect between the US and NATO emerged during this process. "There are big implications with calling this a war," said a NATO representative. "Legally under international law that has serious implications. So we checked with the legal team and they agree it's not a war." McChrystal fixed the problem in his review by saying the war was "not a war in a conventional sense." His first draft failed to mention Al Qaeda because it was all but gone from Afghanistan. In the second draft, Al Qaeda was the reason the US was there.[41]

McChrystal submitted his report on August 30, 2009. An extended administration review from September through November debated a counterinsurgency versus a counterterrorism strategy during which someone leaked McChrystal's report. This provoked Obama to speculate on whether the military was trying to "box him in," which wasn't possible as he was the decision-maker and could fire malefactors. The administration debate fixated on troop numbers. Such a means-based approach can produce the tacticization of strategy because it drives the focus to tactical actions, which are then seen as solutions. This ignores the aims, strategy, and obstacles. In the end, Obama dispatched 30,000 troops and asked NATO for 10,000. "We would announce it as a temporary surge," Rhodes wrote, "in eighteen months, the troops would start to draw down. We'd secure Afghanistan's major population centers, then shift to training and counterterrorism – essentially endorsing the Petraeus-McChrystal approach for two years, and then shifting to the Biden-Brennan approach sooner than the military wanted" (Biden and Deputy National Security Advisor John Brennan argued for a light-footprint counterterrorism strategy). Rhodes wrote: "*We are not going to defeat the Taliban*, Obama kept saying. *We need to knock them back to give us a space to go after al Qaeda.*"[42]

THE POLITICAL AIM AND THE GRAND STRATEGY – REDUX

Obama outlined his political aims and grand strategy in a December 9, 2009 speech at West Point resembling March 27's. The aims were: "to disrupt, dismantle, and defeat Al Qaeda in Afghanistan and Pakistan, and to prevent its capacity to threaten America and our allies in the future." The shift to viewing Afghanistan and Pakistan as a single theater recognized reality. "Defeat" is understandable as an aim, though could be clearer. "Disrupt" and "dismantle" are not aims but things one does to achieve them. The aims didn't include destruction or defeat of the Taliban, nor was there a vision of what victory should look like. The grand strategy included gathering more international support; expanding the Afghan army and police; improving Afghan governance; negotiations with the Taliban; a government civilian "surge"; and a military "surge" of 30,000 to clear Taliban-controlled areas and do COIN and nation building. Clinton later described the strategy as "fight, talk and build." The administration's war was governed by troop caps, none based upon whether the number was sufficient to achieve the aim.[43]

During the composition of the Afghan strategy speech, Obama removed "any language that spoke of winning or victory." He also built in an expiration date: eighteen months. Obama would then begin withdrawing. This upset Afghan, US, and NATO officials because it meant the Taliban could choose to wait for America to leave. Others noted a mismatch between the aim and the strategy because it was impossible to achieve his aims in eighteen months with his strategy.[44]

McChrystal planned to go after the Taliban in areas it controlled, particularly in Afghanistan's south and east. He would let the Marines complete the pacification of Helmand as they were already on the job, then clear Kandahar and move east along the Pakistani border. The Marjah offensive began in February 2010 but took longer than expected. Experience here produced slower clearing of Kandahar to ensure the Afghans were better able to work with the US and establish security. Beforehand, McChrystal's command publicized a "government in a box," creating the impression Afghan governance would follow Kandahar's clearing. The plans for this fell apart. Earlier, the Afghans failed to backfill the coalition in Helmand with stable governance. The Afghan army was getting better, but too many of the police units were part of the problem. The civilian surge tripled US personnel to about 1,000 by mid 2010. By 2010's close, ISAF had 131,000 troops from 47 nations.[45]

Neither Obama nor Karzai believed in the strategy and Obama was skeptical of McChrystal's approach. Ambassador to Afghanistan Karl Eikenberry actively opposed it and remained in his job despite the efforts of JCS chair Mullen, Clinton, and Gates to have him removed. Gates concluded Obama didn't believe in his own strategy because otherwise he wouldn't have kept someone who fought it. By June 2010, Biden was trying to undermine it.[46]

McChrystal was relieved in June 2010 after a *Rolling Stone* article printed critical remarks about the administration uttered largely by McChrystal's staff. Petraeus replaced him. In June 2010, Petraeus' advisor, Derek Harvey, told the general the political and military strategies weren't connected and thus wouldn't work, a conclusion based on the fact that pacifying Helmand hadn't produced popular support for the government as had occurred in Iraq. Harvey believed the US could achieve "some transient stability and the appearance of success that will not be enduring, that might provide a window for us to withdraw, and to keep things steady for the next three or four years." American strategy called for the Afghans to then assume responsibility for security, but Harvey doubted their ability to do so. The US "had hoped to lure up to 70 percent of the Taliban to the government side with the promise of jobs." This didn't happen as they distrusted the Afghan government and foreigners. Petraeus believed the Taliban would need to be defeated to convince them to change sides.[47]

The coalition took Helmand and Kandahar from the Taliban, but Afghan weakness holding cleared areas and Taliban resistance remained. Counterinsurgency takes time, but "at the strategic and operational level, doing it right took a back seat to doing it fast." The COIN strategy implemented in Afghanistan was rushed and lacked direction from its leaders. Applying ideas from the Second Iraq War ran up against Afghanistan not being Iraq. For example, the Afghan tribal system was more fragmented and diverse. Some 80 percent of the Afghan population lived in rural areas, and there were more than 20,000 small clan and tribe groups.[48]

REASSESSMENT

The administration did its December 2010 review quietly. Afghan security forces numbered 260,000, doubling since 2007. Military leaders had earlier told Obama they could "clear, hold, and transition to Afghan security forces places where our troops had been deployed within two years," and Obama gave them a two-year deadline. For Helmand province this was July 2011, which coincided with Obama's eighteen-months promise in his December 2009 speech. By fall 2010, "about a third of the country and an even higher percentage of the population had in fact already been transitioned." Military leaders disliked the deadline, but Gates agreed to it. "I could understand Obama's insistence on keeping to the commitment. If we couldn't get the job done in two years, how many years would it take?" In mid November 2010, the administration and NATO agreed to Karzai's suggestion that foreign troops end combat roles by the close of 2014.[49]

The signs of progress revealed in the December review helped convince Obama it was time to emphasize political reconciliation with the Taliban. But an assessment that the US would need to support the Kabul government for ten to fifteen years at $6–8 billion annually convinced him the political aim needed changing. White House staff suggested aiming for "good enough" and the aim became an Afghanistan "that did not harbor terrorists capable of striking the United States and one with a government sufficiently supported by the people that it could remain stable into the future." The descriptor became "Afghan good enough," something Panetta found "insulting to the Afghans" and that he believed "sounded defeatist and therefore not sufficiently respectful of all those who had died in the war."[50]

On January 20, 2011, Obama launched a review to discuss the July troop drawdown and the post-2014 US presence. What ensued were months of wrangling over the Afghan army's size, Obama's complaints about military leaders trying to game him (particularly after Petraeus cast doubts on the July withdrawal date), and Biden attacking Petraeus and the strategy in Afghanistan. A frustrated Gates wrote: *"The president doesn't trust his commanders, can't stand Karzai, doesn't believe in his own strategy, and doesn't consider the war to be his. For him, it's all about getting out."*[51]

On June 22, 2011, Obama announced the drawdown would begin in July, citing his December 2009 eighteen-months promise: 10,000 troops were to depart by 2011's close, 23,000 others by summer 2012. Obama wanted to run for reelection on having ended "Bush's Wars" and needed to show the troops heading home by November 2012. The aim became: "No safe haven from which al Qaeda or its affiliates can launch attacks against our homeland or our allies." Counterterrorism became the new strategy. US forces began moving to combat support; the nation-building role shrank. Transition to Afghan control was to occur by 2014's end. "America," Obama said, "it is time to focus on nation building here at home." "By the end of 2011, some 1,234 American soldiers had been killed since the start of the Obama presidency, compared with 630 in the previous seven years." And in a war Obama never intended to win.[52]

Obama's speech marked a change in the relationship with Pakistan. Numerous events caused this but discovering Osama Bin Laden living in Abbottabad near Pakistan's West Point was key. After its May 2, 2011 raid that killed Bin Laden, the administration was no longer interested in coddling Islamabad, which supported the Taliban. Washington temporarily suspended military aid in summer 2011 (it resumed in 2013). In November 2011, US troops responded heavily to Pakistani fire, one of numerous such incidents. The Pakistanis refused American requests to stop – until a US airstrike killed twenty-four of them. Obama refused to apologize, and Pakistan closed its borders to American logistical support passing to Afghanistan. Both sides admitting "mistakes" defused matters. In September 2012, Mullen's Congressional testimony noted Pakistan's support of the Taliban and the insurgency.[53]

PART IV: RETREAT AND DEFEAT

Obama's March 27, 2009 speech mentioned negotiations, but the administration initially refused direct talks, fearing it would look weak. Holbrooke pushed unsuccessfully for two years. But in February 2011, the administration seized upon his plan. It first succumbed to an earlier Afghan War British error – being taken in by an impostor – then circumvented Karzai, resulting in a Taliban office in Qatar in June 2013. Karzai threatened to abandon any peace talks and the office closed. Afghanistan dropped far down the list of administration priorities.[54]

Both the White House and Karzai wanted the war ended. But Panetta, now secretary of defense, didn't want to repeat administration Iraq withdrawal errors (examined shortly). They inked an agreement for a gradual drawdown and transition to a small training and advising force. Panetta thought possible "an Afghanistan that can secure and govern itself and never again become a safe haven for terrorists." On May 1, 2012, Obama and Karzai signed the Enduring Strategic Partnership Agreement. Obama said they could "achieve our goal of destroying Al Qaeda and denying it a safe haven" as they "wind down this war and usher in a new era of peace here in Afghanistan." In 2012, the White House was managing the drawdown and handing off to the Afghans. CENTCOM commander Mattis believed the administration now had no real aims or strategy in Afghanistan or the Middle East.[55]

OBAMA'S "COMPREHENSIVE COUNTERTERRORISM STRATEGY"

On May 23, 2013, Obama outlined a "comprehensive counterterrorism strategy." He made the Afghan War part of this, insisting the combat mission had ended and US troops were coming home, while (without admitting the contradiction) a counterterrorism force (troops) and training and assistance groups remained. The "counterterrorism force" would ensure "al Qaeda can never again establish a safe haven to launch attacks against us or our allies." He also mentioned other areas where he was conducting counterterrorism operations – "wars": Somalia, Yemen, and Mali. Special Forces carried America's combat brunt.[56]

Obama called intensified use of drones and Special Forces "lethal, targeted action" and mentioned it as a tactic while reserving the right to act where nations granted sanctuary to groups like Al Qaeda. Obama tightly controlled drone use, even selecting individuals targeted. The administration conducted 25,000 drone strikes by 2015, five times Bush's, a number partly resulting from increased drone numbers and capabilities. This proved effective against Al Qaeda's leaders but demonstrated a common problem in protracted wars: tactical actions begin substituting for strategy. The symptoms are attacked but the failure to convince the opponent to abandon his political aim isn't addressed.[57]

In May 2013, Obama committed to addressing the underlying causes of "extremism." He offered engagement and support for transitions to democracy, especially in Egypt, Libya, and Tunisia, strengthening for Syria's opposition, help resolving the Israeli–Palestinian conflict, and economic and educational modernization via foreign aid. Obama summed up this new approach: "Targeted action against terrorists, effective partnerships, diplomatic engagement and assistance – through such a comprehensive strategy we can significantly reduce the chances of large-scale attacks on the homeland and mitigate threats to Americans overseas." The "targeted action" continued, but little came of the rest. In 2013, Musa Qala and part of Helmand fell again under Taliban sway.[58]

On May 27, 2014, Obama declared he would bring the Afghan War to "a responsible end" by 2014's close; America's combat mission would cease with the year's conclusion. In an address mixing political aims with strategy, Obama announced the US would disrupt Al Qaeda, advise the Afghans, and conduct counterterrorism, but Afghanistan would be responsible for its own security. The US troop drawdown would continue. The roughly 32,000 were scheduled to become 9,800 by the beginning of 2015, become half this by year's end, and decline to an embassy force and a small security assistance team by the end of 2016. Obama said: "this is how wars end in the 21st century – not through signing ceremonies, but through decisive blows against our adversaries, transitions to elected governments, security forces who take the lead and ultimately full responsibility." Obama didn't consult the Taliban; its summer and fall 2014 offensives focused on Helmand province and attacked provincial capitals and Kabul itself.[59]

The "torturous" negotiations with Karzai on the Bilateral Security Agreement defining the post-2014 US presence demonstrated the relationship's deterioration. Karzai blamed the US for Afghanistan's ills. Rice told him that if he didn't sign, the US and NATO would leave by 2014's end. Karzai still refused. His successor, Ashraf Ghani, agreed in September 2014. By 2014, American aid to Afghanistan totaled $100 billion, plus $4 billion annually promised post-2014 by the US and NATO. Perhaps 15 percent went where it was supposed to: "The rest was siphoned off by Western agencies, warlords, local contractors, petty criminals, and at times the Taliban." Thousands of failed development projects dotted the country. Perhaps 32,000 people had died; 600,000 had become refugees.[60]

PART IV: RETREAT AND DEFEAT

The fighting in 2015 intensified, and the survival of the Afghan government appeared threatened by a combination of the Taliban, Al Qaeda, and a branch of Islamic State. The Taliban temporarily captured Kunduz in September 2015 and seized parts of northern Afghanistan where their influence had previously been minimal. They were also establishing shadow governments. Over 4,000 members of the Afghan security forces were killed in the year's first seven months. By the end of 2015, the Taliban held more of Afghanistan than at any time since 2001.[61]

The counterterrorism strategy Biden long demanded (largely a tactical bundle) was failing and Afghan forces still needed an American backstop. In October 2015, Obama altered his withdrawal schedule. Now, 5,500 US troops would remain after his term. Stationed at Bagram, Kandahar, and Jalalabad, they continued to train Afghans and mount counterterrorism strikes. By April 2016, the Taliban controlled or contested control of 20 percent of Afghanistan. In June, Obama authorized US forces to accompany Afghans on combat missions and loosened the rules for air support. The tactical focus remained. The withdrawal schedule slowed and in July 2016, after pleas from Afghan President Ghani and NATO leaders, Obama decided 8,400 troops would remain. Afghan forces continued to perform inadequately, pressure from the Taliban increased, and by October 2016, they controlled 85 percent of Helmand province.[62]

Obama never addressed Pakistani support and sanctuary for the insurgents. This made it almost impossible to stabilize Afghanistan. Obama also never seriously tried to defeat the Taliban or force them to negotiate a settlement. One can certainly question the possibility of any of this, but not doing it ensured Obama wouldn't win the war. But he never intended to.

OBAMA'S IRAQ WAR, 2009-11

When Obama was inaugurated, the Iraqi insurgency had been largely defeated and the country was on the road to self-rule, but the threat of backsliding remained. Obama ordered a review his first day in office, which General Raymond Odierno and Ambassador to Iraq Ryan Crocker conducted. In February 2009, after the review, Obama decided the combat mission in Iraq would end in nineteen months. Remaining US forces would then advise and assist. The number of troops would fall to 50,000 by August 31, 2010, bases to 30 from 350. At its peak, the US had 170,000 troops in Iraq at more than 500 bases. There were 4,000 on three bases at 2011's close.[63]

POLITICAL AIMS AND GRAND STRATEGY

On February 27, 2009, Obama announced the aim would be "an Iraq that is sovereign, stable, and self-reliant." "To achieve that goal," he said, "we will work to promote an Iraqi government that is just, representative, and accountable, and that provides neither support nor safe-haven to terrorists." Obama said policing their nation was an Iraqi responsibility, that Washington couldn't bear these costs indefinitely, insisted it was up to Iraqis to grasp the chance given them, and promised a US troop withdrawal by the end of 2011. He linked Iraq actions to his regional "comprehensive engagement" strategy, which included obtaining peace between Israel and its Arab neighbors and preventing Iran from developing nuclear weapons. Because he didn't mention it, Iraqi politicians wondered if Obama remained committed to a democratic Iraq.[64]

Obama followed Bush's December 2008 agreement for reducing US forces. Al Qaeda and some Shia groups continued bombings and small attacks. Maliki began reducing support for the Sunni Sons of Iraq while persecuting opponents real and imagined, usually Sunni. The March 7, 2010 Iraqi elections produced a victory by Iraqiya, a Sunni–Shia coalition party. Maliki refused to accept the outcome, charged fraud, and began undermining the result. Odierno believed Washington should allow Iraqi election law, which gave the victorious party the right to form a coalition, to work. US Ambassador to Iraq Chris Hill told Odierno Iraq wasn't ready for democracy and needed "a Shia strongman" like Maliki. In the negotiations for a government over the next months, the Iranians worked hard for a Shia administration aligned with Tehran while the US embassy did nothing.[65]

In mid July 2010 Biden, Obama's Iraq point man, told the two parties – Iraqiya and State of Law Coalition – to make a deal within two weeks or both had to step aside. The same week, he began backing Maliki. Many Iraqi leaders wondered why Washington wanted the same man as Tehran, something Biden knew. Others were upset by Washington picking the president in a country that was supposed to be a democracy. Eyewitness and Middle East expert Emma Sky wrote: "The Obama administration wanted to see an Iraqi government in place before the US mid-term elections in November. Biden believed the quickest way to form a government was to keep Maliki as prime minister, and to cajole other Iraqis into accepting this."[66]

Odierno warned Biden of Maliki's increasing sectarianism and Iraqi fears of his suppressing non-Shia. Sky told Biden the new Iraqi leaders were trying to move beyond sectarianism and stressed the importance of the people seeing a peaceful, democratic transition of power, something never witnessed in the Arab world. Biden refused to listen. Meanwhile, *Iran* convinced Shia leader Muqtada al-Sadr "to accept a second Maliki term as prime minister." Maliki's attacks on Sunni opponents and protesters followed, payments to Sunni tribes that had fought Al Qaeda ended, and Islamic State posed as the Sunni defender against a corrupt, sectarian government.[67]

On August 31, 2010, Obama announced the end of America's combat mission and Iraq's assumption of security responsibility. Some forces remained to advise and assist, but Obama said these would leave by the end of 2011. The next day, Odierno handed command to General Lloyd Austin, who led a training and advising mission of 50,000. Obama had declared combat over, but US troops fought insurgents alongside Iraqi forces a week later.[68]

The Second Iraq War's final act concerned whether US troops remained after 2011. This required a new Status of Forces Agreement (SOFA). Many US military and civilian leaders wanted a continued presence, partially because of Maliki. The key sticking point was administration insistence Iraq's parliament approve immunity to Americans from Iraqi prosecution. Panetta believed withdrawal endangered America's achievement and warned Obama Iraq could slide into chaos and host groups plotting terrorist attacks against the United States. CENTCOM commander Mattis warned Biden about Maliki's unreliability and predicted too early removal of US troops would see Washington committing them again. The White House offered 3,500 troops, with no reasoning for this number, *if* the Iraqi parliament gave them immunity. Mattis wrote: "The White House knew that the fractious Iraqi parliament could never unite and agree to those terms. We had other legal ways of protecting American troops from such prosecution. But that made no difference." Obama's approach was smoke and mirrors. Undersecretary of Defense Michèle Flournoy concluded "the president had made up his mind and he didn't want any US troops to remain in Iraq." Obama used SOFA negotiations as cover.[69]

In March 2013, Mattis retired. He wrote of the Middle East: "I was leaving a region aflame and in disarray. The lack of an integrated regional strategy had left us adrift, and our friends confused. We were offering no leadership or direction. I left my post deeply disturbed that we had shaken our friends' confidence and created vacuums that our adversaries would exploit." He later said: "It was like clutching defeat from the jaws of victory."[70]

THE THIRD IRAQ WAR OR THE ISLAMIC STATE WAR, 2014–17

The Third Iraq War arose partly from Iraqi premier Maliki's anti-Sunni sectarianism, which drove many into the arms of Islamic State. Also known as ISIL, ISIS, IS, and Daesh, Islamic State (IS) evolved from Zarqawi's Al Qaeda in Iraq. It was heavily damaged in 2007 and 2008 but continued making attacks. Abu Bakr al Baghdadi became its leader in April 2010, and the outbreak of the Syrian civil war in 2011 brought opportunities for expansion. In July 2013, IS stepped up attacks on Iraqi soldiers and began taking territory. On December 30, it captured Fallujah and areas of Ramadi. It took Raqqa, Syria, in January 2014. In June 2014, IS began an offensive that carried them to the gates of Baghdad. Mosul fell on June 10, Tikrit the next day (though part of it was recaptured by an Iranian-supported Iraqi counterattack). Key border crossings with Syria and Iraqi towns fell as IS pushed into Kurdish areas. This created a flood of refugees, particularly among Iraq's Yazidi, who suffered slavery, mass murder, and mass rape. On June 29, Baghdadi announced the establishment of an Islamic caliphate. At its height in 2015, it controlled "about a third of Syria and 40 percent of Iraq."[71]

Obama resisted new involvement in Iraq and underestimated IS. He refused 2013 Iraqi requests for drone strikes against IS and called them "the jayvee team," meaning the "junior varsity team." The administration misread IS and the Iraqi army, much of which collapsed, but was awakened by Mosul's fall, the capture of Mosul's dam, the IS advance toward Baghdad, and its march on Erbil with its US consulate and UN offices. In June 2014, Obama dispatched 650 troops as advisors and support. He granted approval for airstrikes in July, primarily to support Kurdish forces, but refused to support the Iraqi government until Maliki resigned. This didn't happen until mid August. The US began air attacks on August 7, 2014, hoping to stem IS's genocidal assault on the Yazidis besieged on Mount Sinjar. Kurdish troops broke the siege in mid December. Combined Joint Task Force Operation INHERENT RESOLVE was established on October 7, 2014, ostensibly to run the war.[72]

Obama didn't seek UN or Congressional approval as both Bushes had done for their Iraq wars. Some accused him of waging war unconstitutionally (the US hadn't been attacked). Obama said at the end of August 2014 that he didn't have time to approach Congress because of the danger to US personnel in Erbil. He shocked listeners later in August by saying "we don't have a strategy yet," but committed to going to Congress once they did. The administration failed to get Congressional agreement for a new AUMF [Authorization for the Use of Military Force] and then insisted it could fight its war based upon the 2001 AUMF. When Iraq chose a new prime minister in September 2014, Washington began deploying trainers and combat aircraft. Obama, Rhodes wrote, "placed strict caps on the numbers of these troops, and on what they could do, prompting another series of complaints about Obama 'micromanaging' the Pentagon."[73]

Obama explained on September 10, 2014 that the security of the United States demanded action against the "terrorist threat." Islamic State was its new face. The US political aim was to "degrade, and ultimately destroy" Islamic State "through a comprehensive and sustained counter-terrorism strategy." It included airstrikes in Iraq and Syria; more troops advising; building a Sunni National Guard and supporting Syrian rebels; convincing other nations to stop the flow of foreign fighters; and humanitarian assistance – all supported by a coalition. The administration intended to first deal with IS in Iraq, believing this would take thirty-six months, leaving the Syrian IS forces for the next administration.[74]

"Degrade" isn't an aim but what one does to achieve an aim. The strategy depended upon coalition partners that had failed and whose forces had been wrecked. Obama essentially delivered a trimmed version of his 2009 West Point Afghanistan speech and insisted this strategy built around eliminating terrorists "while supporting partners on the front lines" had delivered success in Yemen and Somalia. Later, in 2015, the administration closed the embassy in Yemen and removed its 100 troops as order collapsed in the face of Houthi rebel, Al Qaeda, and IS attacks. One critic said of the administration's Yemen war: "A military operation that lacks clear courses of action, coherent objectives, or an intended end state is nothing more than the random, purposeless application of force against some enemy."[75]

The administration remained reluctant to admit it was at war or address the reality. Obama said on September 10, 2014: "These American forces will not have a combat mission; we will not get dragged into another ground war in Iraq." The next day, Secretary of State Kerry said the US was not at war with Islamic State but conducting "a major counter-terrorism operation." This denial continued in postmodernist fashion with Obama's press secretary stressing that the US was in a "narrative fight" with Islamic State.[76]

The struggle against IS was complicated by the fraught US relationship with Syria. In October 2014, Secretary of Defense Chuck Hagel complained that the political aim toward the Assad regime was unclear, injuring the implementation of strategy. Military leaders at the Pentagon and on the ground grumbled about "micromanagement" of the IS war and the Syrian rebel training program. National Security Advisor Rice insisted upon maintaining control over even minor details. One analyst said: "Nobody thinks the president really wants to do anything on Syria." Hagel pressed the administration for direction and was being pushed by America's NATO allies for clear aims. The White House was unhappy with his request. Hagel resigned in November and was replaced by Ash Carter.[77]

Carter clarified the political aim against Islamic State on February 4, 2015: the administration sought the "lasting defeat" of Islamic State, but the problem of strategy remained. Carter didn't think inserting large American forces was the answer, insisting it better to play to America's technological and other advantages. Doing otherwise might keep Iraqis and Syrians from doing the job themselves. Carter "gradually concluded that the United States and its coalition partners lacked a comprehensive, achievable plan for success." It was December 2015 before Washington had one. Carter wrote: "It's fair to say that we took longer than we should have to get our act together." American generals eventually branded how the US was fighting the "by, with, and through" strategy because "operations were carried out against a common foe *by* a diverse array of local allies, *with* support from American forces and their coalition partners, and *through* a U.S. legal and diplomatic framework."[78]

Meanwhile, IS captured Ramadi in May 2015. In June, Obama raised eyebrows again by saying the administration didn't have "a complete strategy." His message was part of an effort to pressure Iraqis to build a more inclusive government and convince nations to do more to staunch the flow of foreign fighters feeding Islamic State. But no one ran the war, a problem Carter was exceptionally slow to correct. Carter inherited a situation in which General John Allen held a nebulous position as State Department special envoy on Islamic State matters. Despite this, Allen and Brett McGurk assembled a sixty-five-nation coalition while engineering restrictions on the flow of money and foreign fighters to IS and helping Baghdad stabilize its finances. In July 2015, Carter told JCS chair General Martin Dempsey "to draft plans for consolidating the campaign under a single operational commander." This became Lieutenant General Sean MacFarland, who wasn't put in the job until September 2015. In August 2016, Lieutenant General Steve Townsend succeeded him, commanding until September 2017.[79]

The planning was also troubled. In July 2015, Carter was briefed by CENTCOM commander Austin on a plan to recapture Mosul that was unworkable because the Iraqi forces it required didn't yet exist. Carter inherited plans to train and equip anti-IS forces in Syria that collapsed in scandal amidst revelations that millions of dollars had been spent to train sixty soldiers. In the last half of 2015, the administration added forces in small numbers. In October, Obama approved inserting Special Operations

Forces into Syria to train and equip the Syrian Arab Coalition serving under the Syrian Kurds (which caused problems with Turkey), and some anti-IS forces in southern Syria.[80]

The administration still refused to say it was fighting a war. Moreover, Obama admitted at a November 16, 2015 press conference that he wasn't interested in "pursuing some notion of American leadership or America winning," One critic said: "I don't know that we've ever had a president who didn't really care about America winning – and who announced it to the public." Worsening Obama's situation was his insisting IS was contained the day before its devastating November 13, 2015 Paris attacks.[81]

Criticism mounted, even from his own party, and Obama was pushed to act more aggressively. Half-measures and slow movement increased civilian suffering. National Security Advisor Rice wrote: "In December 2015, Obama internally mandated that this administration 'put ISIS in a box' by the end of his term." On December 14, Carter and JCS chair General Joseph Dunford briefed Obama and the NSC on their war plan: essentially a two-pronged drive against Islamic State. A primarily Iraqi force would recapture Fallujah, then isolate and take Mosul, but this first required training and refitting additional units, including Kurdish forces. Subsidiary attacks would clear the western desert communities and cut IS supply lines with Syria. The second prong was based upon training and equipping the Syrian Democratic Forces (SDF). They would clear IS areas in Syria's north, advance on Dabiq, then isolate and take Raqqa, a move also intended to break the flow of IS operatives to the west.[82]

During the war, America had to "deconflict" with Russian forces helping Assad in Syria and balance between the Turks and Kurds. In June 2016, Iraqi forces recaptured Fallujah. In July, the airfield at Qayyarah West (Q-West) was taken and became the campaign's logistics hub. The US then dispatched another 500 troops, most for securing this. By January 2017, Iraqis were clearing Mosul and SDF forces neared Raqqa. By the end of Obama's tenure, the coalition had recaptured 60 percent of Iraq and 30 percent of Syria lost to IS. The administration deployed 5,200 US troops to "train, advise, and equip" Iraqis.[83] Kurdish and Iraqi forces bore the brunt of the fighting, which continued.

There were four key weaknesses in Obama's prosecution of his Iraq war: kicking the can down the road, a failure to provide the forces for achieving his declared aims, a focus on tactical matters (exemplified by concentration on airstrikes and Special Forces), and White House micromanagement. Combined with this was obfuscation on whether the US was at war and public denial of this.

MILITARY STRATEGY – OTHER FACTORS

Retrenchment included defense cuts. Spending dropped, and the military suffered under the Budget Control Act of 2011, known as sequestration, which was scheduled to slice $1 trillion from defense over ten years. Obama's 2011 national defense strategy built upon the 2010 *NSS* and the *QDR*. It stressed "countering violent extremism," deterrence, the ability to defeat foes, and working with partner nations to strengthen regional security. Alliance relationships, building partner capacity, and halting WMD proliferation played key roles. Panetta's "defense strategy for the twenty-first century" followed in January 2012. Its key elements were: 1) a smaller, more agile and deployable force; 2) a "rebalance" of forces to Asia, which was seen as a more likely conflict arena; 3) "rotational deployment," meaning smaller forces doing training and conducting operations with other nations instead of large, long-term deployments; 4) maintaining the ability to fight two wars, one actively while "freezing" the other; and 5) investment in key capabilities such as expanded Special Operations Forces (SOF), space, cyber, drones, and technology. It also cut the army to 490,000. In 2010, it was 565,000. The 2012 Defense Strategic Guidance declared "US forces will no longer be sized to conduct large-scale, prolonged stability operations."[84]

The 2015 *NSS* stressed using all elements of national power and was grounded on two planks: "Respect for universal values at home and around the world," and "A rules-based international order advanced by US leadership."[85] But not all nations have the same values, nor do they agree on international rules.

CONCLUSION

The administration's declared pursuit of democracy overseas was neither enthusiastic nor consistent, while it acted in ways reminiscent of the Cold War by subverting democratic processes in Afghanistan and Iraq. The administration's greatest weakness was its domination by domestic political concerns. No political leader – particularly in a democracy – can ignore public opinion, but the unyielding supremacy of this produced tightly controlled tactical solutions to strategic matters. This extends rather than solves problems and rarely achieves political aims. One analyst insisted Obama's diplomacy "seems primarily motivated by what he wants to avoid rather than what he wants to achieve" and branded it "avoidant foreign policy" plagued by a failure to match ends with means. Retrenchment has dangers, and "there was a feeling of mixed messages received in capitals, and an unmistakable sense overseas that the United

States was disengaging from much of its traditional role in the world."[86] The administration often alienated friends and won over no enemies.

Obama was the nation's first two-term president to be at war during his entire tenure. He inherited wars in Iraq and Afghanistan and left with the same war in Afghanistan and a new one in Iraq. He overthrew the Libyan regime but left the country a basket case. Troop caps were a norm as the administration consistently constrained both the means and the time it allotted military commanders to deliver the purposes the administration insisted it wanted achieved, while never supplying the means these commanders thought necessary. The result: "The Obama administration would not wage wars; it would manage them."[87]

Perhaps the most apt portrayal of the Obama administration is one describing the French Bourbon monarchy after its 1815 restoration: "They had learned nothing and forgotten nothing." It was an administration professing to understand its predecessor's mistakes, but then repeated them with no awareness it was doing so.

20

RETRENCHMENT, ENGAGEMENT, AND WEAKNESS: TRUMP AND BIDEN, 2017–2022

INTRODUCTION

The election of celebrity real estate mogul and reality television star Donald J. Trump as president shocked the political establishment. Though critical of his predecessor, Trump followed Obama's retrenchment path. But in the realm of grand strategy, Bill Clinton and George W. Bush were forerunners; the president and his national security apparatus moved on different lines. Trump brought no government experience to the office. His successor, Joseph Biden, brought decades. One of the few matters upon which they agreed was America's war in Afghanistan.

THE ASSESSMENT

Trump viewed America as overextended and burdened by allies who didn't carry their weight. Friends couldn't depend on Washington because of Obama's actions; America's rivals didn't respect it; nations were taking advantage of America, "free riders" on a system Washington underpinned. One advisor insisted Trump "represented a return to realpolitik: blunt, hard-charging, and transactional pragmatism on the world stage." Journalist Peter Bergen noted that "In his first months in office, when Trump encountered a national security problem, he tended to ask the same five questions: 'Why do we care?' 'Why does it matter to the American people?' 'Why can't others do it?' 'Who's paying for it?' 'Why can't others pay?'" Trump had one more for Afghanistan: "Why are we there sixteen years later?" These were "unsettling questions for many in the foreign policy and national security establishments in Washington because they had not been asked in a long time." But to Trump, economics mattered most.[1]

The administration explicitly based aims and strategy upon what it saw as America's interests and noted there was no "global community" but a global arena where states "compete for advantage." Lieutenant General H. R. McMaster, Trump's second national security advisor (the first lasted twenty-two days), ordered a reassessment focused on "great power competition," "transnational terrorist organizations," North Korea and Iran, and "complex arenas of competition from space to cyberspace, to cyber-enabled information warfare to emerging disruptive technologies."[2]

THE POLITICAL AIMS

Administration documents have the standard terminological problems, but clear aims appeared immediately. A January 28, 2017 directive reads: "As President, my highest priority is to ensure the safety and security of the United States and the American people." Another aim was protecting American sovereignty, a foundation of the liberal democratic order. A twist was connecting sovereignty to other states. Trump said: "We will pursue this beautiful vision – a world of strong, sovereign, and independent nations ... thriving side-by-side in prosperity, freedom, and peace." Not respecting sovereignty brought problems such as Russia's Ukraine war, Chinese expansion in the South China Sea, and Iran destabilizing neighbors.[3]

Trump insisted America veered off course "with the dangerous idea that we could make Western democracies out of countries that had no experience or interest in becoming a Western democracy." But Secretary of State Rex Tillerson said in a February 1, 2018 speech on Latin America that the administration possessed the "same goals as the visionary leaders before us: to eliminate tyranny and further the cause of economic and political freedom throughout our hemisphere." The administration consistently pressured the authoritarian Venezuelan and Cuban regimes. It also sought "a free and open Indo-Pacific." By February 2020, Trump was publicly pushing establishment of democratic governments in Cuba, Nicaragua, and Venezuela.[4]

"WE'RE AMERICA, BITCH" – A TRUMP DOCTRINE?

In mid 2018, "a senior White House official" insisted: "The Trump Doctrine is 'We're America, Bitch.'" The same official said: "Obama apologized to everyone for everything. He felt bad about everything." Trump "doesn't feel like he has to apologize for anything America does." The closest Trump came to declaring his own doctrine was perhaps his campaign slogan: "Make America Great Again," or maybe "America First," which Trump believed voters saw as optimistic. FDR struck this tone in his inaugural. Democrat George McGovern's 1972 and Republican Patrick Buchanan's

1992 presidential campaigns hit similar notes. Secretary of Defense Jim Mattis reassured allies that "America first does not mean America alone," a message echoed by Tillerson and Trump.[5]

OBSTACLES

Creating and implementing grand strategy faced obstacles. Trump didn't grasp the effects of presidential behavior and statements. One administration veteran said: "Trump is history's greatest troll." Every word a president utters can shift relations with other states or drive the bureaucracy. Altering course via Twitter pronouncements – with no prior notification – created an image of an administration adrift and can produce chaos within the government itself. A Special Assistant wrote:

> Trump believes he alone, often through sheer force of will, can solve certain problems.... Layered on top of that is his belief that all of life is a negotiation, and that every negotiation is a zero-sum game.... Layered on top of that is his belief that personal relationships are paramount, taking precedence in all negotiations, even over mutual interests. And layered on top of that is his belief that creating chaos gives him an advantage because he's more comfortable in the mayhem than anyone else.

Creating chaos among enemies can be advantageous, but something tactically useful in business can be injurious strategically in government. It worked against increasing what Trump's *National Security Strategy* insisted was important: American influence.[6] Other nations – particularly America's allies – look to Washington and the president for stability, not chaos.

The cascade of leaks from Federal bureaucrats and administration officials, especially initially, undermined the government's ability to protect the country. In late 2019, the leaking aligned with Trump's Clintonesque lack of self-control when a US army officer on the NSC staff illegally released the transcript of a clumsy, ethically questionable (though not lawbreaking) conversation between Trump and Ukraine's president. This gave the Democratic Party the opportunity to do what some of its leaders urged even before his inauguration: impeach him.[7] This occurred on December 19, 2019; the Republican Senate acquitted him.

After losing his 2020 reelection bid, Trump made history by being impeached (and acquitted) a second time, on January 13, 2020. He publicly refused to accept his electoral defeat and charged fraud. On January 6, 2021, he addressed supporters gathered in Washington to protest Congress' certification of the election and urged them to march to the Capitol Building to pressure Congressional Republicans to vote against certification of the election. William Barr, Trump's last attorney general, wrote: "Trump seized on a harebrained legal theory that instead of counting electoral votes as cast by the states, as the Constitution required, the Vice President could unilaterally send votes back to state legislators for further proceedings." He added: "Orchestrating a mob to pressure Congress is inexcusable." Rioting protestors broke into the Capitol and Congress fled; several people died. The year 2020 was wracked by progressive–left protests and riots producing murders, much looting, and seizure of part of Portland, Oregon. A conservative–right mob now added to the nation's disorders. Trump did nothing to discourage violence until too late.[8]

The administration's grand strategy suffered from dependence upon a trio of poor ideas that seeped from the defense community during the previous decade, all rooted in the same means-based analysis that produced the "limited war" ideas contributing to defeat in Vietnam. "Hybrid war" was portrayed as a new form of war but demonstrated a failure to understand that war, particularly at the tactical level, has always mixed conventional and irregular elements with subversion and crime. The "gray zone" emerged into general usage in 2015 largely as a broken way of examining Russia's actions during its war against Ukraine. It imagined a "gray zone" between peace and war, unaware that states have always used subversion during both war and peace. Gray-zone proponents unwittingly described what others branded "great-power competition." The Gerasimov Doctrine, or Russian New Generation Warfare myth, arose after the Libya War when Russian Chief of the General Staff Valery Gerasimov penned his incoherent assessment of the modern operational environment. Western analysts spun his ramblings into a supposed new Russian approach to war after Putin's subsequent and unconnected Crimea invasion and then recanted.[9]

The result: an ahistorical *tactical* idea (hybrid war) and *two things that do not exist* (the gray zone and the Gerasimov Doctrine) became underpinnings for American strategy and that of its allies. The 2017 *National Security Strategy* doesn't mention "gray zone," but its composers considered this central to understanding the China and Russia threats. Hybrid-war ideas influenced Mattis' *National Military Strategy*. NATO developed a strategy for countering so-called hybrid warfare in 2015.[10]

The creation of grand strategy and reassessment were hindered by intelligence figures publicly criticizing Trump during his campaign. These included Michael Morrell, the former CIA second in command, former CIA director and retired general Michael Hayden, and Obama's CIA director, John Brennan. Morrell lamented his failure to consider the unintended effects of his actions and said that such attacks, combined with immediate leaking by intelligence officials of details from Trump's initial intelligence briefing when he was the Republican nominee, undoubtedly proved to Trump that the government's intelligence officials were acting along political lines.[11]

Trump and some administration members suffered an unprecedented assault from Obama administration veterans and the government bureaucracy. The core false charge was that Trump had colluded with Russia, an accusation for which a two-year special counsel investigation found no evidence and was later revealed to have originated in the campaign of Trump's Democratic presidential rival, Hillary Clinton. Many American news outlets commonly branded Trump a Russian tool, and the conspiratorial nature of the attacks proved so long-lasting, intense, and unfounded that progressive *Rolling Stone* journalist Matt Taibbi branded it "a permanent coup." Trump called it "Obamagate."[12]

Trump retrenched like Obama, but Trump's views and administration practices more resembled Clinton's. Both saw national security as defined by economic power and military strength. Both lacked personal discipline and sometimes acted on one line while their respective national security arms moved on another. This is not to say that Trump was detached. Participants are clear that key documents reflected his priorities. Retired Marine general John Kelly, Trump's White House chief of staff for eighteen months, ensured "Trump had access to multiple streams of detailed information before he made a decision."[13]

THE NATIONAL SECURITY STRATEGY

Trump's 2017 *National Security Strategy* was an effort "to extend the logic of America First into a strategic framework." It rested on four pillars: 1) protecting the homeland; 2) economic growth; 3) building military strength (seeking to preserve "peace through strength"); and 4) expanding America's influence. The authors understood one grand strategy doesn't fit all. Two key aspects were "great-power competition" and how to address it: "principled realism." The emphasis would shift from combating organizations using terrorism to the dominant threats: China and Russia. The *NSS* also addressed North Korea, Iran, and transnational jihadists, and noted the engagement strategy with China had failed. Principled realism, the *NSS* said,

> is realist because it acknowledges the central role of power in international politics, affirms that sovereign states are the best hope for a peaceful

world, and clearly defines our national interests. It is principled because it is grounded in the knowledge that advancing American principles spreads peace and prosperity around the globe. We are guided by our values and disciplined by our interests.[14]

ECONOMIC STRATEGY

Trump saw economic strength as an end rather than a tool for achieving aims. His economic strategy had domestic and foreign prongs. The threat at home was "excessive regulations and high taxes." Trump ordered the elimination of two regulations for each new one and emphasized energy production to make the US an energy exporter and allowed construction of the Keystone and Dakota Access Pipelines blocked by Obama. Corporate tax rates fell from 35 to 21 percent. Restricted immigration would increase the wages of the lowest paid by removing competition.[15]

The external threat was unfair foreign trade and Trump shattered America's free-trade consensus. He disliked America's enormous trade deficit – $566 billion in 2017, the most since 2008 – particularly with China. Nations with trade deficits "must rely on foreign direct investment or borrow money to make up the difference ... persistent trade deficits lower the total demand for goods and services in a country, reducing growth and employment." "Trade must be fair and reciprocal," Trump insisted. America would no longer be taken advantage of by nations refusing to open their economies as the US had done. Many experts agreed with Trump's diagnosis of America's trade problems, particularly with China. The administration's free traders initially slow-walked Trump's tariff moves, about which Trump gave no notice to friends or enemies, then lost the fight. Trump used the national security provision of Section 232 of the Trade Expansion Act to impose tariffs. Simultaneously, he opposed protectionism. In March 2017, he forced the G-20 to abandon its protectionism commitment. In May, he called on the G-7 countries to abandon protectionism, tariffs, barriers, and government subsidies.[16] They refused.

Trump promised to renegotiate or cancel the North American Free Trade Agreement (NAFTA). The United States–Mexico–Canada Agreement (USMCA), announced on October 1, 2018, updated it. Trump promised withdrawal from the Trans-Pacific Partnership (TPP) and delivered; Americans turned against such deals after the 2008–09 recession. He withdrew from the unratified Paris Climate Agreement on June 1, 2017. It was viewed as infringing US sovereignty, possibly giving grounds for suits if Washington didn't meet standards beyond those required of others while committing America to pay for other states to transition to renewables. Trump believed it disadvantageous to US workers and industry. His successor rejoined it his first day in office.[17]

It is difficult to judge the economic effects of Trump's actions so close to events, and to determine why Trump secured better pre-COVID GDP and wage growth than Obama. The key differences were Trump's lower business tax rates and aggressive deregulation. Unemployment, 4.7 percent after Trump's election, fell to 3.5 percent before the pandemic. African-American and Hispanic-American unemployment rates reached record lows: 5.9 percent and 4.2 percent, respectively. Pre-COVID annualized GDP growth was higher than under Obama, though not dramatically: 2017, 2.2 percent; 2018, 3.18 percent; and 2019, 2.33 percent. Critics argue Trump's tariffs did nothing to decrease the trade deficit or produce reshoring of jobs. Both administrations buried the nation in debt ($27 trillion by November 2020), and it's impossible to see how either supports a Keynesian multiplier effect.[18]

DIPLOMATIC STRATEGY

A Trump assistant wrote: "Everything was personal to Trump – *everything*. In international affairs, he believed his personal relationship with foreign leaders was more important than shared interests or geopolitics." Because of this, Trump's approach to dealing with dictators mirrored FDR's: he tried to schmooze them, with the same lack of success. Trump followed Obama's example of being willing to talk to any leader but questioned the value of America's alliances.[19] "Engagement" describes diplomatic strategy.

NORTH KOREA

Tensions over North Korea's nuclear and ballistic missile programs boiled over. Trump responded to Pyongyang's threats by promising to destroy North Korea if the US was forced to defend itself. The administration sought North Korea's denuclearization and Trump approved in March 2017 a multinational strategy of "maximum pressure." The administration linked diplomatic and military strategy, refused to duplicate the previous American error of rewarding Pyongyang "just for talking," and rejected sanctions loosening before denuclearizing was clear. North Korean missile tests helped the administration secure four additional UN Security Council Resolutions increasing economic pressure and imposing more US sanctions. Trump shocked many by accepting a summit with North Korea's dictator, Kim Jong-un, something he did from belief in his own negotiating skills. Trump offered sanctions removal for denuclearization; Kim refused. "Maximum pressure" continued, but China remained the hole in the sanctions wall.[20]

THE MIDDLE EAST

Trump's regional political aims in the Middle East included destruction of Islamic State's caliphate and removing safe havens for groups using terrorism. After an assessment, the administration determined that most of the region's northern rungs had been lost to Iranian influence: an Iranian proxy, Hezbollah, controlled Lebanon, Iran helped Assad secure his throne, and Iraq was under Tehran's sway. The administration adopted a version of the two-pillars strategy, one resting on Israel and Saudi Arabia. A Trump advisor said: "Our plan was to annihilate the physical caliphate of ISIS in Iraq and Syria – not attrition, annihilation – and to roll back the Persians. And force the Gulf states to stop funding radical Islam."[21]

The administration wanted regional change and thought Saudi Crown Prince Mohammed bin Salman could help bring it. In May 2017, Saudi Arabia hosted a summit of fifty-five Muslim-majority nations. The administration pushed them to stop funding Islamic terrorism; the Saudis, Qataris, and others promised to fight extremism; and the Saudis agreed to fund a jointly run counterterrorism center. In late May 2017, the Saudis, Emiratis, and Bahrain severed diplomatic relations with Qatar and blockaded it because of its close Tehran ties and its funding terror-using groups like Hezbollah and the Muslim Brotherhood. Trump tweeted support, blindsiding Tillerson and Mattis, who objected to Trump's backing. The intelligence community thought Qatar stopped funding terrorism in 2014 and "Trump realized that the Saudi claims about perfidy of the Qataris were massively overblown." Trump recognized Jerusalem as Israel's capital and moved the US embassy in accord with the 1995 Jerusalem Embassy Act. Disaster was predicted. None occurred. The administration also tried to develop an Israeli–Palestinian peace plan.[22]

By January 2018, the administration was implementing engagement to demonstrate continued regional commitment, while trying to deter Iran and block its ambitions. Tillerson insisted the US wouldn't repeat Obama's 2011 mistake of leaving Iraq too early and would see the war against Islamic State to its conclusion. Trump said "Ultimately, it is up to the nations of the region to decide what kind of future they want for themselves and their children." But to help with this, the administration sought (unsuccessfully) a regional alliance between Jordan, Egypt, and the Gulf Cooperation Council states. The administration continuously tackled terrorism and

Iranian influence. Secretary of Defense Mark Esper said in December 2019: "The United States strategy in the Middle East seeks to ensure the region is not a safe haven for terrorists, is not dominated by any power hostile to the United States and contributes to a stable global energy market." The administration secured the Abraham Accords in August and September 2020, normalizing Israel's relations with the United Arab Emirates, Bahrain, Sudan, and Morocco.[23]

SYRIA

On April 4, 2017, Assad attacked a Syrian village with a nerve agent. Trump enforced Obama's "red line" on April 7 with cruise missile strikes to "restore deterrence against the use of chemical weapons" and injure Syria's ability to mount such attacks from the air. Trump gave the launch order while in Mar-a-Lago, Florida, with Chinese dictator Xi Jinping. After McMaster gave Trump a note announcing the attack, "As Xi was eating a piece of chocolate cake, Trump leaned over to him and told him about the strikes." A former Singaporean official wrote: "Trump understood power, albeit instinctively. And he wielded it crudely, and sometimes incoherently. But when he bombed Syria over the use of chemical weapons while at dinner with Xi Jinping, he did much to restore the credibility of American power."[24]

The attack didn't restrain Assad; he launched a similar attack on April 7, 2018. Mattis wanted Congressional approval before acting; Trump refused to wait. A combined US–British–French strike occurred on April 13. The attack was intended to end Syria's "ability to use chemical weapons," while "deterring the use and spread of such weapons and sending a message to two of Syria's international patrons, Russia and Iran." National Security Advisor John Bolton hoped it would deter repetition. Assad struck again on May 19, 2019.[25]

These US attacks exemplify a modern version of nineteenth-century punitive expeditions and are a way of fighting extremely short wars for limited political aims. From 2018, the US sought in Syria a negotiated settlement to its civil war and the removal of Iranian forces. Sanctions were the primary tool against Assad.[26]

IRAN

After a review, Trump announced the administration's Iran strategy on October 13, 2017. The assessment considered Iran's decades of malign behavior, its ideological and political motivations, and extensive terrorism use. Trump cited Iran's violations of the Joint Comprehensive Plan of Action (JCPOA) and announcements it wouldn't allow inspectors in all nuclear sites. The administration sought to prevent Iran from developing nuclear weapons, to convince Tehran to change its behavior toward other states, and "to roll back Iran's activities." Later, the political aim was changing Iran's behavior. The strategy was called "maximum pressure," essentially an aggressive form of containment. Sanctions provided the major plank. Others were working with allies to restrain Iranian proxies and halting Iran's spreading of weapons in the region.[27]

The administration insisted upon the JCPOA's renegotiation, stressing the sunset clauses that removed restrictions on Iran by 2025 and its failure to address Iranian ballistic missile capabilities, further development of which the administration wished to prevent. The Iranians cheated systematically, and the verification system didn't work because it allowed Iranian self-inspection of sites. On May 8, 2018, Trump canceled the agreement and reimposed sanctions, hitting Iran's funds for weapons development, terrorism, and foreign wars. Informationally, the administration tried to expose Tehran's corruption, brutality, and oppression, hoping to show the world Tehran denied its people basic rights and freedoms. The door to negotiations remained open. Deterrence was the military strategy. In December 2018, Secretary of State Mike Pompeo promised to hold Tehran responsible for attacks on the US and its forces, including Iranian proxies. The Bush administration looked the other way as the Iranians killed or wounded more than 600 American soldiers in Iraq between 2004 and 2009.[28]

The cancelation of the JCPOA was controversial, even within the administration. Figures aware of Iran's violations believed it important to keep an international commitment. McMaster thought remaining provided leverage to fix flaws, while withdrawal could make it harder to increase Iran's costs. The JCPOA had a provision for reimposing sanctions if Iran was in violation. In August 2020, the administration asked the UN Security Council to reimpose multilateral sanctions the JCPOA had removed. Its members refused. Washington had left the deal and lacked legal standing. An alternative course was publicizing Iranian violations, having the sanctions reimposed, and then killing the deal. Relatedly, Obama's former secretary of state John Kerry met several times with Iran's foreign minister; the administration saw this as undermining its strategy.[29]

The sanctions were hurting Iran by summer 2019. Its GDP went from 3.7 percent annual growth to 3.9 percent annual shrinkage, and oil exports fell from 3.9 million barrels daily in 2018 to 1.1. million in March 2019.

Inflation leapt to 40 percent from 9 percent. Iran cut funding to proxies and removed some troops from Syria. In June 2019, Iran threatened to exit the deal. In July, the Iranians breached the JCPOA by enriching uranium beyond the agreed 3.67 percent threshold to 4.5 percent. Weapons require 90 percent. In January 2021, Iran announced enrichment to 20 percent, its sixth breach.[30]

In May 2019, the Iranians attacked four ships in the Persian Gulf and Straits of Hormuz, then followed with drone strikes on the Saudi oil industry and a missile attack from Yemeni Houthi proxies on a Saudi airport. Trump sent a message to Iran's dictator Khamenei in June. Khamenei refused to reply. The Islamic Revolutionary Guard Corps (IRGC) navy mined a Japanese tanker, then shot down a US drone in international air space on June 19. Trump approved retaliatory strikes for June 20 but cancelled them because of a DoD casualty estimate of 150 dead. Trump said: "Too many body bags," and "Not proportionate." Trump was told a disproportionate response was illegal. It isn't. Trump didn't want to attack Iran but also succumbed to a security community fallacy. Proportionality is irrelevant. Responses should be sufficient to achieve the aim. Trump imposed more sanctions while expressing doubts Iran intentionally downed the drone. Trump's now former national security advisor McMaster wrote: "the lack of a response emboldened Iranian leaders. It seemed as if President Trump were trying to give the Iranians an out."[31]

Iranian proxies fired rockets at a US base in Iraq on December 27, 2019, killing an American contractor and wounding other Americans. Washington bombed five posts of Iranian-backed Shia militia in reply, and Pompeo suggested killing Qasem Soleimani, head of Iran's IRGC Quds Force. Similar Iranian proxies attacked the US embassy in Baghdad on December 31 while Soleimani prepared further attacks against Americans. Khamenei told Trump: "You can't do anything." On January 3, 2020, Soleimani was killed by a US missile strike launched to prevent his attacks and "restore deterrence." Khamenei promised revenge and the IRGC fired missiles at two Iraqi bases with US troops, killing none but inflicting traumatic brain injuries on over 100, something unknown to administration officials until a week later. Trump took no military action in reply. Afterwards, Schelling's flawed "signaling" idea reared its head as an explanation for some of Iran's action. But Iran had signaled nothing. Washington and Tehran negotiated the entire time through the Swiss, a practice begun in 1979. Shia protests in Iraq followed, as did a non-binding Iraqi resolution for US withdrawal and Iraqi calls for Iran to do the same.[32] Trump said he had acted to prevent a war, but he had just fought one.

PART IV: RETREAT AND DEFEAT

CHINA AND THE INDO-PACIFIC REGION STRATEGY

Trump's most important strategic shift concerned China. Trump abandoned the failed engagement strategy and took a harder line. During April 2017 meetings with China at Mar-a-Lago, the administration relayed concerns about Chinese island-building in the South China Sea and made it clear Washington no longer accepted predatory Chinese trade. Trump insisted a "trade war" had been long underway but now America was fighting back (it wasn't war but competition) to make China play by the rules and "slow its rise." The administration wanted to help US businesses, strengthen America's industrial base, create jobs, and "stop other countries from growing at America's expense." This required reducing Chinese imports.[33]

Tariffs on China were part of the strategy. They protected American industry from discriminatory rules forcing companies to surrender technology to do business in China while Beijing subsidized global expansion of Chinese firms. Making it more expensive to export from China was to convince companies to take their technology and leave. By October 2018, the administration imposed tariffs on half of the $505 billion in Chinese imports; $300 billion more followed a year later. The administration signed its Phase One trade agreement with China in January 2020. China committed to end currency manipulation, buy more US goods, open to additional US products, and protect intellectual property rights. It's unlikely Western powers can end unfair Chinese trade practices such as subsidies, but some Western businesses decoupled from China because of the risks of doing business in a totalitarian state. Some small companies applauded the tariffs. They were excluded from China by its 25 percent tariff, while Chinese firms faced a 2.5 percent US tariff or even none.[34] China's Nazi Germany–like corporatist government–business economic system ensures its firms don't have to compete in a free market.

In early November 2017, administration principals decided to seek "a free and open Indo-Pacific region and adopt a clear-eyed approach to China," taking a concept from Japan's prime minister, Shinzo Abe. Other aims included ensuring North Korea was no longer a threat to the US or its allies and partners, and that the peninsula was free of WMD. This would be achieved by exerting continuous economic and political pressure against Pyongyang and strengthening South Korea and Japan. The administration developed a regional grand strategy under the *NSS*'s auspices that Trump approved in February 2018. The document suffers the standard confusions and is rare in mentioning primacy, specifically "strategic primacy." "Primacy" and "hegemony" generally only arise in *ex post facto* discussions of American actions, bereft of definition amidst uncertainty regarding whether either is an aim or a strategy. "Strategic primacy" in this case meant ensuring America remained the most powerful nation in the Indo-Pacific, thus enabling achievement of aims. The biggest challenge to the political and economic order was China; North Korea co-starred. Another aim was maintaining alignment with Washington of island confederations such as Melanesia. It lacks a political aim toward China.[35]

The grand strategy proposed mirrors elements of Reagan's toward the Soviet Union and was an "all of government" approach. The most important key for delivering success was America retaining its preeminent position diplomatically, economically, and militarily, enabling it to ensure a stable regional environment marked by respect for sovereignty, the rule of law, and free markets. Moreover, "US security and prosperity depend on free and open access to the Indo-Pacific region, which will remain an engine of US, regional, and global economic growth." Diplomatic strategy was multilateral engagement via strengthening relationships with partners, allies, and regional powers to counter China's growing influence. Diplomacy with China would be "high-level" and "results-oriented." Informationally, the administration would seek to "puncture the narrative that Chinese regional domination is inevitable" while promoting American freedoms and their benefits to counter Beijing's propaganda. Washington would back reformers, underwrite development of means for Chinese to communicate uncensored, and grow American and partner capabilities to block Chinese intelligence-gathering and subversion. Economically, the US would work with partners to prevent China from acquiring militarily useful technology. Trade relations would be pursued with states sharing similar standards and that shrank "the region's economic reliance on China." Washington would "Build an international consensus that China's industrial policies and unfair trading practices are damaging the global trading system." Asian economic cooperation would create an alternative to China's One Belt One Road initiative, in which China sought, among other things, to tie countries to Beijing economically and politically. Safeguarding free markets was critical.[36]

In the intermingled military-diplomatic realm, the US would create a "quadrilateral security framework," the US, India, Australia, and Japan the "principal hubs." The administration encouraged deeper partnerships with Japan, Australia, South Korea, and India to make it a "Major Defense Partner." It would strengthen friends such as Taiwan and grow relationships with "emerging partners" such as Bangladesh, Sri Lanka, and the Maldives, and "reinvigorate" relationships with Thailand and the Philippines, and expand those with Indonesia, Malaysia, Singapore, and Vietnam.

Strengthened allies such as South Korea were encouraged to act outside their geographic confines, and Washington would assist Japan's military modernization to help it assume a greater role. The US hoped to deter China's use of military force "against the United States and US allies and partners," while being strong enough to respond against Chinese moves, particularly an attack on the "first island chain," the island eastern rim of the East and South China Seas from Japan to Taiwan, to the Philippines, to Borneo. Preventing nuclear proliferation and the spread of delivery means, and opposing Islamic State branches in Asia, were also critical.[37]

In his speech rolling out a declassified version of the strategy, Trump focused almost exclusively on trade, whereas the strategy was broader and economic issues took a backseat. In July 2020, Secretary of State Pompeo addressed the problem of what to do next about China. Many suggested a version of containment strategy. Pompeo pointed out the problems: "The USSR was closed off from the free world. Communist China is already within our borders." Pompeo suggested an alliance of democracies to counter China.[38]

HUMAN RIGHTS

The administration initially had little interest in using human rights as part of a diplomatic strategy and told Middle East partners they wouldn't be pressed here. But as its tenure lengthened, the administration broadcast authoritarian regimes' human rights abuses. This became a plank of Iran strategy in 2018. Trump criticized Pyongyang in his 2018 State of the Union Address but backed away after the 2018 Singapore Summit. In October 2018, the administration criticized China's persecution of Muslim Uighurs, Tibetans, and Christians, and declared China's Uighur persecution "genocide," making the US the first country to do so.[39]

MILITARY STRATEGY AND DEVELOPMENTS

Trump was consistently either against the use of military force or used it in a restrained manner. The administration devolved warfighting back to the Pentagon from the White House and moved the NSC back to the smaller Scowcroft model. One of its earliest directives – January 27, 2017 – stated that "To pursue peace through strength" the US would rebuild its armed forces. Trump pushed for a year to establish a new military branch – Space Force – but Mattis, Trump's first secretary of defense, was among those arguing this mission should remain with the air force. Trump announced the

Space Force as a sixth military branch in June 2018 – without telling Mattis. The administration also put in motion a plan to expand the navy to 355 combat ships.[40]

Mattis believed the "administration inherited a strategy-free situation" and thought it needed a strategy using all elements of national power. By the end of 2017, Mattis and his team crafted the *National Defense Strategy*, a mandated replacement for the *Quadrennial Defense Review*. Mattis said it "articulates our strategy to compete, deter, and win," and was part of his quest to restore the military budget, saying "a strategy without the budget to enact it is just a hallucination." It was created within the *NSS* framework and considered the same threats: Russia, China, Iran, North Korea, and groups like Al Qaeda and Islamic State. Defense would concentrate on three lines of effort: lethality; strengthening alliances and creating new partnerships; and reforming the Defense Department's business practices.[41]

EUROPE AND NATO

Trump doubted the utility and value of America's alliances, believed allies and partners had ripped off Washington for decades, saw NATO as obsolete, and told advisors he was considering leaving. Trump wasn't NATO's only critic. Some joked that NATO stood for "No Action, Talk Only." Trump publicly blasted its members for failing to meet their 2014 commitment to spend 2 percent of GDP on defense by 2024. Only six of twenty-nine NATO nations were hitting the goal: the US, Great Britain, Greece, Poland, Estonia, and Romania. Trump angered NATO's members, but alliance spending increased by $130 billion. This, and making China a NATO concern, were his most significant effects on Europe. One critic cogently argues that NATO basing its defense upon spending 2 percent of GDP "ignores every real aspect of strategy" as it says "nothing about whether a given ally's efforts are currently effective." Trump eventually admitted NATO had some strategic value but wanted it to pay more.[42]

NATO's July 2018 Brussels summit identified threats from terrorism and focused on deterrence. NATO adopted the "Four Thirties" initiative: ensuring it could respond to a Russian attack with "30 air squadrons, 30 naval ships, 30 combat battalions all available to fight within 30 days." The administration answered Russian aggression by reestablishing the Second Fleet (Atlantic) and deploying missile defense systems to Central Europe. In June 2020, Supreme Allied Commander Europe (SACEUR) approved the Concept for Deterrence and Defense for the Euro Atlantic Area, a precursor for replacing NATO's 1969 war plan.[43]

Mattis was particularly concerned the EU had embraced Russia and feared US actions were worsening things. At a July 2018 NATO meeting, Trump complained about Germany spending billions on oil and gas deals with Russia, against which the US was protecting it. In 2005, German Chancellor Gerhard Schröder had inked the Nord Stream pipeline deal for transporting natural gas from Russia to Germany and headed the shareholder's committee upon leaving office. The Nord Stream 2 deal for a pipeline running under the Baltic Sea, intentionally bypassing Ukraine and other Eastern and Central European states, was signed in April 2017. Detractors feared it giving Russia too much leverage over Germany. Merkel rebuffed criticism by branding it a business issue, which didn't work with Trump. Congress sanctioned companies working on Nord Stream 2 in early 2020, further straining US–German relations. Berlin's continued support for Nord Stream 2 was one reason Trump shrank US forces in Germany from 34,000 to 25,000, as was Germany's failure to meet its defense commitments.[44]

RUSSIA

Trump mentioned easing tensions with Russia and repairing US relations with Moscow when running for president. Tillerson hoped his personal connections would pay dividends and sanctions induce Russian departure from Ukraine and from Syria. This proved forlorn. The administration was hindered by a conspiracy theory insisting Trump was Putin's pawn, but Trump's actions played into his political enemies' hands. At a July 16, 2018 Helsinki meeting, Trump and Putin mainly discussed Syria; Putin did 90 percent of the talking, but Trump caused a stir with his public refusal to blame Putin for election interference while disagreeing with his intelligence agencies on this point. Trump's aversion to anything tainting his election explains his response, as do the well-documented efforts of US intelligence and law enforcement agencies and officials to undermine his presidency.[45]

Trump was tougher on Russia than Obama or Bush, though there was a disconnect between Trump's rhetoric and his administration's actions. The administration approved $40 million in arms sales to Ukraine in January 2018. Sixty Russian diplomats were expelled in March 2018. February 7, 2018 saw Russian mercenaries and Assad-linked forces launch a disastrous attack against American and Syrian Democratic Forces in Syria. The *NSS* branded Russia a threat, and in early 2018 McMaster made clear Russia's subversion and campaign interference menaced America's sovereignty.

The administration sanctioned more than 100 companies and individuals because of Russian aggression in the Crimea and Ukraine, and passed the Global Magnitsky Human Rights Accountability Act and the Countering America's Adversaries through Sanctions Act. The administration completed withdrawal from the 1987 Intermediate-Range Nuclear Forces (INF) Treaty in August 2019; Russia had long been in breach.[46]

THE THIRD IRAQ WAR, OR THE ISLAMIC STATE WAR CONTINUED, 2017–21

Trump inherited Obama's Third Iraq War – the war against Islamic State. When campaigning for president, Trump gave destruction of Islamic State as a political aim and promised that within thirty days after his inauguration the generals would have a new plan.[47]

THE ASSESSMENT AND THE POLITICAL AIM

Brett McGurk and retired lieutenant general Terry Wolff, the war's overseers for Obama, told the transition team that the war could go quickly by ending Obama's tight controls, and presented a well-received war plan. At the time of Trump's inauguration, Islamic State had lost 50 percent of its territory. On his first day as president, Trump told Mattis and McGurk he wanted Islamic State quickly and completely destroyed. Mattis needed more autonomy for military commanders. Trump granted it. A week after his inauguration, Trump declared: "It is the policy of the United States that ISIS be defeated." The administration ordered a new strategy completed within thirty days, including diplomacy, cyber, and information, any needed revisions to the rules of engagement, action against IS funding, and identifying additional allies.[48]

THE GRAND STRATEGY

The administration largely adopted the strategy and war plan developed under Obama but eliminated constraints such as forcing CENTCOM's commander to clear combat operations with the White House. Trump publicly differentiated his approach from Obama's, and Mattis made clear they intended IS's destruction. The strategy relied on airstrikes, coalition forces that included 4,000 non-Americans from 26 nations, and shutting the flow of foreign fighters. The Iraqis and Syrian Democratic Forces (SDF) carried the combat burden, the latter then completing the isolation of Raqqa.

American advisors began working more closely with Iraqi forces, including in combat operations the Iraqis had launched against Mosul in October 2016. Trump approved in May 2017 a plan for arming Kurds fighting IS in Syria. McGurk directed stabilization operations in cleared areas. After Raqqa's fall, the coalition intended to target the caliphate's remains in Syria's Euphrates River Valley Deir al-Zour province.[49]

The organizational shifts and the removal of constraints accelerated the war, producing the destruction of IS's physical caliphate by October 2017. It lost some 95 percent of its territory by December. The coalition eventually included seventy-nine states and international organizations. Between 2014 and 2017, 26,000 Iraqi soldiers were killed, and 17 US military personnel. But the war wasn't over. By August 2018, IS controlled perhaps 2 percent of what it once ruled, but estimates of its manpower in Iraq and Syria ran to 30,000, and it had transitioned down Mao's phases to a weakened insurgency in phase one. Simultaneously, Trump worried about Iranian influence in Iraq. Many of the Shia militia the Iraqi government used to stay in power – the Popular Mobilization Forces – were headed by Iranian agents and served as Tehran's proxies and levers on the Iraqi government. Trump, though, remained uninterested in giving Iraq more aid when this was suggested as a way to help consolidate victory over IS.[50]

In April 2018, Trump told the military to begin planning to leave and hand the war to America's Arab allies. Mattis and others "worried that despite territorial defeat, ISIS could reconsolidate. Trump had listened to conventional wisdom from his generals and agreed to push back withdrawal every six months since assuming office, but now he was ready to leave." In this war fought for an unlimited political aim – destruction of Islamic State – the Trump administration repeated a mistake America commonly makes in its wars for limited political aims: failing to use force long enough and with sufficient decisiveness to end the war. The US also "dithered over troop levels and military commitments to staying in the Gulf." Trump wanted out and balked at the projected costs of suggested postwar stabilization or reconstruction operations.[51]

In late 2018, the US had 2,000 advisors helping the Kurds when Turkey's Recep Erdoğan began threatening to attack Kurdish forces in Syria. Trump was advised to tell Ankara US troops would "fire on the Turkish military if they attacked the Kurdish forces." Trump refused. On December 14, Trump told Erdoğan that if Turkey could finish IS, America would leave. The deal was struck. Pompeo, Bolton, and Mattis tried to dissuade Trump. McGurk publicly warned: "We have to maintain pressure on these networks really, for a period of years." Trump tweeted the withdrawal announcement on December 19.[52]

Trump's decision was portrayed as unexpected and the result of a conspiratorial deal between Trump, Erdoğan, or Putin. But both Defense and State had already been told to prepare. State had been working this since at least March 2018. Trump had granted the military several extensions on prosecuting the war against Islamic State (there was apparently a deadline). The Kurds, though not given a date, knew this was in the works. What is true is that there was no interagency review beforehand or discussion with allies (neither are required; both are recommended).[53] Trump's actions here mirrored Obama's in Iraq and Afghanistan, but with less stick-to-it-iveness.

Trump's decision produced McGurk's resignation. Mattis' followed on December 20, 2018, after he failed to get Trump to change his mind, even though he believed Trump was generally making America stronger. Trump soon backpedalled. He committed to protecting the Kurds and warned Erdoğan against attacking them. During a January 2019 trip to Iraq, Trump agreed to a military plan to clear remaining IS areas within two to four weeks and learned that remaining in Iraq pressured Iran, which he liked. National Security Advisor Bolton said on January 6, 2019 that the US would continue in Syria until IS was fully defeated and Turkey was clear it wouldn't attack America's Kurdish friends. Secretary of State Pompeo tried to reassure allies Washington wasn't quitting the fight.[54]

Others pressed Trump to stay. Retired general Jack Keane told Trump on February 12, 2019 that leaving Syria meant the airspace would be controlled by Syria and Russia while Iran controlled the ground and took the oilfields, giving them more money to fund their proxies while reducing the effect of US sanctions. Trump replied: "That's a big deal." Meanwhile, Bolton and the Pentagon tried to assemble a multinational force as a buffer between the Turks and Syrian Kurds. Trump was told on February 20 that no nation would participate unless a few hundred Americans were present. Trump agreed to leave several hundred troops in Syria. Ambassador James Jeffrey, the president's new special envoy, admitted that he and other officials afterward routinely lied to the president about US troop numbers in Syria. It was higher than the 200 Trump committed to leave. The multinational force never materialized but IS lost its last territorial stronghold in Syria in March 2019.[55]

On October 6, 2019 – without warning – Trump ordered US forces out of Syria after a call with Erdoğan, who invaded the Kurdish areas of Syria on October 9. Trump's move was widely criticized as abandoning an ally and many Kurds felt betrayed. This exposed some Kurdish forces to potential Turkish attack, a danger to which Trump replied by threatening via Twitter to "obliterate" the economy of Turkey – a NATO ally. As before, Trump backtracked, announcing on October 21 that US troops would protect Syria's oilfields from IS. The entire event injured American credibility and drove the Syrian Kurds to align with Assad.[56]

The coalition forces shifted to advising and assisting the Iraqis via Security Force Assistance Brigades, but the US still mounted airstrikes and raids against IS remainders. Problems with Iran drove a reduction in the US footprint. In August 2020, the drawdown began. The Iraq troop level fell from 5,200 to 3,500 concentrated in Baghdad and Erbil. Some 300 coalition and 900 American troops remained at al-Tanf near Syria's southern border. Islamic State forces were still operating in cells of five to fifteen fighters. On October 9, 2020, Trump ordered the 3,000 troops reduced to 2,500 by year's end. By March 31, 2019, the Department of Defense had spent $765 billion on the Iraq and Islamic State wars. A commentator noted about Trump: "it is striking how successful his own appointees have been at slow rolling him on a withdrawal of US troops from Syria."[57]

THE AFGHAN WAR CONTINUED, 2017–21

Trump considered the Afghan War pointless, and his first instinct was withdrawal. Some feared raising Afghanistan with him because they thought he might order immediate departure. Others warned that leaving risked repeating Obama's 2011 Iraq mistake. Trump was convinced to keep the American commitment partially from fear of Afghanistan becoming a haven for Al Qaeda and similar groups.[58]

THE ASSESSMENT

The Afghanistan of 2017 was dramatically different from that of 2001. Kabul's population grew from 1 to nearly 5 million. There were free elections, though tainted. The number of children in school rose from fewer than 1 million to 9.3 million. Three hundred thousand students attended universities, one-third women, and 80 percent of Afghans had mobile phones.[59]

National Security Advisor McMaster led a review in early 2017. The Taliban probably controlled 10 percent of the population and contested control of perhaps 30 percent of the country. Thirty-nine nations contributed to the coalition; Afghan forces carried the combat weight. There were twenty groups using terrorism operating in the Afghanistan–Pakistan region, including ISIS-Khorasam (ISIS-K). Defense was executing Obama's drawdown plan and US troop strength was around 8,400. The US operated under a troop cap that bore no relation to the aims they were supposed to achieve, and the diplomatic and military efforts were unconnected.[60]

McMaster found no real strategy, that US actions weren't directed at delivering peace, and that intermittent talks with the Taliban were partially based upon two illusions: that the Taliban would abandon its goal of a Sharia-based Afghan government and that it had no significant links with Al Qaeda. Other misconceptions he identified included Pakistan ending its Taliban support in exchange for US aid and that the "counterterrorism-only approach" could work. McMaster believed one reason America was losing was it had been "operating under a withdrawal strategy for eight years." "The previous approach was, we're not going to fight the Taliban. We're not going to have them as a declared enemy and we're going to tell them we're leaving and we're going to try to negotiate a deal with them while they're in the ascendancy militarily."[61]

In mid June 2017, Trump delegated to Mattis the decision on increasing US troop numbers. Mattis declined any changes until he knew what Trump wanted to do there. Trump loosened Obama's rules of engagement, which had essentially restricted US forces to defending themselves against Taliban attacks. They could now take the war to the enemy. Trump questioned whether the war was in America's interest. This became connected to the larger issue of the value of overseas forces. Trump insisted subordinates justify projecting military power globally and a contentious administration debate raged through the summer. The final meeting on a new Afghanistan strategy was held at Camp David on August 18, 2017. Trump agreed to the military's plan to increase US troop levels and gave a speech on his South Asia strategy three days later. Such major public speeches are important internal communication tools for disseminating the administration's aims and strategy throughout the bureaucracy. But since these speeches have input from around the administration, the heads of the government branches such as Defense and State use them to secure things they want and parameters for action.[62]

THE POLITICAL AIMS AND THE GRAND STRATEGY

Trump's team grew Obama's Afghanistan–Pakistan strategy to a South Asia strategy, announcing this on August 21, 2017. The US sought victory in Afghanistan and defined it as: "attacking our enemies, obliterating ISIS, crushing al Qaeda, preventing the Taliban from taking over Afghanistan, and stopping mass terror attacks against America before they emerge."[63] Destroying ISIS and Al Qaeda and securing the Afghan state are understandable aims, but "attacking our enemies" is part of achieving them.

The grand strategy involved the US using its military, diplomatic, and economic power while not imposing a withdrawal timeline, which would be driven by Afghanistan's conditions. The US would seek additional NATO backing and pressure Pakistan to stop supporting and providing sanctuary for the Taliban and others, while deepening relations with India and enlisting its development and economic help in Afghanistan. The Afghans were expected to bear the burden. Trump stressed no nation building and said: "Military power alone will not bring peace to Afghanistan or stop the terrorist threat arising in that country. But strategically applied force aims to create the conditions for a political process to achieve a lasting peace."[64]

The strategy was branded R4+S: Regionalize, Realign, Reinforce, Reconcile, and Sustain. "Regionalize" meant seeking the participation of India, Pakistan, China, and Russia. "Realign" meant pushing active advising to a lower level and having advisors help with air support. The Afghans fielded 320,000 soldiers and police, but the US still had 11,000 troops, while NATO and others supplied 6,800. "Reinforce" meant 3,000 troops. "Reconcile" was the Taliban making peace with the Afghan government. This, Mattis said, was "the desired outcome from our military operations." "Sustain" meant working with the Afghans and coalition partners to ensure "this campaign is politically, fiscally, and militarily sustainable." The strategy was supposed to drive the Taliban to the negotiating table. It upset them because it appeared the US would stay and try to win. Their internal discussions urged serious efforts at peace negotiations.[65]

McMaster told Pakistan America might stop supporting it because Washington was essentially subsidizing the war against itself as the money it gave Islamabad funded groups fighting coalition forces in Afghanistan. In January 2018, the US cut security assistance funding and demanded Pakistan eliminate Taliban sanctuary; it didn't. McMaster believed the Afghan strategy was working. The financial and blood costs were falling, the government improving, and the Afghans doing most of the fighting.[66]

As always with Afghanistan, there are differing views. The Special Inspector General for Afghanistan Reconstruction (SIGAR) was created by Congress in 2008. Its May 2018 report "found the stabilization strategy and the programs used to achieve it were not properly tailored to the Afghan context, and successes in stabilizing Afghan districts rarely lasted longer than the physical presence of coalition troops and civilians." Others argue the Trump administration never committed to its strategy. By August 2018, some US commanders considered the war a stalemate and believed the Taliban contested control of over 60 percent of Afghanistan. Pakistan's behavior remained unchanged. The Taliban ruled with an iron fist in areas it controlled. Those who could fled to government-controlled regions. The focus became negotiating the war's end. CENTCOM commander Joseph Votel remarked in early August 2018 that the US planned to continue using various means to drive the Taliban to the negotiating table, while seeking to destroy IS elements. Khalilzad, appointed in September 2018 to negotiate with the Taliban, met them in Doha, Qatar, in October 2018. The administration continued development and anticorruption efforts in Afghanistan while pressuring Pakistan, eventually cancelling billions in aid, to no effect.[67]

Trump was convinced the strategy was failing and angered by the Inspector General report showing Taliban gains and massive waste of US funds. On November 8, 2018, Trump gave his advisors until February 14, 2019 to withdraw. The date became January 20. It changed several times and proved arbitrary. Trump didn't want to wait for Khalilzad to make a deal. He wanted to end the war before the conclusion of his second year in office because it would become his war if he didn't. On December 10, he ordered withdrawal but was convinced to backtrack after Mattis' resignation.[68]

On February 5, 2019, Trump announced a strategy focused on diplomacy in the form of negotiations with the Taliban. If the US secured a deal, it would draw down and conduct counterterrorism operations. One obstacle was the disconnect between State and Defense. State was trying to follow Trump's instruction that troops should leave while Defense had been told to plan for post-agreement counterterrorism action. Additionally, Washington had to secure a deal ending one mission while laying groundwork for another. Washington sought assurances Afghanistan wouldn't be a base for groups using terrorism. In return, it would remove its troops. But Washington first wanted an agreement on post-US governance. The Taliban refused. Their key demand was the departure of all US troops. Meanwhile, the negotiations excluded the Afghan government. The US faced the difficulty of securing Taliban agreement while shrinking its forces and thus its leverage. Ambassador Crocker compared the process – correctly – to what the US had done in Vietnam.[69]

The Taliban agreed, among other things, to not provide haven for Al Qaeda and to publicly break with it. But after a September 7, 2019 Taliban suicide bombing in Kabul killed several people, including an American soldier, Trump broke off negotiations, promising to intensify the war to force them to make peace. But he also made clear his belief America had stayed long enough and that the Afghans should take responsibility for themselves. Later talks produced the Doha Agreement. The Taliban promised Afghanistan wouldn't be a base for attacks on the US and agreed to a timeline for withdrawing foreign troops and the March 10, 2020 start of Taliban–Afghan government peace talks to discuss ceasefire arrangements and Afghanistan's future political organization. The US agreed to complete withdrawal within 14 months (May 2021), and to lower its troop strength to 8,600 within 135 days. Afghan president Ghani complained that Khalilzad kept him in the dark about the talks.[70]

The deal wasn't a peace treaty. One of its weaknesses was that, in theory, the US would withdraw while the Taliban and the Afghan government were still at war. Moreover, the US saw this "as a way to enlist the Taliban in the fight against the Islamic State," which was considered a bigger threat and had an Afghanistan presence. The agreement was inked on February 29, 2020; the drawdown began ten days later. The situation would be reassessed when the force level hit 8,600. The administration said it would keep the fourteen-month deadline – "if security conditions are met." Secretary of Defense Mark Esper said in March 2020 that peace in Afghanistan would allow the US to focus more on China but said in May that "neither the Taliban nor the Afghan government is abiding by the agreement."[71]

The failure of the Afghans to resolve a dispute over their presidential election threatened the deal and the beginning of talks between the Taliban and Kabul. The Trump administration cut $1 billion in aid in March 2020 to pressure Kabul and threatened more cuts the next year. From 2001 to 2019, the Departments of State and Defense and USAID appropriated or spent for Afghanistan and Pakistan between $934 and $978 billion in inflation-adjusted 2019 dollars. During the same period 2,300 Americans died there.[72]

The war continued during the talks. In October 2020, the Taliban launched an offensive in Helmand that displaced thousands of families. Afghan and US forces counterattacked. Meanwhile, Trump tweeted that all US troops would be withdrawn by the end of the year. Officials said they had no orders for this. US troop numbers fell to 2,500 by January 2021, with complete withdrawal scheduled by May 2021. The idea of a full withdrawal was smoke and mirrors. The administration's last defense secretary, Christopher Miller, called Trump's full-withdrawal promise a "play" and said the administration hoped to convince Ghani to quit or accept a "power-sharing agreement with the Taliban" that permitted an American counterterrorism presence of around 800 troops to go after groups like Islamic State.[73]

On November 11, 2021, four days after losing reelection, Trump ordered a complete American troop withdrawal from Afghanistan and Somalia.

In Somalia, a small number of US troops had been fighting an Al Qaeda wing, Al Shabaab, since 2007, and training local forces. The US mounted similar combat operations in Yemen, Niger, the West Sahel, and other places during Trump's tenure. Citing a failure to follow the chain of command in the issuance of the orders, officials insisted they lacked the legal ability to comply and didn't.[74]

Trump didn't deliver victory in Afghanistan. One critic offered this reason: "Trump, like Obama, was never committed to winning in Afghanistan."[75]

CONCLUSION

Political scientist Jacob Shively wrote that under Trump "US grand strategy had become a mix of unpredictable, often short-lived, eruptions coupled with steady, relatively conventional policy work."[76] Mark Esper, Trump's second defense secretary, wrote:

> Trump's instincts weren't always wrong about the policy or end state he wanted to achieve. However, the odds of success were spoiled or the goal tarnished by the process he often followed (little to none); the strategy he usually pursued (narrow and incomplete); the consensus he normally built behind it (minimal and insufficient); and the manner in which he generally communicated it (coarsely and divisively). In short, the ends he often sought rarely survived the ways and means he typically pursued to accomplish them. This often made the difference.[77]

One would add the disconnect between what Trump wanted and said, and the actions of his appointees. The fact that Trump's advisors pushed engagement while he worked to retrench, and his failure to exert his will over them, demonstrate his weakness as a president.

Security and prosperity were Trump's priorities. The Trump administration had successes, especially economically, and the tight labor market pushed up wages. The economy generally boomed – until the COVID shutdowns. Trump broke the nearly eighty-year bipartisan consensus that the near-unilateral opening of the US market to foreign goods was the best approach. His administration completed the destruction of the Islamic State caliphate, though failed to properly end the war – America's third such error in Iraq.[78] He didn't embroil the US in a war of his own making, a rare achievement for a US president in the post–Cold War era.

Trump both weakened and strengthened America's strategic position in the world. He shifted more of the defense burden to partners by driving them to increase outlays for their own defense and reimburse Washington more for what it pays to station deterrence forces abroad. His administration repaired the defense budgeting sequestration debacle. But Trump, like Obama, often injured America's relations with allies via ill-treatment. They needed to do more, but family quarrels are best had behind closed doors. Trump's greatest foreign relations achievement – and his most important contribution to American grand strategy – was to shift America's strategic focus toward a rising China. The administration's greatest success was "Operation Warp Speed," which developed COVID-19 vaccines.

THE JOSEPH BIDEN ADMINISTRATION, 2021-?

Joseph Biden brought a long political résumé to the presidency. He was a Delaware senator for thirty-six years and Obama's vice president. He was 78 when inaugurated, the oldest president yet to enter office, and assumed the mantle in the midst of the global COVID pandemic that saw most nations closing much of their respective economies, at least for a time. COVID vaccines had just become available, but the entire globe still struggled against the plague. It is unfair to judge an administration before it's finished, and everything said here is tentative, but the pivotal events of Biden's first year make examination necessary.

ASSESSMENT

The Biden team saw the international order as endangered and identified four primary threats. China was the top, followed by Russia, Iran, and North Korea. Terrorism was also a danger. China was considered a near-peer competitor and the primary challenge. The administration saw democracy as besieged by internal and external threats and perceived "a world of rising nationalism, receding democracy, growing rivalry with China, Russia, and other authoritarian states, and a technological revolution that is reshaping every aspect of our lives."[79]

National Security Advisor Jake Sullivan, a long-time Hillary Clinton advisor, believed the global situation demanded "a new and broader understanding of national security." He wanted a strategy concentrating on domestic renewal which was influenced by his coedited work *Making US Foreign Policy Work Better for the Middle Class*. Sullivan said: "Everything we do in our foreign policy and national security will be measured by a basic metric: Is it going to make life better, safer, and easier for working families?"[80]

This is a weak lens for analyzing strategic decisions, not least because of the difficulty of defining "middle class." It is subjective, short term, and ignores that strategy is for delivering political aims. It also potentially creates an impossible, self-imposed constraint. For example, logically, the US couldn't do anything that imposes costs in blood or treasure upon the middle class because this could be deemed as not in their interests. Plus, what if something is in the interest of the working class rather than the middle class, should that be ignored? Again, whether or not an action helps to deliver the political aim, preferably with acceptable costs and risks, is a better metric.

POLITICAL AIMS

Secretary of State Antony Blinken, a State Department and NSC veteran, revealed the administration's political aims in May 2021. It sought to defend, improve, and grow the "international rules-based order." This is the international system of sovereign nations linked by international law and organizations such as the UN and the World Trade Organization. Blinken insisted Washington would "continue to push back forcefully" against states that "undermine the international order, pretend that the rules we've all agreed to don't exist, or simply violate them at will." Additionally, the March 2021 *Interim National Security Strategic Guidance* (*INSSG*) insisted: "It is our most solemn obligation to protect the security of the American people."[81]

GRAND STRATEGY

Like its predecessor, the administration saw similar revisionist threats from China and Russia. Blinken said the administration would protect the "international rules-based order" by ensuring nations kept their commitments, that respect for human rights remained an international norm, and that states respected the sovereignty of other nations (this is continuity from the Trump administration) by not forcibly redrawing borders, undermining their elections, or targeting them with misinformation. But there was also a "need to address legitimate grievances – particularly unfair trading practices – that have provoked a backlash against an open international economic order in many countries, including in the United States." The US would do these things via multilateralism, as this was "still our best tool for tackling big global challenges and building coalitions," and would include non-traditional partners, meaning entities other than states.[82]

To defend American security, the *INSSG* said the country should: "Defend and nurture the underlying sources of American strength, including our people, our economy, our national defense, and our democracy at home"; "Promote a favorable distribution of power to deter and prevent adversaries from directly threatening the United States and our allies, inhibiting access to the global commons, or dominating key regions"; and "Lead and sustain a stable and open international system, underwritten by strong democratic alliances, partnerships, multilateral institutions, and rules."[83]

Militarily, the *INSSG* said Washington "should not, and will not, engage in 'forever wars' that have cost thousands of lives and trillions of dollars." Instead, the administration would "work to responsibly end America's longest war in Afghanistan while ensuring that Afghanistan does not again become a safe haven for terrorist attacks against the United States." The US would seek to deter adversaries, work with partners, have its most "robust" presence "in the Indo-Pacific and Europe," and "right-size" its Middle East "military presence to the level required to disrupt international terrorist networks, deter Iranian aggression, and protect other vital US interests" after its "Global Posture Review."[84]

Implementation required engaging the world, strengthening alliances, reengaging with international organizations such as the UN, and revitalizing democracy. Strengthening allies and partners would "also deter Chinese aggression and counter threats to our collective security, prosperity, and democratic way of life." Overall, the *INNSG* insisted "Taken together, this agenda will strengthen our enduring advantages, and allow us to prevail in strategic competition with China or any other nation."[85] In October 2021, the Biden team abandoned "great-power competition" for "strategic competition."

In February 2022, the administration added its Indo-Pacific Strategy. This suffered the standard confusion of aims and strategy and differed little substantively from Trump's approach. It also lacked an aim directed at China but made clear it is intended to deliver "an Indo-Pacific that is free and open, connected, prosperous, secure, and resilient," something necessary to "Our vital interests and those of our closest partners." It gives five "objectives" that are actually elements of strategy; the first, "Advance a free and open Indo-Pacific," mixes strategy and the aim. "Advance" implies action to achieve an aim or objective. Indo-Pacific freedom would be secured by: building regional connections; increasing "regional prosperity"; growing regional security; and increasing "regional resilience to transnational threats." Securing success demanded "unprecedented cooperation." The US would use diplomacy, strengthen allies and partners and attract new ones, grow economic ties, strengthen the Quad (US, India, Japan, Australia), increase its own role, and "build support for rules-based approaches to the maritime domain, including in the South China Sea and the East China Sea." On China, Washington would "seek to manage competition with the PRC [People's Republic of China] responsibly. We will cooperate with our allies and partners while seeking to work with the PRC in areas like climate change and nonproliferation."[86]

The administration's *National Security Strategy*, released in October 2022, built upon the *INSSG*. Its declared political aim was "a free, open, prosperous, and secure international order." It identified competition between democracies and autocracies as the primary challenge to the global order. Russia and China took center stage, but other authoritarian states, terrorism, global economic problems, and climate change were also denoted. The key elements of grand strategy were investment in internal sources of American power, international coalition-building, and military modernization.[87]

INTEGRATED DETERRENCE

The idea tying together the Biden administration's strategic strands was "integrated deterrence." Its author is unclear, but a Defense Department official said Secretary of Defense Lloyd Austin began using the term in January 2021. The concept underpinned the administration's new *National Defense Strategy*. "Integrated deterrence" meant integrating national power and capabilities across what were identified as air, maritime, land, space, and cyber domains across "the whole of government" while also "using the capability and capacity" of "our partners and allies." This applied "across the spectrum of conflict from high intensity warfare to the gray zone." The Department of Defense recognized China as the most significant threat and it was toward this that the new defense strategy was primarily directed, but it didn't ignore other dangers. Combined, this would "ensure that the United States, alongside our allies and partners, can dissuade or defeat aggression in any form or domain."[88]

Several theoretical problems undermined the grand strategy. The Indo-Pacific Strategy document has a box insert that is supposed to paint a picture of the administration's regional strategy by using the Ends-Ways-Means construct but does it incorrectly. For example, the point labeled "Strategic Ends" says this is "Advance a free and open Indo-Pacific that is more connected, prosperous, secure, and resilient." But the "End" should be the political aim being sought. Moreover, one doesn't advance aims (Ends): one pursues them. The administration also duplicated a Trump administration error: belief in a supposed gray zone between war and peace. This, along with the "spectrum of conflict" view, fails to acknowledge the critical distinction between war and peace, leading to impoverished analysis of both and increasing the chances of poor decisions. "Gray zone" appears in the *INSSG* as well and reached its apotheosis when Biden used it in a January 2022 speech to describe the 2014 Russian invasion of the Crimea and the Donbas. Things here were always black and white to the Ukrainians and Russians. The October 2022 *National Security Strategy* recapped integrated deterrence.[89]

ECONOMIC STRATEGY

Like everything early in the administration, the COVID pandemic was a backdrop. The *INSSG* said "We have an enduring interest in expanding economic prosperity and opportunity, but we must redefine America's economic interests in terms of working families' livelihoods, rather than corporate profits or aggregate national wealth." Such thinking informed the administration's failed effort to pass a multi-trillion-dollar bill to expand the Federal government's role in American life likened to 1960s efforts. Biden did secure a bipartisan $1 trillion infrastructure bill and a $1.9 trillion COVID stimulus package. The San Francisco Federal Reserve determined the latter helped fuel short-term inflation, which reached a forty-year high – 7.5 percent annually. Biden acknowledged this pushed up prices by giving people money to spend. Federal debt hit $30 trillion by January 2022, fueled by $5 trillion in COVID-related spending by Biden and Trump. Federal indebtedness reached $31 trillion in October 2022. Economist Larry Summers, formerly a Clinton administration Treasury secretary and head of Obama's Council of Economic Advisors, blamed growing inflation on Biden's "massively expansionary policies relevant to the size of the GDP gap," a "fiscal stimulus … five times as large as it had been during the financial crisis, and at the same time, massively accommodative monetary policies" with "the Fed [Federal Reserve] growing its balance sheet rapidly and maintaining very low real interest rates even as the inflation rate accelerated." The US added jobs as it emerged from the COVID shutdowns, unemployment soon dropped to 4 percent, and the administration cut a deal with the EU to lower some Trump-era US tariffs on steel and aluminum in return for adjustments from Europe.[90]

DIPLOMACY AND WAR

The administration insisted "We will lead with diplomacy" and seek "to boldly engage the world to keep Americans safe, prosperous, and free." Though the administration had many Obama administration veterans, it didn't completely duplicate Obama's approach to an Iranian nuclear deal. Both Blinken and Sullivan had shifted their views and "Instead of treating the nuclear deal apart from Iran's other malign behavior," thought "any new deal with Tehran should address Iran's missile program and terrorist activities across the region." But the administration backed away from Trump's hard line. In late 2021, it waived sanctions on Iran selling electricity to Iraq before negotiations began. The timing led to accusations of doing so to secure talks or "offering concessions to Tehran to generate goodwill." In January 2022, Iran mounted drone and rocket strikes on US bases in Iraq, without inflicting casualties, to pressure America during the nuclear negotiations ongoing in Vienna. Iran also wanted to force the US out of the region. Biden ordered retaliatory attacks in both February and July.[91]

The administration maintained much of Trump's approach to China. Its key figures realized engagement had failed and that Beijing was a competitor with global ambitions. Instead of the standard initial review, the administration early met with allies to inform them Washington would take a hard line. A State Department official said: "It's a competition, and we intend to win it." The administration kept Trump's tariffs and stood against Chinese attempts at intimidation such as sanctioning twenty-eight former Trump officials and its aggressive actions against US officials, all launched in a failed effort to pressure the administration to roll back Trump's moves. Washington added sanctions because of China's continued genocide against the Uyghurs and its suppression of democracy in Hong Kong, and refused to look the other way on issues merely because Beijing cooperated on items of common interest. The administration maintained "strategic ambiguity" regarding whether or not America would defend Taiwan, but in September 2021 solidified a regional alliance – AUKUS (Australia, United Kingdom, United States).[92]

THE THIRD IRAQ WAR, OR ISLAMIC STATE WAR CONTINUED, 2021-22

Islamic State remained active and dangerous. US ground and air forces continued to support partners fighting them in Syria and Iraq, and the administration made a deal with Iraq to end America's combat role by December 31, 2021. Iraq announced the official conclusion of this in early December. Remaining US forces were to "fully transition to a [sic] training, advising, assisting, and intelligence-sharing" and have no combat role. But American troop numbers didn't change: around 2,500 remained in Iraq and about 900 in Syria. The US also still fought, and killed Islamic State's new caliph in February 2022. The war against Al Qaeda also continued, and included the July 30, 2022 killing of 9/11 mastermind Ayman al-Zawahiri.[93]

LOSING THE AFGHAN WAR, 2021[94]

On April 14, 2021, President Biden announced America would withdraw its forces from Afghanistan by September 11, 2021, the twentieth anniversary of the September 11 attacks that brought America to Afghanistan. Biden inherited a Trump administration commitment to depart by May 1, 2021, but announced this would instead begin on May 1. Biden pledged continued support for Afghanistan, including its security forces, promised an "over the horizon" counterterrorism strategy to answer any emerging threat in Afghanistan, and told the Taliban to expect American retribution if they interfered with the withdrawal.[95]

Biden insisted he was bound by Trump's February 2020 Doha Agreement, one the Taliban had broken by refusing to separate from Al Qaeda and failing to seriously negotiate with Kabul's democratically elected government. Biden insisted the US couldn't stay in Afghanistan, where the US had only 2,500 troops, and needed to depart to meet the China challenge. Biden had long wanted a withdrawal and promised this during his presidential campaign. This desire remained despite the US implementing a version of the light-footprint counterterrorism strategy he advocated at the beginning of Obama's administration. It was "highly unlikely," Biden insisted, that the Taliban would take over Afghanistan.[96]

American military commanders argued against withdrawal, insisting the US needed to maintain 2,500 troops to keep the Taliban at bay and prevent Afghanistan from again becoming a haven for groups using terrorism. Biden overrode them. Both JCS chair General Mark Milley and CENTCOM's commander, General Kenneth McKenzie, wanted a continued presence. On July 13, 2021, two dozen American diplomats at the Kabul embassy warned Blinken in a memo that US withdrawal meant Afghanistan's collapse. Neither Biden's White House nor Sullivan and his NSC saw the memo; Sullivan read about it in the *Wall Street Journal* a month after its dispatch. It also offered advice (unheeded) for speeding evacuation.[97]

A few days before, on July 8, 2021, Biden announced a new withdrawal date: August 31. The reason for the change isn't immediately clear, but many remarked that it stepped away from September 11. Biden noted that staying longer in Afghanistan meant the Taliban would renew attacks on US troops, forcing the dispatch of additional troops. Milley revealed later that if the US didn't leave by August 31, the Taliban might renew fighting against the Americans, which would require committing 30,000 more US troops. Milley still advised keeping 2,500 troops in Afghanistan.[98]

The US began withdrawing in May and the situation fell apart more quickly than the administration expected. Afghanistan's army and police had a paper strength of 300,000. But this number was inflated by "ghost soldiers" carried on the books. Undermining the force was extensive corruption and leadership incompetence. Additionally, as America transitioned to Afghan control over the previous decade, Afghan leaders in Kabul focused on personal enrichment, not good governance.[99]

The Taliban, meanwhile, slowly increased its strength in the countryside and established shadow governments in areas they controlled that undermined the authority and credibility of Kabul's government. They established ties with provincial elders and Kabul officials, building a strong position for negotiating with enemy forces and leaders when they thought it time, and filling the ruling and security vacuum they created. The Taliban had long laid the foundation for the Kabul government's collapse by undermining the will of the Afghan forces and government. The Doha Agreement had disillusioned the already weak army and police, and the American withdrawal announcement "shattered the confidence" of the Kabul government and its forces. Even the Taliban was shocked by the speed and ease of their advance.[100]

Without its American backstop, the Afghan will to fight broke under Taliban pressure. It was a force designed to fight with American backing, particularly air support, intelligence, and logistics. When the US removed contractors providing maintenance and intelligence, the Afghan security forces began coming apart. The Afghans could no longer support their 400 positions throughout the country, many of which required air resupply.[101]

Biden said in the press conference following his July 8 speech that he trusted the Afghan forces to hold up against the Taliban and didn't see Afghanistan's fall as inevitable. CIA Director William Burns said in a July 22, 2021 interview that "The Taliban are making significant military advances; they're probably in the strongest military position that they've been in since 2001." The administration stayed the course. Biden insisted the collapse came much sooner than anticipated, but some intelligence assessments given both the Trump and Biden administrations predicted collapse could come in days.[102]

The first Afghan provincial capital, Zaranj, fell to the Taliban on August 6, 2021. For much of August 7, as Afghanistan collapsed into Taliban hands, President Ghani sat on the lawn at the presidential palace reading a book. President Biden played golf in Delaware. On August 8, the

US embassy advised Americans to leave as soon as possible. There was no sense of urgency anywhere. The Taliban offensive unrolled with stunning rapidity as Kabul's forces fled, surrendered, or switched sides. By August 10, Afghan officials were resigning and fleeing the country. The city of Ghazni surrendered without a fight on August 12, opening the Taliban's path to Kabul from the south. Afghan officials saw this as a turning point. The State Department had already ordered the destruction of "sensitive" documents. August 12 also saw the defenses of both Herat and Kandahar evaporate. On August 13, panic hit Kabul. Ghani and key government members fled on August 15 as Taliban forces entered the capital. Afghanistan's democratically elected government was dead.[103]

The collapse of the Afghan army and the Taliban's quick final campaign destroyed American evacuation plans. The administration had intended to leave 650 troops to guard the embassy. This meant there were insufficient troops to also hold the key Bagram airport. Biden approved its closure, which meant operating out of Kabul. Biden's push for a rapid withdrawal put Defense and State on different paths, and Milley accused State of waiting too long to order an evacuation. This, combined with the quick collapse of Kabul's army, forced the administration to launch an evacuation mission entailing the dispatch of 6,000 US troops to secure Kabul's airport. An August 26 suicide bombing killed thirteen American service members supporting the evacuation. The administration received abundant intelligence that such an attack might occur.[104]

The US and others evacuated 124,000 people by August 31 but left behind perhaps 200 Americans and most of the tens of thousands of Afghans who had helped the Americans. France's Emmanuel Macron, Germany's Angela Merkel, and Great Britain's Boris Johnson all pressed Biden to extend the August 31 deadline. He refused.[105]

On August 31, 2021, 11:59pm Kabul time, the commander of the 82nd Airborne Division, Major General Chris Donahue, the last American soldier in Afghanistan, boarded the last American transport aircraft in Kabul. America's twenty-year war in Afghanistan was over. The United States was leaving in defeat. Its NATO partners were already gone. In total, 2,461 American military personnel were killed in the Afghan War. Perhaps 69,000 Afghan soldiers and police died, and perhaps 47,000 civilians. The US spent $824.9 billion, an average of $3.4 billion a month. Comparisons with America's 1975 evacuation of Hanoi quickly emerged, but instead of the image of helicopters departing the US embassy roof, the picture was of Afghans falling to their deaths from American aircraft fleeing Kabul. CNN journalist Peter Bergen wrote: "Biden is presiding over a debacle entirely of his own making in Afghanistan." Biden later defended his actions: the mission had been accomplished – Bin Laden was dead, and Afghanistan wasn't a base for global terror. China, COVID, cyberspace, and climate change were, he insisted, more important.[106]

RUSSIA'S UKRAINE WAR

In June 2021, the NATO summit communiqué reiterated Ukraine's right to join NATO. On November 10, "the US and Ukraine signed a Charter on Strategic Partnership, which asserted America's support for Kyiv's right to pursue membership in the North Atlantic Treaty Organization." Putin made clear in public statements in 2007, 2012, and July 2021 that to him "the Ukraine–NATO question wasn't negotiable." But it was ultimately Putin's decision to resort to force. His own paranoia drove him to war. Neither Ukraine nor NATO were Russia's enemies.[107]

On February 18, 2022, Defense Secretary Austin noted, in the midst of growing concern about potential Russian aggression as Moscow massed troops near Ukraine, that "you have seen a preview of that strategy [strategic deterrence] begin to play out here, as we address this most recent crisis."[108] On February 24, Putin intensified the Ukraine war he had launched in 2014. Biden stepped up the supplying of arms to Ukraine begun under Trump and intensified economic sanctions on Russia. An international coalition rallied to support Ukraine with arms, and with financial and material support.

If the administration's grand strategy – strategic deterrence – was intended to uphold the rules-based international order, critics – particularly Republican ones – judged it as having failed with the advent of Russia's effort to conquer Ukraine.[109] Biden's critics also insisted it was his weakness and the damage dealt to his and American credibility by the Afghanistan defeat that convinced Putin he could escalate in Ukraine. This can't yet be proven or disproven and it is too early to render judgment, but it must be considered, as American defeat in Vietnam emboldened the Soviet Union and convinced Bin Laden and others of American weakness.

CONCLUSION

It will be many years before we can hazard definitive conclusions on the actions of the Trump or Biden administrations and their effects. But financial profligacy, weakness abroad, susceptibility to flawed strategic concepts, poor assessment of foes, and a lost war are things we clearly see.

CONCLUSION

WHAT SHOULD AMERICAN GRAND STRATEGY BE? THIS IS THE WRONG QUESTION

We're awash in works urging America's pursuit of specific grand strategies such as "liberal hegemony" and "offshore balancing." I've spent little time on suggestions such as these because there's no evidence for the United States ever attempting them. These discussions also generally neglect the fundamental question of political purpose and thus lack a basis for analysis. The aims America pursues vary. This means how power is used varies. Any insistence upon a blanket "doctrine" or grand strategy to address the totality of America's place in the world takes insufficient account of the complexity of the geopolitical picture.

THE WAY WE THINK AND HOW WE GOT HERE

The influence of academia upon American strategic thinking has been mixed. Its first large-scale impact arrived in the form of Professor Woodrow Wilson. As we have seen, he brought with him to Versailles a group known as "The Inquiry," a convocation of academics, journalists, and attorneys to help plan for the postwar period and do preparatory labor for the Versailles conference. This is generally considered a failure. Franklin Roosevelt had what was known as his "brain trust," a collection of professors largely from Harvard and Columbia who focused on domestic actions and helped construct the New Deal. This failed as well. The Second World War efforts proved more successful, particularly those concentrating on science and industrial projects such as the Manhattan Project that built the atomic bomb.[1]

In the 1950s, a new professional foreign relations elite was emerging. Through the 1940s, 1950s, and 1960s, America's top universities developed deep ties to the Federal government and became knowledge production venues to help the US manage its new post–Second World War responsibilities. Washington poured funding on them.[2] This also launched

CONCLUSION

an era where America's leaders often seized upon flawed strategic ideas, invariably means-based and thus lacking foundations for clear analysis. We received the concepts that failed in Vietnam: modernization theory, signaling theory, and so-called "limited war" ideas. The last two are widely taught as valuable despite their failure when applied in the real world. And one never sees discussion of independent or dependent variables where strategy is crafted or implemented.

What we branded the "Cold War" inadvertently helped confuse us about the differences between peace and war. It was neither cold nor a war. But to many it *felt* like a war. A lack of clarity in regard to US actions in Korea and Vietnam fed our misconceptions. These misunderstandings carried over to the post–Cold War era, birthing errors such as hybrid war and the gray zone, ideas arising from misreading history and an inability to do systematic strategic analysis. They infiltrated the Obama administration, underpinned some Trump administration strategic thinking, and damaged Biden's. Americans should stop unquestioningly accepting every "new" "strategic idea." Why do we? Insufficient knowledge of history and theory.

SOME CORE MISTAKES

Some urge the US to go abroad in search of monsters to slay, and sometimes the US must. But this isn't easy. American power has never been as overwhelming as both its critics and proponents insist, and only develops in relation to the value of the political aim being pursued. When America does go abroad to slay monsters, this should be undertaken with a grim seriousness tempered by the awareness that this is almost always harder, bloodier, longer, and far more costly financially and politically than anyone thinks.

We have seen the problems of administrations lacking clear political aims or a concrete vision for where they want to go. The Carter administration initially flailed. The Obama administration dwelt upon the tactical. This contrasts greatly with the James Monroe–John Quincy Adams approach, and Reagan's. They possessed vision, developed clear aims, and had leaders dedicated to achieving them. No American president surpasses Eisenhower for having clear aims and offering solid strategic direction. FDR provided a clear, wartime purpose. Dangerous opponents gave both Ike and FDR targets against which to focus, but other administrations had this and failed to perform as well. There is also the opposite problem of being too ambitious. Wilson and George W. Bush are examples.

Sometimes having clear aims doesn't matter. This has proven particularly true in wartime. The US possessed clear aims in South Vietnam and in

CONCLUSION

Iraq in 2003 but didn't consider sufficiently the value of these aims in the eyes of the respective opponents, the difficulty of their achievement, how long it would take, the costs, the means required, or the effects from third-party actors. Lincoln possessed clear aims, and eventually secured them, but it was far from smooth or easy. The American revolutionaries had clear aims but needed help to achieve them. Wilson knew for what purpose he wished to use American power but was unrealistic and insufficiently considered America's allies, which he needed to achieve his aims.

The use of American power in war since the Second World War has been too often blundering. Entering wars such as Korea unprepared continued an American tradition marked by the War of 1812, the Mexican War, the Spanish–American War, and virtually every conflict against the American Indians. But the failure to understand or admit when the nation was at war, something true for Truman in Korea, Kennedy and Johnson in Vietnam, and Obama in Libya and Iraq, worsened situations. The perpetual American stumbling on ending wars, particularly the 2003–11 Iraq War, the Iraq War launched in 2014 that continues today, and the two-decade conflict in Afghanistan, demonstrates poor American understanding of the use and limits of American military power and the political complexities accompanying its use. American leaders – particularly political leaders – haven't understood what is required to win the wars into which they take the United States, a part of the job now forgotten.

Our most moralistic presidents – Wilson, Carter, George W. Bush, Obama – conducted foreign relations in a manner that seems hypocritical at best and uninformed at worst. When one compares, for example, their support for tyrannical regimes abroad or use of military force one finds little difference with administrations without moralistic pretensions. Obama's sins extended to the subversion of democracy in Iraq and Afghanistan. They also often held America's friends to a higher standard than America's enemies. This was particularly true of Wilson, Carter, and Obama, as well as Trump. The "realists" (so-called) often founder on the shoals of contradiction while the "idealists" (so-called) are often buried by the reality of national self-interest.

SOME CORE SUCCESSES

There have been problems and failures but, overall, America has enjoyed national success. German Chancellor Otto von Bismarck quipped that "God has a special providence for fools, drunkards, and the United States of America." For two and a half centuries, US leaders have kept America secure and protected its sovereignty. American democracy has prospered, and American freedom continually expanded. This is no mean feat. Economic prosperity and advantages have generally increased, though with bumps. America began as a trading nation and remains one. It is a place where native and immigrant entrepreneurs can build better, more prosperous lives; they remain an engine of American affluence. America's military power has continued unmatched for decades, and the flexibility and innovative spirit of the American system allows it to produce increasingly effective and technologically superior inventions and weaponry. America remains a font of ideas and enjoys a broad stream of intelligent and skilled people willing to serve voluntarily in America's armed forces and other arms in a professional and self-sacrificial manner. Because of American power, the world is freer than it has ever been, and freer than it would be without it. But past success doesn't guarantee future performance.

THE PURPOSE OF POWER?

The United States should continue protecting its sovereignty and security. Democracy abroad is greatly in the US interests as these states become partners (and competitors) instead of rivals, but assuming it can be imposed quickly and cheaply is wishful thinking. This can work, but it requires enormous amounts of time, treasure, and blood. It is best if this can be encouraged to arise from within, but that takes homegrown efforts. Since the Second World War, achieving security and stability in a foreign nation has been possible generally only in states capable of doing it themselves.[3] Whether or not the US becomes involved abroad, and how, will be a tough call for whoever sits in the Oval office.

But how to use America's power?

DIPLOMATIC STRATEGY

One can't stress enough the value of solid, realistic diplomacy based upon clear assessments of other states. America has often been quite effective here and continuously involved in the world. Interestingly – and this pains me to say – overall, the lawyers and bankers who dominated American diplomacy before the Second World War seem to have performed more solidly than those trained in politics, history, and economics overlooking the postwar order. America was involved in the world without exhausting itself. Its actions were imperfect, but US tragedies were few. This can be debated, and the conditions have certainly changed, but the impression is there.

CONCLUSION

The US should continue strengthening and expanding its alliance commitments, particularly with democratic countries, but America's allies and partners *must* carry more of the burden. There's no political tolerance in the US for them doing otherwise. Publicly rebuking them as did Obama and Trump is not the best way of securing this. It's also the case that sometimes allies must be shed. If they won't keep their commitments in peacetime, can they be relied upon to keep them in wartime?

Protests by totalitarian states against American power should be vigorously rebutted. Our allies should be pushed to do the same and be punished if they refuse. Moreover, public criticism of US actions by the officials of our allies should not pass unaddressed. Neither should US administrations conduct themselves in an ill-mannered fashion. There will be times when no agreement is possible, and allies will do what they believe they need to do. That's when disappointed officials in the other camp should be silent or speak behind closed doors. One complaint will be that the US is discriminating against non-democratic states. Yes. That's how it should be as those states won't play by the same rules and work against the interests of America and its partners. This doesn't mean the US shouldn't work with them, but the rules are different. Ideology matters and shouldn't be forgotten.

One of the many wrongheaded ideas to enter the American diplomatic realm is that engagement with other states – particularly rivals or competitors – is sure to produce behavioral changes Washington desires. The implementation of engagement takes many forms – political discussions, cultural exchanges, and so on. But the dominating concept has been economic cooperation. The failed, more than forty-year experiment with China should kill Western illusions that authoritarian or totalitarian regimes will become "just like us" because we want them to. Indeed, one could argue it emboldened China because a grand strategy dominated by engagement looks weak. American leaders forget that the political trumps the economic.

We had an example of this from Republican William Howard Taft. His administration pursued Dollar Diplomacy – economic reform and investment by American firms – particularly in Latin America and China, believing this would produce economic rehabilitation, and then political stability, particularly because factions wanted foreign investment. Taft worked from the false assumption that economic development was more important than politics. Dollar Diplomacy died as Latin American leaders pursued political power, and Japan and Russia pushed America from China.

CONCLUSION

ECONOMIC STRATEGY

Economic strategy is the most complex strategic realm and one with little agreement. All comments here are cautionary. The most consistent American mistake has been pursuing economic growth as an aim in itself. A nation should build economic strength to have a tool for achieving its political purposes. Failing to do this doesn't preclude economic success. But for what purpose?

Economic strategy should have internal and external components, which will often intertwine. Taxes and regulation should be as low as possible to spur economic growth. The level of government regulation might be more important as lessening it removes economic friction. Lower corporate tax rates seem more influential than personal ones as the former spur business reinvestment and expansion and thus job growth. Keeping government spending in line and thus out of the bond market as Clinton did does at times help spur growth. This also means the nation isn't accumulating debt, the servicing of which consumes greater proportions of the budget as it expands, thus requiring more revenue. In January 2022, Federal debt was $30 trillion.

In a purely economic sense (meaning no political effects or consequences), with all things being equal, free trade is best. But we don't live in a pure economic world, and nothing is equal. From 1815 to the Great Depression, American tariffs were intended to protect and encourage the growth of American industry. Moreover, barring a few years dominated by income from selling land, tariffs provided 80–90 percent of US Federal income before 1913's income tax. Some tariffs can work for the US because of the large internal market, though consumers might pay more. To insist a protectionist tariff is always wrong is as great an error as arguing it is always good. When facing a predatory power seeking to expand its industrial strength at your expense, whether Great Britain in the late eighteenth century or China since the end of the Cold War, tariffs can help bring the nation through the danger zone and preserve its critical industrial base. This is vital for defense, and protects industrial jobs and the nation's sovereignty. A great power with weak industry won't remain a great power. But the adjunct problem is tariffs from other nations. None of this is easy.

In the post–Second World War era, the US enjoyed enormous economic growth. One reason was much of the world's economic structures had been destroyed, leaving many markets to the United States. That was reversing by the 1960s. China in some respects has repeated America's postwar economic boom and done so partially by becoming the world's producer as America did. Countering this is difficult.

MILITARY STRATEGY

More often than not, when the US has gone to war it has been successful, and the nation has often been fortunate in its wartime political and military leaders. There are certainly problems and defeats, but America has enjoyed far more professionals in high commands than blunderers.

Deterrence should remain the basis of military strategy. The US needs to deter attacks on its homeland, its allies, and partners. But deterrence only succeeds if an aggressor knows belligerency faces a response, one greater than it wishes to bear. Strong, decisive leaders are required for the first, abundant military and economic power for the latter. How much depends upon the enemies and their power. But the US must avoid past mistakes, particularly misreading and underestimating its opponents, entering wars unprepared, and failing to have a plan for victoriously ending the war.

INFORMATION STRATEGY

The US had a sustained Cold War effort to promote the American system and the benefits of democracy, freedom, and free markets. Some of these instruments, like Voice of America (VOA), are still around but need sharpening. This, like everything, is exceedingly difficult and complex, but also necessary. China is selling itself and its system and doing so with little restraint. America must be its own best advocate to compete in the global idea marketplace. The world is not marching toward democracy, and freedom doesn't preserve itself. And the US needs to stop being outperformed in the information realm, particularly by groups as pitiful as Islamic State.[4]

A FINAL WORD...

The United States in 2023 faces new challenges resembling old ones: Russia, China, and Iran – expansionist, revisionist, totalitarian states determined to reshape the world. America has often been accused – falsely – of seeking hegemony, mostly by other Americans. Putin's Russia seeks a regional form of this, as does Iran. Communist China is chasing it globally. American leaders must provide direction and vision by constructing rational aims for the US to achieve at home and abroad, particularly in regard to these three powers, and especially China. This requires clear-eyed assessments based upon an awareness of the opponent's aims (if possible), an understanding of their ideological underpinnings, their power, and how they might use it. Just as important is to appreciate America's own strengths and weaknesses and how the nation can exercise its power in pursuit and defense of its purposes. This must be done with no illusions and unencumbered by broken ideas. Doing less could prove fatal.

Acknowledgements

I am grateful to the staff of the libraries of Marymount University, George Mason University, Georgetown University, and especially Irma Fink of the Naval Postgraduate School's Dudley Knox Library in Monterey, California. Despite the complications of the COVID pandemic, she secured many needed books and articles. I could not have done my work without her efforts and those of numerous other librarians.

I have incurred innumerable debts in the course of researching and writing this book. Guidance on sources and a willingness to read chapters proved particularly important. My gratitude goes out to Kevin Benson, Hal Blanton, Patrick Brady (who read the entire manuscript), Llewellyn Cook, John Ferling, Edward Lengel, Branden Little, James Goldgeier, Samuel Helfont, Mike Jones, Joseph Ledford, Lukas Milevski, Gary Ohls, Jacob Shively, Craig Whiteside, James Graham Wilson, Tom Young, those interviewed on background, and two insightful referees. My apologies to those I've forgotten.

Soli Deo Gloria

Notes

THINKING ABOUT GRAND STRATEGY IN PEACE AND WAR

1 One example that does: Scott A. Silverstone, "American Grand Strategy and the Future of Landpower in Historic Context," in Joseph Da Silva et al., eds., *American Grand Strategy and the Future of US Landpower* (Carlisle: Army War College Press, 2014), 62.
2 Stephen Walt, *The Hell of Good Intentions: America's Foreign Policy Elite and the Decline of US Primacy* (New York: Farrar, Straus, and Giroux, 2018), xi.
3 John Lewis Gaddis, *Strategies of Containment: A Critical Appraisal of Postwar American National Security* (Oxford: Oxford University Press, 2005), 233.
4 Robert Art, *A Grand Strategy for America* (Ithaca: Cornell University Press, 2003), 45.
5 Bernard Brodie, *War and Politics* (New York: Macmillan, 1973), 2, quoted in Tami Davis Biddle, *Strategy and Grand Strategy: What Students and Practitioners Need to Know* (Carlisle: Army War College Press, 2015), 18.
6 Art, *Grand Strategy*, 46.
7 John A. Thompson, *A Sense of Power: The Roots of America's Global Role* (Ithaca: Cornell University Press, 2015), 37–39.
8 Julian E. Zelizer, *The Arsenal of Democracy: The Politics of National Security – From World War II to the War on Terrorism* (New York: Basic Books, 2010), 4–5.
9 Gordon S. Wood, *Empire of Liberty: A History of the Early Republic, 1789–1815* (Oxford: Oxford University Press, 2009), 260; Alan Taylor, *The Civil War of 1812: American Citizens, British Subjects, Irish Rebels, and Indian Allies* (New York: Knopf, 2011); Gail Chaddock, "On Iraq War, Senate Leader Harry Reid in Cross Hairs," *Christian Science Monitor* (April 27, 2007), www.csmonitor.com/2007/0427/p01s02-uspo.html.
10 Carl von Clausewitz, *On War*, Michael Howard and Peter Paret, trans. and eds. (Princeton: Princeton University Press, 1984), 69, 80, 579; Julian Corbett, *Some Principles of Maritime Strategy* (Annapolis: Naval Institute Press, 1988), 41–44.
11 Clausewitz, *On War*, 484, 579; Sun Tzu, *The Art of War*, Samuel Griffith, trans. (London: Oxford University Press, 1961), 71; Robert Strassler, ed., *The Landmark Thucydides: A Comprehensive Guide to the Peloponnesian War* (New York: Touchstone, 1996), 44.
12 Clausewitz, *On War*, 585–86.

13 Ibid., 94, italics in the original.
14 Michael Fuchs, "America Doesn't Need a Grand Strategy," *Foreign Policy* (July 2019), 40–45; James Carden, "Grand Strategy Is Bunk," *The American Conservative* (December 3, 2014), www.theamericanconservative.com/articles/grand-strategy-is-bunk/?print=1.
15 Lukas Milevski, *The Evolution of Modern Grand Strategic Thought* (Oxford: Oxford University Press, 2016), 1–2.
16 Examples: Art, *Grand Strategy*, 3–4; William C. Martel, *Grand Strategy in Theory and Practice: The Need for an Effective American Foreign Policy* (Cambridge: Cambridge University Press, 2015), 32–34.
17 Leon Fuerth, "Grand Strategy," in Sheila Ronis, ed., *Forging an American Grand Strategy: Securing a Path through a Complex Future. Selected Presentations from a Symposium at the National Defense University* (Carlisle: Army War College Press, 2013), 11.
18 Barry R. Posen and Andrew L. Ross, "Competing Visions for US Grand Strategy," *International Security*, 21:3 (winter 1996/97), 7.
19 B. H. Liddell Hart, *Strategy*, 2nd ed. (New York: Meridian, 1991), 322; Biddle, *Strategy*, 4; Hal Brands, *What Good Is Grand Strategy? Power and Purpose in American Statecraft from Harry S. Truman to George W. Bush* (Ithaca: Cornell University Press, 2014), 4; Terry L. Deibel, *Foreign Affairs Strategy: Logic for American Statecraft* (Cambridge: Cambridge University Press, 2007), 8; Richard Rosencrance and Arthur Stein, "Beyond Realism: The Study of Grand Strategy," in Richard Rosencrance and Arthur Stein, eds., *The Domestic Bases of Grand Strategy* (Ithaca: Cornell University Press, 1993), 4.
20 Milevski, *Evolution*, 98.
21 Peter Trubowitz, *Defining the National Interest: Conflict and Change in American Foreign Policy* (Chicago: University of Chicago Press, 1998), 6.
22 Foster Rhea Dulles, *America's Rise to World Power, 1898–1954* (New York: Harper, 1955), xvii–xviii; John Lewis Gaddis, *Surprise, Security, and the American Experience* (Cambridge: Harvard University Press, 2004), 24; Walter A. McDougall, *Promised Land, Crusader State: The American Encounter with the World since 1776* (New York: Houghton Mifflin, 1997), 50–51; Jonathan R. Dull, *A Diplomatic History of the American Revolution* (New Haven: Yale University Press, 1985), 94.
23 McDougall, *Promised*, 39–40, 104, 117; Robert Seager II, *Alfred Thayer Mahan: The Man and His Letters* (Annapolis: Naval Institute Press, 1977), 225; Christopher Hemmer, *American Pendulum: Recurring Debates in US Grand Strategy* (Ithaca: Cornell University Press, 2015), 7, 27–28; George W. Bush, *The National Security Strategy of the United States* (Washington: White House, 2006), ii.
24 Joseph S. Nye Jr., *Soft Power: The Means to Success in World Politics* (New York: Public Affairs, 2004), x, 2–7, 11, 99; Peter Layton, *Grand Strategy* (Australia: Peter Layton, 2018), 59; Martel, *Grand Strategy*, 12.
25 Reginald Stuart, *War and American Thought: From the Revolution to the Monroe Doctrine* (Kent: Kent State University Press, 1982), 1.
26 Biddle, *Strategy*, 11.

27 George W. Baer, *One Hundred Years of Sea Power: The US Navy, 1890–1990* (Stanford: Stanford University Press, 1993), 147–49.
28 Stuart, *War*, 1.
29 Alfred E. Eckes Jr., *Opening America's Market: US Foreign Trade Policy since 1776* (Chapel Hill: UNC Press, 1995), xvii, 7.
30 Thompson, *Power*, 14, 17–19.
31 The operational and tactical realms relayed in Figure 0.1 lay outside our discussion.

1 THE FIGHT FOR SOVEREIGNTY, 1775–1801

1 Jonathan R. Dull, *A Diplomatic History of the American Revolution* (New Haven: Yale University Press, 1985), 9.
2 Robert Allison, *The American Revolution: A Concise History* (Oxford: Oxford University Press, 2011), 5–8, 10–14.
3 Ibid., 17–19; Maurice Matloff, ed., *American Military History* (hereafter *AMH*), (Washington: Office of the Chief of Military History, 1969), 42; Christopher Ward, *The War of the Revolution* (New York: Macmillan, 1952), 1:17–18.
4 Allison, *Revolution*, 19; *AMH*, 42–43; Victor Brooks and Robert Hohwald, *How America Fought Its Wars: Military Strategy from the American Revolution to the Civil War* (Conshohocken: Combined Publishing, 1999), 18–19.
5 Jeremy Black, *War for America: The Fight for Independence, 1775–1783* (London: Wrens Park, 1991), 83–86.
6 Carl von Clausewitz, *On War*, Michael Howard and Peter Paret, trans. and eds. (Princeton: Princeton University Press, 1984), 81, 92, 579; Robert Middlekauff, *The Glorious Cause: The American Revolution, 1763–1789* (Oxford: Oxford University Press, 2007), 283–85; John Ferling, *Almost a Miracle: The American Victory in the War for Independence* (Oxford: Oxford University Press, 2009), 70–71; Allison, *Revolution*, 21–22, 32; Dull, *Diplomatic*, 11–12; The Declaration as Adopted by Congress [July 6, 1775], https://founders.archives.gov/?q=Declaration%20of%20the%20Causes%20and%20Necessity%20of%20Taking%20Up%20Arms%20&s=1111311111&sa=&r=6&sr=.
7 Dull, *Diplomatic*, 11–12, 54; Richard Morris, *The Forging of the Union, 1781–1789* (New York: Harper and Row, 1987), 64–65.
8 Piers Mackesy, *The War for America, 1775–1783* (Lincoln: Bison Books, 1993 [1964]), 29, 33–34, 71; Piers Mackesy, "British Strategy in the War of American Independence," *The Yale Review* (June 1963), 541–42.
9 John Shy, *A People Numerous and Armed: Reflections on the Military Struggle for American Independence* (Ann Arbor: University of Michigan Press, 1990), 32–34, 37–38; *AMH*, 55.
10 Edward Lengel, *General George Washington: A Military Life* (New York: Random House, 2005), 91; Middlekauff, *Glorious*, 36, 92–93, 287; *AMH*, 55, 57; Mackesy,

War, 29; Ricardo A. Herrera, "The King's Friends: Loyalists in British Strategy," in Donald Stoker, Kenneth Hagan, and Michael McMaster, eds., *Strategy in the War of American Independence: A Global Approach* (London: Routledge, 2010), 100.
11 Dull, *Diplomatic*, 14–15, 43–44, 47; Mackesy, *War*, 29.
12 *AMH*, 44; Middlekauff, *Glorious*, 287–98.
13 Middlekauff, *Glorious*, 286; *AMH*, 50; *Warren-Adams Letters. Being Chiefly a Correspondence Among John Adams, Samuel Adams, and James Warren* (Boston: Massachusetts Historical Society, 1917), 1:52–53; Philander Chase et al., eds., *The Papers of George Washington, Revolutionary War Series* (hereafter *PWR*) (Charlottesville: University Press of Virginia, 2002), 1:42–43, 43n.1; Don Higginbotham, *The War of American Independence: Military Attitudes, Policies, and Practice, 1763–1789* (New York: Macmillan, 1971), 108; Ferling, *Miracle*, 69.
14 *PWR*, 1:331–33, 2:396–97, 397n.1; *AMH*, 50; Middlekauff, *Glorious*, 313.
15 *PWR*, 1:21–22, 3:3–4, 4n.1; Lengel, *Washington*, 93, 105–6; Joseph Ellis, *His Excellency: George Washington* (New York: Vintage, 2005), 77–78; Don Higginbotham, "The American Militia: A Traditional Institution with Revolutionary Responsibilities," in Don Higginbotham, ed., *Reconsiderations on the Revolutionary War: Selected Essays* (Westport: Greenwood, 1978), 90.
16 Thomas Frothingham, *Washington: Commander in Chief* (Boston: Houghton Mifflin, 1930), 84–86; John Steele Gordon, *An Empire of Wealth: The Epic History of American Economic Power* (New York: HarperCollins, 2004), 61; Kenneth J. Hagan, *This People's Navy: The Making of American Sea Power* (New York: Free Press, 1991), 2–19.
17 *PWR*, 1:21–22, 2:24–30; Middlekauff, *Glorious*, 314–17.
18 Antulio J. Echevarria II, *Reconsidering the American Way of War: US Military Practice from the Revolution to Afghanistan* (Washington: Georgetown University Press, 2014), 65; Mackesy, *War*, 36, 58.
19 Lengel, *Washington*, 97; Mackesy, *War*, 60, 82.
20 Ferling, *Miracle*, 111–14, 117–18.
21 Declaration of Independence, July 4, 1776, www.archives.gov/founding-docs/declaration-transcript.
22 Alfred E. Eckes Jr., *Opening America's Market: US Foreign Trade Policy since 1776* (Chapel Hill: UNC Press, 1995), 4–5.
23 Ellis, *Excellency*, 93; *PWR*, 4:21–22, 111–13.
24 *PWR*, 5:253–54, 258–60, 610–14, 625–28, 6:70–71, 248–52; Ellis, *Excellency*, 77; Lengel, *Washington*, 105.
25 Mackesy, *War*, 83–85; Ferling, *Miracle*, 129–30; Clausewitz, *On War*, 357.
26 *PWR* 6:98, 123–24, 124n.1; Ferling, *Miracle*, 130–36, 209.
27 *PWR*, 6:248–52; Michael I. Handel, *Masters of War; Classical Strategic Thought*, 3rd ed. (London: Frank Cass, 2001), 46, 353–60.
28 Ferling, *Miracle*, 157–60.
29 Richard Showman et al., eds., *The Papers of Nathanael Greene* (hereafter *Greene Papers*) (Chapel Hill: UNC Press, 1976), 1:294–95.

30 Theodore Thayer, *Nathanael Greene: Strategist of the American Revolution* (New York: Twayne Publishers, 1960), 214–15; B. H. Liddell Hart, *Strategy*, 2nd ed. (New York: Meridian, 1991), 26–27.
31 *PWR*, 6:248–52; John Fitzpatrick, ed., *The Writings of George Washington* (hereafter *WW*) (Washington: USGPO, 1937), 6:27n.27.
32 Harold Syrett et al., eds., *The Papers of Alexander Hamilton* (New York: Columbia University Press, 1961), 1:274–77.
33 *PWR*, 9:323–24; Sun Tzu, *The Art of War*, Samuel Griffith, trans. (London: Oxford University Press, 1961), 144; Lengel, *Washington*, 15; J. E. A. Crake, "Roman Politics from 215 to 209 BC," *Phoenix*, 17:2 (summer 1963), 126.
34 *PWR*, 6:279–81, 280n.2, 288–89, 289n.4, 308–9, 7:96–98, 102–5, 105–6n.10, 115–16, 161–62n.1, 162–65, 165n.4, 168–69n.9; *Collections of the New York Historical Society for the Year 1778* (New York: New York Historical Society, 1879), 404–5; Thayer, *Greene*, 124.
35 Ferling, *Miracle*, 142–46; *AMH*, 63, 65; *PWR*, 7:1–3n.1, 102–5, 105n.2.
36 *PWR*, 7:245, 262–64, 334, 339, 366–68; *WW*, 6:414–16.
37 *PWR*, 2:346–47, 347n.3; 5:280; Capitaine de Jeney, *The Partisan: or, The Art of Making War in Detachment*, J. Berkenhout, trans. (London: n.p., 1760).
38 Ferling, *Miracle*, 168–69; *PWR*, 7:382–86.
39 *PWR*, 7:197n.2, 425, 425n.1, 439, 468, 495, 499–500; David Hackett Fischer, *Washington's Crossing* (Oxford: Oxford University Press, 2004), 346–62; Ferling, *Miracle*, 209.
40 Mackesy, *War*, 111–18.
41 Ibid., 121–23.
42 *PWR*, 10:170–72, 198–99; Thayer, *Greene*, 200–4; Mackesy, *War*, 121–23; Ferling, *Miracle*, 246; Ellis, *Excellency*, 101.
43 Brooks and Hohwald, *How America*, 71–75; Middlekauff, *Glorious*, 377–79; *AMH*, 77–79; Mackesy, *War*, 131–41.
44 Mackesy, *War*, 132, 143–44; Ellis, *Excellency*, 109–18.
45 Dull, *Diplomatic*, 89–91.
46 Ibid., 89–94, 98–100; Richard Morris, *The Peacemakers: The Great Powers and American Independence* (New York: Harper and Row, 1965), 15–17; James Pritchard, "French Strategy in the American Revolution: A Reappraisal," in Stoker et al., *Strategy in the War of American Independence*, 144.
47 Victor Enthoven, "Dutch Maritime Strategy," in Stoker et al., *Strategy in the War of American Independence*, 181–85; Ferling, *Miracle*, 564; Dull, *Diplomatic*, 110–12.
48 Morris, *Forging*, 34–35; Hugh Rockoff, *America's Economic Way of War: War and the US Economy from the Spanish-American War to the Persian Gulf War* (Cambridge: Cambridge University Press, 2012), 21; Paul Koistinen, *Beating Plowshares into Swords: The Political Economy of American Warfare* (Lawrence: University Press of Kansas, 1996), 18–21.
49 Morris, *Forging*, 40, 153; Eckes, *Opening*, 6–7.
50 Ferling, *Miracle*, 267–68.

51 Ibid., 351; Ellis, *Excellency*, 122.
52 Ferling, *Miracle*, 346, 351–54; Ellis, *Excellency*, 123–24.
53 Ferling, *Miracle*, 267–68; Shy, *People*, 198–201.
54 Mackesy, *War*, 340–42; Middlekauff, *Glorious*, 446–55; Ferling, *Miracle*, 423–27, 435–37; David Mattern, *Benjamin Lincoln and the American Revolution* (Columbia: University of South Carolina Press, 1995), 94; Donald Stoker and Michael Jones, "Colonial Military Strategy," in Stoker et al., *Strategy in the War of American Independence*, 18–19. Prisoner numbers vary.
55 Shy, *People*, 209; Middlekauff, *Glorious*, 455–58; Ferling, *Miracle*, 437–38; Mackesy, *War*, 342–43.
56 Shy, *People*, 210–11; Mackesy, *War*, 342–45; Middlekauff, *Glorious*, 467–68.
57 Thayer, *Greene*, 243, 261, 279, 282–85.
58 *Greene Papers*, 6:543; Thayer, *Greene*, 282–83, 290–92.
59 *Greene Papers*, 7:74–75.
60 Ibid., 6:549.
61 Ibid., 7:175.
62 Thayer, *Greene*, 303–15; Mackesy, *War*, 404–5.
63 Thayer, *Greene*, 315–21, 326–30; Lawrence Babits, "Greene's Southern Campaign," in Maarten Ultee, ed., *Adapting to Conditions: War and Society in the Eighteenth Century* (Tuscaloosa: University of Alabama Press, 1986), 147.
64 Mackesy, *War*, 406–9; Babits, "Greene's," 147.
65 Ellis, *Excellency*, 133; Mackesy, *War*, 410–11, 422–27; Griffith, *War*, 647–48, 656.
66 Mackesy, *War*, 461, 465, 469–73.
67 Morris, *Peacemakers*, 45.
68 Gregg Lint, "Preparing for Peace: The Objectives of the United States, France, and Spain in the War of the American Revolution," in Ronald Hoffman and Peter Albert, eds., *Peace and the Peacemakers: The Treaty of 1783* (Charlottesville: United States Capitol Historical Society, 1986), 31–32; Morris, *Peacemakers*, 302, 309–10, 382–85, 462–64.
69 Gordon, *Empire of Wealth*, 63; George Herring, *From Colony to Superpower: US Foreign Relations since 1776* (Oxford: Oxford University Press, 2011), 12–13, 16.
70 Peter Maslowski, "To the Edge of Greatness: The United States, 1783–1865," in Williamson Murray et al., eds., *The Making of Strategy: Rulers, States, and War* (Cambridge: Cambridge University Press, 1996), 207; Herring, *Colony*, 6; C. Vann Woodward, "The Age of Reinterpretation," *The American Historical Review*, 66:1 (October 1960), 2.
71 *AMH*, 101; Morris, *Forging*, 53; Allan Millett et al., *For the Common Defense: A Military History of the United States from 1607 to 2012*, 3rd ed. (New York: Free Press, 2012), 88.
72 Eckes, *Opening*, 9; Michael Green, *By More Than Providence: Grand Strategy and American Power in the Asia Pacific since 1783* (New York: Columbia University Press, 2019), 21–22; Herring, *Colony*, 37–38.
73 Eckes, *Opening*, 10–11; Gordon, *Empire of Wealth*, 64–65; Herring, *Colony*, 48–51.

74 Maslowski, "To the Edge," 207–11; Herring, *Colony*, 51, 53; Morris, *Forging*, 87–88, 152; Eckes, *Opening*, 11.
75 Herring, *Colony*, 58–59.
76 Eckes, *Opening*, 14–15.
77 Edward Mead Earle, "Adam Smith, Alexander Hamilton, Friedrich List: The Economic Foundations of Military Power," in Edward Mead Earle, ed., *Makers of Modern Strategy: Military Thought from Machiavelli to Hitler* (Princeton: Princeton University Press, 1971), 133, 136.
78 Ron Chernow, *Alexander Hamilton* (New York: Penguin, 2005), 286–87, 294–96, 347; Gordon, *Empire of Wealth*, 73–75.
79 Douglas Irwin, *Clashing over Commerce: A History of US Trade Policy* (Chicago: University of Chicago Press, 2017), 68–71.
80 Irwin, *Clashing*, 77–78; Eckes, *Opening*, 13–14; Gordon, *Empire of Wealth*, 68–73.
81 Earle, "Adam Smith," 134; Gordon S. Wood, *Empire of Liberty: A History of the Early Republic, 1789–1815* (Oxford: Oxford University Press, 2009), 76–79, 98–99.
82 Earle, "Adam Smith," 130–32, 136; George Washington, Eighth Annual Address to Congress, December 7, 1796, www.presidency.ucsb.edu/ws/?pid=29438; Wood, *Empire of Liberty*, 101–2; Irwin, *Clashing*, 82–85.
83 Gordon, *Empire of Wealth*, 75; Irwin, *Clashing*, 79.
84 Thomas Bailey, *A Diplomatic History of the American People* (New York: Appleton-Century-Crofts, 1964), 83–84; Chernow, *Hamilton*, 435–36.
85 Walter A. McDougall, *Promised Land, Crusader State: The American Encounter with the World since 1776* (New York: Houghton Mifflin, 1997), 29.
86 Irwin, *Clashing*, 95–97; Herring, *Colony*, 74–80; Koistinen, *Beating*, 42.
87 Earle, "Adam Smith," 134–35; Wood, *Empire of Liberty*, 111.
88 Craig Symonds, "Defining an American Navy, 1783–1812," in Kenneth Hagan and Michael McMaster, eds., *In Peace and War: Interpretations of American Naval History* (Westport: Praeger, 2008), 20–23.
89 Wood, *Empire of Liberty*, 112–14.
90 Ibid., 126; Colin Calloway, *The American Revolution in Indian Country: Crisis and Diversity in Native American Communities* (Cambridge: Cambridge University Press, 1995), 273, 277–78, 288–89; Francis Paul Prucha, *The Sword of the Republic: The United States Army on the Frontier, 1783–1846* (London: Macmillan, 1969), 8, 18–19.
91 Wood, *Empire of Liberty*, 114–16, 121–23, 126.
92 Calloway, *American*, 280–82, 285, 290; *AMH*, 110; Francis Paul Prucha, *The Great Father: The United States Government and the American Indian* (Lincoln: University of Nebraska Press, 1988), 16–17.
93 Wood, *Empire of Liberty*, 126–29; Calloway, *American*, 283–84; *AMH*, 110; Prucha, *Great Father*, 16–17; Prucha, *Sword*, 18–19.
94 *AMH*, 110–11; George Washington, First Annual Address to Congress, January 8, 1790, www.presidency.ucsb.edu/ws/index.php?pid=29431; Prucha, *Sword*, 20–22; *AMH*, 111–12; Wood, *Empire of Liberty*, 129.

95 *AMH*, 112–13; Prucha, *Sword*, 30–35; Calloway, *American*, 289; Wood, *Empire of Liberty*, 131–34.
96 Wood, *Empire of Liberty*, 131; Calloway, *American*, 290; Millett et al., *Common*, 87.
97 Earle, "Adam Smith," 132; Robert Kagan, *Dangerous Nation: America's Place in the World from Its Earliest Days to the Dawn of the Twentieth Century* (New York: Knopf, 2006), 113–15.
98 George Washington, Farewell Address, September 17, 1796, http://avalon.law.yale.edu/18th_century/washing.asp.
99 Ibid.
100 Ibid.
101 David McCullough, *John Adams* (New York: Touchstone, 2001), 474.
102 John Adams, Inaugural Address, March 4, 1797, https://millercenter.org/the-presidency/presidential-speeches/march-4-1797-inaugural-address; John Adams, Special Session Message to Congress, May 16, 1797, https://millercenter.org/the-presidency/presidential-speeches/may-16-1797-special-session-message-congress-xyz-affair.
103 Wood, *Empire of Liberty*, 239–40.
104 Ibid., 240–44; McCullough, *Adams*, 489.
105 Herring, *Colony*, 86; Wood, *Empire of Liberty*, 245; Maslowski, "To the Edge," 220; Symonds, "Defining," 23–25.
106 Clausewitz, *On War*, 75; Gregory E. Fehlings, "America's First Limited War," *Naval War College Review*, 53:3 (summer 2000), 101, 118–19.
107 Wood, *Empire of Liberty*, 263–67; Maslowski, "To the Edge," 221.
108 Wood, *Empire of Liberty*, 247–51, 260; Maslowski, "To the Edge," 220.
109 McCullough, *Adams*, 523–28, 531, 538–39; Herring, *Colony*, 88–89.
110 Symonds, "Defining," 25; Herring, *Colony*, 90–91; McCullough, *Adams*, 531.
111 Herring, *Colony*, 91.

2 EXPANSION, SOVEREIGNTY, AND WAR, 1801–1817

1 Gordon S. Wood, *Empire of Liberty: A History of the Early Republic, 1789–1815* (Oxford: Oxford University Press, 2009), 287, 357–58; Thomas Jefferson, First Inaugural Address, March 4, 1801, https://millercenter.org/the-presidency/presidential-speeches/march-4-1801-first-inaugural-address.
2 Wood, *Empire of Liberty*, 626–28; Alfred E. Eckes Jr., *Opening America's Market: US Foreign Trade Policy since 1776* (Chapel Hill: UNC Press, 1995), 3.
3 Wood, *Empire of Liberty*, 293, 295–98; John Steele Gordon, *An Empire of Wealth: The Epic History of American Economic Power* (New York: HarperCollins, 2004), 81.
4 Donald Hickey, *The War of 1812: A Forgotten Conflict* (Urbana: University of Illinois Press, 1989), 8; Wood, *Empire of Liberty*, 292; Jefferson, First Inaugural.

5 Kevin McCranie, *Utmost Gallantry: The US Navy and the Royal Navies at Sea in the War of 1812* (Annapolis: Naval Institute Press, 2011), 17; Craig Symonds, "Defining an American Navy, 1783–1812," in Kenneth Hagan and Michael McMaster, eds., *In Peace and War: Interpretations of American Naval History* (Westport: Praeger, 2008), 2; Antulio J. Echevarria II, *Reconsidering the American Way of War: US Military Practice from the Revolution to Afghanistan* (Washington: Georgetown University Press, 2014), 72.

6 Kenneth J. Hagan, *This People's Navy: The Making of American Sea Power* (New York: Free Press, 1991), 54–56; Allan Millett et al., *For the Common Defense: A Military History of the United States from 1607 to 2012*, 3rd ed. (New York: Free Press, 2012), 93.

7 Hagan, *People's Navy*, 58–61; Echevarria, *Reconsidering*, 72–73.

8 Hagan, *People's Navy*, 61; Echevarria, *Reconsidering*, 73.

9 Symonds, "Defining," 28–29; Hickey, *1812*, 8–9; Wood, *Empire of Liberty*, 293; McCranie, *Utmost*, 17.

10 *AMH*, 113–14; Francis Paul Prucha, *The Sword of the Republic: The United States Army on the Frontier, 1783–1846* (London: Macmillan, 1969), 40–42; Woods, *Empire of Liberty*, 675.

11 Wood, *Empire of Liberty*, 358, 366.

12 Ibid., 367–69.

13 Ibid., 369, 377; Thomas Jefferson, Second Inaugural Address, March 4, 1805, https://millercenter.org/the-presidency/presidential-speeches/march-4-1805-second-inaugural-address.

14 McCranie, *Utmost*, 13–14; Hickey, *1812*, 11.

15 McCranie, *Utmost*, 12–14.

16 Ibid., 14–16; Douglas Irwin, *Clashing over Commerce: A History of US Trade Policy* (Chicago: University of Chicago Press, 2017), 102–11, 116.

17 Irwin, *Clashing*, 116–17; Hickey, *1812*, 22–23; McCranie, *Utmost*, 16.

18 Echevarria, *Reconsidering*, 73–74; Hickey, *1812*, 26–28.

19 J. C. A. Stagg, *Mr Madison's War: Politics, Diplomacy, and Warfare in the Early American Republic, 1783–1830* (Princeton: Princeton University Press, 1983), 143–44; Hickey, *1812*, 28–34.

20 Hickey, *1812*, 34–39, 49–50; Stagg, *Madison's*, 151–52; Wood, *Empire of Liberty*, 673.

21 Hickey, *1812*, 42.

22 Ibid.; Special Message to Congress on the Foreign Policy Crisis – War Message, June 1, 1812, https://millercenter.org/the-presidency/presidential-speeches/june-1-1812-special-message-congress-foreign-policy-crisis-war.

23 Stagg, *Madison's*, 4; Hickey, *1812*, 72; Alan Taylor, *The Civil War of 1812: American Citizens, British Subjects, Irish Rebels, and Indian Allies* (New York: Knopf, 2011), 137–39.

24 Stagg, *Madison's*, 6, 39–40; Carl von Clausewitz, *On War*, Michael Howard and Peter Paret, trans. and eds. (Princeton: Princeton University Press, 1984), 94.

25. Peter Maslowski, "To the Edge of Greatness: The United States, 1783–1865," in Williamson Murray et al., eds., *The Making of Strategy: Rulers, States, and War* (Cambridge: Cambridge University Press, 1996), 223.
26. *AMH*, 125–26.
27. Taylor, *Civil*, 140–41.
28. Hickey, *1812*, 48–49.
29. Stagg, *Madison's*, 227–31.
30. Taylor, *Civil*, 155–57.
31. Ibid., 157.
32. Ibid., 150; *AMH*, 124–26.
33. *AMH*, 127.
34. Ibid.; Hickey, *1812*, 151–52.
35. J. C. A. Stagg, *The War of 1812: Conflict for a Continent* (Cambridge: Cambridge University Press, 2012), 1; Millett et al., *Common*, 99.
36. McCranie, *Utmost*, 24–27, 52–53; Linda Maloney, "The War of 1812: What Role for Sea Power?" in Hagan and McMaster, eds., *In Peace and War*, 35–36.
37. Taylor, *Civil*, 139; *AMH*, 127; Stagg, *Madison's*, 201.
38. Taylor, *Civil*, 151–52.
39. Ibid. 151–52, 172–73; *AMH*, 128–31.
40. Taylor, *Civil*, 182, 187; *AMH*, 128–29.
41. *AMH*, 128; Taylor, *Civil*, 182, 187; Stagg, *Madison's*, 247.
42. *AMH*, 128–29; Taylor, *Civil*, 188–89.
43. *AMH*, 129; Taylor, *Civil*, 193, 196.
44. Taylor, *Civil*, 180–81, 191–92; Stagg, *Madison's*, 268; Hickey, *1812*, 88; *AMH*, 129–30.
45. Stagg, *Madison's*, 275–76; Hickey, *1812*, 105–6.
46. McCranie, *Utmost*, 116.
47. Hickey, *1812*, 127–28, 131.
48. Ibid., 106–7; Stagg, *Madison's*, 282–83.
49. Stagg, *Madison's*, 283–86; Hickey, *1812*, 127.
50. Stagg, *Madison's*, 279–82, 298; Taylor, *Civil*, 201.
51. Stagg, *Madison's*, 286; Hickey, *1812*, 129.
52. *AMH*, 131–32.
53. Ibid., 132.
54. Ibid., 134; Hickey, *1812*, 135; Stagg, *Madison's*, 321–22; Maloney, "1812," 44.
55. Hickey, *1812*, 139; *AMH*, 134; Stagg, *Madison's*, 330.
56. Stagg, *Madison's*, 337–38.
57. Taylor, *Civil*, 269–276.
58. Ibid., 279–82.
59. Ibid., 283–90; Stagg, *Madison's*, 338–46.
60. Maloney, "1812," 38; Hickey, *1812*, 173–74; Stagg, *Madison's*, 375–76, 384–85.
61. Maloney, "1812," 41; McCranie, *Utmost*, 196–97, 206–7.
62. Stagg, *Madison's*, 388–89; Taylor, *Civil*, 292–93; Robert Leckie, *The Wars of America* (Edison: Castle Books, 1998), 279.

63 Stagg, *Madison's*, 390.
64 Ibid., 400–1.
65 Ibid., 400–3.
66 Ibid., 403–7.
67 Ibid., 407, 412–13.
68 McCranie, *Utmost*, 115, 218–19; Wayne Lee, "Plattsburgh 1814: Warring for Bargaining Chips," in Matthew Moten, ed., *Between War and Peace: How America Ends Its Wars* (New York: Free Press, 2011), 43–44, 52.
69 Lee, "Plattsburgh," 52–53; Millett et al., *Common*, 103–4; McCranie, *Utmost*, 229–30.
70 Lee, "Plattsburgh," 44, 53–57.
71 Taylor, *Civil*, 416.
72 Stagg, *Madison's*, 348, 354–55.
73 Ibid., 353.
74 Ibid., 355–56.
75 Ibid., 358–61.
76 Ibid., 487; *AMH*, 144–46.
77 Millett et al., *Common*, 105; Stagg, *Madison's*, 489–90; *AMH*, 144–46.
78 Taylor, *Civil*, 412–13; Daniel Walker Howe, *What Hath God Wrought: The Transformation of America, 1815–1848* (Oxford: Oxford University Press, 2007), 72.
79 Taylor, *Civil*, 413–14.
80 Ibid., 415–16.
81 Ibid., 417–19; Robert V. Remini, *Andrew Jackson and the Course of American Empire, 1767–1821* (New York: Harper and Row, 1977), 1:300; Howe, *What Hath*, 75.
82 Stagg, *Madison's*, 270–71.
83 Remini, *Jackson and Empire*, 1:298–99; Taylor, *Civil*, 421.
84 Howe, *What Hath*, 90.
85 Ibid., 78; Echevarria, *Reconsidering*, 73.
86 Howe, *What Hath*, 81–88; Irwin, *Clashing*, 122–26.

3 SEEKING A CONTINENT: EXPANSION, INDIAN REMOVAL, AND THE MEXICAN WAR, 1817–1849

1 George Herring, *From Colony to Superpower: US Foreign Relations since 1776* (Oxford: Oxford University Press, 2011), 138–39.
2 Ibid., 134; Daniel Walker Howe, *What Hath God Wrought: The Transformation of America, 1815–1848* (Oxford: Oxford University Press, 2007), 107; Walter LaFeber, ed., *John Quincy Adams and American Continental Empire* (Chicago: Quadrangle, 1965), 36, 39–41.
3 Charles Edel, *Nation Builder: John Quincy Adams and the Grand Strategy of the Republic* (Cambridge: Harvard, 2014), 120–21, 128–29.

4 Ibid., 129–32, 160–63; Walter A. McDougall, *Promised Land, Crusader State: The American Encounter with the World since 1776* (New York: Houghton Mifflin, 1997), 66–67; John Quincy Adams, Speech to the US House of Representatives on Foreign Policy, July 4, 1821, https://millercenter.org/the-presidency/presidential-speeches/july-4-1821-speech-us-house-representatives-foreign-policy.
5 Edel, *Nation*, 122–23.
6 John Quincy Adams, Inaugural Address, March 4, 1825, https://avalon.law.yale.edu/19th_century/qadams.asp.
7 Edel, *Nation*, 8–9, 63, 123, 134–35; Robert V. Remini, *Andrew Jackson and the Course of American Empire, 1767–1821* (New York: Harper and Row, 1977), 1:304.
8 Michael Green, *By More Than Providence: Grand Strategy and American Power in the Asia Pacific since 1783* (New York: Columbia University Press, 2019), 27.
9 Ibid., 28–29; McDougall, *Promised*, 61–62.
10 Howe, *What Hath*, 112–13; Edel, *Nation*, 174–76; McDougall, *Promised*, 69.
11 Edel, *Nation*, 178–82.
12 James Monroe, Seventh Annual Address to Congress (the Monroe Doctrine), December 2, 1823, https://millercenter.org/the-presidency/presidential-speeches/december-2-1823-seventh-annual-message-monroe-doctrine.
13 Green, *Providence*, 29; Edel, *Nation*, 183; Howe, *What Hath*, 113, 116; McDougall, *Promised*, 74.
14 James Monroe, Inaugural Address, March 4, 1817, https://avalon.law.yale.edu/19th_century/monroe1.asp; Edel, *Nation*, 9.
15 E. A. J. Johnson and Herman E. Krooss, *The Origins and Development of the American Economy: An Introduction to Economics* (New York: Prentice-Hall, 1953), 18–19; John Steele Gordon, *An Empire of Wealth: The Epic History of American Economic Power* (New York: HarperCollins, 2004), 94–96; Alfred E. Eckes Jr., *Opening America's Market: US Foreign Trade Policy since 1776* (Chapel Hill: UNC Press, 1995), 18, 22–23.
16 Johnson and Krooss, *Origins*, 113; Eckes, *Opening*, 18–20.
17 Eckes, *Opening*, 17.
18 Edel, *Nation*, 84–85; Herring, *Colony*, 141–43.
19 Eckes, *Opening*, 20–22; Johnson and Krooss, *Origins*, 113–14.
20 Allan Millett et al., *For the Common Defense: A Military History of the United States from 1607 to 2012*, 3rd ed. (New York: Free Press, 2012), 108–9, 113; Monroe, Inaugural; Green, *Providence*, 31; Peter Maslowski, "To the Edge of Greatness: The United States, 1783–1865," in Williamson Murray et al., eds., *The Making of Strategy: Rulers, States, and War* (Cambridge: Cambridge University Press, 1996), 226–27.
21 Francis Paul Prucha, *The Sword of the Republic: The United States Army on the Frontier, 1783–1846* (London: Macmillan, 1969), 135–37, 153.
22 Edel, *Nation*, 101, 103, 136.
23 Various dates are given for the First Seminole War.
24 Robert Remini, *Andrew Jackson and His Indian Wars* (New York: Penguin, 2001), 131–33; Howe, *What Hath*, 98; Prucha, *Sword*, 131.

25 Remini, *Jackson Indian Wars*, 132–33, 137–38; Howe, *What Hath*, 98–99; H. W. Brands, *Andrew Jackson: His Life and Times* (New York: Anchor, 2005), 323–24.
26 Remini, *Jackson Indian Wars*, 141–54; Howe, *What Hath*, 101–2.
27 Remini, *Jackson Indian Wars*, 157–62; Howe, *What Hath*, 102.
28 Edel, *Nation*, 140–49; Gregory E. Fehlings, "America's First Limited War," *Naval War College Review*, 53:3 (summer 2000), 119–26.
29 Edel, *Nation*, 143–47.
30 Ibid., 154–57; Herring, *Colony*, 137.
31 Monroe, Inaugural.
32 S. Lyman Tyler, *A History of Indian Policy* (Washington: Department of the Interior, 1973), 54–56; Francis Paul Prucha, *The Great Father: The United States Government and the American Indian* (Lincoln: University of Nebraska Press, 1988), 65–66.
33 Remini, *Jackson Indian Wars*, 167–77; Prucha, *Great Father*, 65–68; Robert Remini, *The Life of Andrew Jackson* (New York: Harper Perennial, 2010), 112.
34 Remini, *Jackson Indian Wars*, 190–91, 194–205.
35 Edel, *Nation*, 211–14, 229, 242–43, 247.
36 Adams, Inaugural Address; Stanley Engerman and Kenneth Sokoloff, "Technology and Industrialization, 1790–1914," in Stanley Engerman and Robert Gallman, eds., *The Cambridge Economic History of the United States: The Long Nineteenth Century* (Cambridge: Cambridge University Press, 2000), 2:400; Herring, *Colony*, 164; Johnson and Krooss, *Origins*, 115–17, 117n.1.
37 Brands, *Jackson*, 122–28, 435; Donald Cole, *The Presidency of Andrew Jackson* (Lawrence: University Press of Kansas, 1993), 156.
38 Andrew Jackson, First Annual Message to Congress, December 8, 1829, https://millercenter.org/the-presidency/presidential-speeches/december-8-1829-first-annual-message-congress; Cole, *Jackson*, 122–28; Herring, *Colony*, 166–68.
39 Brands, *Jackson*, 508–22.
40 Remini, *Jackson Indian Wars*, 226–29, 279.
41 Jackson, First Annual Message.
42 Remini, *Jackson Indian Wars*, 233–39, 268–71, 277, 281.
43 Millett et al., *Common*, 120–25.
44 Prucha, *Sword*, 341–64; Major Wilson, *The Presidency of Martin Van Buren* (Lawrence: University Press of Kansas, 1984), 189.
45 Herring, *Colony*, 170–71.
46 Prucha, *Sword*, 211–18; Cole, *Jackson*, 112.
47 Prucha, *Sword*, 218–24.
48 Ibid., 224–30; Cole, *Jackson*, 112.
49 Prucha, *Great Father*, 80–82; Remini, *Jackson Indian Wars*, 272–73.
50 Andrew Birtle, *US Army Counterinsurgency and Contingency Operations Doctrine, 1860–1941* (Washington: Center of Military History, 2009), 9–10; Remini, *Jackson Indian Wars*, 275–77; Millett et al., *Common*, 127; John Hall, "'A Reckless

Waste of Blood and Treasure': The Last Campaign of the Second Seminole War," in Matthew Moten, ed., *Between War and Peace: How America Ends Its Wars* (New York: Free Press, 2011), 64–65.
51 Hall, "'Reckless,'" 66–67; Remini, *Jackson Indian Wars*, 274–75; Cole, *Jackson*, 133.
52 Hall, "'Reckless,'" 68–69; Remini, *Jackson Indian Wars*, 275.
53 Hall, "'Reckless,'" 69–70; Wilson, *Van Buren*, 181–82.
54 Wilson, *Van Buren*, 182–84; Hall, "'Reckless,'" 64, 70–71; Prucha, *Sword*, 290–91.
55 Prucha, *Sword*, 293–96; Hall, "'Reckless,'" 72–73.
56 Hall, "'Reckless,'" 73–77.
57 Ibid., 78–81; Wilson, *Van Buren*, 183–84.
58 Wilson, *Van Buren*, 3.
59 Eckes, *Opening*, 18–23; Brands, *Jackson*, 433–34.
60 Brands, *Jackson*, 440–41, 479.
61 Ibid., 445–49, 476–79.
62 Ibid., 481; Eckes, *Opening*, 23.
63 Cole, *Jackson*, 56–58; Brands, *Jackson*, 468–70.
64 Cole, *Jackson*, 98, 103–4; Brands, *Jackson*, 473, 496–97.
65 Brands, *Jackson*, 498–503; Cole, *Jackson*, 190–91, 197–99, 217.
66 Wilson, *Van Buren*, 33, 152.
67 Ibid., xii, 41, 147–49, 187–89.
68 David B. Cole, *Martin Van Buren and the American Political System* (Princeton: Princeton University Press, 1984), 292–93; Wilson, *Van Buren*, 43; Douglas Irwin, *Clashing over Commerce: A History of US Trade Policy* (Chicago: University of Chicago Press, 2017), 183.
69 Wilson, *Van Buren*, 147, 157–69.
70 Ibid., xii, 149–53.
71 Edward P. Crapol, *John Tyler: The Accidental President* (Chapel Hill: UNC Press, 2006), 2, 5, 38.
72 Ibid., 41–42, 106–7; Herring, *Colony*, 178.
73 Johnson and Krooss, *Origins*, 126–27; Eckes, *Opening*, 17.
74 Crapol, *Tyler*, 25, 91, 95–96, 108–12, 119–21.
75 Ibid., 36, 42, 130, 136, 154–62.
76 Ibid., 141, 176–77, 198, 202, 218–22.
77 Paul K. Bergeron, *The Presidency of James K. Polk* (Lawrence: University Press of Kansas, 1987), xii, 17.
78 Ibid., 66–67.
79 Ibid., 65; McDougall, *Promised*, 76–77; Anders Stephanson, *Manifest Destiny: American Expansionism and the Empire of Right* (New York: Hill and Wang, 1995), ix.
80 Bergeron, *Polk*, 67–68; James Knox Polk, Inaugural Address, March 4, 1845, https://avalon.law.yale.edu/19th_century/polk.asp.
81 Herring, *Colony*, 190–92.

82 James K. Polk, Second Annual Message to Congress, December 8, 1846, https://millercenter.org/the-presidency/presidential-speeches/december-8-1846-second-annual-message-congress; James K. Polk, Third Annual Message to Congress, December 7, 1847, https://millercenter.org/the-presidency/presidential-speeches/december-7-1847-third-annual-message; Milo Quaife, ed., *The Diary of James K. Polk during His Presidency, 1845 to 1849* (Chicago: A. C. McClurg, 1910), 1:71, 496–97 (hereafter Polk, *Diary*); Bergeron, *Polk*, 81–82.

83 Bergeron, *Polk*, 68–72; Polk, *Diary*, 1:33–35; Timothy Henderson, *A Glorious Defeat: Mexico and Its War with the United States* (New York: Hill and Wang, 2007), 151–54.

84 Bergeron, *Polk*, 62–63, 74–75; Polk, *Diary*, 1:8–12; Maslowski, "To the Edge," 230; K. Jack Bauer, *The Mexican War, 1846–1848* (Lincoln: University of Nebraska Press, 1992), 37–38; Henderson, *Glorious*, 154–55.

85 Henderson, *Glorious*, 148, 150; Bauer, *Mexican*, 42–43, 48–63; Bergeron, *Polk*, 78.

86 Polk, *Diary*, 1:484–87; Bergeron, *Polk*, 76–77; Bauer, *Mexican*, 68–69.

87 Joseph G. Dawson III, "The US War with Mexico: The Difficulties of Concluding a Victorious Peace," in *Between War*, 87–88; Millett et al., *Common*, 130.

88 Irving Levinson, "A New Paradigm for an Old Conflict: The Mexico–United States War," *The Journal of Military History*, 73 (April 2009), 396; Howe, *What Hath*, 746, 749–51.

89 Dawson, "War," 85; Bergeron, *Polk*, 78; Bauer, *Mexican*, 70; Howe, *What Hath*, 750.

90 Bergeron, *Polk*, 77, 86, 89–91; McDougall, *Promised*, 95; Maslowski, "To the Edge," 231–32.

91 Polk, *Diary*, 1:395–96, 400–4, 409–11, 429, 437–38, 443; Bergeron, *Polk*, 79–81.

92 Polk, *Diary*, 1:407–8, 413–16, 484; Timothy Johnson, *A Gallant Little Army: The Mexico City Campaign* (Lawrence: University of Kansas Press, 2007), 12–13.

93 Bergeron, *Polk*, 83–86.

94 Ibid., 91; Elbert Smith, *The Presidencies of Zachary Taylor and Millard Fillmore* (Lawrence: University Press of Kansas, 1988), 36–37; Henderson, *Glorious*, 163.

95 Henderson, *Glorious*, 163–65; Smith, *Taylor*, 37–38.

96 Howe, *What Hath*, 753–55.

97 Ibid., 756–57.

98 Bauer, *Mexican*, 233–35; Bergeron, *Polk*, 91; Johnson, *Gallant*, 10–17, 299n.7.

99 Johnson, *Gallant*, 14–15; Bergeron, *Polk*, 91–93.

100 Bergeron, *Polk*, 95–97; Johnson, *Gallant*, 3, 7, 10–11, 26, 45–46.

101 Johnson, *Gallant*, 19, 48, 54–55.

102 Ibid., 34, 57–58; Levinson, "Paradigm," 398–99.

103 Johnson, *Gallant*, 61.

104 Bergeron, *Polk*, 97–98.

105 Johnson, *Gallant*, 61–62.

106 Ibid., 64–68, 96–97; Henderson, *Glorious*, 165–77.

107 Johnson, *Gallant*, 102–4; Levinson, "Paradigm," 399–401; Henderson, *Glorious*, 168.
108 Levinson, "Paradigm," 405–6; Johnson, *Gallant*, 108–9, 112.
109 Johnson, *Gallant*, 110, 116–17.
110 Ibid., 130, 137–40.
111 Ibid., 112–15, 142–44; Bauer, *Mexican*, 271; Henderson, *Glorious*, 168–69.
112 Johnson, *Gallant*, 147–48.
113 Ibid., 148–49, 154–57.
114 Ibid., 194–95.
115 Henderson, *Glorious*, 169–70.
116 Johnson, *Gallant*, 197–201; Bergeron, *Polk*, 100.
117 Henderson, *Glorious*, 171–72; Johnson, *Gallant*, 200–1, 239–42.
118 Henderson, *Glorious*, 172–74.
119 Johnson, *Gallant*, 241–53; Levinson, "Paradigm," 403.
120 Johnson, *Gallant*, 266–67; Henderson, *Glorious*, 174–75; Bergeron, *Polk*, 101–2.
121 Bergeron, *Polk*, 102; Polk, Third Annual Message.
122 Johnson, *Gallant*, 267–68; Bergeron, *Polk*, 103, 106; Henderson, *Glorious*, 177–78; Levinson, "Paradigm," 410, 413–14.
123 Johnson, *Gallant*, 3.
124 Howe, *What Hath*, 749.
125 Ibid., 752; Henderson, *Glorious*, 180–81.

4 SCHISM, CIVIL WAR, AND RECONSTRUCTION, 1849–1877

1 Elbert Smith, *The Presidencies of Zachary Taylor and Millard Fillmore* (Lawrence: University Press of Kansas, 1988), 38–42, 52.
2 Inaugural Address of Zachary Taylor, March 5, 1849, https://avalon.law.yale.edu/19th_century/taylor.asp.
3 Smith, *Taylor*, 50, 75–85; George Herring, *From Colony to Superpower: US Foreign Relations since 1776* (Oxford: Oxford University Press, 2011), 214.
4 Herring, *Colony*, 214, 217; Larry Gara, *The Presidency of Franklin Pierce* (Lawrence: University Press of Kansas, 1991), 26–28.
5 Francis Paul Prucha, *The Great Father: The United States Government and the American Indian* (Lincoln: University of Nebraska Press, 1988), 114–18; Edward B. Westermann, *Hitler's Ostkrieg and the Indian Wars: Comparing Genocide and Conquest* (Norman: University of Oklahoma Press, 2017), 117.
6 Gara, *Pierce*, 21–22; Smith, *Taylor*, 190–92, 199–200.
7 Herring, *Colony*, 214–16, 222; Smith, *Taylor*, 227–30; Gara, *Pierce*, 127–28.
8 Herring, *Colony*, 207–9; Smith, *Taylor*, 225–27.
9 Gara, *Pierce*, xii, 127–33; James McPherson, *Battle Cry of Freedom: The Civil War Era* (Oxford: Oxford University Press, 1988), 121–25; Prucha, *Great Father*, 118–19.

10 Gara, *Pierce*, 146–49; Michael Green, *By More Than Providence: Grand Strategy and American Power in the Asia Pacific since 1783* (New York: Columbia University Press, 2019), 34; Herring, *Colony*, 215.
11 Green, *Providence*, 40, 53.
12 Ibid., 41, 48–50, 66–67; Gara, *Pierce*, 135.
13 Gara, *Pierce*, 133–34.
14 Elbert Smith, *The Presidency of James Buchanan* (Lawrence: University of Kansas Press, 1975), 65, 74–75.
15 Ibid., 76–78.
16 Roy P. Basler, ed., *The Collected Works of Abraham Lincoln* (hereafter *CWL*) (New Brunswick: Rutgers University Press, 1953), 4:149–50; Donald Stoker, *The Grand Design: Strategy and the US Civil War* (Oxford: Oxford University Press, 2010), 18–19.
17 Smith, *Buchanan*, 129, 138, 143, 148–51.
18 *CWL*, 4:262–71.
19 James Richardson, ed., *The Messages and Papers of Jefferson Davis and the Confederacy Including Diplomatic Correspondence, 1861–1865* (New York: Chelsea House, 1966), 1:67, 82; Lynda Lasswell Crist et al., eds., *The Papers of Jefferson Davis* (hereafter *Davis Papers*) (Baton Rouge: LSU Press, 1979–2015), 7:43–44, 64–65; Burton Hendrick, *Statesman of the Lost Cause: Jefferson Davis and His Cabinet* (New York: Literary Guild of America, 1939), 46–47.
20 James McPherson and William J. Cooper Jr., "Introduction," in James McPherson and William J. Cooper Jr., eds., *Writing the Civil War: The Quest to Understand* (Columbia: University of South Carolina Press, 1998), 5.
21 Edwin C. Fishel, *Secret War for the Union* (Boston: Houghton Mifflin, 1996), 16; *CWL*, 4:323–24, 324n.1; Russell Weigley, *A Great Civil War: A Military and Political History, 1861–1865* (Bloomington: Indiana University Press, 2000), 20–21; McPherson, *Battle*, 271–72, 272n.78.
22 *CWL*, 4:331–32; Weigley, *Civil War*, 24–25.
23 Winfield Scott, *Memoirs of Lieut.-Gen. Winfield Scott* (New York: Sheldon, 1864), 2:625–28, Charles Winslow Eliot, *Winfield Scott: The Soldier and the Man* (New York: Macmillan, 1937), 696–98; Clifford Dowdey and Louis Manarin, eds., *The Wartime Papers of R. E. Lee* (hereafter *Lee Papers*) (Boston: Little Brown, 1961), 15, 96.
24 Herman Hattaway and Archer Jones, *How the North Won: A Military History of the Civil War* (Urbana: University of Illinois Press, 1991), 114; Stoker, *Grand*, 23.
25 Weigley, *Civil War*, 35; E. A. J. Johnson and Herman E. Krooss, *The Origins and Development of the American Economy: An Introduction to Economics* (New York: Prentice-Hall, 1953), 118–23; Peter Maslowski, "To the Edge of Greatness: The United States, 1783–1865," in Williamson Murray et al., eds., *The Making of Strategy: Rulers, States, and War* (Cambridge: Cambridge University Press, 1996), 232; Richard Current, "God and the Strongest Battalions," in David Herbert Donald, ed., *Why the North Won the Civil War* (New York: Harper, 1996), 33; Jefferson Davis, *The Rise and Fall of Confederate Government* (New York: Thomas Yosseloff, 1958), 1:316.

26 Weigley, *Civil War*, 35; Davis, *Rise and Fall*, 1:315; Hattaway and Jones, *How*, 58–59; Richard Beringer, Herman Hattaway et al., *Why the South Lost the Civil War* (Athens: University of Georgia Press, 1986), 118–19.
27 Stoker, *Grand*, 30–31, 263.
28 Ibid., 28–30.
29 Ibid., 35; Max Gideonse, "Foreign Trade and Commercial Policy," in Harold Williamson, ed., *The Growth of the American Economy*, 2nd ed. (New York: Prentice-Hall, 1951), 535–36.
30 Donald Stoker, "There Was No Offensive-Defensive Confederate Strategy," *The Journal of Military History*, 73 (April 2009), 177–208; *Supplement to the Official Records of the Union and Confederate Armies* (hereafter *ORS*) (Wilmington: Broadfoot, 1994–99), 94:194–97; Robert Scott, ed., *The War of the Rebellion: A Compilation of the Official Records of the Union and Confederate Armies* (Washington: GPO, 1880–1901), Phillip Oliver, ed., *The Civil War CD-ROM* (Zionsville: Guild Press of Indiana, 1996–2000) (hereafter *OR*), series 1 (series 1 unless otherwise noted), 10/2:458–9, 16/1:1088–94, 1109–12, 22/1:24–6, 32/3:536, 34/1:30, 43/1:448–52; Stoker, *Grand*, 65.
31 Stoker, *Grand*, 22–23, 26–27.
32 *Davis Papers*, 8:58–62; Archer Jones, *Confederate Strategy from Shiloh to Vicksburg* (Baton Rouge: LSU Press, 1991), 20–21; Robert Tanner, *Retreat to Victory? Confederate Strategy Reconsidered* (Washington: Scholarly Resources, 2002), 3; Alfred Thayer Mahan, *The Influence of Sea Power upon History, 1660–1783* (New York: Dover Publications, 1987 [1890]), 42–44.
33 *OR*, 51/1:369–70, 386–87; Eliot, *Scott*, 696–97, 727; Theodore Pease, ed., *The Diary of Orville Hickman Browning* (Springfield: Illinois State Historical Library, 1925), 1:447–48; *CWL*, 4:338–39, 346–47, 432–33, 487–89; *OR*, 2:718–21; *Report of the Joint Committee on the Conduct of the War, 1863* (Washington: GPO, 1863), 2:35–36; Robert Johnson and Clarence Buell, eds., *Battles and Leaders of the Civil War* (hereafter *B&L*) (Edison: Castle, 1995), 2:144; T. Harry Williams, *Lincoln and His Generals* (New York: Knopf, 1952), 20–21. Williams incorrectly insists the Union aimed at Richmond.
34 Weigley, *Civil War*, 40; McPherson, *Battle*, 284.
35 *CWL*, 4:531–33; Emory Thomas, *Confederate Nation, 1861–1865* (New York: Harper, 1979), 89.
36 Stoker, *Grand*, 46–48.
37 *ORS*, 93:377–78; *OR*, 3:687–88, 4:180–81, 188, 396–97; *Davis Papers*, 7:325; Stoker, *Grand*, 48–51.
38 *OR*, 5:7–8.
39 *OR*, 5:6.
40 Stephen Sears, ed., *The Civil War Papers of George B. McClellan: Selected Correspondence, 1860–1865* (hereafter *McClellan Papers*) (New York: Ticknor and Fields, 1989), 95–97, 114–18, 147–48; *OR*, 5:9–10.

41 Kevin Weddle, "The Blockade Board of 1861 and Union Naval Strategy," *Civil War History*, 48:2 (2002), 125–26, 134, 139n.49, 139–42; William Barney, *Flawed Victory: A New Perspective on the Civil War* (New York: Praeger, 1975), 33–35; Stoker, *Grand*, 93–95.
42 Stoker, *Grand*, 95–102.
43 Ibid., 103–4.
44 Ibid., 104–5.
45 Williams, *Lincoln*, 47–48; *OR*, 7:447, 450–52, 8:382, 408.
46 *CWL*, 5:98–99, 111–12; *OR*, 7:928–29.
47 Ulysses S. Grant, *Personal Memoirs of U. S. Grant, 1839–1865* (New York: Literary Classics, 1990), 189–90; John Simon, ed., *The Papers of Ulysses S. Grant* (Carbondale: Southern Illinois University Press, 1967–2005), 4:99, 99–100nn; *McClellan Papers*, 160n.1; *OR*, 7:571, 577, 586–87.
48 *OR*, 6:826–7, 11/3:405–8; *Davis Papers*, 8:67–69, 69nn.
49 *OR*, 7:257–61; *Davis Papers*, 8:92–94.
50 *OR*, 7:671, 678, 668–69, 10/1:920–21, 10/2:111, 115, 124–26, 619–20, 16/2:679; Steven E. Woodworth, *Jefferson Davis and His Generals: The Failure of Confederate Command in the West* (Lawrence: University Press of Kansas, 1990), 126–28; *CWL*, 5:155.
51 *McClellan Papers*, 167–70; *CWL*, 5:155.
52 Carl von Clausewitz, *On War*, Michael Howard and Peter Paret, trans. and eds. (Princeton: Princeton University Press, 1984), 595–97, 617–19.
53 John Marszalek, *Commander of All Lincoln's Armies: A Life of General Henry Wager Halleck* (Cambridge: Belknap, 2004), 123–25; *OR*, 10/1:902–3, 10/2:98–99, 117, 618, 15:447–50, 52/2:330; US Congress, *Official Records of the Union and Confederate Navies in the War of the Rebellion* (Washington: GPO, 1894–1922) (hereafter *ORN*), ser. 1, 18:8–9, 498–99, 502, 519–21, 558–59, 588–90, 593, 636, 23:86, 121; McPherson, *Battle*, 418–21.
54 *OR*, 17/2:91; Gideon Welles, *The Diary of Gideon Welles* (Boston: Houghton and Mifflin, 1911), 1:113; Michael Burlingame and John Ettlinger, eds., *Inside Lincoln's White House: The Complete Civil War Diary of John Hay* (Carbondale: Southern Illinois University Press, 1997) (hereafter Hay, *Diary*), 38–9; *CWL*, 5:509–10.
55 *OR*, 16/1:1087–8, 17/1:375–82, 19/2:590–91; William J. Cooper Jr., ed., *Jefferson Davis: The Essential Writings* (New York: Modern Library, 2003), 260–62; Grady McWhiney, *Braxton Bragg and Confederate Defeat* (Tuscaloosa: University of Alabama Press, 1991), 335; Stoker, *Grand*, 187–91.
56 John Nicolay and John Hay, eds., *Abraham Lincoln: Complete Works* (New York: Century, 1907), 2:479; Allen Guelzo, *Lincoln's Emancipation Proclamation: The End of Slavery in America* (New York: Simon and Schuster, 2004), 151–53.
57 *OR*, 17/2:757–58; Stoker, *Grand*, 236–44.
58 *OR*, 17/2:757–58, 20/2:487–88, 23/2:613–14, 626–27, 52/2:404; *Davis Papers*, 9:19.

59 *Davis Papers*, 9:189; Craig Symonds, *Joseph E. Johnston: A Civil War Biography* (New York: Norton, 1992), 207–8; *OR*, 24/1:216–17, 220–23, 24/3:888–90.
60 Allen Guelzo et al., "An Alternative Strategy," *North and South*, 11:4 (August 2009), 15, 20.
61 *Wartime Papers*, 507–10, 569–70; Davis, *Rise and Fall*, 2:437–38; Gary Gallagher, ed., *Lee the Soldier* (Lincoln: University of Nebraska Press, 1996), 13–14; *ORS*, 5:432–35; Walter H. Taylor, *General Lee: His Campaigns in Virginia, 1861–1865, with Personal Reminiscences* (Norfolk: Nussbaum, 1906), 180; William Allan, "Campaigns in Virginia, Maryland, and Pennsylvania, 1862–1863," May 9, 1887, in *Papers of the Military Historical Society of Massachusetts* (Boston: Military Historical Society of Massachusetts, 1903), 3:446–47.
62 *OR*, 27/1:82–83, 27/3:605; *CWL*, 6:319.
63 *OR*, 24/3:513, 528, 546–47, 26/1:659, ser. 3, 3:735; *CWL*, 6:354–55, 355n.1; Mark Grimsley, *The Hard Hand of War: Union Military Policy toward Southern Civilians* (Cambridge: Cambridge University Press, 1997), 159–63; Stoker, *Grand*, 319–31.
64 Stoker, *Grand*, 338–44.
65 *CWL*, 7:36–56.
66 *Grant Papers*, 10:141–42nn.
67 Roy Basler, ed., *The Collected Works of Abraham Lincoln. Supplement, 1832–1865* (Westport: Greenwood, 1974), 226; Donald Herbert Donald, *Lincoln* (New York: Touchstone, 1996), 490–91; *Grant Papers*, 9:541.
68 *OR*, 34/1:8–9, 34/2:610–11.
69 *OR*, 32/3:245–47, 33:794–95, 821, 827–29, 874–75, 885–89, 904–5, 1017–18, 34/1:10–11, 13, 34/3:740–41, 36/2:328–29; Hattaway and Jones, *How*, 554, 574–75; *Wartime Papers*, 792–93.
70 Hay, *Diary*, 194; *OR*, 32/3:246–47, 312–14; *OR*, 34/1:8–9, 34/2:610–11.
71 George A. Bruce, "The Strategy of the Civil War," in *Civil and Mexican Wars, 1861, 1846. Papers of the Military Historical Society of Massachusetts* (Boston: The Military Historical Society of Massachusetts, 1913), 13:437; *Davis Papers*, 10:392, n.14; *OR*, 34/1:10; Hattaway and Jones, *How*, 539, 545; E. P. Alexander, *Fighting for the Confederacy: The Personal Recollections of General Edward Porter Alexander*, Gary Gallagher, ed. (Chapel Hill: UNC Press, 1989), 346.
72 Russell F. Weigley, *The American Way of War: A History of United States Military Strategy and Policy* (Bloomington: Indiana University Press, 1977), 143–45; *OR*, 34/1:9; Hattaway and Jones, *How*, 558–67, 570; Grant, *Memoirs*, 512.
73 William T. Sherman, *Memoirs of General W. T. Sherman* (New York: Literary Classics, 1990), 520–23; McPherson, *Battle*, 750.
74 *OR*, 38/5:882–85, 888.
75 *CWL*, 7:380, 381–82nn.
76 *CWL*, 7:506–8.
77 Stoker, *Grand*, 186; Cooper, ed., *Essential*, 260–62; Larry E. Nelson, *Bullets, Ballots, and Rhetoric: Confederate Policy for the United States Presidential Contest of 1864* (Tuscaloosa: University of Alabama Press, 1980), xi, 18–20, 24, 89, 110–11.

78 Nelson, *Bullets*, 28, 129; Grant, *Memoirs*, 632–33.
79 Sherman, *Memoirs*, 544, 573, 577; McPherson, *Battle*, 754–55, 774; Hattaway and Jones, *How*, 623.
80 *OR*, 39/2: 202, 658–61.
81 *Wartime Papers*, 801; Grant, *Memoirs*, 630–31.
82 Stoker, *Grand*, 397.
83 Ibid., 397–98.
84 *CWL*, 8:1–2.
85 *OR*, 34/1:48–50.
86 *OR*, 34/1:51, 46/3:332, 509–10; *CWL*, 8:377–78; *Wartime Papers*, 933–34.
87 *Davis Papers*, 11:552, 558–59; *OR*, 47/3:823–34.
88 Donald, *Lincoln*, 594–99; *Davis Papers*, 11:562n.12, 15; *OR*, 47/3:835–36, 843–44; Sherman, *Memoirs*, 844–51; Albert Castel, *The Presidency of Andrew Johnson* (Lawrence: Regents Press of Kansas, 1979), 23; Davis, *Rise and Fall*, 2:698.
89 Castel, *Johnson*, 11–14, 38; J. David Hacker, "A Census-Based Count of the Civil War Dead," *Civil War History*, 57:4 (December 2011), 307–48.
90 Fareed Zakaria, *From Wealth to Power: The Unusual Origins of America's World Role* (Princeton: Princeton University Press, 1998), 57–58, 75; Herring, *Colony*, 251.
91 Andrew Birtle, *US Army Counterinsurgency and Contingency Operations Doctrine, 1860–1941* (Washington: Center of Military History, 2009), 25–26; Castel, *Johnson*, 18.
92 Castel, *Johnson*, 25; Erik Foner, *Reconstruction: America's Unfinished Revolution* (New York: Harper and Row, 1988), ix; Andrew Birtle, *US Army Counterinsurgency and Contingency Operations Doctrine, 1860–1941* (Washington: Center of Military History, 2009), 55–56.
93 Foner, *Reconstruction*, 178–80; Castel, *Johnson*, 21.
94 Foner, *Reconstruction*, 182–84, 188–89; Castel, *Johnson*, 26, 47–48, 51.
95 Andrew Johnson, First Annual Message, December 4, 1865, https://millercenter.org/the-presidency/presidential-speeches/december-4-1865-first-annual-message; Foner, *Reconstruction*, 239–40; Castel, *Johnson*, 59–60.
96 Foner, *Reconstruction*, 247–50, 260; Castel, *Johnson*, 70–71, 74–75.
97 Foner, *Reconstruction*, 190–91.
98 Ibid., 276–77; Allan Millett et al., *For the Common Defense: A Military History of the United States from 1607 to 2012*, 3rd ed. (New York: Free Press, 2012), 230; Birtle, *Counterinsurgency, 1860–1941*, 56.
99 Foner, *Reconstruction*, 333–36, 426; Richard White, *The Republic for Which It Stands: The United States during Reconstruction and the Gilded Age, 1865–1896* (Oxford: Oxford University Press, 2017), 91–92.
100 Foner, *Reconstruction*, 425–26; Millett et al., *Common*, 231.
101 Millett et al., *Common*, 231–32.
102 Ibid., 232; Birtle, *Counterinsurgency, 1860–1941*, 56.
103 White, *Republic*, 330–32.

104 Foner, *Reconstruction*, 333; Millett et al., *Common*, 231–32; Martin Alexander and John Keiger, "Limiting Arms, Enforcing Limits: International Inspections and the Challenges of Compellance in Germany Post-1919, Iraq Post-1991," *Journal of Strategic Studies*, 29:2 (2006), 361–64.
105 Birtle, *Counterinsurgency, 1860–1941*, 57.

5 CONQUERING A CONTINENT: THE INDIAN WARS, 1865–1897

1 George Herring, *From Colony to Superpower: US Foreign Relations since 1776* (Oxford: Oxford University Press, 2011), 275; Walter A. McDougall, *Promised Land, Crusader State: The American Encounter with the World since 1776* (New York: Houghton Mifflin, 1997), 102; John A. Thompson, *A Sense of Power: The Roots of America's Global Role* (Ithaca: Cornell University Press, 2015), 4.
2 Fareed Zakaria, *From Wealth to Power: The Unusual Origins of America's World Role* (Princeton: Princeton University Press, 1998), 57–59, 63–64; Michael Green, *By More Than Providence: Grand Strategy and American Power in the Asia Pacific since 1783* (New York: Columbia University Press, 2019), 62; Herring, *Colony*, 255–57; Andrew Johnson, Third Annual Message to Congress, December 3, 1867, https://millercenter.org/the-presidency/presidential-speeches/december-3-1867-third-annual-message-congress.
3 Zakaria, *Wealth*, 57; Herring, *Colony*, 256; Green, *Providence*, 57–61.
4 John Lewis Gaddis, *Surprise, Security, and the American Experience* (Cambridge: Harvard University Press, 2004), 29; Albert Castel, *The Presidency of Andrew Johnson* (Lawrence: Regents Press of Kansas, 1979), 39–42; Herring, *Colony*, 252; Daniel Walker Howe, *What Hath God Wrought: The Transformation of America, 1815–1848* (Oxford: Oxford University Press, 2007), 116.
5 Green, *Providence*, 62; Herring, *Colony*, 257–58; Zakaria, *Wealth*, 59–62, 64–67.
6 Zakaria, *Wealth*, 67.
7 Ibid., 68–69; Herring, *Colony*, 259–60; Ulysses Simpson Grant, State of the Union, December 5, 1870, www.let.rug.nl/usa/presidents/ulysses-simpson-grant/state-of-the-union-1870.php.
8 Zakaria, *Wealth*, 70–74.
9 Ibid., 74–75; Green, *Providence*, 68; Herring, *Colony*, 262–63.
10 Douglas Irwin, *Clashing over Commerce: A History of US Trade Policy* (Chicago: University of Chicago Press, 2017), 221; Stanley Engerman and Kenneth Sokoloff, "Technology and Industrialization, 1790–1914," in Stanley Engerman and Robert Gallman, eds., *The Cambridge Economic History of the United States: The Long Nineteenth Century* (Cambridge: Cambridge University Press, 2000), 2:399; Thompson, *Power*, 17; McDougall, *Promised*, 103–4.
11 Richard Bensel, *The Political Economy of American Industrialization, 1877–1900* (Cambridge: Cambridge University Press, 2000), 457–59, 465.

12 Richard White, *The Republic for Which It Stands: The United States during Reconstruction and the Gilded Age, 1865–1896* (Oxford: Oxford University Press, 2017), 260–70; Herring, *Colony*, 286.
13 Edward Ellis, *The Indian Wars of the United States: From the First Settlement in Jamestown, in 1607, to the Close of the Great Uprising of 1890–91* (New York: Cassell, 1892), iii.
14 C. E. Callwell, *Small Wars: Their Principles and Practice*, 3rd ed. (Lincoln: University of Nebraska Press, 1996), 27; Edward B. Westermann, *Hitler's Ostkrieg and the Indian Wars: Comparing Genocide and Conquest* (Norman: University of Oklahoma Press, 2017), 174–79.
15 Andrew Birtle, *US Army Counterinsurgency and Contingency Operations Doctrine, 1860–1941* (Washington: Center of Military History, 2009), 78; Westermann, *Ostkrieg*, 119.
16 Birtle, *Counterinsurgency, 1860–1941*, 76–77.
17 Ibid., 58; Allan Millett et al., *For the Common Defense: A Military History of the United States from 1607 to 2012*, 3rd ed. (New York: Free Press, 2012), 224; Westermann, *Ostkrieg*, 121; Paul Wellman, *The Indian Wars of the West* (New York: Indian Head, 1992), 10; Peter Cozzens, *The Earth Is Weeping: The Epic Story of the Indian Wars for the American West* (New York: Vintage, 2006), 10, 16.
18 Birtle, *Counterinsurgency, 1860–1941*, 59–60.
19 Robert Wooster, *The Military and United States Indian Policy, 1865–1903* (Lincoln: University of Nebraska Press, 1988), 4, 23.
20 Birtle, *Counterinsurgency, 1860–1941*, 60.
21 Ibid., 67–69.
22 Ibid., 62.
23 Westermann, *Ostkrieg*, 22–23, 125–28; S. Lyman Tyler, *A History of Indian Policy* (Washington: Department of the Interior, 1973), 88; Millett et al., *Common*, 227–28.
24 Robert Utley and Wilcomb Washburn, *The American Heritage History of the Indian Wars* (New York: Barnes & Noble, 1992), 222–23.
25 Tyler, *Indian*, 83; Westermann, *Ostkrieg*, 71; Wooster, *Indian Policy*, 123–24.
26 Utley and Washburn, *Indian Wars*, 223, 230–32; Cozzens, *Weeping*, 26.
27 Cozzens, *Weeping*, 26–27; Utley and Washburn, *Indian Wars*, 234–35.
28 Cozzens, *Weeping*, 28–29; Utley and Washburn, *Indian Wars*, 235–36.
29 Wellman, *Indian Wars*, 295, 307–13; Utley and Washburn, *Indian Wars*, 226–29.
30 Cozzens, *Weeping*, 28–29, 61–62.
31 Ibid., 54, 62.
32 Millett et al., *Common*, 225; "The Snake War, 1864–1868," *Idaho State Historical Society Reference Series* (1966), https://history.idaho.gov/wp-content/uploads/0236.pdf.
33 Ibid.; Millett et al., *Common*, 226.
34 Cozzens, *Weeping*, 29, 33.

35 Ibid., 32–40; Westermann, *Ostkrieg*, 67.
36 Westermann, *Ostkrieg*, 67; Cozzens, *Weeping*, 40–41.
37 Cozzens, *Weeping*, 76–78; Utley and Washburn, *Indian Wars*, 244.
38 Cozzens, *Weeping*, 44–45; Wellman, *Indian Wars*, 67.
39 Westermann, *Ostkrieg*, 70, 120; William T. Sherman, *Memoirs of General W. T. Sherman* (New York: Literary Classics, 1990), 926; Tyler, *Indian*, 86; Wellman, *Indian Wars*, 103–4; Wooster, *Indian Policy*, 123–24; Cozzens, *Weeping*, 197, 200.
40 Cozzens, *Weeping*, 64–65; Utley and Washburn, *Indian Wars*, 241; Wooster, *Indian Policy*, 120–21.
41 Cozzens, *Weeping*, 65–73; Utley and Washburn, *Indian Wars*, 241.
42 Cozzens, *Weeping*, 78–84; Utley and Washburn, *Indian Wars*, 244.
43 Cozzens, *Weeping*, 86, 111; White, *Republic*, 108.
44 Cozzens, *Weeping*, 91–92.
45 Ibid., 94–95, 98, 103–6, 110–12; Wellman, *Indian Wars*, 88–89; Utley and Washburn, *Indian Wars*, 257–58.
46 Utley and Washburn, *Indian Wars*, 258; Ulysses Grant, State of the Union, December 6, 1869, www.let.rug.nl/usa/presidents/ulysses-simpson-grant/state-of-the-union-1869.php; Grant, State of the Union, 1870; Westermann, *Ostkrieg*, 70–75, 79.
47 Westermann, *Ostkrieg*, 70–73; Grant, State of the Union, 1869; Tyler, *Indian*, 80.
48 Tyler, *Indian*, 84; Cozzens, *Weeping*, 118.
49 Cozzens, *Weeping*, 112–13, 121–23.
50 Ibid., 123–26, 129–32; Utley and Washburn, *Indian Wars*, 262–63.
51 Westermann, *Ostkrieg*, 122–24; Utley and Washburn, *Indian Wars*, 264.
52 Cozzens, *Weeping*, 140–46; Wooster, *Indian Policy*, 23.
53 Cozzens, *Weeping*, 146–49.
54 Ibid., 150–54.
55 Millett et al., *Common*, 226; Westermann, *Ostkrieg*, 130; Utley and Washburn, *Indian Wars*, 266; Wellman, *Indian Wars*, 124–26.
56 Cozzens, *Weeping*, 218–20; Westermann, *Ostkrieg*, 130.
57 Cozzens, *Weeping*, 214–17; Millett et al., *Common*, 226; Westermann, *Ostkrieg*, 130–31.
58 Millett et al., *Common*, 226–27; Birtle, *Counterinsurgency, 1860–1941*, 67; Westermann, *Ostkrieg*, 131–33.
59 Westermann, *Ostkrieg*, 133–34; Cozzens, *Weeping*, 247; Millett et al., *Common*, 227.
60 Westermann, *Ostkrieg*, 136–37, 139–41; Cozzens, *Weeping*, 273–79, 287, 311.
61 Ari Hoogenboom, *The Presidency of Rutherford B. Hayes* (Lawrence: University Press of Kansas, 1988), 154–56.
62 Ibid., 156–57.
63 Ibid., 157–58.
64 Ibid., 158–60.
65 Wooster, *Indian Policy*, 179; Cozzens, *Weeping*, 346–56.

66 Cozzens, *Weeping*, 174–75; Francis Paul Prucha, *The Great Father: The United States Government and the American Indian* (Lincoln: University of Nebraska Press, 1988), 170.
67 Cozzens, *Weeping*, 177, 179; Utley and Washburn, *Indian Wars*, 247; Westermann, *Ostkrieg*, 214.
68 Cozzens, *Weeping*, 183–87; Utley and Washburn, *Indian Wars*, 247.
69 Cozzens, *Weeping*, 189–90; Utley and Washburn, *Indian Wars*, 311.
70 Utley and Washburn, *Indian Wars*, 311–13; Cozzens, *Weeping*, 359–62; Westermann, *Ostkrieg*, 216.
71 Utley and Washburn, *Indian Wars*, 324–25; Wellman, *Indian Wars*, 419.
72 Utley and Washburn, *Indian Wars*, 325–26; Westermann, *Ostkrieg*, 221.
73 Utley and Washburn, *Indian Wars*, 326; Westermann, *Ostkrieg*, 223–24; Wellman, *Indian Wars*, 439–41.
74 Cozzens, *Weeping*, 405–7.
75 Wellman, *Indian Wars*, 442–45; Utley and Washburn, *Indian Wars*, 326–27.
76 Cozzens, *Weeping*, 421–24; Hoogenboom, *Hayes*, 160–65.
77 Cozzens, *Weeping*, 424–27, 452–56, 459, 462–67.
78 Antulio J. Echevarria II, *Reconsidering the American Way of War: US Military Practice from the Revolution to Afghanistan* (Washington: Georgetown University Press, 2014), 94; Millett et al., *Common*, 228.
79 Herring, *Colony*, 264, 271–77.
80 Zakaria, *Wealth*, 75–76; Hoogenboom, *Hayes*, 173, 187–90; Jerald Combs, *American Diplomatic History: Two Centuries of Changing Interpretations* (Berkeley: University of California Press, 1983), 67–68.
81 Samuel Flagg Bemis, *A Diplomatic History of the United States*, 5th ed. (New York: Holt, Rinehart, and Winston, 1965), 479–80; Zakaria, *Wealth*, 76–77; Green, *Providence*, 68–69.
82 Zakaria, *Wealth*, 76; Herring, *Colony*, 288; Green, *Providence*, 10–11.
83 Thompson, *Power*, 39; Zakaria, *Wealth*, 76–79.
84 Herring, *Colony*, 288–89; Richard E. Welch Jr., *The Presidencies of Grover Cleveland* (Lawrence: University Press of Kansas, 1988), 84; Homer Socolofsky and Allan Spetter, *The Presidency of Benjamin Harrison* (Lawrence: University Press of Kansas, 1987), 119–20.
85 Welch, *Cleveland*, 159–60; McDougall, *Promised*, 101; Zakaria, *Wealth*, 80–81.
86 Socolofsky and Spetter, *Harrison*, 125–28; Zakaria, *Wealth*, 136–37; Herring, *Colony*, 278–79.
87 Thompson, *Power*, 35–36; Socolofsky and Spetter, *Harrison*, 115–18; Zakaria, *Wealth*, 138–39; Charles Calhoun, *Benjamin Harrison* (New York: Times Books, 2005), 79.
88 Herring, *Colony*, 289–90.
89 Socolofsky and Spetter, *Harrison*, 125–26, 146–51; Zakaria, *Wealth*, 140–41.
90 Herring, *Colony*, 285, 300–1; George Mowry, *The Era of Theodore Roosevelt, and the Birth of Modern America, 1900–1912* (New York: Harper, 1958), 8.

91　Welch, *Cleveland*, 170–71; Zakaria, *Wealth*, 142–46.
92　McDougall, *Promised*, 109, 117; Welch, *Cleveland*, 180–86.
93　Welch, *Cleveland*, 194–96.
94　Green, *Providence*, 70.
95　Millett et al., *Common*, 232–33.
96　Wooster, *Indian Policy*, 74–75.
97　Ibid., 84–87; Millett et al., *Common*, 242–45; Socolofsky and Spetter, *Harrison*, 104; Steven T. Ross, *American War Plans, 1890–1939* (London: Frank Cass, 2002), 4.
98　Justus Doenecke, *The Presidencies of James A. Garfield and Chester A. Arthur* (Lawrence: Regents Press of Kansas, 1981), 145–46; Socolofsky and Spetter, *Harrison*, 95–96; Grant, State of the Union, 1870.
99　Doenecke, *Garfield*, 146–47; Green, *Providence*, 74.
100　Doenecke, *Garfield*, 147–52; Green, *Providence*, 74–75; Ross, *War Plans, 1890–1939*, 5–6.
101　Socolofsky and Spetter, *Harrison*, 96–98; Ross, *War Plans, 1890–1939*, 6.
102　Ross, *War Plans, 1890–1939*, 10–11.
103　Azar Gat, *A History of Military Thought* (Oxford: Oxford University Press, 2001), 442–50; Warren Zimmerman, *First Great Triumph: How Five Americans Made Their Country a World Power* (New York: Farrar, Straus, and Giroux, 2002), 107.
104　Gat, *History*, 449; Ross, *War Plans, 1890–1939*, 6–7.
105　Alfred Thayer Mahan, *The Influence of Sea Power upon History, 1660–1783* (New York: Dover Publications, 1987 [1890]), 29–50.
106　Ibid., 29–89.
107　Ibid., 88–89.
108　Ibid., 487, 514, 535, 539–40; Margaret Sprout, "Mahan: Evangelist of Sea Power," in Edward Mead Earle, ed., *Makers of Modern Strategy: Military Thought from Machiavelli to Hitler* (Princeton: Princeton University Press, 1971), 432–34; William E. Livezey, *Mahan on Sea Power* (Norman: University of Oklahoma Press, 1981), 51.
109　Green, *Providence*, 75; Zimmerman, *Triumph*, 93, 97, 101.

6 AMERICAN EMPIRE, 1897–1913

1　Warren Zimmerman, *First Great Triumph: How Five Americans Made Their Country a World Power* (New York: Farrar, Straus, and Giroux, 2002), 13; John Lewis Gaddis, *Surprise, Security, and the American Experience* (Cambridge: Harvard University Press, 2004), 29; Walter A. McDougall, *Promised Land, Crusader State: The American Encounter with the World since 1776* (New York: Houghton Mifflin, 1997), 106, 118.
2　Lewis Gould, *The Presidency of William McKinley* (Lawrence: Regents Press of Kansas, 1980), 33–34; *AMH*, 321.

3 Zimmerman, *Triumph*, 248–49; *AMH*, 320; Hugh Rockoff, *America's Economic Way of War: War and the US Economy from the Spanish-American War to the Persian Gulf War* (Cambridge: Cambridge University Press, 2012), 52; McDougall, *Promised Land*, 111.
4 Gould, *McKinley*, 59–64; Philip Zelikow, "Why Did America Cross the Pacific? Reconstructing the US Decision to Take the Philippines, 1898–99," *Texas National Security Review*, 1:1 (December 2017), 39; Zimmerman, *Triumph*, 215–16.
5 Gould, *McKinley*, 64–65, 68–69.
6 Ibid., 69–71.
7 Ibid., 71–75; *AMH*, 321.
8 *AMH*, 321–22; Gould, *McKinley*, 74–75; Joseph G. Dawson III, "William T. Sampson and Santiago: Blockade, Victory, and Controversy," in James Bradford, ed., *Crucible of Empire: The Spanish-American War and Its Aftermath* (Annapolis: Naval Institute Press, 1993), 50.
9 Gould, *McKinley*, 78–80, 84–86; *AMH*, 322.
10 *AMH*, 322; Gould, *McKinley*, 88.
11 Charles Olcott, *The Life of William McKinley* (Boston: Houghton Mifflin, 1916), 2:4, 31–34; Gould, *McKinley*, 50, 69; Ephraim Smith, "William McKinley's Enduring Legacy: The Historiographical Debate on the Taking of the Philippine Island," in Bradford, ed., *Crucible*, 209; Zimmerman, *Triumph*, 263; McDougall, *Promised*, 111.
12 Antulio J. Echevarria II, *Reconsidering the American Way of War: US Military Practice from the Revolution to Afghanistan* (Washington: Georgetown University Press, 2014), 98; *AMH*, 322.
13 Zelikow, "Why," 43; Mark Hayes, "War Plans and Preparations and Their Impact on US Naval Operations in the Spanish-American War," *Naval History and Heritage Command* (March 1998), www.history.navy.mil/research/library/online-reading-room/title-list-alphabetically/s/spanish-american-war-war-plans-and-impact-on-u-s-navy.html; Gould, *McKinley*, 94–95.
14 Hayes, "War Plans"; Steven T. Ross, *American War Plans, 1890–1939* (London: Frank Cass, 2002), 14–17; Olcott, *McKinley*, 2:4; *AMH*, 322.
15 Zimmerman, *Triumph*, 277.
16 Gould, *McKinley*, 91–93, 102; McDougall, *Promised*, 111; Zelikow, "Why," 47.
17 Hayes, "War Plans"; Kenneth J. Hagan, *This People's Navy: The Making of American Sea Power* (New York: Free Press, 1991), 214–16; Dawson, "Sampson," 50; Zimmerman, *Triumph*, 277.
18 Zelikow, "Why," 44–45; Hayes, "War Plans"; Hagan, *People's Navy*, 220; Brian Linn, *The Philippine War, 1899–1902* (Lawrence: University of Kansas Press, 2002), 5.
19 Linn, *Philippine War*, 6–8; Zelikow, "Why," 45; James Holmes, *Theodore Roosevelt and World Order: Police Power in International Relations* (Washington: Potomac Books, 2006), 140; *AMH*, 336; Hagan, *People's Navy*, 222.

20 *AMH*, 324–25; Zelikow, "Why," 46–47.
21 Zelikow, "Why," 47–49.
22 Dawson, "Sampson," 50, 54–55, 60; *AMH*, 327; Zimmerman, *Triumph*, 277–78.
23 *AMH*, 328–29, 332; Dawson, "Sampson," 55.
24 *AMH*, 332–33.
25 Ibid., 332–34; Dawson, "Sampson," 55–58.
26 *AMH*, 334; Zimmerman, *Triumph*, 281, 293; Dawson, "Sampson," 61.
27 Zimmerman, *Triumph*, 313–14; *AMH*, 334; Olcott, *McKinley*, 2:67–74; Smith, "McKinley's Enduring," 209.
28 Zelikow, "Why," 50–60.
29 Zimmerman, *Triumph*, 321–23; Marc Leepson, "The Philippine War," *Military History* (November 2007), 62.
30 Rockoff, *Economic*, 57–61, 84.
31 McDougall, *Promised*, 118–19.
32 Ibid., 119–20.
33 John A. Thompson, *A Sense of Power: The Roots of America's Global Role* (Ithaca: Cornell University Press, 2015), 31; Michael Green, *By More Than Providence: Grand Strategy and American Power in the Asia Pacific since 1783* (New York: Columbia University Press, 2019), 89.
34 Green, *Providence*, 90–91; McDougall, *Promised*, 112–14.
35 Echevarria, *Reconsidering*, 103; Linn, *Philippine War*, 15–16.
36 Leepson, "Philippine War," 62–63; Linn, *Philippine War*, 20–22; Zimmerman, *Triumph*, 305.
37 Linn, *Philippine War*, 25–30, 36, 40–42; Andrew Birtle, *US Army Counterinsurgency and Contingency Operations Doctrine, 1860–1941* (Washington: Center of Military History, 2009), 119; Leepson, "Philippine War," 65.
38 Linn, *Philippine War*, 42, 47, 52, 61–62.
39 Ibid., 88.
40 Ibid., 88–90, 100–1.
41 Ibid., 92–93.
42 Ibid., 93–99, 104–6, 109.
43 Ibid., 109–11, 116.
44 Ibid., 117, 129–30; Holmes, *Roosevelt*, 154.
45 Birtle, *Counterinsurgency, 1860–1941*, 116–17; Linn, *Philippine War*, 197, 203.
46 Linn, *Philippine War*, 130–31.
47 Ibid., 139–48, 159, 169, 180–81.
48 Ibid., 136–38, 148, 184–87.
49 Ibid., 191–93, 196.
50 Ibid., 72–73, 127, 169–74, 197, 211; Birtle, *Counterinsurgency, 1860–1941*, 117–22.
51 Birtle, *Counterinsurgency, 1860–1941*, 113–14, 120–21; Linn, *Philippine War*, 199–202.
52 Linn, *Philippine War*, 206; Birtle, *Counterinsurgency, 1860–1941*, 113–14.

53 Linn, *Philippine War*, 208–10.
54 Ibid., 9, 211–12; Birtle, *Counterinsurgency, 1860–1941*, 131.
55 Birtle, *Counterinsurgency, 1860–1941*, 119–20, 124–26; Linn, *Philippine War*, 213.
56 Linn, *Philippine War*, 210–16; Birtle, *Counterinsurgency, 1860–1941*, 126–27.
57 Birtle, *Counterinsurgency, 1860–1941*, 127–32; Linn, *Philippine War*, 214–15, 295.
58 Birtle, *Counterinsurgency, 1860–1941*, 122–23; Linn, *Philippine War*, 216–17.
59 Birtle, *Counterinsurgency, 1860–1941*, 132–35; Linn, *Philippine War*, 218–19; Leepson, "Philippine War," 67; Echevarria, *Reconsidering*, 103.
60 Birtle, *Counterinsurgency, 1860–1941*, 135–36; Echevarria, *Reconsidering*, 103; Ross, *War Plans, 1890–1939*, 23; Green, *Providence*, 91.
61 George Herring, *From Colony to Superpower: US Foreign Relations since 1776* (Oxford: Oxford University Press, 2011), 329–34; George Mowry, *The Era of Theodore Roosevelt, and the Birth of Modern America, 1900–1912* (New York: Harper, 1958), 181; *AMH*, 340; Samuel Flagg Bemis, *A Diplomatic History of the United States*, 5th ed. (New York: Holt, Rinehart, and Winston, 1965), 484–87.
62 *AMH*, 340–42; Echevarria, *Reconsidering*, 104–5; Bemis, *Diplomatic*, 486–87.
63 Smith, "McKinley's Enduring," 225; Thompson, *Power*, 30–31; Gaddis, *Surprise*, 28; Ross, *War Plans, 1890–1939*, 23; Birtle, *Counterinsurgency, 1860–1941*, 103.
64 Ross, *War Plans, 1890–1939*, x.
65 Ibid., 27–28; Robert Wooster, *The Military and United States Indian Policy, 1865–1903* (Lincoln: University of Nebraska Press, 1988), 201–2.
66 Edmund Morris, *Theodore Rex* (New York: Modern Library, 2001), 215–16; Thompson, *Power*, 32, 51–52; Theodore Roosevelt, First Annual Message, December 3, 1901, https://millercenter.org/the-presidency/presidential-speeches/december-3-1901-first-annual-message; Theodore Roosevelt, Third Annual Message, December 7, 1903, https://millercenter.org/the-presidency/presidential-speeches/december-7-1903-third-annual-message.
67 Roosevelt, First Annual Message; Theodore Roosevelt, Fifth Annual Message, December 5, 1905, https://millercenter.org/the-presidency/presidential-speeches/december-5-1905-fifth-annual-message.
68 Herring, *Colony*, 291–92; Morris, *Theodore Rex*, 25–26.
69 Mowry, *Roosevelt*, 146; Holmes, *Roosevelt*, 169; Roosevelt, First Annual Message; Theodore Roosevelt, Second Annual Message, December 2, 1902, https://millercenter.org/the-presidency/presidential-speeches/december-2-1902-second-annual-message; Morris, *Theodore Rex*, 115–16.
70 Morris, *Theodore Rex*, 238–43, 264; Holmes, *Roosevelt*, 170.
71 Morris, *Theodore Rex*, 264–65, 268, 273.
72 Ibid., 273–75, 292–94; Bemis, *Diplomatic*, 514–15.
73 Bemis, *Diplomatic*, 515–18; Holmes, *Roosevelt*, 173–74; Mowry, *Roosevelt*, 149, 154.
74 Mowry, *Roosevelt*, 146; Morris, *Theodore Rex*, 177–79.
75 Morris, *Theodore Rex*, 186–87.

76 Ibid., 187–91.
77 Ibid., 191, 201, 204–5, 208.
78 Herring, *Colony*, 370–71; Lester Langley, *The Banana Wars: United States Intervention in the Caribbean, 1898–1934* (Lexington: University Press of Kentucky, 1985), 58; Theodore Roosevelt, Fourth Annual Message, December 6, 1904, https://millercenter.org/the-presidency/presidential-speeches/december-6-1904-fourth-annual-message; Morris, *Theodore Rex*, 325–26; Holmes, *Roosevelt*, 165.
79 Morris, *Theodore Rex*, 317–19; Mowry, *Roosevelt*, 158–60.
80 Morris, *Theodore Rex*, 461–64; Birtle, *Counterinsurgency, 1860–1941*, 168–74; Holmes, *Roosevelt*, 163–65; Zimmerman, *Triumph*, 442.
81 Mowry, *Roosevelt*, 146, 181; Green, *Providence*, 103.
82 Morris, *Theodore Rex*, 228–29.
83 Ibid., 389–91; Mowry, *Roosevelt*, 184–85; Denis Warner and Peggy Warner, *The Tide at Sunrise: A History of the Russo-Japanese War, 1904–1905* (Abingdon: Routledge, 2004), 175; Green, *Providence*, 98; Bemis, *Diplomatic*, 492, 494; Zimmerman, *Triumph*, 470.
84 Morris, *Theodore Rex*, 397; Green, *Providence*, 98–102; Mowry, *Roosevelt*, 186–89.
85 Green, *Providence*, 101; Mowry, *Roosevelt*, 149; Morris, *Theodore Rex*, 180–81.
86 Morris, *Theodore Rex*, 493–95, 509; Hagan, *People's Navy*, 238–39.
87 Morris, *Theodore Rex*, 115, 206–8; Mowry, *Roosevelt*, 133.
88 Gould, *McKinley*, 40–43; Mowry, *Roosevelt*, 126–29; Roosevelt, First Annual Message.
89 Theodore Roosevelt, Sixth Annual Message, December 9, 1908, https://millercenter.org/the-presidency/presidential-speeches/december-9-1908-eighth-annual-message.
90 Mowry, *Roosevelt*, 233–34.
91 William Taft, Inaugural Address, March 4, 1909, https://millercenter.org/the-presidency/presidential-speeches/march-4-1909-inaugural-address; Mowry, *Roosevelt*, 278.
92 Lester Langley, *The United States and the Caribbean, 1900–1970* (Athens: University of Georgia Press, 1980), 58; Langley, *Banana Wars*, 65; McDougall, *Promised*, 116; Bemis, *Diplomatic*, 531–33; William Taft, Fourth Annual Message, December 3, 1912, https://millercenter.org/the-presidency/presidential-speeches/december-3-1912-fourth-annual-message.
93 Mowry, *Roosevelt*, 242–46.
94 Langley, *Banana Wars*, 59–62; Langley, *Caribbean*, 50.
95 Langley, *Banana Wars*, 63–64.
96 Ibid., 53–61.
97 Ibid., 66–75; Langley, *Caribbean*, 58.
98 Green, *Providence*, 118–20.
99 Ibid., 118–21; McDougall, *Promised*, 116.
100 Green, *Providence*, 118, 122; Mowry, *Roosevelt*, 275.

7 STEPPING UPON THE GLOBAL STAGE, 1913–1921

1 Lester Langley, *The United States and the Caribbean, 1900–1970* (Athens: University of Georgia Press, 1980), 62; Lester Langley, *The Banana Wars: United States Intervention in the Caribbean, 1898–1934* (Lexington: University Press of Kentucky, 1985), 77; John A. Thompson, *A Sense of Power: The Roots of America's Global Role* (Ithaca: Cornell University Press, 2015), 40; Walter A. McDougall, *Promised Land, Crusader State: The American Encounter with the World since 1776* (New York: Houghton Mifflin, 1997), 127; Andrew Birtle, *US Army Counterinsurgency and Contingency Operations Doctrine, 1860–1941* (Washington: Center of Military History, 2009), 191.
2 Samuel Flagg Bemis, *A Diplomatic History of the United States*, 5th ed. (New York: Holt, Rinehart, and Winston, 1965), 547; Saladin Ambar, "Woodrow Wilson: Foreign Affairs," *Miller Center*, https://millercenter.org/president/wilson/foreign-affairs.
3 George C. Herring, *The American Century: US Foreign Relations, 1893–2014* (Oxford: Oxford University Press, 2017), 81–83; Thompson, *Power*, 5, 37; McDougall, *Promised*, 130.
4 Douglas Irwin, *Clashing over Commerce: A History of US Trade Policy* (Chicago: University of Chicago Press, 2017), 331–32, 338–39; Woodrow Wilson, Message regarding Tariff Duties, April 8, 1913, https://millercenter.org/the-presidency/presidential-speeches/april-8-1913-message-regarding-tariff-duties.
5 Herring, *American*, 81–82.
6 Ibid., 87.
7 McDougall, *Promised*, 129; [William Jennings] Bryan, March 12, 1913, *Foreign Relations of the United States with the Address of the President to Congress, December 2, 1913* (hereafter *FRUS*) (Washington: USGPO, 1920), https://history.state.gov/historicaldocuments/frus1913/d7; Langley, *Banana Wars*, 8; Herring, *American*, 88.
8 Herring, *American*, 83–84.
9 Ibid., 88–90; Langley, *Caribbean*, 71–77; Langley, *Banana Wars*, 140; James McCrocklin, *Garde d'Haiti: Twenty Years of Organization and Training by the United States Marine Corps, 1915–1934* (Annapolis: Naval Institute Press, 1956), v, 21–22.
10 Langley, *Banana Wars*, 78–83.
11 Ibid., 84–85; McDougall, *Promised*, 130.
12 Langley, *Banana Wars*, 85–86.
13 Ibid., 87, 90–100; McDougall, *Promised*, 131.
14 Langley, *Banana Wars*, 102; Steven T. Ross, *American War Plans, 1890–1939* (London: Frank Cass, 2002), 74; Birtle, *Counterinsurgency, 1860–1941*, 193, 196–97.
15 Langley, *Banana Wars*, 108–13.
16 Birtle, *Counterinsurgency, 1860–1941*, 199–201.
17 Ibid., 201–4; Ross, *War Plans, 1890–1939*, 74.
18 Birtle, *Counterinsurgency, 1860–1941*, 203–6, 226–30; Ross, *War Plans, 1890–1939*, 75–76.
19 Langley, *Banana Wars*, 117, 121–22.

20 Ibid., 150–54; Langley, *Caribbean*, 77–84; Ross, *War Plans, 1890–1939*, 24–25.
21 Louis A. Pérez Jr., *Intervention, Revolution, and Politics in Cuba* (Pittsburgh: University of Pittsburgh Press, 1978), 40–42, 48, 78–80, 88–93.
22 Langley, *Caribbean*, 110–13.
23 Herring, *America*, 85–86; Michael Green, *By More Than Providence: Grand Strategy and American Power in the Asia Pacific since 1783* (New York: Columbia University Press, 2019), 123–27; McDougall, *Promised*, 129.
24 Thompson, *Power*, 26; Ross Gregory, *The Origins of American Intervention in the First World War* (New York: Norton, 1973), 3.
25 Gregory, *Origins*, 14; David Woodward, *Trial by Friendship: Anglo-American Relations, 1917–1918* (Lexington: University Press of Kentucky, 1993), 10–11.
26 Ibid., 26–43, 55, 71–72; Woodrow Wilson, Message on Neutrality, August 20, 1914, https://millercenter.org/the-presidency/presidential-speeches/august-20-1914-message-neutrality.
27 Gregory, *Origins*, 22, 49–55, 71–72; Paul G. Halpern, *A Naval History of World War I* (Annapolis: Naval Institute Press, 1994), 293–95.
28 Gregory, *Origins*, 11, 57–65; Halpern, *Naval*, 299; Herring, *American*, 104.
29 Woodward, *Trial*, 15; McDougall, *Promised*, 132; Gregory, *Origins*, 78–82.
30 Gregory, *Origins*, 91–95; Woodrow Wilson, Message regarding German Actions, April 19, 1916, https://millercenter.org/the-presidency/presidential-speeches/april-19-1916-message-regarding-german-actions; Halpern, *Naval*, 307–8.
31 Woodward, *Trial*, 21, 27–31; Gregory, *Origins*, 108–15.
32 Gregory, *Origins*, 115; Herring, *American*, 109; Woodrow Wilson, "A World League for Peace" Speech, January 22, 1917, https://millercenter.org/the-presidency/presidential-speeches/january-22-1917-world-league-peace-speech; McDougall, *Promised*, 134–35.
33 Halpern, *Naval*, 335–40; Gregory, *Origins*, 117, 120–24.
34 Gregory, *Origins*, 124–26.
35 Ibid., 126–29; McDougall, *Promised*, 136.
36 Woodward, *Trial*, 18–20, 33; David Trask, *The United States in the Supreme War Council: American War Aims and Inter-Allied Strategy, 1917–1918* (Middletown: Wesleyan University Press, 1961), 8–9; Ross, *War Plans, 1890–1939*, 25.
37 Trask, *Supreme*, 9–11.
38 Hugh Rockoff, *America's Economic Way of War: War and the US Economy from the Spanish-American War to the Persian Gulf War* (Cambridge: Cambridge University Press, 2012), 115, 125; Colin Dueck, *Reluctant Crusaders: Power, Culture, and Change in American Grand Strategy* (Princeton: Princeton University Press, 2006), 46.
39 Woodward, *Trial*, 37, 42.
40 Gregory, *Origins*, 15; Woodrow Wilson, Address to Congress Requesting a Declaration of War against Germany, April 2, 1917, https://millercenter.org/the-presidency/presidential-speeches/april-2-1917-address-congress-requesting-declaration-war.

41 Trask, *Supreme*, 7–8. Italics in quoted original.
42 Thompson, *Power*, 1.
43 Woodward, *Trial*, 60–61, 139.
44 Ibid., 43, 55–59; Trask, *Supreme*, 11–12.
45 Trask, *Supreme*, 12; Halpern, *Naval*, 343–56.
46 Halpern, *Naval*, 357–59; Woodward, *Trial*, 65.
47 Halpern, *Naval*, 360–66; Ross, *War Plans, 1890–1939*, 88.
48 Woodward, *Trial*, 117–19, 198–99.
49 Trask, *Supreme*, 14.
50 Ibid., 13; Woodward, *Trial*, 82–83.
51 Woodward, *Trial*, 83–85, 88–90.
52 Ibid., 93.
53 Ibid., 88, 109; Trask, *Supreme*, 24–26; Meghan McCrae, *Coalition Strategy and the End of the First World War: The Supreme War Council and War Planning, 1917–1918* (Cambridge: Cambridge University Press, 2019), 13–14.
54 Trask, *Supreme*, ix, 4, 38, 41, 46, 50.
55 Ibid., 15–18.
56 Woodward, *Trial*, 121–24.
57 Woodrow Wilson, Fifth Annual Message, December 4, 1917, https://millercenter.org/the-presidency/presidential-speeches/december-4-1917-fifth-annual-message.
58 Trask, *Supreme*, 46; Woodrow Wilson, Wilson's "Fourteen Points," January 8, 1918, https://millercenter.org/the-presidency/presidential-speeches/january-8-1918-wilsons-fourteen-points; McDougall, *Promised*, 132.
59 Trask, *Supreme*, 54–55, 111; Woodward, *Trial*, 156–57.
60 Trask, *Supreme*, 51–52; Woodward, *Trial*, 153–55.
61 Trask, *Supreme*, 62–64, 69; Woodward, *Trial*, 155, 165.
62 Trask, *Supreme*, 95; Woodward, *Trial*, 134–37, 159, 169, 172.
63 Woodward, *Trial*, 166, 172; Trask, *Supreme*, 131.
64 Woodward, *Trial*, 140–42, 178–81; Trask, *Supreme*, 100, 117–18, 124, 127.
65 Woodward, *Trial*, 181, 190, 200–1, 213–14; Hew Strachan, *The First World War* (New York: Penguin, 2003), 315–16.
66 David Stevenson, *Cataclysm: The First World War as Political Tragedy* (New York: Basic Books, 2004), 382–84; Michael Neiberg, "To End All Wars? A Case Study of Conflict Termination in World War I," in J. Boone Bartholomees Jr., ed., *US Army War College Guide to National Security Issues: National Security Policy and Strategy*, 5th ed. (Carlisle: Strategic Studies Institute, 2012), 2:339; Woodward, *Trial*, 202, 208–9; Trask, *Supreme*, 95, 153.
67 Gideon Rose, *How Wars End: Why We Always Fight the Last Battle* (New York: Simon and Schuster, 2010), 21; Trask, *Supreme*, 156–57.
68 Trask, *Supreme*, 157–58.
69 Ibid., 160–62; Neiberg, "End," 2:340–41.

70 Neiberg, "End," 2:344; Trask, *Supreme*, 165–71; Paul Pillar, *Negotiating Peace: War Termination as a Bargaining Process* (Princeton: Princeton University Press, 1983), 31; Stevenson, *Cataclysm*, 391, 404.
71 Neiberg, "End," 2:342–43.
72 Trask, *Supreme*, 8.
73 Raymond Sontag, *A Broken World, 1919–1939* (New York: Harper, 1971), 2–3; Martin Alexander and John Keiger, "Limiting Arms, Enforcing Limits: International Inspections and the Challenges of Compellance in Germany Post-1919, Iraq Post-1991," *Journal of Strategic Studies*, 29:2 (2006), 386.
74 Trask, *Supreme*, 173; Strachan, *First World War*, 310; Woodward, *Trial*, 213.
75 Woodward, *Trial*, 212–14; Strachan, *First World War*, 333.
76 Strachan, *First World War*, 326–27.
77 Alexander and Keiger, "Limiting Arms," 355.
78 McDougall, *Promised*, 139–40; Rose, *How Wars*, 41, 43–46.
79 Sontag, *Broken*, 4.
80 Ibid., 11, 15; John Lewis Gaddis, *Surprise, Security, and the American Experience* (Cambridge: Harvard University Press, 2004), 40; Dueck, *Reluctant*, 47, 61; McDougall, *Promised*, 140.
81 Neiberg, "End," 2:343.
82 McDougall, *Promised*, 140–41; Dueck, *Reluctant*, 61; Sontag, *Broken*, 17.
83 McDougall, *Promised*, 143–44; Dueck, *Reluctant*, 49–50, 53.
84 McDougall, *Promised*, 144; Sontag, *Broken*, 17–21.
85 Strachan, *First World War*, 152–53, 333–34.
86 Green, *Providence*, 128–29.
87 Rockoff, *Economic*, 141–43; Sontag, *Broken*, 24–25.
88 Alexander and Keiger, "Limiting Arms," 359–62.
89 Dueck, *Reluctant*, 2; Rose, *How Wars*, 49.
90 Woodward, *Trial*, 202; Bernadotte Schmitt and Harold Vedeler, *The World in the Crucible, 1914–1919* (New York: Harper & Row, 1984), 255.

8 THE INTERWAR INTERLUDE, 1921–1939

1 Foster Rhea Dulles, *America's Rise to World Power, 1898–1954* (New York: Harper, 1955), 108; John A. Thompson, *A Sense of Power: The Roots of America's Global Role* (Ithaca: Cornell University Press, 2015), 3; Walter A. McDougall, *Promised Land, Crusader State: The American Encounter with the World since 1776* (New York: Houghton Mifflin, 1997), 124–25.
2 George C. Herring, *The American Century: US Foreign Relations, 1893–2014* (Oxford: Oxford University Press, 2017), 137–41; Eugene Trani and David Wilson, *The Presidency of Warren G. Harding* (Lawrence: Regents Press of Kansas, 1977), 1–3.
3 Trani and Wilson, *Harding*, 14–17.

4 Ibid., 144; David Kennedy, *Freedom from Fear: The American People in Depression and War, 1929–1945* (Oxford: Oxford University Press, 1999), 29–30.
5 L. Ethan Ellis, *Republican Foreign Policy, 1921–1933* (New Brunswick: Rutgers University Press, 1968), 10, 59; Michael Green, *By More Than Providence: Grand Strategy and American Power in the Asia Pacific since 1783* (New York: Columbia University Press, 2019), 137–38; Herring, *American*, 144–45.
6 Warren G. Harding, Inaugural Address, March 4, 1921, https://millercenter.org/the-presidency/presidential-speeches/march-4-1921-inaugural-address; Warren G. Harding, Nationalism and Americanism, March 31, 1921, https://millercenter.org/the-presidency/presidential-speeches/march-31-1921-nationalism-and-americanism.
7 Calvin Coolidge, Inaugural Address, March 4, 1925, https://millercenter.org/the-presidency/presidential-speeches/march-4-1925-inaugural-address; Calvin Coolidge, Fourth Annual Message to Congress, December 7, 1926, https://millercenter.org/the-presidency/presidential-speeches/december-7-1926-fourth-annual-message; Calvin Coolidge, Sixth Annual Message to Congress, December 4, 1928, https://millercenter.org/the-presidency/presidential-speeches/december-4-1928-sixth-annual-message; Calvin Coolidge, First Annual Message, December 6, 1923, https://millercenter.org/the-presidency/presidential-speeches/december-6-1923-first-annual-message.
8 John Vinson, "Charles Evans Hughes," in Norman Graebner, ed., *An Uncertain Tradition: American Secretaries of State in the Twentieth Century* (New York: McGraw-Hill, 1961), 128–31; Herring, *American*, 143; Merlo Pusey, *Charles Evans Hughes* (New York: Macmillan, 1952), 2:439.
9 Pusey, *Hughes*, 2:421–24; Alan McPherson, "Herbert Hoover, Occupation Withdrawal, and the Good Neighbor Policy," *Presidential Studies Quarterly*, 44:4 (December 2014), 629–30.
10 Colin Dueck, "Hoover and Offshore Foreign Policy, 1921–1933," *Orbis* (winter 2016), 9–10.
11 Trani and Wilson, *Harding*, 13–14, 54–55, 61, 80, 94; Peter Temin, "The Great Depression," in Engerman and Gallman, eds., *Cambridge Economic History*, 3:302–3; Herring, *American*, 146; Ellis, *Republican*, 10–11.
12 Trani and Wilson, *Harding*, 74; Pusey, *Hughes*, 2:570–74.
13 Pusey, *Hughes*, 2:563–65; Joseph Brandes, *Herbert Hoover and Economic Diplomacy: Department of Commerce Policy, 1921–1928* (Pittsburgh: University of Pittsburgh Press, 1962), x, 3–8.
14 Robert Ferrell, *The Presidency of Calvin Coolidge* (Lawrence: University Press of Kansas, 1998), 42, 61–62, 70, 74; Calvin Coolidge, Fifth Annual Message to Congress, December 6, 1927, https://millercenter.org/the-presidency/presidential-speeches/december-6-1927-fifth-annual-message; Calvin Coolidge, Second Annual Message, December 3, 1924, https://millercenter.org/the-presidency/presidential-speeches/december-3-1924-second-annual-message; Coolidge, Sixth Annual Message; Kimberly Amadeo, "1920s Economy," *The*

Balance, April 13, 2020, www.thebalance.com/roaring-twenties-4060511#:~:text=The%201920s%20is%20the%20decade,of%20being%20a%20global%20power.

15 Akira Iriye, *The Globalizing of America, 1913–1945.* The Cambridge History of American Foreign Relations (Cambridge: Cambridge University Press, 1993), 3:79–80; Herring, *American,* 152; Dueck, "Hoover," 10; Pusey, *Hughes,* 2:431, 439; Trani and Wilson, *Harding,* 142, 146–49; Ferrell, *Coolidge,* 79–80.

16 Herring, *American,* 171; Lester Langley, *The Banana Wars: United States Intervention in the Caribbean, 1898–1934* (Lexington: University Press of Kentucky, 1985), 169; Lester Langley, *The United States and the Caribbean, 1900–1970* (Athens: University of Georgia Press, 1980), 96; McPherson, "Hoover," 625; Pusey, *Hughes,* 2:531.

17 Pusey, *Hughes,* 2:530–31, 535–37; Vinson, "Hughes," 147; Trani and Wilson, *Harding,* 134–35.

18 Langley, *Caribbean,* 107–8.

19 Pusey, *Hughes,* 2:530–31; Trani and Wilson, *Harding,* 135–36.

20 Langley, *Caribbean,* 96; Trani and Wilson, *Harding,* 137–38; Dueck, "Hoover," 8; Herring, *American,* 150–51, 172–73.

21 Trani and Wilson, *Harding,* 128–32; Herring, *American,* 176–78; L. Ethan Ellis, "Frank B. Kellogg," in Graebner, ed., *Uncertain,* 159–61; Ferrell, *Coolidge,* 125–30.

22 Pusey, *Hughes,* 2:533–34; Langley, *Caribbean,* 97–101.

23 Langley, *Caribbean,* 101–5; James McCrocklin, *Garde d'Haiti: Twenty Years of Organization and Training by the United States Marine Corps, 1915–1934* (Annapolis: Naval Institute Press, 1956), 186–87, 207, 228.

24 McPherson, "Hoover," 634–36; Langley, *Banana Wars,* 219; Langley, *Caribbean,* 136.

25 Langley, *Caribbean,* 177–80; Pusey, *Hughes,* 2:532.

26 Trani and Wilson, *Harding,* 119; Pusey, *Hughes,* 2:527–28; Herring, *American,* 165–66.

27 Herring, *American,* 145–46, 166–68.

28 Ibid., 166–67; Warren G. Harding, First Annual Address, December 6, 1921, https://millercenter.org/the-presidency/presidential-speeches/december-6-1921-first-annual-message; Trani and Wilson, *Harding,* 118, 122–23; McDougall, *Promised,* 176.

29 Herring, *American,* 153; Pusey, *Hughes,* 2:463.

30 Ferrell, *Coolidge,* 75–76.

31 Green, *Providence,* 138–39; Herring, *American,* 154, 156.

32 Steven T. Ross, *American War Plans, 1890–1939* (London: Frank Cass, 2002), 102–3; Ferrell, *Coolidge,* 76–78; Pusey, *Hughes,* 2:572–73; Green, *Providence,* 136–37, 140; Herring, *American,* 155; Warren G. Harding, Second Annual Address, December 8, 1922, https://millercenter.org/the-presidency/presidential-speeches/december-8-1922-second-annual-message.

33 Green, *Providence,* 144–48.

34 Herring, *American,* 168–70.

35 Ibid., 170–71.
36 Ibid., 157; Dueck, "Hoover," 13–14.
37 Herring, *American*, 138, 158–62; Detlev Peukert, *The Weimar Republic* (New York: Hill and Wang, 1992), 59–60.
38 Herring, *American*, 159–62; Hugh Rockoff, *America's Economic Way of War: War and the US Economy from the Spanish-American War to the Persian Gulf War* (Cambridge: Cambridge University Press, 2012), 144.
39 Herring, *American*, 161–62.
40 Ibid., 144; Pusey, *Hughes*, 2:613; Ellis, "Kellogg," 151, 153–56.
41 Ellis, "Kellogg," 164–66; Herring, *American*, 178–79.
42 Herring, *American*, 182; Rockoff, *Economic*, 144.
43 Langley, *Banana Wars*, 183–84.
44 Ibid., 184–85, 204–5; Langley, *Caribbean*, 118.
45 Langley, *Banana Wars*, 183, 186, 190.
46 Ibid., 186–88.
47 Ellis, "Kellogg," 156–57; Langley, *Banana Wars*, 191–93.
48 Langley, *Banana Wars*, 193–94, 197–99.
49 Ibid., 200–3.
50 Ibid., 204–5.
51 Ibid., 201–3.
52 Ibid., 206–11.
53 Ibid., 206–8, 211–14.
54 Ibid., 214–17; McPherson, "Hoover," 633; Bryce Wood, "How Wars End in Latin America," *The Annals of the American Academy of Political and Social Science*, 392 (November 1970), 47–49.
55 Trani and Wilson, *Harding*, 11–12.
56 Ibid., 145; Herring, *American*, 140–41; Coolidge, First and Second Annual Messages.
57 Green, *Providence*, 142; Herring, *American*, 181.
58 Ross, *War Plans, 1890–1939*, 86, 94–100; Lukas Milevski, *The Evolution of Modern Grand Strategic Thought* (Oxford: Oxford University Press, 2016), 36; Green, *Providence*, 135, 143.
59 Herbert Hoover, First State of the Union Address, December 3, 1929, https://millercenter.org/the-presidency/presidential-speeches/december-3-1929-first-state-union-address.; McPherson, "Hoover," 629.
60 Herbert Hoover, Message Regarding International Peace, September 18, 1929, https://millercenter.org/the-presidency/presidential-speeches/september-18-1929-message-regarding-international-peace; Hoover, First State of the Union.
61 Herbert Hoover, Principles and Ideals of the United States Government, October 22, 1928, https://millercenter.org/the-presidency/presidential-speeches/october-22-1928-principles-and-ideals-united-states-government; Hoover, First State of the Union; Green, *Providence*, 138.

62 Richard Current, "Henry L. Stimson," in Graebner, ed., *Uncertain*, 171–78; Herbert Hoover, Inaugural Address, March 4, 1929, https://millercenter.org/the-presidency/presidential-speeches/march-4-1929-inaugural-address; Herring, *American*, 190–92.
63 Langley, *Caribbean*, 115; McPherson, "Hoover," 623–25; Paul Drake, "From Good Men to Good Neighbors, 1912–1932," in Abraham Lowenthal, ed., *Exporting Democracy: The United States and Latin America* (Baltimore: Johns Hopkins University Press, 1991), 29; Langley, *Banana Wars*, 205–6.
64 McPherson, "Hoover," 624–27, 632–33, 637; Langley, *Caribbean*, 127–31; Current, "Stimson," 176.
65 Kennedy, *Freedom*, 11–13, 47–48.
66 Ibid., 35–36, 39–41.
67 Ibid., 37–40; Temin, "Great Depression," 305.
68 Kennedy, *Freedom*, 52–55, 58–59.
69 Ibid., 65–67.
70 Ibid., 68, 77–78; Temin, "Great Depression," 305, 311–13.
71 Kennedy, *Freedom*, 79–82.
72 Ibid., 82–83.
73 Ellis, *Republican*, 21; Kennedy, *Freedom*, 17–19, 43–44.
74 Ellis, *Republican*, 21; Hoover, First State of the Union; Herbert Hoover, Message Regarding the Smoot-Hawley Tariff Act, June 16, 1930, https://millercenter.org/the-presidency/presidential-speeches/june-16-1930-message-regarding-smoot-hawley-tariff-act; Kennedy, *Freedom*, 49–50, 49n.12; McPherson, "Hoover," 637.
75 Kennedy, *Freedom*, 49n.12; Alfred E. Eckes Jr., *Opening America's Market: US Foreign Trade Policy since 1776* (Chapel Hill: UNC Press, 1995), 106–9; Temin, "Great Depression," 305–6; Ellis, *Republican*, 22.
76 Kennedy, *Freedom*, 86–87, 94–95.
77 Herring, *American*, 146–48.
78 Ibid., 149, 183–84.
79 Dueck, "Hoover," 19–21.
80 Ibid., 7.
81 Kennedy, *Freedom*, 9, 131–36, 162–63; Michael Sherry, *In the Shadow of War: The United States since the 1930s* (New Haven: Yale University Press, 1995), 15–17.
82 Kennedy, *Freedom*, 107, 120–22.
83 Ibid., 103, 115–18; Robert Dallek, *Franklin D. Roosevelt and American Foreign Policy, 1931–1945* (New York: Oxford University Press, 1979), 24.
84 Kennedy, *Freedom*, 127–28.
85 Herring, *American*, 193.
86 Kennedy, *Freedom*, 107, 118, 138–39, 365.
87 Ibid., 154–57; Franklin Roosevelt, Inaugural Address, March 4, 1933, https://millercenter.org/the-presidency/presidential-speeches/march-4-1933-first-inaugural-address; Herring, *American*, 186, 193–96; Dallek, *Roosevelt*, 54–55.

88 Kennedy, *Freedom*, 123–24, 140–41, 200–4.
89 Ibid., 144, 202–9, 213; Dallek, *Roosevelt*, 45.
90 Kennedy, *Freedom*, 149–52, 178, 185–91.
91 Ibid., 177, 197, 199.
92 Ibid., 144–45, 170–71.
93 Ibid., 144, 147–49.
94 Ibid., 153, 366–68.
95 Dallek, *Roosevelt*, 33; Eckes, *Opening*, 140–48, 153; Kennedy, *Freedom*, 389; Herring, *American*, 200–2; Price Fishback, "US Monetary and Fiscal Policy in the 1930s," *National Bureau of Economic Research* (October 2010), 38, www.nber.org/papers/w16477; Green, *Providence*, 185.
96 Ellen McGrattan, "Capital Taxation during the US Great Depression," *National Bureau of Economic Research* (December 2010), 13–15, www.nber.org/papers/w16588; Fishback, "Monetary," 31, 38; Roy Blakey and Gladys Blakey, *The Federal Income Tax* (Clark: Lawbook Exchange, 2006), 347.
97 Kennedy, *Freedom*, 149, 153, 214.
98 Ibid., 216, 245–49, 248n.5, 258.
99 Ibid., 249–53, 257.
100 Ibid., 258–60, 264–65, 271–73.
101 Ibid., 278–79, 286, 325–38, 339–43.
102 Ibid., 275–76, 285, 288–89; Michael Bernstein, *The Great Depression: Delayed Recovery and Economic Change in America, 1912–1939* (Cambridge: Cambridge University Press, 1987), 108, 192.
103 Kennedy, *Freedom*, 350–55.
104 Ibid., 357–60.
105 Ibid., 361, 364.
106 Dallek, *Roosevelt*, 23, 32; Roosevelt, Inaugural; Herring, *American*, 194.
107 Dallek, *Roosevelt*, 65, 122, 133; Herring, *American*, 198, 201.
108 Dallek, *Roosevelt*, 78, 101; McDougall, *Promised*, 147–50; Herring, *American*, 202–4; Kennedy, *Freedom*, 386–90.
109 Dallek, *Roosevelt*, 102–3, 106–8, 117–18, 120, 137; Ross, *War Plans, 1890–1939*, 161; Kennedy, *Freedom*, 393–94; Herring, *American*, 208.
110 Dallek, *Roosevelt*, 127–28, 135–37, 159–60, 177–78; Ross, *War Plans, 1890–1939*, 161.
111 Dallek, *Roosevelt*, 148–54 157.
112 Ibid., 157–58, 162–65, 171–75; Herring, *American*, 216.
113 Dallek, *Roosevelt*, 175–77, 182–85, 187, 192.
114 Ibid., 35–36, 47–48, 66–69, 75–76, 90; C. Vann Woodward, "The Age of Reinterpretation," *The American Historical Review*, 66:1 (October 1960), 4; Ross, *War Plans, 1890–1939*, 163; George W. Baer, *One Hundred Years of Sea Power: The US Navy, 1890–1990* (Stanford: Stanford University Press, 1993), 134–35.

9 MOVING ASTRIDE THE WORLD: THE SECOND WORLD WAR, 1939–1945

1 Robert Dallek, *Franklin D. Roosevelt and American Foreign Policy, 1931–1945* (New York: Oxford University Press, 1979), 199.
2 Ibid., 199–205, 213, 224–36, 242–49, 289.
3 Ibid., 221–24.
4 Ibid., 224, 252–60; Julian E. Zelizer, *The Arsenal of Democracy: The Politics of National Security – From World War II to the War on Terrorism* (New York: Basic Books, 2010), 1–2, 49; Jeffrey Taliaferro, "Strategy of Innocence or Provocation? The Roosevelt Administration's Road to World War II," in Jeffrey Taliaferro et al., eds., *The Challenge of Grand Strategy: The Great Powers and the Broken Balance between the World Wars* (Cambridge: Cambridge University Press, 2013), 209.
5 Dallek, *Roosevelt*, 265, 267; Taliaferro, "Strategy," 214.
6 Dallek, *Roosevelt*, 276, 278–80, 293–98.
7 Ibid., 193–95; 236–37; Michael Green, *By More Than Providence: Grand Strategy and American Power in the Asia Pacific since 1783* (New York: Columbia University Press, 2019), 177.
8 Dallek, *Roosevelt*, 237–42.
9 Ibid., 269–74; Louis Morton, "Germany First: The Basic Concept of Allied Strategy in World War II," in Kent Roberts Greenfield, ed., *Command Decisions* (Washington: Center of Military History, 2000), 33; Taliaferro, "Strategy," 214; Louis Morton, "Japan's Decision for War," in Greenfield, ed., *Command*, 104–5; Green, *Providence*, 180.
10 Dallek, *Roosevelt*, 299, 303–10; Taliaferro, "Strategy," 213–19; Gerhard Weinberg, *A World at Arms: A Global History of World War II*, 2nd ed. (Cambridge: Cambridge University Press, 2005), 255.
11 Arthur A. Stein, "Domestic Constraints, Extended Deterrence, and the Incoherence of Grand Strategy: The United States, 1938–1950," in Richard Rosencrance and Arthur Stein, eds., *The Domestic Bases of Grand Strategy* (Ithaca: Cornell University Press, 1993), 97; Hugh Rockoff, *America's Economic Way of War: War and the US Economy from the Spanish-American War to the Persian Gulf War* (Cambridge: Cambridge University Press, 2012), 181.
12 George W. Baer, *One Hundred Years of Sea Power: The US Navy, 1890–1990* (Stanford: Stanford University Press, 1993), 147–49.
13 Morton, "Germany First," 21–24, 46–47.
14 Ibid., 35–36, 40; James Lacey, "Toward a Strategy: Creating an American Strategy for Global War, 1940–1943," in Williamson Murray et al., eds., *The Shaping of Grand Strategy: Policy, Diplomacy, and War* (Cambridge: Cambridge University Press, 2011), 185–86; Taliaferro, "Strategy," 208; Maurice Matloff, "Allied Strategy in Europe, 1939–1945," in Peter Paret, ed., *Makers of Modern Strategy: From Machiavelli to the Nuclear Age* (Princeton: Princeton University Press, 1984), 683.

15 Rockoff, *Economic*, 163–64.
16 Alfred E. Eckes Jr., *Opening America's Market: US Foreign Trade Policy since 1776* (Chapel Hill: UNC Press, 1995), 153–55.
17 Lacey, "Strategy," 187–91.
18 Rockoff, *Economic*, 164–67, 171, 175, 177.
19 Ibid., 183; David Rigby, *Allied Master Strategists: The Combined Chiefs of Staff in World War II* (Annapolis: Naval Institute Press, 2012), 99–100.
20 Taliaferro, "Strategy," 213; Franklin Roosevelt and Winston Churchill, The Atlantic Charter, August 14, 1941, www.nato.int/cps/en/natohq/official_texts_16912.htm?; Dallek, *Roosevelt*, 281–84.
21 Dallek, *Roosevelt*, 284–90.
22 Ibid., 311–12.
23 Franklin Roosevelt, State of the Union Address, January 6, 1942, www.presidency.ucsb.edu/ws/?pid=16253.
24 Mark Stoler, "The Grand Alliance in World War II," in Peter Mansoor and Williamson Murray, eds., *Grand Strategy and Military Alliances* (Cambridge: Cambridge University Press, 2018), 138–44; Rigby, *Allied*, 68–69.
25 Stoler, "Grand Alliance," 139; Green, *Providence*, 192–93; Ronald Spector, *Eagle against the Sun: The American War with Japan* (New York: Vintage, 1985), 142; Rigby, *Allied*, 71.
26 Green, *Providence*, 191–92.
27 Kent Roberts Greenfield, *American Strategy in World War II: A Reconsideration* (Malabar: Krieger, 1982), 3.
28 Morton, "Germany First," 11; FRUS, *The Conferences at Washington, 1941–1942, and Casablanca, 1943* (Washington: USGPO, 1958), 210–11.
29 Matloff, "Allied Strategy," 681.
30 Ibid., 684; Stoler, "Grand Alliance," 142.
31 Matloff, "Allied Strategy," 685–86; Lacey, "Strategy," 191–93; Mark A. Stoler, "The 'Second Front' and American Fear of Soviet Expansion, 1941–1943," *Military Affairs*, 39:3 (October 1975), 136–37.
32 Eric Larrabee, *Commander in Chief: Franklin Delano Roosevelt, His Lieutenants, and Their War* (New York: Harper and Row, 1987), 414–21, 448; John Wukovits, *Eisenhower: A Biography* (New York: St. Martins, 2006), 103.
33 Matloff, "Allied Strategy," 685–86; Lacey, "Strategy," 193–97; Greenfield, *American Strategy*, 12–13, 41; Weinberg, *World*, 356–59.
34 Lacey, "Strategy," 197–98; Douglas Porch, *The Path to Victory: The Mediterranean Theater in World War II* (New York: Farrar, Straus, and Giroux, 2004), 332; Weinberg, *World*, 359–60.
35 Williamson Murray and Allan Millett, *A War to Be Won: Fighting the Second World War* (Cambridge: Belknap/Harvard, 2000), 270–71; Weinberg, *World*, 360–62, 432–33.
36 Weinberg, *World*, 433–36.
37 Greenfield, *American Strategy*, 5; Weinberg, *World*, 436–37, 441–43, 446–47.

38 Lacey, "Strategy," 198, 201–2.
39 Ibid., 202–6.
40 Greenfield, *American Strategy*, 6, 31; Lacey, "Strategy," 204; Stoler, "Grand Alliance," 150–51; Weinberg, *World*, 380, 437–38.
41 Lacey, "Strategy," 207; Stoler, "Grand Alliance," 149–50; Rigby, *Allied*, 58–59; Weinberg, *World*, 438–39.
42 Weinberg, *World*, 439–40, 592; Rigby, *Allied*, 107, 126, 141.
43 Weinberg, *World*, 591, 593–96; Murray and Millett, *War*, 298; Greenfield, *American Strategy*, 5–6.
44 Weinberg, *World*, 596–601.
45 Stoler, "Grand Alliance," 152–55; Weinberg, *World*, 592, 628–30; Greenfield, *American Strategy*, 40–41.
46 Rigby, *Allied*, 138; Stoler, "Grand Alliance," 156; Weinberg, *World*, 611–14, 625–29; Greenfield, *American Strategy*, 43–45.
47 Baer, *One Hundred*, 190–94, 202.
48 Ibid., 194–99; Weinberg, *World*, 378.
49 Baer, *One Hundred*, 187–88, 202–3; Weinberg, *World*, 370–71, 377–79; Richard Overy, *Why the Allies Won* (New York: Norton, 1995), 50–58.
50 Rigby, *Allied*, 198; Weinberg, *World*, 375; Baer, *One Hundred Years*, 199–200.
51 Rigby, *Allied*, 96; Weinberg, *World*, 387; Baer, *One Hundred*, 204–5; Overy, *Allies*, 58.
52 David MacIsaac, "Voices from the Central Blue: The Air Power Theorists," in Paret, ed., *Makers*, 630–34; Overy, *Allies*, 105; William R. Emerson, "Operation POINTBLANK: A Tale of Bombers and Fighters," in *The Harmon Memorial Lectures in Military History, 1959–1987* (Washington: Office of Air Force History, 1988), 451.
53 Emerson, "POINTBLANK," 448–50; MacIsaac, "Voices," 634.
54 Overy, *Allies*, 108–10.
55 Ibid., 111–13; Weinberg, *World*, 419.
56 Emerson, "POINTBLANK," 442.
57 Ibid., 442–46, 460, 462, 464–68.
58 Murray and Millett, *War*, 328–29; Overy, *Allies*, 123–24.
59 Murray and Millett, *War*, 330–31.
60 Emerson, "POINTBLANK," 446–47; Weinberg, *World*, 663.
61 Overy, *Allies*, 125, 129–33.
62 Ibid., 128; Rockoff, *Economic*, 203–4, 207.
63 Gideon Rose, *How Wars End: Why We Always Fight the Last Battle* (New York: Simon and Schuster, 2010), 71.
64 Larrabee, *Commander*, 441–49; Greenfield, *American Strategy*, 37–40.
65 Larrabee, *Commander*, 441–43.
66 Ibid., 441; Greenfield, *American Strategy*, 42; Murray and Millett, *War*, 413.
67 Murray and Millett, *War*, 413, 416; Larrabee, *Commander*, 448–50; T. L. Cubbage II, "The German Misapprehensions Regarding Overlord: Understanding Failure

in the Estimative Process," in Michael I. Handel, ed., *Strategic and Operational Deception in the Second World War* (London: Frank Cass, 1987), 116–17, 154–56.
68 Larrabee, *Commander*, 450, 453–55.
69 Murray and Millett, *War*, 418–21.
70 Dieter Ose, "Rommel and Rundstedt: The 1944 Panzer Controversy," *Military Affairs*, 50:1 (January 1986), 8, 10; Larrabee, *Commander*, 448; Horst Boog, Gerhard Krebs, and Detlef Vogel, *Germany and the Second World War: The Strategic Air War in Europe and the War in the West and East Asia, 1943–1944/5* (Oxford: Clarendon, 2006), 496–98.
71 Murray and Millett, *War*, 420–25.
72 Ibid., 428–33; Weinberg, *World*, 694; Martin Blumenson, "General Bradley's Decision at Argentan (13 August 1944)," in Greenfield, ed., *Command*, 401, 404–17.
73 Weinberg, *World*, 658; Murray and Millett, *War*, 448–52.
74 Weinberg, *World*, 695; Maurice Matloff, "The Anvil Decision: Crossroads of Strategy," in Greenfield, ed., *Command*, 392–95; Murray and Millett, *War*, 433.
75 Ronald G. Ruppenthal, "Logistics and the Broad-Front Strategy," in Greenfield, ed., *Command*, 420–23; Murray and Millett, *War*, 437; Weinberg, *World*, 698, 762–63.
76 Murray and Millett, *War*, 438; Larrabee, *Commander*, 480.
77 Larrabee, *Commander*, 475–76; Stoler, "Grand Alliance," 156; Dennis Showalter, *Patton and Rommel: Men of War in the Twentieth Century* (New York: Berkley, 2006), 374.
78 Weinberg, *World*, 701; Murray and Millett, *War*, 439–43.
79 Murray and Millett, *War*, 463–70; Weinberg, *World*, 765–69; Showalter, *Patton*, 374; Maurice Matloff, "The 90-Division Gamble," in Greenfield, ed., *Command*, 380.
80 Murray and Millett, *War*, 477–88.
81 D. Clayton James, "America and Japanese Strategies in the Pacific," in Paret, ed., *Makers*, 705; Morton, "Japan's Decision," 100.
82 Morton, "Japan's Decision," 100–1, 105; Paul Kennedy, *Strategy and Diplomacy, 1870–1945* (London: Fontana, 1984), 183; James, "Strategies," 705–6.
83 Morton, "Japan's Decision," 110, 122–23; Kennedy, *Strategy*, 184–85; Meirion and Susie Harries, *Soldiers of the Sun: The Rise and Fall of the Imperial Japanese Army* (New York: Random House, 1991), 299; John Ellis, *Brute Force: Allied Strategy and Tactics in the Second World War* (New York: Viking, 1990), 42, 444–45; James, "Strategies," 707; Gerhard Krebs, "Super Sunrise? Japanese-United States Peace Feelers in Switzerland, 1945," *The Journal of Military History*, 69:4 (October 2005), 1081–82.
84 Morton, "Japan's Decision," 104–5, 119.
85 Harries, *Soldiers*, 316.
86 Ellis, *Brute*, 453; Baer, *One Hundred*, 206–10, 234; Edwin P. Hoyt III, *Japan's War: The Great Pacific Conflict, 1853 to 1952* (New York: McGraw-Hill, 1986), 329–30.

87 Baer, *One Hundred*, 206–7; Ellis, *Brute*, 470–71, 474, 512.
88 Spector, *Eagle*, 142–44.
89 Ibid., 187; Baer, *One Hundred*, 214.
90 Baer, *One Hundred*, 212.
91 Ellis, *Brute*, 450; John Parshall and Anthony Tully, *Shattered Sword: The Untold Story of the Battle of Midway* (Washington: Potomac Books, 2005), 26–34.
92 Ibid., 36–38, 42–44.
93 Ellis, *Brute*, 450; Harries, *Soldiers*, 396–97.
94 Baer, *One Hundred*, 218–19; Parshall and Tully, *Shattered Sword*, 60–61.
95 Spector, *Eagle*, 167; Ellis, *Brute*, 456–57.
96 Spector, *Eagle*, 157; Baer, *One Hundred*, 182, 220–21; Ellis, *Brute*, statistical Appendix Tables 47 and 57, np.
97 Hoyt, *Japan's War*, 302–3; Kennedy, *Strategy*, 188; Baer, *One Hundred*, 232.
98 Baer, *One Hundred*, 237–38; Ellis, *Brute*, 459n; Spector, *Eagle*, 144–45.
99 Baer, *One Hundred*, 211; Spector, *Eagle*, 185–87; Ellis, *Brute*, 502.
100 Hoyt, *Japan's War*, 305–6; Stoler, "Grand Alliance," 147; Ellis, *Brute*, 460–61, 465–67.
101 Hoyt, *Japan's War*, 319, 321.
102 Ibid., 321; Rigby, *Allied*, 61–62, 73–74; Spector, *Eagle*, 255.
103 Ellis, *Brute*, 500; Rigby, *Allied*, 79–80.
104 Ellis, *Brute*, 510–51.
105 Spector, *Eagle*, 252–54.
106 Ibid., 277–78; Rigby, *Allied*, 76–78; Weinberg, *World*, 439–41.
107 Green, *Providence*, 219–20; Baer, *One Hundred*, 240.
108 Spector, *Eagle*, 279–80.
109 Ellis, *Brute*, 485.
110 David Horner, "General MacArthur's War: The Southwest and Southwest Pacific Campaigns," in Daniel Marston, ed., *The Pacific War: From Pearl Harbor to Hiroshima* (Oxford: Osprey, 2005), 128; Hoyt, *Japan's War*, 327; Rigby, *Allied*, 81; Murray and Millett, *War*, 206–7; Spector, *Eagle*, 226, 230, 232; Tony R. Mullis, "Douglas MacArthur," in James Wilbanks, ed., *Generals of the Army: Marshall, MacArthur, Eisenhower, Arnold, Bradley* (Lexington: University Press of Kentucky, 2013), 90.
111 Kennedy, *Strategy*, 189.
112 Spector, *Eagle*, 254–56; Baer, *One Hundred*, 239–40, 242.
113 Hoyt, *Japan's War*, 340; Rigby, *Allied*, 80; Spector, *Eagle*, 259–61.
114 Spector, *Eagle*, 268, 270–72; Rigby, *Allied*, 70.
115 Spector, *Eagle*, 279, 282–85; Hoyt, *Japan's War*, 327–28, 340–42.
116 Hoyt, *Japan's War*, 343; Ellis, *Brute*, 480–81; Spector, *Eagle*, 292–94.
117 Baer, *One Hundred*, 241; Ellis, *Brute*, 480–81; Kennedy, *Strategy*, 189–90; Hoyt, *Japan's War*, 347.
118 Spector, *Eagle*, 365–67; Green, *Providence*, 211, 214; Baer, *One Hundred*, 267–69; Hoyt, *Japan's War*, 379–81.

119 Robert Smith, "Luzon versus Formosa," in Greenfield, ed., *Command*, 461; Spector, *Eagle*, 418–19; Ellis, *Brute*, 481.
120 Ellis, *Brute*, 481; Spector, *Eagle*, 441–42.
121 Spector, *Eagle*, 440; Ellis, *Brute*, 491; Baer, *One Hundred*, 265–67.
122 Hoyt, *Japan's War*, 366; Millett and Murray, *War*, 370, 496–503.
123 Smith, "Luzon," 476; Baer, *One Hundred*, 262–66; Hoyt, *Japan's War*, 380, 396.
124 Richard Frank, "Ending the Pacific War: 'No Alternative to Annihilation,'" in Marston, ed., *The Pacific War*, 230.
125 Ibid., 230–31, 237–38.
126 Hoyt, *Japan's War*, 393–97; Kennedy, *Strategy*, 193; Frank, "Ending," 231–36.
127 Frank, "Ending," 232–34, 237–40.
128 Ibid., 242; Hoyt, *Japan's War*, 398–99; Weinberg, *World*, 888–89.
129 Kennedy, *Strategy*, 194; Weinberg, *World*, 890; Frank, "Ending," 243.
130 Frank, "Ending," 244–45; Weinberg, *World*, 891–92.
131 Stoler, "Grand Alliance," 160; Fred Charles Iklé, *Every War Must End* (New York: Columbia University Press, 1971), xiii.
132 The Atlantic Charter, August 14, 1941; Rose, *How Wars*, 62; Weinberg, *World*, 591–92.
133 Stoler, "Grand Alliance," 150, 164; Green, *Providence*, 165, 192–94; Rose, *How Wars*, 66–69, 75–76, 110–11.
134 Rose, *How Wars*, 69.
135 Ibid., 61–62.
136 Ibid., 75; Green, *Providence*, 151–53.
137 Rockoff, *Economic*, 223–25; Rose, *How Wars*, 62–63.
138 Stoler, "Grand Alliance," 159–60; Green, *Providence*, 215–18; Weinberg, *World*, 802–5, 836–41.
139 Green, *Providence*, 205–7, 222.

10 THE HOT PEACE AND THE KOREAN WAR, 1945–1953

1 George Orwell, "You and the Atom Bomb," *Tribune* (October 19, 1945), www.orwellfoundation.com/the-orwell-foundation/orwell/essays-and-other-works/you-and-the-atom-bomb/; Julian E. Zelizer, *The Arsenal of Democracy: The Politics of National Security – From World War II to the War on Terrorism* (New York: Basic Books, 2010), 69–70.
2 Chiara Libiseller and Lukas Milevski, "War and Peace: Reaffirming the Distinction," *Survival*, 63:1 (2021), 106–7.
3 John Lewis Gaddis, *Strategies of Containment: A Critical Appraisal of Postwar American National Security* (Oxford: Oxford University Press, 2005), 10–11.
4 Vladislav Zubok and Constantine Pleshakov, *Inside the Kremlin's Cold War: From Stalin to Khrushchev* (Cambridge: Harvard University Press, 1996), 11–17; Gaddis, *Strategies*, 11.

5 Melvyn Leffler, *A Preponderance of Power: National Security, the Truman Administrations, and the Cold War* (Stanford: Stanford University Press, 1992), 14; Gaddis, *Strategies*, 15.
6 Zelizer, *Arsenal*, 4–5, 66, 79–80; Colin Dueck, *Reluctant Crusaders: Power, Culture, and Change in American Grand Strategy* (Princeton: Princeton University Press, 2006), 11–12.
7 Leffler, *Preponderance*, 40–42.
8 Ibid., 16; Gaddis, *Strategies*, 19.
9 Leffler, *Preponderance*, 31–33; Gaddis, *Strategies*, 16–18.
10 John Lewis Gaddis, *George F. Kennan: An American Life* (New York: Penguin, 2011), 216–22; Gaddis, *Strategies*, 18–20; Kennan to Secretary of the State, February 22, 1946, https://nsarchive2.gwu.edu//coldwar/documents/episode-1/kennan.htm.
11 Gaddis, *Strategies*, 20; Gaddis, *Kennan*, 219, 222.
12 Gaddis, *Strategies*, 22–23; Zelizer, *Arsenal*, 66; John Lewis Gaddis, *The Cold War: A New History* (New York: Penguin, 2005), 31; Harry S. Truman, The Truman Doctrine, March 12, 1947, https://avalon.law.yale.edu/20th_century/trudoc.asp; Dueck, *Reluctant*, 100–1; Leffler, *Preponderance*, 447.
13 Howard Jones, *"A New Kind of War": America's Global Strategy and the Truman Doctrine* (New York: Oxford University Press, 1989), vii; Gaddis, *Strategies*, 23; Gaddis, *Kennan*, 257; Steven T. Ross, *American War Plans, 1945–1950: Strategies for Defeating the Soviet Union* (London: Frank Cass, 1996), 11.
14 Gaddis, *Cold War*, 31; Hal Brands, *What Good Is Grand Strategy? Power and Purpose in American Statecraft from Harry S. Truman to George W. Bush* (Ithaca: Cornell University Press, 2014), 24–25; *FRUS, 1947, General, The United Nations* (Washington: USGPO, 1973), 1:733–34.
15 Gaddis, *Strategies*, 24–25; X [George Kennan], "The Sources of Soviet Conduct," *Foreign Affairs*, 25:4 (July 1947), espec. 575, 581–82.
16 Marc Trachtenberg, *History and Strategy* (Princeton: Princeton University Press, 1991), 103–6; Colin Gray, "Harry Truman and the Forming of American Grand Strategy in the Cold War, 1945–1953," in Williamson Murray et al., eds., *The Shaping of Grand Strategy: Policy, Diplomacy, and War* (Cambridge: Cambridge University Press, 2011), 215.
17 Gaddis, *Strategies*, 24–86; Gray, "Truman," 234.
18 Brands, *What Good*, 26–27, 30–31; Zelizer, *Arsenal*, 72–75; Dueck, *Reluctant*, 101; Hal Brands, *The Promise and Pitfalls of Grand Strategy* (Carlisle: Army War College Press, 2012), 18–19.
19 Walter A. McDougall, *Promised Land, Crusader State: The American Encounter with the World since 1776* (New York: Houghton Mifflin, 1997), 180; Hugh Rockoff, *America's Economic Way of War: War and the US Economy from the Spanish-American War to the Persian Gulf War* (Cambridge: Cambridge University Press, 2012), 221; Brands, *What Good*, 29.
20 Brands, *What Good*, 32–33.

21 Leffler, *Preponderance*, 12; NSC 20/4, November 23, 1948, https://history.state.gov/historicaldocuments/frus1948v01p2/d60; Ross, *War Plans, 1945–1950*, 111–19.
22 Harry Truman, Annual Message to the Congress on the State of the Union, January 5, 1949, www.presidency.ucsb.edu/documents/annual-message-the-congress-the-state-the-union-21; McDougall, *Promised*, 181–82; Benjamin Miller, with Ziv Rubinovitz, *Grand Strategy from Truman to Trump* (Chicago: University of Chicago Press, 2020), 94.
23 Alfred E. Eckes Jr., *Opening America's Market: US Foreign Trade Policy since 1776* (Chapel Hill: UNC Press, 1995), 157–58.
24 Ibid., 159–66; John A. Thompson, *A Sense of Power: The Roots of America's Global Role* (Ithaca: Cornell University Press, 2015), 17.
25 Gaddis, *Strategies*, 60.
26 Dueck, *Reluctant*, 102; Brands, *What Good*, 32–33.
27 Gaddis, *Cold War*, 34; Cyril Black et al., *Rebirth: A History of Europe since World War II* (Boulder: Westview, 1992), 84; Gaddis, *Strategies*, 150n.
28 Charles J. Pach Jr., *Arming the Free World: The Origins of the United States Military Assistance Program* (Chapel Hill: UNC Press, 1991), 5; Dueck, *Reluctant*, 92.
29 Gaddis, *Strategies*, 72; Zubok and Pleshakov, *Inside*, 51; David Miller, *The Cold War: A Military History* (New York: St. Martin's, 1998), 332; Brands, *What Good*, 34, 41.
30 Dueck, *Reluctant*, 106.
31 Leffler, *Preponderance*, 84–87.
32 Michael Green, *By More Than Providence: Grand Strategy and American Power in the Asia Pacific since 1783* (New York: Columbia University Press, 2019), 255–58; Harold Tanner, "Guerrilla, Mobile, and Base Warfare in Communist Military Operations in Manchuria, 1945–1947," *The Journal of Military History*, 67 (October 2003), 1206; Ernest May, "1947–48: When Marshall Kept the US out of the War in China," *The Journal of Military History*, 66 (October 2002), 1005.
33 Green, *Providence*, 260; Brands, *What Good*, 30; May, "1947–48," 1008.
34 Green, *Providence*, 255–58; Tanner, "Guerrilla," 1206; Brands, *What Good*, 37–38.
35 Green, *Providence*, 259–60; Edward Dreyer, *China at War, 1901–1949* (London: Longman, 1995), 319–20.
36 Clay Blair, *The Forgotten War: America in Korea, 1950–1953* (New York: Anchor, 1989), 67; John Haynes and Harvey Klehr, *Venona: Decoding Soviet Espionage in America* (New Haven: Yale University Press, 1999), 12.
37 Alan Millett, *The War for Korea, 1950–1951: They Came from the North* (Lawrence: University Press of Kansas, 2010), 206; Sergei Goncharov et al., *Uncertain Partners: Stalin, Mao, and the Korean War* (Palo Alto: Stanford University Press, 1993), 157.
38 Steve Yetiv, *The Absence of Grand Strategy: The United States in the Persian Gulf, 1972–2005* (Baltimore: Johns Hopkins University Press, 2008), 28; Brands, *What Good*, 39.

39 George Herring, *America's Longest War: The United States and Vietnam, 1950–1975*, 3rd ed. (New York: McGraw-Hill, 1996), 14–17; Brian VanDeMark, *Road to Disaster: A New History of America's Descent into Vietnam* (New York: HarperCollins, 2018), 117–18.
40 *The Pentagon Papers: The Secret History of the Vietnam War* (New York: Racehorse, 2017), 28–29; Herring, *America's Longest*, 17, 24.
41 Brands, *What Good*, 55; Dueck, *Reluctant*, 91.
42 Ross, *War Plans, 1945–1950*, ix, 3, 6; Brands, *What Good*, 27–28.
43 Zelizer, *Arsenal*, 71–73, 76; Ross, *War Plans, 1945–1950*, ix–x; *FRUS, 1947, General; The United Nations*, 1:760–61; John Gans, *White House Warriors: How the National Security Council Transformed the American Way of War* (New York: Liveright, 2019), 3, 5, 13.
44 Allan Millett et al., *For the Common Defense: A Military History of the United States from 1607 to 2012*, 3rd ed. (New York: Free Press, 2012), 448–50; Blair, *Forgotten*, 11–13, 17.
45 Gray, "Truman," 243–44; Blair, *Forgotten*, 12.
46 Gregory Pedlow, "The Evolution of NATO Strategy, 1949–1969," in Gregory Pedlow, ed., *NATO Strategy Documents, 1949–1969* (Brussels: NATO Archives, 1999), xi, xiv–xv.
47 DC 13, March 28, 1950 (and decision of April 1, 1950), and MC 14/1, December 9, 1952, in *NATO Strategy*, 117–20, 195, 201–2, 205, 212.
48 Ross, *War Plans, 1945–1950*, 12–14.
49 Ibid., 15–19, 74–75; Gray, "Truman," 245–46.
50 Brands, *What Good*, 36.
51 Ibid., 43; Ross, *War Plans, 1945–1950*, 103, 108–10; Brands, *Promise*, 18; Arthur A. Stein, "Domestic Constraints, Extended Deterrence, and the Incoherence of Grand Strategy: The United States, 1938–1950," in Richard Rosencrance and Arthur Stein, eds., *The Domestic Bases of Grand Strategy* (Ithaca: Cornell University Press, 1993), 97.
52 Gaddis, *Strategies*, 87–88.
53 The Executive Secretary on the United States Objectives and Programs for National Security, April 14, 1950, "NSC-68: A Report to the National Security Council," *Naval War College Review* (May/June 1975), 58, 105, 107 (hereafter NSC 68); NSC 20/4, November 23, 1948. NSC 68 often uses "policy" when "strategy" is more appropriate.
54 NSC 68, 68–71, 77, 80, 94, 96.
55 Ibid., 108; Libiseller and Milevski, "War and Peace," 106–7.
56 NSC 68, editor's note, 52; Brands, *What Good*, 47; Alonzo Hamby, "Harry S. Truman: Foreign Affairs," https://millercenter.org/president/truman/foreign-affairs.
57 Blair, *Forgotten*, 36–37; Green, *Providence*, 266.
58 Blair, *Forgotten*, 40–43; Green, *Providence*, 266–68; Goncharov et al., *Uncertain*, 131–32; Alan R. Millett, *The War for Korea, 1945–1950: A House Burning* (Lawrence: University Press of Kansas, 2005), 135, 142.

59 Michael Hunt, "Beijing and the Korean Crisis, June 1950–June 1951," *Political Science Quarterly*, 107:3 (autumn 1992), 457; Goncharov et al., *Uncertain*, 133, 140–41, 147–49; Millett, *Korea, 1945–1950*, 193–95, 212–13; Millett, *Korea, 1950–1951*, 46–47; Edgar O'Ballance, *Korea: 1950–1953* (Malabar: Krieger, 1985), 24–26.

60 Zubok and Pleshakov, *Inside*, 62–64; William Stueck, *Rethinking the Korean War: A New Diplomatic and Strategic History* (Princeton: Princeton University Press, 2002), 73.

61 Millett, *Korea, 1950–1951*, 48; Goncharov et al., *Uncertain*, 140–41, 145–46.

62 Millett, *Korea, 1950–1951*, 12, 50–51.

63 O'Ballance, *Korea*, 30–37; Terry Sandler, *The Korean War: No Victors, No Vanquished* (Lexington: University Press of Kentucky, 1999), 52.

64 Goncharov et al., *Uncertain*, 155; UN Resolutions 82 and 83, June 25, 27, 1950, http://unscr.com/en/resolutions/doc/82; Steven Nerheim, *NSC-81/1 and the Evolution of US War Aims in Korea, June–October 1950* (Carlisle: US Army War College, 2000), 5–6; Gary Hess, *Presidential Decisions for War: Korea, Vietnam, and the Persian Gulf* (Baltimore: Johns Hopkins University Press, 2001), 23, 25; Anne Pierce, *Woodrow Wilson and Harry Truman: Mission and Power in American Foreign Policy* (New Brunswick: Transaction, 2007), 249.

65 Paul Edwards, *The Korean War* (Malabar: Krieger, 1999), 27.

66 Zelizer, *Arsenal*, 99; Gaddis, *Cold War*, 41.

67 Dueck, *Reluctant*, 107; Millett, *Korea, 1950–1951*, 116–19; Harry Truman, *Memoirs by Harry S. Truman* (New York: Doubleday, 1955), 2:335–37, 340; Zelizer, *Arsenal*, 99; John Mueller, *Retreat from Doomsday: The Obsolescence of Major War* (New York: Basic Books, 1989), 122.

68 J. Lawton Collins, *War in Peacetime: The History and Lessons of Korea* (Boston: Houghton Mifflin, 1969), vii; Hess, *Presidential*, 34.

69 Hess, *Presidential*, 35–37, 116.

70 Ibid., 34–37; Millett, *Korea, 1950–1951*, 121–22; Dean Acheson, *The Korean War* (New York: Norton, 1971), 26, 32–34; US Government, Department of State, "Authority of the President to Repel the Attack in Korea," Department of State Memorandum of July 3, 1950, *Department of State Bulletin*, 23 (July 31, 1950), 173–77.

71 Collins, *War*, 32.

72 Marilyn Young. "Limited War, Unlimited," Library of Congress Lecture, Washington, July 8, 2009, www.loc.gov/today/cyberlc/feature_wdesc.php?rec=4683, minute 23:00; Hess, *Presidential*, 20–27; The President's News Conference of June 29, 1950, https://teachingamericanhistory.org/library/document/the-presidents-news-conference-of-june-29-1950/; Millett, *Korea, 1950–1951*, 124; Truman, *Memoirs*, 2:331–464. The only example I found here of Truman calling the war in Korea a war is in his Atlee meeting account, ibid., 2:406.

73 Hess, *Presidential*, 38; Gregory E. Fehlings, "America's First Limited War," *Naval War College Review*, 53:3 (summer 2000), 121; Zelizer, *Arsenal*, 107; Sandler, *Korean*, 54.

74 Collins, *War*, 23; Sandler, *Korean*, 55–56, 58–59, 63.

75 Millett, *Korea, 1950–1951*, 86, 126, 170; Taewoo Kim, "Limited War, Unlimited Targets: US Air Force Bombing of North Korea during the Korean War, 1950–1953," *Critical Asian Studies*, 44:3 (2012), 489; Collins, *War*, 18–19; James Schnabel, *Policy and Direction: The First Year* (Washington: Center of Military History, 1992), 76.

76 David Zabecki, "Stand or Die – 1950 Defense of Korea's Pusan Perimeter," *Historynet* [n.d.], www.historynet.com/stand-or-die-1950-defense-of-koreas-pusan-perimeter.htm.

77 Millett, *Korea, 1950–1951*, 132–33; Collins, *War*, 81–82; Omar Bradley and Clay Blair, *A General's Life* (New York: Simon and Schuster, 1983), 546.

78 Schnabel, *Policy*, 139–42, 145–72; Mathew B. Ridgway, *The War in Korea: How We Met the Challenge, How All-Out Asian War Was Averted, Why MacArthur Was Dismissed, Why Today's War Objectives Must Be Limited* (London: Barrie and Rockliff, 1967), 38–39; Bradley and Blair, *General's Life*, 544–46.

79 Schnabel, *Policy*, 172–77; Goncharov et al., *Uncertain*, 171–72; Millett, *Korea, 1950–1951*, 273–74; Nerheim, *NSC-81/1*, 10.

80 National Security Council Report, NSC 81/1, United States Courses of Action with Respect to Korea, September 9, 1950, History and Public Policy Program Digital Archive, Truman Presidential Museum and Library, http://digitalarchive.wilsoncenter.org/document/116194.pdf?v=b5f4cbf0ae773fe6970014edb854029e.

81 Acheson, *Korean War*, 57–59; Bernard Brodie, *War and Politics* (New York: Macmillan, 1973), 70–71; George Herring, *From Colony to Superpower: US Foreign Relations since 1776* (Oxford: Oxford University Press, 2011), 641; Millett, *Korea, 1950–1951*, 145, 147.

82 Matthew Ridgway, *The Korean War* (New York: Da Capo, 1967), 44; Douglas MacArthur, *Reminiscences* (New York: McGraw-Hill, 1964), 358; Hess, *Presidential*, 45; Collins, *War*, 149; *FRUS, 1950, Korea* (Washington: USGPO, 1976), 7:393–95, 458–61, 502–10, 600–3, 712–21, 781–82.

83 Hess, *Presidential*, 38, 44–45; John M. Pruitt Jr., "Limited War: A Model for Entry, Conduct, and Termination" (MA thesis, Naval Postgraduate School, 1984), 124; *FRUS, 1950, Korea*, 7:272 and n.3; Dan Reiter, *How Wars End* (Princeton: Princeton University Press, 2009), 67, 79.

84 Nerheim, *NSC-81/1*, 13, 16, 20–21; Stueck, *Rethinking*, 94–96, 98; Bradford Lee, "Strategic Interaction: Theory and History for Practitioners," in Thomas Mahnken, ed., *Competitive Strategies for the 21st Century* (Palo Alto: Stanford University Press, 2012), 44n.9; Reiter, *How Wars*, 63, 67–68, 76; NSC 81/1; *FRUS, 1950, Korea*, 7, doc. 640, https://history.state.gov/historicaldocuments/frus1950v07/d640; Collins, *War*, 147.

85 NSC 81/1; Truman, *Memoirs*, 2:345.

86 Schnabel, *Policy*, 183–84; Millett, *Korea, 1950–1951*, 274–75; Goncharov et al., *Uncertain*, 171.

87 Stueck, *Rethinking*, 89; Millett, *Korea, 1950–1951*, 279–82; Billy Mossman, *Ebb and Flow, November 1950–July 1951* (Washington: Center of Military History, 1990), 20; Millett, *Korea, 1950–1951*, 285, 289–90.

88 Stueck, *Rethinking*, 100; D. Clayton James, with Anne Sharp Wells, *Refighting the Last War: Command and Crisis in Korea* (New York: Free Press, 1993), 17; Christopher M. Gacek, *The Logic of Force: The Dilemma of Limited War in American Foreign Policy* (New York: Columbia University Press, 1994), 55; Acheson, *Korean War*, 55; Truman, *Memoirs*, 2:361–62; Paul Nitze et al., *From Hiroshima to Glasnost: At the Center of Decision – A Memoir* (New York: Grove Weidenfeld, 1989), 108; Millett, *Korea, 1950–1951*, 283; Hess, *Presidential*, 54; Nathan Yu-jen Lai, "United States Policy and the Diplomacy of Limited War in Korea, 1950–1951" (PhD dissertation, University of Massachusetts, 1974), 147–48; Collins, *War*, 175.

89 Goncharov et al., *Uncertain*, 174–75, 180–81; Stueck, *Rethinking*, 102–3, 108; Hunt, "Beijing," 464–65.

90 Jian Chen, "China's Changing Aims during the Korean War, 1950–1951," *The Journal of American-East Asian Relations*, 1:1 (spring 1992), 19, 40; Hunt, "Beijing," 463; Shu Guang Zhang, *Mao's Military Romanticism: China and the Korean War, 1950–1953* (Lawrence: University Press of Kansas, 1995), 87–88; Goncharov et al., *Uncertain*, 182.

91 Zhang, *Mao's*, 101; Millett, *Korea, 1950–1951*, 311–16, 339–40, 344–47, 354; Xiaobing Li, *China's Battle for Korea: The 1951 Spring Offensive* (Bloomington: Indiana University Press, 2014), 45–46, 52; Richard Stewart, ed., *American Military History: The United States Army in a Global Era, 1917–2008* (Washington: Center of Military History, 2010), 2:232–33. The numbers given for Chinese and UN forces vary widely.

92 Hess, *Presidential*, 59–62; Conrad Crane, "To Avert Impending Disaster: American Military Plans to Use Atomic Weapons during the Korean War," *Journal of Strategic Studies*, 23:2 (June 2000), 77; Bernard Brodie, *The Meaning of Limited War* (Santa Monica: RAND, 1958), 13–14; Robert Saundby, "The Doctrine of Proportional Force," *Military Review*, 37 (October 1957), 88.

93 Crane, "Avert," 75–76; Larry Elowitz, "Korea and Vietnam: Limited War and the American Political System" (PhD dissertation, University of Florida, 1972), 214; Colin F. Jackson, "Lost Chance or Lost Horizon? Strategic Opportunity and Escalation Risk in the Korean War, April–July 1951," *Journal of Strategic Studies*, 33:2 (2010), 276–77; James, *Refighting*, 18–19; MacArthur, *Reminiscences*, 337; James M. Gavin, "Why Limited War?" *Ordnance*, 42 (April 1958), 809.

94 Schnabel, *Policy*, 240–47; Kim, "Limited," 489; Elowitz, "Korea," 215; Gacek, *Logic*, 58–60; Edmund Traverso, ed., *Korea and the Limits of Limited War* (Menlo Park: Addison-Wesley Publishing, 1970), 35; MacArthur, *Reminiscences*, 331.

95 Kim, "Limited," 489; Rosemary Foot, *A Substitute for Victory: The Politics of Peacemaking at the Korean Armistice Talks* (Ithaca: Cornell University Press, 1990), 213–14.

96 Collins, *War*, 205–6, 233–34.

97 Ibid., 235–36; Zhang, *Mao's*, 217–18; Li, *China's*, 53; Stewart, ed., *American*, 2:234–35.

98 Collins, *War*, 246–248, 252; Ridgway, *Korean War*, 82.

99 Collins, *War*, 263–65; Gacek, *Logic*, 66; *FRUS, 1951, Korea and China* (Washington: USGPO, 1983), 7/1:174–75.
100 Stewart, ed., *American*, 2:235–37; Li, *China's*, 58–60.
101 Stewart, ed., *American*, 2:238.
102 Ibid., 2:238–39; Millett, *Korea, 1950–1951*, 420–26.
103 William Kaufmann, *Policy Objectives and Military Action in the Korean War* (Santa Monica: RAND, 1956), 16n.12.
104 Collins, *War*, 298–300; Schnabel, *Policy*, 380–87, 392–96.
105 Collins, *War*, 303–6; NSC 48/5, *FRUS, Asia and the Pacific* (Washington: USGPO, 1977), 1/1:33–34; Schnabel, *Policy*, 395–96; Mossman, *Ebb*, 490; Carter Malkasian, "Toward a Better Understanding of Attrition: The Korean and Vietnam Wars," *The Journal of Military History*, 68:3 (July 2004), 922; Hunt, "Beijing," 465–68.
106 Kaufmann, *Policy*, 16.
107 Hunt, "Beijing," 467; Li, *China's*, 62–64; Schnabel, *Policy*, 389–90.
108 Jackson, "Lost," 256 and n.5, 257, 269–71; C. Turner Joy, *How Communists Negotiate* (New York: Macmillan, [1955] 2013), 166; Foot, *Substitute*, 36; James Van Fleet, "The Truth about Korea: Part 1. From a Man Now Free to Speak," *Life*, 34:19 (May 11, 1953), 127, 132.
109 Zhang, *Mao's*, 220, 225–26; Jackson, "Lost," 273–74; Stueck, *Rethinking*, 138–39; Sun Tzu, *The Art of War*, Samuel Griffith, trans. (London: Oxford University Press, 1961), 120.
110 Jackson, "Lost," 256–74; Henry Kissinger, *Nuclear Weapons and Foreign Policy* (New York: Harper, 1957), 152; Brodie, *Meaning*, 12; Raymond Aron, "Can War in the Atomic Age Be Limited?" *Confluence*, 5 (July 1956), 104.
111 Paul Pillar, *Negotiating Peace: War Termination as a Bargaining Process* (Princeton: Princeton University Press, 1983), 55; Acheson, *Korean War*, 119–22; Collins, *War*, 327–30; Ridgway, *Korean War*, 182; Truman, *Memoirs*, 2:456–59.
112 James Van Fleet, "The Truth about Korea: Part II. How We Can Win with What We Have," *Life* (May 8, 1953), 164; Joy, *How Communists*, 30–31.
113 Walter Hermes, *Truce Tent and Fighting Front* (Washington: Center of Military History, 1992), ix, 23, 32–34, 44–45, 51.
114 Ridgway, *Korean War*, 190–93; Joy, *How Communists*, 128–29, 139–40, 165–66.
115 Steven Casey, *Selling the Korean War: Propaganda, Politics, and Public Opinion in the United States, 1950–1953* (Oxford: Oxford University Press, 2008), 359; Bruce Lesh, "Limited War or Rollback of Communism?: Truman, MacArthur, and the Korean Conflict," *OAH Magazine of History*, 22:4 (October 2008), 50; Hess, *Presidential*, 70, 227; Bernard Brodie, "Learning to Fight a Limited War," in William Gerbering and Bernard Brodie, eds., *The Political Dimension in Strategy: Five Papers* (Los Angeles: UCLA Press, 1968), 30–31; Leffler, *Preponderance*, 447.
116 Paul Lashmar, "Stalin's 'Hot' War," *New Statesman and Society*, 9:388 (February 2, 1996), 4; Zubok and Pleshakov, *Inside*, 70–71; Stueck, *Rethinking*, 157–58, 171; Avram Agov, "North Korea's Alliances and the Unfinished Korean War," *The Journal of Korean Studies*, 18:2 (fall 2013), 237–38; Millett, *Korea, 1950–1951*, 14.

117 Foot, *Substitute*, 215; Collins, *War*, 331; Joy, *How Communists*, 165–66.
118 Gideon Rose, *How Wars End: Why We Always Fight the Last Battle* (New York: Simon and Schuster, 2010), 140–42, 150; James, *Refighting*, 99.
119 Joy, *How Communists*, 160; Fred Charles Iklé, *Every War Must End* (New York: Columbia University Press, 1971), 90.
120 Conrad C. Crane, *American Airpower Strategy in Korea, 1950–1953* (Lawrence: University Press of Kansas, 2000), 116–28.
121 Zhang, *Mao's*, 187, 216; James, *Refighting*, 123–25.
122 James, *Refighting*, 111; Crane, *American*, 155–57.
123 Millett, *Korea, 1950–1951*, 122.
124 Zhang, *Mao's*, 233; James, *Refighting*, 116–17.
125 Crane, "Avert," 72–73.
126 Allan Millett, *Their War for Korea: American, Asian, and European Combatants and Civilians, 1945–1953* (Dulles: Brassey's, 2002), 111; Reiter, *How Wars*, 89; Yafeng Xia, *Negotiating with the Enemy: US–China Talks during the Cold War, 1949–1972* (Bloomington: Indiana University Press, 2006), 71.
127 Hermes, *Truce*, 419–20; Gacek, *Logic*, 73–75.
128 Gacek, *Logic*, 76–77; Crane, *American*, 158–59; Foot, *Substitute*, 213.
129 Kim, "Limited," 487–90.
130 Gacek, *Logic*, 79–81; Rose, *How Wars*, 135–36; Foot, *Substitute*, 178; Crane, *American*, 281; Hermes, *Truce*, 430–32.
131 Gacek, *Logic*, 81; Rose, *How Wars*, 136; Stueck, *Rethinking*, 174–76, 189–92, 230–31; Foot, *Substitute*, 184–85; Millett, *Their War*, 6; James, *Refighting*, 112–14; Zhang, *Mao's*, 242–43.
132 James, *Refighting*, 25, 114–15; Gacek, *Logic*, 81; Rose, *How Wars*, 156.
133 Douglas MacArthur, Farewell Address to Congress, April 19, 1951, www.americanrhetoric.com/speeches/douglasmacarthurfarewelladdress.htm.
134 Rockoff, *Economic*, 246–49, 253–54; James, *Refighting*, 109.
135 Dueck, *Reluctant*, 103; Millett, *Korea, 1950–1951*, 206.
136 Dueck, *Reluctant*, 104.
137 Thomas C. Schelling, *Arms and Influence* (New Haven: Yale University Press, 1966), 136.
138 Gray, "Truman," 227, 238; Blair, *Forgotten*, 4.
139 Truman, *Memoirs*, 2:290.

11 THE HOT PEACE: THE EISENHOWER, KENNEDY, AND JOHNSON YEARS, 1953–1969

1 Julian E. Zelizer, *The Arsenal of Democracy: The Politics of National Security – From World War II to the War on Terrorism* (New York: Basic Books, 2010), 146–47; George C. Herring, *The American Century: US Foreign Relations, 1893–2014* (Oxford: Oxford University Press, 2017), 354.

2 Steven Metz, *Eisenhower as Strategist: The Coherent Use of Military Power in War and Peace* (Carlisle: Strategic Studies Institute, 1993), 47–50.
3 John Lewis Gaddis, *Strategies of Containment: A Critical Appraisal of Postwar American National Security* (Oxford: Oxford University Press, 2005), 128–33; Metz, *Eisenhower*, 67–68; NSC 153/1, *FRUS, 1952–1954, National Security Affairs* (Washington: USGPO, 1984), 2/1:378–85; NSC 5501, January 7, 1955, *FRUS, 1955–1957, National Security Policy* (Washington: USGPO, 1999), 19:25. NSC 153/1 was supplanted in October 1953 by NSC 162/2, which was itself superseded by NSC 5501 in January 1955.
4 *FRUS, 1952–1954, National Security Affairs*, 2/1:323–26, 349–54, 360–66; Gaddis, *Strategies*, 143–44.
5 NSC 162/2, *FRUS, 1952–1954, National Security Affairs*, 2/1:578–82; NSC 5501, *FRUS, 1952–1954, National Security Policy* (Washington: USGPO, 1990), 19:30; Gaddis, *Strategies*, 138; NSC 174, *FRUS, 1952–1954, Eastern Europe; Soviet Union; Eastern Mediterranean* (Washington: USGPO, 1988), 8:110–16; Herring, *American*, 366.
6 Marc Trachtenberg, *History and Strategy* (Princeton: Princeton University Press, 1991), 141; Metz, *Eisenhower*, 62.
7 Metz, *Eisenhower*, 52.
8 Ibid., 54, 68–69; D. Clayton James, with Anne Sharp Wells, *Refighting the Last War: Command and Crisis in Korea* (New York: Free Press, 1993), 117; Douglas Kinnard, *President Eisenhower and Strategy Management: A Study in Defense Politics* (Lexington: University Press of Kentucky, 1977), 26; John Foster Dulles, Speech before the Council of Foreign Relations, January 12, 1954, https://babel.hathitrust.org/cgi/pt?id=umn.31951d024881358&view=1up&seq=4; Gaddis, *Strategies*, 144–45.
9 Trachtenberg, *History*, 132–34.
10 Metz, *Eisenhower*, 69–70; Gaddis, *Strategies*, 164–65, 173.
11 Gaddis, *Strategies*, 151; Metz, *Eisenhower*, 71.
12 Gaddis, *Strategies*, 146–47, 165, 178; Herring, *American*, 363–65, 374–75; Metz, *Eisenhower*, 72.
13 Zelizer, *Arsenal*, 138–43; Gaddis, *Strategies*, 184–87.
14 Gaddis, *Strategies*, 163; Trachtenberg, *History*, 40.
15 Gaddis, *Strategies*, 157, 187, 195; Vladislav Zubok and Constantine Pleshakov, *Inside the Kremlin's Cold War: From Stalin to Khrushchev* (Cambridge: Harvard University Press, 1996), 157, 164, 174–77; Odd Arne Westad, *The Global Cold War: Third World Interventions and the Making of Our Times* (Cambridge: Cambridge University Press, 2011), 69–70.
16 Gaddis, *Strategies*, 149, 167–69, 188–89, 192–93; Zelizer, *Arsenal*, 129–31; Herring, *American*, 364–65.
17 Gaddis, *Strategies*, 174–76; Metz, *Eisenhower*, 74; Westad, *Global*, 131–32.
18 Westad, *Global*, 123–26; Herring, *American*, 375–78.
19 Herring, *American*, 378–80; David Miller, *The Cold War: A Military History* (New York: St. Martin's, 1998), 225.

20 Westad, *Global*, 146–48.
21 Gaddis, *Strategies*, 152–55; Metz, *Eisenhower*, 72–74; Zelizer, *Arsenal*, 136–37.
22 Metz, *Eisenhower*, 72; Gaddis, *Strategies*, 155–57; Herring, *American*, 379.
23 Metz, *Eisenhower*, 72; James Patterson, *Grand Expectations: The United States, 1945–1974* (New York: Oxford University Press, 1996), 312.
24 Alfred E. Eckes Jr., *Opening America's Market: US Foreign Trade Policy since 1776* (Chapel Hill: UNC Press, 1995), 167–70, 175; Westad, *Global*, 26.
25 George Herring, *America's Longest War: The United States and Vietnam, 1950–1975*, 3rd ed. (New York: McGraw-Hill, 1996), 26–27; Gaddis, *Strategies*, 128–29.
26 Seth Jacobs, *Cold War Mandarin: Ngo Dinh Diem and the Origins of America's War in Vietnam, 1950–1963* (Lanham: Rowman and Littlefield, 2006), 39–42, 98–99; Herring, *America's Longest*, 27, 43–44, 53, 61–62; Herring, *American*, 363; Brian VanDeMark, *Road to Disaster: A New History of America's Descent into Vietnam* (New York: HarperCollins, 2018), 126.
27 Jacobs, *Mandarin*, 39–42; VanDeMark, *Road*, 124–26, 129; Allan Millett and Peter Maslowski, *For the Common Defense: A Military History of the United States of America*, 2nd ed. (New York: Free Press, 1994), 572–73; NSC 5429/2, *FRUS, 1952–1954, East Asia and the Pacific* (Washington: USGPO, 1984), 12/1:770–74; Dale Walton, *The Myth of Inevitable US Defeat in Vietnam* (Abingdon: Routledge, 2002), 14–15.
28 Summary, *FRUS, 1964–1968, National Security Policy* (Washington: USGPO, 2001), 10:summary; NSC 5906/1, *FRUS, 1958–1960, National Security Policy, Arms Control and Disarmament* (Washington: USGPO, 1996), 8:293–313.
29 Gaddis, *Strategies*, 160, 170.
30 Ibid., 162.
31 Ibid., 169–74.
32 Ibid., 171; Donald Stoker, *Why America Loses Wars: Limited War and US Strategy from the Korean War to the Present* (Cambridge: Cambridge University Press, 2019), 113–17. An example: Henry A. Kissinger, *Nuclear Weapons and Foreign Policy* (New York: Harper, 1957), 174–202.
33 VanDeMark, *Road*, 8–9; Gary Hess, *Presidential Decisions for War: Korea, Vietnam, and the Persian Gulf* (Baltimore: Johns Hopkins University Press, 2001), 81.
34 Gaddis, *Strategies*, 200–2.
35 Ibid., 202–4; John F. Kennedy, Special Message to the Congress on the Defense Budget, March 28, 1961, presidency.ucsb.edu/documents/special-message-the-congress-the-defense-budget.
36 Westad, *Global*, 136, 162–63.
37 William Rosenau, "The Kennedy Administration, US Foreign Internal Security Assistance, and the Challenge of 'Subterranean War,' 1961–63," *Small Wars and Insurgencies*, 14:3 (2003), 66, 73–74; Zelizer, *Arsenal*, 154; W. W. Rostow, *The Stages of Economic Growth: A Non-Communist Manifesto* (Cambridge: Cambridge University Press, 1960).
38 B. H. Liddell Hart, "War, Limited," *Harper's*, 192:1150 (March 1946), 193–203 and *The Revolution in Warfare* (New Haven: Yale University Press, 1947), 36;

Stoker, *Why*, 29–36; Arthur E. Brown, "The Strategy of Limited War," in Arthur F. Lykke Jr., ed., *Military Strategy: Theory and Application* (Carlisle: Army War College Press, 1993), 221.

39 *FRUS, 1961–1963, National Security Policy* (Washington: USGPO, 1996), espec. 8:1–11, 14–15.

40 Ibid., 8:19–20, 33; Gaddis, *Strategies*, 199, 213; Francis Gavin, "The Myth of Flexible Response: United States Strategy in Europe during the 1960s," *International History Review*, 23:4 (December 2001), 849.

41 Gaddis, *Strategies*, 200; Herring, *American*, 403; *FRUS, 1961–1963, National Security Policy*, 8:222; NSC 5906/1, *FRUS, 1958–1960, National Security Policy*, 8:293.

42 John F. Kennedy, Special Message to the Congress on the Defense Budget, March 28, 1961, presidency.ucsb.edu/documents/special-message-the-congress-the-defense-budget; Gaddis, *Strategies*, 199.

43 Aaron L. Friedberg, *In the Shadow of the Garrison State: America's Anti-Statism and Its Cold War Grand Strategy* (Princeton: Princeton University Press, 2000), 141–43.

44 Gaddis, *Strategies*, 216, 224–25.

45 Ibid., 214–15, 219; Gavin, "Myth," 855–65; Millett and Maslowski, *Common*, 2nd ed., 531–32.

46 Gaddis, *Strategies*, 217; Francis Gavin, *Nuclear Statecraft* (Ithaca: Cornell University Press, 2012), 4, 23–24; Trachtenberg, *History*, 14 and n.21, 45–46. A brief overview of so-called "limited nuclear war" theory (with the standard definitional weaknesses): Andrew L. Ross, "The Origins of Limited Nuclear War Theory," in Jeffrey Larsen and Kerry Kartchner, eds., *On Limited Nuclear War in the 21st Century* (Stanford: Stanford University Press, 2014), 21–48.

47 Trachtenberg, *History*, 43; Gavin, "Myth," 850–53; Gaddis, *Strategies*, 218.

48 Gaddis, *Strategies*, 205–7, 226, 228.

49 Ibid., 220, 222.

50 Herring, *American*, 415–17; Westad, *Global*, 134–43.

51 Herring, *American*, 414–15.

52 Ibid., 417–20.

53 Gaddis, *Strategies*, 223–24.

54 Hugh Rockoff, *America's Economic Way of War: War and the US Economy from the Spanish-American War to the Persian Gulf War* (Cambridge: Cambridge University Press, 2012), 284–86; Friedberg, *Shadow*, 134, 145–47.

55 Friedberg, *Shadow*, 147; Rockoff, *Economic*, 286, 290.

56 VanDeMark, *Road*, 23–27.

57 Ibid., 30–45; Zelizer, *Arsenal*, 149–50.

58 VanDeMark, *Road*, 50–55.

59 Herring, *American*, 409–11; Zubok and Pleshakov, *Inside*, 248–53; John Lewis Gaddis, *We Now Know: Rethinking Cold War History* (Oxford: Oxford University Press, 1998), 143–49.

60 Herring, *American*, 408; VanDeMark, *Road*, 56, 64, 77–78; Zelizer, *Arsenal*, 160–65.

61 Zelizer, *Arsenal*, 169; VanDeMark, *Road*, 99, 103, 109.
62 VanDeMark, *Road*, 11–12.
63 Herring, *American*, 424–25, 432; Zubok and Pleshakov, *Inside*, 272–74.
64 James T. Patterson, *Restless Giant: The United States from Watergate to Bush v. Gore* (Oxford: Oxford University Press, 2007), 525–30.
65 Herring, *American*, 432–33; Philip Short, *Mao: A Life* (New York: Henry Holt, 1999), 504–5.
66 Lyndon Johnson, State of the Union Address, January 10, 1967, www.infoplease.com/primary-sources/government/presidential-speeches/state-union-address-lyndon-b-johnson-january-10-1967; Justin Vaïsse, *Zbigniew Brzezinski: America's Grand Strategist*, Catherine Porter, trans. (Cambridge: Harvard University Press, 2018), 93; Herring, *American*, 443, 457.
67 Herring, *American*, 457–58; Black et al., *Rebirth*, 123–24.
68 Herring, *American*, 433–37; Robert Doughty et al., *Warfare in the Western World: Military Operations since 1871* (Lexington: D. C. Heath, 1997), 2:967; David Coleman, "Lyndon Johnson and the Dominican Intervention of 1965," *National Security Archive*, April 28, 2015, https://nsarchive2.gwu.edu/NSAEBB/NSAEBB513/.
69 Herring, *American*, 447–49, 452.
70 Ibid., 443; Gavin, "Myth," 865–70.
71 Herring, *American*, 445–46; Michael Green, *By More Than Providence: Grand Strategy and American Power in the Asia Pacific since 1783* (New York: Columbia University Press, 2019), 317–18.
72 Patterson, *Restless*, 530–32, 542–48, 584; David Kaiser, *American Tragedy: Kennedy, Johnson, and the Origins of the Vietnam War* (Cambridge: Belknap Harvard, 2000), 284–85.
73 Patterson, *Restless*, 532–542, 569–77, 589.
74 Friedberg, *Shadow*, 147.
75 Rockoff, *Economic*, 287.
76 Ibid., 287–88, 294, 296; Herring, *American*, 459.

12 THE VIETNAM WAR, 1961–1969

1 Max Hastings, *Vietnam: An Epic Tragedy* (New York: HarperCollins, 2018), 102; Lien-Hang T. Nguyen, *Hanoi's War: An International History of the War for Peace in Vietnam* (Chapel Hill: UNC Press, 2012), 2–3; Van Nguyen Duong, *The Tragedy of the Vietnam War: A South Vietnamese Officer's Analysis* (Jefferson: McFarland, 2008), 45.
2 Mao Tse-Tung, "The Three Stages of Protracted War," in Committee for the Publication of the Selected Works of Mao Tse-tung, Central Committee of the Communist Party of China, eds., *Selected Military Writings* (Peking: Foreign Language Press, 1967), 210–19; Ian Beckett, *Modern Insurgencies: Guerrillas and Their Opponents since 1750* (London: Routledge, 2001), 73–76; Rod Paschall, "Low-Intensity Conflict Doctrine: Who Needs It?" *Parameters*, 15:3 (fall 1985), 34.

3 Douglas Pike, *PAVN: The People's Army of Vietnam* (Novato: Presidio, 1986), 213–53.
4 Richard Hunt, *Pacification: The American Struggle for Vietnam's Hearts and Minds* (Boulder: Westview, 1995), 12–15; Cecil Currey, *Victory at Any Cost: The Genius of Viet Nam's Gen. Vo Nguyen Giap* (Washington: Brassey's, 1997), 234; William Duiker, *The Communist Road to Power*, 2nd ed. (Boulder: Westview, 1996), 184–86; Nguyen, *Hanoi's War*, 31, 45–51; Harry G. Summers Jr., *Historical Atlas of the Vietnam War* (New York: Houghton Mifflin, 1995), 70.
5 George Herring, *America's Longest War: The United States and Vietnam, 1950–1975*, 3rd ed. (New York: McGraw-Hill, 1996), 83, 91, 94.
6 *FRUS, Vietnam, 1961–1963, Vietnam, 1961* (Washington: USGPO, 1988), 1:95; NSAM 52, May 11, 1961, https://fas.org/irp/offdocs/nsam-jfk/nsam-52.htm; *FRUS, 1961–1963, Vietnam*, 1:1–11.
7 *FRUS, 1961–1963, Vietnam, 1961*, 1:3; NSAM 111, November 22, 1961, https://fas.org/irp/offdocs/nsam-jfk/nsam111.htm; Herring, *America's Longest*, 94–96, 101–2; Brian VanDeMark, *Road to Disaster: A New History of America's Descent into Vietnam* (New York: HarperCollins, 2018), 135–36.
8 Summers, *Atlas*, 74; Hunt, *Pacification*, 20–24; Duiker, *Communist*, 230–31; Seth Jacobs, *Cold War Mandarin: Ngo Dinh Diem and the Origins of America's War in Vietnam, 1950–1963* (Lanham: Rowman and Littlefield, 2006), 125–27; David Milne, *America's Rasputin: Walt Rostow and the Vietnam War* (New York: Hill and Wang, 2008), 106–7; Herring, *America's Longest*, 94–95, 98–99; Gregory Daddis, *Westmoreland's War: Reassessing American Strategy in Vietnam* (Oxford: Oxford University Press, 2014), 49.
9 Nguyen, *Hanoi's War*, 59–61.
10 George C. Herring, *The American Century: US Foreign Relations, 1893–2014* (Oxford: Oxford University Press, 2017), 409; Dale Walton, *The Myth of Inevitable US Defeat in Vietnam* (Abingdon: Routledge, 2002), 72–74; Herring, *America's Longest*, 86; Daddis, *Westmoreland's*, 53.
11 John Gans, *White House Warriors: How the National Security Council Transformed the American Way of War* (New York: Liveright, 2019), 27–28; Herring, *America's Longest*, 116–17; VanDeMark, *Road*, 166–72.
12 Milne, *Rasputin*, 126.
13 Nguyen, *Hanoi's War*, 63–66; VanDeMark, *Road*, 135.
14 Herring, *America's Longest*, 126–30; NSAM 273, November 26, 1963, https://fas.org/irp/offdocs/nsam-lbj/nsam-273.htm; VanDeMark, *Road*, 362; David Kaiser, *American Tragedy: Kennedy, Johnson, and the Origins of the Vietnam War* (Cambridge: Belknap Harvard, 2000), 288.
15 Kaiser, *Tragedy*, 289–90, 295–96, 304, 309–10, 319.
16 Herring, *America's Longest*, 133–35; VanDeMark, *Road*, 242–44.
17 Kaiser, *Tragedy*, 336; VanDeMark, *Road*, 243–45; Herring, *America's Longest*, 136–37; Gary Hess, *Presidential Decisions for War: Korea, Vietnam, and the Persian Gulf* (Baltimore: Johns Hopkins University Press, 2001), 86–88; George Herring,

"'Cold Blood': LBJ's Conduct of Limited War in Vietnam," *The Harmon Memorial Lectures* (Colorado Springs: US Air Force Academy, 1990), 11.

18 Bruce Kuklick, *Blind Oracles: Intellectuals and War from Kennan to Kissinger* (Princeton: Princeton University Press, 2006), 140; Thomas Schelling, *Arms and Influence* (New Haven: Yale University Press, 1966), 141–51.

19 Hess, *Presidential*, 181; David Milne, "'Our Equivalent of Guerrilla Warfare': Walt Rostow and the Bombing of Vietnam, 1961–1968," *The Journal of Military History*, 71:1 (January 2007), 187.

20 VanDeMark, *Road*, 136–43; Bernard Brodie, "Learning to Fight a Limited War," in William Gerbering and Bernard Brodie, eds., *The Political Dimension in Strategy: Five Papers* (Los Angeles: UCLA Press, 1968), 31.

21 Herring, "'Cold Blood,'" 3, 5, 8–9, 22.

22 *FRUS, 1964–1968, Vietnam, 1964* (Washington: USGPO, 1992), 1:153–54, 172–73, 970, 984.

23 Mark Clodfelter, *The Limits of Air Power: The American Bombing of North Vietnam* (New York: Free Press, 1989), 74; Harry G. Summers Jr., *On Strategy: A Critical Analysis of the Vietnam War* (Novato: Presidio, 1984), 105.

24 Kaiser, *Tragedy*, 347–48.

25 Ibid., 348–51.

26 Ibid., 354–56, 379–82; Hess, *Presidential*, 225–26.

27 VanDeMark, *Road*, 204, 260–63; Hess, *Presidential*, 84; Herring, "'Cold Blood,'" 2; Herring, *America's Longest*, 126; Walton, *Myth*, 22.

28 Christopher M. Gacek, *The Logic of Force: The Dilemma of Limited War in American Foreign Policy* (New York: Columbia University Press, 1994), 195; Daddis, *Westmoreland's*, 61; Bernard Fall, "The Theory and Practice of Insurgency and Counter-Insurgency," *Military Review* (September–October 2015), 45–46.

29 Daddis, *Westmoreland's*, 60, 73; Jeffrey Record, *Beating Goliath: Why Insurgencies Win* (Washington: Potomac Books, 2007), 5.

30 William Rosenau, "The Kennedy Administration, US Foreign Internal Security Assistance, and the Challenge of 'Subterranean War,' 1961–63," *Small Wars and Insurgencies*, 14:3 (2003), 66, 73–74; Herring, "'Cold Blood,'" 4, 23; Marc Trachtenberg, *History and Strategy* (Princeton: Princeton University Press, 1991), 43; Walton, *Myth*, 109.

31 Allan Millett and Peter Maslowski, *For the Common Defense: A Military History of the United States of America*, 2nd ed. (New York: Free Press, 1994), 577; Stephen Rosen, "Vietnam and the American Theory of Limited War," *International Security*, 7:2 (fall 1982), 91.

32 Esther-Mirjam Sent, "Some Like It Cold: Thomas Schelling as a Cold Warrior," *Journal of Economic Methodology*, 14:4 (December 2007), 465; George Quester, "Wars Prolonged by Misunderstood Signals," *The Annals of the American Academy of Political and Social Science*, 392 (November 1970), 35; Thomas Schelling, "Bargaining, Communication, and Limited War," *Conflict Resolution*, 1:1 (March 1957), 19–36, and *The Strategy of Conflict* (Cambridge: Harvard University Press, 1963).

33 Milne, "Our Equivalent," 185; Kuklick, *Blind,* 145; VanDeMark, *Road,* 266–68; Phillip Davidson, *Vietnam at War: The History: 1946–1975* (Novato: Presidio, 1988), 366; Robert Pape, *Bombing to Win: Air Power and Coercion in War* (Ithaca: Cornell University Press, 1996), 175, 178–80; Clodfelter, *Limits,* 75–76.
34 Milne, "Our Equivalent," 184–85.
35 Pape, *Bombing,* 178–79; Clodfelter, *Limits,* 92–107; U. S. G. Sharp, *Strategy for Defeat: Vietnam in Retrospect* (Novato: Presidio Press, 1998), 65–66.
36 Pape, *Bombing,* 183–84; Clodfelter, *Limits,* 107–12.
37 Pape, *Bombing,* 185, 192; Clodfelter, *Limits,* 119; Milne, "Our Equivalent," 171, 190; Sharp, *Strategy,* 107.
38 Foot, *Substitute,* 221; Gacek, *Logic,* 400n.19; Jonathan Haslam, *Russia's Cold War: From the October Revolution to the Fall of the Wall* (New Haven: Yale University Press, 2011), 225.
39 Millett and Maslowski, *Common,* 2nd ed., 585; Pape, *Bombing,* 193; Matthew Ridgway, *The Korean War* (New York: Da Capo, 1967), 75; Sharp, *Strategy,* 134.
40 Millett and Maslowski, *Common,* 2nd ed., 578; Guenter Lewy, *America in Vietnam* (Oxford: Oxford University Press, 1978), 42; VanDeMark, *Road,* 269, 271–73.
41 Lewy, *America,* 42; Rosen, "Vietnam," 93.
42 VanDeMark, *Road,* 274.
43 Ibid., 279–81; NSAM 328, April 6, 1965, https://fas.org/irp/offdocs/nsam-lbj/nsam-328.htm; Sharp, *Strategy,* 70–72; Davidson, *Vietnam,* 345.
44 Davidson, *Vietnam,* 345–47; VanDeMark, *Road,* 274.
45 VanDeMark, *Road,* 284–88; Milne, "Our Equivalent," 188.
46 VanDeMark, *Road,* 289–90 and note.
47 Daddis, *Westmoreland's,* 60, 67, 76–78; Carter Malkasian, "Toward a Better Understanding of Attrition: The Korean and Vietnam Wars," *The Journal of Military History,* 68:3 (July 2004), 931–32.
48 George Herring, *From Colony to Superpower: US Foreign Relations since 1776* (Oxford: Oxford University Press, 2011), 739; Hunt, *Pacification,* 31–32; Malkasian, "Attrition," 929; William S. Turley, *The Second Indochina War: A Concise Political and Military History,* 2nd ed. (Lanham: Rowman and Littlefield, 2009), 96; Nguyen, *Hanoi's War,* 116, 128.
49 Gregory A. Daddis, "CORDS in Charge: Organizing for Pacification Support in the Vietnam War," in Ty Seidule and Jacqueline Whitt, eds., *Stand Up and Fight! The Creation of US Security Organizations, 1942–2005* (Carlisle: Army War College Press, 2015), 139; Malkasian, "Attrition," 933–34; Walton, *Myth,* 53; Andrew F. Krepinevich Jr., *The Army and Vietnam* (Baltimore: Johns Hopkins University Press, 1986), 165; VanDeMark, *Road,* 302; Daddis, *Westmoreland's,* 72, 78.
50 Malkasian, "Attrition," 937–38; Davidson, *Vietnam,* 351, 400; Gregory Daddis, *No Sure Victory: Measuring US Army Effectiveness and Progress in the Vietnam War* (Oxford: Oxford University Press, 2011), 6.
51 Hunt, *Pacification,* 32–33.

52 Davidson, *Vietnam*, 351–53; Walton, *Myth*, 48–50, 54; Millett and Maslowski, *Common*, 2nd ed., 580; Krepinevich, *Army*, 179.
53 Lewy, *America*, 56–57; Davidson, *Vietnam*, 360–62; Malkasian, "Attrition," 936.
54 Lewy, *America*, 57–59, 64–70.
55 Walton, *Myth*, 50, 54, 58; Millett and Maslowski, *Common*, 2nd ed., 580–81.
56 Lewy, *America*, 65, 99–108; Krepinevich, *Army*, 198, 259.
57 VanDeMark, *Road*, 343–44; Qiang Zhai, *China and the Vietnam Wars, 1950–1975* (Chapel Hill: UNC Press, 2000), ix–x, 153.
58 Davidson, *Vietnam*, 461–62; Charles F. Brower IV, "Strategic Reassessment in Vietnam: The Westmoreland 'Alternative Strategy' of 1967–1968," *Naval War College Review*, 44:2 (spring 1991), 25–33; Daddis, *Westmoreland's*, 86–87; *Pentagon Papers*, 539–40, 577–78; Herring, *America's Longest*, 192.
59 *Pentagon Papers*, 547–48, 594–97; Davidson, *Vietnam*, 462; George C. Herring, *LBJ and Vietnam: A Different Kind of War* (Austin: University of Texas Press, 1995), 54; Brower, "Strategic Reassessment," 30, 33; David Schmitz, *Richard Nixon and the Vietnam War: The End of the American Century* (Lanham: Rowman and Littlefield, 2014), 62; Herring, "'Cold Blood,'" 9–10.
60 Gacek, *Logic*, 158–78.
61 Hunt, *Pacification*, 31, 45, 47; Daddis, "CORDS," 143; Gregory A. Daddis, *Withdrawal: Reassessing America's Final Years in Vietnam* (Oxford: Oxford University Press, 2017), 83.
62 Daddis, "CORDS," 142; Hunt, *Pacification*, 36–39, 42, 59.
63 Hunt, *Pacification*, 63–74.
64 Ibid., 75–88, 93, 99–100, 117, 121, 248; NSAM 362, May 9, 1967, www.discoverlbj.org/item/nsf-nsam362. HES's value is disputed.
65 Krepinevich, *Army*, 172–77; Hunt, *Pacification*, 108; Theodore Easterling, "Keeping the Fish out of the Water: United States Marine Corps Combined Action Platoons in the Vietnam War" (PhD dissertation, University of Akron, 2016), 290; T. P. Schwartz, "The Combined Action Program: A Different Perspective," *Marine Corps Gazette*, 83:2 (February 1999), 65, 70; Daddis, *Withdrawal*, 21; Daddis, *Westmoreland's*, 81.
66 Ibid., 39–40, 49, 60–62, 118, 130–32; Daddis, *Westmoreland's*, 67–68.
67 Daddis, *Westmoreland's*, 134; Lewy, *America in Vietnam*, 93.
68 George W. Baer, *One Hundred Years of Sea Power: The US Navy, 1890–1990* (Stanford: Stanford University Press, 1993), 385–86, 390–92.
69 Herring, "'Cold Blood,'" 10–14, 17–18; Lyndon Johnson, State of the Union, January 10, 1967, https://millercenter.org/the-presidency/presidential-speeches/january-10-1967-state-union-address.
70 Herring, "'Cold Blood,'" 16–17; Rosen, "Vietnam," 134; Hess, *Presidential*, x; Walton, *Myth*, 35.
71 Sun Tzu, *The Art of War*, Samuel Griffith, trans. (London: Oxford University Press, 1961), 73.
72 Millett and Maslowski, *Common*, 2nd ed., 585–86.

73 Nguyen, *Hanoi's War*, 79–80, 89–91, 98–101.
74 Ibid., 113; Daddis, *Westmoreland's*, 142; Millett and Maslowski, *Common*, 2nd ed., 588.
75 Nguyen, *Hanoi's War*, 112–16, 122, 128–30, 148.
76 Hunt, *Pacification*, 137–39.
77 Ibid., 141–42; Daddis, *Westmoreland's*, 89; Daddis, *Withdrawal*, 34; VanDeMark, *Road*, 449–51; Krepinevich, *Army*, 244–45.
78 Davidson, *Vietnam*, 514; Hess, *Presidential*, 142–43; Daddis, *Withdrawal*, 34; Hunt, *Pacification*, 141–42.
79 Daddis, *Withdrawal*, 9; Hess, *Presidential*, 145–46; Davidson, *Vietnam*, 524–25; Millett and Maslowski, *Common*, 2nd ed., 588.
80 Hess, *Presidential*, 147–48; Daddis, *Withdrawal*, 49–50; Herring, *LBJ*, 174; Schmitz, *Nixon*, 36–37; Josh Zeitz, "Worried about a Rigged Election? Here's One Way to Handle It," *Politico* (October 27, 2016), www.politico.com/magazine/story/2016/10/donald-trump-2016-rigged-nixon-kennedy-1960-214395.
81 Daddis, *Withdrawal*, 37–40.
82 Ibid., 90–92; Hunt, *Pacification*, 154–59, 172, 193.
83 Hunt, *Pacification*, 197–203; Eric Bergerud, *The Dynamics of Defeat: The Vietnam War in Hau Nghia Province* (Boulder: Westview, 1991), 236–37.
84 Hunt, *Pacification*, 212.

13 DÉTENTE AND DEFEAT: NIXON, FORD, AND VIETNAM, 1969–1977

1 Hal Brands, *What Good Is Grand Strategy? Power and Purpose in American Statecraft from Harry S. Truman to George W. Bush* (Ithaca: Cornell University Press, 2014), 59–64.
2 Ibid., 64–65.
3 Ibid., 65–67, 73; John Lewis Gaddis, *Strategies of Containment: A Critical Appraisal of Postwar American National Security* (Oxford: Oxford University Press, 2005), 275–76, 282–83.
4 *Public Papers of the Presidents of the United States: Richard Nixon, 1970* (Washington: USGPO, 1971), 117; Richard M. Nixon, First Inaugural Address, January 20, 1969, https://millercenter.org/the-presidency/presidential-speeches/january-20-1969-first-inaugural-address; Gaddis, *Strategies*, 303.
5 George C. Herring, *The American Century: US Foreign Relations, 1893–2014* (Oxford: Oxford University Press, 2017), 463; James Patterson, *Grand Expectations: The United States, 1945–1974* (New York: Oxford University Press, 1996), 678–709, 716–17.
6 *Nixon, 1970*, 117; Gaddis, *Strategies*, 303; Jeffrey Kimball, *Nixon's Vietnam War* (Lawrence: University Press of Kansas, 1998), 66.
7 Herring, *American*, 465; John Gans, *White House Warriors: How the National Security Council Transformed the American Way of War* (New York: Liveright, 2019), 37.

8 Gaddis, *Strategies*, 278–81; Hal Brands, *The Promise and Pitfalls of Grand Strategy* (Carlisle: Army War College Press, 2012), 31.
9 Michael Green, *By More Than Providence: Grand Strategy and American Power in the Asia Pacific since 1783* (New York: Columbia University Press, 2019), 337; Brands, *What Good*, 76–77; Gaddis, *Strategies*, 277, 295–96.
10 Green, *Providence*, 337–40; Richard M. Nixon, Address to the Nation on the War in Vietnam, November 3, 1969, https://millercenter.org/the-presidency/presidential-speeches/november-3-1969-address-nation-war-vietnam; Brands, *What Good*, 73–74.
11 Raymond Garthoff, *Détente and Confrontation: American–Soviet Relations from Nixon to Reagan* (Washington: Brookings Institution, 1985), 25; Gaddis, *Strategies*, 280–81, 286–87.
12 Brands, *What Good*, 67–69; Gaddis, *Strategies*, 287–90, 301, 310–11.
13 Dan Caldwell, "The Legitimation of the Nixon–Kissinger Grand Design and Grand Strategy," *Diplomatic History*, 33:4 (September 2009), 646–47; Brands, *What Good*, 82, 90–91.
14 Brands, *What Good*, 69–71; Gaddis, *Strategies*, 280, 292–94; Green, *Providence*, 347.
15 Brands, *What Good*, 79–80; Gaddis, *Strategies*, 295; Green, *Providence*, 344–45, 350.
16 Gaddis, *Strategies*, 283.
17 Ibid., 285; Brands, *What Good*, 91–92; Steve Yetiv, *The Absence of Grand Strategy: The United States in the Persian Gulf, 1972–2005* (Baltimore: Johns Hopkins University Press, 2008), 28–31.
18 Brands, *What Good*, 75–76, 94–95; Gaddis, *Strategies*, 333.
19 Brands, *What Good*, 95.
20 Ibid., 75; Gaddis, *Strategies*, 304; Green, *Providence*, 358–59.
21 Green, *Providence*, 360–61.
22 Ibid., 362; Address by President Gerald R. Ford at the University of Hawaii, December 7, 1975, https://china.usc.edu/address-president-gerald-r-ford-university-hawaii-december-7-1975.
23 Gaddis, *Strategies*, 339; Brands, *What Good*, 92–93; Hal Brands, *Making the Unipolar Moment: US Foreign Policy and the Rise of the Post-Cold War Order* (Ithaca: Cornell University Press, 2016), 45; Green, *Providence*, 355.
24 Brands, *What Good*, 85; Gaddis, *Strategies*, 316–17.
25 Gaddis, *Strategies*, 297–300, 305.
26 Caldwell, "Legitimation," 638–43.
27 Brands, *What Good*, 97; Herring, *American*, 465–66; Gans, *Warriors*, 46–47, 56; Caldwell, "Legitimation," 648.
28 Brands, *Unipolar*, 18; Hugh Rockoff, *America's Economic Way of War: War and the US Economy from the Spanish-American War to the Persian Gulf War* (Cambridge: Cambridge University Press, 2012), 300.
29 Brands, *Unipolar*, 20–21.

30 Ibid., 18–20, 58; Rockoff, *Economic*, 289, 299; David Schmitz, *Richard Nixon and the Vietnam War: The End of the American Century* (Lanham: Rowman and Littlefield, 2014), 132; Patterson, *Grand*, 740–41.
31 Brands, *What Good*, 69, 84; Gaddis, *Strategies*, 292, 309, 311–13.
32 Brands, *What Good*, 68–69, 74; Gaddis, *Strategies*, 275–78.
33 Gaddis, *Strategies*, 330; NSDM 133, September 22, 1971, https://fas.org/irp/offdocs/nsdm-nixon/nsdm-133.pdf; NSDM 242, January 17, 1974, Policy for Planning the Employment of Nuclear Weapons, https://fas.org/irp/offdocs/nsdm-nixon/nsdm_242.pdf.
34 *Nixon, 1970*, 117; Gaddis, *Strategies*, 295 and note, 319–21, 326; Allan Millett and Peter Maslowski, *For the Common Defense: A Military History of the United States of America*, 2nd ed. (New York: Free Press, 1994), 568; Rockoff, *Economic*, 302.
35 Kimball, *Nixon's Vietnam*, 62, 66–67, 88–89, 100–1; Gregory A. Daddis, *Withdrawal: Reassessing America's Final Years in Vietnam* (Oxford: Oxford University Press, 2017), 105; Schmitz, *Nixon*, 42.
36 Schmitz, *Nixon*, 43.
37 Ibid., 23–24, 44; Daddis, *Withdrawal*, 56–57; NSSM 1, *FRUS, 1969–1976, Vietnam, January 1969–July 1970* (Washington: USGPO, 2006), 6:4–10; Kimball, *Nixon's Vietnam*, 91–96.
38 *FRUS, 1969–1976, Vietnam, January 1969–July 1970*, 6:131.
39 Schmitz, *Nixon*, 30; George Herring, *America's Longest War: The United States and Vietnam, 1950–1975*, 3rd ed. (New York: McGraw-Hill, 1996), 243; Kimball, *Nixon's Vietnam*, 62, 66–67; *Public Papers of the Presidents of the United States: Richard Nixon, 1969* (Washington: USGPO, 1971), 230–31; Robert Dallek, *Nixon and Kissinger: Partners in Power* (New York: HarperCollins, 2007), 68, 105–6.
40 *FRUS, 1969–1976, Vietnam, July 1970–January 1972*, 7:doc. 190; Kimball, *Nixon's Vietnam*, 12; Richard Nixon, Address to the Nation Announcing an Agreement on Ending the War in Vietnam, January 23, 1973, https://millercenter.org/the-presidency/presidential-speeches/january-23-1973-address-nation-announcing-agreement-ending-war.
41 Schmitz, *Nixon*, 24–27, 33; Kimball, *Nixon's Vietnam*, 72–73, 97–99.
42 Kimball, *Nixon's Vietnam*, 97.
43 Schmitz, *Nixon*, 43–44.
44 Ibid., 33; Kimball, *Nixon's Vietnam*, 86.
45 Kimball, *Nixon's Vietnam*, 103–4; David Prentice, "Choosing 'the Long Road': Henry Kissinger, Melvin Laird, Vietnamization, and the War over Nixon's Vietnam Strategy," *Diplomatic History*, 40:3 (2016), 459.
46 Kimball, *Nixon's Vietnam*, 99, 105, 111; Daddis, *Withdrawal*, 53; Schmitz, *Nixon*, 43.
47 Kimball, *Nixon's Vietnam*, 74–77, 99, 107–8, 151–53; Daddis, *Withdrawal*, 51–52; Schmitz, *Nixon*, 46–47, 50.
48 Kimball, *Nixon's Vietnam*, 133–37; Daddis, *Withdrawal*, 56; Schmitz, *Nixon*, 47–50.

49 Daddis, *Withdrawal*, 60; Dale Van Atta, *With Honor: Melvin Laird in War, Peace, and Politics* (Madison: University of Wisconsin Press, 2008), 176–78; Prentice, "Choosing," 452–55.
50 *FRUS, 1969–1976, Vietnam, January 1969–July 1970*, 6:111.
51 Ibid., 6:112–17.
52 Daddis, *Withdrawal*, 112–15; Henry Kissinger, *White House Years* (New York: Little Brown, 1979), 444.
53 Prentice, "Choosing," 460–61; Schmitz, *Nixon*, 55–56; Daddis, *Withdrawal*, 102; Gaddis, *Strategies*, 296.
54 NSSM 36, April 10, 1969, https://fas.org/irp/offdocs/nssm-nixon/nssm_036.pdf; Prentice, "Choosing," 455–62; Daddis, *Withdrawal*, 61; Schmitz, *Nixon*, 56, 100–3; Kimball, *Nixon's Vietnam*, 139.
55 Daddis, *Withdrawal*, 36; Jeffrey Clarke, *Advice and Support: The Final Years, 1965–1973* (Washington: Center of Military History, 1988), 362–63.
56 Daddis, *Withdrawal*, 21, 42; Prentice, "Choosing," 462; Kimball, *Nixon's Vietnam*, 128; Richard Hunt, *Pacification: The American Struggle for Vietnam's Hearts and Minds* (Boulder: Westview, 1995), 230–31.
57 Kimball, *Nixon's Vietnam*, 151; Harry G. Summers Jr., *On Strategy: A Critical Analysis of the Vietnam War* (Novato: Presidio, 1984), 104.
58 Prentice, "Choosing," 466; Daddis, *Withdrawal*, 164.
59 Prentice, "Choosing," 463–71; Nixon, Address to the Nation, November 3, 1969; Schmitz, *Nixon*, 70; Kimball, *Nixon's Vietnam*, 172–74.
60 Daddis, *Withdrawal*, 11–12, 22, 69, 71, 78, 100; Dale Walton, *The Myth of Inevitable US Defeat in Vietnam* (Abingdon: Routledge, 2002), 49; Millett and Maslowski, *Common*, 2nd ed., 590.
61 Hunt, *Pacification*, 152–54, 253–58, 278; Daddis, *Withdrawal*, 23, 99.
62 Daddis, *Withdrawal*, 22–23, 92–93, 128, 181; Jefferson Marquis, "The 'Other War': An Intellectual History of American Nation Building in South Vietnam, 1954–1975" (PhD dissertation, Ohio State University, 1997), 192; Hunt, *Pacification*, 265–66.
63 Daddis, *Withdrawal*, 79–80.
64 Hunt, *Pacification*, 212–13.
65 Ibid., 215; Daddis, *Withdrawal*, 88–95.
66 Daddis, *Withdrawal*, 85, 91–92, 97, 101–2; Hunt, *Pacification*, 252; Marquis, "Other War," 189.
67 Daddis, *Withdrawal*, 84, 90–91.
68 Ibid., 102–3; Hunt, *Pacification*, 252–55.
69 Daddis, *Withdrawal*, 86–87; Kevin Dougherty, *The United States Military in Limited War: Case Studies in Success and Failure* (Jefferson: McFarland, 2012), 94; Hunt, *Pacification*, 267–68, 279.
70 Kimball, *Nixon's Vietnam*, 125–26.
71 Green, *Providence*, 333; Walton, *Myth*, 75.
72 Green, *Providence*, 333–34; Daddis, *Withdrawal*, 120–25.

73 Daddis, *Withdrawal*, 124–27, 131–32; Kimball, *Nixon's Vietnam*, 219, 224; NSSM 99, August 17, 1970, https://fas.org/irp/offdocs/nssm-nixon/nssm_099.pdf; NSDM 89, *FRUS, 1969–1976, Vietnam, July 1970–January 1972* (Washington: USGPO, 2010), 7:doc. 61.

74 Kimball, *Nixon's Vietnam*, 211; Daddis, *Withdrawal*, 128–29; Green, *Providence*, 334–35.

75 Bruce Kuklick, *Blind Oracles: Intellectuals and War from Kennan to Kissinger* (Princeton: Princeton University Press, 2006), 201–2; Esther-Mirjam Sent, "Some Like It Cold: Thomas Schelling as a Cold Warrior," *Journal of Economic Methodology*, 14:4 (December 2007), 406.

76 Green, *Providence*, 332–35; Daddis, *Withdrawal*, 166–67, 175.

77 Lien-Hang T. Nguyen, *Hanoi's War: An International History of the War for Peace in Vietnam* (Chapel Hill: UNC Press, 2012), 163–65.

78 Daddis, *Withdrawal*, 169–75; Kimball, *Nixon's Vietnam*, 242; Gregory Daddis, "Out of Balance: Evaluating American Strategy in Vietnam, 1968–72," *War and Society*, 32:3 (2013), 263.

79 Kimball, *Nixon's Vietnam*, 242–48; Nguyen, *Hanoi's War*, 203; Daddis, *Withdrawal*, 176; *FRUS 1969–1976, Vietnam, July 1970–January 1972*, 7:doc. 190.

80 Schmitz, *Nixon*, 104; Walton, *Myth*, 136; *FRUS, 1969–1976, Vietnam, July 1970–January 1972*, 7:doc. 76.

81 Daddis, *Withdrawal*, 73, 182, 185; Schmitz, *Nixon*, 62, 71, 84, 114–15, 132–33; Prentice, "Choosing," 469.

82 Jussi Hanhimaki, "Selling the 'Decent Interval': Kissinger, Triangular Diplomacy, and the End of the Vietnam War, 1971–73," *Diplomacy and Statecraft*, 14:1 (2003), 163, 166; Schmitz, *Nixon*, 113–14.

83 Hanhimaki, "Selling," 167; Daddis, *Withdrawal*, 180.

84 Hanhimaki, "Selling," 173–78. Italics in source.

85 Ibid., 171, 174; Nguyen, *Hanoi's War*, 218, 228, 233, 243–45.

86 Nguyen, *Hanoi's War*, 245; Phil Haun and Colin Jackson, "Breaker of Armies: Air Power in the Easter Offensive and the Myth of Linebacker I and II in the Vietnam War," *International Security*, 40:3 (winter 2015–16), 148.

87 Kimball, *Nixon's Vietnam*, 306–9.

88 Ibid., 302–5; Mark Clodfelter, "Nixon and the Air Weapon," in Dennis Showalter and John Albert, eds., *An American Dilemma: Vietnam, 1964–1973* (Chicago: Imprint Publications, 1993), 157–58; Haun and Jackson, "Breaker," 139, 160–61, 166–71; Nguyen, *Hanoi's War*, 245, 270.

89 Daddis, *Withdrawal*, 185, 189; Haun and Jackson, "Breaker," 167–71; Marquis, "Other War," 185.

90 Hanhimaki, "Selling," 179.

91 Paul Pillar, *Negotiating Peace: War Termination as a Bargaining Process* (Princeton: Princeton University Press, 1983), 52, 198; Gideon Rose, *How Wars End: Why We Always Fight the Last Battle* (New York: Simon and Schuster, 2010), 172; Herring, *America's Longest*, 275; Nguyen, *Hanoi's War*, 212.

92 Nguyen, *Hanoi's War*, 259–61; Clodfelter, "Nixon," 172–73; Haun and Jackson, "Breaker," 171.
93 Haun and Jackson, "Breaker," 171–72; Nguyen, *Hanoi's War*, 280–85; Hanhimaki, "Selling," 180; Rose, *How Wars*, 160–61.
94 Schmitz, *Nixon*, 141; Clodfelter, "Nixon," 174–77; Nguyen, *Hanoi's War*, 288–89, 294.
95 Haun and Jackson, "Breaker," 172; Rose, *How Wars*, 174; Hanhimaki, "Selling," 186; Clodfelter, "Nixon," 177–80; Nguyen, *Hanoi's War*, 295–97; Agreement on Ending the War and Restoring Peace in Vietnam, January 17, 1973, https://treaties.un.org/doc/Publication/UNTS/Volume%20935/volume-935-I-13295-English.pdf; Daddis, *Withdrawal*, 287n.157.
96 Nixon, Address to the Nation, January 23, 1973; Agreement on Ending the War, January 17, 1973.
97 William S. Turley, *The Second Indochina War: A Concise Political and Military History*, 2nd ed. (Lanham: Rowman and Littlefield, 2009), 151–54; Henry Kissinger, *Diplomacy* (New York: Simon and Schuster, 1994), 674–77.
98 Schmitz, *Nixon*, 143–44; Walton, *Myth*, 137; Millett and Maslowski, *Common*, 2nd ed., 601; Rose, *How Wars*, 189; Fred Charles Iklé, *Every War Must End* (New York: Columbia University Press, 1971), xix.
99 Brian VanDeMark, *Road to Disaster: A New History of America's Descent into Vietnam* (New York: HarperCollins, 2018), 326; Millett and Maslowski, *Common*, 2nd ed., 570–71; Brands, *What Good*, 88.
100 Melvin Laird, "Iraq: Learning the Lessons of Vietnam," *Foreign Affairs*, 84:6 (November–December 2005), 25.
101 *FRUS, Vietnam, 1964–1968*, 1:153–54, 172–73; Harry G. Summers Jr., *Historical Atlas of the Vietnam War* (New York: Houghton Mifflin, 1995), 183.
102 Rose, *How Wars*, 192–94; VanDeMark, *Road*, 336.

14 FOR WANT OF A VISION: THE CARTER YEARS, 1977–1981

1 Hal Brands, *Making the Unipolar Moment: US Foreign Policy and the Rise of the Post-Cold War Order* (Ithaca: Cornell University Press, 2016), 1–2, 17, 36; John Lewis Gaddis, *Strategies of Containment: A Critical Appraisal of Postwar American National Security* (Oxford: Oxford University Press, 2005), 343, 348; Michael Green, *By More Than Providence: Grand Strategy and American Power in the Asia Pacific since 1783* (New York: Columbia University Press, 2019), 364.
2 Green, *Providence*, 364.
3 Ibid., 365; John Gans, *White House Warriors: How the National Security Council Transformed the American Way of War* (New York: Liveright, 2019), 58–60; Justin Vaïsse, *Zbigniew Brzezinski: America's Grand Strategist*, Catherine Porter, trans. (Cambridge: Harvard University Press, 2018), 8, 47, 189, 195–96.
4 Vaïsse, *Brzezinski*, 273, 280–82, 350; Green, *Providence*, 366–67.

5 Betty Glad, *Outsider in the White House: Jimmy Carter, His Advisors, and the Making of American Foreign Policy* (Ithaca: Cornell University Press, 2009), 1; Jimmy Carter, *Keeping Faith: Memoirs of a President* (Toronto: Bantam, 1982), 20.
6 Interview with Zbigniew Brzezinski et al., February 18, 1982, 66, http://web1.millercenter.org/poh/transcripts/ohp_1982_0218_brzezinski.pdf; Vaïsse, *Brzezinski*, 282, 294–95; Zbigniew Brzezinski, *Power and Principle: Memoirs of the National Security Adviser, 1977–1981* (New York: Farrar, Straus, Giroux, 1983), 53–56.
7 Brzezinski, *Power*, 56.
8 *FRUS, 1977–1980, Foundations of Foreign Policy* (Washington: USGPO, 2014), 7:65–67.
9 Jimmy Carter, State of the Union Address, January 19, 1978, https://millercenter.org/the-presidency/presidential-speeches/january-19-1978-state-union-address.
10 Carter, State of the Union, January 19, 1978; "Speech of the President on Soviet-American Relations at the US Naval Academy," *NYT* (June 8, 1978), www.nytimes.com/1978/06/08/archives/speech-of-the-president-on-sovietamerican-relations-at-the-us-naval.html.
11 James T. Patterson, *Restless Giant: The United States from Watergate to Bush v. Gore* (Oxford: Oxford University Press, 2007), 111.
12 "Text of President's Commencement Address at Notre Dame on Foreign Policy," *NYT* (May 23, 1977), www.nytimes.com/1977/05/23/archives/text-of-presidents-commencement-address-at-notre-dame-on-foreign.html.
13 David Schmitz and Vanessa Walker, "Jimmy Carter and the Foreign Policy of Human Rights: The Development of a Post-Cold War Foreign Policy," *Diplomatic History*, 28:1 (January 2004), 113; Interview with Jimmy Carter, November 29, 1982, http://web1.millercenter.org/poh/transcripts/ohp_1982_1129_carter.pdf.
14 Vaïsse, *Brzezinski*, 298–300; PRM/NSC 10, February 18, 1977, https://fas.org/irp/offdocs/prm/prm10.pdf.
15 "Address at Notre Dame."
16 PD/NSC 18, US National Strategy, August 26, 1977, https://fas.org/irp/offdocs/pd/pd18.pdf; Vaïsse, *Brzezinski*, 340.
17 Green, *Providence*, 385; *FRUS, 1977–1980, Human Rights and Humanitarian Affairs* (Washington: USGPO, 2013), 2:215 (italics in original); Schmitz and Walker, "Carter," 121.
18 PD/NSC 30, *FRUS, 1977–1980, Human Rights and Humanitarian Affairs*, 2:405–6.
19 Ibid.: Walter A. McDougall, *Promised Land, Crusader State: The American Encounter with the World since 1776* (New York: Houghton Mifflin, 1997), 197.
20 Green, *Providence*, 366; Allan Millett et al., *For the Common Defense: A Military History of the United States from 1607 to 2012*, 3rd ed. (New York: Free Press, 2012), 570–77; Vaïsse, *Brzezinski*, 324, 340; Patterson, *Restless*, 121.
21 George W. Baer, *One Hundred Years of Sea Power: The US Navy, 1890–1990* (Stanford: Stanford University Press, 1993), 424–25; John Hattendorf, *The*

Evolution of the US Navy's Maritime Strategy, 1977–1986 (Newport: Naval War College Press, 2004), 17–21.
22 Vaïsse, *Brzezinski*, 275; "Address at Notre Dame."
23 Vaïsse, *Brzezinski*, 263–64, 279–80.
24 Ibid., 279–80.
25 Ibid., 282, 296–97, 302–3; Gaddis, *Strategies*, 345–47; "Speech of the President on Soviet-American Relations."
26 Vaïsse, *Brzezinski*, 33, 297–98, 302–3; Brands, *Unipolar*, 37.
27 Vaïsse, *Brzezinski*, 315–20; Millett et al., *Common*, 574.
28 Green, *Providence*, 369, 374–75; Vaïsse, *Brzezinski*, 369–71.
29 Green, *Providence*, 371–72.
30 Ibid., 367, 377–79.
31 Ibid., 380–81.
32 "Address at Notre Dame"; Vaïsse, *Brzezinski*, 282, 296–97.
33 Steve Yetiv, *The Absence of Grand Strategy: The United States in the Persian Gulf, 1972–2005* (Baltimore: Johns Hopkins University Press, 2008), 36; Vaïsse, *Brzezinski*, 335–36.
34 PRM/NSC 8, January 21, 1977, https://fas.org/irp/offdocs/prm/prm08.pdf.
35 Vaïsse, *Brzezinski*, 325–27.
36 Ibid., 296, 327; Hal Brands, *What Good Is Grand Strategy? Power and Purpose in American Statecraft from Harry S. Truman to George W. Bush* (Ithaca: Cornell University Press, 2014), 43; "Address at Notre Dame"; Brands, *Unipolar*, 48–49; Carter, *Keeping*, 155.
37 Brands, *Unipolar*, 49–50; McDougall, *Promised*, 197.
38 George C. Herring, *The American Century: US Foreign Relations, 1893–2014* (Oxford: Oxford University Press, 2017), 544–45.
39 Brands, *Unipolar*, 55; "Address at Notre Dame."
40 Carter, State of the Union, January 19, 1978.
41 Brands, *Unipolar*, 63.
42 Jimmy Carter, "Crisis of Confidence" Speech, July 15, 1979, https://millercenter.org/the-presidency/presidential-speeches/july-15-1979-crisis-confidence-speech; Carter, *Keeping*, 91, 96, 122–23; Brands, *Unipolar*, 54.
43 Brands, *Unipolar*, 60–61; Patterson, *Restless*, 112, 115.
44 Vaïsse, *Brzezinski*, 321, 336; Brands, *Unipolar*, 49–50; Yetiv, *Absence*, 37, 43–44; McDougall, *Promised*, 197.
45 Vaïsse, *Brzezinski*, 336; Yetiv, *Absence*, 44–45; Gans, *Warriors*, 59–60; McDougall, *Promised*, 197; Patterson, *Restless*, 126; Carter, *Keeping*, 4–5, 11.
46 Brands, *Unipolar*, 21; Yetiv, *Absence*, 37–40, 45.
47 Vaïsse, *Brzezinski*, 310; "Brzezinski: 'Oui, la CIA est entrée en Afghanistan avant les Russes,'" *Le Nouvel Observateur* (January 5–21, 1998), 76, www.voltairenet.org/article165889.html.
48 Brands, *Unipolar*, 28, 38; Vaïsse, *Brzezinski*, 310; Yetiv, *Absence*, 46.

49 Vaïsse, *Brzezinski*, 310; Jimmy Carter, State of the Union Address, January 23, 1980, https://millercenter.org/the-presidency/presidential-speeches/january-23-1980-state-union-address. Carter also declared three additional things as political aims, but they do not equate to such.
50 Brands, *Unipolar*, 36.
51 Carter, State of the Union, January 23, 1980; Patterson, *Restless*, 123–24.
52 PD/NSC 62, January 15, 1981, https://fas.org/irp/offdocs/pd/pd62.pdf.
53 Carter, State of the Union, January 23, 1980; PD/NSC 63, January 15, 1981, https://fas.org/irp/offdocs/pd/pd63.pdf; Vaïsse, *Brzezinski*, 311.
54 Vaïsse, *Brzezinski*, 313; Brands, *Unipolar*, 32–33.
55 PD/NSC 63.
56 Vaïsse, *Brzezinski*, 291–92, 340; Brands, *Unipolar*, 35–38.
57 PD/NSC 59, July 25, 1980, https://fas.org/irp/offdocs/pd/pd59.pdf; Vaïsse, *Brzezinski*, 312; Millett et al., *Common*, 573,
58 PD/NSC 59; Vaïsse, *Brzezinski*, 312–13; Millett et al., *Common*, 573. "Counterforce strategy" is sometimes mistakenly used to label the administration's approach to the Third World, see Westad, *Global*, 331.
59 Brands, *Unipolar*, 30, 33–35; Vaïsse, *Brzezinski*, 298.
60 Green, *Providence*, 374–75.
61 Vaïsse, *Brzezinski*, 332.
62 Ibid., 332, 339–40; Patterson, *Restless*, 127, 148.
63 Schmitz and Walker, "Carter," 143; Brands, *Unipolar*, 52; McDougall, *Promised*, 197.

15 WINNING THE HOT PEACE: REAGAN'S GREAT-POWER COMPETITION, 1981–1990

1 Hal Brands, *Making the Unipolar Moment: US Foreign Policy and the Rise of the Post-Cold War Order* (Ithaca: Cornell University Press, 2016), 1–2; Hal Brands, *What Good Is Grand Strategy? Power and Purpose in American Statecraft from Harry S. Truman to George W. Bush* (Ithaca: Cornell University Press, 2014), 105.
2 Brands, *Unipolar*, 7, 72; Justin Vaïsse, *Zbigniew Brzezinski: America's Grand Strategist*, Catherine Porter, trans. (Cambridge: Harvard University Press, 2018), 264; John Lewis Gaddis, *Strategies of Containment: A Critical Appraisal of Postwar American National Security* (Oxford: Oxford University Press, 2005), 349–52.
3 Gaddis, *Strategies*, 350–52; Brands, *What Good*, 103, 109–10; Peter Schweizer, *Victory: The Reagan Administration's Secret Strategy That Hastened the Collapse of the Soviet Union* (New York: Atlantic Monthly Press, 1994), xiv.
4 Gaddis, *Strategies*, 351; Brands, *What Good*, 107; Reagan campaign speech draft, "State of the Union," March 13, 1980, in Kiron Skinner et al., eds., *Reagan in His Own Hand: The Writings of Ronald Reagan That Reveal His Revolutionary Vision for America* (New York: Free Press, 2001), 476–77; NSSD 1-82, February 5, 1982, https://fas.org/irp/offdocs/nssd/nssd-1-82.pdf; NSDD 32, May 20, 1982, https://fas.org/irp/offdocs/nsdd/nsdd-32.pdf.

5 Brands, *Unipolar*, 75; Michael Green, *By More Than Providence: Grand Strategy and American Power in the Asia Pacific since 1783* (New York: Columbia University Press, 2019), 391–92; Schweizer, *Victory*, xvii; Joseph Ledford email to author, January 22, 2021.
6 Brands, *What Good*, 110.
7 Brands, *Unipolar*, 72–75; Ronald Reagan, First Inaugural Address, January 20, 1981, https://millercenter.org/the-presidency/presidential-speeches/january-20-1981-first-inaugural-address; Ronald Reagan, Speech on the Strategic Arms Reduction Talks, November 18, 1981, https://millercenter.org/the-presidency/presidential-speeches/november-18-1981-speech-strategic-arms-reduction-talks.
8 Ronald Reagan, Address at University of Notre Dame, November 17, 1981, https://millercenter.org/the-presidency/presidential-speeches/may-17-1981-address-university-notre-dame; Robert Pee, "Democracy Promotion, National Security, and Strategy during the Reagan Administration, 1981–1986" (PhD dissertation, University of Birmingham, 2013), 113; Robert Pee, "Containing Revolution: Democracy Promotion, the Cold War, and US National Security," *International Politics*, 55 (2018), 693–94; Ronald Reagan, Address to the British Parliament, June 8, 1982, https://millercenter.org/the-presidency/presidential-speeches/june-8-1982-address-british-parliament.
9 NSDD 54, September 2, 1982, https://fas.org/irp/offdocs/nsdd/nsdd-54.pdf.
10 NSDD 75, January 17, 1983, https://fas.org/irp/offdocs/nsdd/nsdd-75.pdf; Schweizer, *Victory*, 131; Gaddis, *Strategies*, 118.
11 NSDD 75.
12 Reagan, Address to the British Parliament.
13 Chester Pach, "The Reagan Doctrine: Principle, Pragmatism, and Policy," *Presidential Studies Quarterly*, 36:1 (March 2006), 75; Ronald Reagan, State of the Union Address, February 6, 1985, https://millercenter.org/the-presidency/presidential-speeches/february-6-1985-state-union-address.
14 NSDD 75; Gaddis, *Strategies*, 356–57.
15 Ronald Reagan, Republican National Convention, July 17, 1980, https://millercenter.org/the-presidency/presidential-speeches/july-17-1980-republican-national-convention.
16 Reagan, First Inaugural, January 20, 1981; Ronald Reagan, First Press Conference, January 29, 1981, https://millercenter.org/the-presidency/presidential-speeches/january-29-1981-first-press-conference; Ronald Reagan, State of the Union Address, January 26, 1982, https://millercenter.org/the-presidency/presidential-speeches/january-26-1982-state-union-address; Reagan, State of the Union, February 6, 1985.
17 Brands, *Unipolar*, 57; James T. Patterson, *Restless Giant: The United States from Watergate to Bush v. Gore* (Oxford: Oxford University Press, 2007), 154–55.
18 Reagan, Republican National Convention; Patterson, *Restless*, 156–57.
19 Patterson, *Restless*, 158–59, 166–68.
20 Reagan, First Inaugural, January 20, 1981; Patterson, *Restless*, 127, 162–63, 189.

21 Green, *Providence*, 408–11.
22 NSDD 75.
23 Schweizer, *Victory*, 71–73, 106–11, 123–25, 140.
24 Ibid., 41–46, 77–79, 163–65, 194–95, 200, 216, 248; Brands, *Unipolar*, 84.
25 NSDD 66, November 29, 1982, https://fas.org/irp/offdocs/nsdd/nsdd-066.htm; Schweizer, *Victory*, 73–74; Brands, *Unipolar*, 84–84.
26 Brands, *Unipolar*, 64.
27 Reagan, Speech on the Strategic Arms Reduction Talks, November 18, 1981; NSDD 32; Brands, *What Good*, 111; Brands, *Unipolar*, 72–75.
28 NSDD 75.
29 NSDD 32.
30 NSDD 75; NSDD 32; Brands, *Unipolar*, 77–78; Brands, *What Good*, 112.
31 George W. Baer, *One Hundred Years of Sea Power: The US Navy, 1890–1990* (Stanford: Stanford University Press, 1993), 418, 429–30, 442; Walter A. McDougall: "History and Strategies: Grand, Maritime, and American," in Michael Gerson and Alison Russell, eds., *American Grand Strategy and Seapower: Conference Report* (Arlington: CNA, 2011), 41; Green, *Providence*, 401.
32 Brands, *What Good*, 111; Allan Millett et al., *For the Common Defense: A Military History of the United States from 1607 to 2012*, 3rd ed. (New York: Free Press, 2012), 580; Schweizer, *Victory*, 195–96.
33 NSDD 32; NSDD 12, October 1, 1981, https://fas.org/irp/offdocs/nsdd/nsdd-12.pdf; NSDD 13, [October 1, 1981], https://fas.org/irp/offdocs/nsdd/nsdd-13.pdf. This superseded PD 59.
34 Gaddis, *Strategies*, 352, 357–58; Ronald Reagan, Second Inaugural Address, January 21, 1985, https://millercenter.org/the-presidency/presidential-speeches/january-21-1985-second-inaugural-address.
35 Gaddis, *Strategies*, 358; Brands, *What Good*, 112; NSDD 12; NSDD 85, March 25, 1983, www.hsdl.org/?view&did=463005; NSDD 119, January 6, 1984, https://fas.org/irp/offdocs/nsdd/nsdd-119.pdf; NSDD 153, January 1, 1985, https://fas.org/irp/offdocs/nsdd/nsdd-153.pdf.
36 Gaddis, *Strategies*, 358; Schweizer, *Victory*, 133–36; Brands, *Unipolar*, 89–90.
37 Gaddis, *Strategies*, 359–61; Brands, *What Good*, 124; Brands, *Unipolar*, 92–94.
38 Boaz Ganor, "Defining Terrorism – Is One Man's Terrorist Another Man's Freedom Fighter?" *International Institute for Counterterrorism* (January 1, 2010), www.ict.org.il/Article/1123/Defining-Terrorism-Is-One-Mans-Terrorist-Another-Mans-Freedom-Fighter#gsc.tab=0; NSDD 138, April 3, 1984, https://fas.org/irp/offdocs/nsdd/nsdd-138.pdf; NSDD 207, January 20, 1986, https://fas.org/irp/offdocs/nsdd/nsdd-207.pdf.
39 NSDD 277, June 15, 1987, https://fas.org/irp/offdocs/nsdd/nsdd-277.pdf.
40 NSDD 75.
41 Ibid.; Brands, *Unipolar*, 80.
42 Gaddis, *Strategies*, 359; Brands, *Unipolar*, 73; NSDD 75; Brands, *What Good*, 117.

43 Brands, *Unipolar*, 81–82; NSDD 45, July 15, 1982, https://fas.org/irp/offdocs/nsdd/nsdd-45.pdf; Brands, *What Good*, 120–21.
44 NSDD 75; Brands, *What Good*, 115–16; Brands, *Unipolar*, 82.
45 Schweizer, *Victory*, xvi–xvii, 11, 100; Brands, *What Good*, 114, 120; Brands, *Unipolar*, 82–83.
46 Schweizer, *Victory*, 172.
47 Vincent Bzdek, *The Kennedy Legacy: Jack, Bobby, Ted, and a Family Dream Fulfilled* (New York: Palgrave Macmillan, 2009), 193–94; Text of KGB Letter on Senator Ted Kennedy, in Paul Kengor, *The Crusader: Ronald Reagan and the Fall of Communism* (New York: Regan HarperCollins, 2006), 317–20.
48 Schweizer, *Victory*, 116.
49 Ibid., 9, 116, 153; Odd Arne Westad, *The Global Cold War: Third World Interventions and the Making of Our Times* (Cambridge: Cambridge University Press, 2011), 354; NSDD 166, March 27, 1985, https://fas.org/irp/offdocs/nsdd/nsdd-166.pdf.
50 Schweizer, *Victory*, 26–27, 29.
51 NSDD 105, October 4, 1983, https://fas.org/irp/offdocs/nsdd/nsdd-105.pdf; Robert Leckie, *The Wars of America* (Edison: Castle Books, 1998), 1090–91.
52 NSDD 110, October 21, 1983, https://fas.org/irp/offdocs/nsdd/23-2169t.gif; NSDD 110A, October 23, 1983, https://fas.org/irp/offdocs/nsdd/23-2171t.gif; Leckie, *Wars*, 1091.
53 Millett et al., *Common*, 583; Leckie, *Wars*, 1091–92; Patterson, *Restless*, 205.
54 Westad, *Global*, 340–43; Brands, *Unipolar*, 79–80.
55 NSDD 17, January 4, 1982, https://fas.org/irp/offdocs/nsdd/nsdd-17.pdf; NSDD 82, February 24, 1983, https://fas.org/irp/offdocs/nsdd/nsdd-82.pdf.
56 Westad, *Global*, 345; Brands, *Unipolar*, 90.
57 NSDD 100, July 28, 1983, https://fas.org/irp/offdocs/nsdd/nsdd-100.pdf; NSDD 124, February 7, 1984, https://fas.org/irp/offdocs/nsdd/nsdd-124.pdf.
58 NSDD 264, February 27, 1987, https://irp.fas.org/offdocs/nsdd/23-2972a.gif.
59 Andrew Marvin, "Operation EARNEST WILL: The US Foreign Policy behind US Naval Operations in the Persian Gulf, 1987–89: A Curious Cause," *Naval War College Review*, 73:2 (spring 2020), 89; Steve Yetiv, *The Absence of Grand Strategy: The United States in the Persian Gulf, 1972–2005* (Baltimore: Johns Hopkins University Press, 2008), 54–57; Brands, *Unipolar*, 114; Richard Sobel, "Contra Aid Fundamentals: Exploring the Intricacies and the Issues," *Political Science Quarterly*, 110:2 (summer 1995), 289–90.
60 Pach, "Reagan," 84; Brands, *What Good*, 120; Westad, *Global*, 346–47.
61 Brands, *Unipolar*, 143–50.
62 Marvin, "Operation," 89; NSDD 99, July 12, 1983, https://fas.org/irp/offdocs/nsdd/nsdd-99.pdf.
63 Yetiv, *Absence*, 47; Marvin, "Operation," 83–86.
64 Yetiv, *Absence*, 51–53; Marvin, "Operation," 84.

65 Schweizer, *Victory*, 31, 93, 99, 203; NSDD 114, November 26, 1983, https://fas.org/irp/offdocs/nsdd/nsdd-114.pdf; NSDD 141, May 25, 1984, https://fas.org/irp/offdocs/nsdd/nsdd-141.pdf; Schweizer, *Victory*, 242–43.
66 Marvin, "Operation," 82–84, 88, 91–95; Yetiv, *Absence*, 62.
67 Marvin, "Operation," 96; John Mearsheimer, "Imperial by Design," *National Interest*, 111 (January–February 2011), 18, 32.
68 John Gans, *White House Warriors: How the National Security Council Transformed the American Way of War* (New York: Liveright, 2019), 68–69.
69 Ibid., 70–71, 74–79; Lou Cannon, *President Reagan: The Role of a Lifetime* (New York: PublicAffairs, 2000), 357–59; Millett et al., *Common*, 581.
70 NSDD 103, September 10, 1983, https://fas.org/irp/offdocs/nsdd/nsdd-103.pdf; Gans, *Warriors*, 81–82; Millett et al., *Common*, 582.
71 Gans, *Warriors*, 84; Statement by Secretary of Defense Weinberger at National Press Club, "The Uses of Military Power," November 28, 1984, http://insidethecoldwar.org/sites/default/files/documents/Statement%20by%20Secretary%20of%20Defense%20Weinberger%20at%20National%20Press%20Club,%20November%2028,%201984.pdf.
72 "Powell's Doctrine, in Powell's Words," *Washington Post* (October 7, 2001), www.washingtonpost.com/archive/opinions/2001/10/07/powells-doctrine-in-powells-words/e8fd25c5-a97f-4550-8cbd-0588eb4a9d8e/.
73 Millett et al., *Common*, 583; NSDD 138, April 3, 1984; NSDD 205, January 8, 1986, https://fas.org/irp/offdocs/nsdd/nsdd-205.pdf.
74 Millett et al., *Common*, 582; NSDD 224, April 12, 1986, https://fas.org/irp/offdocs/nsdd/nsdd-224.pdf.
75 NSDD 234, August 16, 1986, https://fas.org/irp/offdocs/nsdd/nsdd-234.pdf.
76 Green, *Providence*, 389–90, 394–96.
77 Ibid., 397.
78 Ibid., 389; NSDD 120, January 9, 1984, https://fas.org/irp/offdocs/nsdd/23-2192t.gif.
79 Green, *Providence*, 390–91, 399–400.
80 Ibid., 403–4, 414–15; NSDD 147, October 11, 1984, https://fas.org/irp/offdocs/nsdd/nsdd-147.pdf.
81 Green, *Providence*, 415–20.
82 NSDD 187, September 7, 1985, https://fas.org/irp/offdocs/nsdd/23-2642a.gif; NSDD 273, May 7, 1987, www.reaganlibrary.gov/sites/default/files/archives/reference/scanned-nsdds/nsdd273.pdf; NSDD 272, May 7, 1987, www.reaganlibrary.gov/sites/default/files/archives/reference/scanned-nsdds/nsdd272.pdf; Pach, "Reagan," 85.
83 Gaddis, *Strategies*, 362; Brands, *What Good*, 104.
84 NSDD 238, September 2, 1986, https://irp.fas.org/offdocs/nsdd/nsdd-238.pdf.
85 Ibid.
86 Ibid.
87 Ibid.

88 Ibid.
89 Ibid.
90 Baer, *One Hundred*, 442; Millett et al., *Common*, 588–89; James Graham Wilson, "The Emergence of a Post-Cold War US National Security Strategy, 1982–1993," Paper for SHAFR, Philadelphia, June 22, 2018, 4–5.
91 Wilson, "Emergence," 1–2.
92 Ronald Reagan, *The National Security Strategy of the United States* (Washington: White House, 1987).
93 Ronald Reagan, *The National Security Strategy of the United States* (Washington: White House, 1988).
94 Brands, *Unipolar*, 98–99, 106–7; Brands, *What Good*, 127–28; Westad, *Global*, 364, 367–72.
95 Brands, *What Good*, 126, 129–31; Gaddis, *Strategies*, 365; NSDD 270, May 1, 1987, https://fas.org/irp/offdocs/nsdd/nsdd-270.pdf.
96 Brands, *Unipolar*, 101–2, 107–9; Ronald Reagan, Address from the Brandenburg Gate, June 12, 1987, https://millercenter.org/the-presidency/presidential-speeches/june-12-1987-address-brandenburg-gate-berlin-wall.
97 Brands, *What Good*, 130–31; Brands, *Unipolar*, 100, 104–5; Gaddis, *Strategies*, 364–67.
98 Gaddis, *Strategies*, 378; Brands, *Unipolar*, 107, 111.
99 George C. Herring, *The American Century: US Foreign Relations, 1893–2014* (Oxford: Oxford University Press, 2017), 601; Patterson, *Restless*, 218–19; Derek Chollet and James Goldgeier, *America between the Wars: From 11/9 to 9/11* (New York: PublicAffairs, 2008), 8–9; Brands, *Unipolar*, 276–77.
100 Christopher Hemmer, *American Pendulum: Recurring Debates in US Grand Strategy* (Ithaca: Cornell University Press, 2015), 115; National Security Review (NSR) 3, February 15, 1989, https://fas.org/irp/offdocs/nsr/nsr3.pdf; NSR 4, February 15, 1989, https://fas.org/irp/offdocs/nsr/nsr4.pdf; NSR 5, February 15, 1989, https://fas.org/irp/offdocs/nsr/nsr5.pdf; Timothy Lynch, *In the Shadow of the Cold War: American Foreign Policy from George Bush Sr. to Donald Trump* (Cambridge: Cambridge University Press, 2020), 23; Hal Brands, "Choosing Primacy: US Strategy and Global Order at the Dawn of the Post-Cold War Era," *Texas National Security Review*, 1:2 (March 2018), 12–14.
101 George H. W. Bush, Remarks at the United States Coast Guard Academy Commencement Ceremony in New London, Connecticut, May 24, 1989, https://bush41library.tamu.edu/archives/public-papers/448; Brands, *Unipolar*, 278; George H. W. Bush, Address at Texas A&M, May 12, 1989, https://millercenter.org/the-presidency/presidential-speeches/may-12-1989-commencement-address-texas-am-university.
102 Bush, Remarks at the Coast Guard Academy; Bush, Address at Texas A&M.
103 Bush, Address at Texas A&M; George H. W. Bush, *The National Security Strategy of the United States* (Washington: White House, 1990), 2–3.
104 John Lewis Gaddis, *The Cold War: A New History* (New York: Penguin, 2005), 241–46.

105 Ibid., 246–47.
106 *NSS*, 1990, 5, 9, 11.
107 Melvyn Leffler, *Safeguarding Democratic Capitalism: US Foreign Policy and National Security, 1920–2015* (Princeton: Princeton University Press, 2017), 251–52; NSD 23, September 22, 1989, https://fas.org/irp/offdocs/nsd/nsd23.pdf.
108 Leffler, *Safeguarding*, 254–55; Brands, *Unipolar*, 283–87.
109 Brands, *Unipolar*, 289–97; Leffler, *Safeguarding*, 255–57; James Goldgeier, "Bill and Boris: A Window into a Most Important Post-Cold War Relationship," *Texas National Security Review*, 1:4 (August 2018), 48.
110 NSD 8, May 1, 1989, https://fas.org/irp/offdocs/nsd/nsd8.pdf; *NSS* 1990, 12.
111 Lynch, *Shadow*, 45–46; Patterson, *Restless*, 219, 226, 246–47, 253; *NSS*, 1990, 22.
112 *NSS*, 1990, 23; Patterson, *Restless*, 229 and n.27.
113 Joshua Itzkowitz Shifrinson, "Deal or No Deal? The End of the Cold War and the US Offer to Limit NATO Expansion," *International Security*, 40:4 (spring 2016), 11, 31–40; *NSS*, 1990, 10.
114 Patterson, *Restless*, 226–27; Leckie, *Wars*, 1097–98; Joe Pichirallo, "Indictments Depict Noriega as Drug-Trafficking Kingpin," *Washington Post* (February 6, 1988), www.washingtonpost.com/archive/politics/1988/02/06/indictments-depict-noriega-as-drug-trafficking-kingpin/1a1675d6-88ec-449a-9147-07f55c78a326/; NSD 21, September 1, 1989, https://fas.org/irp/offdocs/nsd/nsd21.pdf; NSD 32, September 30, 1989, https://fas.org/irp/offdocs/nsd/nsd32.pdf.
115 George H. W. Bush, Address to the Nation on Panama, December 20, 1989, https://millercenter.org/the-presidency/presidential-speeches/december-20-1989-address-nation-panama; Lynch, *Shadow*, 31; Patterson, *Restless*, 227; Millett et al., *Common*, 593.
116 NSD 20, August 29, 1989, https://fas.org/irp/offdocs/nsd/nsd20.pdf.
117 NSD 3, February 13, 1989, https://fas.org/irp/offdocs/nsd/nsd3.pdf; Peter Tomsen, *The Wars of Afghanistan: Messianic Terrorism, Tribal Conflicts, and the Failures of Great Powers* (New York: PublicAffairs, 2011), 453; Seth Jones, *In the Graveyard of Empires: America's War in Afghanistan* (New York: Norton, 2009), 48.
118 Tomsen, *Afghanistan*, 483–84, 524; Millett et al., *Common*, 624.
119 Lynch, *Shadow*, 26–28, 49; Herring, *American*, 603.
120 Herring, *American*, 604–5; *NSS*, 1990, 12.
121 Zachary Karabell, "Backfire: US Policy toward Iraq, 1988–2 August 1990," *Middle East Journal*, 49:1 (winter 1995), 28–32; Yetiv, *Absence*, 65–70, 79, 202; NSD 26, October 2, 1989, https://fas.org/irp/offdocs/nsd/nsd26.pdf.
122 Hemmer, *Pendulum*, 104–7; Gaddis, *Cold War*, 252–54.
123 Lynch, *Shadow*, 41; Gaddis, *Cold War*, 254–57.
124 George H. W. Bush, State of the Union Address, January 29, 1991, https://millercenter.org/the-presidency/presidential-speeches/january-29-1991-state-union-address; Christopher Hemmer, *American Pendulum: Recurring Debates in US Grand Strategy* (Ithaca: Cornell University Press, 2015), 107.

125 Colin Gray, "Harry Truman and the Forming of American Grand Strategy in the Cold War, 1945–1953," in Williamson Murray et al., eds., *The Shaping of Grand Strategy: Policy, Diplomacy, and War* (Cambridge: Cambridge University Press, 2011), 229.
126 Brands, *What Good*, 119.
127 Brands, *Unipolar*, 42–44; Patterson, *Restless*, 195.

16 THE GULF WAR, OR FIRST IRAQ WAR, 1990–1991

1 Melvyn Leffler, *Safeguarding Democratic Capitalism: US Foreign Policy and National Security, 1920–2015* (Princeton: Princeton University Press, 2017), 258; Lawrence Freedman and Efraim Karsh, *The Gulf Conflict, 1990–1991: Diplomacy and War in the New World Order* (Princeton: Princeton University Press, 1995), xxix.
2 Freedman and Karsh, *Gulf*, 21–27, 39, 45–47.
3 Ibid., 33–36, 51–62; Timothy Lynch, *In the Shadow of the Cold War: American Foreign Policy from George Bush Sr. to Donald Trump* (Cambridge: Cambridge University Press, 2020), 33–36.
4 Freedman and Karsh, *Gulf*, 73–76; George H. W. Bush, Address on Iraq's Invasion of Kuwait, August 8, 1990, https://millercenter.org/the-presidency/presidential-speeches/august-8-1990-address-iraqs-invasion-kuwait; George H. W. Bush, Address to the United Nations, October 1, 1990, https://millercenter.org/the-presidency/presidential-speeches/october-1-1990-address-united-nations; Derek Chollet and James Goldgeier, *America between the Wars: From 11/9 to 9/11* (New York: PublicAffairs, 2008), 9; Hal Brands, *Making the Unipolar Moment: US Foreign Policy and the Rise of the Post-Cold War Order* (Ithaca: Cornell University Press, 2016), 302; NSD 45, August 20, 1990, https://fas.org/irp/offdocs/nsd/nsd45.pdf; Kevin Woods, *The Mother of All Battles: Saddam Hussein's Strategic Plan for the Persian Gulf War* (Annapolis: Naval Institute Press, 2008), 125; George H. W. Bush, Address before a Joint Session of Congress, September 11, 1990, https://millercenter.org/the-presidency/presidential-speeches/september-11-1990-address-joint-session-congress.
5 Chollet and Goldgeier, *America*, 11; Freedman and Karsh, *Gulf*, 232.
6 Freedman and Karsh, *Gulf*, 85–88, 93–94.
7 Bush, Address on Iraq's Invasion; Bush, Address before a Joint Session.
8 Richard Swain, "The Gulf War, 1990–1991: A Coalition of Convenience in a Changing World," in Peter Mansoor and Williamson Murray, eds., *Grand Strategy and Military Alliances* (Cambridge: Cambridge University Press, 2011), 348; NSD 45; Bush, Address on Iraq's Invasion; Leffler, *Safeguarding*, 259.
9 Freedman and Karsh, *Gulf*, 79–83, 111, 190; Woods, *Mother*, 159; NSD 45; Bush, Address on Iraq's Invasion; Swain, "Gulf War," 348, 355.
10 NSD 45; Gary Hess, *Presidential Decisions for War: Korea, Vietnam, and the Persian Gulf* (Baltimore: Johns Hopkins University Press, 2001), 201 and note; Swain, "Gulf War," 351–52.

11 Freedman and Karsh, *Gulf*, 358; Peter Layton, *Grand Strategy* (Australia: Peter Layton, 2018), 101–2; Hugh Rockoff, *America's Economic Way of War: War and the US Economy from the Spanish-American War to the Persian Gulf War* (Cambridge: Cambridge University Press, 2012), 309; Swain, "Gulf War," 358.
12 NSD 54; W. Andrew Terrill, *Escalation and Intrawar Deterrence during Limited Wars in the Middle East* (Carlisle: SSI, 2009), 73–74; Swain, "Gulf War," 367–68; Lynch, *Shadow*, 37; Freedman and Karsh, *Gulf*, 234, 241, 255–57; Woods, *Mother*, 159.
13 George H. W. Bush and Brent Scowcroft, *A World Transformed* (New York: Vintage, 1999) 417–18, 435, 446; Freedman and Karsh, *Gulf*, 294; James T. Patterson, *Restless Giant: The United States from Watergate to Bush v. Gore* (Oxford: Oxford University Press, 2007), 233.
14 NSD 54.
15 Bush and Scowcroft, *World*, 432–33; Leffler, *Safeguarding*, 259.
16 NSD 54; Bush and Scowcroft, *World*, 433.
17 NSD 54.
18 Swain, "Gulf War," 347; Freedman and Karsh, *Gulf*, 202; Allan Millett et al., *For the Common Defense: A Military History of the United States from 1607 to 2012*, 3rd ed. (New York: Free Press, 2012), 596–97.
19 Freedman and Karsh, *Gulf*, 203; Michael Gordon and Bernard Trainor, *The Generals' War: The Inside Story of the Conflict in the Gulf* (New York: Back Bay, 1995), 33–34.
20 Carl von Clausewitz, *On War*, Michael Howard and Peter Paret, trans. and eds. (Princeton: Princeton University Press, 1984), 595–96, 618; John A. Warden III, *The Air Campaign: Planning for Combat* (Washington: NDU Press, 1988), 40.
21 Gordon and Trainor, *Generals' War*, 78; John A. Warden III, "The Enemy as a System," *Air Power Journal*, 9:1 (1995), 42.
22 Gordon and Trainor, *Generals' War*, 79–80; Rick Atkinson, *Crusade: The Untold Story of the Persian Gulf War* (Boston: Houghton Mifflin, 1993), 59; Benjamin S. Lambeth, *The Transformation of American Air Power* (Ithaca: Cornell University Press, 2000), 105.
23 Gordon and Trainor, *Generals' War*, 82–84; Atkinson, *Crusade*, 60.
24 Gordon and Trainor, *Generals' War*, 132, 135–38; Atkinson, *Crusade*, 61–65; Lambeth, *Transformation*, 106–7.
25 Gordon and Trainor, *Generals' War*, 124–27.
26 Ibid., 129, 138–52, 160–62, 172; Freedman and Karsh, *Gulf*, 204–5.
27 Gordon and Trainor, *Generals' War*, 153–54.
28 Norman Schwarzkopf and Peter Petre, *It Doesn't Take a Hero* (New York: Bantam, 1992), 382.
29 Ibid., 382–83; Robert Scales, *Certain Victory: The US Army in the Gulf War* (Washington: Office of the Chief of Staff, US Army, 1993), 128–29, 145–46; Gordon and Trainor, *Generals' War*, 306–8.
30 Schwarzkopf and Petre, *Hero*, 383; Bush and Scowcroft, *World*, 469; Freedman and Karsh, *Gulf*, 301.

31 Woods, *Mother*, 125, 129, 134–49, 163, 177–83, 192, 200–1; Freedman and Karsh, *Gulf*, xxiii; Gordon and Trainor, *Generals' War*, 345.
32 George H. W. Bush, Address to the Nation on the Invasion of Iraq, January 16, 1991, https://millercenter.org/the-presidency/presidential-speeches/january-16-1991-address-nation-invasion-iraq; William Thomas Allison, *The Gulf War, 1990–91* (New York: Palgrave Macmillan, 2012), 98; Freedman and Karsh, *Gulf*, 285–88, 320–21; Woods, *Mother*, 150–52, 155–56.
33 Freedman and Karsh, *Gulf*, 300–1, 313, 327; Gordon and Trainor, *Generals' War*, 326; Woods, *Mother*, 185–87, 202–3; Bush and Scowcroft, *World*, 454.
34 Woods, *Mother*, 4–5; Allison, *Gulf*, 108–9; Freedman and Karsh, *Gulf*, 303, 320–24; Gordon and Trainor, *Generals' War*, 331, 351–52; Samuel Helfont, "The Gulf War's Afterlife: Dilemmas, Missed Opportunities, and the Post-Cold War Order Undone," *Texas National Security Review*, 4:2 (spring 2021), 30–31; Richard G. Davis, *Decisive Force: Strategic Bombing in the Gulf War* (Washington: Air Force History and Museums Program, 1996), 54–68.
35 Woods, *Mother*, 14–21, 129, 137–39, 196–97; Gordon and Trainor, *Generals' War*, 165, 267–88.
36 Woods, *Mother*, 149–51; Gordon and Trainor, *Generals' War*, 228–48; Freedman and Karsh, *Gulf*, 331–32.
37 Woods, *Mother*, 181, 210; Schwarzkopf and Petre, *Hero*, 434–36; Millett et al., *Common*, 601, 604; Allison, *Gulf*, 126.
38 Schwarzkopf and Petre, *Hero*, 436, 453–57, 560; Allison, *Gulf*, 130–33.
39 Woods, *Mother*, 227–38.
40 Schwarzkopf and Petre, *Hero*, 461–63, 466; Allison, *Gulf*, 135–38.
41 Schwarzkopf and Petre, *Hero*, 464–65; Allison, *Gulf*, 136.
42 Allison, *Gulf*, 138.
43 Gideon Rose, *How Wars End: Why We Always Fight the Last Battle* (New York: Simon and Schuster, 2010), 222–23; Bush and Scowcroft, *World*, 235; Colin Powell, *My American Journey* (New York: Random House Ballantine, 1996), 519; Christian Alfonsi, *Circle in the Sand: Why We Went back to Iraq* (New York: Doubleday, 2006), 154–55.
44 Allison, *Gulf*, 139.
45 Ibid., 139; Powell, *Journey*, 519–23; Gordon and Trainor, *Generals' War*, 422–23; Bush and Scowcroft, *World*, 485–86.
46 Bush and Scowcroft, *World*, 484; Powell, *Journey*, 523.
47 Woods, *Mother*, 240–43; Bush and Scowcroft, *World*, 486–87.
48 Powell, *Journey*, 523; NSD 54; Gordon and Trainor, *Generals' War*, 423–26; Kenneth Pollack, *The Threatening Storm* (New York: Random House, 2002), 69–70, 88.
49 Schwarzkopf and Petre, *Hero*, 473, 476–78.
50 Woods, *Mother*, 244–45; Schwarzkopf and Petre, *Hero*, 479–80.
51 Schwarzkopf and Petre, *Hero*, 479–80; Allison, *Gulf*, 141–42.
52 Allison, *Gulf*, 143; Schwarzkopf and Petre, *Hero*, 488–89; Bush and Scowcroft, *World*, 488; Robert Gates, *Duty: Memoirs of a Secretary of State* (New York: Knopf, 2014), 26.

53 Allison, *Gulf*, 146; Gordon and Trainor, *Generals' War*, 444; Schwarzkopf and Petre, *Hero*, 480.
54 Clausewitz, *On War*, 611.
55 NSD 54.
56 Rose, *How Wars*, 217–18.
57 Gordon and Trainor, *Generals' War*, 435, 443; Bush and Scowcroft, *World*, 471–72.
58 Bush and Scowcroft, *World*, 472; Brands, *Unipolar*, 314; Gordon and Trainor, *Generals' War*, 477.
59 NSD 54; Gordon and Trainor, *Generals' War*, 84.
60 Allison, *Gulf*, 146; Bush and Scowcroft, *World*, 489–90.
61 Gordon and Trainor, *Generals' War*, 447.
62 Faleh Abd al-Jabbar, "Why the Uprisings Failed," *Middle East Report*, 176 (May–June 1992), 9–12.
63 Ibid., 11; Lynch, *Shadow*, 40; Allison, *Gulf*, 147.
64 Allison, *Gulf*, 146; Brands, *Unipolar*, 323.
65 Pollack, *Threatening*, xxiv–xxviii; Allison, *Gulf*, 146.
66 Martin Alexander and John Keiger, "Limiting Arms, Enforcing Limits: International Inspections and the Challenges of Compellance in Germany Post-1919, Iraq Post-1991," *Journal of Strategic Studies*, 29:2 (2006), 361–64, 386.
67 Patterson, *Restless*, 235; Allison, *Gulf*, 144; Lynch, *Shadow*, 39.
68 Swain, "Gulf War," 344.

17 THE NEW WORLD DISORDER: BUSH AND CLINTON, 1991–2001

1 George H. W. Bush, Address before a Joint Session of Congress, September 11, 1990, https://millercenter.org/the-presidency/presidential-speeches/september-11-1990-address-joint-session-congress; Hal Brands, *Making the Unipolar Moment: US Foreign Policy and the Rise of the Post-Cold War Order* (Ithaca: Cornell University Press, 2016), 319–23, 327; Melvyn Leffler, *Safeguarding Democratic Capitalism: US Foreign Policy and National Security, 1920–2015* (Princeton: Princeton University Press, 2017), 259–60; Hal Brands, "Choosing Primacy: US Strategy and Global Order at the Dawn of the Post-Cold War Era," *Texas National Security Review*, 1:2 (March 2018), 17–18.
2 George H. W. Bush, *The National Security Strategy of the United States* (Washington: White House, 1991), v, 1, 8; Brands, *Unipolar*, 325; Kristina Spohr, *Post Wall, Post Square: Rebuilding the World after 1989* (Glasgow: William Collins, 2019), 465.
3 *NSS*, 1991, 9, 14–15, 19–21, 25–27, 31; Brands, "Choosing," 15.
4 Brands, *Unipolar*, 327, 331; Robert Art, *A Grand Strategy for America* (Ithaca: Cornell University Press, 2003), 88–89; Eric Edelman, "The Strange Career of the 1992 Defense Planning Guidance," in Melvyn Leffler and Jeffrey Legro, eds., *In Uncertain Times: American Foreign Policy after the Berlin Wall and 9/11* (Ithaca: Cornell University Press, 2011), 62–63.

5 Dale Vesser, FY 94–95 Defense Planning Guidance Sections for Comment, February 18, 1992, https://nsarchive2.gwu.edu/nukevault/ebb245/doc03_extract_nytedit.pdf.
6 Vesser, Defense Planning Guidance; George H. W. Bush, Remarks at the United States Coast Guard Academy Commencement Ceremony in New London, Connecticut, May 24, 1989, https://bush41library.tamu.edu/archives/public-papers/448; Samuel Huntington, "Why International Primacy Matters," *International Security*, 17:4 (spring 1993), 69.
7 Brands, *Unipolar*, 331; Dick Cheney, *Defense Strategy for the 1990s: The Regional Defense Strategy (RDS)*, (Washington: Department of Defense, 1993), 1–6, 11, 14.
8 Don Snider, *The National Security Strategy: Documenting Strategic Vision*, 2nd ed. (Carlisle: SSI, 1995), 9; George H. W. Bush, *The National Security Strategy of the United States* (Washington: White House, 1993), ii, 3, 21.
9 Brands, *Unipolar*, 323.
10 Timothy Lynch, *In the Shadow of the Cold War: American Foreign Policy from George Bush Sr. to Donald Trump* (Cambridge: Cambridge University Press, 2020), 43; James T. Patterson, *Restless Giant: The United States from Watergate to Bush v. Gore* (Oxford: Oxford University Press, 2007), 225–26.
11 George H. W. Bush, Address on Somalia, December 4, 1992, https://millercenter.org/the-presidency/presidential-speeches/december-4-1992-address-somalia; Lynch, *Shadow*, 46–48.
12 Derek Chollet and James Goldgeier, *America between the Wars: From 11/9 to 9/11* (New York: PublicAffairs, 2008), 40.
13 Ibid., 32–33.
14 Ibid., 37, 42; James Boys, *Clinton's Grand Strategy: US Foreign Policy in a Post-Cold War World* (London: Bloomsbury, 2015), 16–17, 22; Bill Clinton, A New Covenant for American Security, December 12, 1991, http://web.archive.org/web/20030525033427/http://www.ndol.org/print.cfm?contentid=250537; Bill Clinton, First Inaugural Address, January 20, 1993, https://millercenter.org/the-presidency/presidential-speeches/january-20-1993-first-inaugural.
15 Leon Panetta, with Jim Newton, *Worthy Fights: A Memoir of Leadership in War and Peace* (New York: Penguin, 2014), 123; Chollet and Goldgeier, *America*, 81–82; Christopher Hemmer, *American Pendulum: Recurring Debates in US Grand Strategy* (Ithaca: Cornell University Press, 2015), 116–17, 122; Boys, *Clinton's*, 41–42.
16 Chollet and Goldgeier, *America*, 47–50; Eagleburger to Warren, Parting Thoughts: US Foreign Policy in the Years Ahead, January 5, 1993, https://carnegieendowment.org/pdf/back-channel/1993MemotoChristopher.pdf.
17 Eagleburger, Parting Thoughts; Lynch, *Shadow*, 57; John Lewis Gaddis, *Surprise, Security, and the American Experience* (Cambridge: Harvard University Press, 2004), 76–77; Francis Fukuyama, "The End of History?" *The National Interest*, 16 (summer 1989), 4–5.
18 Strobe Talbott, *The Russia Hand: A Memoir of Presidential Diplomacy* (New York: Random House, 2002), 133–34; Boys, *Clinton's*, 82; Gaddis, *Surprise*, 77; Hal

Brands, *The Promise and Pitfalls of Grand Strategy* (Carlisle: Army War College Press, 2012), 15; John Lewis Gaddis, *George F. Kennan: An American Life* (New York: Penguin, 2011), 680.
19 Boys, *Clinton's*, 52–53; Lynch, *Shadow*, 52; Bill Clinton, Address before a Joint Session of Congress, February 17, 1993, https://millercenter.org/the-presidency/presidential-speeches/february-17-1993-address-joint-session-congress.
20 Chollet and Goldgeier, *America*, 151–62; Boys, *Clinton's*, 163–66, 169–72, 176–77; Bill Clinton, State of the Union Address, February 4, 1997, https://millercenter.org/the-presidency/presidential-speeches/february-4-1997-state-union-address; Bill Clinton, Remarks on the Signing of NAFTA, December 8, 1993, https://millercenter.org/the-presidency/presidential-speeches/december-8-1993-remarks-signing-nafta.
21 Boys, *Clinton's*, 171; Douglas Irwin, *Clashing over Commerce: A History of US Trade Policy* (Chicago: University of Chicago Press, 2017), 643; Alfred E. Eckes Jr., *Opening America's Market: US Foreign Trade Policy since 1776* (Chapel Hill: UNC Press, 1995), 287.
22 Chollet and Goldgeier, *America*, 248.
23 Ibid., 252; Boys, *Clinton's*, 167; Patterson, *Restless*, 331–33.
24 Fukuyama, "End," 4–5; Boys, *Clinton's*, 55–56.
25 Lynch, *Shadow*, 61; Bill Clinton, Remarks on Operation Restore Hope, May 5, 1993, https://millercenter.org/the-presidency/presidential-speeches/may-5-1993-remarks-operation-restore-hope; Boys, *Clinton's*, 56; Allan Millett et al., *For the Common Defense: A Military History of the United States from 1607 to 2012*, 3rd ed. (New York: Free Press, 2012), 614–15; Chollet and Goldgeier, *America*, 74; Hemmer, *Pendulum*, 120.
26 Chollet and Goldgeier, *America*, 73–75; Madeleine Albright, with Bill Woodward, *Madam Secretary* (New York: Hyperion, 2003), 180–82; Millett et al., *Common*, 615.
27 Chollet and Goldgeier, *America*, 77–76; Albright, *Madam Secretary*, 183; Boys, *Clinton's*, 57–58; Bill Clinton, Address on Somalia, October 7, 1993, https://millercenter.org/the-presidency/presidential-speeches/october-7-1993-address-somalia.
28 Chollet and Goldgeier, *America*, 75; Bill Clinton, Remarks to the 48th Session of the United Nations General Assembly, September 27, 1993, https://2009-2017.state.gov/p/io/potusunga/207375.htm.
29 Albright, *Madam Secretary*, 183–84.
30 Colin Dueck, *Reluctant Crusaders: Power, Culture, and Change in American Grand Strategy* (Princeton: Princeton University Press, 2006), 142.
31 Lynch, *Shadow*, 62–63; Chollet and Goldgeier, *America*, 78.
32 Boys, *Clinton's*, 83.
33 Lynch, *Shadow*, 57–58; Chollet and Goldgeier, *America*, 67; Hemmer, *Pendulum*, 111; Samuel Huntington, "The Clash of Civilizations?" *Foreign Affairs*, 72:3 (summer, 1993), 22–49; Remarks of Anthony Lake, "From Containment to

Enlargement," Washington, September 21, 1993, www.mtholyoke.edu/acad/intrel/lakedoc.html (hereafter Lake Remarks).
34 Lake Remarks; Boys, *Clinton's*, 85, 91–92; Clinton, Remarks to the 48th Session; Bill Clinton, State of the Union Address, January 25, 1994, https://millercenter.org/the-presidency/presidential-speeches/january-25-1994-state-union-address.
35 Lake Remarks.
36 Ibid.
37 Ibid.; Boys, *Clinton's*, 46, 85–86, 268; Jeremi Suri, "American Grand Strategy from the Cold War's End to 9/11," *Orbis* (fall 2009), 622; Chollet and Goldgeier, *America*, 69, 79–83; Anthony Lake, Oral History, 2002, https://millercenter.org/the-presidency/presidential-oral-histories/anthony-lake-oral-history-2002.
38 Boys, *Clinton's*, 268; William Clinton, *A National Security Strategy of Engagement and Enlargement* (Washington: White House, 1994), i–ii; William Clinton, *A National Security Strategy of Engagement and Enlargement* (Washington: White House, 1995); William Clinton, *A National Security Strategy of Engagement and Enlargement* (Washington: White House, 1996).
39 Boys, *Clinton's*, 217–22; PDD/NSC 28, September 8, 1994, https://fas.org/irp/offdocs/pdd/pdd-28.pdf.
40 Chollet and Goldgeier, *America*, 81; Lynch, *Shadow*, 64.
41 Boys, *Clinton's*, 187–88; Lake, Oral History, 2002; Leffler, *Safeguarding*, 272.
42 Chollet and Goldgeier, *America*, 258–60; Boys, *Clinton's*, 188–90.
43 Chollet and Goldgeier, *America*, 137; Remarks by Samuel Berger, Council on Foreign Relations, New York, June 6, 1997, www.mtholyoke.edu/acad/intrel/bergchin.htm.
44 Chollet and Goldgeier, *America*, 93–95; Albright, *Madam Secretary*, 579–80; Lynch, *Shadow*, 63–65; Brendan Taylor, *Sanctions as Grand Strategy* (Abingdon: Routledge, 2010), 27; "A Timeline of North Korea's Nuclear Tests," *CBS News*, updated September 3, 2017, www.cbsnews.com/news/north-koreas-nuclear-tests-timeline/.
45 Chollet and Goldgeier, *America*, 119–20; Boys, *Clinton's*, 185; Lynch, *Shadow*, 58–59.
46 Chollet and Goldgeier, *America*, 125; Rajan Menon and William Ruger, "NATO Enlargement and US Grand Strategy: A Net Assessment," *International Politics*, 57 (2020), 373–75; Boys, *Clinton's*, 132–45; James Goldgeier, "Bill and Boris: A Window into a Most Important Post-Cold War Relationship," *Texas National Security Review*, 1:4 (August 2018), 48.
47 Goldgeier, "Bill and Boris," 49, 52; Chollet and Goldgeier, *America*, 125; Boys, *Clinton's*, 145.
48 Lynch, *Shadow*, 72; Menon and Ruger, "NATO," 373–74; Boys, *Clinton's*, 141.
49 Chollet and Goldgeier, *America*, 95–98; Lynch, *Shadow*, 63–64.
50 George C. Herring, *The American Century: US Foreign Relations, 1893–2014* (Oxford: Oxford University Press, 2017), 628–30; Allan Millett et al., *For the Common Defense: A Military History of the United States from 1607 to 2012*, 3rd

ed. (New York: Free Press, 2012), 618–21; Boys, *Clinton's*, 239–42; "Powell's Doctrine, in Powell's Words," *Washington Post*, October 7, 2001, www.washingtonpost.com/archive/opinions/2001/10/07/powells-doctrine-in-powells-words/e8fd25c5-a97f-4550-8cbd-0588eb4a9d8e/.

51 Boys, *Clinton's*, 59, 238, 243–46; Chollet and Goldgeier, *America*, 126; Albright, *Madam Secretary*, 228–29; Robert Lieber, "Eagle without a Cause: Making Foreign Policy without a Soviet Threat," in Robert Lieber, ed., *Eagle Adrift: American Foreign Policy at the End of the Century* (New York: Longman, 1997), 14.

52 Boys, *Clinton's*, 246–47; Chollet and Goldgeier, *America*, 127; Lynch, *Shadow*, 70; Albright, *Madam Secretary*, 233–35.

53 Chollet and Goldgeier, *America*, 127–28, 133; Boys, *Clinton's*, 249; Albright, *Madam Secretary*, 241; Millett et al., *Common*, 621.

54 Albright, *Madam Secretary*, 239–41; Millett et al., *Common*, 621–22; Bill Clinton, Address on Bosnia, November 27, 1995, https://millercenter.org/the-presidency/presidential-speeches/november-27-1995-address-bosnia; Chollet and Goldgeier, *America*, 132.

55 Lieber, "Eagle," 15.

56 Chollet and Goldgeier, *America*, 97–100, 112–15; Michael Mandelbaum, "Foreign Policy as Social Work," *Foreign Affairs*, 75:1 (January–February 1996), 16–17, 20–21.

57 Lynch, *Shadow*, 78–79; Chollet and Goldgeier, *America*, 147–49.

58 William Clinton, *A National Security Strategy for a New Century* (Washington: White House, 1997). The text consulted lacks page numbers.

59 Bill Clinton, *A National Security Strategy for a New Century* (Washington: White House, 1998); Bill Clinton, *A National Security Strategy for a New Century* (Washington: White House, 1999); William J. Clinton, *A National Security Strategy for a Global Age* (Washington: White House, 2000), 1–3, 67; Hemmer, *Pendulum*, 118.

60 Dueck, *Reluctant*, 144; Leffler, *Safeguarding*, 291; Boys, *Clinton's*, 53, 85, 123–28.

61 Clinton, State of the Union, January 25, 1994; *NSS*, 1994, 10.

62 William Cohen, *Report of the Quadrennial Defense Review* (Washington: Department of Defense, 1997), 6–8.

63 Ibid., iv, 5, 9–14.

64 *Joint Doctrine for Military Operations Other than War*, Joint Pub 3–07, June 16, 1995, www.bits.de/NRANEU/others/jp-doctrine/jp3_07.pdf; PDD/NSC 56, May 20, 1997, https://fas.org/irp/offdocs/pdd/pdd-56.pdf.

65 Lynch, *Shadow*, 55–56; PDD/NSC 39, June 21, 1995, https://fas.org/irp/offdocs/pdd/pdd-39.pdf; Boys, *Clinton's*, 135, 138–39.

66 Peter Tomsen, *The Wars of Afghanistan: Messianic Terrorism, Tribal Conflicts, and the Failures of Great Powers* (New York: PublicAffairs, 2011), 524–25, 543–44, 550; Millett et al., *Common*, 627–28.

67 Tomsen, *Afghanistan*, 523–24, 550–51; Chollet and Goldgeier, *America*, 244–45; Boys, *Clinton's*, 139.

68 David Crist, *The Twilight War: The Secret History of America's Thirty-Year Conflict with Iran* (New York: Penguin, 2012), 392; Boys, *Clinton's*, 85; Lynch, *Shadow*, 93–95.
69 Steve Yetiv, *The Absence of Grand Strategy: The United States in the Persian Gulf, 1972–2005* (Baltimore: Johns Hopkins University Press, 2008), 91, 99–103, 107–8; Crist, *Twilight*, 391; Boys, *Clinton's*, 62–66; Samuel Helfont, "The Gulf War's Afterlife: Dilemmas, Missed Opportunities, and the Post-Cold War Order Undone," *Texas National Security Review*, 4:2 (spring 2021), 37–45.
70 Boys, *Clinton's*, 62–63; Chollet and Goldgeier, *America*, 149; Yetiv, *Absence*, 96.
71 Yetiv, *Absence*, 101–2; Boys, *Clinton's*, 272; Crist, *Twilight*, 401–6, 409–15.
72 Boys, *Clinton's*, 60–61; Yetiv, *Absence*, 100–2.
73 Lynch, *Shadow*, 80; Chollet and Goldgeier, *America*, 185, 203.
74 Boys, *Clinton's*, 272; Yetiv, *Absence*, 111–13; Peter Layton, *Grand Strategy* (Australia: Peter Layton, 2018), 201; Michael Gordon and Bernard Trainor, *The Endgame: The Inside Story of the Struggle for Iraq from George W. Bush to Barack Obama* (New York: Pantheon, 2012), 5.
75 Yetiv, *Absence*, 95, 110; Gordon and Trainor, *Endgame*, 5–6; Lynch, *Shadow*, 80, 85; Chollet and Goldgeier, *America*, 200–2.
76 Gordon and Trainor, *Endgame*, 6–9.
77 Hemmer, *Pendulum*, 125; Chollet and Goldgeier, *America*, 215, 229–30; Millett et al., *Common*, 623.
78 Lynch, *Shadow*, 90; Chollet and Goldgeier, *America*, 215–16.
79 Chollet and Goldgeier, *America*, 216, 220; Ivo Daalder and Michael O'Hanlon, *Winning Ugly: NATO's War to Save Kosovo* (Washington: Brookings, 2000), 2, 18.
80 Daalder and O'Hanlon, *Winning*, 90–93; Independent International Commission on Kosovo, *The Kosovo Report: Conflict, International Response, Lessons Learned* (Oxford: Oxford University Press, 2000), 85–86; Remarks by the President on the Situation in Kosovo, March 22, 1999, https://clintonwhitehouse2.archives.gov/WH/New/html/19990322-5615.html; Bill Clinton, Statement on Kosovo, March 24, 1999, https://millercenter.org/the-presidency/presidential-speeches/march-24-1999-statement-kosovo.
81 Daalder and O'Hanlon, *Winning*, 4–5; Chollet and Goldgeier, *America*, 214, 223–25.
82 Albright, *Madam Secretary*, 523; *Kosovo Report*, 86, 259–60; Len Hawley and Dennis Skocz, "Advance Political-Military Planning: Laying the Foundation for Achieving Viable Peace," in Jock Covey et al., eds., *The Quest for Viable Peace: International Intervention and Strategies for Conflict Transformation* (Washington: USIP, 2015), 50; Brendan Gallagher, *The Day After: Why America Wins the War But Loses the Peace* (Ithaca: Cornell University Press, 2019), 40–41.
83 Chollet and Goldgeier, *America*, 225; Daalder and O'Hanlon, *Winning*, 4–5.
84 Chollet and Goldgeier, *America*, 218–19.
85 Ibid., 232–34.
86 Walter A. McDougall, *Promised Land, Crusader State: The American Encounter with the World since 1776* (New York: Houghton Mifflin, 1997), 202; Boys, *Clinton's*, 198.

87 McDougall, *Promised*, 202; Boys, *Clinton's*, 250–51.
88 Boys, *Clinton's*, 270; Dueck, *Reluctant*, 143; Lieber, "Eagle," 6.
89 Lynch, *Shadow*, 74, 95; Chollet and Goldgeier, *America*, 258–60.
90 Herring, *American*, 637.

18 WILSONIAN REVOLUTIONARIES: THE BUSH ADMINISTRATION, 2001–2009

1 Timothy Lynch, *In the Shadow of the Cold War: American Foreign Policy from George Bush Sr. to Donald Trump* (Cambridge: Cambridge University Press, 2020), 98; James T. Patterson, *Restless Giant: The United States from Watergate to Bush v. Gore* (Oxford: Oxford University Press, 2007), 422–23; Melvyn Leffler, *Safeguarding Democratic Capitalism: US Foreign Policy and National Security, 1920–2015* (Princeton: Princeton University Press, 2017), 274–75; Derek Chollet and James Goldgeier, *America between the Wars: From 11/9 to 9/11* (New York: PublicAffairs, 2008), 296; Christopher Hemmer, *American Pendulum: Recurring Debates in US Grand Strategy* (Ithaca: Cornell University Press, 2015), 129–31; Colin Dueck, *Reluctant Crusaders: Power, Culture, and Change in American Grand Strategy* (Princeton: Princeton University Press, 2006), 148–50.
2 Dueck, *Reluctant*, 149; Leffler, *Safeguarding*, 275–76; George W. Bush, First Inaugural Address, January 20, 2001, https://millercenter.org/the-presidency/presidential-speeches/january-20-2001-first-inaugural-address; George C. Herring, *The American Century: US Foreign Relations, 1893–2014* (Oxford: Oxford University Press, 2017), 642.
3 Lawrence Wright, *The Looming Tower: Al-Qaeda and the Road to 9/11* (New York: Knopf, 2007), 171–75, 187–89, 223–26.
4 Bob Woodward, *Bush at War* (New York: Simon and Schuster, 2002), 17, 26–27; Leffler, *Safeguarding*, 282; Hemmer, *Pendulum*, 132.
5 George W. Bush, *Decision Points* (New York: Crown, 2010), 189–90.
6 President Bush Addresses the Nation, September 20, 2001, www.washingtonpost.com/wp-srv/nation/specials/attacked/transcripts/bushaddress_092001.html.
7 NSPD 9, October 25, 2001, https://fas.org/irp/offdocs/nspd/nspd-9.pdf; Bush, *Decision*, 396–97.
8 Hemmer, *Pendulum*, 134; Hew Strachan, *The Direction of War: Contemporary Strategy in Historical Perspective* (Cambridge: Cambridge University Press, 2013), 11; John Morrissey, *The Long War: CENTCOM, Grand Strategy, and Global Security* (Athens: University of Georgia Press, 2017), 7.
9 Donald Rumsfeld, Strategic Guidance for the Campaign against Terrorism, October 3, 2001, http://library.rumsfeld.com/doclib/sp/134/2001-10-03%20To%20Deputy%20SecDef%20et%20al%20re%20Strategic%20Guidance%20for%20Campaign%20Against%20Terrorism.pdf.
10 Ibid.

11 Richard Stewart, *Operation ENDURING FREEDOM: The United States Army in Afghanistan, October 2001–March 2002* (Washington: Center for Military History, 2004), 7; Wright, *Looming*, 223, 226; Peter Tomsen, *The Wars of Afghanistan: Messianic Terrorism, Tribal Conflicts, and the Failures of Great Powers* (New York: PublicAffairs, 2011), 556–58.
12 Woodward, *Bush*, 41, 46, 191–92; Allan Millett et al., *For the Common Defense: A Military History of the United States from 1607 to 2012*, 3rd ed. (New York: Free Press, 2012), 640; Authorization for Use of Military Force, September 18, 2001, www.congress.gov/107/plaws/publ40/PLAW-107publ40.pdf; Bush, *Decision*, 194–95.
13 Woodward, *Bush*, 47; Bush, *Decision*, 188; Seth Jones, *In the Graveyard of Empires: America's War in Afghanistan* (New York: Norton, 2009), 88–89; Tomsen, *Afghanistan*, 591–92, 627.
14 Woodward, *Bush*, 41, 45, 62, 98–99, 172, 176; Barry Posen, *Restraint: A New Foundation for US Grand Strategy* (Ithaca: Cornell University Press, 2014), 38; Michael DeLong, with Noah Lukeman, *Inside CENTCOM: The Unvarnished Truth about the Wars in Afghanistan and Iraq* (Washington: Regnery, 2004), 23–24, 28–29, 36.
15 Tomsen, *Afghanistan*, 558; Woodward, *Bush*, 43–44, 153; Donald Rumsfeld, *Known and Unknown: A Memoir* (New York: Sentinel, 2011), 369–71; Bush, *Decision*, 194; Stewart, *ENDURING*, 19; DeLong, *CENTCOM*, 23–25, 35–36, 58–59; Jones, *Graveyard*, 88–91.
16 Bush, *Decision*, 197–98; Stewart, *ENDURING*, 10–11; DeLong, *CENTCOM*, 38–41; Jones, *Graveyard*, 91–92.
17 DeLong, *CENTCOM*, 53; Tomsen, *Afghanistan*, 604–7; Jones, *Graveyard*, 92.
18 Rumsfeld, *Known*, 392; Jim Mattis and Bing West, *Call Sign Chaos: Learning to Lead* (New York: Random House, 2019), 53–58, 65, 67–68; DeLong, *CENTCOM*, 54.
19 Tomsen, *Afghanistan*, 613–14; Stewart, *ENDURING*, 22–25; Jones, *Graveyard*, 68; DeLong, *CENTCOM*, 54–55.
20 Mary Ann Weaver, "Lost at Tora Bora," *NYT* (September 11, 2005); Stewart, *ENDURING*, 26; Jack Fairweather, *The Good War: Why We Couldn't Win the War or the Peace in Afghanistan* (New York: Basic Books, 2014), 47–50.
21 Philip Smucker, *Al Qaeda's Great Escape: The Military and the Media on Terror's Trail* (Washington: Brassey's, 2004), 34; Fairweather, *Good War*, 50–51; Tomsen, *Afghanistan*, 609–10; Mattis and West, *Chaos*, 73–74; Weaver, "Lost."
22 Tomsen, *Afghanistan*, 610–11; Fairweather, *Good War*, 52; Peter Bergen, "The Account of How We Nearly Caught Osama bin Laden in 2001," *The New Republic* (December 29, 2009), https://newrepublic.com/article/72086/the-battle-tora-bora; Weaver, "Lost."
23 Fairweather, *Good War*, 57; Mark Geibel, "Operation Anaconda, Shah-i-Khot Valley, Afghanistan, 2–10 March 2002," *Military Review* (May–June 2002), 72–76; Craig Whitlock, "Stranded without a Strategy," *Washington Post* (December 9, 2019).
24 Jones, *Graveyard*, xxii, 108; Smucker, *Escape*, 88, 205–6; Fairweather, *Good War*, 52; Tomsen, *Afghanistan*, 558, 591–93.

25 Jones, *Graveyard*, 131–32.
26 Fairweather, *Good War*, 51; "Tora Bora Revisited: How We Failed to Get Bin Laden and Why It Matters Today," *A Report To Members of the Committee on Foreign Relations of the United States Senate*, November 30, 2009, www.foreign.senate.gov/imo/media/doc/Tora_Bora_Report.pdf.
27 Fairweather, *Good War*, 41–45.
28 Tomsen, *Afghanistan*, 632; Bush, *Decision*, 197, 205; Woodward, *Bush*, 195.
29 Bush, *Decision*, 205–9; Tomsen, *Afghanistan*, 628, 640–43; Paul Miller, *Armed State Building: Confronting State Failure, 1898–2012* (Ithaca: Cornell University Press, 2013), 156.
30 Tomsen, *Afghanistan*, 630; Jones, *Graveyard*, 240–49; Sharifullah Dorani, *America in Afghanistan: Foreign Policy and Decision Making from Bush to Obama to Trump* (London: I. B. Tauris, 2019), 76–77; Donald Stoker, "Expeditionary Police Advising: A Brief History," in Donald Stoker and Edward Westermann, eds., *Expeditionary Police Advising and Militarization: Building Security in a Fractured World* (Solihull: Helion, 2018), 41–47; Nicholas Kramer and Craig Whiteside, "The Thin Blue Line: Police Advising in Dynamic Environments, Iraq (2003–2014) and Afghanistan (2009–2015)," in Stoker and Westermann, eds., *Expeditionary*, 291; Fairweather, *Good War*, 126–31; DeeDee Derksen, *The Politics of Disarmament and Rearmament In Afghanistan* (Washington: USIP, 2015), 8–11.
31 Jones, *Graveyard*, 176–78; Dorani, *America*, 76.
32 Tomsen, *Afghanistan*, 632–34, 643–46; Fairweather, *Good War*, 60.
33 Fairweather, *Good War*, 61–64, 209–10; Tomsen, *Afghanistan*, 640.
34 Tomsen, *Afghanistan*, 613; Jones, *Graveyard*, 98–108.
35 Fairweather, *Good War*, 54–56; Jones, *Graveyard*, 114–15, 124, 129–32; Hal Brands, *What Good Is Grand Strategy? Power and Purpose in American Statecraft from Harry S. Truman to George W. Bush* (Ithaca: Cornell University Press, 2014), 170; Bush, *Decision*, 207.
36 Fairweather, *Good War*, 102–4, 107–8, 112–14; Hemmer, *Pendulum*, 142.
37 Jones, *Graveyard*, 139–42; Fairweather, *Good War*, 95; Steve Coll, *Directorate S: The C.I.A. and America's Secret Wars in Afghanistan* (New York: Penguin, 2018), 185–86.
38 Coll, *Directorate*, 186; Jones, *Graveyard*, 139, 142; David W. Barno, "Fighting 'The Other War': Counterinsurgency Strategy in Afghanistan, 2003–2005," *Military Review* (September–October 2007), 34–42.
39 Barno, "Fighting," 42; Jones, *Graveyard*, 148–51, 163, 178, 181, 204–6; Tomsen, *Afghanistan*, 620, 656; Bush, *Decision*, 211; Whitlock, "Stranded."
40 Fairweather, *Good War*, 178–84; Tomsen, *Afghanistan*, 648–51.
41 Fairweather, *Good War*, 143–45, 186–88, 222–26; Whitlock, "Stranded."
42 Jones, *Graveyard*, 281–82; Fairweather, *Good War*, 188, 193–94; Brands, *What Good*, 170–71.
43 Fairweather, *Good War*, 231; Bob Woodward, *Obama's Wars* (New York: Simon and Schuster, 2010), 40–44.

44 Lynch, *Shadow*, 111; Steve Yetiv, *The Absence of Grand Strategy: The United States in the Persian Gulf, 1972–2005* (Baltimore: Johns Hopkins University Press, 2008), 124; Leffler, *Safeguarding*, 278; George H. W. Bush, Address before a Joint Session of Congress, September 11, 1990; Carter, State of the Union, January 23, 1980.

45 George W. Bush, State of the Union Address, January 29, 2002, https://millercenter.org/the-presidency/presidential-speeches/january-29-2002-state-union-address; George W. Bush, *The National Security Strategy of the United States* (Washington: White House, 2002), v, 1; Leffler, *Safeguarding*, 277–78, 298; George W. Bush, Remarks on Freedom in Iraq and Middle East, November 6, 2003, https://millercenter.org/the-presidency/presidential-speeches/november-6-2003-remarks-freedom-iraq-and-middle-east; NSPD 58, July 17, 2008, https://fas.org/irp/offdocs/nspd/nspd-58.pdf; President Bush Discusses Importance of Democracy in Middle East, February 4, 2004, georgewbush-whitehouse.archives.gov/news/releases/2004/02/20040204-4.html.

46 *NSS*, 2002, v, 15; Bush, State of the Union, January 29, 2002. The 2002 *NSS* was followed by another in 2006 and the *National Strategy for Combating Terrorism* in 2003 and 2006. Related documents include: Joint Staff, *National Military Strategy Plan for the War on Terrorism* (Washington: Joint Staff, 2002), www.esd.whs.mil/Portals/54/Documents/FOID/Reading%20Room/Joint_Staff/06-F-2573_national_military_strategic_plan_for_the_war_on_terrorism.pdf; Donald Rumsfeld, *The National Defense Strategy of the United States* (Washington: Department of Defense, 2005); Donald Rumsfeld and Peter Pace, *National Military Strategic Plan for the War on Terrorism* (Washington: Chairman of the Joint Chiefs of Staff, 2006).

47 James Steinberg, Michael O'Hanlon, and Susan Rice, "The New National Security Strategy and Preemption," *Brookings Institution* (December 21, 2002), www.brookings.edu/research/the-new-national-security-strategy-and-preemption/; John Lewis Gaddis, *Surprise, Security, and the American Experience* (Cambridge: Harvard University Press, 2004), 21; Leffler, *Safeguarding*, 282, 287; G. John Ikenberry, "America's Imperial Ambition," *Foreign Affairs*, 81:5 (September–October 2002), https://go-gale-.com.ezproxy.liberty.edu/ps/i.do?p=BIC&u=vic_liberty&id=GALE|A90404190&v=2.1&it=r&sid=summon.

48 George W. Bush, Graduation Speech at West Point, June 1, 2002, https://millercenter.org/the-presidency/presidential-speeches/june-1-2002-graduation-speech-west-point.

49 Brands, *What Good*, 160; Hemmer, *Pendulum*, 140, 144; Lynch, *Shadow*, 116.

50 Yetiv, *Absence*, 120; Michael Gordon and Bernard Trainor, *The Endgame: The Inside Story of the Struggle for Iraq from George W. Bush to Barack Obama* (New York: Pantheon, 2012), 8–9; Condoleezza Rice, Iraq: Goals, Objectives, and Strategy, October 29, 2002, Rumsfeld Papers, http://library.rumsfeld.com/doclib/sp/4136/2002-10-29%20From%20Condoleezza%20Rice%20re%20Principals'%20Committee%20Review%20of%20Iraq%20Policy%20Paper.pdf;

George W. Bush, President Discusses the Future of Iraq, February 26, 2003, https://georgewbush-whitehouse.archives.gov/news/releases/2003/02/20030226-11.html.
51 Rumsfeld, *Known*, 499; Rice, Iraq, October 29, 2002, Rumsfeld Papers; Kevin Benson, "Fighting the CENTCOM OIF Campaign Plan: Lessons for the Future Battlefield," *Modern War Institute* (November 6, 2020), https://mwi.usma.edu/fighting-the-centcom-oif-campaign-plan-lessons-for-the-future-battlefield/.
52 Hemmer, *Pendulum*, 145; Bush, Graduation Speech, June 1, 2002.
53 Thomas Ricks, *Fiasco: The American Military Adventure in Iraq* (New York: Penguin, 2006), 58–59; Gideon Rose, *How Wars End: Why We Always Fight the Last Battle* (New York: Simon and Schuster, 2010), 259–60, 264.
54 Hemmer, *Pendulum*, 141; Peter Layton, *Grand Strategy* (Australia: Peter Layton, 2018), 208.
55 Bush, *Decision*, 236; Wright, *Looming*, 295–96; Samuel Helfont, "Saddam and the Islamists: The Ba'thist Regime's Instrumentalization of Religion in Foreign Affairs," *The Middle East Journal*, 68:3 (2014), 362.
56 Walter A. McDougall, *The Tragedy of U.S. Foreign Policy: How America's Civil Religion Betrayed the National Interest* (New Haven: Yale University Press, 2016), 8; Bush, *Decision*, 230, 238–40; Ricks, *Fiasco*, 52–53.
57 Bush, *Decision*, 230, 238; Rose, *How Wars*, 244; George W. Bush, Remarks at the UN General Assembly, September 12, 2002, millercenter.org/the-presidency/presidential-speeches/september-12-2002-remarks-un-general-assembly; Yetiv, *Absence*, 117.
58 Samuel Helfont, "The Iraq War's Intelligence Failures Are Still Misunderstood," *War on the Rocks* (March 28, 2023), https://warontherocks.com/2023/03/the-iraq-wars-intelligence-failures-are-still-misunderstood/; Kevin Woods et al., *Iraqi Perspectives Project: A View of Operation Iraqi Freedom from Saddam's Senior Leadership* (Norfolk: Joint Center for Operational Analysis, 2013), 89–95; Yetiv, *Absence*, 118–19; Bush, *Decision*, 253; George W. Bush, Address to the Nation on Iraq, March 17, 2003, https://millercenter.org/the-presidency/presidential-speeches/march-17-2003-address-nation-iraq.
59 Ricks, *Fiasco*, 46, 63; Bush, *Decision*, 241; Authorization for the Use of Military Force against Iraq, October 16, 2002, www.congress.gov/bill/107th-congress/house-joint-resolution/114/text; Michael Mazarr, *Leap of Faith: Hubris, Negligence, and America's Greatest Foreign Policy Tragedy* (New York: PublicAffairs, 2019), 316–17.
60 Lynch, *Shadow*, 117; Bill Gertz, "Saddam Paid off French Leaders," *Washington Times*, October 7, 2004, www.washingtontimes.com/news/2004/oct/7/20041007-123838-3146r/; Jones, *Graveyard*, 246; Strobe Talbot, "Unilateralism: Anatomy of a Foreign Policy Disaster," *Brookings Institution* (February 21, 2007), www.brookings.edu/opinions/unilateralism-anatomy-of-a-foreign-policy-disaster/; Lionel Beehner, "The 'Coalition of the Willing'," *The Council on Foreign Relations* (February 22, 2007), www.cfr.org/backgrounder/coalition-willing; Layton, *Grand Strategy*, 203; Hemmer, *Pendulum*, 141; Lawrence Freedman, "On War and Choice," *The National Interest* (May–June 2010), 12–13; Richard Haass, *War of*

Necessity, War of Choice: A Memoir of Two Iraq Wars (New York: Simon and Schuster, 2009), 9–11; Melvyn Leffler, "9/11 in Retrospect: George W. Bush's Grand Strategy, Reconsidered," *Foreign Affairs*, 90:5 (September/October 2011), 42.

61 Rose, *How Wars*, 243; Michael Gordon and Bernard Trainor, *COBRA II: The Inside Story of the Invasion and Occupation of Iraq* (New York: Pantheon, 2006), 4; Joel Rayburn and Frank Sobchak, eds., *The US Army in the Iraq War: Invasion, Insurgency, Civil War, 2003–2006* (Carlisle: Army War College, 2019), 1:32; Ricks, *Fiasco*, 33, 37–38.
62 Rayburn and Sobchak, eds., *Army*, 1:35–36, 60.
63 Ibid., 1:55–58, 67; Gordon and Trainor, *Cobra II*, 79–80, 144–45; Ricks, *Fiasco*, 110.
64 Rose, *How Wars*, 244–45; Mazarr, *Leap*, 330; Rayburn and Sobchak, eds., *Army*, 1:67; NSPD 24, January 20, 2003, https://fas.org/irp/offdocs/nspd/nspd-24.pdf; Brands, *What Good*, 175; Gordon and Trainor, *Endgame*, 8–12; Gordon and Trainor, *Cobra II*, 150.
65 Rose, *How Wars*, 245; Rayburn and Sobchak, *Army*, 1:66–68; Ricks, *Fiasco*, 78–81, 101.
66 Rose, *How Wars*, 1–2; Ricks, *Fiasco*, 84; Gordon and Trainor, *Cobra II*, 144–46.
67 Rose, *How Wars*, 261–62; Ricks, *Fiasco*, 96–100; Brands, *What Good*, 163.
68 Rose, *How Wars*, 268; Ricks, *Fiasco*, 221; Brands, *What Good*, 163–64.
69 "Franks Savors Win with War Chiefs," *Tampa Bay Times* (August 31, 2005), www.tampabay.com/archive/2003/04/17/franks-savors-win-with-war-chiefs/; Gordon and Trainor, *Cobra II*, 67, 79; Bob Woodward interview of Rumsfeld, September 20, 2003, Rumsfeld Papers, http://library.rumsfeld.com/doclib/sp/2655/Interview%20with%20Bob%20Woodward%2009-20-2003.pdf#search=%22iraq%22; Jim Hoagl, "The Franks Strategy: Fast and Flexible," *Washington Post* (April 1, 2003), www.washingtonpost.com/archive/opinions/2003/04/01/the-franks-strategy-fast-and-flexible/1ac2f6e6-fb2d-4015-8d19-6893892b4cf1/.
70 Yetiv, *Absence*, 116; Rayburn and Sobchak, eds., *Army*, 1:39; Gordon and Trainor, *Cobra II*, 35–36; Ricks, *Fiasco*, 117.
71 Ricks, *Fiasco*, 117–18.
72 Ibid., 118, 124–27; Colin Powell and Richard Armitage Oral History, March 28, 2017, https://millercenter.org/the-presidency/presidential-oral-histories/colin-l-powell-and-richard-l-armitage-oral-history.
73 Franks to Rumsfeld, April 16, 2003, Rumsfeld Papers, http://library.rumsfeld.com/doclib/sp/323/From%20CENTCOM%20re%20Operation%20Iraqi%20Freedom%2004-16-2003; Rose, *How Wars*, 248.
74 Bush, *Decision*, 256–57.
75 Ibid., 257–58; Fred Charles Iklé, *Every War Must End* (New York: Columbia University Press, 1971), xii–xiv; Ricks, *Fiasco*, 147; Rose, *How Wars*, 247.
76 Gordon and Trainor, *Endgame*, 12–15, 28; Bush, *Decision*, 258; L. Paul Bremer III, with Malcolm McConnell, *My Year in Iraq: The Struggle to Build a Future of Hope* (New York: Simon and Schuster, 2006), 6–8, 12–13.
77 Michael Gordon, "Fateful Choice on Iraq Army Bypassed Debate," *NYT* (March 17, 2008), www.nytimes.com/2008/03/17/world/middleeast/17bremer.html;

Rajiv Chandrasekaran, *Imperial Life in the Emerald City: Inside Iraq's Green Zone* (New York: Vintage, 2006), 88–90; Bremer, *My Year*, 19; Gordon and Trainor, *Endgame*, 14–16, 26–29, 31–34; Frederic Kirgis, "Security Council Resolution 1483 on the Rebuilding of Iraq," *American Society of International Law*, 8:13 (June 6, 2003), www.asil.org/insights/volume/8/issue/13/security-council-resolution-1483-rebuilding-iraq; Rose, *How Wars*, 251.

78 Bremer, *My Year*, 39–42, 48; Chandrasekaran, *Imperial*, 79–83.

79 Chandrasekaran, *Imperial*, 84–86; Mazarr, *Leap*, 341; Gordon, "Fateful"; Walter Slocombe, "To Build an Army," *Washington Post* (November 5, 2003), www.washingtonpost.com/archive/opinions/2003/11/05/to-build-an-army/9c9d470d-9086-450e-be45-58aeb8ee7069/; Peter Slevin, "Wrong Turn at a Postwar Crossroads?" *Washington Post* (November 20, 2003), www.washingtonpost.com/archive/politics/2003/11/20/wrong-turn-at-a-postwar-crossroads/03c9d41f-efa2-4846-8f8d-168879bc029b/; Gordon, "Fateful."

80 Bremer to Rumsfeld, May 19, 2003, Rumsfeld Papers, http://library.rumsfeld.com/doclib/sp/340/2003-05-19%20from%20Bremer%20re%20Dissolution%20of%20the%20Ministry%20of%20Defense%20and%20related%20Entities.pdf; Rodman to Secretary of Defense, [May 24, 2006], Rumsfeld Papers, http://library.rumsfeld.com/doclib/sp/339/2006-05-24%20from%20Rodman%20re%20Disbanding%20the%20Iraqi%20Army.pdf#search=%22from%20peter%20rodman%20disbanding%22; Chandrasekaran, *Imperial*, 86; Powell and Armitage Oral History; Slevin, "Wrong Turn"; Gordon, "Fateful"; Bremer, *My Year*, 54–57, 224.

81 Bremer, *My Year*, 115–16, 128–29; Gordon, "Fateful"; Ricks, *Fiasco*, 165; David Rohde, "After the War: Occupation; Iraqis Were Set to Vote, But US Wielded a Veto," *NYT* (January 19, 2003), www.nytimes.com/2003/06/19/world/after-the-war-occupation-iraqis-were-set-to-vote-but-us-wielded-a-veto.html.

82 Gordon and Trainor, *Endgame*, 18; Brands, *What Good*, 172; Rumsfeld to Bremer, July 8, 2003, Rumsfeld Papers, http://library.rumsfeld.com/doclib/sp/351/To%20Jerry%20Bremer%20re%20Memos%20on%20Iraq%2007-08-2003.pdf.

83 Rose, *How Wars*, 250; Gordon and Trainor, *Endgame*, 18; Powell and Armitage Oral History.

84 Ricks, *Fiasco*, 173–74; Powell and Armitage Oral History; Rose, *How Wars*, 250; L. Paul Bremer III Interview, August 28–29, 2012, Miller Center, https://millercenter.org/the-presidency/presidential-oral-histories/l-paul-bremer-iii-oral-history.

85 Bremer, *My Year*, 104–6.

86 Mattis and West, *Chaos*, 115–16.

87 Gordon and Trainor, *Endgame*, 19.

88 Ibid., 19–24, 44–45; Ahmed Hashim, *Insurgency and Counterinsurgency in Iraq* (Ithaca: Cornell University Press, 2006), 170–76; William Grube, "The Evolution of Combined USMC/Iraqi Army Operations: A Company Commander's Perspective, Fallujah Iraq, September 2005 to April 2006," in Donald Stoker,

ed., *Military Advising and Assistance: From Mercenaries to Privatization, 1815–2007* (London: Routledge, 2008), 212–15; Ricks, *Fiasco*, 215.
89 Gordon and Trainor, *Endgame*, 19; Bush, *Decision*, 268.
90 Ricks, *Fiasco*, 212; Gordon and Trainor, *Endgame*, 26, 33.
91 James Jones, *The Report of the Independent Commission on the Security Forces of Iraq*, September 6, 2007, https://csis-website-prod.s3.amazonaws.com/s3fs-public/070906_isf.pdf; Thom Shanker, "The Struggle for Iraq: The Military: General Says Training of Iraqi Troops Suffered from Poor Planning and Staffing," *NYT* (February 11, 2006), www.nytimes.com/2006/02/11/washington/world/the-struggle-for-iraq-the-military-general-says-training.html; Frederick Kienle, "Creating an Iraqi Army from Scratch: Lessons for the Future," *American Enterprise Institute* (May 2007), 2–3.
92 Ricks, *Fiasco*, 247, 255–56; Gordon and Trainor, *Endgame*, 34–35.
93 Ricks, *Fiasco*, 262–63, 321–23; Bush, *Decision*, 268; Gordon and Trainor, *Endgame*, 48–49.
94 Gordon and Trainor, *Endgame*, 56–64; *Fiasco*, 332–33; Bremer, *My Year*, 334–37; Mattis and West, *Chaos*, 123, 128–30.
95 Gordon and Trainor, *Endgame*, 60–63, 66–69, 73; Ricks, *Fiasco*, 341, 394.
96 "Al Qaeda Spells out Iraq Attack Strategy in Handbook: Report," *Yahoo! News* (June 30, 2004); Gordon and Trainor, *Endgame*, 69–70; Ricks, *Fiasco*, 346–47.
97 Ricks, *Fiasco*, 390–92; Gordon and Trainor, *Endgame*, 88–90, 96; Rayburn and Sobchak, eds., *Army*, 1:319–20; George W. Casey Jr., *Strategic Reflections: Operation Iraqi Freedom, July 2004–February 2007* (Washington: NDU Press, 2012), 20.
98 Casey, *Strategic*, 18, 28–32; Gordon and Trainor, *Endgame*, 97; Rayburn and Sobchak, eds., *Army*, 1:323–28.
99 Gordon and Trainor, *Endgame*, 99–102; Ricks, *Fiasco*, 399–400, 405, 413.
100 Rayburn and Sobchak, eds., *Army*, 1:383–84, 387; Gordon and Trainor, *Endgame*, 137–38; Ricks, *Fiasco*, 413.
101 Rayburn and Sobchak, eds., *Army*, 1:427; Gordon and Trainor, *Endgame*, 158–60; Casey, *Strategy*, 67.
102 Gordon and Trainor, *Endgame*, 161–62.
103 Ibid., 162–63; Casey, *Strategy*, 67–68.
104 Gordon and Trainor, *Endgame*, 163–77; Ricks, *Fiasco*, 413–14, 418.
105 Gordon and Trainor, *Endgame*, 175–77; Rose, *How Wars*, 277.
106 Gordon and Trainor, *Endgame*, 176; *National Strategy for Victory in Iraq* (Washington: National Security Council, 2005), 1.
107 Gordon and Trainor, *Endgame*, 176–77, 180–82, 190, 210–11.
108 *National Strategy*, 1; Bill Sullivan, "Fighting the Long War – Military Strategy for the War on Terrorism," Joint Staff PowerPoint Briefing, 2006; Thomas Hegghammer, "Global Jihadism after the Iraq War," *The Middle East Journal*, 60:1 (winter 2006), 17–18; Gordon and Trainor, *Endgame*, 49, 192–94, 203.
109 Gordon and Trainor, *Endgame*, 208.
110 Robert Gates, *Duty: Memoirs of a Secretary of State* (New York: Knopf, 2014), 38.

111 Bush, *Decision*, 364–67.
112 Ibid., 370–76; Gates, *Duty*, 33–34, 38–39.
113 Gates, *Duty*, 42, 45; Bush, *Decision*, 377–78.
114 Bush, *Decision*, 378; George W. Bush, January 11 [10], 2007, https://millercenter.org/the-presidency/presidential-speeches/january-11-2007-address-military-operations-iraq; Peter Feaver, "The Right to Be Right: Civil-Military Relations and the Iraq Surge Decision," *International Security*, 35:4 (spring 2011), 87.
115 Jake Tapper, "Senate Regrets the Vote to Enter Iraq," *ABC News*, January 5, 2007, https://abcnews.go.com/GMA/Politics/story?id=2771519&page=1; Gordon and Trainor, *Endgame*, 301; Gates, *Duty*, 48–49, 55, 375–76; Bush, *Decision*, 382–84; Gail Chaddock, "On Iraq War, Senate Leader Harry Reid in Cross Hairs," *Christian Science Monitor* (April 27, 2007), www.csmonitor.com/2007/0427/p01s02-uspo.html.
116 David Petraeus, "Getting the Big Ideas Right: The Strategic Concepts That Helped Achieve Substantial Progress in Iraq," *The Heritage Lectures*, No. 1101 (November 13, 2008), 2; Bush, *Decision*, 380–81; Merrit Kennedy, "US Says It Will Cut Number of Troops in Iraq by Nearly Half This Month," *NPR* (September 9, 2020), www.npr.org/2020/09/09/911032406/u-s-says-it-will-cut-number-of-troops-in-iraq-by-nearly-half; Gordon and Trainor, *Endgame*, 335–36, 344–45, 362, 367; Rayburn and Sobchak, eds., *Army*, 2:125–28.
117 Gates, *Duty*, 51; Craig Whiteside, "Nine Bullets for the Traitors, One for the Enemy: The Slogans and Strategy behind the Islamic State's Campaign to Defeat the Sunni Awakening (2006–2017)," *The International Centre for Counter-Terrorism – The Hague*, 9 (2018), 1, 4; Martha Cottam et al., *Confronting al Qaeda: The Sunni Awakening and American Strategy in al Anbar* (Lanham: Rowman and Littlefield, 2016), 92, 94; Gordon and Trainor, *Endgame*, 383–84.
118 Petraeus, "Big Ideas," 2–3, 8–9; Thomas Ricks, *The Gamble: General Petraeus and the American Military Adventure in Iraq* (New York: Penguin, 2010), 303; "Peace Rules as Polls Close in Iraq," *CNN*, January 31, 2009, www.cnn.com/2009/WORLD/meast/01/31/iraq.elections/; David Petraeus, "Gen. Petraeus' Testimony to the Senate Armed Services Comm.," April 8, 2008, www.realclearpolitics.com/articles/2008/04/gen_petraeus_testimony_to_the.html; Ewen MacAskill, "CIA Chief Claims al-Qaida Essentially Defeated in Iraq and Saudi Arabia," *Guardian* (May 30, 2008), www.theguardian.com/world/2008/may/30/usa.alqaida; Gates, *Duty*, 470; Bush, *Decision*, 390.
119 George W. Bush, Address to the Nation on the Department of Homeland Security, June 7, 2002, https://millercenter.org/the-presidency/presidential-speeches/june-7-2002-address-nation-department-homeland-security; DeLong, *CENTCOM*, 69–71.
120 Brands, *What Good*, 173, 182–84.
121 Herring, *American*, 667–70; Bush, *Decision*, 424–26, 432–35; *NSS*, 2002, 29–30.

122 Douglas Irwin, *Clashing over Commerce: A History of US Trade Policy* (Chicago: University of Chicago Press, 2017), 670–73; Brands, *What Good*, 186; Leffler, "9/11," 38; Bush, *Decision*, 427; Nina Silove, "The Pivot before the Pivot: US Strategy to Preserve the Power Balance in Asia," *International Security*, 40:4 (spring 2016), 46–47, 54–67; Donald Rumsfeld, *Quadrennial Defense Review Report* (Washington: Department of Defense, 2001).

123 George W. Bush, Speech on Financial Markets and the World Economy, November 13, 2008, https://millercenter.org/the-presidency/presidential-speeches/november-13-2008-speech-financial-markets-and-world-economy; *NSS*, 2002, 17–18; George W. Bush, *The National Security Strategy of the United States* (Washington: White House, 2006), 25–27; Irwin, *Clashing*, 675–81.

124 *NSS*, 2002, 17; Bush, *Decision*, 442, 445–47.

125 Lynch, *Shadow*, 156–57; Bush, *Decision*. 448–49.

126 Lynch, *Shadow*, 157; Bush, *Decision*, 440, 454; George W. Bush, Remarks on Emergency Economic Stabilization Act of 2008, October 3, 2008, https://millercenter.org/the-presidency/presidential-speeches/october-3-2008-remarks-emergency-economic-stabilization-act; George W. Bush, Remarks on Plan to Assist Automakers, December 19, 2008, https://millercenter.org/the-presidency/presidential-speeches/december-19-2008-remarks-plan-assist-automakers.

127 Jeffrey Anderson, "Economic Growth by President," *The Hudson Institute*, August 8, 2016, www.hudson.org/research/12714-economic-growth-by-president; Historical Debt Outstanding: Annual 2000–2020, *Treasury Direct*, www.treasurydirect.gov/govt/reports/pd/histdebt/histdebt_histo5.htm; Kimberley Amadeo, "GDP Growth by President," *The Balance* (March 27, 2020), www.thebalance.com/gdp-growth-by-president-highs-lows-averages-4801102.

128 Lynch, *Shadow*, 104.

129 Mazaar, *Leap*, 395–401.

130 Leffler, *Safeguarding*, 294; Dueck, *Crusaders*, 141.

19 RETRENCHMENT, ENGAGEMENT, AND WAR: THE OBAMA YEARS, 2009–2017

1 Martin Indyk et al., *Bending History: Barack Obama's Foreign Policy* (Washington: Brookings, 2012), 7–8.

2 Colin Dueck, *The Obama Doctrine: American Grand Strategy Today* (Oxford: Oxford University Press, 2015), 42–43, 48, 106; David Samuels, "The Aspiring Novelist Who Became Obama's Foreign-Policy Guru," *NYT Magazine* (May 5, 2016), www.nytimes.com/2016/05/08/magazine/the-aspiring-novelist-who-became-obamas-foreign-policy-guru.html; William Burns, *The Back Channel: A Memoir of American Diplomacy and the Case for Its Renewal* (New York: Random House, 2020), 246; Timothy Lynch, *In the Shadow of the Cold War: American Foreign Policy from George Bush Sr. to Donald Trump* (Cambridge: Cambridge University Press, 2020), 163, 168, 172; Indyk et al., *Bending*, 4–5; Robert Gates,

Duty: Memoirs of a Secretary of State (New York: Knopf, 2014), 322; Barack Obama, Acceptance Speech at the Democratic National Convention, August 28, 2008, https://millercenter.org/the-presidency/presidential-speeches/august-28-2008-acceptance-speech-democratic-national.

3 Dueck, *Obama*, 6; Kevin Lasher and Christine Rinehart, "The Shadowboxer: The Obama Administration and Foreign Policy Grand Strategy," *Politics & Policy*, 44:5 (2016), 869–70; Gates, *Duty*, 404; Leon Panetta, with Jim Newton, *Worthy Fights: A Memoir of Leadership in War and Peace* (New York: Penguin, 2014), 290; Susan Rice, *Tough Love: My Story of the Things Worth Fighting For* (New York: Simon and Schuster, 2019), 242.

4 Barack Obama, *National Security Strategy, 2010* (Washington: White House, 2010), 4, 9, 37; Barack Obama, *National Security Strategy, 2015* (Washington: White House, 2015), 2; Barack Obama, Address at Cairo University, June 4, 2009, https://millercenter.org/the-presidency/presidential-speeches/june-4-2009-address-cairo-university; Barack Obama, Speech on American Diplomacy in the Middle East and North Africa, May 19, 2011, https://millercenter.org/the-presidency/presidential-speeches/may-19-2011-speech-american-diplomacy-middle-east-and-north.

5 Vali Nasr, *The Dispensable Nation: American Foreign Policy in Retreat* (New York: Doubleday, 2013), 2, 12; Panetta, *Worthy*, 375–76; Indyk et al., *Bending*, 19–20; Gates, *Duty*, 352, 384, 482, 522, 684–87; Josh Rogin and Eli Lake, "Military Hates White House 'Micromanagement' of ISIS War," *Daily Beast* (October 31, 2014), www.thedailybeast.com/military-hates-white-house-micromanagement-of-isis-war; Rice, *Tough*, 424.

6 Dueck, *Obama*, 2–3, 15–16, 31, 35–36, 111–12; Rice, *Tough*, 245; Indyk et al., *Bending*, 23; Gates, *Duty*, 298; *NSS*, 2010, 11; Daniel Drezner, "Does Obama Have a Grand Strategy?" *Foreign Affairs*, 90:4 (July–August 2011), 57–60, 61–64, 65–68.

7 Christopher Hemmer, *American Pendulum: Recurring Debates in US Grand Strategy* (Ithaca: Cornell University Press, 2015), 157–58; Mark Mykelby et al., *The New Grand Strategy: Restoring America's Prosperity, Security, and Stability in the 21st Century* (New York: St. Martin's Press, 2016), vii–x.

8 Jeffrey Goldberg, "The Obama Doctrine," *The Atlantic* (April 2016), www.theatlantic.com/magazine/archive/2016/04/the-obama-doctrine/471525/; Paul Miller, "Reassessing Obama's Legacy of Restraint," *War on the Rocks* (March 6, 2017), https://warontherocks.com/2017/03/reassessing-obamas-legacy-of-restraint/; Ben Rhodes, *The World as It Is: A Memoir of the Obama White House* (New York: Random House, 2018), 67, 122, 277–78; Samuels, "Aspiring"; Jeffrey Goldberg, "Hillary Clinton: 'Failure' to Help Syrian Rebels Led to the Rise of ISIS," *The Atlantic* (August 10, 2014), www.theatlantic.com/international/archive/2014/08/hillary-clinton-failure-to-help-syrian-rebels-led-to-the-rise-of-isis/375832/; David Milne, *Worldmaking: The Art and Science of American Diplomacy* (New York: Farrar, Straus and Giroux, 2015), 513.

9 Indyk et al., *Bending*, 8; Lynch, *Shadow*, 172; Barack Obama, Remarks on the American Recovery and Reinvestment Act, February 7, 2009, https://millercenter.org/the-presidency/presidential-speeches/february-7-2009-remarks-american-recovery-and-reinvestment-act; Katie Fehrenbacher, "Why the Solyndra Mistake Is Still Important to Remember," *Fortune* (August 27, 2015), https://fortune.com/2015/08/27/remember-solyndra-mistake/; Barack Obama, State of the Union Address, January 27, 2010, https://millercenter.org/the-presidency/presidential-speeches/january-27-2010-2010-state-union-address; Werner Neudeck, Professor of International Economics, Diplomatic Academy, Vienna, Austria, 2018.
10 Angie Drobnic Holan and Louis Jacobson, *Politifact*, September 7, 2012, www.politifact.com/factchecks/2012/sep/07/barack-obama/barack-obama-said-hes-cut-taxes-middle-class-famil/; Richard Williams, "How Obama Is Keeping Small Businesses Down," *US News and World Report* (March 25, 2014), www.usnews.com/opinion/economic-intelligence/2014/03/24/obamas-slams-small-businesses-with-excessive-regulations; Fareed Zakaria, "Obama's CEO Problem – And Ours," *Washington Post* (July 5, 2010), www.washingtonpost.com/wp-dyn/content/article/2010/07/04/AR2010070403856.html?hpid=opinionsbox1; Renae Merle, "Obama Criticizes Companies That Leave US for Lower Taxes," *Washington Post* (April 5, 2016), www.washingtonpost.com/business/economy/obama-companies-that-denounce-us-citizenship-for-lower-taxes-are-insidious/2016/04/05/cf43a2bc-fb41-11e5-886f-a037dba38301_story.html; William McBride, "A Comparison of the Camp and Obama International Corporate Tax Proposals," *Tax Foundation* (March 10, 2014), https://taxfoundation.org/comparison-camp-and-obama-international-corporate-tax-proposals/; Bastiaan van Apeldoorn and Naná de Graaff, "Obama's Economic Recovery Strategy, Open Markets, and Elite Power: Business as Usual?" *International Politics*, 54 (2017), 368; Dan Roberts and Ryan Felton, "Trump and Clinton's Free Trade Retreat: A Pivotal Moment for the World's Economic Future," *Guardian* (August 20, 2016), www.theguardian.com/us-news/2016/aug/20/trump-clinton-free-trade-policies-tpp.
11 Bureau of Labor Statistics, "The Recession of 2007–2009," February 2012, www.bls.gov/spotlight/2012/recession/pdf/recession_bls_spotlight.pdf; Bureau of Labor Statistics, February 3, 2017, www.bls.gov/news.release/archives/empsit_02032017.pdf; Courtenay Brown and Danielle Alberti, "How Trump's Economy Stacks Up," *Axios* (February 17, 2020), www.axios.com/presidents-economy-gdp-trump-5d042c64-ace6-4904-8602-40003f917719.html; Jeffrey Anderson, "Economic Growth by President," *Hudson Institute* (August 8, 2016), www.hudson.org/research/12714-economic-growth-by-president#:~:text=From%201947%2Donward%2C%20average%20annual,2015)%20has%20been%203.2%20percent; Hemmer, *Pendulum*, 170; "Donald Trump: Has US Debt Fallen since the President Took Office?" *BBC*, October 17, 2017, www.bbc.com/news/world-us-canada-41596847; Kimberly Amadeo, "US Debt by

President by Dollar and Percentage," *The Balance* (October 20, 2020), www.thebalance.com/us-debt-by-president-by-dollar-and-percent-3306296.

12 Barack Obama, A New Beginning, June 4, 2009, https://obamawhitehouse.archives.gov/the-press-office/remarks-president-cairo-university-6-04-09; Rhodes, *World*, 52–53; Gates, *Duty*, 331; Ryan Lizza, "The Consequentialist," *The New Yorker* (May 2, 2011), www.newyorker.com/magazine/2011/05/02/the-consequentialist.

13 Burns, *Back Channel*, 246, 252–53; Nasr, *Dispensable*, 22–23; Gates, *Duty*, 299.

14 Jeffrey Bader, *Obama and China's Rise: An Insider's Account of America's Asia Strategy* (Washington: Brookings, 2012), 69–70, 80, 104–6, 109–10; *NSS, 2010*, 11; Dueck, *Obama*, 73.

15 Hillary Clinton, "America's Pacific Century," *Foreign Policy* (October 11, 2011), https://foreignpolicy.com/2011/10/11/americas-pacific-century/; Tom Donilon, Remarks by National Security Advisor Tom Donilon, November 15, 2012, https://obamawhitehouse.archives.gov/the-press-office/2012/11/15/remarks-national-security-advisor-tom-donilon-prepared-delivery; Michael Clarke and Anthony Ricketts, "US Grand Strategy and National Security: The Dilemmas of Primacy, Decline, and Denial," *Australian Journal of International Affairs*, 71:5 (2017), 492.

16 Indyk et al., *Bending*, 25, 30, 38; Michael Green, *By More Than Providence: Grand Strategy and American Power in the Asia Pacific since 1783* (New York: Columbia University Press, 2019), 522, 531; Robert Haddick, "America Has No Answer to China's Salami-Slicing," *War on the Rocks* (February 6, 2014), https://warontherocks.com/2014/02/america-has-no-answer-to-chinas-salami-slicing/; Mathew Southerland, "China's Island Building in the South China Sea: Damage to the Marine Environment, Implications, and International Law," April 12, 2016, www.uscc.gov/sites/default/files/Research/China's%20Island%20Building%20in%20the%20South%20China%20Sea_0.pdf.

17 Lasher and Rinehart, "Shadowboxer," 869; Gates, *Duty*, 399–405; Lynch, *Shadow*, 190–91; Dueck, *Obama*, 64–73.

18 Rhodes, *World*, 272; Lynch, *Shadow*, 205, 210; John Kerry, "Interview with David Gregory," *Meet the Press* (March 3, 2014), https://usa.mfa.gov.ua/en/news/18625-interview-of-secretary-of-state-john-kerry-with-david-gregory-of-nbcs-meet-the-press; Rice, *Tough*, 399, 445, 448; Dueck, *Obama*, 70–71.

19 Goldberg, "Obama Doctrine"; Josef Joffe, "How Trump Is Like Obama," *WSJ* (June 13, 2017), www.wsj.com/articles/how-trump-is-like-obama-1497395979; Kęstutis Paulauskas, "On Deterrence" (August 5, 2016), www.nato.int/docu/review/articles/2016/08/05/on-deterrence/index.html.

20 Lynch, *Shadow*, 179–81; Dueck, *Obama*, 77–81; Gates, *Duty*, 506–7; Rhodes, *World*, 104; Barack Obama, Speech on American Diplomacy in the Middle East and North Africa, May 19, 2011, https://millercenter.org/the-presidency/presidential-speeches/may-19-2011-speech-american-diplomacy-middle-east-and-north.

21 Walter Russell Mead, "Our Failed Grand Strategy: American Foreign Policy in the Middle East Made Five Big Miscalculations," *WSJ* (August 24, 2013), C1; Dexter Filkins, "A Saudi Prince's Quest to Remake the Middle East," *The New Yorker* (April 9, 2018), https://longform.org/posts/a-saudi-prince-s-quest-to-remake-the-middle-east; Rhodes, *World*, 57; Obama, Address at Cairo University; "Fed Up, Obama Says Israel 'doesn't know its own best interests,'" *Times of Israel* (January 15, 2013), www.timesofisrael.com/fed-up-with-settlements-obama-has-reportedly-lost-faith-in-israel/.
22 Indyk et al., *Bending*, 158–61; Rhodes, *World*, 111; Barack Obama, Remarks by the President in Address to the Nation on Libya, March 28, 2011, https://obamawhitehouse.archives.gov/the-press-office/2011/03/28/remarks-president-address-nation-libya.
23 Indyk et al., *Bending*, 162–63; Goldberg, "Obama Doctrine"; Gates, *Duty*, 510–22; Rhodes, *World*, 111–12, 115.
24 Rhodes, *World*, 114–15; Indyk et al., *Bending*, 162–63; Obama, Remarks on Libya; Lizza, "Consequentialist"; Lynch, *Shadow*, 184.
25 Rhodes, *World*, 118–19; Gates, *Duty*, 520; Dueck, *Obama*, 142; Lynch, *Shadow*, 184.
26 Ivo Daalder and James Stavridis, "NATO's Victory in Libya: The Right Way to Run an Intervention," *Foreign Affairs* (March 2012), 2–7; Alan Kuperman, "Obama's Libya Debacle: How a Well-Meaning Intervention Ended in Failure," *Foreign Affairs* (March–April 2015); Rhodes, *World*, 120; Joe Quartararo Sr. et al., "Libya's Operation Odyssey Dawn," *PRISM*, 3:2 (March 2012), 145; Jeremiah Gertler, *Operation Odyssey Dawn (Libya): Background and Issues for Congress* (Washington: Congressional Research Service, 2011), summary; Gates, *Duty*, 521; "NATO and Libya," *NATO*, November 9, 2015, www.nato.int/cps/en/natohq/topics_71652.htm.
27 Lizza, "Consequentialist"; Joshua Foust, "Syria and the Pernicious Consequences of Our Libya Intervention," *The Atlantic* (February 6, 2012), www.theatlantic.com/international/archive/2012/02/syria-and-the-pernicious-consequences-of-our-libya-intervention/252631/; Gates, *Duty*, 530; Ryan Browne and Eric Bradner, "Benghazi Scandal: How Did We Get Here?" *CNN*, June 28, 2016, www.cnn.com/2016/06/28/politics/benghazi-scandal-report-hillary-clinton/index.html; "This Week's Transcript: US Ambassador to the United Nations Susan Rice," *ABC News*, September 14, 2012, https://abcnews.go.com/Politics/week-transcript-us-ambassador-united-nations-susan-rice/story?id=17240933; House of Representatives, *Final Report of the Select Committee on the Events surrounding the 2012 Terrorist Attack in Benghazi* (Washington: USGPO, 2016), 416; Rice, *Tough*, 308–9, 326–27; Rhodes, *World*, 183–85.
28 Lynch, *Shadow*, 185; Rice, *Tough*, 293.
29 Rhodes, *World*, 157–58; Goldberg, "Obama Doctrine"; Dueck, *Obama*, 84–85; Lynch, *Shadow*, 202–3; Kilic Bugra Kanat, *A Tale of Four Augusts: Obama's Syria Policy* (Washington: SETA, 2016), 156.

30 Barack Obama, Remarks by the President to the White House Press Corps, August 20, 2012, www.cnn.com/2012/08/20/world/meast/syria-unrest/index.html; Aaron Blake, "Kerry: Military Action in Syria Would Be 'Unbelievably Small,'" *Washington Post* (September 9, 2003), www.washingtonpost.com/pb/news/post-politics/wp/2013/09/09/kerry-military-action-in-syria-would-be-unbelievably-small/?nid=menu_nav_accessibilityforscreenreader&outputType=accessibility; Goldberg, "Obama Doctrine"; Burgess Everett, "Tough Hill Vote on Syria Fades," *Politico* (September 9, 2013), www.politico.com/story/2013/09/congress-syria-vote-096806; Dueck, *Obama*, 85–88, 115, 143; Panetta, *Worthy*, 450; Rice, *Tough*, 364–65; Lasher and Rinehart, "Shadowboxer," 874; "Kerry Fesses up about Obama's 'Red Line,'" *New York Post* (December 5, 2016), https://nypost.com/2016/12/05/kerry-fesses-up-about-obamas-red-line/; Jim Mattis and Bing West, *Call Sign Chaos: Learning to Lead* (New York: Random House, 2019), 228; Seth Mandel, "Disempowered: Review of 'Education of an Idealist: A Memoir' by Samantha Power," *Commentary* (October 2019), www.commentarymagazine.com/articles/disempowered/; Ahmed Al Hendi, "I Saw the Birth, and Bloody Death of the Dream of Syrian Democracy," *Foreign Policy* (November 6, 2019), https://foreignpolicy.com/2019/11/06/hevrin-khalaf-murder-syrian-revolution-jihadis/.

31 Nasr, *Dispensable*, 99–100, 109–14.

32 Ibid., 115–22; Samuels, "Aspiring"; Burns, *Back Channel*, 364; Hemmer, *Pendulum*, 167; Gates, *Duty*, 387–91.

33 Nasr, *Dispensable*, 134–36; President Obama's Full NPR Interview on Iran Nuclear Deal, *NPR*, April 7, 2015, www.npr.org/2015/04/07/397933577/transcript-president-obamas-full-npr-interview-on-iran-nuclear-deal; Burns, *Back Channel*, 368; *Assessing the Iran Deal, Hearing before the Subcommittee on National Security of the Committee on Oversight and Government Reform, House of Representatives, April 5, 2017* (Washington: USGPO, 2017), 58; Nasr, *Dispensable*, 132; William H. Tobey, "Are Iranian Military Bases Off-Limits to Inspection?" *The Belfer Center* (September 8, 2015), www.belfercenter.org/publication/are-iranian-military-bases-limits-inspection; Executive Order, January 16, 2016, https://obamawhitehouse.archives.gov/the-press-office/2016/01/16/executive-order-revocation-of-executive-orders-with-respect-to-Iran; Elise Labott, "John Kerry: Some Sanctions Relief Money for Iran Will Go to Terrorism," *CNN*, January 21, 2016, www.cnn.com/2016/01/21/politics/john-kerry-money-iran-sanctions-terrorism/index.html; Brian Bennett, "Donald Trump Is Right: The US Did Pay Iran $1.7 billion in Cash," *Los Angeles Times* (October 19, 2016), www.latimes.com/nation/politics/trailguide/la-na-trailguide-third-presidential-donald-trump-is-right-the-u-s-did-pay-1476931849-htmlstory.html.

34 Scott Wilson and Al Kamen, "'Global War on Terror' Is Given New Name," *Washington Post* (March 25, 2009), www.washingtonpost.com/wp-dyn/content/article/2009/03/24/AR2009032402818.html; Lynch, *Shadow*, 165; Indyk et al., *Bending*, 14–15; Barack Obama, Acceptance of Nobel Peace Prize, December 10,

2009, https://millercenter.org/the-presidency/presidential-speeches/december-10-2009-acceptance-nobel-peace-prize; Hemmer, *Pendulum*, 154.

35 Nasr, *Indispensable*, 13–14; Panetta, *Worthy*, 251; Donald Stoker, *Why America Loses Wars: Limited War and US Strategy from the Korean War to the Present* (Cambridge: Cambridge University Press, 2019), 67–68.

36 Gates, *Duty*, 336–42; Bob Woodward, *Obama's Wars* (New York: Simon and Schuster, 2010), 63–64, 71, 94–98; Nasr, *Dispensable*, 20.

37 Gates, *Duty*, 340–41, 358; Jack Fairweather, *The Good War: Why We Couldn't Win the War or the Peace in Afghanistan* (New York: Basic Books, 2014), 264–79.

38 Barack Obama, Remarks by the President on a New Strategy for Afghanistan, March 27, 2009, https://obamawhitehouse.archives.gov/the-press-office/remarks-president-a-new-strategy-afghanistan-and-pakistan; Gates, *Duty*, 342–43; Woodward, *Obama's Wars*, 144–46.

39 Gates, *Duty*, 348–50, 356.

40 Ibid., 352–55; Stanley McChrystal, *My Share of the Task: A Memoir* (New York: Portfolio/Penguin, 2014), 308, 323, 329–33, 345, 350–53; Fairweather, *Good War*, 281–82.

41 Craig Whitlock, "Stranded without a Strategy," *Washington Post* (December 9, 2019).

42 McChrystal, *My Share*, 337; Gates, *Duty*, 370–85; Rhodes, *World*, 66, 75, 78; Woodward, *Obama's Wars*, 102.

43 Barack Obama, Remarks by the President in Address to the Nation on the Way forward in Afghanistan and Pakistan, December 1, 2009, www.whitehouse.gov/the-press-office/remarks-president-address-nation-way-forward-afghanistan-and-pakistan; *NSS, 2010*, 19–21; Panetta, *Worthy*, 225; Karen DeYoung, "US Revises Its Strategy for Winding down the Afghan War," *Washington Post* (November 1, 2011), 7; Gates, *Duty*, 362, 384, 572.

44 Rhodes, *World*, 79; Obama, Remarks ... Afghanistan; Whitlock, "Stranded."

45 Fairweather, *Good War*, 283–84, 302, 307; Gates, *Duty*, 485; Peter Tomsen, *The Wars of Afghanistan: Messianic Terrorism, Tribal Conflicts, and the Failures of Great Powers* (New York: PublicAffairs, 2011), 658–59; A. Nicoll, ed., "Clear, Hold, Hand Over: NATO's Afghan Transition Plan," *IISS Strategic Comments*, 17:10 (March 2011).

46 Gates, *Duty*, 483, 486, 496.

47 Ibid., 488–89; Rhodes, *World*, 84; Fairweather, *Good War*, 311–12.

48 Fairweather, *Good War*, 319; Whitlock, "Stranded"; Tomsen, *Afghanistan*, 656.

49 Gates, *Duty*, 375, 497–98; Nancy Youssef, "Under New US Plan, US Troops Will Stay in Afghanistan till 2014," *McClatchy Newspapers* (November 16, 2010), www.mcclatchydc.com.

50 Panetta, *Worthy*, 287–88.

51 Gates, *Duty*, 501, 556–57 (italics in original).

52 Ibid., 501, 556; Barack Obama, Remarks on the Afghanistan Pullout, June 22, 2011, https://millercenter.org/the-presidency/presidential-speeches/june-22-2011-

remarks-afghanistan-pullout; Dueck, *Obama*, 55–56; Rajiv Chandrasekaran, *Little America: The War within the War for Afghanistan* (New York: Knopf, 2012), 323–26; Fairweather, *Good War*, 324.

53 Obama, Afghanistan Pullout; Nasr, *Dispensable*, 65, 83–90; Fairweather, *Good War*, 372n.39.
54 Nasr, *Dispensable*, 35–36, 42; Fairweather, *Good War*, 327–28.
55 Panetta, *Worthy*, 411, 414–19; Fairweather, *Good War*, 326; Mattis and West, *Chaos*, 220.
56 Barack Obama, Remarks by the President at the National Defense University, May 23, 2013, https://obamawhitehouse.archives.gov/the-press-office/2013/05/23/remarks-president-national-defense-university.
57 Obama, Remarks ... National Defense University; Rhodes, *World*, 274; Lasher and Rinehart, "Shadowboxer," 875–76; Nasr, *Dispensable*, 27, 71; Audrey Kurth Cronin, "The 'War on Terrorism': What Does It Mean to Win?" *Journal of Strategic Studies*, 37:2 (2014), 183–85.
58 Obama, Remarks ... National Defense University; Fairweather, *Good War*, 326.
59 Barack Obama, Statement by the President on Afghanistan, May 27, 2014, https://obamawhitehouse.archives.gov/the-press-office/2014/05/27/statement-president-afghanistan; James Lebovic, *Planning to Fail: The US Wars in Vietnam, Iraq, and Afghanistan* (Oxford: Oxford University Press, 2019), 160; Lauren McNally and Paul Bucala, *The Taliban Resurgence: Threats to Afghanistan's Security* (Washington: Institute for the Study of War, 2015), 11–12.
60 Rice, *Tough*, 390–91; Fairweather, *Good War*, xviii.
61 Sharifullah Dorani, *America in Afghanistan: Foreign Policy and Decision Making from Bush to Obama to Trump* (London: I. B. Tauris, 2019), 193; Lebovic, *Planning*, 161.
62 Lebovic, *Planning*, 161; Rice, *Tough*, 394.
63 Michael Gordon and Bernard Trainor, *The Endgame: The Inside Story of the Struggle for Iraq from George W. Bush to Barack Obama* (New York: Pantheon, 2012), 567–75; Panetta, *Worthy*, 398–99.
64 Barack Obama, Responsibly Ending the War in Iraq, February 27, 2009, https://obamawhitehouse.archives.gov/the-press-office/remarks-president-barack-obama-ndash-responsibly-ending-war-iraq; Gordon and Trainor, *Endgame*, 576.
65 Gates, *Duty*, 297; Gordon and Trainor, *Endgame*, 587–88, 591–94, 603, 606–7, 623–24; Emma Sky, "How Obama Abandoned Democracy in Iraq," *Politico* (April 27, 2015), www.politico.com/magazine/story/2015/04/obama-iraq-116708?o=0.
66 Sky, "How Obama"; Gordon and Trainor, *Endgame*, 642.
67 Sky, "How Obama"; Spencer Ackerman, "How Biden Kept Screwing up Iraq – Over and over and over Again," *Daily Beast* (December 14, 2019), www.thedailybeast.com/how-biden-kept-screwing-up-iraq-over-and-over-and-over-again.
68 Barack Obama, Address on the End of the Combat Mission in Iraq, August 31, 2010, https://millercenter.org/the-presidency/presidential-speeches/august-31-2010-address-end-combat-mission-iraq; Gates, *Duty*, 473–74; Gordon and Trainor, *Endgame*, 636–37.

69 Gordon and Trainor, *Endgame*, 652–71; Panetta, *Worthy*, 392–93; Mattis and West, *Chaos*, 206–9; Andrew Payne, "Presidents, Politics, and Military Strategy: Electoral Constraints during the Iraq War," *International Security*, 44:3 (winter 2019/20), 198–99; Ash Carter, *Inside the Five-Sided Box: Lessons from a Lifetime of Leadership in the Pentagon* (New York: Dutton, 2019), 228.
70 Mattis and West, *Chaos*, 223; Guy M. Snodgrass, *Holding the Line: Inside Trump's Pentagon with Secretary Mattis* (New York: Sentinel, 2019), 66.
71 Dexter Filkins, "In Extremists' Iraq Rise, America's Legacy," *The New Yorker* (June 11, 2014), www.newyorker.com/news/news-desk/in-extremists-iraq-rise-americas-legacy; "Timeline: The Rise, Spread, and Fall of Islamic State," *Wilson Center*, October 28, 2019, www.wilsoncenter.org/article/timeline-the-rise-spread-and-fall-of-the-islamic-state; Lynch, *Shadow*, 200; George C. Herring, *The American Century: US Foreign Relations, 1893–2014* (Oxford: Oxford University Press, 2017), 689; Panetta, *Worthy*, 392–93.
72 Ezra Klein, "One Quote That Shows How Badly Obama Underestimated ISIS," *Vox* (August 7, 2014), www.vox.com/iraq-crisis/2014/8/7/5980869/one-quote-that-shows-how-badly-obama-underestimated-isis; Goldberg, "Obama Doctrine"; Rice, *Tough*, 419; Rhodes, *World*, 291; "Obama's Gradual Iraq War," *WSJ* (May 1, 2016), www.wsj.com/articles/obamas-gradual-iraq-war-1462142386; "Iraq Formally Asks US to Launch Air Strikes against Rebels," *BBC*, June 18, 2014, www.bbc.com/news/world-middle-east-27905849; "US Begins Air Strikes against Isis Targets in Iraq, Pentagon Says," *Guardian* (August 8, 2014), www.theguardian.com/world/2014/aug/08/us-begins-air-strikes-iraq-isis; "Mount Sinjar: Islamic State Siege Broken, Say Kurds," *BBC*, December 14, 2014, www.bbc.com/news/world-middle-east-30539170; Operation Inherent Resolve, Naval History and Heritage Command, www.history.navy.mil/browse-by-topic/wars-conflicts-and-operations/middle-east/inherent-resolve.html.
73 Philip Gourevitch, "What Obama Didn't Say," *The New Yorker* (September 11, 2014), www.newyorker.com/news/daily-comment/obama-didnt-say; George Will, "Obama Is Defying the Constitution on War," *Washington Post* (September 17, 2014); Zeke Miller, "Obama Says 'We Don't Have a Strategy Yet' for Fighting ISIS," *Time* (August 28, 2014), https://time.com/3211132/isis-iraq-syria-barack-obama-strategy/; Mary Louise Kelly, "When the US Military Strikes, White House Points to a 2001 Measure," *NPR* (September 6, 2016), www.npr.org/sections/parallels/2016/09/06/492857888/when-the-u-s-military-strikes-white-house-points-to-a-2001-measure; Rice, *Tough*, 419; Rhodes, *World*, 294.
74 Barack Obama, "President Obama's Speech on Combating ISIS and Terrorism," *CNN*, September 10, 2014, www.cnn.com/2014/09/10/politics/transcript-obama-syria-isis-speech/; Julian Robinson, "'ISIS to Outlast Obama's Presidency': Military Campaign to Destroy Terror Group Could Take THREE Years, Senior US Officials Warn," *Daily Mail* (September 8, 2014), www.dailymail.co.uk/news/article-2747640/ISIS-outlast-Obama-s-presidency-Military-campaign-destroy-terror-group-years-senior-U-S-officials-warn.html.

75 See Obama, Remarks... Afghanistan; "Yemen Crisis: US Troops Withdraw from Air Base," *BBC*, March 22, 2015, www.bbc.com/news/world-middle-east-32000970; Micah Zenko, "Make No Mistake – The United States Is at War in Yemen," *Foreign Policy* (March 30, 2015), https://foreignpolicy.com/2015/03/30/make-no-mistake-the-united-states-is-at-war-in-yemen-saudi-arabia-iran/.

76 Obama, Combating ISIS; Mark Landler, *NYT* (September 10, 2014), www.nytimes.com/2014/09/11/world/middleeast/obama-speech-isis.html; "Kerry: US Not at War with ISIS," *Daily Beast* (September 11, 2014), www.thedailybeast.com/cheats/2014/09/11/kerry-u-s-is-not-at-war-with-isis.html; Douglas Ernst, "Josh Earnest: US in a Narrative Fight with Islamic State," *Washington Times* (September 19, 2016), www.washingtontimes.com/news/2016/sep/19/josh-earnest-stresses-narrative-fight-with-isis-wh/.

77 Rogin and Lake, "Military Hates"; Dan De Luce, "Hagel: The White House Tried to 'Destroy' Me," *Foreign Policy* (December 18, 2015), https://foreignpolicy.com/2015/12/18/hagel-the-white-house-tried-to-destroy-me/; Paul Shinkman, "Chuck Hagel Explains Why He Resigned as Secretary of Defense," *US News and World Report* (December 4, 2014), www.usnews.com/news/articles/2014/12/04/chuck-hagel-explains-why-he-resigned-as-secretary-of-defense.

78 Carter, *Inside*, 231, 229–30.

79 Ibid., 234–39; Howard LaFranchi, "Obama Says No 'Complete Strategy' against ISIS: What He's Getting At," *Christian Science Monitor* (June 8, 2015), www.csmonitor.com/USA/Foreign-Policy/2015/0608/Obama-says-no-complete-strategy-against-ISIS-what-he-s-getting-at; Rice, *Tough*, 420.

80 Carter, *Inside*, 230, 235–39.

81 Barack Obama, "Press Conference by President Obama – Antalya," November 16, 2015, www.whitehouse.gov/the-press-office/2015/11/16/press-conference-president-obama-antalya-turkey; Robert Tracinski, "Barack Obama: Worst. President. Ever," *The Federalist* (November 19, 2015), http://thefederalist.com/2015/11/19/barack-obama-worst-president-ever/; Goldberg, "Obama Doctrine."

82 Jim Puzzanghera, "Feinstein Criticizes Obama's Islamic State Strategy, Urges More US Special Forces in Syria," *Los Angeles Times* (November 22, 2015), www.latimes.com/world/la-fg-obama-isis-criticism-20151122-story.html; Anthony Cordesman, *Creeping Incrementalism: US Strategy in Iraq and Syria from 2011 to 2015* (Washington: CSIS, 2015), https://csis-prod.s3.amazonaws.com/s3fs-public/legacy_files/files/publication/151109_Cordesman_Incrementalism_iraq_syria.pdf; Carter, *Inside*, 241–46; Rice, *Tough*, 422–23.

83 Rice, *Tough*, 419–20, 423; Carter, *Inside*, 226, 248–49.

84 Dueck, *Obama*, 94–98, 140–41; Panetta, *Worthy*, 375–76; Mike Mullen, *The National Military Strategy of the United States of America, 2011: Redefining America's Military Leadership* (Washington: Joint Chiefs of Staff, 2011); *Quadrennial Defense Review Report* (Washington: Department of Defense, 2010); Panetta, *Worthy*, 282–85; Leon Panetta, *Sustaining Global Leadership: A Defense Strategy for the 21st*

Century (Washington: Department of Defense, 2012), https://archive.defense.gov/news/defense_strategic_guidance.pdf; Allan Millett et al., *For the Common Defense: A Military History of the United States from 1607 to 2012*, 3rd ed. (New York: Free Press, 2012), 684.
85 *NSS, 2015*, 2, 4.
86 Paul Saunders, "Choosing Not to Choose: Obama's Dithering on Syria," *The National Interest* (December 16, 2015), http://nationalinterest.org/feature/choosing-not-choose-obamas-dithering-syria-14633?page=show; Dueck, *Obama*, 4, 93.
87 Christi Parson and W. J. Hennigan, "President Obama, Who Hoped to Sow Peace, Instead Led the Nation in War," *LA Times* (January 13, 2017), www.latimes.com/projects/la-na-pol-obama-at-war/; Gordon and Trainor, *Endgame*, 574.

20 RETRENCHMENT, ENGAGEMENT, AND WEAKNESS: TRUMP AND BIDEN, 2017–2022

1 Donald Trump, "Trump on Foreign Policy," *National Interest* (April 22, 2016), https://nationalinterest.org/feature/trump-foreign-policy-15960; Background Interview #1 and #3; Donald Trump, Address to the United Nations General Assembly, September 19, 2017, https://millercenter.org/the-presidency/presidential-speeches/september-19-2017-address-united-nations-general-assembly; Cliff Sims, *Team of Vipers: My Extraordinary 500 Days in the Trump White House* (New York: Thomas Dunne, 2019), 126, 232–33; Peter Bergen, *Trump and His Generals: The Cost of Chaos* (New York: Penguin, 2019), 128.
2 Trump, Address to UN, September 19, 2017; Trump, "Trump on Foreign Policy"; Donald J. Trump, *The National Security Strategy of the United States of America* (Washington: White House, 2017), 2; H. R. McMaster, Remarks by LTG H. R. McMaster at the Reagan National Defense Forum: Reclaiming America's Strategic Confidence, December 2, 2017, https://trumpwhitehouse.archives.gov/briefings-statements/remarks-ltg-h-r-mcmaster-reagan-national-defense-forum-reclaiming-americas-strategic-confidence/; H. R. McMaster, *Battlegrounds: The Fight to Defend the Free World* (New York: HarperCollins, 2020), 17–18; H. R. McMaster and Gary Cohn, "America First Does Not Mean America Alone," *WSJ* (May 30, 2017), www.wsj.com/articles/america-first-doesnt-mean-america-alone-1496187426; Jacob Shively, *Make America First Again: Grand Strategy Analysis and the Trump Administration* (Amherst: Cambria, 2020), 136.
3 Trump, "Trump on Foreign Policy"; *NSS*, 2017, i-ii, 1–4; NSPM 2, January 28, 2017, https://fas.org/irp/offdocs/nspm/nspm-2.pdf; NSPM 4, April 4, 2017, https://fas.org/irp/offdocs/nspm/nspm-4.pdf; NSPM 11, May 8, 2018, https://fas.org/irp/offdocs/nspm/nspm-11.pdf; Trump, Address to UN, September 19, 2017; Background Interview #1.

4 Trump, "Trump on Foreign Policy"; Donald Trump, Address to Joint Session of Congress, February 28, 2017, https://millercenter.org/the-presidency/presidential-speeches/february-28-2017-address-joint-session-congress; Rex Tillerson, "US Engagement in the Western Hemisphere," *Texas National Security Review*, 1:2 (March 2018), 129, 133; Donald Trump, State of the Union Address, February 4, 2020, https://millercenter.org/the-presidency/presidential-speeches/february-4-2020-state-union-address; Shively, *Make*, 142; Cabinet Memorandum on the US Strategic Framework for the Indo-Pacific, https://news.usni.org/2021/01/15/u-s-strategic-framework-for-the-indo-pacific.

5 Jeffrey Goldberg, "A Senior White House Official Defines the Trump Doctrine: 'We're America, Bitch,'" *The Atlantic* (June 11, 2018), www.theatlantic.com/politics/archive/2018/06/a-senior-white-house-official-defines-the-trump-doctrine-were-america-bitch/562511/; Franklin Roosevelt, Inaugural Address, March 4, 1933, https://millercenter.org/the-presidency/presidential-speeches/march-4-1933-first-inaugural-address; Derek Chollet and James Goldgeier, *America between the Wars: From 11/9 to 9/11* (New York: PublicAffairs, 2008), 24–25; Shively, *Make*, 84; Guy M. Snodgrass, *Holding the Line: Inside Trump's Pentagon with Secretary Mattis* (New York: Sentinel, 2019), 60; Donald Trump, Address at the World Economic Forum, January 26, 2018, https://millercenter.org/the-presidency/presidential-speeches/january-26-2018-address-world-economic-forum.

6 Sims, *Team*, 41, 113; *NSS*, 2017, 4.

7 Sims, *Team*, 222; Memorandum of Telephone Conversation, July 25, 2019, https://trumpwhitehouse.archives.gov/wp-content/uploads/2019/09/Unclassified09.2019.pdf; "Vindman Reveals in Testimony That He Told an Intelligence Official about Trump's Call with Ukrainian Leader," *Bangor Daily News* (November 19, 2019), https://bangordailynews.com/2019/11/19/news/vindman-reveals-in-testimony-that-he-told-an-intelligence-official-about-trumps-call-with-ukrainian-leader/; William Cummings, "Trump Lawyer Dershowitz Argues President Can't Be Impeached for an Act He Thinks Will Help His Reelection," *USA Today* (January 30, 2020), www.usatoday.com/story/news/politics/2020/01/30/alan-dershowitz-controversial-trump-impeachment-argument/4618461002/; Adam Schiff tweet, December 22, 2016, https://twitter.com/RepAdamSchiff/status/811964588367417345?s=20.

8 Sean Noone and Elyse Russo, "President Trump's Speech ahead of Capitol Riot," *News Nation Now* (updated January 13, 2020), www.newsnationnow.com/us-news/read-the-full-transcript-president-trumps-speech-ahead-of-the-capitol-riot/; Natalie Andrews et al., "President Trump Impeached by the House for a Second Time," *WSJ* (January 13, 2021), www.wsj.com/articles/trump-to-face-impeachment-vote-over-capitol-riot-11610543781?st=qxidqg53rps8ylg&reflink=share_mobilewebshare; Jemima McEvoy, "14 Days of Protests, 19 Dead," *Forbes*, www.forbes.com/sites/jemimamcevoy/2020/06/08/14-days-of-protests-19-dead/?sh=67e11d204de4; Tristan Justice, "28 Times Media and Democrats Excused or Endorsed Violence Committed by Left-Wing Activists," *The Federalist* (January 7,

2021), https://thefederalist.com/2021/01/07/28-times-media-and-democrats-excused-or-endorsed-violence-committed-by-left-wing-activists/; Lee Brown, "Portland's Red House 'Autonomous Zone' Dismantled after Mayor Apologizes," *New York Post* (December 14, 2020), https://nypost.com/2020/12/14/portlands-autonomous-zone-dismantled-after-mayor-apology/.

9 Donald Stoker and Craig Whiteside, "Blurred Lines: Gray-Zone Conflict and Hybrid War – Two Failures of American Strategic Thinking," *Naval War College Review*, 73:1 (2020), https://digital-commons.usnwc.edu/nwc-review/vol73/iss1/4; McMaster, *Battlegrounds*, 26, 40.

10 Background Interviews #1 and #2; *NSS*, 2017, 27–28; NATO Warfighting Capstone Concept: Expert Symposium, Zoom Conference, June 30, 2020.

11 Byron York, "Former Top Spy Rethinks Attacks on President," *State Journal Register* (December 12, 2017), www.sj-r.com/news/20171212/byron-york-former-top-spy-rethinks-attacks-on-new-president.

12 Matt Taibbi, "We're in a Permanent Coup," *Substack* (October 11, 2019), https://taibbi.substack.com/p/were-in-a-permanent-coup; Eli Lake, "The FBI Scandal," *Commentary* (January 23, 2020), www.commentarymagazine.com/articles/eli-lake/the-fbi-scandal/; Philip Ewing, "Mueller Report Finds No Evidence of Russian Collusion," *NPR* (March 24, 2019), www.npr.org/2019/03/24/706385781/mueller-report-finds-evidence-of-russian-collusion; Donald Trump tweet, May 24, 2020, https://twitter.com/realDonaldTrump/status/1264754622830444544; Sean Davis, "DNI Declassifies Handwritten Notes from John Brennan, 2016 CIA Referral on Clinton Campaign's Collusion Operation," *The Federalist* (October 6, 2020), https://thefederalist.com/2020/10/06/breaking-dni-declassifies-handwritten-notes-from-john-brennan-2016-cia-referral-on-clinton-campaigns-collusion-operation/.

13 Bergen, *Trump*, 12; Background Interview #1; Mollie O'Toole, "Outgoing White House Chief of Staff John Kelly Defends His Rocky Tenure," *LA Times* (December 30, 2018), www.latimes.com/politics/la-na-pol-john-kelly-exit-interview-20181230-story.html.

14 Background Interview #1; *NSS*, 2017, ii, 3–4, 37, 45, 55; Donald Trump, Remarks on National Security Strategy, December 18, 2017, https://millercenter.org/the-presidency/presidential-speeches/december-18-2017-remarks-national-security-strategy; Shively, *Make*, 137, 141; McMaster, Remarks at the Reagan Forum.

15 *NSS*, 2017, 2; Donald Trump, Speech at the Unleashing American Energy Event, June 29, 2017, https://millercenter.org/the-presidency/presidential-speeches/june-29-2017-speech-unleashing-american-energy-event; Donald Trump, Address at the World Economic Forum, January 26, 2018, https://millercenter.org/the-presidency/presidential-speeches/january-26-2018-address-world-economic-forum; Trump, Address to Joint Session.

16 Randall Schweller, "Three Cheers for Trump's Foreign Policy: What the Establishment Misses," *Foreign Affairs*, 97:5 (September/October 2018),

www.foreignaffairs.com/articles/world/2018-08-14/three-cheers-trumps-foreign-policy; Donald Trump, Remarks by President Trump to the 73rd Session of the United Nations General Assembly, September 25, 2018, https://trumpwhitehouse.archives.gov/briefings-statements/remarks-president-trump-73rd-session-united-nations-general-assembly-new-york-ny/; Sims, *Team*, 219; Shively, *Make*, 84, 96, 153–54; Stuart Malawer, "Trump's Tariff Wars and National Security: A Political and Historical Perspective," *China & WTO Review*, 2 (2018), 354–55; "Trump at G7: US President Calls for End to Tariffs and Trade Barriers," *BBC*, June 9, 2018, www.bbc.com/news/world-us-canada-44423072.

17 Shively, *Make*, 83–85, 96, 177–78; "US Tariffs on China Aren't a Short-Term Strategy," *WSJ* (October 6, 2018), www.wsj.com/articles/u-s-tariffs-on-china-arent-a-short-term-strategy-1538841600?emailToken=a96b6f4db50a680037f24d655739abeafGz50/mwFwwwsAcs%E2%80%A6; McMaster, *Battlegrounds*, 415–16; Emma Newburger, "President Joe Biden Rejoins the Paris Climate Accord in First Move to Tackle Global Warming," *CNBC*, January 20, 2021, www.cnbc.com/2021/01/20/biden-inauguration-us-rejoins-paris-climate-accord.html.

18 "US GDP Growth Rate, 1961–2020," *Macrotrends*, www.macrotrends.net/countries/USA/united-states/gdp-growth-rate#:~:text=US%20GDP%20Growth%20Rate%20-%20Historical%20Data%20,%20%20-1.31%25%20%2055%20more%20rows%20; Bureau of Labor and Statistics, February 21, 2020, www.bls.gov/news.release/archives/empsit_01102020.pdf; "What Happened to the Economy under Trump before Covid and After," *WSJ* (October 14, 2020), www.wsj.com/articles/what-happened-to-the-economy-under-trump-before-covid-and-after-11602713077; Bureau of Labor and Statistics, Employment Situation News Release, January 10, 2020, www.bls.gov/news.release/archives/empsit_01102020.htm; Maggie Fitzgerald, "Black and Hispanic Unemployment Is at a Record Low," *CNBC*, October 4, 2019, www.cnbc.com/2019/10/04/black-and-hispanic-unemployment-is-at-a-record-low.html; US National Debt Clock, https://usdebtclock.org/; Douglas Irwin, "Trade Truths Will Outlast Trump," *WSJ* (November 19, 2020), www.wsj.com/articles/trade-truths-will-outlast-trump-11605828052; Josh Zumbrun and Rob Davis, "China Trade War Didn't Boost US Manufacturing Might," *WSJ* (October 25, 2020), www.wsj.com/articles/china-trade-war-didnt-boost-u-s-manufacturing-might-11603618203.

19 Sims, *Team*, 100; Snodgrass, *Holding*, 62–65, 69.

20 McMaster, *Battlegrounds*, 350, 362, 365–66, 377–80, 387; Snodgrass, *Holding*, 111; Trump, Address to UN, September 19, 2017; Shively, *Make*, 152–53, 173; Bergen, *Trump*, 216–21; John Bolton, *The Room Where It Happened: A White House Memoir* (New York: Simon and Schuster, 2020), 334.

21 Dexter Filkins, "A Saudi Prince's Quest to Remake the Middle East," *The New Yorker* (April 9, 2018), https://longform.org/posts/a-saudi-prince-s-quest-to-remake-the-middle-east; *NSS*, 2017, 48.

22 Filkins, "Saudi Prince's"; Shively, *Make*, 120, 149–51; Bergen, *Trump*, 177–79, 242; Peter Baker, "An Embassy in Jerusalem? Trump Promises, But So Did Predecessors," *NYT* (November 18, 2016), www.nytimes.com/2016/11/19/world/middleeast/jerusalem-us-embassy-trump.html; Rashid Khalidi, "Trump's Error on Jerusalem Is a Disaster for the Arab World ... and the US Too," *Guardian* (December 6, 2017), www.theguardian.com/commentisfree/2017/dec/06/trump-jerusalem-disaster-arab-world-israel.

23 McMaster, *Battlegrounds*, 269–70; Carla Humud and Christopher Blanchard, *Armed Conflict in Syria: Overview and US Response* (Washington: Congressional Research Service, 2020), 30; Trump, Address to UN, September 25, 2018; Ahmed Charai, "The Victory of Jared Kushner," *The National Interest* (August 14, 2020), https://nationalinterest.org/feature/victory-jared-kushner-166913; Mathew Lee, "Israel, Morocco to Normalize Ties; US Shifts W. Sahara Policy," *Associated Press* (December 10, 2020), https://apnews.com/article/donald-trump-africa-israel-north-africa-morocco-4279242f6f688d242bad5c7a64e29caf.

24 McMaster, *Battlegrounds*, 27; Bergen, *Trump*, 112–14; Bilahari Kausikan, "Watch What You Wish For, Including a Biden Victory," *Nikkei Asia* (November 3, 2020), https://asia.nikkei.com/Opinion/Watch-what-you-wish-for-including-a-Biden-victory.

25 Shively, *Make*, 169; Michael Bender and Louise Radnofsky, "Trump Says Strikes Aimed at Ending Syria's Use of Chemical Weapons, Sending Message to Russia and Iran," *WSJ* (April 13, 2018), www.wsj.com/articles/trump-says-strikes-aimed-at-ending-syrias-use-of-chemical-weapons-sending-message-to-russia-and-iran-1523673529; Bolton, *Room*, 47, 60.

26 Humud and Blanchard, *Armed Conflict*, 30–31.

27 Donald Trump, Remarks on Iran Strategy, October 13, 2017, https://trumpwhitehouse.archives.gov/briefings-statements/remarks-president-trump-iran-strategy/; NSPM 11, May 8, 2018, https://fas.org/irp/offdocs/nspm/nspm-11.pdf; Michael Pompeo, "Confronting Iran: The Trump Administration's Strategy," *Foreign Affairs* (November/December, 2018), www.foreignaffairs.com/articles/middle-east/2018-10-15/michael-pompeo-secretary-of-state-on-confronting-iran; Victoria Coates, A Look at the US Strategy for Iran, February 13, 2019, https://trumpwhitehouse.archives.gov/articles/look-u-s-strategy-iran/; Filkins, "A Saudi Prince's."

28 Shively, *Make*, 113; *Assessing the Iran Deal, Hearing before the Subcommittee on National Security of the Committee on Oversight and Government Reform, House of Representatives, April 5, 2017* (Washington: USGPO, 2017), 15, 18–26, 31–33; McMaster, *Battlegrounds*, 296–99; Trump, Iran Strategy; NSPM 11; Pompeo, "Confronting"; Jim Mattis and Bing West, *Call Sign Chaos: Learning to Lead* (New York: Random House, 2019), 229.

29 Snodgrass, *Holding*, 134; McMaster, *Battlegrounds*, 293–95; Courtney McBride, "U.N. Won't Act on US Effort to 'Snapback' Iran Sanctions, Citing Opposition from Security Council Members," *WSJ* (August 26, 2020), www.wsj.com/

articles/u-n-wont-act-on-u-s-effort-to-snapback-iran-sanctions-citing-opposition-from-security-council-members-11598394152; Lesley Wroughton, "Pompeo Slams Kerry for 'Inappropriate' Meetings with Iran Officials," *Reuters* (September 14, 2018), www.reuters.com/article/us-usa-iran-pompeo/pompeo-slams-kerry-for-inappropriate-meetings-with-iran-officials-idUSKCN1LU2NY.

30 McMaster, *Battlegrounds*, 300; Bergen, *Trump*, 280–83; "Iran Breaches Key Limit on Uranium Enrichment," *United States Institute of Peace* (January 6, 2021), https://iranprimer.usip.org/blog/2021/jan/04/iran-breaches-key-limit-uranium-enrichment.

31 Bergen, *Trump*, 280–82; Bolton, *Room*, 377, 381, 388–404, 410–11; McMaster, *Battlegrounds*, 301–2.

32 McMaster, *Battlegrounds*, 271–72, 324, 334; Donald Trump, Remarks on the Killing of Qasem Soleimani, January 3, 2020, https://millercenter.org/the-presidency/presidential-speeches/january-3-2020-remarks-killing-qasem-soleimani; Mark T. Esper, *A Sacred Oath: Memoirs of a Secretary of Defense during Extraordinary Times* (New York: William Morrow, 2022), 177–78; Meghann Myers, "Esper, on His Way out, Says He Was No Yes Man," *Military Times* (November 9, 2020), www.militarytimes.com/news/your-military/2020/11/09/exclusive-esper-on-his-way-out-says-he-was-no-yes-man/; Tom Nichols, "Iran's Smart Strategy," *The Atlantic* (January 10, 2020), www.theatlantic.com/ideas/archive/2020/01/how-iran-deterred-us/604717/; Rice, *Strong*, 263; Drew Hinshaw et al., "Swiss Back Channel Helped Defuse US-Iran Crisis," *WSJ* (January 10, 2020), www.wsj.com/articles/swiss-back-channel-helped-defuse-u-s-iran-crisis-11578702290; Mike Pompeo, *Never Give an Inch: Fighting for the America I Love* (New York: Broadside, 2023), 148–51.

33 McMaster, *Battlegrounds*, 89–90; "US Edges toward New Cold War Era with China," *WSJ* (October 12, 2018), www.wsj.com/articles/u-s-edges-toward-new-cold-war-era-with-china-1539355839?emailToken=d7ebccbff7d2598660f6f77a070da0a3A8iiF9emsqJJ/OJuCbk%E2%80%A6; *United States Strategic Approach to the People's Republic of China* (Washington: White House, 2020), 1; Annie Lowery, "The 'Madman' behind Trump's Trade Theory," *The Atlantic* (December 2018), 1–3, 6–7.

34 Schweller, "Three Cheers"; "US Tariffs on China"; Bergen, *Trump*, 293–94; McMaster, *Battlegrounds*, 144–46; "Trump Is Right about China Trade," *WSJ* (October 2, 2018), www.wsj.com/articles/trump-is-right-about-china-trade-1538520453?emailToken=1b96f2bc51ffec564e62bef5038f73ce0/7W/+Y7dimQyli9FIpiPWKhQPlvX%E2%80%A6.

35 Robert O'Brien, Assistant to the President for National Security Affairs, A Free and Open Indo-Pacific, January 5, 2021, https://trumpwhitehouse.archives.gov/wp-content/uploads/2021/01/OBrien-Expanded-Statement.pdf; Cabinet Memorandum on the US Strategic Framework for the Indo-Pacific, February 15, 2018; Michael Pompeo, *A Free and Open Indo-Pacific: Advancing a Shared Vision* (Washington: Department of State, 2019), 7. The supporting documents mentioned: *US Strategic Approach to the People's Republic of China*, the *US Strategic*

Framework for Countering China's Economic Aggression, and *US Campaign Plan for Countering China's Malign Influence in International Organizations*. See also *The Indo-Pacific Strategy Report: Preparedness, Partnerships, and Promoting a Networked Region* (Washington: Department of Defense, 2019).
36 Cabinet Memorandum ... Indo-Pacific.
37 Ibid.
38 Remarks by President Trump at APEC CEO Summit, November 10, 2017, https://trumpwhitehouse.archives.gov/briefings-statements/remarks-president-trump-apec-ceo-summit-da-nang-vietnam/; Mike Pompeo, Communist China and the Free World, July 23, 2020, https://2017-2021.state.gov/communist-china-and-the-free-worlds-future-2/index.html.
39 Bergen, *Trump*, 177; Bolton, *Room*, 310–12; McMaster, *Battlegrounds*, 367–68; Cabinet Memorandum ... Indo-Pacific; Walter Russell Mead, "Trump Is No 'Isolationist,'" *WSJ* (October 22, 2018); Pompeo, "Confronting"; Bethany Allen-Ebrahimian, "US Declares China's Actions against Uighurs 'Genocide,'" *Axios*, [January 19, 2020], www.axios.com/us-declares-china-actions-against-uyghurs-genocide-65e19e86-29ad-4c56-922f-d8a060aa2df8.html/.
40 Shively, *Make*, 90; Bergen, *Trump*, 70–71, 245; NSPM 1, January 27, 2017, https://fas.org/irp/offdocs/nspm/nspm-1.html; Snodgrass, *Holding*, 235–36; Katie Rogers, "Trump Orders Establishment of Space Force as Sixth Military Branch," *NYT* (June 18, 2018), www.nytimes.com/2018/06/18/us/politics/trump-space-force-sixth-military-branch.html; Russ Vought and Robert O'Brien, "The Navy Stops Taking on Water," *WSJ* (December 9, 2020), www.wsj.com/articles/the-navy-stops-taking-on-water-11607556845.
41 Snodgrass, *Holding*, 42, 154–55, 180; Joe Gould, "QDR Dead in 2017 Defense Policy Bill," *Defense News* (April 25, 2016), www.defensenews.com/home/2016/04/25/qdr-dead-in-2017-defense-policy-bill/; Jim Mattis, *A Summary of the National Defense Strategy of the United States of America: Sharpening the American Military's Competitive Edge* (Washington: Department of Defense, 2018), https://dod.defense.gov/Portals/1/Documents/pubs/2018-National-Defense-Strategy-Summary.pdf; James Mattis, On US National Defense Strategy, January 19, 2018, www.americanrhetoric.com/speeches/jamesmattisnatsecjohnshopkins.htm.
42 Snodgrass, *Holding*, 57–61, 147, 227–28; Bergen, *Trump*, 11, 245; Schweller, "Three Cheers"; Background Interview #2; Anthony Cordesman, *Ending America's Grand Strategic Failures* (Washington: CSIS, 2020), www.csis.org/analysis/ending-americas-grand-strategic-failures; Robert O'Brien, "Why the US Is Moving Troops out of Germany," *WSJ* (June 21, 2020), www.wsj.com/articles/why-the-u-s-is-moving-troops-out-of-germany-11592757552; Shively, *Make*, 110; Timothy Lynch, *In the Shadow of the Cold War: American Foreign Policy from George Bush Sr. to Donald Trump* (Cambridge: Cambridge University Press, 2020), 237.
43 Brussels Summit Declaration, NATO, July 11, 2018, www.nato.int/cps/en/natohq/official_texts_156624.htm; Ben Warner, "SECDEF Mattis' New 'Four Thirties' Initiative Designed to Reinforce NATO against Russia," *Proceedings*

(August 30, 2018), news.usni.org/2018/08/30/mattis-says-natos-four-thirties-force-structure-shows-political-strength; Background Interview #2.

44 Snodgrass, *Holding*, 64, 230, 277; McMaster, *Battlegrounds*, 58–59; Mathew Karnitschnig, "Germany Blames Trump in Pursuit of Nord Stream 2 Pipeline," *Politico* (August 10, 2020), www.politico.eu/article/germany-plays-trump-card-in-pursuit-of-russian-nord-stream-2-pipeline-dream/; O'Brien, "Why the US."

45 Trump, "Trump on Foreign Policy"; McMaster, *Battlegrounds*, 28, 68; Bergen, *Trump*, 229, 233, 237; Bolton, *Room*, 152–54; Emily Jacobs, "Obama's Top Brass Contradict Public Statements about 'Collusion' under Oath," *New York Post* (May 11, 2020), https://nypost.com/2020/05/11/obamas-top-brass-contradict-statements-about-collusion-under-oath/; Interview, James Clapper, Executive Session Permanent Select Committee on Intelligence, US House of Representatives, Washington, DC, July 17, 2017, 26, https://intelligence.house.gov/uploadedfiles/jc7.pdf.

46 Bergen, *Trump*, 232; *NSS*, 2017, 2–3, 25, 28, 47–48; McMaster, *Battlegrounds*, 27–28, 33–34; Shively, *Make*, 183; Lynch, *Shadow*, 229–30; Bolton, *Room*, 159–64; Background Interview #2.

47 Trump, "Trump on Foreign Policy"; *NSS*, 2017, i; Bergen, *Trump*, 115–16.

48 Bergen, *Trump*, 119; Snodgrass, *Holding*, 127–28; NSPM 3, January 27, 2017, https://fas.org/irp/offdocs/nspm/nspm-3.pdf.

49 Bergen, *Trump*, 119–23; McMaster, *Battlegrounds*, 231; Snodgrass, *Holding*, 128–30; Department of Defense Press Briefing by Secretary Mattis, General Dunford, and Special Envoy McGurk on the Campaign to Defeat ISIS in the Pentagon Press Briefing Room, May 19, 2017, www.defense.gov/Newsroom/Transcripts/Transcript/Article/1188225/department-of-defense-press-briefing-by-secretary-mattis-general-dunford-and-sp/.

50 Snodgrass, *Holding*, 130–31; McMaster, *Battlegrounds*, 226–27, 231; "Timeline: The Rise, Spread, and Fall of Islamic State," *Wilson Center*, October 28, 2019, www.wilsoncenter.org/article/timeline-the-rise-spread-and-fall-the-islamic-state; Hassan Hassan, "ISIS Is Ready for a Resurgence," *The Atlantic* (August 26, 2018), www.theatlantic.com/international/archive/2018/08/baghdadi-recording-iraq-syria-terrorism/568471/.

51 Shively, *Make*, 168–69; Craig Whiteside and Ian Rice, "Ambassador Feisal al-Istrabadi, Former Iraqi Ambassador to the United Nations," *CTX*, 10:2 (summer 2020), 23; Cordesman, *Ending*.

52 Bergen, *Trump*, 248–50; Bolton, *Room*, 194–98.

53 Courtney Kube et al., "US Troops to Leave Syria as President Trump Declares Victory over ISIS," *NBC News*, December 19, 2018, www.nbcnews.com/news/us-news/u-s-troops-leave-syria-president-trump-declares-victory-over-n949806; Mark Perry, "The Blob Is Lying about Trump's Sudden Syria Withdrawal," *Foreign Policy* (January 4, 2019), https://foreignpolicy.com/2019/01/04/the-blob-is-lying-about-trumps-sudden-syria-withdrawal/; Bolton, *Room*, 202.

54 Bergen, *Trump*, 249–51; Snodgrass, *Holding*, 235, 298–300; Bolton, *Room*, 199–202, 206; David Sanger et al., "Bolton Puts Conditions on Syria Withdrawal, Suggesting a Delay of Months or Years," *NYT* (January 6, 2019), www.nytimes.com/2019/01/06/world/middleeast/bolton-syria-pullout.html; "US to Expel Every Last Iranian Boot from Syria – Pompeo," *BBC*, January 10, 2019, www.bbc.com/news/world-middle-east-46828810.

55 Bergen, *Trump*, 254–55; Bolton, *Room*, 209–12; Katie Williams, "Outgoing Syria Envoy Admits Hiding US Troop Numbers; Praises Trump's Mideast Record," *Defense One* (November 12, 2020), www.defenseone.com/threats/2020/11/outgoing-syria-envoy-admits-hiding-us-troop-numbers-praises-trumps-mideast-record/170012/; Humud and Blanchard, *Armed Conflict*, 12.

56 Natasha Turak, "Trump Handing Northern Syria to Turkey Is a 'Gift to Russia, Iran, and ISIS,' Former US Envoy Says," October 7, 2019, *CNBC*, www.cnbc.com/2019/10/07/trump-handing-syria-to-turkey-is-gift-to-russia-iran-isis-mcgu.html?__source=twitter%7Cmain; "Turkey Launches Operation into Northeast Syria – Erdogan," *Reuters* (October 9, 2019), http://news.trust.org/item/20191009125826-y6tof; Bergen, *Trump*, 255; Humud and Blanchard, *Armed Conflict*, 35; Eli Lake, "The Kurds Have Paid Dearly for Trump's Recklessness," *Bloomberg* (September 16, 2020), www.bloomberg.com/opinion/articles/2020-09-17/kurds-have-paid-dearly-for-trump-s-reckless-withdrawal-from-syria?srnd=opinion; Bolton, *Room*, 213.

57 Seth Frantzman, "Is Intercepted Rocket Attack on US Embassy a Game Changer? Analysis," *Jerusalem Post* (July 5, 2020), www.jpost.com/middle-east/is-intercepted-rocket-attack-on-us-embassy-a-game-changer-analysis-633915; Lolita Baldor and Kathy Gannon, "Military Blindsided by Trump's Afghanistan Plan to Withdraw Troops by Year's End," *Realcleardefense* (October 9, 2020), www.realcleardefense.com/articles/2020/10/09/military_blindsided_by_trumps_afghanistan_plan_to_withdraw_troops_by_years_end_580219.html; Gordon Lubold and Michael Gordon, "US to Cut Troop Presence in Iraq by about One-Third, Officials Say," *WSJ* (August 28, 2020), www.wsj.com/articles/u-s-to-cut-troop-presence-in-iraq-by-about-one-third-officials-say-11598625823; Anthony Cordesman, *America's Failed Strategy in the Middle East: Losing Iraq and the Gulf* (Washington: CSIS, 2020), 2–3; Eliot Cohen, "The End of American Power: Trump's Reelection Would Usher in Permanent Decline," *Foreign Affairs* (October 27, 2020), www.foreignaffairs.com/articles/united-states/2020-10-27/end-american-power.

58 Donald Trump, Remarks by President Trump on the Strategy in Afghanistan and South Asia, August 21, 2017, www.whitehouse.gov/briefings-statements/remarks-president-trump-strategy-afghanistan-south-asia/; McMaster, *Battlegrounds*, 155–56; Bergen, *Trump*, 55, 128, 134–35.

59 McMaster, *Battlegrounds*, 188–89.

60 Ibid., 170–74; Bergen, *Trump*, 132–33.

61 McMaster, *Battlegrounds*, 157–59; Bergen, *Trump*, 135.
62 Bergen, *Trump*, 139–40, 157; Sims, *Team*, 153, 158–59; Background Interview #1; Snodgrass, *Holding*, 103.
63 Trump, Strategy in Afghanistan.
64 Ibid.; McMaster, Remarks at the Reagan Forum.
65 Snodgrass, *Holding*, 124–25; Thomas Jocelyn, "Losing a War," *The Weekly Standard* (August 27, 2018), www.weeklystandard.com/thomas-joscelyn/losing-a-war; Bergen, *Trump*, 161.
66 McMaster, *Battlegrounds*, 192–93, 198, 215, 218; Carter Malkasian, *The American War in Afghanistan: A History* (Oxford: Oxford University Press, 2021), 428–29.
67 Craig Whitlock, "Stranded without a Strategy," *Washington Post* (December 9, 2019); Jocelyn, "Losing"; Lolita Baldor, "US Commander: No Need for Major Change in Afghan War Plan as New General Takes Over," *Military Times* (August 8, 2018), www.militarytimes.com/news/your-military/2018/08/08/us-commander-no-need-for-major-change-in-afghan-war-plan-as-new-general-takes-over/; US Department of State, Integrated Country Strategy: Afghanistan, September 27, 2018, www.state.gov/wp-content/uploads/2019/01/ICS-Afghanistan_UNCLASS_508.pdf; McMaster, *Battlegrounds*, 216; Thomas Jocelyn, "The Afghanistan War Is Over. We Lost," *Weekly Standard* (October 28, 2018); Phil Stewart and Idrees Ali, "Pentagon Cancels Aid to Pakistan over Record on Militants," *Reuters* (September 1, 2018), www.reuters.com/article/us-usa-pakistan-military-exclusive/exclusive-pentagon-cancels-aid-to-pakistan-over-record-on-militants-idUSKCN1LH3TA.
68 Bolton, *Room*, 215–21; Bergen, *Trump*, 260; Malkasian, *Afghanistan*, 430–31, 437.
69 Donald Trump, State of the Union Address, February 5, 2019, https://millercenter.org/the-presidency/presidential-speeches/february-5-2019-state-union-address; Bolton, *Room*, 222, 430–31; Bergen, *Trump*, 259–64.
70 Bergen, *Trump*, 267–68; Bolton, *Room*, 440–42; Michael Kugelman, "America Has a New Strategy In Afghanistan, But It Isn't Actually Very New," *Wilson Center: Asia Dispatches* (September 17, 2019); McMaster, *Battlegrounds*, 216–17; Agreement for Bringing Peace to Afghanistan, February 29, 2020, state.gov/wp-content/uploads/2020/02/Agreement-For-Bringing-Peace-to-Afghanistan-02.29.20.pdf; Matthew Lee and Kathy Gannon, "US and Taliban Agree to Truce, Way forward in Afghanistan," *Associated Press* (February 14, 2020), https://apnews.com/fa41245d47d48332b10c8aeadcd6cb73.
71 Robert Burns, "Pentagon Sees Taliban Deal as Allowing Fuller Focus on China," *Associated Press* (March 1, 2020), https://apnews.com/21926f8af b7ccf3599f735d6fb966854; Robert Burns, "US on Track to Pull Troops from Afghanistan Despite Turmoil," *Realcleardefense* (May 16, 2020), www.realcleardefense.com/articles/2020/05/16/us_on_track_to_pull_troops_from_afghanistan_despite_turmoil_115293.html; Lolita Baldor, "US Begins Troop Withdrawal from Afghanistan, Official Says," *Associated Press* (March 9, 2020), https://apnews.com/2e8a815a031e8da37075feec466694c2.

72 Joel Gehrke, "US Slashes Aid to Afghanistan by $1B as Power Struggle Threatens Taliban Peace Deal," *Washington Examiner* (March 23, 2020), www.washingtonexaminer.com/policy/defense-national-security/u-s-slashes-aid-to-afghanistan-by-1-billion-as-power-struggle-threatens-taliban-peace-deal; Whitlock, "At War."

73 Mohsin Mohmand and Ali Latifi, "The US Once Surged into Helmand Province. Now the Taliban Is, Too," *Foreign Policy* (October 20, 2020), https://foreignpolicy.com/2020/10/20/the-u-s-once-surged-helmand-province-afghanistan-taliban/; Zainullah Stanekzai, "Afghan Forces Launch Counter Assault after Taliban Offensive Overshadows Talks," *Reuters* (October 13, 2020), www.reuters.com/article/us-afghanistan-taliban-clashes/afghan-forces-launch-counter-assault-after-taliban-offensive-overshadows-talks-idUSKBN26Y22T; Baldor and Gannon, "Military Blindsided"; "Trump's Pledge to Exit Afghanistan Was a Ruse, His Final SecDef Says," *Defense One* (August 18, 2021), www.defenseone.com/policy/2021/08/trumps-pledge-exit-afghanistan-was-ruse-his-final-secdef-says/184660/.

74 Michael M. Phillips, "America's Other Endless War: Battling al-Shabaab in Somalia," *WSJ* (January 17, 2019), www.wsj.com/articles/americas-other-endless-war-somalia-11547738433; Nancy Youssef and Michael Phillips, "US Will Move Nearly All Troops out of Somalia, Officials Say," *WSJ* (December 4, 2020), www.wsj.com/articles/u-s-will-move-nearly-all-u-s-troops-out-of-somalia-11607114195.

75 Jocelyn, "Losing."

76 Shively, *Make*, 167.

77 Esper, *A Sacred Oath*, 81.

78 *NSS*, 2017, 55; "The Trump Disruption," *WSJ* (August 27, 2020), www.wsj.com/articles/the-trump-disruption-11598570719; Cordesman, *America's Failed*, 2.

79 Greg Myre, "Biden's National Security Team Lists Leading Threats, with China at the Top," *NPR* (April 13, 2021), www.npr.org/2021/04/13/986453250/bidens-national-security-team-lists-leading-threats-with-china-at-the-top; Joseph Biden, *Interim National Security Strategic Guidance* (*INSSG*) (Washington: White House, 2021), 6–8.

80 *INSSG*, 6; *Making US Foreign Policy Work Better for the Middle Class* (Washington: Carnegie Endowment for International Peace, 2020); Elise Labott, "The Sullivan Model," *Foreign Policy* (April 9, 2021), https://foreignpolicy.com/2021/04/09/the-sullivan-model-jake-nsc-biden-adviser-middle-class/; Press Briefing by Press Secretary Jen Psaki and National Security Advisor Jake Sullivan, February 4, 2021, www.whitehouse.gov/briefing-room/press-briefings/2021/02/04/press-briefing-by-press-secretary-jen-psaki-and-national-security-advisor-jake-sullivan-february-4-2021/.

81 Secretary of State Antony Blinken, Virtual Remarks at the UN Security Council Open Debate on Multilateralism, May 7, 2021, https://geneva.usmission.gov/2021/05/07/secretary-blinken-virtual-remarks-at-the-un-security-council-open-debate-on-multilateralism/; *INSSG*, 9.

82 Blinken, Virtual Remarks at the UN.

83 *INSSG*, 9.
84 Ibid., 15.
85 Ibid., 4, 10, 13–14, 19–20.
86 *The Indo-Pacific Strategy of the United States* (Washington: White House, 2022), 5–12, 15–16.
87 Joseph Biden, *National Security Strategy* (Washington: White House, 2022), 6–48.
88 Jim Garamone, "Concept of Integrated Deterrence Will Be Key to National Defense Strategy, DOD Official Says," *DOD News* (December 8, 2021), www.defense.gov/News/News-Stories/Article/Article/2866963/concept-of-integrated-deterrence-will-be-key-to-national-defense-strategy-dod-o/; Jim Garamone, "Austin Says Current Operations Give Hints of New National Defense Strategy," *DOD News* (February 18, 2022), www.defense.gov/News/News-Stories/Article/Article/2940956/austin-says-current-operations-give-hints-of-new-national-defense-strategy/; Teri Cronk, "DOD Official Outlines 2022 National Defense Strategy in CNAS Forum," *DOD News* (December 10, 2021), www.defense.gov/News/News-Stories/Article/Article/2869837/dod-official-outlines-2022-national-defense-strategy-in-cnas-forum/; *Indo-Pacific Strategy*, 12.
89 *INSSG*, 10, 14; Remarks by President Biden before Meeting with the Infrastructure Implementation Task Force, January 20, 2022, www.whitehouse.gov/briefing-room/speeches-remarks/2022/01/20/remarks-by-president-biden-before-meeting-with-the-infrastructure-implementation-task-force/.
90 *INSSG*, 9; Brian Naylor and Deidre Walsh, "Biden Signs the $1 Trillion Bipartisan Infrastructure Bill into Law," *NPR* (November 15, 2021), www.npr.org/2021/11/15/1055841358/biden-signs-1t-bipartisan-infrastructure-bill-into-law; Matt Egan, "Biden's Stimulus Plan Is Fueling Short-term Inflation, SF Fed Paper Finds," *CNN*, October 19, 2021, www.cnn.com/2021/10/19/economy/inflation-biden-stimulus/index.html; Dominic Rushe, "Tackling Inflation Is 'Top Priority', Says Biden in State of the Union Address," *Guardian* (March 1, 2022), www.theguardian.com/us-news/2022/mar/01/tackling-inflation-is-top-priority-says-biden-in-state-of-the-union-address; Alan Rappeport, "US National Debt Tops $30 Trillion as Borrowing Surged amid Pandemic," *NYT* (February 1, 2022), www.nytimes.com/2022/02/01/us/politics/national-debt-30-trillion.html; Steve Nelson, "Biden Concedes His COVID Stimulus Checks Fueled Spike in Inflation," *New York Post* (November 10, 2021), https://nypost.com/2021/11/10/biden-says-covid-stimulus-checks-fueled-spike-in-inflation/; Seoung Min Kim and Jeff Stein, "US Announces Deal with European Union to Ease Steel and Aluminum Tariffs Enacted under Trump," *Washington Post* (October 30, 2021), www.washingtonpost.com/world/2021/10/30/tariffs-us-eu-steel/; Larry Summers, "Is the US Headed for Stagflation?" *The Aspen Institute*, August 10, 2022, www.youtube.com/watch?v=iLxEfg3SeM4, minute 2:58-5:09.
91 *INSSG*, 6; Labott, "Sullivan Model"; Adam Kredo, "Biden Admin Waives Sanctions on Iran as Nuclear Talks Restart," *Washington Free Beacon* (December 3, 2021), https://freebeacon.com/national-security/biden-admin-waives-sanctions-on-

iran-as-nuclear-talks-restart/; Ali Hashem, "Attacks on US in Iraq Meant to Send 'Harsh' Message – Without Spilling Blood," *Al-Monitor* (January 6, 2022), www.al-monitor.com/originals/2022/01/attacks-us-iraq-meant-send-harsh-message-without-spilling-blood; Shelly Kittelson, "Coalition Hits back at Iran-Backed Groups," *Al-Monitor* (January 6, 2020), www.al-monitor.com/originals/2022/01/coalition-hits-back-iran-backed-groups; Matt Seyler and William Mansell, "Biden Orders Airstrikes on Iran-Backed Militias near Iraq-Syria Border in Response to UAV Attacks," *ABC News* (June 27, 2021), https://abcnews.go.com/International/biden-orders-airstrikes-iran-backed-militias-iraq-syria/story?id=78526157.

92 Josh Rogin, "Biden Doesn't Want to Change China. He Wants to Beat It," *Washington Post* (February 10, 2022), www.washingtonpost.com/opinions/2022/02/10/biden-china-strategy-competition/.

93 Jane Arraf and Ben Hubbard, "As Islamic State Resurges, US Is Drawn back into the Fray," *NYT* (January 25, 2022), www.nytimes.com/2022/01/25/world/middleeast/isis-syria.html#:~:text=%E2%80%9CISIS%20is%20not%20over%E2%80%9D%3A,their%20ability%20to%20do%20so; Steve Herman, "Biden Announces End to US Combat Mission in Iraq," *Voice of America*, July 26, 2021, www.voanews.com/a/usa_biden-announces-end-us-combat-mission-iraq/6208745.html; Tara Copp, "The Combat Mission in Iraq Has Ended. But Troops Aren't Coming Home," *Defense One* (December 9, 2021), www.defenseone.com/threats/2021/12/combat-mission-iraq-has-ended-troops-arent-coming-home/187433/.

94 The Afghan War section comes largely from my *Why America Loses Wars*.

95 Joe Biden, Remarks by President Biden on the Way forward in Afghanistan, April 14, 2021, www.whitehouse.gov/briefing-room/speeches-remarks/2021/04/14/remarks-by-president-biden-on-the-way-forward-in-afghanistan/.

96 Lara Seligman et al., "How Biden's Team Overrode the Brass on Afghanistan," *Politico* (April 14, 2021), www.politico.com/news/2021/04/14/pentagon-biden-team-overrode-afghanistan-481556; Peter Bergen, "The Worst Speech of Biden's Presidency," *CNN*, July 9, 2021, https://edition.cnn.com/2021/07/09/opinions/biden-afghanistan-speech-malarkey-bergen/index.html.

97 Seligman et al., "How Biden's"; Ellie Kaufman, "Five Takeaways from Senior Military Leaders' Testimony on Afghanistan," *CNN*, September 28, 2021, www.cnn.com/2021/09/28/politics/five-takeaways-senate-afghanistan/index.html; Jonathan Guyer, "The Unheeded Dissent Cable," *American Prospect* (August 26, 2021), https://prospect.org/world/unheeded-dissent-cable-white-house-misses-afghanistan-warning/

98 Joe Biden, Speech on the Drawdown of US Forces in Afghanistan, July 8, 2021, https://millercenter.org/the-presidency/presidential-speeches/july-8-2021-speech-drawdown-us-forces-afghanistan; Fred Kaplan, "We Now Know Why Biden Was in a Hurry to Exit Afghanistan," *Slate* (September 28, 2021), https://slate.com/news-and-politics/2021/09/biden-afghanistan-exit-troops-milley.html.

99 Chas Danner, "Why Afghanistan's Security Forces Suddenly Collapsed," *New York Magazine* (August 17, 2021), https://nymag.com/intelligencer/2021/08/why-afghanistans-security-forces-suddenly-collapsed.html.
100 Douglas London, "CIA's Former Counterterrorism Chief for the Region: Afghanistan, Not an Intelligence Failure – Something Much Worse," *Just Security* (August 18, 2021), www.justsecurity.org/77801/cias-former-counterterrorism-chief-for-the-region-afghanistan-not-an-intelligence-failure-something-much-worse/; "How the Taliban Engineered 'Political Collapse' of Afghanistan," *Reuters* (August 17, 2021), www.reuters.com/world/asia-pacific/how-taliban-engineered-political-collapse-afghanistan-2021-08-17/; Kaufman, "Five Takeaways."
101 Danner, "Why Afghanistan's."
102 Biden, Speech on Drawdown; Guyer, "Unheeded"; London, "CIA's Former."
103 Michael Gordon et al., "Inside Biden's Afghanistan Withdrawal Plan: Warnings, Doubts But Little Change," *WSJ* (September 5, 2021), www.wsj.com/articles/inside-the-biden-administrations-push-to-exit-afghanistan-11630855499; Yaroslav Trofimov et al., "'The Taliban Are Here': The Final Days before Kabul's Collapse," *WSJ* (August 20, 2021), www.wsj.com/articles/the-taliban-are-here-the-final-days-before-kabuls-collapse-11629505499.
104 Kevin Liptak et al., "'A direct punch in the gut': Inside Biden's Biggest Crisis as He Races to Withdraw from Afghanistan," *CNN*, August 28, 2021, www.cnn.com/2021/08/28/politics/biden-behind-scenes-crisis-attack-kabul-afghanistan/index.html; Jonathan Swan and Zachary Basu, "Scoop: Milley's Blunt Private Blame for the State Department," *Axios* (September 29, 2021), www.axios.com/milley-state-department-afghanistan-evacuation-ebb00a6b-a59d-42b9-b5e0-348b0227b89b.html
105 Joe Biden, Remarks on Situation in Afghanistan, August 16, 2021, https://millercenter.org/the-presidency/presidential-speeches/august-16-2021-remarks-situation-afghanistan; Gordon et al., "Inside Biden's"; Liptak et al., "'A direct punch.'"
106 "Leaving Afghanistan, US General's Ghostly Image Books Place in History," *Reuters* (August 31, 2021), www.reuters.com/world/asia-pacific/leaving-afghanistan-us-generals-ghostly-image-books-place-history-2021-08-31/; Nancy Youssef and Gordon Lubold, "Last US Troops Leave Afghanistan after Nearly 20 Years," *WSJ* (August 30, 2021), www.wsj.com/articles/last-u-s-troops-leave-afghanistan-after-nearly-20-years-11630355853; Peter Bergen, "Biden Deserves Blame for the Debacle in Afghanistan," *CNN*, August 13, 2021, www.cnn.com/2021/08/12/opinions/afghanistan-president-biden-debacle-bergen/index.html; Biden, Speech on the Drawdown.
107 Tunku Varadarajan, "The Two Blunders That Caused the Ukraine War," *WSJ* (March 4, 2022), www.wsj.com/articles/cause-ukraine-war-robert-service-moscow-putin-lenin-stalin-history-communism-invasion-kgb-fsb-11646413200;

Brussels Summit Communiqué, NATO, June 14, 2021, www.nato.int/cps/en/natohq/news_185000.htm.
108 Garamone, "Austin Says."
109 Megan Eckstein, "Congressman Argues US Deterrence Strategy Failed to Protect Ukraine and Could Fail Taiwan Too," *Defense News* (March 3, 2022), www.defensenews.com/congress/2022/03/03/congressman-argues-us-deterrence-strategy-failed-to-protect-ukraine-and-could-fail-taiwan-too/.

CONCLUSION

1 Justin Vaïsse, *Zbigniew Brzezinski: America's Grand Strategist*, Catherine Porter, trans. (Cambridge: Harvard University Press, 2018), 33–34.
2 Ibid., 3, 32–33.
3 Anthony Cordesman, *Creeping Incrementalism: US Strategy in Iraq and Syria from 2011 to 2015* (Washington: CSIS, 2015), https://csis-prod.s3.amazonaws.com/s3fs-public/legacy_files/files/publication/151109_Cordesman_Incrementalism_iraq_syria.pdf, 4.
4 Haroro Ingram and Craig Whiteside, "The Challenge of Outcommunicating the Islamic State," in Andrea Dew et al., eds., *From Quills to Tweets: How America Communicates about War and Revolution* (Washington: Georgetown University Press, 2019), 247.

Index

Each figure (fig.) and map is indicated by its number rather than the page. The abbreviation P. is used for President. Arabic names containing the prefix *al* are filed alphabetically as though the prefix is missing. For example, entries on Al Qaeda are filed under Q.

9/11 attacks, 589–90

Abizaid, John, 615–16, 618, 619, 623
Abrams, Creighton
    Army Chief of Staff appointment, 443–44
    Cambodia and Laos invasion plans, 465, 467–68
    One War strategy, 444, 461
    pacification strategy, 444, 464
Acheson, Dean
    on bipartisan politics, 346, 349
    Cold War strategy, 356–58
    on Japan occupation, 341
    Korean War strategy, 367, 370–71, 374–75, 383
    Press Club speech, 360, 364
    Vietnam War strategy, 431, 442–43
Adams, John, 21–22, 35–37, 46–48
Adams, John Quincy, 57, 73, 77, 156, 191, *See also* Monroe and Adams (6th P.) administrations
Afghan War, Bush (43rd P.) administration
    aims, 592–94, 600
    coalition building and Musharraf's double game, 594–97, 601–602
    counterinsurgency campaigns, 601–602
    early offensives, map 18.1, 595–98
    military strategy, 117, 594–95, 597–98, 600–603, 629
    nation building strategy, 598–601
Afghan War, Obama, Trump and Biden administrations
    aims and grand strategy
    2009–10, 644–48
    2010–12, 648–50
    2013–16, 650–52
    2017–21, 680–85, 688, 692–95
    war situation, initial assessment, 643–44
Afghanistan. *See also* Afghan War entries
    civil war, 530
    Islamic State in, 680–81
    Al Qaeda leaders in, 582–83, 590, 592
    Soviet invasion and war, 485, 491–92, 495, 510, 523, 524
    Taliban, level of control, 652, 680, 693–94
Africa, US diplomatic strategy. *See also* Middle East; individual country names
    anti Communist policies, 395–96, 407, 408
    Carter administration, 489
    Reagan administration, 519–20
Aguinaldo, Emilio, 201–202, 204–207, 211
Ahmad, Hashid, 554–55
Aideed, Mohammed Farah, 568–70
aims, political, 1, 3–7, *See also* democracy promotion aim; expansion aim; human rights promotion aim; security aim; sovereignty aim; war aims
Air Force. *See also* Army; military strategy; Navy
    Eisenhower administration, 393
    Gulf War, strategy and campaign, 542–44, 549–50
    Joint Chiefs of Staff, 302–303, 358, 409, 423
    Korean War bombing campaigns, 369, 383–84, 386

INDEX

pre Second World War, 292
Rapid Deployment Force, 491, 494, 514, 515
Reagan administration, 505
Second World War bombing campaigns, 312–15, 327, 333, 335–36
Truman administration, 349–50, 358–59
Vietnam War bombing campaigns, 426–30, 443, 471–73, 475
in Laos and Cambodia, 459, 461, 467–69
Alaska Purchase, 159
Albright, Madeleine
Balkan Wars, views on, 577–78, 587
military strategy, 568, 573, 579–80
Somalia and Haiti operations, views on, 568–70
Alexander I of Russia, 80, 81
Alger, Russell M., 197, 200
Ali, Hazrat, 596
Allawi, Ayad, 619
Allen, John, 657
Allison, John M., 371
American Civil War. *See* Civil War
American Revolutionary War
British military strategy, 20–21, 27, 30, 31
diplomatic and economy strategy, 21–22, 29–30, 36
French and Spanish support, 21, 28–29, 35, 36
military strategy
first phase, 18–20
second phase, 22–24
shift to Fabian strategy, 24–25, 33, 36
origins, 15–16
peace negotiations and disarmament, 35–37, 42
political aims, 17, 18, 21, 35–36
preparations and resources, 17–19, 28–30
principal offensives, map 1.1
New York and New Jersey, 25–27
northern theater, 18–19, 30–31
Philadelphia and Saratoga, 27–28
southern theater, 31–35
Anaya, Pedro Maria, 112
Andropov, Yuri, 506–507, 509–10
Anglo-French War (1778–83), 28–29, 35
Anglo-French War (1793–1802), 41
Angola, 449, 484, 508, 512, 519–20, 523, 524

anti Communist policies. *See also* Cold War
China, 355–57
domestic policies, 258–59, 356
former European colonies, 395–96, 407, 408
Greece and Turkey, 349, 355, 357, 398–99
Indochina, 357–58, 398–99
Latin America and Caribbean, 397–98, 407–408, 412
Middle East, 355, 357, 396–98, 407, 412–13
Soviet Union, non-recognition, 266
Apache Wars, 177–79
Arab-Israeli relations. *See under* Middle East
Arab Spring uprisings, 634, 639, 641
Arafat, Yasser, 583
Arbenz, Jacobo, 396–97
Argentina, 408
Aristide, Jean-Bertrand, 570, 576–77
Armistead, Walker Keith, 94
Armstrong, John, 66–68, 70–71
Army. *See also* Air Force; military strategy; Navy
Adams (2nd P.) administration, 47–48
Carter administration, 484
Continental Army predecessor, 17, 37
disarmament after wars. *See* disarmament policies
Eisenhower administration, 393
establishment, 41–42, 44
Gilded Age era (1877–97), 180–81, 185–86
Harding and Coolidge administrations, 274–76
Jefferson administration, 52
Joint Army and Navy Board, 213, 275, 302
Joint Chiefs of Staff, 302–303, 358, 409, 423
Kennedy and Johnson (36th P.) administrations, 405
Madison administration, 57, 65, 66
Marine Corps. *See* Marine Corps
McKinley administration, 213
Monroe administration, 83
Polk administration, 105–106
Rapid Deployment Force, 491, 494, 514, 515
Reagan administration, 505

825

INDEX

Army (cont.)
   Roosevelt (32nd P.) administration, 292–93, 296
   Truman administration, 349–50, 358–59, 368–69
   Wilson administration, 240, 257
Arnold, Benedict, 19, 23–24, 28
Arnold, Henry ("Hap"), 332
Arthur, Chester A., 181–82, 187, 215
Articles of Confederation 1781, 36
Asia, US diplomatic strategy. *See also* Middle East; Pacific region; individual country names
   Biden administration, 690–91
   Bush (41st P.) administration, 529–31
   Carter administration, 486–87, 495–96
   Clinton administration, 574–75
   Gilded Age era (1877–97), 181, 185
   Harding and Coolidge administrations, 267–69
   Hoover administration, 277
   Indochina. *See* Indochina
   Jackson administration, 99
   Johnson (17th P.) and Grant administrations, 158, 160
   Nixon and Ford administrations, 451–52
   Obama administration, 637–38
   Pierce and Buchanan administrations, 121, 122
   Polk administration, 101
   Reagan administration, 517–19
   Roosevelt (26th P.) administration, 218–20
   Roosevelt (32nd P.) administration (pre Second World War), 291–92
   Taft administration, 223–24
   Truman administration, 355–58
   Trump administration, 667–68, 672–74
   Wilson administration, 234–35, 256
Aspin, Les, 569, 570, 575
al-Assad, Bashar, 641, 658, 668, 669
Astor, John Jacob (and Fort Astoria), 80, 84
Atlantic Charter 1941, 301, 340, 343
atomic warfare. *See also* Cold War; weapons of mass destruction
   Chinese capability, 446
   countervailing/counterforce strategy, 494–95
   Cuban Missile Crisis, 406, 410–11
   disarmament agreements, 450, 455, 484, 485, 506, 524, 528, 626
   Eisenhower administration strategy, 392–95, 401
   Hiroshima and Nagasaki attacks, 339–40
   Kennedy and Johnson (36th P.) administration strategy, 405–406
   Korean War, threatened use, 374, 384–86
   preemptive strikes to prevent, 350–51, 575
   Reagan administration strategy, 505–507
   Soviet capability, 358, 361, 394, 411, 446, 504, 505
   threat as diplomatic tool, 347–48, 360, 392–93, 401
   MAD (mutually assured destruction), 406, 484, 495, 506
   US capability, 360, 393, 401, 404–406, 696
   Vietnam War, threatened use, 458–59
Attlee, Clement, 374
Austin, Lloyd, 654, 657, 689, 695
Aziz, Tariq, 540, 612

Baden, Prince Max von, 249–50
Baer, George, 298, 611
al Baghdadi, Abu Bakr, 655
Bainbridge, William, 75
Baker Island, 121
Baker, James, 524, 525, 539, 542, 556, 560, 561
Baker, Newton D., 240, 242
Balkan Wars, 563–64, 577–79, 585–87
Ball, George, 424–25, 431
Bank for International Settlements, 271
Bank of the United States, 39–40, 52, 76, 96–98
Banks, Nathaniel, 139, 143
Barbary Wars, 52–53, 75
Barno, David, 601
Baruch, Bernard, 257, 344
Bay of Pigs invasion, 409–10
Baylor, John R., 166
Bell, John, 94
Bergen, Peter, 661, 694–95
Berger, Samuel ('Sandy'), 564, 568, 574–75, 587
Biddle, Nicholas, 97
Biddle, Tami Davis, 9

INDEX

Biden administration
    Afghan War, 688, 692–95
    diplomatic strategy, 690–91
    economic strategy, 667, 690
    grand strategy, 686–90
    Iraq War (Third), 691–92
    political aims, 687
    Russian-Ukrainian War, 1, 690, 695
Biden, Joseph, 607, 639, 643, 646, 647, 649, 653–54, *See also* Biden administration
Bin Laden, Osama. *See also* Al Qaeda
    in Afghanistan, 582–83, 592
    death, 633, 649
    escape from Afghanistan, 596, 597
    Saddam Hussein, links to, 606
    US perceived as weak by, 570, 695
Birkhimer, William, 209–10
Birtle, Andrew J., 155
Bishop, Maurice, 510–11
Bismarck, Otto von, 698
Black Codes and Jim Crow laws, 152, 155, 265
Black Hawk War, 91
Blaine, James G., 183
Blair, Tony, 607, 621
Blinken, Antony, 639, 687, 691, 692
Bliss, Tasker H., 213, 240, 245, 246, 248, 257
Bolton, John, 669, 678, 679
bombing campaigns. *See under* Air Force
Borah, William, 255, 266, 267, 272
Bosnian War, 563–64, 577–79, 587
Boston Tea Party, 16
Boutros-Ghali, Boutros, 568
Boxer Rebellion, China, 212–13
Bradley, Omar
    Korean War strategy, 366, 374–75, 378, 384–85
    in Second World War, 307, 318, 319
    Vietnam War strategy, 431, 442–43
Bragg, Braxton, 135, 137, 138
Brands, Hal, 532
Brazil, 412, 451
Bremer, L. Paul ("Jerry"), 613–19
Brennan, John, 646, 664
Bretton Woods institutions, 342
Brezhnev, Leonid, 411, 412, 470–71, 477
Briand, Aristide, 270–71

Britain. *See* Great Britain
British Guiana boundary dispute, 184–85
British North America. *See* Lower Canada province (Quebec); Upper Canada province
Brock, Sir Isaac, 62–65
Brodie, Bernard, 3, 380, 423
Brown, Harold, 483–84
Brown, Jacob, 70
Brown, John, 122
Bryan, William Jennings, 203, 229, 230, 233–37
Brzezinski, Zbigniew
    Carter administration objectives, development of, 478–79
    China, strategy towards, 486
    Middle East, strategy towards, 490–94
    Obama administration, views on, 636
    Soviet Union, strategy towards, 484–86, 494
    as strategy advisor, 477–78, 483
    Third World, strategy towards, 488
Buchanan, James, 120, 122–23
Buell, Don Carlos, 134–36, 138
buffalo slaughter policy, 164, 169, 170, 173
Bulgaria, 526
Bulge, Battle of the, 320
Bundy, McGeorge, 403–404, 409, 422, 426, 429–30
Bunker, Ellsworth, 461, 467
Buren, Martin van. *See* Van Buren administration
Burgoyne, Sir John, 18, 27, 28
Burns, William, 693
Bush (41st P.) administration
    Asia, diplomatic strategy, 529–31
    Bosnian War, non-intervention, 563–64, 577
    diplomatic strategy generally, 526–28
    economic strategy, 528
    grand strategy, 524–26, 560–63
    Gulf War. *See* Gulf War
    Middle East, diplomatic strategy, 530, 531, 603
    military strategy, 528–29, 537, 561
    Panama War, 529
    security and democracy promotion aims, 525, 528, 561, 562
    Somalia, humanitarian mission, 564

INDEX

Bush (43rd P.) administration
assessment of, 628–29, 697
China, diplomatic strategy, 627
diplomatic strategy generally, 589
economic strategy, 627–28
global war on terror, strategy and aims, 85, 589–92, 603–604, 625–26
political aims, 589, 598, 603
wars. *See* Afghan War, Bush (43rd P.) administration; Iraq War (Second)
Bush, George H.W., 524, 584, *See also* Bush (41st P.) administration
Bush, George W., 589, *See also* Bush (43rd P.) administration
Butler, Benjamin, 143
Butler, Smedley, 222
Byrnes, James F., 347

Calhoun, Henry, 96
Calhoun, John C., 82–84
California
expansionist aims towards, 100–104
Guadalupe Hidalgo Treaty 1848, 116
Mexican War, Californian campaign, 108–109
Call, Richard Keith, 92–93
Callwell, C.E., 161
Cambodia in Vietnam War
bombing operations against, 459, 468–69
creation of state, 399
invasion of, 465–67
North Vietnamese base, 417, 431, 433, 438, 465–66
Cambodia, Khmer Rouge regime, 452, 486, 495–96
Canada, pre Dominion era. *See* Lower Canada province (Quebec); Upper Canada province
Canby, Edward R.S., 173
Caribbean. *See* Latin America and Caribbean
Carleton, J.H., 166
Carleton, Sir Guy, 19, 20, 23–24
Carnegie, Andrew, 183, 203, 222
Carranza, Venustiano, 232–33
Carter administration
Asia, diplomatic strategy, 486–87, 495–96
Cold War strategy, 477, 480–82, 484–85
diplomatic strategy generally, 481–82, 494, 496
economic strategy, 486, 489–90, 494, 496
human rights promotion aim, 479, 485–88
critiqued, 481–83, 486, 495–96
information strategy, 482–83, 485–86
Middle East, diplomatic strategy, 487–88, 490–94, 603
military strategy, 481–84, 493–95
political aims and grand strategy, 478–81, 492, 697
Soviet Union, diplomatic strategy, 484–86, 491–94
strategy advisors, 477–78
Third World, diplomatic strategy, 488–89, 496
Carter Doctrine, 493, 515
Carter, Ash, 657, 658
Carter, Jimmy, 575, 576, 588, *See also* Carter administration
Casey, George, 619–24
Casey, William J., 508, 510
Cass, Lewis, 90
Castro, Cipriano, 217
Castro, Fidel, 397, 449
Ceausescu, Nicolae, 526
CENTO (Central Treaty Organization), 394, 406–407
Central Intelligence Agency. *See* CIA (Central Intelligence Agency)
Cervera, Pascual, 198, 200
Chaffee, Adna R., 211
Chamorro, Emiliano, 271–72
Chandler, William E., 187
Chauncey, Isaac, 65, 70
Cheney, Dick, 542, 545, 590
Chesapeake affair, 56, 58
Cheyenne-Arapaho-Kiowa War (1868), 170–71
Cheyenne-Arapaho-Kiowa-Sioux War (1867), 169–70
Chiang Kai-Shek, 268–69, 308, 355–56
Chile, 183–84, 186–87, 451, 513
China
atomic warfare capability, 446
Boxer Rebellion, 212–13

civil war and Communist revolution, 355–56, 403
Cultural Revolution, 403
diplomatic strategy towards. *See* China, US diplomatic strategy
economic rivalry with US, 1, 627, 666, 672, 701
Japan, invasions by, 277, 291–92, 322–23
in Korean War. *See under* Korean War
Manchuria. *See* Manchuria, China
post-Second World War aid to, 354
in Second World War, 336, 339
Soviet Union, split from, 402–403, 411, 446, 449–50, 508
Taiwan, relations with. *See* Taiwan
Tiananmen Square massacre, 527, 530, 538, 574
Vietnam War, feared entry into, 431
World Trade Organization membership, 574, 627
China, US diplomatic strategy
Biden administration, 691
Bush (41st P.) administration, 530–31
Bush (43rd P.) administration, 627
Carter administration, 486, 495–96
Clinton administration, 574–75
Eisenhower administration, 395
generally, 700–703
Harding and Coolidge administrations, 267–69
Johnson (17th P.) and Grant administrations, 158
Nixon and Ford administrations, 449–51, 459, 469, 486
Obama administration, 637–38
Open Door policy, 212, 223, 235, 256, 267, 268, 297
Pierce and Buchanan administrations, 121, 122
Reagan administration, 517–19
Roosevelt (26th P.) administration, 219
Roosevelt (32nd P.) administration, 291–92, 297, 298
Taft administration, 223–24, 700–701
Truman administration, 355–57
Trump administration, 672–74

Tyler administration, 100–101
Wilson administration, 234–35, 256
Chivington, John, 165
Christopher, Warren, 488, 489, 569, 570, 572–73, 575–76
Churchill, Sir Winston, 301, 302, 308, 313, 499
CIA (Central Intelligence Agency)
in Bush (43rd) administration, 594–95, 607
in Carter administration, 484, 494
Castro regime, Cuba, strategies against, 397, 409–10
in Clinton administration, 583
covert operations generally, 397–98, 407
establishment, 358
in Reagan administration, 508–10
civil rights
Constitutional protections, 152, 153
in interwar period, 258
Kennedy and Johnson (36th P.) administrations, 407, 413–14, 430
Reconstruction era, recognition blocked, 151–52, 154–55
Civil War
Border States in, 130–31
casualties and economic impact, 149–50, 160
commencement, 124
diplomatic strategies, 127
economic strategies and naval blockade, 127–28, 133–34, 142
escalation, 139
Indian Wars during, 165–66
military strategies, 125–26, 149
Confederacy, 128–29, 135–36, 138–40, 146
Union, 129–38, 141–45
origins. *See* slave states, sectional tensions
peace negotiations, 147–49
political aims, 124
preparations and resources, 126–27
presidential election (1864), 145–46
principal offensives, map 4.1
Atlanta and Sherman's march, 126–27, 143–47
Lee's northern offensive, 140–41

INDEX

Civil War (cont.)
    Petersburg and Richmond, 148–49
    Virginia Peninsula, 135–39, 147
    western theater, 136–40
    Reconstruction policies. *See* Reconstruction policies
    slavery abolition, 139, 145, 148, 151
Clark, Mark W., 309, 383–84, 386–87
Clausewitz, Carl von
    military strategy, 6–7, 59, 137, 542–43, 555, 604, 611, 623
    on war, 9, 103, 139, 305, 344, 439
    on war aims, 6, 403, 516–17
Clay, Henry, 57, 58, 73, 74, 82, 83
Clemenceau, Georges, 251, 252, 254
Cleveland, Grover, 179–80, 182, 184–85, *See also* Gilded Age era (1877–97)
Clifford, Clark, 431, 442, 443
Clinch, Duncan, 92
Clinton administration
    Asia, diplomatic strategy, 574–75
    Bosnian War, 577–79, 587
    counterterrorism strategy, 582–84
    diplomatic strategy generally, 573–74, 579
    economic strategy, 566–68, 571, 573–74, 588, 701
    grand strategy, 561, 564–66, 571–73, 580, 587–88
    Haiti, operations in, 570–71, 576–77
    Kosovo War, 585–87
    Middle East, diplomatic strategy, 583–85
    military strategy, 567–68, 575–76, 580–82
    political aims, 565, 571–73, 580, 588
    Rwanda genocide, non-intervention, 574, 577
    Somalia, operations in, 568–70, 578
    strategy advisors and ideas, 564–66, 571, 579–80
Clinton, Bill. *See* Clinton administration
Clinton, Hillary
    Iraq War, Senate voting on, 607, 625
    as Secretary of State, Obama administration, 635, 637–40, 647
    Trump election, Russian interference claim, 665
Clinton, Sir Henry, 18, 31–32, 35
Cochise (Apache leader), 177

Cochrane, Sir Alexander, 71, 73
Colby, William, 444, 464
Cold War
    assessment of US victory, 532–33
    atomic warfare threat. *See* atomic warfare
    CIA operations. *See under* CIA (Central Intelligence Agency)
    'Cold War' term, 344, 362
    Communism spread, policies against. *See* anti Communist policies
    containment strategy, 3, 350–51, 354, 361, 389, 391, 404, 566
    Cuban Missile Crisis, 406, 410–11
    détente strategy, 449–51, 476, 482, 484–85, 497–98
    Eisenhower Doctrine, 396–97
    'hot wars' of. *See* Korean War; Vietnam War entries
    information strategy, 352, 358, 397–98, 400, 408, 702
    New Look strategy, 391–92
    NSC 20/4 and NSC 68 strategies (Truman administration), 352, 361–62, 390–91
    NSC 5906/1 strategy (Eisenhower administration), 399–400
    origins, 345–49
    Sino-Soviet split, 402–403, 411, 446, 449–50, 508
    Soviet agents in US, 356
    Soviet Union and Eastern bloc collapse, 524, 526, 527, 531–32, 560
    Truman Doctrine, 349–50
    weaponization of economics strategy, 499, 503–504, 506
Collins, J. Lawton, 366–67, 372–73, 376–77, 379
Comanche and Red River Wars, 172–73
Communism. *See* anti Communist policies; Cold War
Confederation period, 36–38
Connor, David, 107
containment strategy, Cold War, 3, 350–51, 354, 361, 389, 391, 404, 566
Coolidge Doctrine, 264–65
Coolidge, Calvin. *See* Harding and Coolidge administrations
Coral Sea, Battle of the, 328

INDEX

Corbin, Henry C., 197
Cornwallis, Lord Charles, 28, 32, 34–35
COSSAC (Sir Frederick Morgan), 316
counterterrorism strategy
   Bush (43rd P.) administration, 85, 589–92, 603–604, 625–26
   Clinton administration, 582–84
   Obama administration, 643, 650–52, 656
   Reagan administration, 507, 517
   wars. *See* Afghan War entries; Iraq War (Second); Iraq War (Third)
COVID-19 pandemic, 685, 686, 690
Crazy Horse, 167–68, 174, 175
Creek Wars, 72–73, 91–92
Crocker, Ryan, 624, 625, 652, 683
Croly, Herbert, 202
Crook, George, 162–63, 167, 174–75, 177–79
Cuba
   Castro, CIA plans to depose, 397, 409–10
   Cuban Missile Crisis, 406, 410–11
   diplomatic strategy towards. *See* Cuba, US diplomatic strategy
   independence declaration, 192–96
   war consequence. *See* Spanish-American War
   Reagan administration strategy towards, 508, 510–12
   in Spanish-American War, 197–201
Cuba, US diplomatic strategy
   Bush (41st P.) administration, 528
   Harding and Coolidge administrations, 264
   McKinley administration (post Spanish-American War), 202–203
   preindependence, 120, 160, 182, 183, 185
   Roosevelt (26th P.) administration, 218
   Roosevelt (32nd P.) administration, 290
   Wilson administration, 234
Cullom, Shelby M., 192
Custer, George Armstrong, 171, 175
Czech Republic, 576
Czechoslovakia, 292, 352, 354, 412, 526

Dale, Robert, 52
Davis, Jefferson, 124, 131, 145, 149, 152
   military strategies. *See* Civil War, military strategies

Davis, Jefferson C., 173
Dawes Plan, 269–70
D-Day and Operation OVERLORD, 307, 309–10, 315–22
Dearborn, Henry, 61, 63–67
Decatur, Stephen, 70, 75
Declaration of Independence, 21, 37
democracy promotion aim. *See also* human rights promotion aim
   anti Communist policies. *See* anti Communist policies
   Bush (41st P.) administration, 525, 528, 561, 562
   Bush (43rd P.) administration, 598, 603
   Carter administration, 480
   Clinton administration, 565, 571–73, 588
   generally, 5, 698, 699, 702
   Harding's view of, 262
   Hoover administration, 276, 277
   Nixon and Ford administrations, skepticism towards, 452, 476
   Obama administration, 634, 659, 698
   Reagan administration, 499–501, 512, 513, 519, 522, 532–33
   Truman Doctrine, 349–50
   Trump administration, 662
   Wilson administration, 227–28, 239, 241, 244, 246–47, 252, 257
Deng Xiaoping, 486, 518
détente strategy, Cold War, 449–51, 476, 482, 484–85, 497–98
Dewey, George, 197–99, 201, 204
Díaz, Adolfo, 272
Dickinson, John, 15
diplomatic strategy
   Adams (2nd P.) administration, 46–47
   American Revolutionary War, 21–22, 29, 36
   anti Communist policies. *See* anti Communist policies
   atomic warfare threat as. *See under* atomic warfare
   Biden administration, 690–91
   Bush (41st P.) administration, 526–28
   Bush (43rd P.) administration, 589
   Carter administration, 481–82, 494, 496
   Civil War, 127
   Clinton administration, 573–74, 579

831

INDEX

diplomatic strategy (cont.)
  Coolidge Doctrine, 264–65
  Eisenhower administration, 395–97, 400
  empire-building. *See* Imperialist era (1897–1913)
  generally, 8–9, 699–701
  Gilded Age era (1877–97), 180–85
  Good Neighbor Policy, 262–63, 277, 290, 407
  Harding and Coolidge administrations, 260, 262, 282–83
  Hoover administration, 276–78, 282–83
  isolationism. *See* isolationism
  Jackson administration, 88–89
  Jefferson administration, 54, map 2.1
  Johnson (17th P.) and Grant administrations, 158–60
  Kennedy and Johnson (36th P.) administrations, 406–408, 411–13
  Madison administration, 56–57
  McKinley administration, 191–92, 213
  Mexican War, 104, 107–108
  Monroe and Adams (6th P.) administrations, 78–83
  Monroe Doctrine. *See* Monroe Doctrine
  Nixon and Ford administrations, 451–53, 458–59, 486
  Obama administration, 636–37, 659–60, 667, 698, 700
  Pierce administration, 121
  Reagan administration, 508–509
  Roosevelt (26th P.) administration, 214–15, 217–20
  Roosevelt (32nd P.) administration. *See* Roosevelt (32nd P.) administration
  specific strategies. *See under* individual countries and world regions; individual Presidential administrations
  Taft administration (Dollar Diplomacy), 221–22, 224, 700–701
  Truman administration, 354–58
  Trump administration, 667, 700
  Tyler administration, 100–101
  Van Buren administration, 98
  Washington administration, 40–41, 45–46
  Wilson administration, 229–30

disarmament policies. *See also* Air Force; Army; Navy
  post American Revolutionary War, 37
  post Civil War, 150
  post First World War, 267–68, 275, 282
  post Quasi War, 52
  pre Second World War, 292–93
  post Second World War, 349–50, 358–59
Dodge, Richard I., 163
Dominican Republic, 159–60, 218, 230, 233–34, 265, 408, 412
Donilon, Tom, 637
Dönitz, Karl, 310, 311
Doolittle, James, 168
Douglas, Stephen, 120–21
Douhet, Giulio, 312
Dueck, Colin, 282–83, 629
Dulles, Foster Rhea, 258
Dulles, John Foster, 386, 391, 392, 395, 400

Eagleburger, Lawrence, 565–66
Earle, Edward Meade, 39
East Germany, 354–55, 410, 526–28
Eaton, Paul D., 617
Ebert, Friedrich, 253
Eckes, Alfred, 10
economic panics. *See also* Great Depression
  of 1833, 97
  of 1837, 98
  of 1873, 161
  of 1893, 184
  of 1929–30, 278–79
  of 1933, 283
  of 2007–08, 628, 633
economic strategy
  American Revolutionary War, 21–22, 29–30
  Biden administration, 667, 690
  Bush (41st P.) administration, 528
  Bush (43rd P.) administration, 627–28
  Carter administration, 486, 489–90, 494, 496
  Civil War, 127–28
  Clinton administration, 566–68, 571, 573–74, 588, 701
  Confederation period, 37
  Eisenhower administration, 398, 400–401
  generally, 10–11, 701–702

INDEX

Harding and Coolidge administrations, 260–62, 269, 282, 502
Hoover administration, 276, 278
   Great Depression response, 280–81
Jackson administration, 95–97, 99
Jefferson administration, 50–52
Johnson (17th P.) and Grant administrations, 158, 160–61
Kennedy and Johnson (36th P.) administrations, 408–409, 413–15, 502
Madison administration, 76
Monroe and Adams (6th P.) administrations, 82–83
Nixon and Ford administrations, 453–55
Obama administration, 635–36, 667
Reagan administration, 499, 501–504, 567
Roosevelt (26th P.) administration, 220–21
Roosevelt (32nd P.) administration
   New Deal. *See* New Deal policies
   Second World War, pre US entry, 299–300
   Second World War, post US entry, 300–301
Taft administration (Dollar Diplomacy), 221–22, 224, 700–701
Truman administration, 352–54, 387
   Marshall Plan, 351–52
Trump administration, 666–67, 672, 673, 685
Tyler administration, 99–101
Van Buren administration, 98
Washington administration, 10, 38–41
Wilson administration, 228–29, 237
Edel, Charles, 79
Edmunds, Newton, 165–66
Egypt
   Arab-Israeli War, 449, 451, 454
   Arab Spring and aftermath, 639
   Israel, peace treaty with, 487, 491, 496
   Soviet influence in, 407, 412–13
   Suez Crisis, 396
Eikenberry, Karl, 599, 647
Eisenhower administration
   Cold War grand strategy, 391–92, 399–400, 697
   diplomatic strategy, 395–97, 400
   economic strategy, 398, 400–401

information strategy, 397–98, 400
Korean War, final months, 384–87
military strategy, 390–97, 400–401
security aim, 390, 400
Eisenhower, Dwight D. ("Ike"). *See also* Eisenhower administration
   as Joint Chiefs of Staff Chairman, 359
   as military strategist, 305, 343
   as NATO Supreme Allied Commander Europe, 359
   in Operation OVERLORD, 315–22
   Second World War strategy, 305, 309, 327, 341
El Salvador, 511–12, 523, 524
Ellis, Edward S., 161
Ellsberg, Daniel, 456
empire-building. *See* Imperialist era (1897–1913)
energy crises. *See* oil crises
Erdoğan, Recep, 678–79
Esper, Mark, 669, 684
Estrada, Juan J., 222
Evans, John, 165
expansion aim. *See also* frontier expansion
   American Revolutionary War, 17
   Buchanan administration, 122
   empire-building. *See* Imperialist era (1897–1913)
   generally, 5, 77
   Gilded Age era (1877–97), 183
   Jefferson administration, 50
   Johnson (17th P.) and Grant administrations, 156–59
   Monroe and Adams (6th P.) administrations, 78
   Polk administration, 101–103
   sectional tensions over. *See* slave states, sectional tensions
   Tyler administration, 99, 101
   Wilson administration's shift, 241

Fabian strategy, 24, 25
Fall, Bernard, 425
Farragut, David, 137, 143
Feaver, Peter, 621–22
Feith, Douglas, 609, 613, 614
Feland, Logan, 272

INDEX

Ferguson, Patrick, 32
filibustering (military strategy), 120
Fillmore administration, 119–20
First Bank of the United States, 39–40, 52
First Barbary War, 52–53
First Creek War, 72–73
First Iraq War. *See* Gulf War
First Seminole War, 84–85
First World War, debts and reparations, 269–71
First World War, Wilson administration in
  armistice negotiations, 249–51
    Fourteen Points, 246–47, 249–51, 254, 256
  assessment of, 257
  as coalition partner, 241–43, 245, 247–48
  democracy promotion aim, 239, 241, 244, 246–47
  introduction to topic, 235–36
  military strategy, map 7.1, 244–49, 252–53
  peace treaty negotiations. *See* Versailles Treaty 1919
  preparations and resources, 239–40, 243, 257
  prewar diplomacy, 236–40
  Russia Interlude, 248–49
Fish, Hamilton, 159, 160
Florida
  boundary negotiations with Spain, 44, 48–49
  Creek tribes in, 72, 78, 84
  expansionist aims towards, 54, 72
  Seminole Wars, 84–85, 92–95, map 3.1
Flournoy, Michèle, 654
Foch, Ferdinand, 247–51
Foote, Andrew H., 135
Fordney-McCumber Tariff, 261, 281, 282
foreign policy. *See* diplomatic strategy
Formosa. *See* Taiwan
Fort Astoria, 80, 84
Fort Harmar Treaty 1789, 42–44
Fort Jackson Treaty 1814, 74
Fort Sumter, Battle of, 124
France
  aircraft purchases, 292
  American Revolutionary War, colonialist support, 21, 28–29, 35

  Civil War, position on, 127
  diplomatic strategy towards. *See* France, US diplomatic strategy
  Indochina War, 357, 399
  Iraq War opposition, 608
  Louisiana Purchase, 54, 76, 78, 103
  post Second World War aid to, 353–54, 357–58
  in Second World War, 306–307, 309–10, 315–22
  Suez Crisis, 396
France, US diplomatic strategy
  Adams (2nd P.) administration, 46–47, *See also* Quasi-War
  Madison administration, 55–57
  Washington administration, 40–41
Franco, Francisco, 291
Franklin, Benjamin, 21–22, 29–30, 36
Franks, Frederick, 551
Franks, Tommy
  Afghan War strategy, 594, 596, 597
  Iraq, postwar strategy, 610, 612, 614
  Iraq War strategy, 608, 611
free trade policies. *See also* tariff policies
  in American Revolutionary War, 21–22
  Bush (41st P.) administration, 528, 564
  Bush (43rd P.) administration, 627
  Carter administration, 486, 489
  Clinton administration, 567, 573–74, 588
  Gilded Age era (1877–97), 180–85
  Jackson administration, 99
  Jefferson administration, 50–52, 56
  List on, 100
  Obama administration, 636
  Reagan administration, 503, 567
  Roosevelt (32nd P.) administration, 287, 299, 341
  Washington administration, 10, 39–41
Frémont, John C., 108–109, 130–31
French and Indian War, 4, 15
frontier expansion. *See also* expansion aim
  Alaska Purchase, 159
  California. *See also* Mexican War
    expansionist aims towards, 100–104
    Guadalupe Hidalgo Treaty 1848, 116
  Central American states, 120, 122, 159–60

INDEX

empire-building. *See* Imperialist era (1897–1913)
Florida. *See* Florida
Hawaii annexation, 196, 203
Louisiana, 54, 76, 78
Maine boundary dispute, 98, 100
maps depicting, maps 1.1, 2.1
Native American territories. *See* Indian Wars; Native American territorial losses
New Mexico, 116, 120
Oregon boundary dispute, 100, 103
Pacific island territories, 121, 201–3, 227
railroad construction, 119, 126–27, 161, 165, 168, 169, 184
slave states. *See* slave states, sectional tensions
Texas annexation, 97, 100–103
Fukuyama, Francis, 566, 568, 571
Fulbright, J. William, 460

Gaddafi, Moammar, 517, 626, 639, 640, 642
Gaddis, John Lewis, 497
Gadsden Purchase, 120
Gage, Thomas, 16, 18
Gaines, Edmund, 84, 92
Galbraith, John Kenneth, 315
Gallatin, Albert, 52, 66, 67, 72, 73
Garfield, James, 181, 187
Garner, Jay, 610, 612–14
Garthoff, Raymond, 449
Gates, Horatio, 28, 32
Gates, Robert
   Afghan War strategy, 645–48
   Gulf War strategy, 556
   Iraq War strategy, 624
   Obama administration, views on, 636, 639–40, 644, 649
Gelb, Leslie, 588
Gemayel, Bashir, 515–16
George III of Great Britain, 17, 20, 21, 35
Georgia, Russian invasion, 626, 638, 642
Gerasimov Doctrine, 664
Germain, Lord George, 20, 27, 31, 35
Germany
   Allied occupation, map 9.1b, 322, 342, 359
   First World War. *See* First World War entries; Versailles Treaty 1919
   Pacific region expansionist aims, 195, 201, 230
   post Second World War aid to, 353–54
   reunification, 527–28
   Russia, oil and gas deals with, 676
   Second World War. *See* Second World War entries
   US troop withdrawals from, 405, 413
   Venezuela Crisis, 216–18
   West and East division, 354–55, 410
Geronimo (Chiricahua Chief), 178–79
Gettysburg, Battle of, 140–41
Ghani, Ashraf, 651–52, 684, 693, 694
Ghazni, city, 694
Ghost Dance War, 180
Gibbon, John, 174, 175
Gilbert and Marshall Islands, 334–35
Gilded Age era (1877–97)
   Army reforms, 185–86
   diplomatic and foreign trade strategies, 180–85
   expansion aim, 183
   military strategy generally, 185
   Navy reforms, 181–82, 186–90
Glaspie, April, 537–38
Glass-Steagall Act 1933, 280, 287
global financial crisis, 628, 633
global war on terror. *See* counterterrorism strategy
Glosson, Buster, 544
Goldberg, Jeffrey, 635
Good Friday Agreement, 588
Good Neighbor Policy, 262–63, 277, 290, 407
Gorbachev, Mikhail, 520, 523–24, 526–28, 531–32
Gorgas, Josiah, 134
Goulburn, William, 63
grand strategy
   advisors on, 696–97
   concept, 1, 2–3, 11
   core mistakes, 697–98
   core successes, 698–99
   future directions, 702–703
   interests dimension, 3–4
   national power elements, 7–8, 11, *See also* diplomatic strategy; economic strategy; information strategy; military strategy

INDEX

grand strategy (cont.)
  political aims dimension, 1, 3–7,
    See also democracy promotion
    aim; expansion aim; human rights
    promotion aim; security aim;
    sovereignty aim; war aims
Grant, Ulysses S. *See also* Johnson (17th P.)
  and Grant administrations
  as Civil War commander, 131, 135, 138,
    139, 141
  as Civil War lieutenant general, 132,
    142–44, 146, 148–49
  as peacetime commander, 158–59
Gray, Colin, 389
'gray zone' between war and peace, 664,
  689–90, 697
Greasy Grass, Battle of, 174, 175
Great Britain
  in American Revolutionary War. *See*
    American Revolutionary War
  British Guiana boundary dispute, 184–85
  British North America. *See* Lower Canada
    province (Quebec); Upper Canada
    province
  Civil War, position on, 127–28
  economic dumping policy, 37
  gold standard policies, 278–80
  Good Friday Agreement, 588
  Native American peoples, relations with,
    18–19, 42, 44, 74, 84–85
  in Second World War. *See* Second World
    War entries
  Suez Crisis, 396
  Venezuela Crisis, 216–18
  in War of 1812. *See* War of 1812
  Washington administration, relations
    with, 41
Great Depression
  bank crisis (1933), 283
  causes, purported, 278–81, 283
  defense spending and, 292, 299
  further downturn (1937), 289
  Hoover administration response,
    280–81
  Roosevelt (32nd P.) administration
    response. *See* New Deal policies
Great Sioux War, 174–76

Greece, anti Communist policies towards,
  349, 355, 357, 398–99
Greene, Nathanael, 24–26, 32–35
Greene, Wallace, 435
Gregory, Ross, 239–40
Grenada War, 510–11, 522
Grew, Joseph, 341
Gromyko, Andrei, 381
Guadalupe Hidalgo Treaty 1848, 116
Guam, 201, 202, 299, *See also* Mariana Islands
Guatemala, 396–97
Gulf of Tonkin Resolution, 422, 467
Gulf War
  aims and grand strategy, 539–42, 554,
    556–57, 559
  air power, strategy and campaign, 542–44,
    549–50
  ceasefire decision and terms, 552–58
  coalition building for, 538–40
  ground war, strategy and campaign,
    544–48, 550–52
  Iraqi military strategy, 548–50
  military strategy generally, 542, maps
    16.1a, 16.1b, 545
  origins, 537–38
  United Nations' role, 538–40, 558–59, 561
  US decision to engage, 538, 539
  weapons of mass destruction, feared use,
    540, 541, 549
Guyana (formerly British Guiana), 184–85, 408

Hadley, Stephen, 620–21, 623
Hagel, Chuck, 656–57
Haig, Al, 498, 503, 518
Haig, Douglas, 247, 252
Haiti, 230, 265, 290, 528, 570–71, 576–77
Halleck, Henry Wager, 128, 134, 136–38, 141
Halsey, William F. ("Bull"), 336–37
Hamas, 626
Hamilton, Alexander
  in American Revolutionary War, 24–25, 30
  diplomatic strategy, 40–41, 45, 82
  economic strategy, 10, 38–40, 82
  military strategy, 41–42, 69
  in Quasi-War, 47–48
Hamilton, Paul, 62–63
Hancock, Winfield Scott, 169–70

INDEX

Harding and Coolidge administrations
  Asia, diplomatic strategy, 267–69
  diplomatic strategy generally, 260, 262, 282–83
  economic strategy, 260–62, 269, 282, 502
  Europe, diplomatic strategy, 259, 269–71
  Last Banana War, Nicaragua, 271–74
  Latin America and Caribbean, diplomatic strategy, 262–66
  military strategy, 267–68, 274–76
  sovereignty and security aims, 259–60, 263
  Soviet Union, diplomatic strategy, 266–67
Harding, Warren G. *See* Harding and Coolidge administrations
Harris, Arthur, 313
Harrison, Benjamin, 180, 182–84, *See also* Gilded Age era (1877–97)
Harrison, William Henry, 53–54, 63, 67, 99
Harvey, Derek, 647–48
Hatfield, Mark, 467
Havel, Vaclav, 526
Hawaii
  annexation, 196, 203
  diplomatic strategy towards. *See* Hawaii, US diplomatic strategy
  in Second World War, 297–99
  Pearl Harbor attack, 301–302, 322
Hawaii, US diplomatic strategy
  Fillmore administration, 120
  Gilded Age era (1877–97), 181–84
  Grant administration, 160
  Johnson administration, 158
  Taylor administration, 119
  Tyler administration, 100–101
Hay, John, 212–13, 215
Hayden, Michael, 625, 664
Hayes, Rutherford B., 154–55, 179–81, *See also* Gilded Age era (1877–97)
Helsinki Final Act, 452–53, 485
Hezbollah, 513, 515, 583–84, 616, 668
Hirohito, Emperor of Japan, 339–40
Hiroshima and Nagasaki attacks, 339–40
Hitler, Adolf
  Munich Agreement, 292, 298, 351
  in Second World War. *See* Second World War entries
  Versailles Treaty abrogation, 271, 291
Ho Chi Minh, 256, 357, 399, 416, 462, 475
Holbrooke, Richard, 578, 579, 585, 644, 650
Honduras, 265–66, 512
Hood, John Bell, 145–47
Hoover administration
  democracy promotion aim, 276, 277
  diplomatic strategy, 276–78, 282–83
  economic strategy, 276, 278
  Great Depression response, 280–81
  Haiti, withdrawal of US forces, 265
  Last Banana War, Nicaragua, 271–74
  military strategy, 276
  Wall Street Crash and bank failures, 278–80
  Young Plan on war reparations, 271
Hoover, Herbert, 261, 264, 266, 269, 276–77, *See also* Hoover administration
Hopkins, Harry, 288, 342
Horton, Sir Max, 311
House, Edward M., 236, 246, 251, 252
Howe, Lord Richard, 20
Howe, William, 18, 20–23, 26–28, 30
Huerta, Victoriano, 230–32
Hughes, Charles Evans
  diplomatic strategy generally, 260, 261, 269
  Europe, policy towards, 269
  Latin America and Caribbean, policy towards, 262–65, 273
  Soviet Union, policy towards, 266
  in Washington Treaties negotiations, 267, 268
Hull, Cordell, 287, 341–42
Hull, William, 61, 63, 65
human rights promotion aim. *See also* democracy promotion aim
  Carter administration, 479, 485–88
  critiqued, 481–83, 486, 495–96
  Clinton administration, 574
  Nixon and Ford administrations, skepticism towards, 452
  Obama administration, 634, 637, 698
  Reagan administration, 523
  Trump administration, 674
Hungary, 396, 397, 526, 576

837

INDEX

Hunt, Richard, 437–38
Hunt, William H., 187
Huntington, Samuel, 478, 481, 562, 571
Hussein, Saddam. *See also* Iraq
   collapse of regime, 612
   in Gulf War. *See* Gulf War
   in Iran-Iraq War, 493, 514
   Kurds, persecution of, 558
   overthrow, whether US aim, 541, 556–57, 584, 585, 604, 629
   post-Gulf War uprising against, 558
   Al Qaeda, links to, 607
   US diplomatic relations with, 531
'hybrid war' theory, 664, 689–90, 697

Ia Drang, Battle of, 433
Iklé, Fred Charles, 552
Imperialist era (1897–1913)
   opposition to imperialism, 203
   Panama Canal Zone acquisition, 5, 215–16, 604
   political aims, 191–92, 202
   Progressive era coincident with, 202
   wars. *See* Philippines, War for the; Spanish-American War
India, 451–52, 519, 637, 673, 682
Indian Wars. *See also* Native American peoples; Native American territorial losses
   Black Hawk War, 91
   Creek Wars, 72–73, 91–92
   mid-nineteenth century. *See* Indian Wars, mid-nineteenth century
   Seminole Wars, 84–85, 92–95, map 3.1
   Tecumseh's War, 53–54
Indian Wars, mid-nineteenth century
   aims, 161–63
   Apache Wars, 177–79
   Cheyenne-Arapaho-Kiowa War (1868), 170–71
   Cheyenne-Arapaho-Kiowa-Sioux War (1867), 169–70
   Civil War period, 165–66
   Comanche and Red River Wars, 172–73
   final battles, 179–80
   Grant's peace policy, 171–72
   Great Plains Indians, characteristics, 162–63

Great Sioux War, 174–76
   military strategy, 163–64
   Modoc War, 173–74
   Nez Perce War, 176
   preparations and resources, 163
   Red Cloud War, 167–69
   Snake War, 166–67
   Ute War, 176–77
Indochina. *See also* individual country names
   anti Communist policies towards, 357–58, 398–99
Indochina War (anti-French resistance), 357, 399
SEATO (Southeast Asian Treaty Organization), 394, 399, 406–407, 452
Vietnam War. *See* Vietnam War entries
Indonesia, 397, 413
inflation. *See also* economic strategy
   American Revolutionary War and, 29–30
   Carter administration, 489–90, 496, 497
   Civil War and, 128, 134
   Eisenhower administration, 398
   Kennedy and Johnson (36th P.) administrations, 408, 414–15
   Nixon and Ford administrations, 447, 453–54, 463
   Reagan administration, 497, 502–503
   Roosevelt (32nd P.) administration, 285, 286, 300
information strategy
   American Revolutionary War, 25
   Carter administration, 482–83, 485–86
   Eisenhower administration, 397–98, 400
   generally, 9, 702
   intelligence. *See* CIA (Central Intelligence Agency)
   Kennedy and Johnson (36th P.) administrations, 408, 438–39
   Mexican War, 104, 107, 110
   Nixon and Ford administrations, 453
   Obama administration, 636, 640–41
   Reagan administration, 509–10, 523–24
   Roosevelt (26th P.) administration, 220
   Second World War, 296
   Truman administration, 352, 358
   Tyler administration, 100
interests, national, 3–4

INDEX

International Monetary Fund, 342
interwar period (1921–39), 258–59, 281–83, 293, *See also* Great Depression; Harding and Coolidge administrations; Hoover administration; Roosevelt (32nd P.) administration
Iran
  Arab Oil Embargo and, 451, 487–88
  diplomatic strategy. *See* Iran, US diplomatic strategy
  Iran-Contra Scandal, 513
  Iran-Iraq War, 493, 514–15, 537
  nuclear capability, 626, 642–43, 669–70
  Persian Gulf, US military operations, 514–15
  pre Revolution strategy towards, 397, 412–13, 451, 487–88
  Revolution and US hostage crisis, 490–91, 496
  in Second World War, 357
  terrorism, support for, 583, 643, 668, 670
Iran, US diplomatic strategy
  Biden administration, 690–91
  Bush (41st P.) administration, 531
  Bush (43rd P.) administration, 626
  Clinton administration, 583–85
  Obama administration, 639, 642–43
  Trump administration, 669–72, 674
Iraq
  Bush (41st P.) administration, diplomatic strategy, 531
  Clinton administration, diplomatic strategy, 583
  Gulf War aftermath, 558–59
  Iran-Iraq War, 493, 514–15, 537
  9/11, proposed response against, 590
  Al Qaeda, prewar links to, 607
  sectarianism and Iranian influence, 622, 654, 668, 670, 678
  wars against. *See* Gulf War; Iraq War (Second); Iraq War (Third)
  weapons of mass destruction capability, 559, 584, 606–607
Iraq War (First). *See* Gulf War
Iraq War (Second)
  aims, 604–606, 612, 653
  Bush (43rd P.), reflections on, 8, 612, 617, 623, 624
  coalition building for, 607–608, 619
  counterinsurgency strategy, 619–21, 624–26
  global war on terror consequences, 625–27
  insurgency combat, 616–19, 670
  military strategy, 117, 608–609, 615–17, 623–26, 629
  Obama administration in, 652–54
  Operation IRAQI FREEDOM, 611–12
  postwar failures, 612–17, 626
  postwar planning and strategies, 610–12, 621–22
  Al Qaeda in, 616, 618, 619, 622–23, 625–26
Iraq War (Third), 654–59, 677–80, 691–92
Iroquois Confederation, 30–31
Islamic State. *See also* Al Qaeda
  in Afghanistan, 680–81
  Iraq War (Third) against, 654–59, 677–80, 691–92
  in Libya, 641
  origins of, 625–26, 654–55
  in Syria, 655–58, 678
isolationism
  Adams (6th P.) administration and, 79
  Bush (43rd P.) administration and, 589
  generally, 8–9
  Hoover administration and, 282
  'neo-isolationists', 586
  Roosevelt (32nd P.) administration and, 290
  Truman administration and, 368
  Washington administration and, 45–46
  Wilson administration and, 254–55, 266
Israel
  Arab-Israeli peace process, 583, 588, 639
  Arab-Israeli War, 449, 451, 454
  Egypt, peace treaty with, 487, 491, 496
  Gulf War, feared participation, 542, 550
  Kennedy administration, diplomatic strategy, 407
  Lebanon, invasion of, 515–16
  Palestinian territory elections, 626
  in Suez Crisis, 396
  Six Day War, 412–13
  Trump administration, diplomatic strategy, 668, 669

INDEX

Italy, 291, 308–309
Iwo Jima, Battle of, 337
Izard, George, 70

Jack, Captain (Kintpuash), 173
Jackson administration
  Asia, attempted trade with, 99
  Bank of the United States, battle with, 96–98
  Black Hawk War, 91
  diplomatic strategy, 88–89
  Indian removal policy, 89–90
  military strategy, 90–91
  Second Creek War, 91–92
  Second Seminole War, 92–95, map 3.1
  security aim, 88
  tariff policies and Nullification Crisis, 95–96, 122
Jackson, Andrew. *See also* Jackson administration
  in First Seminole War, 84–85
  Native American territorial seizures, 74, 86–87
  in War of 1812, 72–73, 75
Japan
  China, invasions of, 277, 291–92, 322–23
  diplomatic strategy towards. *See* Japan, US diplomatic strategy
  economic rivalry with US, 503
  Korea annexation, 220, 362
  military strategy respecting, 275–76
  post Second World War aid and investment, 351, 388, 398
  in Second World War
    pre US entry, 296–98
    post US entry. *See* Pacific theater of Second World War
Japan, US diplomatic strategy
  Carter administration, 487
  Gilded Age era (1877–97), 185
  Harding and Coolidge administrations, 267–68
  Hoover administration, 277
  Pierce administration, 121
  Reagan administration, 519
  Roosevelt (26th P.) administration, 219–20

Roosevelt (32nd P.) administration (pre Second World War), 291–93
Taft administration, 223–24
Trump administration, 672–74
Wilson administration, 235, 256
Jay, John, 35–36, 41
Jay's Treaty 1794, 44, 46
Jefferson administration
  diplomatic strategy, 54, map 2.1
  economic strategy, 50–52
  First Barbary War, 52–53
  Fort Astoria, recognition of, 80
  Louisiana Purchase, 54, 76, 78, 103
  military strategy, 52, 53
  Native American affairs, 53–54, 86
  political aims, 50, 55–56
Jefferson, Thomas. *See also* Jefferson administration
  in Adams (2nd P.) administration, 46
  American Revolutionary War, aims, 17
  in Madison administration, 58, 60
  in Monroe and Adams (6th P.) administrations, 82
  in Washington administration, 38, 41
Jeffrey, James, 679
Jessup, Thomas, 93–94
Jim Crow laws and Black Codes, 152, 155, 265
Johnson (17th P.) and Grant administrations
  Alaska Purchase, 159
  diplomatic strategy, 158–60
  economic strategy, 158, 160–61
  expansion aim, 156–59
  Indian Wars. *See* Indian Wars, mid-nineteenth century
  Johnson's appointment, 149
  Reconstruction policies. *See* Reconstruction policies
  sovereignty aim, 150–51
Johnson, Andrew. *See* Johnson (17th P.) and Grant administrations
Johnson, Louis, 368–69
Johnson, Lyndon B., 394, 411, *See also* Kennedy and Johnson (36th P.) administrations
Johnson, Robert B., 568
Johnston, Albert Sidney, 131, 135

INDEX

Johnston, Joseph E., 135–36, 139–40, 144–45, 149
Joint Army and Navy Board, 213, 275, 302
Joint Chiefs of Staff, 302–303, 358, 409, 423
Jomini, Antoine-Henri, 128–29
Jones, William, 65, 69, 72
Jordan, 396
Joseph, Chief, 176
Joy, C. Turner, 381–83

Kansas-Nebraska Act 1854, 120–21
Karzai, Hamid
  in Afghan War, 598, 647, 648, 650, 651
  elected Afghan President, 598, 644
  governance of Afghanistan, 599, 600, 643
  in Pakistan, 595–96
Keane, Jack, 679
Kearny, Stephen W., 106, 109
Kellogg-Briand Pact, 270–71
Kellogg, Frank B., 264, 268–71
Kelly, John, 665
Kennan, George F.
  China, views on, 355–56, 402
  Cold War strategy, 350–51, 355, 361, 390, 391, 566
  in Korean War, 371, 380
  "long telegram" on Soviet aims, 348, 391, 450
  NATO expansion without Russia, views on, 576
Kennedy and Johnson (36th P.) administrations
  Bay of Pigs invasion and Cuban Missile Crisis, 409–11
  civil rights movement, 407, 413–14, 430
  Cold War grand strategy, 403–404, 415
  diplomatic strategy, 406–408, 411–13
  economic strategy, 408–409, 413–15, 502
  information strategy, 408, 438–39
  military strategy, 402, 404–406, 413
  security aim, 402, 404
  strategy advisors and ideas, 401–403, 415, 416, 696–97
  in Vietnam War, 422–23, 426–27, 431, 438, 444–45
  Vietnam War. *See* Vietnam War, Kennedy and Johnson (36th P.) administrations

Kennedy, John F., 411, 420, *See also* Kennedy and Johnson (36th P.) administrations
Kennedy, John P., 121
Kennedy, Robert, 409, 447
Kennedy, Ted, 509–10
Kentucky in Civil War, 130–31, 138
Kerry, John, 607, 625, 638, 642, 643, 656, 670
Keynes, John Maynard, 256, 289
Khalilzad, Zalmay, 598, 601, 613, 620–21, 683, 684
Khalis, Mohammed Younes, 596
Khamenei, Ali, 671
Khatami, Mohammad, 584
Khomeini, Ruhollah, 490, 491
Khrushchev, Nikita, 395, 396, 400, 405, 406, 410, 411
Kidder Massacre, 170
Kim Il Sung, 364, 365, 370, 373, 380
Kim Jong-un, 667–68
King, Ernest
  on Germany First strategy, 305–306, 311
  in Pacific War, 311, 327, 329, 331, 333, 334, 337, 338
King, Martin Luther Jr., 447
Kintpuash (Captain Jack), 173
Kissinger, Henry
  China, secret diplomatic missions to, 450, 469
  criticisms of, 477–78, 497
  as grand strategist, 446–48, 476
  peace, views on, 447–48
  strategies generally. *See under* Nixon and Ford administrations
  Vietnam War diplomatic strategies, 469–70, 472–73
  Vietnam War military strategies, 380, 456–58, 460–62, 468
Knox, Frank, 296
Knox, Henry, 22, 38, 43, 44
Knox, Philander, 222–24
Komer, Robert W., 436–37, 444
Korea, 158, 160, 181, 220, 362–64, *See also* North Korea, US diplomatic strategy; South Korea, US diplomatic strategy

INDEX

Korean War
  armistice negotiations, 380–83, 385–87
  assessment of, 387–89
  atomic weapons, threatened use, 374, 384–86
  China's entry, 372–74
  first phase, 365
  military strategy, 368–69, 372–76, 378–79, 385–86
  nondeclaration or Congressional vote, 366–68, 422
  origins, 3, 10, 360, 362–65
  political aims, 365–66, 370–72, 376–79, 384, 387
  preparations and resources, 364, 368–69, 374–76
  principal offensives, map 10.1
    first Chinese offensives, 373–74
    Inchon landing and Pusan offensive, 369–70
    stalemate period, operations in, 381–84, 386
    38th parallel combat (winter 1950-spring 1951), 376–77, 379–80
Kosovo War, 585–87
Ku Klux Klan, 153–54, 258
Kuwait, Iraqi invasion of, 537–38, *See also* Gulf War

Lacey, James, 307
Laird, Melvin, 458–62, 466, 468, 475
Lake, Anthony
  "democratic enlargement" strategy, 571–73
  Iran, views on, 583
  Somalia and Haiti operations, views on, 568–70
  as strategy advisor, 564–66, 588
Lamont, Thomas J., 268
Lansing, Robert, 236, 237
Laos in Vietnam War
  bombing operations against, 459, 461, 467–69
  creation of state, 399
  diplomacy towards, 419–20
  Ho Chi Minh Trail, 417–18, 420, 428, 467

  invasions, proposed and attempted, 435, 467–68, 470
  North Vietnamese base, 431, 433, 434
Laramie Treaty 1851, 119
Last Banana War, Nicaragua, 271–74
Latimer, Julian, 272
Latin America and Caribbean, US diplomatic strategy. *See also* individual country names
  Bush (41st P.) administration, 528
  Carter administration, 488–89
  Eisenhower administration, 396–97
  Good Neighbor Policy, 262–63, 277, 290, 407
  Harding and Coolidge administrations, 262–66
  Hoover administration, 277–78
  Kennedy and Johnson (36th P.) administrations, 407–408, 412
  Nixon and Ford administrations, 451
  Reagan administration, 508, 510–13
  Roosevelt (32nd P.) administration, 290
  Spanish colonies, 78–79, 120, 160, 182–85, *See also* Philippines, War for the; Spanish-American War
  Taft administration, 221–22, 224, 230–31
  Wilson administration, 229–30
Lavrov, Sergey, 638
Le Duan, 416, 419, 420, 440, 472
Le Duc Tho, 460, 472
League of Nations, 247, 253–55, 262
Lebanon, 396–97, 513, 515–17, 626, 668
Lee, Robert E., 126, 138, 140–41, 144, 148–49
LeMay, Curtis, 336
Lesseps, Ferdinand de, 181
Leyte Gulf, Battle of, 336–37
Liberia, 626
Libya, 517, 626, 639–41
Lieber Code, 209
limited war theory, 388, 401, 403, 415, 426, 444–45, 511
Lincoln, Abraham
  assassination, 149
  Indian Wars. *See* Indian Wars, mid-nineteenth century

INDEX

military strategy and campaigns. *See* Civil War
presidential election (1864), 145–46
slavery, views on, 122, 130–31
Lincoln, Benjamin, 31
List, Friedrich, 100
Little Bighorn, Battle of, 174, 175
Lloyd George, David, 238, 245, 251, 252, 254
Locarno Agreements, 270, 282
Lodge, Henry Cabot, 185, 191, 254, 255
Lodge, Henry Cabot Jr, 436
Lôme, Enrique Dupuy de, 195
Lon Nol, 466, 467–68
Long, John, 197, 198
López de Santa Anna, Antonio, 89, 107–108, 111, 113–14, 120
Lord, Winston, 448
Louisiana
  Battle of New Orleans, 73, 75
  Louisiana Purchase, 55, 76, 78, 103
Lower Canada province (Quebec), 18–19, 59–62, 68–69
Luce, Stephen B., 187–88
Luna, Antonio, 205–207
Lusitania sinking, 237
Lute, Douglas, 602–603

MacArthur, Arthur, 206–207, 209–11
MacArthur, Douglas
  Korean War controversies, 370–71, 374–79, 382, 387, 423
  Korean War offensives, 369–70, 373–74
  Korean War strategy, 365, 369, 371, 372, 374–75
  in Pacific War, 329–31, 333–35, 337
Macdonough, Thomas, 71
Machado, Gerardo, 234
Mackinder, Halford J., 389
Macomb, Alexander, 71
MAD (mutually assured destruction), 406, 484, 495, 506
Madero, Francisco, 230
Madison administration
  diplomatic strategy, 55–57, 69
  economic strategy, 76
  Second Barbary War, 75

War of 1812. *See* War of 1812
Madison, James, 41, 50, *See also* Madison administration
Madriz, José, 222
Mahan, Alfred Thayer, 8, 181, 188–92, 198
Mahan, Dennis Hart, 163
Maine boundary dispute, 98, 100
Malik, Jacob, 380–81
al-Maliki, Nouri, 623–24, 626, 653–55
Mallory, Stephen, 133
Manchuria, China
  Chinese civil war in, 355–56
  Dollar Diplomacy to, 223, 268, 700–701
  Japanese occupation, 277, 322, 337
  Soviet occupation, 339, 342, 355, 362–64
  Yalu River (border with North Korea), 373–74
Mandelbaum, Michael, 579
Manifest Destiny, 101–102, 119, 196
Mann Doctrine, 412
Mantoux, Étienne, 256
Mao Tse-Tung
  Chinese civil war and Communist revolution, 355–56, 403
  Cultural Revolution, 411
  Korean War role, 364, 365, 373, 379, 380, 382, 385, 386
  military strategy, 416–17
  Vietnam War role, 469
Marcos, Ferdinand, 519
Marcy, William L., 106, 107, 112, 121–22
Mariana Islands, 331, 332, 334, 335–36, *See also* Guam
Marine Corps. *See also* Army; Navy
  China, operations in, 355
  generally, 47, 240, 275, 349–50
  in Gulf War, 548, 551–52
  in Korean War, 369–70
  Lebanon, operations in, 396–97
  pre Second World War operations, 212, 222, 230, 234, 264–66, 271–74
  in Second World War, 330, 331, 333–35, 337
  in Vietnam War, 429–35
Marshall and Gilbert Islands, 334–35
Marshall, Andrew, 505

843

INDEX

Marshall, George C.
 China, diplomatic mission to, 355
 as Joint Chiefs of Staff head, 302–303, 329
 Korean War strategy, 371, 372, 374–75, 378
 Marshall Plan, 351–52
 pre Second World War strategy, 297
 post Second World War strategy, 347, 350
 Second World War strategy, 304–308, 331, 338
Marshall, Humphrey, 121
Marshall Plan, 351–52
Masood, Ahmad Shad, 582, 592
Mattis, Jim
 Afghan War strategy, 596, 681, 682
 Iraq War (Second) strategy, 616, 618
 Iraq War (Third) strategy, 677–79
 Obama administration, views on, 650, 654
 as Trump administration strategy advisor, 663, 664, 668, 669, 674–76, 683
May, Stacy, 300
Mayaguez incident, 452
McCarthy, Joseph, 356
McChrystal, Stanley, 645–47
McClellan, George B.
 Civil War military strategy, 131–36
 as Lincoln's political opponent, 145–46
 removal as Union general-in-chief, 136, 137
 Virginia Peninsula campaign, 135–39
McGovern, George, 467
McGurk, Brett, 657, 677–79
McKiernan, David, 602, 609, 612, 614, 644
McKinley administration
 Boxer Rebellion, China, 212–13
 diplomatic strategy, 191–92, 213
 wars. *See* Philippines, War for the; Spanish-American War
McMaster, H.R.
 Afghan War strategy, 680–82
 in Iraq War (Second), 621, 623, 625
 as Trump administration strategy advisor, 661–62, 670, 671, 676
McNamara, Robert
 Cold War strategy, 404–406, 409, 413
 as strategy advisor, 401–402, 423
 on Vietnam War aim, 423–24
 Vietnam War strategy, 427–32, 434
McNaughton, John, 426

McNeill, Dan, 600–602
McPherson, James, 140
Meade, George Gordon, 141, 143
Mearsheimer, John, 515
Merkel, Angela, 639, 676, 694
Merritt, Wesley, 198, 204
Mexican War
 diplomatic strategy, 104, 107–108
 information strategy, 104, 107, 110
 Mexico's military strategy, 105, 114–15
 military strategy, 104–107, 116–17
 opposition to, 106, 109
 peace negotiations, 107–108, 111, 113–16
 political aims, 103–104, 106
 preparations and resources, 105–106
 principal offensives, map 3.2
  California, 108–109
  Mexico City, 111–15
  Veracruz, 108–11
Mexico
 Apache warriors in, 178
 Harding and Coolidge administrations, diplomatic strategy, 264–65
 Mexican War. *See* Mexican War
 NAFTA (North American Free Trade Agreement), 528, 564, 567, 666
 Napoleon III's intervention, 141, 158–59
 Texan independence from, 88–89, 98
 US expansionist aims, 119, 120, 122
 US investment in, 180
 Wilson administration's Mexican Wars, 230–33
 Zimmerman telegram, 239
Middle East. *See also* individual country names
 Arab-Israeli peace process, 583, 588, 639
 Arab-Israeli War and oil embargo, 449, 451, 454
 Arab Spring uprisings, 634, 639, 641
 Carter Doctrine, 493, 515
 CENTO (Central Treaty Organization), 394, 406–407
 diplomatic strategy towards. *See* Middle East, US diplomatic strategy
 Iran-Iraq War, 493, 514–15, 537
 Suez Crisis, 396
 terrorist groups. *See* Hezbollah; Islamic State; Al Qaeda

INDEX

Middle East, US diplomatic strategy
  Bush (41st P.) administration, 530, 531, 603
  Bush (43rd P.) administration, 603
  Carter administration, 487–88, 490–94, 603
  Clinton administration, 583–85
  Eisenhower administration, 396–97
  Kennedy and Johnson (36th P.) administrations, 407, 412–13
  Nixon and Ford administrations, 451
  Obama administration, 636, 639
  Reagan administration, 504, 508–10, 513–17, 521
  Truman administration, 357, 364
  Trump administration, 668–72, 674
Midway, Battle of, 328–29
Mifflin, Thomas, 26
Miles, Nelson, 164, 175, 179, 197–99
military strategy. *See also* war aims; individual war entries
  Adams (2nd P.) administration, 46
  atomic warfare threat. *See* atomic warfare
  Bush (41st P.) administration, 528–29, 537, 561
  Carter administration, 481, 482–84, 493–95
  Clinton administration, 567–68, 575–76, 580–82
  core mistakes, 697–98, 702
  disarmament after wars. *See* disarmament policies
  Eisenhower administration, 390–97, 400–401
  Fabian strategy, 24, 25
  filibustering, 120
  generally, 9–10, 38, 387, 702
  Gilded Age era (1877–97), 185
    Army reforms, 185–86
    Navy reforms, 181–82, 186–90
  Harding and Coolidge administrations, 267–68, 274–76
  Hoover administration, 276
  Jackson administration, 90–91
  Jefferson administration, 52, 53
  Kennedy and Johnson (36th P.) administrations, 402, 404–406, 413
  limited war theory, 388, 401, 403, 415, 426, 444–45, 511
  Mahan on naval strategy, 188–90
  Monroe and Adams (6th P.) administrations, 83–84
  NATO relations. *See* NATO (North Atlantic Treaty Organization)
  Nixon and Ford administrations, 448–49, 455
  Obama administration, 659
  preemptive action, 350–51, 575, 582, 603–604
  Reagan administration, 495, 502, 504–508, 516–17, 521–22
  Roosevelt (26th P.) administration, 214–15, 220
  Roosevelt (32nd P.) administration, 292–93, 298–99, 301
  signaling theory, 422, 426–27, 671
  tacticization of, 23, 646, 650–51
  theorists. *See* Clausewitz, Carl von; Schelling, Thomas; Sun Tzu
  Truman administration, 349–50, 354, 358–62
  Trump administration, 674–76
  unpreparedness tradition. *See* unpreparedness for war tradition
  Van Buren administration, 98
  war strategies. *See under* individual war entries
  Washington administration, 41–42
Miller, Christopher, 684
Milley, Mark, 692–94
Milošević, Slobodan, 585, 586
Missouri Compromise 1820, 85
Mitchel, Ormsby, 136
Mitchell, William ("Billy"), 312
modernization theory, 403, 415, 426, 438, 444–45, 463
Modoc War, 173–74
Moffat, Thomas, 222
Mohammad Reza, Shah of Iran, 451, 487–88, 490
Mondale, Walter, 482–83
Monroe and Adams (6th P.) administrations
  assessment of, 87
  diplomatic strategy, 78–83, *See also* Monroe Doctrine
  economic strategy, 82–83, 87

Monroe and Adams (6th P.) (cont.)
  expansion and security aims, 78
  First Seminole War, 84–85
  grand strategy, 79–80, 697
  Indian removal policies, 85–87
  military strategy, 83–84
Monroe Doctrine
  formulation, 80–82
  Gilded Age era (1877–97), 181, 182, 184–85
  Harding variant, 263
  Johnson (17th P.) and Grant administrations, 159–60
  Polk administration, 103
  Roosevelt Corollary, 214–15, 217–18, 262, 277–78, 290
  Tyler administration, 100
  Wilson variant, 239
Monroe, James, 58, 72–74, 77, *See also* Monroe and Adams (6th P.) administrations
Montgomery, Bernard, 306, 307, 309, 318–20
Montgomery, Richard, 19
Moore, Willy, 595
Morgan, Daniel, 34
Morgan, Sir Frederick (COSSAC), 316
Morrell, Michael, 664–65
Moro, 211
Morris, Robert, 30
Morrow, Dwight, 264
Morsi, Mohamed, 639
Mubarak, Hosni, 639
Mugabe, Robert, 489
Mullen, Mike, 634, 647, 649–50
Munich Agreement, 292, 298, 351
Musharraf, Pervez, 594–97, 601–602
Muskie, Edmund, 487, 494
Mussolini, Benito, 291, 292, 309
mutually assured destruction (MAD), 406, 484, 495, 506

NAFTA (North American Free Trade Agreement), 528, 564, 567, 666
Namibia, 519–20, 524
Napoleon I of France, 56, 62, 69, 71, 73
Napoleon III of France, 141, 158–59
Nasr, Vali, 634

Nasser, Gemal Abdel, 396, 407
national interests, 3–4
National Security Council (NSC)
  establishment, 358
Native American peoples
  British relations with, 18–19, 42, 44, 74, 84–85
  concentration policies, 90, 94, 164–65, 171–72
  Indian Question, 179
  Iroquois Confederation, 30–31
  territorial losses. *See* Native American territorial losses
  wars. *See* Indian Wars
Native American territorial losses
  Fort Jackson Treaty 1814, 74
  Indian removal policies, 85–87, 89–90
  Kansas-Nebraska Act 1854, 120–21
  security aim of, 88
  trail system agreements, 119
  wars over. *See* Indian Wars
  Washington administration, 42–45
NATO (North Atlantic Treaty Organization)
  in Biden administration, 695
  in Bush (41st P.) administration, 527–29, 560, 562
  in Bush (43rd P.) administration, 594, 598, 602
  in Carter administration, 484, 493
  in Clinton administration, 575–76, 578–79, 586–87
  in Eisenhower administration, 390, 394
  establishment and early years, 354, 359–60
  in Kennedy and Johnson (36th P.) administrations, 405, 413
  in Nixon and Ford administrations, 448, 455
  in Obama administration, 638–39, 640
  in Reagan administration, 504, 505, 507, 514
  in Trump administration, 675–76
naval engagements
  of American Revolutionary War, 19–20
  Barbary Wars, 52–53, 75
  Chesapeake affair, 56, 58
  Civil War naval blockade, 133–34, 142
  Mahan on naval strategy, 188–90

INDEX

Quallah Battoo, Battle of, 90–91
Quasi-War, 5, 47–48
   of Spanish-American War, 197–201
   submarine warfare. *See* submarine warfare of Vietnam War, 438
   of War of 1812, 62–63, 65–67, 69, 71
Navy. *See also* Air Force; Army; military strategy
   Carter administration, 484
   Continental Navy predecessor, 17, 19–20, 22, 37
   disarmament after wars. *See* disarmament policies
   Eisenhower administration, 393
   engagements. *See* naval engagements
   establishment, 40, 42, 47
   Gilded Age era (1877–97), 181–82, 186–90
   Harding and Coolidge administrations, 267–68, 274–76
   Hoover administration, 276
   Jackson administration, 90
   Jefferson administration, 53
   Joint Army and Navy Board, 213, 275, 302
   Joint Chiefs of Staff, 302–303, 358, 409, 423
   Marine Corps. *See* Marine Corps
   McKinley administration, 213
   Monroe administration, 83
   Reagan administration, 505
   Roosevelt (26th P.) administration, 214, 220
   Roosevelt (32nd P.) administration, 293
   Truman administration, 349–50, 358–59
   Wilson administration, 240
Negroponte, John, 473, 619
New Deal policies. *See also* Great Depression; Roosevelt (32nd P.) administration
   advisors on, 696
   agricultural sector, 285–86, 288
   assessment of, 287–90
   generally, 284–85, 288–89
   Glass-Steagall Act 1933, 280, 287
   industrial sector, 286
   trade policies, 285, 287, 299
   unemployment relief and job creation, 286–88
New Look strategy, Cold War, 391–92
New Orleans, Battle of, 73, 75
Nez Perce War, 176

Ngo Dinh Diem, 399, 417–20
Nguyen Duc Thang, 436, 437, 438
Nguyen Van Thieu
   appointment as South Vietnamese P., 437, 439, 463
   Land for Tiller program, 464
   South Vietnam, fall of, 474–76
   Vietnam War peace terms, opposition to, 472, 473
   Vietnam War strategy, 444, 458, 467, 468
Nicaragua
   Bush (41st P.) administration, diplomatic strategy, 528
   canal-building schemes, 119, 182, 191, 215, 216
   Last Banana War, 271–74
   Sandinista regime, Carter administration support, 488–89, 496
   Sandinista regime, Reagan administration opposition, 511–13
   Soviet economic aid to, 523, 524
   Taft administration, diplomatic strategy, 222–23
Nimitz, Chester W., 328, 329, 331, 334, 335
Nitze, Paul, 361
Nixon and Ford administrations
   Cold War strategy, 449–53
   democracy promotion, skepticism towards, 452, 476
   diplomatic strategy, 451–53, 458–59, 486
   economic strategy, 453–55
   grand strategy, 446–49, 476
   information strategy, 453
   military strategy, 448–49, 455
   security aim, 447–48, 452
   Vietnam War. *See* Vietnam War, Nixon and Ford administrations
   Watergate scandal, 453, 474
Nixon Doctrine, 448–49
Nixon, Richard, 443, *See also* Nixon and Ford administrations
Noriega, Manuel, 529
North Africa campaign, Second World War, 306–307
North American Free Trade Agreement (NAFTA), 528, 564, 567, 666

INDEX

North Atlantic Treaty Organization. *See* NATO (North Atlantic Treaty Organization)
North Carolina in American Revolutionary War, 32–35
North Korea, US diplomatic strategy
    Bush (43rd P.) administration, 626–27
    Clinton administration, 575
    Trump administration, 667–68, 672, 674
North, Lord Frederick, 16, 29, 35
NSC (National Security Council)
    establishment, 358
nuclear weapons. *See* atomic warfare; weapons of mass destruction
Nullification Crisis, 95–96, 122

Obama administration
    Afghan War. *See* Afghan War, Obama, Trump and Biden administrations
    Asia, diplomatic strategy, 637–38
    assessment of, 633
    counterterrorism strategy, 643, 650–52, 656
    diplomatic strategy generally, 636–37, 659–60, 667, 698, 700
    economic strategy, 635–36, 667
    grand strategy, 634–35, 697
    information strategy, 636, 640–41
    Iraq War (Second), 652–54
    Iraq War (Third), 654–59
    Libyan War, 639–41
    Middle East, diplomatic strategy, 636, 639
    military strategy, 659
    political aims, 633–34, 659
    Russia, diplomatic strategy, 638–40, 642
    Syrian civil war, 641–42
Obama, Barack, 625, *See also* Obama administration
Obregón, Álvaro, 264
Odierno, Raymond, 621, 652, 653
Odom, William, 478
oil crises
    Carter administration, 479–80, 487, 490, 491, 496
    Nixon and Ford administrations, 451, 454
    Reagan administration, efforts to prevent, 514–15

Okinawa, Battle of, 337
Olney, Richard, 185, 191
Open Door policy towards China, 212, 223, 235, 256, 267, 268, 297
Oregon boundary dispute, 100, 103
Ortega, Daniel, 489, 511–13
Osceola (Seminole leader), 92, 94
O'Sullivan, John, 101–102
Otis, Elwell S., 204–209
OVERLORD (invasion of France, Second World War), 307, 309–10, 315–22

Pacific Fur Company, 80
Pacific region. *See also* Asia, US diplomatic strategy; Latin America and Caribbean, US diplomatic strategy; Monroe Doctrine; individual country names
    island territory acquisitions, 121, 201–3, 227
    Pacific Northwest, Russian expansion fears, 80–82
    Panama Canal. *See* Panama Canal
    Philippines, War for the. *See* Philippines, War for the
    Second World War
        pre US entry, 297–99
        post US entry. *See* Pacific theater of Second World War
    Seward's expansionist aims (Johnson administration), 158
    Spanish-American War. *See* Spanish-American War
    Truman's "defensive perimeter" strategy, 360
    Vietnam War, support for, 413
Pacific theater of Second World War
    Allied and US military strategy, 323–27, 329, 331–33, 336
    Japanese aims, 323
    Japanese military strategy, 327–28, 330–31, 334, 337–39
    origins (Japanese invasions of China), 277, 291–92, 322–23
    Pearl Harbor attack, 301–302, 322
    postwar plans, 342–43
    principal offensives, maps 9.2a, 9.2b
        Aleutians operation, 327–28
        bombing raids on Japan, 336

INDEX

Central Pacific drive, 334–37
dual pronged offensive, 331–35
final invasions and atomic bombs, 337–40
Midway operation, 327, 328–29
Philippines liberation, 336–37
Solomon Islands operations, 306, 307, 329–31
Pacific, War of the, 183–84, 186–87
Paine, Thomas, 21, 26, 36
Pakistan
  Afghan War, Musharraf's double game, 594–97, 601–602
  Al Qaeda and Taliban in, 599–602, 644, 649–50, 681, 682
Pakistan, US diplomatic strategy
  Bush (41st P.) administration, 529–30
  Bush (43rd P.) administration, 594
  Carter administration, 493
  Clinton administration, 582–83
  Nixon administration, 451–52
  Reagan administration, 519
  Trump administration, 682, 683
Palestine, 583, 626, 639
Panama, 215–16, 233, 529
Panama Canal
  early plans for, 158, 181, 186
  Second World War defense of, 299
  sovereignty challenged, 412
  sovereignty transferred, 488
  zone acquisition, 5, 215–16, 604
Panetta, Leon, 565, 633, 649, 650, 654, 659
Panikkar, K.M., 372
Paris Climate Agreement, 666–67
Parish, David, 68, 69
Patton, George S., 307, 318
Pearl Harbor attack, 301–302, 322
Pemberton, John, 140
Perot, H. Ross, 564
Perry, Mathew, 121
Perry, Oliver Hazard, 65, 67
Pershing, John J.
  First World War, German unconditional surrender sought, 250, 252
  First World War, military strategy, 242, 244–46, 248, 249, 257
  in Mexican Wars of Wilson administration, 232–33

Pétain, Philippe, 247, 252–53
Petraeus, David, 618–19, 623–25, 647–49
Philippines
  Carter administration, diplomatic strategy, 487
  Reagan administration, diplomatic strategy, 519
  in Second World War, 297, 298, 329, 336–37
  in Spanish-American War, 197–99, 201
  US annexation, 201–204
    war consequence. *See* Philippines, War for the
  US sovereignty conceded, 235
Philippines, War for the
  consequences, 211–13
  conventional warfare, 205–207
  guerrilla warfare, 207–11
  military strategy, 205, 207–10
  origins, 201–204
  outbreak, 204–205
Piegan Massacre, 162, 171–72
Pierce administration, 120–22
Pike, Zebulon, 67
Pillow, Gideon J., 131
Pinckney, Thomas, 44
"plausible deniability", 84
Poinsett, Joel Robert, 90, 94
Poland
  NATO membership, 576
  opposition movements in, 485–86, 494, 499, 509, 526
  postwar territory expansion, 309, 342
  in Second World War, 294, 318
  Wilson's support for Polish independence, 238, 247
political aims, 1, 3–7, *See also* democracy promotion aim; expansion aim; human rights promotion aim; security aim; sovereignty aim; war aims
Polk administration
  expansion aim, 101–103
  Mexican War. *See* Mexican War
Polk, James K. *See* Polk administration
Polk, Leonidas K., 131
Pompeo, Mike, 670, 674, 678, 679
Porter, Peter B., 69

849

INDEX

Powell, Colin
　Afghan War strategy, 594
　Afghanistan democracy plan, 598
　Gulf War ceasefire decision and terms, 552–55
　Gulf War strategy, 538, 542–45
　Haiti, diplomatic mission to, 576
　Iraq War strategy, 606
　9/11 response, views on, 590
　Powell Doctrine, 517, 577
Prague Spring uprising, 412
Preble, Edward, 52–53
preemptive military action, 350–51, 575, 582, 603–604
Preliminary Emancipation Proclamation 1863, 139
Prevost, Sir George, 61–63, 67, 71
Progressive era, 202, *See also* Imperialist era (1897–1913)
Prohibition, 258
protectionism. *See* tariff policies
Puerto Rico, 182, 183, 201, 202
Putin, Vladimir, 1, 575, 638, 640, 641, 676, 695

Qaddafi, Moammar, 517, 626, 639, 640, 642
Al Qaeda. *See also* Islamic State
　Benghazi attacks, 640–41
　in Iraq War, 616, 618, 619, 622–23, 625–26
　Iraq's prewar links to, 607
　leaders. *See* Bin Laden, Osama; Zarqawi, Abu Musab Al
　leaders' escape from Afghanistan, 596, 597
　in Pakistan, 599–602, 644, 649–50
　Taliban support for, 582–83, 590, 592, 683, 692
　terrorist attacks, 582, 589–90, 602
　in Yemen, 626
Qasem Soleimani, 671
Qatar, 668
Quallah Battoo, Battle of, 90–91
Quasi-War, 5, 47–48
Quebec (Lower Canada Province), 18–19, 59–62, 68–69

Raeder, Erich, 310
railroad construction, 119, 126–27, 161, 165, 168, 169, 184

Rapid Deployment Force, 491, 494, 514, 515
signaling theory, 422, 426–27, 671
Raymond, Daniel, 82, 100
Reagan administration
　Africa, diplomatic strategy, 519–20
　Asia, diplomatic strategy, 517–19
　Cold War strategy, 497–98, 500–501, 508–509, 520–21, 532
　　weaponization of economics, 499, 503–504, 506
　diplomatic strategy generally, 508–509
　economic strategy, 499, 501–508, 567
　grand strategy, 498–501, 520–23, 697
　information strategy, 509–10, 523–24
　Latin America and Caribbean, diplomatic strategy, 508, 510–13
　Middle East, diplomatic strategy, 504, 508–10, 513–17, 521
　military strategy, 495, 502, 504–508, 516–17, 521–22
　security and democracy promotion aims, 499–501, 512, 513, 519, 522, 532–33
　Soviet Union, diplomatic strategy, 508–509, 520, 523–24
Reagan, Ronald, 452, 497, *See also* Reagan administration
Reciprocal Trade Agreements Program (RTAP), 287, 299, 353, 398
Reconstruction policies. *See also* Johnson (17th P.) and Grant administrations
　during Civil War, 151
　Ku Klux Klan resistance, 153–54
　presidential election (1876) ending, 154–55
　presidential ("soft") Reconstruction, 151–53
　radical Reconstruction, 153
　Reconstruction as grand strategy, 155
　sovereignty aim, 150–51
Red Cloud War, 167–69
Red River and Comanche Wars, 172–73
Red Scare (1920), 258–59
Reid, Harry, 5, 607, 625
Rensselaer, Stephen van, 63–64
Rhee, Syngman, 364, 381, 386
Rhodes, Ben, 635, 639, 640, 646, 655–56
Rice, Condoleezza, 589, 603, 621, 624

850

INDEX

Rice, Susan, 633–34, 638–41, 651, 658
Richards, David, 601
Ridgway, Mathew B.
  military strategy, 378–81, 429
  on Korean War armistice terms, 381, 383
  as Korean War commander, 376–78
Riedel, Bruce, 644
Rochambeau, Jean-Baptiste, 35
Rodgers, John, 53
ROLLING THUNDER (Vietnam War bombing campaign), 426–30, 443
Romania, 526
Roosevelt (26th P.) administration
  Cuban intervention, 218
  diplomatic and military strategy, 214–15, 217–20
  Dominican Republic Crisis, 218, 233
  economic strategy, 220–21
  information strategy, 220
  Panama Canal Zone acquisition, 5, 215–16, 604
  Philippines, war declared on, 211
  Venezuela Crisis, 216–18
Roosevelt (32nd P.) administration
  bank crisis (1933), 283
  military strategy (pre Second World War), 292–93
  New Deal. *See* New Deal policies
  political aims, 284
  pre Second World War diplomatic strategy, 290, 667
    Asia, 291–92
    Europe, 290–91
    Latin America and Caribbean, 290
  Second World War. *See* Second World War entries
Roosevelt Corollary to Monroe Doctrine, 214–15, 217–18, 262, 277–78, 290
Roosevelt, Franklin D., 280, 284, 322, 340, *See also* Roosevelt (32nd P.) administration
Roosevelt, Theodore. *See also* Roosevelt (26th P.) administration
  early career, 213–14
  on imperialism, 191, 203, 214–15
  in Spanish-American War, 197–99
Root, Elihu, 211, 217, 255

Rosecrans, William S., 139, 141
Rostow, Walt, 403, 404, 426–28, 438
RTAP (Reciprocal Trade Agreements Program), 287, 299, 353, 398
Rumsfeld, Donald
  Afghan War strategy, 594, 595, 597–98, 600, 601, 609
  Afghanistan nation building strategy, 599
  global war on terrorism strategy, 591–92
  Iraq, postwar strategy, 613–15, 621
  Iraq War aims and strategy, 605, 608, 611, 616, 618, 619, 625
  in Reagan administration, 514
Rush-Bagot Agreement 1817, 80
Rusk, Dean, 362, 371, 401, 409, 422, 439
Russia. *See also* Soviet Union
  Alaska Purchase, 159
  diplomatic strategy towards. *See* Russia, US diplomatic strategy
  Georgia invasion, 626, 638, 642
  Gerasimov Doctrine, 664
  German oil and gas deals with, 676
  in First World War, 246–49
  NATO expansion, Russia barred from, 575–76
  Pacific Northwest expansion, US fears, 80–82
  Revolution, 239, 266
  Russo-Japanese War, 219–20
  Trump election interference claim, 665, 676
  Ukraine invasions, 1, 10–11, 638, 664, 676–77, 690, 695
Russia, US diplomatic strategy. *See also* Soviet Union, US diplomatic strategy
  Bush (43rd P.) administration, 626
  Clinton administration, 575–76
  Obama administration, 638–40, 642
  Taft administration, 223–24
  Trump administration, 676–77
Rwanda genocide, 574, 577

Sadat, Anwar, 449, 487
Saddam Hussein. *See* Hussein, Saddam
al-Sadr, Moqtada, 616, 618, 619, 625, 654
Samoa, 160, 181, 183, 203
Sampson, William T., 198, 199

INDEX

Sanchez, Ricardo, 615–17
Sand Creek Massacre, 165
Sandino, Augusto C., 272–74
Santa Anna, Antonio López de, 89, 107–108, 111, 113–14, 120
Santo Domingo, 159–60, *See also* Dominican Republic
Saudi Arabia, US diplomatic strategy
   Bush (41st P.) administration, 538–40, 559
   Carter administration, 487–88, 491
   Eisenhower administration, 396
   Johnson (36th P.) administration, 412–13
   Nixon and Ford administrations, 451
   Obama administration, 639
   Reagan administration, 504, 509, 510, 514
   Truman administration, 355, 357
   Trump administration, 668
Schelling, Thomas, 388, 406, 422, 426–27, 466–67, 671
Schroeder, Gerhard, 676
Schurz, Carl, 177
Schwarzkopf, Norman
   Gulf War ceasefire negotiations, 554–55, 557
   Gulf War, ground war command, 551
   military strategy, 538, 543–45, 553, 554
Scott, Winfield
   in Black Hawk War, 91
   in Civil War, 125–26, 129–30
   in Maine boundary dispute, 98
   in Mexican War, 106, 107, 109–116, 210
   in Second Seminole War, 92
   in War of 1812, 64, 67
Scowcroft, Brent
   Cold War strategy, 527, 538
   Gulf War strategy, 544–45, 553, 556, 557
   as strategy advisor, 525
SEATO (Southeast Asian Treaty Organization), 394, 399, 406–407, 452
Second Bank of the United States, 76
Second Barbary War, 75
Second Creek War, 91–92
Second Iraq War. *See* Iraq War (Second)
Second Seminole War, 92–95, map 3.1
Second World War, pre US entry
   diplomatic strategy, 290–92
   early German victories, 294
   economic strategy, 299–300
   Japan, strategy towards, 297–99
   military strategy, 298–99, 301
   neutrality and Allied assistance, 294–98, 301
   Pearl Harbor attack, 301–302, 322
Second World War, post-US entry
   consequences, 344–45
   economic strategy, 300–301
   military strategy
      air operations, 312–15, 327, 333, 335–36
      Casablanca Conference, 307–308, 313–14, 331
      generally, 302–304, 343
      Germany First, 304, 331
      naval operations, 310–12, 326
      Pacific War. *See under* Pacific theater of Second World War
      Quebec, Tehran and Cairo Conferences, 309–10, 332–33
   postwar order negotiations, 340–43, 345
   principal offensives
      North Africa, 306–307
      OVERLORD (invasion of France), 307, 309–10, 315–22
      Pacific theater. *See* Pacific theater of Second World War
      Sicily and Italy invasions, 308–309
   war aims, 302–303, 308, 340–41
security aim
   Adams (2nd P.) administration, 46
   American Revolutionary War, 18–19
   Bush (41st P.) administration, 525, 562
   Carter administration, 479
   Clinton administration, 565, 571–73
   Eisenhower administration, 390, 400
   generally, 4–5, 77, 699
   Harding and Coolidge administrations, 259–60, 263
   Jackson administration, 88
   Kennedy and Johnson (36th P.) administrations, 402, 404
   League of Nations proposal, opposition to, 254–55
   Monroe and Adams (6th P.) administrations, 78
   Nixon and Ford administrations, 447–48, 452

INDEX

Reagan administration, 499, 522
Roosevelt (32nd P.) administration, 284
Truman administration, 347, 349–50, 389
Washington administration, 38, 40
Seminole Wars, 84–85, 92–95, map 3.1
September 11, 2001 attacks, 589–90
Serbia, 563–64, 577–79, 585–87
Seward, Henry, 127, 147–48, 156–59
Shafter, William, 197, 199–201
Sharp, Ulysses S. Grant, 427–29
Shay's Rebellion, 37
Shelburne, William Petty, 2nd Earl of, 35
Sheridan, Philip, 164, 169–71, 173, 174, 177
Sherman, William Tecumseh
    Army reforms, 185–86
    in Civil War, 126–27, 141, 143–47, 149, 187–88
    "hard hand of war" strategy, 139, 211
    in Indian Wars, 166, 167–72
    in Reconstruction era, 155
Shinseki, Eric, 610
Shively, Jacob, 685
Shultz, George, 498, 506, 508–509, 518
Sibley, Henry Hastings, 165
Sicily and Italy invasions, Second World War, 308–309
Sigel, Franz, 143
signaling theory, 422, 426–27, 671
Sims, William, 243
Singapore, 413
Sioux Uprising, 165
Sioux War, 174–76
Sitting Bull, 174–76
Sky, Emma, 653–54
slave states, sectional tensions. *See also* Civil War
    Missouri Compromise 1820, 85
    Nullification Crisis, 95–96, 122
    Taylor and Fillmore administrations, 119–20
    Tyler administration, 99
    Van Buren administration, 97–98
slavery
    abolition, 139, 145, 148, 151
    Adams (6th P.), opposition to, 77, 82
    Lincoln's views on, 122, 130–31
    Reconstruction era servitude, 151–52, 155

slave numbers (1860 census), 126
Slidell, John, 104
Sloat, John D., 107, 108–109
Slocombe, Walter, 614
Smith, Adam, 39
Smoot-Hawley Tariff, 95, 281
Smyth, Alexander, 64
Snake War, 166–67
Solomon Islands, 306, 307, 329–31
Somalia, 564, 568–70, 578, 684–85
Somoza, Anastasio, 488–89
South Africa, 489, 519
South America. *See* Latin America and Caribbean
South Carolina
    in American Revolutionary War, 31–32, 34
    in Civil War, 124
    Nullification Crisis, 95–96, 122
    secession from Union, 122–23
South Korea, US diplomatic strategy
    Carter administration, 486–87
    Reagan administration, 519
    Trump administration, 672–74
Southeast Asia. *See* Indochina
sovereignty aim
    American Revolutionary War, 17, 21, 35–36
    Clinton administration, 580, 581
    Constitutional protection, 37–38
    generally, 5, 699
    Harding and Coolidge administrations, 259–60
    Jefferson administration, 50, 55–56
    Johnson (17th P.) and Grant administrations, 150–51
    League of Nations proposal, opposition to, 254–55
    Trump administration, 662
    War of 1812, 58
Soviet Union. *See also* Cold War; Russia
    Afghanistan invasion and war, 485, 491–92, 495, 510, 523, 524
    atomic warfare capability, 358, 361, 394, 411, 446, 504, 505
    China, split from, 402–403, 411, 446, 449–50, 508
    collapse, 524, 526, 527, 531–32, 560

INDEX

Soviet Union (cont.)
    diplomatic strategy towards. *See* Soviet Union, US diplomatic strategy
    economic decline, 495, 503–504, 506
    Korean War role, 362–66, 373, 388
    postwar order agreements, 309–10, 322, 342
    in Second World War. *See* Soviet Union in Second World War
    Vietnam War role, 412
Soviet Union in Second World War
    Allied Second Front plans, 304–308, 315–16
    early years, 294
    Germany, attacks against, 309, 318, 338
    Manchuria and Korea occupation, 339, 342, 355, 362–64
    Russian front, 303, 306, 307
    US perspective on, 297, 332–33, 340–41
Soviet Union, US diplomatic strategy. *See also* Russia, US diplomatic strategy
    Bush (41st P.) administration, 527–29
    Carter administration, 484–86, 491–94
    Eisenhower administration, 395
    Harding and Coolidge administrations, 266–67
    Kennedy and Johnson (36th P.) administrations, 406, 411–12
    Nixon and Ford administrations, 449, 459, 469–71
    Reagan administration, 508–509, 520, 523–24
    Roosevelt (32nd P.) administration, 290–91
    Truman administration, 346–49
Spain
    American Revolutionary War, colonialist support, 28–29, 35
    Al Qaeda terrorist attacks, 619
    Spanish Civil War, 291, 642
    Transcontinental Treaty 1819, 85
Spanish colonies, US diplomatic strategy generally, 78–79, 120, 160, 182–85
    Spanish Florida. *See* Florida
    wars. *See* Philippines, War for the; Spanish-American War

Spanish-American War
    consequences, 202–203, 213, *See also* Philippines, War for the
    military strategy, map 6.1, map 6.2, 197–201
    origins, 192–96
    peace negotiations, 201–202
    political aims, 196
    preparations and resources, 196–97
Spooner, John C., 192
Spykman, Nicholas John, 389
Stalin, Josef. *See also* Cold War; Korean War; Soviet Union
    death, 385, 395
    early administration, 266, 290–91
    imperialist expansion aim, 342, 345–46, 352, 354–55
    Korean War role, 364–65, 373, 380, 382, 388
    postwar order agreements, 309–10, 322, 342, 345
    Second World War aims, 302
Stanton, Edwin, 136, 153
Stark, Harold, 297, 299, 326
Stephens, Alexander H., 118
Stewart, Carol, 618
Stimson, Henry
    in Hoover administration, 277–78
    in Nicaragua, 272–74
    in Second World War, 296, 297, 303
Stockton, Robert, 109
Storms, Jane, 110–11
submarine warfare
    First World War, 237–39, 242–43
    Second World War, 296–97, 301, 310–12, 326
Suez Crisis, 396
Sullivan, Jake, 686–87, 691, 692
Sumner, Charles, 159, 160
Sun Tzu, 25, 169, 380, 439, 500
Syria
    chemical weapons use, 641–42, 669
    CIA failed operation in, 397
    in Iraq War (Second), 615
    Islamic State in, 655–58, 678
    Russian support for Assad regime, 658, 676
    withdrawal of US forces from, 678–80, 680

INDEX

tacticization of military strategy, 23, 646, 650–51
Taft administration
  China and Japan, diplomatic strategy, 222–24, 700–701
  Dollar Diplomacy strategy, 221–22, 224, 700–701
  Nicaragua, diplomatic strategy, 222–23
  peace aim, 221
Taft, Robert, 346, 367, 368
Taft, William Howard, 211, *See also* Taft administration
Taibbi, Matt, 665
Taiwan
  diplomatic strategy towards. *See* Taiwan, US diplomatic strategy
  Taipei, 450, 486
  Taiwan Straits Crisis, 395, 400
  US objectives towards, 158, 331, 336, 356–57
  in Vietnam War, 413
Taiwan, US diplomatic strategy
  Biden administration, 691
  Carter administration, 486, 487
  Clinton administration, 574
  Reagan administration, 517–19
  Trump administration, 673
Talbott, Strobe, 566, 585–86
Taliban
  Afghan War, leaders' escape, 596, 597
  Afghanistan, level of control in, 652, 680, 693–94
  in Pakistan, 599–602, 644, 649–50, 681, 682
  Al Qaeda, support for, 582–83, 590, 592, 683, 692
Tarawa, Battle of, 334–35
tariff policies. *See also* free trade policies
  Biden administration, 690
  generally, 701
  Gilded Age era (1877–97), 181, 182
  Harding and Coolidge administrations, 260–61, 281, 282
  Hoover administration, 276, 281
  Jackson administration, 95–96
  Johnson (17th P.) and Grant administrations, 158, 160–61

List on, 100
Madison administration, 76
McKinley and Roosevelt (26th P.) administrations, 220–21
Monroe and Adams (6th P.) administrations, 82, 83, 87
Reagan administration, rejection of, 503
Reciprocal Trade Agreements Program (RTAP), 287, 299, 353, 398
Roosevelt (32nd P.) administration, 285, 287
Taft administration, 222
Truman administration, 353
Trump administration, 666, 667, 672
Tyler administration, 99
Washington administration, 10, 39, 40
Wilson administration, 228–29
Tarleton, Banastre, 31–32, 34
Taylor, Alan, 63
Taylor, Maxwell, 425, 427–30
Taylor, Nathaniel G., 168
Taylor, Zachary
  in Mexican War, 104–109, 111
  presidency, 118–20
  in Second Seminole War, 94
Tecumseh (Shawnee chief), 53–54, 63, 67
Tedder, Arthur, 314
terrorism, strategy against. *See* counterterrorism strategy
Terry, Alfred, 174, 175, 179
Texas
  annexation, 97, 100–103
  border negotiations with Mexico, 85
  Comanche and Red River Wars, 172–73
  independence from Mexico, 88–89, 98
Thatcher, Margaret, 538–40, 558
Third Iraq War, 654–59, 677–80, 691–92
Third World, US diplomatic strategy. *See also* individual country names
  anti Communist policies, 395–96, 407, 408
  Carter administration, 488–89, 496
  Reagan administration, 508
Thucydides, 6
Tiananmen Square massacre, 527, 530, 538, 574
Tilden, Samuel J., 154

INDEX

Tilghman, Tench, 26
Tillerson, Rex, 662, 663, 668, 676
Tōjō, Hideki, 330–31, 333
Tomsen, Peter, 530
Toyoda, Soemu, 336
TPP (Trans-Pacific Partnership), 636, 666
Tracy, Benjamin Franklin, 187
Transcontinental Treaty 1819, 85
Trans-Pacific Partnership (TPP), 636, 666
Trask, David, 213
Treaty of Paris 1783, 35–37, 42
Trenchard, Sir Hugh, 312
Trist, Nicholas, 111–13, 115–16
Truman administration
  atomic bombing of Japan, 339–40
  bipartisan politics, 5, 346–47
  Cold War commencement, 346–49
  Cold War grand strategy, 350–52, 354, 360–62, 389
  diplomatic strategy, 354–58
  economic strategy, 352–54, 387
  Marshall Plan, 351–52
  information strategy, 352, 358
  Korean War. *See* Korean War
  military strategy, 349–50, 354, 358–62
  post Second World War challenges, 344–45, 347
  post Second World War negotiations, 340, 341
  security and democracy promotion aims, 347, 349–50, 353, 389
Trump administration
  Afghan War, 680–85
  Asia, diplomatic strategy, 667–68, 672–74
  diplomatic strategy generally, 667, 700
  economic strategy, 666–67, 672, 673, 685
  grand strategy, 661–63, 665–66, 685–86
  obstacles to delivery, 663–65, 685
  Iraq War (Third), 677–80
  Middle East, diplomatic strategy, 668–72, 674
  military strategy, 674–76
  political aims, 662
  Russia, diplomatic strategy, 676–77
Tuchman, Jessica, 483
Tunisia, 639

Turkey
  Erdoğan's threats against Syrian Kurds, 678–80
  in First World War, 235, 250
  in Iraq War (Second), 609
  US aid to, 349, 355, 493
Tyler administration
  commencement, 99
  diplomatic strategy, 100–101
  economic strategy, 99–101
  expansion aim, 99, 101
  Second Seminole War conclusion, 94–95

Ukraine
  Russian invasions, 1, 10–11, 638, 664, 676–77, 690, 695
  Trump administration, relations with, 663, 676
undeclared wars, 47, 85, 366–68, 422, 540–41, 640, 655
United Kingdom. *See* Great Britain
United Nations
  in Bosnian War, 578
  Eisenhower administration and, 393
  establishment, 341–42
  in Gulf War, 538–40, 558–59, 561
  Kennedy and Johnson (36th P.) administrations and, 407
  in Korean War, 365–67
  Somalia, operations in, 564, 568–70
unpreparedness for war tradition
  American Revolutionary War, 17
  First World War, 239
  generally, 698, 702
  Korean War, 359, 368–69
  Mexican War, 105, 116–17
  Second Seminole War, 95
  Spanish-American War, 196–97
Upper Canada province
  in American Revolutionary War, 17, 18–19, 23–24, 31
  Maine boundary dispute, 98, 100
  Oregon boundary dispute, 100, 103
  Pierce administration trade agreement, 121–22
  rebellion (1837), 98

INDEX

Rush-Bagot Agreement 1817, 80
 in War of 1812. *See* War of 1812, Canadian front
USSR. *See* Soviet Union
Ute War, 176–77

Van Buren administration
 diplomatic strategy, 98
 economic strategy, 98
 Native American affairs, 90, 94
 political aims, 97–98
Van Fleet, James A., 378–81, 384
Vance, Cyrus
 Cold War strategy, 485
 diplomatic strategy, 486, 487
 military strategy, 410, 494
 as strategy advisor, 477, 478, 491
Vandenberg, Arthur, 5, 346
Vandiver, Frank E., 128
Venezuela, 184–85, 216–18
Versailles Treaty 1919. *See also* First World War entries
 advisors to Wilson, 696
 aims of negotiators, 251–54
 Hitler's abrogation, 271, 291
 military strategy, post armistice, 252–53
 terms and enforcement, 253–57, 269–70
 US domestic opposition, 254–55
Vicksburg, Battle of, 139–40
Vietnam, 256–58, 398–99
Vietnam War, Kennedy and Johnson (36th P.) administrations
 aim and grand strategy, 418–19, 421–24, 439
 casualties, 474–75
 financing of, 414–15
 ground war strategy, 429–35
 Gulf of Tonkin Resolution, 422, 467
 military strategy, 416, 418–19, 424–26, 442–44
  advisors and ideas, 422–23, 426–27, 431, 438, 444–45, 463
 naval operations, 438
 Ngo Dinh Diem assassination, 420, 423, 435

North Vietnamese aims and strategy, fig. 12.1, 416–18, 420–21, 440, 475
 opposition to, 5, 387–88, 413, 438–39, 441
 origins, 398–99
 Pacific region support for, 413
 pacification (counterinsurgency) strategy, 418, 420, 424, 432–33, 435–38, 441–42, 444
 ROLLING THUNDER (bombing campaign), 426–30, 443
 Tet Offensive, map 12.1, 433, 434, 438–42, 444, 461
Vietnam War, Laos and Cambodia in. *See* Cambodia in Vietnam War; Laos in Vietnam War
Vietnam War, Nixon and Ford administrations
 aim and grand strategy, 444, 447–48, 455–58, 475–76
 Cambodia invasion, 465–67
 casualties, 474–75
 Easter Offensive, 470–72
 economic consequences, 453–54
 Laos, attempted invasion, 467–68
 military strategy, 450, 458–62, 471–73, 475
 opposition to, 466–67, 471, 473–74
 pacification (counterinsurgency) strategy, 464–65, 470
 peace negotiations, 458–59, 468–73, 475
 South Vietnam, fall of, 474–76
 troop withdrawals, 458, 468–69, 471
 Vietnamization strategy, 460–64
Vinson, Carl S., 293
Virginia
 in American Revolutionary War, 34–35
 in Civil War, 135–38, 147
Volcker, Paul, 489–90, 502
Votel, Joseph, 683

Wait, Stephen, 2
Wake Island, 203, 299, 327
Walker, Robert, 121
Walker, Walton, 369, 374, 376
Wall Street Crash, 278–79, *See also* Great Depression
Wallace, Henry A., 303

INDEX

war aims. *See also* military strategy
  Afghan War, 592–94, 600, 644, 646–49, 681–82
  American Revolutionary War, 17, 18, 21
  Civil War, 124
  Clausewitz on, 6, 403, 516–17
  First World War, 239, 241, 244, 246–47
  generally, 6–7, 10, 697–98
  Gulf War, 539, 541–42, 542, 554, 556–57
  Indian Wars, mid-nineteenth century, 161–63
  Iraq War (Second), 604–606, 612, 653
  Korean War, 365–66, 370–72, 376–79, 384, 387
  Kosovo War, 586, 587
  limited war theory, 388, 401, 403, 415, 426, 444–45, 511
  Mexican War, 103–104, 106
  Second World War, 302–303, 308, 340–41
  Spanish-American War, 196
  Vietnam War, 418, 421, 423–24, 439, 457, 475–76
  War of 1812, 58
  Weinberger and Powell Doctrines, 516–17, 521–22, 577
war concept
  "hybrid war" theory, 664, 689–90, 697
  insurgencies compared, 507
  misapplications of term, 344, 362, 410–11
  war status denials, 367–68, 388, 586, 646, 656, 698
War of 1812
  British military strategy, 62, 71
  Canadian front, 57–63
    Great Lakes campaigns, 65–68
    Montreal campaign, 68–69
    Niagara and Plattsburgh campaigns (1812), 63–65
    Niagara and Plattsburgh campaigns (1814), 69–71
  consequences, 75, 78, 84
  naval engagements, 62–63, 65–67, 69, 71
  origins, 55–57
  peace negotiations, 73–74
  political opposition to, 5, 60, 74–75
  preparations and resources, 58, 60, 65, 69, 72
  southern theater, 72–73, 75
  sovereignty aim, 58
  western theater, 59, 63
War of Independence. *See* American Revolutionary War
war on terror. *See* counterterrorism strategy
Warden, John, 542–44
wars without formal declaration, 47, 85, 366–68, 422, 540–41, 640, 655
Washington administration
  diplomatic strategy, 40–41, 45–46
  economic strategy, 10, 38–41
  frontier expansion, 42–45, 48–49, map 2.1
  military strategy, 41–42
  Native American affairs, 42–45
  political aims, 38–39, 40
Washington Treaties on naval disarmament, 267–68, 275, 282
Washington, George. *See also* Washington administration
  military strategy and campaigns. *See under* American Revolutionary War
  in Quasi-War, 47–48
Watergate scandal, 453, 474
Wayne, Anthony, 44
weaponization of economics strategy, Cold War, 499, 503–504, 506
weapons of mass destruction. *See also* atomic warfare
  global war on terror strategy on, 591–92, 603
  Gulf War concerns about, 540, 541, 549
  Iranian capability, 626, 642–43, 669–70
  Iraqi capability, 559, 584, 606–607
  Libyan capability, 626
  North Korean capability, 575, 626–27, 667–68
  Syria, chemical weapons use, 641–42, 669
Webster, Daniel, 100, 120
Weinberger, Caspar
  Cold War strategy, 498–99, 504, 505
  military strategy, 506, 514–17, 521–22
Weinberger Doctrine, 516–17
Welles, Sumner, 263–64, 265
West Germany, 354–55, 410, 527–28

INDEX

Western Confederacy, war against, 44–45
Westmoreland, William
   Tet offensive and, 439, 461
   Vietnam War ground war strategy, 429–35
   Vietnam War strategy generally, 423–25, 428, 442, 443
Wheeler, Earle, 442
Whiskey Rebellion, 5
Whitman, Walt, 106
Wilderness, Battle of the, 144
Wilhelm II of Germany, 188, 216–17, 250, 251
Wilkinson, James, 68–69
Wilson administration
   Asia, diplomatic strategy, 234–35, 256
   Cuba, diplomatic strategy, 234
   democracy promotion aim, 227–28, 239, 241, 244, 246–47, 252, 257
   diplomatic strategy generally, 229–30
   Dominican Republic War, 233–34
   economic strategy, 228–29, 237
   First World War. *See* First World War, Wilson administration in
   Haiti War, 230
   League of Nations proposal, 247, 253–55, 342
   Mexican Wars, 230–33
   Versailles Treaty. *See* Versailles Treaty 1919
Wilson, James H., 142
Wilson, Woodrow, 5, 182, 224, 227, 416, *See also* Wilson administration
Winder, William, 71
Wolfowitz, Paul
   Gulf War strategy, 542

Iraq, postwar strategy, 610, 613, 615
Iraq War, aims and strategy, 607, 608
9/11 response, views on, 590
Woodward, C. Vann, 36–37
Woodworth, Steven, 140
World Bank, 342
World Trade Center attacks, 582, 589–90
World Trade Organization, China's membership, 574, 627
World War I. *See* First World War entries
World War II. *See* Second World War entries
Worth, William Jenkins, 94–95

Xi Jinping, 669
XYZ affair, 46–47

Yamamoto, Isoroku, 327–29
Yeltsin, Boris, 531, 575, 576
Yemen, 626, 656, 685
Young America movement, 119
Young Plan on war reparations, 271
Yugoslav Wars, 563–64, 577–79, 585–87
Yugoslavia, 354–55, 532

Zaman, Mohammed, 596
Zarqawi, Abu Musab Al, 606, 618, 622–23, 654–55
Zelaya, José Santos, 222
Zelikow, Philip, 621, 624
Zhou Enlai, 469
Zimbabwe, 489
Zimmerman telegram, 239
Zinni, Anthony, 585

For EU product safety concerns, contact us at Calle de José Abascal, 56–1°, 28003 Madrid, Spain or eugpsr@cambridge.org.

www.ingramcontent.com/pod-product-compliance
Lightning Source LLC
LaVergne TN
LVHW092231260326
834689LV00059B/30